URBAN POLITICS

CQ Press, an imprint of SAGE, is the leading publisher of books, periodicals, and electronic products on American government and international affairs. CQ Press consistently ranks among the top commercial publishers in terms of quality, as evidenced by the numerous awards its products have won over the years. CQ Press owes its existence to Nelson Poynter, former publisher of the St. Petersburg Times, and his wife Henrietta, with whom he founded Congressional Quarterly in 1945. Poynter established CQ with the mission of promoting democracy through education and in 1975 founded the Modern Media Institute, renamed The Poynter Institute for Media Studies after his death. The Poynter Institute (www.poynter.org) is a nonprofit organization dedicated to training journalists and media leaders.

In 2008, CQ Press was acquired by SAGE, a leading international publisher of journals, books, and electronic media for academic, educational, and professional markets. Since 1965, SAGE has helped inform and educate a global community of scholars, practitioners, researchers, and students spanning a wide range of subject areas, including business, humanities, social sciences, and science, technology, and medicine. A privately owned corporation, SAGE has offices in Los Angeles, London, New Delhi, and Singapore, in addition to the Washington DC office of CQ Press.

URBAN POLITICS
A Reader

Editor

Stephen J. McGovern
Haverford College

Los Angeles | London | New Delhi
Singapore | Washington DC

Los Angeles | London | New Delhi
Singapore | Washington DC

FOR INFORMATION:

CQ Press

An Imprint of SAGE Publications, Inc.

2455 Teller Road

Thousand Oaks, California 91320

E-mail: order@sagepub.com

SAGE Publications Ltd.

1 Oliver's Yard

55 City Road

London EC1Y 1SP

United Kingdom

SAGE Publications India Pvt. Ltd.

B 1/I 1 Mohan Cooperative Industrial Area

Mathura Road, New Delhi 110 044

India

SAGE Publications Asia-Pacific Pte. Ltd.

3 Church Street

#10-04 Samsung Hub

Singapore 049483

Senior Acquisitions Editor: Michael Kerns

Developmental Editor: Elise Frasier

Editorial Assistant: Zachary Hoskins

Production Editor: Tracy Buyan

Copy Editor: QuADS Prepress Pvt. Ltd.

Typesetter: Hurix Systems (P) Ltd.

Proofreader: Pam Suwinsky

Cover Designer: Anupama Krishnan

Marketing Manager: Amy Whitaker

Printed in the United States of America

ISBN 978-1-5063-1119-7

This book is printed on acid-free paper.

16 17 18 19 20 10 9 8 7 6 5 4 3 2 1

CONTENTS

PART IV: CHANGING DYNAMICS OF URBAN POLITICS

PART V: VISIONS OF URBAN POLITICS TODAY

PREFACE

A number of themes permeate *Urban Politics: A Reader*. First, it is organized on a historical basis. Utilizing a narrative approach has the advantage of making intuitive sense to students who readily grasp the story of the rise, fall, and possible resurrection of U.S. cities. Moreover, proceeding chronologically facilitates learning because to understand how urban politics works now, it is essential for students to know what has happened in the past. Second, this reader highlights the crucial role of societal change in engendering political change within cities. Accordingly, considerable attention is devoted to how industrialization, internal migration, immigration, racial and ethnic transition, deindustrialization, suburbanization, and globalization have affected urban politics. Third, although the influence of broad societal forces is elaborated at length, this reader also strives to illuminate how people—both at an elite level and at the grassroots—make a difference in how a polity is governed; in short, structure and agency matter in elucidating local governance. Fourth, in teaching urban politics I have always tried to expose students to multiple voices with respect to race and ethnicity, class, culture, and ideology. A thorough encounter with the rich variety of perspectives that make up the urban mosaic is necessary for comprehending who wields power and why. A consequence of employing the same approach here is that this book contains more readings than other urban politics readers (but a similar number in comparison to many other readers in urban studies and American politics). My hope is that the depth and breadth of this reader will engage students and stimulate lively discussion and debate.

As for the format of the book, each chapter begins with an essay that provides historical, conceptual, and theoretical context for the readings to follow. Although relatively short, these introductory essays cover a lot of substantive ground while offering guidance for further reading for those who wish to pursue more specialized areas of inquiry.

The selected readings naturally represent the core of the book. They include reflections from familiar and colorful luminaries of the world of urban politics like George Washington Plunkitt, Andrew Dickson White, and Jacob Riis, as well as time-tested analyses from long-respected scholars such as Sam Bass Warner, Robert Merton, Samuel Hays, Michael Katz, Kenneth Jackson, Jon Teaford, Carl Abbott, and Clarence Stone. I have also turned to many scholars from the current generation of urbanists whose path-breaking work has been published in the leading university presses and top journals, including Guian McKee, Jason Hackworth,

Andra Gillespie, Tracy Neumann, Paul O'Hara, Joel Rast, Audrey Singer, Domenic Vitiello, and Thad Williamson. In addition to scholars, there are readings by journalists (Alan Ehrenhalt, Jonathan Kozol, and Karen Paget), activists (Stokely Carmichael, Bayard Rustin, and Saul Alinsky), and politicians (the former mayor of Indianapolis, Stephen Goldsmith). Furthermore, the readings offer a look at a wide array of places that vary by size, demographic composition, and geography. Along with the larger urban centers that tend to garner considerable attention from scholars—New York, Chicago, and Los Angeles—this collection shines an analytical light on understudied cities such as Indianapolis, San Antonio, Portland, Richmond, Gary, and Camden.

After each set of readings on a particular topic, I have added material on the implications for public policy associated with the time period covered and the contemporary era. The Policy Then/Policy Now sections are designed to give students an opportunity to consider more practically how and why urban politics matters to people in their day-to-day lives, often in momentous ways. Each chapter concludes with a list of additional resources and discussion questions. The ultimate goals are to expand students' knowledge of power and politics in American cities, sharpen critical thinking skills, and cultivate a love of learning about urban affairs and a lifelong concern for the vitality and well-being of cities.

Acknowledgments

Many people deserve my sincere gratitude for enabling me to bring this project to fruition. The structure and content of *Urban Politics: A Reader* is in no small measure a product of my teaching experiences during the past two decades, mostly at Haverford College. I am deeply indebted to my students for providing a true partnership in the process of learning about politics in American cities and helping me to think about how and why power dynamics evolve over time. Their insights and feedback have shaped this book in profound ways.

More specifically, urban politics was the first class I taught when I started my career as a visiting assistant professor at Temple University, and many of my core ideas about how to frame the course can be traced to that initial effort. A colleague at the time suggested that I might use my syllabus as the basis for a book, and so the seed was planted very early on. My students at Temple helped me make constructive revisions, and I am particularly grateful to Susan Clampet-Lundquist, Cameron Voss, Marshall King, and Neil Donahue for their encouragement and support; I have not forgotten.

I have had the great pleasure of spending the bulk of my career at Haverford College where I have taught urban politics and related courses for the past sixteen years. There are far too many students to mention by name, but I cannot thank them enough for making classroom experiences there so stimulating, challenging, and rewarding. At a time when institutions of higher learning are under attack, and sometimes for valid reasons, Haverford's commitment to excellence in scholarship and teaching stands as an exemplar of how to do it right. I am also deeply appreciative to the many folks at Haverford who have provided important research, administrative, and technical support, including Margaret Schaus,

Rob Haley, Dawn Heckert, Theresa Donahue, Norm Medeiros, Krista Murphy, and Brian Taylor, as well as my colleagues in the Political Science Department. The College's generous leave policy made this project possible.

Many thanks to SAGE for inviting me to submit a prospectus and then giving me the opportunity to realize a plan that had been percolating for many years. Thanks, in particular, to the anonymous reviewers and to Sarah Calabi, Suzanne Flinchbaugh, Katie Lowry, Sheri Gilbert, Raquel Christie, Tracy Buyan, Rajasree Ghosh, Nancy Matuszak, Matt Byrnie, and especially Elise Frasier. Putting together a reader is a far more complicated job than I had ever anticipated, so I am sincerely grateful to Elise for guiding me through the maze with such intelligence, patience, sensitivity to everyone's preferences, and good humor.

Closer to home, thank you to my two wonderful kids, Jack and Maria, for never complaining when I seemingly disappeared for hours (days?) at a time to work on the book and for bringing so much laughter and joy into our home. I'm so proud of both of you. And finally, none of this would have been possible but for the love, generosity, understanding, and unwavering intellectual and emotional support from my partner in all things, Lisa.

ABOUT THE EDITOR

Stephen J. McGovern is an associate professor in the Political Science Department at Haverford College. He is the author of *The Politics of Downtown Development: Dynamic Political Cultures in San Francisco and Washington, D.C.*, and is the coauthor with Charles C. Euchner of *Urban Policy Reconsidered: Dialogues on the Problems and Prospects of American Cities*. He has also published numerous articles in journals such as *Urban Affairs Review*, *Journal of Urban Affairs*, *Journal of Urban History*, *Housing Policy Debate*, *Journal of Planning History*, and *Journal of Planning Education and Research*. He earned a Ph.D. in Government from Cornell University and a J.D. from New York University School of Law.

To Jack and Maria

Chapter 1

Cities in a Global Era

Introduction

In a book about power and politics in American cities, it is appropriate to ask at the very outset whether cities are relevant in an age of globalization. And even if cities do fulfill a significant function in the transnational flow of capital, labor, and goods, how important is political decision making at the local level? When key actors in the global economy sometimes seem to operate above nation-states in an autonomous and even unaccountable manner, do ordinary citizens living and working in cities have much influence over the big issues that shape their lives? Put simply, does urban politics still matter?

While sweeping societal change would at first blush seem to undermine the place of cities as economic and political entities in the global era, many scholars have contended just the opposite. Saskia Sassen notes the paradox that notwithstanding the worldwide dispersal of economic activities, there has been a simultaneous concentration of economic activities in cities, which have become strategic nodes in the implementation and maintenance of the global economy. In her view, cities are the spatial hub of leading economic sectors such as finance and specialized services for firms. Moreover, they continue to be the primary site of production processes, organizational arrangements, and physical infrastructures. Sassen claims that it is no coincidence that with the rapid growth of the globalized knowledge economy based on information, technology, and innovation, we have seen the marked expansion of cities throughout the world.[1]

However, urbanists agree that globalization has had varying impacts on American cities. In **Reading 1-1**, Richard C. Longworth provides a typology of cities based on their capacity to connect to the global economy. At the top of the hierarchy are the so-called global cities, such as New York, Los Angeles, and Chicago, which are major centers of business and finance, technology, culture, and power and thus are directly linked to global networks trading in capital, information, and expertise. A second tier of cities is somewhat less tied to the world economy, but places like Indianapolis, Denver, and Portland continue to serve as thriving regional centers. All these cities lure newcomers searching for good jobs and economic opportunity. A third tier consists of former industrial dynamos such as Detroit and Akron that lack both strong links to the global economy and regional stature; their future prospects are uncertain at best.[2]

Other commentators believe that changes in society threaten the long-term vitality of all but the most prosperous cities. They point to the revolution in digital communications and how it has transformed how we think about space, community, and urban life. The Internet makes it possible for individuals, groups, and firms to conduct their affairs from virtually anywhere, rendering the age-old need for people to cluster together in urban places much less compelling.[3] But perceptive observers such as Joel Kotkin contend that the digital era may actually be a boon for cities. He argues that while individuals and businesses are increasingly able to settle wherever they wish, their locational decisions hinge more than ever on the particular amenities of any given area. Ironically, "the more technology frees us from the tyranny of place and past affiliation, the greater the need for individual places to make themselves more attractive." As city leaders endeavor to enhance their appeal to mobile citizens and firms, at least some urban places (and Kotkin refers to a wide variety of such places, not just large cities) can be expected to grow and thrive.[4]

Indeed, some cities in the United States are now growing and flourishing—for the first time in many decades. After nearly a century of declining populations, a trend that seriously undermined the economic, social, and cultural condition of urban America, demographers report that the populations of many cities have stabilized while some have experienced a small but significant increase.[5] The recent influx of middle-class people with resources and skills, including young college graduates, empty nesters, and immigrants, has revitalized neighborhoods and boosted the overall prospects of cities. At the same time, African Americans and immigrants have been moving at higher rates to the suburbs. Alan Ehrenhalt calls these recent demographic shifts "The Great Inversion," and he considers their implications in **Reading 1-2**.

Why have many American cities undergone a resurgence after several decades of decline? One explanation is that some cities have benefited by offering an attractive urban lifestyle. Richard Florida has influenced numerous city planners by emphasizing the practical advantages of implementing policies designed to nurture a lively social environment and a culture that promotes diversity, tolerance, and cosmopolitanism. Such a milieu, Florida maintains, entices a "creative class" of well-educated and highly skilled individuals whose collective presence within urban neighborhoods and business districts serves as an incubator of ideas, innovation, and productivity.[6] Cities that have cultivated such environments—Boston, Seattle, and Austin, Texas, to name just a few—have witnessed healthy population spikes and vigorous economic growth.[7]

However, it would be highly misleading to proclaim any kind of broad-based urban renaissance throughout the United States. First, many cities have not experienced a revival. Some cities have been unable to connect to the global economy or develop robust sociocultural spheres that might attract middle-class newcomers. Such places continue to suffer desperate levels of unemployment and poverty.[8] Second, even among those cities with noticeable gains, the fruits of growth have been uneven. While some sectors of the population have prospered, others have been left behind. Inequality has become one of the defining characteristics of American cities, as elaborated by Alan Mallach in **Reading 1-3**.[9]

What is to be done? Cities continue to be the focal point of many of the nation's most intractable problems. Along with the deepening chasm between the affluent and the poor, urbanites confront racial and ethnic tensions; underfunded and underperforming public schools; a dearth of decent, affordable housing; and the stubborn persistence of gangs, drugs, and violent streets. Responding effectively to such issues is the challenge of urban governance. But are the problems too immense for cities to make real headway, especially in the global era? Or are cities uniquely positioned to make significant contributions? After all, citizens are closest to government at the local level and thus have the best opportunity to get directly involved in the political process and shape public policy. The potential for democratic engagement is arguably greatest within the nation's towns and cities. But what factors work against an energetic and active citizenry? And even assuming an engaged public, what forces limit the capacity of city governments to act productively?

This book explores these fundamental issues of urban politics. A core assumption is that much can be learned from the past, and so we begin our analysis by examining how cities were governed at the birth of the United States and then proceed chronologically. In the process, we will discover how cities have evolved over time and how citizens and their leaders have utilized political power to try and improve their societies. Many approaches to urban governance have been employed with varying degrees of success. For our purposes, the "visions of politics" that have emerged at different times and places provide valuable lessons for the contemporary period. By the end of this narrative, we hope that you will have developed the knowledge and skills to judge for yourself how cities today might go about pursuing a brighter future.

Notes

1. Saskia Sassen, *Cities in a World Economy*, 4th ed. (Thousand Oaks, CA: Pine Forge Press, 2012); Saskia Sassen, *The Global City: New York, London, Tokyo* (Princeton, NJ: Princeton University Press, 1991).

2. For another ranking of global cities, see "Global Cities, Present and Future: 2014 Global Cities Index and Emerging Cities Outlook." A.T. Kearney. www.atkearney.com/research-studies/global-cities-index (Accessed February 28, 2015).

3. Refer to William Mitchell, *City of Bits: Space, Place, and the Infobahn* (Cambridge: MIT Press, 1997).

4. Joel Kotkin, *The New Geography: How the Digital Revolution Is Reshaping the American Landscape* (New York: Random House, 2000); see also Edward Glaeser, *Triumph of the City: How Our Greatest Invention Makes Us Richer, Smarter, Greener, Healthier, and Happier* (New York: Penguin Press, 2011).

5. William H. Frey, "Will This Be the Decade of Big City Growth?" www.brookings.edu/research/opinions/2014/05/23, May 23, 2014 (Accessed February 28, 2015).

6. Richard Florida, *The Rise of the Creative Class: And How It's Transforming Work, Leisure and Everyday Life* (New York: Basic Books, 2002); see also Jane Jacobs, *The Economy of Cities* (New York: Random House, 1969). For a critique of Florida, see Jamie Peck, "Struggling with the Creative Class," *International Journal of Urban and Regional Affairs*, 29 (4), 2005.

7. In explaining the appeal of some reviving cities to the creative class, other urbanists emphasize not so much the recent policy initiatives influenced by Richard Florida but the long-term evolution of economic development and growth management strategies that shaped a city's cultural economy. Carl Grodach, "Before and After the Creative City: The Politics of Cultural Policy in Austin, Texas," *Journal of Urban Affairs*, 34 (1), 2012. Another study, in an even sharper departure from Florida, points to high levels of social capital to account for the rising fortunes of a rustbelt city. Meghan Ashlin Rich, "'From Coal to Cool': The Creative Class, Social Capital, and the Revitalization of Scranton," *Journal of Urban Affairs*, 35 (3), 2013.

8. Refer to Charlie LeDuff, *Detroit: An American Autopsy* (New York: Penguin Press, 2013); Sandra L. Barnes, *The Cost of Being Poor: A Comparative Study of Life in Poor Urban Neighborhoods in Gary, Indiana* (Albany: State University of New York Press, 2005).

9. See also Rowland Atkinson and Gary Bridge, eds., *Gentrification in a Global Context: The New Urban Colonialism* (New York: Routledge, 2005).

1-1 "Urban America: U.S. Cities in the Global Era"*

Richard C. Longworth

Journal of International Affairs

"Put the city up; tear the city down; put it up again; let us find a city."

Carl Sandburg[1]

This much we know for sure: cities are the future. Much was made of the recent demographic tipping point, when, for the first time in history, the population of cities and their suburbs accounted for more than half of humanity.[2] Cities are big and getting bigger. In the twenty-first century, cities are and will continue to be where the action is, where business is done, where ideas and innovations spring up, where arts and sciences proliferate. For better or worse, our future is urban.

How exactly our urban future will take shape remains an open question. Clearly not all cities will grow equally. Which cities will grow, which will shrink and why? Will urban patterns in the United States resemble those in Europe or, for that matter, in Asia and Africa? Will most cities remain, as they have been in the past, centers of a limited geographic area, dependent on their physical environment? Or will globalization create a new class of cities, a sort of global Hanseatic League, increasingly divorced from surrounding hinterlands that may wither without them?[3]

What may be evolving is an urban-rural divide between wealthy cities participating in a new global hierarchy and the impoverished others, mired in the lowlands of a supposedly flat world. If cities aspire to global preeminence, they will need to provide the services and amenities for global citizens who, increasingly, can live anywhere.[4] But how will cities pay for these services and amenities? This may be the biggest question of all.

These questions apply to all cities, from London to Lagos to Los Angeles to Lahore. However, globalization affects each in different ways and will assign each of them different roles, just as the industrial era in the United States assigned different roles to Boston, Pittsburgh and Omaha, all of which developed in the same era but evolved differently. Chongqing—booming, thrusting, raw, ambitious—calls itself the Chicago of China.[5] But the Chicago it resembles is the lusty industrial Chicago of the late nineteenth century, not the relatively sedate business center of the early twenty-first century, which has ceded industrial prominence to the Chongqings of the world to establish a new postindustrial niche in the global economy.[6]

One urban size does not fit all, and any attempt to squeeze New York and Nairobi into one grand theory is flawed from the start. Let us focus then on the futures of American cities, a more modest task made easier by the fact that their futures are beginning to be revealed.

Early U.S. Cities and Their Economic Roots

Almost all American cities, like cities throughout history, developed to serve some economic purpose. Invariably, that purpose was place-bound. A port, a mine, or a river provided the *raison d'être* for many cities.[7] Steel mills took root near raw materials. Auto plants grew up near steel mills. Stockyards depended on fields of grain to feed livestock and on railroads to

Source: Richard C. Longworth, "Urban America: U.S. Cities in the Global Era" from *Journal of International Affairs*, vol. 65, no. 2, Spring/Summer 2012, pp. 97–103, 104–110. Reprinted with permission from the School of International Affairs, Columbia University.

*Some text and accompanying endnotes have been omitted. Please consult the original source.

ship them. Oil cities relied on nearby oil fields while trading posts lay astride trade routes. The economic needs that created cities in turn created jobs, and where industries were robust, the workers stayed to build places to live. In some cases these settlements produced small towns comprised of just a few houses, stores, a school and a church, all serving local farmers or miners. In other cases, these economic epicenters spawned great cities—civilizations that grew to a million people or more—with museums, symphonies and universities, all dependent on that original economic *raison d'être;* the port, the steel industry or the auto plants.[8]

Thus grew Chicago, New Orleans, Detroit, Miami, Houston, San Francisco and Boston.[9] Not all great cities grew near water—Atlanta and Denver are landlocked—but most lie near oceans, rivers or the Great Lakes, because trade goods traveled by water, not by rail or air. For all of these major urban centers, a place-based economic role brought them into being and defined their identities.[10]

But in economics, nothing lasts forever. Trade routes shift. The raw materials necessary for mighty industries become scarce or expensive and the labor necessary to run those industries becomes cheaper elsewhere. Cities that rely on location for their livelihoods may discover over time that the fonts of their economies have vanished. When economic opportunities arise elsewhere, how can these cities sustain themselves? This is the question facing many American cities today. Born and reared in the industrial era, they find themselves cast adrift in today's global era, forced to reinvent themselves or wither.

Still, if the global future is urban, the United States is already there. While half the world's population now lives in cities, no less than 82 percent of Americans live in metro areas, generating about 86 percent of the nation's jobs and nearly 90 percent of its gross domestic product.[11]

While geography may not be irrelevant in the information era, it is certainly less important. Increasingly, modern global cities exist in the context of global networks overseeing vast supply chains, far-flung human resources and borderless capital flows. The old assets—iron, coal, water, oil—no longer justify their existence. The future of these cities depends on their ability to attract creative talent and wokers [*sic*]

capable of succeeding in a twenty-first century knowledge economy.[12]

Globalization Reshapes Urbanization

The international economy has been with us for centuries, since before Marco Polo made his trade mission to Cathay and before the Lombard banks began financing Europe in the Middle Ages.[13] This economy ultimately helped shape America. Later, the industrial era marked the ascendance of many U.S. cities. In the postindustrial period, going back about forty years, American cities were transformed, some declining and others gaining strength. We have seen the culmination of this process in the exodus of heavy industry from the Rust Belt to the Sun Belt, with population booms in once-remote cities like Phoenix and Las Vegas and with the new eminence of intellectual centers like Raleigh-Durham, Austin and Seattle.[14]

However, the modern wave of globalization is even more recent. It began with the rise of post-Mao China in the 1980s but flowered after the collapse of Soviet communism in 1989. Around this time, India and Brazil emerged from decades of self-imposed isolation and dirigisme.[15] Suddenly, 1.5 billion workers in developed countries found themselves competing with 2 billion new workers entering the global economy. Since these workers came from relatively poor countries, they did not bring much new money with them, which meant more than twice as many workers were competing for roughly the same amount of money. This had the effect of devaluing labor, which explains the availability of cheap goods in American stores, the offshoring of much of American industry and the decline in American wages. At the same time, new inventions like the Internet made it easy to tie the previously distinct first, second and third worlds into one big economy.[16]

All of a sudden, Chicago and Detroit no longer competed with Atlanta or Birmingham. American cities found themselves competing instead with Shenzhen or Jakarta. Whole industries relocated and, in time, services began to follow. Still in its infancy, this new wave of globalization proved as raw as the industrial era was twenty years after James Watt first improved the steam engine.[17]

Quickly, the service economy gave way to the knowledge economy, with its emphasis on innovation, information, technology and speed. With luck, the refinement of the globalized economy in the coming decades will produce the widely shared economic decency that eventually flowed from the industrial era. But human capital is not what it once was, and the rewards of the knowledge economy are unlikely to be distributed in the same manner they were when industry reigned. Some cities will win and others will lose. This may sound too competitive—too much of a zero-sum game—but the rapid decline of many American cities shows that this is a reality, and there are few indications suggesting the future holds otherwise.[18] Throughout history, cities have flourished or faded according to their ability to cope with new challenges and reinvent themselves. The great cities—London, Paris, Mumbai, Beijing, Cairo—have reinvented themselves many times. Other once-great cities, like Ur and Nineveh, are now no more than ruins, or have declined into backwaters like Venice and Bruges. We can see the same process happening in many U.S. cities today.

New Urban Power Structures

American cities, now and in the future, can be sorted into three categories: global cities, regional capitals and the rest. Global cities are the handful of metropolises that are intimately linked to and help guide the global economy. Regional capitals are healthy cities, magnets for their immediate heartlands, but are weakly linked to the global economy. The rest are mostly the losers, neither healthy nor global, caught in a downward spiral that may be terminal.

Global cities are the true metropolises of a globalizing world. A 2010 listing of the mightiest global cities compiled by the Chicago Council on Global Affairs and A.T. Kearney describes global cities this way:

These are the ports of the global age, the places that both run the global economy and influence its direction. The cities where decisions are made, where the world's movers and shakers come to exchange the latest news and information. . . . They are where you go to do business, yes, but also to see the greatest art, hear the greatest orchestras, learn the latest styles, eat the best food and study in the finest universities. They have global corporations—this goes

without saying. But they also have think tanks, jazz bars and broadband. In a word, they have clout. . . . To be a global city, then, is to belong to the urban elite. Global cities are not always the most beautiful or the most pleasant. Almost by definition, they are busy, crowded, noisy, even frantic. But they are crowded with those who are creating the future, noisy with the clash of deals and ideas, frantic in the race to stay ahead. They have money and power. They know where the world is going because they're already there.[19]

Ranking global cities has become something of an intellectual party game. For the 2010 study, A. T. Kearney and the Chicago Council scored cities using various metrics within five categories: business activity, human capital, information exchange, cultural experience and political engagement.[20] Arbitrary criteria, perhaps, but the results tallied with other similar rankings. New York, always America's most international city, is the leading global city, followed by London, Tokyo and Paris, bunched at the top in a class by themselves.[21]

Of the sixty-five global cities listed, eight other American cities made the cut. Chicago ranked sixth and Los Angeles seventh, in the company of Singapore, Sydney, Seoul and Hong Kong. San Francisco ranked twelfth, the smallest city to rank so highly, followed by Washington, a one-industry town that made the list only because that industry is the world's most powerful government. Boston was nineteenth, Miami thirty-fourth, Houston thirty-eighth and Atlanta fortieth.[22] If the list were longer, Minneapolis, Dallas, Denver and Seattle might also have been included.

The United States led the global rankings with nine cities on the list, while China had six. These nine, already off and running in the global race, are poised to remain global cities in the coming years, though their rankings may slip as they are surpassed by rising Asian cities. All of these global U.S. cities face three crucial questions: What do they have to do to stay competitive, and how will they pay for it? How do they identify—are they regional capitals, American cities, or global cities? Does the mere fact of having gone global give them more in common with cities around the world than with their national neighbors?

Regional capitals are second-rank cities, often prosperous, cultured and pleasant, but more plugged into their immediate surroundings than the wider world. This list includes Indianapolis, Columbus, Little Rock, Oklahoma City, Salt Lake City, Richmond, Kansas City and Portland, among others. These cities are often state capitals, dominating their states and drawing in much of its talent and money, but not much else.[23]

Then there are the rest—winners of the industrial era who are losers in the global era. Many have tried desperately to hold onto the industry that made them rich, but have failed. This failure is evident in their drastically reduced populations, high dropout and poverty rates, depressed housing prices and a "brain drain" that is depleting their intellectual capital. These cities are disproportionately in the Rust Belt—the large manufacturing cities of old—including Detroit, Cleveland, St. Louis, Cincinnati, Rochester, Syracuse, Buffalo and Dayton, as well as Birmingham and New Orleans in the South.[24]

Whether these cities have a future remains an open question. One school of thought argues that when a city has lost more than half its population, it has tipped into inevitable decline.[25] All of the cities mentioned in the previous paragraph stood tall in the industrial age, and to this day they boast the trappings of great civilizations—renowned orchestras in Cleveland and Detroit, professional sports teams in Buffalo and Cincinnati, respected universities in St. Louis and Rochester. These assets stir the civic breast but do not contribute to the economic viability of a city.

It is hard to see what some of the old Rust Belt cities, especially Detroit, can do to reverse their downward fortunes. Most continue to bleed residents: Detroit lost no less than 25 percent of its population in the first decade of this century and Cleveland's population fell by 17 percent.[26] Cities in the knowledge economy need educated and skilled workers; Detroit, Cleveland and the like attract mostly the poor, uneducated and unskilled, guaranteeing that these cities will remain poor, uneducated and unskilled.

However, no matter how decrepit at their cores, these cities are still surrounded by decent suburban areas, though poverty is beginning to overwhelm some inner-ring suburbs.[27] But can a large urban region thrive without a solid core? The answer may be no. The Detroit and Cleveland metro areas, along with Pittsburgh, Buffalo, Dayton and Flint, were among the only cities in the country to shrink in the last census.[28]

Size counts, incidentally, but it is not decisive. If population were all that mattered for global-city status, noisome megacities like Lagos, Mexico City and Kolkata would rank at the top instead of at the bottom. The same holds true in America. Until the housing bubble burst, Phoenix and Las Vegas were two of America's fastest growing cities. But neither had the attributes—human capital, business connections, culture, political clout, great universities—that make a global city.[29] . . .

Global versus Regional Cities

Global cities, which have the size and complexity to be great metropolises of the global economy, are at the center of the American urban future. Some people deny that global cities exist, just as they deny that there is any more to globalization than an intensification of the trade practices of old.[35] But the latest wave of globalization has ushered in a new economy based on cutting-edge technology and a reordering of the very nature of work. It has reversed trade routes, restructured patterns of production worldwide and employed billions of people who, two decades ago, played no role at all in the world economy.

Global cities are the command points of this new economy. Globalization has scattered not only manufacturing but many functions, like sales and research, across the global landscape, and global cities serve as the headquarters for the coordination of these activities. As University of Pennsylvania urbanologist Witold Rybczynski has said, paraphrasing Columbia University sociologist Saskia Sassen: "Global cities . . . are a select group of cities that play key roles in the world economy, particularly as regards the cross-border flow of capital and goods."[36] They are the focal points not only of industries and businesses, but of the many global experts—lawyers, accountants, consultants and the like—who serve them.

The way in which the reins of the global economy have been gathered in the hands of global cities is unexpected. Not so long ago, we thought that digital communications would enable us to escape the crush and noise of cities by taking our computers and our business to the mountains or lakes, where we could keep in touch with the world while enjoying the scenery and breathing fresh air. It has not worked out that way. As Sassen points out, global citizens need not only general information, available through their computers, but the latest information, the news of the next new thing—the sort of information that is only available face-to-face. Modern businesses need to move quickly and to have access to many strands of expertise all at once, in the same room, if possible. Despite the explosion in new communication technologies, business air travel between global cities has boomed, because global citizens have to go to these cities just to stay in the loop. As Sassen writes, global cities "have become home to complexes of producer services."[37]

But this does not tell us which cities will continue to lead. Given the rankings by A.T. Kearney and others, New York, London, Paris, Hong Kong, Tokyo and perhaps Shanghai will remain preeminent. Beyond that, we can only look at present trends. As Rybczynski says, again citing Sassen, global cities "have become global centers for finance, servicing, and management, and . . . the network that binds them together is a trans-national one. In a sense the global cities could be said to form a sort of loose medieval league, but on a global scale."

It is the great survivors like New York that are pacing the new global economy. In the process, they are becoming something new, as Rybczynski says; not autonomous city-states, like the Hanseatic ports, but not strictly national either. They belong to nations and live under their laws and regulations. But at the same time, they are part of a global network that "appears to be supra-national, unaccountable to national control, and strikingly autonomous."

"Global cities," says Rybczynski, "are something less than city-states, but something more than prime cities."[38] Until now, great American cities, apart from New York, have been regional centers. Boston defined New England. Atlanta characterized the South, Chicago the Midwest, and Los Angeles was the epitome of California. Now, increasingly, these cities are global city-states, in the hermaphroditic sense described by Rybczynski. They are the centers of regional markets and still sell to those markets. But as the industry and farming that once supported towns

and smaller regional cities shrivel, money, power and talent flow to the cities.[39] Regional capitals often rely on their states for sustenance. Many lie at crossroads served by interstate highways, making them easily reachable from the rest of the state, and most identify with their states and major institutions in a way that global cities like New York or Chicago do not.

This would seem to give these cities a secure future as the hubs of their respective states, attendant to global trends but not dependent on them. But this is not the sinecure it seems to be. Both American states and their governments are facing an uncertain future, and any city that depends on their state may be in for a rough ride. Across the country, rural areas are emptying out. Nonurban economies are generally losing ground to urban economies.[40] Young people are moving to these regional capitals, putting pressure on public services. At the same time, state governments are falling deeper into debt, eroding their ability to pay for these services. Moreover, many state governments are still dominated by rural interests who are reluctant to spend tax money on urban needs, especially given rural difficulties.[41]

As state governments become increasingly unviable, it would make sense for regional capitals to join forces and leverage their strengths, as is taking place now with the Southern Growth Policies Board.[42] Perhaps these cities will be subsumed into a larger region, a networked "megalopolis."[43] Other candidates for regional networks might include the so-called BosWash corridor, the industrial belt stretching from Milwaukee through Chicago to Pittsburgh, the Piedmont region from Charlotte to Atlanta or the Interstate 35 corridor from San Antonio to Kansas City. But so far, these "megapolitan" regions—a term coined by Robert E. Lang and Dawn Dhavale to describe "integrated networks of metro and micropolitan areas"—owe more to geographers' whimsies than to any economic or political reality.[44]

William Cronon's magisterial book, *Nature's Metropolis*, describes the century-long process in which the Midwest created Chicago by sending it the produce and raw materials that fueled the city's industries and markets, while Chicago in turn created the Midwest by stoking the demand for these goods.[45] Without Chicago, there would be no Midwest, and vice versa. The symbiosis that once characterized such relationships has ended.

At the same time, cities remain tied to their states both legally and financially. Tax money flows from cities to state governments and comes back as financing for urban services. State governments retain much control over city financing, taxation, infrastructure, zoning and schools. But state deficits are forcing cities to seek new ways to finance themselves, making them less beholden to their states, even indifferent to them.[46]

Will cities break away from their states and regions? Not entirely. The federal structure dictates that some ties remain. But states will become less able to meet the needs of their biggest economic engines, and cities with global ties will look elsewhere for sustenance. In addition to the wealth that comes from global partnerships, cities are already seeking new local revenue sources in user fees or through the privatization of public services. But can they find enough, in increased fees or taxes, to pay for the services and amenities that they will need to remain global cities?

Global cities will always attract some businesses and people who can afford to live anywhere. But can these cities, still home to the working and middle-class populations from the industrial era, raise costs without pricing out all but the rich? We already see this happening in cities like New York and Chicago, where wealthy citizens of all nationalities are moving back into the city centers, colonizing neighborhoods once left to the poor and forcing the poor farther out.[47]

What then can we predict about the futures of individual American cities? Which cities will become global and which will not? New York is and will continue to be the quintessential global city. Twice assaulted in the past decade, first by al Qaeda and then by the mortgage meltdown, it has emerged strong and has not been chastened. It remains the true capital of America, its intellectual center, its newsroom, its atelier, its tastemaker. It even wants to be its scientific center.[48] This goal may or may not be realized, but it reveals the sheer ambition of the city.

Most global cities like New York have diversified economies; if one sector dips, other sectors pick up the slack. This raises the question of whether one-industry cities may have put too many eggs in one economic basket. In Europe, the unraveling of the European Union and the devaluation of the euro could foil the global ambitions of Frankfurt and Brussels.[49] Houston is America's oil capital; as the United States weans its economy from carbon-based fuels, will Houston fade? Los Angeles is more than a one-industry town, but the entertainment industry looms so large there that one wonders if it has much to sustain it if that industry should decamp, as Richard Florida has suggested it could.[50]

Chicago frets incessantly about whether it really is a global city (it is, according to the Kearney rankings) and whether it can remain one. The city and its new mayor, Rahm Emanuel, are struggling with a huge civic deficit from the productive but expensive reign of Emanuel's predecessor, Richard M. Daley. It is working to fix a broken school system, to reconfigure its aging public transport system to meet the new needs of a shifting population and to retrofit O'Hare Airport, the city's shabby gateway, to keep Chicago on the itinerary of global travelers.[51]

Chicago, like many American cities, once thrived because it was a key part of the world's most dominant national economy. As America's clout in the world declines, just being an important American city won't be enough in the future. Instead, these cities must shine on their own, as Singapore has done for years and as London has learned to do since Britain's preeminence has declined.

Atlanta, the capital of the Sun Belt, would seem to be a candidate for membership in the global urban league. When the economy shifted to the Sun Belt, Atlanta blossomed. It is still a major center, home to the world's busiest airport. But globalization will challenge its economy. Atlanta's population growth seems to have stalled and, after a half-century of breakneck expansion, it faces severe infrastructure problems, especially in transport. In addition, Atlanta is challenged by a galaxy of growing southern stars—for instance, Raleigh-Durham, North Carolina, Nashville, Tennessee and Charlotte, North Carolina—in a way that midwestern Chicago is not.

Many smaller cities occupy powerful niches in the global economy. Boston, San Francisco, Minneapolis and Seattle all have the brainpower and information-based industries to thrive in a global economy. But San Francisco's cost of living may soon be too high to compete, and the others need serious infrastructure improvements—Minneapolis's bridges, Boston's airport and Seattle's highways, for example.[52]

Conclusion

So far the pull of geography has worked to turn some regional capitals into global cities. Cities like Sydney, Toronto, Johannesburg and São Paulo rank as global cities simply because they dominate substantial regions or countries.[53] The same geographic dominance has propelled the growth of regional metropolises like Chicago, Atlanta and, to a lesser degree, Minneapolis, Ironically, these regional centers have achieved some of their growth at the expense of their less-urban environs.[54] We do not know if this process will continue or, as hinterlands empty out, if regional dominance will decline in importance.

In the end, we come back to the need for global cities to attract talent: educated and creative people of all nationalities who can live anywhere but will settle where they can best use their intellect and skills. This migration is already happening to newer, creative cities like Seattle and Minneapolis and to older, educated cities like New York and Chicago. These cities no longer compete just with each other, but also with global cities like Paris, Shanghai and Mumbai. If their feet rest on American soil, their heads are in cyberspace. If their history is local, their future is global. Not all cities can manage or afford to maintain this balance.

Globalization is brand new. For American cities and their residents, the second act of history has just begun.

Notes

1. Carl Sandburg, "The Windy City," *Slabs of the Sunburnt West* (New York: Harcourt, Brace and Company, 1922), 12.
2. "2009 Revision of World Urbanization Prospects," news release, UN Population Fund, 25 March 2010, http://esa.un.org/unpd/wup/Documents/WUP2009_PressRelease_Final_Revl.pdf.
3. The Hanseatic League was founded by German merchants in the thirteenth century to protect their trading rights and goods. The League controlled much of Northern Europe's international commercial activity into the fifteenth century. *Encyclopaedia Britannica Online*, s.v. "Hanseatic League," accessed 1 February 2012, http://www.britannica.com/EBchecked/topic/254543/Hanseatic-League.
4. Richard C. Longworth, *Caught in the Middle: America's Heartland in the Age of Globalism* (New York: Bloomsbury USA, 2008), 10–13.
5. See, for example, James Kynge, *China Shakes the World: A Titan's Rise and Troubled Future—and the Challenge for America* (New York: Houghton-Mifflin, 2007), 25.
6. Longworth, *Caught in the Middle*; "Chicago in the 1890s," University of Chicago Library, 4 June 2010, http://www.lib.uchicago.edu/e/su/maps/chi1890.
7. Longworth, *Caught in the Middle*, 156–57.
8. Ibid.
9. Though San Francisco's rise was place-based, the Gold Rush, which initiated a population boom and an influx of migrants, made its urbanization trajectory unique. "The excitement, and enthusiasm of Gold Washing still continues—increases," *California Star*, 10 June 1848, http://www.sfmuseum.net/hist6/star.html.
10. Longworth, *Caught in the Middle*, 156–57.
11. Percentages reflect 2010 data. The World *Factbook*, s.v. "North America: United States," Central Intelligence Agency, accessed 19 January 2012, https://www.cia.gov/library/publications/the-world-factbook/geos/us.html; *U.S. Metro Economies: GMP and Employment Forecasts* (Lexington, MA: IHS Global Insight (USA), June 2011), 2, http://www.usmayors.org/metroeconomies/2011/rport.pdf.
12. Adam Davidson, "Small Cities Feed the Knowledge Economy," *Wired*, 31 May 2011; "The Four Pillars of the Knowledge Economy," World Bank, http://go.worldbank.org/5WOSIRFA70.
13. D. G. H. Thorpe, "A history of English clearing banks," British Banking History Society, 2010, http://www.banking-history.co.uk/history.html.
14. The Rust Belt describes areas in the midwestern and northeastern regions of the United States where industrial manufacturing was once prevalent. The Sun Belt refers to regions in the southern United States that made agriculture a major industry, to which manufacturing has now moved. Ramit Plushnick-Masti, "Shrunken Rust Belt city shows grit," Associated Press, 14 March 2008, http://www.thestar.com/Business/article/346139; Longworth, *Caught in the Middle*, 2, 162, 164, 166, 208.
15. "Globalisation and Emerging Economies," OECD Policy Brief, March 2009, 2, http://www.oecd.org/dataoecd/35/34/42324460.pdf; Jake Berliner, "The Rise of the

Rest: How New Economic Powers are Reshaping the Globe," (white paper, NDN, Washington, DC, 23 April 2010), http://ndn.org/essay/2010/04/rise-rest-how-new-economic-powers-are-reshaping-globe.

16. Longworth, *Caught in the Middle*, 78–79.

17. Ibid., 8.

18. Richard Florida, *The Flight of the Creative Class: The New Global Competition for Talent* (New York: HarperCollins, 2006); Longworth, *Caught in the Middle*, 162.

19. *The Urban Elite: The A.T. Kearney Global Cities Index 2010* (Chicago: A.T. Kearney, 2010), 1.

20. Ibid., 2.

21. Ibid., 3. The Knight Frank Global Cities Survey ranks New York, London, Paris and Tokyo as the top four cities, in that order. The same four cities led a ranking by PricewaterhouseCoopers and the Partnership for New York City based on "power indicators." "Tales of the Cities," *The Wealth Report 2011*, Knight Frank, http://www.knightfrank.com/wealthreport/2011/global-cities-survey; *Cities of Opportunity* (New York: PricewaterhouseCoopers-Partnership for New York City, 2011), http://www.pfnyc.org/reports/2011-Cities-of-Opportunity.pdf.

22. *The Urban Elite*, 3.

23. Based on the author's reporting between 2006 and 2011.

24. Dana L. Mitra and William C. Frick, "Civic Capacity in Educational Reform Efforts: Emerging and Established Regimes in Rust Belt Cities," *Educational Policy* 25, no. 5 (September 2011): 810–43.

25. See, for example, a book by Albuquerque's former mayor. David Rusk, *Cities Without Suburbs: A Census 2000 Update* (Washington, DC: Woodrow Wilson Center Press, 2003).

26. Richard C. Longworth, "Shrinking City Syndrome? It's Catching," *Midwesterner* (blog), 12 May 2011.

27. Jennifer Agiesta, "Stark divisions found between Detroit and its suburbs," *Washington Post*, 6 January 2010.

28. Longworth, "Shrinking City Syndrome?"; "State and County QuickFacts," U.S. Census Bureau, accessed 31 January 2012, http://quickfacts.census.gov/qfd/states.

29. Longworth, *Caught in the Middle*, 162–63.

35. Reflects the author's original reporting and analysis.

36. Witold Rybczynski, "Cities and Globalization," *Wharton Real Estate Review 8*, No. 1 (Spring 2004): 100.

37. Saskia Sassen, "A Global City," in *Global Chicago*, Charles Madigan (Urbana: University of Illinois Press, 2004), 131.

38. The three preceding quotations are taken from Rybczynski, "Cities and Globalization," 100.

39. Richard Florida, "How the Crash Will Reshape America," *The Atlantic* (March 2009); *The Urban Elite*, 2.

40. "State Fact Sheets: United States: Population, Income, Food Insecurity, Education, and Employment," U.S. Department of Agricultural Economic Research Service, 17 January 2012, http://www.ers.usda.gov/statefacts/us.htm#pie; *U.S. Metro Economies*.

41. The *Urban Elite*, 2: Jon Bruner, "Interactive: Is Your State A Debt Disaster?" *Forbes*, 20 January 2010; Elena Moya, "$2tn debt crisis threatens to bring down 100 US cities," *Guardian*, 20 December 2010.

42. The Southern Growth Policies Board is a public policy think-tank formed by the governors of thirteen southern states to advance economic development through various public-private partnerships. "About Southern Growth Policies Board," Southern Growth Policies Board, accessed 8 March 2012, http://www.southerngrowth.com/about/about.html.

43. Robert E. Lang and his staff at Virginia Tech are the prime movers behind the megalopolis idea, though it was Jean Gottman who originally coined the term in 1961. Robert E. Lang and Dawn Dhavale, "America's Megapolitan Areas," *Land Lines* 17 (July 2005): 14.

44. Lang and Dhavale. "America's Megapolitan Areas," 1.

45. William Cronon, *Nature's Metropolis: Chicago and the Great West* (New York: W. W. Norton, 1991).

46. Moya, "$2tn debt crisis."

47. Rob Paral, *What Does the 2010 Census Tell Us About Metropolitan Chicago?* (Chicago: Chicago Community Trust, 2011), 10–18.

48. Edward L. Glaeser, "Done Right, New Applied cience Center for New York Makes Sense," *Economix* (blog), *New York Times*, 22 March 2011.

49. Author's opinion, based on experience living in Brussels and reporting from Europe.

50. Florida, *Flight of the Creative Class*, 17.

51. *The Global Edge: An Agenda for Chicago's Future* (Chicago: Chicago Council on Global Affairs, 2007).

52. Based on the author's own reporting in all of these cities.

53. *The Urban Elite*, 3.

54. Florida, "Crash Will Reshape America."

1-2 "The Great Inversion"

Alan Ehrenhalt

Governing

In the midst of the 1980s, at a time when poverty, violence and abandonment had settled over most of the big cities in America, the great urban historian Donald Olsen made an intriguing prediction. "If we are to achieve an urban renaissance," Olsen wrote, "it is the 19th-century city that will be reborn."

It was a cryptic comment, and Olsen is no longer around to be asked precisely what he meant, but he was not the only urbanist of taste and judgment who voiced similar sentiments. Jean-Christophe Bailly, the French architect and critic, looked at cities all across North America around the same time and declared that "the 19th century invented modernity, and it must now be reinvented to make up for the damage done by the systematic negligence of 20th-century urban planners."

Today, more than a quarter century later, at least a part of this vision seems to be coming true.

It would be absurd to make the claim that the great European cities of the late 19th century will reappear in this country in anything like their original form. No American city will create a *Ringstrasse* like the one that circled central Vienna. None could reproduce the city of London even if it wanted to. And it's impossible to imagine a central planner with the powers of Baron Haussmann in Paris (or even Robert Moses in New York) emerging anywhere today.

But it would also be a mistake to deny the relevance of these older cities to the evolving urban experience, or not to notice that Donald Olsen, hyperbole notwithstanding, was onto something.

American cities all but lost their street life in the last decades of the 20th century; anybody walking around downtown Philadelphia, Boston or Chicago after 5 in the afternoon found the sidewalks deserted and dangerous. Today, in various forms, street life is returning. One can walk down Michigan Avenue in Chicago or Walnut Street in Philadelphia long after dark and find them throbbing with activity.

Much of this activity, as in the Paris or Vienna of another time, is clustered around entertainment. In the 21st century, this is less likely to mean performances at an immense concert hall, although a few cities have built them, and more likely to mean plays at storefront black box theaters and live music coming out of the bars that line the street. Most of all, however, street life in the emerging city means restaurant life. Walk along Tryon Street in downtown Charlotte, N.C., that highly untraditional American city, and you will see diners at sidewalk tables on every block. There is little retail shopping in downtown Charlotte, but there are restaurants almost everywhere.

And there are cafés. One can make fun of the ubiquitous presence and the uniformity of Starbucks, but the fact remains that just 20 years ago, the idea of coffeehouses in urban centers seemed a quaint vision of the vanished past. Now one can walk into a Starbucks in the center of any large American city at 10 in the morning or 8 in the evening and find clusters of coffee drinkers deep in conversation, many of them lingering as much to talk as to consume. It is not going too far to say that Starbucks resurrected the coffeehouse experience in present-day America: Small independent cafés have returned to the street along with it. We have not recreated the *Ringstrasse* café, where raconteurs held forth for hours at a time—but we have taken a step in that direction.

Source: Alan Ehrenhalt, "The Great Inversion," *Governing*, 25 (7), April 2012. Reprinted with permission from *Governing* magazine.

We have also taken a step toward the urban diversity and tolerance that prevailed in European cities a hundred years ago. People with widely different backgrounds and modes of living come together on the sidewalks of Boston, Chicago, San Francisco and a growing number of other cities in ways that would have been unthinkable in 1980. American cities are also returning to diversity of use. The idea of zoning for segregation of uses is slowly dying in America. Virtually every city planning official is now looking for ways to promote mixed-use zoning, perhaps not the chaotic jumble of much of 19th-century Paris, but a mixture of uses nevertheless.

At the level of the metropolitan region, modern American urban patterns are coming to resemble older ones in a more dramatic fashion. For most of Western history, affluent people lived in the center of metropolitan areas. The latter half of the 20th century was defined by fast-growing suburbs and shrinking inner cities, where wealth moved to the periphery and poverty was concentrated close to the core. The 21st-century city will be defined by the opposite—affluent inner neighborhoods, striving and sometimes struggling farther-out neighborhoods. In short, American cities are undergoing a full-fledged demographic inversion. Midtown Atlanta, for example, is filling up with upper-middle-class professionals, both black and white, while exurban counties that were all but homogeneous white bastions of cul-de-sacs and shopping malls as recently as 20 years ago now have become magnets for immigration. Similar events are taking place in Boston, Chicago and Washington, D.C. Look closely at the changes under way in or near the center of these cities and the 19th-century flavor of 21st-century urban America becomes clear.

Sheffield is a quiet neighborhood three miles north of downtown Chicago. It is six thirty in the morning, and I'm sitting by the window at a bagel and coffeehouse just off the corner of Sheffield and Armitage, across the street from the Armitage elevated train station. Every few minutes a Brown Line train rumbles by directly overhead, its noise so consistent and regular that it feels like an icon of neighborhood life, not an annoyance of any sort.

Armitage Avenue is no Parisian boulevard; there are no boulevards in Sheffield, only business streets and residential streets. But the buildings are about the same age as those in central Paris. Nearly all of them were built between 1880 and 1910. The Argo Tea Café on the other side of the street reveals the date 1885 in large letters on the second story wall.

A parade of early risers marches down the street in front of me: joggers, men in suits on their way to the train, art students from nearby DePaul University carrying their supplies to the studio. It is the sort of diversity Jane Jacobs saw in Greenwich Village in the 1950s, a diversity of occupations, ages and daily schedules. There are people on their way to 9-to-5 jobs, others returning from night shifts, young singles who jog this route every morning, older people who cover the same route at a slower pace. The one thing you won't notice about Sheffield through the windows of the Chicago Bagel Authority may be the most important thing about the place. It is rich. Actually, very rich.

In 1970, Sheffield was poor, unstable, gang-ridden and dangerous to roam around in. But by the time the 2000 Census was taken in Tract 711, where comparatively modest old houses still fill the residential blocks north of Armitage, the median household income was $93,279. The median home value was $675,532. When mid-decade projections were released in 2007 by Esri, an independent demographic research company, the median household income was up to $133,535, and the median home price had surpassed $1 million. Gentrification is not a word that accurately describes Sheffield. It is a neighborhood of stable and substantial affluence where scarcely any of the people we normally consider gentrifiers can afford to live.

It is easier to demonstrate that Sheffield is rich than to explain why. "At first glance," the *Chicago Tribune* wrote in 2006, "it's hard to see why some of Chicago's most wealthy people have chosen this formerly nondescript area as their new enclave. It doesn't have a lake view. It isn't even that close to the lake." And the land is flat as a pancake.

In fact, Lake Michigan is a little more than a mile from the center of Sheffield, and one can walk there in half an hour at a leisurely pace. But few of the residents do that very often. There are other factors that clearly have something to do with what has happened— the 14-minute train ride to downtown, the presence of DePaul University, the tree-lined streets and pleasingly eclectic stock of houses—but none of these quite suffice as explanations. It is more instructive simply to say that Sheffield's current prosperity reflects a realignment of urban life.

This is a controversial subject. Free market purists argue that once the economic downturn ends, Americans will resume their 20th-century thrust outward and seek ever newer greenfield homes on plots of land further and further from the city, transporting themselves back and forth on longer and longer commutes by means of the automobile.

They have some statistics to back them up. One study in 2009 reported that only a small portion of Generation Y (or the Millennials, born roughly between 1980 and 1995) expressed a preference for urban living over a suburban mode of life. But there are equally compelling results on the other side. A competing study by the consulting firm RCLCO in 2008 revealed an almost precisely opposite result: 77 percent of Generation Y wanted to live some variant of the urban life. "Generation Y's attitudes toward homeownership have been changed by the housing crisis and the recession," the Urban Land Institute found in commenting on the RCLCO study. "The number of people trapped by underwater homes that cannot be sold and the millions of foreclosures are tempering their interest in buying their own homes and they will be renters by necessity rather than by choice for years ahead." In many cases, if not most, that means urban rather than suburban rental.

Between 1990 and 2007, central cities increased their share of housing permits within their metropolitan areas by more than double, the Urban Land Institute found. This continued after the housing recession caused the number of permits to plummet in the outer suburbs. What is more, statistics show, housing in cities and inner suburbs held their value during the recession far better than their exurban counterparts.

Where does the Millennial generation want to live? In many ways, this is the question that will determine the face of metropolitan America in the next 20 years. This seems to me a case in which common sense wins a battle of dueling statistics. Most of the major demographic trends going on right now work in favor of an urban preference, at least among a significant cohort of the emerging adult population—smaller households,

later marriages, decisions not to marry at all, decisions not to have children, the emergence of a huge and active baby boom population in its 60s and 70s—point to some form of reemergence of urban choice.

But suppose one grants many of the predictions made by those who attempt to debunk any significant back-to-the-city movement among the Millennial generation. The generation is simply so large—by one measure, 60 million to 70 million people—that even a respectable minority of this cohort seeking an urban life is bound to change American metropolitan areas dramatically.

In a poll cited by *The New York Times* in 2009, 45 percent of Americans between the ages of 20 and 35 said they would like to live in New York City someday if they could. This is an absurdly large number of people—well more than 20 million, in fact. It's a safe assumption that, other than the ones who already live in New York, not too many of them will ever get there. So the poll does not offer much insight into the future demographics of the nation's largest city. But it says a great deal about the values, tastes and wishes of an enormous cohort of American young people.

There is a thirst for urban life among Millennials. It shows up in polls, in anecdotal conversation, in blogs and other casual writing. It is not based primarily on watching television shows such as *Friends* or *Seinfeld*, though those should not be discounted. It is based on an inchoate feeling that the cul-de-sac suburbia in which millions of them grew up is a cul-de-sac in more ways than one: It cuts off not only streets, but also diversity and the casual outdoor life crucial to meaningful human sociability.

Once again, it is necessary to say that outer suburbs are not going to empty out in the coming generation. They remain home to millions of current residents with families who like the space, are concerned about safety and want to stay put; newcomers to this country who are determined to avoid the crowding they encountered in other parts of the world; and poorer people who simply are able to find acceptable housing on the periphery that is not available in the center.

The inhabitants of the center cities of the 21st century will be largely those with money—those who have the greatest choice about where to live. Those who inhabit the periphery will be for the most part those for whom prices in the center are prohibitive. As the Urban Land Institute concludes, "Once the economy recovers and household formation resumes, the demand for urban housing will greatly outstrip the supply."

For students of cities and community, perhaps the final intriguing question is what will happen to the structure of urban life in general. Will the enhanced street vitality and personal contact that is already occurring in many of America's largest cities bring about a return to the casual social cohesiveness that Jane Jacobs praised in 1961 in *The Death and Life of Great American Cities?* Or will the immense changes in human technological communication diminish the ultimate importance of the street life that seems to be a magnet for so many youthful newcomers in the first place?

When Jacobs wrote her book, there were really only two methods of real-time personal communication. One was the telephone. The other was face-to-face human interaction. The world of communication that the microchip has wrought is so fast and so current as to make detailed explanation unnecessary. The person we run into on the street possibly several times a day—the contact that Jacobs prized—has been compromised by iPads, cellphones, email, social media and other tools Jacobs could not imagine in her wildest dreams. To put the question simply, will technology be a substitute for the regular social contact of Jacobs' day, or will it provide a crucial supplement? As anyone who walks down an urban street knows, a significant proportion of the cellphone conversations that take place are simply logistical arrangements, as people seek to reveal to others where they are in space and how soon they can meet each other at an agreed-upon location. Social media are, among other things, ways for large numbers of people to settle on mutual congregating spaces instantly. The more that people are enabled by technology to communicate with one another while remaining physically solitary, the more they crave a physical form of social life to balance out all the electronics. They are settling in cities—those that have a choice—to experience the things that citizens of Paris and Vienna experienced a century ago: round-the-clock street life, café sociability, casual acquaintances they meet on the sidewalk every day, local merchants who recognize them. This is the direction we are heading in, even if we do not get there for a while.

The 23-year-old student glued to a laptop computer in a corner café in a Chicago neighborhood like Sheffield should not be seen as too different from the Viennese reading his newspaper in a café on Vienna's *Ringstrasse* in 1910. He remains a social animal. He merely expresses the balance between his sociability and his individuality in a different, 21st-century way.

1-3 "The Uncoupling of the Economic City: Increasing Spatial and Economic Polarization in American Older Cities"*

Alan Mallach

Urban Affairs Review

Introduction

America's older industrial cities have in recent years become the subject of a growing number of books (Dewar and Thomas 2012; Mallach 2012b; Ryan 2012) and a steady flow of articles, reports, case studies, and newspaper accounts. While rich in descriptions of historic decline, current physical conditions, and prescriptions for changing those conditions, few of these address the dramatic changes that have taken place in many of these cities in recent years. That is not to suggest that there has not been an extensive and valuable literature on urban change in recent years; the process by which cities, not just in the United States but throughout the developed world, have been transformed by population and economic change has been widely addressed, including important works by Sassen (1991), Smith (1996), and Hackworth (2007). At the same time, significant gaps remain, particularly in our understanding of how those changes are spreading from global cities to what might be called the American hinterland, in particular the secondary cities—historically dominated by manufacturing—such as Detroit, Baltimore, and St. Louis which have experienced dramatic losses in population and economic activity since the end of World War II, sometimes termed *shrinking cities* (Oswalt 2006) or, more recently, *legacy cities* (American Assembly 2011).

This article will attempt to describe those changes, focusing on a particular dimension of change that has received relatively little attention; specifically, how change is affecting the distribution of jobs and job-holders in these cities and the implications of those changes for the economic conditions of these cities' residents. In broad terms, I argue that the economic trends during the past decade within these cities have followed a bipolar pattern in which unprecedented growth in small parts of the cities is paralleled by an ongoing and even accelerating pattern of economic decline elsewhere, and that the decline is being most profoundly experienced by these cities' African-American communities, leading to growing racial as well as spatial disparities.

While the redevelopment of shrinking cities has always been uneven, the past decade has seen an increasingly dichotomized pattern of revival and decline, further exacerbating the economic, spatial, and racial divides that have historically characterized these cities, undermining both the narrative of urban triumphalism exemplified by Grogan and Proscio (2000) and Leinberger (2008), and the parallel opposite narrative of continued decline and decay, reflected most prominently in a cluster of books published about Detroit in recent years (Binelli 2012; LeDuff 2013, among others). This article will attempt to provide an initial framework for exploring these divides by focusing on the way in which patterns of job growth associated with revitalization, and the distribution of those who hold those jobs, have exacerbated rather than relieved inequities within cities.[1] My central proposition is that a spatial redistribution of jobs in formerly industrial American cities is taking place, which reflects a dramatic change in the

Source: Alan Mallach, "The Uncoupling of the Economic City: Increasing Spatial and Economic Polarization in American Older Cities," *Urban Affairs Review,* vol. 51, no. 4, July 2015. Reprinted with permission from SAGE Publications, Inc.

*Endnotes and references have been omitted. Please consult the original source.

relationship between the "economic city,"[2] the city as a locus of jobs and economic activity, and what might be called the "demographic city," the city as a residential community and the people who live there. I refer to this change as the "uncoupling" of the economic city.

The first section of this article will provide the framework for that analysis by describing the growing spatial divide in these cities, followed by a direct exploration of the changing distribution of jobs and jobholders in the reviving city, the findings of which form the basis for my proposition about the uncoupling of the economic city. From there, I look at the racial implications of these trends, focusing specifically on the growing disparities between white and African-American households, while a closing section offers some initial thoughts on the implications of the increasing bipolarity of these cities.

This article is based on preliminary findings from ongoing research in a cluster of 10 cities in the United States, which share two common features: sustained population loss of 25% or more from 1950 to 2000 and a 2010 population of 250,000 or larger. These include cities that are continuing to lose both population and jobs, such as Detroit and Cleveland, as well as a few whose populations have stabilized between 2000 and 2010 such as Philadelphia or Newark, New Jersey; most, however, continue to lose population. While recognizing the interrelationships between these cities and their suburban surroundings, and the significance of changes that cut across municipal boundaries, my focus is on the area within the borders of the central city, rather than metropolitan areas as a whole. In that light, it is worth noting that notwithstanding the recent and well-deserved focus on the growth in suburban poverty (Kneebone and Berube 2013), poverty rates and the social ills associated with concentrated poverty continue to remain far more pervasive in central cities than in their suburban rings, although many if not most metropolitan areas contain at least some suburban areas of high poverty concentration.[3]

These cities are more representative of the generality of American cities than are global cities like New York or the handful of other cities that have featured heavily in the gentrification discourse like Washington, D.C., or San Francisco. Large cities, like Chicago, Kansas City, and Minneapolis, to name but three, are

affected by the same trends, while many cities below my population cutoff point, such as Richmond, Virginia, or Jersey City, New Jersey, as well as even smaller cities, like Wilmington, Delaware, show even more pronounced patterns of spatial, economic, and racial polarization. While some still smaller cities may also be similarly affected, many of the large number of small shrinking cities—as well as many cities, particularly in the Northeastern states, which may not be shrinking but are similarly distressed[4]—are seeing fewer positive trends than the larger cities, so that these effects tend to be less pronounced.

The rising inequality in cities raised in this article forms part of the larger issue of the growth in economic inequality in the United States, reflected in scholarly literature (Saez 2013; Smeedling 2005) and in magazine articles and blogs (Hargreaves 2013; Krugman 2012, among others). This, along with increased inequality in the distribution of wealth (Keister 2000), has justifiably become a matter of increasingly intense public concern. While the dynamics I describe are clearly linked to that larger issue, they are both narrower and broader; I am concerned with how inequality is linked to the economic revival of cities, how economic changes parallel changes in the spatial organization of cities, and with the increasingly tenuous relationship of the urban population to their cities in those cities' role as economic entities.

In contrast to the effects of economic change on residential patterns, which are the subject of an extensive literature, these particular changes have been given less attention, having been noted in a few case studies of individual cities—see Wolf-Powers (2013) on New York City, Zimmerman (2008) on Milwaukee, Madison (2011) on Pittsburgh, and Baumgart and Scruggs (2013) on Wilmington—and having recently drawn the attention of Richard Florida and his Martin Prosperity Institute at the University of Toronto (Florida 2012).[5] They have not, however, been the subject of a systematic investigation. While this article can do no more than scratch the surface of such complex issues, I hope that by so doing, it will not only increase the understanding of the nature of these issues and trends but also foster greater awareness of how these trends are affecting the vitality of cities and regions in which millions of people live. These trends also have powerful implications for public policy at the federal, state, and local levels.

The Spatial Divide

The ideological as well as spatial tension between central city downtowns and neighborhoods has been a long-standing issue in American cities since the days of urban renewal if not even earlier (Bauman 1981; Fogelson 2001). The issue for most of the second half of the past century, however, was not that downtowns were prospering and neighborhoods were not. On the contrary, both were in decline, and the tension was over what priority to give the reinvigoration of downtowns versus other objectives more closely associated with social equity goals such as affordable housing or neighborhood revitalization (Keating and Krumholtz 1991). Well into the 1990s, the downtowns of most older cities, despite the addition of some new office buildings, shopping malls, and apartments, often heavily subsidized with public resources, shared, and even exemplified, the city's distress; the blighted and heavily abandoned downtown was a recurrent trope of the narrative of urban decline (Beauregard 1993).

This is no longer the case. Downtowns or central core areas in secondary cities that otherwise continue to lose population like St. Louis, Baltimore, and Cincinnati are thriving. Central core areas as I use that term here encompass not only these cities' traditional Central Business Districts (CBDs) but also the quasi-downtown areas, such as Pittsburgh's Oakland, Detroit's Midtown, or Cleveland's University Circle, that house these cities' major universities and medical centers, along with a small number of predominately residential areas usually adjacent to or closely linked to CBDs or university/medical complexes such as Cincinnati's Over-the-Rhine or the Central West End in St. Louis.

During the past decade, these areas have seen dramatic growth both in their populations and in their share of their city's population, jobs, and wealth. St. Louis' Washington Avenue, all but abandoned 20 years ago, now regularly prompts descriptions like this:

> If your image of shopping in downtown St. Louis conjures up images of dark empty streets and bargain shops with bars on the windows, then you haven't strolled down Washington Avenue

recently. Completely renovated and now a thriving entertainment district, Washington Avenue is also coming alive with a wide range of designer shops, furniture stores and art galleries.[6]

Midtown Detroit now boasts a Whole Foods Market to accompany the Starbucks that arrived a few years earlier.

The growth in single people and nontraditional households and the manner in which it has fueled central core revitalization in St. Louis, Pittsburgh, and many other cities have been widely celebrated (Bevilaqua 2013; Chang et al. 2013). There is growing evidence that a new generation, the so-called millennial generation, has an affinity for high-density urban living epitomized by areas such as St. Louis' Washington Avenue or Cleveland's Warehouse District (Breen and Rigby 2004; Norris 2012). That generation, and in particular the relatively highly skilled, college-educated members of that generation, has fueled the population growth and economic revival of the central cores of the cities discussed here (Cortright 2005). Most of these cities have seen a sharp increase since 2000 in their number and population share of college-educated adults between 25 and 34 (Mallach 2014). As these areas gain population and Whole Foods Markets, however, the cities taken as a whole continue to lose ground, showing significant increases between 2000 and 2010 in such measures as the number of vacant properties, the number of homeowners, or the percentage of households in poverty.

Many downtowns are gaining residents, while the rest of the city continues to lose population. The five downtowns shown in Table 1 added nearly 24,000 people between 2000 and 2010, for a growth rate of 28%. While these are not large numbers, it is worth noting that as these five cities as a group lost 167,000 people during the same period, downtown growth offset 15% of the population loss taking place elsewhere in the city.[7] With the notable exception of Philadelphia, whose downtown, unusual for American cities, has historically accommodated a large residential population, these areas had little or no residential base, at least since the late nineteenth century (Fogelson 2001).

These disparities are reflected in the spatial distribution of house values. . . . High value census tracts

Table 1 Downtown Population Change 2000–2010 in Selected Cities

City	Downtown Population 2000	Downtown Population 2010	Δn	$\Delta\%$
St. Louis	3,539	8,155	+4,616	+130.4
Cincinnati	5,538	7,397	+1,859	+33.6
Cleveland[a]	8,182	10,861	+2,679	+32.7
Baltimore	15,970	21,854	+5,884	+36.8
Philadelphia	53,216	62,004	+8,788	+16.5
Total	86,445	110,271	+23,826	+27.6

Source: U.S. Census 2000 and 2010.

Note: Designation of downtown tracts and block groups by author.

[a]Downtown and Cleveland Circle areas combined.

are concentrated in the central corridor, a narrow strip including downtown, the University of St. Louis, Barnes Jewish Hospital (a major research hospital), and a handful of adjacent neighborhoods such as the Central West End. North of the corridor, with the exception of a small pocket of gentrification immediately adjacent to downtown, market demand hardly exists. South of the corridor, a handful of strong market "pockets" are noticeable amid generally weak markets; the strongest is Lafayette Square, again adjacent to downtown. The median house sales price in 2012 was $142,000 in the central corridor, compared with $59,000 outside.

Although Delmar Boulevard—the northern border of the central core—is no longer the hard and fast line dividing white and African-American populations that it was for much of the past century (Gordon 2008), it is still a powerful boundary. Houses in neighborhoods south of the line often sell for $300,000 or more when they come on the market; north of Delmar, prices are little more than $10,000, and many houses do not sell at all and are eventually abandoned. Similar patterns, although not always as sharply demarcated, can be seen in the other cities.

This spatial disparity forms the geographic framework for the trends driving the location of jobs within the city. Although quantitative data are hard to come by

for earlier eras, it seems safe to say that from the late nineteenth century through the first two-thirds of the twentieth century, jobs were distributed widely across the city.[8] While downtowns were important job centers, they were only one of many; in 1970, less than 9% of the jobs in the city of St. Louis were located in the city's central business district. CBDs as job centers were often dwarfed by their cities' manufacturing sectors; Buffalo's Lackawanna Works and Bethlehem Steel in Bethlehem, Pennsylvania, each employed over 25,000 workers in their heyday. In Trenton, New Jersey, over 70 separate potteries or ceramic factories, distributed widely across the city, employed nearly 5,000 people in the early years of the twentieth century, a significant number in a city of less than 75,000 population (Potteries of Trenton Society 2001).

Universities and hospitals were modest employers, far from the behemoths they have become in recent decades. Secondary or neighborhood-level commercial nodes and corridors, which provided most city residents with their goods and services, were also a major source of employment until their decimation by suburban automobile-oriented facilities after World War II. While by the mid-twentieth century many suburban workers commuted to downtown jobs, particularly in cities like Philadelphia with strong regional rail networks, most of the cities' workforce was made up of local residents, often people who lived in the neighborhoods that surrounded the factories. In 1960, 91% of all job-holding residents of St. Louis reporting a place of work worked inside the city.[9]

As the factories have closed and secondary commercial districts have declined or disappeared, the relative persistence of downtown office employment coupled with dramatic growth of universities and medical centers has led to a spatial concentration of employment into the central core areas of the city, paralleling the increases in population, wealth, and property values in these areas. The St. Louis Central Corridor, which contains roughly 5% of the city's land area,[10] contained 51% of the city's jobs in 2011, a significant increase from 45% in 2002.[11] Table 2 shows similar data on job concentrations for 2002 and 2011 for selected cities. As the table shows, not only are jobs concentrated in the central core but also the level of concentration increased sharply between 2002 and 2011. In most cases, this represented significant net job growth in the central core taking place at the same time that jobs were disappearing at a comparable pace in the balance of the city; in Detroit, both areas declined, but the decline was far more precipitous outside the central core, thus increasing the central core job share and reinforcing the spatial divide. Jobs in the central core on the whole pay better, and demand more higher education, than jobs in the rest of the city, as shown for selected cities in Table 3.

The central core is not only gaining a growing share of the city's jobs but also a growing share of the city's jobholders, wherever they may work. Between 2002 and 2011, the number of jobholders living in 9 of the 10 cities dropped sharply. Reflecting the growing spatial divide, however, the resident workforce is growing in central core areas and declining elsewhere. Between 2002 and 2011, the number of jobholders living in St. Louis' central corridor increased by 17% or over 2,000, while the number of jobholders living in the city's much larger northside declined by 26% or over 9,000 workers.

The decline in both the city's worker base and its pool of traditional blue-collar jobs, coupled with the growth of jobs and workers in the central core, has led to growing economic inequality among urban families generally, as the number of households in the lowest and highest income ranges grows and those in the middle decline. Table 4 shows this pattern for Pittsburgh; from 1960, when 71% of all families could be considered to be in a broad "middle" range,

Table 2   Distribution of Jobs between Central Core and Balance of City for Selected Cities 2002 and 2011

City	Citywide Job Change 2002–2011	Central Core % of City Land Area	Central Core Job Change 2002–2011	Balance of City Job Change 2002–2011	% Change Central Core	% Change Balance	% of All Jobs in Central Core 2002	% of All Jobs in Central Core 2011
Cleveland	−6,106	5	+11,288	−17,394	+10.0	−11.6	48	54
Detroit	−44,278	2	−8,014	−36,264	−6.0	−25.3	43	48
Milwaukee	+550	4	+13,064	−13,614	+13.0	−7.7	36	41
Newark	−767	4	+3,512	−4,280	+6.2	−5.5	42	45
St. Louis	+1,757	5	+13,326	−11,569	+13.7	−9.8	45	51

Source: OnTheMap.

Note: Central core areas defined by author using OnTheMap interactive features.

Table 3   Characteristics of Workers in Central Core and Balance of City 2011

	% of Workers Earning $40,000+		% of Workers with BA or Higher Degree	
	Core	Balance	Core	Balance
Newark	72	49	38	27
Detroit	61	42	36	23
St. Louis	49	42	26	21

Source: OnTheMap.

earning between 50% and 200% of the citywide median income, that number had dropped to less than 57% by 2011. Over a period during which the city's population declined by 55%, the number of middle-income families (earning 100%–200% of the city median) dropped by 66%, from nearly 58,000 to fewer than 20,000 families. This growing inequality is driven to a significant degree by these cities' job trends.

The Uncoupling of the Economic City

The spatial redistribution of jobs in formerly industrial American cities reflects a dramatic change in the relationship between the "economic city,"[2] the city as a locus of jobs and economic activity, and what might be called the "demographic city," the city as a residential community and the people who live there. This is

most pronounced in the diminishing relationship between the city's jobs and its resident workforce. That workforce is shrinking, income disparities in the city are increasing, and the jobs in the city are increasingly held by commuters rather than city residents. As discussed below, these changes are disproportionately affecting these cities' African-American population.

A historical perspective can illuminate the magnitude of this change. Table 5 shows the relationship between three categories of central city worker over time: (1) people who both live and work in the city, (2) people who live in the city but work elsewhere, and (3) people who commute into the city from its suburbs. In 1960, although the postwar decline of the cities was already under way, the historic pattern in which the overwhelming majority of city residents both worked in the city and filled the majority of the

Table 4   Change in Distribution of Families by Income in Pittsburgh 1960–2011

	1960		2000		2011		Change in Families 1960–2011
Income Range	n	%	n	%	n	%	
<50% of city median	25,774	17.0	17,170	23.0	15,079	23.6	−10,604
50%–99% of city median	50,134	33.0	20,134	27.0	16,792	26.3	−33,336
100%–199% of city median	57,761	38.0	24,438	32.7	19,498	30.5	−38,623
200%+ of city median	18,205	12.0	12,966	17.4	12,498	19.6	−6,707
Total	151,874		74,708		63,867		−88,007

Source: 1960 Census of Population, 2000 Census; 2007–2011 Five-Year American Community Survey.

Table 5   Long-Term Trends in Jobs and Workforce 1960 to 2011

City	% of City Residents Working in City			% of City Jobs Held by City Residents			%Δ in City Residents Working in City		%Δ in Number of Commuters Working in City
	1960	1980	2011	1960	1980	2011	1960–1980	1980–2011	1960–2011
Baltimore	86.8	66.6	46.2	73.4	52.1	33.9	−31.2	−48.0	+92.5
Buffalo	NA	NA	45.2	NA	NA	29.9	NA	NA	NA
Cincinnati	87.9	68.0	42.3	63.8	43.1	22.8	−29.8	−43.4	+81.3
Cleveland	92.3	63.1	46.9	62.4	40.5	24.2	−54.8	−52.3	+11.5
Detroit	81.8	57.1	38.0	65.8	51.2	28.0	−53.7	−69.7	−30.2
Milwaukee	90.1	NA	52.9	74.5	NA	40.8	NA	NA	+83.7
Newark	64.0	NA	28.8	46.6	NA	17.4	NA	NA	+4.6
Philadelphia	91.8	79.4	63.5	76.4	69.1	52.7	−29.4	−30.7	+41.8
Pittsburgh	88.1	73.6	56.6	64.1	40.8	25.1	−31.7	−45.3	+98.9
St. Louis	91.2	67.0	44.1	58.7	37.1	24.7	−52.9	−52.8	−3.5

Source: 1960 and 1980 from U.S. Census of Population, 2011 from OnTheMap.

Note: 1980 Census data were unavailable for Newark and Milwaukee. Data were unusable for Buffalo (data are provided at Standard Metropolitan Statistical Area (SMSA) level, and Buffalo–Niagara SMSA contained two central cities making it impossible to separate Buffalo data).

jobs that the city offered was still largely intact. With the exception of Newark, 80% or more of city-resident jobholders in the 10 cities worked in the city where they lived; on average, they filled roughly two-thirds of the jobs in the city. At least 25%, and in some cases over 40%, of all of the jobs in each city were manufacturing jobs.

By 1980, these cities had undergone traumatic waves of depopulation, demographic change, and deindustrialization; predictably, the role of city residents in the city's economy had declined, yet despite the damage of the 1960s and 1970s to these cities' fabric, the decline was not precipitous. In most cases, two-thirds or more of city residents still worked in the city and filled roughly half of the jobs in the city. Since the 1980s, even as many of these cities have begun to revive their economies and, at least in relative terms, stabilize their populations, the number of city residents working in the city, however, has continued to decline at a rate comparable with that of the period of

these cities' greatest overall economic and population loss. This drop has been far greater than the decline in the total number of jobs in the city and greater than the simultaneous decline in the number of city residents working in the suburbs.

As the number of city residents in the workforce generally and those holding jobs in the city in particular have both declined, the number of suburban commuters to city-based jobs has increased, often in substantial numbers, nearly doubling between 1960 and 2011 in four of the nine cities for which data are available. By 2011, the great majority of jobs in all of the cities except for Philadelphia were held not by residents but by workers who live outside the city and commute to work in the city; 71% of all the jobs in the other nine cities were filled by commuters and only 29% by city residents, a reversal of the historic pattern.

The number of commuters holding jobs in the cities has grown by an average of greater than 10% since 2002. As the cities were not growing jobs to any meaningful extent—only 2 of the 10 showed more than nominal growth in jobs between 2002 and 2011—this growth reflected a zero sum relationship with the resident workforce; during the same period, the number of city residents holding jobs in the city dropped by nearly 180,000 or nearly 17%. This reflects a decline not only in the number of residents working in the city but also in the absolute size of the resident workforce, as the number of residents working outside the city also declined in 7 of the 10 cities, but at a lower rate.

Although it is a subject that requires further investigation, it is likely that the growing share of urban workers reverse-commuting to the suburbs reflects the greater number of low-skill, but also low-wage, jobs being created in the suburbs, in such areas as retail trade, fast food restaurants, or eldercare, as in nursing homes and assisted living facilities. Support for this proposition comes from OnTheMap data that show that city residents working outside the city earned consistently lower wages than those working in the city, as well as that the percentage of workers with BA or higher degrees is consistently higher in central cities than in their surrounding metropolitan areas. This is in marked contrast to 50 years earlier, when city residents working in the suburbs earned substantially more than those working inside the city.

Overall, the number of active workforce participants living in the 10 cities dropped over the past decade at a pace considerably faster than the decline in population; while the cities lost 8% of their population between 2000 and 2010, they lost nearly 16% of their resident workforce between 2002 and 2011. Pittsburgh was the only city to see any growth in the relative size of its resident workforce compared with its total population, while Philadelphia's job base remained more or less stable relative to its population.[12]

As the city's resident workforce has shrunk, the city's employers are becoming progressively less dependent on that workforce as a source of people to fill their jobs. As Table 6 shows, the job base in all 10 cities substantially exceeds the size of the resident workforce; taken as a whole, they show a ratio of 1.48 jobs for each resident worker, with 3 cities—Cincinnati, Cleveland, and Pittsburgh—with job/worker ratios close to or above 2.0. Instead of creating job opportunities for city residents, however, the pool from which employers fill these jobs, particularly those that pay well, is increasingly a suburban pool.

The uncoupling of the city's jobs from its population may be in part a reflection of a skills mismatch, as reflected in the disparity between the number of jobs held by college graduates and the share of college graduates in the resident adult population. It may not necessarily be the case that all of the jobs held by college graduates *require* that level of formal education; as has been suggested elsewhere, employers may be taking advantage of weak job market conditions to upgrade the skill levels of their workforce, crowding out less educated workers who might have filled these positions in years past,[13] or college graduates having difficulty finding jobs in their fields are taking jobs that do not require a degree; a recent study found that that was true for 4 out of 10 new graduates (Stone, Van Horn, and Zukin 2012). At the same time, as jobs increasingly concentrate in education, health services, and other white-collar and professional categories, much of the disparity may reflect actual job requirements.

The skill mismatch varies widely from city to city. The gap is modest in Pittsburgh and only slightly greater in Cincinnati; it is pronounced, however, in many cities—most notably Cleveland, Detroit, and Newark—where the percentage of jobholders with college degrees is roughly three times the percentage of adult city residents with college degrees. The apparent absence of a mismatch in some cities is misleading, however, as it fails to recognize the educational disparity between white and African-American adults in these cities. It is more accurate to say that there is no skill mismatch in cities like Pittsburgh and Cincinnati between the jobs and the city's *white non-Latino* population. The mismatch between the city's job base and its African-American population, however, as will be discussed later, is large and growing. The skill mismatch is far from a complete or even satisfactory explanation, however; the share of suburban workers in these cities' goods-producing sector (essentially, manufacturing and construction), where formal education is a far less important condition of employment, is comparable with and often higher than their share of the total job base.[14]

Shifts in the city's economy away from manufacturing to a new economy rooted in higher education and health services have brought significant growth to these

Table 6 Job Inflow/Outflow Trends

City	Number of Jobs in City			Number of Commuters Holding Jobs in City			Number of Residents Holding Jobs in City			Total City Residents Working (Whether Inside or Outside City)		Jobs/Workers Ratio 2011
	2002	2011	%	2002	2011	Δ	2002	2011	%Δ	n2011	%Δ 2002–2011	
Baltimore	298,539	301,928	+1.1	175,465	199,562	+13.7	123,074	102,366	−16.8	221,496	−17.1	1.34
Buffalo	140,587	134,427	−4.4	88,447	94,241	+6.6	51,140	40,186	−21.4	88,947	−13.3	1.58
Cincinnati	213,424	199,550	−6.5	159,008	153,989	−3.2	64,416	45,561	−29.3	107,808	−23.1	1.98
Cleveland	262,586	256,480	−2.3	179,684	194,320	+8.1	82,902	62,160	−25.0	132,526	−26.5	1.98
Detroit	276,083	231,805	−16.0	160,666	167,010	+3.9	115,417	64,795	−43.9	168,628	−42.6	1.64
Milwaukee	276,906	277,251	+0.1	145,939	160,061	+9.7	114,934	117,190	+2.0	223,573	−10.5	1.24
Newark	135,466	134,699	−0.6	105,593	111,225	+5.3	29,873	23,474	−21.4	81,550	−8.1	1.66
Philadelphia	571,150	624,801	+9.4	238,619	294,518	+23.4	332,521	328,283	−1.3	516,937	−0.9	1.10
Pittsburgh	245,289	266,933	+8.8	174,068	199,942	+14.9	71,216	66,961	−6.0	118,451	−3.7	2.07
St. Louis	215,229	216,986	+0.8	148,264	163,402	+10.2	66,965	53,584	−20.0	121,579	−14.3	1.77
10 cities	2,635,259	2,644,860	+0.4	1,575,753	1,738,270	+10.3	1,052,458	874,560	−16.9	1,781,495	−15.6	1.48

Source: OnTheMap.

cities' central core areas, but that growth has been paralleled by continued erosion of jobs and workforce attachment in much of the rest of the city, reflecting the uncoupling of the city's newly emerging economy from the city's residents. Whether a function of the increased educational requirements for participation in the city's workforce, which have rendered a growing share of the city's population less competitive for the jobs that are available, or for other reasons, the workforce that supports central core job growth is largely, and increasingly, suburban. This is taking place at the same time as the city's resident workforce—whether employed inside the city or outside—is shrinking faster than its population, reflecting the growing marginalization of large parts of these cities' populations. The growing impoverishment of the urban population does not reflect the absence of jobs in the city where they lived; it reflects the growing disconnect between the cities' population, particularly their African-American population, and the jobs that are there.

The Growing Racial Divide

The growing economic divide in older American industrial cities is in many respects a racial divide. While this divide has always been a reality of urban America, over the past decade it has grown wider rather than diminishing. The affluent in-migrants who are repopulating city downtowns and other parts of the central core are predominately white; at the same time, these same cities are seeing a significant attrition of their African-American middle class. The size of the black population, either citywide or in many sections of the city, is declining, and the remaining black households are increasingly likely to be poor or near-poor.

The increase in the racial divide can be seen vividly in the dramatic disparity between white and African-American income growth during the past decade, as shown in Table 7. African-American income growth lagged white income growth in all 10 cities, in most cases by significant margins; as the table indicates, white households saw net income growth in constant dollars in 4 of the 10 cities, while their income growth significantly outstripped the national average in 3 more. African-Americans in all 10 cities saw their median income decline in constant dollars, with those declines pronounced in all cities except for Newark and Baltimore.[15] This growing income disparity is *not*

the continuation of an ongoing trend but reflects the reversal of a widespread trend which had previously led to a narrowing of the gap between white and African-American household incomes. Between 1990 and 2000, the racial income gap narrowed—in some cases significantly—in 8 of the 10 cities, only to widen precipitously in the subsequent decade. . . .

While some households undoubtedly experienced income declines during the decade, the decline in the incomes of African-American households is too pronounced to be credibly accounted for by changes taking place within a static pool of households. Rather, it appears to be heavily driven by the acceleration in the movement of middle-class African-American households from the cities to the suburbs during this past decade. Although this is not a new phenomenon, earlier commentators tended to focus on movement within the city to more historically upscale white neighborhoods (Winsberg 1985) or on the effect of migration on the suburbs (Wiese 2004). Although recent trends in Black migration have received only limited scholarly attention (Clerge and Silver 2012), they have been described in numerous journalistic accounts; in addition to detailed reporting from Philadelphia (Ferrick 2011; Mallowe 2011) and Detroit (Kellogg 2010), a web search identified similar accounts from many other cities, including Birmingham, Dallas, Los Angeles, Memphis, and Oakland.

The existence of this trend is borne out by Table 8, which compares the change between 2000 and 2011 in white and African-American families and nonfamily households (mainly single individuals) as a whole with the change in families and nonfamily households earning $50,000 or more (in 1999 dollars) in 4 of the 10 cities. While the number of Black families in all four cities declined during the decade, the number with family incomes above $50,000—a rough surrogate for middle-class status—dropped far more rapidly. While the number of Black families in Cleveland declined by 18%, the number of Black families with incomes above $50,000 dropped by over 40%. The disparity by income is even more pronounced for nonfamily households.

Many white families also continue to leave the cities. Their numbers, including many working-class survivors of these cities' industrial heyday, are also declining. The data presented in Table 8, however, show sharply different overall migration patterns for

Table 7   Percentage Change in Median Income for White and African-American Households 1999–2011

	All Households (%)	White Households (%)	African-American Households (%)
Baltimore	33.3	54.3	28.1
Buffalo	23.2	37.2	18.2
Cincinnati	15.6	31.9	7.7
Cleveland	5.9	7.9	0.7
Detroit	−5.6	0.7	−7.1
Milwaukee	11.3	20.7	9.6
Newark	32.6	33.2	30.7
Philadelphia	20.2	34.8	14.8
Pittsburgh	30.0	36.5	8.5
St. Louis	26.7	40.5	14.8
The United States	25.6	27.0	21.1

Source: 2000 Census and 2007–2011 Five-Year American Community Survey.

White and African-American households. While African-American out-migration is disproportionately concentrated among higher-earning families, White out-migration is more mixed. While White out-migrants are likely to be replaced by younger, affluent White households, middle-income Black out-migrants are being replaced, if at all, by lower-income households, including particularly large numbers of low-income nonfamily households or single individuals. As a result, in three of the four cities shown in Table 8, a growing share of both White families and nonfamily households is in the middle or upper-income brackets, while the opposite is true of Black families and, even more strongly, Black nonfamily households. As the middle continues to shrink, the economic gap between the conditions of White and African-American households continues to grow.

The income gap is becoming a chasm in the cities which have seen the greatest central core revitalization, such as Pittsburgh and St. Louis, compared with Cleveland, where both White and Black populations are seeing their middle-class share decline. Many of the

10 cities are seeing significant White in-migration; as Table 9 shows, the average annual in-migration of White non-Latino households from outside the state into Baltimore, Cincinnati, Pittsburgh, and St. Louis between 2007 and 2011 exceeded 4% of the total white population base, and in 6 of the 10 cities exceeded 5,000 per year. Conversely, in only 2 cities did African-American out-of-state in-migration exceed 2% of the black population base, Newark and Pittsburgh. White out-of-state in-migration—measured as a percentage of the city's same-race population—exceeded African-American in-migration in *every* city.

A further widening racial divide, which may be even more important in its long-term implications, is that of educational attainment. The relationship between educational attainment and economic achievement has been widely noted (Kodrzycki 2002 and others), while the powerful association between educational attainment and both income and unemployment rate has been well documented (Day and Newburger 2002). The gap in educational attainment between White and African-American households in

CHAPTER 1: CITIES IN A GLOBAL ERA   27

Table 8 Change in Income Distribution by Race for Families and Nonfamily Households 2000–2011 in Selected Cities

	Cincinnati		Cleveland		Pittsburgh		St. Louis	
	2000	**2011**	**2000**	**2011**	**2000**	**2011**	**2000**	**2011**
White households (HHs)								
Families								
%Δ families 2000–2011		−20.3		−26.9		−17.0		−15.2
%Δ families >$50,000 2000–2011		−19.2		−37.8		−12.7		−4.8
% families >$50,000	52.0	52.8	36.2	30.8	44.6	47.0	44.3	49.7
Nonfamily households								
%Δ nonfamily HHs 2000–2011		−14.2		−15.1		−3.8		−3.2
%Δ nonfamily HHs >$50,000 2000–2011		−9.7		−25.3		+3.3		+29.3
% nonfamily HHs >$50,000	22.2	23.3	18.2	16.0	18.2	19.5	18.8	25.1
African-American households								
Families								
%Δ families 2000–2011		−11.1		−18.0		−15.9		−15.4
%Δ families >$50,000 2000–2011		−28.3		−40.6		−28.7		−27.5
% families >$50,000	16.4	12.3	19.5	14.1	20.7	17.6	20.2	17.3
Nonfamily households								
%Δ nonfamily HHs 2000–2011		+4.4		+20.6		+7.8		+13.0
%Δ nonfamily HHs >$50,000 2000–2011		−27.9		−49.4		−31.5		−26.3
% nonfamily HHs >$50,000	9.9	6.8	11.2	4.7	9.3	5.0	10.5	6.9

Source: 2000 Census and 2007–2011 Five-Year American Community Survey.

Table 9   Average Annual Out-of-State In-Migration of White and African-American Population 2007–2011 (Number and As a Percentage of Same-Race Population Base) (See Note)

| | White Non-Latino Individuals | | African-American Individuals | | |
	n	% of Same-Race Population	n	% of Same-Race Population	% Ratio
Baltimore	8,326	5.8	4,271	1.3	.224
Buffalo	1,889	2.2	1,152	1.7	.773
Cincinnati	5,521	4.2	1,852	1.9	.452
Cleveland	2,313	2.0	1,975	1.2	.600
Detroit	2,218	1.9	3,725	0.7	.368
Milwaukee	5,834	2.9	2,095	1.2	.414
Newark	566	2.4	2,380	2.1	.875
Philadelphia	18,110	3.9	6,677	1.3	.333
Pittsburgh	7,696	4.5	1,487	2.3	.511
St. Louis	8,649	5.6	2,311	1.6	.286

Source: 2007–2011 Five-Year American Community Survey.

Note: Includes only migrants from outside state in which city is located.

Table 10   Change in Educational Attainment for White and African-American Adults 25+ 1990–2011

| City | White Non-Latino Adults % with BA/BS or Higher Degree | | | African-American Adults % with BA/BS or Higher Degree | | | Ratio | | |
	1990	2000	2011	1990	2000	2011	1990	2000	2011
Baltimore	23.5	39.6	47.1	8.6	8.8	13.2	0.366	0.222	0.280
Buffalo	18.2	23.0	30.4	10.1	10.2	12.6	0.555	0.443	0.413
Cincinnati	28.9	36.4	44.8	7.9	10.0	11.7	0.273	0.274	0.261
Cleveland	10.2	15.9	20.5	5.0	6.5	7.9	0.490	0.409	0.385
Detroit	12.1	21.8	18.6	8.4	10.1	11.6	0.694	0.463	0.618
Milwaukee	17.6	24.8	33.6	6.9	9.1	10.4	0.392	0.367	0.309
Newark	8.2	11.6	16.2	8.3	8.9	13.4	1.012	0.767	0.827
Philadelphia	19.0	22.8	34.7	9.1	10.3	12.2	0.479	0.452	0.352
Pittsburgh	22.6	28.9	37.5	8.8	12.0	13.6	0.389	0.415	0.363
St. Louis	20.2	28.2	42.0	8.0	8.8	11.7	0.396	0.312	0.279
The United States	21.5	27.0	31.3	11.4	14.3	18.0	0.530	0.530	0.575

Source: 1990 and 2000 Census and 2009–2011 3-Year American Community Survey.

the majority of the cities studied is a huge one, as shown in Table 10. For example, 42% of White adults in St. Louis have college degrees, compared with only 12% for African-American adults. In 6 of the 10 cities, the percentage of white adults with college degrees is higher than the national average for White adults; the same is true in no city for African-American adults. The only two cities to show no more than a modest attainment gap are Detroit and Newark; the narrower disparity in those two cities, however, rather than reflecting greater educational attainment by the city's African-American residents, is the product of *lower* educational levels for those cities' White adults. It is notable that these are two of the cities that have among the lowest levels of current White in-migration and which have seen less central core revitalization than the other cities studied.

While the presence of substantial racial disparities in educational attainment has long-standing historical roots, the *increase* in the size of the attainment gap over the past decade arguably has deeper implications for these cities' future. Although African-American adults in the 10 cities exhibited modest improvement in educational attainment between 2000 and 2011, their progress was far outstripped by much greater improvement in the educational attainment of white adults in these cities. With the exception of Detroit, Newark, and Baltimore, every city saw a widening racial educational attainment gap, in contrast to the nation as a whole, which saw a modest decrease in the gap during the same period. Newark and Baltimore were the only cities in which the gap narrowed between 2000 and 2011 as a result of more than modest progress by African-American households, although in Newark gains made up only a small part of the ground lost during the 1990s.

Looked at differently, between 2000 and 2011, the *rate of increase* in educational attainment for Whites exceeded the national rate for White adults in 9 of the 10 cities; for African-Americans, the same was true, outside of Newark and Baltimore, only in St. Louis. The gap grew significantly wider in St. Louis, however, during the decade because of the even stronger growth in educational attainment by White households. As these cities complete their shift to a postindustrial economy and the educational and skill demands of the emerging economic sectors continue to increase, lack of education becomes a permanent barrier to upward mobility and opportunity, which is likely to have long-term ramifications for these cities' racial divide.

Conclusion

While there is strong evidence of revitalization since 2000 in the central core areas of many cities, the evidence is equally compelling that this revitalization is resulting in little benefit to much of the rest of these same cities and that the residents of these cities, taken as a whole, may be losing ground economically. The city's job base is increasingly becoming concentrated in the central core, while those jobs are increasingly held by commuters rather than city residents. During this period, the size of the city's resident labor force has shrunk at a rate roughly double the overall rate of population loss. In effect, the economic city has become increasingly uncoupled from the people who live in the city, the demographic or social city.

The growing bipolarity of these cities is increasingly racial in character. While these cities have historically had social and economic gaps between their White and their African-American populations, these gaps have widened significantly during the past decade, as shown in two critical measures—increased disparities in income and in educational attainment. Middle-class Black families appear to be leaving the cities at an accelerating pace; although White families also continue to leave the city, not only are White out-migrants not disproportionately from the more affluent middle class, but many cities are seeing an influx of young, affluent White households that far outstrips simultaneous African-American in-migration. The outcome is an increasingly affluent and well-educated—and growing—White population in these cities, juxtaposed against an increasingly poor or near-poor African-American population lacking the education and skills to compete for an increasingly white-collar, college-degree-oriented job base clustered around downtowns and major educational and medical institutions.

Some of these cities are already seeing a reversal of the trend of many decades during which African-American populations grew and White populations declined. This may increase in coming decades, if economic growth continues to draw younger and predominately White professionals to these cities while safety concerns, poor school performance, and inadequate public services continue to draw predominately African-American families to the suburbs. This may lead in turn to the acceleration of a trend already widely visible, the impoverishment of many inner-ring suburbs. This trend is already well advanced in the suburbs of Cleveland, St. Louis, and other cities. This population reversal may also change the political and social dynamics of many cities, including a decline in the political base of Black elected officials. While that change may not have major practical implications in terms of the delivery of services or the allocation of resources, it is fraught with powerful symbolic significance.

These findings strongly indicate that revitalization, at least at the scale and of the character that is being experienced in these cities, does not confer citywide benefits; if anything, it may even redirect jobs, resources, and wealth away from large parts of the city, concentrating them in a smaller area and leaving the rest worse off than before. Large parts of all of these cities, even where downtowns are thriving, are market "deserts," where little sales activity takes place except for the occasional investor or speculator and where vacant lots and abandoned buildings are widespread. While this is not new, it is getting worse rather than better.[16]

The specter of a reviving core largely surrounded by poverty and blight is becoming a reality in many of these cities. To what extent such a spatial pattern is sustainable is an open question. If central core jobs, as well as the amenities associated with the core, grow significantly, housing demand may spread into adjacent or nearby areas; that appears to be happening to a limited extent in a few of the cities discussed here such as Pittsburgh or Baltimore. If that fails to happen, the boundaries between the central core and its surroundings are likely to harden—if not literally—in a manner not unlike the walls that protected the prosperity of the medieval city from its impoverished countryside. If it *does* happen, though, it may merely push the walls gradually outward, rather than materially changing the underlying bipolarity of the city.

From a social justice perspective, it would be appealing to be able to assert unequivocally that this emerging spatial pattern is *not* economically sustainable. While the pattern has not been in place long enough in the cities discussed here to answer the question, the experience of cities in other parts of the world, notably Latin America, suggests that an urban settlement pattern based on extreme spatial and economic inequality can persist seemingly indefinitely; whether that pattern is conducive to strong economic growth and vitality, however, is another matter. Benner and Pastor (2012) argued, based on a substantial body of economic research, that "doing good and doing well can go hand in hand" (p. 2).

Beyond the question of sustainability is that of equity or justice. This is, as Fainstein (2010) pointed out, "obviously value laden." From what might be considered a neoliberal perspective, there is arguably little to fault with the trends described in this article. The market is working. Jobs are growing in those areas with the greatest competitive advantage, while employers are maximizing the quality of their workforce by recruiting from throughout the region. Areas like Oakland in Pittsburgh or Cleveland's Warehouse District have become vibrant hubs of activity, while neighborhoods with competitive market advantages are reviving. The city is drawing young people bringing skills, talent, and energy, while African-American middle-class families are acting out of rational self-interest by leaving a city that, from their perspective, is no longer competitive with suburban jurisdictions with respect to the quality of services it offers or the economic and psychological costs it imposes.

From that perspective, therefore, one can argue that the trends described in this article are not only not a problem but also arguably positive, in that they foster a more efficient use of urban resources and maximize the competitive edge of those parts of the city that are indeed market-competitive. Although the neoliberal paradigm is popular with many private- and public-sector policy makers in twenty-first-century America, it is not the only framework through which one can look at a city. It privileges individual, free market activity over all other activities and fails to recognize the many complex ways in which the different sectors of a city, or a society, are interconnected. It attributes little or no value to core principles such as democracy, opportunity,[17] and social cohesion that have long been part of the American tradition. With Fainstein, I would argue that it is not enough. That perspective is inimical to the vision of a just city that she has articulated, with its focus on equity, diversity, and democracy. Indeed, these trends seem destined to lead to a heightened level of segregation, in which households are segregated by race, by economic status—which, within these cities, is increasingly a function of race—and potentially by demography or life cycle.

Moreover, the implications of these trends for the city as a physical environment, and for the quality of life of a large part of its resident population, are equally problematic. As the number of jobholders in the city declines and of that dwindling number, more and more are commuting long distances to the suburbs for what is more often than not low-paying work, the economic framework for the neighborhoods where they live is likely to weaken, bringing in its train declining property values, increased vacancy, and a deteriorating quality of life. There is strong evidence that this is indeed taking place.[18]

The trends described in this article contain significant implications for public policy, and yet may well be highly resistant to change, at least within the present economic and political environment. While a detailed discussion of policies is beyond the scope of this article, a few comments may be appropriate. Although measures to combat inequality are being widely discussed, many of the measures under consideration, such as increasing the minimum wage or adopting local "living wage" ordinances, while likely to benefit some individuals in low-wage jobs, would have little impact on the process of economic uncoupling taking place in these cities. Measures directly designed to increase access for city residents to jobs may hold more promise.

The most obvious recommendation would be for measures to build human capital and increase the competitive position of the urban workforce, focusing on improving educational outcomes and workforce readiness (Perna 2014).[19] Over and above that, one should advocate for concerted use of public policy levers to link the city's workforce to economic opportunity, reflecting the reality that much job and business growth in urban areas is furthered to varying degrees by public resources, investment, or outright subsidy (Weber and Santacroce 2007; Wolf-Powers 2013). Such strategies can include broad reframing of tax incentives away from broadly available and largely undifferentiated subsidies to targeted

approaches focusing on creation of local workforce opportunities, to specific programs, such as "first source" ordinances, mandating that employers receiving public benefits provide preferential hiring opportunities to qualified local workers. Alternatively, one might acknowledge the growing centrality of the suburban job pool for the urban workforce, and press for improved transportation linkages between urban workers and suburban jobs (Katz and Allen 1999).

One cannot be overly optimistic about the likelihood of initiatives of this sort coming into being, particularly in the older industrial cities discussed in this article. Despite the modest improvements resulting from uneven, limited revitalization, all of these cities are subject to severe resource constraints drastically limiting their ability to undertake new initiatives; moreover, while a uniquely situated city like New York may contemplate limiting business incentives or imposing obligations on its private sector, such steps are far harder for the strapped cities of the rustbelt, few of which are experiencing more than at best anemic job growth and which are in a weak competitive position in the global marketplace (Longworth 2008; Moretti 2012). Moreover, it is unclear that the political will is there to provide the resources any serious attempt to address this issue demands; notwithstanding the rise of mayors like Bill de Blasio in New York and Bill Peduto in Pittsburgh, neither the federal government nor more than at most a handful of state governments appear to have any interest in providing the financial support without which the best local ideas are likely to founder.

Finally, one must ask whether, assuming against all odds that truly effective, sustained strategies were indeed put in place that led to significantly greater opportunities for city residents to gain good, well-paying, jobs, whether those strategies would lead to inadvertent consequences; for the cities where those residents now live [sic]. In the absence of fundamental changes to the quality of life in their neighborhoods, it is not only possible but also likely that large numbers of them would move to the suburbs as their economic conditions improved, further hollowing out the central cities. That may be an acceptable trade-off for the improvement to their lives but cannot be considered an entirely positive outcome.

Conclusion

Public Policy Applications: Neighborhood Revitalization and Gentrification

Policy Then

Globalization and technological advances in communications have intensified the competition among cities for mobile wealth and talent. For many years, the conventional wisdom among economic development planners seeking to promote growth was to lure big employers such as large manufacturing firms and *Fortune* 500 corporations by offering inducements such as tax breaks, sweetheart land sales, and infrastructure improvements. Landing a giant company would then stimulate further investment by smaller industrial enterprises, corporate service firms, and restaurants and retail shops, all of which supply additional job opportunities and tax revenues.

More recently, an alternative approach to promoting economic growth in cities has emerged—one inspired by the economist Richard Florida. Rather than trying to attract new business firms, cities are focusing more on enticing desirable employees—highly educated and skilled individuals who are well endowed in the human capital valued by employers in the postindustrial, information-based economy. The assumption is that if cities succeed in accumulating a quality labor pool, substantial business investment will follow.

The capable employees so prized by companies and urban planners alike—Florida calls them "the creative class"—flock to cities that are rich in lifestyle attributes like a vibrant music scene, dynamic neighborhoods, and plentiful outdoor recreation. Add to the mix a multitude of places such as cafes, bookstores, and brewpubs that encourage social interaction within a diverse, tolerant, and cosmopolitan atmosphere and the result is an environment that breeds creativity, innovation, and productivity.

Economic development policy making becomes a matter of establishing social and cultural amenities in neighborhoods that will attract the creative class in droves—arts districts, lively entertainment corridors, cultural heritage museums, waterfront development, and recreational sports. Success stories are trumpeted in local, glossy magazines that celebrate the latest trendy neighborhood in a prospering city.

Policy Now

One serious limitation to this urban revitalization strategy is that some cities are far better positioned than others to appeal to the creative class. San Francisco, for instance, with its breathtaking natural beauty and large stock of lifestyle assets holds an enormous competitive advantage over an aging Rust Belt city with fewer social and cultural resources. The latter's construction of a multimillion-dollar, state-of-the-art performing arts center in an area pockmarked by obsolete factories and abandoned warehouses is not likely to be a sufficient incentive for the creative class.

Even where such policies have been effective, the price of success may be steep. When the creative class moves into a neighborhood that is increasingly perceived as a beacon of urban vitality, rising housing costs may drive older residents out of their homes. Small-business owners who had long served the neighborhood lose their leases and are replaced by upscale restaurants, wine bars, and boutiques catering to the more affluent newcomers.

It is a thorny problem for policy makers. On the one hand, struggling cities have an interest in fostering neighborhood revitalization that brings in new residents to bolster slumping retail businesses, reinvigorate street life and thus inhibit illicit activity, boost mass transit ridership, and strengthen the city's tax base to better support the many public services that benefit all citizens. On the other hand, if neighborhood revitalization is tantamount to gentrification—the displacement of long-time residents and business owners by a wealthier class of people—then is such a "success" a Pyrrhic victory?

Revitalized neighborhood of Little Five Points, Atlanta, Georgia

Additional Resources

Richard L. Florida, *The Rise of the Creative Class: And How It's Transforming Work, Leisure, Community and Everyday Life* (New York: Basic Books, 2002).

Lance Freeman, *There Goes the 'Hood: Views of Gentrification From the Ground Up* (Philadelphia: Temple University Press, 2006).

"International Making Cities Livable." An international movement devoted to improving the quality of urban life and enhancing community and civic engagement by reshaping the built environment. www.livablecities.org.

Loretta Lees, Tom Slater, and Elvin Wyly. *The Gentrification Reader* (New York: Routledge, 2010).

Joshua Long, *Weird City: Sense of Place and Creative Resistance in Austin, Texas* (Austin: University of Texas Press, 2010).

Mitchell L. Moss, "Reinventing the Central City as a Place to Live and Work," *Housing Policy Debate*, 8 (2), 1997.

"Northeast Passage: The Inner City and the American Dream." Documentary film about gentrification in Portland, Oregon.

Neil Smith, *The New Urban Frontier: Gentrification and the Revanchist City* (New York: Routledge, 1996).

Daniel Monroe Sullivan and Samuel Shaw, "Retail Gentrification and Race: The Case of Alberta Street in Portland, Oregon," *Urban Affairs Review*, 47 (3), 2011.

Sharon Zukin, *Naked City: The Death and Life of Authentic Urban Places* (New York: Oxford University Press, 2010).

Discussion Questions

1. Should local governments try to promote urban revitalization by attracting the creative class to their cities? If so, how?

2. What would motivate you to move to a particular city?

3. Is it possible to encourage neighborhood revitalization while controlling the negative effects? How might urban policy minimize the displacement of longtime residents and small business owners?

4. What can urban policymakers do about the increasing gap between the rich and the poor in American cities? What can urban policymakers do about other forms of inequality related to race and ethnicity, gender, and sexual orientation?

5. How meaningful is citizen participation in urban politics? Is it possible for ordinary citizens to exercise significant influence over public policy at the local level?

6. Who wields power in American cities?

Chapter 2

Politics in the Preindustrial City

Introduction

At the founding of the United States in the late eighteenth century, America was an overwhelmingly rural place. Most people lived on farms and made their living through agriculture. Cities existed—they could be found up and down the Atlantic seaboard—but they were small in terms of population and space. According to the nation's first census in 1790, Philadelphia was the largest city, with about 43,000 residents, followed by New York (33,000), Boston (18,000), Charleston (16,000), and Baltimore (14,000). Only 5.1 percent of the total population of the United States lived in cities with 2,500 or more residents. All cities were spatially compact and could be easily walked from end to end.[1]

Notwithstanding their small size during this time period, America's seaport cities played a crucial role in the nation's economic, social, cultural, and political life.[2] Most important, they functioned as commercial centers linking the vast rural hinterland and Europe. In an economy based on the buying and selling of goods, merchants occupied a pivotal position, organizing the sale of farm produce to city residents and the export of grains, tobacco, livestock, fish, furs, lumber, and minerals to Europe and the West Indies. They also oversaw the distribution of imported goods throughout the surrounding countryside and provided essential credit to farmers and other entrepreneurs. The vibrant commercial economy, in turn, spawned simple manufacturing, often housed in one-room workshops, that included milling, brewing, baking, weaving, and metal work. Much economic activity centered on the cities' bustling ports.[3]

Commerce was hardly new to the preindustrial cities of late-eighteenth-century America. Although history textbooks are full of uplifting stories about Europeans flocking to the New World to escape religious and political persecution, colonization and the establishment of colonial cities was first and foremost a business proposition. Even William Penn, who was intent on starting a colony in Pennsylvania where Quakers and other new settlers could worship freely, was a shrewd real estate developer. He carefully anticipated the future growth of Philadelphia by planning a grid of rectangular streets with a central square and other public parks, subdividing parcels of land to ensure an orderly and spacious development of homes and businesses, aggressively marketing the city as a beautiful "greene country town," and promising investors rapid increases in property values.[4] The pursuit of profit was thus a widely accepted principle underlying the foundation and evolution of American colonies and one that became firmly entrenched in the political culture of the preindustrial cities.

Early in the colonial era when cities were forming and commercial economies were taking off, newcomers to America faced both substantial risks in venturing across the Atlantic Ocean and embarking on a new life and genuine opportunities for advancement within a fluid, fast-changing environment. By the middle of the eighteenth century, however, socioeconomic mobility had stabilized and class divisions had become increasingly apparent based on one's occupation, residence, manner of dress, and mode of behavior.[5] Given their central position in the local economy, merchants were the most wealthy and powerful group. They lived in comfortable townhouses, and many owned country estates just beyond the city that served as a refuge from the summer heat and the periodic outbreaks of yellow fever. Artisans consisting of craftspeople, shopkeepers, and small merchants made up much of the middle class. They possessed a skill, owned property, and had acquired some education. The laboring class often toiled around a city's waterfront performing routine tasks associated with the commercial economy. This group was particularly vulnerable to devastating fluctuations in the economy that might cause poverty rates to soar above 30 percent. Most lived in overcrowded, wood frame houses on the periphery of the city, although in more desperate times, impoverished families took refuge in poor houses while prisons filled with debtors.[6] At the bottom of the social hierarchy were the free blacks and slaves (slavery remained common even in the northern cities in the late eighteenth and early nineteenth centuries). In Philadelphia, free blacks made impressive gains in climbing the socioeconomic ladder amid a period of tolerance and enlightenment during the years following the American Revolution. But increasing white resentment of black achievements eventually led to an upsurge in racist attacks, culminating in a series of race riots in the 1830s and declining fortunes for most black residents.[7]

Local politics largely reflected the stratified nature of urban society. Given their status, educational level, worldly experience, and cosmopolitan outlook, the merchant elite believed that it was only natural and proper that they should exercise power. By and large, the laboring people were inclined to defer to their judgment, allowing them to tend to the administration of municipal affairs. Urban governance in the preindustrial city was thus typically an elite-dominated phenomenon, as evidenced by Allan Tully's portrait of eighteenth-century politics in Pennsylvania in **Reading 2-1**.

But the norm of popular deference to upper-class rule would break down if the citizenry perceived that city leaders had abused their authority. Moreover, during periods of severe economic dislocation, artisans and workers would sometimes take to the streets to voice their discontent, and such mass-based protest might then influence electoral politics in ways that would advance the interests of the laboring classes.[8] The most dramatic departure from the standard condition of elite power occurred during the revolutionary era. Many city workers were suffering through a depression that rocked the colonies following the Seven Years' War in the 1760s and were, therefore, predisposed to participate in street protests. Merchants and professionals, who had borne the brunt of the British Crown's onerous tax policies, supplemented their opposition by instigating further political activism among the already agitated artisans and laborers. Over the years, many urban residents within the middle and lower classes got swept up by the revolutionary rhetoric and fervor of the era, a phenomenon that resulted, at least for a time, in broader participation in politics and more extensive use of governmental authority to advance equitable opportunities.[9]

As the revolutionary era faded, however, urban politics returned to its earlier form with prosperous merchants and professionals once again obtaining firm control over the reins of government. And when the elite did exercise authority, they tended to adhere to what Sam Bass Warner called a "privatist" vision of politics that embraced individual autonomy, a faith in the private sector, and a determination to limit the role of government (**Reading 2-2**). It was assumed that prosperity was more likely to be achieved within the mercantile city of the late eighteenth century if government remained constrained so that individuals would be free to seek private gain. In keeping with this ideal, urban governance often took the form of a committee system composed of the leading citizens who volunteered on a part-time basis to administer routine tasks such as street construction and maintenance, night-watch, and poor relief in the interest of promoting order, stability, and commerce.[10]

Economic growth after the Revolutionary War, along with the constant search for new opportunities for commercial enterprise, propelled the westward expansion of the fledgling nation. Trading posts and fortifications along the Ohio and Mississippi rivers soon evolved into small cities such as Pittsburgh, Cincinnati, Louisville, and St. Louis. These "spearheads of the frontier" then nurtured the more widespread settlement of farmers in the surrounding areas, which further fueled urban development. A similar process led to the emergence of cities along the Great Lakes, including Buffalo, Cleveland, Detroit, Chicago, and Milwaukee.[11] With this initial network of urban centers in place, merchants, promoters, and government officials invested in new transportation technologies to encourage commercial growth. The opening of the Erie Canal in 1825 linked the Great Lakes region with the Atlantic coast, which in turn sparked the founding of numerous cities along that bustling trade route and the remarkable expansion of New York City as the largest and most prosperous city in North America. Other cities rushed to keep up by building their own canals, and later railroads, to tap the wealth of raw materials and produce from the Ohio River Valley and beyond.[12]

Frontier cities did not flourish simply because of their convenient locations along major transportation corridors. City leaders also played a critical role in determining whether an early settlement developed into a thriving city or simply faded into obscurity.[13] In particular, the "upstart businessman" described in Daniel J. Boorstin's essay in **Reading 2-3** was notable for promoting new city charters that would empower municipal governments to raise revenues and borrow money to fund new transportation facilities, schools, hospitals, and parks. With much of their own wealth at stake, such entrepreneurs were motivated to proclaim the virtues of their incipient cities. The practice of civic boosterism solidified the pattern of elite influence in local politics while the fierce competition among cities to attract investment reinforced policy making that was highly attuned to market pressures.

Notes

1. Zane L. Miller and Patricia M. Melvin, *The Urbanization of Modern America: A Brief History*, 2nd ed. (New York: Harcourt, Brace, Jovanovich, 1987); Charles R. Adrian and Ernest S. Griffith, *A History of American City Government: The Formation of Traditions, 1775–1870* (New York: Praeger Publishers, 1976).

2. Carl Bridenbaugh, *Cities in Revolt: Urban Life in America, 1743–1776* (New York: Alfred Knopf, 1955).

3. Howard P. Chudacoff and Judith E. Smith, *The Evolution of American Urban Society*, 3rd ed. (Englewood Cliffs, NJ: Prentice Hall, 1988); Billy G. Smith, *The "Lower Sort": Philadelphia's Laboring People, 1750–1800* (Ithaca, NY: Cornell University Press, 1990).

4. See William Penn's Report, "Town Lots in Philadelphia—A Good Investment: 1684," in *Urban America: A History of Documents*, ed. Bayrd Still (Boston: Little, Brown and Company, 1974).

5. Chudacoff and Smith, *The Evolution of American Urban Society*.

6. Smith, *The "Lower Sort"*; Eric Foner, *Tom Paine and Revolutionary America* (New York: Oxford University Press, 1976).

7. Gary B. Nash, *Forging Freedom: The Formation of Philadelphia's Black Community* (Cambridge, MA: Harvard University Press, 1988).

8. Gary B. Nash, "Artisans and Politics in Eighteenth-Century Philadelphia," in *Race, Class, and Politics: Essays on American Colonial and Revolutionary Society* (Urbana: University of Illinois Press, 1986); Gary B. Nash, *The Urban Crucible: Social Change, Political Consciousness, and the Origins of the American Revolution* (Cambridge, MA: Harvard University Press, 1979).

9. Benjamin L. Carp, *Rebels Rising: Cities and the American Revolution* (New York: Oxford University Press, 2007); Foner, *Tom Paine and Revolutionary America*.

10. Sam Bass Warner Jr., *The Private City: Philadelphia in Three Periods of Its Growth* (Philadelphia: University of Pennsylvania Press, 1968).

11. Richard C. Wade, *The Urban Frontier: The Rise of Western Cities* (Cambridge, MA: Harvard University Press, 1959).

12. Charles N. Glaab and A. Theodore Brown, *A History of Urban America* (New York: Macmillan, 1967).

13. Carl Abbott, *Boosters and Businessmen: Popular Economic Thought and Urban Growth in the Antebellum West* (Westport, CT: Greenwood Press, 1981). See also Don H. Doyle, *New Men, New Cities, New South: Atlanta, Nashville, Charleston, Mobile, 1860–1910* (Chapel Hill: University of North Carolina Press, 1990), for a study of the role of business leaders in developing southern cities during a later time period.

2-1 "The Ruling Elite"*

Alan Tully

William Penn's Legacy: Politics and Social Structure in Provincial Pennsylvania, 1726–1755

One of the important underpinnings of political stability in mid-eighteenth-century Pennsylvania was that society's social and economic structure. Because of the dynamic character of Pennsylvania society, observers have often mistakenly described the social organization of the colony as fragmentary and weak. In fact, Pennsylvania possessed a strong, flexible, and coherent community structure—one that could, without shattering, absorb the kinds of impact potentially disruptive social issues generated, and hence one that was particularly well adapted to the needs of a rapidly changing society. So, too, did the prosperity that Pennsylvanians enjoyed tend to produce political stability. Widespread economic opportunity, a commonly shared belief in the possibility of upward mobility, and a broad consensus on both the worthiness and the most suitable expressions of acquisitive values worked to prevent the accumulation of deep dissatisfactions and to promote the cause of social unity. . . .

Between 1726 and 1755 Pennsylvanians enjoyed sustained economic development and marked prosperity. A variety of indices—such as the growth in the colony's population from 40,000 to 150,000, the organization of five new counties, the founding of twenty new towns (compared to none in the preceding twenty years), and the doubling of the ship tonnage clearing Philadelphia between 1725 and 1739—point this out.[1] Perhaps the most important indicator, however, is the record of trade between England and Pennsylvania. Over the three decades, 1726 to 1755, exports almost quadrupled and imports from England rose from approximately £38,000 to £200,000 per annum.[2] These statistics are worth a good deal of attention because the magnitude of their change underlines the fundamental importance of the export trade to the provincial economy.

The development of overseas and coastal markets had begun early in Pennsylvania's history. In comparison with the period from 1720 through 1755, when most of the immigrants who came to Pennsylvania were relatively poor men,[3] those who arrived in the late seventeenth or very early eighteenth centuries were somewhat better off, and used their capital both to establish productive economic enterprises and to seek out export markets for locally produced goods.[4] Because of their efforts and resources, Pennsylvanians quickly overcame the early economic difficulties that every new colony faced, and by the second quarter of the eighteenth century a solid foundation for further economic growth had been laid in Philadelphia.[5] A powerful merchant community—largely made up of Quakers—had come into existence, and among members of this group both opportunity and motivation for the expansion of business were ever present: their firm religious and kinship ties gave them reliable business contacts in commercial centers across the Atlantic and in North America, their need to repay their overseas suppliers for the increasing number of imported goods Pennsylvanians were purchasing forced them to carry on a never-ending search for lucrative markets for

Source: Tully, Alan. *William Penn's Legacy: Politics and Social Structure in Provincial Pennsylvania, 1726–1755*, pp. 53, 66–67, 73–75, 79–80, 82–85, 119–121. © 1977 The Johns Hopkins University Press. Reprinted with permission of Johns Hopkins University Press.

*Endnotes and references have been omitted. Please consult the original source.

provincial produce, and the promptings of the profit motive were reinforced by their acknowledgment of a Quaker obligation to serve God by diligently following their vocation or "calling. . . ."[6]

The desire to attain wealth certainly existed in Pennsylvania, as did the opportunity to acquire it. Financial means meant leisure time, ease, comfort, and security. It meant the ability to free oneself from the strictures others imposed and to participate fully and independently in provincial society. But despite the heavy rhetorical emphasis of contemporaries on the desirability of economic success as a guarantor of independence, clearly Pennsylvanians quietly accepted a correlated implication. As an individual's economic resources increased, so did his capacity for effective social action—whatever that action might be. On the one hand, the man of wealth, whether he be farmer, miller, builder, or merchant, found that the gates that led to the centers of political and social activities, and that were firmly latched in the face of the poorer man, opened to his touch; on the other, he found that he had considerable leverage over the men who worked his fields, operated his mills, framed his houses, unloaded his ships, or retailed his goods. Wealth conferred power, and as such it commanded respect.

Regard for wealth arose, too, out of the symbolic relationship that existed between affluence and the capitalist ethic. Despite the unwillingness of Quaker spokesmen to view poverty as divine punishment and hence as evidence of moral failure, they widely acknowledged worldly success as a fitting reward for diligence, self-discipline, frugality, sobriety, and honesty.[7] In a society so thoroughly permeated with these values, and so thoroughly acquisitive in its tone, the achievement of wealth could only be interpreted as evidence of ability and virtue, unless in some individual cases there was undeniable evidence to the contrary.[8] Deference to affluence, which very often followed the unreserved acceptance of these values, served to reinforce the legitimacy of those very values. By doffing their caps to wealth, Pennsylvanians were providing for one another the kind of open approbation they sought to sanction the "Puritan ethic" they embraced.

More important, however, than the respect men gained simply as economic successes was the opportunity riches afforded them of assuming new social roles and thereby gaining additional status. With wealth, an ambitious man could surround himself with expensive possessions, gain an acquaintance with the popular books of the day, socialize with the prominent, and acquire a country estate. In short, it allowed the economically successful to adopt a life style that accorded with the most preferred forms of behavior sanctioned by the provincial value system.

Because the merchants of Philadelphia were the most successful businessmen in the colony, and because their presence in the provincial capital allowed them to occupy many of the seats of power, they quickly became the recognized social leaders of the province. The norms that they followed and the values they expressed took observable form in a peculiar local style of subdued extravagance, controlled ostentation, and obvious comfort. The house of a merchant was commodious enough by eighteenth-century standards and was furnished with care: mahogany chests, black walnut desks, finely carved chairs, silver plate, and handsome clocks adorned the interior. Books, both borrowed and bought, stood near a quiet, comfortable corner. In the bed chamber, extensive personal wardrobes were sumptuous and colorful, if not foppish and gaudy. In the dining room epicurean proclivities were fully indulged, while outside landscape gardening and other plantation projects provided suitable outlets for the practical, creative urge and for aesthetic tastes. Tea parties, coffeehouse talk, and other forms of social intercourse filled the increasing leisure hours.

Nor did religious or political differences gain expression in significant deviations from common forms of behavior. Architecturally, and in their furnishings, the houses of rich Anglicans and Quakers duplicated each other far more than they differed. At a time when "public friend" Thomas Story could send to James Logan's family "crystal sleeve buttons set in gold cut brilliant fashion" and "bright red Cornelian buttons set in silver" the differences in personal apparel between a "plain" Quaker and a stylish Anglican were minimal.[9] In general, Philadelphia Anglicans and Presbyterians, many of whom were lapsed Quakers, the offspring of former Quakers, or close associates of Friends, shared the same social tastes as the leading Quaker families.[10]

From the very early years of settlement, Pennsylvania trading magnates had not been content with a narrow, city-oriented merchant life style; they had followed William Penn's example of establishing county seats on private plantations. As Frederick Tolles observed, "Every Quaker [and he might have added non-Quaker] merchant, as soon as he was able to afford it, built a country house outside the city. . . ."[11] Some, like James Logan, Edward Home, and Anthony Palmer, established full-fledged, working country estates, while others were content to build small retreats where they could spend a day or a weekend. No matter the scale; the gesture was the important thing. By expanding the orbit of their activities to include country life, the city merchants were neither merely emulating William Penn nor creating the means to escape Philadelphia's summer heat. Rather, they were expressing allegiance to the customary English pattern of social mobility—a pattern that, over the course of several generations, saw commercial wealth converted into land and a country seat—and, above all, they were trying to reconcile the realities of their dependence on commercial life with the prevailing value system that reserved for the independent country gentleman the highest esteem. . . .

In the social world of mid-eighteenth-century Pennsylvania, deference was relatively high, and access to provincial office was restricted to appropriate members of the colony's elite. The social requisites of Assembly officeholding point out what kinds of criteria narrowed the field of potential officeholders, while the informal means of choosing candidates, the usual nonparty form of electoral competition, the unquestioning acceptance of established means of expressing political differences, and the customary apathy of the eligible voters underline the fundamental orderliness of provincial politics. Inside Pennsylvania's small Assembly, most legislative power was concentrated in a few hands. Contests for a share of that power occurred, of course, but the Assembly was so well insulated, changes in the locus of power so infrequent, and the sense of corporate identity among members so strong, that such contests did not develop into sustained public disputes. Despite the apparently closed character of Assembly affairs, legislators were attentive to the opinions and expressed needs of their constituents. Thus, they defused the potential for instability always inherent in extreme political insularity.

Between 1726 and 1755, deferential attitudes in Pennsylvania were more in evidence than at any other time in the eighteenth century. The colony had an established provincial elite, which by virtue of its members' social pretensions and the willingness of "lesser" men to recognize the legitimacy of those claims, formed a recognizable, if roughly defined, group of "natural" superiors; the basic allocations of political power, which had been the source of much intraelite conflict in Pennsylvania's early years, had been worked out and those compromises sanctioned by time. Provincial society had gained sufficient time to "set," yet the colony had not become so large, dispersed, complex, or specialized that power had become diffused among a great range of individuals, associations or institutions. In fact, an extremely high incidence of overlapping membership characterized the colony's political, religious, and economic elites. Leading provincials commanded deference, not simply because they enjoyed one form of deference entitlement, but because they possessed several. They controlled large fortunes, shared a common life style, exercised political power, spoke with weighty voices in religious affairs, and were educated men. Of course, perfect congruence between the memberships of specific elites did not occur, but kinship connections and associational patterns among occupants of the upper social strata reinforced the concentration of deference entitling properties among a relatively small segment of the population.[12] . . .

According to the rhetoric that accompanied Pennsylvania's annual Assembly elections, the most important qualifications for political officer were independence, virtue, and capacity.[13] Because of the intangible nature of such attributes, they were as difficult for contemporaries to measure as for later observers. But those who became assemblymen did display a number of characteristics that undoubtedly helped to convince voters that they, rather than others, possessed the necessary qualities. Possession of wealth was, certainly, one of the more important means of demonstrating public worthiness. Economic independence was a prerequisite of political independence, and the possession of solid financial resources indicated that a man was no stranger to diligence, sobriety, and virtue, that he was capable in worldly affairs; and that he could afford, intermittently, to sacrifice his private affairs in order to attend to the public business. Of the forty men who served as Chester County assemblymen between 1729 and 1755, thirty-two were in the top decile of the county's property holders, four were at the 80 to 90 percent level, three at the 70 to 80 percent level, and one at the 60 to 70 percent level.[14] Despite, however, the marked tendency for provincial legislators to be among the richest residents in their respective counties, wealth alone assured no one of political office: only a small percentage of the wealthiest men became officeholders, and a sprinkling of assemblymen were not particularly well off.

Closely related to wealth was life style, and, as in the case of wealth, members of the Assembly tended to be exemplars of the country way of life. In Philadelphia County, Isaac Norris, William Allen, and Israel Pemberton moved in the highest circles of society; in the country men such as Jeremiah Langhorne, Samuel Blunston, William Moore, and Joseph Pennock set the style with their large plantations, impressive stone houses, extensive lists of personal property, and rounds of informal socializing. Believing that independent countrymen were best able to protect the freeman's rights, electors naturally chose men who displayed some correspondence with that ideal pattern.

A third way in which men could demonstrate ability was through prominence in religious affairs. Anglicans and Presbyterians had some opportunity to do so by serving as vestrymen, church wardens, or elders, but it was among Quakers that service within the appropriate religious organizations was of greatest importance as a requisite of political officeholding. Of the thirty-six Quaker legislators who sat for Chester County between 1729 and 1755, twenty-five had represented their monthly meetings at the quarterly level and fifteen had been authorized to attend the Philadelphia Yearly Meeting. Nor was Chester County exceptional in this respect: of twenty-five Quakers who represented Bucks County over the same time span, seventeen attended the Yearly Meeting; and in Philadelphia County and City sixteen of the twenty-five Quaker representatives did the same.[15]

The high level of political participation by Quaker religious leaders was not without reason. Despite being dissenters and advocates of separation of church and state, Friends felt that their sect rightly enjoyed a peculiar prominence in Pennsylvania and that society should be directed by closely cooperating centers of religious and civil authority.[16] Tradition, rooted in the colony's early years when Quaker meetings performed all the functions of local government, and principles of mutual aid, which were institutionalized in the practices of local meetings, meant that men rose to prominence in the Quaker hierarchy not simply because they were pious men but because they were capable administrators who understood the needs of local society. It was solid reputations as good Quakers that provided two of Pennsylvania's most successful politicians, minister John Wright of Hempfield and elder Thomas Cummings of Chester, with the base they needed to launch and maintain their political careers.

Local administrative experience, somewhat akin to what many leading Quakers gained by handling meeting affairs, was another obvious means of judging capability for higher office. If the record of Chester County assemblymen is any indication, virtually all of the provincial legislators had served one or more years as township constable, supervisor of highways, or overseer of the poor. Even in the performance of these low-level jobs, there was opportunity to demonstrate ability and concern. On the county level, other more responsible offices could lead to that of legislator. Of the forty assemblymen who served Philadelphia County and City between 1729 and 1755, five had gained prior experience as city or county assessors and an additional six had served terms both as city or county assessor and as county commissioner. In the outlying areas this pattern was less distinct but still recognizable.

A fifth criterion by which prospective assemblymen were judged was that of education. Despite the ostensible aversion of Quakers to higher learning, they did recognize the value of a sound practical education and a thorough acquaintance with contemporary European political literature. It was doubly incumbent on a prospective legislator to be able to meet reasonable educational standards, for not only did day-to-day tasks of the assemblyman require legal knowledge and literary skill, but a basic tenet of the dominant English political culture was that both freemen and representatives should be well educated. Liberty could only be preserved by educated men, who, with the benefit of reading, study, and contemplation, could uncover the sinister and designing plots of power-hungry politicians. Unfortunately, there exists no readily available way of testing just how well educated Pennsylvania's legislators were, but from scattered evidence in wills, inventories, newspapers, and pamphlets, and with due regard for the geographical distribution of assemblymen, it appears that the provincial politicians were among the better-educated men in the province.[17]

The importance of wealth, life style, religious reputation, experience in local office, and education as prerequisites for office suggests that voters measured prospective assemblymen by their achievements as well as by how they conducted themselves in attaining these goals. Nor did reference to past performance stop with the candidate himself; the "merits of his progenitors" were examined to see if family name warranted a legitimate "claim" to "advancements."[18] Even if a man appeared to fulfill all of the most important qualifications for office, including the advantage of having ancestors who played a significant role in provincial affairs or had been men of "parts" in England, his ability to attain Assembly office was severely limited if he did not have close personal or family relationships with the acknowledged Quaker leaders of his county. The nature of those relationships was important evidence of a man's integrity. . . .

By 1726 the basic governmental institutions in Pennsylvania were well established, and a solid framework of laws and legal procedures had long been in operation. Residents had cooperated to support order-creating agencies, they had welcomed the introduction of administrative and judicial practices that provided certainty and regularity, and they had staked out the general limits of acceptable social behavior.[19] Given the solid existence of governmental institutions—or, for those who moved to the Pennsylvania backcountry, the expectation of establishing those institutions— and the existence of acceptable statutory guidelines for governmental officers, the chief concerns of local officials became those of enforcement and of

recommending what adjustments were necessary to further the purposes of the government.

One of the basic purposes of government was to provide protection for person and property, and trying individuals who transgressed those rights occupied much of the time of the judges who sat on the court of quarter sessions.[20] Security of life and property was an essential prerequisite for the kind of self-determination provincial residents desired, and both law enforcement agents and members of the judiciary were determined to offer provincial residents the protection they expected. Security too was the purpose of other pieces of legislation that did not deal with acts of violence or larceny. Regulations governing the construction of bakers' and coopers' shops in Philadelphia, prohibiting the firing of chimneys in the city, and outlawing the firing of guns and the lighting of fireworks in urban areas were framed to protect urban dwellers and their property.[21] In pursuing such ends the assemblymen were assisted by county administrators who enforced their laws and by borough officials who evinced similar concerns. Philadelphia councilmen passed ordinances to regulate the public activities of Negro and white servants and appointed larger numbers of regulators to control street traffic; Lancaster officials ordered an end to horse racing and selling spiritous drinks in the streets and firing guns in the town.[22] Their overriding aim was to make the towns quiet, orderly centers in which inhabitants and visitors could safely mingle.

Attempts to encourage good order in places where people congregated were motivated by more than a mere concern for protection of persons and property. The aims of the borough officers included the creation of conditions that would best facilitate commercial exchange. Lancaster officials were determined to maintain free access to the town market; they ordered pigs and boys off the streets and prohibited the building of fences that might impede commerce.[23] The Philadelphia councilmen tried to keep wharves and market stalls in good repair, expanded the number of market stalls to meet growing needs, and tried to improve the conditions of city streets.[24] Out in the counties the thrust of much administrative work was directed towards complementary ends: commissioners paid bounties on pests in order to reduce their toll on the freeholders' crops and livestock and oversaw the construction and repair of bridges that allowed greater amounts of produce to go to market; justices of the peace laid out new roads that would ease commerce and saw to it that the township supervisor opened them up. Government officials provided these and other important services that lowed individuals to accumulate progressively larger hordes of worldly goods, while institutions like the court of common pleas and the orphan's court helped them to protect those goods and control their disposition.

There were, of course, the usual dissonant notes along with the harmonious chords of order. In deciding standards of acceptable behavior, legislators, judges, and juries designated certain behavior deviant and, therefore, antisocial or disorderly. Occasionally, citizens took it upon themselves to dispute a magistrate's decision as to where a road should be laid out, or the provincial legislators' decision that the building of fish dams across certain streams was unlawful. Together, acting as a mob, they forcibly prevented surveyors and constables from executing their orders.[25] Conflict arose, too, out of competition among government officials. In the 1730s the Philadelphia County commissioners were

still wresting away from the quarter sessions justices their power to decide which of several needed public works projects deserved priority.[26] Such competition could have tragic consequences: while the overseers of the poor in two Philadelphia townships were arguing over whose charge he was, the distraught object of their charity, a poor blind man, hanged himself.[27] Conflict, contention, disorder, and irresponsibility were present as they always had been and always would be in Pennsylvania society, but by 1726 there existed strong local institutions, with officers who could play an effective role in resolving incipient social conflict, quieting disorder, reconciling their own differences, and acknowledging governmental responsibilities.

Despite the obvious concern among government officials for order and security, perhaps the most significant characteristic of public activities in Pennsylvania was their limited scope. In failing to demand a more active, innovative role on the part of their government officials, settlers were accepting eighteenth-century English standards of limited government,[28] while at the same time giving expression to their own predilection for individual freedom and economic opportunity insofar as it was consistent with good order and security. . . .

2-2 "The Environment of Private Opportunity"*

Sam Bass Warner Jr.

The Private City: Philadelphia in Three Periods of Its Growth

American cities have grown with the general culture of the nation, not apart from it. Late eighteenth-century Philadelphia was no exception. Its citizens, formerly the first wave of a Holy Experiment, had been swept up in the tides of secularization and borne on by steady prosperity to a modern view of the world. Like the Puritans of Massachusetts and Connecticut, the Quakers of Pennsylvania had proved unable to sustain the primacy of religion against the solvents of cheap land and private opportunity. Quaker, Anglican, Presbyterian, Methodist, Pietist—each label had its social and political implications—but all congregations shared in the general American secular culture of privatism.[1]

Already by the time of the Revolution privatism had become the American tradition. Its essence lay in its concentration upon the individual and the individual's search for wealth. Psychologically, privatism meant that the individual should seek happiness in personal independence and in the search for wealth; socially, privatism meant that the individual should see his first loyalty as his immediate family, and that a community should be a union of such moneymaking, accumulating families; politically, privatism meant that the community should keep the peace among individual moneymakers, and, if possible, help to create an open and thriving setting where each citizen would have some substantial opportunity to prosper.

To describe the American tradition of privatism is not to summarize the entire American cultural tradition. Privatism lies at the core of many modern cultures; privatism alone will not distinguish the experience of America from that of other nations. The tradition of privatism is, however, the most important element of our culture for understanding the development of cities. The tradition of privatism has always meant that the cities of the United States depended for their wages, employment, and general prosperity upon the aggregate successes and failures of thousands of individual enterprises, not upon community action. It has also meant that the physical forms of American cities, their lots, houses, factories, and streets have been the outcome of a real estate market of profit-seeking builders, land speculators, and large investors. Finally, the tradition of privatism has meant that the local politics of American cities have depended for their actors, and for a good deal of their subject matter, on the changing focus of men's private economic activities.[2]

In the eighteenth century the tradition of privatism and the social and economic environment of colonial towns nicely complemented each other. Later as towns grew to big cities, and big cities grew to metropolises, the tradition became more and more ill-suited to the realities of urban life. The tradition assumed that there would be no major conflict between private interest, honestly and liberally viewed, and the public welfare. The modes of eighteenth-century town life encouraged this expectation that if each man would look to his own prosperity the entire town would prosper. And so it had.

Founded in 1682 under William Penn's liberal instructions, and settled first with Quaker artisans and a few Quaker merchants, the town had since prospered as the capital of a thriving colony.[3] By 1720 Philadelphia was said to have 10,000 inhabitants; by 1775 it had

*Some text and accompanying endnotes have been omitted. Please consult the original source.

more than doubled to 23,700.[4] The townsite bordered the Delaware and Schuylkill rivers, both of which tapped rich forests and excellent farm lands. The line of north-south trade ran nearby, and Philadelphia also lay within reach of the Susquehanna and Potomac rivers openings to the west. Philadelphia, thus, soon excelled in most of the staples of colonial trade, exporting furs, lumber, staves, iron, wheat, and flour, and importing rum, sugar, wine, and English manufactures.

Conditions outside the colony encouraged a heavy immigration of new settlers. Because Pennsylvania had been founded late, by comparison to other Atlantic colonies, west-bound space abounded on ships sailing from Great Britain and the Low Countries. Quakers, of course, fleeing persecution in England came to the colony in large numbers, but by the early eighteenth century their group came to be rivaled by Scotch-Irish and German immigrants. The Act of Union joining Scotland to England opened up the entire British Empire to poor Scots, while Irish wars and famines, and rack-renting landlords drove their fellow Presbyterians from Ulster. On the continent west German peasants fled the destruction of Louis XIV's repeated wars. Finally, in America, the Indian control of upstate New York deflected the flow of westward settlers south to Pennsylvania. The result of all these outside events was a boom in the colony and the town; Pennsylvania and Philadelphia had everything, settlers, natural resources, capital, religious freedom, and comparatively little government.[5]

Within the town three conditions confirmed its privatism—its individualized structure of work, its general prosperity, and its open society and economy. When eighteenth-century Philadelphians spoke of the individual and his search for wealth as the goal of government they were simply basing their political arguments on the common place facts of town life. The core element of the town economy was the one-man shop. Most Philadelphians labored alone, some with a helper or two. A storekeeper tended his shop by himself or with the aid of his family or a servant. Craftsmen often worked with an apprentice, or more rarely with another skilled man.[6]

More than at later times, this Philadelphia was a town of entrepreneurs. Artisans sewed shoes, made wagons, boiled soap, or laid bricks for customers who had already placed an order. Workers did not labor under the close price and time disciplines of manufacture for large-scale inventories or big speculative wholesale markets. Most Philadelphians were either independent contractors hiring out on a job-by-job basis, or they were artisan shopkeepers retailing the products of their work. Even the establishment of a large merchant more resembled a small store than a modern wholesale house. Such a merchant frequently had a partner and the two partners carried on the business with the aid of a full-time clerk and an apprentice or servant to help with errands.[7] When a cargo arrived at the pier the partners would hire some laborers to unload the goods and move them to the storehouse. Thus, a very large proportion of the town's men—artisans, shopkeepers, and merchants—shared the common experience of the individual entrepreneur.

In later years the work groups of factories, offices, stores, and construction crews would have enormous significance for the discipline, acculturation, and education of Philadelphia's residents. Such groups were almost entirely absent from the eighteenth-century town. Shipyard, ropewalk, and distillery workers labored in groups of five and even ten, but theirs were exceptionally large urban production units. In the colonial era the plantation, whether for agriculture or manufacture, was the characteristic place of large work gangs.[8] In 1775, associated with Philadelphia's general run of family enterprises were only about 900 indentured servants, 600 slaves, and perhaps 200 hired servants who lived with their employers.[9] These helpers shared the discipline of family life and work; they did not live by the modes of the work gang. Taken all together the eighteenth-century exceptions to the entrepreneurial role had but little significance for the functioning of the town's society.

A German visitor of 1750 wrote: "Pennsylvania is heaven for farmers, paradise for artisans, and hell for officials and preachers."[10] By the same token, Philadelphia on the eve of the Revolution was a town of freedom and abundance for the common man. For young persons there was a great demand for apprentices in all lines of work. An unskilled laborer without connections could find work with board and wages to begin accumulating a little money for tools. An artisan who wanted to carry a few shopkeeping goods in his shop, or a storekeeper with a good reputation, could get his stock from the merchant and settle for his advance a year later.

The ordinary artisan or shopkeeper, if his health was good, could be assured of a comfortable, if frugal, living. To be sure, houses were small and rents high, and furnishings were spare compared to later levels of living: no carpets, no upholstered furniture, a sand-scrubbed floor, and whitewashed walls. Stoves and fireplaces only partially heated drafty rooms, and in severe winters the cost of firewood or imported coal was a major item of family expense. Nevertheless, at the city's markets food was cheap and plentiful. The earnings of the ordinary artisan and shopkeeper could support a wife and children without their having to take outside employment. The rapid growth of the town and its trade meant regular work and good earnings for artisans and easy business, if not wealth, for shopkeepers.[11]

Although the customary hours of work were long, sunrise to sunset, the pace of work was often easy and varied with the season. Those who worked outside their homes, like men in the building trades, took an hour for breakfast, a break in the middle of the day, and an hour for dinner in the afternoon. Coopers, shoemakers, smiths, and men who practiced their craft in their own houses and yards must have stopped work as customers and friends came in, and a trip or two to the local tavern must also have been usual. Although there were no formal vacations, the traditional English holidays and frequent *ad hoc* town celebrations provided about twenty days off each year.

Franklin's *Autobiography* abounds with injunctions for regular habits, and the reputation for diligence he established by staying at his bench for the entire formal working day suggests that his was an extraordinary pace. For most workers rush seasons of hard work and long hours alternated with slack times. These variations meant days for fishing or spare moments for gossip on the streets and visits to the tavern.

Such a commonplace prosperity, generous at least by eighteenth-century standards, confirmed the privatism of the town and its age. As important a confirmation came from the openness of its economy and society. The failure of the craft guilds to control the trades of the town gave newcomers and resident artisans alike an occupational freedom unknown in Europe. Shopkeepers and artisans—and often one man was both—could take up any craft or open any line of business they wished. Although Philadelphia had inherited English regulations favoring the "freemen" of the town, established artisans could not maintain their control of the town's businesses against newcomers. The carpenters and cordwainers managed to form associations to set prices for their work, but failed when they attempted to close the membership of their trades. In Philadelphia men added trades and lines of goods as they thought demand justified. Although this freedom undoubtedly produced a great deal of incompetent craftsmanship, the importance to the individual artisan or shopkeeper of open trades and plentiful work cannot be overestimated. It meant for the common man that there was always a chance for a fresh start. This chance for a new beginning was the urban equivalent of the contemporary farmer's chance to pick up and try again in the West.[12]

Already in these years the American pattern of social mobility by property obtained. No invidious distinction between land and trade favored some occupations over others. As eighteenth-century Philadelphians grew rich they kept their original occupations, whether they were carpenters, distillers, printers, or lawyers. Whatever a man's occupation, there were only a few channels for investment open to the rising man. Since there were no banks, private money lending was the most important investment opportunity in the town. Houses and land were also a favorite way of using savings both among the rich and those with a little capital. Only 19 percent of the families of Philadelphia owned their houses and therefore home rentals offered a safe investment. Other opportunities were shares in voyages, marine insurance, and, of course, land and farms outside the town.[13]

The prosperity and abundant opportunity of the town should not be confused with an even distribution of wealth. According to the published tax list for 1774 the upper tenth of the taxpaying households owned 89 percent of the taxable property. In this respect late eighteenth-century Philadelphia resembled the later Philadelphias—it was a pyramid of wealth in which about five hundred men guided the town's economic life. Its unique quality lay in the general prosperity of the common artisan and shopkeeper and the widely shared entrepreneurial experience and goals of the artisan, shopkeeper, and merchant.[14]

The wealthy presided over a municipal regime of little government. Both in form and function the town's government advertised the lack of concern for public management of the community. The municipal corporation of Philadelphia, copied from the forms of an old English borough, counted for little. Its only important functions in the late eighteenth-century were the management of the markets and the holding of the Recorder's Court. A closed corporation, choosing its members by co-option, it had become a club of wealthy merchants, without much purse, power, or popularity.

By modern standards the town was hardly governed at all. The constable in each ward and a few watchmen provided an ineffective police, the safety of the house and shop being secured by citizens' helping each other to drive away intruders or pursue thieves.[15] Most streets went unpaved, the public wharves little repaired. There were no public schools, no public water, and at best thin charity.

The enduring contribution of the colonial era to Philadelphia government lay in its inauguration of the committee system of municipal government. This system, if system it may be called in the eighteenth century, consisted of placing the administration of specific tasks in the hands of independent committees, or commissions. The Pennsylvania Provincial Assembly, lacking faith in the municipal corporation, created a number of commissions. First came the Board of Assessors established to raise money to pay the debts of the corporation and to require that wharves and streets be repaired and a workhouse erected. Then came separate street commissioners, next the City Wardens to manage the night watch and the lighting of the streets, and, still later, a Board of Overseers of the Poor. None of these commissions' performance would satisfy modern municipal standards. The commissioners were elected officials, chosen under the colonial fifty-pound, freehold qualification by the voters of Philadelphia. Like the town's fire companies, lending libraries, and tavern clubs these commissions helped train Philadelphians to the habits of committee government, a form of management they would have to call upon when creating a new independent government during the Revolution. Like many of the laws and forms of the colonial era which

passed into the usage of the subsequent Commonwealth of Pennsylvania, the committee system of government was the legacy of colonial municipal life to later Philadelphias.[16]

The real secret of the peace and order of the eighteenth-century town lay not in its government but in the informal structure of its community. Unlike later and larger Philadelphias, the eighteenth-century town was a community. Graded by wealth and divided by distinctions of class though it was, it functioned as a single community. The community had been created out of a remarkably inclusive network of business and economic relationships and it was maintained by the daily interactions of trade and sociability. Because it was small and because every rank and occupation lived jumbled together in a narrow compass the town suffered none of the communications problems of later Philadelphias. . . .

Already in the 1770's the crowding of the land exceeded the sanitary capabilities of the town. The streets and alleys reeked of garbage, manure, and night soil, and some private and public wells must have been dangerously polluted. Every few years an epidemic swept through the town. In the 1790's the city would pay a terrible price in deaths from recurring yellow fever.[22] . . .

The high cost of building kept houses small, cramped, and in short supply. The common artisan's or shopkeeper's house was a narrow structure, about seventeen feet wide and twenty-five feet deep. A story-and-a-half high, it offered about eight hundred square feet of floor space on its ground floor and attic. Most often the owner plied his trade in the largest front room. The Middle Ward records show that although some families had five to seven children, most had few. The average number of children per household was 1.3, and counting servants and slaves the average household was four persons. The small houses, thus, were cramped but not severely crowded. If the artisan or shopkeeper prospered he would add a kitchen ell or more likely move to a house of similar proportion with a kitchen ell at the rear. The house of an ordinary merchant or even a craftsman who had grown rich, would be like the artisan's house with the ell, but would be two and one-half stories instead of one and one-half. Such houses of the prosperous also possessed deep lots for gardens, a shed for a cow and some chickens, and perhaps a horse.[25]

A town of small houses, where most houses also served as stores, offices and workshops, encouraged people to live out upon the streets. Moreover, the pace of work, most of it governed by the seasons or advance orders from customers, was irregular, what one would call today a rural pace. Both the physical structure of the town and the pace of its work thus encouraged a more public, gossipy style of life than could later be sustained when a steady pace of work and larger interiors drove people into sharply defined spaces for work and residence.

The ordinary housewife shopped daily, going to the baker's for her bread, and taking her meat and pies to the baker's oven to be cooked. Street peddlers called her out for fish, eggs, and produce, and twice a week the farmers of Philadelphia County held a full market at the public stalls. As in the nineteenth century with its dark tenements and crowded row houses, sunlight must have been a great source of pleasure for women sewing and spinning and many must have worked at these and other household chores out on their door-steps, as their tenement sisters did years later.

For the husband the eighteenth-century custom of men's gossip at the tavern provided the first Philadelphia's basic cells of community life. Every ward in the city had its inns and taverns. The 1774 tax list recorded 93 tavernkeepers and 72 innkeepers in the city of Philadelphia, Southwark, and the Northern Liberties, approximately one neighborhood drinking place for every 140 persons in the city (23,000/165). The Middle Ward, alone, held 18 inns and taverns. Some must have served purely a neighborhood cus-tom; others, like the London Coffee House or the City Tavern served as central communications nodes for the entire city.

Then, as now, each one had its own crowd of regu-lars and thus each constituted an informal community cell of the city. Out of the meetings of the regulars at the neighborhood tavern or inn came much of the com-monplace community development which preceded the Revolution and proved later to be essential to the gov-ernance of the city and the management of the ward. Regular meetings of friends, or men of common occu-pations, led to clubs of all kinds and of every degree of

formality from regular billiard sessions to fire compa-nies and political juntos. Benjamin Franklin and the many community innovations of his junto showed the potential of these informal tavern groups. They pro-vided the underlying social fabric of the town and when the Revolution began made it possible to quickly gather militia companies, to form effective committees of correspondence and of inspection, and to organize and to manage mass town meetings.

At the center of the town's communications sys-tem stood the merchants' coffee houses. On the eve of the Revolution Philadelphia had two such major meeting places—the old London Coffee House (established 1754), run by William Bradford, the newspaper publisher, and the new City Tavern (established 1773), just founded by a syndicate of merchants. The London Coffee House, located at Front and Market streets, adjacent to the town's principal market stalls and overlooking the Delaware, had been for many years the place where merchants gathered every noon to read incoming newspapers, to discuss prices, and to arrange for cargoes and marine insurance. These noon meetings in time rip-ened into the specialized institutions of exchanges, banks, and insurance companies. As yet, Philadelphia had but one insurance company and its merchants' business depended on the variety of functions of these daily tavern gatherings. For many years ship captains and travelers first stopped at the London Coffee House when they arrived in town, messages were left, auction notices posted and auctions held. Frequently on market days, after a parade through the streets, horses were auctioned in front of the tavern doors. Slaves and indentured servants stood before the same block.

As the town grew the importing merchants no lon-ger had a need to be near the market dealers. The merchant community split into at least two parts. The new City Tavern surpassed the old London Coffee House as a place of fashion with the importing mer-chants, though its function remained that of its com-petitor. On May 19, 1774, Paul Revere brought his news of the closing of the Port of Boston to the City Tavern, and here numerous Revolutionary committees gathered. The still extant Philadelphia Assemblies were held at this new tavern, as was the endless series of banquets and balls which served the town with high entertainment.[26]

Because the merchants' tavern was a public place in a small town, it escaped the limitations of later Philadelphia merchant centers—the exchanges, the Chamber of Commerce, and the gentlemen's clubs. These later gatherings were either meeting places of specialists and thereby encouraged only the brokers' or downtown merchants' view of the city, or they were closed organizations which directed their members' attention inward toward the sociability of the group. The eighteenth-century tavern, however, opened out to all the life of the street and it did not shield the leaders of the town from contact with the life that surrounded them.[27]

It was the unity of everyday life, from tavern, to street, to workplace, to housing, which held the town and its leaders together in the eighteenth century. This unity made it possible for the minority of Revolutionary merchants, artisans, and shopkeepers to hold together, run the town, and manage a share of the war against England, even in the face of Quaker neutrality and Tory opposition.

Notes

1. Quaker historians agree that the Holy Experiment died from materialism and secularization during the eighteenth century, Frederick B. Tones, *Meeting House and Counting House* (Chapel Hill, 1948), 240–243; Sydney V. James, *A People Among Peoples* (Cambridge, 1963), 37–43, 211–215; and see the charges against his contemporaries in John Woolman, *The Journal of John Woolman* (F. B. Tolles, Introduction, New York, 1961).

2. Howard Mumford Jones, *O Strange New World* (New York, 1964), 194–272, treats with this tradition as a blend of Christian and classical ideas.

3. Tolles, *Meeting House*, 41.

4. Carl Bridenbaugh, *Cities in the Wilderness* (N.Y. 1938), 303. . . . Also, James T. Lemon, "Urbanization of the Development of Eighteenth Century Southeastern Pennsylvania," *William and Mary Quarterly*, XXIV (Oct., 1967), 502–542; Hannah B. Roach, "The Planning of Philadelphia," *Pennsylvania Magazine*, XCII (January and April, 1968).

5. Marcus L. Hansen, *Atlantic Migration* (Cambridge, 1940), Ch. II.

6. Comments suggesting an individualized or family work structure, Carl Bridenbaugh, *The Colonial Craftsman* (New York, 1950), 126–129, 136–139, 141–143.

7. Harry D. Berg, "The Organization of Business in Colonial Philadelphia," *Pennsylvania History*, X (July, 1943), 157–177; Arthur H. Cole, "The Tempo of Mercantile Life in Colonial America," *Business History Review*, XXXIII (Autumn, 1959), 277–299.

8. Richard B. Morris, *Government and Labor in Early America* (New York, 1946), 38–40.

9. Indentured servants and slaves. The reconstruction of the Middle Ward as of April 8, 1773 showed seventeen hired servants in residence there. On this basis two hundred such servants were guessed for the city. . . .

10. Gottlieb Mittelberger, *Journey to Pennsylvania* (Oscar Handlin and John Clive, eds., Cambridge, 1960), 48.

11. Jackson Turner Main, *The Social Structure of Revolutionary America* (Princeton, 1965), 74–83, 115–163; Chapter IV; Mittelberger, *Journey*, 48–51, 74–75.

12. Morris, *Government and Labor in Early America*, 2–3, 141–143; the American jack-of-all-trades tradition, Mittelberger, *Journey*, 42–3; artisans' associations, Bridenbaugh, *Colonial Craftsman*, 141–143.

13. Wilbur C. Plummer, "Consumer Credit in Colonial Philadelphia," *Pennsylvania Magazine*, LXVI (October, 1942), 385–409. The homeownership percentage was calculated from the number of homeowners and renters listed in the manuscript version of the Seventeenth Eighteen Penny Provincial Tax of April 8, 1774 (in possession of the Pennsylvania Historical and Museum Commission, Harrisburg). A reconstruction of the Middle Ward as of April 8, 1774 shows holdings of land and houses in small lots, and pairs of structures, not big tracts. Rich men, like Israel Pemeberton, and men of few investments, both participated in the housing market.

14. The published version of the Seventeenth Eighteen Penny Provincial Tax, *Pennsylvania Archives, 3rd Series*, XIV (Harrisburg, 1897), 223–445, was used for a quick calculation of the distribution of taxable wealth. The taxpayers on this published list were arranged in order of the size of their published "assessment." The top ten percent, or 498 names, accounted for 89 percent of the 86,100 pounds of assessment given for Philadelphia, the Northern Liberties, and Southwark. This published list is not a sufficient guide to the distribution of wealth since the tax was largely a real property tax to which a head tax and a few personalty [sic] items were added. The very important property of stock-in-trade and money-on-loan

went untaxed and hence unlisted. Also, the compilers of the published list mixed in many cases the taxes-paid entries with the assessment entries thereby distorting even the assessment distribution.

15. There are charming accounts of private policing in Henry D. Biddle, ed., *Extracts from the Journal of Elizabeth Drinker* (Philadelphia, 1889), robbery in her alley, Dec. 15, 1777; insane soldier wanders into the house June 30, 1778; "saucy Ann" and her soldier, Nov. 25, 26, Dec. 2, 1777, Jan. 4, 1778. A call for more considerate treatment of the town watchmen, Advertisement, *Pennsylvania Gazette*, Jan. 20, 1779.

16. For a description of the colonial government of Philadelphia, Judith M. Diamondstone, "Philadelphia's Municipal Corporation, 1701–1776," *Pennsylvania Magazine*, XC (April, 1966), 183–201; Edward P. Allinson & Boise Penrose, "The City Government of Philadelphia," *Johns Hopkins Studies in Historical and Political Science*, V (Baltimore, 1887), 14–33.

22. Bad conditions in alley "huts" of the poor, presumably one-story houses with a sleeping attic reached by a ladder as in the typical rural one-room cabin. Benjamin Rush, *Autobiography of Benjamin Rush* (American Philosophical Society, *Memoirs*, XXV, 1948), 83–84; cellar of a drunken, perhaps insane oyster seller, *Journal of Elizabeth Drinker*, Sept. 2, 1793; eighteenth century epidemics, small pox, yellow fever, dysentery or typhoid,

John Duffy, *Epidemics in Colonial America* (Baton Rouge, 1953), 78–100, 142–161, 220–230, and Struthers Burt, *Philadelphia Holy Experiment* (New York, 1946), 159.

25. The tax records of 1774 give evidence of a colonial housing shortage, for the ratio of occupied to unoccupied dwellings did not exceed two percent that year. Artisans' houses, Grant M. Simon, "Houses and Early Life in Philadelphia," *Historic Philadelphia*, 282–3; typical house for the prosperous, Advertisement, *Pennsylvania Gazette*, March 17, 1779.

26. The name "coffee house," which had been imported from England, merely designated a genteel tavern. Coffee, tea, lemonade, and beer were served, but the customers favored wines and liquors, Robert F. Graham, "The Taverns of Colonial Philadelphia," *Historic Philadelphia*, 318–323.

27. Graydon tells an amusing story of the confrontation of Benjamin Chew, lawyer for the Penns and then Recorder of the town and an alderman with two drunken British officers, *Memoirs*, 43–44; an excellent review of travellers and visitor's accounts mentions the importance to the social structure of the town of immigrant societies like St. David's and St. Tammany, Whitfield J. Bell, Jr., "Some Aspects of the Social History of Pennsylvania, 1760–1790," *Pennsylvania Magazine*, LXII (July, 1938), 301.

2-3 "The Businessman as City Booster"

Daniel J. Boorstin

The Americans: The National Experience

The American businessman—a product (and a maker) of the upstart cities of the American West between the Revolution and the Civil War—was not an American version of the enterprising European city banker or merchant or manufacturer. Not an American Fugger or Medici or Rothschild or Arkwright, he was something quite different. His career and his ideals are an allegory of an American idea of community, for he was born and bred in the dynamic American urbanism in the period of our greatest growth.

The changing meaning of his very name, "businessman," gives us a clue. In 18th-century England to say someone was a "man of business" was primarily to say he engaged in public affairs. Thus, David Hume in 1752 described Pericles as "a man of business." Before the end of the 18th century the expression had begun to lose this, its once primary meaning, and instead to describe a person engaged in mercantile transactions; it became a loose synonym for "merchant." But our now common word "businessman" seems to have been American in origin. It came into use around 1830 in the very period when the new Western cities were founded and were growing most rapidly. Even a casual look at this early American businessman, who he was, what he was doing, and how he thought of his work, will show how inaccurate it would be to describe him as simply a man engaged in mercantile transactions. We might better characterize him as a peculiarly American type of community maker and community leader. His starting belief was in the interfusing of public and private prosperity. Born of a social vagueness unknown in the Old World, he was a distinctive product of the New.

The new fast-growing city, where nothing had been before, a city with no history and unbounded hopes, was the American businessman's first natural habitat. In the period when he first appeared, his primary commodity was land and his secondary commodity transportation. This transformation of land rights and transport rights from political symbols and heirlooms into mere commodities was also an American phenomenon.

The businessman's characteristics would appear in the story of any one of the thousands who made their fortunes in the early 19th century. "I was born close by a saw-mill," boasted William B. Ogden (1805-77), "was early left an orphan, was cradled in a sugar-trough, christened in a mill-pond, graduated at a log-school-house, and at fourteen fancied I could do anything I turned my hand to, and that nothing was impossible, and ever since, madame, I have been trying to prove it, and with some success." He was destined to be an upstart businessman on a heroic scale. Born into a leading local family in a small town in the Catskills in New York, he was actively dealing in real estate before he was fifteen. Before thirty he was elected to the New York Legislature on a program to construct the New York & Erie Railroad with State aid. He was a great booster for his State, to whose growth he called the new railroad essential. "Otherwise," he argued "the sceptre will depart from Judah. The Empire State will no longer be New York. . . . Philadelphia is your great rival, and, if New York is idle, will gather in the trade of the great west."

But Ogden's enthusiasm for New York was not immovable. In 1835, the very year when the money was appropriated for the New York & Erie Railroad, he met some Eastern investors who had formed the American Land Company. They had already shown the foresight to invest heavily in Chicago real estate. One of these was Charles Butler, a politically and philanthropically minded lawyer of Albany, who married Ogden's sister. Butler himself (once a clerk in the law office of Martin Van Buren) was an energetic promoter of real estate and railroads. A man of wide public interests, he was a founder of Hobart College and of Union Theological Seminary, and an early supporter of New York University, among his other community works. He asked Ogden to go to Chicago to manage his interests. Ogden then joined in the purchase of considerable tracts there.

William B. Ogden arrived in Chicago in June, 1835. The town census showed a population of 3265, almost all of whom had come since 1832 (when the settlement had numbered under a hundred). Quickly Ogden transferred his extravagant hopes from the Empire State to the City of Chicago. In 1837, when Chicago was incorporated, Ogden was elected its first mayor, and the city census counted 4170—an increase of almost thirty per cent in two years.

"He could not forget," one of Ogden's fellow businessmen observed, "that everything which benefitted Chicago, or built up the great West, benefitted him. Why should he?" His commodity was land, whose value rose with the population. And Chicago now grew as few cities had ever grown before. The population approximately trebled, decade after decade: from 29,963 in 1850, to 109,260 in 1860, and to 298,977 in 1870. Chicago held over half a million people in 1880 and over a million by 1890, when it was already the second city on the continent. Meanwhile, real-estate values, especially in choice locations such as those Ogden was shrewd enough to buy, rose even more spectacularly. Men like Ogden proudly recorded their business success as the best evidence of their faith in their city. "In 1844," Ogden recalled, "I purchased for $8000, what 8 years thereafter, sold for 3 millions of dollars, and these cases could be extended almost indefinitely." Property he had bought in 1845 for $15,000 only twenty years later was worth ten million dollars. Successes were so common and so sudden, it was hard to know where fact ended and where fable

began. Some of this purchasing was, of course, sheer speculative mania. The Chicago *American* (April 23, 1836) boasted of a piece of city property sold for $96,700 which, in romanticized arithmetic, they said had "risen in value at the rate of *one hundred per cent per* **DAY,** on the original cost ever since [1830], embracing a period of *five years* and a half."

Not to boost your city showed both a lack of community spirit and a lack of business sense. "Perhaps, the most striking trait of his character," a contemporary remembered of Ogden, "was his absolute faith in Chicago. He saw in 1836, not only the Chicago of today, but in the future the great City of the continent. From that early day, his faith never wavered. Come good times—come bad times—come prosperity or adversity—Chicago booming, or Chicago in ashes, its great future was to him a fixed fact." Quite naturally Ogden became a leader in community affairs, and within a few years Chicagoans called him their "representative man."

There was hardly a public improvement in which he did not play a leading role. He built the first draw-bridge across the Chicago river, laid out and opened many miles of streets in the north and west parts of the city, promoted the Illinois and Michigan Canal and advocated laws for its construction and enlargement, projected and built thousands of miles of railroads serving Chicago, and did a great deal to develop Chicago's water supply, sewage system, and parks. More than a hundred miles of streets and hundreds of bridges were built at the private expense of Ogden and his real-estate clients. He helped introduce the McCormick reaping and mowing machines into the West, and helped build the first large factory for their manufacture. He was the first president of Rush Medical College (the first institution of its kind in Chicago), a charter member of the Chicago Historical Society, president of the Board of Trustees of the first "University of Chicago," and one of the first directors of the Merchants Loan and Trust Company (1857). He was elected to the Illinois Senate by the Republicans in 1860. He supported the Theological Seminary of the Northwest, the Academy of Sciences, and the Astronomical Society. The French historian Guizot only slightly exaggerated when he said Ogden had built and owned Chicago.

Characteristic also was Ogden's interest in improving transportation. An upstart community, a community of boosters measuring itself by its rate of growth, depended on transportation in a new way. Settled communities of the Old World—Bordeaux, Lyon, Manchester, or Birmingham—especially when, as in the early 19th century, they were fast becoming industrial towns, needed transportation to feed raw materials and labor to their factories and to take away finished products. But Chicago and the other upstart cities of the American West needed it for their very lifeblood. In the Old World a city might grow or decline, prosper or languish, depending on its transportation, among other facilities. But here, without transportation there was no city at all.

An American city had to "attract" people. The primary community service was to make it easier, cheaper, and pleasanter for people to join your community. In all this, too, William B. Ogden was a paragon, for he pioneered the railroads. One of the first to run out of Chicago was the Galena & Chicago Union Railroad, built to connect Chicago with the great Mississippi River traffic. Chicago businessmen bought a controlling interest in 1846, and tried to raise money from local citizens to complete the railroad. Ogden worked hard to obtain numerous individual subscriptions in small amounts. This, its first railroad, opened a new era in the life and expansion of Chicago. Citizens subscribed its stock "as a public duty, and not as an investment." "Railroads," one of Ogden's collaborators later boasted, "were built as public enterprises, and not as money-making speculations. They were regarded as great highways constructed by the people, either at the expense of the government or by means of private capital, to accommodate the public, and not for the especial benefit of the stockholders." In April, 1849, the first locomotive started west from Chicago on the Galena line.

Ogden took the lead in promoting many more railroads for Chicago. In 1853 he was a director of the Pittsburg, Ft. Wayne & Chicago Railroad; in 1857, president of the Chicago, St. Paul & Fond-du-Lac Railroad which later became part of the Chicago & Northwestern Railroad, of which he was also president (1859-68). A transcontinental railroad with Chicago as the great junction was, of course, his dream. In 1850

he presided over the National Railway Convention and, on the organization of the Union Pacific Company in 1862, its first president was William B. Ogden.

The Ogden story was re-enacted a thousand times all over America—wherever there were upstart cities. Scenes were different, stakes smaller, and dimensions less heroic, but the plot everywhere was much the same. Here was a new breed: the community builder in a mushrooming city where personal and public growth, personal and public prosperity intermingled.

Another example was Dr. Daniel Drake (1785-1852), born in New Jersey, and raised in Kentucky, whose family sent him when he was only fifteen to study in the offices of a leading physician of the small town of Ft. Washington (later called Cincinnati). Within a few years he himself became the town's most prominent practitioner. He opened a drug store where, in 1816, he pioneered in the sale of artificial mineral water; soon he was also running a general store. His *Picture of Cincinnati in 1815,* with its full statistics, and its vivid account of the archaeology, topography, climate, and promise of the city, was translated and circulated widely abroad. Drake, in his own way, was as much a booster as Ogden; using subtler techniques of precise and calculated understatement, he produced the first detailed account of an upstart city. Many believed him when he concluded that small towns like Cincinnati were "destined, before the termination of the present century, to attain the rank of populous and magnificent cities." Drake had established himself in the high noon of Cincinnati prosperity, before the Panic of 1819.

Drake's boosterism was as energetic as Ogden's. Hoping to make Cincinnati a great medical center in 1819, he founded the Ohio Medical College (later the Medical College of the University of Cincinnati). He did a great deal to promote all kinds of community enterprises: the Commercial Hospital and Lunatic Asylum, the eye infirmary, the circulating library, the teacher's college. He helped plan and develop canals and he promoted railroads leading toward the South, which included the successful municipal line, the Cincinnati Southern Railway.

Still another example with a more western habitat was General William Larimer (1809-75). Born and raised in Pennsylvania, he tried many different businesses around Pittsburgh: a general store, a freight service, horse trading, a coal company, a wholesale grocery, his father's hotel, railroads, and banking. When he lost everything in the depression of 1854, Larimer, quickly resolving to start afresh farther west, was in Nebraska the very next spring. There he too became the instantaneous booster of a town which did not yet exist. We have an intimate record in letters he sent east. On May 23, 1855:

I have taken two claims at La Platte, Nebraska Territory . . . and we are laying out a town. I am elected President of the Company, and secured 1/2 of the town. . . . I like this country very much indeed. . . . I think I can make a big raise here in a few years.

Already he claimed a good chance of being elected to Congress from Nebraska. Within a week his optimism had risen still higher: he planned to pay off his creditors with town lots, for he owned a thousand acres within the proposed city.

Now my plan is this: I intend to live in La Platte City. I intend to open up a large farm. I can raise hemp, corn or anything. . . . I will go on with the farm and if the land is ever wanted for a town it is ready. . . . I intend not only to farm simply but I will open a Commission House. I expect to supply the Territory with iron nails, lumber, etc., this will not only be profitable in itself but will be the great means of building up the city. If I go there I can build the city if I do not go only to sell lots as the city may never rise.

Larimer expected the transcontinental railroad to go through La Platte, but this proved a miscalculation. Then, after a heavy winter, the town suffered deep spring floods. "We were not long in coming to the conclusion that La Platte was doomed as a town site." The pattern of western hope was all-or-nothing.

From La Platte, Larimer moved on to Omaha. There he lived in a prefabricated house that had actually been framed in Pittsburgh, knocked down and shipped out in 1856. When Omaha, too, looked unpromising (as it did within less than two years) he moved to Leavenworth, Kansas. This was in 1858, just in time for him to learn of the discovery of gold at

Cherry Creek by Pike's Peak. Unwilling to wait for the better traveling conditions of the following spring, Larimer and his son immediately made up a party and left that fall. After a forty-seven-day trip, the Larimers were among the first to arrive at the mouth of Cherry Creek, where they found two dozen cabins under construction.

This, the first settlement in Colorado, was named Auraria. Larimer's son recorded the events of November 17, 1858:

On our very first night here, my father, without consulting anyone outside of our own Leavenworth Party, packed his blankets and some provisions, left camp and crossed the Creek to pick out a new site. He left instructions for us to get up the oxen and join him, as he believed the east side of the Creek was much the best location for a town and no one in the country laid claim to it, or if so had abandoned it and left the country. . . . When we finally reached the eastern side of Cherry Creek, we found him near the bank with a camp fire awaiting us. He had 4 cottonwood poles crossed, which he called the foundation of his settlement and claimed the site for a town,—for *the* town which has now grown into the one of which Colorado is the proudest.

This time Larimer chose well. He had located on the site of Denver.

At first there was competition between the sites on either side of Cherry Creek. Then the stockholders combined and became a single city named Denver (in honor of the Virginian who had become Governor of the Kansas Territory) in 1860. "I am Denver City," Larimer wrote in a letter in February 1859. And his whole later career proved the extraordinary ability of the American businessmen of these upstart cities to fuse themselves and their destiny with that of their community—at least so long as the community remained prosperous or promising.

At the beginning Larimer had been put in charge of the town and made "Donating Agent," which authorized him to give two city lots to anyone who would build a cabin there measuring at least 16 by 16 feet. He promoted a good hotel and gave valuable shares to men "who were already or could be induced to become interested in the welfare of the city and might be influential in bringing a stage line into the country with Denver as its objective point." He encouraged the founding of drugstores, general stores, sawmills, and newspapers. Complaining that the town lacked the ultimate convenience, he finally helped organize a cemetery.

Examples could be multiplied. But even these three—Ogden, Drake, and Larimer—suggest the variety of opportunities, motives, and attitudes which created the new species *Businessman Americanus*. None of the characteristics of his American habitat was quite unique but their extreme American form and their American combination were.

Cities with no history. The upstart western cities were the rare examples of a dynamic urban environment where almost nothing had been pre-empted by history. Cities were proverbially the centers of institutions, where records were kept and the past was chronicled, hallowed, and enshrined. They were sites of palaces, cathedrals, libraries, archives, and great monuments of all kinds. The American upstart city, by contrast, had no past. At its beginning, it was free of vested interests, monopolies, guilds, skills, and "No Trespassing" signs. Here was the fluidity of the city—the spatial dimension of cosmopolitanism, movement, diversity, and change—but without the historical dimension. There were no ancient walls between classes, occupations, neighborhoods, and nationalities. The American upstart cities began without inherited neighborhood loyalties, without ghettos. "Everything," recalled Larimer, "was open to us."

Quick growth and high hopes. The pace of growth of the upstart cities fired imaginations. A town where nobody was ten years ago, but which today numbered thousands, might be expected to number tens or hundreds of thousands in a few decades. Mankind had required at least a million years to produce its first urban community of a million people; Chicagoans accomplished this feat in less than a century. Within a few days' wagon ride of Drake's Cincinnati, hundreds of towns were laid out, all guaranteed to have unrivalled advantages. Precisely one week after Larimer cut his four cottonwood poles on the future site of Denver, he wrote his wife back east that "we

expect a second Sacramento City, at least." In 1834, H. M. Brackenridge noted, his Pittsburgh was changing so fast that anyone returned after ten years felt himself a stranger. He confidently foresaw that the settlement which had grown from village to big city in a quarter-century would very soon reach half a million. He could not be surprised that Cincinnati had grown from a forest to a city in thirteen years. He himself had hopes "of attaining, on the Ohio or Mississippi, distinction and wealth, with the same rapidity, and on the same scale, that those vast regions were expanding into greatness." The centennial history of St. Louis in 1876 called the city's site superior to that of any other in the world, and predicted that, when its railroad network was completed, it would outstrip Chicago and the eastern metropolises. "And yet, when this has been said, we have but commenced to tell of the wonders of a city destined in the future to equal London in its population, Athens in its philosophy, art and culture, Rome in its hotels, cathedrals, churches and grandeur, and to be the central commercial metropolis of a continent."

Community before government. On this landscape too it was normal to find communities before governments. Men in sudden urban proximity, bound together by specific, concrete purposes, first felt their common needs. Afterwards they called governments into being. From force of circumstance, then, government became functional. Early Chicagoans, and their upstart counterparts elsewhere, were not confronted with the problem of evading obsolete regulations or of transmuting time-honored tyrannies. They simply combined to provide their own water, their own sewage system, their own sidewalks, streets, bridges, and parks. They founded medical schools and universities and museums. Eager for these and other services, they created municipal governments and enlisted state and federal government aid. An upstart government had neither the odor of sanctity nor the odium of tyranny. It was a tool serving personal and community prosperity at the same time.

Intense and transferable loyalties. In upstart cities the loyalties of people were in inverse ratio to the antiquity of their communities, even to the point of absurdity. Older towns could point only to the facts of limited actual accomplishment, while the uncertain future was, of course, ever more promising. Ogden removed his enthusiasm from New York to Chicago; Larimer removed his from La Platte to Omaha to Leavenworth to Auraria to Denver. Men could do this in the twinkling of an eye, and without so much as a glance over the shoulder. Promise, not achievement, commanded loyalty and stirred the booster spirit. One was untrue to oneself and to the spirit of expanding America if one remained enslaved to a vision which had lost its promise. The ghost town and the booster spirit were opposite sides of the same coin.

Competition among communities. The circumstances of American life in the upstart cities of the West produced a lively competitive spirit. But the characteristic and most fertile competition was a competition among communities. We have been misled by slogans of individualism. Just as the competition among colonial seaboard cities helped diffuse American culture and kept it from becoming concentrated in a European-style metropolis, so the competition among western upstart cities helped create the booster spirit. Where there had been no cities before, where all were growing fast, there was no traditional rank among urban centers. If Lexington, Kentucky, could quickly arise by 1800 to be the most populous city of the West, if St. Louis and Cincinnati and Chicago had so suddenly arisen, might not some new Lexington displace them all? Many of each community's institutions had been founded to give it a competitive advantage. Dr. Drake's medical college helped Cincinnati

keep ahead of Lexington, just as Ogden's streets and bridges and parks helped Chicago lead Cincinnati. Where individual and community prosperity were so intermingled, competition among individuals was also a competition among communities.

The emerging businessman of the upstart cities had much in common with the energetic American of an earlier generation. He was the Franklin of the West. He was the undifferentiated man of the colonial period, but in a more expansive setting. The new language of that day called him a "businessman"; the retrospective language of our century calls him the booster. He thrived on growth and expansion. His loyalties were intense, naive, optimistic, and quickly transferable.

Versatility was his hallmark. He usually had neither the advantages nor the disadvantages of specialized skills or monopolistic protection. In Dr. Drake's Cincinnati, physicians became merchants, clergymen became bankers, lawyers became manufacturers. "The young lawyer," H. M. Brackenridge shrewdly advised the Western seeker after fortune (in one of the first recorded uses of the word "businessman") "should think more of picking up his crumbs, than of flying like a balloon. He must be content to become a *business man*, and leave the rest to fortune." For success in this environment, the specialized skills—of lawyer, doctor, financier, or engineer—had a new unimportance. Rewards went to the organizer, the persuader, the discoverer of opportunities, the projector, the risk-taker, and the man able to attach himself quickly and profitably to some group until its promise was tested.

Conclusion

Public Policy Applications: Response to a Public Health Crisis

Policy Then

A series of yellow fever epidemics broke out in cities along the Atlantic seaboard during the 1790s. The deadliest of these occurred in Philadelphia in 1793. The fever spread rapidly after the first cases appeared near the Delaware riverfront in early August. By September 7, 456 people had died. A state of panic pervaded the city, and thousands who had the means to do so, including most members of Philadelphia's Common Council, fled to country estates or the homes of relatives in the hinterlands. On September 10, Mayor Matthew Clarkson published the following announcement in a city newspaper pleading for "benevolent citizens" to volunteer at a time of crisis (see below).

The mayor's call for service produced a committee of 26 citizens (although four soon disappeared and another four died from the disease) of mostly merchants, artisans, and shopkeepers who met almost every day and functioned as the city's de facto government. The committee borrowed money to establish a hospital outside of the city "to receive and accommodate those who are afflicted with malignant disorders," recruited physicians and nurses to carry out the primary treatments of purging and bloodletting, organized safer burial procedures, and ordered a cleansing of streets and wharves. The committee made a special effort to enlist black nurses and attendants on

THE FOLLOWING ADDRESS WAS PUBLISHED IN
THE NEWS PAPERS.

TO THE BENEVOLENT CITIZENS,

THOSE of the overseers of the poor, who attend to the care of the unfortunate now labouring under the prevailing malignant disorder, are almost overcome with the fatigue which they undergo, and require immediate assistance. This, it is hoped, may be found among the benevolent citizens, who actuated by a willingness to contribute their aid in the present distress, will offer themselves as volunteers to support the active overseers in the discharge of what they have undertaken. For which purpose, those who are thus humanely disposed, are requested to apply to the Mayor, who will point out to them how they may be useful.

SEPTEMBER 10th 1793.

Quaker & Special Collections, Haverford College

Mayor's plea for assistance during the yellow fever epidemic of 1793, Philadelphia

the mistaken assumption that blacks had developed a partial immunity to yellow fever; in actuality, blacks succumbed at the same rate as whites.

Despite the heroic, although sometimes misguided, efforts of the committee, the situation only worsened, reaching a low point during the second week of October when 711 people died. The epidemic subsided only after the first frost later that month, which killed the mosquitoes that had—unbeknownst to the committee and the city's medical establishment—been spreading the disease. The official register listed 4,044 deaths between August 1 and November 9, which constituted approximately 10 percent of Philadelphia's entire population.

Policy Now

Fortunately, few U.S. cities have encountered a public health crisis on the scale of Philadelphia's yellow fever epidemic of 1793. In 2014, however, Americans were confronted with the possibility of widespread fatalities when the highly infectious Ebola virus arrived in this country. Thomas Eric Duncan had flown to Dallas on September 20 to visit his fiancée and other family members from his home in Liberia, where he had been exposed to the virus. A massive outbreak of Ebola in West Africa had already claimed over 6,000 lives. Within a few days, Duncan began to experience headaches and nausea and went to the emergency room at Texas Health Presbyterian Hospital in Dallas. He was given an antibiotic and sent home. Duncan returned two days later with a fever. At that point, hospital staff discovered that the patient was from West Africa and that he was showing some early symptoms of Ebola.

Many Americans assume that in the event of a possible Ebola outbreak, the federal government, led by the Centers for Disease Control and Prevention, intervenes and oversees all efforts to treat those who are afflicted and takes appropriate measures to contain the virus. In fact, responsibility for such actions largely falls on local governments. But who within the local sphere of government in Dallas was in charge was far from certain.

After much initial confusion, a judge who supervises emergency management in Dallas County emerged as the primary point person. However, there were no clear guidelines on how to provide care for Duncan while minimizing risks to others or how to safeguard the apartment where Duncan had been staying during the previous week. The city hired a hazardous waste firm called The Cleaning Guys of Fort Worth to decontaminate the apartment, but no one on the ground seemed to know whether full biohazard protective gear was needed when entering the premises. Moreover, as the media reported on the possible Ebola case and the potential for the virus to spread, there was rising panic in Dallas. Parents began to keep their children home from school; many others avoided going out in public. Health care workers for the city and county joined with epidemiologists from the Centers for Disease Control and Prevention to track down and interview the dozens of people Duncan had come into contact with. In all, 177 people in the Dallas area were placed in a twenty-one-day quarantine, monitored for changes in their health, counseled, and supplied with groceries and other necessities as they were kept in isolation.

Meanwhile, Duncan's condition deteriorated, and he died on October 8. Three days later, the anxiety level in Dallas and elsewhere in the country jumped when a second Ebola case was confirmed. Nina Pham, a nurse who had treated Duncan at the hospital tested positive even though she had been wearing protective gear. On October 13, another nurse, Amber Vinson, was diagnosed with Ebola, triggering widespread alarm. City and county officials scrambled to plan for the worst—a colossal epidemic involving hundreds or thousands of stricken patients overwhelming hospitals and other health care facilities.

However, the virus did not spread after that point. Both nurses recovered and everyone who had been quarantined remained in good health. Dallas emerged from a potential crisis of monumental proportions relatively unscathed, but local government leaders there and elsewhere learned many sobering lessons from this episode about the need for clearer and more detailed protocols regarding the identification of new diseases, handling people who are exposed, establishing appropriate treatment facilities, and determining which governmental entities should take the lead in responding to a major public health crisis.

Additional Resources

Bryan Burrough, "Trial by Ebola," *Vanity Fair* (2015). http://www.vanityfair.com/news/2015/02/ebola-us-dallas-epidemic.

Matthew Carey, *A Short Account of the Malignant Fever, Lately Prevalent in Philadelphia in 1793*, 4th ed., improved (Philadelphia: Carey, 1794).

Simon Finger, *The Contagious City: The Politics of Public Health in Early Philadelphia* (Ithaca, NY: Cornell University Press, 2012).

Eric Klinenberg, *Heat Wave: A Social Autopsy of Disaster in Chicago*, 2nd ed. (Chicago: University of Chicago Press, 2015).

Minutes of the proceedings of the Committee, appointed on 14 September, 1793, by the citizens of Philadelphia (Philadelphia: R. Aitken, 1794).

Gary B. Nash, *First City: Philadelphia and the Forging of Historical Memory* (Philadelphia: University of Pennsylvania Press, 2002).

J. H. Powell, *Bring Out Your Dead: The Great Plague of Yellow Fever in Philadelphia in 1793* (Philadelphia: University of Pennsylvania Press, 1949).

Billy G. Smith, ed., *Life in Early Philadelphia: Documents from the Revolutionary and Early National Periods* (University Park: Pennsylvania State University Press, 1995).

Discussion Questions

1. Is city government best equipped to respond to major public health crises? Should the state and federal governments be expected to step in and oversee the treatment and containment of highly contagious diseases?

2. If city government does play a significant role in such matters, what kinds of officials should assume leadership roles? Professionals with expertise? The mayor and other elected representatives who can be held accountable by the voters?

3. City government officials during the eighteenth century tended to come from the upper classes of society and were often respected for their knowledge, wisdom, and integrity. What does this say about who should govern cities? Do Americans still feel this way?

4. Many Americans indicate that they favor a government that is limited in scope. Perhaps this was desirable when cities were relatively small, but is limited government feasible today when cities are far larger and more complex?

Chapter 3

Machine Politics

Introduction

If American society was primarily rural and agricultural in the eighteenth century, then the nineteenth century brought sweeping changes. This was the era of mass urbanization. Never before and probably never again will we see cities grow as fast as they did during the 1800s. Some brief statistics illustrate the magnitude of the transformation. In 1840, only three cities—New York, Baltimore, and New Orleans—had populations exceeding 100,000; by 1920, 68 cities had populations over 100,000. As late as 1850, only 15 percent of the U.S. population was urban, meaning that only one in ten lived in places with 2,500 residents or more; by 1930, over 56 percent of Americans lived in such places. In less than a century, the United States evolved from being an overwhelmingly rural country into a predominantly urban nation.[1]

What caused this unprecedented growth of cities? The key factor was industrialization. Recall that urban economies prior to the nineteenth century revolved around the buying and selling of goods and production was on a small scale. By the end of the century, urban economies were dominated by industry—the large-scale, mechanized production of goods. Industrialization went hand in hand with urban growth. Factory owners preferred to build new plants in cities to take advantage of rising concentrations of workers and expanding markets for their goods. Meanwhile, the explosion in industrialization reinforced urbanization as more and more people, both from the countryside and other nations, flocked to burgeoning American cities in search of good jobs and opportunity. The clustering of new arrivals proved to be conducive to innovative thinking and scientific discoveries that further impelled the pace of industrial production. Technological advances in transportation, most notably, the development of a national railroad system, enabled factory owners to ship their manufactured goods throughout the United States and beyond. Little did the cowboy roaming the West Texas range know that his hat had been manufactured by the Stetson Hat factory in the densely settled, industrial neighborhood of north Philadelphia. The creation of mass markets, in turn, further sparked mass production, allowing more and more factory workers to be hired. Finally, railroads could be used to supply city residents with food and vital raw materials such as coal and lumber, thus allowing for more urban growth.[2]

A crucial societal trend that fueled both industrialization and urbanization during the nineteenth century was immigration. Industrialists needed workers to operate the booming factories and so they readily supported a liberal immigration policy that brought more than 33 million immigrants to the United States between 1820 and 1920. The impact on many cities was enormous. By 1910, immigrants and their native-born children constituted over 70 percent of the populations of New York City, Chicago, Boston, Buffalo, Cleveland, Detroit, and Milwaukee, and in many other cities the percentage ranged between 50 and 70 percent.[3] Immigration generally proceeded in two massive waves, the first mainly from Germany and famine-stricken Ireland during the 1840s and 1850s and the second from southern and central Europe and Russia during the late nineteenth and early twentieth centuries. At first, immigrants tended to reside in ports of arrival, mostly in the northeast and mid-Atlantic, but over time many spread westward, settling in industrial centers of the ever-expanding midwest.[4]

The massive influx of humanity into cities from the surrounding countryside and other nations placed a huge strain on urban infrastructures. Tens of thousands of new and poor immigrants jammed together into overcrowded tenements that lacked adequate light, ventilation, and heat. With no indoor plumbing, tenants used privies in dismal cellars and back alleys. Many cities lacked sewers. Smaller cities relied on scavenging dogs, goats, and hogs as their primary means of removing kitchen waste and other biodegradable debris. Most streets were unpaved and turned into a swampy, odiferous mix of mud and manure following a heavy rain and became virtually impassable in places.[5] Disease was rampant in immigrant ghettos. Regular outbreaks of typhoid, dysentery, and tuberculosis contributed to alarmingly high mortality rates. In addition to horrendous living conditions, rapid urban growth precipitated a host of other pressing problems. Public schools were overwhelmed; a typical classroom in Boston in 1850 had 55 students. Fires in ramshackle, wood-constructed tenements posed a constant threat to entire neighborhoods. The combination of densely populated communities and rising poverty led to sharp increases in criminal behavior. Gangs of young hoodlums roamed the streets and terrorized neighborhoods. As people continued to pour into urban areas, the situation only grew more desperate with each passing year.[6]

The kind of city government that had evolved from the preindustrial era was simply not up to the challenge posed by mass urbanization. The preference for small government composed of elite gentlemen who volunteered their time by serving on committees organized to address a particular issue such as public safety, water supply, and street maintenance gave way to a proliferation of boards, commissions, and departments established to address the escalating number of serious problems. However, the unprecedented expansion of governmental entities proceeded without any overarching plan for how services were supposed to be delivered to the masses. The fragmentation of government was exacerbated by a lack of leadership. Mayors created boards to deal with a problem, while governors established others to address the same problem. At one point in the 1850s, New York City had two different police departments. Urban governance had become an unwieldy, chaotic mess, and one utterly ill equipped to respond to the mounting urban crisis.[7]

And yet, a condition of crisis may present opportunities as well as constraints. By the 1870s, most large cities witnessed the rise of a new political organization that more or less fulfilled the need for governance and order.[8] The political machine was essentially a political party organization featuring a hierarchical structure with a boss at the top presiding over a vast network of party workers at multiple levels. George Washington Plunkitt's personal reflections in **Reading 3-1** on the day-to-day activities of neighborhood-based precinct captains remain the most colorful and illuminating depiction of machine politics in action.

Machine politics was predicated on an exchange relationship. Machine politicians sought votes, particularly from the masses of poor and working-class immigrants, who could now vote thanks to the abolition of all remaining property requirements during the Jacksonian era and to a speedy naturalization process during the nineteenth century.[9] In return, immigrant voters wanted assistance in adjusting to their new and difficult lives in America. Precinct captains found myriad ways to assist the immigrant masses—meeting new arrivals just off the boat from Ellis Island or at the local train station, offering advice on where to live, dispensing aid in times of emergency, or securing a patronage job. As Robert Merton explains in **Reading 3-2**, the machine served as a precursor to the modern-day welfare state, along with fulfilling other societal functions. City bosses also worked out a cooperative arrangement with many businesses. Machines provided government contracts and franchises and greased the wheels of the administrative process. In exchange, businesses supplied political and financial support and patronage jobs.

Not surprisingly, machine politics was no panacea for the urban crisis of the nineteenth century. Given finite resources, the machine's capacity to furnish material support was always limited. Some immigrant groups benefited more than others and symbolic gestures were far more common than tangible goodies.[10] The most glaring drawback associated with machine rule was widespread corruption, as documented in **Reading 3-3**, Alexander Callow's account of the Tweed Ring in New York City.[11] However, the more effective machines, such as Tammany Hall under the quiet but skillful leadership of Charles Francis Murphy between 1902 and 1924, did not rely on bribery and fraud to win elections and remain in power. They succeeded by being at least partially responsive to the substantial needs of many working-class immigrants while providing a sense of empowerment and pride to a significant subset.[12] In this way, machine politics proved to be remarkably durable, lasting in some northeastern and midwestern cities for decades. Even in the modern era, vestiges of machine politics persist.[13]

Notes

1. Conrad Taeubner and Irene B. Taeubner, *The Changing Population of the United States* (New York: John Wiley & Sons, 1958); see also Eric H. Monkkonen, *America Becomes Urban: The Development of U.S. Cities and Towns, 1780–1980* (Berkeley: University of California Press, 1988); Charles N. Glaab and A. Theodore Brown, *A History of Urban America* (New York: Macmillan, 1967).

2. Blake McKelvey, *The Urbanization of America, 1860–1915* (New Brunswick, NJ: Rutgers University Press, 1963); Alan Pred, *Urban Growth and City-Systems in the United States, 1840–1860* (Cambridge, MA: Harvard University Press, 1980); Thomas C. Cochran, *Frontiers of Change: Early Industrialism in America* (New York: Oxford University Press, 1981); Maury Klein and Harvey A. Kantor, *Prisoners of Progress: American Industrial Cities, 1850–1920* (New York: Macmillan, 1976).

3. Raymond A. Mohl, *The New City: Urban America in the Industrial Age, 1860–1920* (Arlington Heights, IL: Harlan Davidson, 1985).

4. The second wave was supplemented by immigrants from China and Japan who moved to the west coast, French Canadians, who settled in industrial cities in New England, and Mexicans, who concentrated in the southwest and California before many relocated to cities in the midwest. David Ward, *Cities and Immigrants: A Geography of Change in Nineteenth Century America* (New York: Oxford University Press, 1971); Humbert S. Nelli, "European Immigrants and Urban America," in *The Urban Experience*, ed. Raymond A. Mohl and James F. Richardson (Belmont, CA: Wadsworth, 1973).

5. Catherine McNeur, *Taming Manhattan: Environmental Battles in the Antebellum City* (Cambridge, MA: Harvard University Press, 2014); Clay McShane and Joel A. Tarr, *The Horse in the City: Living Machines in the Nineteenth Century* (Baltimore: Johns Hopkins University Press, 2007); Martin V. Melosi, *Garbage in the Cities: Refuse, Reform, and the Environment, 1880–1980* (College Station: Texas A&M Press, 1981).

6. Howard P. Chudacoff and Judith E. Smith, *The Evolution of American Urban Society*, 3rd ed. (Englewood Cliffs, NJ: Prentice Hall, 1988); see also Edward K. Spann, *The New Metropolis: New York City, 1840–1857* (New York: Columbia University Press, 1981); Tyler Anbinder, *Five Points: The 19th Century New York City Neighborhood That Invented Tap Dancing, Stole Elections, and Became the World's Most Notorious Slum* (New York: Free Press, 2001).

7. Chudacoff and Smith, *The Evolution of American Urban Society*.

8. Alan DiGaetano, "The Birthplace of Modern Urban Governance: A Comparison of Political Modernization in Boston, Massachusetts and Bristol, England, 1800–1870," *Journal of Urban History*, 35 (2), 2009.

9. Amy Bridges, *A City in the Republic: Antebellum New York and the Origins of Machine Politics* (New York: Cambridge University Press, 1984).

10. Steven P. Erie, *Rainbow's End: Irish-Americans and the Dilemmas of Urban Machine Politics, 1840–1985* (Berkeley: University of California Press, 1988); Terrence J. McDonald, *The Parameters of Urban Fiscal Policy: Socio-Economic Change and Political Culture in San Francisco, 1860–1906* (Berkeley: University of California Press, 1986).

11. See also Joel A. Tarr, "The Urban Politician as Entrepreneur" in *Urban Bosses, Machines, and Progressive Reformers*, ed. Bruce M. Stave (Lexington, MA: D.C. Heath, 1972).

12. John M. Allswang, *Bosses, Machines, and Urban Voters*, rev. ed. (Baltimore: Johns Hopkins University Press, 1986); see also Terry Golway, *Machine Made: Tammany Hall and the Creation of Modern American Politics* (New York: Liveright, 2014); Nancy Joan Weiss, *Charles Francis Murphy, 1858–1924: Respectability and Responsibility in Tammany Politics* (Northampton, MA: Smith College, 1968).

13. Raymond E. Wolfinger, "Why Political Machines Have Not Withered Away and Other Revisionist Thoughts," *Journal of Politics* 34 (2), 1972; Milton Rakove, *Don't Make No Waves . . . Don't Back No Losers: An Insider's Analysis of the Daley Machine* (Bloomington: Indiana University Press, 1975); Mike Stanton, *The Prince of Providence* (New York: Random House, 2003).

3-1 "To Hold Your District: Study Human Nature and Act Accordin'"

William L. Riorden

Plunkitt of Tammany Hall

There's only one way to hold a district: you must study human nature and act accordin'. You can't study human nature in books. Books is a hindrance more than anything else. If you have been to college, so much the worse for you. You'll have to unlearn all you learned before you can get right down to human nature, and unlearnin' takes a lot of time. Some men can never forget what they learned at college. Such men may get to be district leaders by a fluke, but they never last.

To learn real human nature you have to go among the people, see them and be seen. I know every man, woman, and child in the Fifteenth District, except them that's been born this summer—and I know some of them, too. I know what they like and what they don't like, what they are strong at and what they are weak in, and I reach them by approachin' at the right side.

For instance, here's how I gather in the young men. I hear of a young feller that's proud of his voice, thinks that he can sing fine. I ask him to come around to Washington Hall and join our Glee Club. He comes and sings, and he's a follower of Plunkitt for life. Another young feller gains a reputation as a baseball player in a vacant lot. I bring him into our baseball club. That fixes him. You'll find him workin' for my ticket at the polls next election day. Then there's the feller that likes rowin' on the river, the young feller that makes a name as a waltzer on his block, the young feller that's handy with his dukes—I rope them all in by givin' them opportunities to show themselves off. I don't trouble them with political arguments. I just study human nature and act accordin'.

But you may say this game won't work with the high-toned fellers, the fellers that go through college and then join the Citizens' Union. Of course it wouldn't work. I have a special treatment for them. I ain't like the patent medicine man that gives the same medicine for all diseases. The Citizens' Union kind of a young man! I love him! He's the daintiest morsel of the lot, and he don't often escape me.

Before telling you how I catch him, let me mention that before the election last year, the Citizens' Union said they had four hundred or five hundred enrolled voters in my district. They had a lovely headquarters, too, beautiful roll-top desks and the cutest rugs in the world. If I was accused of havin' contributed to fix up the nest for them, I wouldn't deny it under oath. What do I mean by that? Never mind. You can guess from the sequel, if you're sharp.

Well, election day came. The Citizens' Union's candidate for Senator, who ran against me, just polled five votes in the district, while I polled something more than 14,000 votes. What became of the 400 or 500 Citizens' Union enrolled voters in my district? Some people guessed that many of them were good Plunkitt men all along and worked with the Cits just to bring them into the Plunkitt camp by election day. You can guess that way, too, if you want to. I never contradict stories about me, especially in hot weather. I just call your attention to the fact that on last election day 395 Citizens' Union enrolled voters in my district were missin' and unaccounted for.

I tell you frankly, though, how I have captured some of the Citizens' Union's young men. I have a plan that never fails. I watch the City Record to see when

Source: William L. Riorden, "To Hold Your District: Study Human Nature and Act Accordin'" from *Plunkitt of Tammany Hall: A Series of Very Plain Talks on Very Practical Politics.* New York: E.P. Dutton, 1963, pp. 25–28.

there's civil service examinations for good things. Then I take my young Cit in hand, tell him all about the good thing and get him worked up till he goes and takes an examination. I don't bother about him any more. It's a cinch that he comes back to me in a few days and asks to join Tammany Hall. Come over to Washington Hall some night and I'll show you a list of names on our rolls marked "C.S." which means, "bucked up against civil service."

As to the older voters, I reach them, too. No, I don't send them campaign literature. That's rot. People can get all the political stuff they want to read—and a good deal more, too—in the papers. Who reads speeches, nowadays, anyhow? It's bad enough to listen to them. You ain't goin' to gain any votes by stuffin' the letter boxes with campaign documents. Like as not you'll lose votes, for there's nothin' a man hates more than to hear the letter carrier ring his bell and go to the letter box expectin' to find a letter he was lookin' for, and find only a lot of printed politics. I met a man this very mornin' who told me he voted the Democratic State ticket last year just because the Republicans kept crammin' his letter box with campaign documents.

What tells in holdin' your grip on your district is to go right down among the poor families and help them in the different ways they need help. I've got a regular system for this. If there's a fire in Ninth, Tenth, or Eleventh Avenue, for example, any hour of the day or night, I'm usually there with some of my election district captains as soon as the fire engines. If a family is burned out I don't ask whether they are Republicans or Democrats, and I don't refer them to the Charity Organization Society, which would investigate their case in a month or two and decide they were worthy of help about the time they are dead from starvation. I just get quarters for them, buy clothes for them if their clothes were burned up, and fix them up till they get things runnin' again. It's philanthropy, but it's politics, too—mighty good politics. Who can tell how many votes one of these fires bring me? The poor are the most grateful people in the world, and, let me tell you, they have more friends in their neighborhoods than the rich have in theirs.

If there's a family in my district in want I know it before the charitable societies do, and me and my men are first on the ground. I have a special corps to look up such cases. The consequence is that the poor look up to George W. Plunkitt as a father, come to him in trouble—and don't forget him on election day.

Another thing, I can always get a job for a deservin' man. I make it a point to keep on the track of jobs, and it seldom happens that I don't have a few up my sleeve ready for use. I know every big employer in the district and in the whole city, for that matter, and they ain't in the habit of sayin' no to me when I ask them for a job.

And the children—the little roses of the district! Do I forget them? Oh, no! They know me, every one of them, and they know that a sight of Uncle George and candy means the same thing. Some of them are the best kind of vote-getters. I'll tell you a case. Last year a little Eleventh Avenue rosebud, whose father is a Republican, caught hold of his whiskers on election day and said she wouldn't let go till he'd promise to vote for me. And she didn't.

3-2 "The Latent Functions of the Machine"*

Robert Merton

Social Theory and Social Structure

[I]n large sectors of the American population, the political machine or the "political racket" are judged as unequivocally "bad" and "undesirable." The grounds for such moral judgment vary somewhat, but they consist substantially in pointing out that political machines violate moral codes: political patronage violates the code of selecting personnel on the basis of impersonal qualifications rather than on grounds of party loyalty or contributions to the party war-chest; bossism violates the code that votes should be based on individual appraisal of the qualifications of candidates and of political issues, and not on abiding loyalty to a feudal leader; bribery, and "honest graft" obviously offend the proprieties of property; "protection" for crime clearly violates the law and the mores; and so on.

In view of the manifold respects in which political machines, in varying degrees, run counter to the mores and at times to the law, it becomes pertinent to inquire how they manage to continue in operation. The familiar "explanations" for the continuance of the political machine are not here in point. To be sure, it may well be that if "respectable citizenry" would live up to their political obligations, if the electorate were to be alert and enlightened; if the number of elective officers were substantially reduced from the dozens, even hundreds, which the average voter is now expected to appraise in the course of town, county, state and national elections; if the electorate were activated by the "wealthy and educated classes without whose participation," as the not-always democratically oriented Bryce put it, "the best-framed government must speedily degenerate";—if these and a plethora of similar changes in political structure were introduced, perhaps the "evils" of the political machine would indeed be exorcized. But it should be noted that these changes are often not introduced, that political machines have had the phoenix-like quality of arising strong and unspoiled from their ashes, that, in short, this structure has exhibited a notable vitality in many areas of American political life.

Proceeding from the functional view, therefore, that we should *ordinarily* (not invariably) expect persistent social patterns and social structures to perform positive functions *which are at the time not adequately fulfilled by other existing patterns and structures*, the thought occurs that perhaps this publicly maligned organization is, *under present conditions*, satisfying basic latent functions. A brief examination of current analyses of this type of structure may also serve to illustrate additional problems of functional analysis.

Some Functions of the Political Machine

Without presuming to enter into the variations of detail marking different political machines—a Tweed, Vare, Crump, Flynn, Hague are by no means identical types of bosses—we can briefly examine the functions more or less common to the political machine, as a generic type of social organization. We neither attempt to itemize all the diverse functions of the political machine nor imply that all these functions are similarly fulfilled by each and every machine.

*Some text and accompanying endnotes have been omitted. Please consult the original source.

The key structural function of the Boss is to organize, centralize and maintain in good working condition "the scattered fragments of power" which are at present dispersed through our political organization. By this centralized organization of political power, the boss and his apparatus can satisfy the needs of diverse subgroups in the larger community which are not adequately satisfied by legally devised and culturally approved social structures.

To understand the role of bossism and the machine, therefore, we must look at two types of sociological variables: (1) the *structural* context which makes it difficult, if not impossible, for morally approved structures to fulfill essential social functions, thus leaving the door open for political machines (or their structural equivalents) to fulfill these functions and (2) the subgroups whose distinctive needs are left unsatisfied, except for the latent functions which the machine in fact fulfills.

Structural Context: The constitutional framework of American political organization specifically precludes the legal possibility of highly centralized power and, it has been noted, thus "discourages the growth of effective and responsible leadership. The framers of the Constitution, as Woodrow Wilson observed, set up the check and balance system 'to keep government at a sort of mechanical equipoise by means of a standing amicable contest among its several organic parts.' They distrusted power as dangerous to liberty: and therefore they spread it thin and erected barriers against its concentration." This dispersion of power is found not only at the national level but in local areas as well. "As a consequence," Sait goes on to observe, "when *the people or particular groups* among them demanded positive action, no one had adequate authority to act. The machine provided an antidote."[93]

The constitutional dispersion of power not only makes for difficulty of effective decision and action but when action does occur it is defined and hemmed in by legalistic considerations. In consequence, there developed "a much *more human system* of partisan government, whose chief object soon became the circumvention of government by law. . . . The lawlessness of the extra-official democracy was merely the counterpoise of the legalism of the official democracy. The

lawyer having been permitted to subordinate democracy to the Law, the Boss had to be called in to extricate the victim, which he did after a fashion and for a consideration."[94]

Officially, political power is dispersed. Various well-known expedients were devised for this manifest objective. Not only was there the familiar separation of powers among the several branches of the government but, in some measure, tenure in each office was limited, rotation in office approved. And the scope of power inherent in each office was severely circumscribed. Yet, observes Sait in rigorously functional terms, "Leadership is necessary; and *since* it does not develop readily within the constitutional framework, the Boss provides it in a crude and irresponsible form from the outside."[95]

Put in more generalized terms, *the functional deficiencies of the official structure generate an alternative (unofficial) structure to fulfill existing needs somewhat more effectively.* Whatever its specific historical origins, the political machine persists as an apparatus for satisfying otherwise unfulfilled needs of diverse groups in the population. By turning to a few of these subgroups and their characteristic needs, we shall be led at once to a range of latent functions of the political machine.

Functions of the Political Machine for Diverse Subgroups. It is well known that one source of strength of the political machine derives from its roots in the local community and the neighborhood. The political machine does not regard the electorate as an amorphous, undifferentiated mass of voters. With a keen sociological intuition, the machine recognizes that the voter is a person living in a specific neighborhood, with specific personal problems and personal wants. Public issues are abstract and remote; private problems are extremely concrete and immediate. It is not through the generalized appeal to large public concerns that the machine operates, but through the direct, quasi-feudal relationships between local representatives of the machine and voters in their neighborhood. Elections are won in the precinct.

The machine welds its link with ordinary men and women by elaborate networks of personal relations. Politics is transformed into personal ties. The precinct captain "must be a friend to every man, assuming if he does not feel sympathy with the unfortunate, and utilizing in his good works the resources which the boss puts at his disposal."[96] The precinct captain is forever a friend in need. In our prevailingly impersonal society, the machine, through its local agents, fulfills the important social *function of humanizing and personalizing all manner of assistance* to those in need. Food-baskets and jobs, legal and extra-legal advice, setting to rights minor scrapes with the law, helping the bright poor boy to a political scholarship in a local college, looking after the bereaved—the whole range of crises when a feller needs a friend, and, above all, a friend who knows the score and who can do something about it,—all these find the ever-helpful precinct captain available in the pinch.

To assess this function of the political machine adequately, it is important to note not only that aid *is* provided but *the manner in which it is provided.* After all, other agencies do exist for dispensing such assistance. Welfare agencies, settlement houses, legal aid clinics, medical aid in free hospitals, public relief departments, immigration authorities—these and a multitude of other organizations are available to provide the most varied types of assistance. But in contrast to the professional techniques of the welfare worker which may typically represent in the mind of the recipient the cold, bureaucratic dispensation of limited aid following upon detailed investigation of legal claims to aid of the "client" are the unprofessional techniques of the precinct captain who asks no questions, exacts no compliance with legal rules of eligibility and does not "snoop" into private affairs.

For many, the loss of "self-respect" is too high a price for legalized assistance. In contrast to the gulf between the settlement house workers who so often come from a different social class, educational background and ethnic group, the precinct worker is "just one of us," who understands what it's all about. The condescending lady bountiful can hardly compete with the understanding friend in need. In *this struggle between alternative structures for fulfilling the nominally same function* of providing aid and support to those who need it, it is clearly the machine politician who is better integrated with the groups which he serves than the impersonal, professionalized, socially

distant and legally constrained welfare worker. And since the politician can at times influence and manipulate the official organizations for the dispensation of assistance, whereas the welfare worker has practically no influence on the political machine, this only adds to his greater effectiveness. More colloquially and also, perhaps, more incisively, it was the Boston ward-leader, Martin Lomasny, who described this essential function to the curious Lincoln Steffens: "I think," said Lomasny, "that there's got to be in every ward somebody that any bloke can come to—no matter what he's done—and get help. *Help, you understand; none of your law and justice, but help.*"[98]

The "deprived classes," then, constitute one subgroup for whom the political machine satisfies wants not adequately satisfied in the same fashion by the legitimate social structure.

For a second subgroup, that of business (primarily "big" business but also "small"), the political boss serves the function of providing those political privileges which entail immediate economic gains. Business corporations, among which the public utilities (railroads, local transportation and electric light companies, communications corporations) are simply the most conspicuous in this regard, seek special political dispensations which will enable them to stabilize their situation and to near their objective of maximizing profits. Interestingly enough, corporations often want to avoid a chaos of uncontrolled competition. They want the greater security of an economic czar who controls, regulates and organizes competition, providing that this czar is not a public official with his decisions subject to public scrutiny and public control. (The latter would be "government control," and hence taboo.) The political boss fulfills these requirements admirably.

Examined for a moment apart from any moral considerations, the political apparatus operated by the Boss is effectively designed to perform these functions with a minimum of inefficiency. Holding the strings of diverse governmental divisions, bureaus and agencies in his competent hands, the Boss rationalizes the relations between public and private business. He serves as the business community's ambassador in the otherwise alien (and sometimes unfriendly) realm of government. And, in strict business-like terms, he is well-paid for his economic services to his respectable business clients. In an article entitled, "An Apology to Graft," Lincoln Steffens suggested that "Our economic system, which held up riches, power and acclaim as prizes to men bold enough and able enough to buy corruptly timber, mines, oil fields and franchises and 'get away with it,' was at fault."[99] And, in a conference with a hundred or so of Los Angeles business leaders, he described a fact well known to all of them: the Boss and his machine were an *integral part* of the organization of the economy. "You cannot build or operate a railroad, or a street railway, gas, water, or power company, develop and operate a mine, or get forests and cut timber on a large scale, or run any privileged business, without corrupting or joining in the corruption of the government. You tell me privately that you must, and here I am telling you semi-publicly that you must. And that is so all over the country. And that means that we have an organization of society in which, *for some reason,* you and your kind, the ablest, most intelligent, most imaginative, daring, and resourceful leaders of society, are and must be against society and its laws and its all-around growth."[100]

Since the demand for the services of special privileges are built into the structure of the society, the Boss fulfills diverse functions for this second subgroup of business-seeking-privilege. These "needs" of business, as presently constituted, are not adequately provided for by conventional and culturally approved social structures; consequently, the extra-legal but more-or-less efficient organization of the political machine comes to provide these services. To adopt an *exclusively* moral attitude toward the "corrupt political machine" is to lose sight of the very structural conditions which generate the "evil" that is so bitterly attacked. To adopt a functional outlook is to provide not an apologia for the political machine but a more solid basis for modifying or eliminating the machine, *providing* specific structural arrangements are introduced either for eliminating these effective demands of the business community or, if that is the objective, of satisfying these demands through alternative means.

A third set of distinctive functions fulfilled by the political machine for a special subgroup is that of providing alternative channels of social mobility for those otherwise excluded from the more conventional avenues for personal "advancement." Both the sources of this special "need" (for social mobility) and the respect in which the political machine comes to help satisfy this need can be understood by examining the structure of the larger culture and society. As is well known, the American culture lays enormous emphasis on money and power as a "success" goal legitimate for all members of the society. By no means alone in our inventory of cultural goals, it still remains among the most heavily endowed with positive affect and value. However, certain subgroups and certain ecological areas are notable for the relative absence of opportunity for achieving these (monetary and power) types of success. They constitute, in short, sub-populations where "the cultural emphasis upon pecuniary success has been absorbed, but where there is *little access to conventional and legitimate* means for attaining such success. The conventional occupational opportunities of persons in (such areas) are almost completely limited to manual labor. Given our cultural stigmatization of manual labor,[101] and its correlate, the prestige of white-collar work, it is clear that the result is a tendency to achieve these culturally approved objectives *through whatever means are possible.* These people are on the one hand, "asked to orient their conduct toward the prospect of accumulating wealth [and power] and, on the other, they are largely denied effective opportunities to do so institutionally."

It is within this context of social structure that the political machine fulfills the basic function of providing avenues of social mobility for the otherwise disadvantaged. Within this context, even the corrupt political machine and the racket "represent the triumph of amoral intelligence over morally prescribed 'failure' when the channels of vertical mobility are closed or narrowed *in a society which places a high premium on economic affluence, [power] and social ascent for all its members.*"[102] As one sociologist has noted on the basis of several years of close observation in a slum area:

> The sociologist who dismisses racket and political organizations as deviations from desirable standards thereby neglects some of the major elements of slum life.... *He does not discover the functions they perform for the members* [of the groupings in

the slum]. The Irish and later immigrant peoples have had the greatest difficulty in finding places for themselves in our urban social and economic structure. Does anyone believe that the immigrants and their children could have achieved their present degree of social mobility without gaining control of the political organization of some of our largest cities? The same is true of the racket organization. *Politics and the rackets have furnished an important means of social mobility for individuals, who, because of ethnic background and low class position,* are blocked from advancement in the "respectable" channels.[103]

This, then, represents a third type of function performed for a distinctive subgroup. This function, it may be noted in passing, is fulfilled by the sheer existence and operation of the political machine, for it is in the machine itself that these individuals and subgroups find their culturally induced needs more or less satisfied. It refers to the services which the political apparatus provides for its own personnel. But seen in the wider social context we have set forth, it no longer appears as merely a means of self-aggrandizement for profit-hungry and power-hungry individuals, but as an organized provision for subgroups otherwise excluded from or handicapped in the race for "getting ahead."

Just as the political machine performs services for "legitimate" business, so it operates to perform not dissimilar services for "illegitimate" business: vice, crime and rackets. Once again, the basic sociological role of the machine in this respect can be more fully appreciated only if one temporarily abandons attitudes of moral indignation, to examine in all moral innocence the actual workings of the organization. In this light, it at once appears that the subgroup of the professional criminal, racketeer or gambler has basic similarities of organization, demands and operation to the subgroup of the industrialist, man of business or speculator. If there is a Lumber King or an Oil King, there is also a Vice King or a Racket King. If expansive legitimate business organizes administrative and financial syndicates to "rationalize" and to "integrate" diverse areas of production and business enterprise, so expansive rackets and crime organize syndicates to bring order to the otherwise chaotic areas of production of illicit goods and services. If legitimate business regards the proliferation of small business enterprises as wasteful and inefficient, substituting, for example, the giant chain stores for hundreds of corner groceries, so illegitimate business adopts the same businesslike attitude and syndicates crime and vice.

Finally, and in many respects, most important, is the basic similarity, if not near-identity, of the economic role of "legitimate" business and of "illegitimate" business. *Both are in some degree concerned with the provision of goods and services for which there is an economic demand.* Morals aside, they are both business, industrial and professional enterprises, dispensing goods and services which some people want, for which there is a market in which goods and services are transformed into commodities. And, in a prevalently market society, we should expect appropriate enterprises to arise whenever there is a market demand for certain goods or services.

As is well known, vice, crime and the rackets *are* "big business." Consider only that there have been estimated to be about 500,000 professional prostitutes in the United States of 1950, and compare this with the approximately 200,000 physicians and 350,000 professional registered nurses. It is difficult to estimate which have the larger clientele: the professional men and women of medicine or the professional men and women of vice. It is, of course, difficult to estimate the economic assets, income, profits and dividends of illicit gambling in this country and to compare it with the economic assets, income, profits and dividends of, say, the shoe industry, but it is altogether possible that the two industries are about on a par. No precise figures exist on the annual expenditures on illicit narcotics, and it is probable that these are less than the expenditures on candy, but it is also probable that they are larger than the expenditure on books.

It takes but a moment's thought to recognize that, *in strictly economic terms*, there is no relevant difference between the provision of licit and of illicit goods and services. The liquor traffic illustrates this perfectly. It would be peculiar to argue that prior to 1920 (when the 18th amendment became effective), the provision of liquor constituted an economic service, that from 1920 to 1933, its production and sale no longer constituted an economic service dispensed in a market, and that from 1934 to the present, it once again took on a serviceable aspect. Or, it would be *economically* (not morally) absurd to suggest that the sale of boot-legged liquor in the dry state of Kansas is less a response to a market demand than the sale of publicly manufactured liquor in the neighboring wet state of Missouri. Examples of this sort can of course be multiplied many times over. Can it be held that in European countries, with registered and legalized prostitution, the prostitute contributes an economic service, whereas in this country, lacking legal sanction, the prostitute provides no such service? Or that the professional abortionist is in the economic market where he has approved legal status and that he is out of the economic market where he is legally taboo? Or that gambling satisfies a specific demand for entertainment in Nevada, where it constitutes the largest business enterprise of the larger cities in the state, but that it differs essentially in this respect from motion pictures in the neighboring state of California?

The failure to recognize that these businesses are only *morally* and not *economically* distinguishable from "legitimate" businesses has led to badly scrambled analysis. Once the economic identity of the two is recognized, we may anticipate that if the political machine performs functions for "legitimate big business" it will be all the more likely to perform not dissimilar functions for "illegitimate big business." And, of course, such is often the case.

The distinctive function of the political machine for their criminal, vice and racket clientele is to enable them to operate in satisfying the economic demands of a large market without due interference from the government. Just as big business may contribute funds to the political party war-chest to ensure a minimum of governmental interference, so with big rackets and big crime. In both instances, the political machine can, in varying degrees, provide "protection." In both instances, many features of the structural context are identical: (1) market demands for goods and services; (2) the operators' concern with maximizing gains from their enterprises; (3) the need for partial control of government which might otherwise interfere with these activities of businessmen; (4) the need for an efficient, powerful and centralized agency to provide an effective liaison of "business" with government.

Without assuming that the foregoing pages exhaust either the range of functions or the range of subgroups served by the political machine, we can at least see that *it presently fulfills some functions for these diverse subgroups which are not adequately fulfilled by culturally approved or more conventional structures.*

Several additional implications of the functional analysis of the political machine can be mentioned here only in passing, although they obviously require to be developed at length. First, the foregoing analysis has direct implications for *social engineering.* It helps explain why the periodic efforts at "political reform," "turning the rascals out" and "cleaning political house" are typically (though not necessarily) short-lived and ineffectual. It exemplifies a basic theorem: *any attempt to eliminate an existing social structure without providing adequate alternative structures for fulfilling the functions previously fulfilled by the abolished organization is doomed to failure.* (Needless to say, this theorem has much wider bearing than the one instance of the political machine.) When "political reform" confines itself to the manifest task of "turning the rascals out," it is engaging in little more than sociological magic. The reform may for a time bring new figures into the political limelight; it may serve the casual social function of re-assuring the electorate that the moral virtues remain intact and will ultimately triumph; it may actually effect a turnover in the personnel of the political machine; it may even, for a time, so curb the activities of the machine as to leave unsatisfied the many needs it has previously fulfilled. But, inevitably, unless the reform also involves a "re-forming" of the social and political structure such that the existing needs are satisfied by alternative structures or unless it involves a change which eliminates these needs altogether, the political machine will return to its integral place in the social scheme of things. To *seek social change, without due recognition of the manifest and latent functions performed by the social organization undergoing change, is to indulge in social ritual rather than social engineering.* The concepts of manifest and latent functions (or their equivalents) are indispensable elements in the theoretic repertoire of the social engineer. In this crucial sense, these concepts are not "merely" theoretical (in the abusive sense of the term), but are eminently practical. In the deliberate enactment of social change, they can be ignored only at the price of considerably heightening the risk of failure.

A second implication of this analysis of the political machine also has a bearing upon areas wider than the one we have considered. The paradox has often been noted that the supporters of the political machine include both the "respectable" business class elements who are, of course, opposed to the criminal or racketeer and the distinctly "unrespectable" elements of the underworld. And, at first appearance, this is cited as an instance of very strange bedfellows. The learned judge is not infrequently called upon to sentence the very racketeer beside whom he sat the night before at an informal dinner of the political bigwigs. The district attorney jostles the exonerated convict on his way to the back room where the Boss has called a meeting. The big business man may complain almost as bitterly as the big racketeer about the "extortionate" contributions to the party fund demanded by the Boss. Social opposites meet—in the smoke-filled room of the successful politician.

In the light of a functional analysis all this of course no longer seems paradoxical. Since the machine serves both the businessman and the criminal man, the two seemingly antipodal groups intersect. This points to a more general theorem: *the social functions of an organization help determine the structure (including the recruitment of personnel involved in the structure), just as the structure helps determine the effectiveness with which the functions are fulfilled.* In terms of social status, the business group and the criminal group are indeed poles apart. But status does not fully determine behavior and the inter-relations between groups. Functions modify these relations. Given their distinctive needs, the several subgroups in the large society are "integrated," whatever their personal desires or intentions, by the centralizing structure which serves these several needs. In a phrase with many implications which require further study, *structure affects function and function affects structure.* . . .

Notes

93. Edward M. Sait, "Machine, Political," *Encyclopedia of the Social Sciences*, IX, 658 b [italics supplied]; *cf.* A. F. Bentley, *The Process of Government* (Chicago, 1908), Chap. 2.

94. Herbert Croly, *Progressive Democracy* (New York, 1914), p. 254, cited by Sait, *op. cit.,* 658 b.

95. Sait, *op. cit.,* 659 a. [italics supplied].

96. *Ibid.,* 659 a.

98. *The Autobiography of Lincoln Steffens* (Chautauqua, New York: Chautauqua Press, 1931), 618.

99. *Autobiography of Lincoln Steffens,* 570.

100. *Ibid.,* 572-3 (italics supplied).

102. Merton, "Social structure and anomie," *Social Theory and Social Structure* (New York: The Free Press, 1968).

103. William F. Whyte, "Social organization in the slums," *American Sociological Review,* Feb. 1943, 8, 34-39 (italics supplied).

3-3 "'That Impudent Autocrat'"

Alexander Callow

The Tweed Ring

Skilled to pull wires, he baffles Nature's hope,
Who sure intended him to stretch a rope.
                    —James Russell Lowell, "The Boss"

Americans may disagree over politics and foreign policy, but on one subject there may be consensus. If those who are knowledgeable about the American past were asked to name the most infamous city political machine in our history, it would be a safe bet that most, perhaps all, would cite the Tweed Ring of New York City—William Marcy Tweed, the "Elegant" Oakey Hall, Peter "Brains" Sweeny, and Richard "Slippery Dick" Connolly—who dominated New York politics from 1866 to 1871.

There have been many corrupt city machines more successful and certainly more ruthless than the Tweed Ring, yet to the American imagination, the Tweed Ring is still the most audacious and notorious of them all; indeed, the classic example of municipal fraud. The significance of the Ring, however, was neither in its reputation nor in the grandeur of its larcenies, but in its creation—a big-city political organization. The Tweed Ring produced the first real "city boss" in the United States.[1] Boss Tweed and his three indispensable colleagues became the architects of the first modern city machine in New York and one of the first in the country. The Tweed Ring, then, constituted both a critical episode in the history of a great city and an important chapter in the history of American urban politics. To see how the Ring operated, how it gained and sustained power, how its impact reflected the public's attitudes toward corruption, reform, and urban institutions, should illuminate to some degree those fascinating and gaudy years of post-Civil War America.

The Tweed Ring, like other big city political machines, was a distinct, peculiar American institution, created by clever men out of conditions indigenous not only to the city and state but to the nation as well. From the 1850's through the Civil War the momentum of economic, political, and social change generated problems that baffled and overwhelmed New Yorkers and set the stage for machine rule. In this period, old civic problems were magnified and new ones were created. Housing, employment, welfare services, sanitation, health, and law enforcement demanded responsible government from the city and the state. But expansion was so rapid in economic activity, population, and size that the city outgrew its government, leaving an obsolete city government hopelessly inadequate to cope with the problems of a modern urban-industrial society.

A rurally dominated State legislature either ignored the city's problems or met them only halfway, partly because it was jealous of its power and was reluctant to give the city the necessary authority to deal meaningfully with its growing pains, and partly because it was consumed with an anti-urban bias. Like many State legislatures in America, it was often blind to the creative potentiality of a great city. Instead, it tended to see New York City as a threat to agrarian values, the cesspool of vice, crime, disease, and filth, a refuge for moral cripples, shady politicians, and the irresponsible poor—foreign and domestic.

Well-meaning reformers further compounded the problems of responsible government. Dismayed and distrustful of rapid urbanization, many turned to history and learned the wrong lesson. They tried to mold government to accord with an ideal that typified an

Source: Alexander B. Callow, Jr., "'That Impudent Autocrat'" from *The Tweed Ring*, pp. 3–16, 301. Copyright 1966. Reprinted by permission of Oxford University Press.

older, simpler, and less urban America. Their panacea called for a small, inexpensive, intensely economy-minded government, based on the proposition that the best government was the government that governed least and taxed less. To them responsible government existed when politics was replaced by the standards of business efficiency, when, as it were, politics was taken out of politics. Good government could be managed only by "good" people, the middle and upper classes—the affluent, the well-educated, the virtuous. This urge to escape the often harsh and brutal realities of mid-century America and to recapture the great days of Jeffersonian Arcadia, complicated the task of city government. The ideals of the past were irrelevant to the problems created by the burgeoning growth of the city. Above all, these ideals ignored a profound political, economic, and social change that was creating a new political elite and certainly a different political style that could adapt a political organization to meet at least some of the needs and provide some of the services that city government would and could not.

In effect, the era of the Tweed Ring reflected a transition phase of New York politics that spelled the end to the long rule of the middle and upper classes. The old ruling elite of the "best" people was gradually being evicted from power by a three-pronged attack: by the entrepreneur, demanding favors and a special license for his commercial and industrial interests; by the immigrant, who was seeking a firmer economic and political stake in American life; and by the professional politician, adept in trading jobs for the immigrant vote and special favors for the businessman's bribes.

In this struggle for power, the old middle and upper classes never really presented any formidable competition, primarily because they could not adjust to the political and social changes that were creating for them a new, strange urban world. Seeing themselves as the guardians of Protestant, Anglo-Saxon standards, they regarded the immigrant as a threat to the purity of the Anglo-Saxon stock, its religion, its values of self-reliance and independence. Thus the immigrant was alienated and made more accessible to the professional Tammany politician who understood some of his problems. The old elite's genteel tradition in manners, education, and culture, gave it a marked distaste for personal contact with the masses. Its conception of the proper politician as a gentleman devoted to disinterested public service, made for a disdain that underestimated the wit and ability of a son of a saloonkeeper or livery stable owner turned politician. The middle- and upper-class view of politics as a means to moralize society committed them to the tactics of moral exhortation, and obscured the practical, concrete aspects of organized politics.

Thus the professional politician of humble origin was given greater rein to do the things he knew the best. Steeped in the logistics of grass-roots practical politics, he organized the bleak, sprawling areas of the poor into political strongholds, and devoted himself to the mundane business of building and entrenching a political organization. In one sense, the old ruling classes beat themselves. In another sense, professional politicians, like Messrs. Tweed, Sweeny, Hall, and Connolly, outmaneuvered the old elite by exploiting the growing complexities of urban life.

Another phenomenon that helped make the Tweed Ring possible was a decay in business and political standards. The triumph of big business and the emergence of an age of enterprise coming in the aftermath of the Civil War, produced powerful industrialists like the oil, steel, railroad, traction, and utility kings, unprincipled speculators like Jim Fiske and Jay Gould, who made corrupt alliances with politicians to protect and enlarge their economic stake. Corruption became a national infection in the big cities, the State legislatures, the reconstruction governments in the South, and in the federal government itself, with the scandals of the Grant administration.

Along with this, there was a kind of moral twilight: Americans were tired of great causes. The crusade against slavery before the war, the crusade to maintain the Union during the war, and now the crusade to reconstruct North and South, was almost more than one could bear. Moreover, crusades breed cynicism. Bounty jumpers escaped the army, wartime contractors became millionaires, and now a few city politicians were taking their pickings.

Finally, there was the impact of the big city upon the public's interest in municipal politics. A big city like New York encouraged what could be called aggressive apathy toward city government. Who understood the intricacies, the enormous complications of municipal politics? City government seemed coldly impersonal, remote, a dull business, run by third-raters who could not make a living in a respectable profession. What really counted was not the shabby game of city politics but getting ahead. As the man said right after the Civil War, "You can see it in people's faces, you can feel it in the air, everybody and everything's goin' places."[2]

Out of all these developments emerged a man who by experience and ability was best able to manipulate them to his advantage. William Marcy Tweed had many of the attributes celebrated in post-Civil War America—energy, enterprise, enthusiasm for his work. If we forget for a moment his powers for mischief, we could liken him to a successful businessman of the era. The august *Journal of Commerce* admitted that his executive capacity was extraordinary. George Alfred Townsend said, "But for all, he is a powerful business man, always at work, never wearied out . . . stirring from morn till midnight, doing a great part of this work himself . . . and has gone on from grade to grade until he rules New York."[3] Of all his attributes, however, it was his talent for political organization that was the most outstanding.

William Tweed was a first-rate political manager, an intuitive leader of men, and in some ways, a consummate professional politician. It was his mastery of urban politics, abetted by the political astuteness of the other members of the Ring, that consolidated, centralized, and modernized politics in a way never seen before their time. Contrary to popular opinion, Tammany had never dominated New York politics *before* the Civil War. The Whigs and the Know-Nothings were fierce competition; in the nine years between 1834 and 1843 the Democrats and Whigs were equally balanced in political strength. If the Democrats managed to gain power from 1843 to the war, power was precariously held, always vulnerable to the enemies, Whig, Know-Nothing, and Republican.[4] But with the coming of the Tweed Ring the political face of New York was changed. From the era of the Tweed Ring onward, the Democrats monopolized New York City politics. The Republican party, except for brief moments of glory—and then bolstered by dissident Democrats—was never a serious threat to the warriors of Tammany Hall. A good deal of the credit for this goes to the Tweed Ring who fashioned the classic architecture of Tammany. The Ring eventually fell, but its creation, a modernized city machine, has come down to our own day.

The Tweed Ring built its machine by capturing the four fortresses of power: Tammany Hall, City Hall, the Hall of Justice, and the state capitol. To the victors belonged the spoils—control of the Democratic party and city offices. An empire of patronage was created when 1,000 Tammany followers, who called themselves the Shiny Hat Brigade, were placed in every branch of city government.[5] The police, election officials, and criminals abided by the Ring's whims. Continuing the Tammany tactic of the 1840's, the immigrant was effectively wooed to the Tammany banner. Key executive posts were controlled: John Hoffman was Governor; Oakey Hall was Mayor; Richard Connolly, who manipulated city finances with the finesse of a shell-game shark, was Comptroller; and Tweed himself assumed several public and private positions in order to strengthen the Ring's influence in both politics and the business community. He maintained a firm hand over the city legislature as President of the Board of Supervisors; he controlled a rich source of patronage as Deputy Street Commissioner and as Commissioner of Public Works; he held executive positions in banks, railroads, gas, printing, and insurance companies, and was the third largest owner of real estate in New York. With the 1867 elections, he enlarged the power of the machine in the State legislature by becoming a State Senator, where he became a powerful influence over financial and legislative policy as chairman of the important State Finance Committee, and the leader of the so-called Black Horse Cavalry, a group of politicians of both parties who sold their votes for a price.

And climaxing it all, on election day the Ring mustered an army of renegades—barroom brawlers, thugs, ex-convicts, devoted followers, corrupt election officials—who voted early and often, stuffed ballot boxes, intimidated voters, and miscounted the votes. Masterminding the operation was the Boss himself, who enhanced his reputation by a simple question: "Well," he challenged the reformers, "what are you going to do about it?"[6]

The astonishing thing was that the Tweed Ring was successful despite the fact that at no time did it control a majority of all the voters in the city.[7] Part of its success came from intimidation and repeating at the polls, but the Ring did not always have to cheat. It is misleading to think that machine politics rested entirely on election fraud. For all the efficiency of its organization, the Ring needed and received the votes of people who were not a part of Tammany Hall. And here party partisanship was a staunch buttress to power. After all, the Tweed Ring's Tammany Hall was part of the Democratic party, and it got votes from those local Democrats who always voted for their party, whose parents had always voted for the party; local Democrats who would continue to vote for their party through ideals, habit, apathy, or the feeling that the enemy, the Republicans, should be kept out regardless of machine corruption. In the same era, Republicans in Philadelphia supported their party for the same reasons, even though the city was being sacked by a venal Republican city machine.

The fierce partisanship of the New York press also helped sustain the Ring. Until almost the very end, most of the Democratic papers minimized the corruption of the Ring, just as most of the Republican press underplayed the scandals of the Grant administration.

In addition, small shopkeepers, big businessmen, lawyers, and judges, some of whom had no particular love for Tammany, realized nevertheless they could advance their own self-interests by exploiting the favors of Tammany; and others, in the same group, hated Tammany but were terrified of its power of punishment and did not dare vote against it.

One force, which added the final cohesive element to the Ring's organization, was the character of the Boss himself. Tweed brought a personal touch to the cold, steely world of urban politics, that matched his gifts as a political organizer. The Boss had charm, a personal magnetism that made many men admit, although reluctantly, that he was an immensely likable man. Although capable of erupting into violent outbursts, he was gay and congenial. He had a booming hearty personality that befitted his physique. For William Marcy Tweed looked like something that God hacked out with a dull axe. A craggy hulk of a man, he was nearly six feet tall and weighed almost 300 pounds.

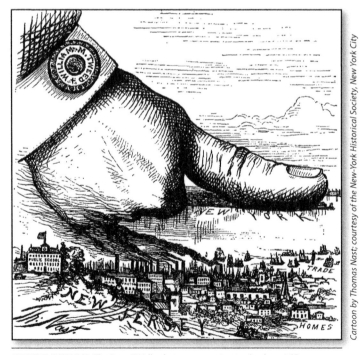

Cartoon by Thomas Nast; courtesy of the New-York Historical Society, New York City

UNDER THE THUMB. The Boss. "Well, what are you going to do about it?"

Everything about him was big; fists, shoulders, head (which sprouted receding reddish-brown hair, like weeds growing from a rock, carved into a mustache, and closely cropped chin whiskers); eyes, blue and friendly; the diamond, which "glittered like a planet on his shirt front"; and his nose, a particularly rocky pinnacle. "His nose is half-Brougham, half-Roman," said one observer, "and a man with a nose of that sort is not a man to be trifled with."[8]

Tweed's sheer physical bulk awed most men into respect. His gift for making friends seemed to go beyond the politician's contrived approach and won the loyalty of some and suspended the suspicion of others. His crudeness and bluster were attractive to roughnecks of the political back alleys of New York, but he could also be suave. Years of being an inveterate clubman—at the rather plush Manhattan, the Americus, the Blossom, the Oriental—social contacts made in holding city offices, had polished him. In the Blossom Club, said a historian of New York clubs, "You will meet Tweed, with his large, grand, good-humored phiz and physique; but here, again, the will of a Roman slumbers under the suavity of a Parisian—for no man so well illustrates the Latin phrase, *Suaviter in modo, fortiter in re*."[9]

Despite his reputation for vulgarity, he numbered friends in every walk of life. He knew Astor, Vanderbilt, and Stewart, Raymond of the *Times*, Bennett of the *Herald*, and Oswald Ottendorfer, an immensely influential German newspaperman. There were tales of drunken orgies on Sunday. If true, it could only suggest that he kept bad company, for Tweed neither drank nor smoked. Like many great scoundrels, he was a good family man, a dutiful husband, a devoted father, although the reformers complained that he carried devotion too far in providing his sons with important city jobs. His charities were legion—to the poor, the hospitals, the schools, the churches, the infirm. This is not to suggest that the proper image of Tweed should be that of a misunderstood Robin Hood, but rather that Tweed was more than the one-dimensional picture of pure evil painted by his critics. He was a rogue, to be sure, but a jolly one at least and a refreshing interlude before his solemn successors—the Kellys, the Crockers, the Murphys, the grim, silent ones.

His talents as an organizer, his gruff charm, his knack of making friends, had a personal rather than a mass appeal. Although accused of being a demagogue, Boss Tweed was not a Huey Long, mesmerizing the rank and file from the public platform. On the many occasions he had to speak—before a torchlight parade in Tweed Plaza, in the State Senate, or at a Tammany Hall Fourth of July celebration—there was no blazing eye or electrifying voice, only a painfully uneasy man whose sputtering delivery made him at times incoherent.

Lack of talent to bewitch the crowd was more than compensated for by one enduring quality, a particular kind of honesty. As Tweed himself identified it: "I challenge any politician in New York to point out one instance where I have broken my word."[10] Unlike his colleague, Slippery Dick Connolly, the Boss could be counted on; a promise was a bond. If, for example, he cut a contractor in on thousands of dollars of graft, the contractor knew Tweed would see to it that he got his money. In his own way, Boss Tweed was honorable. The *New York Telegram*, pondering this strange integrity of the political underworld, guessed that this was the "secret cause" of his great strength.[11] On the day of Tweed's death his secretary tried to sum up, not altogether successfully, this quality in Tweed's character by comparing him to the new leader of Tammany, "Honest" John Kelly. "Tweed was not an honest politician, but a level one," he said. "Kelly is honest but not level."[12]

In the beginning, at least, Tweed did not fit the usual stereotype of a Tammany politician—he was neither Irish, Catholic, nor a ragged slum boy. He was born on April 3, 1823, from a Protestant, third-generation Scottish family. His home at No. 1 Cherry Hill, midway between the East River and City Hall, was a quiet, respectable middle-class neighborhood. His father, "a clever, decent old gentleman," was a solid middle-class manufacturer of chairs, who also had an interest in a brushmaking firm. His mother adored her little boy, and, it was said, spoiled him.[13]

At first Tweed seemed destined for a successful career in business. He studied bookkeeping and joined the brushmaking concern in which his father owned stock. A remarkable executive and organizing ability soon became evident, and within two years he was made a member of the company. He was just nineteen, a strapping young man with fine dark hair and clear blue eyes, almost good-looking. Already he had developed those traits that would be so valuable in later years: amiability, the big smile, an extraordinary memory for faces and names, and financial acumen. But apparently he found the business world too bland.

For every red-blooded young man of Tweed's day who longed for excitement that would relieve the long, boring hours spent as a bookkeeper, clerk, or factory-hand, membership in the New York volunteer firemen offered fun, companionship, danger, and—for those with a taste for it—politics. In 1848 Tweed joined John J. Reilly, a State Assemblyman, and his friends who were organizing a fire company. It was Tweed who suggested the name of the company: the Americus Engine Company, Number 6. It was Tweed who gave it its symbol—a snarling red tiger—a symbol that Thomas Nast, the cartoonist, was later to attach to Tammany Hall. It was Tweed who, as foreman in 1849, became a dashing hero with his brilliant red flannel shirt and white firecoat, and made No. 6, now called the Big Six, into one of the famous fire companies of the day, rivaling other such proud names as the White Ghost, Dry Bones, and Old Junk. And it was the Big Six that gave Tweed his stepping-stone into politics.

New York fire companies, equalitarian, clannish, intensely loyal, were social as well as political organizations. Tweed led an unusually cohesive company of seventy-five men, who could be counted on to vote the Tweed scriptures on issues and candidates, and lend a bully's hand on election day. Each of the partisan seventy-five could himself influence the votes of his family or friends. More were forthcoming from his fame as a fireman. All this, plus Tweed's extensive knowledge of his neighborhood and the people in it, made him important to the politicians of the Seventh Ward. Virtue was rewarded. In 1850 he ran as Democratic candidate for assistant Alderman and was beaten by only a slim margin. In the following year he was nominated for Alderman and won.

As the Honorable William Tweed, he began to learn his trade, for the chambers of the Aldermen was an excellent school in practical politics. Armed with powers over patronage, the city purse, and city improvements, Tweed could consolidate and build a following

in the Seventh Ward, perform favors for businessmen and politicians alike, and generally extend his position in the Democratic party. For example, the Alderman appointed the police of his ward, from patrolman to precinct commander. He granted licenses to saloons and franchises to streetcar lines and ferries, and had the power to override the Mayor's veto if he disapproved. He sat as a Justice in the Mayor's Court which tried all prisoners accused of violations at the polls, and some of the accused might include some overenthusiastic voters from his own ward or the ward of a friend.

If the Board of Aldermen gave an ambitious politician an opportunity to learn some of the fundamentals of urban politics, it also provided basic training in the arts of graft. The Aldermen had a long history of corruption in New York, or as Tweed once described it, "There never was a time when you couldn't buy the Board of Aldermen."[14] Tweed saw his opportunities and took them. He joined a band of political buccaneers whose wholesale corruption earned them the title of the Forty Thieves. His experience with the Forty Thieves was a portent of things to come, for it was as an Alderman that Tweed learned some of the techniques of corruption that would be used in even a grander fashion when the Tweed Ring was formed thirteen years later.

The Aldermen had the power to grant franchises that yielded the greatest amount of graft. The method was simply to sell them to the highest bidder. Schemes involving franchises for the Third Avenue Railroad, the Gansevoort Market property, and the Broadway street-car line brought in thousands of dollars in graft."[15]

Also profitable were city improvements. For example, contracts were given to businessmen for the paving, widening, or extending of city streets, or for building or repairing public offices. The contractors presented padded bills, a percentage of which was split among the Aldermen. A technique of legislative extortion known as "strike" legislation, or "cinch" bills was an added source of income. Legislation was proposed that caused severe hardship to merchants, bankers, insurance companies. To protect their interests, businessmen bribed the Aldermen to kill the legislation. For example, Tweed's colleague, the Honorable Wesley Smith, presented a bill that would save the city money by lowering the fees of the Coroner. Then, in a procedure known as "ringing the bell," Smith called on the Coroner and was reported to have said, "Give me $250 and I'll kill the resolution in committee." The bribe was paid and, as one writer put it, "The bell no longer rang—for the Coroner."[16]

As an Alderman, Tweed served his apprenticeship in politics. He had made money and important friends, but not enough; he had built a local following, but not strong enough to buttress a play for higher stakes. To get what he wanted, he needed more gilt on his political credentials. He decided to run for Congress in 1852, while still serving his term as Alderman.

Tweed spent two unhappy, singularly undistinguished years in the House of Representatives. He disliked the formal nature of Washington, particularly the tradition of merely tolerating first-term Congressmen. In Washington he was nothing. He was assigned to only one committee, the rather unprestigious Committee on Invalid Pensions. He never engaged in Congressional debates. He made only one speech. It was an elegant piece of "platitudes in stained glass attitudes" in favor of the Kansas and Nebraska bill and was intended for home consumption. Nor did he have any ambitions to go on to the United States Senate. He once told a reporter, "If I wanted to go to the Senate, I'd go; but what for? I can't talk, and I know it. As to spending my time in hearing a lot of snoozers discuss the tariff and the particulars of a contract to carry the mails from Paducah to Schoharie, I don't think I'm doing that just now."[17]

At the conclusion of the Thirty-third Congress he did not want to succeed himself in Congress. Disgusted with life in Washington, he decided to resume his promising career in New York. Instead, he found that his luck, his fortune, and New York had changed. He had lived too well in Washington and was almost penniless. His Congressional career, for what it was, had not advanced his reputation, only buried it—New York had forgotten him. He had lost touch with New York politics and, worst of all, New York politicians had lost interest in him. Moreover, Tammany Hall was in unfriendly hands as the city was suffering the painful spasm of the nativistic movement.

Tweed ran again for Alderman, only to be beaten by the Know-Nothings, the anti-Catholic, anti-immigrant

nativist party which was then at the peak of its power. He fought them so well, however, that he became known as the champion of the foreign element, which helped him later, but not in the mid-'fifties. In desperation he accepted an appointment as School Commissioner in 1855, for there were still enough friends and unpaid political debts to muster a dole for the ex-Congressman. But this was offset by a disaster that seemed to signal the end of his political career. He lost control of his own Seventh Ward, a profound humiliation for a professional politician like William Tweed. Alone and deserted, this thirty-one-year-old political hack had come home to New York and failure.

Notes

1. Harold Zink, *City Bosses in the United States*, 1930, p. 96.
2. Eric F. Goldman, *Rendezvous With Destiny*, 1953, p. 30.
3. *New York Times*, May 19, 1871.
4. Charles Garrett, *The La Guardia Years*, 1961, p. 5.
5. Samuel J. Tilden, *The New York City Ring: Its Origin, Maturity and Fall*, 1873, p. 47.
6. Gustavus Myers, *History of Tammany Hall*, 1917, p. 285.
7. Charles Wingate, "Episode in Municipal Government," *North American Review*, Oct. 1874, p. 381, James Bryce, *American Commonwealth* (3rd ed.), Vol. 2, p. 400.
8. Francis G. Fairfield, *The Clubs of New York*, 1873, p. 243.
9. Ibid.
10. *New York Sun*, March 26, 1870.
11. April 14, 1870.
12. Denis Lynch, *Boss Tweed*, 1927, p. 417.
13. Wingate, "An Episode in Municipal Government," *North American Review*, Oct. 5874, p. 361.
14. M. R. Werner, *Tammany Hall*, 1928, p. 108.
15. Lynch, *Boss Tweed*, pp. 67–9, 73–9; Werner, *Tammany Hall*, pp. 107-8; Daniel Van Pelt, *Leslie's History of New York* (4 vols., 1898), Vol. I, p. 435; Wingate, "Episode in Municipal Government," *North American Review*, Oct. 1874, pp. 365–6.
16. Lynch, *Boss Tweed*, p. 73.
17. Werner, *Tammany Hall*, p. 509.

Conclusion

Public Policy Applications: The Administration of City Government

Policy Then

The most common charge leveled against the political machine was its tendency to tolerate and even encourage corruption. In the eyes of its critics, the entire foundation of machine politics—the trading of votes for jobs and other material benefits—was inherently flawed. How could such an exchange relationship advance the common good, as opposed to the particular fortunes of only those groups who had backed the winners of the previous election? Even worse, once in office the machine bosses would often use their authority to enrich themselves while driving up taxes and expanding the city's debt. Expressing the outrage of progressive reformers, Thomas Nast published numerous cartoons like the one below in *Harper's Weekly* magazine, taking aim at the illicit practices of the notorious Tweed Ring, which presided over New York City's Tammany Hall from 1866 to 1871.

And yet, as the sociologist Robert Merton observed, the machine arguably fulfilled important functions, such as assisting immigrants to adapt to a new society under stressful conditions and incorporating them into a democratic system of government. Many had emigrated from countries where democracy was an unknown concept. Machine politics, with its army of ward leaders and precinct captains fanning out all over the city, taught newcomers how to participate in politics and enabled some to secure jobs in city government as a reward for their political support.

Reformers denounced the patronage system as unproductive and corrupt. But many others saw it as a perfectly acceptable form of personnel management, indeed, a much-needed improvement over previous forms of public

WHO STOLE THE PEOPLE'S MONEY? — DO TELL . N.Y.TIMES.   'TWAS HIM.

TWEED CARTOONS BY THOMAS NAST.

Albert Bigelow Paine, Thomas Nast: His Period and His Pictures (New York: Macmillan, 1904)

Thomas Nast cartoon: The Tweed Ring

administration controlled by well-educated, cosmopolitan gentlemen whose formulation and implementation of public policy did not necessarily reflect the wishes of other social classes. The patronage system, for the first time, gave large numbers of immigrant workers access to the reins of government and thus an opportunity to advance the interests of citizens who had often been overlooked. If the machine-led municipal government failed to do its job, then the ensuing election might result in sweeping changes, including—thanks to the patronage system—a fresh influx of administrators incentivized to be more responsive to the voters.

Policy Now

The critics of the patronage system eventually prevailed, as discussed in the following chapter, and succeeded in promoting civil service reform that emphasized the awarding of government jobs based on merit instead of political loyalty. The merit system was intended to enhance professionalism, efficiency, and honesty in municipal government and in many cities notable advances in these areas became evident. However, civil service reform also presented its own drawbacks. Rigid rules and procedures limited the capacity of managers to hire, promote, and reassign employees leading to other manifestations of waste and inefficiency. Others asked how responsive city government bureaucracies were to public opinion.

In recent decades, there has been growing demand for citizen participation in policy-making processes. Empowering ordinary citizens to influence decision making is consistent with the nation's democratic values. It is also seen by advocates as an important check on the power of government administrators. Many municipal governments have, therefore, adopted formal mechanisms to facilitate citizen input. It is possible that the groundwork for mass-based participation in urban politics and governance was established during the several decades when political machines, with their vast network of neighborhood-based politicians, held sway in numerous American cities.

Additional Resources

Sherry Arnstein, "A Ladder of Citizen Participation," *Journal of the American Institute of Planners*, 35 (1969).

Daley: The Last Boss, Documentary film from *The American Experience* series on Mayor Richard J. Daley of Chicago and his control over that city's political machine. PBS Video, 1996.

Domonic A. Bearfield, "What Is Patronage? A Critical Reexamination," *Public Administration Review*, 69 (1), 2009.

Edwin O'Connor, *The Last Hurrah* (Boston: Little, Brown, 1956). Novel loosely based on the life of James Michael Curley.

William M. Rohe, "From Local to Global: One Hundred Years of Neighborhood Planning," *Journal of the American Planning Association*, 75 (2), 2009.

Scandalous Mayor. Documentary film on Mayor James Michael Curley of Boston, one of the last big city bosses. From the series, *The American Experience*. PBS Video, 1991.

Discussion Questions

1. How did political machines benefit working-class immigrants? To what extent did political machines neglect working-class immigrants?

2. Did all immigrants benefit under machine rule?

3. Why were reformers so hostile to political machines?

4. Did political machines strengthen democracy in U.S. cities or undermine it?

5. Why did machines remain in power for so long?

6. Why did machines begin to fade away by the middle of the twentieth century? Are elements of machine politics still visible today?

Chapter 4

Reform Politics

Introduction

The explosive growth of American cities during the nineteenth century became a source of deep concern within some quarters of society. Men and women from middle- and upper-income Protestant backgrounds whose families had resided in the United States for generations looked at the teeming immigrant ghettos of large cities with dismay. In their view, impoverished places like the Lower East Side of New York, with their abundance of saloons, brothels, and gaming houses, had degenerated into breeding grounds of vice and corruption that threatened fundamental values and the American way of life. A vociferous reform movement surfaced by the 1890s intent on, in the words of the historian Paul Boyer, "pulling slum dwellers up to some minimal standard of respectability [and] purifying the entire urban moral climate."[1] Utilizing the tools of governmental authority, the moral reformers launched an all-out crusade against alcohol, prostitution, and gambling. They also viewed schools as a crucial agent of reform and lobbied strenuously for mandatory attendance laws and the establishment of kindergartens, vocational education, and night classes to teach adults English—all with the intention of imposing civic virtues on the immigrant masses.[2]

The moral reformers coupled their drive to expunge vice in urban ghettos by attacking a political system that they believed fostered corrupt behavior. One of their most prominent advocates, Reverend Charles H. Parkhurst, charged that the "thoroughly rotten" moral condition of New York's poorest neighborhoods was attributable to the "slimy, oozy soil of Tammany Hall."[3] To eradicate the despised machine, some of the earliest moral reformers proposed extreme measures. Aware that low-income citizens provided the machine with its electoral base, they called for restrictions on voting, including literacy tests, minimal educational levels, and a revival of property restrictions. However, such disenfranchisement tactics never got off the ground; democratic values and practices had become too entrenched throughout most of the United States.[4]

At this point, a new group of reformers emerged that was just as determined to eviscerate the machine, but one that employed a more sophisticated strategy. These structural reformers sought to undermine machine politicians by overhauling the electoral process and urban government. To minimize fraud, they pushed voter registration laws and the establishment of boards of election to enforce such laws. Voting would be moved out of the saloons and into public schools, and the secret ballot was introduced to protect voters' privacy. Nominations would be taken away from the cigar-chomping bosses meeting in the smoke-filled backrooms of party offices and entrusted to the voters through primary elections. Citizen empowerment would be further advanced through the adoption of the initiative, referendum, and recall. And at-large elections would supplement or replace district elections where neighborhood-based, machine politicians were thought to wield undue influence.[5]

With respect to the reform of municipal government, the most dangerous proposal in the eyes of machine politicians like George Washington Plunkitt was civil service reform. Requiring applicants for city government jobs to take and pass civil service examinations represented a full frontal assault on the patronage system that undergirded the machine's hold on political power.[6] Reformers also sought to remove politics, and thus the influence of machine politicians, as much as possible from the delivery of public services by establishing new structures of municipal government run by appointed city managers with degrees in engineering, planning, or public administration or commissions staffed by professionals.[7]

The reformers succeeded in implementing their initiatives in many U.S. cities, and in some areas of the country—particularly in the south and west where relatively low levels of immigration had inhibited the development of political machines—the structural reforms took hold and shaped local government for decades to come.[8] However, in cities with sizable immigrant populations, the structural reforms typically failed to curtail the power of the bosses. Reformers might manage to ride a wave of popular protest over a machine-related scandal to seize control over city hall, but all too often, their electoral triumph would be short-lived. Once in office, the reformers' preoccupation with honest and efficient government did not satisfy the working-class immigrants who were more inclined to prefer the attention bestowed on them by the machine's precinct captains offering material and symbolic benefits. Plunkitt captured the phenomenon best when he likened the reformers to "morning glories" who "looked lovely in the mornin' and withered up in a short time, while the regular machines went on flourishin' forever, like fine old oaks."[9]

A third group of reformers proved to be more adept at appealing to the urban masses of the early twentieth century. Like the moral and structural reformers, the social reformers were repelled by pervasive corruption in U.S. cities. However, unlike the moral reformers, they did not blame the struggling immigrants for the crisis that afflicted city neighborhoods. Nor did they assume, as did the structural reformers, that simply establishing new institutions and processes of governance would result in sweeping change. Instead, they contended that a thoroughly flawed physical environment was responsible for the poverty, decay, and despair that characterized urban ghettos. The social reformers faulted the bosses and big business for allowing such an environment to develop and fester. Their remedy was an aggressive use of government to transform the environment and thus resolve the seemingly intractable problems of the industrial city. Deplorable living conditions in tenements could be addressed through new housing regulations. Dismal workplaces could be improved through minimum wage and maximum hour laws, as well as through ordinances to promote safer factories and to end child labor. Government could be a force to regulate monopolies, supply unemployment insurance and old-age pensions, and protect union organizing. Reformers who embraced such a program enjoyed broad and lasting electoral support from working-class voters in cities such as Detroit, Cleveland, Toledo, and Milwaukee. In many other cities, shrewd machine politicians recognized the appeal of such reform initiatives, or were pushed to do so by their constituents, and began to adopt them in ways that furthered their own agenda.[10]

The reformers' reliance on state power to effect change marked a significant departure from the libertarian political culture that had pervaded much of America since the founding of the nation. They helped legitimize the notion of using government to improve society. More specifically, the reformers' vision of politics was animated by three core principles. First, only one version of "the public interest" exists; if that one version could be implemented efficiently and honestly, then all citizens would benefit. Second, identification and pursuit of the public interest needs to be entrusted to professionals who have the requisite experience, training, and ability. Government by experts—the well-educated graduate of MIT School of Engineering, as opposed to the undereducated and parochial precinct captain—was the ideal. And third, if the public interest could be identified and executed by skilled professionals, then politics (or the give and take of competing perspectives) should play no role in the actual governing of cities. As much as possible, cities should be run like a business.[11] These principles are evident in **Reading 4-1**, in Andrew Dickson White's 1890 essay on the proper goals of city governance.

How effective was the reform vision? Many of the moral, structural, and social reformers were undoubtedly earnest in their efforts to combat the countless problems endemic to desperately overcrowded and impoverished city slums. Jane Addams dedicated much of her life to providing relief through Hull House in Chicago.[12] Likewise, as elaborated in **Reading 4-2**, Jacob A. Riis sought to expose the horrors of immigrant ghettos and advocated regulatory laws that would bring material improvements in housing, education, and health care. Furthermore, the reformers' emphasis on professional skills often meant that the administration of public services and the provision of new infrastructure—at a time when cities were undergoing explosive growth—were carried out efficiently and effectively. As Stanley Schultz demonstrates in **Reading 4-3**, this represented a marked improvement in comparison to the way government was administered by machine politicians lacking in expertise and integrity.

However, not everyone viewed the reform vision in such positive terms. Many immigrants were put off by the subtle, and sometimes not so subtle, racism and classism underlying the reformers' rhetoric and actions. Moreover, they recognized that the preoccupation with rule by experts had a disempowering effect at a time when machine politics offered an unprecedented opportunity to participate in city government.[13] Finally, scholars like Samuel P. Hays questioned the reformers' avowed commitment to promoting the common good, noting that the use of governmental authority to effect change often worked to the advantage of upper-class businessmen and professionals who had led the reform movement (see **Reading 4-4**).

In sum, the reform approach to urban governance marked a dramatic turn away from machine politics.[14] It resonated with some elements of the public but alienated others. The clash between machine politicians and reformers occupied center stage within city politics for several decades.

Notes

1. Paul Boyer, *Urban Masses and Moral Order: America, 1820–1920* (Cambridge, MA: Harvard University Press, 1978), p. 167.
2. Howard P. Chudacoff and Judith E. Smith, *The Evolution of American Urban Society*, 3rd ed. (Englewood Cliffs, NJ: Prentice Hall, 1988).
3. Boyer, *Urban Masses and Moral Order*, p. 165. See also Charles H. Parkhurst, *Our Fight with Tammany* (New York: Scribner, 1895).
4. Raymond A. Mohl, *The New City: Urban America in the Industrial Age* (Arlington, IL: Harlan Davidson, 1985).
5. Ibid.
6. William L. Riorden, "The Curse of Civil Service Reform," *Plunkitt of Tammany Hall* (New York: E. P. Dutton, 1963), pp. 11–16.
7. Mohl, *The New City*.
8. Amy Bridges, *Morning Glories: Municipal Reform in the Southwest* (Princeton, NJ: Princeton University Press, 1997); Robert B. Fairbanks, *For the City as a Whole: Planning, Politics, and the Public Interest in Dallas, Texas, 1900–1965* (Columbus: Ohio State University Press, 1998).
9. Riorden, *Plunkitt of Tammany Hall*, p. 17.
10. Roy Lubove, *The Progressives and the Slums: Tenement House Reform in New York City, 1890–1917* (Pittsburgh, PA: University of Pittsburgh Press, 1962); Melvin G. Holli, *Reform in Detroit: Hazen S. Pingree and Urban Politics* (New York: Oxford University Press, 1969); John M. Allswang, "Charles Francis Murphy: The Enduring Boss," in *Bosses, Machines, and Urban Voters* (Baltimore: Johns Hopkins University Press, 1986).
11. Chudacoff and Smith, *The Evolution of American Urban Society*. See also Kenneth Finegold, *Experts and Politicians: Reform Challenges to Machine Politics in New York, Cleveland, and Chicago* (Princeton, NJ: Princeton University Press, 1995).
12. Jane Addams, *Twenty Years at Hull House* (New York: Macmillan, 1910). See also Allen F. Davis, *Spearheads for Reform: The Social Settlements and the Progressive Movement* (New York: Oxford University Press, 1967).
13. There were some exceptions to the reformers' preference for elite rule. For example, some of the reform politicians who embraced an activist role for government in remedying urban problems were also inclined to give citizens significant policy-making responsibilities. Mohl, *The New City*. Many settlement house workers saw the battle to improve society as a genuine partnership between themselves and community residents. Louise W. Knight, *Jane Addams and the Struggle for Democracy* (Chicago: University of Chicago Press, 2006); Margaret Kohn, "Public Space in the Progressive Era," in *Justice and the American Metropolis*, ed. Clarissa Rile Hayward and Todd Swanstrom (Minneapolis: University of Minnesota Press, 2011).
14. But see Jessica Trounstine, *Political Monopolies in American Cities: The Rise and Fall of Bosses and Reformers* (Chicago: University of Chicago Press, 2008), who argues provocatively that machine politicians and reformers shared a common desire to hold on to power to the detriment of unrepresented constituencies. For a somewhat different interpretation, see Jon C. Teaford, *The Unheralded Triumph: City Government in America, 1870–1900* (Baltimore: Johns Hopkins University Press, 1983), who contends that the collaboration of machine bosses and reform administrators yielded increasingly effective public services.

4-1 "The Government of American Cities"

Andrew D. White

Forum

Without the slightest exaggeration we may assert that, with very few exceptions, the city governments of the United States are the worst in Christendom—the most expensive, the most inefficient, and the most corrupt. No one who has any considerable knowledge of our own country and of other countries can deny this.

Among our greater municipalities, we naturally look first at New York and Philadelphia. Both are admirably situated; each stands on rising ground with water on both sides; each is happy in position, in climate, in all advantages to be desired by a great metropolis. In each, what is done by individuals is generally well done and sometimes splendidly done; and in each, what is due from the corporate authorities, in matters the most essential to a proper city government, is either wretchedly done or left utterly undone. One has but to walk along the streets of these and other great American cities, to notice at once that some evil principle is at work. Everywhere are wretched wharves, foul docks, inadequate streets, and inefficient systems of sewerage, paving, and lighting. Pavements which were fairly good at the beginning, have been taken up and replaced with utter carelessness, and have been prematurely worn out or ruined. The stranger, seeking to find his way in the first of these great cities, is guided by few signs giving the names of streets; in the most frequented quarters there are generally none at all. Obstacles of all sorts are allowed; tangled networks of wires frequently exist in such masses overhead as to prevent access to buildings in case of fire, and almost to cut off the rays of the sun. Here and there corporations or private persons have been allowed to use the streets in such manner as to close them to the general public. In wet weather many of the most important thoroughfares are covered with reeking mud; in dry weather this mud, reduced to an impalpable dust containing the germs of almost every disease, is blown into the houses and into the nostrils of the citizens.

The city halls of these larger towns are the acknowledged centers of the vilest corruption. They are absolutely demoralizing, not merely to those who live under their sway, but to the country at large. Such cities, like the decaying spots on ripe fruit, tend to corrupt the whole body politic. As a rule, the men who sit in the councils of our larger cities, dispensing comfort or discomfort, justice or injustice, beauty or deformity, health or disease, to this and to future generations, are men who in no other country would think of aspiring to such positions. Some of them, indeed, would think themselves lucky in keeping outside the prisons. Officials intrusted with the expenditure of the vast wealth of our citizens are frequently men whom no one would think of entrusting with the management of his private affairs, or, indeed, of employing in any capacity. Few have gained their positions by fitness or by public service; many have gained them by scoundrelism; some by crime. . . .

All who know anything of American cities, know that these cases are typical. The loss in money is bad; the loss in public health is worse; but worst of all is the loss of character—the corruption and servility thus engendered. This is all the more unfortunate because the city population is so rapidly increasing in comparison with the population of the rural districts. The despotism of bosses seems on the increase; the abject servility of the great mass of citizens seems also on the increase. Now and then, indeed, comes an attack on the men in power, and occasionally something is thus

Source: Andrew D. White, "The Government of American Cities," *Forum*, vol. 10, December 1890, pp. 357–372.

accomplished; but the old order of things returns, for the system itself is vicious. It is the evil tree which must needs bring forth corrupt fruit. . . .

[W]e are attempting to govern our cities upon a theory which has never been found to work practically in any part of the world. Various forms of it were tried in the great cities of antiquity and of the middle ages, especially in the medieval republics of Italy, and without exception they ended in tyranny, confiscation, and bloodshed. The same theory has produced the worst results in various countries of modern Europe, down to a recent period.

What is this evil theory? It is simply that the city is a political body; that its interior affairs have to do with national political parties and issues. My fundamental contention is that a city is a corporation; that as a city it has nothing whatever to do with general political interests; that party political names and duties are utterly out of place there. The questions in a city are not political questions. They have reference to the laying out of streets; to the erection of buildings; to sanitary arrangements, sewerage, water supply, gas supply, electrical supply; to the control of franchises and the like; and to provisions for the public health and comfort in parks, boulevards, libraries, and museums. The work of a city being the creation and control of the city property, it should logically be managed as a piece of property by those who have created it, who have a title to it, or a real substantial part in it, and who can therefore feel strongly their duty to it. Under our theory that a city is a political body, a crowd of illiterate peasants, freshly raked in from Irish bogs, or Bohemian mines, or Italian robber nests, may exercise virtual control. How such men govern cities, we know too well; as a rule they are not alive even to their own most direct interests. I have referred to the work of a legislative committee in supplanting the old murderous system in New York City by the new health board; it fell to my lot to present the report and to take the lead in urging this reform in the Senate of the State. I was successful; and yet had I been recognized, at any time within many months, in the tenement houses where the men, women, and children lived whose lives had thus been saved, my own life would not have been worth an hour's purchase, so bitter was

the feeling of these people in behalf of the political managers who were murdering them, and against those who saved them.

The difference between foreign cities and ours, is that all these well-ordered cities in England, France, Germany, Italy, Switzerland, whether in monarchies or republics, accept this principle—that cities are corporations and not political bodies; that they are not concerned with matters of national policy; that national parties as such have nothing whatever to do with city questions. They base their city governments upon ascertained facts regarding human nature, and upon right reason. They try to conduct them upon the principles observed by honest and energetic men in business affairs. We, on the other hand, are putting ourselves upon a basis which has always failed and will always fail—the idea that a city is a political body, and therefore that it is to be ruled, in the long run, by a city proletariat mob, obeying national party cries.

What is our safety? The reader may possibly expect me, in logical consonance with the statement I have just made, to recommend that the city be treated strictly as a corporate body, and governed entirely by those who have a direct pecuniary interest in it. If so, he is mistaken. I am no doctrinaire; politics cannot be bent completely to logic—certainly not all at once. A wise, statesmanlike view would indicate a compromise between the political idea and the corporate idea. I would not break away entirely from the past, but I would build a better future upon what we may preserve from the past.

To this end I would still leave in existence the theory that the city is a political body, as regards the election of the mayor and common council. I would elect the mayor by the votes of the majority of all the citizens, as at present; I would elect the common council by a majority of all the votes of all the citizens; but instead of electing its members from the wards as at present—so that wards largely controlled by thieves and robbers can send thieves and robbers, and so that men who can carry their ward can control the city—I would elect the board of aldermen on a general ticket, just as the mayor is elected now, thus requiring candidates for the board to have a city reputation. So much for retaining the idea of the city as a political body. In addition to this, in consideration of the fact that the city is a corporation, I would have those owning property in it properly recognized. I would leave to them, and to them alone, the election of a board of control, without whose permission no franchise should be granted and no expenditure should be made. This should be the rule, but to this rule I am inclined to make one exception; I would allow the votes of the board of control, as regards expenditures for primary education, to be overridden by a two-thirds majority of the board of aldermen. I should do this because here alone does the city policy come into direct relations with the general political system of the nation at large. The main argument for the existence of our public schools is that they are an absolute necessity to the existence of our Republic; that without preliminary education a republic simply becomes an illiterate mob; that if illiterate elements control, the destruction of the Republic is sure. On this ground, considering the public-school system as based upon a national political necessity, I would have an exception made regarding the expenditures for it, leaving in this matter a last resort to the political assembly of the people.

A theory resulting in a system virtually like this, has made the cities of Europe, whether in monarchies or republics, what they are, and has made it an honor in many foreign countries for the foremost citizens to serve in the common councils of their cities. Take one example: It has been my good fortune to know well Rudolf Von Gneist, councilor of the German Empire. My acquaintance with him began when it was my official duty to present to him a testimonial, in behalf of the government of the United States, for his services in settling the northwest boundary between the United States and Great Britain. The Emperor William was the nominal umpire; he made Von Gneist the real umpire—that shows Von Gneist's standing. He is also a leading professor of law in the University of Berlin, a member of the Imperial Parliament and of the Prussian Legislature, and the author of famous books, not only upon law, but upon the constitutional history of Germany and of England. This man has been, during a considerable time, a member of what we should call the board of aldermen of the city of

Berlin, and he is proud to serve in that position. With him have been associated other men the most honored in various walks of life, and among these some of the greatest business men, renowned in all lands for their enterprise and their probity. Look through the councils of our cities, using any microscope you can find, and tell me how many such men you discern in them. Under the system I propose, it is, humanly speaking, certain that these better men would seek entrance into our city councils. Especially would this be the case if our citizens should, by and by, learn that it is better to have in the common council an honest man, though a Republican, than a scoundrel, though a Democrat; and better to have a man of ability and civic pride, though a Democrat, than a weak, yielding creature, though a Republican.

Some objections will be made. It will be said, first, that wealthy and well-to-do people do not do their duty in city matters; that if they should, they would have better city government. This is true to this extent, that even well-to-do men are in city politics strangely led away from their civic duties by fancied allegiance to national party men and party issues. But in other respects it is untrue; the vote of a single tenement house, managed by a professional politician, will neutralize the vote of an entire street of well-to-do citizens. Men in business soon find this out; they soon find that to work for political improvement under the present system is time and labor and self-respect thrown away. It may be also said that the proposal is impracticable. I ask, why? History does not show it to be impracticable; for we have before us, as I have shown, the practice of all other great civilized nations on earth, and especially of our principal sister republics.

But it will be said that "revolutions do not go backward." They did go backward in the great cities of Europe when these rid themselves of the old bad system that had at bottom the theory under which ours are managed, and when they entered into their new and better system. The same objection, that revolutions do not go backward, was made against any reform in the tenure of office of the governor and of the higher judiciary in the State of New York; and yet the revolution did go backward, that is, it went back out of doctrinaire folly into sound, substantial, common-sense statesmanship. In 1847 the State of New York so broke away from the old conservative moorings as to make all judgeships elective, with short terms, small pay, and wretched accommodations, and the same plan was pursued as regards the governor and other leading officials; but the State, some years since, very wisely went back to much of its former system—in short, made a revolution backward, if any one chooses to call it so—resuming the far better system of giving our governor and higher judges longer terms, larger salaries, better accommodations, and dignified surroundings. We see, then, that it is not true that steps in a wrong direction in a republic cannot be retraced. As they have been retraced in State affairs, so they may be in municipal affairs.

But it will be said that this change in city government involves a long struggle. It may or it may not. If it does, such a struggle is but part of that price which we pay for the maintenance of free institutions in town, State, and nation. For this struggle, I especially urge all men of light and leading to prepare themselves. As to the public at large, what is most needed in regard to municipal affairs, as in regard to public affairs generally, is the quiet, steady evolution of a knowledge of truth and of proper action in view of it. That truth, as regards city government, is simply the truth that municipal affairs are not political; that political parties as such have nothing to do with cities; that the men who import political considerations into municipal management are to be opposed. This being the case, the adoption of some such system as that which I have sketched would seem likely to prove fruitful of good.

4-2 "Genesis of the Tenement"

Jacob A. Riis

How the Other Half Lives: Studies among the Tenements of New York

The first tenement New York knew bore the mark of Cain from its birth, though a generation passed before the writing was deciphered. It was the "rear house," infamous ever after in our city's history. There had been tenant-houses before, but they were not built for the purpose. Nothing would probably have shocked their original owners more than the idea of their harboring a promiscuous crowd; for they were the decorous homes of the old Knickerbockers, the proud aristocracy of Manhattan in the early days.

It was the stir and bustle of trade, together with the tremendous immigration that followed upon the war of 1812, that dislodged them. In thirty-five years the city of less than a hundred thousand came to harbor half a million souls, for whom homes had to be found. Within the memory of men not yet in their prime, Washington had moved from his house on Cherry Hill as too far out of town to be easily reached. Now the old residents followed his example; but they moved in a different direction and for a different reason. Their comfortable dwellings in the once fashionable streets along the East River front fell into the hands of real-estate agents and boarding-house keepers; and here, says the report to the Legislature of 1857, when the evils engendered had excited just alarm, "in its beginning, the tenant-house became a real blessing to that class of industrious poor whose small earnings limited their expenses, and whose employment in workshops, stores, or about the warehouses and thoroughfares, render a near residence of much importance." Not for long, however. As business increased, and the city grew with rapid strides, the necessities of the poor became the opportunity of their wealthier neighbors, and the stamp was set upon the old houses, suddenly become valuable, which the best thought and effort of a later age have vainly struggled to efface. Their "*large* rooms were partitioned into *several smaller ones*, without regard to light or ventilation, the rate of rent being lower in proportion to space or height from the Street; and they soon became filled from cellar to garret with a class of tenantry living from hand to mouth, loose in morals, improvident in habits, degraded, and squalid as beggary itself." It was thus the dark bedroom, prolific of untold depravities, came into the world. It was destined to survive the old houses. In their new role, says the old report, eloquent in its indignant denunciation of "evils more destructive than wars," "they were not intended to last. Rents were fixed high enough to cover damage and abuse from this class, from whom nothing was expected, and the most was made of them while they lasted. Neatness, order, cleanliness, were never dreamed of in connection with the tenant-house system, as it spread its localities from year to year; while reckless slovenliness, discontent, privation, and ignorance were left to work out their invariable results, until the entire premises reached the level of tenant-house dilapidation, containing, but sheltering not, the miserable hordes that crowded beneath mouldering, water-rotted roofs or burrowed among the rats of clammy cellars." Yet so illogical is human greed that, at a later day, when called to account, "the proprietors frequently urged the filthy habits of the tenants as an excuse for the condition of their property, utterly losing sight of the fact that it was the tolerance of those habits which was the real evil, and that for this they themselves were alone responsible."

Source: Jacob A. Riis, "Genesis of the Tenement," in *How the Other Half Lives: Studies among the Tenements of New York.* New York: Dover Publications, Inc., 1971, pp. 5–6, 8, 11.

Still the pressure of the crowds did not abate, and in the old garden where the stolid Dutch burgher grew his tulips or early cabbages a rear house was built, generally of wood, two stories high at first. Presently it was carried up another story, and another. Where two families had lived ten moved in. The front house followed suit, if the brick walls were strong enough. The question was not always asked, judging from complaints made by a contemporary witness, that the old buildings were "often carried up to a great height without regard to the strength of the foundation walls." It was rent the owner was after; nothing was said in the contract about either the safety or the comfort of the tenants. The garden gate no longer swung on its rusty hinges. The shell-paved walk had become an alley; what the rear house had left of the garden, a "court." Plenty such are yet to be found in the Fourth Ward, with here and there one of the original rear tenements.

Worse was to follow. It was "soon perceived by estate owners and agents of property that a greater percentage of profits could be realized by the conversion of houses and blocks into barracks, and dividing their space into smaller proportions capable of containing human life within four walls. . . . Blocks were rented of real estate owners, or purchased on time, or taken in charge at a percentage, and held for underletting." With the appearance of the middleman, wholly irresponsible, and utterly reckless and unrestrained, began the era of tenement building which turned out such blocks as Gotham Court, where, in one cholera epidemic that scarcely touched the clean wards, the tenants died at the rate of one hundred and ninety-five to the thousand of population; which forced the general mortality of the city up from 1 in 41.83 in 1815, to 1 in 27.33 in 1855, a year of unusual freedom from epidemic disease, and which wrung from the early organizers of the Health Department this wail: "There are numerous examples of tenement-houses in which are lodged several hundred people that have a *pro rata* allotment of ground area scarcely equal to two square yards upon the city lot, court-yards and all included." The tenement-house population had swelled to half a million souls by that time, and on the East Side, in what is still the most densely populated district in all the world, China not excluded,

it was packed at the rate of 290,000 to the square mile, a state of affairs wholly unexampled. The utmost cupidity of other lands and other days had never contrived to herd much more than half that number within the same space. The greatest crowding of Old London was at the rate of 175,816. Swine roamed the streets and gutters as their principal scavengers.[1] The death of a child in a tenement was registered at the Bureau of Vital Statistics as "plainly due to suffocation in the foul air of an unventilated apartment," and the Senators, who had come down from Albany to find out what was the matter with New York, reported that "there are annually cut off from the population by disease and death enough human beings to people a city, and enough human labor to sustain it." And yet experts had testified that, as compared with uptown, rents were from twenty-five to thirty per cent higher in the worst slums of the lower wards, with such accommodations as were enjoyed, for instance, by a "family with boarders" in Cedar Street, who fed hogs in the cellar that contained eight or ten loads of manure; or "one room 12 × 12 with five families living in it, comprising twenty persons of both sexes and all ages, with only two beds, without partition, screen, chair, or table." The rate of rent has been successfully maintained to the present day, though the hog at least has been eliminated.

Lest anybody flatter himself with the notion that these were evils of a day that is happily past and may safely be forgotten, let me mention here three very recent instances of tenement-house life that came under my notice. One was the burning of a rear house in Mott Street, from appearances one of the original tenant-houses that made their owners rich. The fire made homeless ten families, who had paid an average of $5 a month for their mean little cubbyholes. The owner himself told me that it was *fully* insured for $800, though it brought him in $600 a year rent. He evidently considered himself especially entitled to be pitied for losing such valuable property. Another was the case of a hard-working family of man and wife, young people from the old country, who took poison together in a Crosby Street tenement because they were "tired." There was no other explanation, and none was needed when I stood in the room in which they had lived. It was in the attic with sloping ceiling and a single window so far out on the roof that it seemed not to belong to the place at all. With scarcely room enough to turn around in they had been compelled to pay five dollars and a half a month in advance. There were four such rooms in that attic, and together they brought in as much as many a handsome little cottage in a pleasant part of Brooklyn. The third instance was that of a colored family of husband, wife, and baby in a wretched rear rookery in West Third Street. Their rent was eight dollars and a half for a single room on the top-story, so small that I was unable to get a photograph of it even by placing the camera outside the open door. Three short steps across either way would have measured its full extent.

There was just one excuse for the early tenement-house builders, and their successors may plead it with nearly as good right for what it is worth. "Such," says an official report, "is the lack of houseroom in the city that any kind of tenement can be immediately crowded with lodgers, if there is space offered." Thousands were living in cellars. There were three hundred underground lodging-houses in the city when the Health Department was organized. Some fifteen years before that the old Baptist Church in Mulberry Street, just off Chatham Street, had been sold, and the rear half of the frame structure had been converted into tenements that with their swarming population became the scandal even of that reckless age. The wretched pile harbored no less than forty families, and the annual rate of deaths to the population was officially stated to be 75 in 1,000. These tenements were an extreme type of very many, for the big barracks had by this time spread east and west and far up the island into the sparsely settled wards. Whether or not the title was clear to the land upon which they were built was of less account than that the rents were collected. If there were damages to pay, the tenant had to foot them. Cases were "very frequent when property was in litigation, and two or three different parties were collecting rents." Of course under such circumstances "no repairs were ever made."

The climax had been reached. The situation was summed up by the Society for the Improvement of the Condition of the Poor in these words: "Crazy old buildings, crowded rear tenements in filthy yards, dark, damp basements, leaking garrets, shops, out-houses, and stables[2] converted into dwellings, though scarcely fit to shelter brutes, are habitations of thousands of our fellow-beings in this wealthy, Christian city." "The city," says its historian, Mrs. Martha Lamb, commenting on the era of aqueduct building between 1835 and 1845, "was a general asylum for vagrants." Young vagabonds, the natural offspring of such "home" conditions, overran the streets. Juvenile crime increased fearfully year by year. The Children's Aid Society and kindred philanthropic organizations were yet unborn, but in the city directory was to be found the address of the "American Society for the Promotion of Education in Africa."

Notes

1. It was not until the winter of 1867 that owners of swine were prohibited by ordinance from letting them run at large in the built-up portions of the city.

2. "A lot 50 × 60, contained twenty stables, rented for dwellings at $15 a year each; cost of the whole $600."

4-3 "The Engineered Metropolis"*

Stanley Schultz

Constructing Urban Culture: American Cities and City Planning, 1800–1920

At the heart of the engineered metropolis stood a new and expanding profession of municipal engineers. During the post–Civil War years, they were the principal promoters of technological solutions to urban ills. Virtually the only problems successfully attacked by nineteenth-century urban leaders were those susceptible to engineering expertise. As we have seen, for example, many cities dramatically lowered their disease and mortality rates with the construction of paved streets and efficient water-supply and sewage systems.

Municipal engineers solidified their growing reputation as problem-solvers in three ways. First, they made themselves indispensable to officials eager to boost their city's expansion. Second, they proclaimed (and apparently persuaded the public) that they were neutral experts who stood above partisan politics. Third, within their own ranks, they created a professional bureaucracy that outsiders came to admire as a model of efficiency. As an often-cited early twentieth-century text on sanitation and planning observed about the construction and administration of all types of public works, "details have been wisely left to the engineers."[1]

That affirmation was partly wishful thinking, partly admonition. On numerous occasions, urban partisan politics and short-sighted efforts to cut corners and save money had interfered with public works construction. Still, if city officials had not left everything to the engineers, they had often entrusted the details of planning and construction and most of the details of administration to them.

By doing so, officials recognized and supported the growth of a new profession in the United States—municipal engineering—and set in motion processes that would ultimately help restructure municipal government. For local *governments* and the public at large had come to accept the concept of city planning, if not always the actual practice. From citywide water and sewer systems to plans for every feature of the urban physical environment was but a short step of the imagination. A major engineering journal developed this *logic* in 1877: "If the grading, drainage, paving, cleansing, and policing of towns are worthy of careful and systematic control, so are also the general shaping of the towns, the preservation or destruction of the natural features of their sites, and the distribution of their population and residences. Just what are the proper limits of public interference in such matters is a political question upon which we cannot venture; but public neglect has shown itself to be both costly and pernicious."[2]

Engineers shepherded remarkable innovations in technology, helped shape the directions of city planning thought and practice, and laid the groundwork of modern municipal administration. Scrutiny of the emerging profession and its part in reshaping the urban physical environment underscores the importance of engineers in the developing urban culture of the United States.

Engineering a Bureaucracy

The functions of modern municipal administration were inherent in water and wastewater technologies. Sewerage and water supplies required permanent construction and thus necessitated some kind of long-range planning. If engineers did not plan systems to accommodate future growth, the city would have to lay new aqueducts and trunk sewers each time the

Source: "The Engineered Metropolis" from *Constructing Urban Culture: American Cities and City Planning, 1800–1920* by Stanley K. Schultz. Philadelphia: Temple University Press, 1989. Reprinted with permission from the author.

*Endnotes and references have been omitted. Please consult the original source.

population increased even slightly or began to move into new subdivisions. A system that met present needs and anticipated future growth might be expensive in the short run but economical over time. City officials quickly learned these facts and also that disastrous health and financial consequences ensued if they ignored the advice of experts.

Consider several examples. During the early 1870s Alexander Shepard, boss of the District of Columbia, wasted a $5 million bond issue when contractors hired for political reasons built lateral sewers that had to run uphill to empty into the main sewers. In the absence of effective pumping mechanisms (most systems at the time depended upon gravity flow rather than steam pumps), Shepard's system was worse than useless. Partly because of this fiasco, the District lost home rule and became subject to a federally appointed commission that had to include at least one officer of the Army Corps of Engineers. St. Louis had to reconstruct its water-supply system and Cincinnati its sewer system within ten years after completion; both city administrations had rejected engineers' proposals in favor of politically popular decisions to cut costs. Partisan politics and graft counted more than engineering considerations in the construction of Detroit's sewer system, as the city's reform mayor, Hazen Pingree, complained when its concrete pipes began to crumble into dust during his regime in the 1890s. And so the story went from city to city.[3]

Water and sewer systems required centralized construction and administration. There were economies of scale in building only one reservoir and one main aqueduct. An integrated sewer system with a receiving sewer at the lowest grade level and an outfall at a site that minimized pollution also considerably reduced costs over the long haul. The new technologies thus demanded a permanent bureaucracy to acquire land, oversee construction, administer on a day-to-day basis, and plan for long-term needs. Technological and managerial experts who could survey topography, choose appropriate construction materials, and draw readily upon the experiences of their counterparts in other cities gradually gained recognition as the most efficient builders of public works.

Such experts usually had to cope with problems extending beyond the core city. Topography ignored municipal boundaries. An efficient sewer system that followed natural gradients to achieve a gravity flow often had to stretch beyond a city's political limits. The dumping of one community's sewage might and often did pollute the water supply of a neighboring community. Newark, for instance, drew its water supply from the Passaic River at a point below the sewer outflows of Paterson and Passaic. Mill towns in the Merrimac Valley of New Hampshire and Massachusetts were notorious for fouling one another's water supplies. To combat pollution in such locales, the engineering press began urging regional cooperation in water and sewer services during the early 1870s.

Although there were earlier isolated examples of such metropolitan "authorities"—usually public health boards and park planning commissions—permanent administrative bodies arose in the late 1880s and early 1890s in response to pollution. City officials gained state legislative approval to create metropolitan water and sewer districts such as Boston's Metropolitan Sewage Commission (1889) and similar districts in Chicago, the Passaic Valley, and elsewhere. These were the forerunners of such twentieth-century metropolitan authorities as the Port Authority of New York. In most cases, municipal governments vested control of extra municipal projects in their city engineer's office. By the early 1890s, moreover, engineers in a few cities had obtained the power to approve plats in areas beyond city limits to ensure that subdividers' street plans would facilitate travel and accommodate the installation of subsurface utilities. In some cities engineers could abate nuisances beyond city limits, thus gaining authority to protect watersheds and to engage in an early form of zoning regulation as well.[4]

In exercising their increasing responsibilities, municipal engineers raised a banner around which urban reformers could rally. Their own offices were a model of hierarchical, bureaucratic organization that promised greater efficiency in the management of urban problems. They propagated division of responsibility, offered standardized systems for monitoring costs, and suggested new methods of formulating fiscal policies. Well before organizations like the National Conference for Good City Government and the National Municipal League (both founded in 1894) began to publish data on tax and budgetary policies, the engineering press had identified most of the major issues and had shaped the framework for discussion.[5]

Engineers and their projects served to centralize metropolitan administration of public works vital to the health and safety of city dwellers. A substantial minority of engineers active late in the century (almost 28 percent of those born before 1820) had had some legal training, and engineers often advised other city officials on broadly defined administrative and legal questions. In Boston during the 1870s, for example, engineers instigated, drafted, and oversaw enforcement of public welfare laws. Thanks to their successes in public works construction and management, engineers often found city councils receptive to their requests for additional responsibilities. In late nineteenth-century Chicago, the Public Works Department added garbage collection and street cleaning to its specified duties. Gradually, the offices of city engineers and public works boards acquired the reputation of being wise managers who could streamline government operations.[6]

Engineers were apparently the first officials of the emerging administrative bureaucracies to attain anything resembling job security. Ellis Clesbrough, chief engineer of the Chicago Board of Sewerage (1856–61), served as that community's first city engineer from 1861 to 1879, an amazing longevity at a time when most municipal jobs changed hands with every election. Others had equally long terms. E. P North, director of the Croton Water Works for New York City; Robert Moore, municipal engineer of St. Louis; George Benzenberg, city engineer of Milwaukee—all had at least twenty years of continuous service in the same city before 1900. Retention of an engineer familiar with the local system saved money, and in some jurisdictions courts reinforced the tendency toward long tenure by ruling that engineers held title to whatever plans they had drawn. A city that fired its engineer might lose the blueprints to its sewer system.[7]

Still, longevity in office is attributable to factors other than simple cost considerations. Civil service reformers repeatedly praised engineers as models of efficient bureaucrats and the District of Columbia, largely administered by the Army Corps of Engineers from the mid-1870s on, as an example of good city government. European cities with autonomous engineer-administrators, often military officers like Baron Georges E. Haussmann in Paris, also garnered plaudits from American reformers. Engineers, therefore, were among the earliest municipal employees to receive civil service protection under the new laws of the 1880s in a recognition of their role in managing the physical needs of cities. Their political caution, growing stature as problem-solvers, and reputations for fairness all worked to the engineers' advantage.[8]

They bolstered their claim to be neutral experts by institutionalizing the role of consultant. Operating in a cosmopolitan context, engineers were as responsive to their professional peers as to local pressures. George Waring and Rudolph Hering, the two most prominent sanitary engineers of the period, worked almost exclusively as consultants, moving from one city to another. Chesbrough, Benzenberg, Moses Lane of Milwaukee, Joseph P. Davis of Boston, and Colonel Julius W. Adams of Brooklyn were home-based but traveled widely to consult on major projects in other cities. The consultant role reflected both the status of engineers and their aloofness from the pendulum swings of partisan politics. Nineteenth-century city leaders generally viewed their communities as competing with others for economic growth and new population. A reputation for excellence in public works and healthfulness served local boosters well in the wars of urban imperialism. Yet city engineers were so valued as in-house experts that local politicians could not deny them the opportunity to advise rivals.[9]

Engineers secured job tenure through professionalization. At a time when few if any clearinghouses for the exchange of ideas and practices benefited cities nationwide, the engineers built up a remarkable communications network among themselves. Their common training, whether in engineering schools or apprenticeships (usually on the major railroads), bound them together. The practice of review by outside consultants reinforced these connections. Engineers belonged to local and regional professional clubs that corresponded with one another, publishing and exchanging reports about conditions in their respective cities. Numerous professional journals provided forums for discussion and debate.

During the late 1870s and again in the late 1880s, the most prestigious of these journals, the *Engineering News*, printed a lengthy series comparing cities around the country. Reports described water supply, sewerage, streets, parks, housing design, transportation terminals, and other elements of municipal planning. They dealt also with administrative and legal questions. The engineering press also covered European developments, paying particular attention to the important research trips abroad of Chesbrough and Hering. Finally, engineers belonged to the same national organizations. The majority held membership in the American Society of Civil Engineers, which frequently published papers on municipal engineering projects with appended comments from experts throughout the nation. In 1894 professionals involved principally with urban problems formed their own specialized national organization, the American Society for Municipal Improvements.[10]

Engineers were not bashful about asserting their importance to municipal administration. They advertised themselves, one engineer observed, as having "a high reputation for fairness and a capacity to render wise and just decisions." They strongly and repeatedly criticized proposals by citizens' associations for needed public works, stating that such matters were best left to professionals. They even claimed a steward's right to oversee the acts of elected public officials, asserting that the city engineer was "to a certain extent responsible for holding the successive political officials to a consistent, progressive policy. . . . To him, even more than to the successive mayors, falls the duty of serving as the intelligence and brains of the municipal government in all physical matters." Gustavus Karwiese, consulting engineer to the District of Columbia in the late 1870s, capped the claims for his profession when he told Congress that "it is the civil engineer . . . who is, by the silent command of the great Architect, the trustee of human happiness."[11]

That city engineers trumpeted their own importance is not surprising. The core of professionalism is the assertion of knowledge and skills available only to group members. Modern skeptics might doubt the engineers' claims of political neutrality. In some cities, as one scholar has noted, "engineers owed at least their early careers to machine politicians who, in an effort to promote growth and curry voter support, proposed, funded, and completed hundreds of sewer, water, horsecar, railroad, and bridge projects." Engineers' growing importance as managers of the physical

city involved them intimately with elected officials and raised the potential for abuses of power. Yet there is in fact little or no evidence of city engineers' being "on the take," embroiled in the numerous political scandals, large and small, that amused, bemused, or outraged post–Civil War city dwellers. Although they served the immediate interests of local boosters and elected officials, the engineers could claim that over the long run their work benefited all citizens.[12]

The administrative techniques of engineers, along with their reputations as problem-solvers, carried great prestige. Within their specialized functions, engineers had developed centralized agencies capable of long-range, comprehensive planning and staffed by cosmopolitan experts. They had also advocated, with considerable success, the extension of their brand of organization to municipal administration as a whole. Albert F. Noyes, one of the leading city engineers of the period, echoed conventional sentiments in 1894 when he claimed that "the office of the municipal engineer is of the greatest importance to the community. . . . In fact, the city government of today is in a large measure a matter of municipal engineering, and the character of the city engineer's department is a safe index to the intelligence shown in the development of a municipality."[13]

The engineers offered city governments a corps of individuals skilled in the technology and management of large-scale enterprises, experts who could solve the physical problems of the cities. Decades before early twentieth-century political reformers depicted their ideal bureaucrat, municipal engineers embodied all of his characteristics: efficiency, expertise, and professionalism. They had emerged, in Suzanne Keller's telling phrase, as a "strategic elite" in American society.[14] . . .

The City as Sewer

Among major American cities, Baltimore alone put off construction of the kinds of public works projects that sanitarians, landscape architects, and engineers had called for since the 1840s. In 1859, 1881, and again in 1893, commissions appointed by the mayor and led principally by engineers had urged planning and construction to remedy the city's problems. On each occasion the public's reluctance to spend tax dollars, along with partisan politics, had sunk the proposals. Baltimore alone had ignored mounting evidence of the ties between the cleanliness or filth of the environment and rates of disease and mortality among city dwellers. Its citizens paid dearly for the delay. Although the census of 1890 judged Newark, New Jersey, the nation's unhealthiest city, the Chesapeake Bay community did not lag far behind—and Baltimore was two-and-a-half times as populous as Newark, with vastly larger financial resources.[22]

In 1890 Baltimore was one of only seven cities in the United States with a population of 400,000 or more. During the eighties it more than doubled its physical size through annexation, a tool used by every large American city in this period. Annexation, coupled with immigration, boosted Baltimore's population during the eighties by more than 102,000 people. This sudden spurt, paralleled in every other metropolis in the United States, placed stress on Baltimore's ability to provide adequate urban services. Unlike the other large American cities, it would not respond to the problems of development until the close of the first decade of the twentieth century. Between 1890 and roughly 1910, Baltimore remained one of the nation's prime examples of the city as sewer.[23]

Baltimore lines the banks of the Patapsco River, an arm of Chesapeake Bay, with a peninsula splitting the river into a Middle and a Northwest Branch. Along the latter branch as it stretched northward into the city stood factories, grain elevators, warehouses, and the wharves of the nation's third-largest port. Beyond these stood the central business district. Bisecting the city from the north and ending at a harbor formed by the Northwest Branch ran a ravine threaded by a foul stream called Jones Falls. Industrial wastes fed into the stream and poured into the harbor. On one side of Jones Falls lay East Baltimore, housing most of the city's working-class population. Slum tenements huddled in rows along the harbor and the lower sections of the falls. To the north of East Baltimore was most of the land annexed during the 1880s, containing some of the wealthiest sections of the city as well as rapidly growing middle-class suburbs. Immediately west of the core of the city, on the other side of Jones Falls, was the principal black ghetto (next to Washington, Baltimore had the largest Negro population of any American city in 1890). North of the ghetto was a district called Bolton Hill, where lived many of the city's professional and business families. Frequent rainfall, the rolling topography of the city, and the geographic separation of different sections had long hindered provision of an adequate water supply and an effective sewage-disposal system.[24]

During the first half of the nineteenth century, the private Baltimore Water Company supplied the community with water from a number of small reservoirs along Jones Falls. In 1854 the city purchased the water company and expanded service while still depending on Jones Falls for its supply. As population grew and indoor plumbing became popular, that source became inadequate. Between 1875 and 1881, city engineers constructed a new reservoir that tapped a different water source. Although expanded, however, the water supply system, which depended largely on gravity flow, was far from perfected. The houses built during the eighties on hillsides surrounding the Jones Falls valley stood above the reach of existing reservoirs. Baltimore met the problem by building new reservoirs in various districts of the city and installing pumping mechanisms to fill them with water. The pumps often broke down, resulting in water shortages. That was not unusual; other cities at the time faced the same difficulties with the new technology. Nor was it unusual that the new supplies of water were hardly pure. In many large cities thorough filtration and purification of water did not become standard practice until the early 1920s.[25]

Thus, with regard to water supplies, Baltimore's experience was typical—in provision of a municipal water system and in the timing of construction, Baltimore was on track with the rest of urban America. That decidedly was not the case for the city's handling of sewage disposal.

For most of the nineteenth century, Baltimore relied upon "natural" disposal. Rainwater soaked the soil of backyards and the largely unpaved streets, eventually running off through streams. Householders customarily dropped kitchen refuse and domestic wastewater into surface street gutters. Cesspools drained the excrement from privies; in the rainy seasons seepage turned backyards into putrid marshes. As the century wore on, the problems of sewage pollution increased. In some of the wealthier sections, private citizens contracted for the construction of storm drains. There was little or no coordination of these scattered efforts, which served only a small proportion of the city's citizens and polluted nearby streams. Some 15,000 homes owned by the city's elite had privately built sewer lines that funneled raw household wastes into Jones Falls.[26]

Most Baltimoreans periodically had their cesspools cleaned by private companies, notably the inaptly named Odorless Excavating Apparatus Company. The streams, the surface glitters, the private lines, and cesspool seepages all finally dumped their burdens into the harbor, with the predictable result that in spring and summer that body of water was afloat with rotted garbage and the flotsam and jetsam of urban wastes, smelling like "a billion polecats." When prevailing winds shifted, citizens in all parts of the city sensed that they were in for another Baltimore summer. Since most of those who lived on the harbor's hinges were slum dwellers, however, the better classes of Baltimoreans turned up their noses at the problem.[27]

For those who resided in the oldest, most congested parts of the city, the lack of an adequate sewage system was especially acute. Many lived in cellar apartments or in buildings that had earth-packed basement floors. For several months of the year, even under the best of conditions, the "floors" softened into muddy wading-pools of filth. During heavy rainfalls, flooded basements awash with liquid wastes were not uncommon. City inspectors responded to complaints with the helpful suggestion that building owners or residents pave over the dirt. Matters only worsened for the slum dwellers, and to a lesser extent for all Baltimoreans, with the expansion of the city's water supply and the growth of the city's industries.[28]

Wastewater disposal, from all sources, had become a problem of epic dimensions by 1890. "Natural" sewerage had proved an abject failure. The commissioner of health, possessing limited powers to act, could only report of the privies, for example, that "many of them overflow, and the liquid contents flow into yards and gutters, emitting most offensive odors. . . ." These were, he asserted, "a fruitful source of disease, operating indirectly in its production, and directly in lowering the vital stamina of the unfortunates compelled to breathe a polluted atmosphere." The "unfortunates" included most citizens. The privies, he concluded, "are the most dangerous enemies of our lives and happiness." Although his etiology was outmoded, his comments on the prevalence of disease were, as we have seen, pertinent.[29]

In 1890 the death rate from all physical ailments of residents of the nation's twenty-eight largest cities averaged 23.3 persons per thousand. Newark, with a population of 182,000, had a mortality rate of 29 per thousand, highest among American cities with populations of 100,000 or more. Among major cities—those with 400,000 or more citizens—only New York had a higher death rate than Baltimore. By 1900 matters had improved little. Newark's death rate had fallen to 19.8, while Baltimore's had declined to 21 per thousand. Philadelphia, with a rate of 21.2, barely edged the Chesapeake Bay community in the death race, or Baltimore would have stood alone at the top of the heap. Baltimore did capture top honors, however, in 1890 and finished a close second in 1900, for mortality among its colored population.

By the turn of the century, conditions had become so wretched that even well-to-do Baltimoreans could tolerate them no longer. Engineers and sanitarians were no longer alone in calling for the construction of a citywide integrated sewer system. Organizations of prominent, reform-minded citizens, such as the Municipal Art Society and the Reform League, demanded action. Mendes Cohen, a director of the Municipal Art Society and a civil engineer, became chairman in 1893 of a citywide commission to remedy sanitation problems. Aided by two consulting engineers, his commission researched the sewerage systems of the United States and Europe. Its report eventually served as the basis for a city plan prepared by the Olmsted Brothers and privately underwritten by the Municipal Art Society. Businessmen, particularly those whose companies stood in low-lying areas, joined the fray in the late nineties, led by the president of the Merchants' and Manufacturers' Association.[30]

Finally, in 1905, through a series of intricate political maneuvers, a new mayor appointed a blue-ribbon sewerage commission empowered to oversee the building of a comprehensive system. Construction began in 1906 and concluded in 1915. By then, nearly 500 miles of integrated sanitary sewers served more than 100,000 homes. Once stirred into action, the city moved with efficiency and dispatch. In less than a decade, Baltimore transformed itself into one of the best-sewered cities in the nation.[31]

Demands for a host of other public improvements brought about street widening and paving projects, park planning schemes, new transportation networks, and new schools, police stations, and firehouses during the first decade and a half of the twentieth century. In all cases, new administrative procedures governed implementation of city planning proposals. The city charter adopted in 1898 had provided for a five-person Board of Estimates to conduct Baltimore's financial affairs. One of the five was the city engineer, appointed by the mayor. His task was principally to coordinate the activities of several boards charged with administration of various public works and oversee plans for future public improvements.[32]

By the early years of the new century, the city had joined the rest of urban America, which had long since recognized the importance of engineering expertise in the construction and administration of public works projects and city planning. Baltimore's leaders and citizens alike might regret the years of delay, yet take pride in having finally fallen in step with the nation-wide march toward the reforming of cities.

Reforming the Cities

In 1905 Frederic C. Howe, a ten-year veteran of political wars to improve urban government in Cleveland and around the nation, published a self-styled "manual of reform." In *The City: The Hope of Democracy*, he catalogued the concerns of urban reformers of his generation. Like others he denounced immigrant-dominated political machines as economically wasteful and morally indefensible. Boodling politicians, men who cared more about lining their pockets through graft and bribery than serving the public at large, worked hand-in-hand with unscrupulous businessmen in a spoils system that robbed decent citizens of their chances for progress. Or so Howe and other like-minded reformers charged. Wearied by wars against daily greed, Howe outlined a new order of battle, one that presented a practical strategy of technical solutions even as it paraded moral indignation.

For all his diatribes against political bosses and profit-hungry private corporations, Howe identified the "elemental problems" of cities as the building of sewers, streets, transit systems, and public parks. Such public works, he claimed, had become "a necessity to the life, health, comfort, convenience, and industry of the city." They were too important to be left in the hands of private individuals or public officials skilled only at getting themselves elected: these were "executive matters requiring special training or scientific

knowledge of the work to be done." University-trained men—political scholars, scientists, and especially engineers—should lead the cities onto the pathways of progress.[33]

To harness new technologies to meet social needs was the aspiration of many so-called progressives, particularly those enthusiastic about city planning. As the landscape architect John Nolen put it in 1909: "Intelligent city planning is one of the means toward a better utilization of our resources, toward an application of the methods of private business to public affairs, toward efficiency, toward a higher individual and collective life." The watchwords of these reformers, as Nolen suggested, were "conservation," "efficiency," and "social engineering." Each goal required the application of technology to human problems; each demanded innovative methods of administration. Many a reformer championed city planning of one type or another, facilitated by municipal ownership of utilities and administered by new governmental institutions.[34]

Some reformers of this era emphasized one particular planning goal—for example, new transit systems—while others advanced what they called comprehensive planning. Howe expressed the latter in his autobiography. Recalling his enthusiasms, he mused: "I had an architectonic vision of what a city might be. I saw it as a picture. . . . It was a unit, a thing with a mind, with a conscious purpose, seeing far in advance of the present and taking precautions for the future. I had this picture of Cleveland long before the advent of city-planning proposals; it was just as instinctive as any mechanical talent."[35]

It was "instinctive," as other passages of the autobiography made clear, precisely because the young Howe grew up with and was educated by the planning attitudes that had evolved as part of the new urban culture of the nineteenth century. When Howe wrote "long before the advent of city-planning proposals," he meant those of the early twentieth century. He was not ignorant of past efforts. The planning efforts—partial and comprehensive—of Howe's predecessors in the public works crusades had helped shape the reform outlook of the early twentieth century. The reformers' embracing of "comprehensive" planning in the progressive era was in some ways simply a restatement of long-standing attitudes, and in other ways a logical culmination of decades of thought and action.

Many urban political reformers of the early twentieth century found themselves in agreement with Howe. In terms of both process and personnel, changes in the structure of municipal government during the progressive era drew heavily on the technological and administrative skills exhibited by engineers over the last half of the nineteenth century. The cumulative impact of the engineers' contributions helped to create two new professions in early twentieth-century America—city planners and city managers. Both were central in reforming the cities. Both substantially altered the administrative functions of municipal government and its reach into citizens' lives. Both confirmed the maturation of the emerging city culture of the nineteenth century.[36]

Planning and Managing the Cities

In May 1909 a large group of prominent individuals met in the nation's capital to convene the First National Conference on City Planning and the Problems of Congestion. Among them were engineers, landscape architects, public health officials, conservationists, economists, lawyers, social workers, journalists, corporate leaders, and public officials. A sense of urgency pervaded the gathering.

John Nolen denounced present trends in city development as "fatal" and called upon cities to investigate their problems, promote cooperation between public authorities and private individuals, and achieve "prompt and courageous execution of the plan found to be best for all concerned." Benjamin C. Marsh, the era's leading proponent of comprehensive city planning, demanded surveys, publicity, and new legal weapons "against which corporate interests cannot contend." Representing some of those corporate interests (presumably the "responsible" ones) was the financier Henry Morgenthau, who identified congestion as "an evil that breeds physical disease, moral depravity, discontent, and socialism—and all these must be cured and eradicated or else our great body politic will be weakened." Frederick Law Olmsted, Jr., reflecting the views of many other participants, described the glories of town planning in Germany, pointing out that German plans included not only

street layouts "and so forth, but the whole code of building regulations, health ordinances, police rules, and system of taxation in so far as they have a direct influence upon the physical development of the city." Some participants sought to encourage purely local responses to problems, while others called for federal action. But the conference was in full agreement about its final goal—comprehensive planning in and for urban America.[37]

At that first meeting, the noted landscape architect Robert Anderson Pope emphasized the pressing need for "a profession equipped to make city planning the social and economic factor it ought to be." The National Conference on City Planning continued to meet once a year, in a different city each time, advertising principles of comprehensive planning to countless thousands of urban Americans. Gathering together a broad cross-section of people concerned about city problems, the conference served both as an information center for the exchange of practices and ideas and as a public relations outpost for the professionals involved. It also stimulated enthusiasm among some participants for a different forum in which the several varieties of technocrats could discuss and debate technical details of planning that might well bore the general public. In short, the conference sparked commitment to the formal creation of the profession Pope had called for.[38]

The role of engineers in the emerging profession was considerable. New York City's chief engineer, Nelson P. Lewis, author of one of the earliest and most widely consulted texts on city planning, dedicated his 1916 volume "To the Municipal Engineers of the United States, the first men on the ground in City Planning as in City Building." Of the fifty-two charter members of the American Institute of Planners (first called the American City Planning Institute in 1917), thirteen were engineers. Only landscape architecture provided more members (fourteen), and several of them had some engineering training. The newly formed AIP included the individuals who had prepared most of the comprehensive city plans advanced since 1905. In that same year a committee of the American Institute of Architects published a nationwide survey, *City Planning Progress;* its editors noted that "the Committee has laid particular stress on the economic and engineering side of city planning, because it believes that that is fundamental to progress." Mel Scott, historian of the AIP, has calculated that through the 1920s most middle-sized and smaller cities continued to delegate all responsibility for planning to their city engineer's office. With the solitary exception of Delos Wilcox, a political reformer, engineers dominated the most important of the new specialties, transportation planning.[39]

The direct contributions of engineers to municipal administration during the early years of the twentieth century were even more impressive than their role in the growth of the city planning profession. However much political reformers disagreed about the details of structural change, they agreed that the professionalization and bureaucratization of government were steps in the right direction. Members of the National Municipal League left no room for doubt on this point.

In 1899 a subcommittee of the league composed "The Municipal Program," a document promoting theories about the "right organization" of municipal government. The bucket of nineteenth-century Jacksonian democracy—the notion that any common man could govern his fellows—had sprung too many leaks. Cities had to throw it away. Reporting to the tenth annual meeting in 1904, Delos Wilcox declared that one of the core principles of the "Program" was that city officials had to know their business: "It is gradually dawning upon the American mind that special knowledge is required to run the machinery of city government, if we are to avoid a wreck. . . . The complex machinery of a city can be run only by those who know how to do that particular thing. . . . The whole body of municipal officials need special knowledge and long experience to give the city the benefit of good service." Characteristic of progressive-era structural reform was an emphasis on efficiency, specialized training, and administrative accountability. No single political change better reflected those values than the managerial revolution in urban government.[40]

In brief, the progressives wanted to replace ward bosses and corrupt machine politicians with trained, nonpartisan professionals who could carry out the day-by-day administration of government without

regard for the vicissitudes of the political arena. An elected commission or council—having gained office through an at-large, citywide election rather than through the traditional ward-by-ward process—should establish public policies and appoint a skilled professional to handle executive functions. Such a centralized administration would manage municipal services with businesslike efficiency. Reformers repeatedly charged that machine politicians cared not about efficiency but about staying in office to loot the public treasury. Machine leaders controlled elections by garnering the votes of ignorant immigrant dwellers living in the urban core. A favor given here, a job secured there—these were the coins of the realm for exploiting the immigrants for their votes. Meanwhile, the machines failed to represent the interests of the "better sort" of citizens, the middle- and upper-class people who had left the city for the suburbs in an effort to escape the corruption of the core. Or, so the reformers asserted. A city-manager form of government would reduce the voting power wielded by the lower-class central wards while elevating the influence of the business and professional elites living on the urban periphery and in the suburbs. To critics who warned about the dangers to democracy inherent in the scheme, supporters retorted that "democracy need fear no setback through the introduction of this new form of administration; and efficiency . . . can come into her own at last."[41]

The new city-manager form of government first surfaced in Staunton, Virginia, in 1908. The city council appointed Charles E. Ashburner, charging him with improving the community's streets while also holding the line on public expenditures. Within three years, Ashburner had placed the city on a sound financial basis, improved the water and sewage systems, directed installation of effective street lighting, and accelerated the street-paving process tenfold, lifting the community, as one contemporary put it, from "mud to asphalt." Other cities, including communities in both Carolinas, Oregon, and Michigan, soon followed suit. For the most part, these were small cities, and their problems therefore appeared easier to treat than those of larger, more industrialized communities. A more dramatic example was needed.[42]

One came in Dayton, Ohio, in 1913. That city of some 110,000 citizens had governmental problems akin to those of the largest cities. A devastating flood in March focused national attention on Dayton while also revealing the inability of local machine politicians to respond efficiently. Led by John H. Patterson, the wealthy head of the National Cash Register Company, a group of Dayton professionals and businessmen succeeded in gaining election to office, whereupon they drafted a city-manager charter that they sold to the electorate. Early in 1914 the new council appointed Henry M. Waite to the post of city-manager. He not only solved the immediate problems of rebuilding municipal services, but also engaged in social engineering, providing free legal aid, a milk-inspection program in the city's schools, and free medical examinations for children. The "Dayton Plan," as contemporaries called it, spread rapidly throughout the nation over the next few years.[43]

The new city-manager form of government, as attested by the National Municipal League in 1913, promised administrative unity, clear lines of responsibility, expertise at the top of the administration, and discipline and harmony within the ranks of government servants. By 1919 the league had incorporated the position of city manager into its model charter for urban governmental reform. The new professionals brought administrative expertise, a taste for bureaucracy, and the battle cry of "efficiency" to the management of scores of small and middle-sized cities over the first few decades of the twentieth century.[44]

It is not my purpose here to describe in detail the impact of the managerial revolution. Rather, I want to sketch a profile of these new technocrats and look at how their efforts reflected growing public acceptance of the necessity of expertise in planning and managing cities.

A profile of the new profession reveals common backgrounds. The first city managers of Staunton and Dayton, for example, were both practicing civil engineers. Ashburner had worked for railroad and electrical companies and for the Public Roads Administration

of the federal government. Waite came to his Dayton post directly from a highly successful career as city engineer of Cincinnati. The 1919 *Yearbook* of the new City Managers' Association showed that 48 percent of the total membership were engineers. In 1920 a survey of California city managers stated that of the twenty-one listing their backgrounds, thirteen were engineers. Surveys taken during the 1920s and 1930s demonstrated that of those managers with bachelor's degrees, 75 percent had trained as engineers. By the time the "typical" manager assumed his job, he had engaged in practical engineering work and had held one or more posts in government, usually as a department head. As late as 1940, a major nationwide survey related that more than 63 percent of city managers over the previous quarter-century had trained as engineers.[45]

Many contemporaries saw the establishment of the new profession of city manager as the high-water mark of progressive reform in municipal administration. The managers themselves were recruited primarily from another profession that had long since proved its central importance to the orderly functioning of cities. Over the half-century preceding the progressive era, the job of municipal engineer had developed into a profession that had helped reshape the physical landscape of urban America. Of equal significance, it had provided a corps of experienced experts and a model of administrative skill that latter-day progressives would use as a basis for the structural reform of urban government.

In both the technological and the political arenas, municipal engineers played an increasingly important part. Over the last half of the nineteenth century, they stamped their long-range visions of metropolitan planning on the public consciousness. Their demands for political autonomy in solving the physical problems of cities contributed to an ultimate insistence on efficient government run by experts. At the center of physical and political changes in the administration of American cities—indeed, at the very core of city planning by the first decade of the twentieth century—stood the work of municipal engineers.

4-4 "The Politics of Reform in Municipal Government in the Progressive Era"*

Samuel P. Hays

Pacific Northwest Quarterly

In order to achieve a more complete understanding of social change in the Progressive Era, historians must now undertake a deeper analysis of the practices of economic, political, and social groups. Political ideology alone is no longer satisfactory evidence to describe social patterns because generalizations based upon it, which tend to divide political groups into the moral and the immoral, the rational and the irrational, the efficient and the inefficient, do not square with political practice. Behind this contemporary rhetoric concerning the nature of reform lay patterns of political behavior which were at variance with it. Since an extensive gap separated ideology and practice, we can no longer take the former as an accurate description of the latter, but must reconstruct social behavior from other types of evidence.

Reform in urban government provides one of the most striking examples of this problem of analysis. The demand for change in municipal affairs, whether in terms of over-all reform, such as the commission and city-manager plans, or of more piecemeal modifications, such as the development of city-wide school boards, deeply involved reform ideology. Reformers loudly proclaimed a new structure of municipal government as more moral, more rational, and more efficient and, because it was so, self-evidently more desirable. But precisely because of this emphasis, there seemed to be no need to analyze the political forces behind change. Because the goals of reform were good, its causes were obvious; rather than being the product of particular people and particular ideas in particular situations, they were deeply imbedded in the universal impulses and truths of "progress." Consequently, historians have rarely tried to determine precisely who the municipal reformers were or what they did, but instead have relied on reform ideology as an accurate description of reform practice.

The reform ideology which became the basis of historical analysis is well known. It appears in classic form in Lincoln Steffens' *Shame of the Cities*. The urban political struggle of the Progressive Era, so the argument goes, involved a conflict between public impulses for "good government" against a corrupt alliance of "machine politicians" and "special interests."

During the rapid urbanization of the late 19th century, the latter had been free to aggrandize themselves, especially through franchise grants, at the expense of the public. Their power lay primarily in their ability to manipulate the political process, by bribery and corruption, for their own ends. Against such arrangements there gradually arose a public protest, a demand by the public for honest government, for officials who would act for the public rather than for themselves. To accomplish their goals, reformers sought basic modifications in the political system, both in the structure of government and in the manner of selecting public officials. These changes, successful in city after city, enabled the "public interest" to triumph.[1] . . .

In the following account I will summarize evidence in both secondary and primary works concerning the political practices in which municipal reformers were involved. Such an analysis logically can be broken down into three parts, each one corresponding to a step

Source: Samuel P. Hays, "The Politics of Reform in Municipal Government in the Progressive Era", *Pacific Northwest Quarterly*, vol. 55, 1964, pp. 157–169. Reprinted with permission from *Pacific Northwest Quarterly,* University of Washington.

*Some text and accompanying endnotes have been omitted. Please consult the original source.

in the traditional argument. First, what was the source of reform? Did it lie in the general public rather than in particular groups? Was it middle class, working class, or perhaps of other composition? Second, what was the reform target of attack? Were reformers primarily interested in ousting the corrupt individual, the political or business leader who made private arrangements at the expense of the public, or were they interested in something else? Third, what political innovations did reformers bring about? Did they seek to expand popular participation in the governmental process?

There is now sufficient evidence to determine the validity of these specific elements of the more general argument. Some of it has been available for several decades; some has appeared more recently; some is presented here for the first time. All of it adds up to the conclusion that reform in municipal government involved a political development far different from what we have assumed in the past.

Available evidence indicates that the source of support for reform in municipal government did not come from the lower or middle classes, but from the upper class. The leading business groups in each city and professional men closely allied with them initiated and dominated municipal movements. Leonard White, in his study of the city manager published in 1927, wrote:

> The opposition to bad government usually comes to a head in the local chamber of commerce. Business men finally acquire the conviction that the growth of their city is being seriously impaired by the failures of city officials to perform their duties efficiently. Looking about for a remedy, they are captivated by the resemblance of the city-manager plan to their corporate form of business organization.[8]

In the 1930's White directed a number of studies of the origin of city-manager government. The resulting reports invariably begin with such statements as, "the Chamber of Commerce spearheaded the movement," or commission government in this city was a "businessmen's government."[9] Of thirty-two cases of city-manager government in Oklahoma examined by Jewell C. Phillips, twenty-nine were initiated either by chambers of commerce or by community committees dominated by

businessmen.[10] More recently James Weinstein has presented almost irrefutable evidence that the business community, represented largely by chambers of commerce, was the overwhelming force behind both commission and city-manager movements.[11]

Dominant elements of the business community played a prominent role in another crucial aspect of municipal reform: the Municipal Research Bureau movement.[12] Especially in the larger cities, where they had less success in shaping the structure of government, reformers established centers to conduct research in municipal affairs as a springboard for influence.

The first such organization, the Bureau of Municipal Research of New York City, was founded in 1906; it was financed largely through the efforts of Andrew Carnegie and John D. Rockefeller. An investment banker provided the crucial support in Philadelphia, where a Bureau was founded in 1908. A group of wealthy Chicagoans in 1910 established the Bureau of Public Efficiency, a research agency. John H. Patterson of the National Cash Register Company, the leading figure in Dayton municipal reform, financed the Dayton Bureau, founded in 1912. And George Eastman was the driving force behind both the Bureau of Municipal Research and citymanager government in Rochester. In smaller cities data about city government was collected by interested individuals in a more informal way or by chambers of commerce, but in larger cities the task required special support, and prominent businessmen supplied it.

The character of municipal reform is demonstrated more precisely by a brief examination of the movements in Des Moines and Pittsburgh. The Des Moines Commercial Club inaugurated and carefully controlled the drive for the commission form of government.[13] In January, 1906, the Club held a so-called "mass meeting" of business and professional men to secure an enabling act from the state legislature. P. C. Kenyon, president of the Club, selected a Committee of 300, composed principally of business and professional men, to draw up a specific proposal. After the legislature approved their plan, the same committee managed the campaign which persuaded the electorate to accept the commission form of government by a narrow margin in June, 1907.

In this election the lower-income wards of the city opposed the change, the upper-income wards supported it strongly, and the middle-income wards were more evenly divided. In order to control the new government, the Committee of 300, now expanded to 530, sought to determine the nomination and election of the five new commissioners, and to this end they selected an avowedly businessman's slate. Their plans backfired when the voters swept into office a slate of anticommission candidates who now controlled the new commission government.

Proponents of the commission form of government in Des Moines spoke frequently in the name of the "people." But their more explicit statements emphasized their intent that the new plan be a "business system" of government, run by businessmen. The slate of candidates for commissioner endorsed by advocates of the plan was known as the "businessman's ticket." J. W. Hill, president of the committees of 300 and 530, bluntly declared: "The professional politician must be ousted and in his place capable businessmen chosen to conduct the affairs of the city." I. M. Earle, general counsel of the Bankers Life Association and a prominent figure in the movement, put the point more precisely: "When the plan was adopted it was the intention to get businessmen to run it."

Although reformers used the ideology of popular government, they in no sense meant that all segments of society should be involved equally in municipal decision-making. They meant that their concept of the city's welfare would be best achieved if the business community controlled city government. As one businessman told a labor audience, the businessman's slate represented labor "better than you do yourself."

The composition of the municipal reform movement in Pittsburgh demonstrates its upperclass and professional as well as its business sources.[14] Here the two principal reform organizations were the Civic Club and the Voters' League. The 745 members of these two organizations came primarily from the upper class. Sixtyfive per cent appeared in upper-class directories which contained the names of only 2 percent of the city's families. Furthermore, many who were not listed in these directories lived in upper-class areas. These reformers, it should be stressed, comprised not an old but a new upper class. Few came from earlier industrial and mercantile

families. Most of them had risen to social position from wealth created after 1870 in the iron, steel, electrical equipment, and other industries, and they lived in the newer rather than the older fashionable areas.

Almost half (48 per cent) of the reformers were professional men: doctors, lawyers, ministers, directors of libraries and museums, engineers, architects, private and public school teachers, and college professors. Some of these belonged to the upper class as well, especially the lawyers, ministers, and private school teachers. But for the most part their interest in reform stemmed from the inherent dynamics of their professions rather than from their class connections. They came from the more advanced segments of their organizations, from those in the forefront of the acquisition and application of knowledge. They were not the older professional men, seeking to preserve the past against change; they were in the vanguard of professional life, actively seeking to apply expertise more widely to public affairs.

Pittsburgh reformers included a large segment of businessmen; 52 per cent were bankers and corporation officials or their wives. Among them were the presidents of fourteen large banks and officials of Westinghouse, Pittsburgh Plate Glass, U.S. Steel and its component parts (such as Carnegie Steel, American Bridge, and National Tube), Jones and Laughlin, lesser steel companies (such as Crucible, Pittsburgh, Superior, Lockhart, and H. K. Porter), the H. J. Heinz Company, and the Pittsburgh Coal Company, as well as officials of the Pennsylvania Railroad and the Pittsburgh and Lake Erie. These men were not small businessmen; they directed the most powerful banking and industrial organizations of the city. They represented not the old business community, but industries which had developed and grown primarily within the past fifty years and which had come to dominate the city's economic life.

These business, professional, and upper-class groups who dominated municipal reform movements were all involved in the rationalization and systematization of modern life; they wished a form of government which would be more consistent with the objectives inherent in those developments. The most important single feature of their perspective was the rapid expansion of the geographical scope of affairs which they wished to influence and manipulate, a scope which was no longer limited and narrow, no longer within the confines of pedestrian communities, but was now broad and city-wide, covering the whole range of activities of the metropolitan area.

The migration of the upper class from central to outlying areas created a geographical distance between its residential communities and its economic institutions. To protect the latter required involvement both in local ward affairs and in the larger city government as well. Moreover, upper-class cultural institutions, such as museums, libraries, and symphony orchestras, required an active interest in the larger municipal context from which these institutions drew much of their clientele.

Professional groups, broadening the scope of affairs which they sought to study, measure, or manipulate, also sought to influence the public health, the educational system, or the physical arrangements of the entire city. Their concerns were limitless, not bounded by geography, but as expansive as the professional imagination. Finally, the new industrial community greatly broadened its perspective in governmental affairs because of its new recognition of the way in which factors throughout the city affected business growth. The increasing size and scope of industry, the greater stake in more varied and geographically dispersed facets of city life, the effect of floods on many business concerns, the need to promote traffic flows to and from work for both blue-collar and managerial employees all contributed to this larger interest. The geographically larger private perspectives of upper-class, professional, and business groups gave rise to a geographically larger public perspective.

These reformers were dissatisfied with existing systems of municipal government. They did not oppose corruption per se although there was plenty of that. They objected to the structure of government which enabled local and particularistic interests to dominate. Prior to the reforms of the Progressive Era, city government consisted primarily of confederations of local wards, each of which was represented on the city's legislative body. Each ward frequently had its own elementary schools and ward-elected school boards which administered them.

These particularistic interests were the focus of a decentralized political life. City councilmen were local

leaders. They spoke for their local areas, the economic interests of their inhabitants, their residential concerns, their educational, recreational, and religious interests—i.e., for those aspects of community life which mattered most to those they represented. They rolled logs in the city council to provide streets, sewers, and other public works for their local areas. They defended the community's cultural practices, its distinctive languages or national customs, its liberal attitude toward liquor, and its saloons and dance halls which served as centers of community life. One observer described this process of representation in Seattle:

> The residents of the hill-tops and the suburbs may not fully appreciate the faithfulness of certain downtown ward councilmen to the interests of their constituents. . . . The people of a state would rise in arms against a senator or representative in Congress who deliberately misrepresented their wishes and imperilled their interests, though he might plead a higher regard for national good. Yet people in other parts of the city seem to forget that under the old system the ward elected councilmen with the idea of procuring service of special benefit to that ward.[15]

In short, pre-reform officials spoke for their constituencies, inevitably their own wards which had elected them, rather than for other sections or groups of the city.

The ward system of government especially gave representation in city affairs to lower- and middle-class groups. Most elected ward officials were from these groups, and they, in turn, constituted the major opposition to reforms in municipal government. In Pittsburgh, for example, immediately prior to the changes in both the city council and the school board in 1911 in which city-wide representation replaced ward representation, only 24 per cent of the 387 members of those bodies represented the same managerial, professional, and banker occupations which dominated the membership of the Civic Club and the Voters' League. The great majority (67 percent) were small businessmen-grocers, saloonkeepers, livery-stable proprietors, owners of small hotels, druggists-white-collar workers such as clerks and bookkeepers, and skilled and unskilled workmen.[16]

This decentralized system of urban growth and the institutions which arose from it reformers now opposed. Social, professional, and economic life had developed not only in the local wards in a small community context, but also on a larger scale had become highly integrated and organized, giving rise to a superstructure of social organization which lay far above that of ward life and which was sharply divorced from it in both personal contacts and perspective.

By the late 19th century, those involved in these larger institutions found that the decentralized system of political life limited their larger objectives. The movement for reform in municipal government, therefore, constituted an attempt by upper-class, advanced professional, and large business groups to take formal political power from the previously dominant lower- and middle-class elements so that they might advance their own conceptions of desirable public policy. These two groups came from entirely different urban worlds, and the political system fashioned by one was no longer acceptable to the other.

Lower- and middle-class groups not only dominated the pre-reform governments, but vigorously opposed reform. It is significant that none of the occupational groups among them, for example, small businessmen or white-collar workers, skilled or unskilled artisans, had important representation in reform organizations thus far examined. The case studies of city-manager government undertaken in the 1930's under the direction of Leonard White detailed in city after city the particular opposition of labor. In their analysis of Jackson, Michigan, the authors of these studies wrote:

> The *Square Deal*, oldest Labor paper in the state, has been consistently against manager government, perhaps largely because labor has felt that with a decentralized government elected on a ward basis it was more likely to have some voice and to receive its share of privileges.[17]

In Janesville, Wisconsin, the small shopkeepers and workingmen on the west and south sides, heavily Catholic and often Irish, opposed the commission plan in 1911 and in 1912 and the city-manager plan

when adopted in 1923.[18] "In Dallas there is hardly a trace of class consciousness in the Marxian sense," one investigator declared, "yet in city elections the division has been to a great extent along class lines."[19] The commission and city-manager elections were no exceptions. To these authors it seemed a logical reaction, rather than an embarrassing fact that had to be swept away, that workingmen should have opposed municipal reform.[20]

In Des Moines working-class representatives, who in previous years might have been council members, were conspicuously absent from the "businessman's slate." Workingmen acceptable to reformers could not be found. A workingman's slate of candidates, therefore, appeared to challenge the reform slate. Organized labor, and especially the mineworkers, took the lead; one of their number, Wesley Ash, a deputy sheriff and union member, made "an astonishing run" in the primary, coming in second among a field of more than twenty candidates.[21] In fact, the strength of anticommission candidates in the primary so alarmed reformers that they frantically sought to appease labor.

The day before the final election they modified their platform to pledge both an eight-hour day and an "American standard of wages." They attempted to persuade the voters that their slate consisted of men who represented labor because they had "begun at the bottom of the ladder and made a good climb toward success by their own unaided efforts."[22] But their tactics failed. In the election on March 30, 1908, voters swept into office the entire "opposition" slate. The business and professional community had succeeded in changing the form of government, but not in securing its control. A cartoon in the leading reform newspaper illustrated their disappointment; John Q. Public sat dejectedly and muttered, "Aw, What's the Use?"

The most visible opposition to reform and the most readily available target of reform attack was the so-called "machine," for through the "machine" many different ward communities as well as lower- and middle-income groups joined effectively to influence the central city government. Their private occupational and social life did not naturally involve these groups in larger city-wide activities in the same way as the upper class was involved; hence they lacked access to privately organized economic and social power on which they could construct political power. The "machine" filled this organizational gap.

Yet it should never be forgotten that the social and economic institutions in the wards themselves provided the "machine's" sustaining support and gave it larger significance. When reformers attacked the "machine" as the most visible institutional element of the ward system, they attacked the entire ward form of political organization and the political power of lower and middle-income groups which lay behind it.

Reformers often gave the impression that they opposed merely the corrupt politician and his "machine." But in a more fundamental way they looked upon the deficiencies of pre-reform political leaders in terms not of their personal shortcomings, but of the limitations inherent in their occupational, institutional, and class positions. In 1911 the Voters' League of Pittsburgh wrote in its pamphlet analyzing the qualifications of candidates that "a man's occupation ought to give a strong indication of his qualifications for membership on a school board."[23] Certain occupations inherently disqualified a man from serving:

> Employment as ordinary laborer and in the lowest class of mill work would naturally lead to the conclusion that such men did not have sufficient education or business training to act as school directors. . . . Objection might also be made to small shopkeepers, clerks, workmen at many trades, who by lack of educational advantages and business training, could not, no matter how honest, be expected to administer properly the affairs of an educational system, requiring special knowledge, and where millions are spent each year.

These, of course, were precisely the groups which did dominate Pittsburgh government prior to reform. The League deplored the fact that school boards contained only a small number of "men prominent throughout the city in business life . . . in professional occupations . . . holding positions as managers, secretaries, auditors, superintendents and foremen" and exhorted these classes to participate more actively as candidates for office.

Reformers, therefore, wished not simply to replace bad men with good; they proposed to change the occupational and class origins of decision-makers. Toward this end they sought innovations in the formal machinery of government which would concentrate political power by sharply centralizing the processes of decisionmaking rather than distribute it through more popular participation in public affairs. According to the liberal view of the Progressive Era, the major political innovations of reform involved the equalization of political power through the primary, the direct election of public officials, and the initiative, referendum, and recall. These measures played a large role in the political ideology of the time and were frequently incorporated into new municipal charters. But they provided at best only an occasional and often incidental process of decision-making. Far more important in continuous, sustained, day-to-day processes of government were those innovations which centralized decision-making in the hands of fewer and fewer people.

The systematization of municipal government took place on both the executive and the legislative levels. The strong-mayor and city-manager types became the most widely used examples of the former. In the first decade of the 20th century, the commission plan had considerable appeal, but its distribution of administrative responsibility among five people gave rise to a demand for a form with more centralized executive power; consequently, the city-manager or the commission-manager variant often replaced it.[24]

A far more pervasive and significant change, however, lay in the centralization of the system of representation, the shift from ward to city-wide election of councils and school boards. Governing bodies so selected, reformers argued, would give less attention to local and particularistic matters and more to affairs of city-wide scope. This shift, an invariable feature of both commission and city-manager plans, was often adopted by itself. In Pittsburgh, for example, the new charter of 1911 provided as the major innovation that a council of twenty-seven, each member elected from a separate ward, be replaced by a council of nine, each elected by the city as a whole.

Cities displayed wide variations in this innovation. Some regrouped wards into larger units but kept the principle of areas of representation smaller than the entire city. Some combined a majority of councilmen elected by wards with additional ones elected at large. All such innovations, however, constituted steps toward the centralization of the system of representation.

Liberal historians have not appreciated the extent to which municipal reform in the Progressive Era involved a debate over the system of representation. The ward form of representation was universally condemned on the grounds that it gave too much influence to the separate units and not enough attention to the larger problems of the city. Harry A. Toulmin, whose book, *The City Manager*, was published by the National Municipal League, stated the case:

> The spirit of sectionalism had dominated the political life of every city. Ward pitted against ward, alderman against alderman, and legislation only effected by "log-rolling" extravagant measures into operation, mulcting the city, but gratifying the greed of constituents has too long stung the conscience of decent citizenship. This constant treatymaking of factionalism has been no less than a curse. The city manager plan proposes the commendable thing of abolishing wards. The plan is not unique in this for it has been common to many forms of commission government.[25] . . .

Such a system should be supplanted, the argument usually went, with city-wide representation in which elected officials could consider the city "as a unit." "The new officers are elected," wrote Toulmin, "each to represent all the people. Their duties are so defined that they must administer the corporate business in its entirety, not as a hodge-podge of associated localities."

Behind the debate over the method of representation, however, lay a debate over who should be represented, over whose views of public policy should prevail. Many reform leaders often explicitly, if not implicitly, expressed fear that lower- and middle-income groups had too much influence in decision-making. One Galveston leader, for example,

complained about the movement for initiative, referendum, and recall:

> We have in our city a very large number of negroes employed on the docks; we also have a very large number of unskilled white laborers; this city also has more barrooms, according to its population, than any other city in Texas. Under these circumstances it would be extremely difficult to maintain a satisfactory city government where all ordinances must be submitted back to the voters of the city for their ratification and approval.[26]

At the National Municipal League convention of 1907, Rear Admiral F. E. Chadwick (USN Ret.), a leader in the Newport, Rhode Island, movement for municipal reform, spoke to this question even more directly:

> Our present system has excluded in large degree the representation of those who have the city's well-being most at heart. It has brought, in municipalities . . . a government established by the least educated, the least interested class of citizens.
>
> It stands to reason that a man paying $5,000 taxes in a town is more interested in the well-being and development of his town than the man who pays no taxes. . . . It equally stands to reason that the man of the $5,000 tax should be assured a representation in the committee which lays the tax and spends the money which he contributes. . . . Shall we be truly democratic and give the property owner a fair show or shall we develop a tyranny of ignorance which shall crush him.[27]

Municipal reformers thus debated frequently the question of who should be represented as well as the question of what method of representation should be employed.

That these two questions were intimately connected was revealed in other reform proposals for representation, proposals which were rarely taken seriously. One suggestion was that a class system of representation be substituted for ward representation. For example, in 1908 one of the prominent candidates for commissioner in Des Moines proposed that the city council be composed of representatives of five classes: educational and ministerial organizations, manufacturers and jobbers, public utility corporations, retail merchants including liquor men, and the Des Moines Trades and Labor Assembly. Such a system would have greatly reduced the influence in the council of both middle- and lower-class groups. The proposal revealed the basic problem confronting business and professional leaders: how to reduce the influence in government of the majority of voters among middle- and lower income groups.[28]

A growing imbalance between population and representation sharpened the desire of reformers to change from ward to city-wide elections. Despite shifts in population within most cities, neither ward district lines nor the apportionment of city council and school board seats changed frequently. Consequently, older areas of the city, with wards that were small in geographical size and held declining populations (usually lower and middle class in composition), continued to be overrepresented, and newer upper-class areas, where population was growing, became increasingly underrepresented. This intensified the reformers' conviction that the structure of government must be changed to give them the voice they needed to make their views on public policy prevail.[29]

It is not insignificant that in some cities (by no means a majority) municipal reform came about outside of the urban electoral process. The original commission government in Galveston was appointed rather than elected. "The failure of previous attempts to secure an efficient city government through the local electorate made the business men of Galveston willing to put the conduct of the city's affairs in the hands of a commission dominated by state-appointed officials."[30] Only in 1903 did the courts force Galveston to elect the members of the commission, an innovation which one writer described as "an abandonment of the commission idea," and which led to the decline of the influence of the business community in the commission government.[31]

In 1911 Pittsburgh voters were not permitted to approve either the new city charter or the new school board plan, both of which provided for city-wide representation; they were a result of state legislative enactment. The governor appointed the first members of the new city council, but thereafter they were elected. The judges of the court of common pleas, however, and not the voters, selected members of the new school board.

The composition of the new city council and new school board in Pittsburgh, both of which were inaugurated in 1911, revealed the degree to which the shift from ward to city-wide representation produced a change in group representation.[32] Members of the upper class, the advanced professional men, and the large business groups dominated both. Of the fifteen members of the Pittsburgh Board of Education appointed in 1911 and the nine members of the new city council, none were small businessmen or white-collar workers. Each body contained only one person who could remotely be classified as a blue-collar worker; each of these men filled a position specifically but unofficially designed as reserved for a "representative of labor," and each was an official of the Amalgamated Association of Iron, Steel, and Tin Workers. Six of the nine members of the new city council were prominent businessmen, and all six were listed in upper-class directories. Two others were doctors closely associated with the upper class in both professional and social life. The fifteen members of the Board of Education included ten businessmen with citywide interests, one doctor associated with the upper class, and three women previously active in upper-class public welfare.

Lower- and middle-class elements felt that the new city governments did not represent them.[33] The studies carried out under the direction of Leonard White contain numerous expressions of the way in which the change in the structure of government produced not only a change in the geographical scope of representation, but also in the groups represented. "It is not the policies of the manager or the council they oppose," one researcher declared, "as much as the lack of representation for their economic level and social groups."[34] And another wrote:

> There had been nothing unapproachable about the old ward aldermen. Every voter had a

neighbor on the common council who was interested in serving him. The new councilmen, however, made an unfavorable impression on the less well-to-do voters. . . . Election at large made a change that, however desirable in other ways, left the voters in the poorer wards with a feeling that they had been deprived of their share of political importance.[35]

The success of the drive for centralization of administration and representation varied with the size of the city. In the smaller cities, business, professional, and elite groups could easily exercise a dominant influence. Their close ties readily enabled them to shape informal political power which they could transform into formal political power. After the mid-1890's the widespread organization of chambers of commerce provided a base for political action to reform municipal government, resulting in a host of small-city commission and city-manager innovations. In the larger, more heterogeneous cities, whose subcommunities were more dispersed, such community-wide action was extremely difficult. Few commission or city-manager proposals materialized here. Mayors became stronger, and steps were taken toward centralization of representation, but the ward system or some modified version usually persisted. Reformers in large cities often had to rest content with their Municipal Research Bureaus through which they could exert political influence from outside the municipal government.

A central element in the analysis of municipal reform in the Progressive Era is governmental corruption. Should it be understood in moral or political terms? Was it a product of evil men or of particular socio-political circumstances? Reform historians have adopted the former view. Selfish and evil men arose to take advantage of a political arrangement whereby unsystematic government offered many opportunities for personal gain at public expense. The system thrived until the "better elements," "men of intelligence and civic responsibility," or "right-thinking people" ousted the culprits and fashioned a political force which produced decisions in the "public interest." In this scheme of things, corruption in public affairs grew out of individual personal failings and a deficient governmental structure which could not hold

those predispositions in check, rather than from the peculiar nature of social forces. The contestants involved were morally defined: evil men who must be driven from power, and good men who must be activated politically to secure control of municipal affairs.

Public corruption, however, involves political even more than moral considerations. It arises more out of the particular distribution of political power than of personal morality. For corruption is a device to exercise control and influence outside the legal channels of decisionmaking when those channels are not readily responsive. Most generally, corruption stems from an inconsistency between control of the instruments of formal governmental power and the exercise of informal influence in the community. If powerful groups are denied access to formal power in legitimate ways, they seek access through procedures which the community considers illegitimate. Corrupt government, therefore, does not reflect the genius of evil men, but rather the lack of acceptable means for those who exercise power in the private community to wield the same influence in governmental affairs. It can be understood in the Progressive Era not simply by the preponderance of evil men over good, but by the peculiar nature of the distribution of political power.

The political corruption of the "Era of Reform" arose from the inaccessibility of municipal government to those who were rising in power and influence. Municipal government in the United States developed in the 19th century within a context of universal manhood suffrage which decentralized political control. Because all men, whatever their economic, social, or cultural conditions, could vote, leaders who reflected a wide variety of community interests and who represented the views of people of every circumstance arose to guide and direct municipal affairs. Since the majority of urban voters were workingmen or immigrants, the views of those groups carried great and often decisive weight in governmental affairs. Thus, as Herbert Gutman has shown, during strikes in the 1870's city officials were usually friendly to workingmen and refused to use police power to protect strikebreakers.[36]

Ward representation on city councils was an integral part of grass-roots influence, for it enabled diverse urban communities, invariably identified with particular geographical areas of the city, to express their views more clearly through councilmen peculiarly receptive to their concerns. There was a direct, reciprocal flow of power between wards and the center of city affairs in which voters felt a relatively close connection with public matters and city leaders gave special attention to their needs.

Within this political system the community's business leaders grew in influence and power as industrialism advanced, only to find that their economic position did not readily admit them to the formal machinery of government. Thus, during strikes, they had to rely on either their own private police, Pinkertons, or the state militia to enforce their use of strikebreakers. They frequently found that city officials did not accept their views of what was best for the city and what direction municipal policies should take. They had developed a common outlook, closely related to their economic activities, that the city's economic expansion should become the prime concern of municipal government, and yet they found that this view had to compete with even more influential views of public policy. They found that political tendencies which arose from universal manhood suffrage and ward representation were not always friendly to their political conceptions and goals and had produced a political system over which they had little control, despite the fact that their economic ventures were the core of the city's prosperity and the hope for future urban growth.

Under such circumstances, businessmen sought other methods of influencing municipal affairs. They did not restrict themselves to the channels of popular election and representation, but frequently applied direct influence-if not verbal persuasion, then bribery and corruption. Thereby arose the graft which Lincoln Steffens recounted in his *Shame of the Cities*. Utilities were only the largest of those business groups and individuals who requested special favors, and the franchises they sought were only the most sensational of the prizes which included such items as favorable tax assessments and rates, the vacating of streets wanted for factory expansion, or permission to operate amid antiliquor and other laws regulating personal behavior. The relationships between business and formal government became a maze of accommodations, a set of political arrangements which grew up because effective power had few legitimate means of accomplishing its ends.

Steffens and subsequent liberal historians, however, misread the significance of these arrangements, emphasizing their personal rather than their more fundamental institutional elements. To them corruption involved personal arrangements between powerful business leaders and powerful "machine" politicians. Just as they did not fully appreciate the significance of the search for political influence by the rising business community as a whole, so they did not see fully the role of the "ward politician." They stressed the argument that the political leader manipulated voters to his own personal ends, that he used constituents rather than reflected their views.

A different approach is now taking root, namely, that the urban political organization was an integral part of community life, expressing its needs and its goals. As Oscar Handlin has said, for example, the "machine" not only fulfilled specific wants, but provided one of the few avenues to success and public recognition available to the immigrant.[37] The political leader's arrangements with businessmen, therefore, were not simply personal agreements between conniving individuals; they were far-reaching accommodations between powerful sets of institutions in industrial America.

These accommodations, however, proved to be burdensome and unsatisfactory to the business community and to the upper third of socioeconomic groups in general. They were expensive; they were wasteful; they were uncertain. Toward the end of the 19th century, therefore, business and professional men sought more direct control over municipal government in order to exercise political influence more effectively. They realized their goals in the early 20th century in the new commission and city-manager forms of government and in the shift from ward to citywide representation.

These innovations did not always accomplish the objectives that the business community desired because other forces could and often did adjust to the change in governmental structure and reestablish their influence. But businessmen hoped that reform would enable them to increase their political power, and most frequently it did. In most cases the innovations which were introduced between 1901, when Galveston adopted a commission form of government, and the Great Depression, and especially the city-manager form which reached a height of popularity in the mid-1920's, served as vehicles whereby business and professional leaders moved directly into the inner circles of government, brought into one political system their own power and the formal machinery of government, and dominated municipal affairs for two decades.

Municipal reform in the early 20th century involves a paradox: the ideology of an extension of political control and the practice of its concentration. While reformers maintained that their movement rested on a wave of popular demands, called their gatherings of business and professional leaders "mass meetings," described their reforms as "part of a world-wide trend toward popular government," and proclaimed an ideology of a popular upheaval against a selfish few, they were in practice shaping the structure of municipal government so that political power would no longer be broadly distributed, but would in fact be more centralized in the hands of a relatively small segment of the population. The paradox became even sharper when new city charters included provisions for the initiative, referendum, and recall. How does the historian cope with this paradox? Does it represent deliberate deception or simply political strategy? Or does it reflect a phenomenon which should be understood rather than explained away?

The expansion of popular involvement in decision-making was frequently a political tactic, not a political system to be established permanently, but a device to secure immediate political victory. The prohibitionist advocacy of the referendum, one of the most extensive sources of support for such a measure, came from the belief that the referendum would provide the opportunity to outlaw liquor more rapidly. The AntiSaloon League, therefore, urged local option. But the League was not consistent. Towns which were wet, when faced with a county-wide localoption decision to outlaw liquor, demanded town or township local option to reinstate it. The League objected to this as not the proper application of the referendum idea.

Again, "Progressive" reformers often espoused the direct primary when fighting for nominations for their candidates within the party, but once in control they often became cool to it because it might result in their own defeat. By the same token, many municipal reformers attached the initiative, referendum, and recall to municipal charters often as a device to appease voters who opposed the centralization of representation and executive authority. But, by requiring a high percentage of voters to sign petitions—often 25 to 30 per cent—these innovations could be and were rendered relatively harmless.

More fundamentally, however, the distinction between ideology and practice in municipal reform arose from the different roles which each played. The ideology of democratization of decision-making was negative rather than positive; it served as an instrument of attack against the existing political system rather than as a guide to alternative action. Those who wished to destroy the "machine" and to eliminate party competition in local government widely utilized the theory that these political instruments thwarted public impulses, and thereby shaped the tone of their attack.

But there is little evidence that the ideology represented a faith in a purely democratic system of decision-making or that reformers actually wished, in practice, to substitute direct democracy as a continuing system of sustained decisionmaking in place of the old. It was used to destroy the political institutions of the lower and middle classes and the political power which those institutions gave rise to, rather than to provide a clear-cut guide for alternative action.[38]

The guide to alternative action lay in the model of the business enterprise. In describing new conditions which they wished to create, reformers drew on the analogy of the "efficient business enterprise," criticizing current practices with the argument that "no business could conduct its affairs that way and remain in business," and calling upon business practices as the guides to improvement. As one student remarked:

> The folklore of the business elite came by gradual transition to be the symbols of governmental reformers. Efficiency, system. orderliness, budgets, economy, saving, were all injected into the efforts of reformers who sought to remodel municipal government in terms of the great impersonality of corporate enterprise.[39]

Clinton Rodgers Woodruff of the National Municipal League explained that the commission form was "a simple, direct, businesslike way of administering the business affairs of the city . . . an application to city administration of that type of business organization which has been so common and so successful in the field of commerce and industry."[40] The centralization of decisionmaking which developed in the business corporation was now applied in municipal reform.

The model of the efficient business enterprise, then, rather than the New England town meeting, provided the positive inspiration for the municipal reformer. In giving concrete shape to this model in the strong-mayor, commission, and city-manager plans, reformers engaged in the elaboration of the processes of rationalization and systematization inherent in modern science and technology. For in many areas of society, industrialization brought a gradual shift upward in the location of decision-making and the geographical extension of the scope of the area affected by decisions.

Experts in business, in government, and in the professions measured, studied, analyzed, and manipulated ever wider realms of human life, and devices which they used to control such affairs constituted the most fundamental and far-reaching innovations in decision-making in modern America, whether in formal government or in the informal exercise of power in private life. Reformers in the Progressive Era played a major role in shaping this new system. While they expressed an ideology of restoring a previous order, they in fact helped to bring forth a system drastically new.[41]

The drama of reform lay in the competition for supremacy between two systems of decisionmaking. One system, based upon ward representation and growing out of the practices and ideas of representative government, involved wide latitude for the expression of grass-roots impulses and their involvement in the political process. The other grew out of the rationalization of life which came with science and technology, in which decisions arose from expert analysis and flowed from fewer and smaller centers outward to the rest of society. Those who espoused the former looked with fear upon the loss of influence which the latter involved, and those who espoused the latter looked only with disdain upon the wastefulness and inefficiency of the former.

The Progressive Era witnessed rapid strides toward a more centralized system and a relative decline for a more decentralized system. This development constituted an accommodation of forces outside the business community to the political trends within business and professional life rather than vice versa. It involved a tendency for the decision-making processes inherent in science and technology to prevail over those inherent in representative government. . . .

Notes

1. See, for example, Clifford W. Patton, *Battle for Municipal Reform* (Washington, D.C., 1940), and Frank Mann Stewart, *A Half-Century of Municipal Reform* (Berkeley, 1950).

8. Leonard White, *The City Manager* (Chicago, 1927), ix–x.

9. Harold A. Stone *et al.*, *City Manager Government in Nine Cities* (Chicago, 1940); Frederick C. Mosher *et al.*, *City Manager Government in Seven Cities* (Chicago, 1940); Harold A. Stone *et al.*, *City Manager Government in the United States* (Chicago, 1940). Cities covered by these studies include: Austin, Texas; Charlotte, North Carolina; Dallas, Texas; Dayton, Ohio; Fredericksburg, Virginia; Jackson, Michigan; Janesville, Wisconsin; Kingsport, Tennessee; Lynchburg, Virginia; Rochester, New York; San Diego, California.

10. Jewell Cass Phillips, Operation of the Council-Manager Plan of Government in Oklahoma Cities (Philadelphia, 1935), 31–39.

11. James Weinstein, "Organized Business and the City Commission and Manager Movements," *Journal of Southern History,* XXVIII (1962), 166–82.

12. Norman N. Gill, Municipal Research Bureaus (Washington, 1944).

13. This account of the movement for commission government in Des Moines is derived from items in the De Moines *Register* during the years from 1905 through 1908.

14. Biographical data constitutes the main source of evidence for this study of Pittsburgh reform leaders. It was found in city directories, social registers, directories of corporate directors, biographical compilations, reports of boards of education, settlement houses, welfare organizations, and similar types of material. Especially valuable was the clipping file maintained at the Carnegie Library of Pittsburgh.

15. *Town Crier* (Seattle), Feb. 18, 1911, p. 13.

16. Information derived from same sources as cited in footnote 14.

17. Stone *et al.*, *Nine Cities*, 212.

18. *Ibid.*, 3–13.

19. *Ibid.*, 329.

20. Stone *et al.*, *City Manager Government*, 26, 237–41, for analysis of opposition to city-manager government.

21. Des Moines *Register and Leader,* March 17, 1908.

22. *Ibid.*, March 30, March 28, 1908.

23. Voters' Civic League of Allegheny County, "Bulletin of the Voters' Civic League of Allegheny County Concerning the Public School System of Pittsburgh," Feb. 14, 1911, pp 2–3.

24. In the decade 1911 to 1920, 43 per cent of the municipal charters adopted in eleven home rule states involved the commission form and 35 per cent the city-manager form; in the following decade the figures stood at 6 per cent and 71 per cent respectively. The adoption of citymanager charters reached a peak in the years 1918 through 1923 and declined sharply after 1933. See Leonard D. White, "The Future of Public Administration." *Public Management*, XV (1933), 12.

25. Toulmin, *The City Manager*, 42.

26. Woodruff, *City Government*, 315. The Galveston commission plan did not contain provisions for the initiative, referendum, or recall, and Galveston commercial groups which had fathered the commission plan opposed movements to include them. In 1911 Governor Colquitt of Texas vewed [*sic*] a charter bill for Texarkana because it contained such provisions; he maintained that they were "undemocratic" and unnecessary to the success of commission government. *Ibid.*, 314–15.

27. *Ibid.*, 207–208.

28. Des Moines *Register and Leader,* Jan. 15, 1908.

29. Voters' Civic League of Allegheny County, "Report on the Voters' League in the Redistricting of the Wards of the City of Pittsburgh" (Pittsburgh, n.d.).

30. Horace E. Deming, "The Government of American Cities," in Woodruff, *City Government*, 167.

31. *Ibid.*, 168.

32. Information derived from same sources as cited in footnote 14.

33. W. R. Hopkins, city manager of Cleveland, indicated the degree to which the new type of government was more responsive to the business community: "It is undoubtedly easier for a city manager to insist upon acting in accordance with the business interests of the city than it is for a mayor to do the same thing." Quoted in White, *The City Manager*, 13.

34. Stone *et al.*, *Nine Cities*, 20.

35. *Ibid.*, 225.

36. Herbert Gutman, "An Iron Workers' Strike in the Ohio Valley, 1873–74," *Ohio Historical Quarterly*, LXVIII (1959), 353–70; "Trouble on the Railroads, 1873–1874: Prelude to the 1877 Crisis," *Labor History*, II (Spring 1961): 215·36.

37. Oscar Handlin, *The Uprooted* (Boston, 1951), 209–17.

38. Clinton Rodgers Woodruff of the National Municipal League even argued that the initiative, referendum, and recall were rarely used. "Their value lies in their existence rather than in their use." Woodruff, *City Government*, 314. It seems apparent that the most widely used of these devices, the referendum, was popularized by legislative bodies when they could not agree or did not want to take responsibility for a decision and sought to pass that responsibility to the general public, rather than because of a faith in the wisdom of popular will.

39. J. B. Shannon, "County Consolidation," *Annals of the American Academy of Political and Social Science*, Vol. 207 (January, 1940), 168.

40. Woodruff, *City Government*, 29–30.

41. Several recent studies emphasize various aspects of this movement. See, for example, Loren Baritz, *Servants of Power* (Middletown, 1960); Raymond E. Callahan, *Education and the Cult of Efficiency* (Chicago, 1962); Samuel P. Hays, *Conservation and the Gospel of Efficiency* (Cambridge, 1959); Dwight Waldo, *The Administrative State* (New York, 1948), 3–61.

Conclusion

Public Policy Applications: Investment in Civic Space

Policy Then

The skilled professionals who ran municipal governments during the reform era at the start of the twentieth century employed the powers and resources of the public sector to develop the physical infrastructure of rapidly expanding cities. Along with constructing the streets, sidewalks, bridges, sewers, and utilities necessary for modern urban life, they devoted considerable energy and money to erecting massive public buildings and uplifting civic spaces. The efforts of reformers within the planning profession to improve the appearance and operation of industrial cities, while simultaneously nurturing a sense of pride and moral virtue among the citizenry, came to be known as the City Beautiful Movement. That movement left a lasting legacy in the form of monumental city halls, museums, libraries, cultural venues, fountains, and sculptures along grand boulevards typically located in or around the central business districts of numerous American cities.

In some locales, urban planners channeled public resources toward the development of civic structures and spaces in outlying neighborhoods away from the downtown core. Robert Moses, the longtime planning czar in New York City, was responsible for creating dozens of parks, playgrounds, and swimming pools in Upper Manhattan, Brooklyn, Queens, and the Bronx—projects that benefited countless city residents who had previously lacked adequate recreational facilities. Thanks to Moses's public works initiatives like the immense

Photo of the Astoria Park Pool (Geographic File, PR 020) courtesy of Collection of the New York Historical Society, http://www.nyhistory.org/category/blog/outdoor-pools

Municipal swimming pool in the Astoria neighborhood, Queens, New York

municipal pool in Astoria, Queens, that was completed in 1936, New Yorkers no longer had to resort to diving into the polluted East River to cool off on a hot summer day.

Policy Now

It is rare to see major public investments in civic spaces in U.S. cities today. Ambitious undertakings like those associated with the City Beautiful Movement are now often considered to be technically complicated, prohibitively expensive, and politically controversial. And yet, modern-day manifestations of the impulse to develop large-scale, civic projects surface from time to time. One notable example is Millennium Park in downtown Chicago near Lake Michigan. Built on obsolete, industrial land, which was long controlled by the Illinois Central Railroad, by some of the world's leading architects, planners, and landscape designers, the 24.5 acre park was opened in 2004 at a cost of $475 million. It boasts a state-of-the-art musical pavilion, stunning sculptures and fountains, and beautiful gardens and has been broadly popular with residents, workers, and tourists seeking a welcome respite from the fast pace of city life. Given Millennium Park's success as both a catalyst for further economic development and as a much-desired cultural and recreational amenity, should other cities contemplate similar endeavors? Are such projects only feasible if pursued by relatively prosperous cities with robust public spheres and led by well-trained professionals? Who benefits from civic projects like Millennium Park? Are there alternative approaches to developing civic and recreational spaces that might benefit a wider spectrum of a city's population? Should smaller recreational and cultural amenities be established in multiple neighborhoods as opposed to one huge, downtown-based project? What is the rationale for siting such projects in or near a central business district?

Sergei Melki/Wikimedia Commons

Crown Fountain, Millennium Park, Chicago

Additional Resources

Hilary Ballon and Kenneth T. Jackson, eds., *Robert Moses and the Modern City: The Transformation of New York* (New York: W. W. Norton, 2007).

Chicago Architecture Foundation. An outstanding source regarding urban architecture and planning in a city that is justifiably proud of its architectural heritage: www.architecture.org.

Chicago Public Library's digital photography collection of Millennium Park: www.chipublib.org/archival_post/millennium-park-inc-archives/.

Timothy J. Gilfoyle, *Millennium Park: Creating a Chicago Landmark* (Chicago: University of Chicago Press, 2006).

"The House That Jane Built." Documentary film on Hull House, a settlement house founded in Chicago by the reformer Jane Addams (New York: Cinema Guild, 2007).

Jon A. Peterson, *The Birth of City Planning in the United States, 1840–1917* (Baltimore: Johns Hopkins University Press, 2003).

The Plan for Chicago: A Regional Legacy (2008). One hundred years after the publication of Daniel Burnham's historic and influential plan to shape the future of Chicago, this study offers an assessment of the plan's legacy: http://burnhamplan100 .lib.uchicago.edu/files/content/documents/Plan_of_Chicago_booklet.pdf.

Planetizen. A public-interest information exchange covering a wide range of issues for the urban planning, design, and development community: www.planetizen.com.

William H. Wilson, *The City Beautiful Movement in Kansas City* (Columbia: University of Missouri Press, 1964).

The World That Moses Built. Documentary film from the series *The American Experience*. PBS Video, 1988.

Discussion Questions

1. How much of a premium should be placed on expertise in city government today? What level of expertise is desirable or necessary? In more concrete terms, should city governments only hire job candidates for important policy positions who have advanced degrees from top schools in specialized professions like public administration, planning, engineering, and criminal justice?

2. Are such experts better able to identify and carry out the public interest?

3. Should governmental authority be employed aggressively to address chronic urban problems? Or does an activist government cause more harm than good?

4. If public health experts conclude that secondhand smoke is harmful, would a city government be justified in banning smoking in restaurants, bars, and other indoor public places?

5. If public health experts conclude that large (16 ounces or more) bottled sodas and fountain drinks contribute to obesity, diabetes, and heart disease, would a city government be justified in banning their sale in public schools? What about restaurants?

6. Some urban policymakers eager to promote environmental sustainability have advocated implementing a system of congestion pricing to cut down on vehicular use on city streets and to encourage mass transit ridership. Under such a system, automobiles and trucks entering congested parts of a city at peak times would be charged a congestion fee. The revenue generated from the congestion fees would then be set aside to pay for mass transit improvements. Would this be a positive change in public policy? Is a reform vision of politics more or less likely to engender such policies? Why?

Chapter 5

Suburbanization and the Hollowing of the City

Introduction

If the nineteenth century was the age of mass urbanization, then the twentieth century was the era of mass sub-urbanization. Millions of people, and innumerable businesses, left the cities for the greener pastures of suburbia. The United States went from being primarily an urban nation to a suburban nation, and the implications for cities were far-reaching.

The roots of twentieth-century suburbanization can be traced back to the previous century. Remember that the preindustrial city was spatially compact—city dwellers often lived within walking distance of their jobs. But that began to change about halfway through the 1800s when innovations in transportation enabled citizens with means to flee the congested central cities and move to the periphery. With the rise of industrialization, the center of cities had not only become crowded, but noisy and polluted. Those who could afford the cost of commuting by omnibus or horse-drawn trolley, and later electric trolley or streetcar, jumped at the opportunity to relocate on the outskirts of the city in larger homes on tree-lined streets. So-called streetcar suburbs proliferated in many cities by the late nineteenth century.[1]

This early phase of suburbanization was largely confined to the upper classes and was thus not a broad-based phenomenon. That began to change, however, during the 1920s when, for the first time, the number of people moving to the suburbs exceeded the number of people moving to cities. The middle class was growing in size and affluence, and many chose to invest their new income in suburban real estate. Again, advances in transportation technology facilitated this first substantial flight from cities. The automobile had existed since the turn of the century, but for a while it was just a plaything for the rich. Henry Ford's implementation of the assembly line changed everything by making mass production possible, which significantly lowered the cost of automobiles, making them affordable to the fast-expanding middle class. With their new cars, millions of Americans now had the ability to move to suburbia and commute to their city jobs.[2]

The Great Depression and then World War II all but halted the shift in metropolitan living arrangements, but with the end of the war the United States experienced a veritable explosion in suburban growth. Between 1950 and 1960, the population of American suburbs doubled; suburbs grew nearly five times as fast as cities. By 1970, more than half of all residents of metropolitan areas lived beyond city boundaries.[3]

Why the massive exodus from cities? The most pressing cause was a severe shortage of decent, affordable housing in cities, where residential construction had stalled during the Depression and war years. Meanwhile, the demand for housing soared after 1945 when millions of soldiers and other participants in the war effort returned to the home front to resume their life plans. A marriage boom followed by a baby boom generated a tremendous need for new and bigger homes, a need that suburban developers were happy to fulfill. Young families were inexorably drawn to suburban municipalities. The quality of life seemed better in the suburbs. Homes were more spacious and offered valued amenities, including front and back yards and garages for the family car. Neighborhoods were quiet and peaceful. There was little crime. Public schools, funded mostly through local property taxes, boasted superior resources and facilities in comparison to city schools. Moving to suburbia was seen as a step up the socioeconomic ladder in a status-conscious society, a perception reinforced by popular culture's romanticizing the suburban lifestyle through hit TV shows like *Father Knows Best* and *Leave It to Beaver*. At a time when the United States was experiencing unprecedented prosperity as the dominant economic power in the world, millions tapped their rising incomes to join the tide of humanity fleeing the city and pursue the American dream of buying a home in the suburbs. Kenneth T. Jackson examines further in **Reading 5-1** some of the root causes of mass suburbanization while considering its consequences for social interaction and community in metropolitan areas.[4]

The urban exodus was not confined to residents. Businesses also had reasons to relocate to suburban places. Factory owners seeking to expand their plants found cramped, inner-city neighborhoods increasingly problematic. The process of urban deindustrialization, which will be examined in the next chapter, commenced in the early twentieth century and gained momentum with each passing decade. Many other types of business enterprises also migrated beyond the central city to serve an ever-mounting base of suburban residents. The commercial corridors of towns and villages swelled with the proliferation of drug stores, barbershops, hardware stores, and supermarkets. Professionals—doctors, dentists, lawyers, and accountants—started practices in suburban areas brimming with new clients. Entertainment businesses such as restaurants, pubs, and movie theaters were quick to see the potential for profit. Major department stores such as Sears, Roebuck & Co. built branches in the suburbs. In 1922, the first shopping mall opened outside of Kansas City.[5]

The consequences of the decentralization of residents and jobs were devastating for cities. Two problems stood out. First, suburbanization greatly exacerbated racial and class segregation in metropolitan areas. Although recent scholars have demonstrated that suburbanization was not the virtually exclusive white, middle-class phenomenon suggested in many classic studies[6]—working-class towns, villages, and small cities could be found throughout any metropolitan area and a significant number were populated by blacks, Latinos, and Asian Americans[7]—American suburbs were anything but paragons of racial and class diversity. In general, whites lived with other whites and class stratification was pronounced. Furthermore, while some lower-income families and people of color found their way to suburbs, the vast majority remained behind in central cities that grew steadily poorer and nonwhite.[8]

Second, the hemorrhaging of middle-class taxpayers and businesses eroded the tax base of cities, making it increasingly difficult to finance basic public services. Budgets for police and fire protection, sanitation, recreation, and schools had to be cut, yielding a steady decline in the quality of urban life, which prompted yet a new wave of suburban flight and a deeper decline in the fiscal condition of city government.[9]

Given these serious problems, it is fair to ask whether the outflow of residents and jobs was an inevitable result of societal changes and evolving popular tastes. Most scholars also point to public policies at all levels of government to explain the form of suburbanization and deindustrialization. For instance, federal home mortgage programs that made it much simpler and far less expensive for people to purchase homes starting in the 1930s were administered in ways that blatantly discriminated against people of color. As a result, white, middle-class citizens took advantage of newly affordable mortgages to buy suburban homes, while black, Latino, and Asian residents were denied such opportunities.[10] **Reading 5-2** by Peter Dreier, John H. Mollenkopf, and Todd Swanstrom scrutinizes the role of the federal government in promoting, directly and indirectly, the decentralization of the metropolis—and in ways that exacerbated racial and class segregation.

At the local level, Michael N. Danielson explains in **Reading 5-3** how politically autonomous suburban governments used their land use powers to preserve the racial and class homogeneity of their communities. Zoning codes were the most potent tools of exclusion. Regulations that required sizable single-family homes on relatively large parcels of land while limiting or barring altogether standardized, mass-produced homes, apartment buildings, and mobile homes effectively excluded working-class and poor households.[11] Municipal officials also collaborated with school boards and superintendents to use planning tools to establish and reinforce racially segregated neighborhoods and schools.[12] Where exclusionary zoning did not inhibit people of color from moving into a suburban township or village, realtors commonly steered potential homebuyers who did not conform to the prevailing white, middle-class composition of a community to neighborhoods where they would "feel more comfortable."[13] For the few nonwhite families with the means and fortitude to move into predominantly white, suburban municipalities, life was not easy. All too often, their new neighbors remained at a distance or sometimes engaged in frightening acts of aggression to register their disapproval.[14]

Suburbanization by the white middle class was just one societal trend accounting for the changing racial profile of American cities. At the same time, millions of African Americans were migrating from the rural south to cities all over the country. Historians refer to the "Great Black Migration" that unfolded during the early and middle decades of the twentieth century. That migration was triggered by the desperate poverty that gripped the south after technological advances greatly increased the mechanized production of agricultural goods, thus depriving large numbers of farm workers their jobs. The collapse of the economy coincided with a sharp spike in racial tensions rendering living conditions for blacks in the rural south dismal. Meanwhile, job opportunities in cities were mushrooming because of a jump in wartime production during World War I and by the demand for labor following passage of legislation by Congress at three points during the 1920s that imposed draconian restrictions on immigration. Many rural blacks in the south responded by packing up all of their belongings and moving their families to cities elsewhere in the region, but especially to industrial cities in the midwest and northeast.[15] Black migrants still encountered racism in seeking factory jobs—they were typically relegated to lower-skilled and lower-paying jobs—but this still represented a significant improvement over what they had left behind.[16]

But over time, the material condition of black migrants in U.S. cities deteriorated. Widespread residential segregation forced blacks into a small number of increasingly congested neighborhoods whose borders were clearly defined. As noted earlier, cities neglected to build much new housing during the 1930s and 1940s, and with demand far outstripping supply as black migration accelerated during World War II and the ensuing years landlords responded by subdividing larger apartments into numerous smaller units. These makeshift units were woefully deficient in terms of basic heating, plumbing, and ventilation. Many lacked kitchens and often only one solitary bathroom was available to serve all households on a floor. Like the immigrant ghettos of the previous century, the badly overcrowded and dilapidated tenements of black ghettos became focal points for disease, crime, and poverty. **Reading 5-4** is an excerpt from Arnold R. Hirsch's pathbreaking research that analyzes the formation of inner-city ghettos.[17] Further aggravating an already deplorable situation, slumlords failed to maintain their buildings. Even when individual homeowners tried to invest in the upkeep of their properties, the pervasive redlining of black neighborhoods meant that securing loans for repairs was virtually impossible.[18]

In sum, major demographic trends, along with widespread racist and classist policies and practices, were producing increasingly segregated metropolitan areas—with ominous consequences for cities.

Notes

1. Sam Bass Warner Jr., *Streetcar Suburbs: The Process of Growth in Boston, 1870–1900* (Cambridge, MA: Harvard University Press, 1962).
2. Howard P. Chudacoff and Judith E. Smith, *The Evolution of American Urban Society* (Englewood Cliffs, NJ: Prentice Hall, 1988).
3. Jon C. Teaford, "Suburbia Triumphant, 1945–1964," in *The Twentieth Century American City: Problem, Promise and Reality* (Baltimore: Johns Hopkins University Press, 1986).
4. See also Dolores Hayden, *Building Suburbia: Green Fields and Urban Growth, 1820–2000* (New York: Pantheon Books, 2003); Barbara M. Kelly, *Expanding the American Dream: Building and Rebuilding Levittown* (Albany: State University of New York Press, 1993).
5. Chudacoff and Smith, *The Evolution of American Urban Society.*

6. Refer to Kenneth T. Jackson, *Crabgrass Frontier: The Suburbanization of the United States* (New York: Oxford University Press, 1985); Robert Fishman, *Bourgeois Utopias and the Rise and Fall of Suburbia* (New York: Basic Books, 1987).

7. Refer to Becky M. Nicolaides, *My Blue Heaven: Life and Politics in the Working-Class Suburbs of Los Angeles, 1920–1965* (Chicago: University of Chicago Press, 2002); Andrew Wiese, *Place of Their Own: African American Suburbanization in the Twentieth Century* (Chicago: University of Chicago Press, 2004); Wendy Chang, "The Changs Next Door to the Diazes: Suburban Racial Formation in Los Angeles' San Gabriel Valley," *Journal of Urban History*, 39 (1), 2013.

8. Chudacoff and Smith, *The Evolution of American Urban Society.*

9. Ibid.

10. Mark Gelfand, *A Nation of Cities: The Federal Government and Urban America, 1933–1965* (New York: Oxford University Press, 1975).

11. See also Gerald Frug, "The Legal Technology of Exclusion in Metropolitan America," in *The New Suburban History*, ed. Kevin M. Kruse and Thomas J. Sugrue (Chicago: University of Chicago Press, 2006).

12. Ansley T. Erickson, "Building Inequality: The Spatial Organization of Schooling in Nashville, Tennessee, after *Brown*," *Journal of Urban History*, 38 (2), 2012; see also Bruce D. Haynes, *Red Lines, Black Spaces: The Politics of Race and Space in a Black Middle-Class Suburb* (New Haven: Yale University Press, 2001).

13. David McCallister, "Realtors and Racism in Working-Class Philadelphia, 1945–1970," in *African American Urban History since World War II*, eds. Kenneth L. Kusmer and Joe W. Trotter (Chicago: University of Chicago Press, 2009).

14. Refer to Stephen Grant Meyer, *As Long as They Don't Move Next Door: Segregation and Racial Conflict in American Neighborhoods* (Lanham, MD: Rowman & Littlefield, 2000). But see Nancy C. Carnevale, "Italian American and African American Encounters in the City and in the Suburb," *Journal of Urban History*, 40 (3), May 2014, which describes relatively harmonious racial relations in Montclair, New Jersey.

15. James N. Gregory, "The Second Great Migration: A Historical Overview," in *African American Urban History since World War II*, ed. Kenneth L. Kusmer and Joe W. Trotter (Chicago: University of Chicago Press, 2009).

16. William Julius Wilson, *The Declining Significance of Race: Blacks and Changing American Institutions* (Chicago: University of Chicago Press, 1978).

17. An interesting companion to Hirsch is Joe W. Trotter, *Black Milwaukee: The Making of an Industrial Proletariat, 1915–1945* (Urbana: University of Illinois Press, 1985). It challenges the view of blacks as helpless victims of a hostile white society that decimated community institutions. Instead, Trotter depicts a more complex set of relationships and organizations revealing a higher level of black agency, particularly when Milwaukee's industrial economy remained vibrant.

18. Gregory D. Squires, *Capital and Communities in Black and White: The Intersections of Race, Class, and Uneven Development* (Albany: State University of New York Press, 1994).

5-1 "The Loss of Community in Metropolitan America"

Kenneth T. Jackson

Crabgrass Frontier: The Suburbanization of the United States

A major casualty of America's drive-in culture is the weakened "sense of community" which prevails in most metropolitan areas. I refer to a tendency for social life to become "privatized," and to a reduced feeling of concern and responsibility among families for their neighbors and among suburbanites in general for residents of the inner city. The term "community" implies cooperation. If, for example, the "sense of community" in metropolitan Chicago were strong, then most citizens of Lake Forest, Barrington Hills, Flossmoor, Harvey, South Holland, and two hundred other suburbs would have a clear and positive identification with the Windy City. They would believe that they are united in a way that other citizens of Illinois are not.[1]

Citizen identification with the city is now less than it was a century or more ago. To be sure, nineteenth-century communities were bothered by crime, class rigidity, social unrest, racial prejudice, epidemics, alcohol abuse, and fires. But they possessed a significant sense of local pride and spirit as a result of their struggles with other cities for canals, railroads, factories, and state institutions. In our own time, most observers have noted that alienation and *anomie* are more characteristic of urban life than a sense of participation and belonging.[2]

This is reflected in a general shift in the meaning of the word "suburban." Whereas it once implied a relationship with the city, the term today is more likely to represent a distinction from the city. The nomenclature of peripheral communities provides many clues to this new circumstance. In the nineteenth-century suburbs, names were often adopted that suggested

their direction from the central city, such as North Chicago, South Chicago, or West Chicago. No longer. Rather, the pronounced trend in the twentieth century has been to choose something more suggestive of the countryside than of downtown. In the Chicago area, for example, twenty-four separate communities have taken either "Park" or "Forest" (including both a Park Forest and a Forest Park) in their names; other popular terms are Rolling Meadows, Highland Hills, Sleepy Hollow, River Grove, and Lake Villa. Accurate description is rather less important than bucolic imagery. A good example of the semantic shift was provided in 1973 by East Paterson, New Jersey, which changed its name to Elmwood Park. The former title designated a close spatial relationship with a seedy, industrial city; the second was more suggestive of a quiet residential setting. Similarly, East Detroit became Erin Heights in 1984.

The observant traveler can witness a similar phenomenon in the naming of streets and subdivisions. In the older sections of almost every American city—large and small, east or west—the streets of central areas are numbered. City fathers did this because of their belief that numbered streets were a sign of prominence and promise—were not Philadelphia, New York, Chicago, and Cincinnati famous for their numbered gridiron systems? To live on a Fourteenth Street, therefore conveyed several messages. It meant that your residence was fourteen blocks away from the central business district, and it also meant that you lived in an urban place. Not every nineteenth-century thoroughfare was numbered, obviously, but given names did have a certain logic to them. Many took the title of the city to which they ultimately led, as in Bedford Road, or after an important function or institution that was located there, as in Schoolhouse Road, Dock Street, Market Street, or Railroad Street. Thus, the street layout, the street name, and even the use of the word "street" itself all conveyed an image of urbanity.

Contemporary suburbs, of course, seek to suggest quiet repose rather than commercial importance. Beginning in the middle of the nineteenth century in places like Llewellyn Park, New Jersey, but becoming important only after the 1920s, residential developers began to name streets after the bucolic and the peaceful. They abandoned the grid plan wherever possible and began to name rights-of-way with utter disregard for topography, function, or history. The result is familiar to us all—the enterprising entrepreneur simply combines acceptable word choices (rolling, fields, tall, lake, view, hills, timber, roaring, brook, green, farms, forest) into a three- or four-word combination. The new concoction is never followed by the word "street," but rather by lane, cove, road, way, fairway, or terrace. In California and other parts of the Southwest, Spanish names are substituted for the English, but the intent is the same. History, circumstance, and geography are discarded in a conscious attempt to market houses according to the suburban ideal.

Finally, professional sports nomenclature offers a clue to the demise of community. The designation of a place or a team by a name—a specific name under which fans or residents can unite—is one piece of evidence that a community exists. Until about 1960, professional athletic teams were almost always known by the names of the central cities they represented: the New York Yankees, the Montreal Canadiens, the Boston Celtics, or the Pittsburgh Steelers. In recent years, however, there has been a trend away from naming teams for cities, as if an association with the core city would limit box office appeal. Thus we have the New Jersey Nets, the Minnesota Twins, the Texas Rangers, the Golden State Warriors, the California Angels, and the New England Patriots. At Chavez Ravine, the home of the Los Angeles Dodgers, there are two parking spaces for every seven seats, a telling index of a way of life made possible by the car. In the team's former home, Brooklyn, the "trolley dodgers" had derived their very name from the streetcar system.

Changing town, street, and athletic nomenclature is symptomatic of the deeper and more fundamental fragmentation of metropolitan America. As we have seen, the private automobile has been the most important catalyst for this shift. But there are also three related reasons why this circumstance has come about: the polarization of urban neighborhoods by function, by income, and by race; the failure of municipalities to extend their boundaries through annexation and consolidation; and the changing nature of modern entertainment.

The Polarization of the Metropolis

As we noted earlier, America's large cities underwent a startling spatial transformation between 1815 and 1875. By the 1920s, the exodus of the middle and upper classes from the urban centers had proceeded so far that sociologists at the University of Chicago constructed a concentric zone model to describe the way in which residential neighborhoods improved in quality with increasing distance from the core. This Park-Burgess model has been attacked by two generations of academic urbanologists, but the gist of the disagreement has been about detail, not substance. After 1920, no one could deny that the inner cities were poor and that the suburbs were, relatively speaking, rich. Children learned this at an early age. In 1971 a suburban rabbi confessed that when he was growing up in Brooklyn, the posh Five Towns area of Long Island, even more than Israel, represented "the promised land."[3]

As the suburbs drew off the wealthy, central cities became identified with social problems. Newark offers a good example of this trend. In the nineteenth century, the New Jersey metropolis was one of the nation's leading industrial centers. Its heavy industries, its whirring factories, its prosperous building trades, and its noted public works made it a confident and optimistic community. As late as 1927, a prominent businessman could boast:

> Great is Newark's vitality. It is the red blood in its veins—this basic strength that is going to carry it over whatever hurdles it may encounter, enable it to recover from whatever losses it may suffer and battle its way to still higher achievement industrially and financially, making it

eventually perhaps the greatest industrial center in the world.[4]

Yet the suburban trend was already draining away Newark's most successful and prosperous citizens. In 1925 more than 40 percent of all attorneys whose offices were in Newark were already living in the suburbs; by 1947 the figure had jumped to 63 percent; and by 1965, 78 percent. Members of the city's leading booster association abandoned their home community in even greater numbers. As early as 1932, more than 86 percent of the officers and board members of the Newark Chamber of Commerce lived in the suburbs.[5]

Patterns in other old cities were less startling but similar. In staid Boston, more than half of the Hub's lawyers were living outside the city in 1911, two years before the first car rolled off a moving assembly line. Sixty years of automobility increased the percentage only to three out of four. In New York City 38 percent of the attorneys with offices in Manhattan lived outside the borough in 1908, the year Henry Ford introduced the Model T. On the eve of World War I, the percentage was up to 47, but half a century later it had not risen beyond two-thirds. A profession in the law became more attainable to ordinary people in the course of the twentieth century, as the prestige of an address in one of Manhattan's towering office towers remained. During the day, it was important to operate in the reflected glow of the world's corporate, financial, and communications center, but at night the attorneys traveled to homes in the outer boroughs or, more often, in the suburbs.[6]

It was not inevitable, in Newark or Boston or New York or anywhere else, that the middle and upper classes would gravitate to the urban edges. But, as we have seen, an unusual set of circumstances in the United States helped to insure that suburban areas in the second half of the twentieth century would be segregated by income, race, and lifestyle. The core has become identified in the popular mind with poor people, crime, minorities, deterioration, older dwellings, and abandoned buildings. Middle- and upper-income suburbs convey the opposite impression. The result has been as detrimental to older cities as it has been beneficial to the newer suburbs.

After World War II, the racial and economic polarization of large American metropolitan areas became so pronounced that downtown areas lost their commercial hold on the middle class. Cities became identified with fear and danger rather than with glamour and pleasure. In Memphis the homicide rate in 1984, although deplorably high, was only about half what it was in 1915, when the Bluff City was regionally famous as a "murder capital." Yet Memphis's central business district was bustling and vibrant in 1915, in 1985 it is quiet and forlorn. In Newark the streets are also dismal and deserted in the evening, and a businessman there recently complained: "Since the riots (1967), many people—both black and white—have been afraid to come to Newark at night. We've lost many customers."

The Breakdown of Annexation

A second cause of metropolitan fragmentation has been the inability of cities to extend their boundaries through annexation and consolidation. In the nineteenth century, . . . suburbs typically lost their separate identities because municipal governments adopted the philosophy that "bigger is better" and expanded their populations and area by moving their boundaries outward.

In some metropolitan areas, notably those in the South and West, the addition of new land to the central city has continued. In 1970 Indianapolis became the tenth-largest city in the United States by virtue of its absorption of most of Marion County. In Memphis, Jacksonville, Oklahoma City, Houston, Phoenix, and Dallas a similar annexation process has continued. Thus, these cities registered startling population gains between 1960 and 1980. In actuality, what was called urban growth was the building up and annexation of new residential communities on the edges.[7]

This has not been the experience of most of the large, older cities of the United States. They are no longer bordered by nondescript settlements that can be amalgamated without difficulty. A new suburban consciousness has developed, and residents of outlying areas are now worried about real-estate values, educational quality, and personal safety. On all three counts, they regard cities as inferior. Articulate, affluent, and against big municipal governments, they have chosen to reject political absorption into the larger metropolis. In St. Louis, New York, Pittsburgh, Cleveland, San Francisco, and Philadelphia, for example, city boundaries have not been altered in at least half a century, and the core areas are being strangled by a tight ring of suburbs. In 1972 there were 22,185 local governmental units in the nation's SMSA's, with an average of 86 per Standard Metropolitan Statistical Area. The New York metropolitan region was bordered by an incredible number of 1,400 governments, many with overlapping responsibilities. Chicago followed with 1,100 separate units of government.[8]

The negative consequences of governmental fragmentation are especially evident in Newark. Along with Washington, D.C., Newark is unusual in having lost more territory than it has gained, and its miniscule 24-square mile size is the dominant cause of many of its contemporary problems. Like every other large city, Newark sought to annex its suburbs. And its leaders confidently expected that New Jersey's largest city would follow the example set by many other metropolitan areas. As the mayor of Newark remarked in 1900: "East Orange, Vailsburg, Harrison, Kearny, and Belleville would be desirable acquisitions. By an exercise of discretion we can enlarge the city from decade to decade without unnecessarily taxing the property within our limits, which has already paid the cost of public improvements."[9]

But Newark was stifled. While nearby suburbs prospered, the city increasingly became the home of poor minorities. Perceptive observers realized by the 1930s that the future was bleak. In that decade, Princeton University economist James G. Smith noted that Newark had potential "comparable to the phenomenal growth of Los Angeles." But he predicted, "Newark must create a hegemony over her lesser neighbors or find her great destiny aborted." No such hegemony was forthcoming. The suburbs wanted no part of the industrial city's problems, and in 1933 a Newark City Commissioner told the local Optimist Club:

> Newark is not like the city of old. The old, quiet residential community is a thing of the past, and in its place has come a city teeming with activity. With the change has come something unfortunate—the large number of outstanding citizens who used to live within the community's boundaries has dwindled. Many of them have moved to the suburbs and their home interests are there.[10]

The fact that the peripheral neighborhoods had then and usually have now the legal status of separate communities has given them the capacity to zone out the poor, to refuse public housing, and to resist the integrative forces of the modern metropolis. Thus, the problems of core neighborhoods are usually more serious than those of adjacent suburbs. And because the suburbs are independent and have their own traditions and history, residents of Brookline, or Bronxville, or Lake Forest, or Arcadia, or Ladue tend to offer their primary loyalties to their suburb and to deny responsibility for those who reside a few miles away. In Philadelphia, an angry 1968 letter to the editor expressed just such a view: "It is ridiculous to suppose that those of us in the suburbs have any responsibility to help in the current Philadelphia school crisis. We did not create the problems of the inner city and we are not obligated to help in their solution."

The most conspicuous city-suburban contrast in the United States runs along Detroit's Alter Road. Locals call the street the "Berlin Wall," or the "barrier," or the "Mason-Dixon Line." It divides the suburban Grosse Pointe communities, which are among the most genteel towns anywhere, from the East Side of Detroit, which is poor and mostly black. The Detroit side is studded with abandoned cars, graffiti-covered schools, and burned-out buildings. Two blocks away, within view, are neatly-clipped hedges and immaculate houses—a world of servants and charity balls, two-car garages and expensive clothes. On the one side, says John Kelly, a Democratic state senator whose district awkwardly straddles both neighborhoods, is "West Beirut;" on the other side, "Disneyland."[11]

The answer to America's urban ills obviously does not lie solely in absorbing the Grosse Pointes into the Detroits. As the New York City Department of Sanitation sadly illustrates, mere size is no guarantee of excellence or of efficiency. More governmental functions than we perhaps realize can be handled only on a decentralized, almost neighborhood, basis. But our cities also face problems in transportation, pollution, and unemployment that are genuinely metropolitan or even regional in scope and that cannot be solved by having each community go it alone or by creating additional monstrous and self-serving public agencies like

Perception of Newark

the Port Authority of New York and New Jersey. Some sort of metropolitan or federated government whose planners recognize both the need to keep government human in scale as well as the need to develop citizen awareness of responsibilities beyond the local neighborhood or village is necessary if we are to continue to have great cities. As columnist Tom Wicker noted in the *New York Times* of August 11, 1969:

> The choice, in general, is not between the impersonal coldness of remote bureaucracy and a New England town government for every twenty city blocks. The choice is between a dangerously outmoded concept of the city, leading to abandonment and decay, and a rational development that would restore a congruence between the reach of government and the location of the governed.

The Changing Nature of Modern Entertainment

New attitudes toward leisure and especially the establishment of the home as a self-sufficient entertainment center have also contributed to the weakening of the "sense of community' in metropolitan America. In the nineteenth century, leisure was a precious and rare commodity, and retirement was a little-known concept. But men and women have always had some time of their own, and the use of that time provides one indication of their attitudes toward community life.

Cities, by their very nature, ought to encourage the elevation of the human spirit. Anyone who has ever visited the Piazza San Marco in Venice, shared the happy conviviality of Tivoli Gardens in Copenhagen, witnessed the temptations of the Reeperbahn in Hamburg, strolled at midnight along the Ramblas in Barcelona, or bicycled on Sunday in New York's Central Park knows something of the potentialities and varieties of urban experience. They remind one of Samuel Johnson's telling phrase: "When a man is tired of London, he is tired of life."[12]

American cities boast of concert halls, opera houses, ballet companies, museums, and shopping streets as distinguished as any in the world. But in the United States, as Robert C. Wood has observed, what is most significant is not the influence of urban culture, but the general suburban resistance to it. What is striking in the lives of most residents is the frequency with which they choose not to avail themselves of the variety of experiences the metropolis affords, the manner in which they voluntarily restrict their interests and associations to the immediate vicinity, and the way in which they decline contacts with the larger society.[13]

Suburbanites are of course not completely private in their associations. They participate in an incredible variety of charitable and voluntary activities and campaign and vote in numbers greater than those of either urban or rural dwellers. The more affluent join country clubs, which are almost never in the country, or hunt clubs, which almost never run a fox to ground. In general, however, they focus their energies and their leisure on the home. Indeed, homeownership tends to involve a shift in the maintenance and repair of buildings away from professionals and toward more direct work on the part of the householder. Thus, the rise of a do-it-yourself industry and a shift in leisure-time allocation is a consequence of an increase in homeownership. Our idea of the good life is to build a three-bathroom colonial house such as was never seen in any of the colonies or a ranch-style home such as was never seen on a nineteenth-century ranch. Then, we install a patio or a swimming pool for friendly outdoor living. Many back yards are over equipped, even sybaritic, with hot tubs, gas-fired barbecue grills, and changing cabanas.[14]

The real shift, however, is the way in which our lives are now centered inside the house, rather than on the neighborhood or the community. With increased use of automobiles, the life of the sidewalk and the front yard has largely disappeared, and the social intercourse that used to be the main characteristic of urban life has vanished. Residential neighborhoods have become a mass of small, private islands: with the back yard functioning as a wholesome, family-oriented, and reclusive place. There are few places as desolate and lonely as a suburban street on a hot afternoon.

A century and more ago, despite the vigor with which people such as Andrew Jackson Downing and Catharine Beecher extolled the virtues of suburban life, a house was a place of toil, a scene of production, the locus of food preparation and of laundering and of personal hygiene. During free hours, it was a place to get out of. The ventilation, heat, and lighting were atrocious; it was hot in summer and cold in winter. Window screening, which one observer termed "the most humane contribution the 19th Century made to the preservation of sanity and good temper," was not introduced until the late 1880s; before that time swarms of gnats, mosquitoes, June-bugs, and beetles moved at will through domestic quarters. The result, in both the Old World and the New, was an enthusiasm for the commonality of neighborhood life. To be within the four walls of a house was to be away from the action. Among its few pleasures were reading and making love. The miracles of modern technology have changed some of that.[15]

The evolution of the front porch is a microcosm of the decline of community. In the half-century before World War II verandas were simply de regueur [sic]. They were places for observing the world, for meeting friends, for talking, for knitting, for shelling peas, for courting, and for half a hundred other human activities. The front porch was the physical expression of neighborliness and community. With a much-used front porch, one could live on Andy Hardy's street, where doors need not be locked, where everyone was like family, and where the iceman would forever make deliveries. With a front porch, one could live in Brigadoon, Shangri-La, and Camelot, all in one.[16]

When the automobile appeared, however, the slow-motion world of the front porch began yielding to a new pace. With a car at the curb, youngsters no longer had to sit at home and wait for things to happen; cars could quickly whisk them off to the action. Home industries have largely vanished, and child-rearing, religious instruction, education, and care for the sick have been passed to public institutions. But entertainment has moved indoors. First, with the crank-up phonographs and crystal sets, and more recently with the wide availability of stereophonic music, color television, and video cassette recorders, the private dwelling offers a range of comforts and possibilities, and with the expansion of telephone service, easy and quick communication with outsiders.

Air-conditioning in particular has coincided with a general withdrawal into self-pursuit and privatism. It seduced families into retreating behind closed doors and shut windows, making sidewalk society obsolete and altering the country's character and folkways. Invented in 1906 by textile engineer Willis H. Carrier, who predicted that every day could be a good day, air-conditioning became commonplace in public places and private dwellings in the 1960s. General Electric, Westinghouse, and Carrier designed a sophisticated marketing strategy to appeal to women. Air-conditioned homes, they suggested, were happier, healthier, cleaner homes. By 1980, when the United States (with a mere 5 percent of the world's population) was consuming as much man-made coolness as the whole rest of the earth put together, air-conditioning had become an inalienable right of the middle class. Indeed, the growth of the South and Southwest has been closely linked to the technology of dehumidifiers and air-conditioners. Houston, for example, is an accidental city that was founded on a swamp by speculators who could not have dreamed that it would one day be the nation's fifth largest city and the global headquarters of the energy business. Indeed, without air-conditioning it would not have done so.[17]

No longer forced outside by the heat and humidity, no longer attracted by the corner drugstore, and no longer within walking distance of relatives, suburbanites often choose to remain in the family room. When they do venture out, it is often through a garage into an air-conditioned automobile. Streets are no longer places to promenade and to meet, but passageways for high-powered machines. The cult of domestic privatism, the desire to escape from the warm crowds of city streets, and the turning inward on the family have fully evolved since their articulation by Downing, Beecher, and Vaux a century and more earlier. In fact, more and more people now regard it as a waste of time to go out to a game or a movie, what with the Washington Redskins or *Dynasty* available in the family room. In 1976 the median number of hours per week of television-watching was a staggering twenty-eight hours per week. No large population anywhere has ever spent so much time being entertained. Because the action of the individual is passive and private rather than active and communal, the late Margaret Mead referred to such rooms as giant playpens into which the parents had crawled.[18]

The shift in residential behavior was reflected by several aspects of American popular culture. *Mr. Blandings Builds His Dream House* was perhaps the most widely read of the many postwar novels that explored the world of rising executives and long-distance transfers, of kaffeeklatsches and barbeque pits, of split-levels and station wagons. Eric Hodgins's best-selling 1946 book, which was quickly made into a movie starring Cary Grant and Myrna Loy, was about the pain of city-bred innocents as they encountered the problems and frustrations of battles with pipe-fitters and painters en route to a bloated $56,000 house.

Mr. Blandings Builds His Dream House dealt with the efforts of an upper-class New Yorker to build a country house in exurban Connecticut and was hardly typical of the postwar experience. But the book and the movie obviously struck responsive chords among a population that was buying new houses in record numbers. Other books (many of them also made into movies) took up a somewhat similar theme. Sloan Wilson's *The Man in the Gray Flannel Suit*, Jean Kerr's *Please Don't Eat the Daisies*, John Cheever's *Bullet Park*, John Marquand's *Point of No Return*, Peter De Vries's *The Mackeral Plaza*, and Max Shulman's *Rally Round the Flag, Boys* all poked, either hilariously or scaldingly, at the dream of a green and pleasant oasis not far from the office. If the stereotypical portrait of the suburb as affluent, Republican, and WASPish was somewhat overdrawn, they did at least recognize that the great American land rush after 1945 was one of the largest mass movements in our history.[19]

In the 1950s, when television replaced the motion picture as the primary medium of entertainment in the United States, it was appropriate that one of the longest-running and most popular of all the programs dealt with the trials and pleasures of suburban life. Ozzie and Harriet Nelson became staples across the land as households followed the progress of David and Rickie from infancy through young manhood. The tradition continued in subsequent decades as popular series like *My Three Sons, Father Knows Best, The Brady Bunch, Leave It to Beaver,* and *Life with Riley* suggested that the appropriate setting for family life was the detached home and that the ideal symbol of making it in America was to trade a small suburban house for a large one. Even the hugely successful *I Love Lucy* program shifted locales from urban apartment to suburban house. The front yard, the porch, the street, and the corner grocery had insignificant roles in the new private environment.[20]

Notes

1. This chapter is based upon an article which appeared earlier as Kenneth T. Jackson. "The Effect of Suburbanization on the Cities," in Philip C. Dolce, ed., *Suburbia: The American Dream and Dilemma* (Garden City, 1976), 89–110.

2. Two good examples of the literature on urban imperialism are Richard C. Wade, *The Urban Frontier: The Rise of Western Cities, 1790–1830* (Cambridge, 1959); and Robert R. Dykstra, *The Cattle Towns* (New York, 1968).

3. Mel Ziegler, ed., *Amen: The Diary of Rabbi Martin Siegel* (New York, 1970), 20; or Mel Ziegler, "Diary of a Suburban Rabbi," *New York Magazine,* IV (January 18, 1971), 24–33.

4. Quoted in Kenneth T. and Barbara B. Jackson, *Two Cities: A Comparison and Analysis of White Plains and Newark* (unpublished manuscript, 1974).

5. Paul A. Stellhorn, "Depression and Decline: Newark, N.J., 1929–1941" (Ph.D. dissertation, Rutgers University, 1983).

6. The New York data are included in TABLE A-4 in the Appendix. Additional journey-to-work information may be found in TABLES A-7, A-8, A-9.

7. See, for example, Brett W. Hawkins, *Nashville Metro: The Politics of City-County-Consolidation* (Nashville, 1966).

8. The argument that most problems of American urban government are due to the failure of large cities to expand their boundaries is made most effectively by William G. Colman, *Cities, Suburbs, and States: Governing and Financing Urban America* (New York, 1975).

9. The District of Columbia, which was originally one hundred square miles in area, was reduced to sixty square miles with the loss of the Virginia sections in the nineteenth century.

10. Stellhorn, "Depression and Decline," chapters 2 and 3.

11. *The Wall Street Journal,* October 15, 1982.

12. On life and leisure in an earlier society, see Lawrence Stone, *The Family, Sex, and Marriage in England, 1500–1800* (New York, 1977).

13. Robert C. Wood, *Suburbia: Its People and Their Politics* (Boston, 1958), 107–8.

14. The changing use of spare time in Westchester County is considered in a remarkable volume by George A. Lundberg, et al., *Leisure: A Suburban Study* (New York, 1934). See also, John R. Stilgoe, "The Suburbs," *American Heritage*, XXXV (February-March 1984), 20–36.

15. Philippe Aries, "The Family and the City," in Alice S. Rossi, ed., *The Family* (New York, 1978), 227–35. For an amusing comparison of nineteenth- and twentieth-century standards of comfort, see Allen J. Share, "Good Ol' Summer Time," *Louisville Courier-Journal*, July 25, 1980.

16. "The Front Porch," a late 1983 exhibition at the Craft and Folk Art Museum in Los Angeles evoked the sensation of being on a porch and documented the traditions of the porch throughout America: stoop, portico, gallery, veranda, loggia, dog trot, and arbor. See also, Hugh Stevens, "The Lost Art of Porch-Sitting," *Country Journal*, XI (July 1984), 84–85; and Charles Moore and Gere Kavanaugh, *Home Sweet Home: American Domestic Vernacular Architecture* (New York, 1983).

17. Some medical experts have recently suggested that air-conditioning, by allowing an avoidance of the natural swings in climate, may reduce the average individual's capacity to adapt to stress. See Robert Friedman, "The Air-Conditioned Century," *American Heritage*, XXXV (August–September 1984), 20–33; and "The Great American Cooling Machine," *Time*, August 13, 1979, p. 75.

18. Home builders discovered in the 1970s that families on a limited budget would prefer eliminating the living room rather than doing without the family room. In the South, contractors finessed the problem by calling the main gathering area the "great room."

19. In the 1946 movie, "The Girl Next Door," June Haver "loved every minute" of life in Scarsdale.

20. Equally pervasive was the advertising medium. The American way of life—dishwashers, bicycles, ovens, lawnmowers, and automobiles—has long been depicted as a suburban way of life.

5-2 "The Roads Not Taken: How Federal Policies Promote Economic Segregation and Suburban Sprawl"*

Peter Dreier, John H. Mollenkopf, and Todd Swanstrom

Place Matters: Metropolitics for the Twenty-First Century

Government policies have helped to produce and aggravate metropolitan inequalities. A recent survey asked 149 leading urban scholars to identify the most important influences on American metropolitan areas since 1950. They identified "the overwhelming impact of the federal government on American metropolis, especially through policies that intentionally or unintentionally promoted suburbanization and sprawl."[2] Federal policies have had two major consequences. First, they have consistently favored investment in suburbs and disinvestment from central cities. These policies provided incentives for businesses and middle-class Americans to move to suburbs while deterring poor Americans from doing so. Government policies have also favored concentrating the poor in central cities.

Second, federal (and state) policies encouraged economic competition and political fragmentation *within* metropolitan areas, primarily by allowing "local autonomy" over taxation, land use, housing, and education, but also by failing to provide incentives for regional governance or cooperation. The power of each suburb to set its own rules and the competition among local governments for tax-generating development have powerfully promoted economic segregation and suburban sprawl. Both federal policies and the jurisdictional ground rules have created an uneven playing field that fosters segregation and sprawl. . . .

The Effects of Federal Programs: Stealth Urban Policies

We normally think of urban policies as those directly targeted to cities or the urban poor. But virtually all federal policies, whatever their larger aims, have strong spatial effects that harm or benefit cities. (Acknowledging this, the Carter administration during the 1970s experimented with an "Urban Impact Analysis," which would enable policy makers to anticipate the negative impacts of various policies on cities and thereby lessen them.[32]) Many federal policies with profound impacts on cities and metropolitan development are implicit or indirect urban policies. Because many are invisible to people's political radar, they can be called "stealth urban policies.[33]

For example, when the New Deal initiated a large public works program during the 1930s to lift the nation out of the Depression, its primary goal was to create jobs. But a secondary effect was to lift up the cities, where most of the unemployed were located. Similarly, when the Reagan administration adopted policies to reduce inflation in the early 1980s that brought on a deep national recession, it harmed inner cities far more than other areas.[34] Because cities have a disproportionate share of low-income people, federal efforts to help poor people, such as Medicaid, food stamps, welfare, and job training

Source: "The Roads Not Taken: How Federal Policies Promoted Economic Segregation and Suburban Sprawl" from *Place Matters: Metropolitics for the Twenty-First Century*, 2nd ed., by Peter Dreier, John H. Mollenkopf, and Todd Swanstrom, 2004. Used by permission of the publisher, University Press of Kansas.

*Some text and accompanying endnotes have been omitted. Please consult the original source.

programs, generally benefit cities more than suburbs. And when these programs are cut, poor urban neighborhoods are hurt the most.[35] Similarly, when the Bush administration declared a "war on terrorism" and created a "homeland security" program after the bombing of the World Trade Center on September 11, 2001, it had a disproportionate impact on American cities. The federal government required cities to dramatically increase security measures at airports, ports, and sporting events, and to improve emergency preparations around water systems, the emergency 911 telephone system, public health, and public safety, but failed to provide municipalities with adequate funds to buy equipment, or to add and train staff. Cities spent $70 million a week simply to comply with each "orange alert" security threat warning from the federal Department of Homeland Security.[36]

Here we examine four stealth urban policies: transportation, military spending, federal programs to promote home ownership, and federal efforts to reduce racial discrimination in housing. None of these policies was intended primarily to shape urban development, but each had profound urban impacts. In reality, these federal policies subsidized America's postwar suburban exodus (and still do) by pushing people and businesses out of cities and pulling them into suburbs. The idea that this happened purely as a result of the free market is a powerful myth that distorts our understanding of America's social history.

Transportation Policy: An Arranged Marriage with the Automobile

America's marriage to the automobile began early in the twentieth century. But in many ways, it was an arranged marriage, not just a love affair. Each time the nation courted mass transportation, powerful interests intervened, objecting to the arrangement. The "highway lobby," composed of the automobile, trucking, oil, rubber, steel, and road-building industries, literally paved the way to suburbia by promoting public road building over public transit and by keeping gas taxes low (by European standards).[37] By the 1920s, cars and trucks began to outstrip trolleys and trains as the major form of personal and business transportation.[38] While government officials looked the other way, the major car, truck, and bus companies purchased and dismantled many of the electric trolley lines that urban Americans relied on.[39] State governments earmarked tolls and gas taxes for road construction instead of public transit and launched major road-building programs. In 1934, Congress required states receiving federal highway funds to dedicate state turnpike tolls to road building.[40] The highway lobby was gaining momentum.

The federal Interstate Highway and Defense Act of 1956 sounded the final death knell for alternatives to the car as a major source of metropolitan mobility. Although the ostensible purpose was to promote mobility across the country and get Americans quickly out of crowded cities in case of an enemy attack (this was the height of the cold war), it would also powerfully promote suburbanization by building radial and ring freeways around the major cities. It set up the Highway Trust Fund, which used federal gas tax revenues to pay 90 percent of the freeway construction costs. Trust fund expenditures grew from $79 million in 1946 to $429 million in 1950 to $2.9 billion in 1960. It "ensured that the freeways would be self-propagating, because more freeways encouraged more automobile travel, generating more gasoline revenue that could only be used to build more highways."[41] Ultimately, it built 41,000 miles of roads.[42] Urban scholars ranked this program as the most important influence in shaping America's urban areas in the past half century.[43]

By 1997, the United States was spending $20.5 billion a year through the Highway Trust Fund.[44] But gas taxes by then covered only 60 percent of the cost of maintaining the federal highway system, so federal and state governments made up the rest. (This cost does not include the negative health consequences of pollution or the loss of economic productivity from employees stuck in traffic.) Most other industrial nations fund highways out of general revenues (as they also fund national rail systems and often regional commuter railways), forcing roads to compete with other national priorities.

America's car culture is premised on the belief that automobiles provide a degree of personal freedom and flexibility that public transit cannot. We have shown that the car culture poses many costs, including environmental damage, long commutes, and personal injuries. Even if we discount these costs, the irony of millions of Americans simultaneously exercising their personal freedom by driving their cars, only to end up in traffic jams, has been parodied in such films as *Falling Down* (1993) with Michael Douglas and Jean Luc Godard's French film *Weekend* (1967). Drivers are spending significantly more time stuck in traffic. Since 1982, traffic gridlock (the amount of time drivers spend in congestion) has more than doubled in the nation's metro areas. It has increased 580 percent in Indianapolis, 433 percent in Kansas City, 414 percent in Minneapolis, 400 percent in Salt Lake City, and 333 percent in San Antonio. Even areas with the smallest increases experienced significant traffic congestion.[45] Americans now spend 8 billion hours a year stuck in traffic.[46] According to Jane Holtz Kay, "On the coasts that hold two-thirds of all Americans, the long-suffering 'BosWash' and the newer 'Los Diegos' freeways greet their share of the day's 80 million car commuters, and, with a screech of brakes, the love song of freedom and mobility goes flat."[47]

Throughout the twentieth century, advocates for public transit argued and battled for a more balanced federal transportation strategy. They won a number of victories. In the 1970s, neighborhood groups protested federal and state plans to build a highway through Boston's working-class neighborhoods and persuaded the U.S. Department of Transportation to halt the highway and divert funds to build a subway line. In recent decades, Atlanta, Miami, Baltimore, Buffalo, Detroit, Los Angeles, Washington, DC, and San Francisco built new subway lines using federal funds shared from gas tax revenues. But federal policy had already cast the die in favor of roads and cars. Between 1975 and 1995, the United States spent $1.15 trillion for roads and highways, compared with $187 billion for mass transit and only $13 billion for Amtrak, the nation's interurban train system.[48] Highway construction continues to expand, exacerbating sprawl and undermining the economies of older cities and suburbs.[49] As a result, mass transit ridership is much lower in American cities than in Europe, Japan, and Canada, accounting for only 3 percent of all travel, one-fifth the Western European average.[50]

Our car-dominated transportation system was premised on individual choice, but in many ways it has reduced choice. Most Americans have no choice but to use the automobile. You need one to get to your job, buy groceries, or visit friends. In Canadian and European cities, households make great use of cars but also have the choice to live in pedestrian-friendly neighborhoods where they can rely on mass transit. Many live quite well without using their cars often and can even do without them. The United States chose not to take this road.

Military Spending: More Than Just Defense

Most Americans think that the search for cheaper land and lower taxes, along with the rise of truck transportation, inevitably shifted major manufacturing plants to suburban and outlying locations, or to states (mostly in the South) with lower labor costs. Obviously, government transportation policies had an enormous impact on this trend, but so did the federal government's siting of military facilities and distribution of defense contracts. Throughout the post-World War II period, military spending has accounted for the largest part of the federal budget. Pentagon decisions about where to locate military facilities and where to grant defense contracts greatly influenced regional development patterns. They are America's de facto "industrial policy," a form of government planning that has dramatically shaped the location of businesses and jobs.

Before World War II, almost all manufacturing plants were located in the nation's central cities. When the war began, the federal government took control (though not ownership) of the nation's major manufacturing industries in order to mobilize resources for the war effort. Companies that built commercial airplanes were drafted to produce military aircraft; firms that produced clothing were conscripted to manufacture uniforms; firms that turned out automobiles and freighters began making tanks and battleships for military use. America's business leaders were wary of the potential implications of this government takeover, so to appease them, President Roosevelt appointed corporate executives to run the War Production Board (WPB).

Rather than retool existing plants, many of which sat underutilized during the depression, the WPB executives decided to build new plants and to locate most of them (government funded but privately owned) in suburban areas. "In New York, Detroit, Baltimore, and Pittsburgh, for example, new investment was located outside the central cities twice or more as heavily as before the war. This pattern also held for such Sunbelt cities as Los Angeles, Dallas, Houston and San Diego." The leaders of the nation's largest industrial corporations used "government financing to reconstruct the private sector's capital base along new and more desirable lines." Suburban locations were desirable because they were "largely beyond the reach of the unions," which had a strong presence in the existing factories and were not governed by big-city mayors, who were often sympathetic to unions.[51] These location decisions had a major impact on postwar America.

Mobilization for World War II also strongly affected the regional location of employment (with disproportionate shares of wartime investment being located outside the preexisting industrial base in the urban North) and population (prompting a northward flow of blacks and a westward and southward flow of whites). The Defense Department's support for the aerospace and electronics industries continued these shifts in the cold war era.[52] After World War II, key congressmen continued to utilize the "Pentagon pork barrel" to bring jobs to firms and workers in their districts, disproportionately in suburban areas. The ripple effects of Pentagon spending dramatically changed the population and employment map of the entire country.[53]

Even in the metropolitan areas that won the Pentagon sweepstakes, most Pentagon dollars went to the suburbs, not the central cities. One study compared the military contracts and salaries coming into each city with the amount of federal taxes drained out of each city to the Pentagon. In 1990 alone, eighteen of the twenty-five largest cities suffered a loss of $24 billion. New York City alone lost $8.4 billion a year; Los Angeles, $3.3 billion; Chicago, $3.1 billion; Houston, $1.7 billion; Dallas, $731 million; and Detroit, over $900 million. In Los Angeles, taxpayers sent $4.74 billion to the Pentagon and received $1.47 billion back, for a net loss of $3.27 billion, or $3,000 per family.[54] The employment impact of this drain-off of funds is equally dramatic.

Even those cities gaining dollars and jobs from the Pentagon have discovered that depending on military contracts makes them vulnerable to "downturns in the military spending cycle.[55] Both Seattle (dominated by Boeing, the nation's largest defense contractor) and St. Louis (where defense contractor McDonnell-Douglas—recently purchased by Boeing—is the largest employer) experienced severe economic hard times when the Pentagon reduced its funding for specific weapon systems or selected another contractor. Politics influences the rise and fall of regions and cities as a result of Pentagon spending.[56]

Federal Home Ownership Policies: A Suburban Bias

Federal home ownership policies have also had an enormous impact on metropolitan development patterns. It is widely believed that home ownership benefits society as a whole by encouraging more stable families, higher savings rates, and greater civic participation. By their nature, home ownership policies are biased toward suburbs because, compared with cities, more suburban households own their own homes. But these programs were designed and implemented in ways that exaggerated the bias against cities and accentuated economic segregation and sprawl.

Early federal home ownership policies were shamefully racist. The federal government refused to insure loans for blacks, largely confining them to rental housing in cities and keeping them out of the great suburban migration. Although some minority families may want to live in predominantly minority neighborhoods, surveys consistently show that most minorities want to live in racially integrated neighborhoods. Self-segregation is not the major factor in their residential isolation.[57] Federal policies in some respects initially created and then exacerbated the concentration of poor blacks and Hispanics in ghettos and barrios.[58] Racist behavior and racist policies directly contradict the free-market view of metropolitan development.

In the first half of the twentieth century, overt racial discrimination in housing was widespread. Whites often resorted to violence to keep blacks out of all-white neighborhoods, a practice that persisted into the 1960s, especially in northern metropolitan areas. Local governments enacted racial zoning laws and allowed "restrictive covenants" on deeds that forbade home owners to sell to Jews, blacks, and other groups. Real estate organizations promulgated codes of ethics that sanctioned members who helped blacks buy or rent housing in white neighborhoods. Real estate agents have routinely "steered" blacks and Latinos (regardless of income) to racially segregated neighborhoods, mortgage lenders and insurance firms have redlined urban minority neighborhoods and refuse to treat minority loan applicants equally, and landlords have discriminated against minority tenants.[59] Racial segregation thus stems from the routine practices of the private real estate industry as well as from government policy. From the 1930s through the 1960s, however, the federal government generally ignored and in some cases endorsed these practices.[60]

Early in 1933, in the midst of the Depression, Congress created the Home Owners Loan Corporation (HOLC) to provide low-interest loans to home owners who were in danger of losing their homes to foreclosure. The HOLC set up a rating system to evaluate the risks associated with loans in specific urban neighborhoods. Economically well-off and racially and ethnically homogeneous neighborhoods received the highest ratings. Neighborhoods that were mostly black or were located near black neighborhoods (which typically included Jewish neighborhoods) fell into the lowest categories, which led banks to undervalue these areas and limit loans to them.[61]

The HOLC did not invent these standards. It simply embraced the general practices of the real estate industry. But it put the federal government's stamp of approval on these practices, making racial discrimination part of government policy. Banks used HOLC's system in making their own loans, compounding the disinvestment of black areas and urban neighborhoods by government and the private sector. Equally important, HOLC policy set a precedent for the later Federal Housing Administration (FHA) and Veterans Administration (VA) programs, which played a major role in changing postwar America, pumping billions of dollars into the housing industry.

The FHA was established in 1934 to promote home ownership and stimulate the construction industry, which had almost collapsed with the onset of the Depression. The FHA provided government insurance to banks lending money for approved home mortgages. (Later, a similar program was established by the VA.) With the loan guaranteed in this fashion, lenders could confidently make long-term mortgages available,

thereby reducing consumers' monthly payments and stimulating the housing market. The FHA carried out its mandate in ways that promoted suburbanization and racial segregation at the expense of rebuilding central cities and promoting racial integration.

During the FHA's early years, some housing experts, civil rights groups, and public officials pushed Congress to eliminate racial segregation in federal government housing programs, but they met enormous resistance.[62] In fact, it was official FHA policy to promote racial segregation and unofficial policy to promote suburbanization. Many FHA staff came from the private lending industry, which generally refused to make loans in integrated neighborhoods. In 1938, the official FHA underwriting manual discouraged loans to neighborhoods occupied by "inharmonious racial or nationality groups." It stated that "if a neighborhood is to retain stability, it is necessary that properties shall continue to be occupied by the same social and racial classes."[63] It noted that "a change in social or racial occupancy generally contributed to instability and a decline in values." FHA staff even advised housing developers to use restrictive covenants barring sales to nonwhites before seeking FHA financing as a way to promote neighborhood stability and property values.[64]

Pent up by the Depression and World War II and then unleashed by postwar prosperity, demand for housing exploded in the 1950s and 1960s Many returning veterans sought to gravitate away from their immigrant parents' and grandparents' neighborhoods. As a practical matter, they would find the least costly new housing in the suburban periphery, which was also removed from the growing minority populations in many older central-city neighborhoods. Much of this demand could have been satisfied within the existing city boundaries—for example, in the garden apartment complexes constructed on the outer boundaries of the prewar city. During the Truman administration, however, efforts to pass federal legislation to promote this type of middle-income rental housing in cities failed. The home-building lobby pressured Congress to make it easier to build in outlying areas.[65] The FHA and VA home loan programs became the major vehicles for expanding housing construction, home ownership, and suburbanization. "The power to award or withhold mortgage insurance gave the FHA the hidden leverage to shape the postwar metropolis."[66] The FHA and VA redlined the cities, speeding the migration of the white middle class out of the older central cities. Black families who wished to move to suburbs like Levittown, and could afford to do so, were not allowed.[67] As Robert Fishman notes, "a white home buyer who wished to stay in his old neighborhood had to seek old-style conventional mortgages with high rates and short terms. The same purchaser who opted for a new suburban house could get an FHA-insured mortgage with lower interest rates, longer terms, a lower down payment, and a lower monthly payment."[68]

During the booming 1950s, one-third of all private housing was financed with FHA or VA help.[69] Almost all these homes were built in the suburbs. FHA policy favored the construction of new homes over the remodeling of existing homes, making it "easier and cheaper for a family to purchase a new home than to renovate an older one."[70] It also favored single-family homes over multifamily (apartment) buildings. Between 1941 and 1950, FHA-insured single-family starts exceeded FHA multifamily starts by four to one. In the 1950s, the ratio was over seven to one![71] Suburban zoning laws guaranteed that most FHA-backed apartment buildings would be located in central cities.

The vast majority of FHA and VA mortgages went to white, middle-class families in suburbs. Few went to blacks, city residents, or even whites who wanted to purchase (or renovate) city homes. The FHA underwriting manual viewed mixed-use areas or high-density areas (that is, cities) as bad credit risks. The FHA failed to make *any* loans in some cities. Between 1946 and 1959, blacks purchased less than 2 percent of all housing financed with VA and FHA help. In Miami, only one black family received FHA insurance between 1934 and 1949, and "there is evidence that he [the man who secured the loan] was not recognized as a black."[72] As late as 1966, the FHA had no mortgages in Paterson or Camden, New Jersey, older cities with declining white populations.[73] This treatment contrasts with that of Levittown, New Jersey, one of several planned suburban communities (all called "Levittown") in eastern states that featured thousands of similar single-family homes. When the development opened up in 1958, its homes were marketed and sold to whites only.

The FHA went along with this practice. It took a lawsuit based on New Jersey's antidiscrimination law, seeking to prevent Levittown home buyers from getting FHA insurance, to force the developer to relent. The first black family moved into Levittown in 1960. Starting in the 1970s, under pressure from Congress, the FHA began insuring more single-family home loans in central cities and to racial minorities. But by then, the suburban momentum was well under way.

Home Owner Tax Breaks: Subsidizing Suburbanization

The nation's tax code allows home owners to take mortgage interest and property tax deductions that are not available to renters. These tax breaks have been in the federal tax code since it was enacted in 1912, but they were initially intended to help family farmers, not wealthy home owners. By the 1960s, they were providing billions of dollars of tax subsidies, and by the 1980s, they had become by far the largest federal housing program. Most benefits go to well-off suburban home owners. In 2002, home owner tax breaks totaled more than $106 billion, including mortgage interest deductions ($64 billion), property tax deductions ($22 billion), and exclusions of capital gains on home sales ($19 billion).[74] Between 1978 and 2000, the federal government spent $1.7 trillion (in 2001 dollars) on these breaks, compared with $640 billion on all HUD low-income housing subsidies.[75]

Today, 30 million home owners, almost one-fifth of all taxpayers, receive one or more elements of the home owner deduction. But a highly disproportionate share of these federal tax breaks flows to the highest-income taxpayers with the largest houses and biggest mortgages. For example, 59 percent of the total mortgage deduction goes to the richest 10.2 percent of taxpayers, those with incomes over $100,000.[76] Local property tax deductions are similarly regressive.

These tax breaks have significant geographic and social consequences. They clearly encourage home buyers to buy larger homes in more outlying areas than they otherwise might. Moderate-income home owners, who generally do not get much advantage from this deduction, are concentrated in older suburbs and central cities. The property tax deduction helps both suburban and central-city governments raise revenues, but suburbs get a much greater boost because more of their taxpayers claim the deduction. Tax policy thus powerfully promotes suburbanization, metropolitan sprawl, and geographic segregation by social class and race.[77]

Since the 1960s, many tax and housing experts have recommended correcting this inequity in the tax code by reducing the amount that wealthy home owners can deduct and restricting deductions to only one home. The real estate industry has successfully fought these challenges, claiming that changing the tax law would undermine the American dream of home ownership. In 1984, for example, President Reagan announced that he was planning to introduce a comprehensive tax reform plan that would simplify the tax system and reduce taxes on the well-off. One provision was to eliminate the mortgage interest deduction. The real estate industry quickly sprang into action, and when Reagan filed his bill in Congress (the Tax Reform Act of 1986), it retained the mortgage interest deduction.[78] No president since then has proposed tampering with this regressive tax break for home owners.

Federal Fair Housing Laws: Little Impact on Segregation

It was not inevitable that American metropolitan areas would become as segregated by race and class as they now are. As early as the 1940s, advocates for racial justice and housing reformers proposed laws to challenge racial discrimination and promote racial integration. During the debate over the 1949 Housing Act, progressive members of Congress sought to ban racial segregation in public housing, but their amendment was defeated.[79] Since the 1960s, new laws have been enacted to eliminate these practices, but federal enforcement has often been halfhearted or ineffective. Even if strongly enforced, laws to limit discrimination have little impact on the patterns of residential segregation.

In 1968, the Kerner Commission, appointed by President Johnson in the wake of ghetto riots, recommended enacting a national "open occupancy" law and changing federal housing policy to build more low- and moderate-income housing outside of ghetto areas.[80] Congress passed the Fair Housing Act of 1968 a week after the assassination of Martin Luther King Jr., over the opposition of southern congressmen. This

act addressed the first Kerner Commission recommendation, but not the second. The act prohibited discrimination in housing, including racial steering, redlining, and blockbusting, but it did not promote racial integration in middle-income areas.[81]

The law remains an important symbol of the civil rights movement's success, but its enforcement mechanism was glaringly weak. It gave HUD, or state and local fair housing agencies (where they existed), the right to investigate complaints of housing discrimination by individuals. (State and local governments also began enacting parallel laws during this period.) But neither HUD nor the state and local agencies had the power to issue enforcement orders. They could only refer cases to the Department of Justice for prosecution. Hampered by filing deadlines for complaints, long delays in investigations, and infrequent prosecution, the law had little impact. Many complainants bypassed HUD and these other agencies and went directly to court. Civil rights lawyers won many cases, and courts fined landlords and real estate agents. Although they helped individual victims of discrimination, these time-consuming cases rarely changed housing industry practices. In 1988, the law was amended to give HUD the power to initiate complaints and allow administrative law judges to make rulings.[82]

In the three decades since the Fair Housing Act was passed, a network of private fair housing groups, attorneys with expertise in fair housing law, and state and local government agencies has emerged to utilize the law to promote racial justice. Much money and person power have been spent by these individuals, organizations, and agencies, but the overall impact of this activity is questionable. These federal, state, and local fair housing laws "have had little effect on the overall pattern of racial segregation in most suburban housing."[83]

Only a handful of suburbs have actively and voluntarily embraced racial integration by using reduced mortgages or campaigns against "panic" selling to encourage whites to live in racially mixed neighborhoods.[84] Fair housing and fair lending laws do not challenge the basic policies and practices that lead to racial segregation. Instead, they allow individuals or organizations to seek judicial redress for individual acts of discrimination by landlords, real estate agents, or banks. Legal victories may bring monetary rewards for victims and may deter overt discrimination by landlords, lenders, real estate agents, and insurance companies, but they have not significantly changed patterns of residential segregation. Few housing discrimination cases have been brought against municipalities or major developers for the practices that lead to racial segregation. The federal government has taken some aggressive enforcement actions, but only when such violations were overt and could be proved. . . .

Notes

2. Robert Fishman, "The American Metropolis at Century's End: Past and Future Influences," *Housing Policy Debate* 11, no. 1 (2000): 199–213.

32. Ann R. Markusen, "The Urban Impact Analysis: A Critical Forecast," in *The Urban Impact of Federal Policies*, ed. Norman Glickman (Baltimore: Johns Hopkins University Press, 1979).

33. We borrow this term from Bernard H. Ross and Myron A. Levine, *Urban Politics: Power in Metropolitan America*, 5th ed. (Itasca, IL: F. E. Peacock, 1996), 434.

34. Harold Wolman, "The Reagan Urban Policy and Its Impacts," *Urban Affairs Quarterly* 21, no. 3 (March 1986): 311–35.

35. Bruce Katz and Kate Carnevale, *The State of Welfare Caseloads in America's Cities* (Washington, DC: Brookings Institution Center for Urban and Metropolitan Policy, May 1998).

36. Anya Sostek, "Orange Crush," *Governing* (August 2003): 18–23; Siobham Gorman, "Localities Short on Homeland Security Personnel, Not Equipment," *National Journal*, August 8, 2003; Ben Canada, *State and Local Preparedness for Terrorism: Policy Issues and Options* (Washington, DC: Congressional Research Service, February 5, 2002); Amy Elsbree, "Homeland Security Group Focuses on Federal Funding Flow," *Nation's Cities*, National League of Cities, July 7, 2003.

37. James Plink, *The Car Culture* (Cambridge, MA: MIT Press, 1975); Kenneth Jackson, *Crabgrass Frontier*; Jane Holtz Kay, *Asphalt Nation: How the Automobile Took over America and How We Can Take It Back* (New York: Crown, 1997); Helen Leavitt, *Superhighway-Superhoax* (New York: Doubleday, 1970); Pietro S. Nivola, *Laws of the Landscape: How Policies Shape Cities in Europe and America* (Washington, DC: Brookings Institution Press, 1999).

38. By the mid-1920s, 56 percent of American families owned an automobile, according to Nivola, *Laws of the Landscape*, 11.

39. See Bradford C. Snell, "American Ground Transport: A Proposal for Restructuring the Automobile, Truck, Bus, and Rail Industries" (presented to the Subcommittee on Antitrust and Monopoly of the Committee on the Judiciary, U.S. Senate, February 26, 1974).

40. Nivola, *Laws of the Landscape*, 13.

41. Howard P. Chudacoff and Judith E. Smith, *The Evolution of American Urban Society*, 4th ed. (Englewood Cliffs, NJ: Prentice-Hall, 1994), 260.

42. Fishman, "American Metropolis," 3.

43. Ibid., 2.

44. U.S. Bureau of the Census, *Statistical Abstract of the United States 2000* (Washington, DC: U.S. Government Printing Office, 2000), 625.

45. David Schrank and Tim Lomax, *Urban Mobility Report* (College Station: Texas A&M University, September 2003).

46. Kay, *Asphalt Nation*, 14.

47. Ibid.

48. Nivola, *Laws of the Landscape*, 15.

49. Timothy Egan, "The Freeway, Its Cost and 2 Cities' Destinies," *New York Times*, July 14, 1999.

50. Nivola, *Laws of the Landscape*, 15.

51. John H. Mollenkopf, *The Contested City* (Princeton, NJ: Princeton University Press, 1983), 105.

52. See Mollenkopf, *Contested City*, 102–9, on World War II; Ann Markusen, Peter Hall, Scott Campbell, and Sabrina District, *The Rise of the Gunbelt: The Military Remapping of Industrial America* (New York: Oxford University Press, 1991).

53. Ann Markusen and Joel Yudken, *Dismantling the Cold War Economy* (New York: Basic Books, 1992); Markusen et al., *Rise of the Gunbelt*. . . .

54. Report to the Boston Redevelopment Authority (Lansing, MI: Employment Research Associates, 1992), reported in Steven Greenhouse, "Study Says Big Cities Don't Get Fair Share of Military Spending," *New York Times*, May 12, 1992, A20, and in Marion Anderson and Peter Dreier, "How the Pentagon Redlines America's Cities," *Planners Network* (May 1993): 3–4.

55. Markusen and Yudken, *Dismantling the Cold War Economy*, 173.

56. For example, during the presidential race in September 1992, President George Bush, far behind Governor Bill Clinton in the Missouri polls, traveled to St. Louis to

announce the sale to Saudi Arabia of F-15 jet fighters, which were manufactured by McDonnell-Douglas, the state's largest employer. The sale was highly questionable on defense and foreign policy grounds, but Bush made little pretense of discussing geopolitics. He emphasized the 7,000 local jobs generated by the weapon.

57. Howard Schuman, Charlotte Steeh, and Lawrence Bobo, *Racial Attitudes in America: Trends and Interpretations* (Cambridge, MA: Harvard University Press, 1985); Massey and Denton, *American Apartheid;* Reynolds Farley, "Neighborhood Preferences and Aspirations Among Blacks and Whites," in Kingsley and Turner, *Housing Markets;* George Galster, "Research on Discrimination in Housing and Mortgage Markets: Assessment and Future Directions," *Housing Policy Debate* 3, no. 2 (1992): 639–83; David Dent, "The New Black Suburbs," *New York Times Magazine,* July 14, 1992; Reynolds Farley, Elaine L. Fielding, and Maria Krysan, "The Residential Preferences of Blacks and Whites: A Four-Metropolis Analysis," *Housing Policy Debate* 8, no. 4 (1997): 763–800; Maria Krysan and Reynolds Farley, "The Residential Preferences of Blacks: Do They Explain Persistent Segregation?" *Social Forces* 80, no. 3 (2002): 937–80.

58. Massey and Denton, *American Apartheid;* Arnold Hirsch, *Making the Second Ghetto: Race and Housing in Chicago 1940–1960* (New York: Cambridge University Press, 1983); Arnold R. Hirsch, "Searching for a 'Sound Negro Policy': A Racial Agenda for the Housing Acts of 1949 and 1954," *Housing Policy Debate* 11, no. 2 (2000): 393–442; Thomas J. Sugrue, *The Origins of the Urban Crisis: Race and Inequality in Postwar Detroit* (Princeton, NJ: Princeton University Press, 1996).

59. Margery Austin Turner, "Achieving a New Urban Diversity: What Have We Learned?" *Housing Policy Debate* 8, no. 2 (1997): 295–305; John Yinger, "Housing Discrimination Is Still Worth Worrying About," *Housing Policy Debate* 9, no. 4 (1998): 893–927; *What We Know About Mortgage Lending Discrimination in America* (Washington, DC: U.S. Department of Housing and Urban Development and the Urban Institute, September 1999); Gregory D. Squires, ed., *Insurance Redlining: Disinvestment, Reinvestment, and the Evolving Role of Financial Institutions* (Washington, DC: Urban Institute, 1997); Turner et al., *Discrimination in Metropolitan Housing Markets.*

60. Joe Darden, "Choosing Neighbors and Neighborhoods: The Role of Race in Housing Preference," in *Divided Neighborhoods: Changing Patterns of Racial Segregation,* ed. Gary Tobin (Newbury Park, CA: Sage Publications, 1987); W. Dennis Keating, *The Suburban Racial Dilemma: Housing and Neighborhoods* (Philadelphia: Temple University Press, 1994); Hirsch, "Searching for a 'Sound Negro Policy."

61. Rose Helper, *Racial Policies and Practices of Real Estate Brokers* (Minneapolis: University of Minnesota Press, 1969); Jackson, *Crabgrass Frontier.*

62. Charles Abrams, *Forbidden Neighbors* (New York: Harper and Brothers, 1955); Julia Saltman, *Open Housing as a Social Movement: Challenge, Conflict and Change* (Lexington, MA: Heath, 1971); Keating, *Suburban Racial Dilemma;* Hirsch, "Searching for a 'Sound Negro Policy."

63. Massey and Denton, *American Apartheid,* 54. See also Mara S. Sidney, *Unfair Housing: How National Policy Shapes Community Action* (Lawrence: University Press of Kansas, 2003).

64. Cited in Dennis Judd and Todd Swanstrom, *City Politics: Private Power and Public Policy,* 2nd ed. (New York: Longman, 1998), 198. The U.S. Supreme Court ruled that state courts could not enforce racial covenants in *Shelly v. Kraemer* in 1948. The FHA was forced to change its official policy. It took the FHA until 1950 to revise its underwriting manual so that it no longer recommended racial segregation or restrictive covenants. But the FHA continued to favor racial segregation. It did nothing to challenge racial steering or redlining against blacks. As a result, the Supreme Court's ruling had little impact on racial segregation in private housing. See Keating, *Suburban Racial Dilemma,* 8.

65. Barry Checkoway, "Large Builders, Federal Housing Programs, and Postwar Suburbanization," in *Critical Perspectives on Housing,* ed. Rachel Bratt, Chester Hartman, and Ann Meyerson (Philadelphia: Temple University Press, 1986).

66. Fishman, "American Metropolis," 4.

67. Jackson, *Crabgrass Frontier,* 196–213; Massey and Denton, *American Apartheid,* 42–57.

68. Fishman, "American Metropolis," 4.

69. Cited in Dennis Judd and Todd Swanstrom, *City Politics: Private Power and Public Policy,* original ed. (New York: Harper Collins, 1994), 203.

70. Massey and Denton, *American Apartheid,* 53.

71. Jackson, *Crabgrass Frontier,* 207.

72. Nathan Glazer and David McEntire, eds., *Housing and Minority Groups* (Berkeley: University of California Press, 1960), 140.

73. Massey and Denton, *American Apartheid*, 55.

74. Cusling Dolbeare and Sheila Crowley, *Changing Priorities: The Federal Budget and Housing Assistance 1976–2007* (Washington, DC: National Low Income Housing Coalition, August 2002). . . .

75. During the 1976–2000 period, the federal government also provided $21 billion in low-income housing subsidies through the low-income housing tax credit and $104 billion in low-income housing subsidies through the Department of Agriculture. These figures, calculated from a variety of government sources, are reported and explained in Peter Dreier, "The Truth About Federal Housing Subsidies," in *Housing: Foundation of a New Social Agenda*, ed. Rachel Bran, Chester Hartman, and Michael Stone (Philadelphia: Temple University Press, forthcoming).

76. Only 22.6 percent of the 140 million taxpayers took the mortgage interest deduction, but this varied significantly with income. . . .

77. Joseph Gyourko and Richard Voith, "Does the U.S. Tax Treatment of Housing Promote Suburbanization and Central City Decline?" (Philadelphia: Wharton School, University of Pennsylvania, Real Estate and Finance Departments, September 24, 1997); Thomas Bier and Ivan Meric, "IRS Homeseller Provision and Urban Decline," *Journal of Urban Affairs* 16, no. 2 (1994): 141–54; Richard Voith, "The Determinants of Metropolitan Development Patterns: Preferences, Prices, and Public Policies," in *Metropolitan Development Patterns: Annual Roundtable 2000* (Cambridge, MA: Lincoln Institute of Land Policy, 2000).

78. Jeffrey Birnbaum and Alan Murray, *Showdown at Gucci Gulch: Lawmakers, Lobbyists, and the Unlikely Triumph of Tax Reform* (New York: Random House, 1987); Christopher Howard, *The Hidden Welfare State: Tax Expenditures and Social Policy in the United States* (Princeton, NJ: Princeton University Press, 1997).

79. Abrams, *Forbidden Neighbors*; Richard Davies, *Housing Reform During the Truman Administration* (Columbia: University of Missouri Press, 1966); Nathaniel Keith, *Politics and the Housing Crisis Since 1930* (New York: Universe Books, 1973).

80. National Advisory Commission on Civil Disorders (the Kerner Commission), *Report* (New York: Bantam, 1968).

81. The housing and lending industries argue that even if they do not discriminate, consumers vote with their feet. Whites move out of a neighborhood when they perceive that it is, or could become, "too black." . . .

82. James Kushner, "Federal Enforcement and Judicial Review of the Fair Housing Amendments Act of 1988," *Housing Policy Debate* 3, no. 2 (1992): 537–99.

83. Keating, *Suburban Racial Dilemma*, 14.

84. Keating, in *Suburban Racial Dilemma*, discusses suburbs that have utilized these approaches. See also Philip Nyden, Michael Maly, and John Lukehart, "The Emergence of Stable Racially and Ethnically Diverse Urban Communities: A Case Study of Nine U.S. Cities," *Housing Policy Debate* 8, no. 2 (1997): 491–534.

5-3 "Suburban Autonomy"

Michael N. Danielson

The Politics of Exclusion

Suburbia is essentially a political phenomenon. Political independence is the one thing the increasingly diversified settlements beyond the city limits have in common. Local autonomy means that suburban communities seek to control their own destiny largely free from the need to adjust their interests to those of other local jurisdictions and residents of the metropolis. Since local governments in the United States bear the primary responsibility for the provision of basic public services such as education, police and fire protection, as well as the regulation of housing and land use, independence provides suburbs with considerable control over the vital parameters of community life, including the power to exclude unwanted neighbors. In the differentiated and fragmented metropolis, these powers are exercised by suburban governments which are usually responsive to the interests of their relatively homogeneous constituencies. The result, as Robert C. Wood notes, is the division of the metropolitan population into "clusters homogeneous in their skills and outlook which have achieved municipal status and erected social and political barriers against invasion."[1]

With few exceptions, political autonomy affords suburbanites a potential for exclusion which exceeds that usually available to the resident of the central city. Through zoning, building codes, and other planning powers, suburban communities to a far greater degree than city neighborhoods are able to protect the local turf from undesirable housing and residents. Independence also means that the formal consent of local government must be obtained before most state or federal housing programs for the poor can be initiated,

a power rarely delegated by city hall to its neighborhoods. In addition, exclusionary policies are more easily pursued in small and relatively cohesive political systems than in large ones with diverse constituency interests. To protect itself from unwanted developments, a city neighborhood must keep an eye on a variety of agencies and possess substantial clout in complex political arenas.

By living in a smaller, more homogeneous, and less complex polity, the resident of an autonomous suburb tends to be insulated from unwanted change. Local actions are far less likely to threaten him with lower-income neighbors or other disturbing developments in a jurisdiction where both fellow citizens and public officials share his frame of reference. As a consequence, political independence reduces the chances that suburban dwellers will face the sorts of issues concerning race, status, property values, and community character that frequently confront blue-collar and middle-class neighborhoods in the central city. When suburbanites cannot avoid such challenges, they are more likely to enlist the support of a local government that is closely tuned to their interests and values than is commonly the case in the large and heterogeneous central city.

Because of these considerations, the use of local powers over land, housing, and urban development to promote local social values and protect community character are widely viewed as the most important functions of local governments in suburbia. Residents of upper- and middle-class suburbs in the Philadelphia area ranked maintenance of their community's social characteristics—defined in terms of keeping out

Source: Michael N. Danielson, "Suburban Autonomy" from *The Politics of Exclusion*. New York: Columbia University Press, 1976. Reprinted by permission of the author, Michael N. Danielson, Forbes Professor of Politics and Public Affairs Emeritus, Princeton University.

"undesirables" and maintaining the "quality" of residents—as a more important objective for local government than either the provision of public services or maintenance of low tax rates. In suburbs of lower social rank, maintenance of social characteristics was considered more important than the provision of local services and amenities, and almost as important as keeping down local tax rates.[2]

Exclusionary considerations, of course, are neither the sole nor the most important factor underlying the exodus to the suburbs. Most urban Americans have moved outward in search of better housing, nicer surroundings, social status, and separation from the inner city and its inhabitants. Increasingly, however, political separation has come to be an essential element of the appeal of the suburbs. In the words of a local leader in a blue-collar suburb in the Detroit area, "the most important thing to many people in Warren is just the simple fact that it isn't Detroit."[3] Speaking of the blacks who flocked to East Cleveland during the 1960s, the suburb's black city manager notes that "they feel that at least they are not living in the inner city."[4] Regardless of their reasons for moving outward, most suburbanites quickly discover the utility of local autonomy as a means of protecting their neighborhood, their social standing, their property values, and the racial integrity of the local schools from outside threats. As Daniel J. Elazar notes: "People sought *suburbanization* for essentially private purposes, revolving around better living conditions. The same people sought *suburbs* with independent local governments of their own for essentially public ones, namely the ability to maintain these conditions by joining with like-minded neighbors to preserve those life styles which they sought in suburbanization."[5] In the process, local autonomy and exclusion have become closely intertwined. Political independence greatly strengthens the suburban community's ability to exclude, while the desire to exclude both enhances the attractions of local autonomy and reinforces the suburban commitment to the preservation of local control over the vital parameters of community life.

The Scope of Local Autonomy

In its simplest form, suburban autonomy involves a ring of unincorporated communities lying beyond the city limits, with local governmental services provided by town or county governments. The largest of these "doughnut" types of metropolitan political systems is found in the Baltimore area. Baltimore County, whose 610 square miles and 616,000 inhabitants surround the city of Baltimore and its 895,000 residents, has no incorporated municipalities or elected local officials except for a county executive and a seven-member council.[6] While approximately half of all suburbanites in the United States live in unincorporated areas, arrangements typically are more complex than those in Baltimore County. Rarely does the entire suburban portion of a metropolitan area consist of unincorporated territory. Instead, municipalities are usually scattered amidst the unincorporated neighborhoods. Public services for unincorporated areas tend to be provided by a melange of authorities, school districts, county governments, and state agencies. Regulatory and planning activities affecting land use and housing normally are the responsibility of county governments in unincorporated areas.

Greater control over land, housing, and other key local functions is exercised by suburban communities which have incorporated as municipalities under state law. Municipal governments have more extensive authority than local governments in unincorporated areas to tax, to borrow, to provide services, and to regulate urban development. Another attraction of incorporation is the protection it provides a suburb against absorption into other local jurisdictions. In most states, incorporation guarantees the political independence of a community, since territory in a municipality cannot be annexed by another local government. On the other hand, incorporation usually means more extensive and expensive local services. As a result, many suburbanites prefer unincorporated status, particularly when essential public services are available from other public agencies and when state law protects unincorporated areas from the territorial ambitions of adjacent municipalities.

Incorporation also provides suburbanites with a local government more responsive to community desires than is the case with unincorporated areas. Responsiveness results primarily from size and spatial differentiation. Most suburban municipalities are quite small. In 1967, two-thirds of all incorporated local jurisdictions in metropolitan areas had fewer than 5,000 inhabitants. And half of all suburban municipalities encompassed less than a square mile of land area.[7] Superimposing these small governmental units on the spatially differentiated population of the metropolis commonly results in relatively homogeneous local constituencies. Within these jurisdictions, local government tends to be highly responsive to the wishes of residents, particularly on sensitive issues such as housing and community development. By contrast, constituencies are larger and more diverse in most unincorporated areas in suburbia. In these larger local units, governments generally are less concerned about particular neighborhoods than is the typical small-scale incorporated suburban government.

The desire to secure local control over land use, housing, and urban development has been a common motivation for the incorporation of suburban municipalities. Local land owners, builders, and developers have employed incorporation to secure control over planning and zoning in order to advance or protect their economic interests. On the other hand, residents, particularly in newly suburbanizing areas, have frequently sought to incorporate their communities in order to transfer planning responsibilities and land-use controls from the hands of county and township officials to those of local residents, elected to office by their neighbors. Often with good reason, these larger units of suburban local government are considered to be too sympathetic to development interests and insufficiently concerned with the interests of individual communities. As the leader of a homeowner's group seeking to incorporate a suburban neighborhood in the Chicago area explains: "Our main goal in trying to incorporate is to protect our residents from improper zoning. Present restrictions by the county, which . . . controls zoning within our boundaries, is rather loose."[8]

Another common but usually unvoiced concern which has stimulated incorporation efforts is the desire to exclude blacks and subsidized housing. In the San Francisco area, John H. Denton believes "that one of the principal purposes (if not the entire purpose) of suburban incorporations is to give their populations control of the racial composition of their communities."[9] Municipal status substantially enhances the capability of a suburban community to exclude subsidized housing, and the blacks who might live in such

units. Incorporation permits local officials to decide whether the community will participate in subsidized housing programs. It also provides local residents with control over zoning and other powers which can prevent the construction of subsidized housing.

An illustration of the creation of a suburban municipality to foreclose the construction of subsidized housing is provided by the incorporation of Black Jack, a community of 2,900 in the St. Louis area.[10] Late in 1969, a nonprofit group organized by church organizations in the St. Louis area took an option on a twelve-acre site in an unincorporated section of St. Louis County known as Black Jack. The land in question was part of 67 acres which had been zoned by the county government for multiple-family dwellings; and over 300 apartments already had been constructed by private developers on fifteen of the acres. The church group planned to construct 210 apartments for rental to families earning between $5,700 and $10,200 under the federal government's Section 236 program for moderate-income housing. The site was chosen by the church groups because they "wanted to determine the feasibility of providing subsidized housing for people—black and white—just beginning to climb above the poverty line but still too poor to move to the suburbs."[11]

For residents of the area, almost all of whom were white, middle-income, and living in single-family homes costing between $25,000 and $45,000, the notion of subsidized and integrated housing for lower-income families in their community was not at all feasible. Their reaction was vehement and their actions swift. With local neighborhood associations leading the opposition, circulars were distributed, mass meetings held, and public officials contacted. In addition, a delegation was dispatched to Washington to present petitions to top officials of the Department of Housing and Urban Development. In opposing the project, residents emphasized the lack of public services, overcrowded local schools, poor transportation links with the rest of the metropolis, and the absence of jobs in Black Jack's portion of St. Louis County. Concern also was expressed over the impact on property values and community character if lower-income families, and particularly poor blacks, were to live in Black Jack.

Dissatisfaction with county housing and land-use policies in the Black Jack area had stirred thoughts of incorporation before the subsidized housing project materialized. With the announcement of the project, local residents moved quickly to seek incorporation in order to deny the development of the site for apartments. Two weeks after the federal government agreed to finance the project, over 1,400 residents of the area petitioned the St. Louis County Council for incorporation of 2.65 square miles encompassing the proposed housing. At the request of the county council, the incorporation proposal was evaluated by the county planning department, which opposed the creation of a new municipality "on fiscal, planning, and legal grounds."[12] Far more influential with the county council, however, was the strong local support for incorporation. Black Jack's advocates successfully linked opposition to incorporation with support for subsidized housing. Suburbanites throughout the northern portion of the county were warned by the Black Jack Improvement Association that approval of the project "could open the door to similar projects being located almost anywhere in the North County area. By stopping this project, you would lessen the chance of one perhaps appearing in your neighborhood."[13] Obviously, the way to stop the project was to permit incorporation. Framing the issue in these terms, as one observer notes, rendered the council members "powerless. The housing issue which precipitated the incorporation was too politically sensitive to allow the council to turn down the petition, and thus indirectly sanction" the construction of subsidized housing.[14]

The result was approval by the county council of the creation of the city of Black Jack, the first new municipality in St. Louis County in over a decade. With incorporation, control over land use within Black Jack was transferred from the county to the new municipality. Less than three months after incorporation, Black Jack's City Council enacted a zoning ordinance which prohibited the construction of apartments within the municipality, thus blocking the proposed subsidized housing.[15]

While the powers available to independent local governments provide suburban communities such as Black Jack with the capability to exclude, local autonomy is relative rather than absolute. Local control over land use, housing, and related matters, like all local powers in the United States, is derived from state governments. Autonomy of suburban governments is limited by municipal charters which are granted by the state and by delegation of responsibilities to other units of local government, such as townships and counties by the state constitution or legislature. The states oversee a wide range of local activities and provide local governments with substantial financial assistance, particularly for public education. They also construct most of the major roads and regulate sewer development, a pair of activities which greatly influence the accessibility of land for development. State actions may constrain suburban autonomy, as in the establishment of public agencies empowered to supersede local land-use controls, such as New Jersey's Hackensack Meadowlands Development Commission or New York's Urban Development Corporation.[16] On the other hand, the state may expand the powers of residents of independent suburbs, as have those states which require that public housing proposals be approved by local voters in a referendum.

Local autonomy in the suburbs also is affected by activities of metropolitan and federal agencies, as well as by intervention from the courts. A wide variety of metropolitan agencies exercise responsibility for area-wide planning, major public works, and other activities which affect housing and development patterns within local jurisdictions in the metropolis. The federal government supports housing, highway, water, sewer, planning, and other programs which influence the ability of suburban governments to shape the nature and timing of development within their boundaries. The federal government also has substantial powers to prevent local governments from discriminating against minorities in the development, sale, and rental of housing. In addition, all local authority is subject to review in state courts, and the exercise of many local powers raise [sic] issues which fall within the jurisdiction of federal courts.

In the policy areas of greatest importance for exclusion, however, local autonomy tends to be particularly broad. As Richard F. Babcock notes: "Local control over use of private land has withstood with incredible resilience the centripetal political forces of the last generation."[17] State governments typically have delegated virtually all responsibility for planning, zoning, building codes, and related activities to local governments. Few states even maintain an administrative machinery to oversee local land-use and housing controls. Only in response to environmental problems and pressures have states begun to develop plans and regulatory mechanisms which seek to guide or supercede the land-use activities of local governments. Almost all of these state efforts, however, are limited to areas of critical ecological concern, such as coastal zones and floodplains.[18]

Most states also have done little to enlarge the scale of land-use control in suburbia. County governments usually are limited to regulating unincorporated areas, with few states providing counties with a significant land-use role within suburban municipalities. When states provide for county agencies or regional bodies to review local zoning actions, the review power typically, as Coke and Gargan note, "is advisory only; the reviewing agency has no authority unilaterally to overrun the zoning action."[19] Nor have states necessarily permitted metropolitan governments, in the few areas where they have been created, to exercise land-use controls throughout their jurisdiction. In Miami, as the National Commission on Urban Problems pointed out, "the metropolitan government has zoning authority only in unincorporated territory. In Nashville-Davidson County, several small suburban municipalities continued in existence after the creation of the metropolitan government and retained their zoning powers."[20] The state law creating Unigov in the Indianapolis area also permitted suburban municipalities to continue to control land use.

Local autonomy over housing and land use is bolstered further by the absence of a direct federal role in zoning and other development controls. Moreover, local rather than federal officials determine the location of housing units supported by national subsidy programs.[21] A final factor enhancing the ability of suburban governments to use their autonomy to foster exclusion has been the reluctance of most courts to impose significant constraints on the exercise of local land-use powers.[22]

As a result of these developments, suburban governments have been able to use their autonomy to influence housing opportunities with relatively little outside interference. And because land-use patterns strongly affect local taxes and public services, community character,

and the quality of local schools, zoning has become the essence of local autonomy for most suburbanites.

Using Local Autonomy

Local autonomy, of course, does not guarantee success to suburbanites in their efforts to control development. Great variations exist in the use of local controls. A few suburbs permit almost any kind of development, others seek to exclude practically everything. Most, however, pursue more selective policies which result from the concerns and values of local residents, fiscal realities, environmental constraints, and the pressures for growth and change which constantly test the effectiveness of local controls. Some suburbs are highly skilled in their use of the means available to influence settlement patterns, employing sophisticated planning techniques and acting in a timely fashion to shape the forces of change. Others are far less skillful, and their tardy and piecemeal efforts tend to be overwhelmed by private developers.

Size is a major barrier to the acquisition of planning and zoning expertise in many suburbs. In his analysis of suburban land development in three northeastern metropolitan areas, Marion Clawson emphasizes that:

> Most of these local governments are . . . too small in most instances to engage any full-time employees for any of these functions. Those which do hire usually pay low wages. Only the largest of the local governments have top-ranking jobs that pay enough to attract and hold well-trained professional or technical people. Staffing levels in planning and land-use-related activities are low in relation to numbers of persons engaged in the construction activities affected by their work.[23]

Many suburbs, however, have overcome the handicaps posed by small size and limited resources. Mounting suburban concern over the implications of unregulated development during the 1960s increased local willingness to invest in the acquisition of sophisticated planning capabilities. The financial burdens imposed by these activities were eased by assistance from federal and state planning programs. And the shortage of skilled local employees was offset by the availability of advice from private planning consultants.

Acquisition of planning skills, however, cannot insure that local efforts will strongly influence development. Accessibility, topography, land values, and other physical and market factors play a major role in shaping settlement patterns in suburbs. So do the decisions of metropolitan, state, and federal agencies concerning roads, water supply, sewers, and other major public facilities. Control over land use, the primary power available to local government, is essentially negative. Zoning, subdivision regulations, building codes, and other planning devices may prevent undesirable development, but by themselves cannot induce desired change. Zoning vacant land in a working-class suburb for two-acre estates may foreclose the construction of more tract houses on small lots. In the absence of excellent schools, attractive surroundings, and separation from lower-status neighbors, however, such local action is unlikely to result in construction of expensive housing for an upper-income clientele. Similarly, creation of a commercial or industrial district within a suburb will not attract developers unless the site is desirable in terms of the availability of an adequate tract of land at a competitive price, its proximity to highways and other transportation facilities, and its accessibility to markets, suppliers, and labor force.

The ability of suburban governments to shape urban development is frequently undermined by the very factors which afford growing suburbs an opportunity to influence settlement patterns. Having vacant land and being in the path of development in the decentralizing metropolis often means that growth overwhelms the capacity of small and amateur local governments to cope with the complexities of suburbanization. For some fiscally hard-pressed suburban jurisdictions, the perceived tax benefits of growth outweigh the advantages of effective controls, at least during the crucial initial phases of the development process. Local planning controls often fail to check the private sector because of the dominant influence in newly developing areas of large land owners, real-estate operators, bankers, and related interests. Local officials frequently are closely tied to those who are profiting from suburbanization. In Santa Clara County in California, as in many rapidly developing areas, local "officials and the greedy land speculators and developers . . . were never really opposing interests. With few exceptions the local officials were also

involved in real estate speculation, had other vested interests in the rapid development of the valley, or . . . simply were unable to make a strong stand against the powerful development interests and their allies in local government."[24]

Outright corruption also subverts suburban plans and zoning regulations. The high financial stakes of land development combines with the importance of local land-use controls to produce offers which some suburban officials cannot resist. Illustrative is the experience of Hoffman Estates, a suburb in the Chicago area where three officials were convicted of bribery, conspiracy, and tax evasion in 1973 after taking bribes from Kaufman & Broad Homes, one of the nation's largest homebuilding firms. As Ed McCahill has pointed out, the rewards in this instance were high for both local officials and the developer:

> For about $90,000 in bribes, Kaufman & Broad nearly were able to plop an entire town of 25,000 residents right in the middle of a community which had no hospital or industry to speak of, an inadequate transportation system, and schools filled to capacity. The rezoning proposal allowed 33 housing units per acre when Hoffman Estates had no zoning specifications other than "residential." The $90,000 in bribes paid during the 1960s, when the village had only recently been incorporated and was unaccustomed to planning for subdivisions. One of the incidents that tipped off Hoffman Estates homeowners that something was amiss was when their showers went dry in 1970, as 2,500 new neighbors started tapping into the inadequate water system.[25]

As more and more people move to suburbs residential interests are less likely to be compromised by local governments in contests involving developers. With growth constantly augmenting the ranks of those who seek to use local autonomy to preserve and protect their local community from unwanted change, residents have become increasingly active participants in the politics of suburban development. Doubts, often well founded, concerning the ability or desire of local officials to withstand the pressures and other blandishments of developers has stimulated a great deal of political activity at the grass roots. Neighborhood organizations have been created or politicized to bring pressure to bear on local governments, and to fight adverse land-use actions in the courts.[26] An official of a neighborhood civic organization opposed to more apartment construction in East Brunswick, New Jersey, explains the evolution of his group's political activities as follows: "We were a loose social organization that met for July 4 neighborhood picnics before this zoning dilemma blew up. That action pulled us into legal action, with each of the families contributing money to legally fight the variance before the Zoning Board."[27] To check the discretionary power of local officials, suburbanites in some jurisdictions have sought direct public participation in land-use questions. Voters in Eastlake, a suburb in the Cleveland area, approved an amendment to the local charter in 1971 which required approval of all rezoning actions by 55 percent of those voting in a public referendum. Residential interests supporting the provision "wanted to get the power back to the people" by making it necessary for "a developer to convince the voters he's bringing something good into the city."[28]

Local officials who fail to respond to these residential pressures increasingly face retribution at the polls. In many suburbs, a new generation of office holders is emerging dedicated to using local autonomy to protect residential interests rather than to facilitate developers and land owners. As Fred P. Bosselman notes:

The most important manifestation of the new mood is the changing character of suburban political leaders. Traditionally suburban governments have been dominated by the local businessmen, especially real estate brokers, many of whom owned substantial tracts of vacant land. They naturally saw growth as good for business—as long as it didn't attract "undesirables," of course.

This is changing. . . . [In] many parts of the country in the past few years . . . voters have ousted the incumbents and replaced them with a new type of local official. They are housewives, junior executives, engineers, mechanics, truck drivers—in short, typical suburban homeowners who's [sic] only contact with the community is to live in it, not to make money off it. This might be characterized . . . as "suburbia for the suburbanites."[29]

As a consequence of these developments, more and more public officials in suburbia reflect the values of the relatively homogeneous constituencies which elect them or hire them. Zoning and planning boards increasingly are composed of members sympathetic to the interests of local residents. In Greenwich, Connecticut, as in thousands of suburbs, "no one can get elected unless he swears on the Bible, under the tree at midnight, and with a blood oath to uphold zoning."[30] Suburban city managers, planning directors, and the consultants who provide much of the technical and planning advice in many suburbs commonly adjust their attitudes, proposals, and actions to the limited horizons of the suburban jurisdiction which hires them. As a former suburban mayor emphasizes, "the officials they elect understand that their responsibility is to keep the community the way the people here want it."[31]

Of course, the growing influence of residents in suburban politics does not mean that local controls over housing and land use always are employed to advance residential interests. Residents are not cohesive on every development issue, especially in the larger and more heterogeneous suburban jurisdiction. Moreover, landowners and developers retain considerable influence, particularly in areas in the path of suburbanization where residents often are outnumbered by those who seek to profit from development. Nor does local autonomy protect residents of suburbs from losing battles with state highway departments and other outside agencies which are able to alter the pattern of suburban development without the consent of the affected localities.

Despite these limitations, local autonomy constitutes an effective shield against social change in many suburban jurisdictions. As residential influence mounts, autonomy offers most suburbanites local governmental institutions responsive to their interests. Equally important, political independence provides the legal means to pursue these objectives through the exercise of local planning, land-use, and housing controls. In the typical community, the purposes of local autonomy tend to be defined by the widespread suburban preoccupation with home and school, class and status concerns, racial separation, and the desire to be insulated from the problems of the inner city. Internal consensus on the uses of local autonomy, particularly in smaller and relatively homogeneous suburban jurisdictions, is likely to be high when property values, educational quality, community character, or the influx of blacks or lower-income residents are at issue. The result, in the words of one suburban political leader, is "the politics of the territorial imperative . . . [which] means opposing new housing and new people, anything that might change the status quo."[32]

Maximizing Internal Benefits

Local autonomy combines with limited size, a fairly homogeneous population, and the mobilization of residential interests to provide most suburbanites with a highly parochial perspective on the metropolis. The community tends to be perceived solely in terms of the interests of its current residents, who claim "a right to decide how their town develops."[33] Residents of the suburbs and their local governments rarely take the interests of nonresidents into account. Nor do they consider housing, land use, and other issues in an areawide perspective. Within this narrow frame of reference, the overriding purpose of government in suburbia becomes the protection and promotion of local interests. In defense of "the fact that the poor and middle income people cannot afford to move into Mount Laurel" because of local land use controls, a suburban attorney contends that "the Mount Laurel fathers are trying to do their best for the people of Mount Laurel."[34] Doing their best for constituents usually means that local officials ignore broader issues. For example, when deciding whether to permit the construction of apartment units, suburbanites rarely consider metropolitan housing needs or the growing demand of a diversifying suburban population for multiple-family dwellings. Instead, local debate centers on the costs and benefits of apartments to the community and its residents, and construction commonly is permitted only when the local jurisdiction is convinced that the development will make a net contribution to local revenues. "We must be selective as possible—approving only those applications which are sound in all respects" argues a local committeeman in Mount Laurel. "We can approve only those development plans which will provide direct and substantial benefits to our taxpayers."[35]

Suburban indifference to broader needs, including those created by their own land-use policies, is illustrated by the frequent refusal of jurisdictions which have been successful in attracting industry and commerce to permit the construction of housing within the means of local workers. The presence of the Grumman Corporation with 30,000 workers and the arrival of forty-five new industries during the late 1960s produced no changes in zoning and housing policies in Oyster Bay. This Long Island suburb prohibited apartments except by special exception, required one- and two-acre lots for single-family homes, and had less than 350 units of subsidized housing, most of which had been reserved for the elderly. In New Jersey, Mahwah steadfastly refused to alter its zoning codes to permit the United Automobile Workers Housing Corporation to build subsidized housing within the price range of workers at a Ford Motor Company plant which employed 5,200 in Mahwah. The presence of the automobile factory and other industries gives Mahwah a substantially lower tax rate than neighboring suburbs. Yet the town has been no more willing to open its doors to Ford workers—40 percent of whom are black—than are adjacent suburbs with less industry and higher tax rates. In Mahwah, as in nearby Franklin Lakes, which welcomed a large IBM installation but not garden apartments, the local beneficiaries of nonresidential development see no obligation to provide housing for workers: "There is lots of empty land and cheap housing further out—there's no reason why people should feel that they have to live in Franklin Lakes just because they work here."[36] A member of the planning commission in Oak Brook, an affluent suburb of 4,000 in the Chicago area which attracted $350 million in offices, hotels, research facilities, and shopping centers without providing any low-cost housing, insists that "we are sympathetic to the achievers and the underprivileged," but adds: "We have provided for the achievers, however."[37]

Cooperation among neighboring suburbs to secure adequate housing for the local work force also is rare. In 1970, the zoning ordinances of twenty suburbs in central New Jersey set aside sufficient land for industrial and research purposes to support 1.17 million jobs, but would allow residential development to house only 144,000 families, for an imbalance between new jobs and residences of eight to one.[38] Less than one in five mayors surveyed in a New Jersey study indicated that their communities were willing to cooperate with neighboring jurisdictions on zoning. Even fewer suburbs actually consulted adjacent municipalities in setting land-use policies, leading the study to conclude that "cooperation is almost non-existent" in planning and zoning matters in New Jersey.[39]

Exclusion is a natural concomitant to suburban insularity. Since the community's resources are perceived as belonging to its residents, outsiders cannot share in these resources without local consent. Suburbs commonly employ the local police power to exclude nonresidents from parks, beaches, and other public recreational facilities. In suburban Westchester and Nassau Counties in New York, local governments ban nonresidents from parking lots adjacent to commuter railroad stations, or set parking fees for nonresidents many times higher than those for residents. These policies are justified on the grounds that community facilities belong to local taxpayers, that restrictions are essential to insure enjoyment of public facilities by local residents, and that the locality must be able to protect itself from the crowds, traffic, and other burdens that large numbers of nonresident swimmers, picnickers, or parkers would impose on the limited capabilities of the typical suburb. As a suburban official on Long Island explains, "our town has grown so large there is barely enough beach room for our own people."[40] The same rationale is commonly applied to other facilities by suburbanites. River Hills, an affluent suburb in the Milwaukee area, sought to block the construction of a church, arguing that no need existed because only three members of the congregation were residents of the community. "We are not trying to keep outsiders out," explained the suburb's planning commissioner, "but it is not feasible to have people come in here with things which [serve] no residents from the village."[41] In northern New Jersey, Saddle River sought to block construction of a college because the community was "not the type of town for any large school." According to the suburb's mayor: "This is a residential community, there are no public transportation facilities, and we have no sewage disposal system. We haven't even got a full-time police department and 90 per cent of our roads are private."[42]

Local considerations are of paramount importance in the case of housing and land-use policies which determine who "our own people" are in a particular suburb. Exclusion of those who threaten to change a community's character, lower the status of its residents, jeopardize local property values, or burden public services is widely perceived by suburbanites as an inherent aspect of local autonomy. As Anthony Downs notes, "defenders of residential exclusion argue that any group of citizens ought to be able to establish a physical enclave where certain standards of environmental quality and behavior are required for all residents. The resulting exclusion of those too poor to meet the standards is considered essential to protect the rights of those who established the standards."[43] The more homogeneous a suburb, the more easily it can seek to maximize internal benefits through exclusionary housing policies. And the more successful these policies, the less likely becomes the presence of dissenting voices within the local constituency.

Efforts to maximize internal benefits often go beyond using local autonomy to exclude outsiders. Suburban jurisdictions also have sought, with considerable success [to] get rid of residents deemed undesirable by the local community. Zoning changes, code enforcement, urban renewal, road building, and other governmental actions have eliminated substandard and lower-income housing in many communities. Rarely is adequate housing provided for the displaced. The urban renewal plans of thirteen suburbs in Westchester County in the New York region called for the demolition of over 4200 housing units in 1967, most of which were occupied by lower-income and minority families, and their replacement by less than 700 subsidized units.[44] Displacement without replacement, as in one New Jersey suburb, often reflects the widespread local desire "to clear out substandard housing . . . and thereby get better citizens."[45] Facilitating these efforts in most suburban jurisdictions is the meager political influence of lower-income residents, who usually are outnumbered and almost always lack political resources in contrast with their more affluent neighbors.[46]

Black suburbanites are the most common targets of suburban efforts to displace "undesirables." A study conducted for the U.S. Commission on Civil Rights concluded that "development control activities in Baltimore County over the past ten years have functioned to substantially reduce housing opportunities in the county for low-income, predominantly (but not exclusively) black households."[47] One black residential area was eliminated by rezoning for commercial purposes, another was destroyed by zoning the area for industrial uses. In the St. Louis area, federal urban-renewal funds were used by suburban Olivette to redevelop a black neighborhood for industrial purposes. In the process, all but six of the thirty black families in the community of 10,000 were forced to move away.[48]

Reinforcing suburbia's exclusionary tendencies is the dependence of most local governments on tax sources located within their boundaries. Defending his community's ban on nonresident commuter parking, a suburban mayor in the New York area contends that "there is no way I can morally justify spending the tax revenue of my little village on nonresidents."[49] Speaking of restrictions on the use of Nassau County's recreational facilities, County Executive Ralph G. Caso emphasizes that "it is our residents who pay for them and maintain them through taxes."[50]

Local property taxes, and their relationship to public-school costs and land-use patterns, have an especially important influence on suburban policies affecting housing and urban development. Over 80 percent of all local revenues in the suburbs are derived from property taxes, while 60 percent or more of all public expenditures are for education. Yields from the property tax depend primarily on the extent and value of development within a jurisdiction. School costs are directly related to the density of residential settlement. The logic of these relationships leads suburbs to judge development increasingly in fiscal terms. Speaking of Westchester County, New York's Regional Plan Association notes that in "municipality after municipality, planning to achieve a satisfying local environment has been replaced by planning to meet the school tax bills."[51]

From the perspective of the individual suburb, desirable development generates a profit for the local government and its residents, hopefully at not too high a cost to other things valued by the community, while undesirable development creates a net deficit of tax revenues to local costs. As a result of tax considerations, suburbs both compete for desirable development and are attracted to exclusionary policies designed to foreclose undesirable development. In the words of the U.S. Advisory Commission on Intergovernmental Relations, "the name of the game is cutthroat intergovernmental competition, and the object of the game is to 'zone in' urban resources and to 'zone out' urban problems."[52]

The desire to "zone in" tax resources and "zone out" problems for fiscal reasons influences land-use and housing policies to some degree in most suburban jurisdictions. Few suburbs, and particularly bedroom communities whose tax base is wholly or largely residential, can afford to ignore the fact that most residential development costs local government more than it contributes in taxes. . . . [A] typical four-bedroom house in a Chicago suburb generated approximately $1,200 in school taxes in 1968, but the costs of educating the two school-age children likely to live in the house exceeded $1,600. With more school-age children in the family, or in the case of a cheaper house which would generate less tax revenues, the local deficit would be even greater. In general, the gap between local costs and revenues is greater for subsidized housing occupied by families with children. Such housing typically involves higher residential densities than is the case with conventional single-family housing, as well as lower per capita property tax receipts and greater demands on local public services. Local taxes on subsidized housing financed by the New Jersey Housing Finance Agency, for example, cover 20 percent or less of the public service costs imposed on local governments and school districts by the residents of the projects.

In New Jersey, where local property taxes provide a particularly large share of all local revenues, a state planner believes that most local land-use controls are "designed for the . . . purpose of trying to avoid the costs implied in residential growth and its effect on public school growth."[53] Even in New Jersey, however, relatively few suburbs base their housing and land-use policies solely on tax calculations. Instead, concern over the implications of housing development for local taxes tends to reinforce, and to be reinforced by, exclusionary behavior rooted in community, property-value, class, and racial considerations. Equally important, the workings of the property tax provide suburbanites with a respectable rationale to justify the exclusion of lower-income groups, subsidized housing, and blacks, regardless of the actual mix of motives which underlie a particular local policy.

The same fiscal considerations which lead suburban governments to exclude lower-income families and higher-density residential development induce them to seek commercial and industrial tax ratables as a means of easing the burdens of financing local services. Some affluent suburbs prefer to remain exclusively residential, although their ranks have been thinned in recent years with rapid rises in the costs of local services. Others can afford to be selective, accepting only research or office activities in campus-like settings. Many suburban jurisdictions, however, are sufficiently hardpressed financially that they are willing to take any nonresidential tax ratable they can get, even at considerable cost to local amenities and community character.

Suburbs frequently attempt to reduce the impact of these developments on local residents by restricting large-scale commercial and industrial facilities to areas that are separated from residential neighborhoods within the community by highways or natural features. In the process, costs often are displaced to adjacent communities, which receive no tax benefits from the development. A study by the League of Women Voters in Bergen County, New Jersey, indicated that one "community proposed to zone for heavy industry in an area adjacent to one of the most expensive residential areas of a neighboring town." In another instance, access roads "to a new plant were placed so that the traffic moved along roads in an adjacent community."[54] The principle of beggar-thy-neighbor embodied in the common suburban conception of local autonomy and maximization of internal benefits was succinctly expressed by the former mayor of Wayne in northern New Jersey in explaining the impact of Willowbrook shopping center on residents of his community. "Willowbrook doesn't bother anyone here because it's way on the south border, next to Little Falls Township. It bothers them; they get all the traffic and harassment. We get all the taxes."[55]

Residents of both rich and poor suburbs frequently rue the necessity for local efforts to bolster the tax base with nonresidential development. "Our town is slipping away from us," complains a resident of affluent Greenwich, where 150 companies located during the 1960s.[56] The spread of such feelings, along with the rising influence of residential interests

in suburban politics, has increased resistance to the location of commercial and industrial facilities in suburbs across the nation. For example, Greenwich's Planning and Zoning Commission responded to widespread local opposition late in 1973 by rejecting the application of Xerox for a zoning change needed to construct a $20 million corporate headquarters on a 104-acre site in an area reserved for single-family homes. Reinforcing these concerns over community character and status is the fear that offices and factories will lead to requirements that housing be provided locally for employees and other lower-income families. As an official in New Canaan, another Connecticut suburb, explains, "we would welcome RCA's contribution to the tax base, but not if we have to take the caboose of low income housing as well. . . ."[57]

Notes

1. *Suburbia: Its People and Their Politics* (Boston: Houghton Mifflin, 1958), p. 128.
2. See Oliver P. Williams et al., *Suburban Differences and Metropolitan Policies: A Philadelphia Story* (Philadelphia: Univ. of Pa. Press, 1965), pp. 217–19.
3. See Walter S. Mossberg, "A Blue Collar Town Fears Urban Renewal Perils Its Way of Life," *Wall Street Journal,* Nov. 2, 1970.
4. Gladstone L. Chandler, Jr., city manager, East Cleveland, O., quoted in Paul Delaney, "The Outer City: Negroes Find Few Tangible Gains," *New York Times,* June 1, 1971; reprinted as "Negroes Find Few Tangible Gains," in Louis H. Masotti and Jeffrey K. Hadden, eds., *Suburbia in Transition* (New York: Franklin Watts, 1974), p. 278. East Cleveland had no black residents in the mid-1950s; by 1970, 60 percent of its population was black.
5. "Suburbanization: Reviving the Town on the Metropolitan Frontier," *Publius* 5 (Winter, 1975), p. 59.
6. The Baltimore standard metropolitan statistical area contains four additional counties—Anne Arundel, Carroll, Harford and Howard—which lie beyond Baltimore County.
7. See Allen D. Manvel, "Metropolitan Growth and Governmental Fragmentation," in A. E. Kier Nash, ed., *Governance and Population: The Governmental Implications of Population Change,* Vol. 4, Research

Reports, U.S. Commission on Population Growth and the American Future (Washington: U.S. Government Printing Office, 1972), p. 181.

8. Robert Poltzer, Prospect Heights Improvement Association, quoted in Dan Egler, "Prospect Heights Seeks to Incorporate," *Chicago Tribune*, Oct. 1, 1972.

9. "Phase I Report" to the National Committee Against Discrimination in Housing, U.S. Department of Housing and Urban Development Project, No. Cal. D-8 (n.d.), pt. 3, p. Jc-ll.

10. For a summary of the events leading to the incorporation of Black Jack, see Ronald F. Kirby, Frank de Leeuw, and William Silverman, *Residential Zoning and Equal Housing Opportunities: A Case Study in Black Jack, Missouri* (Washington: Urban Inst., 1972), pp. 17–27.

11. See B. Drummond Ayres, "Bulldozers Turn Up Soil and Ill Will in a Suburb of St. Louis," *New York Times*, Jan. 18, 1971.

12. See *Park View Heights Corporation v. City of Black Jack*, 467 F.2d 1208 (1972) at 1211.

13. Sec William K. Reilly, ed., *The Use of Land: A Citizens' Policy Guide to Urban Growth*, A Task Force Report Sponsored by The Rockefeller Brothers Fund (New York: Thomas Y. Crowell Company, 1973), p. 90.

14. Jerome Pratter, "Dispersed Subsidized Housing and Suburbia: Confrontation in Black Jack," *Land-Use Controls Annual* (Chicago: American Society of Planning Officials, 1972), p. 152.

15. Black Jack's actions were challenged in court by the sponsors of the project, other organizations, and the federal government; see *United States v. City of Black Jack, Missouri*, 372 F. Supp. 319 (1974); *United States v. City of Black Jack, Missouri*, 508 F.2d 1179 (1974); *Park View Heights Corporation v. City of Black Jack*, 467 F.2d 1208; and the discussion of the Black Jack litigation in chapter 7.

16. Suburban opposition to this grant of power to the Urban Development Corporation led the New York legislature to rescind it in 1973; see chapter 10 for a discussion of the New York Urban Development Corporation's turbulent efforts to open the suburbs.

17. *The Zoning Game: Municipal Practices and Policies* (Madison: Univ. of Wis. Press, 1966), p. 19.

18. State land-use activities and their impact on suburban exclusion are discussed in detail in chapter 10.

19. James G. Coke and John J. Gargan, *Fragmentation in Land-Use Planning and Control*, Prepared for the consideration of the National Commission on Urban Problems, Research Report No. 18 (Washington: U.S. Government Printing Office, 1969), p. 6.

20. *Building the American City*, Report of the National Commission on Urban Problems to the Congress and President of the United States, 91st Cong., 1st sess., House Doc. No. 91–34 (Washington: U.S. Government Printing Office, 1968), p. 209.

21. The federal role in suburban exclusion is examined in chapter 8.

22. Judicial attitudes concerning exclusionary zoning and housing policies began to shift in the late 1960s; see chapter 7 for an analysis of the role of the courts in opening the suburbs.

23. *Suburban Land Conversion in the United States: An Economic and Governmental Process* (Baltimore: Johns Hopkins Univ. Press, 1971), pp. 65–66.

24. Leonard Downie, Jr., *Mortgage on America* (New York: Praeger Publishers, 1974), p. 111.

25. "Stealing: A Primer on Zoning Corruption," *Planning* 39 (Dec, 1973), p. 6.

26. For a discussion of suburban neighborhood associations, and their role in land-use politics, sec R. Robert Linowes and Don T. Allensworth, *The Politics of Land Use: Planning, Zoning, and the Private Developer* (New York: Praeger Publishers, 1973), pp. 114–42.

27. George Post, vice president, Prides Wood Civic Association, East Brunswick, N.J., quoted in Ruth Ann Burns, "Apartment Proposal Stirs a Dispute in East Brunswick," *New York Times*, Oct. 8, 1972.

28. See "Eastlake Is Upheld on Requiring Vote in Rezoning Cases," *Cleveland Plain Dealer*, Oct. 31, 1972. Eastlake's ordinance was overturned four years later by the Supreme Court of Ohio; see *Forest City Enterprises, Inc. v. City of Eastlake*, 41 Ohio St.2d 187, 324 N.E.2d, 740 (1975).

29. "The Right to Move, the Need to Grow," *Planning* 39 (Sept., 1973), pp. 10–11.

30. See Ralph Blumenthal, "Pressures of Growth Stir Zoning Battles in Suburbs," *New York Times*, May 29, 1967.

31. Harry J. Butler, Wayne, N.J., quoted in Richard Reeves, "Land Is Prize" in Battle for Control of Suburbs," *New York Times*, Aug. 17, 1971; reprinted as "The Battle Over Land," in Masotti and Hadden, *Suburbia in Transition*, p. 310.

32. John F. English, former chairman of the Democratic Party, Nassau County, N.Y., quoted in *ibid.*, p. 304.

33. James Walsh, chairman. Committee to Aid Lake Mohegan, Yorktown, N.Y., quoted in Paula

R. Bernstein, "Suburbia Learning to Fight Town Hall," *New York Times,* July 15, 1973.

34. John W. Trimble, quoted in Walter H. Waggoner, "State High Court Weighs Attacks by Poor on Zoning," *New York Times,* Mar. 6, 1973. Mount Laurel is in Burlington County, N.J., and lies within the Philadelphia metropolitan area. The comment was made during oral arguments before the New Jersey Supreme Court in litigation which is discussed in chapter 7.

35. See *Southern Burlington County NAACP v. Township of Mt. Laurel,* 119 N.J.Super. 164,290 A.2d 465 (1972) at 468.

36. See National Committee Against Discrimination in Housing, *Jobs and Housing: A Study of Employment and Housing Opportunities for Racial Minorities of the New York Metropolitan Region,* Interim Report, Mar., 1970 (New York, 1970), p. 116.

37. See Robert Cassidy, "Planning for Polo, not People," *Planning* 40 (Apr.–May, 1974), pp. 34–37.

38. See Middlesex-Mercer-Somerset Regional Study Council, *Housing and the Quality of Our Environment,* Research Report (Princeton, N.J., 1970), p. 1.

39. State of New Jersey, County and Municipal Government Study Commission, *Joint Services—A Local Response to Area-wide Problems,* Third Report. Sept., 1970 (Trenton: 1970), p. 26.

40. See John Darnton, "Suburbs Stiffening Beach Curbs," *New York Times,* July, 10, 1972.

41. See "Next Thing You Know They'll Build a Church," *Planning* 37 (Aug., 1971), p. 126. The suburban effort to block construction of the church did not survive a challenge in the courts.

42. Mayor G. Tapley Taylor, Saddle River, N.J., quoted in Richard Johnston, "Act to Ban College," *Newark Evening News,* Mar. 23, 1961.

43. *Opening Up the Suburbs: An Urban Strategy for America* (New Haven: Yale Univ. Press, 1973), p. 65.

44. See Urban League of Westchester County, Housing Council, *Urban Renewal in Westchester County: Its Effect on the General Housing Supply and on the Housing Occupied by Negroes* (White Plains, N.Y., 1967), p. 3.

45. See *Southern Burlington County NAACP v. Township of Mt. Laurel,* 119 N.J.Super. 164, 290 A.2d 465 (1972) at 468.

46. The political weaknesses of lower-income and minority suburbanites are discussed in chapter 5.

47. Yale Rabin, "The Effects of Development Control on Housing Opportunities for Black Households in Baltimore County, Maryland," A Report to the U.S. Commission on Civil Rights, Aug. 1970, p. 2; reprinted in U.S. Commission on Civil Rights, *Hearing Held in Baltimore, Maryland, August 17–19, 1970* (Washington: U.S. Government Printing Office, 1970), p. 701.

48. See Simpson F. Lawson, *Above Property Rights,* U.S. Commission on Civil Rights, Clearinghouse publication #38, Dec, 1972 (Washington: U.S. Government Printing Office, 1972), pp. 21–22; and U.S. Commission on Civil Rights, *Hearing Held in St. Louis, Missouri, January 14–17, 1970* (Washington: U.S. Government Printing Office, 1970), pp. 384–410.

49. Mayor Kevin O'Neill, Irvington, N.Y., quoted in Linda Greenhouse, "Nonresident Autoists Seek Equal Parking Privileges," *New York Times,* Feb. 5, 1973.

50. Quoted in Darnton, "Suburbs Stiffening Beach Curbs."

51. *The Future of Westchester County,* A Supplement to the Second Regional Plan, Bulletin 117, Mar., 1971 (New York, 1971), p. 45.

52. *Urban America and the Federal System,* Commission Findings and Proposals, Oct., 1969 (Washington: U.S. Government Printing Office, 1969), p. 12.

53. Sidney Willis, director, Division of State and Regional Planning, N.J. Department of Community Affairs, quoted in Sharon Rosenhause and Edward J. Flynn, "The What, Why, How of Zoning," *Bergen Record,* Aug. 3, 1970.

54. League of Women Voters of Bergen County, *Where Can I Live in Bergen County? Factors Affecting Housing Supply* (Closter, N.J., 1972), p. 10.

55. Harry J. Butler, Wayne, N.J., quoted in Jack Rosenthal, "Suburbs Abandoning Dependence on City," *New York Times,* Aug. 16, 1971; reprinted as "Toward Suburban Independence," in Masotti and Hadden, *Suburbia in Transition,* p. 295.

56. See "The Battle of Greenwich," *Newsweek* 79 (June 5, 1972), p. 82.

57. See Marc Charney, "RCA's Move to New Canaan Raises Issue of Biased Zoning," *Hartford Times,* July 7, 1971.

5-4 "The Second Ghetto and the Dynamics of Neighborhood Change"*

Arnold R. Hirsch

Making the Second Ghetto: Race and Housing in Chicago, 1940–1960

The period of rapid growth following World War II was the second such period in the city's history. The first, coinciding with the Great Migration of southern blacks, encompassed the years between 1890 and 1930. Before 1900, the earliest identifiable black colony existed west of State Street and south of Harrison; an 1874 fire destroyed much of this section and resulted in the settlement's reestablishment between 22nd and 31st streets. By the turn of the century, this nucleus had merged with other colonies to form the South Side Black Belt. Where, according to Thomas Philpott's meticulously researched *The Slum and the Ghetto*, "no large, solidly Negro concentration existed" in Chicago until, the 1890s, by 1900 the black population suffered an "extraordinary" degree of segregation and their residential confinement was "nearly complete." Almost 3 miles long, but barely a quarter mile wide, Chicago's South Side ghetto—neatly circumscribed on all sides by railroad tracks—had come into being.[9]

By 1920 the Black Belt extended roughly to 55th Street, between Wentworth and Cottage Grove avenues. Approximately 85% of the city's nearly 110,000 blacks lived in this area. A second colony existed on the West Side between Austin, Washington Boulevard, California Avenue, and Morgan Street. More than 8,000 blacks, including some "scattered residents as far south as Twelfth Street," lived here. Other minor black enclaves included the area around Ogden Park in Englewood, Morgan Park on the far South Side,

separate settlements in Woodlawn and Hyde Park, and a growing community on the near North Side. Between 1910 and 1920 three additional colonies appeared in Lilydale (around 91st and State streets), near the South Chicago steel mills, and immediately east of Oakwood Cemetery between 67th and 71st streets.[10]

Ten years later it was possible to speak of an almost "solidly" black area from 22nd to 63rd streets, between Wentworth and Cottage Grove. Whole neighborhoods were now black where, according to Philpott, "only some buildings and some streets and blocks had been black earlier." By 1930 even such gross measuring devices as census tracts documented a rigidly segregated ghetto. In 1920 there were no tracts that were even 90% black; the next census revealed that two-thirds of all black Chicagoans lived in such areas and 19% lived in "exclusively" (97.5% or more) black tracts. The West Side colony grew as well. Although it expanded only two blocks southward to Madison Street, it went from only 45% black to nearly all black in the same period; and a new colony appeared in an area previously occupied by Jews near Maxwell Street. By the time of the Depression, Black Chicago encompassed five times the territory it had occupied in 1900. Its borders were sharp and clear, it had reached maturity, and all future growth would spring from this base.[11]

The Depression, however, marked a relaxation in the pace of racial transition, in the growth of

---

*Some text and accompanying endnotes have been omitted. Please consult the original source.

Chicago's Black Belt. Black migration to the Windy City decreased dramatically, thus relieving the pressure placed on increasingly crowded Black Belt borders. The period of the 1930s, consequently, was an era of territorial consolidation for Chicago's blacks. Over three-quarters of them lived in areas that were more than 90% black by 1940, and almost half lived in areas that were more than 98% black. On the eve of World War II, Chicago's black population was, according to sociologist David Wallace, "very close to being as concentrated as it could get. . . ."[12]

The two decades between 1940 and 1960, and especially the fifteen years following the conclusion of World War II witnessed the renewal of massive black migration to Chicago and the overflowing of black population from established areas of residence grown too small, too old, and too decayed to hold old settlers and newcomers alike. It was during the 1940s and 1950s that the Black Belt's boundaries, drawn during the Great Migration, were shattered. . . .

The census figures for 1950 revealed not a city undergoing desegregation but one in the process of redefining racial borders after a period of relative stability. Black isolation was, in fact, increasing even as the Black Belt grew. Nearly 53% of the city's blacks lived in exclusively black census tracts in 1950 compared with only 49.7% in 1940; more people moved into the Black Belt than were permitted to leave it. As overcrowded areas became more overcrowded, the pressure of sheer numbers forced some blacks into previously all-white areas. Thus, whereas blacks were becoming more isolated from white populations generally, a large number of whites found themselves living in technically "mixed" areas. Segregation was not ending. It had merely become time to work out a new geographical accommodation between the races.[17] . . .

As with any migration, a combination of "push" and "pull" factors produced the movement of blacks across Chicago's racial frontier. The resurgence of large-scale black migration to the city during the war and postwar eras was the most conspicuous force pushing blacks into heretofore white areas. Also of great importance was a housing shortage, which, for blacks, antedated the war and grew increasingly severe throughout the 1940s. The horrendous conditions produced by confining a rapidly growing black population in an already overcrowded, aged, and deteriorating housing supply drove many to seek shelter outside their traditional communities. As long as the housing shortage persisted, though, the situation remained relatively stable. There were simply no vacancies in which to move. The renewal of housing construction on the city's outskirts and in the burgeoning suburbs in the years following World War II, however, indirectly pulled blacks into neighborhoods previously closed to them. As whites in the central city began the trek to Chicago's fringes, vacancies began to appear around the Black Belt. The availability of this housing, and the blacks' ability to pay for it, rendered unstable the old geographical accommodation. The Supreme Court's ruling on restrictive covenants in 1948 simply delivered the final blow to a device that was already growing unequal to the task of preserving the racial homogeneity of white neighborhoods beleaguered by mounting economic and social pressures. Additionally, as migration out of the Black Belt progressed, the conditions that produced it—the desperate need for more black housing, the suburban exodus of middle-class whites, and the increased ability of blacks to compete economically with those who remained—made certain that the growth of Chicago's black community would be a conflict-ridden process.

Chicago's black population grew significantly during the twentieth century. Although the percentage increase was greatest during the initial period of ghetto formation, the largest increase in absolute numbers came during the 1940s and 1950s. Analysts of the 1919 riot never fail to cite the growth of Chicago's black population: more than 148% between 1910 and 1920. Yet, it was the addition of 65,355 new black Chicagoans to a relatively small existing black population that accounted for the large percentage increase. Between 1940 and 1950 Chicago's black population swelled by 214,534; between 1950 and 1960 it grew by 320,372. Although the percentage growth during these two decades cannot compare with that associated with the Great Migration, the absolute numbers of new black residents represented a movement of unprecedented scale.[30] In 1920 Chicago's black population totaled 109,458; between 1940 and 1960 it grew from 277,731 to 812,637 (Table 1).

Most of this increase was due to renewed migration from the South. St. Clair Drake and Horace R. Cayton

Table 1	The black population of Chicago, 1890–1960			
Year	Black population	Increase	Percentage increase	Percentage of total population
1890	14,271			1.3
1900	30,150	15,879	111.3	1.9
1910	44,103	13,953	46.3	2.0
1920	109,458	65,355	148.2	4.1
1930	233,903	124,445	113.7	6.9
1940	277,731	43,828	18.7	8.2
1950	492,265	214,534	77.2	13.6
1960	812,637	320,372	65.1	22.9

Source: U.S. Census Reports 1890–1960.

estimated that 60,000 black migrants seeking jobs in Chicago's labor-hungry war industries entered the city between 1940 and 1944.[31] The migration continued, on an increasingly large scale, and the Chicago Community Inventory estimated an average annual increase in the nonwhite population of 27,000 between 1940 and 1950 and 38,100 between 1950 and 1956. The new in-migration was calculated at 21,000 per year in both periods.[32] When combined with white out-migration, this fresh upsurge in black population took on an even greater significance. Where blacks represented only 4.1% of the city's total population in 1920 and but 8.2% in 1940, they accounted for 13.6% of the city's total in 1950 and 22.9% in 1960. Clearly, this was a population movement that dwarfed the earlier Great Migration.

If Chicago offered the migrants work, however, the city was much less able to provide them with shelter. Aggravating the situation was the shortage of black housing that existed before the wartime migration began. After a building boom in the 1920s, which saw more than 287,000 dwelling units constructed, the Depression brought the housing industry in Chicago to a standstill. From the peak year of 1926, when 42,932 units were built, new construction sank to a low of 137 units in 1933. Throughout the 1930s, only 15,500 homes and apartments, slightly more than 5% of the total built in the 1920s, were constructed. As for the city's less well-to-do inhabitants, the Metropolitan

Housing and Planning Council (MHPC) reported in 1937 that there had been "virtually no new building" for the bottom half of Chicago's population for the "last generation."[33]

Not only was there little construction during the 1930s, but the city began a demolition program in 1934 that destroyed 21,000 substandard housing units; about one-third of the demolition occurred in black areas. Even the steps taken to relieve the poor housing condition of the black population were hardly unmitigated blessings. The construction of the Ida B. Wells public housing project destroyed nearly as many apartments as it supplied. When the project finally opened in 1941, 17,544 applications were received for its 1,662 units.[34]

There was, consequently, a severe housing shortage for Chicago's black community well before the Japanese attack on Pearl Harbor. Administrators of Chicago's relief effort noted that the lack of facilities compelled black welfare recipients to pay two to three times the rent paid by white families on public assistance. The housing shortage was such, a Chicago Urban League executive stated, that it produced the "peculiar phenomena of increasing rents during a depression period." Other tendencies that became painfully evident in the postwar era were apparent earlier to the discerning observer. Overcrowding, for example, was already a serious Black Belt problem. A special 1934 census found that the average black household contained 6.8 persons compared to the 4.7 persons found in the average white household; 66% of the white families studied had fewer than one person per room, whereas only 25.8% of the black families examined met that standard. "Kitchenette" apartments proliferated as real estate speculators and absentee landlords exploited the situation by cutting up large apartments into numerous small ones. These units frequently lacked plumbing and often a solitary bathroom served all the families on a floor. A Chicago Urban League investigation of the Armour Square neighborhood found many homes lacking the most "ordinary conveniences," such as water and toilets, and the widespread use of kerosene lamps. The infant mortality rate for the area was 16% higher than that for the city as a whole, the tuberculosis rate was twice as high, and the general mortality rate was 5% higher. This was the state of black housing in Chicago as World War II and a new wave of black migration began.[35]

Little new construction was undertaken, of course, with the onset of hostilities. Men and material were diverted to the production of the necessities of war. The Chicago Housing Authority did construct several projects such as Lawndale and Altgeld Gardens, and the Cabrini, Brooks, and Bridgeport homes, but these were neither sufficient to meet the incoming flood of war workers, nor a solution to the city's preexisting housing problems. The domestic crisis precipitated by the war effort saw the entire city—not just its black community—struggle under the burden of a severe housing shortage. The 1940 vacancy rate for Chicago was only 3.9%. The Metropolitan Housing and Planning Council believed a 5% rate to be the "danger line" below which a genuine shortage existed. By mid-1941, however, the vacancy rate dropped to 1.5% and plummeted even further, to 0.9%, by April 1942. Conditions deteriorated so rapidly that less than a year after Pearl Harbor the MHPC suggested that homeowners rent out vacant rooms to war workers wherever feasible. They also proposed the "commandeering of empty houses, conversion to add more units, [and] even compulsory billeting."[36]

In the context of the general wartime shortage, the coincidence of plentiful jobs and scarce housing simply produced added frustration within Chicago's Black Belt. For some, lack of money was no longer a serious obstacle to the purchase or rental of new living quarters—but there was no shelter available. The heads of black families, columnist Frayser T. Lane wrote in July 1943, "have sufficient income with which to pay rent but are unable to find suitable places in which to live." A private construction firm building 65 apartments received 12,000 applications from Black Belt residents even though they required an $850 down payment. Fifty-two homes being constructed for blacks in the South Side West Chesterfield neighborhood were literally sold before their blueprints were completed. Even the oldest buildings found many willing to pay for their shelter. The Pythian Temple at 37th Place and State Street stood vacant since the Depression; as a haven for squatters it was condemned as uninhabitable. Yet, with the war, the government bought it and began renovations. In a single day more than 200 people sought information on how to obtain apartments there. Soon the building had a waiting list, which, its operators felt, would "take years" to accommodate.[37]

Moreover, if Chicago's black community was virtually unable to locate new housing, it had to fight tenaciously simply to hold on to its current dilapidated stock. The most notable incident, and one that poignantly illustrates the desperation of the age, involved the Mecca building at 34th and State streets. Built to house visitors to the 1893 World's Columbian Exposition, the Mecca building was obtained by the Ilinois Institute of Technology in 1941 with the understanding that it was to be demolished. Eviction of the Mecca's tenants, however, necessitated turning 1,000 to 1,500 people into the streets. Only the feeling that "rioting would be inevitable if this demolition were carried out" saved the building. The Mecca subsequently became the subject of heated legislative debate in the General Assembly of Ilinois, and later a shelter of last resort for homeless squatters who moved into the structure after the original tenants had departed. It took more than a decade before the Ilinois Institute of Technology could clear the land it desired for campus expansion.[38]

As the war entered its final stages, fearful speculation focused on postwar prospects. The *Defender* shuddered at the thought of a "million Negroes . . . homeless after the war." "In the past we have had occasion to protest holdup rents for ramshackle hovels," the *Defender* wrote. "Today, however, there are no broken down hovels to be had at any price."[39]

There was good reason for concern. As the war ended and the postwar era began, the shortage, for both blacks and whites, grew worse. There were two crises embedded within the desperate housing situation. The first was the long-standing problem of slums. The Chicago Plan Commission documented the existence of 23 square miles of "blight," containing more than 242,000 units, within city boundaries. Another 100,000 substandard units, it was estimated, were scattered outside the designated "blighted" areas. Based on data collected before the tremendous wartime migration, additional aging, overcrowding, and overuse of the city's static housing supply rendered the situation even more grim after the war.[40]

The second problem involved returning veterans. Even before the war had ended, the War Housing Center in Chicago noted that veterans were rapidly surpassing war workers as the group most in need of accommodations. Rental units were "disappearing from the market" as veterans claimed units owned by their families. The winding down of the war also produced an increase in evictions as property owners turned out current occupants in favor of returning family members; fully 25% of all evictions in the summer of 1945 involved such cases. By 1947 more than 175,000 veterans had registered their families with the War Housing Center in the attempt to locate new housing; 140,000 of these (80%) lived doubled-up with others and, when added to the estimated 70,000 families that were living doubled-up even before the war, represented a social problem of catastrophic proportions.[41] To meet this crisis, the city developed an Emergency Veterans Temporary Housing Program, which called for a total of 6,100 units. Of these, only 3,400 were ever constructed. Old military barracks, Quonset huts, and government trailers were converted into temporary "apartments" and filled as soon as they became available. By the end of 1947 the Chicago Commission on Human Relations noted the dearth of real progress; it reported that at least 200,000 new units were needed to meet the city's needs.[42]

The city, however, proved incapable of responding quickly to what was called the "most critical housing shortage since the Chicago fire." Construction continued to lag for a variety of reasons. Only 33,034 new units, an average of only 6,600 per year, were built in Chicago from 1945 through 1949. Even the persistent application of emergency wartime measures, such as the renovation of vacant, condemned, or commercial properties, failed to help.[43]

The most dismal situation, of course, existed in black residential areas. Of 441 "social problems" cases handled by the Chicago Urban League between January 1947 and September 1948, 259 (59%) dealt with housing. Of the 1,686 individuals involved in the total case load, 1,178 (70%) needed shelter. Within the main South Side Black Belt, it was estimated that 375,000 blacks resided in an area equipped to house no more than 110,000. The overcrowding evident before the war was intensified; where previous reports placed fewer than a dozen people in the more crowded rooms, reputable observers now counted fifteen.[44]

The extent of the tragedy, however, was revealed not by cold statistics but by the desperate measures taken by those who sought relief. A variety of "con games" were developed to take advantage of the insatiable demand for housing and the vulnerability of inner-city residents. The more gullible were taken by crude operators such as the man who held "office hours" in his home between 7:00 and 9:00 in the evening and a woman who solicited customers in taverns and beauty shops. Both offered "apartment finding" services at substantial prices. Others bought tax delinquent lots from the city at auction and, misrepresenting them as unencumbered, resold them to unsuspecting buyers. Some went so far as to offer Chicago Housing Authority apartments for sale. Even the more sophisticated and "street-wise" Chicagoans, their resistance broken by an enervating mixture of desperation and hope, proved susceptible to the more polished enterprises. "Vampire" rental agencies opened offices, charged finder's fees, and sometimes collected rent in advance for nonexistent dwellings. One developer actually collected more than $500,000 from 470 blacks for homes that he had no intention of building. The most sophisticated operations were obviously well capitalized as they ran large advertisements in the black press, celebrating the "opening" of new buildings for blacks "east of Cottage Grove" and in other previously all-white areas. Although numerous indictments were returned and court proceedings instituted against the worst of these racketeers, the *Defender* still found it necessary in 1951 to establish a Housing Referral Bureau "to protect prospective home investors from the greedy clutches of unscrupulous speculators." The unprecedented degree to which the housing situation was exploited by the "fast-buck" artists was the best indication of the severity of the shortage.[45]

The persistent victimization of desperate homeseekers was also testimony to the deplorable living conditions that existed. Data collected during 1949 and 1950 reveal that, although the city, as a whole, still staggered under the burden of a housing shortage, there were signs that conditions were beginning to ease for whites, whereas they continued to grow worse for blacks. It was apparent at midcentury that thousands of Chicagoans were still compelled to share accommodations with relatives and friends. The 1950 census uncovered 79,300 married couples without their own households; 64,860 "subfamilies" (groups related to and living with the enumerated primary family) and 32,334 "secondary families" (groups unrelated to but living with the enumerated primary family) were also discovered. It is certain that a substantial number of these people would have lived elsewhere if given the opportunity. Opportunities, though, remained few. The vacancy rate for Chicago stayed at a paltry 0.8%.[46]

By 1950, however, there were also indications that the worst had passed for the city's whites. Whereas the white population actually decreased by 0.1% between 1940 and 1950, the number of dwelling units occupied by whites *increased* by 9.4% during that decade. The number of overcrowded units occupied by whites (defined as those units containing more than 1.51 persons per room) also declined; where 5% of Chicago's whites lived in overcrowded homes in 1940, 4% did so in 1950. The process of "undoubling" the white population had begun.[47]

The same could not be said for Chicago's blacks. Chicago's nonwhite population increased by 80.5% between 1940 and 1950, but the number of dwelling units they occupied increased by only 72.3%. Not unexpectedly, the percentage of nonwhites living in overcrowded accommodations rose from 19% in 1940 to 24% in 1950.[48] In absolute numbers, overcrowded nonwhite households increased by 14,942, whereas overcrowded white households *decreased* by 1,241. Significantly, this more than doubled the number of existing overcrowded nonwhite households. Much of the black population also continued to be squeezed into the ever-increasing number of "kitchenette" apartments. The Chicago Community Inventory estimated that there were at least 80,000 such "conversions" between 1940 and 1950. The white population was becoming less cramped even as blacks became more so.[49]

Such intense overcrowding and the proliferation of "kitchenette" apartments were instrumental in driving people to seek new homes elsewhere. First of all, the division of large apartments meant that only a lucky few would have their own bathrooms. The number of dwelling units lacking private bath facilities went from 85,492 in 1940 to 130,200 in 1950—an *increase* of 36,248 units (52.3%).[50] Sanitary living was also rendered difficult by the amount of garbage produced in homes that housed many more people than they were designed to hold. Building inspections and garbage collection, the Metropolitan Housing and Planning Council noted in 1944, fell "far below the minimum mandatory to healthful sanitation."[51] The demand for housing and the subsequent lack of incentive for landlords to make repairs aggravated an already intolerable situation.

One result, aside from the omnipresent threat of disease, was a plague of rats. Rat attacks on sleeping children were frequent occurrences and it was not uncommon to hear reports of children being maimed or even killed. In 1940 the MHPC succeeded in getting the city to sponsor a massive anti-rat campaign. More than 100 men were taken off relief rolls and given the work of spreading poison in alleys and streets; an estimated 1.5 million rats were killed the first year as 29 tons of the rodents were collected from city thoroughfares.[52] The coming of the war, however, crippled this effort. The employment boom took able-bodied men off the relief rolls and Axis control of the Mediterranean closed the only reliable source of the poison then being used. Rats continued to flourish in Chicago, and by the summer of 1953 the city's rat-control officer estimated that there were as many rats as humans in the city. Tenants unable to cope with the problem were reduced to taking pride in its enormity. Responding to a friend's claim that she had rats "big enough to ride on," another woman commented that her rats came "in teams." "Sometimes," she added boastfully, they "have enough for a ball game."[53]

The threat of fire was another "constant and agonizing worry to thousands of Southside Negroes," especially those confined to the ubiquitous kitchenettes, according to the *Defender*. Divided by partitions that were often themselves flammable, the "rabbit warrens" that filled large old buildings made escape difficult, if not impossible, in time of emergency. Buildings packed with families and their furnishings, which often served as so much kindling, were also rendered vulnerable by their frequent lack of heat and cooking facilities. Gas stoves, routinely kept in closets, served as 24-hour-a-day kitchens and heaters in cold weather. One alderman consequently labeled the entire Black Belt a "gigantic fire trap." Between November 1946 and November 1947 at least 751 fires occurred between 26th and 59th streets and Halsted and the lake. The conflagrations, which left "unnumbered thousands" homeless, amounted in the *Defender's* estimation, to "another Chicago Fire except that it has been on a three-month installment basis." Even more alarming, more than 180 "slum dwellers" died in fires between 1947 and 1953; and at least 63 of the victims were less than ten years old.[54]

Nor were all fires accidental.[55] One landlord, determined to evict his tenants to allow conversion of his building into kitchenettes, set fire to the structure after the tenants refused to vacate. The four children of James Hickman were killed in the blaze. Hickman later fatally shot the landlord in revenge and was eventually sentenced to two years probation for his act.[56] Survivors suffered in other ways as well. With no place to go, the Metropolitan Housing and Planning Council reported, "they moved their smoke-weighted and water-soaked possessions back into rooms with charred walls, without roofs, and without plumbing."[57] The need to escape such conditions was clear. The only question was: Where could one go? . . .

The high degree of residential segregation in Chicago produced a dual housing market: one for whites, another for blacks. The restricted black housing supply and the overwhelming demand for new homes combined to inflate the cost of black housing. Rents in black areas ranged from 15% to 50% higher than that paid by whites for similar accommodations, the Illinois Inter-Racial Commission wrote in 1944. The difference was especially great, they added, in areas just beginning the process of racial succession.[63] By 1960, even after a decade of new construction, the rents paid by blacks were still 10% to 25% higher than those paid by whites for equivalent shelter. Not only were rents higher, but the cost of purchasing housing was greater for blacks. Despite this fact, however, the limits on the black rental market forced many into homeownership—even at the cost of overextending family finances.[64] As whites living around the Black Belt were attracted elsewhere, blacks moved in, for the prices property owners could get for their accommodations were much higher if rented or sold to blacks. The "willingness" and ability to pay higher prices thus destabilized a large portion of Chicago's racial frontier.[65] . . .

The cold fact of racial succession was greatly complicated by the very nature of the process. As the expanding Black Belt approached white residential areas, those neighborhoods entered what realtors called a "stagnant" period. Whites no longer bought homes in the community and blacks had yet to make their first appearance. Rents and purchase prices were lowered in the futile attempt to attract white residents, lending agencies refused to grant mortgages to whites in such "threatened" areas, and, of course, they demurred in providing financing to the first blacks to "break" a block. With the future of the area uncertain and income restricted, landlords and homeowners often cut back on the maintenance of their properties. Deterioration thus frequently set in before blacks moved into the community. Vacancies began to appear and the economic pressures of the dual housing market pushed white property owners to rent or sell to blacks. It was at this point that the real estate speculator entered the neighborhood.[69]

The speculator filled the vacuum created by the reluctant lending agencies and realtors. Whites in transition areas sold their properties to them for several reasons. First, the white seller often did not want to deal directly with blacks or thought he could "save face" in the community by selling to another white.

Second, and probably more important, the speculators had more cash to offer than did the typical black buyer. Fleeing to a new home, the seller required cash for a down payment of his own and was aided by the speculator's desire to complete the transaction quickly.[70] Blacks dealt with speculators because they had difficulty in securing their own financing. A survey of 241 white savings and loan associations found that only one made an initial mortgage to a black family in an all-white area. An examination of 141 commercial banks and 229 life insurance companies revealed that they refused to make "even a token number of conventional mortgages . . . for the typical Negro home buyer."[71] The result was that blacks turned to the speculators as the middlemen who facilitated the transition of property from white to black hands. The speculators provided the property, money, and, needless to say, the terms through which the black demand for housing could be met.

The speculators, of course, played their seemingly essential role because of the huge profits that were available to the brokers who bridged the white and black housing markets.[72] Exploiting the fears held by whites, promising cash and a quick sale, the speculator bought cheaply from transition-area customers. Providing financing and new housing to a literally captive market, they sold dearly to blacks and made profits on both transactions.

The device most frequently used in the sale of property to blacks was the installment land contract. An attorney who studied such dealings estimated that 85% of the property sold to blacks in transition areas was sold on contract. The Chicago Commission on Human Relations corroborated those figures. In a CHR study of one square block in the Englewood area, investigators found that 24 of the 29 parcels of property that underwent a change in ownership between 1953 and 1961 were purchased by installment contracts.[73]

When selling on contract, the speculator offered the home to a black purchaser for a relatively low down payment—often several hundred dollars would suffice. For bringing the home within the reach of a black purchaser, however, the speculator extracted a considerable price. In the Commission on Human Relations study, the percentage increase in the cost of the home from the speculator's purchase price to that of the black consumer ranged from a minimum of 35% to 115%; the average increase was 73%. Also of crucial importance was the fact that the speculator retained title to the property. If purchasers failed to keep current on the installment payments, they were subject to eviction. The tenant had no equity in his home until the terms of the contract were fulfilled. Accordingly, at least one speculator retrieved more than 150% of his original investment in less than a year simply by evicting those who missed installments and collecting successive down payments. In any event, with the speculators' small cash investment and the high monthly payments made by blacks unable to obtain conventional financing, most contract sellers were able to have their entire cash equity returned in two years; payments collected after that were sheer profit.[74]

For blacks, purchasing property under land contract was a way of life. In researching Englewood, representatives of the Commission on Human Relations found that many of the black contract purchasers believed that "the installment contract was the only means by which Negro families . . . could acquire property."[75] If the low down payment permitted the move into new and better quarters, however, the total cost of the home and the high monthly payments created fresh problems. Testifying before the United States Commission on Civil Rights, Frederick D. Pollard, acting executive director of the CHR, told the commissioners that any black who bought on such terms was "going to have to abuse his property in some way to meet this financial burden." Overcrowding, poor maintenance, and illegal conversion were all means through which black contract purchasers tried to save or earn the money to meet their obligations. On Chicago's West Side, Pollard specifically concluded, the "most deteriorating structures" were "almost certainly" those bought on contract from speculators.[76]

In transition areas where apartment buildings, rather than single- or two-family homes, were prevalent, the process of transition was different, but the opportunity for profit and the results were the same. In one area on the near North Side, a real estate operator purchased a large building, which was built in the 1880s. After converting the structure into more than 100 one-room units, he opened it to black tenants.

The building was quickly filled with blacks who were willing to pay more than the previous white occupants. Almost overnight the neighborhood acquired nearly 300 new black residents.[77] Throughout the city, large converted kitchenette buildings proved lucrative investments and there was considerable incentive to purchase, convert, and pack such structures with paying black families. Older middle-class areas with many apartment buildings, such as Hyde Park, felt this sort of pressure most sharply. Those large units not reduced to kitchenettes became paying enterprises through the high rents extracted from middle-class blacks and the money saved by reducing operating costs and upkeep. No matter how it was done, there was considerable money to be made in the racial transition of white neighborhoods.[78]

The conditions produced by this process often resembled those created by contract buying. Those existing in the kitchenettes are well known. But even the middle-class areas began to deteriorate under the pressure of too many people and too little maintenance. One black woman complained bitterly that landlords were "fast making slums" out of middle-class areas and that "we have been urged to take roomers to pay the fantastic rentals." She appealed to the Urban League to "take a stand and publicize what is being done to Negro people who are capable of paying reasonable rents, but cannot have the privilege of maintaining a home . . . in decent apartments without additional roomers."[79] The pressures of the marketplace, however, were too great. In all the census tracts undergoing racial transition, the population increased faster than the number of dwelling units, and the increases in units that did occur were usually the result of conversions rather than new construction. Overcrowding increased as succession progressed.[80]

Theoretically, of course, there was a housing code, building inspectors, and court procedures to assure that no one had to live in overcrowded, unsanitary, or dilapidated buildings. Throughout the 1940s and 1950s, however, the system never posed a serious threat to those who systematically exploited the housing situation. During the war, for example, the city had only a handful of inspectors—eight in 1941, only four for much of 1943. New York, in comparison, had 232.[81]

After the war, the building inspection staff was augmented, but other problems remained to thwart the effective enforcement of the housing code. Responsibility for inspection was fragmented, the city's bureaucracy handled the necessary paperwork sloppily (files on the "hottest" cases were frequently and inexplicably misplaced), and many of those serving as inspectors acquired their jobs because of their political, rather than their professional, abilities.[82] Moreover, a Metropolitan Housing and Planning Council study of the city's worst housing code violators revealed that it was more profitable for slum operators to go to court *even if they lost* than it was to repair their properties. The council discovered that the city's twenty-six worst violators were fined an average of only $32.06 for each suit brought against them; for every $100 in fines requested by the city attorneys, the courts actually fined the defendants $3.12. Nor were these twenty-six operators merely an insignificant number of property owners; they owned 868 buildings during the time of the study (1950–62). With many buildings housing dozens, if not hundreds, of individuals, the scope of their operations accounted for the miserable living conditions endured by uncounted thousands.[83]

The process of racial succession was thus a time of desperation and fear for many whites. It began with the speculators who were better known as "block busters" or "panic peddlers." Some of the more unscrupulous were not above harassing vulnerable homeowners by telephone in the middle of the night or hiring blacks to conspicuously and noisily walk and drive through border areas. But the panic that often ensued was not the sole product of these real estate mavericks. In her study of Chicago realtors, Rose Helper found varying degrees of "respectability" among them. Some of the more proper firms refused to sell property to blacks until 50% or more of the area had "gone." Others utilized successively lower percentages, and some proved willing to do business if only a handful of blacks occupied a previously all-white block. The result was that even though each of the "respectable" realtors adamantly refused to "break" an area, they had a great financial stake in the successful operation of the "panic peddler." Once the "disreputable" dealer had done his job, the more "respectable" flocked to do business in transition neighborhoods where their own particular "black threshold" had been inevitably met. In operation, this produced a "gold rush" effect and reluctant residents were literally besieged by hordes of soliciting realtors. Working virtually, if not covertly, in tandem, the panic peddler and the "respectable" broker earned the greatest profits from the greatest degree of white desperation.[84]

In areas where apartment buildings were being converted to kitchenettes and black tenancy, there was, if anything, a sense of helplessness greater even than the fear and desperation. In these neighborhoods white tenants were often evicted in favor of higher paying blacks. In one Oakland apartment, for example, the space that was rented to one white family at $25 per month was able to house three black families at $100 per month. For the working- and lower-middle-class whites caught in this economic squeeze, there was nowhere to go. The cost of the new accommodations being built on the urban fringe was beyond their means and, lacking the mobility of those who left the inner city by choice, the prospect of being ousted from reasonably priced, centrally located housing inspired dread. Indeed, a contemporary South Side study of attitudes toward racial succession found that among lower status whites it was the fear that they would be dispossessed that inspired the most antiblack sentiment. The vigorous rejection of even (perhaps especially) middle-class blacks by these vulnerable whites stemmed not only from imagined "status" differences that were impervious to the bleaching power of money but also from the fear that they could not compete against such opponents in the "life and death" struggle for housing.[85]

Finally, as racial succession progressed, the conditions produced by real estate speculation and exploitation began to yield visible proof to those who believed that black "invasion" meant slum creation. "The buildings into which the negroes are being moved," Lea Taylor, head resident of the Chicago Commons settlement, wrote in 1945, "are producing such congestion . . . that it . . . is impossible for them to live decently. The inference [in the neighborhoods]

is that that is the way negroes like to live." Even in areas of single-family homes, the effects of contract buying, Frederick Pollard observed, led whites to "accept uncritically the idea that communities deteriorate when Negroes move in."[86] For whites perceiving themselves as the victims of black territorial expansion, the entire process of racial transition, from beginning to end, guaranteed strong responses. . . .

Notes

9. David A. Wallace, "Residential Concentration of Negroes in Chicago" (Ph.D. dissertation, Harvard University, 1953), p. 64; Thomas L. Philpott, *The Slum and the Ghetto: Neighborhood Deterioration and Middle-Class Reform, Chicago, 1880–1930* (New York: Oxford University Press, 1978), pp. 119, 121, 130, 146.

10. Spear, *Black Chicago*, pp. 142, 146; CCRR, *The Negro in Chicago*, pp. 106–8; Otis Duncan and Beverly Duncan, *The Negro Population of Chicago* (Chicago: University of Chicago Press, 1957), p. 92; Wallace, "Residential Concentration of Negroes," p. 69, claims no new communities came into being between 1910 and 1920.

11. Duncan and Duncan, *The Negro Population*, pp. 95–6; Wallace, "Residential Concentration of Negroes," p. 111; Philpott, *The Slum and the Ghetto*, p. 121.

12. Duncan and Duncan, *The Negro Population*, pp. 95–7.

17. Duncan and Duncan, *The Negro Population*, pp. 95–6.

30. For the city as a whole, the demand for new housing was even greater than the raw population data would indicate. Between 1940 and 1949 the number of families increased at more than *twice* the rate of the general population. The formation of new families, deferred during Depression and war, accelerated rapidly in the postwar era. See "A Factual Report on Housing" (mimeographed, April 15, 1950), P. 1, MHPC Papers.

31. Drake and Cayton, *Black Metropolis*, 1:90–1.

32. The difference in total growth for the two periods was due to natural increase. This was calculated at 5,900 per year between 1940 and 1950 and at 17,200 per year between 1950 and 1956. See Chicago Community Inventory, *Population Growth in the Chicago Standard Metropolitan Area* (Chicago: n.p., 1958), p. 12.

33. Carl Condit, *Chicago, 1930–1970* (Chicago: University of Chicago Press, 1974), p. 286; Metropolitan Housing [and Planning] Council, Minutes of the Meeting, October 27, 1937, MHPC Papers.

34. Illinois State Committee on the Condition of the Urban Colored Population, *Report* (n.p., n.d.), p. 81; U.S., Congress, House, Interstate Migration Committee, *Hearings Before the Select Committee to Investigate the Interstate Migration of Destitute Citizens,* 76th Cong., 3d sess., 1940, pt. 3, pp. 1098–9, 1102 (hereafter cited as the Interstate Migration Committee, *Hearings); Chicago Defender,* May 18, June 15, 1940; May 10, 1941.

35. Interstate Migration Committee, *Hearings,* p. 1098; *Chicago Defender,* May 11, 1940; Illinois State Committee on the Condition of the Urban Colored Population, *Report,* pp. 81–9.

36. "Housing News," June 1941; April, June 1942, all in the Graham Aldis Papers, Manuscript Collection, The Library, UIC.

37. *Chicago Bee,* July 4, 1943; May 14, 1944; August 5, 1945; *Monthly Summary of Events and Trends in Race Relations* 2 (November 1944): 94.

38. Metropolitan Housing [and Planning] Council, Minutes of the Regular Meeting of the Board of Directors, April 1, 1943, MHPC Papers; *Chicago Bee,* May 23, June 6, 1943; October 15, 1944; April 25, 1945; *Chicago Defender,* March 6, June 5, 1943; April 7, 1945; May 27, 1950; January 5, 1952.

39. *Chicago Defender,* November 27, 1943.

40. Chicago Plan Commission, *Residential Chicago* (Chicago: City of Chicago, 1943); City of Chicago, *Report to the People* (Chicago: City of Chicago, 1947), pp. 155, 157; Dr. Louis Wirth, "Statement of the MHC-MEHC Meeting, City Council Chambers, April 7, 1947," pp. 1–2, MHPC Papers.

41. Of the veterans registered at the center, approximately 75% were white and 25% were nonwhite. Metropolitan Housing [and Planning] Council, Minutes of the Meeting with the NHA and Veterans Information Center, July 30, 1945; Leonard R. McDonald, "The Truth—Real Facts About the Veterans' Housing Problems," n.d., both in the MHPC Papers; CHR, "Monthly Report of the Executive Director, February 1947," (mimeographed, n.d.), Chicago Urban League Papers (hereafter cited as the CUL Papers), Manuscript Collection, The Library, UIC.

42. Black resistance to "temporary" units, which it was feared would become permanent additions to the ghetto, contributed to the reluctance of the housing authority to use them. See Ferd Kramer to Robert R. Taylor, May 19, June 2, 1944; Robert R. Taylor to Ferd Kramer, May 24, 1944; Ferd Kramer to Louis Wirth, May 31, 1944, all in the MHPC Papers. See also "Temporary Housing Need Confirmed by Survey" (mimeographed, n.d.); Metropolitan Housing Council to James Downs, Jr., June 5, 1946; James Downs to Howard E. Green, June 6, 1946, all in the MHPC Papers; CHR, "Memorandum on the Airport Homes," (mimeographed, n.d.), CUL Papers, p. 11; John Bartlow Martin, "Incident at Fernwood," *Harper's Magazine* 198 (October 1949): 88.

43. U.S. Commission on Civil Rights, *Hearings: Housing* (Washington, D.C.: Government Printing Office, 1959), p. 672; Condit, *Chicago,* p. 287; "Report on Survey of Conversion Program" (mimeographed, February 25, 1947), p. 1; "Chicago Housing Center Closes After Providing Living Accommodations for 400,000 People in 6 Years" (mimeographed, n.d.), pp. 2–3, both in the MHPC Papers.

44. Tabulations of the Chicago Urban League's "social problems" cases were found in the CUL Papers *Chicago Defender,* July 3, 1948; *Chicago Bee,* April 21, August 11, September 1, 1946; "General Housing Situation in Chicago" (mimeographed, n.d.), p. 4, MHPC Papers.

45. Innumerable editions of the *Chicago Defender* from February 1947 through at least May 1954 contain examples of such operations.

46. Duncan and Duncan, *The Negro Population,* p. 80.

47. Leonard Z. Breen, "Chicago: Its Housing Supply and Its Population Change, 1940–1950" (mimeographed, February 29, 1952), pp. 2–4, Aldis Papers; Chicago Community Inventory, "Census Statistics on Housing for Chicago, 1950, 1940" (mimeographed, May 1954), pp. 22, 30–1, The Library, UIC.

48. These figures meant that in 1940 the ratio of nonwhite-to white-occupied overcrowded units was 4 to 1; in 1950 it was 6 to 1. As nonwhites also had a higher proportion of one-person households, the ratio would have been even higher had it been calculated for multi-person households alone. See Duncan and Duncan, *The Negro Population,* p. 79.

49. Breen, "Chicago: Its Housing Supply," pp. 1–12; Chicago Community Inventory, "Census Statistics," pp. 22, 30–1.

50. When broken down by race, it was found that 13% of the white-occupied dwelling units were deficient in plumbing facilities, whereas 40% of the units occupied by nonwhites were similarly lacking. See "A Factual Report on Housing," n.d., p. 5, MI-IPC Papers; Breen, "Chicago: Its Housing Supply," p. 12.

51. Metropolitan Housing [and Planning] Council, *Biennial Report of the Metropolitan Housing Council: Activities in 1943–1944* (Chicago: n.p., 1944), p. 3.

52. Metropolitan Housing [and Planning] Council, The 1942 Annual Report (Chicago: n.p., 1943), pp. 8–9.

53. Metropolitan Housing [and Planning] Council, *Biennial Report . . . 1943–1944*, pp. 14–15, and "Report of the Committee on Substandard Housing to the Board of Governors of the Metropolitan Housing Council," June 24, 1940, pp. 14–15, MHPC Papers. The housing council also put out a pamphlet in 1954 entitled *The Road Back,* which reprinted a series of articles on slum conditions published in the *Chicago Daily News* from June 10, 1953, through the rest of the year.

54. Samplings taken from the *Chicago Bee* and the *Chicago Defender* provide numerous examples. See the *Bee* for February 2, 9, 1947, and the *Defender* for November 5, 12, 26, 1949, to cite just a very few. See also the *Chicago Daily News*, December 9, 1950; September 17, 1953; *Chicago Sun-Times*, December 10, 1950; January 30, February 20, May 14, 1958; *Chicago Tribune*, September 8, 1958; Metropolitan Housing [and Planning] Council, Minutes of the Regular Meeting of the Board of Governors, February 1, 1944, and Minutes of the Executive Committee Meeting, January 31, 1958, both in the MHPC Papers; "Report on 215–219 E. 31st Building," July 1949, CUL Papers; Joel D. Hunter to Mrs. Frederick H. Rubel, March 24, 1944, MHPC Papers.

55. *Chicago Sun-Times,* November 13, 1950; *Chicago Defender,* November 18, December 16, 1950.

56. John Bartlow Martin, "The Hickman Story," *Harper's Magazine* 197 (August 1948): 40–8.

57. Metropolitan Housing [and Planning] Council, *Biennial Report 1943–1944*, p. 3.

63. The rental for a two-room furnished apartment, which shared a kitchen and a toilet, in a tenement converted to black occupancy was $78 per month. In contrast, the rent for an apartment in Mayor Martin H. Kennelly's Gold Coast building, unfurnished but including an in-a-door bed, refrigerator, private bath, and kitchenette, was $74.50. See Weaver, *The Negro Ghetto*, p. 104n.

64. "The Growing Negro Middle Class," p. 2.

65. Illinois Inter-Racial Commission, First Biennial Report (Chicago: n.p., 1945), p. 58; CHR, Fourth Chicago Conference, p. 49; Duncan and Duncan, *The Negro Population*, pp. 9, 15–16, 252, 275; Rose Helper, *Racial Policies and Practices of Real Estate Brokers* (Minneapolis: University of Minnesota Press, 1969), p. 50; U.S. Commission on Civil Rights, Hearings, p. 729, "The Growing Negro Middle Class," p. 2; Metropolitan Housing [and Planning] Council, Housing Committee,

Draft of Statement, p. 10, Stanley Carlson Stevens, "The Urban Racial Border: Chicago, 1960" (Ph.D. dissertation, University of Illinois at Urbana, Champaign. 1972), pp. 87–90.

69. Helper, *Racial Policies*, p. 35; U.S. Commission on Civil Rights, Hearings, pp. 684–5.

70. Helper, *Racial Policies*, pp. 172–6.

71. Ibid., pp. 166–8; U.S. Commission on Civil Rights, *Hearings,* pp. 740–2, 746–7, 753–4, 759, 882.

72. Norris Vitchek, "Confessions of a Block Buster," reprint of a 1962 *Saturday Evening Post* article, Leon M. Despres Papers, CHS.

73. Mark J. Satter, "Land Contract Sales in Chicago: Security Turned Exploitation," Saul Alinsky Papers, Manuscript Collection, The Library, UIC; CHR, *Selling and Buying Real Estate in a Racially Changing Neighborhood: A Survey* (Chicago: n.p., n.d.), pp. 5, 8. See also E. F. Schietinger, "Racial Succession and Changing Property Values in Residential Chicago" (Ph.D. dissertation, University of Chicago, 1953), pp. 208–9, passim.

74. CHR, *Selling and Buying Real Estate,* pp. 9–10, Table 1, and passim; Helper, *Racial Policies,* pp. 177–80; CHR, "Questions and Answers on Housing (Preliminary Draft)," January 1958, *Greater Lawndale Conservation Commission Papers*, CHS.

75. CHR, Selling and Buying Real Estate, p. 10.

76. U.S. Commission on Civil Rights, *Hearings,* pp. 685–6.

77. Lea Taylor to Fred Hoehler, October 12, 1949, Chicago Commons Papers, CHS.

78. Metropolitan Housing and Planning Council, *The Road Back,* p. 17.

79. Lucille Sproggins to Sidney Williams, September 3, 1954, CLJL Papers.

80. Duncan and Duncan, *The Negro Population,* pp. 133–236, 238–40.

81. Metropolitan Housing [and Planning] Council, Report of the Activities for 1941 (Chicago: n.p., 1942), p. 3; Metropolitan Housing [and Planning] Council, Minutes of the Meeting, July 6, 1943; Metropolitan Housing [and Planning] Council, Biennial Report, 1943–1944, pp. 8–9, all in the MHPC Papers; *Chicago Bee*, January 14, 1945.

82. *Chicago Tribune,* July 2, 1953; *Housing News* 2 (November 1942), Aldis Papers; Metropolitan Housing [and Planning] Council, *The 1942 Annual Report* (Chicago: n.p., 1943), p. 7, MHPC Papers; Statement for *Daily News* by Alderman Robert E. Merriam, June 16,

1953, Robert E. Merriam Papers, the Department of Special Collections, University of Chicago Library; Memorandum of Meeting with General Smykal, October 15, 1953; Metropolitan Housing and Planning Council, Minutes of the Meeting of the Committee on the Reorganization of the Building Department, November 19, 1953; Memorandum from Jack Siegel to Earl Kribben, July 2, 1954; Metropolitan Housing and Planning Council, *The Road Back,* p. 29, all in the MHPC Papers.

83. Metropolitan Housing and Planning Council, "Report on the Major Violators of the Housing Code" (mimeographed, n.d.), pp. 1–2, 9, 24, 27, and passim; Memorandum from Jack Siegel to Dorothy Rubel, July 14, 1954; Miscellaneous Comments and Questions about the Housing Violations and the Court, November 15,1958; Joseph Pois to Richard J. Daley, August 25, 1955; Memorandum from Mary Wirth: Comments on the Court Hearings in Branch 31 of the Municipal Court, December 5, 1958; Memorandum from Mary Wirth to Dorothy Rubel, n.d.; Metropolitan Housing and Planning Council, Minutes of the Meeting of the Reorganization and Enforcement Committee with Mr. James Downs, Jr., January 31, 1955; Memorandum from Mary Wirth to the Committee on Enforcement, January 9, 1959, all in the MHPC Papers.

84. Vitchek, "Confessions," not paginated; *Chicago Daily News*, October 13–17, 19–22, 1959; Helper, Racial Policies, pp. 41–2, 182–4, and passim; U.S. Commission on Civil Rights, Hearings, p. 741.

85. *Chicago Defender,* September 11, 1943; March 22, 1947; Alvin Winder, "White Attitudes Towards Negro-White Interaction in an Area of Changing Racial Composition" (Ph.D. dissertation, University of Chicago, 1952), pp. 37–8, 42–3, 58, 87–8, 91, 98–9.

86. Lea Taylor to Dorothy Rubel, June 16, 1945, MHPC Papers; U.S. Commission on Civil Rights, *Hearings,* p. 685.

Conclusion

Public Policy Applications: Racial Exclusion and Remedial Policies

Policy Then

One of the earliest tools used to maintain the racial homogeneity of American suburbs during the first half of the twentieth century was racially restrictive covenants. A restrictive covenant is a provision in the deed to a house that limits how the owner may use the property. Suburban real estate developers often used restrictive covenants when subdividing their land to control future development by ensuring, for instance, that only single-family dwellings would be built or that such dwellings would be set back a certain distance from the street. Restrictive covenants could be enforced by surrounding property owners who had similar covenants in the deeds to their houses.

A racially restrictive covenant is a provision in the deed that explicitly prohibits homeowners to sell or rent their homes to minorities, most commonly African Americans and Jews. In 1926, the U.S. Supreme Court declined to hear a case challenging the constitutionality of racially restrictive covenants on the ground that the Equal Protection Clause of the Fourteenth Amendment only applied to state action, not contractual arrangements between private parties. In light of that ruling, the use of racially restrictive covenants proliferated throughout the country. Below is an example that appeared in the deed to a house in a suburb of Seattle.

It was not until 1948 in the case of *Shelly v. Kraemer* that the Supreme Court changed its mind and struck down racially restrictive covenants as a violation of the Equal Protection Clause, finding that a state court's enforcement of such a clause constituted the requisite state action. But by then the extensive reliance on racially restrictive covenants had established a deeply entrenched pattern of racial segregation in suburban neighborhoods. Even after the ruling in *Shelly v. Kraemer*, housing discrimination remained rampant until Congress passed the Fair Housing Act of 1968, which helped reduce at least the more overt forms of racial exclusion.

Box 5.1   **Restrictive Covenant, Laurelhurst Neighborhood, Seattle**

Seattle Neighborhood: Laurelhurst

Subdivision: Laguna Vista

Restriction: *No person or persons of **Asiatic, African or Negro blood, lineage, or extraction** shall be permitted to occupy a portion of said property, or any building thereon except a domestic servant or servants who may actually and in good faith be employed by white occupants of such premises.*

Source: Courtesy of the Seattle Civil Rights & Labor History Project, "Special Section Segregated Seattle," http://depts.washington.edu/civilr/covenants.htm.

Policy Now

As the pace of suburbanization intensified in the years after World War II, many suburban municipalities utilized their zoning codes to exclude undesired uses of land and undesired groups of people—namely, minorities and the poor. In 1971, a group of African Americans led by a day care teacher named Ethel Lawrence and several civil rights organizations filed a lawsuit against the township of Mount Laurel, New Jersey, a suburb of Philadelphia, after its zoning board had denied a petition for a proposed development of 36 affordable garden apartments. In a landmark decision, the Supreme Court of New Jersey ruled in 1975 that all municipalities in the state, not just Mount Laurel, had an affirmative obligation to provide their "fair share of the present and prospective regional need" for low- and moderate-income housing.

After much foot-dragging and evasion by New Jersey's suburban jurisdictions, the state supreme court reaffirmed its previous decision in a second major ruling in 1983 and this time added incentives for compliance, including a "builder's remedy" that enabled local courts to approve development proposals that contained a sufficient percentage of affordable housing units (usually 20 percent) if a municipality did not have a satisfactory plan to meet its fair share requirement. Critics attacked the decision as blatant judicial activism. But two years later, the New Jersey state legislature enacted legislation that acknowledged the constitutional obligation for municipalities to produce affordable housing and created a state agency to determine each municipality's allotment based on a formula. Under the law, a municipality could transfer up to 50 percent of its fair share obligation to another municipality within the region—often an inner-ring suburb or city—along with a payment negotiated between the two municipalities. The use of so-called regional contribution agreements by some jurisdictions undermined the goal of encouraging economic and racial diversity throughout the state but the policy still led to a substantial increase in overall affordable housing: 60,000 homes for low- and moderate-income households with another 40,000 in the pipeline.

Courtesy of Fair Share Housing Development/Mark Lozier (photographer)

Ethel R. Lawrence Homes, Mount Laurel, New Jersey

Recent research by the sociologist Douglas Massey and his collaborators shows that affordable housing developments like the Ethel R. Lawrence Homes, a complex of 140 single-family homes that opened in Mount Laurel in 2000, have resulted in higher rates of employment and income and significantly reduced welfare dependency for adult residents while improving the educational performance of the children who live there. Meanwhile, the anxieties of neighbors about affordable housing have proved unfounded. Even developments like the Ethel R. Lawrence Homes that target very low-income populations did not lead to higher crime rates, lower property values, or deteriorating schools. With respect to these measures, Massey and his collaborators found that there were no differences between Mount Laurel and other predominantly white suburbs within the region that had not constructed affordable housing.

Additional Resources

Brick by Brick: A Civil Rights Story. Documentary film on racial discrimination in housing and public schools in Yonkers, New York (Kavanagh Productions, 2007).

Richard R. W. Brooks and Carol M. Rose, *Saving the Neighborhood: Racially Restrictive Covenants, Law, and Social Norms* (Cambridge, MA: Harvard University Press, 2013).

Fair Share Housing Center. Web site for the organization that has been in the forefront of implementing the *Mount Laurel* doctrine. http://fairsharehousing.org.

Robert M. Fogelson, *Bourgeois Nightmares: Suburbia, 1870-1930* (New Haven: Yale University Press, 2005).

Douglas S. Massey, Len Albright, Rebecca Casciano, Elizabeth Derickson, and David N. Kinsey, *Climbing Mount Laurel: The Struggle for Affordable Housing and Social Mobility in an American Suburb* (Princeton, NJ: Princeton University Press, 2013).

Evan McKenzie, *Privatopia: Homeowner Associations and the Rise of Residential Private Government* (New Haven: Yale University Press, 1994).

National Fair Housing Alliance. A public interest organization that seeks to eliminate housing discrimination in metropolitan areas. www.nationalfairhousing.org.

Eric J. Oliver, *Democracy in Suburbia* (Princeton, NJ: Princeton University Press, 2001).

Seattle Civil Rights and Labor History Project. Data base of racially restrictive covenants in Seattle, Washington, metropolitan area. http://depts.washington.edu/civilr/covenants.htm.

Discussion Questions

1. To what extent is the racial and class composition of suburbs a consequence of public policy as opposed to the personal preferences and choices of individual citizens and families?

2. What do you think of the *Mount Laurel* doctrine as a way to remedy years of exclusionary zoning in suburban towns and villages? What are the pros and cons of this approach?

3. Is racial and class segregation in metropolitan areas diminishing?

4. What impact does suburbanization have on central cities today?

5. Do Americans perceive of suburbs and cities differently today compared with several decades ago? If so, why might that matter for the future of metropolitan areas?

Chapter 6

Deindustrialization and the Rise of the Postindustrial City

Introduction

During the middle of the twentieth century, cities throughout much of the United States, but particularly in the northeast and midwest, suffered staggering declines in manufacturing jobs. To some extent, this resulted from increasing mechanization of industrial plants to improve efficiency and production. But the main reason for the loss of blue-collar jobs in cities concerned corporate decisions to shut down factories and relocate to outlying suburbs, the Sunbelt, or other countries altogether.

One impetus for plant relocations was the need to ramp up output at a time when the U.S. economy was booming. But expansion and upgrading of the typical, multistory factory in congested, urban neighborhoods would be difficult and expensive. There simply was not enough available land to accommodate the demand for modern plant designs; assembly-line production techniques required sprawling, one-story facilities with ample warehouse space for storage. By contrast, many suburban jurisdictions offered spacious parcels at relatively low cost.[1]

Deindustrialization accelerated during the years after World War II aided in no small measure by the federal government's support for highway construction that greatly facilitated the interstate trucking of manufactured goods. Federal spending on highway construction jumped from $79 million in 1946 to $429 million in 1950 before surging again to $2.9 billion in 1960 following passage of the Interstate Highway Act of 1956. Along with building highways that radiated out from the downtown business district, many states used their federal funds to construct beltways around their central cities and those beltways quickly became magnets for manufacturing firms searching for room to grow and convenient access to interstate commerce. In the first year after the completion of Boston's beltway, Route 128, in 1957, ninety-nine industrial plants employing 17,000 people moved to sites along that transit corridor and hundreds more soon followed.[2]

Some corporations decided to move their plants not just out of the city but out of the region. State and local officials in the Sunbelt launched initiatives to lure factories away from the Snowbelt (or Rustbelt) by dangling a host of incentives such as tax breaks, reduced utility rates, subsidies for land acquisition and infrastructure development, and, most important, relatively low wages in a political environment that had long discouraged union organizing. The practice of "smokestack chasing" became a prominent economic development strategy for the Sunbelt, and one exploited by industrial leaders to keep labor costs and workplace activism under control.[3]

The impact of deindustrialization in Rustbelt cities was crippling. The sociologist William Julius Wilson found that between 1967 and 1987 Detroit lost 108,000 factory jobs while Philadelphia lost 160,000, Chicago 326,000, and New York 520,000. In each of these cities, the manufacturing sector fell between 51 and 64 percent.[4] The full impact of industrial decline extended far beyond the closing of a factory. Local businesses that had provided parts and supplies to the plant had their contracts terminated and often shut down themselves. Retail stores in the neighborhood suffered as employees of the factory no longer solicited their business; as families moved away, the customer base of many stores evaporated. Community institutions such as schools, churches, synagogues, and social clubs suffered immensely. Some urban neighborhoods were so devastated that they came to resemble ghost towns made up of abandoned homes and boarded-up storefronts. Thomas Sugrue's analysis of the causes and effects of deindustrialization in Detroit in **Reading 6-1** captures the wrenching toll that plant closings exacted in numerous cities, with African Americans bearing a particularly heavy burden.[5]

The decentralizing forces that were carrying residents and jobs away from central cities to outlying suburbs had been operating for decades starting in the late nineteenth century. But by the 1940s many city leaders realized, as Jon C. Teaford discusses in **Reading 6-2**, that the twin engines of suburbanization and deindustrialization posed a serious challenge to the vitality, and even survival, of many urban centers.

Faced with such a calamitous situation, civic and business elites came together in a concerted effort to chart a path toward urban revitalization. Many of these prominent leaders were the chief executive officers of major corporations and financial firms, the managing partners of prestigious law firms, the publishers of leading newspapers, the heads of major department stores, and the presidents of universities and hospitals—and most were based in and around the downtown business districts of cities. Hence, it is no accident that such corporate and institutional leaders believed that the key to success was the rejuvenation of downtown and the downtown-based economy. They recognized that downtown business districts had languished because of a lack of investment during the previous two decades. Commercial office construction, for instance, had all but ground to a halt during the Depression and World War II. In their minds, the major cause of declining property values and the largest impediment to new capital infusion were the unsightly factories and warehouses and aging working-class neighborhoods that enveloped the downtown core.[6] Starting in the 1940s and then continuing into the 1950s and 1960s, civic and business leaders coalesced into powerful advocacy organizations to push a common agenda. In **Reading 6-3**, Joel Rast offers an illustrative case study of business advocacy in support of redeveloping downtown Chicago.[7]

The crucial policy embraced by dozens of U.S. cities in response to decentralization came to be known as urban renewal. This sounds like a generic term (like urban redevelopment), but it actually had a more precise meaning and was related to a specific act of federal legislation. Urban renewal programs were authorized and funded by the Housing Act of 1949. The law was intended to remedy the dearth of quality, affordable housing in American cities through a partnership among the federal government, city governments, and private developers. Local redevelopment authorities would designate certain areas characterized by high concentrations of poverty and physically dilapidated buildings as "blighted" and then use their power of eminent domain to obtain legal title to the blighted land. Such "takings" of private property were permissible under the Constitution so long as the governmental entity provided owners with fair market compensation and the resulting use of land was for a "public purpose." The next step in the redevelopment process would involve demolition of frayed or deteriorating homes, apartment buildings, and other structures on land now owned by the city followed by the sale of assembled parcels to private developers who would then construct new, affordable housing.[8]

Cities had a huge incentive to establish urban renewal programs because they were heavily subsidized by Washington, D.C. Under the Housing Act of 1949, the federal government supplied generous grants and loans to write down the cost of acquiring and removing blighted property within designated redevelopment zones. By the same token, private developers were also motivated to participate since city governments were seizing and assembling large parcels of land and then selling them at discounted prices. In short, this was a federal program that galvanized the formation of potent public–private partnerships eager to pursue extensive revitalization.[9]

However, urban renewal did not unfold as housing activists and some planners had originally intended. It soon became apparent that city officials and business leaders were primarily interested in clearing decaying areas around the downtown business district, not to create new subsidized housing, but to promote commercial redevelopment that would enhance property values and spur capital investment. Taking advantage of loopholes in the law, as well as subsequent amendments by Congress, advocates of downtown development in the public and private sectors implemented urban renewal programs that yielded myriad nonresidential projects such as office towers, hotels, convention centers, parking garages, and university and medical complexes. And to further strengthen the downtown business district as the economic hub of the metropolitan area, urban renewal was also used to construct and improve expressways linking downtown with outlying suburbs and the interstate highway system. City leaders championed urban renewal as a smart economic development strategy that anticipated the inevitable shift away from a neighborhood-based, industrial economy to a downtown-centric, postindustrial economy based on corporate services, finance, real estate, insurance, and technology.[10]

The costs of urban renewal soon became painfully apparent. To make room for downtown expansion, local redevelopment authorities employed a loose interpretation of "blighted" in designating areas for acquisition, demolition, and redevelopment. City planners and business leaders typically viewed older but still vibrant, working-class neighborhoods adjacent to downtown business districts as decaying slums, and thus impediments to growth.[11] Such assessments were later contested by scholars such as Herbert Gans, whose ethnographic study of Boston's West End—a neighborhood slated for demolition and redevelopment—revealed a physically worn but thriving community of longtime residents and small business owners.[12] Moreover, redevelopment authorities disproportionately targeted black and Latino neighborhoods for demolition such that critics of the policy grimly came to refer to urban renewal as "Negro clearance."[13] Displaced residents would often be relocated to racially segregated public housing developments in sections of the city characterized by a growing concentration of poverty and limited access to good schools and employment opportunities.[14]

The forced evictions of thousands of residents and the decimation of entire neighborhoods eventually provoked strong opposition from the grass roots. So-called blighted areas marked for demolition became battlegrounds of resistance. As the civil rights movement gained momentum during the 1960s, urban renewal came under increasing attack and gradually faded until it was merged into the Community Development Block Grant program in 1974.[15]

In conclusion, it is important to note that not all cities relied so heavily on downtown-centric revitalization policies in response to the debilitating decentralization of residents and jobs. Guian A. McKee shows in **Reading 6-4**, for example, how Philadelphia embarked on an ambitious program during the 1950s to retain and attract manufacturing firms, a policy that substantially slowed the pace of deindustrialization even though it missed opportunities to address rampant racial discrimination in the industrial sector at a time of mounting civil rights activism. McKee's research suggests that alternative paths to urban revitalization might have been pursued.[16]

Notes

1. John F. Kain, "The Distribution and Movement of Jobs and Industry," in *The Metropolitan Enigma: Inquiries into the Nature and Dimensions of America's "Urban Crisis,"* ed. James Q. Wilson (Cambridge, MA: Harvard University Press, 1968). Another obstacle to plant expansion dates back to the reform era when some municipal governments, influenced by planning principles of the City Beautiful movement, discouraged the spread of manufacturing anywhere near downtown districts to promote grand boulevards, monumental civic institutions, and inspiring public spaces. Domenic Vitello, "Machine Building and City Building: Urban Planning and Industrial Restructuring in Philadelphia, 1894–1928," *Journal of Urban History*, 34 (3), 2008.

2. Howard P. Chudacoff and Judith E. Smith, *The Evolution of American Urban Society*, 3rd ed. (Englewood Cliffs, NJ: Prentice Hall, 1988).

3. For an overview of policy tools used to lure capital investment, see chapter 6, "Supply-Side Incentives to Development: Business Climate Policies" in Peter Eisinger, *The Rise of the Entrepreneurial State: State and Local Economic Development Policy in the United States* (Madison: University of Wisconsin Press, 1988); Thomas J. Sugrue, *The Origins of the Urban Crisis: Race and Inequality in Postwar Detroit* (Princeton, NJ: Princeton University Press, 1996).

4. William Julius Wilson, *When Work Disappears: The World of the New Urban Poor* (New York: Vintage Books, 1996).

5. See also Barry Bluestone and Bennett Harrison, *The Deindustrialization of America: Plant Closings, Community Abandonment, and the Dismantling of Basic Industry* (New York: Basic Books, 1982).

6. Robert M. Fogelson, *Downtown: Its Rise and Fall, 1880–1950* (New Haven: Yale University Press, 2001); see also Alison Isenberg, *Downtown America: A History of the Place and the People Who Made It* (Chicago: University of Chicago Press, 2004).

7. Another key component of the business-led downtown growth coalition were building trades unions anticipating a plethora of construction jobs. See also John H. Mollenkopf, *The Contested City* (Princeton: Princeton University Press, 1983) and Robert H. Salisbury, "The New Convergence of Power in Urban Politics," *Journal of Politics*, 26, 1964.

8. Although downtown business leaders tended to be at the forefront of large-scale urban renewal projects, recent scholars have demonstrated how progressive reformers during the early twentieth century helped lay the foundation for this policy initiative by strongly backing the goals of slum clearance and housing redevelopment, while eradicating the blight connected with the city's industrial past. Refer to Samuel Zipp, "The Roots and Routes of Urban Renewal," *Journal of Urban History*, 39 (3), 2013. Indeed, urban renewal programs sometimes enjoyed the support of liberals and community activists. See Joel Schwartz, *The New York Approach: Robert Moses, Urban Liberals, and the Redevelopment of the Inner City* (Columbus: Ohio State University Press, 1993).

9. The earliest public–private partnership of this type appeared in Pittsburgh when the corporate titan Richard King Mellon mobilized other local business elites and formed the Allegheny Conference on Community Development. That group collaborated with a new mayor, David Lawrence, to transform the city's downtown business district at the confluence of the Allegheny, Monongahela, and Ohio Rivers—an area known as the Golden Triangle. Pittsburgh's path to downtown revitalization was soon emulated by many other U.S. cities. Roy Lubove, *Twentieth-Century Pittsburgh: Government, Business, and Environmental Change* (New York: John Wiley & Sons, 1969).

10. Marc Weiss, "The Origins and Legacy of Urban Renewal" in *Federal Housing Policy and Programs, Past and Present*, ed. J. Paul Mitchell (New Brunswick, NJ: Rutgers University Press, 1985); Mark I. Gelfand, *A Nation of Cities: The Federal Government and Urban America, 1933–1965* (New York: Oxford University Press, 1975); and Scott A. Greer, *Urban Renewal and American Cities: The Dilemmas of Democratic Intervention* (New York: Bobbs-Merrill, 1965).

11. For an early defense of "slum clearance" by one of its most prominent practitioners, see Robert Moses, "Slums and City Planning," *Atlantic Monthly* (January, 1945).

12. Herbert J. Gans, *The Urban Villagers: Group and Class in the Life of Italian-Americans* (New York: The Free Press, 1962).

13. Martin Anderson, *The Federal Bulldozer: A Critical Analysis of Urban Renewal, 1949–1962* (Cambridge: MIT Press, 1964).

14. Samuel Zipp, *Manhattan Projects: The Rise and Fall of Urban Renewal in Cold War New York* (New York: Oxford University Press, 2010). In some cases, leaders of black communities and civil rights organizations endorsed urban renewal projects that called for extensive demolition and displacement on the condition that redevelopment would afford new and improved housing for uprooted residents in desegregated neighborhoods; such promises often went unfulfilled. Refer to Andrew R. Highsmith, "Demolition Means Progress: Urban Renewal, Local Politics, and State-Sanctioned Ghetto Formation in Flint, Michigan," *Journal of Urban History*, 35 (3), 2009.

15. The most famous critique of urban renewal came from Jane Jacobs, *The Death and Life of Great American Cities* (New York: Random House, 1961); for a recent overview of the extensive scholarship on urban renewal, see Eric Avila and Mark H. Rose, "Race, Culture, Politics and Urban Renewal: An Introduction," *Journal of Urban History*, 35 (3), 2009. Another period of extensive inner-city redevelopment characterized by forced evictions, gentrification, and displacement of lower-income residents during the 1990s and 2000s prompted some scholars to argue that the federal government, through policies like HOPE VI (Housing Opportunities for People Everywhere) had essentially returned to the earlier era of urban renewal. Refer to Edward G. Goetz, "Where Have All the Towers Gone? The Dismantling of Public Housing in U.S. Cities," *Journal of Urban Affairs*, 33 (3), 2011; Susan S. Fainstein, "The Return of Urban Renewal," *Harvard Design Magazine*, 22 (2005). Others, however, note key differences such as the less prominent role of the federal government and the mixed outcomes for inner-city residents. Derek S. Hyra, "Conceptualizing the New Urban Renewal: Comparing the Past to the Present," *Urban Affairs Review*, 48 (4), 2012.

16. Other scholars have advanced the argument that a modified industrial development agenda was feasible and might have preserved thousands of working-class jobs. Refer to Joel Rast, "Manufacturing Industrial Decline: The Politics of Economic Change in Chicago, 1955–1998," *Journal of Urban Affairs*, 23 (2), 2001. Indeed, the recent revival of some rustbelt cities that have retained manufacturing as at least one component of their economic development strategy supports the position that deindustrialization was hardly an inevitable outcome. Refer to Henry J. Mayer and Michael R. Greenberg, "Coming Back from Economic Despair: Case Studies of Small- and Medium-Sized American Cities," *Economic Development Quarterly*, 15 (3), 2001; George Hobor, "Surviving the Era of Deindustrialization: The New Geography of the Urban Rust Belt," *Journal of Urban Affairs*, 35 (4), 2013.

6-1 "'The Damning Mark of False Prosperities': The Deindustrialization of Detroit"*

Thomas Sugrue

The Origins of the Urban Crisis: Race and Inequality in Postwar Detroit

The Intersection of Grand Boulevard, John R Street, and the Milwaukee and Junction Railroad, just four miles north of downtown Detroit, seemed the heartbeat of the industrial metropolis in the 1940s. Within a two-square-mile area extending along the Grand Trunk and Michigan Central railroads was one of the most remarkable concentrations of industry in the United States. To the north was Detroit's second largest automobile factory, Dodge Main, which employed over thirty-five thousand workers in a five-story factory building with over 4.5 million square feet of floor space. Studebaker had a plant at the corner of Piquette Avenue and Brush where it produced its luxury sedans. Just to the north, on Russell Street, was a cavernous redbrick building that housed Murray Auto Body, a major independent producer of automobile chassis. Packard Motors produced cars in a sprawling ninety-five-building complex that extended for nearly a mile along East Grand Boulevard. At shift change time, the area came to a virtual standstill, as cars, buses, and pedestrians clogged the streets. The whole area was often covered in a grayish haze, a murky combination of pollutants from the factories and car exhaust. Even at night the area bustled, as the factory windows emitted an eerie "blue-green glow," and echoed with the "screams and clank of the machinery."[1]

By the late 1950s, this industrial landscape had become almost unrecognizable. The Milwaukee-Junction area was hard hit by layoffs and plant closings. Murray Auto Body, Packard, and Studebaker shut down between 1953 and 1957. Dodge Main cut its work force by several thousand in the late 1950s. The shells of several empty multistory factories stood as cavernous hulks on the horizon, unobscured by smoke and haze on all but the foggiest days. Dozens of taverns and restaurants that had catered to workers were boarded up. And the neighborhoods surrounding the plants, which had housed thousands of industrial workers, had quickly become run-down. Property values fell, because plant closings deprived the small frame houses on the East Side of their only real advantage, their proximity to the workplace. Their largely white residents followed the flight of jobs to suburban and exurban areas. Traffic on the new Chrysler and Ford Freeways whisked past the former plants, the drivers oblivious to the blighted landscape around them. Similar rotting industrial areas could be found throughout the city, most notably on the city's far East Side, near Connor Road between Gratiot and Jefferson, where Mack, Briggs, Hudson, and Motor Products plants had closed. Even the area around the enormous Ford River Rouge plant lost some of its luster, as whole sections of the plant were modernized and thousands of workers who had patronized local stores, bars, and restaurants were laid off or transferred.

The 1950s marked a decisive turning point in the development of the city—a systematic restructuring of the local economy from which the city never fully recovered. Detroit's economy experienced enormous fluctuations in the 1950s. Between 1949 and 1960, the city suffered four major recessions. Because the

*Endnotes and references have been omitted. Please consult the original source.

auto industry was tremendously sensitive to shifts in consumer demand it weathered recessions badly. The unpredictability of demand for automobiles, especially in times of economic uncertainty, had serious ramifications for Detroit's working class. A slight shift in interest rates or a small drop in car sales resulted in immediate layoffs.[2] That the auto industry was especially vulnerable to economic vagaries was, however, nothing new. What was new in the 1950s was that auto manufacturers and suppliers permanently reduced their Detroit-area work forces, closed plants, and relocated to other parts of the country.

Looking out onto the city in 1952, social welfare worker Mary Jorgensen observed that "Detroit is in the doldrums." But what she observed, unknowingly, were the first signs of long-term economic problems that beset Detroit, not just a momentary economic lull. More important than the periodic downswings that plagued the city's economy was the beginning of a long-term and steady decline in manufacturing employment that affected Detroit and almost all other major northeastern and midwestern industrial cities. Between 1947 and 1963, Detroit lost 134,000 manufacturing jobs, while its population of working-aged men and women actually increased. Workers who had enjoyed a modicum of stability in the boom years of the 1940s suffered repeated bouts of unemployment in the 1950s. Laid-off workers were also consumers whose loss of buying power rippled throughout the city's economy, affecting local businesses from department stores and groceries to restaurants and bowling alleys. The growing gap between job seekers and job opportunities would have profound ramifications in subsequent decades.[3]

Capital Mobility

The transformation of Detroit's economy in the 1950s is best understood from a long-term perspective. Throughout the nineteenth and early twentieth centuries, American industry followed a pattern of centralization. Considerations of topography, access to transportation routes (either water or railroad), and the availability of raw materials determined plant location. The process of deindustrialization—the closing, downsizing, and relocation of plants and sometimes whole industries—accelerated throughout the twentieth century. Advances in communication and transportation, the transformation of industrial

technology, the acceleration of regional and international economic competition, and the expansion of industry in low-wage regions, especially the South, reshaped the geography of American industrial cities. Beginning with the New Deal, the federal government channeled a disproportionate amount of resources to the South, culminating in the Sunbelt-dominated military-industrial complex of the Cold War era. Postwar highway construction, spurred by state and local expressway initiatives in the 1940s, and federally funded highway construction after 1956, made central industrial location less necessary by facilitating the distribution of goods over longer distances. Companies also moved to gain access to markets in other sections of the country, especially rapidly growing areas like California and the urban West.[4]

The forces of capital mobility reshaped the landscape of industrial America. New factories appeared on rural hillsides, in former cornfields, and in cleared forests, and the shells of old manufacturing buildings loomed over towns and cities that were depopulated when businesses relocated production in more profitable places. In the 1920s, New England textile towns were ravaged by the flight of mills to the Piedmont South, presaging similar shifts of capital that would transform much of the industrial North later in the century. By midcentury, what had been a trickle of manufacturing jobs out of the industrial heartland became a flood. In the 1950s, the flight of industry and the loss of jobs reconfigured the landscape of the most prominent industrial cities across the region that came to be known as the Rust Belt. Detroit, Chicago, New York, Pittsburgh, Philadelphia, Baltimore, Trenton, Boston, Buffalo, and St. Louis all lost hundreds of thousands of manufacturing jobs beginning in the 1950s, as firms reduced employment in center-city plants, replaced workers with new automated technology, and constructed new facilities in suburban and semirural areas, in medium-sized cities, often in less industrialized states or regions, and even in other countries.[5]

Automobile manufacturers were in the vanguard of corporate decentralization. The growth of a national and international market for automobiles led firms like Ford and General Motors to construct plants throughout the country. Technological advances, especially in transportation, made industrial decentralization possible. Yet decentralization was not simply a response to the inexorable demands of the market; it was an outgrowth of the social relations of production itself. Decentralization was an effective means for employers to control increasing labor costs and weaken powerful trade unions. The deconcentration of plants gave employers the upper hand during periods of labor unrest. General Motors, the first firm to deconcentrate production on a wide scale, built new plants in the 1930s in rural parts of the country, as a means of reducing wages and inhibiting union militancy in manufacturing cities like Detroit, Pontiac, and Flint, where most of its facilities had been located. The early decentralization experiments had little impact on Detroit. The city's share of national automobile production remained large throughout the first half of the twentieth century. But the pre-World War II decentralization efforts foreshadowed the auto industry's aggressive efforts to deconcentrate production and reduce its Detroit workforce after World War II.[6]

In the late 1940s and 1950s, Detroit's economy began to feel the effects of the mobility of the Big Three automobile manufacturers—Ford, General Motors, and, to a lesser extent, Chrysler. Between 1946 and 1956, General Motors spent $3.4 billion on new plants and facilities. Equally ambitious in its restructuring plans was Ford, which made aggressive decentralization the central part of its postwar corporate policy. From the end of World War II through 1957, Ford alone spent over $2.5 billion nationwide on a program of plant expansion. Chrysler, whose finances for capital expansion were small compared to its rivals, still spent $700 million on plant expansion in the same period.[7] Between 1947 and 1958, the Big Three built twenty-five new plants in the metropolitan Detroit area, all of them in suburban communities, most more than fifteen miles from the center city.[8] The lion's share of new plants, or "runaway shops," as Detroiters called them, however, went to small- and medium-sized cities in the Midwest, like Lima, Lorain, and Walton Hills, Ohio; Kokomo and Indianapolis, Indiana; and to the South and West, especially California.[9] In 1950, 56 percent of all automobile employment in the United States was in Michigan; by 1960, that figure had fallen to 40 percent.[10] As they expanded in other regions of the country, the major automotive producers reduced employment in their older Detroit-area plants.

A major reason that employers cited for the construction of new plants outside Detroit was the lack of available land for expansion. With new assembly-line technology, auto companies found the multistory plants of the 1910s and 1920s outdated. A few plants in the 1930s, and all new postwar auto plants, were built on one level. As more workers commuted to their jobs by car (71 percent of manufacturing employees in 1955 went to work by private car), firms also looked for large sites to accommodate massive parking lots. In addition, after World War II, Detroit lacked large sites with railroad frontage. A 1951 survey found only 367.5 acres of undeveloped land adjacent to railroad lines. The land was scattered about in 36 parcels, the largest site covering only 54 acres. The entire stretch of land abutting the Detroit Terminal railroad between Highland Park and Dearborn was fully developed; the Wabash Railroad line had only 48.5 acres of undeveloped frontage on the East Side and only 2.1 acres on the West Side. These small sites were simply insufficient for any large-scale factory construction. As a 1956 report noted, expanding firms could find "elbow room" only in the "outlying fringe areas."[11]

First to follow the auto industry out of the city were auto-related industries, in particular machine tool manufacturers, metalworking firms, and parts manufacturers. Between 1950 and 1956, 124 manufacturing firms located on the green fields of Detroit's suburbs; 55 of them had moved out of Detroit. Leading the flight were metals-related firms—manufacturers of metalworking tools, wire, stampings, and dies. These small plants (most with between eight and fifty workers) employed about 20 percent of Detroit-area workers in 1950, forming the second largest category of employment in the city after automobile production. It is impossible to calculate the number of metal and auto parts firms that moved outside the Detroit metropolitan area altogether, but undoubtedly many followed auto plants to their new locations in other parts of the country. The mobility of large auto producers and small firms alike reconfigured Detroit's industrial landscape, leaving empty factories and vacant lots behind, and bringing runaway shops to areas that just a few years earlier had been farms.[12]

Yet it was not foreordained that the auto companies would construct single-story automobile plants and downsize or abandon their older multistory factory complexes, nor was it inevitable that smaller machine tool and parts firms would prefer plants in outlying areas. The assumption that companies in the postwar period had no choice but to move to sprawling suburban and rural sites, surrounded by acres of parking lots and manicured lawns, is wrongly based in an ahistorical argument about the inevitability and neutrality of technological decisions. Industrial location policy was not a neutral response to market forces or an inexorable consequence of economic progress. Corporations made decisions about plant location and employment policy in a specific political, cultural, and institutional context, in the case of postwar Detroit in the aftermath of the rise of a powerful union movement and in the midst of a shop-floor struggle over work rules and worker control.[13]

Automation

The most important force that restructured Detroit's economy after World War II was the advent of new automated processes in the automobile, auto parts, and machine tool industries. In the late 1940s and 1950s, many Detroit industries, ranging from major automobile manufacturers to small tool and die firms, embraced automation. Automation had roots in earlier technological innovations in the automobile industry: it was the most refined application of the Fordist system of production.[14] In the wake of the long General Motors strike of 1946, GM began to experiment with labor-reducing machinery in its Flint Buick plant. Ford, however, led the automotive industry in experimentation with automation. In 1947, Ford set up an "Automation Department" to direct the reorganization of its manufacturing operations; its competitors and many other industries followed suit over the next fifteen years.

Automation offered two major benefits to manufacturers: it promised both to increase output and to reduce labor costs. Chrysler executive Harry R. Bentley described the purpose of automation as the "optimum use of machines to produce high-volume, high-quality products at the lowest possible cost." Although automation's advocates exaggerated its utility and underestimated its costs, automation sometimes did have dramatic effects. Before the introduction of automated engine production at Ford's Cleveland

plant, it took 117 workers to produce 154 engine blocks per hour; after automation the same output required a mere 41 workers.[15]

Industrialists touted automation as a way to improve working conditions and workers' standard of living. Del S. Harder, a Ford vice president and Detroit's most energetic proponent of automation, argued that "the era of automation is nothing more than a continuation of the industrial revolution which greatly increased our national wealth . . . and helped bring about the highest standard of living in the world." In Harder's view, automation would improve working conditions, reduce hours, and improve workplace safety. It was simply "a better way to do the job."[16]

Certainly automated production replaced some of the more dangerous and onerous factory jobs. At Ford, automation eliminated "mankilling," a task that demanded high speed and involved tremendous risk. "Mankilling" required a worker to remove hot coil springs from a coiling machine, lift them to chest height, turn around, and lower them into a quench tank, all within several seconds. In Ford's stamping plants, new machines loaded and unloaded presses, another relatively slow, unsafe, and physically demanding job before automation. Here automation offered real benefits to workers.[17]

Despite these occasional benefits, automation was primarily a weapon in the employers' antilabor arsenal. Through automation, employers attempted to reassert control over the industrial process, chipping away at the control over production that workers had gained through intricately negotiated work rules. Manufacturers hoped that self-regulating, computerized machinery would eliminate worker-led slowdowns, soldiering, and sabotage on the line. Contended one of automation's advocates: "Changing times have raised the idea around Detroit" that in the future, industrialists would look to "how to get the most out of machines rather than how to get the most out of people. Personnel men of the future, they say, may be automation experts." Automation would lower the risk "of considerable damage to parts through worker carelessness." Automation also provided engineers and plant managers a seemingly foolproof way to reduce industry's dependence on labor and reduce labor costs. Above all, automation counteracted the "increasing cost of labor . . . given a sharp hike by recent Reuther assistance."[18]

Corporate leaders bluntly stated that automation would ensure that they retained the upper hand in labor-management relations. Only a little more than a decade after the emergence of the UAW, in a period of tremendous labor strength, automation was a formidable tool for management. A manager in the newly automated Ford engine plant in Cleveland reminded UAW President Walter Reuther that "you are going to have trouble collecting union dues from all of these machines."[19] The reduction of the work force in certain plants after the introduction of automation eviscerated some of the most powerful bastions of labor activism.

Automation had a devastating impact on the work force at the Ford River Rouge plant. Rouge workers were represented by UAW Local 600, one of the most militant in the industry. The plant was also the largest employer of blacks in the Detroit area, and throughout the 1940s, a majority of black workers there consistently supported the left-wing caucus of the UAW. Slowdowns or wildcat strikes at the Rouge could paralyze Ford production nationwide. In key sections of the plant, like the Motor and Plastics buildings, workers had gained a great degree of control over production through a mix of custom and work rules. Ford officials, hoping to weaken union strength on the shop floor, targeted the Rouge for automation. In 1950, Rouge workers assembled all Ford and Mercury engines; by 1954, Ford had shifted all engine production to the new automated Cleveland plant. Rouge workers with seniority were transferred to Cleveland or to the new Dearborn Engine Plant that built engines for Lincolns. Stamping, machine casting, forging, steel production, glassmaking, and dozens of other operations were shifted from the Rouge to new Ford plants throughout the 1950s.[20] As a result, employment at the Rouge fell from 85,000 in 1945, to 54,000 in 1954, to only 30,000 in 1960.[21] . . .

Costs: Labor and Taxes

Automation was not the only force contributing to job loss in Detroit. Smaller firms that did not automate production or suffer automation-related job losses still fled the city in increasing numbers in the 1950s. Labor relations were especially important in motivating firms to relocate outside of Detroit, or to expand facilities outside of the city. Employers left industrial centers with high labor costs for regions where they could exploit cheap, nonunion labor. One such firm, Ex-Cell-O, a major machine tool manufacturer, built six new plants in rural Indiana and Ohio in the 1950s, and none in metropolitan Detroit. Ex-Cell-O's president, H. G. Bixby, argued in 1960 that the reason for the failure of firms like his to expand in metropolitan Detroit was that "there was something seriously wrong with our business climate." Bixby blamed union activity for the flight of industry from Detroit. The "militant and venomous attitude toward industry has and will continue to limit job opportunity. . . . Industries, like people, will not go where they are insulted and vilified daily. If Michigan labor union leadership is seriously interested in job opportunity for their members, they must change their attitude from one of conflict to one of cooperation with industry."[41] Forty-nine percent of Michigan industrialists interviewed in 1961 felt that "the labor situation" was worse in 1960 than it had been ten years earlier.[42]

Wage costs were also an important consideration in plant location, especially for small firms. From the 1950s through the 1970s, high wage costs ranked first in small manufacturers' complaints about the Detroit business climate. One small industrialist lamented that "the unions are so strong that they have more influence than they should have. Make unreasonable demands and get them." In his words, "Unions have killed a lot of small industries. They raise union rates. This means costs go up and then prices have to go up. Then a small firm cannot compete. And that is the end." One small Michigan firm opened a new plant in Alabama, citing "labor demands" and the "wage rate" as reasons for leaving Detroit.[43] Fruehauf Trailer also moved out of Detroit to cut labor costs. In 1950, it laid off its thirty-five hundred Detroit workers, and opened a new plant in Avon Lakes, Ohio, where it reduced the workforce to twenty-five hundred, imposed higher production quotas, and cut wages by 25 cents an hour.[44]

Tax rates also ranked as a major factor in plant location policy, although corporate leaders exaggerated the effect of the tax burden on their operations.

In 1954, The Detroiter, the organ of the Detroit
Chamber of Commerce, stated that the "excessive
burden of taxation on inventories is an important
factor in causing the location of new plants outside
the Detroit city limits."[45] Ex-Cell-O's Bixby also
complained of the high taxes in metropolitan
Detroit. In 1957, General Motors cited tax increases
as a rationale for halting expansion in Michigan.
And in 1959, Chrysler Vice-President W. C. Newberg
warned that taxes "dictate some decisions about
plant location" and hinted that in the absence of a
"fair and even distribution of property taxes,"
Chrysler might leave Detroit.[46] One industrialist
worried that his firm paid "three and four times the
amount of taxes per net worth that our competitors
are paying in Ohio, Pennsylvania, Illinois,
California." Detroit's real and personal property
taxes were particularly galling to members of the
city's business community.[47]

Detroit officials were responsive to fears of high
property taxes: Detroit did not increase its property
tax levy between 1948 and 1958. But business leaders, tempted by lower tax rates in nonmetropolitan
areas, frequently used the threat of mobility to push
for changes in tax laws favorable to industry. In the
meantime, the flight of industry diminished Detroit's
tax base. Runaway shops took with them tax revenue
essential to the provision of city services, and the city
was forced to rely on state and federal aid, running up
a growing deficit. City officials, discouraged by
threatened business flight, attempted to maintain a
tax structure favorable to businesses by keeping property taxes low and shifting the burden to income earn-
ers, who faced a 1 percent levy beginning in 1962.
With an aging infrastructure, an enormous school
district, an expensive city-funded social welfare program, and a growing population of poor people,
Detroit could not reduce its taxes to the level of its
small-town and rural competitors.[48]

Neighboring states took advantage of the plight of
Detroit and other large cities and encouraged panic
over urban tax rates; many held out the promise of
low business taxes as a lure to Michigan firms who
wanted to cut overhead costs. Some state chambers of
commerce and economic development officials placed
advertisements in trade publications trumpeting their
favorable tax climates. According to Bixby, Detroit
taxes "were 2⅓ times as high as the state and local
taxes per plant in Ohio, and 1¾ high as in Indiana."[49]
The combination of low taxes and low-wage labor
markets lured firms away from Detroit to small towns
throughout the Midwest and South.

Federal Policy and Decentralization

The federal government also actively encouraged
industrial deconcentration. Beginning during World
War II, it fostered military-industrial development in
suburban areas at the expense of center cities, in part
as a precaution in case of air attack. Firms also frequently took advantage of federal largesse to subsidize
new plant construction on green-field sites. The
Chrysler Warren Tank Plant, built in 1941 in an undeveloped suburban area fifteen miles north of downtown Detroit, and the enormous Willow Run aircraft
complex, constructed in 1942 on over fifteen hundred
acres of rural land twenty-five miles west of the city,
stood as models to postwar industrial planners.[50]

Government support for industrial decentralization
went even further during the Korean War and afterward. During the Korean War buildup, for example,
only 7.5 percent of $353 million allocated for the
purchase of equipment and new plant construction in
metropolitan Detroit went to firms located within the
city of Detroit; 92.5 percent of the funding went to
"out-lying parts of the region."[51] In addition, the
Department of Defense also pioneered a "parallel
plant" policy, building new defense plants outside of
traditional industrial centers that duplicated existing
production.[52] Chrysler shifted tank engine production
to New Orleans and tank production to Newark,
Delaware. Ford, which had constructed aircraft
engines in Detroit during World War II, shifted production to sites in Chicago and Missouri. And Cadillac
began the manufacture of light tanks in Cleveland.[53]

The growing power of Sun Belt politicians in Congress further diminished Detroit's share of the massive
federal defense budget. By the end of the Korean War,
the northeastern and midwestern share of the Cold
War defense budget had shrunk greatly. Southern
members of Congress, many heading influential committees, steered federal military spending toward their
home states. Between 1951 and 1960, the South's

share of the national defense budget doubled. Even more impressive was the impact of defense dollars on the West. California was the major beneficiary of defense spending. In 1951, it was awarded 13.2 percent of national defense contract dollars; by 1958, its share was 21.4 percent. Detroit and other industrial centers in the Northeast and Midwest, all of which had benefited from the flow of defense dollars during the 1940s, suffered the effects of the Pentagon-financed development of the Sun Belt.[54]

The major automobile manufacturers also contributed to the loss of defense contracts in the immediate postwar years. They quickly reconverted plants from defense to civilian production, in anticipation of high demand for cars after the war, while manufacturers in other regions positioned themselves for continued military research and development and defense production. The result was the Detroit area did not attract new high-technology aircraft and electronics manufacturers that benefited from government largesse during the Cold War.[55]

Detroit, the World War II "arsenal of democracy," had become, in the words of a critic of defense policy, a "ghost arsenal."[56] In 1954 alone, the Detroit area lost nearly 56,000 defense jobs; it lost another 26,000 between 1955 and 1957. By 1957, only 33,000 workers in all of metropolitan Detroit worked in defense industries. At a time when the national military-industrial complex was growing by leaps and bounds, Detroit's share of Defense Department contracts shrunk rapidly. The loss of defense jobs in the city occurred simultaneously with the decline in employment in other industries. Detroit's loss of defense jobs only added to its already deep economic troubles.[57]

The movement of firms out of the city, whether spurred by government subsidies or by market considerations, created a spatial mismatch between urban African Americans and jobs. Persistent housing discrimination combined with job flight to worsen the plight of urban blacks. The mismatch was not as perfect as many theorists have contended; some large suburban plants, as we have seen, did hire blacks. But most smaller firms did not. Tool and die companies that located in the all-white suburbs north of Detroit, for example, tended to rely on local contacts to find new employees. The gap between black workers and

job opportunity grew the further firms moved from the metropolitan area. And increasingly firms, from automobile manufacturers to parts suppliers, relocated in small towns and rural areas with minuscule black populations. Firms that moved to the South seldom broke Jim Crow customs, offering the lion's share of their jobs to white workers. Discrimination combined with nonmetropolitan industrialization to limit black economic opportunity.[58] . . .

Industrial Job Loss and Economic Distress

Detroit seemed to embody American confidence and affluence in the aftermath of the triumph of World War II, but just when the city's boosters proclaimed an industrial rebirth, the destructive forces of industrial capitalism began the process of economic corrosion that made Detroit the epitome of the Rust Belt. Between 1948 and 1967, Detroit lost nearly 130,000 manufacturing jobs. The number of manufacturing jobs fell by almost half in the 1950s (Table 1). The trend of job loss continued through the next four decades, mitigated only slightly by the temporary boom in the local economy and in automobile production from 1964 through 1969. Bolstered by the views of postwar social scientists who emphasized American affluence, the perception of Detroit's decline lagged far behind reality. While social scientists were writing of Detroit as the home of the "embourgeoised" auto worker, the face of industrial Detroit was being transformed by enormous economic upheavals. A growing number of Detroit residents joined the ranks of "displaced workers," dislocated by industrial changes and trapped in the declining metropolis.

The restructuring of Detroit's industrial economy diminished opportunity for several segments of the Detroit work force. First, the loss of manufacturing jobs removed a rung of the ladder of economic opportunity for the poorest workers, especially those with little education and few skills. The testimony of workers who lost their jobs when Detroit's Packard plant shut its doors in 1956 revealed the high costs of industrial decline. "I felt like someone had hit me with a sledge hammer," stated one worker. Recalled a stockhandler with twelve years seniority: "It was such a shock . . . I had been there so long. . . . They just threw

Table 1   Decline in Manufacturing Employment in Detroit, 1947–1977

	1947	1954	1958	1963	1967	1972	1977
Manufacturing Firms	3,272	3,453	3,363	3,370	2,947	2,398	1,954
Total Manufacturing Employment[a]	338.4	296.5	204.4	200.6	209.7	180.4	153.3
Total Production Employment[a]	281.5	232.3	145.1	141.4	149.6	125.8	107.5

Source: U.S. Department of Commerce, Bureau of Census, City and County Data Books (Washington, D.C.: U.S. Government Printing Office, 1949, 1956, 1962, 1972, 1977, 1983).

[a]In thousands.

us out and didn't say nothing . . . they just threw us out on the street." A worker with thirty years of seniority perhaps best summed up the effects of plant closings in the 1950s: "It hit and hit hard, hit the man who was a common assembler the hardest."[66]

In the aftermath of the wartime and postwar boom, the bust of the 1950s was devastating. The city's economy had seemed dynamic and unstoppable, insatiable in its demand for labor. Making the process all the more traumatic, layoffs and plant closings were unpredictable. Seemingly secure jobs could be eliminated without notice when a plant automated. Events in the 1950s reminded workers that even the factory buildings that seemed like permanent landmarks on Detroit's skyline were mortal. Bustling plants were abandoned and boarded up as companies moved production outside the city or went out of business. In the midst of celebratory descriptions of national prosperity, as pundits spoke of embourgeoisement, the gap between rhetoric and reality grew.

If many workers were affected in some way by changes in the city's economy, blacks bore the brunt of restructuring. Persistent racial discrimination magnified the effects of deindustrialization on blacks. Data from the 1960 census make clear the disparate impact of automation and labor market constriction on African American workers. Across the city, 15.9 percent of blacks, but only 5.8 percent of whites were out of work. In the motor vehicle industry, the black-white gap was even greater. 19.7 percent of black auto workers were unemployed, compared to only 5.8 percent of whites. Discrimination and deindustrialization proved to be a lethal combination for blacks. Seniority protected some

black workers from permanent layoffs, but it disproportionately benefited white workers. Blacks had not gained footholds in most plants until after 1943—most were hired in the late 1940s and early 1950s, well after large numbers of white workers had established themselves in Detroit's industries. Thus they were less likely to have accumulated enough seniority to protect their jobs. And because blacks were concentrated in unskilled, dangerous jobs—precisely those affected by automation—they often found that their job classifications had been eliminated altogether.[67]

By the early 1960s, observers noted that a seemingly permanent class of underemployed and jobless blacks had emerged, a group that came to be called the "long-term unemployed." In 1962, the editors of the Michigan Labor Market Letter looked back at the troubled 1950s. The last decade, they noted, had been marked by "significant and sometimes violent changes in our economy." They looked with chagrin on the "creation of a very large and alarmingly consistent list of long-term unemployed." Each year from 1956 to 1962, state officials ranked Detroit as an area of "substantial labor surplus." While black and white workers alike suffered from economic dislocations, black workers faced a particularly gloomy future. Overrepresented in Detroit's labor surplus were two groups of African American workers: older, unskilled workers and youth.[68]

The most poignant stories of unemployment and dislocation involved older workers, those who had seniority at plants that had closed down altogether, or those who did not have enough seniority to qualify for a transfer to new jobs. They often had years of experience working in heavy industry, but few skills easily transferable to other jobs. The experience of older black workers was somewhat worse than that of older whites. A survey of workers unemployed when Detroit's Packard plant closed in 1956 found that black workers suffered longer bouts of unemployment (thirteen months compared to ten for whites; 38 percent unemployed for more than nineteen months compared to 26 percent for whites). Blacks also took more substantial pay cuts than whites when reemployed.[69] When Murray Auto Body closed in 1954, 76 percent of black employees surveyed exhausted their unemployment benefits, compared to only 27 percent of whites. Those blacks who found new employment went "to an average of twice as many places to find work as the sample as a whole," and suffered a wage drop twice that of reemployed white workers.[70]

Less visible, but even more momentous than the emergence of a pool of unemployed older, disproportionately black workers, was the dramatic reduction of entry-level jobs. As a committee investigating the city's labor market in the late 1950s noted, "the real loss comes not so much in lay-offs as in a falling off in the number of new hires." As manufacturing industries restructured, decentralized, and cut back plant work forces, experienced workers protected by seniority moved into jobs that would have earlier been filled by recent migrants to the city and young workers entering the work force for the first time.[71] Firms that were decentralizing and automating saved costs by relying on trained, experienced workers. Whenever possible, employers tried to minimize the union backlash against automation and decentralization by reducing employment through attrition and curbs on new hiring, instead of layoffs. Responding to workers' fears of job loss at the River Rouge plant, Ford managers noted that a reduction of the labor force "can be handled by the simple expedient of not hiring new employees rather than laying off older ones."[72]

The decline in the number of entry-level manufacturing jobs disproportionately affected black migrants and black youth. Black migrants were less likely in the 1950s to find entry-level jobs in manufacturing that had provided security and relatively good pay to their predecessors in the 1940s. Detroit's pool of manufacturing jobs decreased at the same time that the population of working-age black adults continued to rise. In 1959, the Detroit News noted that "Too many Negro families who have moved here to work in the automobile plants are now unemployed. For most there are no prospects of jobs. Many are unemployable and either illiterate or nearly so." They had followed the path of migration to the North, with expectations of entry-level industrial work that required few skills—the sort of work that had attracted blacks to the North since the beginning of the Great Migration. But all too often, upon arrival in Detroit, they found that factories simply were not hiring new workers. "There is little hope for them to regain employment," Urban League vocational counselors reported. "There will be very few employment opportunities open to these people."[73]

The combination of discrimination and deindustrialization weighed most heavily on the job opportunities of young African American men. Young workers, especially those who had no postsecondary education, found that the entry-level operative jobs that had been open to their fathers or older siblings in the 1940s and early 1950s were gone. The most dramatic evidence of the impact of industrial changes on young black workers was the enormous gap between black and white youth who had no attachment to the labor market (Table 2). The exclusion of a generation of young men from the work force, at a vital time in their emergence as adults, prevented them from gaining the experience, connections, and skills that would open opportunities in later years. It also confirmed their suspicions that they were entrapped in an economic and political system that confined them to the very bottom. By the end of the 1950s, more and more black job seekers, reported the Urban League, were demoralized, "developing patterns of boredom and hopelessness with the present state of affairs." The anger and despair that prevailed among the young, at a time of national promise and prosperity, would explode on Detroit's streets in the 1960s.[74]

Only fifteen years after World War II, Detroit's landscape was dominated by rotting hulks of factory buildings, closed and abandoned, surrounded by blocks of boarded up-stores [sic] and restaurants. Older neighborhoods, whose streets were lined with

Table 2 Percentage of Men between Ages 15 and 29 Not in Labor Force, Detroit, 1960		
Age	**White**	**Nonwhite**
15	76.3	76.2
16	56.6	77.7
17	42.3	61.6
18	15.0	41.0
19	8.9	35.3
20	7.8	24.9
21–22	4.9	20.5
23–24	3.4	12.5
25–29	2.3	10.1

Source: Detroit Metropolitan Area Employment by Age, Sex, Color, and Residence, copy in DNAACP, Part II, Box 10, Folder 10–5, ALUA. Those in school are not included in the figures.

the proud homes that middle-class and working-class Detroiters had constructed in the late nineteenth and early twentieth centuries, were now pockmarked with the shells of burned-out and empty buildings lying among rubbish-strewn vacant lots. Deteriorating housing and abandoned storefronts were but signs of the profound social and economic changes that were reshaping the metropolis. . . .

The process of industrial decline had other far-reaching consequences. It imperiled Detroit's fiscal base. As jobs left the city, so too did white workers with the means to move to suburbs or small towns where factories relocated. Wealthier whites also followed investments outward. As a result, Detroit's population began an unbroken downward fall in the 1950s. As Detroit's population shrank, it also grew poorer and blacker. Increasingly, the city became the home for the dispossessed, those marginalized in the housing market, in greater peril of unemployment, most subject to the vagaries of a troubled economy. . . .

6-2 "The Problem Perceived"*

Jon C. Teaford

The Rough Road to Renaissance: Urban Revitalization in America, 1940–1985

The census figures for 1940 confirmed the expectations of most urban experts. During the prior decade, Boston, Philadelphia, Cleveland, and Saint Louis had suffered a decline in population, and most of the nation's other major cities only had inched upward in number of inhabitants. Of the ten largest cities in the nation eight had either lost population or grown at a slower rate than the country as a whole. New York City had barely surpassed the national average, and among the top ten only Los Angeles could claim to be booming. Moreover, this sluggishness was in marked contrast with the pattern just two decades earlier. Whereas, during the 1930s, Cleveland's population had dropped 2.5 percent, between 1910 and 1920 it had risen 42 percent. In the 1930s Detroit had gained a mere 3.5 percent; twenty years earlier it had soared 113 percent. After more than a century of rapidly rising population the growth of the leading cities, especially those in the northeastern quadrant of the United States, seemed to be coming to a halt.

Many urban leaders recognized the dangers inherent in the new figures. A prominent planner in Cleveland ominously argued that "the beginning of an era when Cleveland will have to compete with all other major cities in a race for the 'survival of the fittest' is at hand."[1] Meanwhile, the Saint Louis City Plan Commission claimed that the Missouri metropolis was "fast becoming a decadent city" and with considerable prescience contended that the city of more than 800,000 residents in 1940 was "well on the way toward decline of its total population to 500,000 by 1980 or 1990."[2] Boston's mayor warned that "unless prompt measures are taken the contagion will spread until virtual decay and destruction of the whole city has taken place."[3] Throughout the country observers commented on the gradual disintegration of the urban giants, and few could muster much praise for the metropolitan core in the years immediately preceding World War II. Many wrote of economic "dry rot" in the downtown districts, of deterioration and abandonment in the surrounding slums, and of the threatening spread of decay in the remaining residential ring. No one sought to preserve the largest cities of the Northeast and Midwest in their existing form. Instead, by the close of the 1930s these aging metropolises were perceived as relics in radical need of rehabilitation and restructuring.

Local leaders and urban experts viewed this decline of the central cities largely as a physical rather than a social problem. Supposedly, it did not arise from racial conflict or discrimination, a maldistribution of economic or political power, or an absence of law and order. Thus the answer was not racial integration, social and economic revolution, or tougher police action. Rather, the commonly identified enemy of the late 1930s and early 1940s was "blight." When they spoke of blight, city officials, business leaders, and urban planners meant the process of physical deterioration that destroyed property values and undermined the quality of urban life. Moreover, blight was often referred to as a cancer, an insidious, spreading phenomenon that could kill a city if not removed or forced into remission. It was this malady destroying the physical tissue of urban America that appeared to be the archfoe of older central cities and that aroused fears for their future.

Source: Teaford, Jon C. *The Rough Road to Renaissance: Urban Revitalization in America, 1940–1985*, pp. 10–13, 16–23, 25–29, 42–43. © 1990 The Johns Hopkins University Press. Reprinted with permission of Johns Hopkins University Press.

*Some text and accompanying endnotes have been omitted. Please consult the original source.

But civic leaders were not about to surrender to the forces of blight. When the Saint Louis City Plan Commission asked rhetorically, "Shall we gradually abandon St. Louis?" the expected answer was a resounding "no."[4] A Boston newspaper editorialized that "the population decline need not be accepted with apathy and resignation." Instead, it argued that "with ingenuity and energy the condition can be turned into an occasion for new progress.[5] Meanwhile, in Cincinnati a business leader announced that "obviously the citizens of this metropolitan area do not wish to see Cincinnati retrogress," and consequently "the time is at hand" for "the taking of those steps and the making of those improvements necessary to arrest decline and to assure progress."[6] In one aging central city after another, urban leaders both in the public and private sectors agreed with this conclusion. Decisive action could again put the cities on an upward path.

By the early 1940s, then, business chiefs and municipal officials not only recognized the problem confronting them but also began to make plans to do something about it. Since the perceived problem was one of physical structure rather than of social organization, the perceived answer was physical rejuvenation and reconstruction. The tonic that could revive the aging central cities had to include a healthy dose of new highway and sewer construction, the building of better housing and more modern commercial structures, and the elimination of environmental pollution. The engineer, architect, and contractor and not the social worker or agitator were to cure the city's ills. They were to mix the elixir that would bring new life to Boston, Buffalo, Cleveland, and Chicago.

Since the impetus for the campaign against decay came from businesspeople and public officials at the top of the social and political ladder, it was not surprising that physical solutions proved more attractive than a restructuring of society. Though the residents of decaying neighborhoods may have favored action to curb decline, the loudest crying about the signs of impending doom came from downtown real estate interests threatened by falling property values and harried mayors facing fiscal crisis because of the drop in assessed valuations. In their minds blight was a physical phenomenon, and the best means to combat

it was increased investment in the construction of private and public facilities under their control. Physical rejuvenation would bolster their positions; social change would undermine them. Thus physical solutions seemed most desirable.

World War II diverted capital, labor, and materials to the battle abroad, thwarting immediate realization of the plans for physical renewal. But at home politicians, planners, and civil servants prepared for their upcoming battle for the rehabilitation of the city in the postwar era. By 1945 central-city decline had been the subject of discussion for a number of years, and urban revival was a recognized goal. Leaders of the older central cities were aroused to the dangers before them, and they made ready to take action.

The Emigration of Residents

Among the most serious phenomena facing the older central cities was the migration of residents to outlying suburban municipalities. None of the major metropolitan districts lost population during the 1930s, for in the Boston, Philadelphia, Cleveland, and Saint Louis areas gains in the suburbs more than compensated for losses in the central cities. From the beginning of the century the outward movement had accelerated with the suburban population in the nation's metropolitan districts growing at twice the pace of the central-city population during the 1920s and three times the rate of the urban core in the 1930s. "Decentralization" was the watchword of urban experts as millions of metropolitan Americans dispersed to homes beyond the central-city boundaries.

These migrants may have realized their dreams of a suburban house with a plot of grass and room for a garden, but those concerned for the future of the central city viewed the suburban trend with consternation. In fact, decentralization appeared to be a close ally of blight, clearing the city of residents and thereby preparing the ground for dreaded physical deterioration. In 1940 Harland Bartholomew, the distinguished city planner of Saint Louis, warned that "the whole financial structure of cities, as well as the investments of countless individuals and business firms, is in jeopardy because of what is called 'decentralization.'" If residents kept moving outward causing a depreciation of property in the urban core, the result, according to

Bartholomew, could only be disaster for central-city treasuries dependent on property taxes and for central-city landlords unable to rent their holdings.[7] A year later a leading Cincinnati realtor argued that chief among the nation's urban problems was "the undue acceleration of population flight away from city centers causing rot and decay at their cores." This Cincinnatian warned, "If this movement is permitted to proceed unabated, the loss of wealth will be beyond comprehension, because region after region, still sound for good living, will become blighted."[8]

Especially serious was the migration of the wealthier classes to suburbia. Since World War I a steady stream of middle-class Americans had migrated to suburban municipalities, leaving the central city poorer and the suburbs richer. The growing disparity in wealth between the city and its suburbs was evident in the census statistics for twelve aging central cities in the nation's northeastern quadrant. In eight of the twelve the average monthly rent for housing was higher in the metropolitan area outside the central city than within. The gap between central city and suburbs varied among the metropolitan areas, but it was most notable in Boston, Philadelphia, Cleveland, and Saint Louis, the very cities that had recorded population declines during the 1930s. The extreme example of disparity was in the Cleveland metropolitan district, where the average rent for dwellings in the suburbs was 78 percent higher than in the central city. Whereas the suburban average was $51.42, the highest figure for any ward within the city was $41.77. In other words, the average suburban dwelling was considerably more expensive than the average housing in the "best" central-city neighborhood. . . .

[City planners] also noted that the outward migration of the middle class and the spread of blighted residential areas could add up to dire consequences for the municipal treasuries. Saint Louis's Harland Bartholomew reported that "the older residence districts almost uniformly received public services two and one quarter times in cost the amount paid in taxes." In contrast, "the newer residence district paid approximately twenty-five per cent more in taxes than the cost of city services received."[12] A few years earlier a study of a Cleveland slum found that the tax income from the district was $10.12 per capita whereas the public expenditure in the

area amounted to $61.22 per person. "In other words," the study concluded, "the city of Cleveland subsidized each man, woman and child in this area to an amount of $51.10," which seemed to be "a rather large subsidy for the privilege of maintaining a slum area."[13] Throughout the country surveys computed the cost of slum dwellings to the municipal government, and everywhere the answer was the same. Blighted neighborhoods were a burden on the public treasury and could eventually doom the city to bankruptcy. Thus the central city needed new middle-class housing to boost a property tax base that was declining because of the depreciation of vast tracts of aged buildings.

Critics of decentralization not only recognized the impending drain on the city coffers, they also regretted the siphoning off of leadership talent. As the "best" people moved beyond the municipal limits, central cities lost the human resources that seemed necessary for civic improvement. A spokesman for the Chicago Association of Commerce warned of the "withdrawal from the city of many of the brains and voices best suited to help it help itself."[14] Likewise, a student of metropolitan Cleveland observed that "the lack of trained and efficient officials in the administration of urban affairs is also intensified by the migration of the more competent into the suburbs."[15] A Cincinnati businessman reiterated this sentiment when he claimed that "less and less of the better elements of the population . . . are living in the city proper, so that the political aspects of the older city are becoming dangerous to the ideals of good government."[16] If the central city lost its middle-class population, then the venal political bosses who based their machines on lower-class support would supposedly become even more powerful, and the political hacks in city hall would become even more numerous. To middle-class observers this would increase the problems of the central city and seriously hamper urban efforts at combating blight and obsolescence.

Some commentators even felt that suburban living made the wealthier classes callous and indifferent to the plight of the central city. According to one critic of Philadelphia suburbanites, "the most loyal upper-class Philadelphian will generally admit, freely and with a sort of perverse pride, that the city itself is only a necessary evil, incident to the pursuit of the more gracious life along the [suburban] Main Line."[17] Moreover, these uncaring suburbanites burdened the city treasury without paying their fair share of municipal expenses. Each workday suburban commuters crowded city streets, necessitating costly paving and widening projects and adding to police expenditures. Yet their expensive homes in outlying municipalities were not on the central-city tax rolls. Citing Boston as an example, one observer wrote disparagingly of "dwellers in parasitic dormitory cities" expecting much from the central city but giving little in return.[18] Likewise, the Saint Louis City Plan Commission argued that "the taxpayer of the central city is subsidizing the suburban dweller and that this subsidy continues to grow as the area of urbanization is expanded."[19] In 1937 the federal government's National Resources Committee expressed the mounting fears of many urban experts when it argued that no community "can long remain a sound functioning organism, if those . . . who gain the greatest benefits from it, escape from most of the obligations communal life imposes, and if those who obtain the least . . . amenities of life are left to bear the brunt of civic responsibility and taxation. . . ."[20]

The Specter of Commercial Decline

Even more threatening than residential migration was the likelihood of future commercial decline in the central city. Municipal treasuries needed the revenue from lucrative business properties to compensate for the deficit incurred in servicing tax-poor residential slums. If the owners of factories, stores, and office towers continued to find the central city a desirable location, then the ample property tax receipts from these businesses might well keep the aging municipalities solvent. Thus commerce might prove the needed anchor to keep the city safe and sound while middle-class residents drifted off to suburbia.

Unfortunately for central-city leaders, by the late 1930s and early 1940s there were few signs of commercial vitality in the older urban hubs. In fact, commercial decline seemed to be marching lockstep with residential decline. The central business districts were growing increasingly shabby, and traffic clogged their narrow thoroughfares. Lack of necessary capital during the Depression decade kept many factory owners from moving out of the central city and building new plants, but the growing reliance on truck transport and the

emerging preference for expansive single-story facilities made the highways and wide-open spaces of suburbia seem increasingly attractive. By the close of the 1930s the prospects for marked commercial growth in Boston, Buffalo, Pittsburgh, and Cleveland were no brighter than the prospects for rapid population increase.

The downtown business district was especially vital to the future of the central city. With its soaring skyscrapers and massive department stores, it symbolized the wealth, excitement, and opportunity of urban life. More tangibly, its tax revenues kept the city operating. Though it generally encompassed only 1 percent or 2 percent of the city's area, the downtown accounted for anywhere from 12 percent to 20 percent of the city's total assessed valuation. In one city after another it was a golden asset that subsidized many of the other neighborhoods. For example, Saint Louis's central business district paid two and a half times more in taxes than it cost in municipal services.[24]

This valuable asset to the municipal treasury, however, seemed to be in danger. Between 1930 and 1940 the assessed valuation of the Saint Louis business district dropped $46 million, or 28 percent, whereas the valuation of the city as a whole fell only 19 percent. Likewise, from 1936 to 1946 properties in downtown Pittsburgh, known proudly as the Golden Triangle, decreased in valuation 28 percent whereas the decline for the entire city was only 21 percent. Throughout the country the figures were similar: from 1931 to 1945 the assessed valuation of central Baltimore declined 34 percent; from 1935 to 1944 downtown Boston's taxable worth dropped 24 percent; between 1936 and 1945 the value of Detroit's central business district fell 15 percent.[25] Even during the economic upturn of the early 1940s, downtown valuations did not rebound to earlier levels. For example, the figure for Chicago's central business district dropped from $552 million in 1939 to approximately $481 million in 1947, a fall of 13 percent. During these same years, the figure for Chicago as a whole declined only 3 percent, and the county areas outside of the city increased 6 percent in assessed value.[26] In each of the older urban hubs the downtown seemed to be slipping faster than the remainder of the city, and the possible consequences of this trend for the municipal tax base were ominous.

Many observers commented on the unhappy fate of the formerly prosperous urban core. "A visitor touring downtown St. Louis," wrote one commentator in a national magazine, "is amazed at the desolation and desertion characterizing scores of blocks in the business district."[27] In *Nation's Business*, the usually boosterish publication of the United States Chamber of Commerce, a writer claimed that the same was true of other big cities, all of which were, "economically speaking, . . . rotting at the core." According to this dismal observer, "New York, Chicago, Philadelphia, Boston, St. Louis and others show unmistakable signs of advanced decay in those central sections which 35, 50, or 75 years ago were the hubs of much of their activity."[28] A Philadelphian summed up the sentiments of many when he noted that business leaders had "become increasingly aware that the central business districts have not been progressing" but instead "retrogression is very much in evidence."[29]

Numerous statistics supported this contention. Between 1926 and 1937 the number of persons daily entering the Saint Louis downtown area by vehicle dropped to 233,800 from 272,300. Likewise, between 1927 and 1942 the number of persons arriving daily in Pittsburgh's Golden Triangle fell to 247,000 from 297,000. Similarly, those entering and leaving downtown Detroit and Philadelphia declined 15 percent and 11 percent, respectively, between the late 1920s and the end of the 1930s.[30] Hundreds of thousands of commuters were still jamming the transit lines and thoroughfares leading to the central business districts of the older cities. But their numbers were beginning to thin, and the attraction of downtown as a place of employment and shopping was waning.

Still other grim portents also heightened the fears of downtown decline. Throughout the 1930s the office building vacancy rate had been high, peaking at 27 percent nationwide in 1933. By 1940 it still averaged 17 percent to 18 percent nationwide, and in sluggish Philadelphia the rate was 23 percent, in Boston 25 percent, and in moribund Saint Louis 29 percent.[31] The office buildings of downtown Saint Louis had twenty acres of unleased floor space, and a local newspaper reported that "21 mercantile, loft and miscellaneous structures, with a total of 119 floors," were "completely vacant."[32] With the exception of

Rockefeller Center in New York City, there had been no construction starts on major office buildings in the older central cities since the early 1930s. In 1940 the office towers accenting the skyline of major American cities were ironic monuments to the contrast between appearance and reality in the metropolitan downtown. Though they symbolized business success and the commercial might of the city, floor after floor of the office structures stood empty.

Not only was downtown construction at a standstill, in many cities demolition seemed to be the wave of the future. Rather than pay taxes on empty buildings, many landlords during the 1930s chose to tear them down and convert the space to parking lots. In 1927 less than 9 percent of the lots in Detroit's downtown were vacant; ten years later almost 24 percent had no buildings on them. From 1936 through 1939, ninety-six downtown buildings were demolished in the Motor City, and by 1940, 107 of the 140 blocks in the central business district contained one or more vacant lots. Meanwhile, the number of privately owned downtown parking lots rose from 110, with a total capacity of 7,720 cars in 1927, to 265 lots holding 17,251 cars in 1933. And during the next seven years, the increase in parking spaces continued. In 1940 a national magazine observed that "ten years ago a search for vacant land in downtown Detroit would have gone largely unrewarded; . . . today in the same area, a similar search would be satisfied at almost every turn."[33]

Similarly, in downtown Philadelphia there were between 125 and 375 demolitions each year during the 1930s, and the percentage of the parcels being cleared for rebuilding gradually dropped during the decade, falling to only 9 percent in 1939. Moreover, according to one survey of downtown Philadelphia, a number of merchants viewed "with considerable alarm the increase in the number of parking lots, . . . a few of which occupy almost a city block, and that these parking lots have not been confined to the streets of lesser importance but have invaded the main business thoroughfares."[34]

In Philadelphia, Detroit, and throughout the nation more and more gaps appeared in the downtown streetscape. Once valuable properties on major avenues could no longer attract anyone to build on them, and they were relegated to the storage of idle automobiles. Detroit's Temple Theater, for many years the most successful vaudeville house in the city, fell to the wrecker's ball after only thirty-five years of use, and a parking lot took its place. New York City's famed Hippodrome Theater likewise gave way to a parking lot. Demolition and abandonment of downtown real estate, in the words of one observer, was "a fast spreading epidemic" and was "rapidly becoming Real Estate's No. 1 problem."[35]

Even though the number of parking lots was increasing, parking remained one of the most serious downtown problems, and many urban leaders believed that lack of adequate space for automobiles was a prime source of the perceived decline of the central business district. Whereas the number of persons daily entering downtown Philadelphia dropped 11 percent between 1928 and 1938, the number of passenger automobiles making the trip soared 52 percent.[36] Likewise, the number of persons arriving in downtown Detroit plummeted 30 percent between 1925 and 1936, but the number of cars entering the city's core increased 6 percent.[37] And 7 percent fewer persons converged on the Boston central business district in 1938 than in 1927, but the use of the automobile by downtown visitors and workers rose 47 percent.[38] Thus fewer people but more cars were making the journey downtown, worsening central-city traffic jams and heightening the competition for parking spaces. The traffic congestion and parking problems resulted, in turn, in still fewer downtown customers, exacerbating the downward spiral of business activity. Yet the onslaught of cars continued to mount, for commuters were abandoning the streetcar for the automobile faster than they were abandoning the downtown as a place of employment and shopping. Ironically, by 1940 there were fewer people and buildings in the central business district but more congestion.

Traffic was the chief complaint of downtown business interests, but a close second on the list of criticisms was inequitable taxation. Repeatedly in the late 1930s and early 1940s, leaders in the real estate industry claimed that municipal property taxes were speeding the decline of the central business district. Owing to the optimism and real estate speculation of the 1920s, downtown land values soared to unprecedented heights by 1929, and assessed valuations likewise rose markedly. With the onset of depression and the new glut in office space, however, the market value of downtown office structures plummeted more rapidly than that of residential property. Yet to the consternation of downtown property owners, the drop in assessed valuations usually did not keep pace with the decline in market values. Moreover, office buildings traditionally were assessed at a higher proportion of their sale price than were residences.

According to downtown real estate interests, the result was an overburdened central business district, carrying an inordinate tax bill while also suffering from the ill effects of the automobile. In a report on central Boston a distinguished appraiser complained that "the present combination of excessive valuations with the highest tax rate among the large cities of the United States is gradually sucking all the value out of downtown business property."[39] A member of the Philadelphia Real Estate Board claimed that the same was true in his city and argued that "unquestionably, the large proportion of the city taxes borne by the central city business properties . . . is one of the factors leading to decentralization."[40] In Detroit a leading realtor found that a drop of 50 percent in downtown rental receipts combined with a decrease of only 30 percent in taxes increased the proportion of rental income used to pay taxes from 14 percent in 1929 to 20 percent in 1940.[41] Such facts aroused little concern among the thousands of rank-and-file urban dwellers who did not own office buildings or department stores. But the real estate industry viewed grimly the evidence from Detroit, Philadelphia, and Boston. Prominent downtown business interests recognized that municipal governments needed to attract other tax-rich properties and develop new sources of revenue if the financial burden was to lift from the beleaguered central business district.

The statistics, however, all pointed to commercial decentralization, offering little solace to central-city business leaders. Central-city retailing, for example, was lagging seriously behind the outlying areas in rate of sales growth. In the New York, Chicago, Philadelphia, Detroit, and Cleveland metropolitan areas the percentage increase in suburban retail sales was approximately double that in the central cities.

Throughout the 1930s and early 1940s, retail business in Manhattan, the nation's preeminent shopping district, remained sluggish, and the largest New York stores began to seek greater profits through establishment of suburban branches. In 1937 Peck and Peck founded a branch in Garden City in suburban Long Island, and the following year it opened a store in the posh Connecticut suburb of Greenwich. In 1941 Bonwit Teller sought to tap the lucrative Westchester County market by establishing a branch in suburban White Plains, and in 1942 Best and Company expanded into both northern Long Island and Westchester County when it opened stores in Manhasset, White Plains, and Bronxville. Whereas major New York City retailers founded only eight branch outlets from 1930 through 1936, from 1937 through 1942 they established twenty-four outlying stores.[42] If a shopper wanted to patronize Macy's, Gimbel's, or Bloomingdale's, he or she still had to go to the central city, for these retail giants had not yet moved to suburbia. Moreover, sprawling shopping centers were not yet a feature of the suburban landscape. But the decentralization of retailing had begun. . . .

Responding to Decline

Faced with the symptoms of decline, civic leaders did not resign themselves to inevitable decay and deterioration. Instead, during the early 1940s urban Americans began to fashion the strategy for a grand assault on the forces that were sapping the vitality of the central city. In 1940 the *Saint Louis Post-Dispatch* editorialized, "People will live in St. Louis if St. Louis is made livable," and in the following years proposals for creating a livable city abounded.[48] Leaders in the aging central cities did not expect a return to the days of soaring population growth. Rather, they sought to stabilize the city and halt its downward course by making it an attractive place to live and to conduct business. The *Post-Dispatch* admitted that "St. Louis cannot expect to stop the migration to the county that has come with quick transportation," but "it can slacken that migration by checking its major cause, the spreading blight of the metropolitan center."[49] A Cleveland newspaper summed up the views of many when it observed: "Even if Cleveland is not to be a bigger city, it at least can become a far better city."[50]

To most urban leaders a better city was a physically rejuvenated city. Rather than sponsor programs that tampered with the metropolitan social structure or that redistributed wealth and power, planners, politicians, and the business community believed physical changes were the appropriate weapons against blight. Thus brick, mortar, and asphalt constituted the artillery in this initial offensive against the decline of the central cities. A renewed infrastructure would supposedly save the city from blight and limit the inroads of decentralization.

Leading the initial effort at revitalizing the older cities were central-city real estate interests. Residential neighborhood clubs, labor groups, and political party organizations did not spearhead the movement for renewal. In fact, in the early attack on urban decline their role was minimal or nonexistent. Instead, it was the real estate broker and those with large investments in commercial properties who were in the vanguard. No group had more to lose than the real estate interests if the perceived decline continued. Downtown properties were bringing prices lower than their assessed values, and commercial blight seemed to be robbing landlords of millions of dollars each year. If leaders of the real estate industry wanted to prevent central-city properties from spiraling downward in value, they felt that a program of improvements was necessary. Unless they took some action, their investments appeared doomed.

Recognizing this grim fact, in 1940 the Urban Land Institute, a nonprofit research corporation sponsored by the National Association of Real Estate Boards, began to examine closely the older American cities. The institute was dedicated to discovering the causes of urban decline and to prescribing cures for the malady. According to its statement of purpose, the organization was concerned "not only with means for assuring sound city growth but also with means for conserving values in our present business and residential areas and for opening the way toward sound reconstruction of those areas where decay is far advanced."[51] But it did not expect to solve the problem by itself. Instead, the leaders of the institute believed that the threat of decentralization demanded "action with scope enough to ease the transition and prevent huge unnecessary losses," which would require the "coordinated effort of business groups, owners of residential property, and governmental bodies."[52] This group of leading real estate figures from throughout the nation thus envisioned a joint public-private initiative to curb the consequences of debilitating decentralization.

Among the institute's first projects was a series of reports on downtown problems in a number of cities throughout the country. By September 1942 leading brokers and appraisers had completed surveys of the central business districts of Boston, Cincinnati, Detroit, Louisville, Milwaukee, New York, and Philadelphia.[53] Included in each report were proposals for reviving the downtown. Though these differed somewhat from city to city, a common denominator was the emphasis on traffic and parking. In the opinion of the nation's leading real estate brokers the automobile lay at the root of much central-city decay, and successful revitalization required the adaptation of the downtown business district to the new automotive age. Improved traffic circulation, more parking garages, and expressways feeding into the central business district seemed at least a partial answer to downtown problems. And it was clear that the real estate industry's revitalization program would encompass major improvements to accommodate the growing army of automobiles.[54]

Throughout the country a variety of local groups also shared the Urban Land Institute's concern for the future of the central city. In 1940 the Boston chapter of the American Institute of Architects proposed "a nonprofit, nonpolitical, non-partisan private association" including representatives of various interest groups to study the approaching "crisis of ruinous deterioration."[55] In New York City the Merchants Association drafted an urban redevelopment bill and presented it to the state legislature. The measure proposed government incentives for large-scale private investment in urban redevelopment because, according to the association, it had "already become obvious that sufficient public funds [could not] be made available to do all of the necessary rehabilitation work."[56]

In 1940 a group of downtown businesspeople in Saint Louis began to meet informally to plan the rehabilitation of their central business district. Including the presidents of two of the largest downtown department stores and of one of the city's leading banks, this group retained Harland Bartholomew as a consultant in their incipient effort to revive central

Saint Louis. Concerned Saint Louis leaders proposed such concrete improvements as more parking facilities, express highways, and new middle-income housing close to downtown.[57] In 1941 businesspeople on the north side of Saint Louis organized the Civic Committee on Conservation and Rehabilitation because of fears that the city was "on the decline at a speed that eventually will mean destruction, abandonment, bankruptcy and a ghost city." It too suggested more downtown parking and improved traffic flow as well as an easing of FHA restrictions on loans for the repair and construction of houses in run-down neighborhoods.[58]

That same year the Downtown Committee of Baltimore issued a report that spelled out measures necessary to achieve the group's goal of guaranteeing "the attraction of Downtown Baltimore for shopping, business and amusement—to the end that its economic usefulness and its value to the city will be preserved." This organization of prominent merchants, bankers, and property owners and managers proposed the standard list of new "parking terminals," building face-lifts, tax relief, and reforms to improve traffic circulation.[59] But in Philadelphia the Penn Athletic Club felt that such changes were not sufficient and opted for a policy of boosting local morale. Sponsoring "Talk Philadelphia Week," the club took the offensive against fifth columnists within the city who "sold short" their hometown, and club speakers exhorted the citizenry of the flagging metropolis to be "boosters and builder-uppers."[60]

Not only were business groups and boosters becoming increasingly concerned with curbing central-city decline, so were the private planning organizations in the older metropolises. With a membership drawn largely from the city's elite, these groups now lobbied for improved urban planning as a tool for excising blight. In March 1940 New York's Regional Plan Association helped sponsor a conference in support of the Merchants Association proposal for urban redevelopment.[61] The Buffalo City Planning Association likewise dreamed of a renewed city and discussed proposals for an ideal downtown of the future. The group's president expressed the views of worried Buffalo residents when he noted, "We must plan far ahead . . . to control or avoid decadence."[62]

Similarly, the publications of the Regional Association of Cleveland observed: "The movement of decentralization has already begun. How far will it go? How far ought it to go? How can we control it, for the greater benefit of all concerned?"[63] Imitating its regional planning counterpart in New York, the Cleveland group issued a series of reports and proposals on the creation of a better city, a city that would attract rather than repel people. Like the Saint Louis leaders, Cleveland's private planning organization proposed freeways "designed for the fast car of 1940" and inner-city housing projects serving as a "walk-to-work residence for white-collar workers" employed downtown.[64] Through such physical renewal the regional association hoped to successfully harness the forces of decentralization that were transforming Cleveland and every other major city.

By 1940, then, there was the beginning of a nation-wide movement to revitalize the central city. Aware of the statistical signs of decline and unable to escape the obvious physical decay surrounding them, urban leaders were meeting and organizing for the purpose of studying what could be done. The private sector was becoming aroused and was confronting the public sector with demands for action. Physical rehabilitation through the construction of highways, garages, and inner-city middle-class housing ranked high on the agenda of the private groups, but all this meant millions of dollars in public investment. . . .

Setting the Stage

During the decade before 1945, urban planners, municipal officials, central-city business leaders, and concerned citizens had perceived what they interpreted to be the incipient decline of the urban core. In their minds the dual villains responsible for this decline were decentralization and blight. Spurred on by a growing devotion to the automobile, decentralization drew residents and business from the older central cities, and blight followed closely behind destroying property values and tarnishing the reputation of the metropolis.

The solution most often proposed for this problem was the physical renewal of the city. New central-city expressways and parking garages would adapt the urban core to the automobile age; airports would preserve the role of New York City, Chicago, and Saint Louis as centers of transportation; middle-class housing in the inner city would ensure a ready supply of consumers for downtown retailers; and air pollution controls, sewage disposal plants, and new waterworks would eliminate environmental blight destructive to central-city prestige and commerce. Through such reforms the central city would also acquire some of the attractive attributes of suburban communities and thus trim suburbia's competitive advantage. Moreover, these projects would supposedly bolster the interests of the city's leading business figures and its chief public officials. Downtown department store owners and landlords would profit from improved access to the central business district and better parking facilities. Mayors could take political credit for rebuilding their cities while also shoring up the municipal tax base, and city planners and engineers could realize their dreams of a metropolis that conformed to the latest principles of their professions.

In the years before the attack on Pearl Harbor, private interest groups and city governments both had begun consideration of how specifically to counter the debilitating forces that were undermining the central city in its emerging competition with suburbia. World War II prevented the implementation of schemes for capital investment, but the interlude of war did give planners, politicians, and business people a chance to make copious plans for the future. These proposals included most of the elements of later revitalization schemes. New highways, slum clearance, parking facilities, neighborhood rehabilitation, and even participatory planning as espoused by Cleveland planners were all on the wish list for the postwar world. By 1945 the stage was set for urban America's campaign to renew the cities.

Notes

1. *Cleveland Plain Dealer*, 4 July 1940, p. 18.
2. *Saint Louis after World War II* (Saint Louis: City Plan Commission, 1942), pp. 12–13.
3. *City Record* 33 (11 January 1941): 25.
4. "Rebuilding the Cities," *Business Week*, no. 566 (6 July 1940): 40.
5. *Christian Science Monitor*, 25 July 1940, p. 20.
6. Walter S. Schmidt, *Proposals for Downtown Cincinnati* (Chicago: Urban Land Institute, 1941), p. 1.

7. Harland Bartholomew, "The American City: Disintegration Is Taking Place," *Vital Speeches 7* (1 November 1940): 61.

8. *Urban Land Institute News Bulletin*, no. 2 (14 November 1941): 2.

12. Bartholomew, "American City," p. 63. For similar findings for Boston, see William H. Ballard, *A Survey in Respect to the Decentralization of the Boston Central Business District* (Boston: Urban Land Institute, 1940), p. 58; and *Building a Better Boston* (Boston: City Planning Board, 1941), pp. 8–9.

13. R. B. Navin, William D. Peattie, and F. R. Stewart, *An Analysis of a Slum Area in Cleveland* (Cleveland: Cleveland Metropolitan Housing Authority, 1934), p. 16. See also *Waverly: A Study in Neighborhood Conservation* (Washington, D.C.: Federal Home Loan Bank Board, 1940), p. 2.

14. Leverett S. Lyon, "Economic Problems of American Cities," *American Economic Review* 32 (March 1942 Supplement): 313.

15. Mary C. Schauffler, *The Suburbs of Cleveland: A Field Study of the Metropolitan District outside the Administrative Area of the City* (Chicago: University of Chicago Press, 1945), p. 3.

16. *Urban Land Institute News Bulletin*, no. 2, p. 3.

17. Marquis W. Childs and John Coburn Turner, "The Real Philadelphia Story," *Forum* 103 (June 1940): 290.

18. Lyon, "Economic Problems of American Cities," p. 315.

19. *Saint Louis after World War II*, p. 24.

20. Urbanism Committee to National Resources Committee, *Our Cities: Their Role in the National Economy* (Washington, D.C.: U.S. Government Printing Office, 1937), p. 68.

24. Bartholomew, "American City," p. 63. For data on the central business district's share of the total city assessment, see Richard J. Seltzer, *Proposals for Downtown Philadelphia* (Chicago: Urban Land Institute, 1942), p. 38; Carl S. Wells, *Proposals for Downtown Detroit* (Washington, D.C.: Urban Land Institute, 1942), pp. 7, 20; Milton C. Mumford, "A Review of the Parking Problem with Particular Reference to Chicago," *Urban Land* 6 (June 1947): 3; and *St. Louis Post-Dispatch*, 23 June 1940, p. 1C.

25. *St. Louis Post-Dispatch*, 23 June 1940, p. 1C; Donald H. McNeil, "Pittsburgh's Downtown Parking Problem," *in Proceedings Institute of Traffic Engineers, 1946* (New Haven, Conn.: Institute of Traffic Engineers, 1947), p. 30; and Mumford, "Review of Parking Problem," p. 3.

26. Mumford, "Review of Parking Problem," p. 3.

27. Edmundson, "Saint Louis," p. 201.

28. H. M. Propper, "Saving Our Downtown Areas," *Nation's Business* 28 (May 1940): 20.

29. Seltzer, *Proposals for Philadelphia*, p. 5.

30. *St. Louis Post-Dispatch*, 23 June 1940, p. 1C; Park H. Martin, "Pittsburgh's Golden Triangle," *American Planning and Civic Annual, 1951* (Washington, D.C.: American Planning and Civic Association, 1952), p. 139; McNeil, "Pittsburgh's Parking Problem," p. 30; Wells, *Proposals for Detroit*, p. 10; and Seltzer, *Proposals for Philadelphia*, pp. 27, 30.

31. John R. Fugard, "What Is Happening to Our Central Business Districts?" *in National Conference on Planning, 1940* (Chicago: American Society of Planning Officials, 1940), p. 108; Seltzer, *Proposals for Philadelphia*, p. 20; Ballard, *Survey of Boston Central Business District*, p. 26; and *St. Louis Post-Dispatch*, 23 June 1940, p. 1C.

32. *St. Louis Post-Dispatch*, 23 June 1940, p. 1C.

33. "Traffic Jams Business Out," *Architectural Forum* 72 (January 1940): 64–65; Walter H. Blucher, "The Economics of the Parking Lot," *Planners' Journal* 2 (September-October 1936): 113; and Wells, *Proposals for Detroit*, p. 9.

34. Seltzer, *Proposals for Philadelphia*, pp. 20–21, 53. For information on demolition in downtown Boston, see Ballard, *Survey of Boston Central Business District*, pp. 15–16. Ballard found that for the period between 1930 and 1939 "the value of the properties demolished . . . more than offset new construction with the exception of the year 1930."

35. "Traffic Jams Business Out," *Architectural Forum*, p. 64.

36. Seltzer, *Proposals for Philadelphia*, pp. 27, 30.

37. Wells, *Proposals for Detroit*, p. 10.

38. Ballard, *Survey of Boston Central Business District*, p. 27.

39. "Boston Diagnosis," *Business Week*, no. 594 (18 January 1941): 62; and Ballard, *Survey of Boston Central Business District*, p. 49.

40. Seltzer, *Proposals for Philadelphia*, p. 38.

41. Wells, *Proposals for Detroit*, p. 10.

42. "Suburban Branch Stores in the New York Metropolitan Region," *Regional Plan Bulletin*, no. 78 (December 1951): 1–8.

48. *St. Louis Post-Dispatch*, 18 June 1940, p. 2C.

49. Ibid., 26 December 1940, p. 2B.

50. *Cleveland Plain Dealer*, 26 August 1940, p. 6.

51. "Urban Land Institute," *American Society of Planning Officials News Letter* 6 (June 1940): 42.

52. "Rebuilding the Cities," *Business Week,* p. 40.

53. The reports were: William H. Ballard, *Proposals for Downtown Boston;* Walter S. Schmidt, *Proposals for Downtown Cincinnati;* Carl S. Wells, *Proposals for Downtown Detroit;* A. J. Stewart, *Proposals for Downtown Louisville;* K. Lee Hyder and Howard J. Tobin, *Proposals for Downtown Milwaukee;* Robert H. Armstrong and Homer Hoyt, *Decentralization in New York City;* and Richard J. Seltzer, *Proposals for Downtown Philadelphia.* For a description of the Armstrong and Hoyt study, see *New York Times,* 20 April 1941, sec. 11, pp. 1–2.

54. For a planner's comments on the need to accommodate automobiles, see Gordon Whitnall, "Downtown Disease," *Planning and Civic Comment* 6 (October–December 1940): 23–24. Whitnall observed: "Today the capacity of a business district is in an increasing degree measured in terms of automobiles and not in persons."

55. Henry H. Saylor, "The Diary," *Architectural Forum* 74 (February 1941): 131.

56. *New York Times,* 15 December 1940, sec. 12, p. 3.

57. *St. Louis Post-Dispatch,* 23 June 1940, pp. 1C, 3C.

58. Ibid., 12 February 1941, p. 4A.

59. *Downtown Study—Baltimore* (Baltimore: Industrial Corporation, 1941), pt. 2, p. 1.

60. *New York Times,* 19 May 1940, sec. 4, p. 10.

61. "Approval of Neighborhood Unit Development Plan Advances Regional Program of Rehabilitation," *Regional Plan Bulletin,* no. 51(1 July 1940): 1–8.

62. "Downtown Buffalo in 1949," *American City* 55 (February 1940): 57. See also *Urban Land Institute Bulletin,* no. 10 (October 1942): 3–4.

63. John T. Howard, *What's Ahead for Cleveland?* (Cleveland: Regional Association of Cleveland, 1941), p. 10. See also *Regional Association of Cleveland Plan Bulletin,* no. 7 (10 September 1941).

64. Howard, *What's Ahead for Cleveland?* pp. 24, 33.

6-3 "Creating a Unified Business Elite: The Origins of the Chicago Central Area Committee"*

Joel Rast

Journal of Urban History

In August 1958, the *Chicago Tribune* published a story by reporter Thomas Buck on a new development plan for Chicago's downtown area. The plan—a twenty-two-year, $1.5 billion blueprint for "modernizing" Chicago's central area—was unveiled in Mayor Richard J. Daley's office in front of a large group of business and civic leaders.[1] The new plan included a number of improvements for Chicago's central business district, the Loop. However, its principal focus was the roughly ten-square-mile area surrounding downtown.[2] Land use in this area—dominated at the time by manufacturing, commercial development, rail freight operations, and low-income housing—was said to have produced an "unsound" relationship between the Loop and its immediate surroundings.[3] Under the plan, large portions of this area would be transformed into middle-income residential neighborhoods that would better complement the corporate and retail functions in the central business district, providing downtown businesses with both a nearby customer base and a pool of qualified workers.

Fifty years after its publication in 1958, the *Development Plan for the Central Area of Chicago* appears prophetic. In a pattern replicated in cities around the country, near-downtown loft buildings that once housed printing establishments, apparel manufacturers, and other light industries have been converted to residential dwellings for downtown office workers. The construction of new high-rise condominiums in areas surrounding the Loop continues at a brisk pace, fueling a downtown population boom that added nearly twenty thousand new residents to the central area from 1990 to 2000.[4] The new downtown residents are overwhelmingly middle class. Gentrification has pushed most low-income families outside the central area, creating a middle-class residential buffer between the Loop and impoverished neighborhoods to the south and west of downtown in much the way that planners in 1958 imagined.

The 1958 Development Plan was a collaboration between the Daley administration and a newly formed civic organization called the Chicago Central Area Committee. Created in 1956 to provide a unified voice for business leaders in redevelopment planning for the downtown area, the Central Area Committee played a key role both in the preparation of the plan and in the development process that followed. Similar organizations formed in cities across the country following World War II, providing the cohesive business leadership necessary for the formation of powerful urban regimes, or "growth coalitions."[5] In partnership with city government, groups such as the Chicago Central Area Committee, Pittsburgh's Allegheny Conference on Community Development, the Greater Baltimore Committee, and the Boston Coordinating Committee pioneered corporate-centered development strategies that transformed downtowns and their surrounding neighborhoods.[6]

Studies of postwar urban regimes have focused on the activities of downtown business groups such as these and the influence they exercised over development policy.[7] However, far less attention has been paid

Source: Joel Rast, "Creating a Unified Business Elite: The Origins of the Chicago Central Area Committee," *Journal of Urban History*, vol. 37, no. 4, July 2011, pp. 583–605. Reprinted with permission from SAGE Publications, Inc.

*Endnotes and references have been omitted. Please consult the original source.

to the origins of such groups. How was a unified business elite created? In many cities, the challenges of the postwar era revealed important divisions among business leaders that would have to be bridged before plans for redevelopment could move forward. Some business leaders favored urban renewal and redevelopment; others were more complacent, concerned that new downtown projects would benefit their competitors or bring in outside firms that would challenge their dominance.[8] Even among those who supported redevelopment, disagreements sometimes arose between those favoring aggressive public sector intervention, including the use of subsidies, and those advocating a more passive government role.[9] Ambitious redevelopment efforts such as Chicago's 1958 Development Plan could be advanced only if forward-looking, progrowth business elites could convince enough of their more conservative counterparts to play along. How such agreements were reached, in Chicago and other places, is a development that needs to be explained. The presence of a unified business elite in postwar cities cannot simply be assumed.

Some studies have pointed to economic pressures as the key cause of business unity. That is, the formation of downtown business groups was a response to deteriorating economic conditions—particularly central business district decline, the spread of blight in near-downtown areas, and white flight—that most cities were experiencing following World War II. Concerned for their survival in an increasingly hostile economic climate, business leaders came together to address these challenges, and their alliance with city hall set the stage for urban redevelopment.[10]

While economic conditions clearly played a role in the formation of downtown business groups following World War II, there are problems with explanations that rely principally or exclusively on economic factors. For one thing, cities faced similar economic challenges as the war came to a close in 1945. Yet many downtown business groups did not form until the mid- or late 1950s, while others were already in existence by the war's end.[11] If economic pressures were the key motivation for the formation of such groups, why did they not form at roughly the same time? Moreover, even if economic concerns were a key motivation, this still does not explain how historic

rivalries and divergent political preferences among business leaders were overcome to present a united business front on urban redevelopment. How did business elites come to recognize their common interests as a class?

This study argues that declining economic conditions in Chicago failed to produce a unified business response during the years immediately following World War II. Instead, various actors, including certain downtown business leaders, sought to influence the agenda for urban redevelopment, often disagreeing among themselves over key goals and objectives. The Central Area Committee was as much a product of these political contests as a response by business elites to urban economic decline. Its formation was, in part, a defensive reaction by downtown business leaders designed to seize control of a development process in which nondowntown actors played a significant role. I argue that the narrow coalition that emerged between the Daley administration and the Central Area Committee suppressed and overwhelmed alternative development strategies in which the interests of neighborhood actors and institutions were privileged over those of downtown business elites. Business unity was forged through political struggles over concrete policies and initiatives in which business elites became increasingly cognizant of their collective interests.

The Origins of Postwar Redevelopment

Chicago entered the post–World War II era facing challenges similar to those of other older industrial cities at the time. Suburbanization of the city's white population was accompanied by a renewed influx of mostly low-income blacks, boosting the city's African American population from 277,731 to 492,265 between 1940 and 1950.[12] Centrally located neighborhoods, particularly those within the city's Black Belt, grew increasingly distressed. A 1943 report by the Chicago Plan Commission designated a twenty-three-square-mile corridor surrounding the central business district as "blighted" or "near-blighted."[13] Downtown was suffering as well, with assessed valuations of property in the central business district falling 13 percent from 1939 to 1947 and no significant building activity since the 1920s.[14]

Despite these conditions, the city's political and civic leaders were, for the most part, slow to respond.

Mayor Edward Kelly, in office since 1933, was a political boss whose approach to governance assumed a caretaker orientation emphasizing basic services and sound fiscal policies.[15] Business elites and other civic leaders were less complacent. However, their ability to act was hampered by institutional fragmentation and a lack of consensus about what should be done. Downtown interests were represented by several organizations, including the Chicago Association of Commerce, the Commercial Club, the Civic Federation, and the State Street Council.[16] Each group had its own agenda, which it pursued independently, and none could claim to speak for the downtown area as a whole. [17] In a 1947 interview with the *Chicago Tribune*, State Street Council executive secretary Randall Cooper insisted that "blighted areas must be rebuilt" but identified work on the "all important parking problem" downtown as the organization's major focus of activity.[18] The Civic Federation was more skeptical of proposals for redevelopment, arguing against any plans that would increase tax assessments or include a public housing component.[19] The Chicago Association of Commerce established a Blighted Areas, Housing and Redevelopment Committee, but by 1947 the group had done little aside from recommending certain changes to the city's building code.[20]

Ultimately, it was a civic group called the Metropolitan Housing and Planning Council (MHPC), working in collaboration with several downtown business leaders, that initiated the push for change in Chicago.[21] Founded in 1934 to provide civic leadership in planning and development policy, MHPC was governed by a thirty-eight-member board dominated by downtown corporate leaders but also including academics, industrialists, and even neighborhood leaders such as Saul Alinsky.[22] The organization's president was Ferd Kramer, a prominent real estate developer. As Arnold Hirsch has described, MHPC worked closely with several members of the downtown business community to develop a response to Chicago's postwar economic crisis.[23] Key among these were Holman Pettibone, president of Chicago Title and Trust; Hughston McBain, president of Marshall Field & Co.; and Milton Mumford, an assistant vice president at Marshall Field.[24] While certain downtown business leaders were included in this group, it did not constitute a unified business elite. Many prominent business leaders were not participants, and MHPC represented a wider set of interests than downtown alone.

For MHPC and its allies, Chicago's most urgent problem was the spread of "blight" during the past several decades, a development that threatened both downtown and healthy residential neighborhoods.[25] The solution devised by MHPC and its partners involved a combination of slum clearance and redevelopment carried out through public-private partnerships. Local government would take the lead on slum clearance, assembling blighted property through eminent domain powers and demolishing existing structures. The cleared land would then be sold to private developers at a reduced cost, while displaced residents would be rehoused in new public housing developments.[26] Working closely with Mumford and Pettibone, MHPC successfully lobbied Republican Governor Dwight Green and key state legislators to enact state urban renewal legislation.[27] The Blighted Areas Redevelopment Act and the Relocation Act, signed by the governor in July 1947, extended eminent domain powers to slum clearance projects and provided state funding for slum clearance and public housing. Additional resources became available two years later with the passage of the federal government's Housing Act of 1949.

Redevelopment of the magnitude that MHPC and its partners envisioned would require sophisticated planning. The Chicago Plan Commission, a weak, underfunded agency controlled by the city council, was not up to the task.[28] Instead, planning for redevelopment was initiated by civic groups such as MHPC working in collaboration with business leaders and institutions located in areas of the city designated by the Plan Commission as "blighted" in its 1943 survey. Such groups shared certain assumptions about central city decline and how it should be addressed. In particular, blight was often likened to a cancerous growth that would "infect more and more areas" unless it were removed.[29] This meant that the attack on slums required a citywide strategy. Just as no cancerous tumor can be safely ignored, no blighted neighborhood could be neglected indefinitely, since inaction would allow the disease to spread to healthy areas of the city.

Despite these shared assumptions among proponents of redevelopment planning, early planning efforts suggested two different approaches. One approach, backed by downtown business elites such as Pettibone and McBain, took an explicitly downtown orientation to urban redevelopment. Pettibone in particular believed that redevelopment "should begin as near as feasible to the central business district of the city, working outward from that point."[30] This approach, which anticipated the corporate-center strategy of the 1958 Development Plan, viewed centrally located neighborhoods as appendages to downtown. Such areas were envisioned, not as functionally integrated economic entities containing both housing and job locations, but as residential areas for downtown office workers. The preference for individuals and families "of moderately high income" as future residents of such areas would require displacement of much of the existing population.[31]

A second approach recognized near-downtown neighborhoods as places of both residence and employment, independent of downtown. This approach, pursued by neighborhood planning organizations, industries, and other institutional actors in near-downtown areas, emphasized the economic development potential of centrally located neighborhoods. Instead of an extension of the central business district, the neighborhood was viewed more as a self-contained economic unit. Efforts to promote and revitalize industrial development and other business activity in such areas would expand employment opportunities for local residents, most of whom would work in the neighborhood, not downtown.[32] Some proponents of this approach argued against gentrification, insisting that redevelopment projects be carried out with no displacement of existing residents. Like the corporate-center strategy described above, this approach had the potential to attract investment dollars to inner-city areas. But its vision for redevelopment, centered more on neighborhood areas than downtown, created the potential for conflict with a downtown-oriented approach. . . .

Contested Terrain

Downtown business leaders such as Holman Pettibone and Milton Mumford supported and even participated in efforts to plan and redevelop the Near South Side. Representatives from MHPC, Chicago Title and Trust, and Marshall Field & Co. were members of the South Side Planning Board, and the boards of both IIT [Illinois Institute of Technology] and Michael Reese Hospital included downtown corporate leaders. Yet despite the involvement of downtown interests in South Side planning initiatives, the leadership of these South Side institutions maintained a strong South Side orientation. As the actions described above suggest, the redevelopment efforts they spearheaded were intended principally to revitalize the Near South Side, not to integrate the South Side into plans for downtown redevelopment. As such, the emergence of a coalition of South Side interests capable of sophisticated planning so close to downtown must have given Pettibone, Mumford, and other proponents of downtown revitalization pause. The South Side Planning Board claimed as its area of influence a vast, seven-square-mile swath of the Near South Side extending from 12th Street south to 47th Street (see Figure 1). The northern boundary of this area was barely a fifteen-minute walk from the Loop. The possibility was strong that, at some point, plans developed by South Side interests for the near-Loop portions of this area would conflict with the planning preferences of downtown interests.

It did not take long for such a conflict to surface. In 1948, the South Side Planning Board initiated plans for a follow-up study of the Near South Side. Unlike the earlier *Opportunity* report, which focused primarily on residential redevelopment, the new study would address industrial development. Large sections of the Near South Side, particularly those areas closest to downtown, were devoted to manufacturing, with printing, warehousing and distribution, and related activities representing the largest sectors.[49] While Near South Side industries benefited from the area's proximity to downtown and its excellent transportation infrastructure, the viability of the Near South Side for manufacturing was threatened by poor planning.[50] Haphazard zoning had produced incompatible land uses in many areas. Industrial firms were often located too close to nearby residences or commercial establishments, and there was little space available for industrial expansion. The South Side Planning Board included among its membership several of the major industrial firms in the area. The new report was intended both to "maintain the interest of . . . present industrial members" and to serve as a recruiting tool

Figure 1   Central area planning groups and project areas, 1950

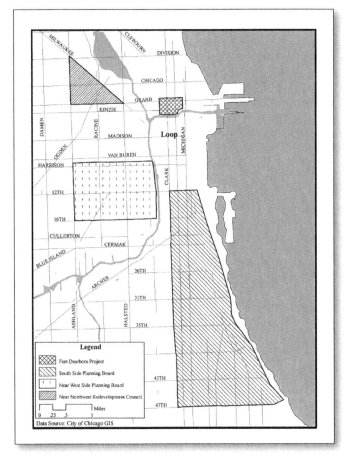

Legend
- Fort Dearborn Project
- South Side Planning Board
- Near West Side Planning Board
- Near Northwest Redevelopment Council

0   .25   .5   1   Miles

Data Source: City of Chicago GIS

the Loop two miles south to Cermak Road. Planners anticipated that the new industrial district would represent a major source of employment for South Side workers and provide a superior operating environment for companies in the area.

The study was well received by labor, industries, and other South Side groups. For downtown interests, however, the new plan was problematic. Redevelopment of the area immediately south of the Loop as an industrial district would perpetuate what many perceived as a dysfunctional relationship that currently existed between the Loop and adjoining areas.[53] Instead of more industrial development, what was needed was middle-class residential development that would provide workers and customers for downtown business establishments.[54] Not surprisingly, when the 1958 Development Plan was released several years later, this area was designated for residential redevelopment, drawing protests from the South Side Planning Board.[55]

In 1955, the South Side Planning Board once again took steps that set up a potential conflict with downtown interests. In this case, the organization announced plans to extend its area of influence north from 12th Street all the way to the Loop.[56] After conferring with institutions in the area, the organization released a land-use plan in 1957 covering portions of the central business district and areas directly south of downtown.[57] The idea was to link planning for these areas to existing planning and redevelopment efforts under way on the Near South Side. This effectively stood the logic of the 1958 Development Plan and its corporate-center strategy on its head. Planning for the central business district would serve the Near South Side instead of the other way around. It was a bold maneuver, invited in part by the failure of the city's corporate leaders to develop a plan of their own for the central area. For downtown business elites such as Pettibone and Mumford, the message was clear: either pull together

with which to expand the organization's industrial membership.[51]

In 1953, the South Side Planning Board released *An Opportunity to Rebuild Chicago through Industrial Development on the Central South Side*, a study the organization hoped would "do for industry" what the previous *Opportunity* report had done for housing on the Near South Side.[52] Identifying the space needs of Near South Side manufacturers as a major concern, the report proposed the creation of a massive industrial district extending from the southern boundary of downtown interests around a plan for the Loop and its immediate surroundings or someone else would fill the void. . . .

Forging an Elite Consensus

By the early 1950s, redevelopment planning for large sections of the central area south and west of downtown was dominated by groups who represented those individual areas, not downtown. No single, overarching vision informed planning for the central area. Instead, planning consisted largely of the uncoordinated efforts of neighborhood planning organizations with few ties to one another and whose principal objective was the revitalization of the areas they served. Even on the South Side, where downtown business leaders at least had a presence in the principal planning organization for the area, planning efforts focused inward on the neighborhood area itself, failing to link developments there to initiatives elsewhere in the city, including downtown. Through partnerships or simple persuasion, business leaders such as Holman Pettibone, Philip Klutznick, and Ferd Kramer sought to reconcile neighborhood planning efforts with the downtown-oriented vision of redevelopment they embraced, but such efforts had been frustrated on multiple occasions.

Downtown business elites might have attempted to assume control over central area planning through development and advocacy of their own plan, but at this stage, there was no consensus on the part of downtown interests around planning for the downtown area. The degree of fragmentation among business leaders at the time was highlighted in 1952 when the Chicago Plan Commission released its plan for a ten-year, $1.5 billion program of public improvements for the central area.[82] The commission proposed a series of projects intended to stimulate private investment in the central area, including street improvements and highway building, new transit facilities, a new downtown railroad terminal consolidating existing passenger and freight facilities, a new civic center to be located on the Near West Side, and several other major public works projects. To finance the improvements, a new public service authority authorized to issue revenue bonds would be established.

In an effort to mobilize support for the proposal, Plan Commission chairman William Spencer made a series of presentations to the city's most influential business organizations.[83] Following a speech to the Commercial Club in December 1951, a special committee appointed by club president Robert Wood to study the issue recommended that club members form a group "which would encourage the accomplishment of such a public works program in every way possible."[84] Soon afterward, a group of downtown business leaders calling itself the Committee for a New Chicago began meeting to discuss a possible action plan. Holman Pettibone was named committee chair. Earl Kribben, vice president for civic affairs at Marshall Field & Co., was appointed secretary. Although the group's immediate task was to mobilize support for the Plan Commission's public works program, early discussions suggested movement toward a broader agenda focused more generally on the city's redevelopment program.[85]

Despite the Commercial Club's endorsement, enthusiasm for the new group among the city's business leaders was not universal, and the committee disbanded following several meetings. In a letter to Pettibone following the group's first meeting, Milton Mumford expressed fears that such an organization, particularly if it assumed a high profile, would "alienate other organizations" such as MHPC, the Civic Federation, the City Club, the Chicago Association of Commerce, and the South Side Planning Board.[86] According to Mumford, such organizations "consider[ed] themselves also qualified and interested in" many of the problems the Committee for a New Chicago would address. In addition, Chicago Association of Commerce president Leverett Lyon warned Pettibone that certain of the Plan Commission's recommendations, including the proposed civic center and downtown rail terminal, would likely provoke "strong disagreement" among business leaders and other groups.[87] Partly for this reason, Lyon concluded that the "formation of a . . . committee or other formal and announced entity at this time would not be the wisest next step."[88]

Although this attempt to unify the city's business leadership around an improvement program for the downtown area ended in failure, developments during the next several years created more favorable conditions for such an effort. In 1954, plans were announced for a 151-acre, $400 million urban renewal project to be located on the north bank of the Chicago River just across the river from the Loop (see Figure 1). The Fort Dearborn project would include five thousand units of middle-income housing in privately built apartment buildings and a $165 million civic center providing office space for federal, state, and local governments.[89] The project was conceived by Arthur Rubloff, a prominent real estate developer whose previous projects included the development of Chicago's "Magnificent Mile" along upper Michigan Avenue.

Although several major urban renewal projects were under way in Chicago by this time, Fort Dearborn was the first of these developments explicitly linked to downtown revitalization. In explaining the rationale for the project, supporters emphasized its positive impact on the Loop. As one supporter put it, the project would "give a north anchor for the Loop which would strengthen the position of the Loop as the commercial and business center of the city."[90] It would do so in part by eliminating what project sponsors described as "a badly blighted section adjacent to and adversely affecting the central business district."[91] Not surprisingly, the Fort Dearborn proposal attracted significant support within the downtown business community. By the time the project was officially launched in March 1954, a team of seven top business executives had been assembled to serve as project sponsors.[92] Both Hughston McBain of Marshall Field and Holman Pettibone were members. Marshall Field vice president Earl Kribben was named project director.

Despite this core of powerful supporters, the Fort Dearborn project quickly became a lightning rod for controversy. The project would require the displacement of nearly ten thousand residents and many commercial establishments north of the Chicago River.[93] As in other portions of the central area targeted for urban renewal, groups representing neighborhood interests opposed plans for slum clearance and displacement. Two planning organizations from the area, the Near North Side Planning Board and the Near Northside Land Use Committee, argued that the announcement of the Fort Dearborn project had destabilized real estate markets in the area by creating uncertainty about the future of the Near North Side.[94] These groups challenged the assertion that the Near North Side was blighted, insisting that profitable

conditions for investment could be restored by removing the prospect of slum clearance in the area.

More importantly, downtown interests could not agree among themselves on the Fort Dearborn project. Retailers and other real estate interests in the South Loop were "less than enthusiastic" about the proposal, fearing that the project would principally benefit the North Loop and the Near North Side.[95] With key members divided over the proposal, downtown business groups such as the Chicago Association of Commerce, the Real Estate Board, the Civic Federation, and the State Street Council avoided taking a position altogether.[96] Eventually, organized opposition to the project within the business community took shape when a group of twenty-eight downtown business leaders dominated by South Loop interests formed the Committee for Government Buildings Downtown.[97] This group opposed the project primarily because of the proposed civic center component. Concerned about the impact on Loop property values of government activities locating or relocating outside the central business district, the committee proposed several downtown locations for new government buildings as alternatives to the Fort Dearborn site.[98]

Opposition to the proposed government center threatened to kill the project, since, without a new civic center as a project anchor, it seemed unlikely that significant new private development activity in the area would materialize.[99]

From the standpoint of business elites, opposition to the Fort Dearborn project within the ranks of the downtown business community did not bode well for the future of downtown redevelopment in Chicago. If business leaders could not agree on this project, what guarantees were there that future projects would not provoke similar dissent? Within this context, Hughston McBain, Holman Pettibone, and several other business leaders resurrected discussions about the formation of a downtown business group.[100] Participants were carefully chosen to incorporate a range of downtown interests. Both South Loop and North Loop interests were represented, including one member of the Committee for Government Buildings Downtown as well as several sponsors of the Fort Dearborn project.[101] These discussions took place over a period of several months and were sufficiently productive that a decision was made to form a new organization. The Chicago Central Area Committee, formally launched in January 1956, would provide a collective voice for downtown business leaders in the planning and redevelopment of the Loop and its immediate surroundings.[102] Holman Pettibone agreed to serve as chairman of the new organization, and a twelve-member executive committee including Hughston McBain and other top business executives was appointed.[103]

With the lessons of the failed Committee for a New Chicago still fresh in his mind, Pettibone took a number of steps to build support for the new organization. First, the Central Area Committee acknowledged the important contributions of the "many fine existing organizations in the Central Area" and the "valuable service" they provided.[104] The Central Area Committee would complement the activities of these groups, not replace them. In addition, the new organization would work largely behind the scenes, brokering agreements among Loop interests and announcing its support for a new project or initiative only after a consensus had been reached.[105] As such, the group took no official position on the Fort Dearborn project until a compromise acceptable to all downtown interests had been worked out.

The Central Area Committee formed during a time when Chicago's governing arrangements were in transition. In April 1955, just months before the organization's official launch date, voters elected Richard J. Daley as mayor. Daley replaced Martin H. Kennelly, a politically weak mayor who had allowed power to gravitate towards the city council.[106] This arrangement had favored neighborhood development groups such as the Near West Side Planning Board and the Near Northwest Redevelopment Council, who, as we saw earlier, formed alliances with aldermen and ward bosses around neighborhood revitalization plans that conflicted with the preferences of downtown actors. Given Kennelly's weakness vis-à-vis the city council, business leaders could not generally look to the mayor for support in conflicts with neighborhood groups. However, Daley's election upset this political balance. Daley was chairman of the Cook County Democratic Party organization, a post he continued to hold after assuming the office of mayor. By serving simultaneously as mayor and party boss, Daley quickly consolidated power over

an undisciplined city council.[107] For downtown business leaders, an alliance with Daley might allow them to prevail in contests with nondowntown actors over the future of the central area, since the mayor rather than ward bosses and aldermen was likely to have the last word in decisions about how or whether redevelopment would go forward.

Daley was, in fact, sympathetic to the development goals of the Central Area Committee, recognizing the economic benefits and prestige that an ambitious, carefully coordinated downtown revitalization program would likely produce.[108] He also recognized the need for a broad business consensus around plans for downtown redevelopment. As such, he refused to take an active role in resolving the controversy surrounding Fort Dearborn and the proposed civic center. Instead, he instructed the Department of City Planning to work with the Central Area Committee on a new plan for the central area that would treat "all of the major problems of the central [area] together."[109] With Pettibone's group playing an active role in the planning process, prospects were good that the new plan would enjoy widespread business support.[110]

The 1958 *Development Plan for the Central Area of Chicago* signaled the triumph of the corporate-centered, downtown approach to central area development over the neighborhood approach advanced by such groups as the South Side Planning Board and the Near West Side Planning Board. The new plan was informed by a vision of development that emerged from downtown in which surrounding neighborhoods were integrated into a comprehensive strategy for downtown revitalization. This vision was explicitly postindustrial. In what the authors of the plan referred to as "probably the most important objective" of the plan, fifty thousand new housing units were recommended for areas surrounding the Loop.[111] New housing developments would replace "blighted industrial and commercial areas" close to downtown and substandard working-class housing.[112] "Special emphasis" would be placed "on the needs of middle-income groups who wish to live in areas close to the heart of the city."[113] In short, land use would be rearranged to accommodate growth of the corporate center at the expense of the commercial and industrial establishments and low-income and working-class residents currently occupying the area.[114]

Predictably, the release of the 1958 Development Plan met with objections from nondowntown planning organizations and other neighborhood groups in the central area. For example, the plan called for a large residential district on the Near South Side extending from the Loop south to 26th Street, an area the South Side Planning Board had designated partially for industrial development. In October 1958, the Planning Board issued a statement critical of the plan, arguing that the area between 16th Street and 26th Street should remain industrial and warning of the disruptive impacts of the plan on existing industrial operations there.[115] According to the statement,

[The plan] can only serve to unsettle these business men and to discourage current plant improvement or expansion plans at existing locations. In fact, it will tend to drive business from the area to a section of the city where it can feel more secure. Since publication of the Central Area Plan random inquiry indicates that a number of companies, including SSPB members, are already giving second thought to long-established programs for growth at a Central South Side location.[116]

The 1958 Development Plan was followed by an explosion of private investment activity downtown, although not of the industrial variety. During the first ten months of 1959 alone, eight major office and residential building projects totaling $130 million were announced.[117] From 1958 to 1963, private construction activity in the central area totaled $662 million.[118] While the downtown construction boom was due in part to favorable economic conditions at the time, both the Central Area Committee and the plan it helped prepare played important roles as well. First, with an established organization representing the development interests of downtown business leaders and a plan in place around which business leaders had coalesced, infighting among downtown commercial and real estate interests over proposals for redevelopment was reduced.[119] New projects were less likely to be sabotaged by factions of the business community motivated largely by self-interest and fearful of the consequences of new development. Second, the work

of the Central Area Committee in planning and promoting the downtown area was said to be "of utmost importance" in renewing investor confidence in the Loop and its immediate surroundings.[120] This renewed optimism represented a "striking change" from the gloomy outlook of previous decades.[121]

Finally, the 1958 Development Plan created a framework for public-private cooperation in the redevelopment of the downtown area. Private investment in the central area was contingent upon government action in the form of land assembly, transportation improvements, new public buildings, use of urban renewal powers, and other activities specified in the plan. As political scientist James Greer observes, it was "the interdependence of public investments, initiatives, and powers, and private investments [that] created the prerequisite" for the building boom that followed.[122] Partnerships among city officials and business leaders necessary to execute complex development projects were facilitated by the business unity that the Central Area Committee provided. Downtown redevelopment created a virtuous, self-reinforcing circle in which new development projects strengthened relationships between business leaders and city officials, creating favorable conditions for additional projects, which further strengthened such relationships, and so on.[123]

As the alliance deepened between the Daley administration and the Central Area Committee, once-influential neighborhood planning organizations such as the South Side Planning Board lost power. By 1958, the South Side group had lost its status as a leader in the city's redevelopment program and was now reduced to fighting a holding action to prevent the further concentration of public housing units on the Central South Side. By this time, twenty-six public housing developments containing 11,617 units (roughly 40 percent of citywide units) were located on the South Side, with more developments in the planning stages.[124] In June 1958, the organization passed a resolution urging the Chicago Housing Authority to withdraw its request for additional units on the South Side to avoid "super-saturation" of public housing developments in the area.[125] Yet public housing had to go somewhere. Locations like the Central South Side within the city's existing Black Belt and well removed from the central business district represented the paths of least resistance.[126] The resolution failed.

With nondowntown planning organizations fading in influence, the Central Area Committee solidified its control over planning for the downtown area. Despite a boom in office building construction during the 1960s, efforts to gentrify the downtown area through new housing development met with less success than hoped for during this time. With the market for middle-income residential development downtown largely untested, developers were reluctant to step forward. A series of closed monthly meetings between city planning officials and the Central Area Committee during the early 1970s culminated in a new plan for the central area released in 1973.[127] The last of fifteen community area reports prepared since 1966, *Chicago 21: A Plan for the Central Area Communities* was written and financed by the Central Area Committee itself. Like the 1958 Development Plan, the new plan emphasized the "physical deterioration" of residential and industrial areas bordering downtown.[128] A highlight of the plan was a proposal for a "new town in town" called Dearborn Park that would eventually house up to 120,000 middle-income residents on a six-hundred-acre site south of the Loop.[129] The hope was that a successful project here would jump-start the gentrification process for the Near South Side and other areas bordering downtown. To finance and oversee the project, the Central Area Committee created the Chicago 21 Corporation, a limited dividend corporation whose board members included Ferd Kramer, Philip Klutznick, and other downtown business leaders.[130] By 1977, stock offerings by the new company had raised $13.7 million for planning, land acquisition, and site preparation.[131]

The Chicago 21 Plan served as rallying point for coordinated opposition by several centrally located neighborhood organizations who perceived the plan as a renewed effort on the part of downtown business leaders to create a *cordon sanitaire* of middle-class residential development around the Loop.[132] However, with support from city officials, implementation of the plan proceeded, and construction of the first phase of Dearborn Park began in 1978. By 1986, 1,500 housing units had been completed, and plans to launch a second phase were under way.[133] Additional middle- and

upper-income residential developments soon followed. River City, located several blocks west of Dearborn Park along the Chicago River, added 2,500 more housing units to the South Loop. West of downtown, the construction of Presidential Towers created 2,460 dwelling units ready for occupancy by 1985. These developments stimulated a wave of residential loft conversions south and west of the Loop that began in the late 1970s and accelerated during 1980s.[134]

It would take decades, but the vision of the Central Area Committee as originally expressed by the 1958 Development Plan and reaffirmed in the Chicago 21 Plan would ultimately be realized. As the 1990s drew to a close, the manufacturing operations, freight yards, and low-income housing that once surrounded the central business district were largely gone, replaced by development that created more synergies with the Loop. The Central Area Committee, established to advance a unified, business-oriented vision for redevelopment of the downtown area, did not single-handedly cause this transformation. However, its planning efforts and close-knit alliance with city officials paved the way for a redevelopment program unprecedented in scale. For neighborhood actors, it was a program that provided little room for the alternative development plans and proposals they supported. Created partly in response to the proliferation of neighborhood planning organizations in the downtown area, the Central Area Committee made such groups redundant. New organizations would eventually surface, but they would struggle to articulate and defend a neighborhood vision on turf that downtown actors had claimed for themselves.

Conclusion

The forging of a unified business elite in postwar cities was a necessary condition for the emergence of postwar growth coalitions and downtown redevelopment efforts that followed. Organizations like the Chicago Central Area Committee created the business consensus necessary for effective partnerships with city government around downtown revitalization. Such efforts were unlikely to succeed where business leaders could not agree among themselves on a course of action, as was initially the case in Chicago. Downtown business groups helped bring together factions of the business community around a common agenda that all could support.

The formation of the Central Area Committee and its counterparts in other cities was partly a result of postwar economic pressures that appeared to threaten the survival of downtown. Yet in Chicago, such pressures alone were insufficient to unite business leaders around a shared redevelopment agenda for the downtown area. Instead, resources available through state and federal urban renewal legislation fostered experimentation in urban redevelopment by various groups, including neighborhood and downtown actors. For business leaders active in redevelopment policy, the results of these ad hoc experiments were unsatisfactory. Neighborhood planning efforts for the central area were, for the most part, neither linked to downtown revitalization nor informed by any unifying logic. The impending collapse of the Fort Dearborn project was the trigger, but the causal forces leading to the formation of the Central Area Committee also include more long-term political contests over the redevelopment of the central area dating back to the late 1940s. The evidence from Chicago thus supports a somewhat more contingent view of postwar urban redevelopment than some have suggested.[135] The downtown-oriented, corporate-center strategy of the 1958 Development Plan succeeded at the expense of neighborhood-level experiments in community development prioritizing different objectives. Had planning efforts and public policies been designed more consistently to nurture and support neighborhood experimentation in redevelopment instead of downtown revitalization, the outcome may have been different. . . .

6-4 "Liberals, Race, and Jobs in Postwar Philadelphia"

Guian A. McKee

The Problem of Jobs: Liberalism, Race, and Deindustrialization in Philadelphia

On a sunny morning in early April 1960, the candy manufacturer Stephen F. Whitman and Son held a groundbreaking ceremony for a new chocolate factory. Only a few months before, the 118-year-old company had been on the verge of moving production of its familiar chocolate sampler boxes from an existing plant in Center City Philadelphia to a suburban location in New Jersey. Whitman and Son had decided instead to remain in the city after the Philadelphia Industrial Development Corporation (PIDC), the city's two-year old quasi-public industrial development authority, organized a transaction that helped the company build a new 400,000-square-foot facility in Philadelphia's Far Northeast section. Although new tract homes, shopping centers, and factories had been developed in the area since World War II, the Far Northeast in 1960 still retained areas of low woods and farms interspersed along the mostly flat plain northwest of the Delaware River. The new Whitman and Son factory was the first plant in what PIDC officials hoped would become a large, planned industrial park on 800 acres of open, city-owned land that surrounded the Northeast Philadelphia Airport. Whitman and Son exemplified the kind of specialty manufacturer that had long formed the core of Philadelphia's industrial base, and the retention of such companies in new city industrial parks was one of PIDC's central goals. At the groundbreaking, city commerce director Frederic R. Mann explained that the Whitman plant was "the beginning of a tremendous development of clean garden-type plants in an area where new homes are being built."[1]

As Mann suggested, the new Whitman factory would rise in a section of Philadelphia that had more in common with nearby suburbs than with much of the inner-city. PIDC, however, was also involved with industrial projects in older, central areas of Philadelphia. Five months to the day after the Whitman groundbreaking, a similar group of local notables attended a second ceremony, this time for the West Wholesale Drug Company. This firm, with PIDC help, planned to build its new facility in a smaller, inner-city industrial park on the site of an abandoned public hospital in the Feltonville area of North Philadelphia. This densely developed urban neighborhood—a motley mix of modern industrial areas and older factories, railroad lines, and brick row houses—had been an important manufacturing center in Philadelphia since the early twentieth century. Although the largely white Feltonville area had not yet experienced racial turnover, it lay barely a mile from the edge of the expanding African American neighborhoods of North Philadelphia. PIDC's success in attracting investment capital to this area—and in building new factories and warehouses there—reflected its extraordinary commitment to solving the economic problems of Philadelphia's aging inner-city neighborhoods.

The "groundbreaking" for West Wholesale Drug, however, was held not at the actual site of the new plant, as the Whitman and Sons ceremony had been, but at the Bellevue-Stratford Hotel in Center City. Instead of traveling to the gritty inner city industrial site, the dignitaries attended a luncheon at the hotel, where they received West Wholesale medicine bottles that had been filled with soil from the construction site and labeled: "This is good medicine for Philadelphia."[2] The figurative distance between these bottles and the actual neighborhood of West Wholesale's new plant symbolized both the boldness and the limitations of Philadelphia's response to deindustrialization: a series of inventive liberal policy strategies brought direct and unexpectedly successful public interventions in the private marketplace, but divisions of race undercut the city's efforts to reshape the process of urban economic transformation.

The contrast between the groundbreaking ceremonies for Whitman and West Wholesale delineated the innovative quality of local liberalism in the postwar United States as well as the constraints that racialized spatial *and* policy boundaries placed on that liberalism. Both companies benefited from strong local interventions in the economy, showing how strands of local governance and state building fundamentally shaped public policy in the postwar United States, and that liberalism in fact deeply influenced multiple levels of the American state. Each case suggests how city officials, business organizations, and community activists in the city drew on American liberalism's rich legacy of policy ideas and experiments to develop a series of local industrial and employment policies that sought to arrest the decline of the city's manufacturing sector.

These local policy initiatives engaged with and, in some cases, relied on the resources and incentives provided by federal programs, but they remained projects of the local state—of liberal policymakers and activists who constructed public, private, and community-based institutions that sought to address the city's loss of industrial jobs. This local state-building project generated significant policy innovation and allowed Philadelphia's postwar liberals to maintain, update, and even expand the engagement with structural economic questions that had typified the most ambitious strands of New Deal and World War II–era liberalism, even as national liberalism moved in significantly different directions.[3] Yet for all of its innovation, Philadelphia's postwar liberalism suffered from a critical flaw. Its core economic strategy bifurcated along racial lines. The resulting division, into parallel, racially defined tracks of industrial and employment policy, ultimately limited the city's ability to respond effectively to the challenges of economic transformation during the post–World War II period.

Postwar Liberalism and Philadelphia

Why does Philadelphia's postwar local liberalism matter? Why is this account of politics and public policy in Philadelphia something more than what anthropologist Clifford Geertz referred to as "another country heard from"?[4] It matters because Philadelphia developed a postwar urban liberalism that differed in crucial ways from national forms of liberalism. In particular, liberals in Philadelphia recognized the problem of deindustrialization at a very early date and used the resources they had available to shape activist, public solutions to crucial economic problems. While they did not always succeed, the vibrancy and creativity of this local liberal response invites a reassessment of the role of urban political actors during this period, and of liberalism generally in the postwar United States.

Philadelphia's local liberalism, of course, evolved within the rich and complex historical context of American liberalism. By the early 1950s—when this study begins—liberalism had followed a varied and shifting course in the United States. Its roots as a political philosophy lay in the seventeenth- and eighteenth-century political and intellectual revolts that rejected the hereditary authority of church and monarchy in favor of constitutional rule and individual liberty in all its forms—property rights, freedom of religious conscience, and political self-determination. By the close of the nineteenth century, the laissez faire tradition of classical liberalism had become dominant in the United States. This version placed almost exclusive emphasis on the rights of private property and individual economic autonomy, including, and even privileging, the rights of corporations. During the first half of the twentieth century, however, the interventions of Progressivism and, most crucially, the New Deal modified classical liberalism almost beyond recognition. While still exhibiting great internal variation, liberalism moved gradually and unevenly toward an acceptance of governmental regulatory intervention in the private sector. It did so on the grounds that in an age of corporate-dominated industrial capitalism, the meaningful preservation of individual social and economic liberty—ideals that lay at the core of classical liberalism—required public constraint of business and provision of at least a limited welfare state, financed primarily through taxation.[5]

By the end of World War II, and for at least two decades afterwards, liberalism attained a position of preeminence as the nation's leading political philosophy. This dominance was buttressed by the Democratic Party coalition of union members, big-city political organizations, racial and ethnic minorities, intellectuals, and Southerners that had built the New Deal. A number of distinctive features characterized this postwar liberalism—some of which Philadelphia's local liberalism shared, and some of which it did not—and set it off from its conservative and radical counterparts. Liberalism's first characteristic consisted of a philosophical and practical commitment to pragmatism, with its emphasis on the importance of empiricism and scientific inquiry in establishing contingent but useful truth claims; this in turn produced an approach to governance that focused on policy experimentation and practical results.[6] The second principle, a staunch endorsement of anti-communism in both foreign and domestic policy, played a far greater role in liberalism nationally than in Philadelphia.[7]

Postwar liberalism's third and fourth characteristics, a reliance on universalist appeals to the common good and a sometimes hesitant engagement in civil rights issues, interacted in powerful and increasingly unstable ways over the postwar decades. Because it is central to my account of postwar Philadelphia, this tension merits elaboration. Postwar liberalism deployed a universalist language that drew on the ethos of the New Deal, which had emphasized the reciprocal obligations of citizens. These obligations included both the duty to aid one another through the mediating, socially ameliorative institutions of government *and* the responsibility of individuals to contribute, primarily through work, to the greater good of society. While partly reflecting solidarity borne of the Depression, this universalism also had an element of opportunism in its tendency to suborn the justice claims of particular groups—especially African Americans—to the Democratic party's need to maintain the political support of its southern wing. Postwar critics increasingly challenged the failures and exclusions of such liberal appeals to the common good and sought redress for those left out of the New Deal paradigm—and

particularly, for its racial exclusions. They focused not on the theoretical ideal of reciprocity, but on community empowerment, grassroots democratization, and attainment of rights for racially marginalized groups.[8]

Increasingly, these insurgencies played out in the context of the civil rights movement. While liberals had maneuvered the Democratic Party into support for civil rights during the 1948 presidential campaign, at the cost of temporarily splitting the party, their actual responsiveness to civil-rights demands remained tepid and slow-moving, particularly for issues where race intersected with economics. The wide embrace of Gunnar Myrdal's sweeping study *An American Dilemma* facilitated this cautious approach to racial problems, as Myrdal explained American racism as a fundamentally cultural and psychological problem, rooted in the hearts and minds of whites and thus amenable to education, positive example, and appeals to morality and fairness. This generated a racial liberalism that viewed discrimination as a problem of the individual and that divorced issues of economic inequality from the structural interplay of race and economics. At times, these ideas shaped key aspects of national civil rights strategies, such as the NAACP Legal Defense Fund's successful effort to challenge the separate but equal doctrine in *Brown v. Board of Education*.[9] Yet at the local level, in Philadelphia and around the nation, civil rights activists continued to assert the centrality of economic issues in the movement *throughout* the postwar period. In cities such as New York during the 1940s, civil rights activists formed alliances with trade unions and, until the Red Scare, communists to fight for both economic and racial gains. By the 1960s, economic concerns emerged as a key focus of the 1963 March on Washington For Jobs and Freedom, as the core of A. Philip Randolph, Bayard Rustin, and Leon Keyserling's 1966 *Freedom Budget for All Americans*, and as the center of much of Martin Luther King Jr.'s work long before he turned north to Chicago in 1966. Meanwhile, from New Orleans to Oakland, from Durham to Brooklyn, and from Las Vegas to Philadelphia, both moderate and radical activists challenged both discriminatory employment practices and, increasingly, economic inequality itself.[10]

The persistence of economic concerns in the civil rights movement suggests the continuing salience of the fifth principle of postwar liberalism—belief in the value of state engagement in the economy. This principle of public economic intervention joins civil rights and liberal universalism as core concerns of this study. Liberals in the early postwar years agreed on the general proposition of such intervention, but the exact policy structures remained the subject of much debate. While most liberals by 1945 had accepted the general principles of Keynesianism, and still shared the New Deal goal of broad economic security, disagreements persisted for decades about whether policy should focus on social spending, such as public investments in job and welfare programs and the redevelopment of depressed areas, or on macroeconomic fiscal policy measures such as tax cuts. "Social Keynesians," who favored the more activist social spending course, suffered two key setbacks during and immediately after the war. The first defeat came in 1943 when congressional conservatives defunded the National Resources Planning Board (NRPB), the body that in a variety of New Deal iterations had developed plans for expansive public works, natural resources development, social welfare, and jobs programs. Many of these would have been managed through new cooperative, intergovernmental economic planning bodies that would have given significant authority to state and local governments. Such decentralized structures offered a model for a "liberal federalism," a thoroughly Americanized vision of how the state might play a more active role in the economy. The social Keynesians' second defeat came when Congress eviscerated the Full Employment Act of 1945, which would have formally committed the federal government to maintaining full employment through the implementation of job and public works projects.[11]

After these setbacks, modified versions of social Keynesianism such as area-redevelopment policy, job training, and even full employment remained on the agenda of many liberals. But by the mid-1960s a policy framework of tax cut–based "commercial Keynesianism" became the dominant strain of liberal economic policy. This approach emphasized the use of fiscal policy to achieve overall economic growth, while rejecting any public intervention in the structure of the economy. President Lyndon Johnson, for example, pursued a significant cut in personal and corporate income taxes, followed by a War on Poverty that

emphasized community political empowerment, reorganization of social services, and the creation of individual connections to existing economic opportunity, but included no significant efforts at structural economic reform or job creation.[12] Throughout this period, however, Philadelphia's local liberals continued to pursue policies associated with the social Keynesian conception of how government should engage the wider economy.

The historical meaning of these postwar economic policy developments, both in Philadelphia and the United States, depends in large part on interpretation of the New Deal and its postwar legacy. In recent decades, historians of New Deal policy have largely divided into two broad groups. The first group argued that while the New Deal actually did possess transformative potential as a step toward American social democracy, a series of compromises with Southern Democrats and corporate business interests undermined this promise. Collectively, adherents of this "end-of-reform" perspective maintain that the New Deal, and by extension postwar liberalism, abandoned any serious effort to address problems of economic structure.[13]

In recent years, other historians have begun to challenge the end-of-reform view of liberalism. New studies have questioned whether the New Deal *ever* possessed truly transformative, social democratic potential, even as they demonstrated that it undertook and accomplished significant *liberal* reform projects. Such work has shown the centrality of public-works programs to the New Deal, not only as immediate employment projects but also and more fundamentally as projects aimed at spurring long-term economic development as a state purpose. Although subject to greater constraint, such efforts continued in the postwar period, with significant public investments in highway construction, urban renewal, and the development of scientific and health care infrastructure.[14] Another strand of argument places a consumer-driven "pocketbook politics" at the center of the New Deal. This regime, which operated through such agencies as the National Recovery Administration's Consumer Advisory Board and the wartime Office of Price Administration, sought to protect purchasing power through policies that promoted low prices and high wages. Although some scholars find a decline in such consumerist liberalism shortly after the war, others see the 1950s and 1960s as its heyday.[15] Another group of studies takes issue with the postwar solidity of the New Deal coalition itself, contending that as early as the late 1940s, it had already begun to splinter on racial lines around issues of access to housing and jobs, especially in the urban North and West.[16] Building on this recognition of early discontent within the New Deal coalition, historians have more recently traced the rise of a powerful new movement conservatism in the 1960s and 1970s, a conservatism rooted in Sunbelt suburbs as well as in white ethnic urban neighborhoods.[17]

Despite these challenges, the end-of-reform thesis continues to shape most accounts of postwar history. Postwar liberalism emerges as intellectually and ideologically enervated even at the moment of its greatest political influence. Unwilling to alter basic economic structures, unable to address noncultural causes of poverty and inequality, and uncertain in challenging systematic dimensions of racism, liberals during the 1940s, 1950s, and early 1960s restricted political life to pluralist bargaining among interest groups, economic policy to a commercial Keynesian focus on overall growth, and antipoverty efforts to remedies for the cultural and behavioral characteristics of the poor themselves. Further, at the local level, liberalism appears to have fractured from within around the issue of race. Most scholarship on the role of localism in the postwar history of liberalism has focused on the frequently bitter narrative of how racial division and violence among the urban working class, along with the rapid growth of segregated suburbs, undermined efforts to achieve residential integration, progressive public housing, and, more broadly, class-based social movements.[18] With liberals seemingly so lacking in imagination and ambition, radicals and conservatives become the only dynamic historical actors, especially at the local level. My difficulty with such accounts lies less with their accuracy in their own field of view, where they offer vitally important insights, but with their failure to account for what I see as the full policy agenda of postwar-urban liberalism, taken on its own terms.

This book tells a different story. It finds not enervation, but a vibrant liberal activism alive and well in the American city. This was a liberalism that adapted the New Deal and wartime tradition of economic engagement for postwar conditions and that focused the power of the state on questions of economic structure and employment. Yet it also moved beyond such 1930s roots. Local liberals in Philadelphia, both in and out of government, developed new mechanisms of state intervention in the economy and shaped civil rights strategies that challenged employment discrimination and demanded economic opportunity for the marginalized. Perhaps most notably, African American activists emphasized a strand of liberal ideology that most critics have missed: an embrace of self-reliance, self-help, and responsibility as core values that liberal policy could and should promote. The state, in this view, had a responsibility to make real resources available to citizens who had none, but those citizens too had a responsibility to then improve themselves and their communities. Philadelphia's local liberalism thus relied on an amalgam of pragmatic approaches: a readiness to experiment, a belief in state activism, a commitment to civil rights, and an incorporation of "mainstream values" that rendered its efforts readily acceptable to a wide and diverse public. This was a relevant and bold American liberalism that has been widely overlooked in histories that emphasize only a national story of pro-growth Keynesianism, group-based rights claims, and anti-communism.

For all its innovation, Philadelphia's postwar local liberalism was not without serious faults. Some liberal initiatives achieved only modest success, some faced significant political obstacles, and others simply failed. More typical, though, was a nuanced pattern in which liberal initiatives worked well in certain key areas, yet left others unaddressed: building new factories in the inner city, for example, but failing to link such projects to job training programs that targeted the city's most needy residents. Above all, divisions of race bifurcated the economic policy initiatives that Philadelphia's postwar liberalism undertook and constrained the results that they achieved. Innovative planning proposals that sought to draw the resulting parallel tracks of liberal policy together failed to achieve implementation. Meanwhile, the wider restructuring of the U.S. economy away from manufacturing and toward services placed increasing pressure on Philadelphia policymakers and activists as the promise of the

1960s faded into the bleakness of the 1970s. Still, liberal activists accomplished much in postwar Philadelphia. Political, business, and community leaders fought back against deindustrialization through local industrial and employment policies that were deeply rooted in the employment-focused liberalism of the New Deal–World War II period, but that took on their own shape as the postwar era unfolded.[19] Most of this story has been lost. When restored, it forces reassessments both of the nature of postwar liberalism in the United States and of the political and social history of American cities.

Clifford Geertz ultimately concluded that detailed studies of the local case mattered because they offered an intellectual path through which "the mega-concepts with which contemporary social science is afflicted . . . can be given the sort of sensible actuality that makes it possible to think not only realistically and concretely *about* them, but, what is more important, creatively and imaginatively *with* them."[20] So it is with the mega-concept of liberalism and the case of Philadelphia. For all its reach, all its power, all its centralization, liberalism for most Americans in the postwar years actually wore a local face. It was in communities across the country that people interacted with their government on a daily basis and that liberalism took on concrete meaning. In cities like Philadelphia, liberalism became lived reality.

The Problem of Jobs

The loss of manufacturing jobs, first as threat and then as reality, posed a fundamental quandary not just for Philadelphia but for American urbanism generally. For centuries, cities in America had offered the promise of plentiful and rewarding work and with it, the prospect of a better life. Generations of migrants and immigrants had left farms and villages to pursue this urban promise. Since the advent of industrialization, this pull had originated with the factory, with manufacturing jobs that offered more regular and higher income than anything available in rural occupations. Reality, of course, had not always matched the ideal of the bountiful city workplace. Many manufacturing jobs had always been dangerous, repetitive, and low-paying. For skilled workers, though, the urban factory often did meet expectations, and after the rise of mass

industrial unionism with the CIO (Congress of Industrial Organizations) organizing drives of the 1930s, even unskilled workers achieved improved working conditions, higher salaries, and benefits such as retirement pensions and health insurance. Regardless of actual factory conditions, however, mass movements of people continued to flow toward the city through the middle of the twentieth century. For most migrants, the implicit promise of work drove their decisions. Industrial work and both its lure and limitations became ingrained in the process of urbanization itself.

This long-standing association of the city with good job opportunities began to unravel after World War II. The loss of industry in Philadelphia and similar cities created a dramatic "problem of jobs" that consisted of the imbalance between the availability of employment, for both men and women, that paid wages sufficient to meet workers' basic economic needs and the size, spatial distribution, and skills of the city's working-age population. Along with the material deprivation that it wrought, this problem of jobs jeopardized a key element of the social and political identity of working people. For many, it even threatened the very basis of citizenship itself, as work had defined the autonomous and independent status that for much of U.S. history had been a prerequisite for full membership in the polity, albeit often along distinct racial and gender lines?[21]

The problem of jobs affected nearly all of the urban working class, but it struck Northern, urban African Americans with particular ferocity. Since the 1890s, but particularly during World War II, African Americans had left the violence and desperate poverty of the Jim Crow South for the lure of industrial jobs in the urban North. With the limited exception of the war years, when huge labor demands opened previously closed manufacturing jobs to blacks, the reality of life in the North had often proved disappointing. Overt racial discrimination in hiring, as well [sic] more subtle discriminatory structures such as closed union hiring and apprenticeship systems, combined to limit blacks to the lowest-paying, dirtiest, and most dangerous jobs. For African American women, at least in peacetime, few openings existed outside of domestic service.[22]

Deindustrialization made such problems dramatically worse, as the pool of manufacturing jobs that had pulled many African Americans north gradually began to shrink. Metropolitan housing discrimination exacerbated the problem still further. White workers, at least those who could save for a down payment or qualify for assistance from the GI bill or other federally assisted home ownership programs, could always follow the jobs to the suburbs (at least when companies remained in business and in the region). Trapped by the "white noose" that excluded them from most new suburban developments around Philadelphia, African Americans, with limited exceptions, could not make such moves.[23] This interplay of racial, economic, and spatial structures meant that the problem of jobs proved particularly devastating for Philadelphia's African Americans. Yet it also generated a range of innovative efforts to solve the problem from within the African American community, efforts that built on the resources of blacks and their institutions but also drew on and sometimes worked with the liberal state. Much of this study focuses on the interaction of Philadelphia's African American liberals with the state, with their white liberal counterparts and sometime partners, and with the city's wider African American community in seeking solutions to the problem of jobs. What they and others found in Philadelphia suggests that devastating as the problem of jobs may have been, potential paths to its resolution did exist. Those paths lay within the field of mid-century U.S. liberalism; yet barriers that would ultimately block those paths lay within liberalism too.

Local Liberalism

The vibrancy, and even the viability, of local liberalism depended on the circumstances. In Philadelphia, such conditions emerged in 1951 when a group of reform-oriented liberals came to power with the support of an often tenuous coalition of civic and political organizations, labor unions, African Americans, Democratic ward organizations, and business groups. This coalition neatly mirrored the national New Deal coalition, with the exceptions that business held a position of greater influence in Philadelphia and that no parallel to the Southern Democrats existed. Originating in the mayor's office under mayors Joseph Clark and Richardson Dilworth but continuing after the reform mayors left office and extending into the sphere of community activism—particularly African American

activism—these Philadelphia liberals pursued policy goals that seemed obsolete to many by the 1950s and 1960s.[24]

Acting in the tradition of pragmatic liberalism that had characterized much of the New Deal, Philadelphia liberals between the 1950s and the 1970s engaged in a series of evolving experiments that infused old approaches with new meanings and possibilities, with the goal of meeting the demands of an altered situation.[25] These liberal policymakers and activists only occasionally linked their efforts to New Deal–wartime liberalism in an explicit way; more often, such ties were demonstrated through policy assumptions, ideological orientations, and intellectual affinities. While liberal leaders and activists drew on the past in their commitment to state intervention in the economy, their reliance on state-sponsored economic development, and their repeatedly frustrated efforts to implement an economic planning agenda, they pushed local liberalism in new directions quite different from its national counterparts.

Such differences emerged especially in three critical policy areas. First, public intervention in private realms of the marketplace moved from bitter controversy to routine administrative procedure in just a few years, as city government entered and transformed the operation of the local industrial real estate market. It did so in a way that sought to maximize the retention of good jobs as well as tax revenue (which supported the reformers' social service agenda). More broadly, it pursued the old reform liberal goal of creating economic order in a key private market. As implemented by the Philadelphia Industrial Development Corporation, Philadelphia's industrial renewal program used federal tax incentives to provide low-cost plant financing for small- and medium-sized firms that made up a large percentage of Philadelphia's industrial base. This strategy . . . reversed the usual pattern of federal subsidy of suburban development and achieved a surprising degree of success, even in the city's aging industrial core.

Second, African American liberals during the 1960s built on the civil rights movement's long-standing engagement with economic concerns even as they reappropriated traditional discourses of self-help and community uplift for liberal purposes. This approach intertwined challenges to racial discrimination with attention to issues of economic structure and class. In the 1960s, a group of black Philadelphia ministers deployed the public resources provided by the War on Poverty to build one of the nation's largest job training and business development programs, the community-controlled Opportunities Industrialization Centers (OIC) and the affiliated Progress Movement. . . . [F]ederal anti-poverty warriors of the period assumed that in a high-growth macroeconomic environment, job training could reduce poverty by improving individual skills and changing behavioral characteristics without addressing the structure of the economy. Faced with the harsh realities of discrimination and limited African American control of capital in the city, OIC soon rejected this central premise of postwar "manpower policy" and expanded its reach to include questions of economic structure and security. Drawing on a well-established base of community support, as well as federal minority contract set-asides and private philanthropy, OIC developed a series of community-owned manufacturing enterprises and commercial businesses. At its core, this effort sought to restructure American capitalism around a model of community control and social responsibility as well as the profit motive. For more than a decade, these efforts succeeded. . . . [T]his on-the-ground evolution of the War on Poverty in Philadelphia indicates that federal inattention to economic structure and employment policy did not preclude a local focus on such issues; careful attention to local policy history thus demonstrates how local actors reshaped federal policy and determined its actual, on-the-ground operation.

Division of these policies along lines of race, however, would prove crucial in determining the effectiveness of Philadelphia's postwar local liberalism at devising solutions to the problem of jobs. Despite the innovations of its local industrial and employment policies, Philadelphia failed to form effective links between publicly funded but community-based programs such as OIC and public-private initiatives such as PIDC. As a result, PIDC and OIC existed as parallel, racially bifurcated tracks of policy in the city. While each track included elements of an effective response to deindustrialization, this racial divide meant that neither could grapple effectively with all aspects of Philadelphia's economic problems.

A third area of liberal activism offered the promise that this racial divide in Philadelphia's industrial and employment policies could be closed. Throughout the 1960s, economic planning remained an ongoing subject of debate among Philadelphia liberals in both the public and private sectors. This local planning discourse . . . transcended the typical physical design concerns of postwar city planning and led to the creation of protean forms of the local planning bodies that had once been called for by the New Deal's National Resources Planning Board.[26] Eventually, these planning efforts forged tentative new ties across the city's racially divided industrial and employment policies. . . . [O]ther inter-racial initiatives during the late 1960s and early 1970s supported both the development of autonomous African American construction contractors and the implementation of the federal "Philadelphia Plan" for integration of the local construction industry—an immediate precursor of affirmative action. This effort not only opened a crucial source of employment in the city to African Americans, but also provided a new source of unity for black and white liberals in Philadelphia. But with these improvements came setbacks. Inter-racial initiatives alienated much of the local labor movement during a period in which the local liberal coalition had come under increasing strain.

Ultimately, this study argues for the continued relevance of localism and place in post–World War II political history. Despite the growth of the federal state during the twentieth century and the attendant, if partial, centralization of state authority, local governments, policymakers, and community activists continued to exert extensive and often defining influence over the implementation and on-the-ground operation of American public policy. This persistent localist strand had both negative and positive characteristics for American governance. Along with the important and well-documented limitations that local racial boundaries and entrenched political cultures placed on federal policy, this study shows that under specific place-based circumstances, local institutions could be sites of significant policy innovation and creative liberal activism. Although often obscured by reactionary qualities of the local state and limited by powerful forces of national and global political economy, this local liberalism is an important but underemphasized piece of recent American political history, the neglect of which impoverishes the sense of political possibility for historians and for Americans generally.

Notes

1. "Whitman Starts Plant; Ground Broken on Roosevelt Blvd.," *PB*, April 7, 1960; Joseph M. Guess, "Whitman's to Build Plant on Boulevard; Chocolate Firm Reverses Its Plan to Move to N.J.," *PB*, January 28, 1960.

2. "Drug Company Abandons Plan to Leave City; West Wholesale to Build New Plant at Front & Luzerne," *PB*, September 8, 1960; Joseph M. Guess, "Firm Decides to Stay in City; PIDC Helps Finance New Drug Plant," *PB*, February 23, 1960.

3. For the continued relevance of the local state in American political history, Thomas J. Sugrue, "All Politics Is Local: The Persistence of Localism in Twentieth Century America," in *The Democratic Experiment: New Directions in American Political History*, ed. Meg Jacobs, William J. Novak, and Julian Zelizer (Princeton: Princeton University Press, 2003), 301–26; Philip J. Ethington, "Mapping the Local State," *Journal of Urban History* 27:5 (July 2001): 686–702; Eric H. Monkkonen, *The Local State: Public Money and American Cities* (Stanford: Stanford University Press, 1995).

4. Clifford Geertz, *The Interpretation of Cultures* (New York: Basic Books, 1973), 23.

5. Paul Starr, *Freedom's Power: The True Force of Liberalism* (New York: Basic Books, 2007); William A. Galston, *Liberal Purposes: Goods, Virtues, and Diversity in the Liberal State* (New York: Cambridge University Press, 1991).

6. David A. Hollinger, *In the American Province: Studies in the History and Historiography of Ideas* (Baltimore: Johns Hopkins University Press, 1989); Gary Gerstle, "The Protean Character of American Liberalism," *American Historical Review* 99:4 (October 1994), 1043–73; Louis Menand, *The Metaphysical Club* (New York: Farrar, Straus and Giroux, 2001); James T. Kloppenburg, *The Virtues of Liberalism* (New York: Oxford University Press, 1998).

7. Robert H. Zieger, *The CIO, 1935–1955* (Chapel Hill: University of North Carolina Press, 199S); Ellen Schrecker, *Many Are the Crimes: McCarthyism in America* (Princeton: Princeton University Press, 1998);

Paul Lyons, *Philadelphia Communists, 1936–1956* (Philadelphia: Temple University Press, 1982); Lyons, *The People of This Generation: The Rise and Fall of the New Left in Philadelphia* (Philadelphia: University of Pennsylvania Press, 2003), 10-11; Sherman Labovitz, *Being Red in Philadelphia: A Memoir of the McCarthy Era* (Philadelphia: Camino Books, 1998).

8. Michael Tomasky, "Party in Search of a Notion," *American Prospect* 17:5 (May 2006), 20–28; Gary Gerstle, "The Protean Character of American Liberalism," *American Historical Review* 99:4 (October 1994), 1043–73; Ira Katznelson, *When Affirmative Action Was White: An Untold History of Racial Inequality in Twentieth Century America* (New York: W. W. Norton, 2005).

9. Gunnar Myrdal, *An American Dilemma: the Negro Problem and Modern Democracy* (New York: Harper & Brothers, 1944); Thomas J. Sugrue, "Affirmative Action from Below: Civil Rights, the Building Trades, and the Politics of Racial Equality in the Urban North, 1945–1969," *Journal of American History* 91 (June 2004): 145–73; Risa L. Goluboff, *The Lost Origins of Civil Rights* (Cambridge, MA: Harvard University Press, 2007).

10. Martha Biondi, *To Stand and Fight: The Struggle for Civil Rights in Postwar New York City* (Cambridge: Harvard University Press, 2003); John D'Emilio, *Lost Prophet: The Life and Times of Bayard Rustin* (New York: Free Press, 2003); Nancy MacLean, *Freedom Is Not Enough: The Opening of the American Workplace* (Cambridge: Harvard University Press, 2006); Thomas F. Jackson, *From Civil Rights to Human Rights: Martin Luther King, Jr., and the Struggle for Economic Justice* (Philadelphia: University of Pennsylvania Press, 2007); Kent Germany, *New Orleans after the Promises: Poverty, Citizenship, and the Search for the Great Society* (Athens: University of Georgia Press, 2007); Robert O. Self, *American Babylon: Race and the Struggle for Postwar Oakland* (Princeton, NJ: Princeton University Press, 2003); Christina Greene, *Our Separate Ways: Women and the Black Freedom Movement in Durham, North Carolina* (Chapel Hill: University of North Carolina Press, 2005); Annelise Orleck, *Storming Caesar's Palace: How Black Mothers Fought Their Own War on Poverty* (Boston: Beacon Press, 2005); Matthew Countryman, *Up South: Civil Rights and Black Power in Philadelphia* (Philadelphia: University of Pennsylvania Press, 2005).

11. Kloppenburg, *The Virtues of Liberalism* (New York: Oxford University Press, 1998); Alice O'Connor, "Swimming against the Tide: A Brief History of Federal Policy in Poor Communities," in William T. Dickens and Ronald F. Ferguson, eds., *Urban Problems and Community Development* (Washington, D.C.: Brookings Institution Press, 1999); Margaret Weir, *Politics and Jobs: The Boundaries of Employment Policy in the United States* (Princeton: Princeton University Press, 1992); Weir, "The Federal Government and Unemployment: The Frustration of Policy Innovation from the New Deal to the Great Society," in *The Politics of Social Policy in the United States*, ed. Weir, Ann Shola Orloff, and Theda Skocpol (Princeton: Princeton University Press, 1988), 149–90.

12. Robert M. Collins, *More: The Politics of Economic Growth in Postwar America* (New York: Oxford University Press, 2000); Gareth Davies, *From Opportunity to Entitlement: The Transformation and Decline of Great Society Liberalism* (Lawrence: University Press of Kansas, 1996); Thomas F. Jackson, "The State, the Movement, and the Urban Poor: The War on Poverty and Political Mobilization in the 1960s," in Michael B. Katz., ed., *The "Underclass" Debate: Views From History* (Princeton: Princeton University Press, 1993), 403–39; Judith Russell, *Economics, Bureaucracy, and Race: How Keynesians Misguided the War on Poverty* (New York: Columbia University Press, 2004).

13. Alan Brinkley, *The End of Reform: New Deal Liberalism in Recession and War* (New York: Alfred A. Knopf, 1995); Steve Fraser and Gary Gerstle, eds., *The Rise and Fall of the New Deal Order, 1930–1980* (Princeton: Princeton University Press, 1989); Colin Gordon, *New Deals: Business, Labor, and Politics in America, 1920–1935* (New York: Cambridge University Press, 1994); Christopher L. Tomlins, *The State and the Unions: Labor Relations, Law, and the Organized Labor Movement in America, 1880–1960* (Cambridge: Cambridge University Press, 1985); Katznelson, *When Affirmative Action Was White*.

14. Jason Scott Smith, *Building New Deal Liberalism: The Political Economy of Public Works, 1933–1956* (New York: Cambridge University Press, 2006); Margaret Pugh O'Mara, *Cities of Knowledge: Cold War Science and the Search for the Next Silicon Valley* (Princeton: Princeton University Press, 2004); Jordan A. Schwartz, *The New Dealers: Power Politics in the Age of Roosevelt* (New York: Alfred A. Knopf, 1993).

15. Meg Jacobs, *Pocketbook Politics: Economic Citizenship in Twentieth-Century America* (Princeton: Princeton University Press, 2005); Lizabeth Cohen, *A Consumers' Republic: The Politics of Mass Consumption in Postwar America* (New York: Alfred A. Knopf, 2003).

16. Thomas J. Sugrue, *The Origins of the Urban Crisis: Race and Inequality in Postwar Detroit* (Princeton: Princeton University Press, 1996); Gary Gerstle, "Race and the Myth of the Liberal Consensus," *Journal of American History* 82:2 (September 1995): 579–86; Arnold R. Hirsch, *Making the Second Ghetto: Race and Housing in Chicago 1940–1960* (New York: Cambridge University Press, 1983).

17. Matthew D. Lassiter, *The Silent Majority: Suburban Politics in the Sunbelt South* (Princeton: Princeton University Press, 2005); Kevin M. Kruse, *White Flight: Atlanta and the Making of Modern Conservatism* (Princeton: Princeton University Press, 2005); Self, *American Babylon*; Becky M. Nicolaides, *My Blue Heaven: Life and Politics in the Working-Class Suburbs of Los Angeles, 1920–1965* (Chicago: University of Chicago Press, 2002); Lisa McGirr, *Suburban Warriors: The Origins of the New American Right* (Princeton: Princeton University Press, 2001).

18. Hirsch, *Making the Second Ghetto*; John F. Bauman, *Public Housing, Race, and Renewal: Urban Planning in Philadelphia, 1920–1974* (Philadelphia: Temple University Press, 1987); Sugrue, *Origins of the Urban Crisis*. For an important reconsideration of such perspectives, Sylvie Murray, *The Progressive Housewife: Community Activism in Suburban Queens, 1945–1965* (Philadelphia: University of Pennsylvania Press, 2003).

19. Industrial policy can be defined as a "menu of subsidies and sanctions" applied to business by government; it focuses on "industrial or producing sectors of the economy" rather than consumers. Aaron Wildavsky, "Industrial Policies in American Political Cultures," in *The Politics of Industrial Policy*, ed. Claude E. Barfield and William A. Schambra (Washington, D.C.: American Enterprise Institute for Public Policy Research, 1986), 27; Harvey A. Goldstein, "Why State and Local Industrial Policy? An Introduction to the Debate," in *The State and Local Industrial Policy Question*, ed. Harvey A. Goldstein (Washington, D.C.: Planners Press, 1987). Employment policy may be defined as any policy designed to

promote employment, ranging from skill training to direct public creation of jobs. Weir, *Politics and Jobs*; Gary Mucciaroni, *The Political Failure of Employment Policy 1945–1982* (Pittsburgh: University of Pittsburgh Press, 1990).

20. Geertz, *Interpretation of Cultures*, 23.

21. Alice Kessler-Harris, *In Pursuit of Equity: Women, Men, and the Quest for Economic Citizenship in 20th-Century America* (New York: Oxford University Press, 2001).

22. James R. Grossman, *Land of Hope: Chicago, Black Southerners, and the Great Migration* (Chicago: University of Chicago Press, 1989); Nicholas Lemann, *The Promised Land: The Great Black Migration and How It Changed America* (New York: Knopf, 1991); James N. Gregory, *The Southern Diaspora: How the Great Migrations of Black and White Southerners Transformed America* (Chapel Hill: University of North Carolina Press, 2005).

23. For an important account of African American suburbs, Andrew Wiese, *Places of Their Own: African American Suburbanization in the Twentieth Century* (Chicago: University of Chicago Press, 2004). James Wolfinger, *Philadelphia Divided: Race and Politics in the City of Brotherly Love* (Chapel Hill: University of North Carolina Press, 2007).

24. Kirk R. Petshek, *The Challenge of Urban Reform: Policies and Programs in Philadelphia* (Philadelphia: Temple University Press, 1973), 8–40, 286–99; William W. Cutler, III, "The Persistent Dualism: Centralization and Decentralization in Philadelphia, 1854–1975," in *The Divided Metropolis: Social and Spatial Dimensions of Philadelphia, 1800–1975*, ed. Cutler and Howard Gillette, Jr. (Westport, CT: Greenwood Press, 1980), 249–84; Bauman, *Public Housing, Race, and Renewal*, 102–3, 118–23; Sam Bass Warner Jr., *The Private City: Philadelphia in Three Periods of Its Growth*, rev. ed. (Philadelphia: University of Pennsylvania Press, 1987), ix–xxvi, 214–23; Carolyn Adams, David Bartelt, David Elesh, Ira Goldstein, Nancy Kleniewski, and William Yancey, *Philadelphia: Neighborhoods, Division, and Conflict in a Postindustrial City* (Philadelphia: Temple University Press, 1991); Walter Licht, *Getting Work: Philadelphia, 1840–1950* (Philadelphia: University of Pennsylvania Press, 1992), 208–19.

25. Petshek, *Challenge of Urban Reform*, 15–16; for Dewey and American liberalism, see Kloppenburg, *The Virtues of Liberalism.*

26. The clearest articulation of these ideas can be found in National Resources Committee, *Our Cities: Their Role in the National Economy* (Washington, D.C.: GPO, 1937), 73–81.

Conclusion

Public Policy Applications: Economic Development

Policy Then

The exodus of residents and manufacturing jobs to surrounding suburbs posed a major threat to the economic vitality of cities in the years after World War II. The response was remarkably similar in most cities. The most prominent downtown business leaders seized the initiative to slow the process of decentralization and encourage new capital investment mainly in the form of *Fortune* 500 corporations and a wide array of firms offering professional services. The success of such an economic development policy, however, hinged on sprucing up the downtown business district as an attractive investment site. The following excerpt from a 1958 master plan to revitalize downtown Providence captures the scope of urban renewal planning, as well as the confidence in the bold leadership of the city's business establishment.

Box 6.1   **Downtown Master Plan for Providence, Rhode Island (1958)**

PHASES I AND II OF A COMPREHENSIVE PLANNING STUDY FOR THE FUTURE OF DOWNTOWN PROVIDENCE

CHAPTER 1: INTRODUCING PROVIDENCE AND THE DOWNTOWN PROJECT

The central business district is the economic, political, and geographic core of most American cities. It is very often the point at which the city began, and around which it grows. Its fortunes are intimately connected with those of the whole community, and often the entire region. It is highly sensitive to changes in population, new methods of production, transportation, selling, and the economic growth of the entire city.

The downtown areas of cities are likely to be their oldest and most intensively developed sections . . . [and] containing the most highly valued land and buildings in the city. In the process of competition, those able to make the greatest use of downtown property at the time come to occupy the central locations. . . .

Background of the Project

. . . In March of 1955, the Greater Providence Chamber of Commerce created the Downtown Business Coordinating Council to represent business, financial, and professional interests in the downtown area. The Downtown Business Coordinating Council then commissioned a study entitled *Attitudes and Practices of Residents of Greater Providence concerning Downtown Providence.* . . .

The results of the Survey, and the growing awareness of the seriousness of the situation led to efforts to begin coordinated renewal work. . . .

(Continued)

(Continued)

CHAPTER 3: REPORT ON RESEARCH FINDINGS . . . .

B. STRUCTURE, LAND AND SPACE USE DATA

Six major categories of building use were identified on the basis of the activities of the majority of the occupants in the building. These major categories are: warehouse, industry, office, retail, public and residential. . . .

Residential and combined residential-retail structures average the lowest land values, with industry almost as low. The highest land values are found under retail, office, combination retail-office, and public buildings. . . .

Residential structures are among the poorest of all downtown buildings in every respect. Fifty percent of permanent residents live in buildings which are more than 60 years old, over 90 percent in structures built before 1920. Nearly 40 percent of the occupants live in frame buildings which average 70 years old, have no fire protection, and very low scores in other respects. Over 50 percent of the permanent residents live in buildings which scored poor or very poor. . . .

F. THE SOCIAL CHARACTERISTICS OF DOWNTOWN PROVIDENCE

An effective plan for downtown Providence must take account of the social and personal characteristics of the residents of the district, and of problem groups and individuals typically found in the downtown areas of most of America's larger cities. Providence, fortunately, has no "skid row" area of flophouses and "bums" sleeping in the streets, but a recent survey indicates a high incidence of certain problems on the downtown fringe. . . .

CHAPTER 5: DESIGN . . .

All the work outlined in Phases I and II of this study has one final purpose: to provide the bases for a downtown master plan. [The study proceeds to present 13 "conclusions"]. . . .

13. Structures classified as being very poor and poor will be considered for removal. Buildings thus demolished will indicate potentially available land on which future buildings can be expected. . . .

Source: Phases I & II of a Comprehensive Planning Study for the Future of Downtown Providence: Demonstration Project with Federal, Municipal and Citizen Participation (Providence, RI: Downtown Master Plan Project, 1958).

Policy Now

Several decades later, economic development continued to be a central preoccupation of American cities still reeling from suburbanization and deindustrialization. Revitalization efforts remained focused on the need to improve the downtown business district as the primary engine of both the city's and region's economy.

By the end of the twentieth century, however, the initiative was led not so much by a citywide or downtown-based business advocacy organization like the Chamber of Commerce; such groups seemed to be fading in stature and political clout. Instead, more localized entities, although ones still dominated by business firms, were assuming influence. Particularly noteworthy was the rise of business improvement districts, or BIDs. They are geographically defined areas in which businesses pay an annual assessment, in addition to their regular taxes, to fund services and activities to improve and promote the district. The core functions of BIDs revolve around cleaning streets and sidewalks and enhanced public safety. Many also engage in capital improvements and beautification projects, marketing, and business development. The idea of using BIDs to make commercial districts safer, cleaner, and

Times Square, New York (circa 1970s)

Times Square, New York (circa 2009)

more inviting for shoppers and pedestrians caught on. Today, there are over 1,000 BIDs nationwide and they exist in virtually every large city.

One of the most prominent examples of a BID rejuvenating a neighborhood involves the Times Square Alliance in New York City. Founded in 1992, it collaborated with city government to revive the city's famed theater district, which, like much of the rest of New York, had fallen on hard times by the 1970s and 1980s. Increasingly overrun by prostitution and drug dealing and its streets marred by litter and graffiti, Times Square became a place to avoid rather than congregate. But then new city ordinances in the mid-1990s led to the closure and scattering of seedy sex shops and X-rated movie theaters while increased policing reduced crime. The Times Square Alliance contributed to the transformation of the area by adding its own security patrols and sanitation crews while improving the streetscape with better lighting and public art. Historic theaters were renovated. The BID's efforts soon paid off. Local residents and tourists alike once again flocked to Times Square, which prompted a striking rise in the construction of new theaters, hotels, retail businesses, and office towers. At the same time, the Times Square Alliance provoked criticism too. Some faulted the organization for mistreating the homeless. Others contended that in its zeal to clean up Times Square, it has produced a sanitized, soulless, and overly commercial district more reminiscent of a Disney-like theme park than the exciting and glittering cultural mecca that it had been decades earlier.

Additional Resources

Center City District. Web site of business improvement district for Center City Philadelphia. www.centercityphila.org.

Peter Dreier, "Jane Jacobs' Radical Legacy," *Shelterforce*, Summer 2006.

Dennis R. Judd and Susan S. Fainstein, eds., *The Tourist City* (New Haven: Yale University Press, 1999).

Bruce Katz and Richard M. Daley, "US Manufacturing's Next Phase," Brookings Institution, May 2012.

Jerry Mitchell, *Business Improvement Districts and the Shape of American Cities* (Albany: State University of New York Press, 2008).

Alexander J. Reichl, *Reconstructing Times Square: Politics and Culture in Urban Development* (Lawrence: University Press of Kansas, 1999).

Discussion Questions

1. What is the utility of business improvement districts today? What are their strengths and weaknesses? Where are they most likely to be effective or ineffective?

2. What is the logic of a downtown-centric economic development policy?

3. Should city governments have devoted more effort to retain and expand manufacturing plants which had long served as the cornerstone of urban economies? Should industrial policy be more pronounced today?

4. For several decades, commercial office development was the principal driver of downtown redevelopment strategies; was this a wise choice? What about arts, entertainment, and tourism as an alternative engine of economic growth for cities? Should all cities try to nurture their own version of Times Square or some variant that is consistent with their own assets?

5. What are the costs of a downtown-centric economic development policy? What groups tend to lose out? How does this happen?

Chapter 7

Race, Protest, and Backlash

Introduction

In the context of the entire sweep of American history, African Americans had made considerable strides in combatting racial oppression by the middle of the twentieth century. Slavery had long been abolished, and legally mandated segregation was confined to the south. For the millions of blacks who had fled the poverty and repression of the rural south and managed to secure factory jobs in other regions of the country, life was better. The sociologist William Julius Wilson documented a marked improvement in the material well-being of black workers starting in the 1940s resulting in a steady expansion of the black middle class.[1]

And yet, even for blacks who had escaped the Jim Crow south and found some measure of monetary gain and relief from the most vicious aspects of racial tyranny, attainment of anything resembling the kind of economic and political security that most white Americans took for granted remained elusive. Indeed, with each passing decade following World War II, the condition of many black Americans seemed to deteriorate, and grievances mounted. Black families that had migrated to industrial cities in search of good jobs were confined to overcrowded, segregated neighborhoods where housing was in a state of neglect.[2] Urban renewal only worsened an already grim situation; black neighborhoods were demolished and residents were displaced to public housing developments, many of which were sited in isolated sections of the city lacking quality public services and schools.[3] At the same time, what had been the primary incentive for migrating to cities in the first place—the availability of manufacturing jobs—had dissipated. Deindustrialization hit blacks particularly hard since they were typically the last hired and first fired.[4] Millions of white urbanites during the postwar period chose to move to prosperous suburbs, an option largely unavailable to blacks due to exclusionary zoning and racial hostility. Many of them were left behind in impoverished and redlined ghettos.[5]

The civil rights movement that emerged in the south during the mid-1950s to demand an end to Jim Crow segregation and electoral disenfranchisement soon stirred the passions of disgruntled blacks elsewhere in the United States. They expressed their anger over rampant discrimination with respect to jobs, housing, schools, and public services. Following the example of civil rights leaders like Martin Luther King Jr., they organized marches and demonstrations and employed tactics of civil disobedience to pressure public officials.[6]

For many blacks and Hispanics, however, the civil rights movement was proving to be a disappointment. They doubted whether the federal government's enactment of landmark legislation such as the Civil Rights Act (1964) and the Voting Rights Act (1965) would alter the dire circumstances that they faced on a day-to-day basis. They grew impatient with what they felt was the slow pace of change. Simmering frustrations boiled over each summer during the mid-1960s when deadly riots, often triggered by an incidence of police abuse or brutality, erupted in numerous American cities. The devastation was breathtaking. In the Los Angeles neighborhood of Watts, dozens of people were killed and property damage was estimated in the hundreds of millions. The commercial and cultural heart of many black communities was utterly wiped out and the physical, economic, and social impacts lingered for decades in the form of burned-out shells of buildings and vacant, garbage-strewn lots.[7]

Under pressure, President Lyndon Johnson formed a high-profile commission chaired by Otto Kerner, the governor of Illinois, to examine the causes of the riots. The Kerner Commission report attracted widespread attention and controversy by finding that white society was at least partly responsible for creating and tolerating pervasive racial inequality. It declared that "our nation is moving toward two societies, one black, one white—separate and unequal" and warned that extensive remedial action was needed to avoid future outbreaks of violence.[8]

Apart from the multitude of riots in inner-city neighborhoods, black grievances were manifested in the political sphere most noticeably with the rise of the Black Power movement in the mid- to late 1960s. Influenced by Malcolm X, Black Power advocates rejected the central goal of the civil rights movement—racial integration—through strategies such as biracial coalitions and peaceful, nonviolent protest. Instead, they contended that blacks first needed to build their own base of power through the development of potent community-based organizations and institutions. Insisting that "power only respects power," Black Power leaders argued that coalitions with whites should only be contemplated after blacks were able to stand firmly on their own and negotiate from a position of strength. In addition, genuine black self-determination would only be advanced when black people "redefine themselves by reclaiming their history or culture."[9] Compared with the civil rights movement, the Black Power movement's rhetoric was more militant and its objectives more radical. **Reading 7-1** is an excerpt from one of the most influential publications about the movement, Stokely Carmichael and Charles V. Hamilton's book, *Black Power*. Impassioned appeals to black power and pride proved to be immensely popular, especially with younger and poorer blacks, and identity-based politics soon spread to other communities, inspiring similar mass-based movements among Chicanos, Asian Americans, and Native Americans.[10]

Others advocated an alternative approach to pursuing racial justice. Respected activists like Bayard Rustin criticized the Black Power movement's emphasis on building community institutions and power bases separate and apart from white society as unrealistic. While agreeing that the ultimate goal was to obtain power, he urged a more robust engagement in mainstream political processes as the most reliable strategy for effecting sweeping policy changes to remedy deepening unemployment and poverty in urban ghettos. But Rustin went on to stress that success within the electoral forum required allies; the need for African Americans to develop strong and lasting coalitions with progressive forces such as labor unions, religious groups, and white liberals was inescapable (see **Reading 7-2**).

The political historian Matthew Countryman's research on racial politics in Philadelphia during this time suggests yet another possible pathway, a blend of elements associated with each of the two previous approaches. Frustrated with the limits of protest, a number of groups within the African American community in Philadelphia formed the Black Political Forum to penetrate the conventional political system and transform the local, white-dominated Democratic Party, which had chronically neglected black interests. While this marked a turn toward mainstream electoral politics, the Black Political Forum continued to be driven by a vision of community control over public institutions and programs. Gaining influence over party structures and eventually the machinery of local government appeared to be the most promising strategy for redirecting the distribution of city jobs and contracts, improving basic service delivery, and combating persistent police misconduct in minority neighborhoods.[11]

This hybrid approach to political empowerment was evident in many other American cities, and it was particularly effective in jurisdictions with a relatively high concentration of minority voters. In such cities, some black candidates embraced certain aspects of the Black Power movement by shining a spotlight on racial inequities and demanding action to remedy generations of racial oppression. Richard Hatcher of Gary, Indiana, and Carl Stokes of Cleveland, Ohio, made history by getting elected as their cities' first black mayors and doing so through bold appeals to racial pride and solidarity.[12]

At the same time, the push for black power in all realms of society and politics was not without cost. It provoked a backlash among many whites anxious about the magnitude and rapidity of social, economic, cultural, and political change. Segments of the white working class voiced their discontent with black activism, condemning, in particular, the lawlessness and disorder associated with the riots and the expansion of the welfare state under President Lyndon Johnson's War on Poverty. In the eyes of white ethnics, Great Society programs disproportionately benefited inner-city blacks and Hispanics while they were expected to foot the bill through steadily rising taxes. Jonathan Rieder's analysis of the political attitudes of working-class Jews and Italian Americans in Brooklyn during the 1960s in **Reading 7-3** reveals an escalating antagonism within some urban neighborhoods.[13]

Whites expressed their discomfort with black gains in city government in various ways. One of the more immediate reactions was white flight. This phenomenon was especially pronounced following court orders to desegregate public schools in numerous cities throughout the country. Many white parents responded to mandatory busing programs by taking their children out of public schools or moving away from the city altogether, an outcome that further intensified racial segregation in metropolitan areas.[14]

Conservative politicians running for president such as George Wallace and Richard Nixon tapped into the festering disenchantment of blue-collar, white voters by promising to restore law and order, reigning in the welfare state, and cutting taxes.[15] Ronald Reagan rode such sentiments to victory in his first campaign for public office—getting elected as governor of California in 1966. And at the local level, populists such as Sam Yorty in Los Angeles and Frank Rizzo in Philadelphia appealed to anxious and angry whites and captured control of city hall. By the late 1960s and early 1970s, racial tensions had infused urban politics.

Notes

1. William Julius Wilson Jr., *The Declining Significance of Race: Blacks and Changing American Institutions* (Chicago: University Press of Chicago, 1978); see also Stephan Thernstrom and Abigail Thernstrom, *America in Black and White: One Nation, Indivisible* (New York: Simon & Schuster, 1997).

2. Albert R. Hirsch, *Making the Second Ghetto: Race and Housing in Chicago, 1940–1960* (Chicago: University of Chicago Press, 1998).

3. John F. Bauman, *Public Housing, Race, and Renewal: Urban Planning in Philadelphia, 1920–1974* (Philadelphia: Temple University Press, 1987); Lee Rainwater, *Behind Ghetto Walls: Black Families in a Federal Slum* (Chicago: Aldine, 1970).

4. Thomas J. Sugrue, *The Origins of the Urban Crisis: Race and Inequality in Postwar Detroit* (Princeton: Princeton University Press, 1996).

5. Michael N. Danielson, *The Politics of Exclusion* (New York: Columbia University Press, 1976); Douglas S. Massey and Nancy Denton, *American Apartheid: Segregation and the Making of the Underclass* (Cambridge, MA: Harvard University Press, 1993).

6. Refer to Thomas J. Sugrue, *Sweet Land of Liberty: The Forgotten Struggle for Civil Rights in the North* (New York: Random House, 2008); Mandi Isaacs Jackson, *Model City Blues: Urban Space and Organized Resistance in New Haven* (Philadelphia: Temple University Press, 2008); James Wolfinger, "'The American Dream—For All Americans': Race, Politics, and the Campaign to Desegregate Levittown," *Journal of Urban History*, 38 (3), 2012.

7. Gerald Horne, *Fire This Time: The Watts Uprising and the 1960s* (Charlottesville: University of Virginia Press, 1995); Sidney Fine, *Violence in the Model City: The Cavanaugh Administration, Race Relations, and the Detroit Riot of 1967* (Ann Arbor: University of Michigan Press, 1989); Robert M. Fogelson, *Violence as Protest: A Study of Riots and Ghettos* (New York: Doubleday, 1971).

8. *Report of the National Advisory Commission on Civil Disorders* (New York: Bantam Books, 1968). For an assessment of the impact of the Kerner Commission report, see Kevin Mumford, "Harvesting the Crisis: The Newark Uprising, the Kerner Commission, and Writings on Riots," in *African American Urban History since World War II*, ed. Kenneth L. Kusmer and Joe W. Trotter (Chicago: University of Chicago Press, 2009); John Charles Boger, "The Kerner Commission Report in Retrospect," in *Race and Ethnicity in the United States: Issues and Debates*, ed. Stephen Steinberg (Malden, MA: Blackwell, 2000).

9. Stokely Carmichael and Charles V. Hamilton, *Black Power: The Politics of Liberation in America* (New York: Random House, 1967); see also Peniel E. Joseph, *Waiting 'Til the Midnight Hour: A Narrative History of Black Power in America* (New York: Henry Holt, 2006); Peniel E. Joseph, ed., *Neighborhood Rebels: Black Power at the Local Level* (New York: Palgrave Macmillan, 2010).

10. Mario T. Garcia, ed., *The Chicano Movement: Perspectives from the Twenty-First Century* (New York: Routledge, 2014); William Wei, *The Asian American Movement* (Philadelphia: Temple University Press, 1993).

11. Matthew J. Countryman, *Up South: Civil Rights and Black Power in Philadelphia* (Philadelphia: University of Pennsylvania Press, 2006).

12. Alex Poinsett, *Black Power: Gary, Style: The Making of Mayor Richard Gordon Hatcher* (Chicago: Johnson Publishing, 1970); Leonard N. Moore, *Carl B. Stokes and the Rise of Black Political Power* (Urbana: University of Illinois Press, 2002).

13. For an intriguing look at another Brooklyn neighborhood during this tumultuous period, but mainly from an African-American perspective, see Wendell Pritchett, *Brownsville, Brooklyn: Blacks, Jews, and the Changing Face of the Ghetto* (Chicago: University of Chicago Press, 2002).

14. For an overview of school desegregation cases, see Gary Orfield, *Public School Desegregation in the United States, 1968–1980* (Washington, DC: Joint Center for Political Studies, 1983). For studies on resulting white flight from public schools and cities, see Christine H. Rossell and Willis D. Hawley, *The Consequences of School Desegregation* (Philadelphia: Temple University Press, 1983); Jack Schneider, "Escape from Los Angeles: White Flight from Los Angeles and Its Schools, 1960–1980," *Journal of Urban History*, 34 (6), 2008.

15. Thomas Byrne Edsall and Mary D. Edsall, *Chain Reaction: The Impact of Race, Rights, and Taxes on American Politics* (New York: W. W. Norton, 1991).

7-1 "Black Power: Its Needs and Substance"*

*Stokely Carmichael** and Charles V. Hamilton*

Black Power: The Politics of Liberation in America

"To carve out a place for itself in the politico-social order," V. O. Key, Jr. wrote in *Politics, Parties and Pressure Groups*, "a new group may have to fight for reorientation of many of the values of the old order." This is especially true when that group is composed of black people in the American society—a society that has for centuries deliberately and systematically excluded them from political participation. Black people in the United States must raise hard questions, questions which challenge the very nature of the society itself: its long-standing values, beliefs and institutions.

To do this, we must first redefine ourselves. Our basic need is to reclaim our history and our identity from what must be called cultural terrorism, from the depredation of self-justifying white guilt. We shall have to struggle for the right to create our own terms through which to define ourselves and our relationship to the society, and to have these terms recognized. This is the first necessity of a free people, and the first right that any oppressor must suspend.

In *Politics Among Nations*, Hans Morgenthau defined political power as "the psychological control over the minds of men." This control includes the attempt by the oppressor to have *his* definitions, *his* historical descriptions, *accepted* by the oppressed. This was true in Africa no less than in the United States. To black Africans, the word "Uhuru" means "freedom," but they had to fight the white colonizers for the right to use the term. The recorded history of this country's dealings with red and black men offers other examples. In the wars between the white settlers and the "Indians," a battle won by the Cavalry was described as a "victory." The "Indians'" triumphs, however, were "massacres." (The American colonists were not unaware of the need to define their acts in their own terms. They labeled their fight against England a "revolution"; the English attempted to demean it by calling it "insubordination" or "riotous.")

The historical period following Reconstruction in the South after the Civil War has been called by many historians the period of Redemption, implying that the bigoted southern slaves societies were "redeemed" from the hands of "reckless and irresponsible" black rulers. Professor John Hope Franklin's *Reconstruction* or Dr. W. E. B. DuBois' *Black Reconstruction* should be sufficient to dispel inaccurate historical notions, but the larger society persists in its own self-serving accounts. Thus black people came to be depicted as "lazy," "apathetic," "dumb," "shiftless," "good-timers." Just as red men had to be recorded as "savages" to justify the white man's theft of their land, so black men had to be vilified in order to justify their continued oppression. Those who have the right to define are the masters of the situation. . . .

Today, the American educational system continues to reinforce the entrenched values of the society through the use of words. Few people in this country

*Endnotes and references have been omitted. Please consult the original source.

**Stokely Carmichael was a prominent leader of the Black Power movement in the United States during the 1960s when he wrote, with Charles V. Hamilton, the highly influential book, *Black Power: The Politics of Liberation in America*. In 1978, he changed his name to Kwame Turé.

question that this is "the land of the free and the home of the brave." They have had these words drummed into them from childhood. Few people question that this is the "Great Society" or that this country is fighting "Communist aggression" around the world. We mouth these things over and over, and they become truisms not to be questioned. In a similar way, black people have been saddled with epithets.

"Integration" is another current example of a word which has been defined according to the way white Americans see it. To many of them, it means black men wanting to marry white daughters; it means "race mixing"—implying bed or dance partners. To black people, it has meant a way to improve their lives—economically and politically. But the predominant white definition has stuck in the minds of too many people.

Black people must redefine themselves, and only *they* can do that. Throughout this country, vast segments of the black communities are beginning to recognize the need to assert their own definitions, to reclaim their history, their culture; to create their own sense of community and togetherness. There is a growing resentment of the word "Negro," for example, because this term is the invention of our oppressor; it is *his* image of us that he describes. Many blacks are now calling themselves African-Americans, Afro-Americans or black people because that is our image of ourselves. When we begin to define our own image, the stereotypes—that is, lies—that our oppressor has developed will begin in the white community and end there. The black community will have a positive image of itself that *it* has created. This means we will no longer call ourselves lazy, apathetic, dumb, good-timers, shiftless, etc. Those are words used by white America to define us. If we accept these adjectives, as some of us have in the past, then we see ourselves only in a negative way, precisely the way white America wants us to see ourselves. Our incentive is broken and our will to fight is surrendered. From now on we shall view ourselves as African-Americans and as black people who are in fact energetic, determined, intelligent, beautiful and peace-loving.

There is a terminology and ethos peculiar to the black community of which black people are beginning to be no longer ashamed. Black communities are the only large segments of this society where people refer to each other as brother—soul-brother, soul-sister. Some people may look upon this as ersatz, as make-believe, but it is not that. It is real. It is a growing sense of community. It is a growing realization that black Americans have a common bond not only among themselves, but with their African brothers. In *Black Man's Burden*, John O. Killens described his trip to ten African countries as follows:

> Everywhere I went people called me brother. . . . "Welcome, American brother." It was a good feeling for me, to be in Africa. To walk in a land for the first time in your entire life knowing within yourself that your color would not be held against you. No black man ever knows this in America.

More and more black Americans are developing this feeling. They are becoming aware that they have a history which pre-dates their forced introduction to this country. African-American history means a long history beginning on the continent of Africa, a history not taught in the standard textbooks of this country. It is absolutely essential that black people know this history, that they know their roots, that they develop an awareness of their cultural heritage. Too long have they been kept in submission by being told that they had no culture, no manifest heritage, before they landed on the slave auction blocks in this country. If black people are to know themselves as a vibrant, valiant people, they must know their roots. And they will soon learn that the Hollywood image of man-eating cannibals waiting for, and waiting on, the Great White Hunter is a lie.

With redefinition will come a clearer notion of the role black Americans can play in this world. This role will emerge clearly out of the unique, common experiences of Afro-Asians. Killens concludes:

> I believe furthermore that the American Negro can be the bridge between the West and Africa-Asia. We black Americans can serve as a bridge to mutual understanding. The one thing we black Americans have in common with the other colored peoples of the world is that we have all felt the cruel and ruthless heel of white supremacy.

We have all been "niggerized" on one level or another. And all of us are determined to "denig-gerize" the earth. To rid the world of "niggers" is the Black Man's Burden, human reconstruction is the grand objective.

Only when black people fully develop this sense of community, of themselves, can they begin to deal effectively with the problems of racism in *this* country. This is what we mean by a new consciousness; this is the vital first step.

The next step is what we shall call the process of political modernization—a process which must take place if the society is to be rid of racism. "Political modernization" includes many things, but we mean by it three major concepts: (1) questioning old values and institutions of the society; (2) searching for new and different forms of political structure to solve political and economic problems; and (3) broadening the base of political participation to include more people in the decision-making process. These notions (we shall take up each in turn) are central to our thinking throughout this book and to contemporary American history as a whole. As David Apter wrote in *The Politics of Modernization*, ". . . the struggle to modernize is what has given meaning to our generation. It tests our cherished institutions and our beliefs. . . . So compelling a force has it become that we are forced to ask new questions of our own institutions. Each country, whether modernized or modernizing, stands in both judgment and fear of the results. Our own society is no exception."

The values of this society support a racist system; we find it incongruous to ask black people to adopt and support most of those values. We also reject the assumption that the basic institutions of this society must be preserved. The goal of black people must *not* be to assimilate into middle-class America, for that class—as a whole—is without a viable conscience as regards humanity. The values of the middle class permit the perpetuation of the ravages of the black community. The values of that class are based on material aggrandizement, not the expansion of humanity. The values of that class ultimately support cloistered little closed societies tucked away neatly in tree-lined suburbia. The values of that class do *not* lead to the creation of an open society. That class *mouths* its preference for a free, competitive society, while at the same time forcefully and even viciously denying to black people as a group the opportunity to compete.

We are not unmindful of other descriptions of the social utility of the middle class. Banfield and Wilson, in *City Politics*, concluded:

> The departure of the middle class from the central city is important in other ways. . . . The middle class supplies a social and political leavening in the life of a city. Middle-class people demand good schools and integrity in government. They support churches, lodges, parent-teacher associations, scout troops, better-housing committees, art galleries, and operas. It is the middle class, in short, that asserts a conception of the public interest. Now its activity is increasingly concentrated in the suburbs.

But this same middle class manifests a sense of superior group position in regard to race. This class wants "good government" for *themselves;* it wants good schools *for its children.* At the same time, many of its members sneak into the black community by day, exploit it, and take the money home to their middle-class communities at night to support their operas and art galleries and comfortable homes. When not actually robbing, they will fight off the handful of more affluent black people who seek to move in; when they approve or even seek token integration, it applies only to black people like themselves—as "white" as possible. *This class is the backbone of institutional racism in this country.*

Thus we reject the goal of assimilation into middle-class America because the values of that class are in themselves anti-humanist and because that class as a social force perpetuates racism. We must face the fact that, in the past, what we have called the movement has not really questioned the middle-class values and institutions of this country. If anything, it has accepted those values and institutions without fully realizing their racist nature. Reorientation means an emphasis on the dignity of man, not on the sanctity of property. It means the creation of a society where human misery and poverty are repugnant to that society, not an indication of laziness or lack of initiative.

The creation of new values means the establishment of a society based, as Killens expresses it in *Black Man's Burden*, on "free people," not "free enterprise." To do this means to modernize—indeed, *to civilize*—this country.

Supporting the old values are old political and economic structures; these must also be "modernized." We should at this point distinguish between "structures" and "system." By system, we have in mind the entire American complex of basic institutions, values, beliefs, etc. By structures, we mean the specific institutions (political parties, interest groups, bureaucratic administrations) which exist to conduct the business of that system. Obviously, the first is broader than the second. Also, the second assumes the legitimacy of the first. Our view is that, given the illegitimacy of the system, we cannot then proceed to transform that system with existing structures.

The two major political parties in this country have become non-viable entities for the legitimate representation of the real needs of masses—especially blacks—in this country. Walter Lippmann raised the same point in his syndicated column of December 8, 1966. He pointed out that the party system in the United States developed before our society became as technologically complex as it is now. He says that the ways in which men live and define themselves are changing radically. Old ideological issues, once the subject of passionate controversy, Lippmann argues, are of little interest today. He asks whether the great urban complexes—which are rapidly becoming the centers of black population in the U.S.—can be run with the same systems and ideas that derive from a time when America was a country of small villages and farms. While not addressing himself directly to the question of race, Lippmann raises a major question about our political institutions; and the crisis of race in America may be its major symptom.

Black people have seen the city planning commissions, the urban renewal commissions, the boards of education and the police departments fail to speak to their needs in a meaningful way. We must devise new structures, new institutions to replace those forms or to make them responsive. There is nothing sacred or inevitable about old institutions; the focus must be on people, not forms.

Existing structures and established ways of doing things have a way of perpetuating themselves and for this reason, the modernizing process will be difficult. Therefore, timidity in calling into question the boards of education or the police departments will not do. They must be challenged forcefully and clearly. If this means the creation of parallel community institutions, then that must be the solution. If this means that black parents must gain control over the operation of the schools in the black community, then that must be the solution. The search for new forms means the search for institutions that will, for once, make decisions in the interest of black people. It means, for example, a building inspection department that neither winks at violations of building codes by absentee slumlords nor imposes meaningless fines which permit them to continue their exploitation of the black community.

Essential to the modernization of structures is a broadened base of political participation. More and more people must become politically sensitive and active (we have already seen this happening in some areas of the South). People must no longer be tied, by small incentives or handouts, to a corrupting and corruptible white machine. Black people will choose their own leaders and hold those leaders responsible to *them*. A broadened base means an end to the condition described by James Wilson in *Negro Politics*, whereby "Negroes tended to be the objects rather than the subjects of civic action. Things are often done for, or about, or to, or because of Negroes, but they are less frequently done *by* Negroes." Broadening the base of political participation, then, has as much to do with the quality of black participation as with the quantity. We are fully aware that the black vote, especially in the North, has been pulled out of white pockets and "delivered" whenever it was in the interest of white politicians to do so. That vote must no longer be controllable by those who have neither the interests nor the demonstrated concern of black people in mind.

As the base broadens, as more and more black people become activated, they will perceive more clearly the special disadvantages heaped upon them as a group. They will perceive that the larger society is growing more affluent while the black society is retrogressing, as daily life and mounting statistics clearly show (see Chapters I and VIII). V. O. Key describes what often happens next, in *Politics, Parties and Pressure Groups:* "A factor of great significance in the setting off of political movements is an abrupt change for the worse in the status of one group relative to that of other groups in society. . . . A rapid change for the worse in the relative status of any group . . . is likely to precipitate political action." Black people will become increasingly active as they notice that their retrogressive status exists in large measure because of values and institutions arraigned against them. They will begin to stress and strain and call the entire system into question. Political modernization will be in motion. We believe that it is now in motion. One form of that motion is Black Power.

The adoption of the concept of Black Power is one of the most legitimate and healthy developments in American politics and race relations in our time. The concept of Black Power speaks to all the needs mentioned in this chapter. It is a call for black people in this country to unite, to recognize their heritage, to build a sense of community. It is a call for black people to begin to define their own goals, to lead their own organizations and to support those organizations. It is a call to reject the racist institutions and values of this society.

The concept of Black Power rests on a fundamental premise: *Before a group can enter the open society, it must first close ranks.* By this we mean that group solidarity is necessary before a group can operate effectively from a bargaining position of strength in a pluralistic society. Traditionally, each new ethnic group in this society has found the route to social and political viability through the organization of its own institutions with which to represent its needs within the larger society. Studies in voting behavior specifically, and political behavior generally, have made it clear that politically the American pot has not melted. Italians vote for Rubino over O'Brien; Irish for Murphy over Goldberg, etc. This phenomenon may seem distasteful to some, but it has been and remains today a central fact of the American political system. There are other examples of ways in which groups in the society have remembered their roots and used this effectively in the political arena. Theodore Sorensen

describes the politics of foreign aid during the Kennedy Administration in his book *Kennedy:*

> No powerful constituencies or interest groups backed foreign aid. The Marshall Plan at least had appealed to Americans who traced their roots to the Western European nations aided. But there were few voters who identified with India, Colombia or Tanganyika.

The extent to which black Americans can and do "trace their roots" to Africa, to that extent will they be able to be more effective on the political scene. . . .

The point is obvious: black people must lead and run their own organizations. Only black people can convey the revolutionary idea—and it is a revolutionary idea—that black people are able to do things themselves. Only they can help create in the community an aroused and continuing black consciousness that will provide the basis for political strength. In the past, white allies have often furthered white supremacy without the whites involved realizing it, or even wanting to do so. Black people must come together and do things for themselves. They must achieve self-identity and self-determination in order to have their daily needs met.

Black Power means, for example, that in Lowndes County, Alabama, a black sheriff can end police brutality. A black tax assessor and tax collector and county board of revenue can lay, collect, and channel tax monies for the building of better roads and schools serving black people. In such areas as Lowndes, where black people have a majority, they will attempt to use power to exercise control. This is what they seek: control. When black people lack a majority, Black Power means proper representation and sharing of control. It means the creation of power bases, of strength, from which black people can press to change local or nation-wide patterns of oppression—instead of from weakness.

It does not mean *merely* putting black faces into office. Black visibility is not Black Power. Most of the black politicians around the country today are not examples of Black Power. The power must be that of a community, and emanate from there. The black politicians must start from there. The black politicians must stop being representatives of "downtown" machines, whatever the cost might be in terms of lost patronage and holiday handouts.

Black Power recognizes—it must recognize—the ethnic basis of American politics as well as the power-oriented nature of American politics. Black Power therefore calls for black people to consolidate behind their own, so that they can bargain from a position of strength. But while we endorse the *procedure* of group solidarity and identity for the purpose of attaining certain goals in the body politic, this does not mean that black people should strive for the same kind of rewards (i.e., end results) obtained by the white society. The ultimate values and goals are not domination or exploitation of other groups, but rather an effective share in the total power of the society.

Nevertheless, some observers have labeled those who advocate Black Power as racists; they have said that the call for self-identification and self-determination is "racism in reverse" or "black supremacy." This is a deliberate and absurd lie. There is no analogy—by any stretch of definition or imagination—between the advocates of Black Power and white racists. Racism is not merely exclusion on the basis of race but exclusion for the purpose of subjugating or maintaining subjugation. The goal of the racists is to keep black people on the bottom, arbitrarily and dictatorially, as they have done in this country for over three hundred years. The goal of black, self-determination and black self-identity—Black Power—is full participation in the decision-making processes affecting the lives of black people, and recognition of the virtues in themselves as black people. The black people of this country have not lynched whites, bombed their churches, murdered their children and manipulated laws and institutions to maintain oppression. White racists have. Congressional laws, one after the other, have not been necessary to stop black people from oppressing others and denying others the full enjoyment of their rights. White racists have made such laws necessary. The goal of Black Power is positive and functional to a free and viable society. No white racist can make this claim.

A great deal of public attention and press space was devoted to the hysterical accusation of "black racism" when the call for Black Power was first sounded. A national committee of influential black churchmen affiliated with the National Council of Churches, despite their obvious respectability and responsibility, had to resort to a paid advertisement to articulate their position, while anyone yapping "black racism" made front-page news. . . .

It is a commentary on the fundamentally racist nature of this society that the concept of group strength for black people must be articulated—not to mention defended. No other group would submit to being led by others. Italians do not run the Anti-Defamation League of B'nai B'rith. Irish do not chair Christopher Columbus Societies. Yet when black people call for black-run and all-black organizations, they are immediately classed in a category with the Ku Klux Klan. This is interesting and ironic, but by no means surprising: the society does not expect black people to be able to take care of their business, and there are many who prefer it precisely that way.

In the end, we cannot and shall not offer any guarantees that Black Power, if achieved, would be non-racist. No one can predict human behavior. Social change always has unanticipated consequences. If black racism is what the larger society fears, we cannot help them. We can only state what we hope will be the result, given the fact that the present situation is unacceptable and that we have no real alternative but to work for Black Power. The final truth is that the white society is not entitled to reassurances, even if it were possible to offer them.

We have outlined the meaning and goals of Black Power; we have also discussed one major thing which it is not. There are others of greater importance. The advocates of Black Power reject the old slogans and meaningless rhetoric of previous years in the civil rights struggle. The language of yesterday is indeed irrelevant: progress, non-violence, integration, fear of "white backlash," coalition. Let us look at the rhetoric and see why these terms must be set aside or redefined.

One of the tragedies of the struggle against racism is that up to this point there has been no national organization which could speak to the growing militancy of young black people in the urban ghettos and the black-belt South. There has been only a "civil rights" movement, whose tone of voice was adapted to an audience of middle-class whites. It served as a sort of buffer zone between that audience and angry young blacks. It claimed to speak for the needs of a community, but it did not speak in the tone of that community. None of its so-called leaders could go into a rioting community and be listened to. In a sense, the blame must be shared—along with the mass media— by those leaders for what happened in Watts, Harlem, Chicago, Cleveland and other places. Each time the black people in those cities saw Dr. Martin Luther King get slapped they became angry. When they saw little black girls bombed to death *in a church* and civil rights workers ambushed and murdered, they were angrier; and when nothing happened, they were steaming mad. We had nothing to offer that they could see, except to go out and be beaten again. We helped to build their frustration.

We had only the old language of love and suffering. And in most places—that is, from the liberals and middle class—we got back the old language of patience and progress. The civil rights leaders were saying to the country: "Look, you guys are supposed to be nice guys, and we are only going to do what we are supposed to do. Why do you beat us up? Why don't you give us what we ask? Why don't you straighten yourselves out?" For the masses of black people, this language resulted in virtually nothing. In fact, their objective day-to-day condition worsened. The unemployment rate among black people increased while that among whites declined. Housing conditions in the black communities deteriorated. Schools in the black ghettos continued to plod along on outmoded techniques, inadequate curricula, and with all too many tired and indifferent teachers. Meanwhile, the President picked up the refrain of "We Shall Overcome" while the Congress passed civil rights law after civil rights law, only to have them effectively nullified by deliberately weak enforcement. "Progress is being made," we were told.

Such language, along with admonitions to remain non-violent and fear the white backlash, convinced some that that course was the *only* course to follow. It misled some into believing that a black minority could bow its head and get whipped into a meaningful position of power. The very notion is absurd. The white society devised the language, adopted the rules and had the black community narcotized into believing that that language and those rules were, in fact,

relevant. The black community was told time and again how *other* immigrants finally won *acceptance:* that is, by following the Protestant Ethic of Work and Achievement. They worked hard; therefore, they achieved. We were not told that it was by building Irish Power, Italian Power, Polish Power or Jewish Power that these groups got themselves together and operated from positions of strength. We were not told that "the American dream" wasn't designed for black people. That while today, to whites, the dream may *seem* to include black people, it cannot do so by the very nature of this nation's political and economic system, which imposes institutional racism on the black masses if not upon every individual black. A notable comment on that "dream" was made by Dr. Percy Julian, the black scientist and director of the Julian Research Institute in Chicago, a man for whom the dream seems to have come true. While not subscribing to "black power" as he understood it, Dr. Julian clearly understood the basis for it: "The false concept of basic Negro inferiority is one of the curses that still lingers. It is a problem created by the white man. Our children just no longer are going to accept the patience we were taught by our generation. We were taught a pretty little lie—excel and the whole world lies, open before you. I *obeyed the injunction and found it to be wishful thinking*" (Authors' italics).[2]

A key phrase in our buffer-zone days was non-violence. For years it has been thought that black people would not literally fight for their lives. Why this has been so is not entirely clear; neither the larger society nor black people are noted for passivity. The notion apparently stems from the years of marches and demonstrations and sit-ins where black people did not strike back and the violence always came from white mobs. There are many who still sincerely believe in that approach. From our viewpoint, rampaging white mobs and white night-riders must be made to understand that their days of free head-whipping are over. Black people should and must fight back. Nothing more quickly repels someone bent on destroying you than the unequivocal message: "O.K., fool, make your move, and run the same risk I run—of dying."

When the concept of Black Power is set forth, many people immediately conjure up notions of violence. The country's reaction to the Deacons for Defense and

Justice, which originated in Louisiana, is instructive. Here is a group which realized that the "law" and law enforcement agencies would not protect people, so they had to do it themselves. If a nation fails to protect its citizens, then that nation cannot condemn those who take up the task themselves. The Deacons and all other blacks who resort to self-defense represent a simple answer to a simple question: what man would not defend his family and home from attack?

But this frightened some white people, because they knew that black people would now fight back. They knew that this was precisely what *they* would have long since done if *they* were subjected to the injustices and oppression heaped on blacks. Those of us who advocate Black Power are quite clear in our own minds that a "non-violent" approach to civil rights is an approach black people cannot afford and a luxury white people do not deserve. It is crystal clear to us— and it must become so with the white society—*that there can be no social order without social justice.* White people must be made to understand that they must stop messing with black people, or the blacks *will* fight back!

Next, we must deal with the term "integration." According to its advocates, social justice will be accomplished by "integrating the Negro into the mainstream institutions of the society from which he has been traditionally excluded." This concept is based on the assumption that there is nothing of value in the black community and that little of value could be created among black people. The thing to do is siphon off the "acceptable" black people into the surrounding middle-class white community.

The goals of integrationists are middle-class goals, articulated primarily by a small group of Negroes with middle-class aspirations or status. Their kind of integration has meant that a few blacks "make it," leaving the black community, sapping it of leadership potential and know-how. As we noted in Chapter I, those token Negroes—absorbed into a white mass— are of no value to the remaining black masses. They become meaningless show-pieces for a conscience-soothed white society. Such people will state that they would prefer to be treated "only as individuals, not as Negroes"; that they "are not and should not be preoccupied with race." This is a totally unrealistic position.

In the first place, black people have not suffered as individuals but as members of a group; therefore, their liberation lies in group action. This is why SNCC— and the concept of Black Power—affirms that helping *individual* black people to solve their problems on an *individual* basis does little to alleviate the mass of black people. Secondly, while color blindness *may* be a sound goal ultimately, we must realize that race is an overwhelming fact of life in this historical period. There is no black man in this country who can live "simply as a man." His blackness is an ever-present fact of this racist society, whether he recognizes it or not. It is unlikely that this or the next generation will witness the time when race will no longer be relevant in the conduct of public affairs and in public policy decision-making. To realize this and to attempt to deal with it does not make one a racist or overly preoccupied with race; it puts one in the forefront of a significant *struggle*. If there is no intense struggle today, there will be no meaningful results tomorrow.

"Integration" as a goal today speaks to the problem of blackness not only in an unrealistic way but also in a despicable way. It is based on complete acceptance of the fact that in order to have a decent house or education, black people must move into a white neighborhood or send their children to a white school. This reinforces, among both black and white, the idea that "white" is automatically superior and "black" is by definition inferior. For this reason, "integration" is a subterfuge for the maintenance of white supremacy. It allows the nation to focus on a handful of Southern black children who get into white schools at a great price, and to ignore the ninety-four percent who are left in unimproved all-black schools. Such situations will not change until black people become equal in a way that means something, and integration ceases to be a one-way street. Then integration does not mean draining skills and energies from the black ghetto into white neighborhoods. To sprinkle black children among white pupils in outlying schools is at best a stop-gap measure. The goal is not to take black children out of the black community and expose them to white middle-class values; the goal is to build and strengthen the black community.

"Integration" also means that black people must give up their identity, deny their heritage. We recall the conclusion of Killian and Grigg: "At the present time, integration as a solution to the race problem demands that the Negro foreswear his identity as a Negro." The fact is that integration, as traditionally articulated, would abolish the black community. The fact is that what must be abolished is not the black community, but the dependent colonial status that has been inflicted upon it.

The racial and cultural personality of the black community must be preserved and that community must win its freedom while preserving its cultural integrity. Integrity includes a pride—in the sense of self-acceptance, not chauvinism—in being black, in the historical attainments and contributions of black people. No person can be healthy, complete and mature if he must deny a part of himself; this is what "integration" has required thus far. This is the essential difference between integration as it is currently practiced and the concept of Black Power.

The idea of cultural integrity is so obvious that it seems almost simple-minded to spell things out at this length. Yet millions of Americans resist such truths when they are applied to black people. Again, that resistance is a comment on the fundamental racism in the society. Irish Catholics took care of their own first without a lot of apology for doing so, without any dubious language from timid leadership about guarding against "backlash." Everyone understood it to be a perfectly legitimate procedure. Of course, there would be "backlash." Organization begets counterorganization, but this was no reason to defer.

The so-called white backlash against black people is something else: the embedded traditions of institutional racism being brought into the open and calling forth overt manifestations of individual racism. In the summer of 1966, when the protest marches into Cicero, Illinois, began, the black people knew they were not allowed to live in Cicero and the white people knew it. When blacks began to demand the right to live in homes in that town, the whites simply reminded them of the status quo. Some people called this "backlash." It was, in fact, racism defending itself. In the black community, this is called "White folks showing their color." It is ludicrous to blame black people for what is simply an overt manifestation of white racism. Dr. Martin Luther King stated clearly that the protest marches were not the cause of the racism but merely exposed a long-term cancerous condition in the society. . . .

7-2 "From Protest to Politics: The Future of the Civil Rights Movement"

Bayard Rustin

Commentary

I

The decade spanned by the 1954 Supreme Court decision on school desegregation and the Civil Rights Act of 1964 will undoubtedly be recorded as the period in which the legal foundations of racism in America were destroyed. To be sure, pockets of resistance remain; but it would be hard to quarrel with the assertion that the elaborate legal structure of segregation and discrimination, particularly in relation to public accommodations, has virtually collapsed. On the other hand, without making light of the human sacrifices involved in the direct-action tactics (sit-ins, freedom rides, and the rest) that were so instrumental to this achievement, we must recognize that in desegregating public accommodations, we affected institutions which are relatively peripheral both to the American socio-economic order and to the fundamental conditions of life of the Negro people. In a highly industrialized, 20th-century civilization, we hit Jim Crow precisely where it was most anachronistic, dispensable, and vulnerable—in hotels, lunch counters, terminals, libraries, swimming pools, and the like. For in these forms, Jim Crow does impede the flow of commerce in the broadest sense: it is a nuisance in a society on the move (and on the make). Not surprisingly, therefore, it was the most mobility conscious and relatively liberated groups in the Negro community—lower-middle-class college students—who launched the attack that brought down this imposing but hollow structure.

The term "classical" appears especially apt for this phase of the civil rights movement. But in the few years that have passed since the first flush of sit-ins, several developments have taken place that have complicated matters enormously. One is the shifting focus of the movement in the South, symbolized by Birmingham; another is the spread of the revolution to the North; and the third, common to the other two, is the expansion of the movement's base in the Negro community. To attempt to disentangle these three strands is to do violence to reality. David Danzig's perceptive article, "The Meaning of Negro Strategy," correctly saw in the Birmingham events the victory of the concept of collective struggle over individual achievement as the road to Negro freedom. And Birmingham remains the unmatched symbol of grass-roots protest involving all strata of the black community. It was also in this most industrialized of Southern cities that the single-issue demands of the movement's classical stage gave way to the "package deal." No longer were Negroes satisfied with integrating lunch counters. They now sought advances in employment, housing, school integration, police protection, and so forth.

Thus, the movement in the South began to attack areas of discrimination which were not so remote from the Northern experience as were Jim Crow lunch counters. At the same time, the interrelationship of these apparently distinct areas became increasingly evident. What is the value of winning access to public accommodations for those who lack money to use them? The minute the movement faced this question, it was compelled to expand its vision beyond race relations to economic relations, including the role of education in modern society. And what also became clear is that all these interrelated problems, by their

Source: "From Protest to Politics: The Future of the Civil Rights Movement" by Bayard Rustin. Reprinted from *Commentary*, February 1964, by permission; copyright © 1964 by Commentary, Inc.

very nature, are not soluble by private, voluntary efforts but require government action—or politics. Already Southern demonstrators had recognized that the most effective way to strike at the police brutality they suffered from was by getting rid of the local sheriff—and that meant political action, which in turn meant, and still means, political action within the Democratic party where the only meaningful primary contests in the South are fought.

And so, in Mississippi, thanks largely to the leadership of Bob Moses, a turn toward political action has been taken. More than voter registration is involved here. A conscious bid for *political power* is being made, and in the course of that effort a tactical shift is being effected: direct-action techniques are being subordinated to a strategy calling for the building of community institutions or power bases. Clearly, the implications of this shift reach far beyond Mississippi. What began as a protest movement is being challenged to translate itself into a political movement. Is this the right course? And if it is, can the transformation be accomplished?

II

The very decade which has witnessed the decline of legal Jim Crow has also seen the rise of *de facto* segregation in our most fundamental socio-economic institutions. More Negroes are unemployed today than in 1954, and the unemployment gap between the races is wider. The median income of Negroes has dropped from 57 per cent to 54 per cent of that of whites. A higher percentage of Negro workers is now concentrated in jobs vulnerable to automation than was the case ten years ago. More Negroes attend *de facto* segregated schools today than when the Supreme Court handed down its famous decision; while school integration proceeds at a snail's pace in the South, the number of Northern schools with an excessive proportion of minority youth proliferates. And behind this is the continuing growth of racial slums, spreading over our central cities and trapping Negro youth in a milieu which, whatever its legal definition, sows an unimaginable demoralization. Again, legal niceties aside, a resident of a racial ghetto lives in segregated housing, and more Negroes fall into this category than ever before.

These are the facts of life which generate frustration in the Negro community and challenge the civil rights movement. At issue, after all, is not *civil rights,* strictly speaking, but social and economic conditions. Last summer's riots were not race riots; they were outbursts of class aggression in a society where class and color definitions are converging disastrously. How can the (perhaps misnamed) civil rights movement deal with this problem?

Before trying to answer, let me first insist that the task of the movement is vastly complicated by the failure of many whites of good will to understand the nature of our problem. There is a widespread assumption that the removal of artificial racial barriers should result in the automatic integration of the Negro into all aspects of American life. This myth is fostered by facile analogies with the experience of various ethnic immigrant groups, particularly the Jews. But the analogies with the Jews do not hold for three simple but profound reasons. First, Jews have a long history as a literate people, a resource which has afforded them opportunities to advance in the academic and professional worlds, to achieve intellectual status even in the midst of economic hardship, and to evolve sustaining value systems in the context of ghetto life. Negroes, for the greater part of their presence in this country, were forbidden by law to read or write. Second, Jews have a long history of family stability, the importance of which in terms of aspiration and self-image is obvious. The Negro family structure was totally destroyed by slavery and with it the possibility of cultural transmission (the right of Negroes to marry and rear children is barely a century old). Third, Jews are white and have the *option* of relinquishing their cultural-religious identity, intermarrying, passing, etc. Negroes, or at least the overwhelming majority of them, do not have this option. There is also a fourth, vulgar reason. If the Jewish and Negro communities are not comparable in terms of education, family structure, and color, it is also true that their respective economic roles bear little resemblance.

This matter of economic role brings us to the greater problem—the fact that we are moving into an era in which the natural functioning of the market does not by itself ensure every man with will and ambition a place in the productive process. The immigrant who came to this country during the late 19th and early 20th centuries entered a society which was expanding territorially and/or economically. It was then possible to start at the bottom, as an unskilled or semi-skilled worker, and move up the ladder, acquiring new skills along the way. Especially was this true when industrial unionism was burgeoning, giving new dignity and higher wages to organized workers. Today the situation has changed. We are not expanding territorially, the western frontier is settled, labor organizing has leveled off, our rate of economic growth has been stagnant for a decade. And we are in the midst of a technological revolution which is altering the fundamental structure of the labor force, destroying unskilled and semi-skilled jobs—jobs in which Negroes are disproportionately concentrated.

Whatever the pace of this technological revolution may be, the *direction* is clear: the lower rungs of the economic ladder are being lopped off. This means that an individual will no longer be able to start at the bottom and work his way up; he will have to start in the middle or on top, and hold on tight. It will not even be enough to have certain specific skills, for many skilled jobs are also vulnerable to automation. A broad educational background, permitting vocational adaptability and flexibility, seems more imperative than ever. We live in a society where, as Secretary of Labor Willard Wirtz puts it, machines have the equivalent of a high school diploma. Yet the average educational attainment of American Negroes is 8.2 years.

Negroes, of course, are not the only people being affected by these developments. It is reported that there are now 50 per cent fewer unskilled and semi-skilled jobs than there are high school dropouts. Almost one-third of the 26 million young people entering the labor market in the 1960's will be dropouts. But the percentage of Negro dropouts nationally is 57 percent, and in New York City, among Negroes 25 years of age or over, it is 68 per cent. They are without a future.

To what extent can the kind of self-help campaign recently prescribed by Eric Hoffer in the *New York Times Magazine* cope with such a situation? I would advise those who think that self-help is the answer to familiarize themselves with the long history of such efforts in the Negro community, and to consider why so many foundered on the shoals of ghetto life.

It goes without saying that any effort to combat demoralization and apathy is desirable, but we must understand that demoralization in the Negro community is largely a common-sense response to an objective reality. Negro youths have no need of statistics to perceive, fairly accurately, what their odds are in American society. Indeed, from the point of view of motivation, some of the healthiest Negro youngsters I know are juvenile delinquents: vigorously pursuing the American Dream of material acquisition and status, yet finding the conventional means of attaining it blocked off, they do not yield to defeatism but resort to illegal (and often ingenious) methods. They are not alien to American culture. They are, in Gunnar Myrdal's phrase, "exaggerated Americans." To want a Cadillac is not un-American; to push a cart in the garment center is. If Negroes are to be persuaded that the conventional path (school, work, etc.) is superior, we had better provide evidence which is now sorely lacking. It is a double cruelty to harangue Negro youth about education and training when we do not know what jobs will be available for them. When a Negro youth can reasonably foresee a future free of slums, when the prospect of gainful employment is realistic, we will see motivation and self-help in abundant enough quantities.

Meanwhile, there is an ironic similarity between the self-help advocated by many liberals and the doctrines of the Black Muslims. Professional sociologists, psychiatrists, and social workers have expressed amazement at the Muslims' success in transforming prostitutes and dope addicts into respectable citizens. But every prostitute the Muslims convert to a model of Calvinist virtue is replaced by the ghetto with two more. Dedicated as they are to maintenance of the ghetto, the Muslims are powerless to affect substantial moral reform. So too with every other group or program which is not aimed at the destruction of slums, their causes and effects. Self-help efforts, directly or indirectly, must be geared to mobilizing people into power units capable of effecting social change. That is, their goal must be genuine self-help, not merely self-improvement. Obviously, where self-improvement activities succeed in imparting to their participants a feeling of some control over their environment, those involved may find their appetites for change whetted; they may move into the political arena.

III

Let me sum up what I have thus far been trying to say: the civil rights movement is evolving from a protest movement into a full-fledged *social movement*—an evolution calling its very name into question. It is now concerned not merely with removing the barriers to full *opportunity* but with achieving the fact of *equality*. From sit-ins and freedom rides we have gone into rent strikes, boycotts, community organization, and political action. As a consequence of this natural evolution, the Negro today finds himself stymied by obstacles of far greater magnitude than the legal barriers he was attacking before: automation, urban decay, *de facto* school segregation. These are problems which, while conditioned by Jim Crow, do not vanish upon its demise. They are more deeply rooted in our socio-economic order; they are the result of the total society's failure to meet not only the Negro's needs, but human needs generally.

These propositions have won increasing recognition and acceptance, but with a curious twist. They have formed the common premise of two apparently contradictory lines of thought which simultaneously nourish and antagonize each other. On the one hand, there is the reasoning of the New York *Times* moderate who says that the problems are so enormous and complicated that Negro militancy is a futile irritation, and that the need is for "intelligent moderation." Thus, during the first New York school boycott, the *Times* editorialized that Negro demands, while abstractly just, would necessitate massive reforms, the funds for which could not realistically be anticipated; therefore the just demands were also foolish demands and would only antagonize white people. Moderates of this stripe are often correct in perceiving the difficulty or impossibility of racial progress in the context of present social and economic policies. But they accept the context as fixed. They ignore (or perhaps see all too well) the potentialities inherent in linking Negro demands to broader pressures for radical revision of existing policies. They apparently see nothing strange in the fact that in the last twenty-five years we have spent nearly

a trillion dollars fighting or preparing for wars, yet throw up our hands before the need for overhauling our schools, clearing the slums, and really abolishing poverty. My quarrel with these moderates is that they do not even envision radical changes; their admonitions of moderation are, for all practical purposes, admonitions to the Negro to adjust to the status quo, and are therefore immoral.

The more effectively the moderates argue their case, the more they convince Negroes that American society will not or cannot be reorganized for full racial equality. Michael Harrington has said that a successful war on poverty might well require the expenditure of a $100 billion. Where, the Negro wonders, are the forces now in motion to compel such a commitment? If the voices of the moderates were raised in an insistence upon a reallocation of national resources at levels that could not be confused with tokenism (that is, if the moderates stopped being moderates), Negroes would have greater grounds for hope. Meanwhile, the Negro movement cannot escape a sense of isolation.

It is precisely this sense of isolation that gives rise to the second line of thought I want to examine—the tendency within the civil rights movement which, despite its militancy, pursues what I call a "no-win" policy. Sharing with many moderates a recognition of the magnitude of the obstacles to freedom, spokesmen for this tendency survey the American scene and find no forces prepared to move toward radical solutions. From this they conclude that the only viable strategy is shock; above all, the hypocrisy of white liberals must be exposed. These spokesmen are often described as the radicals of the movement, but they are really its moralists. They seek to change white hearts—by traumatizing them. Frequently abetted by white self-flagellants, they may gleefully applaud (though not really agreeing with) Malcolm X because, while they admit he has no program, they think he can frighten white people into doing the right thing. To believe this, of course, you must be convinced, even if unconsciously, that at the core of the white man's heart lies a buried affection for Negroes—a proposition one may be permitted to doubt. But in any case, hearts are not relevant to the issue; neither racial affinities nor racial hostilities are rooted there. It is institutions— social, political, and economic institutions—which are the ultimate molders of collective sentiments. Let these institutions be reconstructed *today*, and let the ineluctable gradualism of history govern the formation of a new psychology.

My quarrel with the "no-win" tendency in the civil rights movement (and the reason I have so designated it) parallels my quarrel with the moderates outside the movement. As the latter lack the vision or will for fundamental change, the former lack a realistic strategy for achieving it. For such a strategy they substitute militancy. But militancy is a matter of posture and volume and not of effect.

I believe that the Negro's struggle for equality in America is essentially revolutionary. While most Negroes—in their hearts—unquestionably seek only to enjoy the fruits of American society as it now exists, their quest cannot *objectively* be satisfied within the framework of existing political and economic relations. The young Negro who would demonstrate his way into the labor market may be motivated by a thoroughly bourgeois ambition and thoroughly "capitalist" considerations, but he will end up having to favor a great expansion of the public sector of the economy. At any rate, that is the position the movement will be forced to take as it looks at the number of jobs being generated by the private economy, and if it is to remain true to the masses of Negroes.

The revolutionary character of the Negro's struggle is manifest in the fact that this struggle may have done more to democratize life for whites than for Negroes. Clearly, it was the sit-in movement of young Southern Negroes which, as it galvanized white students, banished the ugliest features of McCarthyism from the American campus and resurrected political debate. It was not until Negroes assaulted *de facto* school segregation in the urban centers that the issue of quality education for *all* children stirred into motion. Finally, it seems reasonably clear that the civil rights movement, directly and through the resurgence of social conscience it kindled, did more to initiate the war on poverty than any other single force.

It will be—it has been—argued that these by-products of the Negro struggle are not revolutionary. But the term revolutionary, as I am using it, does not connote violence; it refers to the qualitative transformation of fundamental institutions, more or less rapidly,

to the point where the social and economic structure which they comprised can no longer be said to be the same. The Negro struggle has hardly run its course; and it will not stop moving until it has been utterly defeated or won substantial equality. But I fail to see how the movement can be victorious in the absence of radical programs for full employment, abolition of slums, the reconstruction of our educational system, new definitions of work and leisure. Adding up the cost of such programs, we can only conclude that we are talking about a refashioning of our political economy. It has been estimated, for example, that the price of replacing New York City's slums with public housing would be $17 billion. Again, a multi-billion dollar federal public-works program, dwarfing the currently proposed $2 billion program, is required to reabsorb unskilled and semi-skilled workers into the labor market—and this must be done if Negro workers in these categories are to be employed. "Preferential treatment" cannot help them.

I am not trying here to delineate a total program, only to suggest the scope of economic reforms which are most immediately related to the plight of the Negro community. One could speculate on their political implications—whether, for example, they do not indicate the obsolescence of state government and the superiority of regional structures as viable units of planning. Such speculations aside, it is clear that Negro needs cannot be satisfied unless we go beyond what has so far been placed on the agenda. How are these radical objectives to be achieved? The answer is simple, deceptively so: *through political power*.

There is a strong moralistic strain in the civil rights movement which would remind us that power corrupts, forgetting that the absence of power also corrupts. But this is not the view I want to debate here, for it is waning. Our problem is posed by those who accept the need for political power but do not understand the nature of the object and therefore lack sound strategies for achieving it; they tend to confuse political institutions with lunch counters.

A handful of Negroes, acting alone, could integrate a lunch counter by strategically locating their bodies so *as directly* to interrupt the operation of the proprietor's will; their numbers were relatively unimportant. In politics, however, such a confrontation is difficult because the interests involved are merely *represented*. In the execution of a political decision a direct confrontation may ensue (as when federal marshals escorted James Meredith into the University of Mississippi—to turn from an example of non-violent coercion to one of force backed up with the threat of violence). But in arriving at a political decision, numbers and organizations are crucial, especially for the economically disenfranchised. (Needless to say, I am assuming that the forms of political democracy exist in America, however imperfectly, that they are valued, and that elitist or putschist conceptions of exercising power are beyond the pale of discussion for the civil rights movement.)

Neither that movement nor the country's twenty million black people can win political power alone. We need allies. The future of the Negro struggle depends on whether the contradictions of this society can be resolved by a coalition of progressive forces which becomes the *effective* political majority in the United States. I speak of the coalition which staged the March on Washington, passed the Civil Rights Act, and laid the basis for the Johnson landslide—Negroes, trade unionists, liberals, and religious groups.

There are those who argue that a coalition strategy would force the Negro to surrender his political independence to white liberals, that he would be neutralized, deprived of his cutting edge, absorbed into the Establishment. Some who take this position urged last year that votes be withheld from the Johnson-Humphrey ticket as a demonstration of the Negro's political power. Curiously enough, these people who sought to demonstrate power through the non-exercise of it, also point to the Negro "swing vote" in crucial urban areas as the source of the Negro's independent political power. But here they are closer to being right: the urban Negro vote will grow in importance in the coming years. If there is anything positive in the spread of the ghetto, it is the potential political power base thus created, and to realize this potential is one of the most challenging and urgent tasks before the civil rights movement. If the movement can wrest leadership of the ghetto vote from the machines, it will have acquired an organized constituency such as other major groups in our society now have.

But we must also remember that the effectiveness of a swing vote depends solely on "other" votes. It derives its power from them. In that sense, it can never be "independent," but must opt for one candidate or the other, even if by default. Thus coalitions are inescapable, however tentative they may be. And this is the case in all but those few situations in which Negroes running on an independent ticket might conceivably win. "Independence," in other words, is not a value in itself. The issue is which coalition to join and how to make it responsive to your program. Necessarily there will be compromise. But the difference between expediency and morality in politics is the difference between selling out a principle and making smaller concessions to win larger ones. The leader who shrinks from this task reveals not his purity but his lack of political sense.

The task of molding a political movement out of the March on Washington coalition is not simple, but no alternatives have been advanced. We need to choose our allies on the basis of common political objectives. It has become fashionable in some no-win Negro circles to decry the white liberal as the main enemy (his hypocrisy is what sustains racism); by virtue of this reverse recitation of the reactionary's litany (liberalism leads to socialism, which leads to Communism) the Negro is left in majestic isolation, except for a tiny band of fervent white initiates. But the objective fact is that *Eastland and Goldwater* are the main enemies— they and the opponents of civil rights, of the war on poverty, of medicare, of social security, of federal aid to education, of unions, and so forth. The labor movement, despite its obvious faults, has been the largest single organized force in this country pushing for progressive social legislation. And where the Negro-labor-liberal axis is weak, as in the farm belt, it was the religious groups that were most influential in rallying support for the Civil Rights Bill.

The durability of the coalition was interestingly tested during the election. I do not believe that the Johnson landslide proved the "white backlash" to be a myth. It proved, rather, that economic interests are more fundamental than prejudice: the backlashers decided that loss of social security was, after all, too high a price to pay for a slap at the Negro. This lesson was a valuable first step in re-educating such people, and it must be kept alive, for the civil rights movement will be advanced only to the degree that social and economic welfare gets to be inextricably entangled with civil rights.

The 1964 elections marked a turning point in American politics. The Democratic landslide was not merely the result of a negative reaction to Goldwaterism; it was also the expression of a majority liberal consensus. The near unanimity with which Negro voters joined in that expression was, I am convinced, a vindication of the July 25th statement by Negro leaders calling for a strategic turn toward political action and a temporary curtailment of mass demonstrations. Despite the controversy surrounding the statement, the instinctive response it met with in the community is suggested by the fact that demonstrations were down 75 per cent as compared with the same period in 1963. But should so high a percentage of Negro voters have gone to Johnson, or should they have held back to narrow his margin of victory and thus give greater visibility to our swing vote? How has our loyalty changed things? Certainly the Negro vote had higher visibility in 1960, when a switch of only 7 per cent from the Republican column of 1956 elected President Kennedy. But the slimness of Kennedy's victory—of his "mandate"—dictated a go-slow approach on civil rights, at least until the Birmingham upheaval.

Although Johnson's popular majority was so large that he could have won without such overwhelming Negro support, that support was important from several angles. Beyond adding to Johnson's total national margin, it was specifically responsible for his victories in Virginia, Florida, Tennessee, and Arkansas. Goldwater took only those states where fewer than 45 percent of eligible Negroes were registered. That Johnson would have won those states had Negro voting rights been enforced is a lesson not likely to be lost on a man who would have been happy with a unanimous electoral college. In any case, the 1.6 million Southern Negroes who voted have had a shattering impact on the Southern political party structure, as illustrated in the changed composition of the Southern congressional delegation. The "backlash" gave the Republicans five House seats in Alabama, one in Georgia, and one in Mississippi. But on the Democratic side, seven segregationists were defeated while all nine Southerners who voted for the Civil Rights Act were re-elected. It may be premature to predict a Southern Democratic party of Negroes and white moderates and a Republican Party of refugee racists and economic conservatives, but there certainly is a strong tendency toward such a realignment; and an additional 3.6 million Negroes of voting age in the eleven Southern states are still to be heard from. Even the *tendency* toward disintegration of the Democratic party's racist wing defines a new context for Presidential and liberal strategy in the congressional battles ahead. Thus the Negro vote (North as well as South), while not *decisive* in the Presidential race, was enormously effective. It was a dramatic element of a historic mandate which contains vast possibilities and dangers that will fundamentally affect the future course of the civil rights movement.

The liberal congressional sweep raises hope for an assault on the seniority system, Rule Twenty-two, and other citadels of Dixiecrat-Republican power. The overwhelming of this conservative coalition should also mean progress on much bottlenecked legislation of profound interest to the movement (e.g., bills by Senators Clark and Nelson on planning, manpower, and employment). Moreover, the irrelevance of the South to Johnson's victory gives the President more freedom to act than his predecessor had and more leverage to the movement to pressure for executive action in Mississippi and other racist strongholds.

None of this *guarantees* vigorous executive or legislative action, for the other side of the Johnson landslide is that it has a Gaullist quality. Goldwater's capture of the Republican party forced into the Democratic camp many disparate elements which do not belong there, Big Business being the major example. Johnson, who wants to be President "of all people," may try to keep his new coalition together by sticking close to the political center. But if he decides to do this, it is unlikely that even his political genius will be able to hold together a coalition so inherently unstable and rife with contradictions. It must come apart. Should it do so while Johnson is pursuing a centrist course, then the mandate will have been wastefully dissipated. However, if the mandate is seized upon to set fundamental changes in motion, then the basis can be laid for a new mandate, a new coalition including hitherto inert and dispossessed strata of the population.

Here is where the cutting edge of the civil rights movement can be applied. We must see to it that the reorganization of the "consensus party" proceeds along lines which will make it an effective vehicle for social reconstruction, a role it cannot play so long as it furnishes Southern racism with its national political power. (One of Barry Goldwater's few attractive ideas was that the Dixiecrats belong with him in the same party.) And nowhere has the civil rights movement's political cutting edge been more magnificently demonstrated than at Atlantic City, where the Mississippi Freedom Democratic Party not only secured recognition as a bona fide component of the national party, but in the process routed the representatives of the most rabid racists—the white Mississippi and Alabama delegations. While I still believe that the FDP made a tactical error in spurning the compromise, there is no question that they launched a political revolution whose logic is the displacement of Dixiecrat power. They launched that revolution within a major political institution and as part of a coalitional effort.

The role of the civil rights movement in the reorganization of American political life is programmatic as well as strategic. We are challenged now to broaden our social vision, to develop functional programs with concrete objectives. We need to propose alternatives to technological unemployment, urban decay, and the rest. We need to be calling for public works and training, for national economic planning, for federal aid to education, for attractive public housing—all this on a sufficiently massive scale to make a difference. We need to protest the notion that our integration into American life, so long delayed, must now proceed in an atmosphere of competitive scarcity instead of in the security of abundance which technology makes possible. We cannot claim to have answers to all the complex problems of modern society. That is too much to ask of a movement still battling barbarism in Mississippi. But we can agitate the right questions by probing at the contradictions which still stand in the way of the "Great Society." The questions having been asked, motion must begin in the larger society, for there is a limit to what Negroes can do alone.

7-3 "The Fenced Land" and "The Lost People"*

Jonathan Rieder

Canarsie: The Jews and Italians of Brooklyn against Liberalism

The Fenced Land

In 1960 Old Canarsie was a sleepy, mainly Italian community, with a remnant of the original Irish, German, and British inhabitants, and some Russian and Polish Jews. Two-thirds of the men were blue-collar workers, many of them operators of machinery or skilled craftsmen. Fewer than 25 percent had graduated from high school. Family income averaged $6,000. . . .

The population of Canarsie soared from 30,000 in 1950 to 50,000 in 1960 to 80,000 in 1970, when it began a gradual decline. Lots marketed at $400 in 1950 went for twenty times that amount fifteen years later. Whites from racially transitional neighborhoods replenished the buying and rental markets through the 1960s and 1970s. In the latter half of the 1970s, Israelis, Russian émigré Jews, mobile Chinese and other Asian Americans, and Orthodox Jews filled some of the vacancies. Middle-class black buyers finally began to crack the racial barrier in Canarsie's northern quadrant during the late 1970s.

For the migrants of the 1960s, at least those attracted by the lure of a new neighborhood rather than reeling from racial change in the old one, moving to Canarsie had simple and complex meanings. The care they invested in the neighborhood reflected their joy at living in a safe place, with good schools and amenities. Homeowners' solicitousness for their properties expressed the sacrifice obliged by mortgage payments and the freshness for many of the experience of ownership. The pride in place also came from a less tangible accomplishment, not the jackpot pledged in some versions of the American mobility creed, but the chance to provide for family, to enjoy simple pleasures, and to live a life no longer pinched by privation.

A Jewish woman who had come to Canarsie from a city project in Brownsville remembered the Depression. "We were so poor in those days, you see, we didn't have very much. We think back to those days a lot. Our children have no idea of what it was like. We didn't need much to make do. There was stoopball and checkers and hopscotch. The ice would melt on the ice wagon, and we'd watch it melt down and change shapes. The kids today would laugh at us." Twenty years passed before she truly believed that the economic ground would not suddenly slide out from under her. The odyssey to Canarsie helped redeem the sacrifices of the 1930s. "Most of us who live in Canarsie came from ghettos. But once we made it to Canarsie, we finally had a little piece of the country. It was like we had moved to a little shtetl," she concluded, using the Yiddish word for village. . . .

Canarsie's rise out of the marshlands of Jamaica Bay symbolized the transformation of the middle classes in the years after World War II. Samuel Lubell penned the classical rendition of that "climbing of Jacob's ladder" by the children of the Depression and the passion for respectability that inspired it. "What makes them so significant politically is that having come to this country in roughly the same period, the so-called 'new' immigrants and their offspring shared common experiences in this country. All have been part of one of the epic population movements in history—of the upsurging out of the slums toward the

Source: "The Fenced Land" and "The Lost People" are reprinted by permission of the publisher from *Canarsie: The Jews and Italians of Brooklyn against Liberalism* by Jonathan Rieder, pp. 15–19, 95–106. Cambridge, Mass.: Harvard University Press, Copyright © 1985 by Jonathan Rieder.

*Some text and accompanying endnotes have been omitted. Please consult the original source.

middle class which has swept our major cities since the turn of the century and which is still going on." Lubell's portrait of the trip from Manhattan's Lower East Side to Forest Hills in Queens holds equally true for the move from Brownsville to Canarsie. "The spanning of that distance was a social revolution. . . . If land hunger was the propelling force behind the agrarian frontier, the drive behind the urban frontier has been the hunger for social status."[1]

A stroll on a summer evening in 1976 suggested the supreme ordinariness of life in Canarsie. Blue skies, hazed over by smog during the day, were shading into the grayish pink pastels of dusk. The Belt Parkway was a sinuous curve between shore and land, humming with commuters heading for Long Island or the outer reaches of Queens and Brooklyn. Earlier that day, out on Canarsie pier, huddles of men in Bermuda shorts sat in beach chairs and kibitzed over cards, the quiet rhythmically broken by the roar of jets landing and taking off at Kennedy Airport a few miles east. Across the parkway in Seaview Village, Orthodox Jews in skullcaps headed for Sabbath services. Grabstein's Deli on Rockaway Parkway, with the neon-orange Hebrew lettering on the window, was crammed with families feasting on blintzes, corned beef, and knishes. Around the corner on Avenue L, stores emblazoned with the red, green, and white of the Italian flag exuded the odors of mortadella and prosciutto. Now teenagers claimed the strip, listening to the pounding beat of disco, as macho boys hustled young girls in halter tops and tight shorts. A mile away, in the heart of Old Canarsie, elderly Italians sat outside their bungalows, enjoying the after-dinner calm. In the receding light, Canarsie fell into a trance. The groups of people seemed suspended for a moment between the abrasions of the work week and the approaching weekend with its promise of small pleasures.

Canarsie is a haven, but the gift of immunity is not given freely. To keep their illusion of refuge the residents sealed out alien races, suspicious people, disturbing forces. They made their community into a fortress, a fenced land. With the exception of two public projects on the edge of Canarsie and three census tracts with two or three dozen blacks, none of the remaining twenty-eight tracts had more than ten blacks out of populations ranging from one thousand to four thousand people. Most blocks were entirely white. Nonetheless, Canarsians felt vulnerable to encroachment from the black communities that form an arc stretching from East Flatbush to the northwest, through Brownsville due north, to East New York in the northeast. Barriers of nature— Jamaica Bay to the south, Paerdegat Basin on the western flank, and Fresh Creek on the eastern flank— protect Canarsie, but those same boundaries limit the residents' options of flight and expansion. . . .

The Lost People

Class Consciousness

Canarsians' feelings of vulnerability violated their expectations that their lives of striving would be rewarded. They felt they had a right to avoid entanglement in the affairs of the larger society. Garry Wills has described Richard Nixon's ingenious appeal to that belief in the frantic election year of 1968. "Nixon's success was not offered in Miami as a theme for mere self-congratulation. It was a pledge to others, a pledge that he would not rob them of the fruits of their success: 'You can see why I believe so deeply in the American dream. For most of us the American Revolution has been won; the American dream has come true.'"[2]

The promise echoed William Jennings Bryan's celebration of a similar notion of privatism. Bryan came to New York City to reassure the 1896 Democratic convention that his intentions were not subversive. Like 1968, 1896 was a time of social upheaval, when the old faiths no longer seemed apt and partisan loyalties had gone slack. "Our campaign has not for its object the reconstruction of society," the Great Redeemer told the convention. "We cannot insure to the vicious the fruits of a virtuous life; we would not invade the home of the provident in order to supply the wants of the spendthrift; we do not propose to transfer the rewards of industry to the laps of indolence."[3]

The speech would have been well received in Canarsie three-quarters of a century later. The residents thought racial quotas transferred the rewards of industry to the laps of indolence, welfare raided the home of the provident to supply the wants of the spendthrift, and rioting was insurance for the vicious. Policies designed to help minorities challenged the social place of middle-income people. The policies were enforced, not by actual muscle, but by the symbolic muscle of government. One aide to a Canarsie elected official, a conservative Democrat who detested "limousine liberals," drew the parallel between threats to physical and to social place in a comment on the impact of the civil rights movement: "The whole middle class is suffering from a proverbial mugging."

The civil rights movement was a heroic phase of American history. In their effort to achieve basic constitutional rights, blacks claimed the title of the injured party. But the more blacks fought for a place in society, the more whites resisted, seizing for themselves the identity of the injured. The reasons for the change in the terms of that racial debate are complex, but in part they stemmed from a shift in the strategy of the civil rights movement. A national consensus in the early 1960s sustained black demands for legal rights and equal opportunity. But as blacks pressed for social and economic equality, complex questions of status, justice, and domination were raised.[4]

Just as Canarsians were closer geographically to the underclasses than were affluent suburbanites, so they were closer socially to the black lower- and middle-income classes.[5] The basic fact of life for the residents of Canarsie was the precariousness of their hold on middle-class status, the recency of their arrival in that exalted position, and the intense fear that it might be taken from them. The cramped quality of lower middle-class life was evident in their abstentions and forfeitures. It galled Canarsians that poor blacks and Hispanics used food stamps to buy "luxury items" while they had to scrimp to get by. "I go to the supermarket and I see the welfare lady splurging and I'm abstaining," complained an insurance salesman. "It makes you mad because you been working so hard, and you have to give up things, and they don't work and get things you can't afford."

"I'd like to take a real vacation," said another man at the pressed margin of the middle class. "What we call a vacation is going to an aunt or uncle or something like that, where there's no hotel expenses. My wife and I, we'd like to go where nobody knows us, go to a show or a nightclub or something, do this or that, that's a vacation, really relaxing." But his take-home pay of $150 a week always seemed to lag behind the spiraling expenses of rent bills, utility bills, feeding the family.

When his wife thought about growing old and getting sick, the future looked grim. The plight of an old Jewish woman whom she and her husband had visited in a city hospital offered a sad portent. The patient lay in her own waste because the nurses wouldn't change the bed linen. "A bowl of soup for a woman who's put her whole life into this country! I know she's not outstanding, but do you have to be an outstanding, well-known person to be taken care of? I'm sure Rockefeller, if anything happened to him, boy, he's not going to want. They'll rush him to the best hospital. Not that I'm saying we need the best hospitals. But they should take care of us properly. We bleed just like Rockefeller bleeds."

Fiscal pressures fortified the feeling of deprivation. An Italian worker offered his own sardonic version of class consciousness. "There is no more middle class any more. I'll give you my interpretation. I don't believe in low, middle and high class. There's high income and there's low income." He argued that thanks to transfer payments, tax policy, and mortgage payments, "The average guy who makes $20,000 a year is basically coming out with the same amount as the guy on welfare. So what does that make him? That makes him low. Middle income is a federal term to make people feel good before they pick their pockets."[6]

Rivalry for jobs dissolved magnanimous impulses. If the employed felt nervous about the security of their jobs, unemployment sometimes produced feelings of white panic and bitterness. An unemployed Jewish salesman saw blacks as his personal tormentors. "The blacks want my job, they want to take my little box of a house, they won't leave me alone!" A Jewish politician explained in 1977, "All over Canarsie, people feel others are eroding what they have gained. Today, with the economy so bad, there's a greater feeling, people are saying, 'Blacks are coming in and taking our jobs.' Of course they had security when only whites were in the job market."

Canarsians saw the workplace as only one of many arenas of threat created by liberal reform, the civil rights movement, and black assertiveness![7] All facets of black and white relations seemed to impose strains on the lower middle classes: on their ability to remain financially solvent, on their ability to believe that life was just, on their ability to withstand privation. A Jewish educator in Canarsie described the pressures placed on his neighbors by the overthrow of white dominance:

> These efforts to help blacks reached a plateau. It's like a rubber band. I don't know the moral or legal limits on stretching the middle class, how far and how much they will pay the price. I don't know, to tell you the truth, if we've stretched the limits far enough. But I do know that since 1964, the vast majority of Canarsie feels that they've been stretched to the limits of their endurance.

The image of being stretched had many variants connoting pressure, discomfort, and pain; blacks were not the only source of hurt. Residents said they were choking from and groaning under and gagging on the costs of efforts to help the poor. Others said they were being "raped," "fucked up the ass," or "screwed" by utility rates, the tax system, or busing. Men sometimes described a vague, malevolent force that was breaking their balls. A sophisticated analyst of lower-middle-class rage captured the dangers that pressed his neighbors. "Canarsie is up against the wall. That's what the lower middle and middle classes feel pressing on them. They feel the pressure, like everything is fading away. It's all in danger: the house you always wanted is in danger, the kids are in danger, the neighborhood is in danger. It's all slipping away."

The real keyword of middle-class lamentation was *squeeze*. A merchant depicted his plight as follows. "Someone is coming in and squeezing us and taking it all away. That is what is unifying our community. The squeezing is wrong, it's so wrong. You are looking at a man who hurts. First, they squeeze my pocketbook, so I can't do anything. Then they come in with busing and squeeze my kids." Squeeze indicated the position of the middle classes betwixt and between the impoverished and the affluent. A self-professed conservative Democrat pinpointed the vulnerability of the middle class:

> It's okay to talk about the welfare classes, but the real problem is the middle-class squeeze. You get it from top and bottom. It's not only welfare, but the multinational corporations who are ripping us off, taking our jobs away and sending employment to the South and the West. The middle

classes are the lost people. We don't have the wherewithal to fight back, because we aren't rich enough, and we're not poor enough to get the advantages that go to the poor. We suffer.

That the elected officials in the Jefferson Democratic Club evinced a hearty progressive streak is not surprising, given their strong New Deal loyalties. Yet Italian leaders in the Republican and Conservative parties voiced similar notions of status radicalism. Whatever else their conservatism entailed, it did not include affection for corporate business. "Oil, steel, insurance, and the banks run this country," exclaimed a Nixon loyalist in the Italian-American Civil Rights League. "I'd go for public ownership of the oil companies if I didn't think the national politicians were a bunch of thieves."

Canarsians' resentment was directed as well at privileged portions of the middle classes. The special perquisites, or "lulus," given to state legislators, the escalator clauses in AFL-CIO union contracts, and the sweetheart deals negotiated by city workers provoked their anger. A dockworker whose union guaranteed him employment did not consider municipal unions instruments of popular justice. "These cops are paid overtime on fringe benefits in their last year before they retire, and that's what they get as a pension. I'm a working guy and I can't imagine getting that. It's not fair. I'm paying money on my house and mortgage, and I just can't make it."

The lines of antagonism, then, were not fixed or simple. Rivalry between blacks and whites, between public and private workers, between business and labor—each was only one of many shifting points of conflict and concord. Canarsians mistrusted privileged blocs of all sorts, including the organized sectors of their own class.

How much squeezing would the citizens absorb before lashing back? Can one detect in the identity of the little man an ominous harbinger of fascism? When a volatile, two-fisted worker used the word, *squeeze* could be the language of the body, unmediated by thought. The word conjures up the image of intense pressure building to a vindictive climax. Historically, the middle classes have felt deeply betrayed when their wants have outpaced expectations or their aspirations have been thwarted by austerity. Betrayal easily turns into soured cynicism or, worse, nationalist mania and race-baiting. Michael Rogin has aptly described the baneful downside of American hopefulness as "the punitive consequences of frustrated optimism." In Seymour Martin Lipset's classic formulation, a crushed middle class succumbs to populist forms of right-wing extremism.[8]

An Italian construction worker warned of the dangerous propensities of riled "average people." "We're working men, and we don't bow our heads in humility. We fight and say to the blacks, 'Keep out of our neighborhood.' We never bullshit. We call a spade a spade." He was equally capable of denouncing large corporations, and the privileged in general, who crushed "little nobodies like us, just average people trying to survive. How the hell can you keep surviving with Con Ed and Brooklyn Gas Company preying on you?" And there were the blacks on welfare, the demands for quotas, and the black felons who paraded across his television on the nightly news. Sometimes it was just too much to endure, and he felt an urge to take out all his different frustrations on one scapegoat. "You know how the Jews were put in concentration camps? Well, people will get angry and reactionary and put the blacks in concentration camps. If we whites are constantly frustrated, there will be a racial conflagration."

One should be wary of a mechanistic equation of strain and right-wing mania. The development of reactionary protest was not a foregone conclusion. Various personal, moral, and political restraints inhibit the direct translation of frustration into authoritarian rage. While racist and nationalist binges remain a latent tendency in American society, that tendency has diminished. Whether middle-class frustration surges to the right or to the left depends significantly on the political leaders and institutions that channel anger. The retributive consequences of frustrated optimism remain a propensity more than a destiny.[9]

Canarsians for decades had felt beleaguered by the forces of corporate avarice and special interests. They had always seen themselves as little people. The forgotten men of the Depression are not that different from the average working people heralded by George Wallace. To the old rhetoric the passions of race added new threats and more vivid culprits. Now Canarsians had to contend with organized minorities and powerful liberalism as well as organized labor and big business. The residents used the categories they inherited from immigrant life and the New Deal, but they stretched them to make room for black and Hispanic rivals and their patrons in academia, the suburbs, the media, the judiciary, the bureaucracy, and the Democratic party.

Welfare

The middle classes hurled blame down on those who enjoyed the indulgence of dependency and up against those who enjoyed the immunities of affluence, yet their focus remained on the minority poor. Before detailing the conceptions of justice and character that shaped their response to the welfare classes, we must examine two major recent changes in the fiscal and political environment that contributed to that fixation. One involves the change in the welfare functions of government and the proportion of those on welfare in Brooklyn and in New York City. As William J. Wilson has argued, competition between blacks and whites has moved from the sphere of jobs to the enjoyment of public goods, like schools and entitlements. The growth in the expense and diversity of claims on municipal and national treasuries, including Aid to Families with Dependent Children and antipoverty programs, enhanced middle-class upset about black dependency. Between 1965 and 1971 the percentage of the population on welfare in minority neighborhoods near Canarsie soared: from 23 percent to 38 percent in Brownsville, from less than 8 percent to a startling 31 percent in East New York.[10]

Changes in publicity accompanied the growth of entitlements; the government's initiatives became more visible, the cries of the claimants louder. The clamor reached a peak in New York City during the 1960s, when the Welfare Rights Organization launched a controversial campaign to enroll eligible clients. "The campaign of disruption was in full swing. There was a three-day sit-in at the commissioner's office, and unruly demonstrators closed [welfare] centers throughout the city. One sit-in reportedly netted $135,000 in new grants." These changes in publicity and dependency gave new meaning to the concept of transfer payments. "Instead of merely granting the poor a continued share of a growing economy, the massive expansion of the rolls began to approach actual redistribution of income from the middle class to the poor."[11]

Canarsians often showed their hostility to people on welfare by contrasting parasites and producers. The head of a conservative civic group wrote in its newspaper, "For years, we have witnessed the appeasement of nonproductive and counter-productive 'leeches' at the expense of New York's middle class work force." He reported on his field trip to the ghetto on "check day." "The first thing that caught my eye . . . was the 8:00 A.M. opening of all the Liquor Stores, who spend their entire morning . . . bracing for the brisk day's business. It's a crude fact that the liquor stores cater to continuous LINES of people, from morning to night on days that welfare checks are received."[12]

A receptive reader could take double pleasure from the editorial. It pledged to exact retribution from the profligate in a disinterested act of upholding morality. And it reminded the readers of their superiority, as plucky bootstrappers, to the hapless leeches, a word that bypassed the equivocations of thought and went right for the guts. A city worker, practically beside himself, exploded, "These welfare people get as much as I do and I work my ass off and come home dead tired. They get up late and they can shack up all day long and watch the tube. With their welfare and food stamps, they come out better than me. . . . So why should I work? I go shopping with my wife and I see them with their forty dollars of food stamps in the supermarket, living and eating better than me. . . . And they got this escalator clause too, so they keep getting more. Let them tighten their belts like we have to."

Was "leeches" an expression of racist contempt? Can an envy of splurging be detected in the animus toward those who lie around and "shack up all day?" Did the call for belt-tightening express a secret wish to squeeze the welfare people as tightly as the speaker felt squeezed by all the privations in his life? Self-denial often produces an attitude of stingy misanthropy. As one man inveighed, "Who's feeling sorry for me? The colored have gotten enough. Let them do for themselves like we do!" His question hinted at the close link between fatiguing sacrifice and greedy self-absorption. The economy of scarcity is emotional as well as political.

The complexity of hostility to welfare becomes lost if we focus on racist passion or on the stinginess induced by financial vulnerability. The first position, which views resentment of the dole as a displacement of inner tensions, succumbs to a false psychologism. The second position, which views the tension between the productive and the dependent classes as a fight for personal advantage, succumbs to a false materialism.[13] Both fail to represent the full range of Canarsians' emotional repertoire. As all the middle-class chants of "It's not fair, it's not right" suggest, one of the key emotions in fiscal backlash is indignation, an emotion born of the perception of injustice. Along with the political and psychic economies of welfare, there is a moral economy of welfare.

The voracity of the word "leech" contrasts sharply with benevolent nurture. It conjures up a creature that sucks the sustenance of others. Unlike those who embrace the ethos of reciprocity, the leech receives without returning, takes but does not give, devours but refuses to contribute. More than a disguise for self-interest, a symptom of envy, or a euphemism for racism, the leech is a symbol of violated justice.

Regardless of where they fell along the spectrum of ideology, most Canarsians reproached what they saw as the deformation of welfare rather than the giving as such. They bemoaned the devolution of a rightful guarantee of subsistence into a pride-corroding, dependency-enhancing system of giveaways. They specifically condemned the way welfare was administered. A liberal Jewish woman argued, "I don't think the problem is we give too much welfare, but how it's handled. We do it poorly. Medicaid and the school lunch program are full of waste and fraud. I worked for the welfare department, and I know that much of it is not proper." The residents said that the aged, the worthy poor, both white and black, and the crippled did not receive adequate recompense. Some of the most conservative enemies of giveaways argued for an expansion of government initiatives in creating jobs, insuring health care, and protecting the environment.[14]

In searching for a model of just giving, the residents cited the system they imagined they knew best. A local civic leader offered this version of the prevailing wisdom. "For scores of years, welfare has served as a dignified alternative to starvation . . . for the individual who has been truly unable to produce, but who obviously would produce if able." The wizardry of the old welfare system was its ability to satisfy a variety of desiderata, both practical and moral. Above all, the man believed, it worked in harmony with, not in opposition to, prized cultural values. "It has served to help our ancestors 'get on their feet' financially after arriving here penniless, so that they could assert their pride and determination, and go on with the business of raising a family and earning a legitimate living."

State aid had sustained many residents of Canarsie, or their friends, relatives, and neighbors. Beneficence, however, did not mean munificence. According to the romance of history, relief extended a modest provision hedged by the client's shame, by the moral sanctions of the local community in which the recipient lived, and by widespread acceptance of the system's authority to place restrictions on giving. An Italian Republican leader said, "Welfare is a necessity, but there are the extravagances, the items allowable. And there's the continuous cycle of generation after generation on welfare."

He migrated back in time. "Years ago my father died and left my mother with eight children. We went on welfare and we were visited by a welfare worker at our home periodically, to see if my mother was buying foolishly." Current talk about forming a union of welfare recipients struck him as arrogant, in contrast to his family's humble deference to the intrusions of a paternalistic state. "We weren't allowed to buy a telephone or linoleum. We had to ask. You need these controls on public funds. When my older sister got a job after she graduated from Midwood High School, they reduced the welfare. And when my second sister went to work, we went off welfare. Welfare helped us, and it was right and just they did. Then we could shift for ourselves."

The ideal of governmental sternness went beyond the chilly withholding of care; it defined the best interests of clients, paralleling folk notions of the best interests of children. The residents saw liberal permissiveness as an abdication of concern, which left children and welfare clients incapable of self-direction and worse off for it. An Italian Reaganite Republican voiced a common opinion: "Blacks have been made the political football of the Democratic party. The Democrats offer the blacks so much welfare that it impairs them. They never give them an opportunity to lift themselves up. Welfare destroys them. They must learn to fend for themselves.

You can't always run to papa." In good universalist fashion, the man applied the same lesson to his children. Would not softness spoil them, he asked, and unfit them for life in a world that required steely character? "A child should begin to stand on his own two feet. Don't hand them everything on a silver platter."

Provincial Italians were convinced that leniency encouraged welfare recipients to make extravagant claims, just as they thought permissive child-rearing encouraged kids to make wild libidinal claims on the world. In both cases, they reasoned, if given one inch, human beings would *naturally* go for the whole foot. "I blame this welfare mess on the government," a policeman said after describing a system that seemed self-perpetuating when it should have been self-canceling. "Now this is only telling me one thing. If you're getting welfare for the first generation, the second generation is just gonna say, 'What the hell do I have to work for? I'll just carry on the same thing,' and it moves down the line. If you're gonna give somebody something for nothing, let's say you tell 'em, 'We'll pay for your house, we'll pay for your rent, we'll pay for your food,' why should you want to work?"

Liberal Democrats in Canarsie were no more enthusiastic about the welfare system than were conservative Republicans. The remnant of Debsean socialists no less than acquisitive vulgarians worshiped self-reliance. Pulling one's own weight was a natural complement to a cooperative society in which all shouldered their burdens. "Bums," "parasites," and "takers" offended that notion of reciprocity, which obliged citizens not to slough off their duties onto others. A leftist saw dependency as a violation of her humanist belief in individual development:

Some of the problems of poor blacks is their cultural background. It's the way they have lived in America. I don't know about Africa, but dependency has become ingrained in their culture. The attitude is, "Let others take care of me." There's a lack of self-reliance. But there has been much black progress despite the bad methods. I see it where I work. People are put into jobs they are not qualified for, but they learn from being in the situation. Learning to contribute makes you less satisfied about being given things.

The division of the world into producers and parasites objectified basic principles of right living. All the adages of lower-middle-class life celebrated the values of get up and go, busting chops, doing for yourself.[15] "Face it," said one Jewish merchant, "the Haitians and the Jamaicans and the other islanders down in Flatbush don't consider themselves black. These island people are producing people, they're up early sweeping their stoops and taking care of their homes. They're producing people like we are! But the black lower element don't contribute to society, they just take. In my view, you should get what you put into. You have to contribute."

Welfare violated notions of distributive as well as contributive justice by circulating burdens and rewards inequitably. When he measured the rewards that accrued to indolence against those produced by effort, an Italian worker felt like a consummate chump. Only his analytic streak and sense of humor saved him from wild resentment. "The average person on welfare, let's say they make $10,000 a year, with all the school benefits and food stamps. I make $20,000 a year. But I am taxed and taxed and taxed, close to $6,000 worth. So I'm down to $14,000 already. You take that fourteen and someone's getting ten, he's making only four thousand less than I am, and he's not working. Interesting idea? I'm just trying to put you in my category."

Garry Wills has argued that "the American fanatic has always suffered moral disorientation at the mere thought of anyone 'getting something for nothing.'" Americans, however, are not the only fanatics. Marcel Mauss wrote, "The essence of potlatch is the obligation of worthy return." Virginia Yans-McGlouglan has written, "The Mezzogiorno peasants were not accustomed to getting 'something for nothing.'"[16] At least the old system of welfare, according to the conventional wisdom, accomplished an implicit trade of something for something. "In essence, the very person that received welfare soon would be paying taxes, so that the city would constantly replace its outlay of funds. He had become a productive citizen."[17] In contrast, the present system seemed to encourage multigenerational welfare families, undermining the public's trust in eventual symbolic or material repayment.

Resentment of the injustice of the tax system reinforced the image of one-sided exchange. Canarsians believed that tax penalties were heaped on working people while the affluent got off scot-free. "The very poor have nothing economically," claimed a housewife, "but they reap the benefits of our hard work. My husband works hard, and the taxes keep going up. The taxes go to the poor, not to us. And the rich have their tax accountants. The middle-income people are carrying the cost of liberal social programs on their backs. The rich can afford to be liberal. They won't be touched by liberalized programs. . . ."

Notes

"The Fenced Land"

1. Samuel Lubell, *The Future of American Politics*, 2nd ed. (Garden City, New York: Doubleday, 1956), pp. 71, 74–75.

"The Lost People"

2. Garry Wills, *Nixon Agonistes: The Crisis of the Self-Made Man* (Boston: Houghton Mifflin, 1970), p. 310.

3. Quoted in Richard Hofstadter, *The American Political Tradition* (New York: Alfred Knopf, 1948), p. 190.

4. Seymour Martin Lipset and Earl Raab, *The Politics of Unreason: Right-Wing Extremism in America, 1790–1977*, 2nd ed. (Chicago: University of Chicago Press, 1978), chaps. 9–13; Nathan Glazer and Daniel Patrick Moynihan, *Beyond the Melting Pot: The Negroes, Puerto Ricans, Jews, Italians, and Irish of New York City*, 2nd ed. (Cambridge, Mass.: MIT Press, 1970), pp. vii–lxxvi.

5. Threats to social and to physical place have much in common. In both cases the magnitude of threat, the resilience of the threatened, and the availability of techniques of fending off threat all determine susceptibility. . . .

6. The perception and the actuality of fiscal privation vary a good deal from nation to nation and also, within nations, from region to region. Harold Wilensky describes the intensity of the welfare backlash in New York and California in *The Welfare State and Equality: Structural and Ideological Roots of Public Expenditures* (Berkeley: University of California Press, 1975), pp. 32–34.

7. Some social theorists argue that racial antagonism provides a distraction, urged on by corporate leaders, from genuine conflicts of interest between workers and owners. Racist passion appears in that telling

as a charade, a surrogate for "real" grievances. A number of things are wrong with this analysis. . . .

8. Michael Paul Rogin, *The Intellectuals and McCarthy: The Radical Specter* (Cambridge: MIT Press, 1967), p. 47; Seymour Martin Lipset, *Political Man: The Social Basis of Politics*, expanded ed. (Baltimore: Johns Hopkins University Press, 1981), pp. 127–183. For a more recent application of the concept of center extremism to Ronald Reagan's 1980 coalition, see Kevin Phillips, *Post-Conservative America: People, Politics, and Ideology in a Time of Crisis* (New York: Random House, 1982).

9. Frustration-aggression theory is predicated on a simple hydraulic logic that suggests a more mechanistic conception of human behavior than is warranted. A number of conditions must be fulfilled before frustration is translated into right-wing reaction. Above all, political entrepreneurs must exploit those feelings of deprivation, and their ability to do so depends on the larger constellation of political forces and opportunities in the polity at large.

10. William J. Wilson, *The Declining Significance of Race: Blacks and Changing American Institutions* (Chicago: University of Chicago Press, 1979), especially chaps, 1, 6, and 7. The figures on the proportion of families on welfare are drawn from Egon Mayer, *From Suburb to Shtetl: The Jews of Boro Park* (Philadelphia: Temple University Press, 1979). Charles Morris observes, "During Lindsay's first term the welfare caseload more than doubled and spending jumped from 8400 million to $1 billion, with about a third of the total coming from city resources; and because welfare clients were also eligible for the new Medicaid program, total welfare and welfare related health costs rose to more than $2 billion." *The Cost of Good Intentions: New York City and the Liberal Experiment, 1960–1975* (New York: W. W. Norton, 1980), p. 71.

11. Morris, *Cost of Good Intentions*, pp. 70, 71. The militance of minority demands naturally drew attention to the pressures emanating from the poor. They formed a vivid figure against the ground of timeless privileges exercised by the powerful, to which Canarsians reconciled themselves with resignation as much as with any ideological enthusiasm. The invisibility of organized producer groups protects them from public scrutiny. See Frances Fox Piven, "The Urban Crisis: Who Got What and Why," in Richard A. Cloward and Frances Fox Piven, *The Politics of Turmoil: Poverty, Race, and the Urban Crisis* (New York: Vintage Books, 1975), p. 324.

12. Alan Erlichman, "Chairman's Message," *Citizens News*, Fall 1975, p. 4.

13. In James O'Connor's words, "The fiscal crisis will continue to divide all those groups and strata that today fight in dismal isolation for a greater share of the budget or for a smaller share of the tax burden." *The Fiscal Crisis of the State* (New York: St. Martin's Press, 1973), p. 255.

14. See Seymour Martin Lipset and Earl Raab, "The Message of Proposition 13," *Commentary* 66 (September 1978).

15. Among the many New York City Jews who favored cuts in welfare levels in the late 1960s, the two statements endorsed most often were "get them off welfare, should be working" and "create jobs for people on welfare." Louis Harris and Bert Swanson, *Black-Jewish Relations in New York City* (New York: Praeger, 1970), p. 169.

16. Wills, *Nixon Agonistes*, p. 537; Marcel Mauss, *The Gift: Forms and Functions of Exchange in Archaic Societies* (New York: Norton, 1967), p. 40; Virginia Yans-McLaughlin, *Family and Community: Italian Immigrants in Buffalo, 1880–1930* (Ithaca, N.Y.: Cornell University Press, 1977), p. 134.

17. Alan Erlichman, "Chairman's Column," *Citizens News*, Fall 1975, p. 4.

Conclusion

Public Policy Applications: Self-Determination in Black Communities

Policy Then

One of the most provocative images of black rebellion against white racism during the 1960s was a snarling, ferocious-looking black panther, ~~~~~~~~ ready to pounce. Introduced by a Black Power organization in Alabama, it was soon adopted as ~~~~~~~~ Black Panther Party, a black nationalist group founded in 1966 by Huey Newton and Bobby ~~~~~~~~ The Black Panthers initially sought to confront police brutality by following pol~~~~~~~~ ~~~~~~~~borhoods—and doing so while car- rying loaded guns (under state l~~~~~~~~ ~~~or shotgun so long as it was openly displayed and not ~~~~~~~~ abuse and encourage black communities to embrace ~~~~~~~~ l news when 26 Black Panthers brandishing guns m~~~~~~~~ to prohibit the public carrying of loaded guns.

In subsequent months, t~~~~~~~~ sweeping policy changes regarding jobs, housing, an~~~~~~~~ including free health clin- ics, drug and alcohol reha~~~~~~~~ fast for Children Program that provided meals for t~~~~~~~~ ol year. By 1969, the Black Panther Party had sprea~~~~~~~~ Panthers in their uniform of

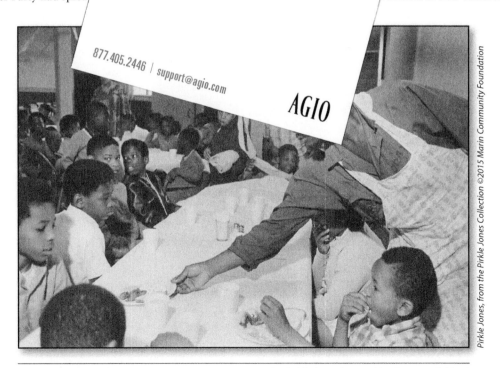

Charles Bursey serving children, St. Augustine's Episcopal Church, the Black Panther Breakfast Program, Oakland, California, 1969

Pirkle Jones, from the Pirkle Jones Collection ©2015 Marin Community Foundation black pants, black leather jackets, and black berets—and holding guns—captured the angry and defiant mood of millions of African Africans, particularly poor, young males, while simultaneously unnerving millions of white Americans.

The decline of the Black Panther Party was nearly as rapid as its ascent. Huey Newton was convicted of voluntary manslaughter in late 1968 for the death of an Oakland police officer following a traffic stop altercation (the conviction was later overturned). The Federal Bureau of Investigation launched a sustained campaign of surveillance, harassment, and violence against the Black Panthers. Several members were killed in shoot-outs with police in different cities. Meanwhile, internal divisions led to mistrust and purges. There was a brief and mostly unproductive flirtation with electoral politics in Oakland in the mid-1970s before the organization faded away.

Policy Now

Police–community interaction remains a highly contentious issue in minority neighborhoods. The potential for intense conflict is heightened in minority-majority cities in which whites still dominate municipal government and the local police force. Such was the situation in Ferguson, Missouri, a small city just outside of St. Louis, during the summer of 2014.

On August 9, an eighteen-year-old black man, Michael Brown, stole a box of cigars from a convenience store and shoved a store clerk in the process. A few minutes later, a police officer, Darren Wilson, who was patrolling the neighborhood in a cruiser, spotted Brown walking down the middle of a street with another black man and told them to move to the sidewalk. At that point, Wilson realized that Brown matched the robbery suspect description. He backed up the cruiser but was prevented from exiting the vehicle by Brown who had blocked the door. A struggle ensued with each man grabbing hold of the other. Wilson sustained a bruised face before he fired his gun; the shot likely struck Brown in the hand. Brown and his companion then fled. Wilson pursued Brown, who stopped and faced the officer. Eyewitness accounts vary on what happened next. Some testified that Brown raised his hands and said, "Hands up, don't shoot." Others stated that Brown started to move toward Wilson in a threatening manner. Wilson fired a total of twelve shots at Brown, hitting him at least six times. The last shot, which struck him in the head, was fatal. Brown had been unarmed. His lifeless body remained on the street for four hours.

The shooting sparked both peaceful and violent protests in Ferguson. Vandalism, looting, and arson prompted the imposition of nightly curfews and an aggressive response from law enforcement authorities equipped with riot gear, tear gas, and armored vehicles. The case was brought before a grand jury to determine whether there was probable cause to indict Wilson. On November 24, the grand jury decided not to bring an indictment. That decision, along with questions regarding some unorthodox procedures employed during the grand jury proceeding, triggered a renewed burst of violence in Ferguson, as well as protests in dozens of other American cities.

Even if there was insufficient evidence to justify an indictment against Wilson (according to reports, the witnesses who challenged the officer's account offered inconsistent testimony that conflicted with the forensic evidence in contrast to the exculpatory testimony that was deemed more reliable), the shooting in Ferguson raises troubling issues about the criminal justice system. Was there a pattern in the use of excessive force by an overwhelmingly white police department (50 of the 53 police officers in Ferguson were white in August 2014) in a city whose resident population was two-thirds African American? Did police officers in Ferguson systematically engage in racial profiling when approaching and interacting with citizens suspected of wrongdoing? What does it suggest about race relations in the United States when a Pew Charitable Trusts poll shows that 80 percent of blacks felt that the unrest in Ferguson "raises important issues about race" while only 37 percent of whites agreed? In March 2015, the U.S. Department of Justice cleared Wilson of civil rights offenses but issued a highly critical report accusing the Ferguson police of disproportionately ticketing and arresting African Americans for traffic violations and then relying heavily on the fines to maintain the city's fiscal well-being. The report also faulted the city for tolerating excessive use of force by the police and the ill treatment of prisoners in local jails.

Additional Resources

The Black Panthers: Vanguard of the Revolution. Documentary film on the Black Panther Party. Directed and produced by Stanley Nelson (Firelight Films, 2015).

Joshua Bloom and Waldo E. Martin Jr., *Black against Empire: The History and Politics of the Black Panther Party* (Berkeley: University of California Press, 2013).

Thomas D. Boston, "The Role of Black-Owned Businesses in Black Community Development," in *Jobs and Economic Development in Minority Communities*, ed. Paul Ong and Anastasia Loukaitou-Sideris (Philadelphia: Temple University Press, 2006).

Christopher Caldwell, "No Law, No Order," *The Weekly Standard*, 19 (47), September 1, 2014.

Eyes on the Prize: America's Civil Rights Years. Documentary film series on the civil rights movement (WGBH Boston, 1986).

Freedom Riders. Documentary film on civil rights activists. Written, produced, and directed by Stanley Nelson (Firelight Media Productions, 2011).

Charles E. Jones Jr., ed., *The Black Panther Party (reconsidered)* (Baltimore: Black Classic Press, 2005).

Rizzo. Documentary film on Philadelphia's populist mayor, a symbol of white backlash against the Black movement. Produced by Ed Cunningham (Philadelphia: WHYY, 1999).

Richard Rothstein, "The Making of Ferguson," *The American Prospect*, 25 (5), Fall 2014.

Discussion Questions

1. Are community–police relations in Ferguson, Missouri, representative of what occurs in other U.S. cities? Or was the unrest associated with events in August 2014 an aberration?

2. How should black residents respond to a pattern of perceived mistreatment by police officers? Is protest appropriate? If so, what form should it take?

3. What kinds of policy reforms might lead to improved community–police relations? What are the pros and cons of community policing in which police officers are expected to get out of their patrol cars (at least for some part of the day), walk the streets, and get to know community residents and stakeholders on a more personal basis?

4. The Black Power movement sought to promote black self-determination by building community-based organizations and institutions that would be powerful enough to thrive in a white-dominated society and culture. Was this a viable strategy for group advancement in the 1960s? Should something like this be pursued today, especially in places like Ferguson? What are your thoughts about the Black Lives Matter Movement today?

5. The civil rights movement is often depicted in history textbooks as being more successful than the Black Power movement. Why then is the latter still more enthusiastically embraced by many African Americans?

6. Is the potential for white backlash against race-based mobilization a compelling reason to avoid such an initiative?

Chapter 8

Crisis

Introduction

Cities seemed to absorb the most pernicious effects of powerful societal changes of the mid-twentieth century. Suburbanization, deindustrialization, rising racial conflict, and deepening poverty, welfare dependency, and crime all severely undermined the quality of urban life. By the 1960s and 1970s, many citizens and scholars believed that cities were in a state of crisis.[1] **Reading 8-1** by Paul S. O'Hara considers popular perspectives on the plight of Gary, Indiana, and shows how explanations for the source of decline are "largely in the eye of the beholder." Interestingly, he notes how the residents of Gary did not necessarily view their circumstances as dire as did outsiders. Consistent with that observation, a number of scholars have criticized the urban decline narrative, arguing that the picture of doom and gloom painted by many observers overstated the extent of problems while underestimating the ability of residents and business owners to revitalize their communities.[2]

Keeping in mind the perspectives of urban residents who never lost faith in their city's long-term prospects, there is no denying that many American cities experienced hard times. One clear manifestation was the extent to which local officials struggled to balance their budgets. Indeed, by the 1970s, numerous cities confronted grave fiscal crises, with some slipping to the very edge of bankruptcy.[3] The most obvious cause of fiscal instability was the decentralization of residents and jobs. As middle-class residents and industry relocated to the suburbs and the Sunbelt, many cities in the northeast and midwest lost valuable sources of revenue; the tax base diminished at an alarming rate. Meanwhile, expenditures soared as crushing job losses yielded increasing poverty and dependence on public assistance and other social services.

Some scholars, however, contended that the fiscal crisis that enveloped many cities was not entirely the product of demographic and economic changes. The political scientist Martin Shefter maintained that intense fiscal pressures were primarily caused by groups with rising levels of political power asserting their claims on city officials who were either allied with such groups or unwilling to resist. Specifically, community organizations based in black and Hispanic neighborhoods mobilized by the civil rights movement pressed for sharp hikes in spending for schools, welfare, and hospitals while municipal employee unions demanded higher wages and benefits. Politicians seeking political support for election and reelection campaigns gave in, notwithstanding an ever-widening gap between revenues and expenditures. In response to what was at root a political crisis, Shefter recounted how New York City resorted to creative accounting and the fiscally dubious practice of borrowing to finance its bulging expenditures. It would then pay off its old debt by issuing new municipal bonds in what was essentially a Ponzi scheme. Banks quietly began to sell off their New York City notes and bonds, which had the effect of saturating the market and putting the nation's largest city on the brink of bankruptcy.[4] At that point, the state legislature, under intense pressure from the financial sector, which had a huge stake in the city's solvency since many banks still held New York City securities in their portfolios, established two public entities authorized to issue bonds to cover the city's debts and prepare a three-year plan that would put the city back on a firm financial footing. The price of the rescue was steep. The newly created public entities were empowered to take substantial powers away from the city's elected officials and impose an agenda of austerity and retrenchment that fell disproportionately on the beneficiaries of social service programs and municipal employees.[5]

Some scholars reject the argument that fiscal crises are actually political crises rooted in the tendency of politicians to cave in to the strident demands of certain well-organized constituencies. They point out that city officials often did not have much of a choice in how they responded to events and phenomena beyond their control. For instance, New York City's loss of 600,000 jobs, mostly in the manufacturing sector, between 1969 and 1975, had astounding repercussions in terms of lost revenue and increased expenditures. In addition, since the 1970s, local governments have been increasingly obligated to comply with costly federal and state regulations to, for example, reduce air pollution by installing expensive scrubbers on municipal incinerators or reconstruct sidewalks, streets, and public facilities to improve accessibility for disabled citizens. Such unfunded mandates from higher levels of government added to the already difficult challenges facing urban policymakers.[6]

In any case, New York City's fiscal woes during the 1970s were far from unusual. Many other U.S. cities struggled to balance their budgets amid the decentralizing forces of suburbanization and deindustrialization and to some extent the ill-advised policy decisions of elected officials.[7] The crucial point is that the condition of urban America steadily deteriorated during the 1960s and 1970s. Frequent targets of city budget cutting included police and fire protection, sanitation, mass transit, health care and municipal hospitals, parks and recreation, libraries, and public schools. While all city residents were adversely affected by reduced services, the most damaging blows were inflicted on the poorest and the least politically powerful groups.

Research by the policy analyst Paul Jargowsky disclosed an increasing concentration of poverty in inner-city neighborhoods between 1970 and 1990. Residents of such neighborhoods faced bleak prospects in trying to overcome the cumulative effects of extreme economic deprivation, oppressive isolation, and the incessant threat of violence.[8] The slashing of public outlays for social services to care for the physically and mentally disabled, substance abusers, and ex-offenders placed new strains on the already overwhelmed low-income neighborhoods.[9] Crime rates in cities had been rising since the 1950s, but budget cuts in law enforcement contributed to an additional surge during the 1970s and 1980s. Popular culture depicted impoverished urban neighborhoods as virtual war zones.[10] Jonathan Kozol provides a painfully clear account of the devastating impact of draconian reductions in spending on public schools in Camden, New Jersey, in **Reading 8-2**.

By the mid-1970s, numerous American cities were overwhelmed by immense problems and hampered by a shrinking fiscal capacity to respond. A pervasive sense of doom about the future prospects of cities began to settle in. One scholar, Theodore Hershberg, remarked that "all of America's cities are on greased skids. What differentiates one from another is the angle of descent."[11] A political scientist who had served under Mayor John Lindsay in New York during the 1960s and 1970s published a book in 1977 with the ominous title *The Ungovernable City*.[12]

Probably the most influential scholarly book to surface at this time came from another political scientist, Paul Peterson, who stopped short of arguing that cities were ungovernable. However, his aptly titled *City Limits* emphasized the degree to which city officials were constrained in policy options to deal with the urban crisis. Peterson warned against redistributive policies that might motivate households and businesses that experience higher taxes or reduced services as a result to relocate to another municipality with a better tax–service ratio. The threat of capital flight, according to Peterson, is especially pronounced for city governments because of the relatively porous boundaries between cities and surrounding jurisdictions. Because local borders are so permeable, cities are forced to compete with one another for mobile wealth. Peterson, therefore, contended that cities have a "unitary interest" in eschewing redistributive policies and, instead, pursuing developmental policies that foster a "favorable climate" to attract and retain capital investment.[13] Refraining from redistributive policies may impose substantial burdens on the neediest populations, but Peterson insisted that doing the opposite would yield even greater hardships over the long term. By the same token, cities that implement developmental policies will eventually generate significant economic growth benefiting all residents. Peterson's argument, which is elaborated in **Reading 8-3**, provoked considerable debate among other scholars.[14] However, his logic proved to be influential with urban policymakers who perceived few viable options given the ongoing exodus of residents and businesses from cities.

An important exception to the crisis atmosphere that pervaded many U.S. cities during this time concerns metropolitan areas within the Sunbelt.[15] Many of those areas experienced steady and in some cases spectacular growth and relative prosperity. As Carl Abbott notes in **Reading 8-4**, five of the twelve largest metropolitan areas were located in the Sunbelt states of California, Texas, Georgia, and Florida according to the 2000 census; fifty years earlier, only one of those areas was ranked in the top twelve. This demographic shift was driven by a rapidly expanding economy in the Sunbelt, along with technological innovations such as the development of air conditioning and commercial airline travel. The proliferation of family tourism, convention business, and retirement communities further fueled mass migration from the Snowbelt to the Sunbelt. As with other societal trends, this one was also impelled by federal government policies such as the disproportionate channeling of funds for military defense and highway and infrastructure development to the Sunbelt, a trend that reflected the increasing political clout of lawmakers from that part of the country.[16] Finally, urban politics in Sunbelt cities during this period was all about the imperative of economic growth. Business leaders and white-collar professionals exercised firm control over municipal governments that energetically promoted capital investment by keeping taxes and regulatory burdens to a minimum and financing infrastructure development to accommodate the influx of residents and jobs. In contrast to the struggles of the Frostbelt cities, many metropolitan areas of the Sunbelt were booming.[17]

Notes

1. Irwin Isenberg, ed., *The City in Crisis* (New York: H. W. Wilson, 1968). But see also Robert A. Beauregard, *Voices of Decline: The Postwar Fate of U.S. Cities*, 2nd ed. (New York: Routledge, 2003), which illuminates how discourse about the "urban crisis" has shaped popular beliefs about the inevitability of urban decline, with important ramifications for public policy.

2. Refer to Heather Ann Thompson, *Whose Detroit? Politics, Labor, and Race in a Modern American City* (Ithaca, NY: Cornell University Press, 1996).

3. Irene S. Rubin, *Running in the Red: The Political Dynamics of Urban Fiscal Stress* (Albany: State University of New York Press, 1982); Roger E. Alcaly and David Mermelstein, eds., *The Fiscal Crisis of American Cities: Essays on the Political Economy of Urban America* (New York: Vintage Books, 1977); Robert B. Pettengill and Jogindar S. Uppal, *Can Cities Survive? The Fiscal Plight of American Cities* (New York: St. Martin's Press, 1974).

4. Such actions suggest that the financial sector bears some responsibility for the panic that precipitated the fiscal crisis. Moreover, some contended that bankers and brokers were well aware of the city's problematic fiscal practices and may have even encouraged them. They stood to profit from commissions on bond sales, as well as from marketing bonds that carried high interest rates to investors. Refer to Jack Newfield and Paul DuBrul, *The Abuse of Power: The Permanent Government and the Fall of New York* (New York: Viking Press, 1977).

5. Martin Shefter, *Political Crisis/Fiscal Crisis: The Collapse and Revival of New York City* (New York: Basic Books, 1985). For other studies of the New York City fiscal crisis and its aftermath, see Charles R. Morris, *The Cost of Good Intentions: New York City and the Liberal Experiment* (New York: W. W. Norton, 1980); John H. Mollenkopf, *A Phoenix in the Ashes: The Rise and Fall of the Koch Coalition in New York City Politics* (Princeton: Princeton University Press, 1992).

6. Ester Fuchs, *Mayors and Money: Fiscal Policy in New York and Chicago* (Chicago: University of Chicago Press, 1992); Robert W. Bailey, *The Crisis Regime: The MAC, the EFCB, and the Political Impact of the New York City Financial Crisis* (Albany: State University of New York Press, 1984); Edward I. Koch, "The Mandate Millstone," *Public Interest*, 61 (Fall 1980).

7. In 1978, Cleveland's fiscal crisis was so severe that it actually defaulted on its loans and was forced to file for bankruptcy, the first major U.S. city to do so since the Depression. Todd Swanstrom, *The Crisis of Growth Politics: Cleveland, Kucinich, and the Challenge of Urban Populism* (Philadelphia: Temple University Press, 1985).

8. Paul Jargowsky, *Poverty and Place: Ghettos, Barrios, and the American City* (New York: Russell Sage Foundation, 1997). Concentrated poverty remains disproportionately centered in inner-city neighborhoods today, but it is increasingly found

in suburbs too. Elizabeth Kneebone, "The Growth and Spread of Concentrated Poverty, 2000 to 2008–2012," Brookings Institute, July 31, 2014. www.brookings.edu/research/interactives/2014/concentrated-poverty#/M10420. But see also Stephen Steinberg, "The Myth of Concentrated Poverty," in *The Integration Debate: Competing Futures for American Cities*, ed. Chester Hartman and Gregory D. Squires (New York: Routledge, 2010), which questions the premise that concentrated poverty exacerbates the adverse consequences of poverty.

9. Michael J. Dear and Jennifer R. Wolch, *Landscapes of Despair: From Deinstitutionalization to Homelessness* (Princeton: Princeton University Press, 1987).

10. Popular films during this time period included *Fort Apache, the Bronx* and *Death Wish*. See Robert Zecker, *Metropolis: The American City in Popular Culture* (Westport, CT: Praeger, 2008); Steve Macek, *Urban Nightmares: The Media, the Right, and the Moral Panic over the City* (Minneapolis: University of Minnesota Press, 2006).

11. Quoted in Stephen Goldsmith, *The Twenty-first Century City: Resurrecting Urban America* (Washington, DC: Regnery Publishing, 1997), p. 6.

12. Douglas Yates, *The Ungovernable City: The Politics of Urban Problems and Policy Making* (Cambridge: MIT Press, 1977); but see also Barbara Ferman, *Governing the Ungovernable City: Political Skill, Leadership, and the Modern Mayor* (Philadelphia: Temple University Press, 1985). Writing about Philadelphia's flirtation with fiscal collapse in the early 1990s in *A Prayer for the City*, the journalist Buzz Bissinger praised the herculean efforts of the new mayor, Ed Rendell, but hinted that even a leader with Rendell's energy and talent required divine intervention. Buzz Bissinger, *A Prayer for the City* (New York: Random House, 1997).

13. Examples of developmental policies include policies that (a) minimize taxes on capital and profits from capital investment, (b) reduce the costs of capital investment by providing infrastructure and public land at discounted prices, (c) lower the cost of doing business by minimizing government regulation, and (d) discourage union organizing to keep labor costs low.

14. Refer to Clarence N. Stone and Heywood Sanders, eds., *The Politics of Urban Development* (Lawrence: University Press of Kansas, 1987); Todd Swanstrom, "Semisovereign Cities: The Politics of Urban Development," *Polity*, 21 (Fall 1988).

15. The Sunbelt, a term used by many scholars since the 1970s, refers to the southern tier of the United States and generally includes North Carolina, Tennessee, Arkansas, Oklahoma, New Mexico, southern Nevada, and southern California, and all states south. Refer to Kirkpatrick Sale, *Power Shift: The Rise of the Southern Rim and Its Challenge to the Eastern Establishment* (New York: Random House, 1975); Richard M. Bernard and Bradley R. Rice, eds., *Sunbelt Cities: Politics and Growth since World War II* (Austin: University of Texas Press, 1983). The Sunbelt is contrasted to the Snowbelt or Rustbelt, which consist of states from the northeast and midwest.

16. Refer to Ann R. Markusen, *The Rise of the Gunbelt: The Military Remapping of Industrial America* (New York: Oxford University Press, 1991).

17. Carl Abbott, *The New Urban America: Growth and Politics in Sunbelt Cities*, rev. ed. (Chapel Hill: University of North Carolina Press, 1987); for a critique of growth politics in a major Sunbelt city, see Joe R. Feagin, *Free Enterprise City: Houston in Political-Economic Perspective* (New Brunswick, NJ: Rutgers University Press, 1988).

8-1 "'The Very Model of Urban Decay': Outsiders' Narratives of Industry and Urban Decline in Gary, Indiana"*

Paul S. O'Hara

Journal of Urban History

"For all the hosannas sung to it in The Music Man," began *Time* magazine in a 1972 article, "Gary, Ind., is not one of those garden spots that perennially win community-service awards." "Indeed," the magazine concluded, "it is in some respects the very model of modern urban decay." In so doing the magazine established a narrative of the rise and fall of the steel city. What had once been a site defined by steel production and European ethnicity had become a site of violence and crime defined by race. "The sons and daughters of the Poles and Slovaks, and Croats, who for generations have worked the foundries," the magazine states:

> form a decided minority. Most of the blacks, who make up the town's majority, are law abiding citizens, but a few of them have lately terrorized Gary with mob shootouts that rival New York City's Mafia battles in sanguinary savagery.

The danger, according to *Time*, came from the gang members who called themselves "The Family." Identifiable by their "wide-brimmed hats, black leather jackets, high-heeled boots, and bell-bottom pants," these gangs sought to control the trade in heroin. Commenting on an attempted killing, one investigator pined for the days of "organized" and orderly crime and vice. "These guys are hardly professional," he said evoking Gary's criminal past. "Can you imagine a Syndicate murderer not waiting around to make sure the guy is dead?" The article provided, for its 1972

audience, a fairly simple tale of urban crisis and decline attributed largely to racial divisions and racial violence.[1]

Yet the story of urban crisis and decline for Gary was never this simple. Indeed, the *Time* article from 1972 was not the first epitaph written for Gary, especially in terms of intractable racial division. When white students of Froebel High School walked out of classes in 1945 to protest the integration of their school, Gary captured the public imagination. For many, Gary was a chance to advocate a new postwar paradigm of race relations. Frank Sinatra, who had become a sort of ambassador for postwar race relations due to his hit song "The House I Live in," flew to Gary to offer this new vision of toleration.[2] Yet only two years after Sinatra's visit, students from another Gary high school walked out to protest integration. Calling the city a "crucible of steel and humanity," *Time* concluded that there had been no change in Gary. "Two years ago Crooner Frank Sinatra flew from Hollywood to Gary to try to persuade Froebel High students to end a strike over Negro pupils," the magazine concluded, "the bobby-soxers squealed with delight but didn't take any of his line of reasoning." What had been possibility for racial change had again become intractable division.[3]

The unchangeable fact of racial divisions within Indiana's industrial northwest corner was still a basic public assumption by the mid-1960s. Indeed, politically, Lake County was supposed to be a minefield for Democrats in the 1968 primary. This was, after all, a county

Source: Paul S. O'Hara, "'The Very Model of Urban Decay': Outsiders' Narratives of Industry and Urban Decline in Gary, Indiana," *Journal of Urban History*, vol. 37, no. 2, March 2011, pp. 135–154. Reprinted with permission from SAGE Publications, Inc.

*Some text and accompanying endnotes have been omitted. Please consult the original source.

that Alabama Governor George Wallace had carried in the 1964 primary. Many journalists and other commentators began to talk about the politics of "white backlash" as a new political paradigm.[4] Given four years of nationwide white flight, urban riots, contentious race relations, the independent campaign of Wallace, and the law and order mantra of Richard Nixon, Democrats seemed to face a difficult trial in the industrial Calumet. Failure to address these issues, warned Rowland Evans and Robert Novak of the *Washington Post*, might mean that not only would the county but perhaps the whole state might tip Republican in the general election. So too did Joseph Kraft predict that Lake County would test Democrats', especially Robert Kennedy's, ability to wed black politics with the politics of white backlash.[5]

Yet when Robert Kennedy visited the steel city in 1968 and took a tour of its streets, a very different picture emerged. "At the Gary city line, two men climbed into Robert Kennedy's open car, and stood on either side of him, for the wild hour it took to navigate the clogged, happy streets," remembered Jack Newfield. "One was Tony Zale, the former middleweight boxing champion from Gary, who was a saint to the East Europeans who worked in the steel mills. The other was Richard Hatcher, the thirty-four-year-old Negro Mayor of Gary." Symbolizing for Newfield, and perhaps for the city of Gary, "the Kennedy alliance that might have been," this combination of Gary's white ethnic identity and its newfound black power was all the more remarkable given the support Wallace had received in 1964 and the possibility of white backlash in 1968. Yet here were the three men "standing on the back seat of the convertible, waving to the cheering citizens of the city that so recently seemed at the edge of a race war."[6]

These three snapshots of the industrial city of Gary from 1945, 1968, and 1972 should trace the origins of urban crisis and the moment of urban decline. As Thomas Sugrue has shown in his study of Detroit in the same period, the so-called urban crisis, often attributed to racial violence, white flight, and riot, had its roots in economic and political decisions that transformed the social structure of the city long before the 1967 riots. For Gary, then, Sinatra's visit in 1945 should have represented the postwar optimism that so defined the "Arsenal of Democracy" Detroit; the backlash of white voters in 1968 should have defined the

splintering of the Democratic party; and the violence and crime of 1972 should epitomize the racial division and decay of late twentieth-century urbanism.

But the narratives of decline and crisis in Gary are quite different. Far from a clear chronological arc, the stories of decline in Gary have no clear chronology. The stories told in 1945, 1968, and 1972 all contained the same basic elements of contradiction.

In all of the aforementioned snapshots, Gary held both social possibility and unchangeable decay, whether that be Sinatra's postwar vision of inclusion vis-à-vis Froebel students' reluctance to integrate or Kennedy's cross-racial appeal vis-à-vis Wallace's popularity. Even in 1972, the year that *Time* declared Gary the "very model of urban decay," the city was also host to the National Black Political Convention. Advocates and activists from across the civil rights spectrum came to Gary to discuss the future of black politics, because the city, according to Imamu Amiri Baraka, was "expressive of most of the contradictions existing in Black politics and the Black movement because we consciously tried to draw every element to the convention that we could."[7]

Much of this ambiguity was made possible by the city's unique origins. Gary had long held the seemingly paradoxical potential to be whatever people wanted it to be. It was a site of limitless potential for ordered industrialism and urban chaos and disorder. Because of its conception as a company town in 1906 and the ambiguity and interpretative room of its meaning, the city of Gary had long been shaped by the visions and images others, particularly outsiders, placed upon it. Thus the city had always been about contradictions and paradoxes. It was part model industrial city, part disposable mill town, and part industrial periphery at the edge of Chicago's urban reach. At the same time, Gary's "urban crisis" also differed from Detroit's because unlike the narrative arc of the arsenal's rise and fall, the city of Gary, while it may have been a model city of efficiency and industrial production, was never envisioned as a model of industrial democracy or patriotic Americanism. Indeed as early as 1912, three years after US Steel began production in its newest steel center, Woodrow Wilson campaigned against the city as an un-American site of unchecked monopolistic power.[8] Other critiques throughout the century would vary between accusations against US Steel and its fiat city to the foreign makeup of the population and their strange habits. For many, Gary never seemed quite fully American, and unlike Detroit, Gary always seemed to be in decline. Indeed, by the late 1920s and early 1930s, people had already begun to write of Gary as paradoxically the youngest city in the world yet already old and in decay.

The stories outsiders chose to tell about Gary mattered because for much of the twentieth century, Gary was at the center of American narratives about industrialism. Its place, however, was far more complex than the "Arsenal of Democracy" imagery that emerged out of Detroit. Gary was far more problematic. For some observers, the experiences of Gary were quintessentially American, for others Gary remained exotically strange and foreign. Even for those who saw the city as "America writ small," Gary was not an example of American triumphs but rather its failures and problems as well as its possibilities. People spoke of Gary because they saw Gary as representative of the larger American experience, the "crucible of humanity." At the same time, however, most stories about Gary were narratives of decline. Each contained a moment where the city went wrong and the Americanism represented in Gary became a corrupted Americanism. Every story had its own turning point. For some it was the moral decay of the 1950s, for others it was the rise of black power and politics in the 1960s, for still others it was the white backlash against civil rights in the 1970s. Some saw in Gary possibilities for reform, others saw inevitable decline. Some saw a microcosm of America, some saw a dangerous cauldron of race and ethnicity. Some saw in Gary a lost opportunity, others looked at Gary as it was and voiced nostalgia for what it had been. The source of decline, the origins of the urban crisis, and thus the parameters of the crisis itself were largely in the eye of the beholder.

This article traces the changing attitudes outsiders held toward Gary from the middle of the twentieth century through the period of deindustrialization at the end of the century. Gary stood at the center of debates and discussions about American industrialism, because people read through Gary their changing expectations and anxieties about industry and industrial spaces. Scholars have long noted the extensive physical and social nature of this transformation—centered especially in late nineteenth-and early twentieth-century America, this is particularly true of Gary whose social and political history has been well documented.[9] Fewer, however, have explored industrialism's cultural manifestations, especially the way people understood the changes that were going on around them. This article uses the Indiana steel city to examine the ways individuals from different classes and backgrounds understood industrial transformation and the meanings of American industrialism in the twentieth century because people themselves used Gary to understand these narratives. Just as industrialization created wealth, class divisions, and segregated cities, it also generated a diverse set of images that explained the course of industrial and urban change throughout the twentieth century.

"The Very Emblem of the Industrial Twentieth Century": Narratives of Industry

If within American society, Detroit represented the "Arsenal of Democracy," Gary in the immediate postwar period held a very different national reputation because it was a very different place. Indeed most commentators saw Gary as a very strange and exotic place, which needed thick descriptions of its smells, environments, peoples, and social realities. At the same time, its exotic nature gave rise to tales of vice, corruption, violence, and illicit sexuality. In sum, the Gary of these stories was indeed a strange place filled with strange people and strange smells, yet it was a city that somehow worked. It was an emblem of what American industry, with all its warts, looked liked [sic], not the positive industrial democracy of Detroit, but rather the darker and more complicated version. Such narratives were not tales of declension per se, but rather tales of an exotic industrial city. Indeed many observers would look back upon this era of ethnic criminal organizations and the local Democratic machine run by George Chacharis with declension tinged nostalgia.

Although his essay focused upon the ramifications on unchecked corporate power in a one-industry town, James O'Gara's piece on the steel settlement in 1949 begins with just such a vivid description of his journey into Gary: an ugly trip into an ugly place that is seemingly uninhabited:

> Much of the area immediately south of Chicago looks like a plot by the Christian anti-industrialists to win friends and influence people. Smokestacks, rather than steeples, dominate this land. When industry is going full blast, a haze of smoke and soot usually obscures the sun. The locomotives which pull long trains of tank and freight cars in and out of the district are pygmied beside towering structures of bizarre shaped [*sic*] and sizes, whose very purpose is obscure to the layman. Normally the casual observer cannot even see the men who serve the giant machines or who labor near the blast furnaces. This lack of anything recognizably human in the scene provides an added air of unreality.

The story then becomes almost mystical and inspiring of both awe and fear.

> By night, however, much of the drabness of industrialism is concealed, and one travels through a land still mysterious but no longer ugly. For the steel towns on the fringes of Chicago, every night is the Fourth of July. The sky glows red as it reflects the flames of the giant furnaces and the white heat of molten steel. Giant torches blaze high into the night sky, and showers of sparks erupt into the darkness as the hot steel is poured. Silhouetted against this display of industrial fireworks, some of the odd structures which seemed so obscure in purpose by day take on that austere sort of beauty possible only to the starkly functional. The trip which was an act of penance by day can by night be an unforgettable expedition.

"Gary is a steel town," O'Gara concludes. "When you have said that, you have just about covered the ground." Yet this conclusion comes with dire consequences. "Without steel in general and Big Steel in particular, Gary would be a ghost town," he writes, "the steel strike did not succeed in making Gary a ghost town. But the strike did show to a frightening degree how real that threat is to Gary and any town like it." As

firm as the future of the mill seems, "the house the steel workers live in is built upon shifting sand."[10]

For some, the experience of traveling through the industrial sites of the Calumet Region were represented by visceral smells, still others were moved by the realization that they had moved into some new realm, whether that meant moving from the pastoral country into the city or from the environs of Chicago into someplace else. Yet for others, the region provided awe at the industrial might and scale of the place. The narrator of Philip Roth's *I Married a Communist*, for instance, feels great comfort when passing through the Calumet.

> Coming as I did from industrial north Jersey, I confronted a not unfamiliar landscape. . . . In Newark we had the big factories and the tiny job shops, we had the grime, we had the smells, we had the crisscrossing rail lines and the lots of steel drums and the hills of scrap metal and the hideous dump sites. We had the black smoke rising from high stacks, a lot of smoke coming up everywhere, and the chemical reek, and the malt reek and the Secaucus pig-farm reek sweeping over our neighborhood when the wind blew hard. And we had trains like this one that ran up on the embankments through the marshes, through bulrushes and swamp grass and open water. We had the dirt and we had the stink.

Yet here was also something quite different and foreign.

> Concentrated here was the power of the Midwest. What they had here was a steelmaking operation, miles and miles of it stretching along the lake through two states and vaster than any other in the world. . . . This was an America that I was not a native of and never would be and that I possessed as an American nonetheless. While I stared from the train window—took in what looked to me to be mightily up-to-date, modern, the very emblem of the industrial twentieth century, and yet an immense archeological site—no fact of my life seemed more serious than that.

The narrator then juxtaposes this industrial might with the "block after block of soot-covered bungalows, the steelworkers' houses." Such a sight reminded the narrator of the realities of "a steelworker's everyday world, its crudity, its austerity, the obdurate world of people who were always strapped, in debt, paying things off." Here reconfirmed was the difference between the crucible of steel and the crucible of humanity. While one was an awe-inspiring if somewhat intimidating and perhaps outdated triumph, the other was a depressing reminder of the ramifications of industrialism. . . .[11]

"To Keep Gary from Disintegrating Altogether": Narratives of Racial Strife

If the tales of postwar industrialism imagined an exotic but functional space, the narratives of racial politics and racial animosities that came to replace them were different in their construction. As the nation grappled with the issues of civil rights, segregation, and racial politics, the language of race came to define most discussions of Gary. Race not only became the meta-language of Gary but it also reduced the possible declensions of Gary into a single storyline; the moment Gary became a black city.[21] Such tales not only made the story of Gary one of race, but it also made Gary into a very American place. Indeed Gary became, in the eyes of many, a cauldron of race. Yet only some of these narratives were declension, many others saw in Gary a great deal of hope and possibility. It held the possibility for racial pride as well as racial animosity, moderate black politics along with radical black power. If the national question was one of race, then Gary sat at the center of that discussion.

By the mid-1960s, anxieties and aspirations on both sides played out on the political arena. At the same time that George Wallace's presidential primary campaign strained the New Deal coalition, black voters and politicians also began to sever traditional ties to white Democratic candidates. These trends combined in the 1967 mayoral campaign. In the traditionally Democratic city of Gary, incumbent A. Martin Katz had received the endorsement of both the Democratic party and the United Steelworkers; support that normally would have guaranteed him a victory. In

1967, however, the rules of Gary politics changed. Instead of supporting Katz in the primary, African American voters overwhelmingly supported black candidate Richard Gordon Hatcher. The primary campaign between Katz and Hatcher was fierce and highly racialized. After Hatcher's victory, significant numbers of white voters switched parties and supported the Republican candidate in the general election. At the same time, the Democratic political machine in Gary, which was largely run by Eastern European ethnics, cut off Hatcher and refused to support or fund his campaign. Democratic party boss John Krupa explained this abandonment in terms of radical politics not race. "I'm not against Dick Hatcher because of his color," he told *Time* magazine, "unless it's because he's a Red." The magazine also points out that along with his color, Hatcher frightened the Democratic machine because he refused their demands for patronage and pledged to clean up corruption. In spite of all the official opposition, Hatcher won the election and became along with Carl Stokes of Cleveland the first black mayors of major American cities.[22]

For the national media the election of Hatcher and Stokes represented a triumph not only for black voters but also for moderate reform. "Shouting, dancing Negroes weaved wildly through the six downtown blocks of Gary, Ind.," reported *Time*. "It was not a riot but a rip-roaring victory celebration; their chant was not 'Black power!' but 'We beat the machine!'" Lauding the "non-incendiary power of the ballot box," the magazine presented Hatcher as a candidate of moderate reform and integration, although it also pointed out that the white backlash that helped Wallace in his primary campaign probably helped Hatcher as well. "Openly appealing to anti-Negro voters," it reported, "a third candidate, Bernard Konrady, siphoned off more than 13,000 votes that most likely would have gone to Katz." For the most part, Hatcher was hailed in the press specifically because he was not a "fanatical leader" of black power but rather an advocate of the more moderate and more integrationist "black pride."[23]

Hatcher's election, however, touched off a dramatic series of events for Gary. Marshall Frady of *Harper's* reported that fear of a city run by a black mayor had led many white residents to move out of Gary, thus creating a rash of white flight of both capital and population. "I been here all my life," reported one white resident to Frady:

I got me a house I paid $35,000 for, but I'm leavin' it. . . . It's not that I hate the colored or anything, but I'm dumpin' it all. Who the hell wants to live this way, I ask you. Bein' scared somebody'll hit you on the head all the time, you can't go out of the house after dark. You work all your life for something, and then they start movin' in, and suddenly you don't have anything—it's not yours anymore. First person that makes me any kind of half-ass offer on that house now, it's his, and I'm gone. With one exception—I'm not sellin' to no goddam colored, I'd put a torch to it first.

Frady quoted other residents who said much the same thing. "Mr. Hatcher, We are a big group of women, who would like to know a few answers," stated one letter to the new mayor:

We have nothing against the colored people but we would not like to have them live next door to us. Yet it seems that the colored people are always pushing. . . . Please can you explain to us why the black people want to be near us when we don't want them deep from our hearts & never will.

"Jesus, what do they want, I ask you what do they want?" asked another resident. "We've passed every law under the sun we could think of for them, they've got their welfare, they even got themselves a Mayor now, but they're still raisin' hell." He concluded, "If the coloreds keep on they gonna find themselves on reservations one of these days just like the Indians. I even predict that. It has about come to that. . . ."[24]

The narratives about Gary also mattered for residents of the Calumet Region because they came to shape the way that they viewed themselves and the city. In his study of the folklore of the Calumet Region of northwest Indiana, Richard Dorson determined that every city possessed its own image within the minds of others. "Gary," he states, "is the black city where nobody goes anymore because of crime, particularly drug crime." Interviewed by Dorson in 1976, Dorothy Gale, a white liberal who had chosen to live in Gary, explained the shocked response she would receive upon disclosing her residence. "I was tired of getting that reception when I said that I was from Gary," she remarked, "because people acted as if you were a leper. I have never heard anything good said about Gary, even on TV." With the election of Hatcher and the ensuing white flight, Gary's image transformed into a black city with the inner-city problems of crime, violence, and drugs. "Gary has declined tremendously," a white resident of neighboring East Chicago told Dorson, "the crime over there is fantastic. I haven't been to Gary in years. I wouldn't go to Gary if I had an armored guard of marines to guard me over there."[26]

For its black residents, however, the city was, for the most part, a special place. After conducting his interviews, Dorson concluded that while "the blighted city [was] spoken of with such fear and disgust by dwellers in other parts of the region . . . these black speakers see a shining metropolis in the inner city. . . . This is the heart of Black Gary, which teems with its own life."[27] This self-pride was perhaps most evident when Gary hosted the 1972 National Black Political Convention. The city greeted the delegates to the convention with banners that read: "Welcome Home to Gary." "What was proposed as the Unity of Gary, presumably was the culmination of a year's worth of meeting," wrote Imamu Amiri Baraka in 1972. What had begun as a discussion of "a Black leadership conference" soon became a call for a broader national black political convention. Reporting for the Black Panthers, Lloyd Barbee stated that:

the quality and quantity of delegates, leaders, and observers in Gary, March 10, 11 and 12 was impressive despite usual convention falderal and confusion. Individualists, collectivists, militants and moderates all had their say and way. . . . In summary, Blacks met together, set up a structure to keep together for the benefit of Black political effectiveness. This was an accomplishment worthy of historical note.[28]

When asked in an interview what impressed him about the current politics of black America, David Maphumzana Sibeko, Head of the Pan Africanist Congress, responded that he had "seen also the meeting that has taken place in Gary, Indiana where the African-American people worked for an agreement on a single presidential candidate, and to see that the voices of the African-American voter were no longer misused by the racist politicians who merely need them to gain office." He concluded, "This great desire to unite in a common National struggle is one of the most important developments."[29]

Other participants were slightly less enthusiastic about the outcomes of the convention. Commenting upon the "state of black unity in Gary, Indiana," Bobby Seale stated that "although, on an overall basis, the theme of the Convention had stressed the need for unity in the Black community, the racist U.S. government press attempted in every way, through a bombardment of propaganda, to present a picture of disunity among Black people."[30] Despite some disappointments, some conflicts, and what Seale and others took to be unfair press coverage, Baraka and others still remained positive about just what the convention in Gary meant. "Gary was successful in a great many ways," Baraka concluded. "The fact that so many Black People did come together, out of so many different bags, and had to seriously consider each other's opinions, is success enough. . . . What was important about Gary, aside from the agenda, was the functioning of Black people together as a *national community*."[31] Indeed, looking back from several years distance, Baraka fondly recalled everyone's participation. "In Gary, Indiana, in 1972, 8,000 Black People came together to roar our solidarity, our willingness to struggle," he wrote. "And though we did suffer from some of the same lack of science and thorough analysis, we did possess the burning spirit without which, armed even with the best of theories, we could not win !"[32]

Of course the national coverage of Gary almost always defined these events differently. Upon his election Hatcher was hailed by the press as a moderate black reformer who offered an alternative to radical black power. Yet by 1969 opinion had changed toward Hatcher. Two years into this term, Hatcher had been beset by problems, and according to many,

black power in office was beginning to fail. Likewise, national coverage of the 1972 convention stressed how disorganized the delegates were and how frail the connections had been between the various different groups and ideologies. Stories about heroin, crime, and gangs painted a picture of a lawless and dangerous city, and these narratives often stressed the racial background of the city. Gary was, in the national eye, a decaying industrial city and a dangerous black city. Calling the choice of Gary as an "odd place for a convention," the *Washington Post* confirmed much of this thinking in its coverage. "Gary, with its belching smoke stacks and oil refineries, its city streets rutted by railroad tracks and flanked by drab buildings," it concluded, "is not a place where people usually come for conventions." Yet it was the Hatcher administration that made the city "particularly symbolic and appropriate to what this convention is all about."[33] Here were the various conflicting images of the city: industrially polluted and potentially dangerous; a cauldron of racial antagonism or a working city of opportunity, self-government, and racial pride. . . .

Conclusion: "In Search of America"

These outsider narratives did not represent the whole truth of Gary, but in many ways they were never supposed to. These were not stories about Gary so much as stories about industrialism's complications and contradictions. Outsiders read onto the city their own fears and assumptions about industry, race, corruption, and crime. The narratives of industry in Gary framed the various ways Americans understood industrialism and industrial spaces. As the concerns and obsessions shifted throughout the twentieth century, so did the narratives of Gary that the larger American public saw. Thus, it has been left to Gary's residents to represent a larger truth. The extensive oral histories compiled by historian James Lane remind us that residents have long presented another version of Gary's history. People in Gary have understood their city's problems and possibilities, but they have also understood the ways in which their city was imagined and used.

Thus when the city of Gary announced in 2000 that it would host the Miss USA pageant to help showcase the city's new developments and postindustrial potential, the outside reviews were not kind. "Where will the 51 contestants frolic during the parts of the TV broadcast devoted to their nights on the town?" asked *US News & World Report*, "In gritty steel mills?" For city officials, however, the televised pageant meant that Gary might be able to reinvent itself as something other than classic Rust Belt decay. "The people of this nation are going to have to find someone else to pick on," stated Ben Clement, the economic development director for Gary, "because they won't be able to pick on Gary, Indiana, any longer." As ABC News pointed out, "the young women competing in the pageant have a lot at stake, but their event may well mean even more to Gary."[54]

In 2002 as part of their series "In Search of America," Peter Jennings and ABC News returned to Gary to tell its story. Despite residents' hopes that a more real, and fair, story of the city might be told, the episode, titled "The Great Divide," repeated many of the standard twentieth-century narratives about the city. It was a slum, the episode declared, racked by drug violence and poverty; problems that a beauty pageant could not solve. Because of the somber and, to the eyes of many residents, inaccurate portrayal of the city, the episode triggered a furious reaction within the city. "Mayor King felt betrayed," writes Lane, ". . . 'it was a predetermined hatchet job' he concluded."

One resident complained, "it portrays Gary as just another slum city with no prosperous, upright citizens." Why no mention of young people developing their talents at Emerson School for the Performing Arts, Lisa DeNeal wondered. Or the activities of block clubs and community centers. Nate Cain wrote: "To indicate that all the good people have left was extremely disrespectful to the hard-working, tax-paying, family-oriented citizens of the community. For every criminal you show me, I'll show you 100 solid citizens. For every boarded-up building, I'll show you a block of well-maintained, residential homes."[55]

Like all of the narratives of declension throughout the twentieth century, the story told by Jennings fell back upon old narratives of decline and decay. Yet for every outsider voice lamenting the decline of the steel city, there were other voices who echoed Gary local Garry Joel August's defense of his city in 1929, "Gary is America. Every American city is Gary writ large and small."[56]

Notes

1. "Godfather in Gary," *Time*, November 12, 1972.
2. "As the Twig Is Bent," *Time*, October 8, 1945.
3. "No Gain," *Time*, September 15, 1947.
4. Austin Wehrwein, "Democrats Hail Welsh's Victory," *New York Times*, May 7, 1964; John Pomfret, "Gary, Ind.: Supposed Center of Backlash Appears to Be Heavily for Johnson," *New York Times*, September 9, 1964.
5. Roland Evans and Robert Novak, "Failure to Heed Gary Racial Tensions Could Shift Indiana to Republicans," *Washington Post*, January 17, 1968; Joseph Kraft, "County Tests Kennedy's Skill to Wed Ghetto and Backlash," *Washington Post*, May 2, 1968.
6. Jack Newfield, *Robert Kennedy: A Memoir* (New York: EP Dutton and Co., 1969), 260.
7. Thomas Sugrue, *The Origins of the Urban Crisis: Race and Inequality in Postwar Detroit* (Princeton: Princeton University Press, 1996); Imamu Amiri Baraka, "Toward the Creation of Political Institutions for All African Peoples," *Black World* (Boulder, CO: Johnson Publishing Company, 1972), 54–78; Lloyd Barbee, "Let's Stay Together," *Black Panther* 8 (April 15, 1972), 54.
8. Library of Congress, Manuscript Division, Ray Stannard Baker Papers; Transcription, Swem Notes; as excerpted in Woodrow Wilson, "The Fear of Monopoly," *Annals of American History*. [http://www.america.eb.com/america/rticle?articleId=386648]
9. For social histories of Gary see Raymond Mohl and Neil Betten, *Steel City: Urban and Ethnic Patterns in Gary, Indiana, 1906–1950* (Teaneck: Holmes and Meier Publishers, 1986); James Lane, *City of the Century: A History of Gary, Indiana* (Bloomington: Indiana University Press, 1978); Ronald Cohen, *Children of the Mill: Schooling and Society in Gary, Indiana, 1906–1960* (Bloomington: Indiana University Press, 1990); Ruth Crocker, *Social Work and Social Order: The Settlement Movement in Two Industrial Cities, 1889–1930* (Champaign: University of Illinois Press, 1992); James Lewis, *The Protestant Experience in Gary, Indiana, 1906–1975* (Knoxville: University of Tennessee Press, 1992); Andrew Hurley,

Environmental Inequalities: Class, Race, and Industrial Pollution in Gary, Indiana, 1945–80 (Chapel Hill, NC: University of North Carolina Press, 1995).

10. James O'Gara, "Big Steel, Little Town: The Recent Steel Settlement has not[sic] Settled Everything," *Commonwealth*, November 25, 1949.

11. Philip Roth, *I Married a Communist* (New York: Vintage, 1999), 225–26.

21. Evelyn Brooks Higginbotham, "African-American Women's History and the Metalanguage of Race," *Signs* 17 (1992), 255.

22. "Plea from Gary," *Time*, September 15, 1967. On the 1967 election and the role of race in Gary's politics, see Alex Poinsett, *Black Power: Gary Style; the Making of Mayor Richard Gordon Hatcher* (Chicago: Johnson Publishing Co., 1970); "Social Trends and Racial Tensions During the Nineteen Sixties," *Steel Shavings* 25 (1996); Robert Catlin, *Racial Politics and Urban Planning: Gary, Indiana, 1980–1989* (Lexington: University of Kentucky Press, 1993); Edward Greer, *Big Steel: Black Politics and Corporate Power in Gary, Indiana* (New York: Monthly Review Press, 1979).

23. "Vote Power," *Time*, May 12, 1967; "Black Power & Black Pride," *Time*, December 1, 1967; "Real Black Power," *Time*, November 17, 1967.

24. Marshall Frady, "Gary, Indiana: For God's Sake Let's Get Ourselves Together," *Harper's*, August 1969.

26. Richard Mercer Dorson, *Land of the Millrats* (Cambridge, MA: Harvard University Press, 1981), 11, 18, 24.

27. Dorson, *Land of the Millrats*.

28. Imamu Amiri Baraka, "Toward the Creation of Political Institutions for All African Peoples," in *Black World* (Boulder, CO: Johnson Publishing Company, 1972), 54–78; Lloyd Barbee, "Let's Stay Together," *Black Panther* 8 (April 15, 1972), 54.

29. Donn Davis, "Unity in All Oppressed Communities," *Black Panther* 8 (March 25, 1972).

30. "A State of Black Unity in Gary, Indiana," *Black Panther* 7 (March 18, 1972).

31. Baraka, "Toward the Creation of Political Institutions for All African Peoples," 64, 66.

32. Imamu Amiri Baraka, *Eulogies* (New York: Marsilio Publishers, 1996), 13.

33. Herbert H. Denton, "Gary: Odd Place for a Convention," *Washington Post*, March 11, 1972.

54. Warren Cohen, "Gary's New Beauties: Hoping for a Makeover," *US News and World Report* (March 13, 2000): 27; "A Tired Town's Beauty Queen Solution," ABC News, February 28, 2001.

55. James B. Lane, *Gary's First Hundred Years: A Centennial History of Gary, Indiana* (Home Mountain Printing, 2006), 269.

56. Lane, *Gary's First Hundred Years*, 89.

8-2 "Children of the Invincible City: Camden, New Jersey"

Jonathan Kozol

Savage Inequalities: Children in America's Schools

Camden, New Jersey, is the fourth-poorest city of more than 50,000 people in America. In 1985, nearly a quarter of its families had less than $5,000 annual income. Nearly 60 percent of its residents receive public assistance. Its children have the highest rate of poverty in the United States.

Once a commercial and industrial center for the southern portion of New Jersey—a single corporation, New York Shipyards, gave employment to 35,000 people during World War II—Camden now has little industry. There are 35,000 jobs in the entire city now, and most of them don't go to Camden residents. The largest employer, RCA, which once gave work to 18,000 people, has about 3,000 jobs today, but only 65 are held by Camden residents. Camden's entire property wealth of $250 million is less than the value of just one casino in Atlantic City.

The city has 200 liquor stores and bars and 180 gambling establishments, no movie theater, one chain supermarket, no new-car dealership, few restaurants other than some fast-food places. City blocks are filled with burnt-out buildings. Of the city's 2,200 public housing units, 500 are boarded up, although there is a three-year waiting list of homeless families. As the city's aged sewers crumble and collapse, streets cave in, but there are no funds to make repairs.

What is life like for children in this city?

To find some answers, I spent several days in Camden in the early spring of 1990. Because the city has no hotel, teachers in Camden arranged for me to stay nearby in Cherry Hill, a beautiful suburban area of handsome stores and costly homes. The drive from Cherry Hill to Camden takes about five minutes. It is like a journey between different worlds.

On a stretch of land beside the Delaware River in the northern part of Camden, in a neighborhood of factories and many abandoned homes, roughly equidistant from a paper plant, a gelatine factory and an illegal dumpsite, stands a school called Pyne Point Junior High.

In the evening, when I drive into the neighborhood to find the school, the air at Pyne Point bears the smell of burning trash. When I return the next day I am hit with a strong smell of ether, or some kind of glue, that seems to be emitted by the paper factory.

The school is a two-story building, yellow brick, its windows covered with metal grates, the flag on its flagpole motionless above a lawn that has no grass. Some 650 children, 98 percent of whom are black or Latino, are enrolled here.

The school nurse, who walks me through the building while the principal is on the phone, speaks of the emergencies and illnesses that she contends with. "Children come into school with rotting teeth," she says. "They sit in class, leaning on their elbows, in discomfort. Many kids have chronic and untreated illnesses. I had a child in here yesterday with diabetes. Her blood-sugar level was over 700. Close to coma level. . . ."

A number of teachers, says the nurse, who tells me that her children go to school in Cherry Hill, do not have books for half the students in their classes. "Black teachers in the building ask me whether I'd put up with this in Cherry Hill. I tell them I would not. But some of the parents here make no demands. They don't know how much we have in Cherry Hill, so they do not know what they're missing."

The typing teacher shows me the typewriters that her students use. "These Olympia machines," she says, "should have been thrown out ten years ago. Most of them were here when I had parents of these children in my class. Some of the children, poor as they are, have better machines at home." The typewriters in the room are battered-looking. It is not a modern typing lab but a historical museum of old typewriters. "What I need are new electrics," says the teacher. When I ask her, "Why not use computers as they do in other schools?" she says, "They'd love it! We don't have the money."

I ask her if the children take this class with a career in mind. Are there any offices in Camden where they use typewriters? "I tell them, 'We are in the age of the computer,'" she replies. "'We cannot afford to give you a computer. If you learn on these typewriters, you will find it easier to move on to computers if you ever have one.' The keyboard, I explain to them, is virtually the same."

In a class in basic mathematics skills, an eighth grade student that I meet cannot add five and two. In a sixth grade classroom, brownish clumps of plaster dot the ceiling where there once were sound-absorbing tiles. An eighth grade science class is using workbooks in a laboratory without lab equipment.

In another science class, where half of the ceiling tiles are missing and where once again there are no laboratory stations, children are being taught about the way that waves are formed. The teacher instructs them to let a drop of water fall into a glass of water and observe the circles that are formed. Following a printed lesson plan, she tells them to drop the water from successive levels—first six inches, then 12 inches, then a higher level—and "observe the consequences." The answer in her lesson plan is this: "Water forms a circle that spreads out until it reaches the circumference of container." When they drop the water from a certain level they should see the ripples spread out to the edge of the container, then return back toward the center.

The children hold eyedroppers at the levels they are told and, when the teacher tells them, they release a water drop. "Describe the phenomena," the teacher says.

Several children write down in their notebooks, "Water splashes."

The teacher insists they try again until they get the answer in her lesson plan. I stand behind a row of children and observe them as they drop the water. The students are right: No ripples can be seen. There is a splash and nothing more.

The problem is that the children do not have the right equipment. In order to see ripples form, they need a saucer with a wide circumference. Instead, as a cost-saving measure, the school system has supplied them with cheap plastic cocktail glasses. There is so little water surface that there is no room for waves to form. The water surface shakes a bit when water drops descend from a low level. When the water droppers are held higher, there is a faint splash. Doggedly persisting with the lesson plan, the teacher tells the children: "Hold the dropper now at 18 inches. Release one drop. Describe the consequence." Students again write "Water splashes" or "The water surface shakes."

What the science lesson is intended to deliver to the children is an element of scientific process. "Controlling for variables" is the description of this lesson in a guide prepared by the New Jersey Board of Education. But, because the children do not have appropriate equipment, there are no variables to be observed. Children in water play in a prekindergarten class would learn as much of scientific process as these eighth grade kids are learning. As I leave, the children are being instructed by the teacher to "review the various phenomena we have observed."

Vernon Dover, principal of Pyne Point Junior High, who joins me as I'm heading up the stairs, tells me a student was shot twice in the chest the day before. He says the boy is in a trauma unit at a local hospital.

Two boys race past us as we're standing on the stairs. They leave the building and the principal pursues them out the door. "These are older kids who ought to be in high school," he explains when I catch up with him outside. The playing field next to the school is bleak and bare. There are no goalposts and there is no sports equipment. Beyond the field is an illegal dumpsite. Contractors from the suburbs drive here, sometimes late at night, the principal says, and dump their trash behind the school. A medical lab in Haddon, which is a white suburb, recently deposited a load of waste, including hypodermic needles, in the field. Children then set fire to the trash.

In the principal's office, a fire inspector is waiting to discuss a recent fire. On the desk, as an exhibit, is a blackened bottle with a torn Budweiser label. The bottle is stuffed with paper that was soaked in kerosene. The inspector says that it was found inside the school. The principal sighs. He says there have been several recent fires. The fire alarm is of no use, he says, because there is a steam leak in the boiler room that sets it off. "The fire alarm has been dysfunctional," he says, "for 20 years. . . .

"A boy named Joselito and his brother," says the principal, "set the science room on fire. Another boy set fire to the curtains in the auditorium. He had no history of arson. He was doing well in school. . . . It puzzles me. This school may be the safest place in life for many of these children. Why do they set fires? They do these things and, when I ask them, they do not know why."

He speaks of the difficulty of retaining teachers. "Salaries are far too low," he says. "Some of my teachers have to work two jobs to pay the rent." Space, he tells me, is a problem too. "When we have to hold remedial classes in a woodshop, that's a problem." Up to 20 percent of children in the school, he says, will not go on to high school. "If 650 enter in sixth grade, I will see at least 100 disappear before ninth grade."

I ask him if desegregation with adjacent Cherry Hill has ever been proposed. "Desegregation in New Jersey means combining black kids and Hispanics," he replies. "Kids in Cherry Hill would never be included. Do you think white people would permit their kids to be exposed to education of this nature? Desegregation? Not with Cherry Hill. It would be easy, a seven minute ride, but it's not going to happen."

Camden High School, which I visit the next morning, can't afford facilities for lunch, so 2,000 children leave school daily to obtain lunch elsewhere. Many do not bother to return. Nonattendance and dropout rates, according to the principal, are very high.

In a twelfth grade English class the teacher is presenting a good overview of nineteenth-century history in England. On the blackboard are these words: "Idealism . . . Industrialization . . . Exploitation . . . Laissez-faire. . . ." The teacher seems competent, but, in this room as almost everywhere in Camden, lack of funds creates a shortage of materials. Half the children in the classroom have no texts.

"What impresses me," the teacher says after the class is over, "is that kids get up at all and come to school. They're old enough to know what they are coming into."

I ask, "Is segregation an accepted fact for children here?"

"You don't even dare to speak about desegregation now. It doesn't come up. Impossible. It's gone."

He's a likable man with horn-rimmed glasses, a mustache, very dark skin, sensitive eyes, a gentle smile. I ask him where he lives.

"I just moved my family out of Camden," he replies. "I grew up here and I pledged in college I'd return here, and I did. Then, a month ago, I was in school when I was told my house was broken into and cleaned out. I packed my bags.

"I'm not angry. What did I expect? Rats packed tight in a cage destroy each other. I got out. I do not plan to be destroyed."

"President Bush," says Ruthie Green-Brown, principal of Camden High, when we meet later in her office, "speaks of his 'goals' and these sound very fine. He mentions preschool education—early childhood. Where is the money? We have children coming to kindergarten or to first grade who are starting out three years delayed in their development. They have had no preschool. Only a minute number of our kids have had a chance at Head Start. This is the *most* significant thing that you can do to help an urban child if your goal is to include that urban child in America. Do we *want* that child to be included?

"These little children cry out to be cared for. Half the population of this city is 20 years old or less. Seven in ten grow up in poverty. . . .

"There is that notion out there," she goes on, "that the fate of all these children is determined from their birth. If they fail, it's something in themselves. That, I believe, is why Joe Clark got so much praise from the white media. 'If they're failing, kick 'em out!' My heart goes out to children in this city. I've worked in upper-middle-class suburban schools. I know the difference.

"I had a little girl stop in to see me yesterday. A little ninth grade girl. 'It's my lunch hour. I wanted to visit you,' she said. There is so much tenderness and shyness in some children. I told her I was glad she came to visit and I asked her to sit down. We had our sandwiches together. She looked at my desk. 'I'd like to have an office like this someday.' I said to her, 'You can!' But I was looking at this little girl and thinking to myself, 'What are the odds?'" . . .

"Our students are innocent of the treachery of the world," she says. "They do not yet understand what is in store for them."

"My first priority, if we had equal funding," says the principal when I return to see her at the end of school, "would be the salaries of teachers. People ask me, 'Can you make a mediocre teacher better with more money?' I am speaking of the money to *attract* the teachers. In some areas where I run into shortages of staff—math and science, in particular—I get provisional teachers who are not yet certified but sometimes highly talented, exciting people. As soon as he or she becomes proficient—squat!—where is she? Out to the suburbs to earn $7,000 more. . . . So this gives you a sense perhaps of the unfairness that we face.

"I am asked to speak sometimes in towns like Princeton. I tell them, 'If you don't believe that money makes a difference, let your children go to school in Camden. *Trade* with our children—not beginning in the high school. Start when they're little, in the first or second grade.' When I say this, people will not meet my eyes. They stare down at the floor. . . .

"I have a brochure here. It is from—" she names a wellknown private school. "They want me to accept a nomination as headmistress. I'm skimming through this and I see—alumni gifts, the colleges that they attend, 99 percent of children graduating, a superb curriculum. . . . The endowment of this school is $50 million. . . . You are left with no choice but to think, 'My God! Am I preparing children to compete with this? And do they even have a *chance*?'"

At night two teachers from the high school meet me at a restaurant in Cherry Hill because, they say, there is no place in Camden to have dinner. At 8:00 P.M. we drive back into Camden.

As we drive, they speak about the students they are losing. "Six hundred children enter ninth grade," says one of the teachers, Linnell Wright, who has been at Camden High School for six years. "By eleventh grade

we have about 300. I am the eleventh grade adviser so I see the difference. I look out into the auditorium when the freshman class comes in. The room is full. By the time they enter the eleventh grade, the same room is half empty. The room is haunted by the presence of the children who are gone. . . .

"This," she tells me as we pass an old stone church, "is supposed to be the church attended by Walt Whitman. I don't know if he cared much for churches, but he did reside in Camden in the last years of his life." A sign on the door indicates that it is now a homeless shelter.

A block from the church, we pass two ruined houses with their walls torn out. A few blocks more and we are at the waterfront, next to the Delaware.

"That darkened building is the Campbell's plant," the other teacher, Winnefred Bullard, says. "Campbell's just announced that they'll be closing down."

On the roof of the shuttered factory is an illuminated soup can: red and white, the Campbell's logo. Now the company is leaving town. General Electric, Mrs. Bullard tells me, may be leaving too. Its RCA division had a major operation here for many years, but Mrs. Bullard says that it is virtually shut down. As we pass the RCA plant on the silent waterfront, I see the lighted symbol of that corporation too: the faithful dog attending to his master's voice. The plants are closing and the jobs are disappearing, but the old familiar symbols are still there for now.

"The world is leaving us behind in Camden," Mrs. Bullard says.

Before us, over the darkened water of the Delaware, are the brightly lighted high-rise office buildings and the new hotels and condominiums of Philadelphia. The bridges that cross the river here in Camden bear the names of Whitman and Ben Franklin. History surrounds the children growing up in Camden, but they do not learn a lot of it in school. Whitman is not read by students in the basic skills curriculum. Few children that I met at Camden High, indeed, had ever heard of him.

Before the announcement of the closing of the Campbell's plant, says Mrs. Bullard, there had been high hopes for a commercial rebirth on the waterfront of Camden. Plans for a riverfront hotel had been announced. Land had been cleared and several buildings were destroyed. Now it is an endless parking lot.

Mrs. Bullard turns the car around so that the Delaware is just behind us. A turn to the left, and one to the right, and just ahead of us there is a huge, white, modern building. It's the first new structure I have seen in Camden. Brilliantly illuminated, it resembles a hotel.

"It may be the closest we will come to a hotel in Camden," Mrs. Bullard says. "This is the new Camden County jail."

On the street beside the jail, several black women in white gloves are making gestures with their hands to men whose faces can be seen behind the windows. "They are making conversation with their men," says Mrs. Bullard. Directly across the street is the two-story wooden house in which Walt Whitman wrote the final manuscript of *Leaves of Grass* and in which he died, in 1892. One block away, the south face of the Camden City Hall bears Whitman's words: "In a dream I saw a city invincible."

The city, Mrs. Bullard tells me, has the highest tax rate in the area. "But," she says, "in order to get more businesses to settle here, we have to give them tax relief. The result is that we don't gain anything in taxes. But, even with that, we can't attract them."

The major industries, apart from RCA and Campbell's, are a trash incinerator and a sewage-treatment plant (neither of which pay taxes to the city), scrapyards (there are ten of them) and two new prisons. A third prison, intended for North Camden near the Pyne Point neighborhood, was halted by the pressures brought by local activists. According to Father Michael Doyle, pastor of Sacred Heart Church in North Camden, "55 million gallons of the county's sewage come into Camden every day. It's processed at the treatment plant, a stone's throw from my church. Five blocks south, on the other side, they're finishing a new incinerator for the county." The incinerator tower, some 350 feet in height, rises above the church and soon will add its smoke to air already fouled by the smell of sewage.

"The stench is tremendous," says Lou Esola, an environmentalist who lives in neighboring Pennsauken. "Sacred Heart is in the midst of it. I went down to talk with Father Doyle. I stepped out of my car and saw the houses and the children and I wondered, 'How can people live here?' They would never dare to put these things in Cherry Hill. It simply would not happen."

"Anything that would reduce the property values of a town like Cherry Hill," says Father Doyle, "is sited here in Camden." In this way, he notes, the tax base for the schools of Cherry Hill remains protected while the tax base for the schools of Camden is diminished even more. Property values in the city are so low today that abandoned houses in North Camden can be purchased for as little as $1,000.

Camden, he says, once had more industry per capita than any city in the world. "The record industry had its start here. Enrico Caruso first recorded here in Camden. Now we have to settle for scrap metal, sewage treatment and incinerators [sic]. When you're on your knees, you take whatever happens to come by. . . ."

Everyone who could leave, he says, has now departed. "What is left are all the ones with broken wings. I can't tell you what it does to children to grow up amid this filth and ugliness. The toxic dangers aren't the worst. It is the aesthetic consequences that may be most damaging in the long run. What is the message that it gives to children to grow up surrounded by trash burners, dumpsites and enormous prisons? Kids I know have told me they're ashamed to say they come from Camden.

"Still, there is this longing, this persistent hunger. People look for beauty even in the midst of ugliness. 'It rains on my city,' said an eight-year-old I know, 'but I see rainbows in the puddles.' It moved me very much to hear that from a child. But you have to ask yourself: How long will this child look for rainbows?" . . .

8-3 "The Interests of the Limited City"

Paul Peterson

City Limits

Like all social structures, cities have interests. Just as we can speak of union interests, judicial interests, and the interests of politicians, so we can speak of the interests of that structured system of social interactions we call a city. Citizens, politicians, and academics are all quite correct in speaking freely of the interests of cities.[1]

Defining the City Interest

By a city's interest, I do not mean the sum total of the interests of those individuals living in the city. For one thing, these are seldom, if ever, known. The wants, needs, and preferences of residents continually change, and few surveys of public opinion in particular cities have ever been taken. Moreover, the residents of a city often have discordant interests. Some want more parkland and better schools; others want better police protection and lower taxes. Some want an elaborated highway system; others wish to keep cars out of their neighborhood. Some want more inexpensive, publicly subsidized housing; others wish to remove the public housing that exists. Some citizens want improved welfare assistance for the unemployed and dependent; others wish to cut drastically all such programs of public aid. Some citizens want rough-tongued ethnic politicians in public office; others wish that municipal administration were a gentleman's calling. Especially in large cities, the cacophony of competing claims by diverse class, race, ethnic, and occupational groups makes impossible the determination of any overall city interest—any public interest, if you like—by compiling all the demands and desires of individual city residents.

Some political scientists have attempted to discover the overall urban public interest by summing up the wide variety of individual interests. The earlier work of Edward Banfield, still worth examination, is perhaps the most persuasive effort of this kind.[2] He argued that urban political processes—or at least those in Chicago—allowed for the expression of nearly all the particular interests within the city. Every significant interest was represented by some economic firm or voluntary association, which had a stake in trying to influence those public policies that touched its vested interests. After these various groups and firms had debated and contended, the political leader searched for a compromise that took into account the vital interests of each, and worked out a solution all could accept with some satisfaction. The leader's own interest in sustaining his political power dictated such a strategy.

Banfield's argument is intriguing, but few people would identify public policies as being in the interest of the city simply because they have been formulated according to certain procedures. The political leader might err in his judgment; the interests of important but politically impotent groups might never get expressed; or the consequences of a policy might in the long run be disastrous for the city. Moreover, most urban policies are not hammered out after great controversy, but are the quiet product of routine decision making. How does one evaluate which of these are in the public interest? Above all, this mechanism for determining the city's interest provides no standpoint for evaluating the substantive worth of urban policies. Within Banfield's framework, whatever urban governments do is said to be in the interest of their communities. But the concept of city interest is used most persuasively when there are calls for reform or innovation. It is a term used to evaluate existing programs and to discriminate between promising and undesirable new ones. To equate the interests of cities with what cities are doing is to so impoverish the term as to make it quite worthless.

The economist Charles Tiebout employs a second approach to the identification of city interests.[3] Unlike Banfield, he does not see the city's interests as a mere summation of individual interests but as something which can be ascribed to the entity, taken as a whole. As an economist, Tiebout is hardly embarrassed by such an enterprise, because in ascribing interests to cities his work parallels both those orthodox economists who state that firms have an interest in maximizing profits and those welfare economists who claim that politicians have an interest in maximizing votes. Of course, they state only that their model will assume that firms and politicians behave in such a way, but insofar as they believe their model has empirical validity, they in fact assert that those constrained by the businessman's or politician's role must pursue certain interests. And so does Tiebout when he says that communities seek to attain the optimum size for the efficient delivery of the bundle of services the local government produces. In his words, "Communities below the optimum size seek to attract new residents to lower average costs. Those above optimum size do just the opposite. Those at an optimum try to keep their populations constant."[4]

Tiebout's approach is in many ways very attractive. By asserting a strategic objective that the city is trying to maximize—optimum size—Tiebout identifies an overriding interest which can account for specific policies the city adopts. He provides a simple analytical tool that will account for the choices cities make, without requiring complex investigations into citizen preferences and political mechanisms for identifying and amalgamating the same. Moreover, he provides a criterion for determining whether a specific policy is in the interest of the city—does it help achieve optimum size? Will it help the too small city grow? Will it help the too big city contract? Will it keep the optimally sized city in equilibrium? Even though the exact determination of the optimum size cannot presently be scientifically

determined in all cases, the criterion does provide a most useful guide for prudential decision making.

The difficulty with Tiebout's assumption is that he does not give very good reasons for its having any plausibility. When most economists posit a certain form of maximizing behavior, there is usually a good commonsense reason for believing the person in that role will have an interest in pursuing this strategic objective. When orthodox economists say that businessmen maximize profits, it squares with our understanding in everyday life that people engage in commercial enterprises for monetary gain. The more they make, the better they like it. The same can be said of those welfare economists who say politicians maximize votes. The assumption, though cynical, is in accord with popular belief—and therefore once again has a certain plausibility.

By contrast, Tiebout's optimum size thesis diverges from what most people think cities are trying to do. Of course, smaller communities are often seeking to expand—boosterism may be the quintessential characteristic of small-town America. Yet Tiebout takes optimum size, not growth or maximum size, as the strategic objective. And when Tiebout discusses the big city that wishes to shrink to optimum size, his cryptic language is quite unconvincing. "The case of the city that is too large and tries to get rid of residents is more difficult to imagine," he confesses. Even more, he concedes that "no alderman in his right political mind would ever admit that the city is too big." "Nevertheless," he continues, "economic forces are at work to push people out of it. Every resident who moves to the suburbs to find better schools, more parks, and so forth, is reacting, in part, against the pattern the city has to offer."[5] In this crucial passage Tiebout speaks neither of local officials nor of local public policies. Instead, he refers to "economic forces" that may be beyond the control of the city and of "every resident," each of whom may be pursuing his own interests, not that of the community at large.

The one reason Tiebout gives for expecting cities to pursue optimum size is to lower the average cost of public goods. If public goods can be delivered most efficiently at some optimum size, then migration of residents will occur until that size has been reached. In one respect Tiebout is quite correct: local governments must concern themselves with operating local services as efficiently as possible in order to protect the city's economic interests. But there is little evidence that there is an optimum size at which services can be delivered with greatest efficiency. And even if such an optimum did exist, it could be realized only if migration occurred among residents who paid equal amounts in local taxes. In the more likely situation, residents pay variable prices for public services (for example, the amount paid in local property taxes varies by the value of the property). Under these circumstances, increasing size to the optimum does not reduce costs to residents unless newcomers pay at least as much in taxes as the marginal increase in costs their arrival imposes on city government.[6] Conversely, if a city needs to lose population to reach the optimum, costs to residents will not decline unless the exiting population paid less in taxes than was the marginal cost of providing them government services. In most big cities losing population, exactly the opposite is occurring. Those who pay more in taxes than they receive in services are the emigrants. Tiebout's identification of city interests with optimum size, while suggestive, fails to take into account the quality as well as the quantity of the local population.

The interests of cities are neither a summation of individual interests nor the pursuit of optimum size. Instead, policies and programs can be said to be in the interest of cities whenever the policies maintain or enhance the economic position, social prestige, or political power of the city, taken as a whole.[7]

Cities have these interests because cities consist of a set of social interactions structured by their location in a particular territorial space. Any time that social interactions come to be structured into recurring patterns, the structure thus formed develops an interest in its own maintenance and enhancement. It is in that sense that we speak of the interests of an organization, the interests of the system, and the like. To be sure, within cities, as within any other structure, one can find diverse social roles, each with its own set of interests. But these varying role interests, as divergent and competing as they may be, do not distract us from speaking of the overall interests of the larger structural entity.[8]

The point can be made less abstractly. A school system is a structured form of social action, and therefore it has an interest in maintaining and improving its material resources, its prestige, and its political power.

Those policies or events which have such positive effects are said to be in the interest of the school system. An increase in state financial aid or the winning of the basketball tournament are events that, respectively, enhance the material well-being and the prestige of a school system and are therefore in its interest. In ordinary speech this is taken for granted, even when we also recognize that teachers, pupils, principals, and board members may have contrasting interests as members of differing role-groups within the school.

Although social roles performed within cities are numerous and conflicting, all are structured by the fact that they take place in a specific spatial location that falls within the jurisdiction of some local government. All members of the city thus come to share an interest in policies that affect the well-being of that territory. Policies which enhance the desirability or attractiveness of the territory are in the city's interest, because they benefit all residents—in their role as residents of the community. Of course, in any of their other social roles, residents of the city may be adversely affected by the policy. The Los Angeles dope peddler—in his role as peddler—hardly benefits from a successful drive to remove hard drugs from the city. On the other hand, as a resident of the city, he benefits from a policy that enhances the attractiveness of the city as a locale in which to live and work. In determining whether a policy is in the interest of a city, therefore, one does not consider whether it has a positive or negative effect on the total range of social interactions of each and every individual. That is an impossible task. To know whether a policy is in a city's interest, one has to consider only the impact on social relationships insofar as they are structured by their taking place within the city's boundaries.

An illustration from recent policy debates over the future of our cities reveals that it is exactly with this meaning that the notion of a city's interest is typically used. The tax deduction that homeowners take on their mortgage interest payments should be eliminated, some urbanists have argued. The deduction has not served the interests of central cities, because it has provided a public subsidy for families who purchase suburban homes. Quite clearly, elimination of this tax deduction is not in the interest of those central city residents who wish to purchase a home in the suburbs. It is not in the interest of those central city homeowners (which in some cities may even form a majority of the voting population), who would then be called upon to pay higher federal taxes. But the policy might very well improve the rental market in the central city, thereby stimulating its economy—and it is for this reason that the proposal has been defended as being in the interest of central cities.

To say that people understand what, generally, is in the interest of cities does not eliminate debate over policy alternatives in specific instances. The notion of city interest can be extremely useful, even though its precise application in specific contexts may be quite problematic. In any policy context one cannot easily assert that one "knows" what is in the interest of cities, whether or not the residents of the city agree. But city residents do know the kind of evidence that must be advanced and the kinds of reasons that must be adduced in order to build a persuasive case that a policy is in the interest of cities. And so do community leaders, mayors, and administrative elites.

Economic Interests

Cities, like all structured social systems, seek to improve their position in all three of the systems of stratification—economic, social, and political—characteristic of industrial societies. In most cases, improved standing in any one of these systems helps enhance a city's position in the other two. In the short run, to be sure, cities may have to choose among economic gains, social prestige, and political weight. And because different cities may choose alternative objectives, one cannot state any one overarching objective—such as improved property values—that is always the paramount interest of the city. But inasmuch as improved economic or market standing seems to be an objective of great importance to most cities, I shall concentrate on this interest and only discuss in passing the significance of social status and political power.

Cities constantly seek to upgrade their economic standing. Following Weber, I mean by this that cities seek to improve their market position, their attractiveness as a locale for economic activity. In the market economy that characterizes Western society, an advantageous economic position means a competitive edge in the production and distribution of desired commodities relative to other localities. When this is present, cities can export goods and/or services to those outside the boundaries of the community.

Some regional economists have gone so far as to suggest that the welfare of a city is identical to the welfare of its export industry.[9] As exporters expand, the city grows. As they contract, the city declines and decays. The economic reasoning supporting such a conclusion is quite straightforward. When cities produce a good that can be sold in an external market, labor and capital flow into the city to help increase the production of that good. They continue to do so until the external market is saturated—that is, until the marginal cost of production within the city exceeds the marginal value of the good external to the city. Those engaged in the production of the exported good will themselves consume a variety of other goods and services, which other businesses will provide. In addition, subsidiary industries locate in the city either because they help supply the exporting industry, because they can utilize some of its by-products, or because they benefit by some economies of scale provided by its presence. Already, the familiar multiplier is at work. With every increase in the sale of exported commodities, there may be as much as a four- or fivefold increase in local economic activity.

The impact of Boeing Aircraft's market prospects on the economy of the Seattle metropolitan area illustrates the importance of export to regional economies. In the late sixties defense and commercial aircraft contracts declined, Boeing laid off thousands of workmen, the economy of the Pacific Northwest slumped, the unemployed moved elsewhere, and Seattle land values dropped sharply. More recently, Boeing has more than recovered its former position. With rapidly expanding production at Boeing, the metropolitan area is enjoying low unemployment, rapid growth, and dramatically increasing land values.

The same multiplier effect is not at work in the case of goods and services produced for domestic consumption within the territory. What is gained by a producer within the community is expended by other community residents. Residents, in effect, are simply taking in one another's laundry. Unless productivity increases, there is no capacity for expansion.

If this economic analysis is correct, it is only a modest oversimplification to equate the interests of cities with the interests of their export industries. Whatever helps them prosper redounds to the benefit of the community as a whole—perhaps four and five times over. And it is just such an economic analysis that has influenced many local government policies. Especially the smaller towns and cities may provide free land, tax concessions, and favorable utility rates to incoming industries.

The smaller the territory and the more primitive its level of economic development, the more persuasive is this simple export thesis. But other economists have elaborated an alternative growth thesis that is in many ways more persuasive, especially as it relates to larger urban areas. In their view a sophisticated local network of public and private services is the key to long-range economic growth. Since the world economy is constantly changing, the economic viability of any particular export industry is highly variable. As a result, a community dependent on any particular set of export industries will have only an episodic economic future. But with a well-developed infrastructure of services the city becomes an attractive locale for a wide variety of export industries. As older exporters fade, new exporters take their place and the community continues to prosper. It is in the city's interest, therefore, to help sustain a high-quality local infrastructure generally attractive to all commerce and industry.

I have no way of evaluating the merits of these contrasting economic arguments. What is important in this context is that both see exports as being of great importance to the well-being of a city. One view suggests a need for direct support of the export industry; the other suggests a need only for maintaining a service infrastructure, allowing the market to determine which particular export industry locates in the community. Either one could be the more correct diagnosis for a particular community, at least in the short run. Yet both recognize that the future of the city depends upon exporting local products. When a city is able to export its products, service industries prosper, labor is in greater demand, wages increase, promotional opportunities widen, land values rise, tax revenues increase, city services can be improved, donations to charitable organizations become more generous, and the social and cultural life of the city is enhanced.

To export successfully, cities must make efficient use of the three main factors of production: land, labor, and capital.[10]

Land

Land is the factor of production that cities control. Yet land is the factor to which cities are bound. It is the fact that cities are spatially defined units whose boundaries seldom change that gives permanence to their interests. City residents come and go, are born and die, and change their tastes and preferences. But the city remains wedded to the land area with which it is blessed (or cursed). And unless it can alter that land area, through annexation or consolidation, it is the long-range value of that land which the city must secure—and which gives a good approximation of how well it is achieving its interests.

Land is an economic resource. Production cannot occur except within some spatial location. And because land varies in its economic potential, so do the economic futures of cities. Historically, the most important variable affecting urban growth has been an area's relationship to land and water routes.

On the eastern coast of the United States, all the great cities had natural harbors that facilitated commercial relations with Europe and other coastal communities. Inland, the great industrial cities all were located on either the Great Lakes or the Ohio River–Mississippi River system. The cities of the West, as Elazar has shown, prospered according to their proximity to East-West trade flows.[11] Denver became the predominant city of the mountain states because it sat at the crossroads of land routes through the Rocky Mountains. Duluth, Minnesota, had only limited potential, even with its Great Lakes location, because it lay north of all major routes to the West.

Access to waterways and other trade routes is not the only way a city's life is structured by its location. Its climate determines the cost and desirability of habitation; its soil affects food production in the surrounding area; its terrain affects drainage, rates of air pollution, and scenic beauty. Of course, the qualities of landscape do not permanently fix a city's fate—it is the intersection of that land and location with the larger national and world economy that is critical. For example, cities controlling access to waterways by straddling natural harbors at one time monopolized the most valuable land in the region, and from that position they dominated their hinterland. But since land and air transport have begun to supplant, not just supplement, water transport, the dominance of these once favored cities has rapidly diminished.

Although the economic future of a city is very much influenced by external forces affecting the value of its land, the fact that a city has control over the use of its land gives it some capacity for influencing that future. Although there are constitutional limits to its authority, the discretion available to a local government in determining land use remains the greatest arena for the exercise of local autonomy. Cities can plan the use of local space; cities have the power of eminent domain; through zoning laws cities can restrict all sorts of land uses; and cities can regulate the size, content, and purpose of buildings constructed within their boundaries. Moreover, cities can provide public services in such a way as to encourage certain kinds of land use. Sewers, gas lines, roads, bridges, tunnels, playgrounds, schools, and parks all impinge on the use of land in the surrounding area. Urban politics is above all the politics of land use, and it is easy to see why. Land is the factor of production over which cities exercise the greatest control.

Labor

To its land area the city must attract not only capital but productive labor. Yet local governments in the United States are very limited in their capacities to control the flow of these factors. Lacking the more direct controls of nation-states, they are all the more constrained to pursue their economic interests in those areas where they do exercise authority.

Labor is an obvious case in point. Since nation-states control migration across their boundaries, the industrially more advanced have formally legislated that only limited numbers of outsiders—for example, relatives of citizens or those with skills needed by the host country—can enter. In a world where it is economically feasible for great masses of the population to migrate long distances, this kind of restrictive legislation seems essential for keeping the nation's social and economic integrity intact. Certainly, the wage levels and welfare assistance programs characteristic of advanced industrial societies could not be sustained were transnational migration unencumbered.

Unlike nation-states, cities cannot control movement across their boundaries. They no longer have walls, guarded and defended by their inhabitants. And as Weber correctly noted, without walls cities no longer have the independence to make significant choices in the way medieval cities once did.[12] It is true that

local governments often try to keep vagrants, bums, paupers, and racial minorities out of their territory. They are harassed, arrested, thrown out of town, and generally discriminated against. But in most of these cases local governments act unconstitutionally, and even this illegal use of the police power does not control migration very efficiently.

Although limited in its powers, the city seeks to obtain an appropriately skilled labor force at wages lower than its competitors so that it can profitably export commodities. In larger cities a diverse work force is desirable. The service industry, which provides the infrastructure for exporters, recruits large numbers of unskilled workers, and many manufacturing industries need only semiskilled workers. When shortages in these skill levels appear, cities may assist industry in advertising the work and living opportunities of the region. In the nineteenth century when unskilled labor was in short supply, frontier cities made extravagant claims to gain a competitive edge in the supply of ordinary labor.

Certain sparsely populated areas, such as Alaska, occasionally advertise for unskilled labor even today. However, competition among most cities is now for highly skilled workers and especially for professional and managerial talent. In a less than full-employment economy, most communities have a surplus of semi-skilled and unskilled labor. Increases in the supply of unskilled workers increase the cost of the community's social services. Since national wage laws preclude a decline in wages below a certain minimum, the increases in the cost of social services are seldom offset by lower wages for unskilled labor in those areas where the unemployed concentrate. But even with high levels of unemployment, there remains a shortage of highly skilled technicians and various types of white collar workers. Where shortages develop, the prices these workers can command in the labor market may climb to a level where local exports are no longer competitive with goods produced elsewhere. The economic health of a community is therefore importantly affected by the availability of professional and managerial talent and of highly skilled technicians.

When successfully pursuing their economic interests, cities develop a set of policies that will attract the more skilled and white collar workers without at the same time attracting unemployables. Of course, there are limits on the number of things cities can do. In contrast to nation-states they cannot simply forbid entry to all but the highly talented whose skills they desire. But through zoning laws they can ensure that adequate land is available for middle-class residences. They can provide parks, recreation areas, and good-quality schools in areas where the economically most productive live. They can keep the cost of social services, little utilized by the middle class, to a minimum, thereby keeping local taxes relatively low. In general, they can try to ensure that the benefits of public service outweigh their costs to those highly skilled workers, managers, and professionals who are vital for sustaining the community's economic growth.

Capital

Capital is the second factor of production that must be attracted to an economically productive territory. Accordingly, nation-states place powerful controls on the flow of capital across their boundaries. Many nations strictly regulate the amount of national currency that can be taken out of the country. They place quotas and tariffs on imported goods. They regulate the rate at which national currency can be exchanged with foreign currency. They regulate the money supply, increasing interest rates when growth is too rapid, lowering interest rates when growth slows down. Debt financing also allows a nation-state to undertake capital expenditures and to encourage growth in the private market. At present the powers of nation-states to control capital flow are being used more sparingly and new supranational institutions are developing in their place. Market forces now seem more powerful than official policies in establishing rates of currency exchange among major industrial societies. Tariffs and other restrictions on trade are subject to retaliation by other countries, and so they must be used sparingly. The economies of industrialized nations are becoming so interdependent that significant changes in the international political economy seem imminent, signaled by numerous international conferences to determine worldwide growth rates, rates of inflation, and levels of unemployment. If these trends continue, nation-states may come to look increasingly like local governments.

But these developments at the national level have only begun to emerge. At the local level in the United

States, cities are much less able to control capital flows. In the first place, the Constitution has been interpreted to mean that states cannot hinder the free flow of goods and monies across their boundaries. And what is true of states is true of their subsidiary jurisdictions as well. In the second place, states and localities cannot regulate the money supply. If unemployment is low, they cannot stimulate the economy by increasing the monetary flow. If inflationary pressures adversely affect their competitive edge in the export market, localities can neither restrict the money supply nor directly control prices and wages. All of these powers are reserved for national governments. In the third place, local governments cannot spend more than they receive in tax revenues without damaging their credit or even running the risk of bankruptcy. Pump priming, sometimes a national disease, is certainly a national prerogative.

Local governments are left with a number of devices for enticing capital into the area. They can minimize their tax on capital and on profits from capital investment. They can reduce the costs of capital investment by providing low-cost public utilities, such as roads, sewers, lights, and police and fire protection. They can even offer public land free of charge or at greatly reduced prices to those investors they are particularly anxious to attract. They can provide a context for business operations free of undue harassment or regulation. For example, they can ignore various external costs of production, such as air pollution, water pollution, and the despoliation of trees, grass, and other features of the landscape. Finally, they can discourage labor from unionizing so as to keep industrial labor costs competitive.

This does not mean it behooves cities to allow any and all profit-maximizing action on the part of an industrial plant. Insofar as the city desires diversified economic growth, no single company can be allowed to pursue policies that seriously detract from the area's overall attractiveness to capital or productive labor. Taxes cannot be so low that government fails to supply residents with as attractive a package of services as can be found in competitive jurisdictions. Regulation of any particular industry cannot fall so far below nationwide standards that other industries must bear external costs not encountered in other places. The city's interest in attracting capital does not mean utter subservience to any particular corporation, but a sensitivity to the need for establishing an overall favorable climate.

In sum, cities, like private firms, compete with one another so as to maximize their economic position. To achieve this objective, the city must use the resources its land area provides by attracting as much capital and as high a quality labor force as is possible. Like a private firm, the city must entice labor and capital resources by offering appropriate inducements. Unlike the nation-state, the American city does not have regulatory powers to control labor and capital flows. The lack thereof sharply limits what cities can do to control their economic development, but at the same time the attempt by cities to maximize their interests within these limits shapes policy choice.

Local Government and the Interests of Cities

Local government leaders are likely to be sensitive to the economic interests of their communities. First, economic prosperity is necessary for protecting the fiscal base of a local government. In the United States, taxes on local sources and charges for local services remain important components of local government revenues. Although transfers of revenue to local units from the federal and state governments increased throughout the postwar period, as late as 1975–76 local governments still were raising almost 59 percent of their own revenue.[13] Raising revenue from one's own economic resources requires continuing local economic prosperity. Second, good government is good politics. By pursuing policies which contribute to the economic prosperity of the local community, the local politician selects policies that redound to his own political advantage. Local politicians, eager for relief from the cross-pressures of local politics, assiduously promote goals that have widespread benefits. And few policies are more popular than economic growth and prosperity. Third, and most important, local officials usually have a sense of community responsibility. They know that, unless the economic well-being of the community can be maintained, local business will suffer, workers will lose employment

opportunities, cultural life will decline, and city land values will fall. To avoid such a dismal future, public officials try to develop policies that assist the prosperity of their community—or, at the very least, that do not seriously detract from it. Quite apart from any effects of economic prosperity on government revenues or local voting behavior, it is quite reasonable to posit that local governments are primarily interested in maintaining the economic vitality of the area for which they are responsible.

Accordingly, governments can be expected to attempt to maximize this particular goal—within the numerous environmental constraints with which they must contend. As policy alternatives are proposed, each is evaluated according to how well it will help to achieve this objective. Although information is imperfect and local governments cannot be expected to select the one best alternative on every occasion, policy choices over time will be limited to those few which can plausibly be shown to be conducive to the community's economic prosperity. Internal disputes and disagreements may affect policy on the margins, but the major contours of local revenue policy will be determined by this strategic objective. . . .

Notes

1. Flathman 1966.
2. Banfield 1961, chapter 12.
3. Tiebout 1956.
4. Ibid., p. 419.
5. Ibid., p. 420.
6. Bruce Hamilton, "Property Taxes and the Tiebout Hypothesis: Some Empirical Evidence," and Michelle J. White, "Fiscal Zoning in Fragmented Metropolitan Areas," in Mills and Oates 1975, chapters 2 and 3.
7. See Weber, "Class, Status, and Power," in Gerth and Mills 1946.
8. For a more complete discussion of roles, structures, and interests, see Greenstone and Peterson 1976, chapter 2.
9. Cf. Thompson 1965.
10. I treat entrepreneurial skill as simply another form of labor, even though it is a form in short supply.
11. Elazar 1970.
12. Weber 1921.
13. United States Department of Commerce, Bureau of the Census 1977.

8-4 "Urbanizing the South"

Carl Abbott

Magazine of History

From *Dallas* to *Designing Women*, from *Baywatch* to *Miami Vice* to *CSI: Crime Scene Investigation*, images of Sunbelt cities have been prominent on prime-time television for the past generation. With their depictions of cities full of fast-paced, colorful, sophisticated, and sometimes dangerous city people, they offer powerful corrections to that other television Sunbelt inhabited by Andy Griffith and the folks of Mayberry, by the *Dukes of Hazzard*, and by *Walker: Texas Ranger.*

No matter which measure you choose, Sunbelt cities now dominate urban growth in the United States. Ranked by simple size, five of the twelve largest metropolitan regions in 2000 were located in the Sunbelt states of California, Texas, Georgia, and Florida (1). In 1950, only one of these urban areas would have made the list. If we look at recent growth, the census reports that during the 1990s alone, five United States metropolitan areas added more than one million people. Four of them were in the Sunbelt: Los Angeles, Atlanta, Dallas, and Phoenix. Sixteen of the twenty fastest growing metropolitan areas were also in the Sunbelt (the others were in Rocky Mountain states with many economic similarities). Las Vegas was at the head of the class with an astonishing 83 percent increase.

The urbanization of the Sunbelt over the last two generations has involved growth at three levels. First, supercities like Los Angeles, Houston, and Atlanta have emerged to challenge—if not yet surpass—older cities like New York, Philadelphia, and Chicago. Second, growing second-level cities are filling in the middle of the urban system. Places like Charlotte, Jacksonville, Austin, and Albuquerque are now the peers of Cincinnati, Providence, Hartford, and Dayton. Finally, smaller cities have grown into new metropolitan areas in their own right. More than three-fifths of the Sunbelt's one hundred twenty-one metropolitan areas in 2000 were too small for metropolitan status fifty years earlier. Examples range from Santa Barbara, California, and Flagstaff, Arizona, to Huntsville, Alabama, and Myrtle Beach, South Carolina.

The Sunbelt was not always an urban powerhouse. At the beginning of the twentieth century, the South and Southwest held small and ambitious cities, but the weight of the nation's urban economy and society resided in the great industrial belt of the Northeast and Midwest. Americans tried to understand the character of city life and read the future from the growth of Pittsburgh and Chicago.

The Sources of Sunbelt Urbanization

What changed? One answer is air conditioning and air travel. The development and marketing of home and business air cooling systems opened up the steamy Gulf Coast and the sun-baked valleys of southern Arizona with their 110-degree summers, allowing small resort communities and farm market centers to attract foot-loose corporations and year-round residents. The spread of air travel with the introduction of commercial jetliners let growing southern and western cities participate in national networks. It allowed, for example, the geographic dispersal of professional sports, pioneered by the move of the Dodgers from Brooklyn to Los Angeles and the Giants from New York to San Francisco in 1957. No longer slowed by train schedules, major league baseball, the National Football League (NFL), and the National Basketball Association

Source: Carl Abbott, "Urbanizing the Sunbelt," *The Magazine of History*, vol. 18, no. 1, October 2003, pp. 11–16. Reproduced with permission from the Organization of American Historians.

(NBA) have been able to treat every large urban area as a potential market since the 1960s, not just cities in one quadrant of the nation. In 2002, the NFL played in eleven Sunbelt cities and the NBA in ten (2).

Deeper economic changes lie behind the regional rebalancing: the defense economy, globalization, the leisure economy, and industrial innovation. These are points that I develop for western cities in *The Metropolitan Frontier* (1993), but they apply as well to the Southeast.

During World War II and after, the Sunbelt became the most military-dependent part of the United States. Military planners concentrated bases and training facilities in places with warm climates. Between 1940 and 1990, it contained three of the nation's premiere military cities, with Honolulu, San Diego, and San Antonio (3). Military bases and employment were a powerful presence in many smaller cities such as Corpus Christi, Texas, Pensacola, Florida, or Fayetteville, North Carolina. War production brought new workers to Los Angeles, Dallas, Atlanta, and New Orleans and confirmed the importance of Sunbelt cities in airframe production. Nuclear weapons production fueled the growth of Albuquerque, Las Vegas, and Denver.

Second, Sunbelt cities have also reintroduced the United States to the world, further spurring their own growth. Caribbean, Mexican, and Asian immigration soared after the Immigration Reform Act of 1965 effectively ended the national quota system that had favored immigrants from Europe. In the last two decades of the twentieth century, approximately 40 percent of documented immigrants have come from Asia and another 40 percent from Latin America. For both groups, southern and western cities have been the major points of arrival. Mexicans constitute the largest immigrant group in the cities of Texas, Arizona, Colorado, and California. Temporary workers, shoppers, visitors, legal migrants, and illegal migrants fill neighborhood after neighborhood in El Paso, San Antonio, San Diego, and Los Angeles, creating bilingual labor markets and downtowns.

The same cities have been in the forefront of changing patterns of foreign trade and investment. The value of American trade across the Pacific passed that of transatlantic trade in the early 1980s, felt especially by the vast port complex of Los Angeles-Long Beach. *Maquiladora*, manufacturing in northern Mexico

since the 1970s, has created "twin" cities divided by the United States-Mexico border, such as El Paso-Juarez, and San Diego-Tijuana, a pattern that has been accentuated by the North American Free Trade Act of 1993. Sunbelt cities have also engaged the world economy as the sources for industrial expertise (Houston and the petroleum industry) or locations for foreign investment in production for the American market (Spartanburg, South Carolina).

Third, the effects of the American leisure economy are obvious in many Sunbelt cities. Family tourism, business and fraternal conventions, and retirement all contribute to their growth. Disneyland helped to transform Orange County, California, into a vast urbanized region; Walt Disney World has had a similar effect on Orlando. John Findlay's *Magic Lands* (1992) and Richard Foglesong's *Married to the Mouse: Walt Disney World and Orlando* (2001) are good introductions to the origins of these two Disney resorts. No developer would build a "Blizzard City" retirement town outside Buffalo and expect to compete with places such as Sun City outside Phoenix. Meanwhile, the sometimes forgotten Sunbelt city of Honolulu looked to Asia as well as the continental United States for business and tourism.

Finally, the Sunbelt has benefitted from the expansion of manufacturing in two ways (4). On the one hand, American corporations began to shift the routine production of standardized products from the expensive northeast core to alternative locations: smaller Sunbelt cities, northern Mexico, and overseas. On the other hand, Sunbelt cities were innovation centers for *new* high-technology aerospace and electronics industries. The United States space program has been a Sunbelt program centered in Melbourne-Titusville, Florida, Huntsville, Alabama, and Houston, Texas. Efforts to devise weapons control systems triggered the takeoff of the postwar electronics industry in the "Silicon Valley" between San Francisco and San Jose in the 1950s. As these industries moved on to civilian applications, advanced semiconductors and computer productions diffused to new industrial complexes around Austin, Phoenix, Dallas, and Albuquerque. Because the Pentagon has been the single best customer for the aerospace, nuclear, and electronics industries since the 1940s, this final point brings us full circle to the importance of the defense budget for Sunbelt cities.

The Sunbelt Catches Up

From the 1950s into the 1970s, scholars understood the growth of Sunbelt cities in terms of the "catch up" thesis. That is, the West and South were viewed as regions whose development retraced that of the Northeast, but with a time lag of a generation or more. Their rapid growth, beginning with the 1940s, suggested that they were finally closing the gap and catching up to the rest of the nation.

For the West and Southwest, the lag was described in economic terms. In the 1930s, writer Bernard DeVoto called the West a "plundered province" that was little more than a colony of New York and Chicago, shipping out raw materials from mines, farms, and forests and buying them back from eastern factories. Since the 1940s, however, western cities, and especially those of California, enjoyed a steady shift of economic power. By developing local production of manufactured goods and accumulating their own sources of capital, they caught up with the industrial core.

For the South, "catching up" was seen more broadly as a process of modernization. The South in the 1930s was poor and culturally different, but rapid urban growth helped the region become richer, more middle class, less isolated, more "American." This interpretation stressed the ways in which World War II reduced regional differences by mixing people from all regions in the military and in war production work. The Civil Rights Era of 1950s and 1960s, during which the South dismantled racial segregation by law and, thus, became more "northern," also supported the idea of convergence. So did the moderating voice of the business community in many southern cities (for example, Atlanta's reputation as a "city too busy to hate"). This interpretation shaped much of the scholarship on southern politics and society and framed some early efforts to look systematically at the history of regional urbanization.

Continuity as Well as Change

In more recent years, scholars have emphasized continuity as well as transformation in the development of Sunbelt cities. World War II and the postwar boom may

have accelerated economic changes, for example, but the changes were built on foundations from previous decades. In the South, postwar economic development efforts extended work already underway in many states and cities, as examined in James Cobb's *The Selling of the South* (1993). For the Southwest, Roger Lotchin, in *Fortress California* (1992), demonstrates that city leaders had long courted military bases and that the militarization of a city like San Diego crowned efforts begun in the 1910s. Los Angeles had similarly emerged as a major manufacturing city early in the twentieth century, creating deep roots for its postwar boom.

David Goldfield's important summary of southern urbanization, *Cottonfields and Skyscrapers* (1982), notes the continuities of southern culture and values that keep southern cities distinct from northern counterparts. He finds that southern cities were marked by continuities of a rural lifestyle, by the prominent role of religion, and by racial division. He shows how urban social institutions were adapted to preserve a biracial system and argues that the neglect of public services in many southern cities reflects the influence of evangelical religion and rural values.

Students of racial and ethnic relations in cities across the Sunbelt increasingly emphasize continuities from before to after the Civil Rights Movement of the 1950s and 1960s. Ron Bayor, Howard Gillette, Chris Silver, and John Moeser have all shown the ways in which early twentieth-century decisions about black-white relations continued to shape the politics and society of southern cities. Similarly, political and economic gains of Mexican Americans in Texas and California cities in recent decades have built on long years of institution building at the community level and political organizing (5).

In short, the Sunbelt did catch up, but in its own way. Its cities have converged economically and demographically, but they remain culturally distinct. Los Angeles is not Boston, New Orleans is not Chicago, San Antonio is not Cleveland, Tampa is not Baltimore.

Special Places/Leading Edges

Several Sunbelt cities stand out as representing important trends in contemporary urban growth. Atlanta shows the classic themes of American city-building with a Sunbelt twist. The power of business leadership in U.S. cities is a well-told story, but Atlanta adds the twist of a delicate balancing act between growth politics and racial politics. Its patterns of development are a model of urban sprawl—indeed, one of the most extreme in the nation. And its economy demonstrates the continuing power of transportation. If nineteenth-century Atlanta was a city made by railroads (one reason it was such a prize during the Civil War), the city of the later twentieth century prospered because it was the hub for Interstate Highways in the Southeast and became a national and international air travel center. Atlanta thus consolidated its role as the center of a fast-growing region like a sort of new Chicago and used direct European air routes to become a headquarters center for international businesses and organizations, serving as an alternative to New York (6).

Across the continent, the Los Angeles urban area elicits strong loyalties and excites deep antipathies. It is variously viewed as emblematic and exceptional, as the pattern for twentieth-century urbanization and the model for the urban future. As featured player in scores of movies and backdrop in hundreds of others, Los Angeles takes much of its imagery from the film writers and directors who call it home. Critics who do not like what they see in Los Angeles "prove" their point with references to the dark dystopia of *Bladerunner* (1982), the violent alienation of *Falling Down* (1993) or *Pulp Fiction* (1994), and old and new noir of *The Big Sleep* (1946), *Chinatown* (1974), and *L.A. Confidential* (1997). Those taken by the metropolis find the choice a bit more strained: *Speed* (1994) as a parable of social cooperation, *Clueless* (1995) as a more appealing vision of everyday life.

For many scholars, Los Angeles has been the representative city for the twentieth century. Both historian Sam Warner, in *The Urban Wilderness* (1995), and geographer James Lemon, in *Liberal Dreams and Nature's Limits* (1996) use it as such. A readable but highly opinionated introduction to Los Angeles politics is Mike Davis's *City of Quartz* (1992), which frames the city's history as the work of an economic elite. Davis's polemic can be balanced with the case studies of land development in William Fulton, *The Reluctant Metropolis* (1997; second edition 2001).

For other scholars, the city is the prototype for the twenty-first century. A "Los Angeles School" of urban analysis argues that the vast southern California metropolis is a new, postmodern urban form and dynamic. Cityscape, economy, and society are each described as fragmented, flexible, and fluid. Political fragmentation, industrial flexibility, and racial variety make Los Angeles a laboratory for examining the complex interactions of Anglos, African Americans, Mexicans, Central Americans, Chinese, Japanese, Koreans, southeast Asians, and many others. Good introductions to these ways of thinking are the essays in *Postsuburban California* (1991), edited by Rob Kling, Spencer Olin, and Mark Poster, and *The City: Los Angeles and Urban Theory at the End of the Twentieth Century* (1996), edited by Allen J. Scott and Edward Soja.

Miami represents yet another city that has been testing new international connections and patterns of ethnic relations since the 1960s (7). The arrival of more than eight hundred thousand refugees from Cuba, as well as large number of refugees from Haiti, fundamentally altered traditional patterns of race relations. In the three-sided tension of white, black, and Cuban, the latter group achieved political dominance and substantial economic power, as explored in Alex Stepnick's and Alejandro Portes's *City on the Edge* (1993). As transnational politics intruded into daily life, Miami became the major economic contact point between the United States and the Caribbean. Many Cuban Americans now argue that their presence and entrepreneurship have made Miami a global city that handles $6 billion of trade with nations to the south.

And then there is Las Vegas, fast emerging as the nation's next supercity. Hal Rothman's *Neon Metropolis: How Las Vegas Started the Twenty-First Century* (2002) and Hal Rothman's and Mike Davis's *The Grit Beneath the Glitter* (2002), trace the evolution of Las Vegas from "sin city" to a diversified metropolis. Entertainment and real estate development for retirees and second homes have replaced gambling as its economic heart, while major banks and pension funds rather than mob money finance the new fantasy land casinos. Far from a deviant sideshow, Las Vegas is increasingly a mainstream city wrestling with labor-management conflict, sprawl, and ethnic conflict. At the same time, the desert city may be a precursor of a new pattern of urban growth in which isolated centers function together as a single dispersed metropolis. In many ways, then, Las Vegas becomes a detached piece of greater Los Angeles.

Endnotes

1. The figure is seven of twelve if we include San Francisco-Oakland-San Jose and Washington-Baltimore, both of which lie north of the commonly accepted Sunbelt boundary but which share many characteristics with other Sunbelt cities. All of the statistics in this section are based on that same boundary that starts along the North Carolina-Virginia border and extends along the same latitude to Monterey Bay. A number of cities that lie north of the line share many economic and demographic patterns with Sunbelt cities. Examples include Norfolk-Virginia Beach and Richmond in Virginia, Colorado Springs and Denver in Colorado, and Reno in Nevada.

2. The total was fifteen for both the American and National Leagues, accounting for shared markets. Major league baseball teams played in nine Sunbelt cities.

3. The fourth major military metropolis, Norfolk-Virginia Beach-Newport News, is within the commonly understood Sunbelt boundary.

4. Economists talk about the product cycle. A cluster of innovations creates a new set of products that stimulate a complex of new companies in a particular region, such as Detroit's automobile complex or aircraft in Los Angeles. As new products gradually become standardized, their manufacture can be shifted to other locations for cheaper land and labor or better access to customers. In the last half century, Sunbelt cities have benefitted both from the decentralization of customers, such as [the] automobile industry, and the fortuitous location of new, fast-growing industries like electronics. In Texas, for example, El Paso has grown for the first reason and Austin for the second.

5. For Los Angeles, for example, see George Sanchez, *Becoming Mexican American: Ethnicity, Culture, and Identity in Chicano Los Angeles, 1900–1945* (New York: Oxford University Press, 1993) and Edward Escobar, *Race, Police, and the Making of an Ethnic Identity: Mexican Americans and the Los Angeles Police Department 1900–1945* (Berkeley, Calif.: University of California Press, 1999).

6. A good source on Atlanta for classroom use is Chris Moser, Gary G. Moss, Dana F. White, and Timothy Crimmins, *The Making of Modern Atlanta* (Atlanta:

WPGA, 1991–199), a set of eight half-hour videos available from the Georgia Humanities Council.

7. Comparisons between Miami and Los Angeles arc pursued in "Orange Empires," *Pacific Historical Review* 68 (May 1999).

References

Abbott, Carl. *The New Urban America: Growth and Politics in Sunbelt Cities.* Chapel Hill, N.C.: University of North Carolina Press, 1981.

———. *The Metropolitan Frontier: Cities in the Modern American West.* Tucson, Ariz.: University of Arizona Press, 1993.

Bayor, Ronald H. *Race and the Shaping of Twentieth Century Atlanta.* Chapel Hill, N.C.: University of North Carolina Press, 1996.

Bernard, Richard M., and Bradley R. Rice. *Sunbelt Cities: Politics and Growth since World War II.* Austin, Tex.: University of Texas Press, 1983.

Cobb, James C. *The Selling of the South: The Southern Crusade for Industrial Development, 1936–1980.* Baton Rouge, La.: Louisiana State University Press, 1982.

Davis, Mike. *City of Quartz: Excavating the Future in Los Angeles.* New York: Verso, 1990.

Escobar, Edward. *Race, Police and the Making of a Political Identity: Mexican Americans and the Los Angeles Police Department, 1900–45.* Berkeley, Calif.: University of California Press, 1999.

Findlay, John. *Magic Lands: Western Cityscapes and American Culture after 1940.* Berkeley, Calif.: University of California Press, 1992.

Foglesong, Richard. *Married to the Mouse: Walt Disney World and Orlando.* New Haven, Conn.: Yale University Press, 2001.

Fulton, William. *The Reluctant Metropolis: The Politics of Urban Growth in Los Angeles.* Point Arena, Calif.: Solano Press Books, 1997.

Gillette, Howard, Jr. *Between Justice and Beauty: Race, Planning, and the Failure of Urban Policy in Washington, D.C.* Baltimore, Md.: Johns Hopkins University Press, 1995.

Goldfield, David. *Cotton Fields and Skyscrapers: Southern City and Region, 1607–1980.* Baton Rouge, La.: Louisiana State University Press, 1982.

——— and Blaine Brownell, eds. *The City in Southern History: The Growth of Urbanization in the South.* Port Washington, N.Y.: Kennikat Press, 1977.

Jacoway, Elizabeth and David Colburn, eds. *Southern Businessmen and Desegregation*. Baton Rouge, La.: Louisiana State University Press, 1982.

Kling, Rob, Spencer Olin, and Mark Poster, eds. *Postsuburban California: The Transformation of Orange County since World War II*. Berkeley, Calif.: University of California Press, 1991.

Lemon, James. *Liberal Dreams and Nature's Limits: Great Cities of North America since 1600*. New York: Oxford University Press, 1996.

Lotchin, Roger. *Fortress California, 1910–1961: From Welfare to Warfare*. New York: Oxford University Press, 1992.

———, ed. *The Way We Really Were: The Golden State in the Second Great War*. Urbana, Ill.: University of Illinois Press, 2000.

Rothman, Hal. *Neon Metropolis: How Las Vegas Started the Twenty-First Century*. New York: Routledge, 2002.

———and Mike Davis, eds. *The Grit Beneath the Glitter*. Berkeley, Calif.: University of California Press, 2002.

Sanchez, George. *Becoming Mexican American: Ethnicity, Culture, and Identity in Chicano Los Angeles, 1900–45*. New York: Oxford University Press, 1993.

Scott, Allen, and Edward Soja, eds. *The City: Los Angeles and Urban Theory at the End of the Twentieth Century*. Berkeley, Calif.: University of California Press, 1996.

Silver, Christopher and John Moeser. *The Separate City: Black Communities in the Urban South, 1940–68*. Lexington, Ky.: University Press of Kentucky, 1995.

Portes, Alejandro and Alex Stepick. *City on the Edge: The Transformation of Miami*. Berkeley, Calif.: University of California Press, 1993.

Warner, Sam Bass. *The Urban Wilderness: A History of the American City*. New York: Harper and Row, 1972.

Conclusion

Public Policy Applications: Public Housing

Policy Then

A key component of Franklin Delano Roosevelt's New Deal, as it applied to cities, was the Housing Act of 1937, which laid the foundation for the nation's public housing program for decades to come. Under the law, local housing authorities were established to issue bonds, acquire land designated for redevelopment, and retain private developers to construct public housing. This marked the first time that the federal government had intervened to produce affordable housing for people who urgently needed shelter.

By the 1960s and 1970s, however, critical problems with the public housing program had become apparent. A new approach to the design of public housing had emphasized clusters of high-rise, high-density buildings with open spaces for leisure and recreation (see photo). Although these "towers in the park" could accommodate more households, they also proved vulnerable to illicit behavior and were poorly maintained. Moreover, the physical separation of public housing developments from surrounding neighborhoods, an attempt to distinguish the new housing as superior to the old housing, came to have the opposite effect.

A change in the class and racial composition of public housing residents also contributed to a shift in popular perceptions of the program. Originally, most public housing residents were working-class families suffering through a particularly harsh depression. But housing advocates persuaded Congress to revise the rules so that the limited supply of affordable housing would be set aside for the poor or the poorest of the poor. Meanwhile, as millions of African Americans migrated to cities during the postwar period just as urban renewal led to a

United States Geological Survey, via Wikimedia Commons

Pruitt-Igoe Public Housing Development, St. Louis (circa 1955)

contraction of affordable housing, many had no alternative but to move into public housing developments that were increasingly located in predominantly black neighborhoods, often at considerable distance from central business districts and other areas of economic opportunity.

The combination of these factors was responsible for a rapid deterioration in the physical condition of public housing in many, but not all, U.S. cities. Such developments often became notorious centers of concentrated poverty, unemployment, welfare dependency, substance abuse, and crime—the epitome of urban decay and demoralization.

Policy Now

In 1992, Congress passed legislation to establish the HOPE VI program, a fresh approach to place-based public housing predicated on the dismantling of concentrated poverty. Under the program, the federal government awarded grants to local housing authorities funding the demolition of more than 150,000 units of distressed public housing and the construction of 224 new public housing developments between 1993 and 2004. The old high-rise, high-density towers were replaced by low-rise, lower-density structures intended to appeal to a broader mix of people, including working-class and even middle-class households.

HOPE VI housing often took the form of attached townhouses or duplexes featuring bay windows, gabled roofs, and modest ornamental flourishes. The new developments were also designed to blend in with nearby neighborhoods to minimize or eliminate perceptions that public housing was different or in any way inferior. To that end, each unit contained popular amenities such as dishwashers, central air conditioning, and washers and dryers. Another important design change sought to enhance safety by giving residents more private spaces such as front porches and enclosed back yards instead of larger common areas that are harder to monitor and control. Finally, HOPE VI projects were often sited near downtown or other thriving neighborhoods to enhance their appeal. All of these policy changes were aimed at reversing the social isolation and prodigious barriers to educational and economic opportunity associated with much public housing of the postwar era.

Progress toward many of these goals was made, but one significant criticism directed at the HOPE VI program concerns its inability to provide replacement housing for all residents displaced by the demolition of the older structures. To some extent, this is a predictable consequence of the policy preference for smaller-scale, mixed-income developments. HOPE VI projects have fewer (and sometimes far fewer) public housing units than the ones they replaced. Indeed, only about half of the public housing units demolished under HOPE VI have been replaced with new public housing. This cost is mitigated somewhat by the fact that not all of the units in the older structures had been occupied; many had deteriorated so badly that they were no longer habitable. Nevertheless, not all residents of older public housing have benefited under HOPE VI. Critics also question the value of promoting mixed-income housing, a policy that has contributed to gentrification in some places and reduced the capacity of the federal government to provide decent, affordable shelter for the poor and the very poor—the people who are most in need. In short, whether HOPE VI has attained its ultimate purpose of reducing concentrated poverty remains a source of debate.

Additional Resources

Nicholas Dagen Bloom, *Public Housing That Worked: New York in the Twentieth Century* (Pittsburgh: University of Pittsburgh Press, 2008).

Xavier de Souza Briggs, Susan J. Popkin, and John Goering, *Moving to Opportunity: The Story of an American Experiment to Fight Ghetto Poverty* (New York: Oxford University Press, 2010).

Edward G. Goetz, *New Deal Ruins: Race, Economic Justice, and Public Housing Policy* (Ithaca, NY: Cornell University Press, 2013).

Paul A. Jargowsky, *Poverty and Place: Ghettos, Barrios, and the American City* (New York: Russell Sage Foundation, 1997).

"The New Old Urban Renewal," Cato Institute, Daily Podcast, April 26, 2010. www.cato.org/multimedia/daily-podcast/new-old-urban-renewal.

Oscar Newman, *Defensible Space: Crime Prevention through Urban Design* (New York: Macmillan, 1972).

Poverty & Race Research Action Council. www.prrac.org.

The Pruitt-Igoe Myth. Documentary film on the public housing complex in St. Louis (Columbia, MO: Unicorn Stencil, 2011).

U.S. Department of Housing and Urban Development. http://www.hud.gov.

William J. Wilson, *The Truly Disadvantaged: The Inner City, the Underclass, and Public Policy* (Chicago: University of Chicago Press, 1987).

Discussion Questions

1. Is deconcentrating the poor a worthwhile strategy to address concentrated poverty and its many related problems? What might be some of the pitfalls of encouraging low-income people to relocate to more economically diverse environments? What might be some of the benefits?

2. One obvious solution to the problem of insufficient replacement housing in the HOPE VI program is simply to build more affordable housing. Should city governments contribute more funds to make that possible for local residents? If so, how should city governments pay for that? Higher taxes? What consequences might flow from that course of action?

3. Should the federal government shoulder more of the financial burden for providing public housing, as well as for funding other social welfare programs? Why does it not do so?

4. Who is responsible for the urban crisis? Does the answer to that question suggest who should bear the burden of trying to ameliorate the crisis?

5. Is there still an urban crisis?

Chapter 9

Cities in a Federal System

Introduction

For much of American history, cities had been virtually absent from the national policy agenda. This was both a reflection of the country's preference for limited government and its lack of enthusiasm for any substantial governmental involvement in promoting cities in particular. Notwithstanding the steady growth of urban areas, most Americans remained culturally and emotionally attached to rural and small-town life and ambivalent at best about the value of cities.[1]

The Great Depression of the 1930s changed everything. That unprecedented crisis prompted President Franklin Delano Roosevelt (FDR) to launch dozens of federal programs to stabilize the economy, provide emergency relief, and put people back to work. For the first time, Americans were able to turn to Washington, D.C., for answers to their problems.[2] Cities benefited from this transformation in the role of the federal government. Many of the relief and public works programs aided urban residents, who gratefully rewarded FDR with their political support in his reelection bid in 1936. Recognizing how crucial urban voters had become to his New Deal coalition, FDR further strengthened the federal government's commitment to cities by issuing a report—"Our Cities: Their Role in the National Economy"—and by pushing the first significant federal legislation aimed at urban revitalization; the Housing Act of 1937 offered grants to local housing authorities to help fund slum clearance and public housing construction. The federal government's engagement with cities expanded with the enactment of the Housing Act of 1949, which spurred a multitude of urban renewal programs all over the United States (see Chapter 6).[3]

By the 1960s, however, the decentralizing forces of suburbanization and deindustrialization had overwhelmed earlier federal initiatives to improve urban conditions. Even before the outbreak of extensive rioting during the mid-1960s, scholars warned of a looming urban crisis and John F. Kennedy, while campaigning for president in 1960, called attention to cities as a pressing issue in American politics.[4] In June 1963, President Kennedy appointed a task force to propose a wide-ranging program to attack poverty in both rural and urban areas and in a televised speech to the nation asked Congress to pass a landmark civil rights bill.[5] After Kennedy was assassinated later that year, his successor, Lyndon Baines Johnson, strongly embraced these initiatives and took them to a new level. In his initial State of the Union Address, Johnson declared "an unconditional war on poverty in America" and during the presidential campaign of 1964 promised to work toward creating a "Great Society" that would ensure civil rights and economic security for all.[6]

Building on FDR's New Deal, Johnson's Great Society programs further solidified an expansive place for the federal government in the lives of Americans. But this time, cities stood to gain even more directly. In March 1965, Johnson delivered a major speech to Congress titled "The Nation's Cities," the first time any president had singled out cities so prominently in a congressional address. He also successfully advocated for the establishment of a cabinet-level department, Housing and Urban Development, which would take the lead in administering numerous urban revitalization programs such as Model Cities and Community Action. A dramatically heightened role for the federal government, with all of its resources and powers, seemed to be the remedy for the urban crisis.[7]

Such hopes and expectations did not last long. The strong Democratic majorities in Congress that had backed Johnson's Great Society dissolved following the 1966 midterm elections, and a Republican, Richard Nixon, won the presidential election two years later promising a new direction. A number of difficulties—some programmatic, some political—undermined Johnson's urban agenda. First, many Americans believed that the War on Poverty was designed to benefit primarily minorities in the inner city; although untrue, that perception stoked resentment, especially among white, working-class voters who felt slighted and burdened by rising taxes and began to abandon the Democratic Party.[8] Second, despite the lofty vision of a Great Society, not enough resources were ever allocated to the War on Poverty, and the funds that were appropriated were spread thinly among as many as 150 cities (a departure from the original plan to concentrate scarce resources in a small number of so-called demonstration projects to showcase their effectiveness). The combination of grandiose rhetoric and limited gains engendered disappointment and a falloff in popular support. Finally, mayors and other government officials objected to policy designs that (a) required federal funds to be channeled directly to community-based organizations, thus bypassing them, and (b) encouraged the participation of local residents in the formation and implementation of programs.[9] City officials viewed this arrangement as a vehicle to mobilize previously disempowered groups and thus as an unacceptable threat to their authority.[10]

President Nixon capitalized on the concerns of city officials and many citizens who regarded the War on Poverty with suspicion by vowing to rein in "federal bureaucrats" who were allegedly trying to impose their vision of society. Nixon pleased state and local government leaders by maintaining intergovernmental assistance while offering those officials much broader discretion over how federal funds could be utilized. The practical result of Nixon's New Federalism—a move away from categorical grants with specific conditions to general revenue sharing—was a diffusion of federal money away from antipoverty programs designated for inner-city neighborhoods to other parts of the city and state, as well as a tendency by cash-starved municipal governments to use their federal money to fund conventional services and normal operating expenses.[11]

The decline of federal support for urban revitalization in the 1970s was more than just the result of a partisan shift in control over the White House. When Jimmy Carter, a Democrat, was elected president in 1976, his administration continued Washington's retreat from cities. An influential presidential commission had warned that any federal policy that attempted to interfere with the nation's long-term transition away from an urban-based, industrial economy and toward a more decentralized, service-based economy would be an exercise in futility. Accordingly, it recommended that while Washington, D.C., should continue to promote national economic growth, it should do so in a place-neutral manner that accorded no preferential treatment for cities.[12] As Tracy Neumann explains in **Reading 9-1**, the Carter administration took the lead in scaling back federal urban programs.

The retrenchment of federal urban programs that began under Nixon and continued under Carter greatly accelerated after Ronald Reagan was elected president in 1980. Reagan's vision of a smaller government appealed to an electorate that had grown weary of several decades of New Deal/Great Society liberalism and disgruntled about a sluggish economy hampered by high inflation and unemployment. In his inaugural address, Reagan turned FDR's faith in government on its head by asserting: "Government is not the answer to your problems. Government is the problem." His drive to downsize the federal government (at least domestic programs) resulted in deep cuts to a wide array of urban initiatives.[13]

The Reagan years were a grim period for city officials who had come to rely on Washington, D.C., as a critical funding source at a time when local revenues were drying up. But if they expected a revival of federal support for cities once Democrats regained power, then their hopes were soon dashed. Subsequent Democratic presidents Bill Clinton and Barack Obama, a one-time community organizer in the south side of Chicago, each backed relatively minor urban revitalization programs but neither chose to draw public attention to chronic problems in cities or propose any major initiatives as Johnson once had. In **Reading 9-2**, Peter Eisinger considers the multiple impacts of the federal government's withdrawal from cities since the 1970s on urban politics and policy.[14]

As Karen M. Paget discusses in **Reading 9-3**, the shift in federal urban policy is likely the product of a cold political calculation. After several decades of suburbanization, the center of political power in the United States had moved away from cities and toward suburbs. Even Democratic candidates who had long benefited from the electoral support of urban voters have concluded that to gain control of the White House, winning over white, middle-class voters in the suburbs was a higher priority.[15]

If the utility of the federal government as an engine of urban revitalization seems to have diminished in recent decades, some scholars and public officials have proposed an alternative pathway—regional governance. A collaborative approach to resolving problems that affect an entire metropolis would seem to offer benefits for all potential partners. Urban leaders are eager to tap the broader tax base of suburban jurisdictions and thus devise a more equitable arrangement for addressing problems that sweep well beyond city borders. Suburbanites, especially those living and working in inner-ring suburbs, increasingly recognize that they are grappling with many of the same issues that arise in cities, issues that might be more effectively confronted through a unified response. More and more, influential organized groups representing business, environmental, and transit interests have called for metropolitan-wide solutions to regional problems.[16]

One key obstacle is the political fragmentation of metropolitan areas in the United States, which are typically composed of dozens of municipal governments, county governments, school districts, special service districts, and other public entities. The plethora of jurisdictions alone is a deterrent to rational and comprehensive planning. In addition, cooperation is hard to achieve when so many jurisdictions are actually competing with one another to attract new middle-class residents and business investment while avoiding such negative externalities of regional growth as landfills, subsidized housing, and substance abuse clinics. Suspicions abound. Suburbanites are leery about taking on problems that they see as emanating from the urban core and whose remedies would impose heavy costs. They fear that regional approaches might disrupt homogeneous communities and a common lifestyle. For their part, city leaders are reluctant to relinquish political power as part of a move toward metropolitan government, particularly if that might entail a return to control by white majorities. All groups worry about a loss of power and the capacity of citizens to shape decision making. Given the practical and political impediments to regionalism, it should not be surprising that there have been few instances of the establishment of formal structures of metropolitan governance.[17]

However, there have been many cases of more informal cooperation among urban and suburban jurisdictions to address common problems. Carl Abbott demonstrates in **Reading 9-4** how Portland, Oregon, has long been a leader in fashioning regional strategies to curtail suburban sprawl, most notably through the adoption of an urban growth boundary that has preserved forests and farmland twenty miles from the downtown center. Metropolitan-wide planning has also enabled the Portland area to develop one of the most heavily used light-rail transit systems in the United States as a means of reducing automobile congestion and air pollution. The success of regional planning regarding these issues has raised hopes that the approach might be applied to other problems as well.[18]

Notes

1. Alfred Kazin, "Fear of the City," *American Heritage*, February/March 1983; Morton White and Lucia White, "The American Intellectual versus the American City," in *American Urban History: An Interpretative Reader and Commentaries*, ed. Alexander B. Callow Jr. (New York: Oxford University Press, 1982); Steve Conn, *Americans against the City: Anti-urbanism in the Twentieth Century* (New York: Oxford University Press, 2014).

2. William E. Leuchtenberg, *Franklin Delano Roosevelt and the New Deal, 1932–1940* (New York: Harper & Row, 1963).

3. Mark I. Gelfand, *A Nation of Cities: The Federal Government and Urban America, 1933–1965* (New York: Oxford University Press, 1975).

4. Ibid.

5. Michael Harrington's *The Other America: Poverty in the United States* (New York: Macmillan, 1962), which documented widespread poverty within an otherwise affluent society, troubled Kennedy and motivated his desire for new policy initiatives. The escalation of civil rights activism during the spring of 1963 also put pressure on the administration to act. Doug McAdam, *Political Process and the Development of Black Insurgency, 1930–1970* (Chicago: University of Chicago Press, 1982).

6. Robert Dallek, *Flawed Giant: Lyndon Johnson and His Times, 1961–1973* (New York: Oxford University Press, 1998).

7. Gelfand, *A Nation of Cities.*

8. Jonathan Rieder, *Canarsie: The Jews and Italians of Brooklyn against Liberalism* (Cambridge, MA: Harvard University Press, 1985); Thomas Byrne Edsall and Mary D. Edsall, *Chain Reaction: The Impact of Race, Rights, and Taxes on American Politics* (New York: W. W. Norton, 1991).

9. Federal administrators intentionally adopted this approach because they believed that local officials had long excluded inner-city residents from policy-making decisions. Providing direct infusions of federal funds while promoting the "maximum feasible participation" of community residents was seen as the best hope for genuine popular empowerment. Dennis R. Judd and Todd Swanstrom, *City Politics: Private Power and Public Policy* (New York: HarperCollins, 1994).

10. Frances Fox Piven and Richard A. Cloward, *Regulating the Poor: The Functions of Public Welfare* (New York: Random House, 1971). Notwithstanding the increasing political opposition to some elements of Lyndon Johnson's Great Society, there is considerable evidence that the War on Poverty achieved much success, including a substantial decrease in the nation's poverty rate from 22 percent in 1960 to 11 percent in 1973. In addition, impressive advances were made with respect to infant mortality, child malnutrition, early education, health care for the poor and elderly, job training, and housing. See John E. Schwarz, *America's Hidden Success: A Reassessment of Public Policy from Kennedy to Reagan*, rev. ed. (New York: W. W. Norton, 1988).

11. Timothy J. Conlan, *From New Federalism to Devolution: Twenty-five Years of Intergovernmental Reform* (Washington, DC: Brookings Institution Press, 1998).

12. President's Commission for a National Agenda for the Eighties, *A National Agenda for the Eighties* (Washington, DC: Government Printing Office, 1980).

13. George E. Peterson and Carol W. Lewis, eds., *Reagan and the Cities* (Washington, DC: The Urban Institute, 1986); Timothy Barnekov, Robin Boyle, and Daniel Rich, *Privatism and Urban Policy in Britain and the United States* (New York: Oxford University Press, 1989).

14. For a comprehensive overview of federal urban policy since the end of World War II, see Roger Biles, *The Fate of Cities: Urban America and the Federal Government, 1945–2000* (Lawrence: University of Kansas Press, 2011); see also Robert A. Beauregard, *Voices of Decline: The Postwar Fate of U.S. Cities*, 2nd ed. (New York: Routledge, 2003).

15. See also William Schneider, "The Suburban Century Begins: The Real Meaning of the 1992 Election," *Atlantic Monthly*, July 1992. For an analysis of how suburbanization invigorated the conservative movement in American politics, see Matthew D. Lassiter, *The Silent Majority: Suburban Politics in the Sunbelt South* (Princeton: Princeton University Press, 2006); Kevin M. Kruse, *White Flight: Atlanta and the Making of Conservativism* (Princeton: Princeton University Press, 2005).

16. Richard C. Feiock, ed., *Metropolitan Governance: Conflict, Competition, and Cooperation* (Washington, DC: Georgetown University Press, 2004).

17. But see also Myron Orfield, *American Metropolitics: The New Suburban Reality* (Washington, DC: Brookings Institution Press, 2002).

18. Recent research has identified factors that may increase the likelihood that regional governance strategies may be productive. On the role of regional organizations, see Sung-Wook Kwon and Sang-Chul Park, "Metropolitan Governance: How Regional Organizations Influence Interlocal Land Use Coordination," *Journal of Urban Affairs*, 36 (5), 2014; on the role of federal and state grants, economic crisis, and private-sector leadership, and the involvement of both senior levels of government and local officials, see Jen Nelles, "Regionalism Redux: Explaining the Impact of Federal Grants on Mass Public Transit Governance and Political Capacity in Metropolitan Detroit," *Urban Affairs Review*, 49 (2), 2013.

9-1 "Privatization, Devolution, and Jimmy Carter's National Urban Policy"*

Tracy Neumann

Journal of Urban History

Two weeks before securing the Democratic presidential nomination, Jimmy Carter assured members of the U.S. Conference of Mayors that if he became president, they would have a friend in the White House.[1] On the campaign trail, seeking support from the urban Democratic voters who had sustained liberal social programs from the New Deal to the Great Society, Carter talked about halting urban decay and stimulating growth to make U.S. cities once again "worthy of the greatest nation on earth."[2] After the election, the mayors who had supported Carter's presidential bid immediately began to pressure him to make good on his campaign promise to focus on urban policy. In March 1978, Carter presented *A New Partnership to Conserve America's Communities* to local, state, and federal officials who had gathered at the White House—to an underwhelming response.[3]

Although marketed as the nation's first "comprehensive" urban policy, *A New Partnership* neither introduced major new federal programs nor substantially increased funding for existing urban programs. Instead, Carter offered "a working alliance of all levels of government, with the private sector of our economy and with our citizens in their communities and neighborhoods."[4]

The "incentives," "leverage," and "catalysts" for private sector activity included in *A New Partnership* posed less of a political liability for Carter than increased direct federal expenditures in troubled central cities.[5] As Chief Domestic Policy Advisor Stuart Eizenstat told Carter in early 1978, national urban policy was a "politically unappealing concept" because it "excite[d] the worst prejudices of suburban and rural constituents" and exacerbated "Sun Belt-Snow Belt antagonisms."[6] Eizenstat cautioned that "*political realities appear to be at odds with most of the policies and programs that our analysis suggests make the most sense from a substantive point of view*"— policies that would require suburban areas to share tax revenue with inner cities, or encourage urban residents to relocate to suburbs or the Sun Belt. Eizenstat recognized that whatever the content of the urban policy, Carter would be criticized from both left and right, and he bemoaned the "national consensus" in favor of antiurban policies reflected in Congress. While most Americans were sympathetic to the urban poor, Eizenstat flatly stated, "few indeed feel sympathy for New York."[7]

Predicated on privatization and devolution through decentralization, voluntarism, and self-help, the long-awaited national urban policy reflected Carter's deeply held Evangelical Christian values as well as moderate Democrats' rejection of liberal social programs. Carter's distrust of special interest groups and affinity with the concerns of the "forgotten" white middle class led him to reject large-scale federal programs, to oppose increased federal urban spending, and to endorse the capacity of the private sector to solve urban problems.[8] Moreover, for a process-oriented president like Carter, devolution and privatization were logical extensions of his desire to reduce both the size of the federal bureaucracy and the federal budget.

Source: Tracy Neumann, "Privatization, Devolution, and Jimmy Carter's National Urban Policy," *Journal of Urban History*, vol. 40, no. 2, March 2014, pp. 283–300. Reprinted with permission from SAGE Publications, Inc.

*Some text and accompanying endnotes have been omitted. Please consult the original source.

Shifting responsibility for urban development to the private sector and state and local governments seemed politically expedient as well, because Carter's advisors assured him that Democratic voters shared his world-view. Deputy White House Chief of Staff Les Francis characterized "post-'72" Congressional Democrats as "Jimmy Carter Democrats" rather than New Deal liberals. "They are suspicious of big government. They are interested in results and are not afraid to abandon programs which have failed," he wrote. "And they know that this new brand of Democratic philosophy is very popular back home."[9]

As activists on both the left and right rejected the perceived excesses of liberal social programs, national debates about urban policy came to reflect popular efforts to redefine the boundaries of liberalism. Indeed, historians have shown, the reduction of federal funding for and oversight of urban programs and the privatization of urban and economic development, which are often associated with the "Reagan Revolution," preceded that particular political moment.[10] By the late 1970s, ideas about urban governance had narrowed among public and private sector actors until federal policymakers saw devolution and privatization as the only politically viable options for national urban policy.

But Carter's pivotal role in making privatization and devolution the cornerstones of federal urban policy is only part of the story, which when taken by itself has led some scholars to conclude that privatization and devolution were top-down changes imposed on unwilling state and local officials by the federal government.[11] Instead, the larger story is one in which state and local government officials competed with each other and with neighborhood activists and private sector groups for increased influence over urban policy and for control of federal urban and economic development funds. Carter and his advisors received repeated demands from state officials and local voluntary organizations to devolve urban policymaking authority away from federal agencies toward state and local governments and neighborhood organizations. Lobbying from neighborhood groups, state and local officials, and for- and non-profit private sector organizations for greater autonomy from what they described as a bloated federal bureaucracy and for federal incentives for public–private partnerships encouraged and legitimated federal policies that devolved and privatized the federal role in urban development. These demands and lobbying efforts were particularly visible in the activities in support of *A New Partnership* and two other federal initiatives, the National Commission on Neighborhoods ("NCN," 1977–1979) and the White House Conference on Balanced Growth and Economic Development ("WH Conference," 1977–1978).

The Neighborhood Movement and the National Urban Policy

A New Partnership was largely the product of negotiations between the Department of Housing and Urban Development (HUD), which oversaw the policy process through Carter's Urban and Regional Policy Group (URPG), and Carter's Domestic Policy Staff (DPS).[12] URPG formed following a March 1977 memo in which Carter directed HUD Secretary Patricia Harris to convene a cabinet-level working group to "conduct a comprehensive review" of federal urban and regional development programs, consult with state and local government officials, and develop administrative and legislative reform recommendations.[13] The working group also included the secretaries of Commerce; Health, Education, and Welfare (HEW); Labor; Transportation; and Treasury, and Carter asked Eizenstat and Jack Watson, Assistant to the President for Intergovernmental Affairs, to serve as White House liaisons. In practice, however, HUD and URPG staff were one and the same.[14]

Carter, like Richard Nixon before him, sought to impose order on what he saw as an outsized federal bureaucracy. And like Nixon, he intended to reduce the size of the federal government by streamlining federal programs and transferring federal power to state and local governments.[15] At the same time, Carter's cabinet was bitterly split over how to manage an inflationary economy. The Treasury and the Office of Management and Budget (OMB) advocated for federal belt-tightening, creating tension between those agencies and Labor, HEW, the Environmental Protection Agency, and congressional staff who did not want to alienate union leaders and farmers, fought to preserve environmental and health and safety requirements, and supported expansionary policies. Moderates like Eizenstat were caught in the middle of warring cabinet heads, arguing in favor of restraining inflation without causing economic contraction or alienating the "base."[16] Cabinet-level conflicts over public expenditures and political expediency seem to have spilled over into the urban policy deliberations. The 178-page *A New Partnership*, which Thomas Sugrue has described as "remarkable in its turgidity and length," was the product of similar interagency bickering over the scope, administrative jurisdiction, and fiscal outlays for more than seventy proposed programs, forty-three of which made it into the final report.[17]

From the outset of the urban policy deliberations, Carter evinced a preference for a strategy that privileged decentralization, industrial tax incentives, and partnerships between the government, the private sector, and community organizations.[18] DPS staff and Democratic mayors were skeptical of a neighborhood-based urban strategy that reduced mayoral control over federal aid, but Carter saw community control and government restructuring as complementary undertakings.[19] Because HUD staffed URPG, the first draft of the urban policy, "Toward Cities and People in Distress," reflected that agency's interest in new housing construction and metropolitan development strategies aimed at the nation's most distressed cities, and called for $20 billion in new federal expenditures.[20] In response to the draft urban policy, Carter informed Eizenstat and Harris that the final version should not require new federal outlays. Further, he instructed them to focus on increasing the role of state governments, the private sector, and neighborhoods.[21] In his handwritten comments on a memorandum about the content of the final urban policy report, Carter spilled the most ink on a section outlining assistance to community organizations. He urged Eizenstat to develop the theme of self-help and suggested that increased federal money for cities would discourage voluntarism and private responsibility.[22]

Under Carter, what Suleiman Osman has called "neighborhoodism" ruled in Washington, providing a language for and legitimation of federal urban policies based on volunteerism, individual choice, local control, and market-driven reform.[23] Organizing at the neighborhood level to confront urban problems and

make demands on local government had begun with settlement houses and community centers in the late nineteenth century, and continued into the 1950s through neighborhood improvement associations (not all of which shared the progressive goals of settlement houses).[24] Neighborhood-based activism around urban development took shape in response to urban renewal programs in the 1950s and accelerated after 1964, when as part of the Equal Opportunity Act, Lyndon Johnson created Community Action Programs to empower the poor through their "maximum feasible participation" in determining how local governments spent federal funds allocated through the War on Poverty and the Great Society.[25]

By the 1970s, disparate groups of local activists—African Americans who came of age with the Black Power movement, young liberals who worked with Great Society programs, Left intellectuals, and white-collar gentrifiers—formed a loose neighborhood movement that was, politically, neither left nor right. The members of the emerging neighborhood movement rejected the centralized planning and technocratic expertise typical of New Deal liberalism, trusting neither the government nor corporations. Politicians with roots in the neighborhood movement formed coalitions with white-collar professionals, blue-collar white ethnics, and black activists.[26] Some, like Dennis Kucinich, won mayoral elections in major cities. But paradoxically, it was Richard Nixon's 1973 moratorium on federal funding for HUD housing programs and his subsequent termination of urban renewal and Model Cities programs that permitted the "remarkable flowering" of block improvement associations, neighborhood federations, community revitalization projects, and nonprofits such as Neighborhood Housing Services.[27] By 1977, forty-three city governments had formally recognized neighborhood organizations as part of the "local governing process."[28]

The neighborhood movement had two fierce advocates in the Carter Administration: Monsignor Geno Baroni and Marcy Kaptur. Baroni, then HUD Assistant Secretary for Neighborhood Development and head of URPG's Neighborhood Task Force, had a long history in neighborhood empowerment. In 1970, he founded the National Center for Urban Ethnic Affairs (NCUEA), a Washington advocacy group sponsored by the U.S. Catholic Conference to promote citizen involvement in neighborhood-based organizations. Staffers for the organization were instrumental in establishing NCN and wrote important federal legislation such as the Home Mortgage Disclosure Act of 1975 and the 1977 Community Reinvestment Act.[29] Kaptur, who had worked as Baroni's Director of Planning at NCUEA, joined him in the Carter administration as a domestic policy advisor on Eizenstat's staff.

Harris, Baroni, Eizenstat, and Kaptur were among the most important voices in the urban policy formulation, and debates between them reflected the conflict between local government officials and proponents of the neighborhood movement inside and outside of the federal government. Harris and Eizenstat focused on pragmatic, politically feasible solutions to urban problems, which sometimes did and other times did not involve neighborhood empowerment.[30] Baroni and Kaptur typically advocated for policies that privileged "community" interests over individual interests, even though Baroni cautioned URPG that the National League of Cities and the U.S. Conference of Mayors were deeply resistant to the idea of the federal government directly funding neighborhood groups to undertake activities that municipal officials saw as their purview.[31]

While neighborhood empowerment was not the central focus of URPG deliberations, Baroni and Kaptur, emboldened by Carter's enthusiasm for voluntarism and self-help, worked to make neighborhood-based solutions central to national urban policy, despite resistance from within DPS and from Democratic mayors.[32] Baroni recommended that Carter publicly articulate a strategy for public–private partnerships that would allow neighborhood and voluntary associations to "alleviate the alienating effects of big government, big industry, and big institutions."[33] For Kaptur, government was "suspect from the federal level on down," and urban revitalization could only come from the neighborhoods and from the for- and not-for-profit private sector. She advocated for urban initiatives that would "replicate and assist where necessary" the scores of neighborhood-based voluntary associations and community development corporations (CDCs) in operation by the late 1970s.[34]

Even as URPG worked on the first draft of the policy, which privileged distressed communities and presumed

the continuation of existing federal-municipal relationships, Eizenstat and Kaptur encouraged Carter to adopt the language of "partnership" that formed the basis of the final urban policy. To prepare Carter for a speech in Detroit in the fall of 1977, Eizenstat and Kaptur noted Detroit's "bleak" history with federal intervention, and suggested that Carter emphasize self-help and voluntary organizations, rather than government, as a means of confronting the city's problems. Eizenstat and Kaptur reminded Carter that "our urban policy should be aimed at unleashing local forces of self-help by encouraging partnerships between the public, private and community sectors," and argued that the federal government should seek to build the capacity of "mediating institutions" such as churches, voluntary groups, and neighborhood associations to serve as brokers between individuals and the government.[35] They also urged Carter to mention the formation of NCN, which they hoped would identify successful and easily replicable models for public–private partnerships.[36]

URPG also considered several neighborhood-related policy recommendations, most of which sought to directly transfer greater portions of federal urban development funds to neighborhood-based organizations. A typical (unrealized) proposal was a Neighborhood Self-Help Development Fund, a demonstration program through which grants would be awarded to "sophisticated" neighborhood organizations—those with three to five years of neighborhood revitalization, housing, or economic development experience—rather than "confrontational" grassroots groups.[37] In an effort to forestall mayoral objections, applicants to the Fund would be required to supply a letter from the mayor's office confirming that all plans were consistent with local urban and economic development goals. The Fund would devolve control of urban development to a quasi-governmental neighborhood unit as well as encourage privatization by prioritizing applicants who proposed private-sector partnerships.[38] The Fund proposal explicitly rejected the idea that any level of government could, or should, undertake development on its own, stipulating instead that the federal government should serve as an "enabler" for neighborhood initiatives.[39]

The circulation of proposals on the model of the Self-Help Fund among URPG and DPS staffers spoke to the Carter Administration's deep interest in tying self-help to devolution through neighborhood empowerment. In broad strokes, national leaders of the neighborhood movement and their lobbyists favored devolution and privatization as a means to achieve local control, but neighborhood advocates outside of the Administration were not convinced that Carter's vision of "partnership" was in their best interests, as they felt that it did not devolve authority far enough. Consequently, the particularities of the Administration's proposals caused some concern.[40] URPG members and White House staff held a series of meetings with neighborhood movement lobbyists such as Milton Kotler, the Executive Director of the National Association of Neighborhoods, to discuss the first draft of the urban policy.[41] Representatives of neighborhood organizations worried that federal interference might create tension in existing partnerships between neighborhood groups and local governments. At the same time, they cautioned Harris and Eizenstat that their years of experience with public and private sector partners had taught them that private industry and city and state governments could not be counted on to undertake neighborhood development, and that mayors would not willingly give up long-held patronage networks.[42]

Neighborhood leaders dismissed the first draft of the urban policy as "little more than a desk blotter used to soak up the ink of the League of Cities and the National Conference of Mayors, who, for all sorts of political reasons, vehemently oppose federal direct funding of community organizations."[43] The neighborhood groups, by contrast, wanted to know when Congress might be persuaded to pass legislation that would allow direct federal funding of neighborhood and community organizations, demanded greater federal subsidies for CDCs, and complained that city governments absorbed as overhead too large a share of the federal money already earmarked for neighborhood and community organizations. What the neighborhood movement wanted, Eizenstat told them, was likely politically impossible.[44]

Urban Policy and Intergovernmental Relations

Neighborhood organizations were not alone in seeking greater control over urban development in the 1970s. While Carter and neighborhood advocates in and outside of his Administration hoped to see neighborhoods empowered to direct urban policy and administer federal aid, state government officials saw the urban policy deliberations as an opportunity to seize greater control over local urban and economic development. State governments had lobbied hard in the postwar years for an increased role in administering and distributing federal funds within their state boundaries. Even though municipalities exist as legal entities of the state rather than federal government, the grants-in-aid formula of federal funding that emerged from the New Deal allowed federal agencies to provide grants directly to cities or to local public authorities. For the forty years between the New Deal and the introduction of the Community Development Block Grant (CDBG) Program in 1974, federal urban and economic development programs bypassed state governments almost entirely.[45] And for most of those forty years, state government officials, either unilaterally or through national organizations such as the National Governors' Association (NGA) and the National Conference of State Legislatures, actively sought to insinuate themselves in the middle of federal–local relationships—a move mayors resisted, jealously guarding their share of federal funding from state houses as well as from community organizations.

Throughout the postwar period, state governments enacted administrative reform efforts intended to demonstrate their capacity to administer federal programs.[46] As early as 1956, the Council of State Governments recommended that every state establish an agency able to oversee urban and rural development. Under pressure from increasingly activist governors, the Advisory Council on Intergovernmental Relations recommended in 1964 that state agencies administer federal grants-in-aid to cities if the agencies established appropriate mechanisms through which to carry out those responsibilities, and if state governments provided financial and technical assistance to local governments. Two years later, the NGA resolved that federal agencies should require state-level review and coordination of all federal funds for local or regional development.[47]

While national organizations pursued a formal role for state governments in urban development, governors and state legislatures worked independently to create intermediary positions for themselves between federal funding and local governments. In 1971, HUD commissioned a study on possible state roles in CDBG programs, which found that federal programs like Model Cities had already helped "build new channels of communication" between state and local governments. The report characterized state officials as increasingly eager to involve themselves in urban affairs and noted that, in most states, large cities and state governments had informally established "a 'pass-through' kind of relationship" for federal funds.[48] When Nixon's New Federalism stimulated interest in creating state "partners" to which the federal government could shift the fiscal and regulatory burden for urban development, HUD proposed a "States First" strategy predicated on federal–state cooperation in transportation, energy, housing, health, education, welfare, equal opportunity, and community development.[49] The strategy was entirely devolutionary— "States First" meant that states would assume the burden of managing growth and development and the federal government would merely work "at the margin" to influence the "character" of national growth through tax and financial incentives to the private sector.[50]

It was no surprise, then, that URPG—staffed by HUD—created a States and Metropolitan Regions Task Force to investigate ways to increase states' responsibility for urban development. In a 1977 report, "Toward a Federal-State Urban Partnership," the task force recommended that federal agencies involved in development establish a demonstration program to finance state urban development strategies and provide incentives to states willing to commit to "pro-city" development policies. Upon federal certification of a state's urban development strategy, the federal government would supply additional "financial and administrative incentives" for its implementation.[51] The National Conference of State Legislatures, especially pleased with the task force's suggestion that executive–legislative committees develop state strategies, enthusiastically endorsed the plan.[52]

The NGA, however, was more critical of the "vague and noncommittal" language of federal–state partnerships. At URPG's request, Michael Dukakis, in his role as president of the NGA, drafted a proposal for a new state role in urban policy. URPG sought a "broad and substantial" consultative role for governors in the development of the urban policy and the NGA was eager to see the states made "full partners" in the process.[53] But

governors were unwilling to absorb the financial and administrative burdens of the urban crisis. Instead, the NGA expected the federal government to take responsibility for meeting the "extraordinary needs of the nation's most distressed cities," while state governments would play a supportive role by using federal incentives for state urban development strategies—the reverse of the recommendations put forth in HUD's "States-First" proposal.[54] Still, the NGA believed state governments could ensure the urban policy's success in a way that the federal government could not: "Strong Presidential leadership and clear policy guidelines cannot ensure that all federal officials in all agencies will conform to a national urban policy," Dukakis argued. "Governors and the state legislatures, by contrast, can respond directly with the kind of investment coordination, fiscal modernization, and local capacity building that can make a national urban policy work."[55]

Already displeased with hints that the urban policy would directly fund neighborhood organizations, the U.S. Conference of Mayors, the National League of Cities, and the National Association of Counties found the idea of increased state control over urban development unacceptable. Mayors and county officials interpreted URPG's devolutionary proposals as a threat to the close relationships they had enjoyed with federal officials since the New Deal. Lobbyists for each of the these national advocacy organizations argued that city and county governments, respectively, should take greater responsibility for urban policy and for the funds that would inevitably accompany new or reconstituted federal programs.[56] Bernard Hillenbrand, Executive Director of the National Association of Counties, characterized neighborhood participation as "ginger peachy" but cautioned Eizenstat that "the mechanisms for distributing and accounting for monies and coordinating neighborhood activities with overall plans must not be removed from the hands of local elected mayors, city councilmen and county commissioners."[57] He predicted that every state and local official in the country would oppose direct funding to neighborhood organizations and warned that county officials, particularly those in the less urbanized western United States, would not support increased funding for central cities at the expense of suburban and rural areas. Any federal proposal to increase funds to central cities, he assured

Eizenstat, "would be a very sharp political liability."[58] While the U.S. Conference of Mayors agreed that state governments held the power to legitimate a national urban policy, its representatives were satisfied with the existing relationship between cities and the federal government and insisted that installing states as intermediaries between local and federal governments "would result in the frustration of Federal/local efforts towards the achievement of national goals."[59] Similarly, the Executive Director of the National League of Cities complained that proposed state or regional strategies "would bind city governments."[60]

Mere weeks before URPG finalized the urban policy, Richard Hoyer, the president of the Texas Municipal League, admonished the federal government to get its own house in order before meddling with the existing relationship between states and cities. Hoyer pointedly noted that state–city relations varied dramatically by region, and a policy that suited Boston would not work in Houston. Moreover, "local governments are not the problem," he exhorted. "*The federal establishment is the problem.*"[61] Invoking popular imagery of booming Sunbelt cities and declining Northeast urban centers, Hoyer argued that Texas had a long tradition of home-rule, "an attitude of local self-reliance," and its cities were not distressed. He tartly suggested that "perhaps Governor Dukakis and the Administration could devise an urban strategy which applies only to Massachusetts, and doesn't try to impose Massachusetts-based solutions on Texas."[62] Lloyd Hackler, president of the American Retail Federation, wrote to Eizenstat to make sure he understood that "the situation in Texas" was dire.[63] The Texas Municipal League, together with similar organizations from at least twenty-two other states, planned to pressure the National League of Cities to "strongly oppose" any state or regional urban development strategies proposed by URPG. Hoyer had mobilized nearly eight hundred city governments, the governor, and most of the Texas Congressional delegation against the urban policy. Hoyer had also met with lobbyists representing banking, industry, retail, and construction, as well as the powerful president of the Houston Chamber of Commerce (and former mayor of Houston), who had promised to secure the support of other state and local Chambers of Commerce for Hoyer's campaign.[64]

Hoyer's letter was dated March 1, 1978—the same day the *Washington Post* ran a front-page article with the headline, "States, Cities in Tug of War for U.S. Aid."[65] The *Post* detailed the NGA's dire prognostications that "any urban policy that excluded 'full partnership by the states would be doomed to failure,'" while Syracuse Mayor Lee Alexander informed the *Post* that the U.S. Conference of Mayors "forcefully objected" to the Administration's proposals for both state incentives and neighborhood-based programs.[66] In drafting the national urban policy, URPG members were caught between the demands of neighborhood advocates, city and county officials, and state governments, and bound by urban–rural and sectional tensions. Capturing the Administration's ambivalence about the nature and extent of the urban policy, Carter's Deputy Assistant for Domestic Affairs Bert Carp suggested that the theme of the urban policy should be revised to emphasize that "we cannot solve the problems of distressed communities from the federal level—the problems are too deep, and both our resources and understanding of the solutions are too limited."[67] Rather than decide among a host of competing constituencies, the Administration ultimately promised only that the federal government would "provide more effective tools" with which to empower "*local* leaders—mayors, the business community, neighborhood groups" to take initiative with the support of state governments."[68] The activism of neighborhood groups and city and state officials, together with the activities of NCN and the WH Conference, served to validate *A New Partnership*. . . .

Conclusion

. . . Carter and the emerging New Democratic coalition in Congress did not impose devolution and privatization on unwitting cities from above. Instead, the interests of states, counties, local governments, and community organizations seeking greater self-determination, less federal oversight, more flexible policies and, of course, more access to federal money aligned with the Carter administration's desire to implement small-scale, relatively inexpensive programs administered at the local level. It is unlikely that most advocates for local control and public–private partnerships in the 1970s desired or anticipated the extent of devolution and privatization that would in part result from efforts to gain increased autonomy. They were unequal partners in the process, to be sure, but state and local officials and neighborhood advocates were complicit in establishing and legitimating the urban policies that reoriented the federal relationship to cities in the 1970s.

Carter's most meaningful efforts to influence urban development actually occurred outside of the framework of the national urban policy. He attacked redundant programs and excessive paperwork, shifted a greater share of CDBG funds from suburbs and the south and southwest to northeastern and midwestern cities and passed along as much oversight as possible for urban development to state and local governments. He rejected large-scale job creation programs and housing subsidies in favor of comparatively cheap undertakings such as a $35 million National Endowment for the Arts program sponsoring public art projects.[100] In a more ambitious move, Carter signed the Housing and Community Development Act of 1977, which provided $12.5 billion for those activities, created the Community Reinvestment Act to end redlining and monitor bank lending practices in low-income and minority areas, and introduced Urban Development Action Grants (UDAGs). Observers have described UDAGs as a "private-sector-led version of urban renewal" that won support from mayors and business interests alike because the program made federal funds available for large-scale downtown revitalization programs, contingent upon the commitment of a private developer.[101]

With lukewarm support from Congress and the president himself, no substantial new urban programs or funding commitments emerged from the national urban policy. Because of political expediency—Carter knew he would need to attract both the suburban and Southern vote in 1980—the urban policy statement sought to "encourage" desired policy outcomes through the private sector or through other levels of government.[102] Carter sent 15 bills related to the national urban policy to Congress in 1978; the only one that passed was a mass transit provision included in a highway bill.[103] The most tangible result of the national urban policy, four executive orders issued in 1978, directed federal agencies to locate facilities in urban areas, emphasize procurement set-asides in areas with high unemployment, consider the impact of programs on urban areas, and establish an inter-agency council to implement the urban

policy.[104] Roger Biles has suggested that the legislative package attached to the *New Partnership* "languished" on Capitol Hill because liberal Democrats were unhappy about limits to federal oversight, because of bipartisan political opposition to targeting aid to distressed cities, and because of concern over the financial implications of the proposed programs in an era of "lingering" stagflation and tax revolts.[105] More importantly, with his focus on foreign policy and the economy, Carter did not push Congress to support the proposed legislation.[106]

While it paid lip service to neighborhoods through decentralization and public–private partnerships, *A New Partnership* did not, in the final analysis, provide the robust federal framework (or financing) for neighborhood empowerment that Kaptur, Baroni, and the NCN Commissioners had envisioned. Instead, it served primarily as an intellectual justification for Carter to download existing federal responsibilities for social service provision and for urban, economic, and industrial development to other political jurisdictions and to the private sector. Incremental decentralization and privatization shaped a policy environment which, by the early 1980s, made it difficult for local governments, community groups, and labor unions to appeal to the federal government to intervene in social and economic disinvestment in cities. Instead, local officials were left to their own devices as state governments struggled to develop and finance programs to counter the urban crisis without substantial new federal support.[107]

Notes

1. Susanna McBee, "Cities Await Carter's Urban Policy," *Pittsburgh Press*, March 25, 1978.
2. Quoted in Roger Biles, *The Fate of Cities: Urban America and the Federal Government, 1945–2000* (Lawrence: University Press of Kansas, 2011), 224.
3. For general information on urban policy under Carter, see Biles, *The Fate of Cities*; Demestrios Caraley, "Carter, Congress, and the Cities," in *Urban Policy Making*, ed. Dale Rogers Marshall (Beverly Hills: Sage, 1979), 71–98; Peter Eisinger, "The Search for a National Urban Policy: 1968–1990," *Journal of Urban History* 12 (November 1985): 3–23; F. J. James, "President Carter's Comprehensive National Urban Policy: Achievements and Lessons Learned," *Environment and Planning C: Government and Policy* 8 (1990): 29–40; Stuart Meck and Rebecca Retzlaff, "President

Jimmy Carter's Urban Policy: A Reconstruction and an Appraisal," *Journal of Planning History* 11 (August 2012): 242–80; Yvonne Scruggs-Leftwich, *Consensus and Compromise: Creating the First National Urban Policy under President Carter* (New York: University Press of America, 2006); Thomas J. Sugrue, "Carter's Urban Policy Crisis," in *The Carter Presidency: Policy Choices in the Post-New Deal Era*, ed. Gary M. Fink and Hugh Davis Graham (Lawrence: University Press of Kansas, 1998); Harold L. Wolman and Astrid E. Merget, "The President and Policy Formulation: President Carter and the Urban Policy," *Presidential Studies Quarterly* 10 (Summer 1980): 402–15.

4. Jimmy Carter, "National Urban Policy Remarks Announcing the Policy," March 27, 1978, Online by Gerhard Peters and John T. Woolley, *The American Presidency Project*, http://www.presidency.ucsb.edu/ws/?pid=30566.

5. Sugrue, "Carter's Urban Policy Crisis," 148.

6. Memo, Stuart Eizenstat to the President, January 9, 1978 (draft), "Urban Policy [CF, O/A 51] [6]" folder, Box 306, Domestic Policy Staff (DPS)-Eizenstat Files, Jimmy Carter Library (JCL).

7. Ibid.

8. On the Carter's presidency and his ambivalent commitment to New Deal liberalism, see Biles, *The Fate of Cities*; Jefferson R. Cowie, *Stayin' Alive: The 1970s and the Last Days of the Working Class* (New York: The New Press, 2010); W. Carl Biven, *Jimmy Carter's Economy: Policy in an Age of Limits* (Chapel Hill: University of North Carolina Press, 2002); Gary M. Fink and Hugh Davis Graham, eds., *The Carter Presidency: Policy Choices in the Post-New Deal Era* (Lawrence: University Press of Kansas, 1998); Laura Kalman, *Right Star Rising: A New Politics, 1974–1980* (New York: W. W. Norton, 2010); Burton I. Kaufman and Scott Kaufman, *The Presidency of James Earl Carter* (Lawrence: University Press of Kansas, 2006); Judith Stein, *Pivotal Decade: How the United States Traded Factories for Finance in the Seventies* (New Haven: Yale University Press, 2010); and Sugrue, "Carter's Urban Policy Crisis."

9. Memo, Les Francis to Stuart Eizenstat, Bert Carp, Bo Cutter, and Harrison Wellford, January 5, 1978, "Urban Policy [CF, O/A 50] [8]" folder, Box 304, DPS-Eizenstat Files, JCL.

10. Biles, *The Fate of Cities*; Sugrue, "Carter's Urban Policy Crisis"; Jane Berger, "'There Is Tragedy on Both Sides of the Layoffs': Privatization and the Urban Crisis in Baltimore," *International Labor and Working-Class History* 71 (Spring 2007): 29–49.

11. See, e.g., Biles, *The Fate of Cities*; Sugrue, "Carter's Urban Policy Crisis."

12. On the politics of the national urban policy and debates between and within URPG and DPS over its content, see especially Scruggs-Leftwich, *Consensus and Compromise* and Meck and Retzlaff, "President Jimmy Carter's Urban Policy."

13. Meck and Retzlaff, "President Jimmy Carter's Urban Policy," 243.

14. Scruggs-Leftwich, *Consensus and Compromise*, 49. See also, Meck and Retzlaff, "President Jimmy Carter's Urban Policy."

15. Sugrue, "Carter's Urban Policy Crisis," 141.

16. Bruce J. Schulman, "Slouching toward the Supply Side," in *The Carter Presidency: Policy Choices in the Post-New Deal Era*, ed. Gary M. Fink and Hugh Davis Graham (Lawrence: University Press of Kansas, 1998), 57–58.

17. Sugrue, "Carter's Urban Policy Crisis," 148.

18. Biles, *The Fate of Cities*, 232.

19. Sugrue, "Carter's Urban Policy Crisis," 144.

20. Biles, *The Fate of Cities*, 236; Meck and Retzlaff, "President Jimmy Carter's Urban Policy," 251.

21. Biles, *The Fate of Cities*, 236.

22. Sugrue, "Carter's Urban Policy Crisis," 151.

23. Suleiman Osman, "The Decade of the Neighborhood," in *Rightward Bound: Making America Conservative in the 1970s*, ed. Bruce J. Schulman and Julian E. Zelizer (Cambridge: Harvard University Press, 2008), 111–13.

24. On the origins of neighborhood-based activism, see Patricia Mooney-Melvin, "Before the Neighborhood Revolution: Cincinnati's Neighborhood Improvement Associations, 1890–1940," in *Making Sense of the City: Local Government, Civic Culture, and Community Life in American Cities*, ed. Robert B. Fairbanks and Patricia Mooney-Melvin (Columbus: Ohio State University Press, 2001), 95–118; and Alexander von Hoffman, *House by House, Block by Block: The Rebirth of America's Urban Neighborhood, 1850–1920* (New York: Oxford University Press, 2003).

25. On citizen participation and neighborhood-based responses to urban renewal and Model Cities programs, see Richard L. Cole, "Citizen Participation in Municipal Politics," *American Journal of Political Science* 19 (November 1975): 761–81; J. David Greenstone and Paul E. Peterson, *Race and Authority in Urban Politics: Community Participation and the War on Poverty* (Chicago: University of Chicago Press, 1976); Andrew R. Highsmith, "Demolition Means Progress: Urban Renewal, Local Politics, and State-Sanctioned

Ghetto Formation in Flint, Michigan," *Journal of Urban History* 35 (March 2009): 346–68; Irene V. Holiman, "From Crackertown to Model City? Urban Renewal and Community Building in Atlanta, 1963–1966," *Journal of Urban History* 35 (March 2009): 369–86; Daniel Patrick Moynihan, *Maximum Feasible Misunderstanding: Community Action in the War on Poverty* (New York: Free Press, 1969); Bret A. Weber and Amanda Wallace, "Revealing the Empowerment Revolution: A Literature Review of the Model Cities Program," *Journal of Urban History* 38 (January 2012): 177–80; Douglas Yates, *Neighborhood Democracy: The Politics and Impacts of Decentralization* (Lexington, MA: Lexington Books, 1973).

26. Osman, "The Decade of the Neighborhood," 111–15.

27. National Commission on Neighborhoods, "Neighborhoods in the President's National Urban Policy," unpublished report, n.d., p. 1, "Baltimore—Everything from Hearing, 2/3/78—2/5/78" folder, Box 16, Records of the National Commission on Neighborhoods (NCN), RG 220, JCL. On the history of neighborhood movements, see Harry C. Boyte, *The Backyard Revolution: Understanding the New Citizen Movement* (Philadelphia: Temple University Press, 1980); Benjamin Looker, "Visions of Autonomy: The New Left and the Neighborhood Government Movement of the 1970s," *Journal of Urban History* 38 (May 2012): 577–98; Osman, "The Decade of the Neighborhood"; Jon C. Teaford, *The Rough Road to Renaissance: Urban Revitalization in America, 1940–1985* (Baltimore: Johns Hopkins University Press, 1990), Chapter 6.

28. Leopold W. Bernhard and Milton Kotler, "Self-Governing Neighborhoods as an Emerging Unit of Governance: How Do They Fit into Government Reorganization?" Paper presented at the Conference on Government Reorganization, Woodrow Wilson International Center for Scholars, Washington, D.C., 1977, "Urban Policy in General 4/77–10/77 [O/A 4413]" folder, Box 42, Office of Public Liaison (OPL)-Costanza Files, JCL.

29. On Baroni's role in the neighborhood movement, see J. A. Kromkowski and J. D. Kromkowski, "An American Catholic Perspective on Urban Neighborhoods: The Lens of Monsignor Geno C. Baroni and the Legacy of the Neighborhood Movement," *American Journal of Economics and Sociology* 71 (2012): 1095–1141.

30. On factions within URPG, see Biles, *The Fate of Cities*; Scruggs-Leftwich, *Consensus and Compromise*; and Sugrue, "Carter's Urban Policy Crisis."

31. "Summary Minutes of the Business Meeting of the National Commission on Neighborhoods," March 11, 1978, p. 2, Washington D.C. Business Meeting folder, box 16, Records of the National Commission on Neighborhoods, JCL.

32. Sugrue, "Carter's Urban Policy Crisis," 144.

33. Memo, Geno C. Baroni to Robert C. Embry, September 13, 1977, "Urban & Regional Policy Group [O/A 6346] [2]" folder, Box 311, DPS-Eizenstat, JCL.

34. Memo, Marcy Kaptur to Bill Johnston, December 6, 1977, "Urban Policy [CF, O/A 732]" folder, Box 302, DPS-Eizenstat, JCL.

35. Memo, Stuart Eizenstat and Marcia Kaptur to the President, October 17, 1977, "Urban Policy (2) 10/77 [O/A 6346] [2]" folder, Box 308, DPS-Eizenstat, JCL.

36. Ibid.

37. "Rationale for Direct Federal Funding to Neighborhood Development Organizations," unpublished report, n.d., "Urban Policy [CF, O/A 50] [5]" folder, Box 304, DPS-Eizenstat, JCL.

38. Ibid.

39. "A New Focus on Neighborhood Programs," unpublished report, n.d., "Urban Policy [CF, O/A 50] [5]" folder, Box 304, DPS-Eizenstat, JCL.

40. Minutes of Meeting on the Urban and Regional Policy with Representatives of Neighborhood and Community Organizations, December 21, 1977, "HUD-Baroni, [Geno]" folder, Box 2, NCN, JCL.

41. Memo, "Seymour" to "Ed," November 28, 1977, "Neighborhoods, 3/77–3/78 [O/A 4609]" folder, Box 29, OPL-Costanza, JCL.

42. Ibid.

43. Ibid.

44. Ibid.

45. On state governments, urban development, and federal–local relations, see especially Peter K. Eisinger, *The Rise of the Entrepreneurial State: State and Local Economic Development Policy in the United States* (Madison: University of Wisconsin Press, 1988); Bruce J. Schulman, *From Cotton Belt to Sunbelt: Federal Policy, Economic Development, and the Transformation of the South, 1938–1980* (Durham: Duke University Press, 1994); Jon C. Teaford, *The Rise of the States: Evolution of American State Government* (Baltimore: Johns Hopkins University Press, 2002).

46. Eisinger, *The Rise of the Entrepreneurial State*.

47. "The States and Urban Problems: A Staff Study for the Committee on State-Urban Relations of the National

Governors' Conference," October 1967, unpublished report, 133–34, Urban Information and Technical Assistance Files of the Program Regulation Division 1967–72, General Records of the Department of Housing and Urban Development (HUD Records), Record Group 207, National Archives at College Park (NARA).

48. Memo, Peter C. Labovitz to Floyd Hyde, February 16, 1971, "Plans, Programs and Evaluations" folder, Community Planning and Management Records, 1961–71, Textual Records (General) 1934–70, HUD Records, NARA.

49. George W. Wright, "Balanced Growth and Community Development Strategies in Federal and State Perspective" speech, September 19–21, 1975, "National Growth and Development—National Growth Policy, 1971–1975" folder, Box 15, David O. Meeker Papers, Gerald R. Ford Library, Ann Arbor.

50. Ibid.

51. Memo, Lawrence O. Houston to Robert C. Embry, November 3, 1977, "Urban Policy [CF, O/A 49] [5]" folder, Box 302, DPS-Eizenstat, JCL.

52. Report of the Task Force on State and Metropolitan Regions of the Urban and Regional Policy Group, November 3, 1977, "Urban Policy [CF, O/A 49] [5]" folder, Box 302, DPS-Eizenstat, JCL.

53. Michael Dukakis, "A Proposal to Encourage the States to Become Full Partners in a National Urban Policy," ca. 1978, "Urban Policy [CF, O/A 49] [10]" folder, Box 302, DPS-Eizenstat, JCL.

54. Ibid., 7–8.

55. Ibid.

56. Letter, Bernard F. Hillenbrand to Stuart Eizenstat, February 15, 1978, "Urban Policy [CF, O/A 51] [4]" folder, Box 306, DPS-Eizenstat, JCL; Report of the Task Force on State and Metropolitan Regions of the Urban and Regional Policy Group, November 3, 1977.

57. Ibid.

58. Ibid.

59. Report of the Task Force on State and Metropolitan Regions of the Urban and Regional Policy Group, November 3, 1977.

60. Ibid.

61. Letter, Richard J. Hoyer to Stuart Eizenstat, March 1, 1978, "Urban Policy [CF, O/A 50] [4]" folder, Box 304, DPS-Eizenstat, JCL.

62. Ibid.

63. Letter, Lloyd Hackler to John White or Stuart Eizenstat, March 3, 1978, "Urban Policy [CF, O/A 50] [4]" folder, Box 304, DPS-Eizenstat, JCL.

64. Ibid.

65. Warren Brown and David Broder, "States, Cities in Tug of War for U.S. Aid," *Washington Post*, March 1, 1978.

66. Ibid.

67. Memo, Bert Carp to Stuart Eizenstat, November 23, 1977, "Urban Policy [CF, O/A 732]" folder, Box 302, DPS-Eizenstat, JCL.

68. Ibid.

100. Sugrue, "Carter's Urban Policy Crisis."

101. Susan Fainstein and Norman Fainstein, "The Ambivalent State: Economic Development Policy in the U.S. Federal System under the Reagan Administration," *Urban Affairs Quarterly* 25, no. 1 (September 1989): 44 and Biles, *The Fate of Cities*, 232.

102. Sugrue, "Carter's Urban Policy Crisis," 148.

103. Biles, *The Fate of Cities*, 237.

104. Meck and Retzlaff found that "altogether the policy proposed more than 160 changes in 38 existing federal programs. However, only 30 components of the plan required new legislation," and that "in one and a half years after the urban policy was released, the Carter administration submitted nineteen urban-related proposals, and Congress enacted 13 of them. Another 100 changes were made to program rules." Meck and Retzlaff, "President Jimmy Carter's Urban Policy," 257.

105. Biles, *The Fate of Cities*, 237.

106. Biles, *The Fate of Cities*, 261.

107. According to Meck and Retzlaff, "The Carter administration transmitted a 'State Community Conservation and Development Act of 1978' to Congress in May 1978. The act authorized a pair of competitive incentive programs, funded at $200 million for FY 1979 and 1980 (originally proposed at $400 million for two years, but reduced by President Carter), for state fiscal and governmental reform strategies, and public investment strategies for community and economic development. But the Carter administration apparently did not push hard for it, and the legislation never passed Congress." Ibid., 261.

9-2 "City Politics in the Era of Federal Devolution"

Peter Eisinger

Urban Affairs Review

The effort that began more than 25 years ago to construct what might be called a New Federal Order is still very much a work in progress. President Clinton and most members of Congress have clearly embraced some of the elements that differentiate this federal arrangement from its New Deal-Great Society predecessor such as diminishing federal intergovernmental aid, block grants, and formal devolution of federal responsibilities. But the scope and details of implementation of this latest iteration of the federal arrangement are not yet fully worked out. The bare walls of the edifice have been erected, but there is little interior decoration.

As members of the tripartite federal partnership that came to its fullest expression in the Great Society and the years immediately following, local governments have a deep interest in the process and outcomes of federal realignment. As the outlines of the New Federal Order of the 1990s have taken shape, it is clear that the implications for urban government are manifold. Nevertheless, even though many of the problems and issues that are reshaping federalism are concentrated in urban areas, much is uncertain about what precise role the cities will play in the emerging intergovernmental environment. Curiously, city representatives and city interests have been, according to Weir (1996, 1), "conspicuously absent from the congressional debate about devolution."

Certain developments in national politics make this an appropriate moment to take stock and to speculate about the future of the cities in the New Federal Order. In summer 1996, Congress passed, and the president signed, the new welfare law, converting cash support for the poor from an open-ended federal entitlement to a fixed block grant to the states. Devolution through block granting is the focus of debate in other areas of public policy, from law enforcement to highway funding and from job training to housing, all policy domains in which the local government role is clearer and more formalized than in the welfare realm. Not only is there now broad interest in devolving power through block grants but the intergovernmental aid reductions put in place in Republican Washington in the 1980s are no longer resisted by deficit-averse Democrats. In this article, then, I explore what is known about cities in the New Federal Order, what their future role might be, and what the effects on cities of the changes in the federal arrangement have been.

I suggest that to the extent that cities are increasingly cut off from federal aid and program initiatives, mayors must focus more and more on making the most of the resources they control. Thus the arts of public management are becoming the primary tasks of local political leadership. This represents an important change in the moral climate of local politics, because city hall is far less likely to be used these days as the bully pulpit from which mayors once sought to exercise leadership on major social, racial, and economic issues.

The New Federal Order

I define the New Federal Order as that rearrangement of federal relationships that began with President Richard Nixon's efforts to devolve authority from Washington to subnational governments through block grants and general revenue sharing and continues today as Congress, the president, and the

Source: Peter Eisinger, "City Politics in the Era of Federal Devolution," *Urban Affairs Review*, vol. 33, no. 3, January 1998, pp. 308–325. Reprinted with permission from SAGE Publications, Inc.

governors combine to contract the role of the federal government in domestic policy. Although the initial efforts in the 1970s to transform the New Deal-Great Society federal system were seen as partisan attempts to diminish Washington's influence, both parties seem to agree today not only that the era of big government is over but that the proper locus of policy invention and administration is at the state and local level. For example, even before the passage of the welfare reform bill of 1996, the Clinton administration had approved 78 state welfare demonstration projects. More generally, the president's urban policy, according to his assistant secretary of the Department of Housing and Urban Development (HUD) at the time, "recognizes that the most pressing problems facing older cities can no longer be addressed through countercyclical grant-in-aid programs" (Stegman 1996). Where do the cities fit, then, in the New Federal Order?

It is important to begin by distinguishing several different aspects of the process of creating the New Federal Order. One aspect is simply the contraction of federal intergovernmental aid. This trend represents the devolution by default of fiscal responsibility to states and localities. A second aspect is the formal devolution of power from Washington to subnational government, a rearrangement of responsibilities that, for the most part, has not yet greatly increased the powers and responsibilities of city governments. A third feature concerns the indirect consequences of devolution to the states. These spin-off fiscal and political effects are manifold, and they affect the cities in important ways.

Fiscal Contraction

Federal assistance to cities is much diminished since the late 1970s. The contraction of aid has been so dramatic that the federal government's loss of interest in urban affairs is one of the signal stories of the great transformation to the New Federal Order. Yet a focus on the big picture alone may be somewhat misleading: Cities have not been entirely cut adrift fiscally to live on their own resources.

In 1977, the year before federal aid contraction began, municipal governments looked to Washington for 15.9% of their total revenues. By 1992, federal assistance had decreased to only 4.7% of local revenues (Chernick and Reschovsky 1997; see also Wallin 1996). In 1991, combined federal grants in aid to state and local governments regained their high watermark of 1978 (in constant dollar terms), but the functional distribution of intergovernmental fiscal assistance had changed in ways particularly disadvantageous to the cities. Although grants for education, job training, and social services, many of which are allocated to local governments, accounted for 23.9% of federal intergovernmental aid in 1980, the figure had decreased to 15.8% by 1994. Community development assistance decreased during this period from 7.1% to 2.9% of federal aid, and grants for sewer and water construction and environmental cleanup went from 5.9% to 2.0%. Meanwhile, health-related grants, mainly Medicaid, which is channeled through the states to individuals, rose from 17.2% of all federal intergovernmental assistance to 42.1% (Advisory Commission on Intergovernmental Relations 1994, 31). In short, a much smaller proportion of federal aid is devoted to urban programs than was true just a decade and a half ago.

An analysis by the U.S. Conference of Mayors ([USCM] 1994) of funding of key urban programs shows how severe the cuts have been from the perspective of the cities. Between 1981 and 1993, funding of community development block grants, urban development action grants, general revenue sharing, mass transit aid, employment and training programs, clean-water construction, assisted housing, and the various programs of the Economic Development Administration decreased by 66.3% in real dollar terms (see Table 1).

State governments did little to make up for the evaporation of federal monies for their municipalities. Reeling from the losses of federal aid that they themselves were experiencing, especially with the end of the state portion of general revenue sharing in 1980, state governments significantly reduced the rate of growth of aid to their local governments. Altogether, state aid to local governments as a proportion of local revenues decreased from 25.4% to 21.2% of local revenues between 1977 and 1992 (Chernick and Reschovsky 1997).

Although urban-oriented federal aid had dropped substantially by the mid-1990s, the federal government in the Clinton era has not abandoned the cities. Beginning with fiscal year 1995, the USCM began tracking

Table 1 Federal Funds for Cities, 1981–1993 (in billions of constant 1993 dollars)

Program	FY 1981 ($)	FY 1993 ($)	% Real Cut
Community Development Block Grant	6.3	4.0	−36.5
Urban Development Action Grant	0.6	0.0	−100.0
General revenue sharing	8.0	0.0	−100.0
Mass transit	6.9	3.5	−49.3
Employment and training	14.3	4.2	−70.6
Economic Development Administration	0.6	0.2	−66.7
Assisted housing	26.8	8.9	−66.8
Clean-water construction	6.0	2.6	−56.7

Source: U.S. Conference of Mayors (1994).

federal funding of a range of specific "municipal programs."[1] Table 2 presents the funding history for these programs for three consecutive years and the percentage change from 1995 to 1997. Dollar figures are not adjusted for inflation. Of the 80 programs tracked over the three-year period by the USCM, 27 showed decreases, 8 were unchanged, and 45 received increases in funding. Of those 45, however, only 26 received funding increases that equaled or exceeded the inflation rate.

The data indicate, however, that with a few exceptions, municipal programs did not experience the huge cuts in the middle Clinton years that they had suffered in the earlier decade. Federal funding of programs that benefit cities could be described as approaching a steady state, with substantial changes only at the tails of the distribution. One implication for the cities is that although they do not stand to lose even more federal dollars, it is unlikely that a return to the patterns of the pre-Reagan era will occur. Nothing in the patterns of federal aid in the 1990s suggests that city governments will be able to relax their habits of fiscal self-reliance.

Formal Devolution

The principal definition of the term devolution in the context of U.S. federalism is the reallocation of specific responsibilities and authority from Washington

to subnational governments. Since 1980, devolution has primarily involved a shift from national to state government. Such a rearrangement lay at the heart of President Reagan's New Federalism, one of the elements of which involved a failed proposal to carry out the so-called Great Swap: Washington would assume full responsibility for Medicaid in return for complete state takeover of the Aid to Families with Dependent Children (AFDC) and Food Stamps programs.

Reagan's effort to shape the New Federal Order was not entirely in vain, however: He did succeed in persuading Congress to consolidate 77 categorical grants-in-aid into 10 broad block grants to the states. The consequence was to strip Congress of the authority to designate specific uses of federal assistance for a variety of mainly health and education programs. State governments could now establish their own priorities within the broad boundaries of these new block grants. As in the current era, however, the interests of cities were scarcely considered in this federal reordering. Indeed, the new state power came directly at the expense of the cities: Of the categorical programs consolidated into block grants to the states, 47 had previously delivered funds directly to local governments (Ladd 1994, 219).

The Reagan federalism reforms failed to stem the growth of categorical grants, the number of which had

Table 2   Federal Funding for Municipal Programs, FY 1995–FY 1997 (in millions of dollars)

Program	1995	1996	1997	Percentage Change 1995–1997
Programs with decreased funding				
Student financial assistance	7,586.0	6,259.0		−100.0
Youthbuild	40.0	20.0		−100.0
Community service employment	396.0	373.0		−100.0
Section 202 elderly	1,176.0	1,013.0	639.0	−45.7
Transit—operation	710.0	400.0	400.0	−43.7
National Endowment for the Arts	162.0	99.5	99.5	−38.6
National Endowment for the Humanities	172.0	110.0	110.0	−36.0
Substance abuse prevention	238.0	92.0	156.0	−34.5
PATH formula grants	29.0	20.0	20.0	−31.0
Section 108 loan guarantees	2,054.0	1,500.0	1,500.0	−27.0
Homeless assistance	1,120.0	823.0	823.0	−26.5
Emergency food and shelter	130.0	100.0	100.0	−23.1
Museum grants	28.0	21.0	22.0	−21.4
AmeriCorps/Corporation for National Service	470.0	403.0	403.0	−14.3
Education for homeless children	29.0	23.0	25.0	−13.8
Public housing modernization	2,885.0	2,500.0	2,500.0	−13.3
AMTRAK	794.0	635.0	695.0	−12.5
Social Services Block Grant	2,800.0	2,381.0	2,500.0	−10.7
Adult job training	997.0	850.0	895.0	−10.2
Economic Development Administration	383.0	348.5	348.5	−9.0
Healthy Start	104.0	93.0	96.0	−7.7
Administration on Aging	876.0	833.0	836.0	−4.6
Food stamps	25,576.0	25,467.0	24,912.0	−2.6
Preventive Health Block Grants	158.0	145.0	154.0	−2.5
Airport facilities and equipment	1,960.0	1,918.0	1,938.0	−1.1
Superfund	1,354.0	1,302.0	1,348.0	−0.4
Maternal and child health	684.0	679.0	681.0	−0.4
Programs with no change in funding				
HOME Investment Partnership	1,400.0	1,400.0	1,400.0	0.0
HUD Drug Elimination	290.0	290.0	290.0	0.0

(Continued)

Table 2   Continued

Program	1995	1996	1997	Percentage Change 1995–1997
Community Development Block Grant	4,600.0	4,600.0	4,600.0	0.0
Youth training	127.0	127.0	127.0	0.0
Housing opportunities for people with AIDS	171.0	171.0	171.0	0.0
Sexually transmitted diseases	225.0	224.0	225.0	0.0
Public housing operating subsidies	2,900.0	2,800.0	2,900.0	0.0
Community development financial institution	50.0	45.0	50.0	0.0
Programs with increased funding				
Transit-capital	1,574.0	1,491.0	1,578.0	0.3
Impact aid	728.0	693.0	730.0	0.3
Summer youth	867.0	625.0	871.0	0.5
Low-income home energy assistance	1,000.0	1,080.0	1,005.0	0.5
Airport improvement	1,450.0	1,450.0	1,460.0	0.7
Clean-water loans	1,885.0	1,848.0	1,900.0	0.8
Immunization	464.0	468.0	468.0	0.9
Substance abuse treatment	1,442.0	1,324.0	1,466.0	1.7
Medicaid	96,391.0	91,990.0	98,542.0	2.2
Child Care Block Grant	935.0	935.0	956.0	2.2
Family planning	193.0	193.0	198.0	2.6
Medicare	189,097.0	174,168.0	194,179.0	2.7
Centers for Disease Control Prevention	590.0	684.0	617.0	4.6
Dislocated workers assistance	1,229.0	1,100.0	1,293.0	5.2
Lead poisoning	36.0	36.0	38.0	5.6
Federal aid highways	17,192.0	17,708.0	18,198.0	5.9
Community health services	757.0	750.0	802.0	5.9
Job Corps	1,089.0	1,094.0	1,154.0	6.0
Title 1 Education for the Disadvantaged	7,228.0	7,228.0	7,698.0	6.5
Refugee and entrant assistance	400.0	413.0	427.0	6.8
Community Services Block Grant	458.0	389.0	489.0	6.8
Vocational and adult education	1,380.0	1,347.0	1,494.0	8.3
Community policing	1,300.0	1,400.0	1,420.0	9.2
Airport operations	4,573.0	4,646.0	5,000.0	9.3

Table 2 Continued

Program	1995	1996	1997	Percentage Change 1995–1997
Severely distressed public housing	500.0	480.0	550.0	10.0
Transit-discretionary	1,725.0	1,665.0	1,900.0	10.1
Headstart	3,534.0	3,569.0	3,981.0	12.6
WIC	3,450.0	3,715.0	3,975.0	15.2
Juvenile justice	155.0	149.0	180.0	16.1
Child nutrition	7,477.0	8,469.0	8,713.0	16.5
AFDCffANF	16,025.0	16,735.0	18,834.0	17.5
Anti-drug enforcement	450.0	600.0	561.0	24.7
Safe and Drug Free Schools	441.0	438.0	553.0	25.4
Bilingual and immigrant education	207.0	188.0	262.0	26.6
Goals 2000	372.0	350.0	491.0	32.0
One-Stop Career Centers	100.0	110.0	150.0	50.0
Ryan White CARE	633.0	757.0	996.0	57.3
School to Work	123.0	170.0	200.0	62.6
Section 8 renewals	2,159.0	4,008.0	3,600.0	66.7
Preservation	175.0	624.0	350.0	100.0
Commodity assistance	190.0	316.0	422.0	122.1
Drug courts	12.0	18.0	30.0	150.0
Lead-based paint demonstration	15.0	65.0	60.0	300.0
Violence against women	28.0	228.0	259.0	825.0

Source: Data obtained from U.S. Conference of Mayors (1995–1997).

reached an all-time high of 618 by 1995. Yet, contrary to the legislative trend, interest in devolution has remained high, both in Washington and in the state houses, fueled by the increasingly bipartisan conviction that in most matters of domestic policy, government closest to the people governs best. For proponents of devolution, the decade of the 1990s began in a promising way with the passage of the Intermodal Surface Transportation Efficiency Act (ISTEA), which greatly expands the ability of state and local governments alike to reallocate transportation funds among specific modes. Thus, in 1995, for example, more than $800 million was shifted by subnational governments from one purpose to another, such as the New York City Transit Authority's transfer of money initially designated for highways to mass transit projects, including station upgrades and signal modernization.[2]

Another significant devolutionary initiative during the Clinton years was the 1996 Personal Responsibility and Work Opportunity Reconciliation Act, better known as welfare reform, which created the Temporary Assistance to Needy Families (TANF) block grant. Henceforth, states will receive a fixed amount of funding from which to provide income support and work programs. State governments will now be responsible for establishing eligibility requirements and time limits. The shift of welfare responsibility to the states creates no formal local role, however, although there are clearly indirect implications for the cities that will be discussed later.

In no analysis of the urban implications of the changing distribution of responsibilities and authority in the federal system can one ignore two other initiatives of the mid-1990s: the Empowerment Zone and Enterprise Cities Act of 1993 and the Unfunded Mandates Reform Act of 1995. Neither devolves specific powers to subnational governments that they did not have before, but unlike most earlier devolutionary reforms, they both promise to expand the scope of local self-determination.

Along with providing some tax and regulatory relief, the Empowerment Zone and Enterprise Cities Program offers selected communities grants under the Title XX Human Services block grant program that may be used for an expanded range of social services and economic development. The Title XX block grant is made to the states, which in turn pass the funds on to their winning communities. In the first round, the few big winners received grants of $100 million each over a 10-year period, and a larger number of cities won smaller grants.

The program does not represent a devolution of new programmatic authority and responsibility in the field of economic and community development; these already rest primarily at the subnational level. Rather, the empowerment zone program devolves additional *capacity* to facilitate initiatives devised at the local level. Indeed, HUD is explicit in its implementation guidelines that programs are to be the product of strategic plans developed in the neighborhoods rather than in Washington (U.S. Government Accounting Office 1996, 3, 5).

The Unfunded Mandates Reform Act of 1995 has less obvious consequences but holds out the potential for curbing the growth rate of federal intergovernmental regulation and oversight and the imposition on states and localities of enforceable duties, as they are

called in the act. The relief from mandates provided by Congress is oblique: The purpose of the act is to "assist Congress in its consideration of proposed legislation . . . containing Federal mandates . . . by providing for development of information about the nature and size of mandates, [by promoting] informed and deliberate decisions by Congress on the appropriateness of Federal mandates in any particular instance, [and by requiring] that Congress consider whether to provide funding" to help subnational governments comply with the mandates (Unfunded Mandates Reform Act of 1995, P.L. 104–4). Members of Congress may be called upon to vote explicitly to include any mandate in a new program. The act is thus designed not so much to bar unfunded mandates as to discourage Congress by making the decision to impose a new mandate a thoroughly self-conscious and transparent action. If the intent of the act is realized, state and local governments may find over time that they may exercise unregulated governance over a slightly larger range of functions.

Although it is evident that little formal devolution from Washington to the cities has yet occurred, there are various proposals on the political agenda that would expand the urban role in the New Federal Order. During his term as the head of HUD, Secretary Henry Cisneros recommended creating a block grant through the consolidation of existing programs that would go to local governments to serve the homeless. Cisneros was said to believe that "homelessness is a local problem that is best solved . . . at the local level. . . . The most Washington can do is show the way" (Rapp 1994, 80). There has also been talk in Washington of consolidating 60 current HUD programs into three block grants for housing assistance, housing production, and community development. Another proposal, put forth by congressional Republicans after they won control of the House in the 1994 elections, was to eliminate the Community Oriented Policing Services program and substitute a $10 billion block grant to localities for law enforcement purposes, but President Clinton vetoed the appropriations bill that threatened to transform this signature program.

As these examples make clear, devolution is increasingly a shared goal of both political parties. Unlike the devolution of the Reagan years, the expansion of state authority is not the sole focus of federal reform. Although little formal authority has yet been transferred to local governments, some of the groundwork has been laid by forcing city governments to rely more heavily on their own resources. City governments may anticipate playing an even more central role in the federal rearrangement in the future.

Indirect Consequences of Devolution

As federal devolution proceeds at the end of the century, cities are increasingly subjected to a variety of indirect effects. Some of these are a function of the increased burdens on state governments; others stem from the cities' growing fiscal self-reliance. There are at least three categories of indirect consequences. First, there are the looming fiscal effects of welfare devolution. Second, there will be some shifting of burdens in a variety of functional areas as federal aid reductions force cities to provide services now supported by shared funding. Finally, there are a number of consequences, already evident, for the nature of local politics and political leadership. In particular, political reputation and success increasingly rest on public management skills rather than on the ability to exercise moral suasion on matters of social policy or to promote a racial agenda. These latter effects, already strongly in evidence, are signs of a deep change in the texture of urban politics. . . .

Public Management as Urban Politics

The most important impact on the cities of the shifting balance in the federal arrangement has been to change what could be called the moral tenor of urban politics. In short, good public administration has displaced the urban social and racial agendas that had dominated local politics since the 1960s. By increasingly forcing local leaders to make do with less intergovernmental aid and by making them husband what resources can be raised locally, the New Federal Order has placed a premium on local public management skills and discouraged grand visions of social and racial reform. As an official from the USCM explained, "In the last few years, our attention has shifted from trying to increase aid to cities in any form to trying to streamline it and make it more effective. *Let's talk about how we can make better use of what we' re getting*" (Stanfield 1996, 1802, emphasis added).

Some scholars see this simply as part of a broad national trend toward conservatism, one that, as Sonenshein, Schockman, and DeLeon (1996, 1) put it, reaches down "even into the generally safe Democratic and minority reaches of urban leadership." Others see a more complex phenomenon taking place; for example, Clark (1994, 23) argued that a New Political Culture has emerged in the cities, one that features lifestyle and consumption concerns (especially lower taxes) rather than redistribution and material issues like housing and community development for the disadvantaged. He traced the crystallization of this middle-class urban politics to the decline of federal and state grants, many of which were targeted to poverty clienteles. Thus the contraction of federal aid has not only meant less money for the cities, but less policy guidance.

In a political climate in which the fear of taxpayer revolts is always present and the continuing flight of the middle class is a constant threat to urban health, leaders must first and foremost demonstrate skills in managing scarce resources. Social issues may or may not be present on current mayoral agendas, but if they are a matter of concern, the new mayors make clear that they can best be addressed by better management. This set of management tasks contrasts significantly with the mayoral challenge of the 1960s and 1970s, the dimensions of which were laid out most clearly by the Kerner Commission (National Advisory Commission on Civil Disorders 1968, 298): "Now, as never before, the American city has need for the personal qualities of strong democratic leadership" to address racial polarization, slum clearance, housing, police misconduct, poverty, and unemployment.

The prototype mayors of this earlier period were people like John Lindsay of New York, Jerome Cavanagh of Detroit, Kevin White of Boston, and Richard Lee of New Haven. They excelled in grantsmanship, and they understood how to use city hall as a bully pulpit in their efforts to bridge racial and class divisions. As Sonenshein, Schockman, and DeLeon (1996, 5) described, "Sympathetic to the urban poor, supported by private philanthropy and federal aid, seeking redevelopment, these liberal mayors redefined the mayoral role." In the political climate of the 1990s, however, mayors seek guidance to accomplish their leadership tasks not first by reference to the moral compass of liberal reform but rather from the more neutral market. According to Gurwitt (1994, 26), Mayor Steven Goldsmith of Indianapolis, who exemplifies the new mayoral type, argues that market forces and competition ultimately serve the citizens of his city better than the government monopoly. Mastery of the market, he believes, requires the ingenuity of the entrepreneur and the management skills of a corporate executive officer (CEO).

The new mayors seem at ease with their fiscal self-reliance. The mayor of Nashville, quoted in an editorial in *The Wall Street Journal* ("Cities Discover Federalism" 1995), professed that "it's not all bad [that] Washington is busy extricating itself from . . . responsibility for well-being [in the cities]." Cities now have more freedom to experiment. John Norquist, mayor of Milwaukee, made a similar point about the freeing effects of federal divestment: Federal grants, he says, "are only costing us more money, because they force us to . . . do things we wouldn't otherwise do" (quoted in Osborne 1992, 63).

The new mayors speak the language of modern public management and run their administrations accordingly. They believe in reinvention, innovation, privatization, competition, strategic planning, and productivity improvements. They favor economic development and low taxes, partnership with the business sector, and good housekeeping. As Mayor Norquist reportedly said ("A Genuine New Democrat" 1996), his success is a function of performance, not ideology.

The issue of privatization illustrates how the commitment to the new public management crosses partisan and racial boundaries. Although Mayor Goldsmith, a Republican who once declared that he wanted to become the CEO of Indianapolis, is noted for his leadership in privatizing public services, the same policies have been pursued with equal fervor by Mayor Richard Daley, Jr. of Chicago, a Democrat, and by successive black mayoral administrations in Detroit (see Smith and Leyden 1996; Jackson and Wilson 1996). Daley has been particularly vigorous in contracting formerly public responsibilities to private firms, including, among others, the parking garage at O'Hare Airport, sewer cleaning, office janitorial services, the management of public golf courses, water customer billing,

abandoned automobile collection, parking ticket enforcement, and tree stump removal.

The change in the moral tenor of urban politics is perhaps nowhere more evident than in the cities governed by black mayors. "New black leaders," such as Michael White of Cleveland, Kurt Schmoke of Baltimore, Marc Morial of New Orleans, and others, are characterized as "technopoliticians" in contrast to such "champions of the race" as Coleman Young of Detroit and Marion Barry of Washington (Barras 1996, 20). According to Barras (p. 19), "They have moved beyond rallies and protest marches, replacing talk with action and ushering in a new era of competent, professional stewardship in cities."

Young's successor in Detroit provides an example. Peirce (1993, 3013) wrote that Mayor Dennis Archer's agenda is to fashion a "reinvented" city government "that pays its bills on time," improves its low bond rating, and "picks up garbage on time and keeps the streetlights on all night." Archer, who established close ties to the white business establishment in pursuit of economic development objectives, is contrasted with Young for "rejecting the politics of class and race." Similarly, Barras (1996) compared Bill Campbell, mayor of Atlanta, to the civil rights giants Maynard Jackson and Andrew Young, who preceded him in city hall.[5] Although Campbell is a strong supporter of affirmative action, he reportedly sees himself

> as the vanguard of a new generation of black leaders who embrace a less conspicuous brand of racial politics. . . . His agenda is less about the fight for black empowerment than about paving potholes, encouraging job growth, making neighborhoods safer and building downtown housing. (Sack 1996)

Two decades ago, the social agendas of both black and white mayors captured the attention of the news media and urban observers, but today, the public spotlight is on the new public managers. Eggers (1993) claimed that "America's boldest mayors" were Edward Rendell of Philadelphia, Milwaukee's Norquist, and Indianapolis's Goldsmith. What was bold about these urban leaders was their management initiatives: Rendell's Private Sector Task Force on Management and Productivity, which saved the city more than $150 million; Norquist's strategic budget process; and Goldsmith's introduction of competitive bidding between city service providers and private firms.

Leadership as public management is what urban electorates apparently want in this age of local fiscal self-reliance. In fact, America's boldest mayors hardly stand out from their colleagues in other cities. Mayor Richard Riordan of Los Angeles, a businessman turned politician, runs his city in the style of a CEO—nonideological, managerial, eschewing the "arts of political leadership and public appeals" (Sonenshein, Schockman, and DeLeon 1996, 15). Even Rudolph Giuliani of New York, an aggressive and brash former public prosecutor, came to office promising to "reinvent" city government by cutting and streamlining its massive size (Gurwitt 1995, 23).

The New Federal Order Brings New City Limits

In the New Federal Order, the fiscal links between Washington and the cities have become significantly attenuated. More than at any time since the early Great Society years, city governments can spend only what they can raise. It is possible to imagine several responses to this local fiscal autonomy. One response is to raise taxes to maintain the array of service responsibilities that people have come to expect. To some modest extent, this is what city governments have done. Beginning in 1982 and continuing through the decade, city governments increased per capita tax revenues to offset rising expenditure burdens (Bahl et al. 1991, Table 7). Another response is to engage vigorously in economic development activities, seeking to raise additional revenues by growing the indigenous tax base. There is strong evidence that this has been done in cities too (Clarke and Gaile 1989).

Another response, ever sensitive to citizen resistance to higher taxes, is to husband the resources that cities control through more careful management strategies characterized by contracting out, strategic planning, downsizing, and reorganizing. There is strong evidence that this, too, has been a major response in the cities to the New Federal Order.

The resultant emergence of a public management agenda in place of a social reform platform—what Sonenshein, Schockman, and DeLeon (1996) called the platform of multiethnic liberalism—might be seen as a narrowing of political vision. In a different light, better, more innovative management of the scarce resources under local control may be seen as simply a realistic response to a fiscal world very different from that of a quarter of a century ago. In a sense, the absence of a growing stream of federal dollars has meant that city political leaders cannot afford, fiscally or politically, to push an agenda of social and racial reform financed by local taxpayers alone. Nor can municipal leaders find much encouragement for defying these realities: Left to confront the great urban racial and economic polarities, few elected officials would be so foolhardy as to risk inevitable failure by initiating solutions based solely on the modest and limited resources that they themselves can raise. It is far easier—and the outcome more certain—to lower taxes, reduce government employment, and fill potholes. City limits have never been more in evidence.

Notes

1. The definition of municipal is somewhat broad. In its analysis, the USCM included Food Stamps, AFDC, Headstart, and National Endowment for the Arts grants, none of which, by any account, would be regarded as particularly municipal in character. But it also included various homeless assistance grants, a broad range of assisted housing programs, mass transit, community policing, and other such programs that have a strong urban component. Prior to 1995, the USCM tracked funding for a mix of specific programs and general categories of programs (see Table 1).

2. Testimony of Secretary of Transportation Federico Peña in the *Reauthorization of ISTEA* hearings before the Committee on Transportation and Infrastructure, U.S. House of Representatives, 2 May 1996.

5. In a national survey of 1,211 black Americans conducted in 1992 for the *Detroit News*, researchers found that 94% of the respondents believed that the people who came to power during the civil rights era were out of touch with the real concerns of ordinary African-Americans. Such leaders continue to cite racism as the most pressing issue facing blacks, but the black citizenry is concerned about crime, employment, and economic prospects (Barras 1996, 19).

References

Advisory Commission on Intergovernmental Relations. 1994. *Significant features of fiscal federalism, 1994.* Vol. 2. Washington, DC: Government Printing Office.

Bahl, R., J. Martinez, D. Sjoquist, and L. Williams. 1991. The fiscal conditions of U.S. cities at the beginning of the 1990s. Paper presented at the Urban Institute Conference on Big City Governance and Fiscal Choices, Southern California University, Los Angeles, June.

Barras, J. R. 1996. From symbolism to substance: The rise of America's new generation of black political leaders. *New Democrat* 8 (November–December): 19–22.

Burke, V. 1996. *New welfare law: Comparison of the new block grant program with Aid to Families with Dependent Children.* Congressional Research Service Report to Congress, 26 August.

Chernick, H., and A. Reschovsky. 1997. Urban fiscal problems: Coordinating actions among governments. In *The urban crisis: Linking research to action,* edited by B. Weisbrod and J. Worthy, 131–76. Evanston, IL: Northwestern Univ. Press.

Cities discover federalism. 1995. *The Wall Street Journal,* 8 December.

Clark, T. N. 1994. Race and class versus the New Political Culture. In *Urban Innovation,* edited by T. N. Clark, 21–78. Thousand Oaks, CA: Sage.

Clarke, S., and G. Gaile. 1989. Moving toward entrepreneurial economic development policies: Opportunities and barriers. *Policy Studies Journal* 17 (spring): 574–98.

Eggers, W. D. 1993. City lights: America's boldest mayors. *Policy Review* (summer): 67–74.

Gurwitt, R. 1994. Indianapolis and the Republican future. *Governing* 7 (February): 24–28.

———1995. The trials of Rudy Giuliani. *Governing* 8 (June): 23–27.

———1996. Detroit dresses for business. *Governing* 8 (April): 38–42.

Jackson, C., and D. Wilson. 1996. Service delivery in Detroit, Michigan. Paper presented at the annual meeting of the Midwest Political Science Association, Chicago, IL, April.

Ladd, H. 1994. Big-city finances. In *Big-city politics, governance, and fiscal constraints,* edited by G. Peterson, 201–66. Washington, DC: Urban Institute.

National Advisory Commission on Civil Disorders. 1968. *Report of the National Advisory Commission on Civil Disorders.* New York: Bantam.

Osborne, D. 1992. John Norquist and the Milwaukee experiment. *Governing* 5 (November): 63.

Peirce, N. 1993. Motor City's "Mayor Realtor." *National Journal,* 18 December, 3013.

Rapp, D. 1994. A program for Billy Yeager. *Governing* 7 (July): 80.

Sack, K. 1996. Mayor finds old issue emerging in new way. *The New York Times,* 15 July.

Smith, D., and K. Leyden. 1996. Exploring the political dimension of privatization: A tale of two cities. Paper presented at the annual meeting of the Midwest Political Science Association, Chicago, IL, April.

Sonenshein, R., E. Schockman, and R. DeLeon. 1996. Urban conservatism in an age of diversity. Paper presented at the 1996 annual meeting of the Western Political Science Association, San Francisco, California, March.

Stanfield, R. 1996. Mayors are the soul of the new machine. *National Journal* 28 (24 August): 1801–1802.

Stegman, M. 1996. Speech presented at Rutgers University, Princeton, NJ, 28 February.

U.S. Conference of Mayors (USCM). 1994. *The federal budget and the cities.* Washington, DC: Government Printing Office.

———1995–1997. Funding levels for key municipal programs. Annual releases. Washington, DC: Author.

U.S. Government Accounting Office. 1996. *Community development: Status of urban empowerment zones.* Report to the chair of the Subcommittee on Human Resources and Intergovernmental Relations, Committee on Government Reform and Oversight, House of Representatives, Washington, DC, December.

Wallin, B. 1996. Federal retrenchment and state-local response: Lessons from the past. Paper presented at the annual meeting of the American Political Science Association, San Francisco, 30 August.

Weir, M. 1996. Big cities confront the New Federalism. Paper presented at Columbia University, New York, 12 April.

9-3 "Can Cities Escape Political Isolation?"

Karen M. Paget

The American Prospect

In the past three decades, most cities outside the Sunbelt have experienced economic contraction, population decline, and increasing concentrations of poverty. For some, like Detroit, the descent has been catastrophic. Dozens of smaller, once vibrant manufacturing and commercial cities like Newark, Cleveland, Buffalo, and St. Louis face similar conditions. Three decades after the wave of urban conflagrations, countless neighborhoods that once housed a productive lower middle class still look as if 1968 happened yesterday. Others, such as New York, Chicago, and Los Angeles, tell tales of two cities—glittering economic resurgence coexisting with deepening deprivation.

The loss of good blue-collar jobs, the flight of the middle class to suburbia, and the urban concentration of minorities and the poor are not a new story. What is relatively new, however, is the political isolation of cities and a related decline in federal and state aid. Public policy once recognized that cities faced a terrible mismatch between local resources and local need. But cities today have more expensive social problems, a stressed local tax base, and less intergovernmental help. "The contraction of aid has been so dramatic that Washington's loss of interest in urban affairs is one of the signal stories of the great transformation to the New Federal Order," says urban scholar Peter Eisinger of the University of Wisconsin's Robert M. La Follette Institute of Public Affairs.

This new reality reflects the conjuncture of several factors. The bipartisan commitment to budge balance, coupled with an aversion to raising taxes, has constrained federal outlay across the board. Within this general climate of fiscal scarcity, the sanctity of Social Security and the bipartisan collusion to avoid cutting defense have imposed disproportionate cuts on the discretionary portion of the budget, which includes urban aid. In this zero-sum game, as a National League of Cities analysis observes, the reduced funds flowing to cities go into a local "shark tank where they will compete directly against each other—the growth in any one program important to cities will only come at the expense of another."

The fiscal isolation of cities also reflects a political deterioration. Many older suburbs, as well as rural small towns, face similar economic and social problems. But where cities were once central to a broader coalition that believed in social remediation through public outlay—whether for rural development or urban antipoverty—cities are now increasingly on their own.

Is there any prospect for reversing these trends, or are cities doomed to go it alone for the foreseeable future? Why have city voices been so muted politically, even among Democrats who rely on urban voters? Can one imagine the revival of a public spending coalition that would unite voters from cities, less affluent suburbs, and needy rural areas? Or is this strategy doomed by the politics of budget balance?

A great urban awakening occurred in the 1960s. Intergovernmental aid, which previously had favored suburbs and rural development, began rising—and flowing increasingly to cities. With the War on Poverty and the Great Society, federal policy sought to compensate for the disparity between urban problems and urban resources. Though Richard Nixon's New Federalism changed the form of the funding to block grants often funneled through states, the stream of federal money continued.

According to the Advisory Commission on Intergovernmental Relations (ACIR), an immensely useful research body crippled by the Reagan administration in the mid-1980s, in 1957 cities at the center of metro areas got just 19 percent of their total expenditures from intergovernmental aid, compared to 26 percent for suburban and rural communities in the same metro areas. By 1970, intergovernmental aid had increased dramatically to 31 percent for cities and 33 percent for adjacent communities. By the peak in 1977, center cities were depending on federal and state aid for fully 44 percent of their outlays, outpacing nonurban areas, which were getting 41 percent.

State governments also became more conscious of the need to redistribute resources to fiscally stressed cities. Frank Mauro, director of the Fiscal Policy Institute near Albany, recalls the successful 1969 campaign waged by New York City Mayor John Lindsay and five upstate mayors to alter formulas that had biased state education aid against urban areas. The mayors' success in achieving formula changes has been gradually reversed in the last two decades, first by changing the aid criteria in ways detrimental to cities, and then by outright cuts. "What was understood so much better then [in the 1960s] was that there was a mismatch between resources and needs, and that the higher level of government had the broadest tax base," Mauro says.

Defining Devolution Down

Since the late 1970s, there has been a sharp reversal. Both the amount of intergovernmental aid and the share going to center cities have declined. Aggregate data comparable to the ACIR's earlier series are not available, since ACIR scaled back its publications during the 1980s before finally being effectively eliminated at the end of fiscal year 1996. . . .

According to a study by the U.S. Conference of Mayors, between 1981 and 1993 funding of community development block grants, urban development action grants, general revenue sharing, mass transit aid, employment, and the various programs of the Economic Development Administration fell by a total of 66.3 percent in real dollar terms. During nearly two decades of federal disinvestment, state aid to cities has also declined. Economists Howard Chernick of Hunter College and Andrew Reschovsky of the University of Wisconsin at Madison estimate that state aid to local government, as a portion of local revenues, dropped from 25.4 percent to 21.2 percent of local revenues between 1997 and 1992.

"Devolution," in Republican hands, has not just meant giving lower levels of government greater responsibility, as Nixon's New Federalism did, but a dramatic cut in resources. Richard Nathan, a longtime scholar of federalism, observes that today's proposals stand the original principles of devolution of program responsibility on their head. In a 1996 speech to California legislators, Nathan noted that Nixon's New Federalism was based on "the theory that income transfer programs should be centralized and other programs should be convened into block grants."

Nixon's proposed family assistance program would have had the federal government take over welfare. In health care, Nixon proposed requiring employers to provide insurance to their employees. Even Ronald Reagan's proposals partly reflected similar principles. Reagan's proposed "swap" would have had the federal government take over Medicaid and the states take over Aid to Families with Dependent Children. Thus, Republicans as well as Democrats once recognized that a state or local tax base was insufficient to provide necessary social supports to its citizenry, and that only the federal government was large enough to raise and redistribute adequate resources.

Falling Aid, Rising Need

If these cuts in aid to cities had occurred against a backdrop of broadly rising prosperity, they would be less painful. But in the past two decades, poverty has become more concentrated and more urban. The Annie E. Casey Foundation's recent report, "City Kids Count," assessed how children were faring in the nation's 50 largest cities. Using ten key indicators, ranging from low birth weight to school dropout rates and unemployment figures, the report found: "For every measure the average value for the 50 cities shows that kids living in large cities are more likely to be worse off than kids in the nation as a whole" and that poverty rates for children in cities are increasing disproportionately.

"Between 1969 and 1989, the child poverty rate in the 50 largest cities increased from 18 to 27 percent, while the national child poverty rate grew from 15 to 18 percent," the foundation reported. The percentage of children living in distressed neighborhoods in the 50 largest cities increased between 1970 and 1990 from 3 percent to 17 percent. These averages understate the condition of the most distressed cities. For instance, the percentage of children under age 15 living in Detroit's distressed neighborhoods increased from 3 percent in 1970 to 37 percent in 1980 to 62 percent in 1990. Several cities, including Buffalo, Cleveland, and St. Louis, now have 40 percent or more of children under 15 living in distressed neighborhoods. Twenty years earlier, these percentages were all 10 percent or less.

The decline in federal housing aid illustrates how shifts in federal spending patterns compound urban poverty. Since the 1930s, Washington has invested in housing for the poor, either directly with construction grants or through mortgage interest subsidies, and more recently with vouchers. This policy had bipartisan support, acknowledging that poor households, especially in cities where real estate is costly, simply cannot afford market rentals. Even the Reagan administration approved an average of 80,000 new subsidized housing units annually. Few if any new subsidized housing units are included in the current budget, and Washington is actually shedding subsidized units as old mortgages are paid off and public housing projects are downsized.

These budget figures do not take into account the level of unmet need. The number of affordable housing units—defined as a unit that a low-income household can afford without spending more than 30 percent of its income on rent—is shrinking nationwide, while needs are increasing. Using 1993 Housing and Urban Development (HUD) data, the Center on Budget and Policy Priorities estimates there is currently an affordable housing gap of approximately five million units. Comparable 1970 HUD data showed roughly 700,000 units in excess of low-income need.

There is often an important, interactive relationship between two or more federal programs. For instance, ending "welfare as we know it" will end the ability for some unknown number of low-income individuals to pay their rent—just as subsidized housing is becoming more scarce. As welfare reform bites, voluntary agencies dealing with the homeless report huge increases in the number of homeless people seeking shelter.

According to the *Flint* (Michigan) *Journal,* one agency, Love, Inc., reported a 44 percent rise in the number of people seeking food or clothing between July 1996 and July 1997 despite a generally improving economy. Since cities house a disproportionate number of welfare recipients, they will experience most of these multiple effects, all of which make cascading claims on city budgets.

Lost Political Clout

Disinvestment trends in the face of growing poverty are not simply the consequence of scarce resources. They reflect a steady loss of power by cities, in both Congress and state legislatures. While suburban population growth is an old story, its political effects are relatively recent—and intensifying. Suburbs have become the battleground for swing voters, often at the expense of policies that benefit cities.

Suburbanites were a majority of presidential voters for the first time in 1992. In that election, Clinton narrowly beat George Bush among suburban voters, 41 to 39, with Perot getting 21 percent. In 1996, President Clinton increased his suburban vote, winning 47 percent to Dole's 42 percent and Perot's 9 percent. Fourteen states, including California and Florida, have populations with suburban majorities. In 1996, Clinton won 13 of the 14, and his wins included suburban districts that had not been won by a Democrat since the 1960s.

This capacity to carry the suburbs may be good partisan news for the Democrats, but it carries an ominous message for cities. The grain of truth in the battle for "suburban soccer moms" lies in the gender breakdown for 1996, and illustrates just how critical women voters have become: While suburban men vote 62 percent Republican to 37 percent Democrat, suburban women, by contrast, voted Democratic, 53 to 47. While women have emerged as a key Democratic bloc, the battle for the swing suburban female vote reinforces the general suburban tilt of presidential politics and the impulse to neglect urban voters.

Congressional Democrats, however, ran behind Clinton. In 1994, when they lost control of the House, Democrats lost suburban voters to Republicans, 43 percent to 57 percent. In 1996, a come-back year for Democrats, Clinton won the suburban vote by five points, but House Democrats lost the suburbs by four points, 48 to 52. Democrats may yet be competitive in the suburbs—but at the expense of policies that address cities.

Until the Republicans took control of Congress in 1994, central city representatives, though declining in number, had one huge advantage. Largely Democrats with safe seats and hence seniority, they controlled a disproportionate number of leadership positions. That advantage, of course, depended on Democratic control of Congress, and was wiped out in 1994. Central city representation fell from 30.5 percent to 10.1 percent of committee and subcommittee chairs, while suburban representatives increased their leadership positions from 45.7 to 69.7 percent.

Politically, cities are trapped in a vicious circle. It is a staple of political science literature that lower income voters are less likely to vote because they feel less of a sense of efficacy and have less confidence that politics will make a difference. This dynamic has intensified in recent years. The political system has delivered less to cities—and urban voters have reciprocated. So while cities have lost population, they have lost even more voters. Voting turnout has declined generally in recent years, but most sharply among the poor. New York's fifteenth and sixteenth districts, representing Harlem and the South Bronx, had turnouts of 33 and 29 percent in 1996. A few miles away, the third and fourth districts, on suburban Long Island, had turnouts of 58 and 55 percent. According to Curtis Gans, director of the Committee for the Study of the American Electorate, the sharpest decline of all has occurred among voters earning under $15,000, with a 20 percent decline between 1990 and 1994 alone.

Cities are experiencing a parallel loss of clout in state legislatures as well because of similar population shifts. Prior to the Supreme Court decision in *Baker v. Carr* (1962), which required legislative districts to roughly reflect population size, state legislatures were dominated by rural interests, and cities were vastly underrepresented. While *Baker v. Carr* forced a more equitable distribution of seats, by the time its effect was felt, suburbs, not cities, were the beneficiaries. In many states, the full political impact was delayed, because longtime control of the legislature gave Democrats critical influence in the reapportionment

process. In 1994, Democratic representation in state legislatures was as its lowest level since before *Baker v. Carr*, and rebounded only slightly in 1996.

Consider Chicago and New York. In 1950, according to Margaret Weir of the Brookings Institution, 69.5 percent of people in the greater Chicago metro area lived in the center city, Chicago. By 1990, that figure had dropped to 31.9. New York City's comparable population share fell from 81.1 percent in 1950 to 63.9 percent in 1990.

"For much of the postwar era," Weir observes, "Chicago was able to exercise power in the state legislature by striking bargains with downstate rural Republicans and Democrats, and the suburbs were generally left out of such deals." While that coalition had been unraveling for awhile, "the final blow was the 1991 redistricting that eliminated the city's advantage in the legislature." After the 1992 elections, the suburbs held the majority of seats in the house, 37 percent, compared to Chicago's 19 percent, and 37 percent in the Senate, compared to Chicago's 15 percent. Suburban representatives immediately exercised their muscle by denying Chicago a major economic development project and by slashing general welfare assistance for the urban poor, 80 percent of whom lived (in 1992) in Chicago.

Likewise, New York City's influence in Albany traditionally relied on the sheer number of city voters. According to Weir, the consequences of New York City's shrinking electorate became evident during Governor Mario Cuomo's tenure. Cuomo "spoke out in favor of the city's interests and occasionally proposed such policies as state takeover of Medicaid and more aid for urban school districts, but . . . was often criticized for not following through in the legislature," which had already, become suburbanized. By contrast, Republican Governor George Pataki, Cuomo's successor, was elected "on a wave of support from upstate voters . . . who were deeply antagonistic to state spending, which they believed favored the city at their expense."

Two reporters for the *Buffalo News*, Sue Schulman and Jerry Zremski, spent months investigating why the upstate cities of Buffalo, Syracuse, Rochester, Niagara Falls, Schenectady, Troy, and Utica were faring so badly. Buffalo typifies the dynamics of urban fiscal and political decline. Buffalo has had massive population loss (46 percent since 1950), accompanied by a loss of federal and state aid. Federal aid dropped from 26 percent of the city's budget in 1980 to 14 percent in 1995. In the same period, state aid dropped from 24 percent to 18 percent. Buffalo is so broke that the city is selling off assets and exploring a merger with Erie County.

Schulman and Zremski concluded that reapportionment, which redrew legislative district lines in accordance with suburban population shifts, compounded Buffalo's loss of political influence. Today, only one state legislator out of ten in the state assembly and senate who represent parts of Buffalo represents exclusively the city; the other legislators who represent part of Buffalo have a majority of suburban voters in their districts, and frequently vote against legislation sought by city officials. The *Buffalo News* quotes public Opinion polls indicating suburbanites believe Buffalo "should take care of its own problems."

In a recent paper, political scientists Harold Wolman of the University of Maryland at Baltimore County and Lisa Marckini of Wayne State University examined changes in central city, suburban, and nonmetropolitan congressional districts between 1964 and 1994. The drop in districts with a majority of central city voters, while evident (18 percent), is not nearly so dramatic as the growth of majority suburban districts (228 percent) and the drop in nonmetropolitan seats (54 percent decline).

Wolman and Marckini explored the relationship between place and liberal attitudes and found a consistent correlation, with representatives from cities the most liberal, from suburbs less so, and from nonmetropolitan areas the least. That finding is not unexpected, but Wolman and Marckini also found that place itself made a difference, independent of party affiliation or other factors: "Something about representing a central city, apart from the actual constituency characteristics of the district and party affiliation, had a discernible impact on voting."

The Search for Allies

There are essentially two available possible strategies for reversing these trends: either the development of new forms of regionalism, which would broaden cities' fiscal and political bases, or the revival of even broader coalition politics. David Rusk, former mayor of Albuquerque, has written a provocative book, *Cities without Suburbs*, in which he argues that "the real city is the total metropolitan area—city and suburb." He classifies American cities into two categories: elastic and inelastic. Elastic cities either have vacant land to develop within their city limits or can expand by annexing adjacent land. Inelastic cities can do neither. Thus, elastic cities can capture some of the regional growth that occurs beyond their boundaries, while inelastic cities mainly reap the social costs.

Inelastic cities, Rusk reports, have everything from greater concentrations of poverty, more segregation, and greater urban-suburban income gaps, to lower bond ratings. Inelastic cities, unable to grow, do not just not remain static; they "start shrinking," losing their people, tax base, and fiscal capacity. Inelastic cities lacking development land, or amenities to attract or renew a middle class, lose most of their middle class to adjacent suburbs. Thus, the city of Detroit is in near-terminal decline, while surrounding suburbs are healthy and even affluent.

Rusk identified 24 cities as having "passed the point of no return," those with major population loss (20 percent or more), a disproportionate minority population (typically 30 percent or more), and average income levels of less than 70 percent of suburban income levels. These cities simply cannot "escape the grip of ghetto poverty solely by their own efforts." Further, he argues, "no city past the point of no return has ever closed the economic gap with its suburbs by as much as a single percentage point." Yet many of these poorest cities are surrounded by some of the wealthiest suburbs. Therefore, regional economic development is an insufficient strategy to help these cities.

Rusk advocates metropolitan or regional solutions as the key to coping with dwindling growth, diminished fiscal capacity, and growing concentrations of poverty. If cities can annex suburbs, as New York and Boston did around the turn of the last century—or make an equivalent claim on tax base and economic resources—then the fruits of growth can be distributed more evenly. While a few cities, such as Indianapolis, have recently succeeded in annexing suburbs, most suburbs neither wish to be annexed nor to share their tax base in other ways. Commuter taxes and other proposals to allow cities to capture suburban tax bases are mostly political nonstarters. The more that suburbs become politically ascendant, the less chance such proposals have.

Another strategy has been proposed by Myron Orfield, an urban planner and state legislator from Minnesota. Orfield is a leading proponent of metropolitan government, having sponsored and passed legislation that yokes together the fate of center cities and suburbs. Until a decade ago, Orfield writes in his book, *Metropolitics: A Regional Agenda for Community and Stability*, the Twin Cities were thought to be "immune to urban decline, inner-suburban decay, urban sprawl—and the polarization that has devastated and divided older, larger regions." But, as the 1980s unfolded, all the patterns that describe Chicago, Detroit, and Milwaukee developed in Minneapolis-St. Paul. Orfield says education is always a bellwether of a downward spiral. Between 1982 and 1994, the Twin Cities' percentage of children on free or reduced-cost lunch went from 33 percent to 52 percent. School enrollment went from 34 percent to 59 percent minority, and "both central cities lost one-third of their pre-school white children." Crime rates grew, including a 1995 murder rate that was "higher than New York City."

Concluding that there was no "federal urban policy left," Orfield introduced legislation to give greater taxing capacity to a previously created Metropolitan Council. Through an ingenious use of mapping, Orfield showed fellow legislators a geographical distribution of social and economic problems, including the increased concentrations of poverty and racial segregation. He also mapped the geographical distribution of state and federal subsidies. Not surprisingly, the maps revealed that those suburbs with the most wealth and resources received significant government subsidies, while many working- and middle-class suburbs, or "inner-ring" suburbs, shared many of the same needs and social problems of the Twin Cities, but had fewer government resources.

Orfield concluded that a regional tax could produce a substantial increase in resources for affordable housing. Again through the use of mapping techniques, he demonstrated that most of the suburbs that ring the Twin Cities (roughly 80 percent) would be net beneficiaries of such a regional tax; that is, they would receive back more than they contributed to a common

pool. Only a handful of the wealthiest suburbs, such as Edina or Eden Prairie, would experience a net loss.

Since 1993, a legislative majority has twice approved Orfield's proposed regional property tax on assessed values over $200,000. The Republican governor, Arne Carlson, vetoed it both times. Whether or not the Orfield-inspired coalition will hold hasn't been tested a third time, and likely won't be until there is a different governor.

National economic studies confirm that the economic health of cities and their suburbs is closely tied together, though casual empiricism displays dynamic suburbs ringing decaying cities. What is important is that Orfield proposes a commonality based on self-interest, not altruism. Politically, a coalition of the central city with inner-ring or less affluent suburbs is the polar opposite of the more typical dynamic where a few central city representatives fight suburban legislators over scarce resources. An Orfield-style coalition broadens the urban base to include needed suburban allies. Orfield is convinced that the potential for new political coalitions is not limited to the peculiarities of the Twin Cities or the progressivism of Minnesota, and is helping to advise Cleveland, Chicago, Philadelphia, and Portland, Oregon. In fact, Orfield says every organizer needs to have the following slogan taped to his or her desk: "It's the older suburbs, stupid."

Some elements of Orfield's overall argument are controversial, especially his contention that inner-city poverty is more pathological because it is so concentrated. And some of his remedies face more political opposition than his proposal for a regional tax. Orfield supports transportation and housing policies that literally move people from the inner city to the suburbs where jobs are going begging. Such plans require dispersing low-income housing throughout the region—just the kind of proposal that draws objections from both sides of the racial divide. Racial and ethnic populations often view with suspicion efforts to break up culturally cohesive neighborhoods, even if poverty-stricken; in some cases, dispersal threatens minority political power. Conversely, white suburbanites remain hostile to an influx of racial minorities.

While states could authorize cities to diversify their tax base, they seldom have granted this authority. Wealthy potential taxpayers can usually find friends in the legislature. In one stunning case, a state legislature withdrew its authorization for a city to tax itself in order to provide for low-income housing, even though state coffers weren't out a penny. Washington state legislators passed legislation that enabled Seattle to impose a real estate tax on property transactions. It was short-lived because realtors and developers, who hate this tax, complained to their legislative friends. City representatives, shy of allies, watched as the state revoked its permission.

New Political Coalitions

American history suggests the basis of a broader coalition politics. For all the difference between urban progressives and rural populists, the basis of their alliance was economic. They expressed a common antagonism against "the interests," who ranged from railroad owners, bankers, and grain dealers to timber and mining corporations. Party alliances, in turn, were backed by the institutional strength of both urban labor and rural farmer's unions, the fullest expression of which is Minnesota's Democratic Farmer-Labor Party (DFL). Throughout the West and Midwest, this alliance produced both progressive Republicans and liberal Democrats, such as Republican George Norris of Nebraska, and Democrats Warren Magnuson of Washington, George McGovern of South Dakota, and Frank Church of Idaho.

Even today, North Dakota's Byron Dorgan, Iowa's Tom Harkin, and Minnesota's Paul Wellstone are beneficiaries of this (albeit now considerably weakened) tradition. What's missing today is the mass organizational base that sent such representatives to Washington (and to state capitals). The rural social underpinning of this political alliance is substantially gone, with the demise of small farmers as a major political force, the weakening of unions, and the reduction of federal outlay as a source of economic development. In its place, Samantha Sanchez, who tracks money in Western states, sees a rise of rural conservative populism ("black helicopter types") often allied with corporate interests such as the "wise use movement" financed by extractive industries to counter environmentalists [see Samantha Sanchez, "How the West Is Won: Astroturf Lobbying and the 'Wise Use' Movement," *TAP*, March–April 1996].

So long as the political problem is narrowly defined as cities versus the suburbs, little progress toward rebuilding political coalitions can be made. But the persistence of rural poverty and the growing diversity of suburbs may contain the seeds of new political alliances. A dramatic example of change in suburban demographics is the election of Loretta Sanchez to the House of Representatives from Orange County, one of the most conservative areas in the country. In 1996, she replaced Robert "B-1 Bomber" Dornan, who, as of this writing, is still protesting her narrow victory.

This review of the growing fiscal and political isolation of cities suggests one more political price of the bipartisan obsession with budget balance and tax reduction. It is hard to imagine a new public spending coalition in which cities share, if public spending itself is off the table. The old spending coalition included outlays that were place-specific (urban renewal, public housing, rural electrification, public works, farm supports) as well for the broad citizenry (Social Security, Medicare.) Some of the latter programs, such as Head Start, Medicaid, and food stamps, were targeted to the poor and hence benefited the urban poor. Public spending, as a function of government, had broad legitimacy, and cities were considered legitimate claimants. The shift in political power to the suburbs now inhibits the role of place-specific remedies.

There are obvious limits to public spending. But other advanced democracies spend at least ten percentage points more of their gross domestic product than the United States does, and with it they purchase a more equitable society. To restore a spending coalition that cares about urban problems, cities and their advocates need to move on all fronts—to pursue the regional strategies commended by people like Orfield, to restore links with coalition partners, and to energize a constituent base.

For the most part, progressive organizations have had their base in central cities, which are now politically isolated. With the exception of environmental and good-government groups, few progressive organizations seriously pursue the suburbs. Beyond regional alliances, any renaissance of advocacy on behalf of cities requires a broader national agenda that renews the legitimacy of public outlays.

9-4 "The Portland Region: Where City and Suburbs Talk to Each Other—and Often Agree"*

Carl Abbott

Housing Policy Debate

Introduction

Portlanders are proud of themselves. Like residents of many other U.S. cities, residents of Portland, OR, can be formidable promoters of their home community. Ask around town and you will learn that Portland is special for its climate ("mild," not rainy), its views of snow-capped Mount Hood, its small-town ambiance and "just folks" style, and its success at fending off many of the problems of urban sprawl and congestion. In this self-satisfied picture of achievement by avoidance, Los Angeles has long been damned, Seattle has sold its soul, and only Portland still treads the straight path to good planning.

Outsiders might freely dismiss these claims as the standard wares of local boosters were they not shared by many well-informed observers around the nation. Portland enjoys a strong reputation in the circles of urban planning and policy as a well-planned and livable metropolitan community. The city and region gained initial attention in the late 1970s and 1980s and have enjoyed a surge of positive commentary in the 1990s. Inspection junkets have become a steady contributor to the Portland tourist economy as journalists try to discover "how Portland does it" (Langdon 1992; see Goldberg 1994 for an example) and civic delegations make the rounds of Portland's leaders in search of lessons for their own cities.

Portland as a Planning Model

The admiration starts at the center. According to its press clippings, Portland is an urban mecca (Ortega 1995) and one of the few large cities in the United States "where it works" ("Town Planning" 1990). Over the past 20 years, it has frequently appeared near the top of urban livability rankings. An informal poll of planning and design experts in 1988 rated Portland's efforts to deal with urban design issues among the best in the United States (Laatz 1988), and the city makes regular appearances on lists of the nation's best-managed cities (McEnery 1994).

At the regional scale, the Portland area is a prime exhibit for innovative institutions in managing metropolitan growth and services. In a burst of institutional creativity in the 1970s, the Oregon legislature crafted a statewide system for mandated land use planning (Abbott and Howe 1993; Knaap and Nelson 1992; Leonard 1983), and the voters of the three core metropolitan counties created an elected regional government now known as Metro (Abbott and Abbott 1991; Nelson 1996). The U.S. Department of Housing and Urban Development (HUD) recently credited regionwide cooperation for supporting a successful transition from traditional manufacturing to a knowledge-based economy (Tripp 1996).

Given this level of attention, it is worth taking a serious look at exactly what other communities might learn from Portland. This article addresses four questions that other cities might ask in considering Portland's reputation and record:

1. What are Portland's major accomplishments?
2. What led to these accomplishments?

3. What are the potential costs associated with compact urban growth in the Portland area?
4. What lessons might other cities draw from the Portland experience?

Analysis of these issues leads to two broad conclusions about the politics of good planning. *What* Portland has accomplished centers on decisions about *urban design and the physical shape* of the central city and its related communities. *How* Portlanders have shaped their cityscape and metroscape has to do most essentially with *politics—with* public values, leadership, the capacity of planning agencies and local governments, and the quality of civic discourse.

To summarize the "what" question, Portland is one of a limited number of U.S. metropolitan areas that measure favorably against the model of good urban form that increasingly dominates the contemporary literature of urban planning and design. As summarized in recent publications (Bank of America 1995; Congress of the New Urbanism 1996; Downs 1994; Rusk 1993), this model embraces several normative prescriptions about the characteristics of a balanced metropolis. First, it assigns high value to the maintenance of strong downtowns in order to nurture cultural vibrancy, promote social cohesion, and support nationally competitive advanced service industries. Closely related is the neotraditional turn in neighborhood planning, which also stresses small-scale planning and mixed land use (Calthorpe 1993; Katz 1994; Kunstler 1993; Langdon 1994). The third goal is tightly knit metropolitan regions. Since the famous report *The Costs of Sprawl* (Real Estate Research Corporation 1974), opponents of urban sprawl have had practical justifications for their argument that the centered metropolis should also be compact. The concentration of urbanization at relatively high density within a contiguous territory and circumscribed satellite centers presumably preserves green spaces and farmland, reduces energy consumption, and keeps infrastructure affordable (Frank 1989; Persky and Wiewel 1996; U.S. Congress 1995).

In exploring the second, or "how," question, an analysis of the ways metropolitan Portland has pursued the goals of centeredness and compactness confirms the truism that planning is a political process.

Good design and planning do not happen simply because they are good ideas. They happen because a community talks itself into putting ideas into action, and because that same community creates an infrastructure of governmental systems and civic institutions to support and implement those decisions. In short, it makes a difference where and how a community talks about its future.

Portland as a Compact Metropolis

What distinguishes Portland-area growth patterns from those elsewhere is the compactness of the city's urban development. Unlike many fast-growing metropolitan areas in the American West—such as Phoenix, Houston, and Las Vegas—Portland is still best understood from the inside out (see table 1). The metropolitan area remains strong at its center, whether the standard is regional economic leadership, cultural creativity, or political clout.

Economic Context

Portland has developed as a regional metropolis for the Pacific Northwest. Historically it grew as a transportation, finance, and wholesaling center with a moderate-sized manufacturing sector turning regional

Table 1	Portland Metropolitan Population, 1950 to 1995

Year	City of Portland	Metropolitan Area*
1950	374,000	705,000
1960	373,000	822,000
1970	382,000	1,007,000
1980	365,000	1,245,000
1990	437,000	1,478,000
1995	498,000	2,024,000

Source: For 1950 to 1990: U.S. Census of Population; for 1995: Center for Population Research and Census, Portland State University.

*Four counties in 1950–80, five-county consolidated metropolitan statistical area in 1990, eight-county consolidated metropolitan statistical area in 1995.

raw materials into foodstuffs, clothing, paper, and wood products. The metropolitan economy added a homegrown electronics industry in the 1960s and boomed in the 1970s. The 1980s, in contrast, began with a severe downturn as a national recession hit the regional timber industry especially hard. Between 1981 and 1985, the metropolitan area lost more residents than it gained through migration.

The economic picture a decade later offered a sharp contrast. The mid-1980s brought a recovery in regional service businesses and a new surge of growth in electronics. The combination of affordable land, available skilled workers, and convenience to California and the Pacific nations made the region very attractive to outside firms. Led by Intel, seven major electronics manufacturers announced plans to locate in or expand to Portland in 1994–95 (Barnett 1995). Between 1983 and 1993, export-oriented manufacturing (primarily electronics) grew by 23,000 jobs in the metropolitan area, and overseas exports soared (Ertel 1996). Whether measured by job growth or unemployment rates, the region outperformed the U.S. economy as a whole every year from 1985 to 1996.

The downside of the boom has been uneven distribution of benefits and downward pressure on wages. In effect, migration of potential workers—attracted by the economy and regional amenities—has outpaced the needs of high-wage manufacturing. As a result, traditionally low-paying personal service jobs grew by 59 percent during the 1983–93 period, twice the rate of export manufacturing jobs. The result has been that real annual income per worker has not recovered from its mid-1980s trough while the demand for housing has increased (Ertel 1996).

Downtown

Metropolitan Portland is anchored by a strong and viable central core, as might be expected in a regional finance and business center. The downtown is walkable and attractive. Visitors to the city nearly always start at the center. *Time* (Henry 1988), the *Atlantic Monthly* (Langdon 1992), *Architecture* (Canty 1986), and the *Los Angeles Times* (Kaplan 1989) have all reported on the strength of the downtown design, the careful conservation of a sense of place, and the enhancement of the downtown with public art. The *New Yorker* pointed to "closely controlled

new building, the carefully monitored rehabilitation of worthy old buildings, [and] the vigorous creation of open space" as key factors in creating a city of "individuality and distinction" (Roueche 1985, 42). Downtown design earned a City Livability Award from the U.S. Conference of Mayors in 1988 and an Award for Urban Excellence from the Bruner Foundation in 1989 (Peirce and Guskind 1993).[1]

Beyond its attractions of place, central Portland has retained economic and institutional dominance in the metropolitan area. The central office core has increased its job total and upgraded average job quality over the past 20 years; the number of jobs in five core census tracts increased from 89,000 in 1980 to 104,000 in 1994. Downtown and adjacent districts claim nearly all the major metropolitan institutions and gathering places: museums (art, history, and science), a performing arts center, several major hospitals, a public university, a medical school, a stadium, a convention center, a new privately funded arena for the Trail Blazers of the National Basketball Association, Pioneer Courthouse Square for political rallies, and Waterfront Park for community festivals.

Business statistics also depict a prosperous downtown. Downtown Portland has an unusually high share of office space within its region. In 1989, it had 66 percent of the class A space in its metropolitan area, second only to downtown Pittsburgh and far above the 40 percent for all large office markets taken together (Hughes, Miller, and Lang 1992). Retailing data are harder to obtain because of a lack of sales tax data. Downtown's share of total area sales is declining, but core retailing remains strong overall. The 1995 vacancy rate for downtown retail space was 4 percent, and the store mix has become increasingly upscale in the 1990s, with Saks Fifth Avenue and Banana Republic arriving and JCPenney and Newberry's leaving.

Inner Ring

Portland lacks the "dead zone" of derelict industrial districts and abandoned neighborhoods that surrounds the high-rise core of many cities. Nearly 40 years ago, Hoover and Vernon (1959) identified the problem of "gray areas" in older cities—the old transitional zones that seemed to be falling out of the real estate market. Since then, most inner-ring districts throughout the United States have followed an up-or-out pattern, in which the only options are gentrification and abandonment.

Portland, however, has seen essentially no abandonment and only scattered gentrification. Many areas have retained old functions and attracted gradual reinvestment. Downtown Portland is bordered by viable residential neighborhoods at several economic scales, by neighborhoods in the making on waterfront industrial and rail-yard sites, and by strong industrial-wholesaling districts.

Several of the industrial-wholesaling districts were incorporated into the Central City Plan of 1988 rather than being excluded as irrelevant to a growing downtown. The Central City Plan identified which areas adjacent to the downtown to appropriate for intensified development for information industries and information workers (Lloyd District and portions of the west bank of the Willamette) and which to stabilize for blue-collar jobs. In effect, the plan recognized that a seaport and regional trade center needs to push both paper and payloads. An innovative industrial sanctuary policy uses a zoning overlay to protect inner manufacturing and warehousing districts from incompatible uses such as big-box retailing. This industrial sanctuary policy is a powerful tool for avoiding the mismatch between the locations of jobs and housing that afflicts many metropolitan areas. In 1994, major employment centers within two miles of downtown added roughly 100,000 jobs to those in the central business district.

Middle Ring

Beyond the inner ring of apartment neighborhoods and industry lie Portland's streetcar suburbs, the residential districts that first developed between 1890 and 1940. In most cases, a third generation of families filled these neighborhoods in the 1970s, 1980s, and 1990s. These neighborhoods support an unusually prosperous set of neighborhood business districts and strong public schools. The public school system that serves the city of Portland enrolls 92 percent of school-age children in its district, and suburban systems enroll even higher percentages. Median Scholastic Aptitude Test scores for the Portland schools compare favorably with statewide figures and exceed national medians.[2] In the face of substantial revenue reductions caused by statewide voter-mandated property tax cuts, there is yet no evidence of middle-class exodus to private schools.

The conservation of older neighborhoods is most striking in the West Hills, a large crescent of upscale houses draped across the steep hills to the west of downtown. Initially opened to residential development by cable cars, the West Hills became Portland's elite district with the advent of family automobiles in the 1910s and 1920s. For three generations, the affluent highlanders of King's Heights, Arlington Heights, Willamette Heights, Portland Heights, and Council Crest have enjoyed views of Mount Hood and 10-minute commutes to downtown offices. A good indicator of social status is education level; in 1990, more than two-thirds of the adult residents (age 25 or older) in the half-dozen neighborhoods that overlook downtown from the west and southwest had college degrees. Protected by elevation from the lower-income residents and mixed uses of the downtown fringe, successful businessmen, ambitious professionals, and heirs of moneyed families have been able to maintain social status and leafy living without needing to flee to suburbia.

Outer Ring

Portland's suburbs have plenty of people (65 percent of those in the primary metropolitan statistical area [PMSAD]), plenty of jobs (45 percent of those in the PMSA), and large stretches of standard postwar cityscapes. Workers leave standard model subdivisions and apartment tracts to battle clogged suburban highways in order to reach jobs in commercial strips and office parks. Power retail stores compete with precast concrete manufacturing boxes and landscaped corporate headquarters for prime acreage. Mile by mile, much of Washington and Clackamas Counties looks like the suburbs of Seattle or Denver.

In contrast to many other metropolitan areas, however, Portland's outer ring lacks metrowide public facilities and concentrated employment centers that rival those of the historic downtown. There is no equivalent to Houston's Galleria—Post Oak district or the Tysons Corner complex in the Virginia suburbs of Washington, DC. Specialists on the multinodal city can identify only one "edge city" (Garreau 1991) or "suburban activity center" (Cervero 1989), and those are flimsy examples at best.[3] Instead, the outer ring of the metropolitan area remains closely tied to the core through a radial highway system and a developing radial rail system.

Indeed, the key structural reason that the Portland suburbs remain supplementary employment and consumption arenas is the lack of a suburban beltway. In the 1950s, highway engineers decided to bring the city's first limited-access freeways into the center of the city and connect them with a tight freeway loop that hugged the edges of the central business district. The route took advantage of available or easily acquired rights of way and avoided the steepest parts of the West Hills. The economic consequence was to maintain downtown Portland and its nearby neighborhoods as the most accessible parts of the metropolitan area after the demise of streetcars and interurban railways (Dotterrer 1974). The eastern half of a suburban freeway bypass through the less fashionable side of the metropolitan area did not open until the 1980s. Plans for a southwestern quadrant recently stalled in political traffic, and a northwestern quadrant that would violate parks and open spaces and require multiple bridges across the Columbia River is even less likely.

Minority Neighborhoods

Distant from both the rural South and Latin America, Portland in the 20th century has had small minority populations. Federally identified minorities (Asian, Native American, black, and Hispanic) constituted only 7.8 percent of the population in the three core counties of Multnomah, Washington, and Clackamas in 1980. By 1990, the figure had grown to 11.4 percent, largely as a result of large Asian and Hispanic migration. Portland is thus one of the "whitest" metropolitan areas in the nation.

As late as 1940, Portland's African-American population totaled only 2,000. The black community grew to 20,000 during the shipbuilding boom of World War II and inched upward to 38,000 in 1990—8 percent of the central-city population and only 3 percent of the metropolitan-area population. Most of these new Portlanders replaced European immigrants in working-class neighborhoods on the east side of the Willamette River, where they were physically isolated from downtown Portland (Portland Bureau of Planning 1993). Since 1980, however, the black suburban population has increased more rapidly than the black concentration in north-northeast

Portland, which accounted for roughly 75 percent of the total in 1990.

Partly because of their small numbers, racial groups are relatively well integrated on the neighborhood scale. Portland in 1990 had only six census tracts that were more than 50 percent African American (Abbott 1991a). Hispanics are scattered through lower-income city neighborhoods and live in large numbers on the rural fringe of the metropolitan area. Vietnamese are concentrated on the east side of Portland, while a substantial Korean population has settled in Washington County. The index of dissimilarity was 0.63 for black/nonblack, 0.21 for Asian/non-Asian, and 0.18 for Hispanic/non-Hispanic. . . .

Lessons from Portland

What is there in the Portland story that other communities might want to imitate, and what problems or complications might they seek to avoid? Which aspects of Portland's planning and growth management efforts realistically hold the potential for imitation?

The preceding discussion has repeatedly singled out civic consensus and political will as the forces that have pulled policy fragments into a coherent and effective strategy for Portland metropolitan development. It is clear that most American cities have access to the technical and policy tools they need to maintain centered metropolitan areas. The achievement of a compact and efficient urban form is a solvable issue of the sort that James Q. Wilson wrote about 25 years ago:

> These problems . . . fiscal imbalance, traffic congestion, air pollution, the movement of jobs away from minority groups . . . are susceptible to rather precise formulation and study; alternative ways of coping with them can be conceived and evaluated with a certain rigor; the obstacles to remedial action are primarily political (and to a certain degree economic) . . . what is most important, something *can* be done. (Wilson 1970, 398)

With Wilson's challenge in mind, what advice might other cities draw from Portland's admittedly peculiar history of municipal and regional policy making? Are there useful lessons for Louisville civic leaders, pointers for Pittsburgh politicians?

In looking for generalizable lessons in Portland's history of planning and policy making, it is useful to bear in mind that Portland in the aggregate is not a unique metropolitan area. Many aspects of its economic base, social geography, and demography certainly set it apart from the typical city of the South or Northeast. However, it is not sui generis, despite its "whiteness" and its muted class divisions. In particular, Portland bears many similarities to a number of "middle American" cities, including Indianapolis, Des Moines, Minneapolis–St. Paul, Omaha, Denver, Salt Lake City, Sacramento, and Seattle.

Variability of Housing Tastes

Economic models of housing and land markets tend to project past consumer preferences into the future. We know from other consumption arenas, however, that tastes and behaviors change—that millions of Americans can decide to grind out their cigarettes, or that four-cylinder Hondas can push Roadmasters and Rocket-88s out of American driveways.

Portland in the 1990s shows that tastes for housing are similarly flexible and that suburban large-lot housing fails to satisfy a large segment of the market. Although standard suburban housing has remained plentiful, old neighborhoods with tightly packed houses have also become hot spots. New row houses, small-lot subdivisions, and upscale downtown condominiums jump off the market. A series of demonstration projects and market subdivisions in 1995 and 1996 have successfully offered a variety of configurations of individually owned small-lot housing. One example is a suburban development of freestanding houses on 2,500-square-foot lots that have sold out before completion. Another is a demonstration project on a vacant half-block in a middle-income Portland neighborhood. Its 18 row house, courtyard, and duplex units with average floor area of 1,200 square feet sold within months.

Anecdotal evidence from other cities also shows the breadth of the housing market. Many households still prefer freestanding houses on relatively large lots. However, the range of preferences for alternative styles and configurations is more varied than appraisers and bankers are willing to allow, especially as the structure of households becomes more varied. A yet undetermined proportion of home buyers are willing to trade extensive private space for high-quality public space.

UGBs as Planning Tools

UGBs in various forms have become popular solutions to metropolitan planning problems, frequently proposed in tandem with the principles of neotraditional design and the new urbanism. UGBs or their equivalents are found in several state planning systems, such as those in Washington and New Jersey, and have been adopted or advocated for cities as diverse as Boulder, CO, and San Jose, CA. In fast-growing metropolitan areas, they can prevent explosive deconcentration of urban activities. In stagnant regions, they can maintain market focus on areas that are already urbanized and perhaps slow class segregation.

The Portland experience offers several additional suggestions about the use of UGBs. First is the reminder that growth boundaries are long-term commitments, not quick fixes. They work best when they are part of a planning implementation package that includes public transit investment, infill development, and affordable housing strategies. In Oregon, such coordination is formally mandated through a planning program in which growth containment operates in conjunction with efforts to achieve 13 other statewide planning goals.

Like all planning tools, UGBs need to be flexible enough to respond to changing circumstances. In Portland in the mid-1990s, the UGB has become a symbol as well as a tool. Many residents now regard it as a metaphor for the region's ability to control its own future in the face of global market forces. If the idea of a "frozen" UGB becomes a politically untouchable absolute, however, the region will lose adaptability and may invite future problems of congestion or housing affordability.

Value of Incrementalism

Portland has built its particular urban form and its supportive institutions of planning and growth management through a series of small decisions. The decisions and institution building that have shaped the Portland of 1996 had their beginnings in the late 1960s. During these three decades, residents of the Portland area have moved one step at a time, addressing problems in sequence rather than trying for a comprehensive onetime solution to a complex set of concerns. They have also built public institutions incrementally. An example is the evolution of Metro from the Columbia Region Association of Governments (CRAG) in 1966, addition of the Metropolitan Service District (MSD) in 1970, modification of CRAG in 1974, merger of CRAG and MSD into Metro in 1978, and further expansion of Metro's authority and independence in 1992.

Other cities might also think about the value of incremental approaches to growth management. It is common wisdom among community organizers that it is vital to start with small but winnable issues to build community confidence and political momentum before tackling the hard problems. The Portland experience suggests that an analogous approach may be relevant for citywide and regional planning and growth management.

A Habit of Planning

Incremental policy making has allowed Portlanders to develop a habit of planning. Portland's civic community is comfortable and familiar with planning processes, issues, and terminologies. Planning issues are part of the civic discourse and a staple of local news reporting to an extent unusual in other cities. As Department of Land Construction and Development staffer Mitch Rohse puts it, "the ethos or culture of land-use planning has absolutely permeated the population" (Hylton 1995; see also Abbott 1994).

Metropolitan areas frequently take a single well-publicized swing at defining a regional agenda. Examples in recent years have been the Civic Index Project of the National Civic League and newspaper-sponsored reports on metropolitan issues by Neal Peirce. The Portland experience suggests the importance of following such highly visible activities with continued discussion through ongoing newspaper coverage and through conferences, meetings, and specialized publications sponsored by local institutions. These institutions might be urban universities, government agencies, or nonprofit advocacy organizations (such as 1000 Friends of Oregon or the Regional Planning Association of New York).

This conclusion draws support from the experiences of other cities where repeated discussion and

promotion of a set of policy alternatives and the underlying public values have shifted the center of political discourse over time. An example is the gradual acceptance of neighborhood-based growth management in San Francisco after 1975 (DeLeon 1992; McGovern 1993). The appropriate forums and sponsors and the most pressing issues will vary from one metropolitan area to the next, but the principle of gradual and persistent education is constant.

Institutionalizing Good Ideas

The impacts of civic discussion and education can be reinforced by the creation of institutional or organizational homes for good planning ideas, making the procedures of planning and growth management into everyday routines. In 1973, for example, the Oregon legislature followed the Progressive Era tactic of depoliticizing governmental decisions in the interest of "good government" when it placed the state planning system under an independent commission. The Portland area offers other examples of the bureaucratization of good planning, including the regular participation of neighborhood associations in Portland planning decisions (Adler and Blake 1990), the application of design review to downtown development (Abbott 1991b), and the depoliticizing of metropolitan transportation decisions (Edner and Adler 1991).

In the Portland area, planning bureaucracies have brought strong community movements into regular relationships with other interests. They have helped to channel high levels of public concern into accepted procedures designed to implement a community consensus. At best, such procedures equalize access to public decision making and tend to reduce the privileges of wealth. In their turn, the presence of strong municipal and regional institutions for planning and policy formulation facilitates the good-government habit (Lewis 1996).

Coalition Building

The central point of the preceding analysis is the importance of building stable political coalitions for moving a metropolitan regional agenda. Portlanders share a political culture that considers policy alliances and team building to be the normal way of doing public business. Nurtured in nonpartisan political institutions for local government, the Portland style prefers protracted discussion and negotiation to ideological battles and electoral confrontation. At its worst, coalition politics ignores and isolates pockets of dissent in favor of a soft middle ground. At its best, it involves a search for a common public good that transcends the summation of individual and group interests.

As described for metropolitan Portland, city-level coalitions nest within regional coalitions. An important result of Portland's city-level planning initiatives, for example, has been an ability to avoid viewing downtown and neighborhoods as rivals in a zero-sum game. Urban politics nationwide has frequently pitted advocates of neighborhood needs against proponents of downtown development, with both sides fighting for the attention and resources of city hall. Examples of this polarization can be drawn from every part of the country—from Chicago (Suttles 1990) to San Antonio (Abbott 1987), Seattle (Bello 1993), and Los Angeles (Davis 1992). Since the 1960s, in contrast, Portlanders have recognized that the Goldschmidt strategy makes every district within five miles of the central business district into a winner. The city-suburban coalition has a similar basis—a belief that there is enough growth for both city and suburbs to negotiate equitable cuts and to make such potentially explosive issues as fair-share housing politically palatable.

Portland's bias toward centrist coalitions can be framed in the perspectives of urban political theory. In Peterson's terminology (1981), neighborhood and downtown interests unite around a carefully balanced developmental agenda rather than fighting over redistribution of resources. In the terms of Logan and Molotch (1987), downtown and neighborhood interests come together as parts of a mild-mannered growth machine. The same analyses apply to the city-suburban growth management coalition.

It is unlikely that the basis for coalition building will be the same in other metropolitan areas, where different issues may be foremost in the public mind. Another commonly suggested catalyst for assembling a metropolitan coalition, for example, is equitable sharing of city and suburban tax resources (as in the Minneapolis–St. Paul region). In a different community, it might be the creation of political bridges across racial divides. Whatever the issue, the need for long-term commitments to a broad public interest argues strongly for networks of community support that outlast the short-term election cycle. Self-conscious coalitions built on shared visions of a community's future potentially have the necessary staying power.

Conclusion

An appropriate headline to capture the Portland experience would be "City and Suburbs Talk to Each Other—and Often Agree!" The growth management process in Portland in the late 1990s reflects a political culture that values coalition building over electoral confrontation and balances the brokering of economic and political interests with a serious regard for rational argument. Portland's ethos also assumes that it is possible to find common goals and goods (if not necessarily a unitary public interest). Mayor Gussie McRobert of Gresham (the second-largest city in the Portland area) comments, "In Oregon we have a tradition of being able to set aside our individual interest for the broader good of the community" (Hylton 1995, 117). A few years earlier, a prominent economic and civic leader challenged an audience of citizens to hold fast to a "moral obligation to the idea of Oregon" (Abbott 1994, 205). The point is not that Portlanders are saints, but that the political culture allows such statements to be part of the dialogue.

The organization and character of the public realm are thus the key variables that make Portland different. This analysis is not intended to be self-congratulatory. This discussion has made clear that the Portland consensus has significant limits and blind spots. Nevertheless, the experience suggests that the specifics of policy and planning decisions need to be embedded in a "thick" environment of discourse and debate and to be thought through as civic choices by citizens and officials. In concert with recent ideas about social and civic capital (Putnam 1993), these discussions should engage multiple groups and utilize multiple forums—the formal citizen participation process for public agencies, neighborhood associations, civic organizations, and a wide range of issue-advocacy groups.

One of Portland's key lessons is thus less about growth management than about democracy. Its planning debates are about specific goals, but an underlying function has been to build a sense of community and to provide opportunities for exploring common interests. Other metropolitan areas might emulate what is best about Portland by engaging in rich and vigorous democratic discussion about *their* most salient issues—about ethnicity and equity, or economic transition, or fair sharing of public resources.

These suggestions resemble the theoretical work of Habermas (1984) and its adaptation to planning by Forester (1989) and Innes (1995, 1996). Habermas's theory of communicative rationality places reiterative discussion at the center of civic life. Experts learn from citizens and citizens from experts in a continual refining of ideas; the public realm takes on a life and value of its own. The achievement of consensus becomes a valuable and positive product in itself—not a compromise among conflicting interests, but an understanding of common needs and goals. In this light, the Portland experience is ultimately an argument for the value of talk and the power of democracy.

Notes

1. A not surprising reaction to all this good ink is a skeptical recharacterization of downtown Portland as a Disney-like theme park rather than a "real" place (Robert Shibley, quoted in Peirce and Guskind 1993, 80; Bruegmann 1992).

2. Portland median scores (math/verbal) in 1996 were 522/514. Oregon medians were 521/523. U.S. medians were 508/505.

3. Garreau identifies the Beaverton-Tigard-Tualatin triangle and Cervero the 1–5 corridor from Tigard to Wilsonville. These are overlapping areas in the western suburbs.

References

Abbott, Carl. 1987. *The New Urban America: Growth and Politics in Sunbelt Cities*. Rev. ed. Chapel Hill, NC: University of North Carolina Press.

Abbott, Carl. 1991a. *Ethnic Minorities in Portland: A 1990 Census Profile*. Portland, OR: Center for Urban Studies, Portland State University.

Abbott, Carl. 1991b. Urban Design in Portland, Oregon, as Policy and Process, 1960–1989. *Planning Perspectives* 6(1):1–18.

Abbott, Carl. 1994. The Oregon Planning Style. In *Planning the Oregon Way*, ed. Carl Abbott, Deborah Howe, and Sy Adler, 205–26. Corvallis, OR: Oregon State University Press.

Abbott, Carl, and Margery Post Abbott. 1991. *Historical Development of the Metropolitan Service District*. Portland, OR: Metro Home Rule Charter Commission.

Abbott, Carl, and Deborah Howe. 1993. The Politics of Land-Use Law in Oregon: Senate Bill 100, Twenty Years After. *Oregon Historical Quarterly* 94(1):5–35.

Adler, Sy, and Gerald Blake. 1990. The Effects of a Formal Citizen Participation Program on Involvement in the Planning Process: A Case Study of Portland, Oregon. *State and Local Government Review* 22(1):37–43.

Bank of America. 1995. *Beyond Sprawl: Patterns of Growth to Fit the New California*. San Francisco.

Barnett, Jim. 1995. The New Silicon Forest. *Oregonian*, October 1.

Bello, Mark Richard. 1993. Urban Regimes and Downtown Planning in Portland, Oregon, and Seattle, Washington, 1972–1992. Ph.D. dissertation. Portland State University.

Bruegmann, Robert. 1992. New Centers on the Periphery. *Center: A Journal for Architecture in America* 7:25–43.

Calthorpe, Peter. 1993. *The Next American Metropolis: Ecology, Community, and the American Dream*. Princeton, NJ: Princeton Architectural Press.

Canty, Donald. 1986. Portland. Architecture: *The MA Journal* 75(7):32–47.

Cervero, Robert. 1989. *America's Suburban Centers: The Land Use-Transportation Link*. Boston: Unwin Hyman.

Congress of the New Urbanism. 1996. *Charter of the New Urbanism*. World Wide Web page <http://www.arc.miami.edu/cnu/charter.htm> (last modified September 16).

Davis, Mike. 1992. *City of Quartz: Excavating the Future on Los Angeles*. New York: Vintage.

DeLeon, Richard. 1992. *Left Coast City: Progressive Politics in San Francisco, 1975–1991*. Lawrence, KS: University Press of Kansas.

Dotterrer, Steve. 1974. *Cities and Towns. In Space, Style, and Structure: Building in Northwest America*, ed. Thomas Vaughan and Virginia Ferriday, 494–611. Portland, OR: Oregon Historical Society.

Downs, Anthony. 1994. *New Visions for Metropolitan America*. Washington, DC: Brookings Institution.

Edner, Sheldon, and Sy Adler. 1991. *Challenges Confronting Metropolitan Portland's Transportation Regime*. Washington, DC: National Academy Press.

Ertel, Chris. 1996. Revenge of the Baristas: Economic Growth and Income Stagnation in Portland, 1983–1993. *Metroscape*, Spring, pp. 7–12.

Frank, James E. 1989. *The Costs of Alternative Development*. Washington, DC: Urban Land Institute.

Garreau, Joel. 1991. *Edge City: Life on the New Frontier*. New York: Doubleday.

Goldberg, David. 1994. Two Cities, Two Routes to the Future. *Atlanta Constitution*, August 28.

Habermas, Jürgen. 1984. *The Theory of Communicative Action*. Boston: Beacon.

Henry, William A., III. 1988. Portland Offers a Calling Card. *Time*, December 12, p. 88.

Hoover, Edgar, and Raymond Vernon. 1959. *Anatomy of a Metropolis*. Cambridge, MA: Harvard University Press.

Hughes, James W., K. Tyler Miller, and Robert Lang. 1992. *The New Geography of Services and Office Buildings*. New Brunswick, NJ: Center for Urban Policy Research.

Hylton, Thomas. 1995. *Save Our Land, Save Our Towns: A Plan for Pennsylvania*. Harrisburg, PA: RB Books.

Innes, Judith. 1995. Planning Theory's Emerging Paradigm: Communicative Action and Interactive Practice. *Journal of Planning Education and Research* 14(3):128–35.

Innes, Judith. 1996. Planning through Consensus Building: A New View of the Comprehensive Planning Ideal. *Journal of the American Planning Association* 62(4):460–72.

Kaplan, Sam Hall. 1989. Portland Sets Example in Urban Design. *Los Angeles Times*, September 24.

Knaap, Gerrit, and Arthur C. Nelson. 1992. *The Regulated Landscape: Lessons on State Land Use Planning from Oregon*. Cambridge, MA: Lincoln Institute of Land Policy.

Krumholz, Norman, and W. Dennis Keating. 1994. Downtown Plans of the 1980s: The Case for More Equity in the 1990s. *Journal of the American Planning Association* 57(2):136–52.

Kunstler, James Howard. 1993. *The Geography of Nowhere: The Rise and Decline of America's Man-Made Landscape*. New York: Simon and Schuster.

Laatz, Joan. 1988. Urban Experts Like Portland's Style. *Oregonian*, May 6.

Langdon, Philip. 1992. How Portland Does It. *Atlantic Monthly*, November, pp. 134–41.

Langdon, Philip. 1994. *A Better Place to Live*. Amherst, MA: University of Massachusetts Press.

Leonard, R. Jeffrey. 1983. *Managing Oregon's Growth*. Washington, DC: Conservation Foundation.

Lewis, Paul G. 1996. *Shaping Suburbia: How Political Institutions Organize Urban Development*. Pittsburgh: University of Pittsburgh Press.

Logan, John R., and Harvey Molotch. 1987. *Urban Fortunes: The Political Economy of Place*. Berkeley, CA: University of California Press.

McEnery, Tom. 1994. *The New City-State: Change and Renewal in America's Cities*. Niwot, CO: Roberts Rinehart.

McGovern, Stephen. 1993. Transforming the Politics of Downtown Development: A Cultural Analysis of Political Change in American Cities. Ph.D. dissertation. Cornell University.

Nelson, Arthur C. 1996. Portland: The Metropolitan Umbrella. In *Regional Politics*, ed. H. V. Savitch and Ronald K. Vogel, 253–71. Thousand Oaks, CA: Sage.

1000 Friends of Oregon. 1996. *Making the Land Use, Transportation, Air Quality Connection: Vol. 5, Analysis of Alternatives*. Portland, OR.

Ortega, Bob. 1995. Urban Mecca. *Wall Street Journal*, December 26.

Peirce, Neal R., and Robert Guskind. 1993. *Breakthroughs: Re-Creating the American City*. New Brunswick, NJ: Center for Urban Policy Research.

Persky, Joseph, and Wim Wiewel. 1996. Central City and Suburban Development: Who Pays and Who Benefits? Working paper. Great Cities Institute, University of Illinois at Chicago.

Peterson, Paul. 1981. *City Limits*. Chicago: University of Chicago Press.

Portland Bureau of Planning. 1993. *The History of Portland's African American Community*. Portland, OR.

Putnam, Robert (with Robert Leonardi and Raffaella Y. Nanetti). 1993. *Making Democracy Work: Civic Traditions in Modern Italy*. Princeton, NJ: Princeton University Press.

Real Estate Research Corporation. 1974. *The Costs of Sprawl: Environmental and Economic Costs of Alternative Residential Development Patterns at the Urban Fringe*. Washington, DC: U.S. Government Printing Office.

Roueche, Berton. 1985. A New Kind of City. *New Yorker*, October 21, pp. 42–53.

Rusk, David. 1993. *Cities without Suburbs*. Baltimore: Johns Hopkins University Press.

Suttles, Gerald. 1990. *The Man-Made City: The Land Use Confidence Game in Chicago*. Chicago: University of Chicago Press.

Town Planning: Where It Works. 1990. *Economist*, September≈1, pp. 24–25.

Tripp, Julie. 1996. Feds Cite Portland as Example of Vibrant Economy. *Oregonian*, October 16.

U.S. Congress, Office of Technology Assessment. 1995. *The Technological Reshaping of Metropolitan America*. Washington, DC: U.S. Government Printing Office.

Wilson, James Q. 1970. Urban Problems in Perspective. In *The Metropolitan Enigma*, ed. James Q. Wilson, 386–409. New York: Anchor.

Conclusion

Public Policy Applications: Federal Policy toward Cities

Policy Then

At the depth of the urban crisis in the 1970s, when the federal government was most needed to help cities manage the debilitating effects of suburbanization, deindustrialization, and racial conflict, Washington, D.C., retreated from any substantial commitment to urban revitalization. Nothing symbolized the federal government's stance better than President Gerald Ford's reaction to New York City's desperate plea for assistance at the peak of its fiscal crisis in 1975. In a speech before the National Press Club on October 29, Ford vowed to veto any fiscal relief package passed by Congress to prevent the city's defaulting on its debt. The president blamed the city's government for years of profligate spending and insisted that it put its own house in order. At that point, bankruptcy seemed inevitable. The memorable headline in the *New York Daily News* the next day caught the feeling of despair that pervaded the city.

Behind the scenes, however, leaders in New York's political and financial sectors stepped up their pressure on the federal government, warning of disastrous consequences if the nation's largest city were to default. Two months after Ford's speech, and just days before the city intended to file for bankruptcy, the president changed his mind and agreed to a plan providing $2.3 billion in federal funds. Bankruptcy was avoided and the city implemented an austerity program that in time produced consistently balanced budgets.

Nevertheless, New Yorkers never forgot Ford's initial decision in their hour of need. In the 1976 presidential election, Democratic challenger Jimmy Carter narrowly defeated Ford, aided in no small measure by his winning New York's 41 electoral votes. Ford always believed that the *Daily News* headline cost him the election.

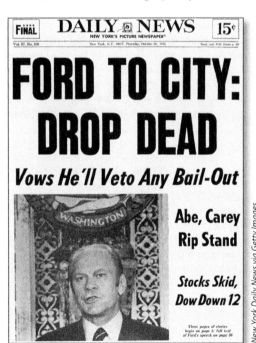

New York Daily News *headline, October 30, 1975*

Policy Now

Few U.S. cities currently confront the gloomy prospects of bankruptcy and yet most continue to struggle with intractable problems such as concentrated poverty, homelessness, underfunded and overstressed schools, crumbling infrastructure, and violent crime. Local governments seem incapable of remedying the inner-city blight that has scarred urban landscapes for decades. The federal government today demonstrates virtually no inclination to lead any effort to revitalize such long-neglected areas. Even Barack Obama, the first president from a city in generations and a former community organizer from the south side of Chicago, has been surprisingly reticent about calling attention to the plight of inner-city neighborhoods and proposing remedial policies. His primary policy initiatives have not targeted cities per se, although some, such as the Affordable Care Act's provision of health insurance to millions of previously uninsured citizens, may disproportionately benefit urban (and rural) residents.

For the most recent federal policy aimed at urban revitalization, it is necessary to go back to the Reagan era.

Inspired by a program that originated in Margaret Thatcher's Great Britain, the concept of enterprise zones involved designating a distressed area within a city and then minimizing the role of government there by slashing taxes and regulations in an attempt to entice business investment. The conservative notion of shrinking the presence of government so that economic activity would blossom and thereby benefit local residents appealed to the Reagan administration. A dubious Congress controlled in part by Democrats blocked federal legislation, but enterprise zones were adopted by many state and local governments eager to try any new approach to aid inner-city neighborhoods. In general, the programs did not work as intended. Tax and regulatory relief were not sufficient incentives to motivate businesses to relocate to zones characterized by high crime rates, decaying infrastructure, and unskilled workers.

However, a substantially revised form of the program was implemented under President Bill Clinton under the name "empowerment zones." The renaming was not just a cosmetic change. It was meant to signify the federal government's desire to create a program that empowered local residents to formulate strategic plans to improve their own neighborhoods. Empowerment zones also envisioned a broader role for government by making the zones more attractive to businesses through expanded public investment in infrastructure repair, law enforcement, job training, and day care, along with greater use of the tax code to encourage incoming firms to hire locally.

Under the Clinton administration, a total of nine empowerment zones were established, six of which were located in large cities. Each zone received $100 million over a ten-year period for grants and loans and an additional $250 million over ten years to finance tax incentives to lure business investment. Some cities made headway in promoting economic growth in their zones while others struggled to meet unreasonably elevated expectations. The key drawback of the empowerment zone program was its limited scope. Only a handful of neighborhoods within a half dozen cities benefited, leaving myriad inner-city communities throughout the country untouched.

Additional Resources

Robert Bruegmann, *Sprawl: A Compact History* (Chicago: University of Chicago Press, 2005).

Congress for the New Urbanism. A prominent organization founded by planners committed to creating compact, pedestrian-friendly, mixed-use, and sustainable communities with lively civic spaces. www.cnu.org.

Department of Housing and Urban Development, Office of Policy Development and Research. A source of abundant information on housing and urban development. www.huduser.org.

Peter Gordon and Harry W. Richardson, "Are Compact Cities a Desirable Planning Goal?" *Journal of the American Planning Association*, Winter 1997.

Bruce Katz, "The Metropolitan Moment," *The Atlantic: Cities*, September 15, 2011. www.theatlanticcities.com/jobs-and-economy/2011/09/metropolitan-moment/108.

Nicholas Lemann, "The Myth of Community Development," *The New York Times Magazine*, January 9, 1994.

Michael Porter, "The Competitive Advantage of the Inner City," *Harvard Business Review*, May/June 1995.

Michael J. Rich and Robert P. Stoker, *Collaborative Governance for Urban Revitalization: Lessons for Empowerment Zones* (Ithaca, NY: Cornell University Press, 2014).

Gregory D. Squires, "Urban Sprawl and the Uneven Development of Metropolitan America," in *Urban Sprawl: Causes, Consequences and Policy Responses*, ed. Gregory D. Squires (Washington, DC: Urban Institute Press, 2002).

Discussion Questions

1. Does it make sense to have place-based revitalization programs that target cities? In other words, should there be a national urban policy to revitalize cities? Or, alternatively, should there just be policies to help individuals in need wherever they happen to live?

2. Why has President Obama been so reluctant to highlight urban problems and propose appropriate policies, especially given his ties to Chicago and his experience organizing distressed neighborhoods in that city after he graduated from law school?

3. Is there any reason to believe that future presidents might be more willing to promote urban revitalization?

4. Have recent demographic changes altered the potential political clout of cities in American politics?

5. How has regional planning to limit suburban sprawl affected central cities?

6. How have changing conditions in metropolitan areas increased the likelihood of intergovernmental cooperation in addressing regional problems?

Chapter 10

Grassroots Activism

Introduction

With the quality of life in American cities steadily deteriorating during the middle decades of the twentieth century due to suburbanization, deindustrialization, racial strife, and declining public services, it is hardly surprising that many urban residents had become disgruntled. The most visible and dramatic manifestation of anger came from poor blacks and Latinos in inner-city neighborhoods each summer during the mid-1960s. Fed up with years of police brutality, discriminatory delivery of city services, and oppressive poverty, they rioted in the streets of their own neighborhoods with deadly and destructive consequences.[1]

Other urban groups also had ample reason to feel frustrated and angry. White, working-class residents complained about shrinking job opportunities and wages, as well as declining schools, poorly maintained parks and playgrounds, and unsafe streets. They criticized new federal programs that seemed to benefit blacks and Latinos while ignoring them. And they condemned federal judges who ordered mandatory busing to desegregate public schools, especially when that meant busing their children to schools in distant neighborhoods. From the vantage point of blue-collar ethnics, their neighborhoods were under siege, and they blamed elites in city hall, the downtown business leaders, federal judges, and bureaucrats in Washington, D.C., for their predicament.[2]

For too long, residents in a wide variety of urban neighborhoods had come to feel alienated and disempowered. By the 1960s and 1970s, many resolved to take matters into their own hands, not by violent riots but through a relatively new strategy of community organizing. The core idea was to encourage disenchanted individuals and groups to come together around shared grievances and utilize their collective power to force city hall to pay attention and take corrective action.

The most influential practitioner of community organizing was a young labor activist from the south side of Chicago who had decided in the late 1930s that certain concepts and tactics that he had learned as a union organizer might be effectively applied to empower residents, small-business owners, and other stakeholders of urban neighborhoods. Saul Alinsky succeeded in organizing the Back of the Yards neighborhood, a working-class community composed mainly of Eastern European immigrants who worked in nearby slaughterhouses for paltry wages amid squalid conditions. The Back of the Yards Neighborhood Council managed to wring concessions from the factory owners and obtain new benefits for the community from the city government. Alinsky was not shy about sharing his thoughts on empowering community residents and disseminating a distinctive model of community organizing. That model emphasized the importance of professional organizers who would enter communities that had been neglected and identify indigenous leaders capable of building a broad-based, inclusive, community organization committed to gaining power. The organization would be prepared to engage in any tactics necessary to win its battles short of violence. For Alinsky, the end justified the means, and he urged organizations to be creative, aggressive, and confrontational in challenging power brokers. He also advised against imposing any particular political ideology on residents. Instead, Alinsky stressed the need to let the people decide on their goals, interests, strategies, and tactics. A fervent democrat, he had confidence that empowering the people would lead to positive change. Alinsky presents his provocative views on community organizing in **Reading 10-1**, which is a series of excerpts from his influential book *Reveille for Radicals*.[3]

Community organizing was hardly a panacea for urban decline. Alinsky's own Back of the Yards Neighborhood Council remained a potent organization, but it evolved into a deeply conservative, even reactionary, entity whose empowered white members were primarily intent on protecting their neighborhood from intrusive outsiders, namely black families who wished to move in. Critics argued that the Alinsky model was flawed. Some charged that it bred an enclave mentality among local residents and thus unwittingly fostered racist and xenophobic attitudes and behavior. Others contended that Alinsky's unconditional faith in the judgment of ordinary people was naive, that perhaps professional organizers needed to provide some form of political education such as the desirability of racial inclusion and cooperation.[4]

Although he was dismayed by the racism exhibited by the Back of the Yards Neighborhood Council, Alinsky continued to organize other communities of varied racial and ethnic identities in Chicago and other cities and with considerable success. After his death in 1974, his followers adopted his model of community organizing and applied it in new contexts. In **Reading 10-2**, Mark R. Warren describes how a neo-Alinsky model was developed by an organization called Communities Organized for Public Service in San Antonio, Texas, that emphasized faith-based organizing in Latino communities where the Catholic Church was a major presence, and that approach quickly spread throughout the southwestern United States.[5]

Others excited about the potential of grassroots organizing in cities turned to other models altogether. For some, Alinsky's confrontational approach was problematic because some troubled neighborhoods preferred to avoid the risk of burning bridges with city hall. Wishing to maintain working relationships with city officials who had the power to reward and punish entire communities, they opted for more cooperative forms of organizing.[6] Other community leaders embraced the organizing model of the Brazilian educator and activist Paulo Freire, who preached the value of individual growth and leadership development through emotional and cultural exchange.[7] In sum, grassroots activists in cities have adopted a broad range of organizing models to mobilize their communities and to fight for change in specific policy arenas such as housing and education.[8]

Community organizing has been an important strategy in enabling previously disempowered urban groups to fight for their interests in trying times and places. It should be noted, however, that many scholars see community organizing as a useful but limited tool in effecting change. While mobilizing residents and other community groups may work to bring about policy changes that directly affect that community, such changes tend to be on a fairly small scale. To address the root causes of deep-seated urban problems requires action at higher levels of government and mass mobilization well beyond the borders of any one urban neighborhood.[9] The best of community organizers, whether associated with Alinsky, Freire, or others, recognize the need to form coalitions across cities, regions, and nations, and some organizations, such as the Industrial Areas Foundation, the Association of Community Organizations for Reform Now, or Pacific Institute of Community Organizing, have endeavored to do so.[10] Yet most maintain that organizing at the community level is an essential starting point for engaging citizens.

Another constraint on community-based activism involves city leaders who are wary of challenges to their authority from the grassroots. Such leaders believe that they have an interest in containing community-based mobilization, or better yet, preventing it from surfacing in the first place. One scholar, J. Phillip Thompson, has written that "the dirty little secret" of urban politics is that even liberal mayors avoid promoting popular empowerment of disengaged residents for fear of sparking organized opposition to their leadership.[11] In **Reading 10-3**, Michael B. Katz explores various "techniques" employed by elites to pacify populations who might otherwise be expected to vent their anger through community mobilization, street protest, and even violence.[12]

Finally, for city residents who have become deeply disenchanted with the urban condition, one more option exists in addition to community organizing or political protest. Apart from voicing their dissatisfaction, they may also register their discontent by exiting the city.[13] The exit option may take two forms. First, urban residents and businesses may simply move out of the city, much as the political scientist Paul Peterson predicted that they would if faced by an unfavorable tax–service ratio.[14] Second, it is possible for the residents of entire communities to join forces and try to separate their community altogether from a city that seems chronically incapable of responding to their needs and interests. Secession is a very uncommon strategy of grassroots rebellion and one that rarely succeeds because groups that pursue this option are often an isolated minority whose campaign to establish a separate municipality or join another are easily defeated by a majority of a city's population. However, if disgruntled communities can find ways to overcome traditional divisions along racial, ethnic, class, or cultural lines, then threats of secession may become a somewhat more viable form of political opposition.[15]

Notes

1. Gerald Horne, *Fire This Time: The Watts Uprising and the 1960s* (Charlottesville: University of Virginia Press, 1995); Sidney Fine, *Violence in the Model City: The Cavanaugh Administration, Race Relations, and the Detroit Riot of 1967* (Ann Arbor: University of Michigan Press, 1989); Robert M. Fogelson, *Violence as Protest: A Study of Riots and Ghettos* (New York: Doubleday, 1971).

2. Anthony J. Lukas, *Common Ground: A Turbulent Decade in the Lives of Three American Families* (New York: A. A. Knopf, 1985).

3. For a good analysis of the Alinsky model of community organizing, see Robert Fisher, *Let the People Decide: Neighborhood Organizing in America* (Boston: Twayne Publishers, 1984). For a firsthand account of organizing with Alinsky by one of his most trusted partners, see Nicholas Von Hoffman, *Radical: A Portrait of Saul Alinsky* (Philadelphia: Nation Books, 2010).

4. Refer to Sidney Plotkin, "Community and Alienation: Enclave Consciousness and Urban Movements," in *Breaking Chains: Social Movements and Collective Action*, ed. Michael P. Smith (New Brunswick, NJ: Transaction Publishers, 1991); Mark Santow, "Running in Place: Saul Alinsky, Race, and Community Organizing," in *Transforming the City: Community Organizing and the Challenge of Political Change*, ed. Marion Orr (Lawrence: University Press of Kansas, 2007).

5. Mark R. Warren, *Dry Bones Rattling: Community Building to Revitalize American Democracy* (Princeton: Princeton University Press, 2001).

6. Michael Eichler, "Consensus Organizing: Sharing Power to Gain Power." *National Civic Review* Summer/Fall 1995.

7. Celina Su, *Streetwise for Book Smarts: Grassroots Organizing and Education Reform in the Bronx* (Ithaca, NY: Cornell University Press, 2009).

8. Refer to Susan Stall and Randy Stoecker, "Community Organizing or Organizing Community? Gender and the Craft of Empowerment," *Gender and Society*, 12 (6), 1998; Marion Orr and John Rodgers, eds., *Public Engagement for Public Education: Joining Forces to Revitalize Democracy and Equalize Schools* (Stanford, CA: Stanford University Press, 2011); Harry Boyte, *The Backyard Revolution* (Philadelphia: Temple University Press, 1980).

9. Refer to James DeFilippis, Robert Fisher, and Eric Shragge, "Community Organizing Theory and Practice: Conservative Trends, Oppositional Alternatives," in *The People Shall Rule: ACORN, Community Organizing and the Struggle for Economic Justice*, ed. Robert Fisher (Nashville: Vanderbilt University Press, 2009).

10. Heidi J. Swarts, *Organizing Urban America: Secular and Faith-Based Progressive Movements* (Minneapolis: University of Minnesota Press, 2008); Richard L. Wood, "Higher Power: Strategic Capacity for State and National Organizing," in *Transforming the City: Community Organizing and the Challenge of Political Change*, ed. Marion Orr (Lawrence: University Press of Kansas, 2007); and Robert Fisher, ed., *The People Shall Rule: ACORN, Community Organizing and the Struggle for Economic Justice* (Nashville: Vanderbilt University Press, 2009).

11. J. Phillip Thompson, *Double Trouble: Black Mayors, Black Communities, and the Call for a Deep Democracy* (New York: Oxford University Press, 2006).

12. See also Adolph Reed Jr., "Demobilization in the New Black Political Regime: Ideological Capitulation and Radical Failure in the Post-Segregation Era," in *The Bubbling Cauldron: Race, Ethnicity, and the Urban Crisis*, ed. Michael Peter Smith and Joe R. Feagin (Minneapolis: University of Minnesota Press, 1995).

13. Albert O. Hirschman, *Exit, Voice, and Loyalty: Responses to Decline in Firms, Organizations, and States* (Cambridge, MA: Harvard University Press, 1970).

14. Paul Peterson, *City Limits* (Chicago: University of Chicago Press, 1981).

15. Refer to Michen Andrew Connor, "'Those Communities Have the Most to Gain from Valley Cityhood': Color-Blind Rhetoric of Urban Secession in Los Angeles, 1996–2002," *Journal of Urban History*, 40 (1), 2014.

10-1 Excerpts from *Reveille for Radicals*

Saul D. Alinsky

Reveille for Radicals

The Program

The present power age defines and evaluates everything in terms of power. To this common and accepted view the field of organization has been no exception. It is universally assumed that the function of a People's Organization is similar to that of any other kind of organization, which is to become so strong, so powerful, that it can achieve its ends. The question as to what constitutes these ends is countered with some general statement like, "Why, the people's program, of course." If we persist in our inquiry as to what is meant by a people's program, raising a series of questions— "Who thought up the program?" "Where did it come from?" "Who worked in its creation?" and other similar queries—we rapidly discover that too often the program is not a people's program at all but the product of one person, five persons, a church, a labor union, a business group, a social agency, or a political club—in short, a program that can be traced to one or two persons or institutions, but not to the people themselves. The phrase "people's program" has become well worn with lip service, but whether such a program actually exists in practice is something else again. The words have become like the word "democracy," a common carrier of so many different meanings that they are meaningless.

Under such circumstances it behooves us to raise the simple question, "What is a people's program?" The question itself leads to the obvious and true answer that a people's program is whatever program the people themselves decide. It is a set of principles, purposes, and practices which have been commonly agreed upon by the people.

What has been completely forgotten and cannot be overemphasized is that a People's Organization carries within it two major functions. Both are equally important. One is the accepted understanding that organization will generate power which will be controlled and applied for the attainment of a program. The second is the realization that only through organization can a people's program be developed. When people are brought together, or organized, they get to know each other's point of view; they reach compromises on many of their differences, they learn that many opinions which they entertained solely as their own are shared by others, and they discover that many problems which they had thought of only as "their" problems are common to all. Out of all this social interplay emerges a common agreement, and that is the people's program. Then the other function of organization becomes important: the use of power in order to fulfill the program.

This does not mean that the organizer cannot state certain general principles during the initial stages of organization. These are general issues of the kind that all people support, such as medical care, full employment, good housing, good schools, equal opportunities, and above all the opportunity to create their own program. The chance to work out their own program will be found to be one of the greatest motivating forces in the building of a People's Organization. This fact in itself bears witness to both the desire of the people to work out their own destiny and the scarcity of opportunities to do so.

But the objective of securing a people's program absolutely precludes the organizer's going beyond these broad general principles into a detailed blueprint for the future. That kind of program can and must come only from the people themselves. The actual projection of a completely particularized program by a few persons is a highly dictatorial action. It is not a democratic program but a monumental testament to lack of faith in the ability and intelligence of the masses of people to think their way through to the successful solution of their problems. It is not a people's program, and the people will have little to do with it.

There should not be too much concern with specifics or details of a people's program. The program items are not too significant when one considers the enormous importance of getting people interested and participating in a democratic way. *After all, the real democratic program is a democratically minded people*—a healthy, active, participating, interested, self-confident people who, through their participation and interest, become informed, educated, and above all develop faith in themselves, their fellow men, and the future. The people themselves are the future. The people themselves will solve each problem that will arise out of a changing world. They will if they, the people, have the opportunity and power to make and enforce the decision instead of seeing that power vested in just a few. No clique, or caste, power group or benevolent administration can have the people's interest at heart as much as the people themselves. . . .

Native Leadership

The building of a People's Organization can be done only by the people themselves. The only way that people can express themselves is through their leaders. By *their* leaders we mean those persons whom the local people define and look up to as leaders. Native or indigenous leadership is of fundamental importance in the attempt to build a People's Organization, for without the support and co-operative efforts of native leaders any such venture is doomed to failure from the very beginning.

These indigenous leaders are in a very true sense the real representatives of the people of the community. They have earned their position of leadership among their people and are accepted as leaders. A People's Organization must be rooted in the people themselves: if a People's Organization were to be thought of as a tree, the indigenous leaders would be the roots and the people themselves the soil. To rest on the soil and be nourished by the soil, the tree must be deeply and well rooted.

To organize the people means to talk with them, to get them together so that they can talk with one another and arrive at a common agreement. But it is obviously impossible to get all of the people to talk with one another. The only way that you can reach people is through their own representatives or their own leaders. You talk to people through their leaders, and if you do not know the leaders you are in the same position as a person trying to telephone another party without knowing the telephone number. Knowing the identity of these natural leaders is knowing the telephone number of the people. Talking with these natural leaders is talking with the people. Working with them is working with the people, and building with them is the building of a People's Organization.

Most attempts at community organization have foundered on the rock of native leadership. The conventional community council has evinced little knowledge or understanding of the significance of indigenous leadership. Such organizations have largely confined themselves to coordinating professional, formal agencies which are first superimposed upon the community and subsequently never play more than a superficial role in the life of the community. It is rare to discover a community organization in which the indigenous interest groups and action groups of the community not only participate but play a fundamental role.

Practically all of these community organizations that talk of native leadership think in terms of token representation by community leaders. Even in their token representation one finds residents of the local community but very few, if any, of its leaders. The fact is that almost none of the professional or formal outside agencies that have been active in the field of community organization have any realistic appreciation of the meaning of indigenous leadership. They talk glibly of it but understand and use little of it. If they have accepted local representation, they have generally *selected* persons whom they defined as leaders rather than those persons whom the people have defined and accepted as leaders.

To a certain extent this is a natural, expected reaction. Formal agency representatives who have started community activities have usually regarded themselves as of the "leadership" type. It is the natural egotism of most people to think of themselves in such terms. Therefore when the workers of formal organizations enter a community and search for indigenous leadership they look for persons as similar to themselves as possible. That is one reason why so many of these little organizations known as neighborhood civic committees, community councils, or neighborhood leagues include local people who are of the professional class—doctors, dentists, lawyers, social workers, businessmen and bankers. These types of neighborhood people, usually by virtue of educational background and personal manners, have much more in common with the representatives of the formal agencies than do the rank and file of the area. The organizers themselves feel much more at home with these people, and find them more articulate and more able to talk in terms and values that the outside agency representatives are comfortable with.

Substantially what it amounts to is that the formal agencies' representatives, conceiving of themselves as leaders, hunt for those community persons with whom they can most readily identify. But with rare exception those local professional or business people who are selected by the formal agencies as community leaders may possess a legitimate claim to being native to the community [sic] but no valid claim to being a leader. As to being native to the community, it will often be found that most of them are only half-time natives in that they work within the community and live outside in a more desirable residential area. Furthermore, having very little real relationship with the people (not being part of the people themselves), the actual extent of their being "native" to the community really boils down to their being physically native, whereas on the basis of their thoughts, their aspirations, their hopes, their desires, their sharing the tragedies of the people, these physically native professional and business people are as foreign to the local residents as are outside formal agencies. They have not only never been accepted by the people as leaders, they have never even been thought of in those terms. They possess no following to speak of, and a community council made up of ten of them would in actuality be an organization of ten people—and that's all it would be. It wouldn't even be ten generals and no army, because they are generals only by self-appointment.

Thus it becomes obvious why these alleged community councils very shortly deteriorate into monthly social get-togethers for a small group of professional people who wallow in their egos as self-anointed saviors

of the people and commiserate with one another on the poor benighted people of the neighborhood who don't have sufficient intelligence to know what is good for them and ignore this proffered leadership. These community councils soon shrivel up and disappear.

The understanding of what constitutes a genuine native, indigenous leader is rarely found among conventional social do-gooders. The latter are to be found either in professional positions working with various outside agencies or else on the boards of typical community houses. A vivid demonstration of the wide gap in the understanding of leadership between the community people and these outside do-gooders was found in a conference between some of the representatives of the board of a community center and the leaders of the neighborhood People's Organization. The board representatives consisted of economically comfortable persons residing in a good residential section who devoted one evening a month to meeting in the center, where they reviewed all of the purported good that they were doing in the community. This center was represented in the community by a building and nothing more. It did not participate in the life of the community and was not recognized as a neighborhood factor by any of the significant neighborhood groups.

During one discussion some of the leaders of the People's Organization were trying to explain what they meant by native leadership, and they pointed out that those persons holding positions of leadership on the board of the local community center knew very little of the problems of the community and had less real interest in their solution. From the point of view of the People's Organization these outside board members were unknown to the local community, their services were unsolicited, their interest was questionable, and generally their method of doing things *for* rather than *with* the people was resented. So the leaders of the People's Organization inquired as to just what place these outsiders had within the community. (It cannot be too strongly emphasized that when they used the word "outsiders" the People's Organization thought much more in terms of persons whose interests and objectives were outside the community than in terms of geographical location.) At this stage a board member of the local center, a rather young academician specializing in education and personal pompousness, declared, "You people are really isolationists. You don't understand when you talk about leadership or representation just what we represent. We represent the City of Chicago."

This statement convinced the leaders of the People's Organization of the futility of continuing the meeting. Immediately after the meeting they discussed the professor's views:

"Now, that professor says that he and the other guys with him represent the City of Chicago. What the hell are they talking about? When we talk about representing men we really mean representing them. I don't know what they mean by their words. Now take John here [a local labor leader]. When he goes into a factory and organizes the people for his union he says he represents them. He can bargain for them. The employer knows that if John feels that the workers should go out on strike, they will go out on strike—and if John says they ought to end the strike, they'll go back to work. The boss knows that John really represents the people, but this professor who says he represents Chicago—if he even got into a fight with anybody, who else, outside of his second cousin and maybe a couple of friends of his, would get behind him? Who does he represent? He says, 'the City of Chicago.' What the hell is he talking about? The poor guy, maybe he really believes it. He doesn't mean wrong, he's just nuts!"

Since representatives of formal agencies judge leadership according to *their own* criteria, evaluate what is good or bad in the community according to *their own* standards, and understand life in the community only when interpreted according to *their own* code or standards—it is crystal clear that they don't know the meaning of indigenous leadership, let alone the identities of these natural leaders. . . .

Conflict Tactics

A People's Organization is a conflict group. This must be openly and fully recognized. Its sole reason for coming into being is to wage war against all evils which cause suffering and unhappiness. A People's

Organization is the banding together of large numbers of men and women to fight for those rights which insure a decent way of life. Most of this constant conflict will take place in orderly and conventionally approved legal procedures—but in all fights there come times when "the law spoke too softly to be heard in such a noise of war."

The building of a People's Organization is the building of a new power group. The creation of any new power group automatically becomes an intrusion and a threat to the existing power arrangements. It carries with it the menacing implication of displacement and disorganization of the status quo.

Agnes E. Meyer of the *Washington Post* pointed this out in a study of a People's Organization in Chicago:

These serious-minded inhabitants of Packingtown have never picked a fight, nor have they avoided one when great issues and principles were involved. They have fought because in a competitive city like Chicago, any new power group has to go through battles if it is going to survive. Their thinking on pressure is very simple.

"We believe that democracy is a government constantly responding to the pressure of its people," a group of council members said to me. "The biggest hope for democracy is that Americans will overcome their lethargy and that more and more people and groups will become articulate and formulate their needs."[1]

A People's Organization is not a philanthropic plaything or a social service's ameliorative gesture. It is a deep, hard-driving force, striking and cutting at the very roots of all the evils which beset the people. It recognizes the existence of the vicious circle in which most human beings are caught, and strives viciously to break this circle. It thinks and acts in terms of social surgery and not cosmetic cover-ups. This is one of the reasons why a People's Organization will find that it has to fight its way along every foot of the road toward its destination—a people's world.

Because the character of a People's Organization is such that it will frequently involve itself in conflict, and since most attempts at the building of

People's Organizations have been broken by the attacks of an opposition which knows no rules of fair play or so-called ethics, it is imperative that the organizers and leaders of a People's Organization not only understand the necessity for and the nature and purpose of conflict tactics, but become familiar with and skillful in the use of such tactics.

A People's Organization is dedicated to an eternal war. It is a war against poverty, misery, delinquency, disease, injustice, hopelessness, despair, and unhappiness. They are basically the same issues for which nations have gone to war in almost every generation.

A war is not an intellectual debate, and in the war against social evils there are no rules of fair play. In this sense all wars are the same. Rules of fair play are regulations upon which both sides are in mutual agreement. When you have war, it means that neither side can agree on anything. The minimum agreements of decency that either side may display stem not from decency but from fear. Prisoners are treated according to certain minimum standards and both sides hesitate, to use certain inhuman weapons simply because of fear of reprisal.

In our war against the social menaces of mankind there can be no compromise. It is life or death. Failing to understand this, many well-meaning liberals look askance and with horror at the nakedness with which a People's Organization will attack or counterattack in its battles. Liberals will settle for a "moral" victory; radicals fight for victory. These liberals cannot and never be able to understand the feelings of the rank-and-file people fighting in their own People's Organization any more than one who has never gone through combat action can fully grasp what combat means. The fights for decent housing, economic security, health programs, and for many of those other social issues for which liberals profess their sympathy and support, are to the liberals simply intellectual affinities. They would like to see better housing, health, and economic security, but *they* are not *living* in the rotten houses; it is not *their* children who are sick; it is not *they* who are working with the specter of unemployment hanging over their heads; they are not fighting their *own* fight.

It is very well for bystanders to relax in luxurious security and wax critical of the tactics and weapons used by a People's Organization whose people are fighting for their own children, their own homes, their own jobs, and their own lives. It is very well under those circumstances for liberals who have the time to engage in leisurely democratic discussions to quibble about the semantics of a limited resolution, to look with horror on the split-second decisions, rough-and-ready, up-and-down and sideways swinging and cudgeling of a People's Organization. Unfortunately conditions are not always such that a board of directors can leisurely discuss a problem, refer it to a committee, and carry through with all of Robert's Rules of Order. That luxury is denied to the people who suddenly find themselves subjected to a lightning attack, of what liberals would call a foul character, by the opposition. The people in a People's Organization cannot afford simply to stew in righteous feelings of indignation. They are in a fight for everything that makes life meaningful—and attack by the enemy calls for counterattack.

The People's Organization does not live comfortably and serenely in an ivory tower where it not only can discuss controversial issues but actually possesses the choice of whether or not to take a hand in the controversy. In actual life, conflict, like so many other things that happen to us, does not concern itself too much with our own preferences of the moment any more than it does with our judgment as to whether or not it is time to fight.

A People's Organization lives in a world of hard reality. It lives in the midst of smashing forces, clashing struggles, sweeping cross-currents, ripping passions, conflict, confusion, seeming chaos, the hot and the cold, the squalor and the drama, which people prosaically refer to as life and students describe as "society. . . ."

Popular Education

In the last analysis the objective for which any democratic movement must strive is the ultimate objective implicit within democracy—*popular education*. Thomas Jefferson's confidence in the eventual realization of the full potentialities of democracy was based on popular education: "enlighten the people generally, and tyranny and oppression of body and mind will vanish like spirits at the dawn of day."

The very purpose and character of a People's Organization is educational. The bringing together of the many diversified elements of the American population results in the acquisition of knowledge and a consequent changing of attitudes on the part of all of these various elements. Businessmen, labor leaders, religious leaders, heads of nationality, racial, fraternal, and athletic groups all get to know each other. Through constant exchange of views and by sharing common experiences there comes not a so-called "better understanding" between these various groups, but simply *an understanding*. This mutual understanding is accompanied by a new appreciation and definition of social issues.

During hard times the businessmen of the community assume that the problem of unemployment is mainly the burden of business; that when people are unemployed the businessmen have to pay taxes for relief and at the same time suffer from lack of business. There are many labor unions, on the other hand, that feel that unemployment is mainly a burden on labor because unemployed men can't pay dues and are constantly requesting financial aid from the union. The churches feel that unemployment is primarily the heavy cross of the church because when men are unemployed they are wholly concerned with the fundamental job of getting bread for themselves and their families—and in addition there are not only few contributions coming in to support the church but an ever increasing flow of supplications for help from the church.

Through the People's Organization these groups discover that what they considered primarily their individual problem is also the problem of the others, and that furthermore the only hope for solving an issue of such titanic proportions is by pooling all their efforts and strengths. That appreciation and conclusion is an educational process.

More important is the fact that leaders of groups that have seemingly conflicting interests get to know each other as human beings by working together on joint programs of mutual concern. They get to know each other as Johnny and Fred. They learn that they both admire the same ball team. They both cuss when they have a flat tire. They both are filled with the cute sayings of their three- and four-year-olds and essentially they both want just about the same things out of life. Where they differ is in the means to be used in achieving the end.

One of the most common experiences during the early days of a People's Organization is the constant reactions of leaders from various groups along these lines: "Well, Freddy, I had no idea that you guys felt that way about it. Of course, I never knew about how you fellows saw it, but you've certainly got something on

your side too." This educational process represents one of the cardinal premises of a People's Organization.

The Organization is convinced that when people get to know one another as human beings instead of as symbols or statistics, a human relationship—carrying with it a full constellation of human attitudes—will inevitably result. It would seem that this point is so patent that it is unnecessary to elaborate, and yet, as with many fundamental precepts, it is so obvious that while we talk about it we completely overlook its significance for practical purposes. A simple illustration is in the reading of the morning paper as part of our breakfast routine. The front page carries a detailed account of the threat of starvation facing millions of people in India. We continue to turn the pages and suddenly our attention is riveted by a small item on page 19 that informs us that one of our friends has been seriously injured in an automobile accident. The emotional impact brings about a sudden cessation of our breakfast enjoyment. Our reaction is one of shock and sorrow. Here is one individual injured in an accident that evokes all of the human sympathy within us. But the millions of Indians have no relationship to us and mean nothing to us. The millions of Indians add up to impersonal digits, but that one friend of ours is not a symbol or a digit, but a warm human being whom we know as a person. We know our friend suffers pain just as we do; in essence, our knowing him as a human being serves as a strong bond of identification. That is the human relationship.

You obviously cannot get everyone in the community to know everyone else on a personal, human basis, but you can get the hundreds of little local leaders to know one another on a human basis. These little local leaders may be shop stewards in their union. They may be active in the P.T.A. They may be officials in their religious organizations. They may be heads of athletic groups. They may be bartenders, precinct captains, or small businessmen. They are the people we referred to earlier in our discussion of native leadership—the "Little Joes." They are the Little Joes that have some thirty or forty followers apiece. Their attitudes significantly shape and determine the attitudes of their followers.

Any labor organizer knows of the Little Joes. When a man is being solicited to join a union he will usually respond along these lines: "Everything you say sounds pretty good, Mister, but before I sign up I want to know if Joe has signed up." If the organizer says he has, the reply will be, "Well, if Joe has signed up, what are we waiting for?" If the organizer says that Joe has not joined, the potential member will answer, "Well, I think you're right, Mister, but I want to think it over and I'll let you know some time tomorrow." The organizer knows full well that the prospect is not going to reach a decision until he talks it over with Little Joe that night. He knows also that Little Joe's decision that night will be the prospect's decision the next day.

These Little Joes are usually totally ignored in all programs superimposed by well-meaning outside agencies, whether they be in the field of reaction or adult education. *But these Little Joes, are the natural leaders of their people, the biggest blades in the grass roots of American democracy.* These Little Joes present not only the most promising channels for education, but in certain respects the only channels. As the Little Joes get to know one another as human beings, prejudices are broken down and human attitudes are generated in this new relationship. These changes are reflected among their followers, so that the understanding or education begins to affect the attitudes of thousands of people. . . .

Note

1. "Orderly Revolution," *Washington Post*, June 4, 1945.

10-2 "A Theology of Organizing: From Alinsky to the Modern IAF"*

Mark R. Warren

The Community Development Reader

On a winter's day in 1975 George Ozuna's grandmother asked him to accompany her shopping in downtown San Antonio.[1] The high school senior got his shoes and began the long walk from the Hispanic south side of town to Joske's Department Store, the largest retail establishment in the city. When the pair arrived, George immediately realized something was going on. Hundreds of Hispanic grandmothers, housewives and churchgoers had gathered outside the store. They entered en mass and began trying on clothes. And they didn't stop. They continued to try on clothes all day, grinding store operations to a halt. The protesters were all members of Catholic parishes active in Communities Organized for Public Service (COPS), a new organization fighting to improve conditions in San Antonio's impoverished and long neglected south and west side neighborhoods. While they disrupted business, COPS leaders and its organizer Ernesto Cortes, Jr., met with the store's owner. They demanded that he use his influence on San Antonio's city council to pass COPS' $100 million budget proposal for infrastructural improvements and increased services to Mexican American neighborhoods.

The next day COPS supporters disrupted banking operations on a busy Friday afternoon at the central branch of Frost National Bank by continuously exchanging pennies for dollars and vice versa. Upstairs COPS leaders and organizer Cortes met with Tom Frost, Jr., one of the most influential men in San Antonio. The Joske Department Store manager had refused COPS' demand for assistance and now Frost, although polite, declined to call the mayor as well. Cortes, as the organizer, was supposed to let COPS leaders do the negotiating; but he watched them fold as Frost stalled.

As Cortes later recounted in a speech to farm workers, "My leaders freeze, and they don't do anything. I believe in the Iron Rule of organizing: never do anything for anybody that they can do for themselves. But they ain't doing for themselves! They're collapsing; they're folding. Our people are downstairs waiting with no instruction, no word and they don't know what to do. I decide I've got to do something, so I move my chair over to Mr. Frost, and he's got a blood vessel that's exposed, and I focus on it and look at it. I just keep moving, he moves away, and I move closer with the chair. Then finally he says something, and I say, 'Mr. Frost, that's a bunch of balderdash. You're the most arrogant man I've ever met.' And he gets up. We have a priest there and Mr. Frost says, 'Father, you better teach your people some manners and some values.' And finally the priest says, 'Well, Mr. Frost, I don't know about that, but you know, you're apathetic and I think that's much worse.'"

Despite little initial success, COPS continued its protests and the tide began to turn. Prime time television crews started covering the actions, scaring away paying customers. Pressure mounted on business leaders. The head of the Chamber of Commerce came to negotiate with Cortes. But the organizer made him wait until COPS leaders could be rounded up to participate. COPS eventually won the city's commitment for $100 million worth of desperately needed improvements to its neighborhoods. For the first time, Mexican Americans had flexed their political muscle in San Antonio, and they gained new drainage projects, sidewalks, parks and libraries for their efforts.

Militant, direct action tactics geared towards winning put COPS squarely in the tradition started by Saul Alinsky and codified in his books *Rules for*

Source: Mark Warren, "A Theology of Organizing: From Alinsky to the Modern IAF," in *The Community Development Reader*, eds. James DeFillippis and Susan Saegert. Published in 2008 by Routledge. Reprinted by permission of Taylor & Francis LLC Books.

Radicals and *Reveille for Radicals*. After his encounter with Cortes, the banker Tom Frost bought a case of these books and distributed them among the power elite of San Antonio so that they could better prepare to deal with COPS. COPS and the IAF are still known for these militant tactics. The casual observer who sees only these tactics, however, will miss the fundamental changes to Alinsky's way of organizing that Cortes began to make with his work in San Antonio. Twenty years after the tie-up at his bank, Frost, now an influential figure in Texas state politics as well, gave this author his last remaining copy of *Rules for Radicals*, claiming it was no longer relevant. According to Frost, "I told Ernie [Cortes] he's now working out of another book. And I asked him just what is that book? Ernie said he's still writing it."

Considered the "father of community organizing" Alinsky was the first to attempt to mobilize industrial workers and their families into direct action where they lived, as opposed to where they worked.[2] Although Alinsky's organizing projects scored impressive victories, most were short-lived or failed to maintain the progressive vision and participatory character upon which they were founded. Trained under the IAF in the early seventies, Cortes began organizing COPS using Alinsky's methods. Almost immediately, though, he began to revise Alinsky's approach. The modern IAF would come to base its local organizations in the institutions and values of faith communities. Its organizers would become a permanent feature of local affiliates using relational organizing to reach beyond pastors to foster the participation of lay leaders. And the IAF would come to link these leaders across racial lines, attempting to build broad-based organizations that would help ensure a commitment to the common good, rather than narrow group interests. While Alinsky took a rather utilitarian view of churches as repositories of money and people to be mobilized, the modern IAF developed a close collaboration with people of faith, fusing religious traditions and power politics into a theology of organizing.

Saul Alinsky and the Origins of the IAF

Saul Alinsky founded his first community organization, the Back of the Yards Neighborhood Council (BYNC), on Chicago's southwest side in 1939. Since that time, despite Alinsky's impressive achievements, and the significant legacy he left to American populist organizing, the local organizations he built largely failed to sustain themselves as participatory political institutions. By the early seventies, the IAF could count many individual successes, at least in the short run. But neither the local organizations it formed, nor the IAF itself, had found a way to establish long-lasting institutions that could sustain broad participation and an independent base of power for poor communities.

Upon Alinsky's death, Ed Chambers took over as director of the IAF, and began to make some significant changes to Alinsky's organizing approach. To stabilize the IAF's precarious financial situation, Chambers moved to extend contracts with community organizations after the initial two to three year start-up period. Chambers wanted to develop long-term relationships with local organizations, both to keep the flow of money into the IAF and also because he thought community organizations needed the kind of extended training that the IAF could provide. Chambers also systematized the training of organizers themselves and promoted the professionalization of the occupation by upgrading pay. While Alinsky liked to run a one-man show, Chambers set up a cabinet of senior organizers to provide collective supervision to the IAF's efforts.

Chambers put the IAF on a new road that held out the possibility of mutual interaction and collaboration between professional organizers on the one hand and community leaders from local organizations on the other. Although Chambers had the germ of these ideas in his head, the new model of organizing would be initiated in practice through the organizing work of Ernesto Cortes. Cortes began to organize Communities Organized for Public Service (COPS) in San Antonio. Through that effort, and in coordination with Chambers and IAF efforts in other parts of the country, Cortes began to write the new book on organizing to which the banker Tom Frost alluded.

Communities Organized for Public Service (COPS)

Ernesto Cortes, Jr., arrived back to his home town of San Antonio in 1973. His goal was to build an organization to give voice to poor and working Mexican Americans in San Antonio's forgotten west and south sides. Within a few short years he and a group of committed Catholic clergy and lay leaders had built a powerful organization that broke the Anglo elite's monopoly on political power in San Antonio. In the process, the modern IAF came to base its organizing work almost exclusively in religious congregations and to reach deeply into religious networks to build organizations based upon religious values as much as material interests. By doing so, the IAF began to build organizations meant to last and to maintain participation over time.

While Hispanics made up a majority of San Antonio's nearly one million residents by the early seventies, they were almost entirely excluded from political representation at city hall. The city displayed an old-fashioned colonial atmosphere, as the growing Hispanic community, reaching a majority of the city's population by 1970, remained a "sleeping giant" (Rogers, 1992). Cortes, however, thought the sleeping giant might be ready to wake up.

At first, Cortes followed Alinsky's methods and attempted to recruit to COPS a variety of neighborhood social organizations, including churches, PTAs and social clubs. About twenty-five Catholic parishes, however, soon emerged as the bedrock of COPS, while the other institutions proved too unstable or unsuited for the ensuing political conflict. The Catholic Church hierarchy provided both funds and encouragement of pastoral support for COPS. As COPS became established, the largest part of its budget came from dues paid by member parishes, the funding principle followed by all IAF affiliates.

Support by the Archdiocese of San Antonio for COPS represented the culmination of several trends both in the larger Catholic Church and in the diocese of San Antonio. Vatican II heralded a greater openness in the church, encouraged lay participation, and pushed the church to address concerns for social justice and the plight of the poor. In many ways the diocese of San Antonio was ahead of these trends. In addition to the support of San Antonio's bishops, a movement of Hispanic clergy contributed to the development of COPS. Tapping the funds, legitimacy and institutional leaders from the Catholic Church conformed to traditional Alinsky methods. But in organizing COPS, Cortes began to make a profound innovation. He went beyond the priests and the

usually male presidents of parish councils and began to reach more deeply into the networks of lay leaders that spread out from the church. He started with priests, got the names of potential supporters from them and moved through the community. He recruited leaders, now mostly women, from the ranks of parish councils, fund-raising committees, and church-goers who were active in PTAs and social clubs. These were people connected to parishes and rooted in the dense networks of extended families and friends that constituted San Antonio's Hispanic neighborhoods. Rather than activists committed to the cause, COPS leaders cared primarily about the needs of their families and the religion that bound them together.

Reflecting on the early years of COPS, Cortes explains that "we tried to bust the stereotypes . . . to see leaders not necessarily as someone who could speak or persuade a crowd. We wanted to see leaders as people who have networks, relationships with other people." These leaders were often women, and many of them were excited about the opportunities the new organization offered. Once Cortes found someone whom he thought had potential to be a COPS leader, he could be dogged in pursuit. He first met Beatrice Cortes (no relation) at a parents meeting about the closing of a neighborhood school. In 1981 Mrs. Cortes became COPS' fourth president.

In COPS the IAF began to develop a different strategy than Alinsky to recruit lay leaders, a strategy the IAF would come to call relational organizing. Rather than mobilize people around an issue, Cortes engaged people's value commitments to their community. He got community leaders to talk with each other about community needs first, before identifying an issue around which to act. Specific plans for action emerged out of conversations at the bottom, rather than issues identified by activists at the top. Relational organizing worked to bring community leaders together to find a common ground for action and to develop the capacity to act in the interests of the broader community. By reaching beyond institutional leaders, the IAF unleashed the deeper capacities of the communities within these churches. By continuing to recruit from these networks, the IAF generated a continual stream of new leaders to bring fresh energy and new ideas into local organizations.

To unleash the leadership capabilities of these women, however, the IAF needed to innovate again. The organization could not be led by a coalition of official representatives from member social institutions, as Alinsky's organizations had been run. Room had to be made for the leadership of the lay parishioners Cortes was recruiting, many of whom were women traditionally excluded from official church positions. As a result, COPS created a hybrid organizational form. Its members were institutions, that is, churches. But the organization was not a coalition, composed of institutional representatives. Its leadership was drawn more broadly from the membership of those institutions, and leaders operated together in a single organization. COPS' structure allowed member parishes and neighborhood leaders to take action for the needs of their own particular neighborhoods at the same time as the organization could also act with a single will, as something more than the sum of its parts.

COPS mobilized its strong church base to challenge the power monopoly of the Anglo elite. In these early battles for recognition, COPS acquired a reputation for pursuing militant and confrontational tactics. Because COPS leaders were embedded in social relationships, they could consistently provide large turnouts of hundreds of Mexican Americans to these actions, something never accomplished before in San Antonio. The militant tactics proved successful, and COPS began to win important victories.

While mass mobilization provided one key source of COPS' power, the organization quickly began to see the importance of voter turn-out as well. In 1976 it allied with environmentalists to block the construction of a large shopping mall over the Edwards Aquifer, the city's only source of drinking water. By mobilizing their friends and neighbors, COPS leaders provided crucial votes to block the project and quickly became a force to reckon with on important public issues facing the city. With increased voting by Hispanics and sufficient support from Anglos and African Americans, Henry Cisneros won election in 1981 as the first Mexican American mayor of San Antonio since 1842 and the first Hispanic mayor of a large American city. Meanwhile, COPS expanded its role in determining city policy through its influence on the councilors elected from the five districts where it was concentrated.

During this period the IAF institutionalized what came to be known as "accountability sessions." As COPS mobilized supporters through its church base, candidates would face audiences of potential voters numbering in the hundreds, and sometimes thousands. After the meeting, COPS informed its supporters about the candidate's stand on the issues, thereby influencing the outcome of the election without a formal endorsement. If COPS had gained a public commitment from a successful candidate at an accountability night, the organization pressured the official to make good on that promise after the election. Once the IAF standardized this routine in COPS' electoral campaigns, it extended the format to all its large public actions in all its affiliates, whether the invited guest was a candidate for office, a current public official or a business leader. City bonds came to represent another source of public funds for COPS' projects and, eventually, an important venue for building alliances. The state of Texas requires municipalities to hold elections for voters to approve the sale of city bonds. Bond elections became a way for COPS to build alliances with development oriented interests and city officials who wanted the city to fund capital projects. Since middle class voters in established neighborhoods often resist the tax implications of large bond campaigns, COPS could supply the inner city votes required to pass bond packages. In return, COPS got its share of these funds, as well as leverage for its other proposals.

The IAF's explicit emphasis on organization building helped COPS move from issue to issue. IAF organizers trained COPS leaders not to think primarily about the cause or the issue, but to consider whether that action would build the capacity of the organization. In this way, when an issue campaign was over, the organization could build upon the capacity generated in that campaign to begin to initiate another. There was yet another way that COPS' approach marked a clear change from at least some of Alinsky's projects and helped to sustain its participatory character. COPS did not administer the programs it campaigned for itself. COPS refused to accept any government money directly. Instead, COPS would allow public agencies to handle the administration, while its leaders carefully watched to make sure the programs went as planned.

Rather than administration, COPS organizers and leaders remain focused on organizing.

COPS now had an organizing approach that proved powerful in gathering many kinds of resources for its neighborhoods. COPS combined careful research and planning by its leaders with large-scale mobilizations to public actions, and demonstrated its ability to turn out voters too when necessary to win its campaigns. By the organization's twentieth anniversary convention in 1994, COPS had channeled to its neighborhoods close to $1 billion from a wide variety of sources. Pragmatic and willing to compromise, COPS seldom made proposals beyond its political means, and consequently did not suffer many losses. But its most serious failures came when the organization, concerned that the needs of its constituents were being overlooked, attempted to oppose the plans of powerful developers—without proposing constructive projects of its own.

Bringing Values and Interests Together

In 1976 Ernesto Cortes left San Antonio to begin an organizing project in the largely Mexican American community of East Los Angeles. He founded the United Neighborhoods Organization (UNO), which became a powerful community organization active in the IAF network to this day. In the past, under Alinsky's direction, the IAF would have left COPS leaders on their own to continue their efforts upon Cortes' departure. But this time, in keeping with the new emphasis placed by IAF director Ed Chambers on continuing a financial relationship between affiliates and the organizing staff, the IAF sent organizer Arnold Graf to San Antonio.

While continuing a contractual relationship between the IAF and its local organizations contributed to keeping the IAF itself financially viable, it had a much deeper significance. It placed local affiliates and IAF organizers in a long-term relationship, where each could be influenced by the other. IAF organizers would now be present to ensure that its local affiliates did not violate the network's broad principles. Continual influence by an organizer connected to the larger IAF network helped to broaden the outlook of local leaders and expand their capacity for action. Moreover, having organizers who were accountable to a larger authority, the IAF itself, for the development of new leaders, made it less likely that local affiliates could become

dominated by a small group of entrenched officials, a problem that also plagued Alinsky's projects.

Through their long-term relationship with people of faith, IAF organizers became interested in religious traditions in a way that Alinsky never did. A self-interested motivation may have been sufficient for the kind of short-term campaigns that Alinsky's projects pursued. But the IAF wanted to build institutions that would last for the long term, not rise and fall around one issue. To sustain people's participation, something more than self-interest would be necessary.

The new women leaders of COPS, like Beatrice Cortes, demonstrated the viability of this new approach to organizing. The power and status that came with her election to its presidency may have given her extra drive. But leaders like Mrs. Cortes ranted about their involvement in faith terms, as part of their religious responsibility to the community. Meanwhile, if religion helped motivate leaders to action, that political experience deepened and clarified religious commitment.

Contact with the priests in COPS and UNO reignited Ernesto Cortes' earlier interest in theology. Cortes was raised in the Catholic Church and had begun to study theology seriously in graduate school. There he read mostly Protestant theologians, like Reinhold Niebuhr, Paul Tillich, Karl Barth, Dietrich Bonhoefer and Harvey Cox. Cortes brought these theological concerns with him to IAF training in Chicago. But Ed Chambers was initially skeptical. An ex-seminarian himself, Chambers had been involved with the Catholic Worker movement in New York before allying with Alinsky. But he had adopted Alinsky's tough, secular brand of power politics. Nevertheless, now that he was at the helm of a weak IAF network, Chambers was open to considering Alinsky's limitations and trying new approaches. Chambers himself began to argue that political organizing should emerge from the intertwined values of family and religion (Rogers, 1992).

When Cortes moved to East Los Angeles to organize the United Neighborhoods Organization, he continued his effort to ground IAF organizing in religious traditions, and to confront the tensions that arose in combining practical politics with faith ideals. He found many religious traditions that spoke powerfully about the obligations of people of faith to intervene in public life. Cortes and UNO priests developed a workshop that drew upon the stories of Pentecost and Sinai to strengthen lay leaders' commitment to the UNO effort. In the UNO context, these central events in people's religious traditions became symbols for the decision to draw from faith to take action to build a community. Over the course of the next twenty years, retelling stories from a largely Christian tradition and identifying potent symbols of community building became a central organizing tool for the IAF.

The ferment in Catholic social thought in the seventies motivated many priests and women from religious orders to get involved in the IAF. These women, including Sisters Christine Stephens, Maribeth Larkin, Pearl Caesar and others, became key organizers for the expanding Texas network. Catholic social thought emphasized that the root cause of evil lay in unjust economic and social institutions, and emphasized the responsibility of the church to work for social justice. Catholic teachings therefore provided a way to link religious responsibility with the self-interest of poor communities, precisely what IAF organizing came to be about (Chambers, 1978).

Relational Organizing and Institution Building

IAF organizing in San Antonio built upon the strong social fabric of Hispanic Catholic communities and the viability of their parish institutions. But in East Los Angeles, the Hispanic communities were newer, more transient and more fragmented. Lay leaders in UNO did not have the kind of well-established and expansive social networks available to COPS leaders. The IAF could not simply mobilize existing networks, it had to build them as well. But this task was beyond the capacity of IAF organizers alone to accomplish. The IAF staff decided to try, for the first time, to train UNO leaders in relational organizing themselves. In other words, leaders learned how to conduct the individual, relationship-building meetings IAF organizers used to recruit leaders. UNO leaders began holding these meetings with each other, in order to deepen collective bonds, as well as with their fellow parishioners and neighbors, in order to forge broader support for the organization's efforts.

In addition to individual meetings, UNO leaders also began conducting house meetings, which then became a standard part of IAF organizing as well. Cesar Chavez had used house meetings to organize farm workers in California. The IAF realized such meetings could help bring disconnected community residents together to talk about common concerns and develop plans of action. House meetings and individual meetings became ways to strengthen community and undertake political action—and to link the two together for mutual benefit.

In the mid-seventies a group of Protestant ministers in Houston, impressed by the success of COPS, invited the IAF to organize in their city. The new Houston sponsoring committee convinced Cortes to return to Texas from East Los Angeles in 1978 to organize.

In the late seventies Houston was a boomtown. Business dominated the city from its founding, and Houston was still run by a small group of economic elites. Business was used to getting its way in a city that had no zoning laws, poorly funded public services and weak public institutions. But while much of Houston boomed in the seventies, a large part of its African American and rapidly growing Hispanic populations lived in poverty.

Organizing in Houston posed a different kind of challenge to the IAF than it had faced in San Antonio. There, COPS operated in a relatively compact geographic area containing a well-established Hispanic community with a common history. But Houston was a huge, sprawling city that lacked many clearly definable neighborhoods with shared histories. Houston's Hispanic community was much newer, dispersed around the city, and quite diverse, as it included many Central Americans as well as Mexican immigrants.

African Americans in Houston's fifth ward did form a historic community. But, unlike the parish priests on the Hispanic west and south sides of San Antonio who were largely uninvolved in politics prior to COPS, black ministers in the fifth ward were deeply intertwined with electoral politics. They regularly endorsed candidates, supplying the votes of their members in exchange for some resources to their community. Although these resources were perhaps rather meager, many ministers feared the loss of any desperately needed funds that might come if they disrupted electoral relationships by joining the nonpartisan IAF effort. The IAF had to convince these ministers to engage their faith traditions in a different kind of politics and in an untested organization. For many African American ministers, the IAF represented a gamble. Moreover, although many admired the IAF's achievements in COPS, they saw the organization as one committed primarily to Hispanics.

In Houston, though, the IAF effort did have one unusual source of strength in its efforts to build a base in the black community. Many African Americans had come to Houston from Louisiana and so were Catholics. With the strong backing of Houston's Bishop John Markovsky, the Houston IAF affiliate, The Metropolitan Organization (TMO) attracted several black Catholic churches along with Hispanic Catholics and Anglo Protestants. TMO made it a point to address concerns in the black community and began to have a number of small, but important victories in fighting high electric bills, improving public transportation and combating drugs in school. Eventually some black Protestant ministers saw the benefits of TMO to the black community and took the first steps towards involvement.

In Houston the IAF faced the problem that many of the individual religious institutions within TMO were weak. They had too few members, insufficient finances, and a small leadership base which often barely extended beyond the pastor and a few key church officials. Although the Texas economy boomed in the seventies, when the oil crisis hit in the early eighties, IAF organizing throughout the state had to confront the rapid deterioration of social institutions. For IAF organizing to succeed, it could not assume the existence of healthy base institutions. Although the IAF had always argued that political action would redound to the benefit of communities, it now had to pay closer attention to institution building within communities.

In response to these conditions, the IAF offered the services of its organizers for "parish development." The term reveals its Catholic roots, but was meant to apply to churches in all denominations. To accomplish these goals, IAF organizers used the network's relational organizing technique of conversation leading to action. Parish development processes helped to identify new leaders, build a consensus and forge collective leadership for the church.

Not all Catholics, however, accepted the IAF's challenge to engage the church in political action. The IAF effort in Houston nearly collapsed when a prominent group of wealthy and conservative Catholics opposed the church's involvement in TMO. Led by George Strake, later the chairman of the state Republican Party, the group tried to squash the IAF effort. Bishop Markovsky, however, held firm in his support and the effort continued.

At its height, TMO had sixty congregations representing about 75,000 families. Despite the gains made from parish development work, TMO struggled with Houston's sprawling size and weak neighborhoods. It simply could not achieve the kind of power and prominence that COPS had attained in San Antonio.

Building Broad-Based Organizations

While the IAF experimented with multiracial and interfaith organizing in Houston, COPS was struggling to break out of the confines of the Hispanic west and south sides of San Antonio. In the late seventies the IAF began to look beyond the Hispanic west and south sides of San Antonio to build a base among African Americans concentrated on the city's east side. Conditions seemed ripe for organizing among African Americans. The predominantly black east side suffered from high levels of poverty and had, like the Hispanic west and south sides, been long neglected by the city government. Moreover, many black pastors were tremendously impressed by the accomplishments of COPS. In fact, they were jealous of growing Hispanic power. In their eyes, COPS was an organization that really worked to bring power to poor people of color, but it was all going to Mexican Americans.

Perhaps even more so than in Houston, however, African American Protestants in San Antonio were hesitant to become part of an IAF operation they saw as Hispanic and Catholic. African Americans constituted a relatively small share of the city's population, about 8 percent. Since COPS was so big and powerful, many black pastors feared they would be dominated by the Hispanic giant and that their concerns as African Americans would be ignored by the IAF. Many of these ministers hoped to build their own black church-based network instead. In order to give the black community more independence and autonomy within the IAF, the network decided to build a separate organization for San Antonio's African Americans, founding the East Side Alliance (ESA) in 1983. Although this tactic helped assuage the most immediate fears of African Americans that they would be dominated by the Hispanic COPS, the fundamental problem remained. In 1980, the IAF formed the Metropolitan Congregational Alliance (MCA) among mainly white, and to a lesser extent Hispanic, congregations on the north side. The theologically based organizing appealed to many clergy and lay leaders in these congregations, both Anglo as well as Hispanic, Protestant as well as Catholic. The religiously motivated MCA leaders, however, struggled to tap the self-interest of their relatively affluent congregants. To them, the IAF was for poor Hispanics.

Despite the obstacles each organization faced, MCA and ESA persisted and won victories on a number of issues. In the late eighties MCA and ESA merged into the Metro Alliance, making one stronger organization. Metro Alliance became a tri-racial organization, roughly one third each Anglo, Hispanic, and African American. Composed of Catholic, Methodist, Unitarian, Episcopalian, Lutheran and Baptist denominations throughout the east side and north side of San Antonio, Metro Alliance covered (albeit sparsely) the five city council districts outside of COPS areas. Without giving up its independence, the Metro Alliance gained the political muscle of COPS to make its efforts more successful.

The weaknesses of organizations formed separately by race and neighborhood in San Antonio, and the subsequent difficulties of uniting them, taught the Texas IAF an important lesson. From now on, the IAF would establish its Texas affiliates as what it called broad-based organizations. All organizations would now be metropolitan-wide and multiracial, as representative as the population as a whole.

Conclusion: A Synergy of Faith and Politics

By the early eighties Cortes and the IAF had written a good part of that "new book" which revised Alinsky's model of organizing in a number of significant ways, allowing the IAF to build and sustain local organizations with broad participation in a growing number of cities across Texas. The new model served as the framework for the modern IAF's organizing efforts across the country and pushed community organizers in other networks to take faith, values and relational organizing seriously as well.

In San Antonio, Cortes began to reach beyond institutional leaders into the social fabric of the churches on the west and south sides of the city. He chose not to start with an issue around which to mobilize. Instead, he asked lay leaders to talk amongst themselves to identify their concerns and find a basis for cooperative action. By doing so, he unleashed the capacity of indigenous leaders, particularly women who were immersed in and often responsible for community life. These women cared about their families, their communities and their faith as much as about any particular issue. Where Alinsky emphasized self-interest, and saw his base religious institutions solely as repositories of hard resources like money and people, the IAF began to take faith traditions, and the relational strengths of women lay leaders, seriously.

IAF organizers began to talk about two kinds of power, unilateral and relational (Loomer, 1976). Unilateral power represents "power over" others, the kind of power Alinsky generated in his projects. But the new IAF sought to create relational power as well, that is, the "power to" act collectively together. While the faith/politics and values/interest combination proved powerful in founding and sustaining IAF organizations, it was not without its inherent tensions. Too strong an emphasis on faith and values led to idealism, and sometimes failures. Too much emphasis on interests and pragmatic politics, however, led to alliances with development interests that some found unappealing. Another kind of tension between faith and politics resulted in religious opposition to IAF organizing, as happened in Houston. Despite the tensions, the IAF was able to build a powerful synergy between faith and politics, and other community organizers around the country began to take notice. The Pacific Institute for Community Organizing (PICO), led by organizers trained in the Chicago Alinsky tradition, had built a number of organizations along the west coast that pursued issue-based and neighborhood organizing. Struggling with instability in their efforts and learning from the IAF experience, PICO adopted a faith-based organizing strategy in the eighties.

Through its organizing the IAF also began to establish an institutional structure to mitigate the kind of narrowness that plagued Alinsky's projects. A foundation of religious caring for the community gave IAF organizations stability, so that they could persist beyond one issue and build their capacity over time. Meanwhile, the IAF organizers, permanently attached to local organizations, served as a counterweight against domination by narrow groups of leaders. In addition, the IAF began to build organizations in Texas that reached beyond one constituency, whether by neighborhood or race. Broad-based organizations required leaders from any one community to broaden their perspectives as they attempted to cooperate with people from other traditions. By the nineties, the synergy of faith and politics that Ernie Cortes began to create in San Antonio in 1973 had thoroughly transformed Alinsky organizing.

Notes

1. Sources for all accounts of events can be found in the full version of this chapter, Chapter 2 in *Dry Bones Rattling: Community Building to Revitalize America*. Princeton, NJ: Princeton University Press, 2001.
2. Discussion of Alinsky draws on S. D. Horwitz (1989) *Let Them Call Me Rebel*. New York: Alfred A. Knopf; P. D. Finks (1984) *The Radical Vision of Saul Alinsky*. New York: Paulist Press; R. Slayton (1986) *Back of the Yards*. Chicago: University of Chicago Press; R. J. Bailey (1974) *Radicals in Urban Politics: The Alinsky Approach*. Chicago: University of Chicago; D. C. Reitzes and D. C. Reitzes (1987) *The Alinsky Legacy: Alive and Kicking*. Greenwich, CT: JAI Press; N. Betten and M. J. Austin (1990) The conflict approach to community organizing in N. Betten and M. J. Austin (eds.) *The Roots of Community Organizing, 1917-1939*. Philadelphia: Temple University Press; R. Fisher (1984) *Let the People Decide: Neighborhood Organizing in America*. Boston: Twayne Publishers.

References

Alinsky, Saul D. (1969) *Reveille for Radicals*. New York: Vintage.

Alinsky, Saul D. (1971) *Rules for Radicals*. New York: Random House.

Chambers, E. (1978) Organizing for *Family and Congregation*. Hyde Park, NY: Industrial Areas Foundation.

Loomer, B. (1976) Two conceptions of power. *Criterion* (Winter): 12–29.

Rogers, Mary Beth (1992) *Cold Anger: A Story of Faith and Power Politics*. Denton: University of North Texas State Press.

10-3 "Why Don't American Cities Burn Very Often?"*

Michael B. Katz

Journal of Urban History

The question why widespread civil violence failed to recur [in American cities] is legitimate because a number of the conditions thought to have precipitated the eruption of civil violence in the 1960s have either persisted or grown worse. Consider the 1968 analysis of the National Advisory Commission on Civil Disorders (the Kerner Commission), appointed by President Lyndon Johnson. The commission unequivocally—and to the intense displeasure of the president—dismissed the idea that civil disorders—its term for civil violence—reflected Communist agitation.[7] In almost every instance, police actions had ignited long-standing grievances whose roots lay in racism and economic deprivation. The commission's "basic conclusion" was the memorable and arresting observation: "Our nation is moving toward two societies, one black, one white—separate and unequal."[8]

Thomas J. Sugrue and Andrew P. Goodman point out that added to these grievances was a sense that institutions had failed. Government, schools, police, and the economy: none of these delivered on their promises. In the 1960s, the stunning disjunction between the ideals of equal justice and opportunity embodied in American political rhetoric and the reality of everyday life undercut the legitimacy of institutions, loosening the hold of social control, facilitating the eruption of rage and frustration on the nation's streets. . . .

No single reason explains why American cities did not burn. Rather, the relative absence of civil violence resulted from the concatenation of several factors. These fall under three broad headings: the ecology of power, the management of marginalization, and the incorporation and control of immigrants.

The Ecology of Power

Attempts to breach the boundaries that separate hostile groups activate collective violence. Boundary change, writes Charles Tilly, "strongly affects the likelihood, intensity, scale, and form of collective violence."[22] Boundaries matter because they guard both identities and interests. They reinforce relations—"you-me and us-them"—that structure identities which, in turn, solidify over time. At the same time, cross-boundary inequalities accelerate the accumulation of advantages and resources through a process Tilly calls "opportunity hoarding." That is why attempts to break through boundaries inevitably result in conflict.[23] Throughout the history of American cities, boundary challenges often precipitated collective violence when, for example, white protestants attacked Irish Catholics in antebellum Philadelphia and Boston, or when African Americans tried to breach racial segregation in 1920s Detroit and 1940s Chicago.[24] The northward migration of African Americans after World War II constituted the greatest challenge yet to ethnic boundaries within predominantly white cities. Between 1950 and 1970, the black population of many cities skyrocketed: in Newark from 17 percent to 54 percent, in Chicago from 14 percent to 34 percent, and in Detroit from 16 percent to 44 percent.[25] The number of African Americans in Los Angeles soared from 63,744 to 763,000 between 1940 and 1970. The city's African American population spiked so rapidly, writes historian Josh Sides, "that even the most determined could not ignore it. Whites were now forced to interact with blacks to a degree unimaginable in prewar Los Angeles, a situation that generated unprecedented racial conflict. . . ."[26] To

Source: Michael B. Katz, "Why Don't American Cities Burn Very Often?" *Journal of Urban History*, vol. 34, no. 2, January 2008, pp. 185–208. Reprinted with permission from SAGE Publications, Inc.

*Some text and accompanying endnotes have been omitted. Please consult the original source.

many white residents, black migrants threatened to raise taxes for social services, overwhelm public schools, depress property values, and inject a rough new culture into daily life. To preserve existing boundaries, whites often turned to violence—a response documented with painful detail by historians.[27] The point for this discussion is that civil violence erupted at the height of urban boundary challenge, when huge numbers of African Americans had moved in and whites had not yet moved out.

In the years following the Great Migration, as boundary challenges receded, the ecology of urban power was rearranged. Whites left central cities for suburbs where they found ways to erect new and effective borders, and many cities became majority or near-majority minority. In places such as Boston where the white working class remained strong—the African American population only increased from 5 percent to 16 percent between 1950 and 1970—civil violence sometimes erupted, especially in protests over school busing, but remained spatially contained and narrowly targeted.[28] Elsewhere, whites decamped for the suburbs and ceded effective political control of cities to African Americans, retaining only a hold on commerce and finance and gentrified pockets of downtown. After the Voting Rights Act of 1965, the number of black elected officials jumped from 100 to 1,813 in 1980.[29] Between 1970 and 2001, the number of African American county and municipal officials rose 960 percent and 619 percent, respectively.[30] African Americans also made inroads into the police, the most visible and, often, hated agents of the local state. Cities hired African American police chiefs only in the years after the 1960s civil violence—in Cleveland in 1970, Detroit in 1976, and Chicago in 1983. In the same years, city police forces hired more African Americans, although not in numbers that matched their share of the population. In Detroit, for example, African Americans as a fraction of the police force increased from 22.3 percent in 1975 to 48.0 percent in 1987 while African Americans comprised 64.2 percent of the city's population.[31] A survey of 254 American cities found that minorities, as a share of police, increased between 1970 and 1981 from 5.1 percent to 11.6 percent while minorities as a share of total population rose from 16.7 percent to 27.6 percent—an improvement in the ratio from 3.2 to 2.3, but still a

decided under-representation.[32] The irony, of course, is that African Americans inherited city governments at the moment when de-industrialization, cuts in federal aid, and white flight were decimating tax bases and job opportunities while fueling homelessness, street crime, and poverty. Newly African American-led city governments confronted escalating demands for services and the repair of crumbling infrastructures with shrinking resources and power curtailed by often hostile state governments. They were, truly, as a political scientist described in 1969, a "hollow prize."[33] Nonetheless, with so many whites gone, boundaries became less contentious, eroding one major source of civil violence. . . .

In the 1980s, massive immigration from Latin America and Asia re-ignited urban boundary conflicts, particularly in the gateway cities where most immigrants entered. The civil violence that exploded in southwest Los Angeles in 1992 marked the first major boundary conflict since the 1960s. As the nation's major immigrant city, with Los Angeles International Airport (LAX) the Ellis Island of the late twentieth century, Los Angeles was the natural site for civil violence reflecting the nation's new demography. Despite widespread fear, however, events in Los Angeles proved singular, not the first spark of a long fuse stretching across urban America.[36] Why did it prove so hard to ignite civil violence throughout the nation? The answer lies partly in a set of mechanisms that complemented the new ecology of urban power. Collectively, these mechanisms deflected civil violence by managing marginalization.

The Management of Marginalization

In one way or another, civil violence in American history usually has involved marginalized populations. They have served both as objects of attack, as in lynching, and as active participants, as in Watts in 1965. By marginalized, I mean groups largely excluded from the prerogatives and rewards that accompany full citizenship, including employment, housing, consumption, social benefits, and equal justice. Before the 1950s or 1960s, nearly all African Americans remained marginalized in one way or another. In the last half of the twentieth century, a significant fraction moved into the American middle class. But a large share lacked work in the regular labor market, access to the best benefits of the welfare state, and the ability to match white

Americans in the consumption of housing, education, and other goods. The same can be said of Puerto Ricans and many immigrants. Since the 1960s, however, deprivation rarely has translated into civil violence. Americans have learned to manage marginalization. Five mechanisms have proved crucial: selective incorporation, mimetic reform, indirect rule, consumption, repression, and surveillance. Together, they set in motion a process of de-politicization that undercuts the capacity for collective action.[37]

In recent decades, gateways to better education, jobs, income, and housing have opened to a significant fraction of African Americans and other minorities. This is what I mean by selective incorporation. As a result, African American social structure resembles the social structure of white America, albeit with a smaller middle class and fewer wealthy. Incorporation did not happen unaided. It was not the inevitable product of market forces or the working of America's democratic institutions and assimilative processes. Rather, it resulted from government and private sector sponsorship. The civil violence of the 1960s, the Civil Rights Movement, and affirmative action all encouraged selective incorporation, which depended heavily on public or quasi-public employment (that is, employment in private agencies largely dependent on public funds). These proliferated as a result of the War on Poverty and Great Society social spending. Municipal bureaucracies increasingly controlled by African Americans provided many jobs, as did state and federal governments, where affirmative action took hold most quickly. In 2000, approximately 43 percent of African American women and 19 percent of black men worked in public or quasi-public sector jobs. Among Mexican Americans born between 1945 and 1954, the share in public or publicly funded employment was 37 percent for women and 17 percent for men. In 1970, government jobs, many funded by Great Society programs, employed 57 percent of black male college graduates and 72 percent of female college graduates.[38] Many private sector firms, prompted by affirmative action and the commercial value of diversity, also increased minority employment.

For the most part, selective incorporation constructed limited ladders of social mobility.[39] African American men entering the professions, for example, clustered largely in the human services, not in law, medicine, or the top ranks of corporate America. African American women professionals worked disproportionately as technicians, the lowest rung on the professional ladder.[40] Nonetheless, these limited ladders of mobility proved very important, fracturing African American communities along lines of class and gender (women fared far better than men) and eroding the potential for collective protest by holding out the promise of economic and occupational achievement and spreading a modest prosperity more widely than ever before—a prosperity, it should be noted, that was extremely fragile because it depended so heavily on public sector jobs.[41] When the Community Service Administration was abolished in 1981, for example, 60 percent of the 9,000 workers who lost their jobs were black.[42]

Mimetic reform also dampened the potential for collective violence. By mimetic reform, I mean measures that respond to insurgent demands without devolving real power or redistributing significant resources.[43] Mimetic reform cools out insurgencies; it does not resolve the problems that underlie them. Consider, for instance, Ira Katznelson's account of how in New York City in the late 1960s the Lindsay administration redirected demands for community control of schools in northern Manhattan to conservative ends. Through two new institutions, the Neighborhood Action Program and District School Board, the administration "refocused neighborhood politics in traditional directions . . . by appearing to be responsive to the period's demands for community control. But their activity, at a moment of social and political crisis, not only absorbed the energies of insurgents, it also transformed their protests and rendered them harmless." The triumph of the "mimetic policy formula" substituted decentralization for community control, elections for protest, and "modest but sufficiently tantalizing distribution" for redistribution. "The noise of schooling now signified nothing."[44] Another example is corporate leadership's deflection of civil violence and black protest and its cooptation of protest leaders, described in Julia Rabig's history of the politics of urban development in Newark, New Jersey. A third is Rebuild LA, which promised to reconstruct South Central Los Angeles after the 1992 civil violence, but delivered very little.[45]

Together, white abandonment, selective incorporation, and mimetic reform resulted in indirect rule.[46] Like colonial British imperialists who kept order through the exercise of authority by indigenous leaders, powerful white Americans retained authority over cities through their influence on minorities elected to political office, appointed to public and social service bureaucracies, and hired in larger numbers by police forces. Despite African American ascension to public office, however, real power lay elsewhere. In law cities are creatures of state government,[47] and state legislatures retain effective control of city finances, a situation underlined by the appointment of financial control boards when New York and other cities faced bankruptcy. States exercise control over cities in many other ways as well, as in education when the Illinois legislature mandated radical change in Chicago's school system or when the Pennsylvania legislature replaced Philadelphia's school board. In Pennsylvania, the state legislature in the 1990s also overturned a modest gun control law passed by the city council. Cities are profoundly influenced, too, by federal spending and regulations. In the mid-1970s, for example, the federal government flexed its muscle by setting stringent conditions for urban fiscal bailouts and drastically cutting money for public housing. Corporations also limited the autonomy of city governments by threatening to exit, taking with them needed jobs.

Thus, city leaders remained trapped between constituents who elected them and the state, national, and corporate authorities who supplied funds for their campaigns and circumscribed their actions. But indirect rule meant that civil violence or other claims on city government increasingly would be directed toward African American elected officials, African American public bureaucrats, and African American police.

The private sector also helped dampen the potential for civil violence by incorporating potential insurgents into America's Consumers' Republic.[48] In the 1960s, corporate America discovered the newly urbanized black consumer. Between 1940 and 1960, the proportion of African Americans living in urban areas increased from 48.6 percent to 73.2 percent. Corporations, recognizing a new market, quickly responded. The 1960s, writes Robert E. Weems, Jr., in *Desegregating the Dollar*, "witnessed a virtual explosion of

'how-to' articles in various advertising and trade journals offering advice on selling to African-Americans." Advertising revenues in *Ebony* magazine tripled from $3,630,804 in 1962 to $9,965,898 in 1969.[49]

With more spare cash than ever before, targeted by advertising, African Americans bought the material symbols of the good life. By 1993, the black consumer electronics market had reached $2,582 million. In the late twentieth century, the spending patterns of African Americans did not differ very much from whites (although blacks did spend less per capita on alcoholic beverages). Blacks had less income, but spent it in roughly the same way. In the early twenty-first century, the average income of white "consumer units" was $50,742 compared to $35,994 for blacks. Blacks spent $4,186 on food, $1,124 on entertainment, $488 on personal care products, and $1,704 on apparel compared to $5,349, $2,148, $529, and $1,716, respectively, for non-Hispanic whites.[50]

In their turn toward consumption, African Americans joined post–World War II Americans who had created what historian Lizabeth Cohen calls the Consumers' Republic, an "economy, culture, and politics built around the promises of mass consumption, both in terms of the material life and the more idealistic goals of freedom, democracy, and equality."[51] The story is full of irony. Consumption demands—equal access to public accommodation, entertainment, shopping, and transportation—comprised key goals in the Civil Rights Movement.[52] They also, as Alison Isenberg has shown, helped precipitate the civil disorders of the 1960s.[53] The National Welfare Rights Movement made full membership in the Consumers' Republic—the means to enjoy an American standard of consumption—a key demand.[54] "The Consumers' Republic," claims Cohen, "in prizing broad participation in mass consumer markets, provided a wide range of black Americans—differing in locale, class, and ideology—with an available and legitimate recourse for challenging racial discrimination, particularly as other avenues—such as desegregated neighborhoods, schools, voter registration lists, and jobs—were often blocked." But the Consumers' Republic also undermined black protest. Its "focus on winning access to public accommodations and markets inevitably limited the civil rights movement, particularly in the North, because it favored those demands that grew out of, and intersected with, the mainstream discourse and assumptions of the nation, braiding the experience of black Americans with those of whites." In the process, alternatives based on black nationalism or social democratic visions of economic justice receded. "Articulating black discontent in the language of a liberal struggle to pursue individual rights in a free capitalist marketplace and then successfully securing those rights . . . only reinforced the legitimacy of the capitalist order as a way of organizing economic life."[55]

The Consumers' Republic embraced more than the black middle class. Corporations responded to the bifurcation of black social structure with segmented products and advertising. "This market segmentation," claims Weems, "prompted corporate marketers to develop class-specific advertising aimed at African Americans." In the 1970s, "blaxploitation" films, for example, "stimulated conspicuous consumption as young black males sought to emulate the lifestyles of these dubious film icons." Although the blaxploitation films proved "an extremely effective means to more fully incorporate blacks as American consumers," concludes Weems, "the millions of dollars spent visiting a fantasy world of African American triumph and achievement might have been better spent trying to effect changes in the real world."[56] As it defined the good life in terms of the endless acquisition of material goods, this relentless pursuit of consumption turned Americans, both white and black, away from politics and, especially, from the politics of the common good. "If integration and desegregation were the call to arms of the civil rights movement," points out anthropologist Elizabeth Chin, "self-esteem claims equal prominence in contemporary discussions of racial problems and their solutions." What she terms the "commodification of race and the racialization of commodities" have accompanied "a turning away from the emphases of civil-rights oriented movements."[57] Among both black and white Americans consumption masked widening inequality, environmental degradation, and heightened insecurity with a blanket of inexpensive clothes, jewelry, and electronics, available to nearly everyone through the magic of credit. The result was the blossoming of consumer debt and bankruptcy—which reached previously

unimagined heights—rather than mobilization expressed through politics or other forms of collective action. Between 1999 and 2005, credit card debt almost tripled. The average African American debt was $8,319 compared to $8,992 for whites, who had higher incomes. In 2005, 84 percent of African American cardholders, compared to 50 percent of whites, carried a balance.[58] This disparity highlights one more irony in the relation of African Americans to the Consumers' Republic: the inability of formally equal access to consumption, like formally equal access to schools or housing, to overcome historic inequalities of class and race. Full participation in the Consumers' Republic required not only desegregated shopping, but the means with which to enjoy it. As long as African Americans remained economically behind whites, they would remain second-class citizens, disproportionately dependent on plastic to acquire not just luxuries, but the very means of survival. . . .[59]

By facilitating the rise of the Consumers' Republic, the private sector developed an indirect mechanism for deflecting the potential for civil violence. Public authorities deployed more direct mechanisms that relied on law enforcement. In 1968, Congress passed the Omnibus Crime Control and Safe Streets Act, which created the Law Enforcement Assistance Administration (LEAA), "the largest and longest federal effort to respond to the problem of crime in America."[61] Prompted by an increasing crime rate in the early 1960s, the LEAA had sought unsuccessfully to pass a crime bill. Civil violence on the nation's streets and campuses, as well in cities around the world, quickly changed the political calculus.[62] The LEAA, according to one historian, "provided a law-and-order alternative to the social, cultural, and economic perspective of the Kerner Commission."[63] The LEAA, operating mainly through block grants to states, gave money to police forces and other parts of the criminal justice system.[64] The legislation specified that no more than one-third of federal grants go to personnel—a requirement that excluded manpower intensive programs, including most of those based in communities or social work practice. "The police, on the other hand," point out criminologists, Alan R. Gordon and Norval Morris, "could easily meet the requirements through expenditures on hardware, such as vehicles, helicopters, computers, communications equipment, and antiriot gear."[65] Thus, much LEAA money supplied technologies of repression and control. Lynn A. Curtis, president of the Eisenhower Foundation, reported:

In its early days, LEAA distributed many grants for police hardware and command-and-control systems. The San Diego police acquired a submarine to patrol the waterfront, and Mobile, Alabama, received tanks for crowd control . . . in our crime-control policy as in our policy in Southeast Asia, we sought to resolve problems that were social and communal in nature through high technology and big money.[66]

In 1970, an amendment to the LEAA, one of several before its abolition in 1980, eliminated the one-third requirement. Although the LEAA spent about $7.5 billion between 1969 and 1980—an unprecedented federal commitment to law enforcement—its funds, at their peak, never amounted to more than 5 percent of total spending on criminal justice.[67]

State and local governments continued to bear most of the responsibility and expense for law enforcement. Like the federal government, in the aftermath of the 1960s civil violence, they also ramped up spending. Local spending on police protection leaped from $2,001 million in 1965 to $3,803 in 1970 and $6,813 in 1975. By 1995, it had reached $58,768.[68] More money allowed local police to adopt military practices, as historian Robert Fogelson describes:

In addition to employing the rhetoric of the 'war on crime' and stressing the martial arts in the training academies, these [police] departments ordered grenade launchers, infrared screening devices, and other weapons that were more appropriate for a military or paramilitary outfit than for a civilian police force. Chief Ed Davis even asked the Los Angeles City Council to appropriate funds for two jet helicopters. . . . In the aftermath of the 1960s riots, which overwhelmed the police forces in Los Angeles, Newark, Detroit, and several other cities, many departments attempted to turn groups of ordinary officers who were accustomed to working on

their own into highly centralized and tightly disciplined riot control units. Following recommendations proposed by the FBI and the army, the departments taught these units how to form lines, circles, diamonds, wedges, and other formations that were designed to disperse unruly crowds.[69]

While local governments paid most of the cost of police, state governments picked up the largest share of the escalating cost of incarceration, which, notes criminologist Elliot Currie, since the mid-1970s has been "the strategy most consistently adopted against crime in America."[70] As a consequence, in the late twentieth century a vast carceral state, described with chilling detail by political scientist Marie Gottschalk, spread throughout the nation. State costs for correction increased from $632 million in 1965 to $1,051 million in 1970, $2,193 million in 1975, and $4,258 million in 1980.[71]

What impact did increased funding and militarized policing have on crime? Most analyses claim that the LEAA failed to reduce crime.[72] As for incarceration, even optimistic accounts, claims Currie, leave us "at best, with a remarkably meager payoff for the enormous, costly, and disruptive investment of social resources involved."[73] Indeed, crime rates, which had been increasing during the early 1960s, soared *after* the episodes of civil violence. Despite increased federal, state, and local funding, violent crime increased per 100,000 population, from 160.9 in 1960 to 200.2 in 1965, 363.5 in 1970, 487.8 in 1975, and 596.6 in 1980.[74] Nonetheless, with few exceptions, the civil violence of the 1960s did not recur. Did the militarization of policing and mass incarceration help authorities break up potential insurgencies, respond more effectively to ones that occurred, and prevent them from spreading to other cities?

In *City of Quartz*, Mike Davis limns a connection between police repression and the end of civil violence. In what he calls the August 1965 "festival of the oppressed," Davis claims, "formerly hostile [gang] groups forgot old grudges and cheered each other on against the hated LAPD and the National Guard." To everyone's surprise, the "ecumenical movement of the streets and 'hoods lasted for three or four years. Community workers, and even the Los Angeles Police Department (LAPD) themselves, were astonished by the virtual cessation of gang hostilities as the gang leadership joined the Revolution." This "aspiration for unity and militancy" did not sit well with authorities. Together, "the FBI's notorious COINTELPRO program and the LAPD's Public Disorder Intelligence Division . . . concentrated on destroying Los Angeles's Black Power vanguards." In this, they succeeded, but the result was not what they had hoped or predicted. "As even the *Times* recognized, the decimation of the Panthers led to a recrudescence of gangs in the early 1970s." This, Davis emphasizes, "was not merely a gang revival, but a radical permutation of Black gang culture" led by the Crips, who "blended a penchant for ultra-violence with overweening ambition to dominate the entire ghetto." In the 1970s, Davis writes, the Crips evolved "into a hybrid of teen cult and proto-Mafia."[75] The "recrudescence of gangs," he argues, also contributed to the de-politicization of ghetto youth.

> Teenagers, who today flock to hear Easy-E rap, 'It ain't about color, it's about the color of money, I love that green'—then filled the Sports Arena to listen to Stokely Carmichael, H. Rap Brown, Bobby Seale and James Forman adumbrate the unity program of SNCC and the Panthers.[76]

In Los Angeles in August 1992, two major gangs, the Crips and the Bloods, entered into a truce with the hopes of both lessening violence and opening work opportunities. For a time the truce held. Measured against 1991, by June, homicides had dropped 88.2 percent, attempted murder 45 percent, and robberies 13.2 percent. "As far as I know," said Los Angeles police lieutenant John Dinkin, "there have been no drive-by shootings between gangs in south and central Los Angles since the [April 1992] riots."[77] A barbecue chef whose restaurant had been under siege reported, "It's a big change in only 100 days. People can walk and not be scared of being hit by the spray."[78] The truce even extended beyond African American gangs and South Central Los Angeles, embracing Latino gangs in the San Fernando Valley while "individual efforts to initiate and maintain the truce soon developed into community-based organizations. . . ." One gang member observed,

"Instead of shooting each other, we decided to fight together for black power."[79]

Instead of welcoming the truce, officials reacted skeptically, with law enforcement authorities claiming the truce "was an excuse for young gang members to unify against the police," and they constantly harassed truce leaders, even arresting a "respected leader of Homidos Uniodos, a truce organization" and, in violation of a city order that prohibited police from arresting someone solely because they suspected a federal immigration violation, handing him to the Immigration and Naturalization Service (INS), which sought to deport him. (He successfully fought the charge.)[80] Nor did authorities get the message about opportunity. Job progress remained virtually non-existent for youths over the age of twenty-one. One commentator warned, gangs "made the first step to come together in peace, to stop the madness, to stop the killing. Now they have to have some help, some training, some educational assistance."[81] He might as well have been talking to the wind, as the sad failure of Rebuild LA, the effort to reconstruct violence-torn neighborhoods solely through the private sector, soon revealed.[82]

Since then, public authorities have worked to prevent any resurgence of legitimate political activity by gangs. In 1993 and 1994, when gang summits met in a number of cities to discuss joining together around issues of economic justice, politicians and the media quickly dismissed their actions as nothing more than transparent ploys by criminals. Commenting on the response to a gang summit in Chicago, a newspaper reporter observed, "Most reports of the gang meeting have been negative. Chicago's local and national politicians have called the peace effort a joke. . . . Alderwoman Dorothy Tillman called the new movement a scam."[83] But Jesse Jackson proved supportive. In Chicago, he "embraced the leaders of the gang peace movement . . . calling their efforts 'the centerpiece of a new urban policy.'"[84]

Fewer black men, in fact, could participate in politics, even if they wanted to, because they were felons. Felony disenfranchisement laws had long been on the books in most states, but their consequences became more severe as aggressive law enforcement, including draconian drug laws, created unprecedented numbers of felons, who were disproportionately black. Adding together incarcerated felons and former inmates barred from voting effectively disenfranchised about 1.4 million, or 13 percent, of African American men, a rate seven times the national average. Looking ahead to younger men, the situation appears even bleaker. With the current rate of incarceration, at some point in their lives 30 percent of the next generation of black men, points out The Sentencing Project, will face disenfranchisement, a fraction that rises to a possible stunning 40 percent of black men who live in states that permanently bar ex-offenders from voting.[85] Many black men, moreover, evading warrants or just fearful of potential arrest, avoid the institutions and agents of the state, thereby eliminating themselves from participation in political action.[86]

That a share of the responsibility for the turn toward criminal violence and de-politicization among African American youth rests with public authorities remains a hypothesis—intriguing, explosive in its implications, and in need of much research. Indeed, the lack of research on the question—and on the social history of policing post-1960—remains stunning and surprising. Clearly, though, the turn from politics also reflected other influences. Among the most important were disillusionment with the achievements of civil rights liberalism and Black Power. In his history of civil rights and Black Power in Philadelphia, Matthew J. Countryman writes, "A decade after it began, the Black Power movement dissipated as African Americans experienced a series of clear lessons about the limitation of their ability to change public policy at the national and local level." At the heart of the matter, observes Countryman, "Black Power advocates were never able to convince other elements of the New Deal coalition to bear the cost of its agenda for racial justice."[87] In his ethnography of the informal economy in a Chicago neighborhood, Sudhir Alladi Venkatesh shows how, even at the height of Harold Washington's mayoral administration, poor Southside Chicagoans learned a similar lesson as they found their political influence and patronage cutoff by the city's now black administration, which depended increasingly on a coalition of black middle and upper class supporters. The result was the "gradual withdrawal of grassroots persons from the mainstream black political scene."[88]

The frustrations and failed hopes that turned young African Americans away from politics and protest reflected dashed expectations among former radicals in Europe as well as the United States. "Now more cynical than idealistic," claims Suri, "dissidents learned to live under what they perceived as illegitimate—or at least deeply flawed—governments. Many turned away from their former political activism to a self-imposed isolation from what they saw as the corrupt world of state power."[89] For black Americans, the sources of disillusionment proved especially strong. In the 1970s and 1980s, as the spread of black poverty turned vast areas of cities into reservations for the black poor, as fewer black men found work in the regular labor market, as mass incarceration locked unprecedented numbers of them away, young African Americans had reason to look with skepticism at civil rights liberalism, Black Power, and, indeed, politics in general.[90]

Other factors already discussed—the Consumers' Republic, selective incorporation, and indirect rule—also facilitated de-politicization, without which the management of marginalization would have proved far more difficult. In the 1960s, black Americans lacked channels through which to make effective claims on the state. They were underrepresented in Congress, state legislatures, city councils, police forces, and in influential positions in private corporations. Other than through collective action—whether sit-ins or violence—they had few ways to force their grievances onto public attention or persuade authorities to respond. This changed as the new demography of urban politics, the victories of the Civil Rights movement, and affirmative action combined to open new channels of access. As selective incorporation bifurcated African American social structure, unprecedented numbers of African Americans found themselves elected public officials, public bureaucrats, and administrators of social service agencies. New channels of access removed one powerful justification for violent protest. African Americans who once might have led protests now held positions from which they could argue that civil violence was both unnecessary and counterproductive. Others remained in America's inner cities, struggling to get by, disenfranchised, wary of the state, disillusioned with politicians, and lacking leadership or vision strong enough to mobilize them once again to make claims on the state. . . .

Notes

7. *The Kerner Report: the 1968 Report of the National Advisory Commission on Civil Disorders* (New York: Pantheon, 1988), 9.

8. Ibid., 1.

22. Charles Tilly, *Identities, Boundaries, and Social Ties* (Boulder and London: Paradigm Publishers, 2005), 147. See also, Tilly, *Politics of Collective Violence*, 75.

23. Tilly, *Identities*, 8–9.

24. Kevin Boyle, *Arc of Justice: A Saga of Race, Civil Rights, and Murder in the Jazz Age* (New York: Henry Holt, 2004); Arnold R. Hirsch, *Making the Second Ghetto: Race and Housing in Chicago 1940–1960* (New York: Cambridge University Press, 1983).

25. Campbell Gibson and Kay Jung. *Historical Census Statistics on Population Totals by Race, 1790 to 1990, and by Hispanic Origins, 1970 to 1990, For Large Cities and Other Urban Place in the United States.* U.S. Census Bureau. Population Division. Working Paper no. 76. February 2005.

26. Josh Sides, *L.A. City Limits: African American Los Angeles from the Great Depression to the Present* (Berkeley and Los Angeles: University of California Press, 2003), 2, 44.

27. Hirsch, *Making the Second Ghetto*; Thomas J. Sugrue, *Origins of the Urban Crisis: Race and Inequality in Postwar Detroit* (Princeton: Princeton University Press, 1986).

28. Gerald Gamm, *Urban Exodus: Why the Jews Left Boston and the Catholics Stayed* (Cambridge: Harvard University Press, 1999); J. Anthony Lukas, *Common Ground: A Turbulent Decade in the Lives of Three American Families* (New York: Knopf, 1985); Lillian B. Rubin, *Busing and Backlash: White Against White in a California School District* (Berkeley: University of California Press, 1972); Ronald P. Formisano, *Boston Against Busing: Race, Class, and Ethnicity in the 1960s and 1970s* (Chapel Hill: University of North Carolina Press, 1991).

29. Ball-Rokeach and Short, "Collective Violence," 161.

30. "Tracking Change: a Look At the Growth of Black Elected Officials in the United States, Based on Reports by the Joint Center for Political and Economic Studies." Chart. *New York Times.* March 29, 2006.

31. W. Marvin Dulaney, *Black Police in America* (Bloomington and Indianapolis: Indiana University Press, 1996), 121–22.

32. Ball-Rokeach and Short, "Collective Violence," 163.

33. H. Paul Friesema, "Black Control of Central Cities: The Hollow Prize," *Journal of the American Institute of Planners* (March 1969), 75.

36. I recall some stores in West Philadelphia, where I live, boarding up their windows in anticipation of rioting, which did not occur.

37. I use mechanisms in Charles Tilly's definition as a "form of delimited class of events that change relations among specified sets of elements in identical or closely similar ways over a variety of situations" and processes as "frequently occurring combinations or sequences of mechanisms." Charles Tilly, *Identities, Boundaries, and Social Ties* (Boulder and London: Paradigm Publishers, 2005), 28.

38. Ball-Rokeach and Short, "Collective Violence," 162. On African American public employment, see also Roger Waldinger, *Still the Promised City? African-Americans and New Immigrants in Post-Industrial New York* (Cambridge: Harvard University Press, 1996).

39. For the concept of limited ladders of mobility, I am indebted to John Foster, "Nineteenth Century Towns: A Class Dimension," in H. J. Dyos, *The Study of Urban History* (London: St. Martin's, 1968), 281–399.

40. Katz and Stern, *One Nation Divisible*, 92.

41. Sides, *L.A. City Limits*, 88, 91.

42. Ball-Rokeach and Short, "Collective Violence," 160.

43. For the idea of mimetic reform, I am indebted to Katznelson, *City Trenches*, 177, 187.

44. Katznelson, *City Trenches*, 179, 187.

45. Julia Rabig, "Broken Deal: Devolution, Development, and Civil Society in Newark, New Jersey: 1960–1990," Ph.D. dissertation, University of Pennsylvania, 2007, ch. 2.

46. The idea of indirect rule applied to African American ghettos was developed as part of the theory of internal colonialism advanced by black writers in the late 1960s. See, for example, Stokely Carmichael and Charles V. Hamilton, *Black Power: The Politics of Liberation in America* (New York: Random House, 1967).

47. Gerald E. Frug, *City Making: Building Communities Without Building Walls* (Princeton: Princeton University Press, 1999).

48. The term is from Lizabeth Cohen, *A Consumers' Republic: The Politics of Mass Consumption in Postwar America* (New York: Knopf, 2003).

49. Robert E. Weems, Jr., *Desegregating the Dollar: African American Consumption in the Twentieth Century* (New York: New York University Press, 1998), 71, tables 4.1, 75.

50. Weems, *Desegregating the Dollar*, 107; The 1993/94 report on the Buying Power of Black America (Chicago: Target Market News Group, Inc., 1993), 22; *Household Spending: Who Spends How Much on What* (Ithaca, NY: New Strategies and Publications, 2005), 125–26.

51. Cohen, *Consumers' Republic*, 7.

52. In his history of youth in post-war West Philadelphia, Carl Nightingale claims that, rather than being disaffected from the American mainstream, in their frustrated aspirations as consumers young African-Americans are the most American of Americans. Carl Husemoller Nightingale, *On the Edge: A History of Poor Black Children and Their American Dreams* (New York: Basic Books, 1993).

53. Alison Isenberg, *Downtown America: A History of the Place and the People Who Made It* (Chicago and London: University of Chicago Press, 2004), 203–54.

54. Felicia Kornbluh, "To Fulfill Their 'Rightly Needs': Consumerism and the National Welfare Rights Movement," *Radical History Review* 69 (Fall 199), 76–112.

55. Cohen, *Consumers' Republic*, 7, 88–89, 90.

56. Weems, *Desegregating the Dollar*, 90, 100.

57. Elizabeth Chin, *Purchasing Power: Black Kids and American Consumer Culture* (Minneapolis and London: University of Minnesota Press, 2001), 168–69.

58. Tamara Dracut et al., The Plastic Safety Net: Findings from a National Survey of Credit Card Debt Among Low- and Middle-Income Households (Demos and Center for Responsible Lending, 2005), 8; Jennifer Wheary, *The Future of the Middle Class: African Americans, Latinos, and Economic Opportunity* (New York: Demos, 2006), 22.

59. The way inequality structures consumption is a major theme of Chin in *Purchasing Power*.

61. Alan R. Gordon and Norval Morris, "Presidential Commissions and the Law Enforcement Administration" in Lynn A. Curtis ed., *American Violence and Public Policy: An Update of the National Commission on the Causes and Prevention of Violence* (New Haven: Yale University Press, 1985), 117.

62. Kenneth O'Reilly, "The FBI and the Politics of Riots, 1964–1968," *Journal of American History*, 75:1 (June 1988), 91–114; Suri, *Power and Protest*, 182–212.

63. Ibid, 113.

64. Fogelson, *Big City Police*, 220.

65. Gordon and Morris, "Presidential Commissions," 125.

66. Lynn A. Curtis, "Introduction," in Curtis, *American Violence*, 7–8.

67. Robert A. Diegeleman, "Federal Financial Assistance for Crime Control," *Journal of Criminal Law and Criminology*, 73:3 (Autumn 1982), 1001.

68. Richard Sutch, "Criminal Justice Expenditures, by Level of Government: 1902–1996" in S. Carter, S. S. Gartner et al., *Historical Statistics of the United States Millennial Edition Online* (New York: Cambridge University Press, 2006 [http://husu/-Cambridge.org]), Table Ec1159–1178.

69. Fogelson, *Big City Police*, 220.

70. Elliott Currie, "Crimes of Violence and Public Policy: Changing Directions," in Curtis, *American Violence*, 44.

71. Sutch, "Criminal Justice Expenditures."

72. Congressional Budget Office, "Federal Law Enforcement Assistance: Alternative Approaches," April 1978, xii. See also, Malcolm M. Feeley and Austin D. Surat, *The Policy Dilemma: Federal Crime Policy and the Law Enforcement Assistance Administration, 1968–1978* (Minneapolis: University of Minnesota Press, 1980).

73. Currie, "Crimes of Violence," 45.

74. "Estimated rates of crime known to police, by type of offense, 1960–1997," *Historical Statistics*, Series Ec11–20.

75. Mike Davis, *City of Quartz: Excavating the Future in Los Angeles* (New York: Vintage, 1992), 297–300.

76. Davis, *City of Quartz*, 298.

77. Haya El Nasser and Jonathan T. Lovitt, "Frustration Makes Gang Truce More Tenuous," *USA Today*, August 6, 1992, 9A.

78. Op. cit.

79. Gottlieb et al., *The Next Los Angeles*, 126.

80. Gottlieb et al., *Next Los Angeles*, 126–27.

81. Nasser and Lovitt, "Frustration."

82. Gottlieb et al., *Next Los Angeles*, 178–83.

83. Don Terry, "Guardian America: Youth Power Hits the Streets," *The Guardian* (London), October 28, 1993, 16.

84. Paul Shepard, "Gang Peace Leaders Need Jackson's Pull, Most Say, Want Policy-Makers to Provide Job Training, Employment," *Plain Dealer* (Cleveland), October 25, 1993, 5A. See also: Seth Mydans, "Gangs Go Public in New Fight for Respect," *New York Times*, May 2, 1993. Section 1, 1; Peter Leyden, "Gang Chiefs End Summit," *Star Tribune* (Minneapolis), July 19, 1993, 1A; Don Terry, "Chicago Group, Extends Turf, Turns to Politics,"

New York Times, October 25, 1993, Section A, 12; Dennis R. Roddy and Lamont Jones Junior, "Gang Summit: An Invitation to Hope or Disaster?" and "Gang Summit Opens Despite Cold Shoulder," *Pittsburgh Post-Gazette*, March 6, 1994, A1 and May 27, 1994, A1.

85. The Sentencing Project, "Felony Disenfranchisement Laws in the United States" [http://www.sentencingproject.org/pdfs/1046.pdf. Accessed November 16, 2006].

86. For this point, as well as for directing me toward the impact of felony disenfranchisement, my thanks to Alice Goffman.

87. Matthew J. Countryman, *Up South: Civil Rights and Black Power in Philadelphia* (Philadelphia: University of Pennsylvania Press, 2006), 328–30.

88. Sudhir Alladi Venkatesh, *Off the Books: The Underground Economy of the Urban Poor* (Cambridge: Harvard University Press, 2006), 240–44.

89. Suri, *Power and Protest*, 215.

90. See the interesting article, Lisa Y. Sullivan, "The Demise of Black Civil Society: Once Upon a Time When We Were Colored Meets the Hip-Hop Generation," *Social Policy* (Winter 1996: 27, 2): 6–10.

Conclusion

Public Policy Applications: Mass Transit

Policy Then

In the middle of the twentieth century, Los Angeles was the quintessential Sunbelt city. Sprawling across a vast stretch of land, the "city" was really a seemingly endless conglomeration of suburbs of single-family homes with front and back yards and two-car garages punctuated by multiple commercial/retail centers and connected by wide boulevards and even wider freeways. Angelenos loved their cars and the freedom that they afforded to travel wherever they wanted, fast and in style.

But by the 1960s, the costs of a decentralized automobile-centric landscape became painfully apparent. Feverish growth had resulted in horrendous traffic congestion and air pollution that for months at a time obscured the once sun-kissed hills and mountains that envelop the region. As gasoline prices soared in the 1970s, many realized that a new direction in transit planning was needed.

In 1980, voters in Los Angeles County approved a ballot initiative that raised the sales tax by 0.5 percent to fund a rail-based mass transit system centered in the downtown business district. Construction began in 1985. By 1991, a 22-mile light rail line from downtown to Long Beach had opened, followed soon after by a heavy rail subway running 4 miles from downtown and later extended an additional 11 miles to Hollywood. Another 13-mile light rail line was completed in 1995, with more light and heavy rail lines under construction after 2000.

Building a rail-based mass transit system was expensive. To help pay for it, the Metropolitan Transit Authority (MTA) began to divert funds away from bus transportation. Los Angeles's 350,000 bus riders, who were overwhelmingly working-class people of color with no other way to get to work, soon felt the impact of the service cuts in the form of long waits at bus stops and overcrowded buses. Resentment deepened over the fact that 70 percent of the MTA's capital budget had been allocated to rail transit even though suburban rail commuters constituted only 6 percent of the system's total ridership. The last straw came in 1994 when the MTA announced that it had budgeted $123 million for the first phase of construction of a light rail line to Pasadena to serve higher-income white commuters while imposing a fare hike and further service cuts on bus riders totaling $126 million.

A formidable grassroots organization, the Bus Riders Union (BRU), emerged and turned inequities in transit funding into a civil rights issue. It engaged in disruptive protest and then joined a coalition of groups in filing a class action lawsuit in 1994 that charged the MTA with discriminating against minorities in violation of the Civil Rights Act and the Equal Protection Clause of the Fourteenth Amendment to the U.S. Constitution. The case was settled in 1996 when the MTA entered into a consent decree in which it promised to reduce overcrowding by specified amounts by a series of set deadlines. When the MTA failed to comply with the consent decree, the BRU organized a strike in which bus riders refused to pay fares on overcrowded buses. The "no seat, no fare" strike remained in effect until the MTA agreed to put another 1,600 buses on the streets. The BRU continued to criticize the MTA in subsequent years for giving preferential treatment to an expanding rail-based transit system over inner-city bus riders of color.

Policy Now

The BRU remains active in the politics of transportation policy in Los Angeles today. In 2012, it played a key role in defeating a ballot measure that would have generated more revenue to support further expansion of the city's rail lines, which the BRU viewed as taking money away from the underfunded bus transit system. The initiative won 66.1 percent, just short of the two-thirds of the vote necessary under state law to raise taxes.

Notwithstanding the narrow defeat of Proposition J, a consensus seems to be emerging in Los Angeles around the need to support a mass transit system that offers ample, reliable, and affordable bus *and* rail service. The drawbacks of Los Angeles's car-centered culture are starker than ever. Freeways remain clogged with traffic as the region's population continues to swell and sensitivity to global climate change increases with each passing year. Surveys show that young people are less attached to automobiles than ever before.

Much evidence suggests that popular support for mass transit is climbing. Passage of an earlier initiative in 2008 to increase the sales tax to fund extensions of two existing rail lines has resulted in 28.4 miles of new tracks and thirty more stations. As of September 2013, the two heavy rail lines averaged a weekday ridership of 164,214, making it the fourth busiest system per track length in the United States after New York, Boston, and Washington, D.C. Los Angeles's light rail system, with 202,500 daily weekday boardings, is the second-most used in the nation.

Rail lines, both new and old, have also spurred vigorous development within downtown Los Angeles and along the transit corridors. Planners try to encourage relatively dense, mixed-use "transit-oriented development," or TODs, as a way of rejuvenating stagnating or distressed areas while boosting potential ridership of mass transit. The synergistic effect of rail line extension and the spread of TODs is seen by policymakers as conducive to economic growth and environmental protection.

One concern, however, is the tendency of TODs to spur rising property values and thus gentrification. The desirable goal of building new rail lines not just in communities that benefit white, middle-class suburbanites commuting to downtown jobs but also in a broad range of neighborhoods with diverse populations is undercut if the expansion of mass transit leads to the displacement of longtime residents and small-business owners.

Visitor7 (http://creativecommons.org/licenses/by-sa/3.0), via Wikimedia Commons

Subway station at Hollywood and Highland, Los Angeles

Additional Resources

Robert Cervero, "Transit-Oriented Development in America: Strategies, Issues, Policy Directions," in *The New Urbanism and Beyond: Designing Cities for the Future*, ed. Tigran Haas (New York: Rizzoli, 2008).

Ethan N. Elkind, *Railtown: The Fight for the Los Angeles Metro Rail and the Future of the City* (Berkeley: University of California Press, 2014).

Eyes on the Prize: America's Civil Rights Movement: Keys to the Kingdom, 1974–1980. Segment of documentary film series on community-based protest against court-ordered busing to desegregate public schools in Boston (WGBH Boston, 2006).

Joe Grengs, "Community-Based Planning as a Source of Change: The Transit Equity Movement of Los Angeles's Bus Riders Union," *Journal of the American Planning Association*, 68 (2), 2002.

Industrial Areas Foundation. Founded by Saul Alinsky, the IAF is the nation's oldest and largest network of local faith and community-based organizations. www.industrialareasfoundation.org.

J. Anthony Lukas, *Common Ground: A Turbulent Decade in the Lives of Three American Families* (New York: A. A. Knopf, 1985).

PICO National Network. Another long-standing and effective faith-based, community-organizing network. www.piconetwork.org.

Shelterforce. The nation's oldest continually published community development magazine and a valuable resource for community activists. www.shelterforce.org.

James Q. Wilson, "Cars and Their Enemies," *Commentary*, July 1997.

Discussion Questions

1. What is the appropriate mix of trains and buses in an urban public transit system? What factors should be considered in striking a balance in a given city?

2. Why has rail-based transit become so popular in recent years even though it is considerably more expensive than bus-based transit?

3. Grassroots organizing typically originates in communities where people live. Why is this a useful place to mobilize citizens? What are the limitations of community-based organizing?

4. What models of community organizing are likely to be most effective in influencing urban policy making? Why?

5. Community organizations sometimes struggle to establish coalitions with like-minded groups across the city. What strategies might be employed to build and maintain such coalitions? Why has the Los Angeles Bus Riders Union been so successful in its citywide activism?

Chapter 11

Regime Politics

Introduction

Governing cities in late-twentieth-century America was a challenge at best and an exercise in futility at worst. A shrinking tax base, struggling economies, and persistent racial tensions severely limited how mayors and other city officials could deliver on promises made to voters during their election campaigns. Influential scholars like Paul Peterson asserted that mayors had no real choices other than to pursue developmental policies aimed at attracting and retaining capital investment; any attempt to ameliorate inequities through redistributive policies would ensure only a deeper slide into fiscal oblivion. The implication flowing from this set of circumstances was that urban politics—the process of determining who gets what, when, where, and how in U.S. cities—essentially would vanish.[1] There is no meaningful debate about policy directions. Desperate cities are compelled to nurture a business-friendly environment and embrace a pro-growth agenda favoring the downtown business district.[2]

Many scholars disputed Peterson's constricted view of urban politics, contending that within the constraints set by societal trends there was still room for city officials to maneuver and chart alternative paths.[3] The leading voice within this school of thought belonged to Clarence N. Stone, who observed that while city officials are limited by economic factors, particularly the threat of capital mobility, political pressures also constrain what city leaders can do. Politicians need to get elected and reelected and business interests require the support of governmental authority to pursue their pro-growth goals. According to Stone, the crucial entity that accommodates the competing forces arising from popular control over the state and private influence over the market is the *regime*. He defined a regime as the informal partnership between public officials and private groups that allows an administration to advance an agenda. The most valuable, and thus the most influential, regime partners are the ones who possess substantial material resources that can be utilized to win elections and get things done once the election is over by bringing together diverse groups within an otherwise disjointed society. Regimes, therefore, provide a vehicle for mayors facing extraordinarily difficult conditions to govern effectively.[4]

Reading 11-1 summarizes Stone's regime theory and its application to the city of Atlanta. His book, *Regime Politics: Governing Atlanta, 1946–1988*, reveals how a succession of mayors over a forty-year period worked closely with downtown business interests seeking to revitalize the central business district *and* leaders of the black middle class who sought advances in civil rights and economic opportunity. Each member of Atlanta's governing coalition benefited from the cooperative relationship, and together that coalition provided the leadership and resources to move the city forward in an effective manner.[5]

Raphael J. Sonenshein's research on urban politics in Los Angeles during the 1970s and 1980s is not explicitly grounded in regime theory. Instead, Sonenshein was more interested in explaining how biracial coalitions might be forged and maintained amid a broader climate of racial tension. But Sonenshein's analysis of Tom Bradley's five terms as mayor of Los Angeles in **Reading 11-2** offers valuable insights into the formation and durability of a governing coalition based on common interests, a unifying ideology, and skilled leadership. As in Atlanta, a smoothly functioning biracial regime with crucial support from business leaders presided over a sustained period of economic growth and racial harmony.[6]

Regime theory showed how effective and stable governance was possible in the face of trying circumstances. However, some questioned whether it lived up to its promise of offering multiple pathways to varied forms of governance, particularly regimes willing and able to promote equitable growth.[7] In practice, the scope of possibilities appeared to be surprisingly narrow. Many case studies of urban politics confirmed that business elites held a dominant position in governing coalitions that prioritized downtown expansion over neighborhood revitalization. The result was a recurring pattern of uneven development and ever-deepening inequality across the urban landscape.[8] Even when alternative regimes did emerge, policy changes intended to assist neglected communities often proved to be limited and temporary.[9]

Stone's own analysis of Atlanta revealed that when the city's first black mayor, Maynard Jackson, tried to establish a more inclusive administration and a fairer distribution of the benefits of growth through policies like affirmative action, he encountered stiff opposition from downtown interests and a withdrawal of resources necessary to implement his desired programs. Before long, Jackson concluded that he needed "to go along to get along" and gravitated back into the orbit of the downtown-led coalition.[10]

Doubts about regime theory's capacity to elucidate how more equitable regime governance is possible have reinforced scholarly perspectives that minimize the role of political agency in cities. Apart from market centrists like Peterson, structural Marxists have long argued that the imperatives of capitalist development systematically overwhelm mechanisms of popular control.[11] In **Reading 11-3**, Jason Hackworth makes the case that the public–private partnerships at the heart of regime theory are not simply "salves for market failures" but function aggressively as "market facilitators." This represents a sharp break from scholars who highlight the agency of urban policymakers. By shifting the focus beyond the immediate local context to incorporate the broader political economy, Hackworth aims to explicate "the regime's role as an agent of capitalism."[12]

Structural constraints may be particularly onerous for so-called secondary cities located within the penumbra of primary cities that are active in the global economy or are major forces within a regional economy. Such municipalities are subject not only to the fierce competition of the marketplace but also to the sometimes stifling economic and political influences of the dominant regional city. Alan Lessof's research illuminates how a secondary city like Corpus Christi struggled to chart its own path of economic development that was independent of larger cities in the region such as San Antonio and Houston. Indeed, Lessof finds that secondary cities that dare to reinvent themselves risk overreaching and incurring significant, long-term costs.[13]

At the same time, attention to how structural conditions may limit policymakers in some cities prompted other scholars to investigate how alternative conditions may open up possibilities for policies that are usually opposed by prominent business interests. In **Reading 11-4**, Paul Kantor and H. V. Savitch consider how a wide range of "market conditions" may influence the ability of city officials to bargain effectively with downtown business elites. For example, businesses in San Francisco might accept a neighborhood-oriented policy agenda that entails more taxation and regulation because of that city's spectacular natural beauty. Similarly, corporate interests and trade associations in Washington, D.C., may tolerate a less-than-friendly business climate to remain within close proximity of the federal government. In such cases, locational advantages significantly reduce the threat of capital mobility and, presumably, the impetus in favor of pro-business policy making.[14]

However, enduring alternative regimes do not spring up simply because a city happens to enjoy a number of place-based attributes that may justify a higher cost of doing business. Kantor and Savitch also point to "popular-control systems" or local political institutions and processes that strengthen the influence of groups in the electorate whose interests may clash with those of the downtown business establishment. In such cities, potent and sustained activism at the grassroots may play a critical role. Some scholars see this as a serious conceptual gap in regime theory. They argue that with their focus on elite-level politics, regime theorists tend to neglect the conditions under which community groups and social movement organizations might develop political coalitions capable of challenging the neoliberal priorities of downtown business interests.[15] Stone was certainly aware of such a possibility and always claimed that the composition and direction of regimes may take many forms, but he also underscored the difficulty of organizing a governing coalition led by community groups given their lack of material resources and the extent to which they are often riven by racial, ethnic, class, and cultural divisions.[16]

Notwithstanding such obstacles, neighborhood-oriented groups contesting the downtown-centric agenda favored by business elites have mobilized successfully, won key elections, and established viable governing coalitions in cities such as Chicago, Boston, and San Francisco.[17] How exactly such community-oriented regimes form and endure, and whether such regimes are replicable in cities lacking locational advantages, requires further careful attention.[18]

Notes

1. This classic definition of politics first appeared in Harold D. Lasswell, *Politics: Who Gets What, When, How* (New York: McGraw-Hill, 1935).

2. Paul Peterson, *City Limits* (Chicago: University of Chicago Press, 1981). For Peterson, the only alternative available to city leaders who wished to address the dire conditions within inner-city neighborhoods was to turn to Washington, D.C., but retrenchment of federal programs directed at cities was already under way by the early 1970s, and with the election of Ronald Reagan in 1980 that source of funding was no longer reliable. Refer to George E. Peterson and Carol W. Lewis, eds., *Reagan and the Cities* (Washington, DC: The Urban Institute, 1986).

3. Refer to Todd Swanstrom, "Semisovereign Cities: The Politics of Urban Development," *Polity*, 21 (Fall 1988); John R. Logan and Todd Swanstrom, *Beyond the City Limits: Urban Policy and Economic Restructuring in Comparative Perspective* (Philadelphia: Temple University Press, 1990); John H. Mollenkopf, *A Phoenix in the Ashes: The Rise and Fall of the Koch Coalition in New York City Politics* (Princeton: Princeton University Press, 1992).

4. Clarence N. Stone, *Regime Politics: Governing Atlanta, 1946–1988* (Lawrence: University Press of Kansas, 1989); Clarence N. Stone, "Urban Regimes and the Capacity to Govern: A Political Economy Approach," *Journal of Urban Affairs*, 15, 1993. See also Stephen L. Elkin, *City and Regime in the American Republic* (Chicago: University of Chicago Press, 1987).

5. Business-led regimes emerged in other U.S. cities such as Dallas, Albuquerque, and Baltimore. Clarence N. Stone and Heywood T. Sanders, *The Politics of Urban Development* (Lawrence: University Press of Kansas, 1987); Bernard J. Frieden and Lynne B. Sagalyn, *Downtown, Inc.: How America Rebuilds Cities* (Cambridge: MIT Press, 1989).

6. Raphael J. Sonenshein, *Politics in Black and White: Race and Power in Los Angeles* (Princeton: Princeton University Press, 1993). However, as in Atlanta, questions arise over the extent and depth of Los Angeles's good fortunes. Prosperity certainly did not extend to all segments of the city's population and perceptions of racial tranquility were shattered with the brutal beating of a black man, Rodney King, by four white police officers in 1991 and the uprising that ensued in South Central Los Angeles immediately after those officers were exonerated. For a scathing critique of inequality and repression in Los Angeles, see Mike Davis, *City of Quartz: Excavating the Future in Los Angeles* (New York: Verso, 1990).

7. Refer to Jonathan S. Davies, "Urban Regime Theory: A Normative-Empirical Critique," *Journal of Urban Affairs*, 24 (1), 2002.

8. Gregory D. Squires, ed., *Unequal Partnerships: The Political Economy of Urban Redevelopment* (New Brunswick, NJ: Rutgers University Press, 1989); Scott Cummings, ed., *Business Elites and Urban Development: Case Studies and Critical Perspectives* (Albany: State University of New York Press, 1988); Marc V. Levine, "Downtown Redevelopment as an Urban Growth Strategy: A Critical Appraisal of the Baltimore Renaissance," *Journal of Urban Affairs*, 9 (2), 1987.

9. William Sites, "The Limits of Urban Regime Theory: New York City Under Koch, Dinkins, and Giuliani," *Urban Affairs Review*, 32 (4), March 1997.

10. Stone, *Regime Politics*.

11. Refer to David Harvey, *Social Justice and the City* (Baltimore: Johns Hopkins University Press, 1973); David Harvey, *The Urbanization of Capital* (Baltimore: Johns Hopkins University Press, 1985).

12. For another study of neoliberalism in a contemporary American city, see John P. Koval, ed., *The New Chicago: A Social and Cultural Analysis* (Philadelphia: Temple University Press, 2006). Other scholars maintain that even smaller municipalities retain the capacity to respond effectively to global forces such as those that precipitated the foreclosure crisis following the financial crisis of 2008. Refer to Garrett Glasgow, Paul G. Lewis, and Max Neiman, "Local Development Policies and the Foreclosure Crisis in California: Can Local Policies Hold Back National Tides?" *Urban Affairs Review*, 48 (1), 2012.

13. Alan Lessoff, "Corpus Christi, 1965–2005: A Secondary City's Search for a New Direction," *Journal of Urban History*, 35 (1), 2008.

14. In a related vein, fluctuations in the national or regional economy may expand or constrict opportunities to pursue policies that might normally be opposed by business interests.

15. Refer to Gerry Stoker, "Regime Theory and Urban Politics," in *Theories of Urban Politics*, ed. David Judge, Gerry Stoker, and Harold Wolman (London: Sage, 1995).

16. By contrast, the downtown business community typically commands an imposing stockpile of material resources far in excess of whatever may be available to community-based organizations and is relatively cohesive with respect to socio-economic class and overall goals. Stone, *Regime Politics*.

17. Pierre Clavel, *Activists in City Hall: The Progressive Response to the Reagan Era in Boston and Chicago* (Ithaca, NY: Cornell University Press, 2010); Richard E. DeLeon, "San Francisco: The Politics of Race, Land Use, and Ideology," in *Racial Politics in American Cities*, ed. Rufus P. Browning, Dale R. Marshall, and David H. Tabb, 3rd ed. (New York: Longman, 2003); Stephen J. McGovern, *The Politics of Downtown Development: Dynamic Political Cultures in San Francisco and Washington, D.C.* (Lexington: University Press of Kentucky, 1998); Peter Dreier and Bruce Ehrlich, "Downtown Development and Urban Reform: The Politics of Boston's Linkage Policy," *Urban Affairs Quarterly*, 26 (3), 1991; Pierre Clavel, *The Progressive City: Planning and Participation, 1969–1984* (New Brunswick, NJ: Rutgers University Press, 1986).

18. The future prospects of progressive regimes in urban politics, even in cities lacking strong locational advantages, may be on the rise with the declining presence and political impact of downtown businesses. Scholars have noted that in recent years organized business advocacy has diminished with the spread of mergers and acquisitions, resulting in the relocations or closings of corporate offices in many cities. Elizabeth Strom, "Rethinking the Politics of Downtown Development," *Journal of Urban Affairs*, 30 (1), 2008; Royce Hanson et al., "Corporate Citizenship and Urban Problem Solving: The Changing Civic Role of Business Leaders in American Cities," *Journal of Urban Affairs*, 32 (1), 2010. The resulting vacuum may create opportunities for community-based organizations to exercise more leadership within urban regimes.

11-1 "Urban Regimes: A Research Perspective" and "Conclusion"*

Clarence N. Stone

Regime Politics: Governing Atlanta, 1946–1988

Urban Regimes: A Research Perspective

What makes governance in Atlanta effective is not the formal machinery of government, but rather the informal partnership between city hall and the downtown business elite. This informal partnership and the way it operates constitute the city's regime; it is the means through which major policy decisions are made.

The word "regime" connotes different things to different people, but in this book regime is specifically about the *informal arrangements* that surround and complement the formal workings of governmental authority. All governmental authority in the United States is greatly limited—limited by the Constitution, limited perhaps even more by the nation's political tradition, and limited structurally by the autonomy of privately owned business enterprise. The exercise of public authority is thus never a simple matter; it is almost always enhanced by extra formal considerations. Because local governmental authority is by law and tradition even more limited than authority at the state and national level, informal arrangements assume special importance in urban politics. But we should begin our understanding of regimes by realizing that informal arrangements are by no means peculiar to cities or, for that matter, to government.

Even narrowly bounded organizations, those with highly specific functional responsibilities, develop informal governing coalitions.[1] As Chester Barnard argued many years ago, formal goals and formal lines of authority are insufficient by themselves to bring about coordinated action with sufficient energy to accomplish organizational purposes;[2] commitment and cooperation do not just spring up from the lines of an organization chart. Because every formal organization gives rise to an informal one, Barnard concluded, successful executives must master the skill of shaping and using informal organization for their purposes.

Attention to informal arrangements takes various forms. In the analysis of business firms, the school of thought labeled "transaction cost economics" has given systematic attention to how things actually get done in a world full of social friction—basically the same question that Chester Barnard considered. A leading proponent of this approach, Oliver Williamson,[3] finds that what he terms "private orderings" (as opposed to formal and legal agreements) are enormously important in the running of business affairs. For many transactions, mutual and tacit understanding is a more efficient way of conducting relations than are legal agreements and formal contracts. Williamson quotes a business executive as saying, "You can settle any dispute if you keep the lawyers and accountants out of it. They just do not understand the give-and-take needed in business."[4] Because informal understandings and arrangements provide needed flexibility to cope with nonroutine matters, they facilitate cooperation to a degree that formally defined relationships do not. People who know one another, who have worked together in the past, who have shared in the achievement of a task, and who

---

Source: "Urban Regimes: A Research Perspective" from *Regime Politics: Governing Atlanta, 1946–1988*, by Clarence N. Stone, 1989. Used by permission of the publisher, University Press of Kansas.

*Some text and accompanying endnotes have been omitted. Please consult the original source.

perhaps have experienced the same crisis are especially likely to develop tacit understandings. If they interact on a continuing basis, they can learn to trust one another and to expect dependability from one another. It can be argued, then, that transactions flow more smoothly and business is conducted more efficiently when a core of insiders form and develop an ongoing relationship.

A regime thus involves not just any informal group that comes together to make a decision but an informal yet relatively stable group *with access to institutional resources* that enable it to have a sustained role in making governing decisions. What makes the group informal is not a lack of institutional connections, but the fact that the group, *as a group*, brings together institutional connections by an informal mode of cooperation. There is no all-encompassing structure of command that guides and synchronizes everyone's behavior. There is a purposive coordination of efforts, but it comes about informally, in ways that often depend heavily on tacit understandings.

If there is no overarching command structure, what gives a regime coherence? What makes it more than an "ecology of games"?[5] The answer is that the regime is purposive, created and maintained as a way of facilitating action. In a very important sense, *a regime is empowering*. Its supporters see it as a means for achieving coordinated efforts that might not otherwise be realized. A regime, however, is not created or redirected at will. Organizational analysis teaches us that cognition is limited, existing arrangements have staying power, and implementation is profoundly shaped by procedures in place.[6] Shrewd and determined leaders can effect purposive change, but only by being attentive to the ways in which existing forms of coordination can be altered or amplified.[7]

We can think of cities as organizations that lack a conjoining structure of command. There are institutional sectors within which the power of command may be much in evidence, but the sectors are independent of one another.[8] Because localities have only weak formal means through which coordination can be achieved, informal arrangements to promote cooperation are especially useful. *These informal modes of coordinating efforts across institutional boundaries are what I call "civic cooperation."* In a system of weak formal authority, it holds special importance. Integrated with the formal structure of

authority into a suprainstitutional capacity to take action, any informal basis of cooperation is empowering. It enables community actors to achieve cooperation beyond what could be formally commanded.

Consider the case of local political machines. When ward politicians learned to coordinate informally what otherwise was mired in institutional fragmentation and personal opportunism, the urban political machine was created and proved to have enormous staying power.[9] "Loyalty" is the shorthand that machine politicians used to describe the code that bound them into a cohesive group.[10] The political machine is in many ways the exemplar of governance in which informal arrangements are vital complements to the formal organization of government. The classic urban machines brought together various elements of the community in an informal scheme of exchange and cooperation that was the real governing system of the community.

The urban machine, of course, represents only one form of regime. In considering Atlanta, I am examining the governing coalition in a nonmachine city. The term "governing coalition" is a way of making the notion of regime concrete. It makes us face the fact that informal arrangements are held together by a core group—typically a body of insiders—who come together repeatedly in making important decisions. Thus, when I refer to the governing coalition in Atlanta, I mean the core group at the center of the workings of the regime.

To talk about a core group is not to suggest that they are of one mind or that they all represent identical interests—far from it. "Coalition" is the word I use to emphasize that a regime involves bringing together various elements of the community and the different institutional capacities they control. "Governing," as used in "governing coalition," I must stress, does not mean rule in command-and-control fashion. Governance through informal arrangements is about how some forms of coordination of effort prevail over others. It is about mobilizing efforts to cope and to adapt; it is not about absolute control. Informal arrangements are a way of bolstering (and guiding) the formal capacity to act, but even this enhanced capacity remains quite limited.

Having argued that informal arrangements are important in a range of circumstances, not just in cities, let me return to the specifics of the city setting. After all, the important point is not simply that there are informal arrangements; it is the particular features of urban regimes that provide the lenses through which we see the Atlanta experience. For cities, two questions face us: (1) Who makes up the governing coalition—who has to come together to make governance possible? (2) How is the coming together accomplished? These two questions imply a third: What are the consequences of the *who* and *how*? Urban regimes are not neutral mechanisms through which policy is made; they shape policy. To be sure, they do not do so on terms solely of the governing coalition's own choosing. But regimes are the mediating agents between the ill-defined pressures of an urban environment and the making of community policy. The *who* and *how* of urban regimes matter, thus giving rise to the further question of *with what consequences*. These three questions will guide my analysis of Atlanta.

Urban Regimes

As indicated above, an urban regime refers to the set of arrangements by which a community is actually governed. Even though the institutions of local government bear most of the formal responsibility for governing, they lack the resources and the scope of authority to govern without the active support and cooperation of significant private interests. An urban regime may thus be defined *as the informal arrangements by which public bodies and private interests function together in order to be able to make and carry out governing decisions.* These governing decisions, I want to emphasize, are not a matter of running or controlling everything. They have to do with *managing conflict* and *making adaptive responses* to social change. The informal arrangements through which governing decisions are made differ from community to community, but everywhere they are driven by two needs: (1) institutional scope (that is, the need to encompass a wide enough scope of institutions to mobilize the resources required to make and implement governing decisions) and (2) cooperation (that is, the need to promote enough cooperation and coordination for the diverse participants to reach decisions and sustain action in support of those decisions).

The mix of participants varies by community, but that mix is itself constrained by the accommodation of two basic institutional principles of the American political economy: (1) popular control of the formal machinery of government and (2) private ownership of business enterprise.[11] Neither of these principles is pristine. Popular

control is modified and compromised in various ways, but nevertheless remains as the basic principle of government. Private ownership is less than universal, as governments do own and operate various auxiliary enterprises from mass transit to convention centers. Even so, governmental conduct is constrained by the need to promote investment activity in an economic arena dominated by private ownership. This political economy insight is the foundation for a theory of urban regimes.[12]

In defining an urban regime as the informal arrangements through which public bodies and private interests function together to make and carry out governing decisions, bear in mind that I did not specify that the private interests are business interests. Indeed, in practice, private interests are not confined to business figures. Labor-union officials, party functionaries, officers in nonprofit organizations or foundations, and church leaders may also be involved.[13]

Why, then, pay particular attention to business interests? One reason is the now well-understood need to encourage business investment in order to have an economically thriving community. A second reason is the sometimes overlooked factor that businesses control politically important resources and are rarely absent totally from the scene. They may work through intermediaries, or some businesses may even be passive because others represent their interests as property holders, but a business presence is always part of the urban political scene. Although the nature of business involvement extends from the direct and extensive to the indirect and limited, the economic role of businesses *and the resources they control are* too important for these enterprises to be left out completely.

With revived interest in political economy, the regime's need for an adequate institutional scope (including typically some degree of business involvement) has received significant attention. However, less has been said about the regime's need for cooperation—and the various ways to meet it.[14] Perhaps some take for granted that, when cooperation is called for, it will be forthcoming. But careful reflection reminds us that cooperation does not occur simply because it is useful.

Robert Wiebe analyzed machine politics in a way that illustrates an important point: "The ward politician . . . required wider connections in order to manage many of his clients' problems. . . . Therefore clusters of these men allied to increase their bargaining power in city affairs. But if logic led to an integrated city-wide organization, the instinct of self-preservation did not. The more elaborate the structure, the more independence the ward bosses and area chieftains lost."[15] Cooperation can thus never be taken as a given; it must be achieved and at significant costs. Some of the costs are visible resources expended in promoting cooperation—favors and benefits distributed to curry reciprocity, the effort required to establish and maintain channels of communication, and responsibilities borne to knit activities together are a few examples. But, as Wiebe's observation reminds us, there are less visible costs. Achieving cooperation entails commitment to a set of relationships, and these relationships limit independence of action. If relationships are to be ongoing, they cannot be neglected; they may even call for sacrifices to prevent alienating allies. Forming wider connections is thus not a cost-free step, and it is not a step that community actors are always eager to take.

Because centrifugal tendencies are always strong, achieving cooperation is a major accomplishment and requires constant effort. Cooperation can be brought about in various ways. It can be induced if there is an actor powerful enough to coerce others into it, but that is a rare occurrence, because power is not usually so concentrated. More often, cooperation is achieved by some degree of reciprocity.

The literature on collective action focuses on the problem of cooperation in the absence of a system of command. For example, the "prisoner's dilemma" game instructs us that noncooperation may be invited by a number of situations.[16] In the same vein, Mancur Olson's classic analysis highlights the free-rider problem and the importance of selective incentives in inducing cooperation.[17] Alternatively, repeated interactions permit people to see the shortcomings of mutual noncooperation and to learn norms of cooperation.[18] Moreover, although Robert Axelrod's experiments with TIT FOR TAT computer programs indicate that cooperation can be instrumentally rational under some conditions, the process is not purely mechanical.[19] Students of culture point to the importance of common identity and language in facilitating interaction and promoting trust.[20] Size of group is also a consideration, affecting the ease of communication and bargaining among members; Michael Taylor, for example, emphasizes the increased difficulty of conditional cooperation in larger groups.[21]

What we can surmise about the urban community is thus twofold: (1) cooperation across institutional lines is valuable but far from automatic; and (2) cooperation is more likely to grow under some circumstances than others. This conclusion has wide implications for the study of urban politics. For example, much of the literature on community power has centered on the question of control, its possibilities and limitations: to what extent is domination by a command center possible and how is the cost of social control worked out. The long-standing elitist-pluralist debate centers on such questions. However, my line of argument here points to another way of viewing urban communities; it points to the need to think about cooperation, its possibilities and limitations—not just any cooperation, but cooperation of the kind that can bring together people based in different sectors of a community's institutional life and that enables a coalition of actors to make and support a set of governing decisions.

If the conventional model of urban politics is one of social control (with both elitist and pluralist variants), then the one proposed here might be called "the social-production model." It is based on the question of how, in a world of limited and dispersed authority, actors work together across institutional lines to produce a capacity to govern and to bring about publicly significant results.

To be sure, the development of a system of cooperation for governing is something that arises, not from an unformed mass, but rather within a structured set of relationships. Following Stephen Elkin, I described above the basic configuration in political-economy terms: popular control of governmental authority and private ownership of business activity. However, both of these elements are subject to variation. Populations vary in characteristics and in type of political organization; hence, popular control comes in many forms. The economic sector itself varies by the types of businesses that compose it and by the way in which it is organized formally and informally. Hence there is no one formula for bringing institutional sectors into an arrangement for cooperation, and the whole process is imbued with uncertainty. Cooperation is always somewhat tenuous, and it is made more so as conditions change and new actors enter the scene.

The study of urban regimes is thus a study of who cooperates and how their cooperation is achieved across institutional sectors of community life. Further, it is an examination of how that cooperation is maintained when confronted with an ongoing process of social change, a continuing influx of new actors, and potential break-downs through conflict or indifference.

Regimes are dynamic, not static, and regime dynamics concern the ways in which forces for change and forces for continuity play against one another. For example, Atlanta's governing coalition has displayed remarkable continuity in the post–World War II period, and it has done so despite deep-seated forces of social change. Understanding Atlanta's urban regime involves understanding how cooperation can be maintained and continuity can prevail in the face of so many possibilities for conflict. . . .

Prologue to the Atlanta Narrative

Structuring in Atlanta is a story in which race is central. If regimes are about who cooperates, how, and with what consequences, one of the remarkable features of Atlanta's urban regime is its biracial character. How has cooperation been achieved across racial lines, particularly since race is often a chasm rather than a bridge? Atlanta has been governed by a biracial coalition for so long that it is tempting to believe that nothing else was possible. Yet other cities followed a different pattern. At a time when Atlanta prided itself on being "the city too busy to hate," Little Rock, Birmingham, and New Orleans pursued die-hard segregation and were caught up in racial violence and turmoil. The experience of these cities reminds us that Atlanta's regime is not simply an informal arrangement through which popular elections and private ownership are reconciled, but is deeply intertwined with race relations, with some actors on the Atlanta scene able to overcome the divisive character of race sufficiently to achieve cooperation.

Atlanta's earlier history is itself a mixed experience, offering no clear indication that biracial cooperation would emerge and prevail in the years after World War II. In 1906, the city was the site of a violent race riot apparently precipitated by inflammatory antiblack newspaper rhetoric.[28] The incident hastened the city's move toward the economic exclusion and residential segregation of blacks, their disenfranchisement, and

enforcement of social subordination; and the years after 1906 saw the Jim Crow system fastened into place. Still, the riot was followed by modest efforts to promote biracial understanding, culminating in the formation in 1919 of the Commission on Interracial Cooperation.

Atlanta, however, also became the headquarters city for a revived Ku Klux Klan. During the 1920s, the Klan enjoyed wide support and was a significant influence in city elections. At this time, it gained a strong foothold in city government and a lasting one in the police department.[29] In 1930, faced with rising unemployment, some white Atlantans also founded the Order of Black Shirts for the express purpose of driving blacks out of even menial jobs and replacing them with whites. Black Shirt protests had an impact, and opportunities for blacks once again were constricted. At the end of World War II, with Atlanta's black population expanding beyond a number that could be contained in the city's traditionally defined black neighborhoods, another klanlike organization, the Columbians, sought to use terror tactics to prevent black expansion into previously all-white areas. All of this occurred against a background of state and regional politics devoted to the subordination of blacks to whites—a setting that did not change much until the 1960s.

Nevertheless, other patterns surfaced briefly from time to time. In 1932, Angelo Herndon, a black Communist organizer, led a mass demonstration of white and black unemployed protesting a cutoff of work relief. Herndon was arrested, and the biracial following he led proved short-lived. Still, the event had occurred, and Atlanta's city council did in fact accede to the demand for continued relief.[30] In the immediate postwar period, a progressive biracial coalition formed around the successful candidacy of Helen Douglas Mankin for a congressional seat representing Georgia's fifth district. That, too, was short-lived, as ultra-conservative Talmadge forces maneuvered to reinstitute Georgia's county-unit system for the fifth district and defeat Mankin with a minority of the popular vote.[31]

It is tempting to see the flow of history as flux, and one could easily dwell on the mutable character of political alignments. The Atlanta experience suggests that coalitions often give expression to instability. Centrifugal forces are strong, and in some ways disorder is a natural state. What conflict does not tear asunder, indifference is fully capable of wearing away.

The political incorporation of blacks into Atlanta's urban regime in tight coalition with the city's white business elite is thus not a story of how popular control and private capital came inevitably to live together in peace and harmony. It is an account of struggle and conflict—bringing together a biracial governing coalition at the outset, and then allowing each of the coalition partners to secure for itself an advantageous position within the coalition. In the first instance, struggle involved efforts to see that the coalition between white business interests and the black middle class prevailed over other possible alignments. In the second instance, there was struggle over the terms of coalition between the partners; thus political conflict is not confined to "ins" versus "outs." Those on the inside engage in significant struggle with one another over the terms on which cooperation will be maintained, which is one reason governing arrangements should never be taken for granted.

Atlanta's urban regime therefore appears to be the creature of purposive struggle, and both its establishment and its maintenance call for a political explanation. The shape of the regime was far from inevitable, but rather came about through the actions of human agents making political choices. Without extra economic efforts by the city's business leadership, Atlanta would have been governed in a much different manner, and Atlanta's urban regime and the policies furthered by that regime might well have diverged from the path taken. History, perhaps, is as much about alternatives not pursued as about those that were.

Conclusion

The Political Ramifications of Unequal Resources

. . . From Aristotle to Tocqueville to the present, keen political observers have understood that politics evolves from and reflects the associational life of a community. How people are grouped is important—so much so that, as the authors of the *Federalist* essays understood, the formation and reformation of coalitions is at the heart of political activity. Democracy should be viewed within that context; i.e., realizing that people do not act together simply because they share preferences on some particular issue.

Overlooking that long-standing lesson, many public-choice economists regard democracy with suspicion. They fear that popular majorities will insist on an egalitarian redistribution of benefits and thereby interfere with economic productivity. As worded by one economist, "The majority (the poor) will always vote for taxing the minority (the rich), at least until the opportunities for benefiting from redistribution ran out."[17] In other words, majority rule will overturn an unequal distribution of goods and resources. This reasoning, however, involves the simple-minded premise that formal governmental authority confers a capacity to redistribute at the will of those who hold office by virtue of popular election. The social-production model of politics employed here offers a contrasting view. Starting from an assumption about the costliness of civic cooperation, the social-production model suggests that an unequal distribution of goods and resources substantially modifies majority rule.

In operation, democracy is a great deal more complicated than counting votes and sorting through the wants of rational egoists. In response to those who regard democracy as a process of aggregating preferences within a system characterized by formal equality, a good antidote is Stein Rokkan's aphorism, "Votes count but resources decide."[18] Voting power is certainly not insignificant, but policies are decided mainly by those who control important concentrations of resources. Hence, governing is never simply a matter of aggregating numbers, whether for redistribution or other purposes.

How governing coalitions are put together is the focus of this book. An underlying question throughout has been why one alignment has prevailed over others. The Atlanta case suggests that a key factor is control of resources in a quantity and of a kind that can lead groups to ally with one set of arrangements instead of another. Thus any element of the community that has a unique capacity to promote action—whether by making side payments, affording small opportunities, or some other means—has a claim on membership in the governing coalition.

Of course, the election of key public officials provides a channel of popular expression. Since democracy rests on the principle of equal voting power, it would seem that all groups do share in the capacity to become part of the governing regime. Certainly the vote played a major role in the turnaround of the position of blacks in Atlanta. Popular control, however, is not a simple and straightforward process. Much depends on how the populace is organized to participate in a community's civic life. Machine politics, for example, promotes a search for personal favors. With electoral mobilization dependent upon an organizational network oriented toward patronage and related considerations, other kinds of popular concerns may have difficulty gaining expression.[19] The political machine thus enjoys a type of preemptive power, though the party organization is only one aspect of the overall governing regime.

On the surface, Atlanta represents a situation quite different from machine politics. Nonpartisan elections and an absence of mass patronage have characterized the city throughout the post–World War II era. Yet it would hardly be accurate to describe civic life in Atlanta as open and fluid. Nonpartisanship has heightened the role of organizations connected to business, and the newspapers have held an important position in policy debate. At the same time, working-class organizations and nonprofit groups unsupported by business are not major players in city politics.

Within Atlanta's civic sector, activities serve to piece together concerns across the institutional lines of the community, connecting government with business and each with a variety of nonprofit entities. The downtown elite has been especially adept at building alliances in that sector and, in doing so, has extended its resource advantage well beyond the control of strictly economic functions. Responding to its own weakness in numbers, the business elite has crafted a network through which cooperation can be advanced and potential cleavages between haves and have-nots redirected.

Consider what Atlanta's postwar regime represents. In 1946, the central element in the governing coalition was a downtown business elite organized for and committed to an active program of redevelopment that would transform the character of the business district and, in the process, displace a largely black population to the south and east of the district. At the time, with the end of the white primary that same year, a middle-class black population, long excluded from power, mobilized its electoral strength to begin an assault on a firmly entrenched Jim Crow system. Knowing only those facts, one might well have predicted in 1946 that these two groups would be political antagonists. They were not. Both committed to an agenda of change, they worked out an accommodation and became the city's governing coalition. The alliance has had its tensions and even temporary ruptures, but it has held and demonstrated remarkable strength in making and carrying out policy decisions.

To understand the process, the Atlanta experience indicates that one must appreciate institutional capacities and the resources that various groups control. That is why simple preference aggregation is no guide to how coalitions are built. The downtown elite and the black middle class had complementary needs that could be met by forming an alliance, and the business elite in particular had the kind and amount of resources to knit the alliance together.

Politics in Atlanta, then, is not organized around an overriding division between haves and have-nots. Instead, unequally distributed resources serve to destabilize opposition and encourage alliances around small opportunities. Without command of a capacity to govern, elected leaders have difficulty building support around popular discontent. That is why Rokkan's phrase, "Votes count but resources decide," is so apt.

Unequal Resources and Urban Regimes

Regimes, I have suggested, are to be understood in terms of: (1) who makes up the governing coalition and (2) how the coalition achieves cooperation. Both points illustrate how the unequal distribution of resources affects politics and what differences the formation of a regime makes. That the downtown elite is a central partner in the Atlanta regime shapes the priorities set and the trade-offs made. Hence, investor prerogative is protected practice in Atlanta, under the substantial influence of the business elite *within* the governing coalition. At the same time, the fact that the downtown elite is part of a governing coalition prevents business isolation from community affairs. Yet, although "corporate responsibility" promotes business involvement, it does so in a way that enhances business as patron and promoter of small opportunities.

Similarly, the incorporation of the black middle class into the mainstream civic and economic life of Atlanta is testimony to its ability to use electoral leverage to help set community priorities. The importance of the mode of cooperation is also evident. Although much of what the regime has done has generated popular resistance, the black middle class has been persuaded to go along by a combination of selective incentives and small opportunities. Alliance with the business elite enabled the black middle class to achieve particular objectives not readily available by other means. This kind of enabling capacity is what gives concentrated resources its gravitational force.

The pattern thus represents something more than individual cooptation. The black middle class as a group benefited from new housing areas in the early postwar years and from employment and business opportunities in recent years. Some of the beneficiaries have been institutional—colleges in the Atlanta University system and a financially troubled bank, for example. Because the term "selective incentives" implies individual benefits (and these have been important), the more inclusive term "small opportunities" provides a useful complement. In both cases, the business elite is a primary source; they can make things happen, provide needed assistance, and open up opportunities. At the same time, since the downtown elite needs the cooperation of local government and various community groups, the elite itself is drawn toward a broad community-leadership role. Although its bottom-line economic interests are narrow, its community role can involve it in wider concerns. Selective incentives, however, enable the elite to muffle some of the pressure that might otherwise come from the larger community.

Once we focus on the regime and the importance of informally achieved cooperation, we can appreciate better the complex way in which local politics actually functions. Public-choice economists, fearful that democracy will lead to redistribution, misunderstand the process and treat politics as a causal force operating in isolation from resources other than the vote. That clearly is unwarranted. Atlanta's business elite possesses substantial slack resources that can be and are devoted to politics. Some devotion of resources to political purposes is direct, in the form of campaign funds, but much is indirect; it takes on the character of facilitating civic cooperation for those efforts deemed worthy.

The business elite is small and homogeneous enough to use the norms of class unity and corporate responsibility to maintain its cohesion internally. In interacting with

allies, the prevailing mode of operation is reciprocity, reinforced in many cases by years of trust built from past exchanges. The biracial insiders have also been at their tasks long enough to experience a sense of pride in the community role they play. Even so, the coalition is centered around a combination of explicit and tacit deals. Reciprocity is thus the hallmark of Atlanta's regime, and reciprocity hinges on what one actor can do for another. Instead of promoting redistribution toward equality, such a system perpetuates inequality.

Reciprocity, of course, occurs in a context, and in Atlanta, it is interwoven with a complex set of conditions. The slack resources controlled by business corporations give them an extraordinary opportunity to promote civic cooperation. Where there is a compelling mutual interest, as within Atlanta's downtown elite, businesses have the means to solve their own collective-action problem and unite behind a program of action. Their resources also enable them to create a network of cooperation that extends across lines of institutional division, which makes them attractive to public officials and other results-oriented community groups. In becoming an integral part of a system of civic cooperation, Atlanta's business elite has used its resource advantage to shape community policy and protect a privileged position. Because the elite is useful to others, it attracts and holds a variety of allies in its web of reciprocity. The concentration of resources it has gathered thus enables the elite to counter demands for greater equality.

Social Learning versus Privilege

Instead of understanding democratic politics as an instance of the equality (redistribution)/efficiency (productivity) trade-off, I suggest an alternative. Policy actions (and inactions) have extensive repercussions and involve significant issues that do not fit neatly into an equality-versus-efficiency mold. There is a need, then, for members of the governing coalition to be widely informed about a community's problems, and not to be indifferent about the information. That is what representative democracy is about.

For their part, in order to be productive, business enterprises need a degree of autonomy and a supply of slack resources. It is also appropriate that they participate in politics. However, there are dangers involved in the ability of high-resource groups, like Atlanta's business elite, to secure for themselves a place in the governing coalition and then use that inside position along with their own ample resources to shape the regime on their terms. Elsewhere I have called this "preemptive power,"[20] and have suggested that it enables a group to protect a privileged position. The ability to parcel out selective incentives and other small opportunities permits Atlanta's business elite to enforce discipline on behalf of civic cooperation by vesting others with lesser privileges—privileges perhaps contingently held in return for "going along."

The flip side of discipline through selective incentives is a set of contingent privileges that restrict the questions asked and curtail social learning. Thus one of the trade-offs in local politics can be phrased as social learning versus privilege. Some degree of privilege for business may be necessary to encourage investment, but the greater the privilege being protected, the less the incentive to understand and act on behalf of the community in its entirety.

The political challenge illustrated by the Atlanta case is how to reconstitute the regime so that both social learning and civic cooperation occur. The risk in the present situation is that those who govern have only a limited comprehension of the consequences of their actions. Steps taken to correct one problem may create or aggravate another while leaving still others unaddressed. Those who govern can discover that only, it seems, through wide representation of the affected groups. Otherwise, choices are limited by an inability to understand the city's full situation.

No governing coalition has an inclination to expand the difficulties of making and carrying out decisions. Still, coalitions can be induced to attempt the difficult. For example, Atlanta's regime has been centrally involved in race relations, perhaps the community's most difficult and volatile issue. Relationships within the governing coalition have been fraught with tension; friction was unavoidable. Yet the coalition achieved a cooperative working relationship between the black middle class and the white business elite. In a rare but telling incident, black leaders insisted successfully that a 1971 pledge to build a MARTA spur to a black public-housing area not be repudiated. The newspaper opined that trust within the coalition was too important to be sacrificed on the altar of economizing. Thus the task of the governing regime was expanded beyond the narrow issue of serving downtown in the least expensive manner possible; concerns *can* be broadened.

Although no regime is likely to be totally inclusive, most regimes can be made more inclusive. Just as Atlanta's regime was drawn into dealing with race relations, others can become sensitive to the situations of a larger set of groups. Greater inclusiveness will not come automatically nor from the vote alone. Pressures to narrow the governing coalition are strong and recurring. Yet, if civic cooperation is the key to the terms on which economic and electoral power are accommodated, then more inclusive urban regimes can be encouraged through an associational life at the community level that reflects a broad range of perspectives. The problem is not an absence of associational life at that level but how to lessen its dependence on business sponsorship, how to free participation in civic activity from an overriding concern with protecting insider privileges, and how to enrich associational life so that nonprofit and other groups can function together as they express encompassing community concerns.

This step is one in which federal policy could make a fundamental difference. In the past, starting with the urban-redevelopment provision in the 1949 housing act and continuing through the Carter administration's UDAG program, cities have been strongly encouraged to devise partnerships with private, for-profit developers, thus intensifying already strong leanings in that direction. Since these were matters of legislative choice, it seems fully possible for the federal government to move in another direction and encourage nonprofit organizations. The federal government could, for example, establish a program of large-scale assistance to community development corporations and other nonprofit groups. Some foundations now support such programs, but their modest efforts could be augmented. Programs of community service required by high schools and colleges or spawned by a national-level service requirement could increase voluntary participation and alter the character of civic life in local communities. It is noteworthy that neighborhood mobilization in Atlanta was partly initiated by VISTA (Volunteers in Service to America) workers in the 1960s and continued by those who stayed in the city after completing service with

VISTA. This, however, is not the place to prescribe a full set of remedies; my aim is only to indicate that change is possible but will probably require a stimulus external to the local community.

Summing Up

If the slack resources of business help to set the terms on which urban governance occurs, then we need to be aware of what this imbalance means. The Atlanta case suggests that the more uneven the distribution of resources, the greater the tendency of the regime to become concerned with protecting privilege. Concurrently, there is a narrowing of the regime's willingness to engage in "information seeking" (or social learning). Imbalances in the civic sector thus lead to biases in policy, biases that electoral politics alone is unable to correct.

A genuinely effective regime is not only adept at promoting cooperation in the execution of complex and nonroutine projects, but is also able to comprehend the consequences of its actions and inactions for a diverse citizenry. The promotion of this broad comprehension is, after all, a major aim of democracy. Even if democratic politics were removed from the complexities of coordination for social production, it still could not be reduced to a set of decision rules. Arrow's theorem shows that majority choices cannot be neutrally aggregated when preference structures are complex,[21] as indeed they are bound to be in modern societies.

Democracy, then, is not simply a decision rule for registering choices; it has to operate with a commitment to inclusiveness. Permanent or excluded minorities are inconsistent with the basic idea of equality that underpins democracy. That is why some notion of social learning is an essential part of the democratic process; all are entitled to have their situations understood. Thus, to the extent that urban regimes safeguard special privileges at the expense of social learning, democracy is weakened.

Those fearful that too much community participation will lead to unproductive policies should widen their own understanding and consider other dangers on the political landscape. Particularly under conditions of an imbalance in civically useful resources, the political challenge is one of preventing government from being harnessed to the protection of special privilege. The social-production model reminds us that only a segment of society's institutions are under the sway of majority rule; hence, actual governance is never simply a matter of registering the preferences of citizens as individuals.

The character of local politics depends greatly on the nature of a community's associational life, which in turn depends greatly on the distribution of resources other than the vote. Of course, the vote is significant, but equality in the right to vote is an inadequate guarantee against the diversion of politics into the protection of privilege. If broad social learning is to occur, then other considerations must enter the picture. "One person, one vote" is not enough.

Notes

"Urban Regimes: A Research Perspective"

1. James G. March, "The Business Firm as a Political Coalition," *Journal of Politics* 24 (November 1962): 662–678.
2. Chester I. Barnard, *The Functions of the Executive* (Cambridge, Mass: Harvard University Press, 1968).
3. Oliver E. Williamson, *The Economic Institutions of Capitalism* (New York: Free Press, 1985).
4. Ibid., 10.
5. See Norton E. Long, "The Local Community as Ecology of Games," *American Journal of Sociology* 64 (November 1958): 251–261.
6. Cf. Graham T. Allison, *Essence of Decision* (Boston: Little, Brown, 1971).
7. See Philip Selznick, *Leadership in Administration* (New York: Harper & Row, 1957).
8. Cf. Bryan D. Jones and Lynn W. Bachelor, *The Sustaining Hand* (Lawrence: University Press of Kansas, 1986).
9. See especially Martin Shelter, "The Emergence of the Political Machine: An Alternative View," in *Theoretical Perspectives on Urban Politics*, by Willis D. Hawley and others (Englewood Cliffs, N.J.: Prentice-Hall, 1976).
10. Clarence N. Stone, Robert K. Whelan, and William J. Murin, *Urban Policy and Politics in a Bureaucratic Age*, 2d ed. (Englewood Cliffs, N.J.: Prentice-Hall, 1986), 104.
11. Stephen L. Elkin, *City and Regime in the American Republic* (Chicago: University of Chicago Press, 1987).
12. See ibid.
13. Cf. Jones and Bachelor, *Sustaining Hand*, 214–215.

14. But see Elkin, *City and Regime;* Martin Shelter, *Political Crisis/Fiscal Crisis: The Collapse and Revival of New York City* (New York: Basic Books, 1985); and Todd Swanstrom, *The Crisis of Growth Politics* (Philadelphia: Temple University Press, 1985).

15. Robert H. Wiebe, *The Search for Order, 1877–1920* (New York: Hill and Wang, 1967), 10.

16. Russell Hardin, *Collective Action* (Baltimore: Johns Hopkins University Press, 1982); and Michael Taylor, *The Possibility of Cooperation* (Cambridge: Cambridge University Press, 1987).

17. Mancur Olson, Jr., *The Logic of Collective Action* (Cambridge, Mass.: Harvard University Press, 1965).

18. Hardin, *Collective Action.*

19. Robert Axelrod, *The Evolution of Cooperation* (New York: Basic Books, 1984).

20. Hardin, *Collective Action;* and David D. Laitin, *Hegemony and Culture* (Chicago: University of Chicago Press, 1986).

21. Taylor, *Possibility of Cooperation.*

28. Michael L. Porter, "Black Atlanta: An Interdisciplinary Study of Blacks on the East Side of Atlanta, 1890–1930" (Ph.D. diss., Emory University, 1974); Walter White, *A Man Called White* (New York: Arno Press and the New York Times, 1969); and Dana F. White, "The Black Sides of Atlanta," *Atlanta Historical Journal* 26 (Summer/Fall 1982): 199–225.

29. Kenneth T. Jackson, *The Ku Klux Klan in the City, 1915–1930* (New York: Oxford University Press, 1967); and Herbert T. Jenkins, *Forty Years on the Force: 1932–1972* (Atlanta: Center for Research in Social Change, Emory University, 1973).

30. Charles H. Martin, *The Angelo Herndon Case and Southern Justice* (Baton Rouge: Louisiana State University Press, 1976); Kenneth Coleman, ed., *A History of Georgia* (Athens: University of Georgia Press, 1976): 294; and Writer's Program of the Workers Progress Administration, *Atlanta: A City of the Modern South* (St. Clairshores, Mich.: Somerset Publishers, 1973) 69.

31. Lorraine N. Spritzer, *The Belle of Ashby Street: Helen Douglas Mankin and Georgia Politics* (Athens: University of Georgia Press, 1982).

"Conclusion"

17. John Bonner, *Introduction to the Theory of Social Choice* (Baltimore: Johns Hopkins University Press, 1986), 34.

18. Stein Rokkan, "Norway: Numerical Democracy and Corporate Pluralism," in *Political Oppositions in Western Democracies*, ed. Robert A. Dahl (New Haven, Conn.: Yale University Press, 1966), 105; see also Erie, *Rainbow's End.*

19. Matthew A. Crenson, *The Un-Politics of Air Pollution* (Baltimore: Johns Hopkins University Press, 1971); see also, Edwin H. Rhyne, "Political Parties and Decision Making in Three Southern Counties," *American Political Science Review* 52 (December 1958): 1091–1107.

20. Clarence N. Stone, "Preemptive Power: Floyd Hunter's 'Community Power Structure' Reconsidered." *American Journal of Political Science* 32 (February 1988): 82–104.

21. Norman Frohlich and Joe A. Oppenheimer, *Modern Political Economy* (Englewood Cliffs, N.J.: Prentice Hall, 1978), 19–31.

11-2 "Conclusions and Implications: Toward a New Contract for Biracial Politics"

Raphael J. Sonenshein

Politics in Black and White: Race and Power in Los Angeles

Los Angeles—where political life has been rarely studied—provides a remarkably useful case study of minority incorporation. Despite a relatively small population, Los Angeles' African-Americans were surprisingly successful in obtaining an important share of municipal power. Until the early 1960s, Blacks had held very little political clout in Los Angeles. They had elected no officeholder in city government, and were excluded from citywide coalitions.

Between 1961 and 1963, Blacks succeeded in eroding some of the barriers to their participation. In 1963, three Black candidates rode a wave of Black mobilization into council seats. In the three decades since, African-Americans have held these three seats, a higher share of the fifteen-member council than the Black share of the population (by the 1990 census, Los Angeles was only 13 percent African-American).

In 1973, the city elected a Black mayor, Tom Bradley, who was reelected in 1977, 1981, 1985, and 1989. With Bradley's election, Los Angeles Blacks obtained a core role in the dominant citywide coalition. Shifts in the city council expanded the base of that coalition over time. Black-supported candidates won all citywide offices.

The initial victories in city council races were largely conducted under African-American leadership appealing to a Black mass base. Bradley's citywide victory was part of a wider coalition with white liberals, principally Jews. This coalition was highly stable. Joint membership in this citywide liberal coalition has meant that Blacks have had more than representation; they have had incorporation.

Significant policy changes occurred in city government as a result of Black incorporation. The first real limits were placed on police conduct in the minority community after years of city hall subservience to the department. Substantial amounts of federal aid were obtained for social service programs, in contrast to Los Angeles's lackluster previous record.

Higher proportions of minorities were appointed to city commissions, including the most important posts. Substantial increases occurred in the city's minority hiring. While these changes often fell short of the expectations of the coalition's supporters, they represented a great improvement over the previous conservative practices. Opportunities for upward mobility increased for previously excluded groups.

The goal of economic equality for minority and poor neighborhoods, however, was not achieved through the economic revitalization of the downtown. As a result of restrictive federal policies, changing demographics, and the limited equalizing benefits of downtown redevelopment, the city's economic life is not more equal today than when the regime came to power. The shocking violence that hit South Central Los Angeles in 1992 underscored the inequality that remains.

The political alliance that underlay Black incorporation combined Black mobilization and white liberal support. Secondary assistance came from the Latino and Asian-American communities. Downtown business and labor became pillars of the incumbent coalition, as redevelopment policies favored their interests.

At the mass level, the persistence of ideological division among whites was remarkable. The pattern can be seen as far back as the 1964 vote on Proposition 14, which sought to preserve housing discrimination, and as recently as the 1992 vote to reform the LAPD. Over a wide range of elections, high-turnout white liberal areas differed significantly from high-turnout white conservative areas. When combined with the heavily mobilized and unified Black vote and less-mobilized Latinos, the multiracial liberal community in Los Angeles attained extraordinary electoral strength.

When these communities divided, particularly over growth issues, the coalition substantially weakened. The rise of Latino and Asian-American aspirations has profoundly challenged the biracial coalition, as have the decline in federal aid and tensions from within.

At the elite level, the coalition was effectively created, managed, and preserved by an alliance of Black and white liberal activists who had known each other for many years. Their ties dated back to Bradley's election to the city council in 1963 in the biracial Tenth District. From within the Black community, leadership came from a progressive faction based in the upwardly mobile areas of the community. Elite trust provided an essential bridge over troubled waters that might have sunk another coalition. These cross-racial leadership ties were important reasons why Black-Jewish conflict rarely threatened coalition survival.

Elite alliance in the political sphere was strengthened by sharing a common goal—winning elections and changing public policies. Relatively equal status enhanced the ability of people from different sides of the racial divide to work together.

In short, the Los Angeles case casts doubt on the widely accepted notion that elite and mass coalitions between Blacks and white liberals are dead. They have shown, in Los Angeles, substantial signs of life.

A small Black population in a big city wins substantial political power, and then shares in the development of new city policies benefiting minorities. Is this a unique phenomenon, or indicative of some broader pattern? Bradley's electoral victories are often presented in the urban literature as inexplicable exceptions to the rule of racial polarization. In reality, the Los Angeles story differs in degree but not in kind from the evidence gathered in other American cities. It is part of the history of the movement for Black empowerment. It is a key signpost in a broader model of biracial coalition politics than has yet been brought into the literature.

Among western cities, the Los Angeles case study offers strong confirmation of the patterns Browning, Marshall, and Tabb (1984) found in ten northern California cities. In each of their cities, conservative coalitions had been dominant until 1960, and minority representation had been extremely limited. In the 1960s and 1970s, Blacks and Latinos obtained power and policy change at a very different level in the ten cities. The key factors were the extent of Black mobilization and unity, and the level of white liberal support. Latinos joined Black-liberal coalitions as secondary partners.

The city in which African-Americans attained the highest level of incorporation, Berkeley, followed a path surprisingly similar to that of Los Angeles. In Berkeley, Blacks organized in the late 1950s and early 1960s to win initial incorporation; then, in alliance with white liberal reformers, they formed a citywide progressive coalition able to win full incorporation. As in Los Angeles, the coalition elected a Black mayor. Substantial policy change (much more than in moderate Los Angeles) followed the development of a winning coalition.

In sum, Los Angeles stands as the first big-city confirmation of a model peculiarly suited to western, reform-dominated cities. It also shows that the model works in conservative southern California as well as in more liberal northern California.

This research suggests that a western model of biracial politics deserves much more attention than it has received. In settings where reform structures are strong, where the African-American population is of moderate size, where conservative regimes frustrate liberal aspirations, and where racial antipathy is relatively low, the path to liberal biracial coalition seems relatively auspicious. In such settings, the likelihood of biracial politics seems greater than in the eastern and midwestern cities that generally frame the discussion.

In western communities, the opportunities for white liberals and Black activists to meet in political situations where they are peers—a crucial precondition for biracial elite linkages—may be greater as well. Yet these conditions are more fragile in the 1990s, and much exploration needs to be done about the prospects for coalitions in the postincorporation era.

How does the Los Angeles case fit with those of other large cities in the East and Midwest, which have been the basis of the polarization model? Applicability does not have to be limited to western states where parties are weak and African-American populations are relatively small. In other words, there may be elements that unify both the crossover and polarization models into a more general model of biracial coalitions.

A unified model accepts that Black mobilization and white liberal support are core factors in the success of Black incorporation. In many polarized cities, the slice of white support for Black incorporation is much smaller than in Los Angeles, and the Black population much larger. But the pattern is much the same. Pettigrew (1971) found that Black mayoral candidates in Gary, Newark, and Cleveland received white support from similar populations as in Los Angeles. The difference was in the degree of white support. The same result was found in Ransom's (1987) Philadelphia and Kleppner's (1985) Chicago.

The intensity of racial conflict is so great in cities such as Chicago that it tends to overshadow ideological conflict among whites. But that ideological division can be a significant—even a determining—factor in outcomes. Harold Washington's 1983 victory in Chicago was made possible by overwhelming Black (and Latino) support and a slice of white liberal voting. The 1989 mayoral election between an incumbent Black mayor and challenger Richard M. Daley depended heavily on the votes of white liberals. This group had provided the key swing voters for Harold Washington's victories in 1983 and 1987. With Black and white voters so evenly divided, the small slice of ideologically liberal whites became extremely important, and eventually handed the mayoralty to Daley.

In short, the difference between Los Angeles's crossover politics and the polarization model of eastern and midwestern cities is in part a difference of degree and emphasis. If the two models share a common framework—Black mobilization and unity combined with white liberal support—they differ significantly in the emphasis on each element. Los Angeles represents one "bookend," in which white liberal support is a truly major share of the equation. Chicago represents another, opposite "bookend," in which the overwhelming need is for Black unity, with some small increment of white support.

These differences in degree matter, because they affect the tone and direction of city politics. In Los Angeles, coalition politics is always in the air and is the

beginning of all citywide strategy; in Chicago, it may be the last consideration. Even Harold Washington did not get around to cultivating a white liberal base until after he had won the 1983 Democratic primary.

In both models, African-American mobilization and biracial coalition are needed in order to achieve minority incorporation. The situation is particularly complex in New York City, where the Black population percentage is higher than in Los Angeles but lower than in Chicago. Minority strategists have often seemed caught in the middle between mobilization and coalition, sometimes achieving neither. With the election of David Dinkins as mayor of New York City in 1989, the largest U.S. city now constitutes a sort of bridge between the polarization and crossover wings of a broader model of interracial politics. The racial experience of New York City has strong elements in common with both Chicago and Los Angeles.

New York City has been more polarized than Los Angeles, but it has a much deeper white liberal base than Chicago. The biracial coalition behind Dinkins is broader (if more precarious) than the late Harold Washington's but quite a bit weaker than Tom Bradley's. Perhaps the New York City experience, which has until now been one of the main arguments against the viability of biracial coalitions, will someday help in the process of devising a new, expanded view of biracial politics that incorporates both the polarization and crossover experiences.

In national perspective, Los Angeles represents (along with other western cities) one end of a broad continuum of Black mobilization and white liberal support. For too long, the other end of the continuum (polarization) has been treated as the whole continuum. Placing the second-largest U.S. city in its correct place therefore helps shift the weight of the analysis of minority incorporation and biracial coalitions.

New Thinking on Biracial Coalitions

If biracial coalitions between Blacks and white liberals are not dead, then the widely held belief that the civil rights movement died in 1965 must be reexamined. Clearly the ideological alliance that provided the basis for the civil rights movement did not disappear with the completion of its legislative agenda. But that alliance did undergo a profound shift that has been unrecognized by either Blacks or white liberals.

After 1965, the racial coalition became much narrower, at least in terms of white participation, and the role of Black mobilization became much greater. This shift is of considerable importance because it has been overemphasized by African-Americans and underemphasized by whites. In short, the role of whites in the modern movement for Black political incorporation is qualitatively different than it was in the civil rights movement. But it still exists, and is crucial.

The civil rights movement was a broad coalition around a series of agreed-upon issues of great moral force. It was oriented toward changing government policy through external pressure and protest. The whole nature of the modern enterprise is different. While moral force and persuasion are parts of the new movement, they share the stage with an overt plan to obtain minority political empowerment. The new movement is aimed not only at changing policies but at gaining the political power to make policies. It also involves much straightforward politics, seeking to win and hold public office. More than the civil rights movement, the new era is about both morality and politics.

This presents both an opportunity and a problem. It is an opportunity because politics is an activity with enough specific goals to make common goals possible. The problem is that if the civil rights movement model does not evolve, it cannot easily survive when politics are involved.

If the broad model explaining minority incorporation in the 1960s and 1970s is a combination of Black mobilization and white liberal support, then many things need to be rethought. The whole accepted basis of biracial coalitions needs to be reexamined. Previous efforts have failed to take into account the paradoxical nature of a phenomenon with two distinctive elements.

The most widely discussed liberal views of biracial coalitions tend to emphasize what amounts to a philanthropic model, derived from the civil rights movement. In this view, racial progress emerges from the goodwill of liberal whites, who choose to offer assistance to Blacks. This model suggests that ideology is the basis of biracial politics. The failings of this model lie in two areas.

White liberals often fail to acknowledge the leading role of the African-American community in the search for racial equality. It is all too easy to redraw history to portray Blacks as victims and whites as saviors. Studies of Black mayors may highlight their relationships with the white community, rather than the African-American community base that has been essential to their self-reliance and political success.

The liberal model is also at a loss to explain conflict between Blacks and white liberals. If biracial politics is about ideology, what happens when there is a conflict of interest between the two groups? Sometimes the conflict is denied, or explained away. Liberals may withdraw from the struggle for equality, unable to confront the apparent contradiction. It is equally hard to acknowledge evidence that white benefits derive from minority political efforts. Ideological politics can break down when interest conflicts cause groups, and their leaders, to defend their threatened interests.

White liberals ought to understand that many minority activists are justifiably cautious about committing themselves to biracial coalitions that may founder when hard, divisive issues arise. Where liberalism is too strong, as perhaps has been the case in New York City and San Francisco, it may even inhibit the development of independent minority politics. Thus, the health of a Black-liberal coalition—indeed, of any minority-liberal alliance—may depend on a balance of strength.

The best biracial politics is not a form of philanthropy; when liberal support seems like charity, baffled liberals may find their hands bitten by the "ungrateful" recipient. As Hamilton (1979) has pointed out, votes provide reciprocity; mutual need can add a reliable and dignified glue to good intentions. While the Black Power argument too quickly dismisses the consistent support of white liberals, liberals tend to understate the importance of realistic group conflict and pragmatic cooperation.

In 1967, Carmichael and Hamilton sought to create a new model of biracial coalitions that would overcome the inadequacies of the liberal model. They intended to move beyond the sentimentality of the civil rights movement into a more pragmatic focus on African-American interests. For the first time they presented biracial coalition as a conscious political choice made by Blacks, thereby fundamentally altering the terms of the discussion. They constructed a listing of preconditions for biracial coalitions that emphasized Black self-determination.

Carmichael and Hamilton argued that whites played too dominant a role in the civil rights movement, and that when their own interests were threatened, such whites would desert the Black cause. The only answer was to abandon alliances of ideology in favor of interest-based coalitions.

The Black Power movement fractured the confidence of advocates of biracial coalitions. Instead of being seen as philanthropic, white liberals were characterized as patronizing and domineering. The removal of white liberals from the leadership of civil rights organizations became a painful issue. Now African-Americans saw themselves as picking and choosing coalition partners, rather than asking for the benevolent assistance of whites.

Since the publication of *Black Power* in 1967, many have emphasized the role of Black unity as the cause of Black empowerment. Full credit for African-American empowerment is given to the Black community, with other supporters banished to the fine print, unless the allies are nonwhite. Evidence of racial polarization is reemphasized in order to downplay any role for whites in the sharing of credit for success.

The pain engendered on both sides by the fracturing of the old coalition has meant that the opening presented by Carmichael and Hamilton has been inadequately extended and tested. Generally, the subject gets addressed in the course of Black-Jewish conflict, often with reference to alliance efforts several decades old. Such battles do not encourage people to devote full attention to a new understanding of the relationship.

Carmichael and Hamilton had hit on a crucial point. Their argument could be read as saying that there had been an implicit contract in the early coalition, in which white liberals felt noble and Blacks got needed political support. In *Black Power*, Carmichael and Hamilton sought to devise a new, more explicit contract that would end the "patron-client" relationship.

The problem is that their hard-eyed view is, in its own way, just as myopic about the nature of biracial coalitions as the more romantic liberal view. Goodwill alone is not enough, but neither is cold self-interest. But the debate largely ended with the publication of *Black Power* in 1967. It is long past time to reopen that discussion, with a new perspective beyond the sentimental and the cynical.

Black Power argued that Blacks had been overshadowed in the civil rights movement, and that liberal alliances were generally useless. It argued instead for alliances based on economic issues and links to the Third World. It should be obvious that there is a direct line from *Black Power* to the Jesse Jackson presidential campaigns. Jackson's campaigns presented an important alternative to liberal coalitions, and his approach came right off the pages of Carmichael and Hamilton's book. Such a coalition would begin with racial consciousness among Blacks, and the candidate would openly act as the Black candidate. Allies would then be sought in areas of common economic interest—white workers, Latinos, and others.

Only the most progressive whites—those able to support the candidate's agenda in full—would be incorporated. No effort would be made to accommodate those whites, such as Jews, who had reservations about some aspects of the program. Finally, strong linkages would be forged with Third World peoples. Combined in a single package, these elements of the rainbow coalition fit all the preconditions for successful coalitions offered in *Black Power*.

But virtually every case of Black political incorporation since the publication of *Black Power* has followed a model substantially different from Jackson's model. These victories were built on Black mobilization and the careful cultivation of white liberal support.

The main problem with *Black Power* is not its theory of Blacks, but rather its theory of whites. The book performed a tremendous service by highlighting the necessity for African-American independent action and political self-reliance. (In its argument against white domination of the civil rights movement, however, the book made the same mistake that many whites have made: underestimating the actual Black leadership role. In Los Angeles and other cities, Blacks were creating an independent political base long before 1967.) The theory set out a highly dignified role for Blacks, based on the pursuit of their group interest, but then confined whites to a role that is highly unrealistic and close to demeaning.

Carmichael and Hamilton (1967:77, emphasis in original) indicated that a coalition must be based on the following premise: "All parties to the coalition must perceive a *mutually* beneficial goal based on the conception of *each* party of his *own* self-interest." However, in the sections that followed, they did not apply this notion to liberal whites. Liberal whites who defended their own interests were defined as betrayers. In fact, Carmichael and Hamilton specifically defined an appropriate role for white progressives, without regard for whether such a role would be acceptable to them: "There is a definite, much-needed role whites can play . . . educative, organizational, supportive" (81).

Whites were then urged to rid themselves of racist values and bring other whites to the correct view: "[T]hey might also educate other white people to the need for Black Power" (82). Culturally, whites must seek to overthrow their own way of living because it is dead and jaded. Those whites who are devoted to racial justice are actually escapees from sick environments: "They have sought refuge among blacks from a sterile, meaningless, irrelevant life in middle-class America. They have been unable to deal with the stifling, racist, parochial, split-level mentality of their parents, teachers, preachers and friends. . . . Anglo-conformity is a dead weight on their necks, too" (83).

When biracial coalitions are to be formed, they must be wholly directed by African-Americans:

> It is our position that black organizations should be black-led and essentially black-staffed, with policy being made by black people. White people can and do play very important supportive roles in those organizations. . . .

> There are white lawyers who defend black civil rights workers in court, and white activists who support indigenous black movements across the country. Their function is not to lead or to set policy or to attempt to define black people to black people. Their role is supportive. (83–84)

Even with due allowance for the period in which this was written, the role defined in such coalitions for white liberals is constricting. They are invited to open for inspection their cultural values, renounce their families and communities, act in a supporting role without input into policy, and, in effect, ask permission to be part of a progressive movement. How could such a process produce healthy politics? How could such whites ever be expected to deliver a bloc of white support?

In this light, the conflicts between Jesse Jackson and the Jewish community can be seen in a new light. With their strong sense of community and family, Jews are unlikely to accept as terms of participation in progressive politics the agenda laid out in *Black Power*. To do so would be to violate the very conditions for strong coalition laid out in that book. As Carmichael and Hamilton stated, no coalition can survive that is not based on the survival and protection of the groups involved. Both must be able to prosper through coalition.

Thus, *Black Power* made a major contribution by laying to rest a naive view that goodwill will solve everything. But it left the job of constructing a realistic biracial coalition unfinished. It is to that task that I now turn.

We now know that African-American political incorporation (a political expression of the doctrine of Black Power) came about over the last several decades through a combination of Black mobilization and white liberal support. Blacks and liberals often saw these events differently. Blacks tended to see the great effort put toward Black unity. White liberals often noticed how at the crucial junctures, the support of whites like themselves put the Black movement over the top.

Coalitions can certainly survive the different interpretations of their members. Such differing perspectives may be crucial to coalition survival (Downs 1957). But when the views pull too far apart, how people understand their contributions to coalitions can actually affect the chances for coalition success.

For example, if African-Americans feel that white liberals are generally hypocrites, they will fail to cultivate ideological support. If white liberals fail to appreciate the Black political base and its importance, they may place pressures on a Black leader that he or she can ill afford.

It is therefore time to try to draw up a new contract for biracial politics—one in which both sides can thrive. The philanthropic model underestimates the role of Blacks, and the Black Power model underestimates the role of whites. Is there a new model that can serve the interests of all parties, and can allow coalitions to be built on a solid foundation? Can such an approach be helpful in forming new coalitions among Blacks, Latinos, Asian-Americans and liberal whites in the postincorporation era? Such a foundation will, of course, be built among leaders. But leaders affect the masses through their statements and actions.

The first element of a fair contract is to give credit where credit is due. Thus it is fair to indicate that the political successes of the past decades are due to both Black political mobilization and white liberal support.

Liberals need to recognize that the African-American movement precedes their involvement; and Blacks need to recognize that without white liberals, many of their greatest victories would not have taken place.

Objectively, white liberals are, indeed, very different from white conservatives. The differences are obvious, in polls and in elections. Denial of the evidence is useless. Without a split among whites on ideological grounds, Black political mobilization would be unable to succeed. That split can be cultivated. It is crucial for white liberals, however, not to take more than their fair share of credit. Revising history to accentuate the white role is highly damaging, as is ignorance of the leading Black role in the development of minority incorporation.

Biracial politics should be understood on both sides as a mixed-motive game. The sentimental liberal view holds that ideology is everything; Black Power theorists see hypocrisy in liberalism whenever there is a conflict of interest. But most coalitions between groups are based on both conflict and cooperation.

Even when ideology draws groups together, there are numerous opportunities for conflict of interest. One would not realistically conclude that therefore the ideological affinity is meaningless. Rather, one would seek to manage or isolate the conflict of interest if the coalition were on balance successful. Caditz (1976) wisely suggested that white liberals should be realistic about their own racial ambivalence. She considered this an antidote to liberal "rigidification." They should avoid the tendency to ascribe only the loftiest of motives to their own political actions. On the other hand, others should also be realistic about liberalism.

Given the cynicism with which Black Power theorists view liberals, it is striking how disappointed they are when liberals define their own interests. If ideology does not matter, why would a progressive be expected to sacrifice his or her own interests and take full direction from others? The realism about coalitions shown in *Black Power* should be extended: white liberals are much more inclined than white conservatives to support the African-American movement, except when their own interests are threatened. These interests are not always threatened, and sometimes are advanced by the Black movement. In this view, a biracial coalition need not collapse because of a conflict of interest—unless

both sides have developed, without knowing it, an overly sentimental view of coalitions.

There is no weakness in cultivating a coalition partner. White liberals may believe that they have a claim on the Black community, but this is not realistic. Coalition is a choice, not an end in itself, and there are times not to coalesce. For instance, in 1961 Blacks went for Sam Yorty while liberals hated him. Latinos have fought both Blacks and white liberals—their ideological allies—to win changes in the Los Angeles council reapportionment.

Conversely, it is only good politics to cultivate liberals to participate in the minority movement. It is surely not strength, for instance, to purposely alienate Jews from a coalition on racial equality. All ethnic groups who have used politics have also allied with other groups; that is a sign of strength.

Is there in fact a contradiction between Black Power and biracial coalition? On the rhetorical level, there may be a severe conflict. The public stances that define each position may often be in opposition. But in real politics, not only is there not a contradiction—there is a mutuality of philosophy and interest.

Generally speaking, biracial coalition building is likely to be undertaken as a result of successful minority mobilization. It is the outcome of an internal process of, as Carmichael and Hamilton (1967:vii) put it, how "black people in America must get themselves together." The early stages of Black political incorporation are spent forging unity. This means nominating conventions, the development of Black media themes, and the building of street-level precinct organizations.

In Berkeley and Los Angeles, citywide biracial coalitions were built on top of existing African-American political movements of great strength and duration. In Los Angeles, the Black community became even stronger politically as a result of the citywide coalition. After several elections, it was clear that the Black community was the single most important factor in citywide elections. Black power was at the heart of all the mobilization efforts behind African-American mayoral candidates. Yet as a part of the electoral effort, these candidates built biracial coalitions. This was not out of weakness, but due to the proximity of victory.

Where Black power is weak, there tends to be a corresponding atrophy of biracial coalition. For example, in New York City the Black and Jewish communities together comprise nearly half the city's population. Yet until Dinkins's election in 1989, there had never been a serious Black mayoral candidate. One crucial reason for the failure of Black incorporation in New York City has been the stultification of an independent Black movement. For many reasons, New York City did not become a site for such activism. Hamilton (1979) complained that New York City Blacks had failed to go after electoral power, settling instead for a patron-client relationship with federally funded agencies.

Not surprisingly, the city also failed to develop the sort of biracial coalition that Los Angeles did. In fact, conflicts of interest between Blacks and Jews escalated rapidly without the moderating influence of citywide politicians. Thus, New York City's biracial coalition politics would have been greatly advanced by a substantial dose of Black power.

It is necessary to accept the distance that separates Blacks and white liberals. One of the problems of the civil rights movement was that the attempt to bridge the distance through human relations alone was insufficient. When whites were involved in the definition and leadership of the African-American movement, it was inevitable that there would be severe strains. Human relations will be most effective as a supplement to activities that recognize the distinct interests and identities of groups.

In the same manner, the view that there is only one progressive movement, led by Blacks, omits the ability of white liberals to define their own progressivism. The recognition that Blacks and white liberals have distinct, overlapping movements can be liberating. The same will undoubtedly be true in the long effort to build alliances between Blacks and Latinos.

The bridge building does not need to be conducted at the mass level, where such bridges are notoriously open to misinterpretation. Coalitions are more likely to succeed when leaders, operating as peers in a competitive political environment, form relationships of mutual trust and respect. These leadership groups can be highly successful in muting the sort of conflicts that can be devastating to a biracial coalition.

In the best of all possible worlds, African-American unity is forged and leaders arise who can translate this unity into alliance. White liberals are themselves in need

of political power after being excluded. An alliance is forged that is both ideological and pragmatic—an alliance of both shared beliefs and shared ambitions. One can imagine no better conditions for biracial coalition. These were the conditions in Los Angeles. But even where racial polarization has burned its way into the heart of a city, the possibilities for biracial alliance remain.

It is time to lay to rest the notion that the development of the African-American political community stands in opposition to a broad progressive movement among white liberals. As long as white liberals do not try to define the minority movement, and as long as Blacks do not seek to narrowly circumscribe the political expression of white liberals, the outlines of a powerful coalition for change can be seen. It will be stymied by conflicts of interest, but will be pushed ahead by shared ideology. When interests are shared under certain political circumstances, major victories with lasting value will be won.

References

Browning, Rufus P., Dale Rogers Marshall, and David Tabb. 1984. *Protest Is Not Enough: The Struggle of Blacks and Hispanics for Equality in City Politics*. Berkeley: University of California Press.

Caditz, Judith. 1976. *White Liberals in Transition: Current Dilemmas of Ethnic Integration*. Holliswood, NY: Spectrum Publications.

Carmichael, Stokely and Charles V. Hamilton. 1967. *Black Power: The Politics of Liberation in America*. New York: Random House.

Downs, Anthony. 1957. *An Economic Theory of Democracy*. New York: Harper and Row.

Hamilton, Charles V. 1979. The Patron-Recipient Relationship and Minority Politics in New York City. *Political Science Quarterly* 94 (Summer): 211–28.

Kleppner, Paul. 1985. *Chicago Divided: The Making of a Black Mayor*. DeKalb: Northern Illinois University Press.

Pettigrew, Thomas F. 1971. When a Black Candidate Runs for Mayor: Race and Voting Behavior. In Harlan Hahn, ed. *People and Politics in Urban Society*, 99–105. Beverly Hills, CA: Sage Publications.

Ransom, Bruce. 1987. Black Independent Electoral Politics in Philadelphia: The Election of Mayor W. Wilson Goode. In Michael B. Preston, Lenneal J. Henderson, Jr., and Paul L. Puryear, eds., *The New Black Politics: The Search for Political Power*, 2nd ed., 256–89. New York and London: Longman.

11-3 "The Public-Private Partnership"

Jason Hackworth

The Neoliberal City: Governance, Ideology, and Development in American Urbanism

One of the foundations of neoliberal governance at the local level is public-private cooperation. These alliances can vary considerably in form, but city governments are increasingly expected to serve as market facilitators, rather than salves for market failures. Cities have moved from a managerialist role under Keynesianism to an entrepreneurial one under neoliberalism (Harvey 1989b). No longer are cities as able to establish regulatory barriers to capital; on the contrary, they are expected to lower such barriers. An entire body of academic literature—regime theory—has arisen to address public-private partnerships and such entrepreneurial behavior, but knowledge of how such alliances function within multiscalar capitalism is underdeveloped. In particular, regime theory and much of the mainstream literature on public-private alliances tend to be highly localist in its orientation. That is, it says very little about how local regimes are connected to broader policy shifts, such as the current fervor for federal devolution in the United States. Regime theory also says very little about the market influence and behavior of public-private coalitions, choosing instead to conceptualize the local state and local capital as more or less autonomous entities that just happen to be coalescing around a particular set of development concerns. This chapter attempts to address both gaps by linking the concept of urban regimes to wider policy changes and by considering the local effects of coalitions that have no obvious barriers between public and private. The goal is to examining regime theory critically through the use of a case study of such cooperation in New Brunswick, New Jersey, during the past thirty years.

Regime Theory and the Local State

Urban regimes are collectives of public and private interests that join forces to initiate development or retard disinvestment in a particular city. Their public participants include city hall, development authorities, housing authorities, and the like, while their private participants can range from wealthy individuals to influential local corporations. Regime theory is helpful in understanding neoliberal urban governance insofar as it emphasizes the increasingly murky boundaries between private and public institutions in the land development process, but there are serious deficiencies in its approach, as a brief history of the literature shows.

Stone's study of urban development in Atlanta, Georgia, is often cited as the nominal beginning of regime theory (1989), but important antecedents were undertaken several years earlier by Norman and Susan Fainstein (1983, 1985) in their work on the changing role of the local state in New York City. Regime theory is best understood intellectually as a rapprochement of competing local state theories and empirically as a set of ideas about the future of local government amidst widespread urban decline following the 1970s. During the 1950s and 1960s, one of the more salient debates in urban studies addressed the general question of who governs at the local level. Generally, there were two strands of thought on this subject: pluralism and elitism. Pluralists argued that power at the local level was not the domain of any one group or constituency but rather was formed through political coalitions. Postwar metropolitan fragmentation in the United States, which divided power into smaller geographical units, fueled this sentiment. Power was "up for grabs" according to pluralists, and the mechanism of the general election was the chief (though not the only) mechanism for achieving this power. Dahl's *Who Governs* is a classic articulation and defense of pluralist local political theory (1961). In this book, Dahl chronicles the formation of a mayor-centered electoral coalition in New Haven, Connecticut, that was eventually responsible for redeveloping the downtown area of the city. The importance of economic restructuring, the financial power of coalition participants, and the links to wider processes are generally missing in this and other pluralist narratives.

The work of Dahl and the pluralists more generally was criticized by practitioners of elite theory[1] as being blind to an existing economic power structure that places enormous power in the hands of elite business-people. To elite theorists, local power is not open to all who are organized enough to reach for it but rather is an obvious by-product of economic power. Miliband's instrumentalist model of the local state was in line with elite conceptions when it posited a veritable conspiracy between local business elites and local political elites (1969; see also Clark and Dear 1981). The argument runs that elites from both worlds (business and politics) exchange roles freely—business elites become political elites, and vice versa. Miliband and some other elite theorists thus suggested that a real understanding of local politics is actually more economic than that proposed by Dahl and the pluralists. In the elite model, we need only understand the individual career behavior of a locality's most economically powerful people.[2]

Regime theory developed initially as an attempt to reconcile the strength of both pluralist and elitist notions of local power. The regime literature during the 1980s was composed primarily of case study research, but more recently some practitioners have developed general theoretical statements so that we can begin to speak more clearly about the idea of regimes (Horan 1991; Stone 1993; Stoker 1995; Lauria 1997b). Regime theory emphasizes the following: (a) the importance of coalition building, a central tenet of pluralist theory; (b) the ability to provide leadership in a complex and changing environment; and (c) the importance of economic and institutional power. In essence, as Stone explains, "regime analysis concedes to pluralism the unlikelihood that any group can exercise comprehensive social control but also holds that the absence of monolithic control is so universal as to be uninteresting" (1993, p. 8). In contrast to elite theory, though, "regime theory recognizes that any [one] group is unlikely to be able to exercise comprehensive social control in a complex world" (Stoker 1995, p. 59). That is, regime theory recognizes that political actors are beholden at least in part to the economy and more specifically to economic actors but at the same time attempts to steer clear of the economic determinism of elite theory by arguing that power is more complicated than simple access to resources. Power, according to regime theory, is dependent also upon electoral power, the nature of coalitions in a locality, and technical knowledge (ibid., p. 60).

While most general statements on regime theory tend to explain it in relation to pluralism and elitism, Brown (1999) has argued that regime theory's emphasis on the nexus between the public and private is reminiscent of the commercial republic, which is a product of classical liberal thought. Brown's placement of regime theory into the liberal tradition relates it more closely with the pluralist model, which emphasizes individual choice and diffuse electoral democracy. Though some have refuted this conception of regime theory (see in particular Feldman 1997), at a minimum it is true that its tendency to focus on the uniqueness of individual coalitions in particular places blinds us to the ways in which such coalitions are connected to broader restructuring processes. Stone's work provides a good (but by no means the only) example of this tendency (1989). In his study of coalition building in Atlanta, Stone presents a relatively liberal notion of local politics. He argues that a regime was formed whose core was a coalition between the sizeable black middle class and downtown business elites, particularly those associated with Coca-Cola. His emphasis on this coalition was an important contribution for understanding the group psychology of a power alliance in a city undergoing restructuring. Yet because of this emphasis on the power created by this coalition, Stone struggles to represent adequately the nonlocal sources of economic and political power that were driving the regime in question (see Lauria 1997b). "Consequently," as Lauria points out, "the abstraction of theoretical insights [in this case and others] becomes confined to behavioral microeconomic, and possibly pluralistic, explanations of the social production of cooperation and political coalition building" (ibid., p. 5). To this extent, then, Brown is not alone in his concern that regime theory devolves into a liberal pluralist and often highly local understanding of public-private cooperation.

But orthodox regime theory is not the only source of insight on public-private cooperation. Some scholars have taken a wider view of regimes and have thus been able to think more clearly about their connections to broader activity. Norman and Susan Fainstein's attempts to understand the state in urban development (1983, 1985) and more recently Lauria's project to weave regulation theory into regime theory (1997a) are two important examples of this approach. Lauria's project culminated in an edited collection of mostly neo-Marxian pieces that debated the relative merits of weaving the hitherto very local regime theory with the nation-state–scaled regulation theory. Regulation theory posits that forms of governance are created at the national level to ensure economic stability and peace between capital and labor. The idea with the marriage was to move beyond the relatively simplistic assumptions of individual choice that had characterized the urban regime literature. While raising important issues, however, Lauria was only partially successful at using regulation theory as a way to "structuralize" and "de-localize" regime theory (1997c). Though both literatures developed out of a similar set of conditions, their empirical foci are so radically different that such a rapprochement is very difficult to achieve. Perhaps the most important insight that emerged from this exercise was that certain important antecedents to the literature—particularly the work of Norman and Susan Fainstein—may provide a better model for how to do this than previously thought. The time has come, Lauria suggests (1997b, p. 5) to "revert back to a Fainsteinesque approach that focuses on the connections to external economic relations."

Though they did not themselves use the language of "regimes," Fainstein and Fainstein developed an important historical (and multiscalar) typology of postwar urban development coalitions that provides an early framework for how to understand local variability, and demonstrated how such alliances are constrained by the imperatives of the capitalist urban system in the United States (1983, 1985). They argued that federal urban policies were particularly important at shaping the local coalitions during the twentieth century, and that three observable periods of regime formation could be identified: (1) the Directive Period, 1950–64; (2) the Concessionary Period, 1965–74; and (3) the Conserving Period, 1975–84. By basing their typology on the experience of five very different cities,[3] they were able to develop the typology without falling into the trap of a "one size fits all" economic determinism. Their comparison highlights how local politics matter, because they use larger political and economic change as the starting point rather than as a tangential side-note buried in their conclusions. Their typology is a useful framework for understanding the activities of contemporary public-private alliances,[4] so it will be explained here.

Local coalitions formed during the Directive Period were typically intent upon sustaining postwar growth and restoring the vitality of downtown areas, which in many cities had fallen into physical disrepair. Federal urban policies encouraged slum clearance as a means to achieve these goals, and local participation was minimal, as vast areas of major urban cores were eviscerated in this political context. In New York City, for example, prominent officials like Robert Moses and powerful institutions like the Port Authority of New York and New Jersey demolished neighborhoods mainly to make way for freeways and bridges (Warf 1988; Caro 1975). Over time, local protest, primarily emanating from minority neighborhoods—frequent targets of slum clearance—became effective at stopping such activity. Federal urban policy was forced to change in the 1960s along with local coalitions as the social costs of this form of slum clearance became clear.

The Concessionary Period emerged from the ashes of the Directive Period. It is largely defined by the mildly redistributive programs that developed under President Johnson's "Great Society" and "War on Poverty" initiatives. The 1964 Civil Rights Act and rising minority (particularly African-American) power in cities essentially forced the shift. During the Concessionary Period, coalitions at the local level focused on community development more than on community replacement, housing more than freeways. These coalitions were facilitated by a spate of regional programs and institutions established to revive inner city areas with new housing. For example, the New York State's Urban Development Corporation (UDC) was formed in 1968 to provide public and affordable housing for the urban minority poor in the state. It was given enormous power to override local zoning restrictions and opposition and to issue bonds in order to site such facilities. The UDC was, however, among the first regional government agencies to realize that without a parallel change in the federal redistribution of income, their goals were unprofitable. They were effectively bankrupt by 1975, forced to shift their focus to more profitable real estate activities. The experience of the UDC is emblematic of the larger historical regime typology that the Fainsteins developed.

Largely because of such financial hardship, regime formation, they argue, moved into a third phase in 1975: the Conserving Period. During the conserving period, cities were forced to respond to the harsh fiscal realities of the mid-1970s by focusing more attention on property tax generation than on social service provision. Agencies like the UDC shifted to highly profitable commercial redevelopments, while at the federal level New Deal and Great Society safety net reforms were slowly unraveled. "Entrepreneurial coalitions"—also known as public-private alliances—formed in this era as a response to economic restructuring (Fainstein and Fainstein 1985; Harvey 1989b; Leitner 1990). These alliances were varied in purpose and extent but generally involved the deployment of local statecraft in ways that differed from the Keynesian era. As Susan Fainstein would later remark, "Cities, like private corporations, are increasingly in the business of making deals. But the kinds of deals public officials can make are limited to what conforms to business strategies" (1995, p. 38).

According to Harvey, four development foci emerged among entrepreneurial coalitions after the 1970s (1989b). First, cities attempted to enhance their ability to compete within the increasingly global division of labor by defraying costs of technology and labor force training for capital. Universities and research centers became the predominant vehicles for pursuing this strategy. Second, cities attempted to enhance their position within the spatial division of consumption, particularly in areas of upscale retail and tourism. With manufacturing income on the ebb, many cities opted for consumption-oriented, tourist-friendly inner cities. Third, cities attempted to attain "command functions" within the global economy (Sassen 1991). That is, they attempted to lure corporations and interests with global reach to their municipality by offering tax breaks and other incentives—the idea being, of course, to "ground" some of the profits being experienced by global finance capital. Finally, as Harvey points out, there was some continuance of the erstwhile goal of competing for federal redistribution of one sort or another (1989b). Competition for defense industry contracts and military bases during the Reagan buildup of the 1980s was a particularly acute example of this strategy in action.

Urban Regimes in a Devolved Context

The structural conditions prodding local governments to behave in a more entrepreneurial way sharpened in 1994 with the Republican Contract with America—a highly devolutionary tract partially built on the ideas of classical liberalism (Staeheli et al. 1997; Eisinger 1998).[5] The ostensible goal of devolving federal power was to give states and localities more political autonomy (Staeheli et al. 1997), but most local governments were relatively powerless on their own at realizing the "autonomy" that sat before them. Capital was relatively well-situated to acquire the devolved power (Kodras 1997), but it could not work alone either, and it often depended upon the local state to defray some of its self-imposed costs. Zoning enforcement, neighborhood policing, and utility costs are all typically beyond the capacity of individual fractions of capital to absorb, so the local state is often deployed to cover them. In essence, then, it is neither the local state nor capital which stood *ipso facto* to gain from federal devolution; rather, an organized relationship between the two entities would be necessary. Urban regimes thus became increasingly important institutional mechanisms for acquiring power released from the federal state.

As mentioned earlier, contemporary regime theory evolved from case studies that correctly assumed that the local state is embedded in a larger economic context (for example, see Stone 1989; Jones and Bachelor 1993) but devoted enormous attention to *extra-economic* concerns like race and culture to demonstrate why local coalitions matter (Fainstein 1995; Stoker 1995; Brown 1999). Because of this extra-economic bias, we still know little about how regimes behave as capitalist agents at the local level and, perhaps more important, about how they relate to the larger political economy (Jessop et al. 1999; MacLeod and Goodwin 1999). Such issues are assumed rather than explained in this literature (Lauria 1997b), so it is important to return to a more basic political economy literature for answers. We know, for example, that capitalism is wrought with internal contradictions that collide to form an unevenly developed socioeconomic landscape (Harvey 1985; N. Smith 1990; 1996). Uneven development is derived in particular from the tension between capital's need to equalize the conditions of production (to expand), on the one hand, and its conflicting need to differentiate those conditions (to exclude), on the other (Plotkin 1987; N. Smith 1990). As a dialectic, exclusion and expansion are at once in opposition to one another and at the same time necessitate each other's continued presence. "In capitalism," as Sidney Plotkin observes, "the logic is inescapable: expansion is the condition of exclusion just as exclusion is the condition of expansion" (1987, p. 10). We know, furthermore, that the state intervenes at several scales to manage the spatial effects of this contradiction. Land-use zoning, for example, is an explicit attempt by the state to protect real estate capital's need to differentiate economic space. As Eisinger has pointed out, the recent devolution in federal power has required local states to ally with capital (in the form of regimes) even more directly than before (1998). However, because the *raison d'être* of regime theory has thus far been to focus on extra-economic political behavior to understand uneven development, there has been little explicit attempt to understand regimes as capitalist agents within this dialectic. Though a more materialist understanding of urban regimes in the United States has been needed since the mid-1970s, it has become increasingly important since the mid-1990s, as the federal state has restructured.

Regime Formation in New Brunswick, New Jersey

The following case study describes the formation of an urban regime in New Brunswick, New Jersey, within the context of the capitalist expansion-exclusion dialectic to illustrate both the connections to wider-scale politico-economic restructuring and the capacity of public-private coalitions to become more or less autonomous participants in the market. A regime was formed in New Brunswick to redevelop the city's central business district (CBD) after years of disinvestment. One ancillary goal of the regime has been to

demolish a nearby public housing complex as a way to protect local property values in the adjacent CBD. An exploration of this case highlights the way in which local regimes become locked into the maelstrom of expansion and exclusion and how, as a result, geographic scale gets produced and dissolved. This process is most easily understood by breaking the history of redevelopment in New Brunswick into three phases.

1975–1981

Like many cities in the northeastern United States, by the mid-1970s New Brunswick had found itself embroiled in a fiscal crisis. Its main employers were fleeing to areas where labor and land were cheaper and where regulations and taxes were more relaxed (Beauregard and Holcomb 1984; Holcomb 1997). The primary circuit of the larger regional economy was in crisis, so a revival of manufacturing seemed an improbable strategy for increasingly desperate city leaders to pursue. A strategy that could tap into the enormous transfer of capital into the built environment that was afoot (Harvey 1978) was more likely to be successful. Yet the regional profitability landscape was grossly uneven by the mid-1970s, so there were significant barriers to real estate investment in New Brunswick. The city had rent control, high taxes, and relatively expensive labor; on top of that, its volatile race politics had been chronicled in the infamous *Kerner Commission Report* several years earlier (1968). Investors were squeamish about planting their capital in New Brunswick during the mid-1970s because of barriers—both perceived and material—in the regionally differentiated profit landscape.

Just as things apparently could not get worse for city officials, the city's largest private sector employer, Johnson and Johnson, began serious deliberation on whether they should join the exodus from New Brunswick and move their headquarters closer to their manufacturing facilities in Texas. In a vote that was eventually decided by the chairman of the corporation, Johnson and Johnson decided to stay in New Brunswick, but only on the condition that the city devote itself more seriously to removing the aforementioned obstacles to real estate reinvestment in the downtown area. Some of the obstacle removal would necessarily involve the local state, while other goals were dependent on capital, so a public-private coalition was formed to facilitate the redevelopment. The coalition was named The New Brunswick Development Corporation (DevCo), and, along with a sister organization called New Brunswick Tomorrow (NBT), it was responsible for facilitating the redevelopment of downtown New Brunswick and devising more privatized methods of service provision. A regime was thus born to handle the increasingly complex task of governance in an economically devastated city. It is interesting to note that, although its primary focus was on a very specific geographic area—the central business district of New Brunswick—few leaders of the regime actually lived in New Brunswick, much less near the downtown. This membership structure remained intact largely because neither of the two key public-private organizations had democratically elected boards (Beauregard and Holcomb 1984).

With the institutional apparatus for redevelopment in place, Johnson and Johnson affirmed its commitment to the city by constructing corporate headquarters complex in 1978 costing $70 million. This investment served as an important material foundation to the more ethereal business-friendly atmosphere that was sought by the public-private coalition. The new headquarters building directly encouraged the construction of the Hyatt Regency Hotel and indirectly encouraged the Trenton-assisted beautification of George Street and the construction of Ferren Mall and the Plaza II Building. These initial projects improved investor confidence—an important condition for tapping into the wider property boom that would arrive in the 1980s.

1982–1989

During the second phase of New Brunswick's redevelopment, the real estate capital planted in phase one expanded southward within the CBD. . . . [R]eal estate capital had become implanted in the northern portion of the CBD and was now migrating southward. The growth occurred because of the regime's, and particularly DevCo's, continued efforts at removing barriers to reinvestment vis-a-vis surrounding cities. This continued to be the primary governance motive throughout the second period, and it was met with continued success as reinvestment poured into the area. Yet precisely because an expansion was occurring within its jurisdiction, the local regime became confronted with

the need to exclude. That is, after the implantation of real estate capital and some growth during the late 1970s, it became necessary to differentiate the central business district as a means of facilitating growth within it—to exclude in order to expand.

The year 1982 marks the onset of the second phase for precisely this reason. In that year, the city's mayor, John Lynch—a key figure in the extant regime—publicly announced for the first time the city's intent to demolish the nearby New Brunswick Memorial Homes Complex (Rubin 1990; NBHA 1996). The complex sat at the fringe of the putative central business district and was seen as an obstacle to urban redevelopment in the area. The removal of the complex was therefore proposed, but because the Department of Housing and Urban Development (HUD) prohibited local demolition plans that could not guarantee one-to-one unit replacement, the local regime could not afford to follow through. Despite its growing power, the regime did not possess the resources necessary to overcome the regulatory constraints on its activities. For a demolition plan to take place, 246 housing units would have had to be built elsewhere in New Brunswick, so the mayor and his supporters eventually withdrew the proposal. With obstacles to removing the Memorial Homes seemingly insurmountable, regime participants concentrated on other more veiled forms of exclusion to protect and expand real estate capital in the central business district, such as the establishment of the City Market Special Improvement District in 1987. The district served to protect local real estate capital by assuring that the CBD was more attractive, better-served, and safer than the rest of the city. The emphasis on protecting CBD real estate investment at the expense of nearby residents generated a more public (and racialized) form of social conflict in the city. One local activist angrily summarized the tension that was developing between city residents and regime participants; while castigating Mayor John Lynch at a meeting during the 1980s, activist David Harris stated, "There is a substantial minority presence downtown. After each of your projects there is none at all. That disturbs me" (quoted in Todd 1989, p. Al). Exclusion as a means of expansion was plainly unacceptable to nearby residents, but because their electoral power was being progressively eroded by the material power of real estate capital in the regime, New Brunswick residents became even more marginal in city politics than they had been at the beginning of the decade.

1990–Present

If exclusive measures that facilitated expansion characterized the second phase of New Brunswick's redevelopment, the capital expansion that produced exclusion is the identifying theme of the third phase. The dialectical sea change took place in 1990 with the formal announcement of an expansion beyond the current CBD. Lynch, still mayor of the city and key participant of the regime, proudly announced that the central business district was going to leap-frog Route 18 and expand into the waterfront park. The Riverwatch Luxury Housing Complex, built on several sites, was going to form the cornerstone of the expansion (Parisi and Holcomb 1995; Patterson 1997). Several months later, Lynch unveiled the requisite exclusionary piece of the expansionary puzzle: a formal funded plan to demolish the Memorial Homes Complex (Wallace 1990). The complex was adjacent to the only bridge linking the existing central business district to the waterfront and was seen as an obstacle to expansion. Lynch summarized the regime's exclusionary sentiment in his characteristically unvarnished way. "It is clear," he noted, "that from a marketing standpoint, you would not be able to market the waterfront with the presence of the Memorial Homes" (quoted in Rubin 1990, p. Al).

The demolition proposal included public and private money to rebuild and scatter the existing Memorial Homes units throughout the city (Fazzi 1990). The fact that local capital was even willing to help finance such an expensive plan is a telling gauge of how threatening the Memorial Homes were to the CBD expansion. Yet while construction on the Riverwatch portion of the plan began almost immediately after the 1990 announcement, the private financing for the demolition plan began to evaporate as the early 1990s recession took hold. The first phase of Riverwatch eventually opened in 1993, the nadir of the recession for regional housing markets, so support for this portion of the plan eventually began to evaporate too. For Riverwatch to expand, the recession would have to

abate, and the local regime would once again have to find a way to underwrite the replacement of the units in the Memorial Homes, because HUD still required one-for-one unit replacement.

Several years after the completion of Riverwatch's first phase, the recession finally subsided. The southward progression of real estate investment within the central business district resumed, and the waterfront tracts were redeveloped for a possible expansion. . . . Yet the expensive project of replacing the 246 units in the Memorial Homes still remained an onerous obstacle for the local regime. Just as it was beginning to appear that Riverwatch's expansion was going to necessitate the enormously expensive project of moving several hundred very poor families, the devolution of the federal state gave the local regime the requisite power to expand without the extant requirement. As part of HUD's "reinvention"—itself part of the larger federal devolution—the one-to-one unit requirement for local demolition plans was removed. Furthermore, the HOPE VI program had begun encouraging demolition nationwide by providing funding for such plans. With this regulatory hurdle absent and a possible funding source in place, the New Brunswick Housing Authority, in regular consultation with local regime leaders (Clarke 1997a), submitted a HOPE VI proposal to HUD in 1996. In line with the new, less stringent regulations, this plan only sought to replace 102 of the 246 existing units with newly built houses (NBHA 1996). HUD eventually rejected the proposal, so the New Brunswick Housing Authority submitted a similar plan the following year, which drew upon local capital for demolition costs (Clarke 1997b). HUD approved this iteration of the plan but offered only housing vouchers (no new units) as a means of replacement. Because the New Brunswick affordable housing market is saturated by Rutgers University students, this virtually guaranteed that most Memorial Homes residents would be forced to relocate elsewhere. In effect, the local regime had acquired the lever of exclusion to complement its power to expand and, in so doing, effectively eliminated a perceived threat to local real estate growth. The complex was demolished on August 18, 2001, and development has begun on the Boyd Park area of the city. As Mayor Cahill blithely pointed out in 2002, the gentrification

Table 1   Redevelopment phase by predominant spatial strategy

Redevelopment phase	Spatial goals of the regime		
	Primary	**Secondary**	**Tertiary**
1975–1981	Capital enticement		
1982–1989	Capital enticement	CBD exclusion	CBD expansion
1990–present	CBD expansion	CBD exclusion	Capital enticement

of inner New Brunswick during the previous ten years had been nothing short of astonishing: "In 1991, if one were to have said that New Brunswick, over the course of the next ten or so years, would see the development of over 1,000 upscale and luxury housing units, the demolition of Memorial Homes, . . . and the realization of over 1.1 billion dollars of investment within our revitalization efforts, most would have thought that individual was dreaming" (Cahill 2002).

The Expansion-Exclusion Dialectic

The real estate capital that was expanding within New Brunswick's CBD during the 1980s began to expand beyond its boundaries during the 1990s. The local regime aggressively facilitated this expansion by attempting to finance the removal of the nearby Memorial Homes complex. Yet only with federal devolution was the regime given the effective power to realize this particular goal. Expansion was deemed possible only through exclusion, yet the effective power to exclude prior to 1995 was still embedded in the federal state. After this power was devolved, the regime was empowered to manipulate more directly the expansion-exclusion dialectic in and around the central business district.

The New Brunswick case demonstrates capital's need to exclude in order to expand (and vice versa) and its ability to do so through the mechanism of an urban regime. The initial motivation of the regime was to dissolve the barriers to real estate investment that had built up over time—to entice capital. . . . With the initial goal of constructing a scale of profitability successfully met, the regime's spatial strategy diversified and shifted (see Table 1). A more localized—and thus more controllable—expansion-exclusion dialectic

took hold as the regime and its participants acquired more power. The regime's survival became virtually dependent on facilitating the expansion of this scale— a goal that could be accomplished only through the exclusion of perceived threats in the landscape.

The regime's acquisition of power over time and its subsequent immersion into the contradictions of the urban land market were accelerated by events occurring at higher political scales, especially the devolution of the federal state in 1994–95. It is thus reasonable to conclude that the New Brunswick case is not anomalous and that urban regimes elsewhere are increasingly better understood according to the calculus of capitalism than according to the extra-economic behavior of their participants. If carefully done, this understanding can be achieved without returning to the economistic cul-de-sac of state theory's past, but it does involve a reversal of the classic emphasis in regime theory. Rather than assume that regimes operate in a murky economic context while describing their unique political attributes, it has become increasingly important to assume that such local details exist while devoting more attention to the regime's role as an agent of capitalism.

Notes

1. Some, such as Lauria (1997b), have deemed this school of thought "structuralism" rather than elite theory.
2. This view was disputed on the left by Poulantzas, who argued that while economically powerful people often become politically powerful, the relationship is more structural than interpersonal or cronyistic per se (1969). That is, it is the position of economic power within liberal capitalism that confers political power,

not the particular connection of individuals currently residing in those positions.

3. New Haven, Detroit, New Orleans, Denver, and San Francisco, and later New York City.

4. They were certainly not arguing—nor am I—that these phases descended upon cities at *exactly* the same time, with exactly the same consequences. The phases highlight, and are only meant to highlight, a generalized structural context for regime formation.

5. It is important to note that this document and the politics that led to it were motivated by concerns that included, but were not limited to neoliberalism. In particular, there is a strong social conservatism that pervades this document and the American Right in general. This social conservatism, though frequently allying with neoliberal politics, is nonetheless a different strand of political thought, with a different genealogy.

References

Beauregard, R., and B. Holcomb. 1984. "New Brunswick." *Cities*, February, pp. 215–20.

Brown, M. 1999. "Reconceptualizing Public and Private in Urban Regime Theory: Governance in AIDS Politics." *International Journal of Urban and Regional Research* 23: 70–87.

Cahill, J. 2002. "New Brunswick State of the City Address 2002." www.cityofnewbrunswick.org/mayorsoffice/stateofthecity2002.asp. Accessed January 15, 2002.

Caro, R. 1975. *The Power Broker: Robert Moses and the Fall of New York*. New York: Vintage.

Clark, G. and M. Dear. 1981. "The State in Capitalism and the Capitalist State." In *Urbanization and Urban Planning in Capitalist Society*, edited by M. Dear and A. Scott. London: Methuen.

Clarke, J. 1997a. Interview by the author with the executive director of the New Brunswick Housing Authority. August 25.

Clarke, J. 1997b. Interview by the author with the executive director of the New Brunswick Housing Authority. December 12.

Dahl, R. 1961. *Who Governs?* New Haven: Yale University Press.

Eisinger, P. 1998. "City Politics in an Era of Federal Devolution." *Urban Affairs Review* 33: 308–25.

Fainstein, N. and S. Fainstein. 1983. "Regime Strategies, Communal Resistance, and Economic Forces." In *Restructuring the City: The Political Economy of Urban Redevelopment*, edited by S. Fainstein, N. Fainstein, R. C. Hill, D. Judd, and M. P. Smith. New York: Longman.

Fainstein, N. and S. Fainstein. 1985. "Is State Planning Necessary for Capital? The U.S. Case." *International Journal of Urban and Regional Research* 9 (4): 485–507.

Fainstein, S. 1995. "Politics, Economics, and Planning: Why Urban Regimes Matter." *Planning Theory* 14: 34–41.

Fazzi, R. 1990. "City Sets Sights on Housing Sites." *Home News and Tribune* December 12, A1–A2.

Feldman, M. 1997. "Spatial Structures of Regulation and Urban Regimes." In *Reconstructing Urban Regime Theory: Regulating Urban Politics in a Global Era*, edited by M. Lauria. Thousand Oaks, CA: Sage Publishing.

Harvey, D. 1978. "The Urban Process under Capitalism: A Framework for Analysis." *International Journal of Urban and Regional Research* 2: 101–31.

Harvey, D. 1985. *The Urbanization of Capital: Studies in the History and Theory of Capitalist Urbanization*. Baltimore: The Johns Hopkins University Press.

Harvey, D. 1989. "From Managerialism to Entrepreneurialism: The Transformation of Urban Governance in Late Capitalism." *Geografiska Annaler* 71: 3–17.

Holcomb, B. 1997. "New Brunswick Walk." Unpublished notes. Department of Urban Studies, Rutgers University.

Horan, C. 1991. "Beyond Governing Coalitions: Analyzing Urban Regimes in the 1990s." *Journal of Urban Affairs* 13: 119–35.

Jessop, B., J. Peck, and A. Tickell. 1999. "Retooling the Machine: Economic Crisis, State Restructuring, and Urban Politics." In *The Urban Growth Machine: Critical State Perspectives Two Decades Later*, edited by A. E. G. Jonas and D. Wilson. Albany: State University of New York Press.

Jones, B. and L. Bachelor. 1993. *The Sustaining Hand: Community Leadership and Corporate Power*. Lawrence: University of Kansas Press.

Kerner Commission. 1968. *Report of the National Advisory Commission of Civil Disorders*. Washington, D.C.: U.S. Government Printing Office.

Kodras, J. 1997. "Restructuring the State: Devolution, Privatization, and the Geographic Redistribution of Power and Capacity in Governance." In *State Devolution in America: Implications for a Diverse Society*, edited by L. Staeheli, J. Kodras, and C. Flint. Thousand Oaks, CA: Sage Publishing.

Lauria, M., ed., 1997a. *Reconstructing Urban Regime Theory: Regulating Urban Politics in a Global Era.* Thousand Oaks, CA: Sage Publishing.

Lauria, M., 1997b. "Introduction." In *Reconstructing Urban Regime Theory: Regulating Urban Politics in a Global Era.* Thousand Oaks, CA: Sage Publishing.

Lauria, M., 1997c. "Regulating Urban Regimes: Reconstruction or Impasse?" In *Reconstructing Urban Regime Theory: Regulating Urban Politics in a Global Era.* Thousand Oaks, CA: Sage Publishing.

Leitner, H., 1990. "Cities in Pursuit of Economic Growth: The Local State as Entrepreneur." *Political Geography Quarterly* 9: 146–70.

MacLeod, G. and M. Goodwin, 1999. "Space, Scale and State Strategy: Rethinking Urban and Regional Governance." *Progress in Human Geography* 23 (4): 503–27.

Miliband, R. 1969. *The State in Capitalist Society.* New York: Basic Books.

New Brunswick Housing Authority [NBHA]. 1996. "HOPE VI Application," An unpublished funding proposal submitted to the Department of Housing and Urban Development in September of 1996.

Parisi, P. and B. Holcomb. 1995. "Symbolizing Place: Journalistic Narratives of the City: *Urban Geography* 15: 379–94.

Patterson, G. 1997. Interview by the author with the Head of New Brunswick Community Planning Department, December 12.

Plotkin, S. 1987. *Keep Out: The Struggle for Land Use Control:* Berkeley: University of California Press.

Poulantzas, N. 1969. "The Problem of the Capitalist State." *New Left Review* 58: 67–78.

Ruben, H. 1990. "Memorial Homes Fate Murky." *Home News and Tribune*, February 14, A1, A8.

Sassen, S. 1991. *The Global City: New York, London, Tokyo.* Princeton: Princeton University Press.

Smith, N. 1990. *Uneven Development: Nature, Capital, and the Production of Space.* Oxford, UK: Blackwell Publishing.

Smith, N. 1996. *The New Urban Frontier: Gentrification and the Revanchist City.* New York: Routledge.

Staeheli, L., J. Kodras, and C. Flint., eds. 1997. *State Devolution in America: Implications for a Diverse Society.* Thousand Oaks, CA: Sage Publishing.

Stoker, G. 1995. "Regime Theory and Urban Politics." In *Theories of Urban Politics*, edited by D. Judge, G. Stoker, and H. Wolman. London: Sage Publishing.

Stone, C. 1989. *Regime Politics: Governing Atlanta, 1946–1988.* Lawrence: University Press of Kansas.

Stone, C. 1993. "Urban Regimes and the Capacity to Govern: A Political Economy Approach." *Journal of Urban Affairs* 15: 1–28.

Todd, S. 1989. "Uneasy Wait for New Homes." *Home News and Tribune*, September 17, A1, A6.

Wallace, E. 1990. "Riverwatch Plans Aired: Project Touted as City's New 'Gateway,'" *Home News and Tribune*, February 14, A1, A9.

Warf, B. 1988. "The Port Authority of New York-New Jersey." *Professional Geographer* 40: 287–97.

11-4 "Can Politicians Bargain with Business? A Theoretical and Comparative Perspective on Urban Development"

Paul Kantor and H. V. Savitch

Urban Affairs Quarterly

In the summer of 1989, United Air Lines [*sic*] announced it was planning a new maintenance hub that would bring nearly a billion dollars in investment and generate over 7,000 jobs for the region lucky enough to attract it. Within a few short months, officials in over 90 localities were competing for the bonanza and were tripping over one another in an effort to lure United. Denver offered $115 million in incentives and cash, Oklahoma City sought to raise $120 million, and localities in Virginia offered a similar amount. The competition for United was so keen that cities began to bid against one another and asked that their bids be kept secret.

United was so delighted at the level of bidding that it repeatedly delayed its decision in anticipation the offers would get even better. Nearly two years later, city officials in nine finalists were enhancing their incentives, courting United executives, and holding their breaths. Reflecting on the competition, Louisville Mayor Jerry Abramson quipped, "We haven't begun to offer up our firstborn yet, but we're getting close. Right now we are into siblings."[1]

Except for the extremity of the case, there is nothing new about cities questing for private capital. Cities compete with one another for tourism, foreign trade, baseball franchises, and federal grants. Yet, there is another side to this behavior. Although 93 cities competed for the United hub, many others did not, and some cities would have resisted the corporate intrusion (Etzkowitz and Mack 1976; Savitch 1988). When United stalled and raised the ante, Kentucky's governor angrily withdrew, complaining that he would "not continue this auction, this bidding war. There is a

point at which you draw the line ("Governor turns down UAL," *Courier-Journal*, 18 October 1991). In Denver, the legislature's majority leader protested, saying, "United has a ring and is pulling Colorado by the nose." With those remarks and heightening resentment, public opinion began to pull the state away from the lure of United ("UAL bidding goes on," *Courier Journal*, 22 October 1991).

Such cases do not seem uncommon. Although many cities are willing to build sports stadia, others have turned down the opportunity. For instance, when Fort Wayne, Indiana, declined to go beyond its offer of a short-term low-interest loan to obtain a minor-league baseball team, the franchise was taken elsewhere (Rosentraub and Swindell 1990). Although officials in some cities trip over one another in efforts to attract business by lowering taxes, officials in others raise them. Over the last three years, Los Angeles, New York, and Denver have increased business taxes. Notwithstanding high taxes and locational costs, business continues to seek out such cities as San Francisco, Tokyo, London, Toronto, and Frankfurt.

Nevertheless, the literature on urban politics has not systematically examined such "nondecisional" cases (Bachrach and Baratz 1962) to probe the precise circumstances under which local governments can influence the capital investment process. In *City Limits* Peterson (1981) suggested a *market-centered* view of the urban development process that compared cities to private corporations, each responding to the discipline of economic competition to maximize its revenue base. In this view, cities bear considerable political

Source: Paul Kantor and H. V. Savitch, "Can Politicians Bargain with Business? A Theoretical and Comparative Perspective on Urban Development," *Urban Affairs Quarterly*, vol. 29, no. 2, December 1993, pp. 230–55. Reprinted with permission from SAGE Publications, Inc.

limitations, are at a disadvantage in dealing with private capital, and ought to be cautious about their ability to pursue policies of their own choosing. In a related vein, even scholars writing in the neo-Marxist tradition have also emphasized how conflicts over class and inequality generated by the capitalist system enable business to dominate development outcomes.

In contrast, critics of these views have offered more *state-centered* perspectives that argue that local development decisions are not as driven by business and markets as scholars like Peterson (1981) suggest. They point out that political judgments and pressures are part of the urban development process (Stone and Sanders 1987; Logan and Swanstrom 1990; Dreier and Keating 1990; Squires 1988). In particular, Stone (1989) stressed that governing regimes must be formed to enable the "social production" of development decisions to occur. Other analysts even suggest that the state possesses sufficient autonomy from economy and society to promote developmental objectives that reflect interests that are essentially internal to the state (Gurr and King 1987).

Although this debate has yielded valuable insights, it has not brought scholars very close to understanding how and when local government can shape business development. Regime theory shows that politics matters, but it offers little guidance about how much, and when, it matters. The regime concept does not account for how local policy is constrained by different economic contexts. A city's development is shaped by local, regional, and even global economic dynamics, as well as by local governing coalitions (Horan 1991). Similarly, theories of state autonomy do not specify the circumstances under which interests that are peculiar to the state are likely to drive the development process. Further, the notion of state-driven policy is complicated by the fact that there is little agreement among theorists about the meaning of state autonomy (Evans, Rueschemeyer, and Skocpol 1985; Nordlinger 1981; Krasner 1984; Benjamin and Elkin 1985) and its realworld, as opposed to theoretical, referents (Almond 1988).

State and Business in a Liberal-Democratic Political Economy

In view of the theoretical dead ends posed by market-centered and state-centered theorizing, we pursue a more modest objective. We outline a framework that suggests ways that local government can influence private decisions concerning development. We propose that questions of how, when, and why local government can influence economic development are best answered by treating political control as something that springs from bargaining advantages that the state has in political and economic exchange relationships with business. Variations in local-government influence are strongly tied to the ways in which the larger political economy distributes particular bargaining resources between the public and private sectors.

Following Lindblom (1977), we find that it is useful to regard this context as a liberal-democratic system in which there is a division of labor between business and government (Kantor 1988; Elkin 1987). The private sector is responsible for the production of wealth in a market system in which choices over production and exchange are determined by price mechanisms. For its part, the public sector is organized along polyarchal lines (Dahl 1971; Dahl and Lindblom 1965) in which public decisions are subject to popular control. Public officials may be viewed as primarily responsible for the management of political support for governmental undertakings; business leaders can be considered essentially managers of market enterprises.

This perspective suggests that even though public and private control systems are theoretically separate, in reality they are highly interdependent. So far as government is concerned, the private sector produces economic resources that are necessary for the well-being of the political community—including jobs, revenues for public programs, and political support that is likely to flow to public authorities from popular satisfaction with economic prosperity and security. For business, the public sector is important because it provides forms of intervention into the market that are necessary for the promotion of economic enterprise but that the private sector cannot provide on its own. Such interventions include inducements that enable private investors to take risks (tax abatements and tax credits), the resolution of private conflicts that threaten social or economic stability (courts, mediation services), and the creation of an infrastructure or other forms of support (highways, workforce training).

Configuring Bargaining Advantages

Conceptualized in this manner, business and government must engage in exchange relationships (bargaining) to realize common goals. This is done by using bargaining advantages that derive from three dimensions or spheres of interdependence: market conditions, popular-control systems, and publicintervention mechanisms.

Market conditions consist of the circumstances or forces that make cities more or less appealing to private investors. The market position that results is a source of bargaining advantages or disadvantages for government. Market conditions may be site specific, as when localities find they are desirable because of innate features that have become critical (e.g., Washington, D.C., as an important organizational locale or Singapore as a gateway for investment in Asia). Market conditions are also reflected in larger economic fluctuations that put urban investment at a premium (e.g., the office-building boom of the 1980s) or put urban investment at risk (e.g., the savings-and-loan bust of the 1990s). We posit that cities with strong market positions obtain influence over the capital investment process.

Popular-control systems are the polyarchal processes through which public-sector decisions that affect urban development are legitimized. Such processes may vary along several dimensions, including the scope of public participation, the extent to which participation is organized, and the effectiveness of electoral mechanisms in ensuring accountability in the process of legitimization. We posit that popular-control systems that motivate and enable elected political leaders to exercise influence over the process of legitimizing economic development decisions enhance local-government control over business investment.

Public-intervention mechanisms are relationships and methods used by state institutions to regulate the marketplace. The kinds of policy instruments available to government and the way in which it uses them can affect the distribution of bargaining advantages between business and government. We posit that governmental systems that centralize or coordinate power as well as financial support are better able to regulate economic development and shape the marketplace. These systems enhance local governmental influence over investment.

Although we are unable to test all of these propositions systematically, we seek to illustrate their reality in the pages that follow. Our analysis suggests that there is substantial variation among local governments in their ability to bargain. We also suggest that bargaining advantages tend to be cumulative—that is,

the more advantages a city holds, the greater its ability to bargain. Finally, we suggest that because bargaining is a product of political and economic circumstance, so is urban development. Although it may not be possible for a city to manipulate all the variables affecting its bargaining position, most cities can manipulate some and thereby shape its own future.

Table 1 describes how differences in market conditions, popular-control systems, and public-intervention mechanisms furnish bargaining advantages or disadvantages to cities. Each of these bargaining components are examined here. In our analysis, public-sector influence over capital investment is indicated by distinct kinds of outcomes. When bargaining relationships put local government at a persistent disadvantage, the public sector tends to absorb greater costs and risks of private enterprise (Jones and Bachelor 1986). Cities in a weak position also are more inclined to accommodate private-sector demands, even at the cost of maintaining or expanding programs that serve nonbusiness groups.

When bargaining relationships put local governments at a persistent advantage, an altogether different set of outcomes are likely (Logan and Molotch 1987; Capek and Gilderbloom 1992). Public actors tend to impose costs for the privilege of doing business in the locality or to place other demands on the private investor. They may levy differential taxes on businesses located in high-density commercial districts, charge linkage fees on downtown development (which can be invested elsewhere), demand amenity contributions that are applied toward the enhancement of city services, or impose inclusionary zoning, requiring developers to set aside a number of low- or moderate-income rental units in market-rate housing. More often than not, cities will be somewhere between such bipolar situations of a weak or strong bargaining position. Table 2 indicates the kinds of outcomes that are related to the three kinds of bargaining components.

Markets and Public Control of Urban Development

There is little doubt that businesses' greatest bargaining resource in urban development is its control over private wealth in the capital investment process. It is this dimension of business-government relations that Peterson's (1981) market-centered model of local

Table 1 System Characteristics

Sphere of Activity	Characteristics Determining Governmental Bargaining Advantages	
	Low	**High**
Market condition	Competitive	Noncompetitive
	Nondiversified	Economic diversity
	Company towns	Economies of agglomeration
	Flexible capital	Fixed capital
	Mobile investment	Sunk investments
Popular control	Low party competition	Competitive parties
	Unstable partisanship	Stable partisanship
	Low ideological cohesion	High ideological cohesion
	Nonprogrammatic parties	Programmatic parties
	Fragmented party organization	High party discipline
	Few channels for citizen participation	Multiple channels for citizen participation
Public intervention	Particularistic policies	General market regulation
	Side payments	Spending on infrastructure, subsidies
	Decentralized	Centralized
	Local borrowing	National borrowing
	Finance: dependence on private investment	Finance: autonomous investment

politics describes. The logic of this model is that cities compete for capital investment by seeking to attract mobile capital to the community; failure to meet the conditions demanded by business for investment leads to the "automatic punishing recoil" (Lindblom 1982) of the marketplace as business disinvests. This notion has been variously interpreted to suggest that business inherently holds a dominant position (Fainstein et al. 1986; Mollenkopf 1983; Logan and Molotch 1987; Jones and Bachelor 1986; Kantor 1988).

Although the market-centered model is a powerful tool for analyzing development politics, it does not fully capture the bargaining relationships that logically derive from it. Specifically, the market perspective tends to highlight only those advantages that accrue to business. Yet, the marketplace works in two directions, not one. If we look at specific market conditions and bargaining demands, it becomes apparent that government also can use the market to obtain leverage over business. Thus we will present a number of common market-centered arguments and show their other side.

The Cities-Lose-If-Business-Wins Argument

In the market model, public and private actors represent institutions that compete to achieve rival goals. Business pursues public objectives only insofar as they serve private needs; if important business needs are not met, local government experiences the discipline of the marketplace as capital and labor seek alternative locations.

Table 2	Bargaining Components

Bargaining Yields	
Market Conditions	
Unfavorable	Inducement to business: Cash outlays, tax exemptions, aid to capital projects, loan guarantees, free land, and large-scale condemnating
Favorable	Demands on business: Development fees (linkage), public amenities (refurbished train stations, bus shelters, pedestrian walkways), higher business taxes, stiffer architectural requirements (building setbacks), and restrictive zoning requirements
Mixed	Negotiations with business: Extent of tax abatements, public-private contributions to capital projects, payments for land, and capital improvements to land
Popular Control	
Weak	Acquiescent, uninvolved public—bargaining takes place exclusively between elites—increasing number of side payments, low accountability, exclusionary zoning
Strong	Institutionalized land-use review policies, employment concessions for local residents and minorities, contract setasides for local firms or minority contractors, rent control or stabilization laws, inclusionary zoning
Policy Intervention	
Dispersed	Absence of zoning or loose zoning laws, tax code enforcement, intense competition between localities, significant sublocal disparities
Integrated	Highly restrictive zoning laws, strict code enforcement, extensive infrastructure investments, frequent public-private compacts.

Yet, in this description of market dynamics, cases in which local government and business may also share the same goals (as distinct from the same interests) are ignored; in such instances the market model no longer indicates business advantage in the development process. Thus a local government may have an interest in raising public revenue by increasing retail sales while shopkeepers and investors have an interest in maximizing profits. Though their interests are different, they may share the common goal of bringing about higher sales through expanded development. When this happens, bargaining between government and business shifts from rivalry over competing goals to settling differences over how to facilitate what already has been agreed on. This kind of scenario enhances the value of bargaining resources that are mostly owned by the public sector. Development politics focuses on such things as the ability to amass land, grant legal privileges and rights, control zoning, provide appropriate infrastructure, and-not leastenlist public support. Because alternative means of promoting growth are important choices (Logan and Swanstrom 1990), substantial bargaining leverage over development outcomes is placed in the hands of those who manage the governmental process, a point that Mollenkopf (1983) underscored in his study of urban renewal politics.

Yet, this partial escape from the market often is not recognized. Peterson (1981) considered the sharing of interests and goals to be one and the same. Other scholars have often assumed that there is an inherent conflict between private and public goals (Stone and Sanders 1987; Logan and Swanstrom 1990; Swanstrom 1986). However, a strong case can be made that business and government often share common goals. Although they cannot logically share interests, public officials, motivated by different stakes, frequently choose to pursue economic objectives that are also favored by business (Cummings 1988). Although some critics reject progrowth values, these values tend to be supported broadly by local electorates (Logan and Molotch 1987, 50–98; Vaughn 1979; Crenson 1971).

To take a different tack on former head of General Motors Charles Wilson's aphorism, scholars may be too anxious to suggest that if it is good for General Motors, it must be bad for Detroit. Yet, local officials and their publics do not always share this logic. When government and business perceive common goals, such perceptions can have a powerful effect on opportunities for political control over the urban economy. Under these conditions, the ability of political authorities to create political support for specific programs and their willingness to use public authority to assist business can become important bargaining resources for achieving their own interests. At the very least, the extent to which agreement between business and local government is a by-product of political choice rather than of economic constraint should be a premise for empirical investigation instead of an a priori conclusion.

The Capital Mobility Argument

This argument encompasses an assumption that bargaining advantages accrue to business as it becomes more mobile. Historically, private capital was more dependent on the local state than it is today (Kantor 1988). Technological advances in production, communications, and transportation have enhanced the ability of business to move more easily and rapidly. Changes in the organization of capital, especially the rise of multilocational corporations, have increased business mobility and made urban locations interchangeable. Automation, robotics, and the postindustrial revolution are supposed to enhance capital mobility. Fixed capital has been nudged aside by a new postindustrial technology of flexible capital (Hill 1989; Parkinson, Foley, and Judd 1989).

It would seem to follow that increasing capital mobility must favor business interests. Yet, this conclusion does not always follow, if one considers specific cities and businesses that are caught up in this process of economic globalization. Capital is, in fact, not always very portable. Although cities are frequently viewed as interchangeable by some corporations, many cities retain inherent advantages of location (e.g., Brussels), of agglomeration (e.g., New York), of technological prowess (e.g., Grenoble), or of political access (e.g., Washington, D.C.). The dispersion of capital has triggered a countermovement to create centers that specialize in the communication, coordination, and support of far-flung corporate units. Larger global cities have captured these roles. Much of postindustrial capital has put enormous sunk costs into major cities. One of the more conspicuous examples is the Canadian development firm of Olympia and York, which has invested billions of dollars in New York, London, Ontario, and a host of other cities. As Olympia and York teeters on the edge of collapse, banks, realty interests, and mortgage brokers are also threatened. It is not easy for any of these interests to pull up stakes.

There has been a fairly stable tendency for corporate headquarters operations, together with the ancillary services on which headquarters depend, to gravitate to large cities that have acquired the status of world business centers (Sassen 1988; Noyelle and Stanback 1984). New York's downtown and midtown, London's financial district and its docklands, Paris's La Defense, and Tokyo's Shinjuku are some outstanding examples of postindustrialism that has generated billions in fixed investments. Movement by individual enterprises away from such established corporate business centers is unlikely for various reasons, including that this kind of change imposes costs on those owning fixed assets in these locations and disrupts established business networks.

Cities that have experienced ascendant market positions have not been reluctant to cash in on this. When property values and development pressures rose in downtowns, local politicians used the advantage to impose new planning requirements and demand development fees. In San Francisco, a moratorium on highrise construction regulates the amount and pace of investment (Muzzio and Bailey 1986). In Boston and several other large cities, linkage policies have exacted fees on office development to support moderate-income housing (Dreier 1989). In Paris, differential taxes have been placed on high-rise development and the proceeds used to support city services (Savitch 1988). One should also recognize that market conditions are not immutable.

Local governments may be subject to the blandishments of business at an early stage of development, when there is great eagerness for development and capital has wide investment choices. However, once business has made the investment, it may be bound for the long term. Thus bargaining does not stop after the first deal is struck, and the advantages may shift.

This occurred in Orlando, Florida, where Disney World exacted early concessions from the local governments, only to be faced with new sets of public demands afterward (Fogelsong 1989). Prior to building what is now a vast entertainment complex near Orlando, Disney planners capitalized on their impending investment and won huge concessions from government (including political autonomy, tax advantages, and free infrastructure). However, as Disney transformed the region into a sprawling tourist center, local government demanded that the corporation relinquish autonomy and pressured it to pay for physical improvements. Disney struggled to defeat these demands but eventually conceded. With huge sunk investments, Disney executives had little choice but to accommodate the public sector.

So although some industries have grown more mobile, others have not. The issue turns on the relative costs incurred by business and by government when facilities, jobs, and people are moved. How relative costs are assessed and the likelihood that businesses will absorb them influence the respective bargaining postures of business and government.

The City-Cannot-Choose Argument

In the market model, business makes investment choices among stationary cities; because cities cannot move, powerful bargaining advantages accrue to business in the urban development process and supposedly this enables them to exact what they want from local governments. Although this is sometimes the case, it is also true that local communities may have investment choices as well. Some local governments can make choices among alternative types of business investment. In particular, economic diversification enables local political authorities to market the community in a particular economic sector (e.g., as a tourist city, as a research or technical center, or as a sound place in which to retire). Further, economic diversification enhances a locality's ability to withstand economic pressure from any particular segment of the business community. This has occurred in cities as far ranging as Seattle, Singapore, and Rome, enabling them to maintain powerful market positions for years, despite profound changes in the world and national economies.

Experience teaches city officials to sense their vulnerabilities and develop defenses against dominance by a single industry. Through diversification, these cities can gain a good deal of strength, not only in weathering economic fluctuations but in dealing with prospective investors. Houston's experience after oil prices crashed moved city leaders to develop high-technology and service industries (Feagin 1988). Pittsburgh's successful effort to clean its air gave that city a new economic complexion. Louisville's deindustrial crisis was followed by a succession of new investments in health services, a revival in the transportation industry, and a booming business in the arts (Vogel 1990). Diversification, which was so instrumental in strengthening the public hand, was actually made possible by government coalitions with business.

The advantages of diversification are most apparent when these cities are compared to localities that are prisoners of relatively monopolistic bargaining relations with business. Officials in single-industry towns are strongly inclined to accommodate business demands on matters of development because they lack alternative sources of capital investment. Crenson (1971) found this pattern in Gary, Indiana, where local officials resisted proposals for pollution control because they feared that U.S. Steel would lay off workers. Similarly, Jones and Bachelor (1986) described how Detroit leaders weakened their market position when they sought to preserve the city's position as a site for automobile manufacturing. When worldwide changes in the auto industry eroded Detroit's traditional competitive advantages, political leaders fought to subsidize new plants and to demolish an otherwise viable residential neighborhood.

Neither Gary's steel-centered strategy nor Detroit's auto-centered strategy has stemmed their economic decline. The lesson for urban politicians is clear: Instead of vainly hanging on to old industry, go for new, preferably clean business. More than most politicians, big-city mayors have learned well and are fast becoming major economic promoters (Savitch and Thomas 1991).

The City-Maximizes-Growth Argument

Although the market model is built on the supposition that it is in the interest of cities to promote economic growth, not all localities seek to compete in capital markets. To the extent that communities ignore participation in this market, they do not have to bargain with business over demands that they might choose to bring to the bargaining table. Santa Barbara, Vancouver, and Stockholm are cities that have resisted growth and instituted extensive land-use controls. These cities are in enviable positions as they deal with business and developers.

Aside from major cities, there are smaller communities that do not seek to compete for capital investment such as suburban areas and middle-size cities that after years of expansion, now face environmental degradation. Even if these localities have a stake in maintaining competitive advantages as bedroom communities or steady-state mixed commercial/residential locales, their bargaining relationship with business is more independent than in relatively growth-hungry urban communities (Danielson 1976). University towns, in which a self-sustaining and alert population values its traditions, have managed to resist the intrusions of unwanted industry. Coastal cities, which seek to preserve open space, have successfully acquired land or used zoning to curtail development.

Moreover, there are cities in which governmental structures reduce financial pressure and are able to resist indiscriminate development. Regionalism and annexation have enabled cities to widen their tax nets, so that business cannot easily play one municipality off against another. Minneapolis-St. Paul, Miami-Dade, and metro Toronto furnish examples of localities banding together to strengthen their fiscal positions and turn down unwanted growth. In Western European and other non-American nations, cities are heavily financed by central government, thereby reducing and sometimes eliminating the pressure to

attract development. For these cities, growth only engenders liabilities.

Popular-Control Systems and Urban Development

Democratic political institutions not only provide means of disciplining public officials, but they constrain all political actors who seek governmental cooperation or public legitimation in the pursuit of their interests. The reality of this is suggested by the fact that business development projects frequently get stopped when they lack a compelling public rationale and generate significant community opposition. This has occurred under varying conditions and in different types of cities. In Paris, neighborhood mobilization successfully averted developers (Body-Gendrot 1987); in London, communities were able to totally redo urban renewal plans (Christensen 1979); in Amsterdam and Berlin, local squatters defied property owners by taking over abandoned buildings; after the recent earthquake in San Francisco, public opinion prevailed against the business community in preventing the reconstruction of a major highway. The existence of open, competitive systems of elections and other polyarchal institutions affords a means by which nonbusiness interests are able to influence, however imperfectly, an urban development process in which business power otherwise looms large.

But do institutions of popular control afford political authorities with a valuable bargaining resource in dealing with business? Are democratic institutions loose cannons that are irrelevant to political bargaining over economic development? From our bargaining perspective, it would appear that these institutions can provide a resource upon which political leaders can draw to impose their own policy preferences when the three conditions described in the following paragraphs are satisfied.

First, public approval of bargaining outcomes between government and business must be connected to the capital-investment process. This is often not the case because most private-sector investment decisions are virtually outside the influence of local government. Even when the characteristics of private projects require substantial public-sector cooperation, many decisions are only indirectly dependent on processes of political approval. Economic-development decisions have increasingly become insulated from the mainstream political processes of city governments as a result of the proliferation of public-benefit corporations (Walsh 1978; Kantor 1993). As power to finance and regulate business development has been ceded to public-benefit corporations, the ability of elected political leaders to build popular coalitions around development issues has shrunk because it makes little sense to appeal to voters on matters that they cannot influence.

On the other hand, the importance of this bargaining resource increases as issues spill over their ordinary institutional boundaries and into public or neighborhood arenas. When this occurs, elected political authorities gain bargaining advantages by putting together coalitions that can play a vital role in the urban development game. Consequently, even the most powerful public and private developers can be checked by politicians representing hostile voter coalitions.

In New York, Robert Moses's slide from power was made possible by mounting public discontent with his later projects and by the intervention of a popular governor who capitalized on this to undercut Moses's position (Caro 1974); Donald Trump's plans for the Upper West Side of Manhattan incurred defeats by a coalition of irate residents, local legislators, and a hostile mayor (Savitch 1988); a major highway (Westway) proposal, sponsored by developers, bankers, and other business interests, was defeated by community activists who skillfully used the courts to question the project's environmental impact.

Second, public authorities must have the managerial capability to organize and deliver political support for programs sought by business. Credible bargaining requires organizing a stable constituency whose consent can be offered to business in a quid pro quo process. However, political authorities clearly differ enormously in their capacity to draw on this resource. In the United States, the decline of machine politics, the weakening of party loyalties and organizations, and the dispersal of political power to interest groups have weakened the capacity of elected political authorities. To some extent, this has been counterbalanced by grassroots and other populist-style movements that have provided a broad base for mayors and other political leaders (Swanstrom 1986; Dreier and Keating 1990; Savitch and Thomas 1991; Capek and Gilderbloom 1992).

In contrast, in Western European cities, the stability and cohesion displayed by urban party systems more frequently strengthen political control of development. In Paris, extensive political control over major development projects is related to stable and well-organized political support enjoyed by officials who dominated the central and local governments (Savitch 1988). In London, ideological divisions between Conservative and Labour parties at the local and national levels limit the ability of business interests to win a powerful role, even in cases involving massive redevelopment such as Covent Garden, the construction of motorways, and the docklands renewal adjacent to the financial city. For example, changes in planning the docklands project were tied to shifts in party control at both the national and local levels. Given the political significance of development issues to both major British parties, it was difficult for nonparty interests to offer inducements that were capable of splitting politicians away from their partisan agendas (Savitch 1988).

Similarly, even highly fragmented but highly ideological political party systems seem capable of providing a powerful bargaining resource to elected governmental authorities. In Italy, many small parties compete for power at the national and local levels. Although this is sometimes a source of political instability, the relatively stable ideological character of party loyalties means that elected politicians are assured of constituency support. Consequently, this base of political power offers substantial bargaining advantages in dealing with business. According to Molotch and Vicari (1988), this enables elected political authorities to undertake major projects relatively free from business pressure. In Milan, officials planned and built a subway line through the downtown commercial district of the city with minimal involvement of local business.

Third, popular-control mechanisms are a valuable bargaining resource when they bind elected leaders to programmatic objectives. If political authorities are not easily disciplined for failure to promote programmatic objectives in development bargaining, business may promote their claims by providing selective incentives (side payments), such as jobs, campaign donations, and other petty favors, to public officials in exchange for their cooperation. When this happens, the bargaining position of city governments is undermined by splitting off public officials from their representational roles—and the process of popular control becomes more of a business resource.

In America, where partisan attachments are weak and where ethnic, neighborhood, and other particularistic loyalties are strong, political leaders are inclined to put a high value on seeking selective benefits to the neglect of programmatic objectives. Although populist mayors have sometimes succeeded in overcoming these obstacles (Swanstrom 1986; Dreier and Keating 1990), the need to maintain unstable political coalitions that are easily undermined by racial and ethnic rivalries limits programmatic political competition. For example, in Detroit and Atlanta, black mayors have relied heavily on economic development to generate side payments that are used to minimize political opposition; this is facilitated by the symbolic importance that these black mayors enjoy among the heavily black electorates in the two cities. Consequently, they have been able to hold on to power without challenging many business demands (Stone 1989; Hill 1986). In contrast, in Western Europe, where political-party systems more frequently discipline public officials to compete on programmatic grounds, bargaining with business is less likely to focus on side payments. As suggested earlier, in France, Italy, and Britain, votes are more often secured by partisan and ideological loyalties and reinforced by programmatic competition than by generating selective incentives for followers.

In sum, city governments vary enormously in their capacity to draw on the popular-control process in bargaining over development. The proximity of electoral competition to development, the capability of officials to organize voter support, and the extent of competition over programmatic objectives are crucial factors that weaken or enhance the resources of city governments. . . .

Are Bargaining Resources Cumulative?

Essentially, our survey suggests that bargaining and development are likely to follow state-centered patterns (favorable to government) when market conditions are favorable, popular control is strong, and policy intervention is nationally integrated. Market-centered patterns (favorable to the private sector) are likely to emerge when market conditions are unfavorable to city

governments, when popular control is weak, and when policy intervention is dispersed and competitive. Although it seems likely that bargaining advantages are cumulative in impact (the more advantages a city government holds, the greater its ability to bargain), we are unable to test this proposition systematically. However, tentative support is suggested by various studies of 15 cities in Western Europe, North America, and Japan that we evaluated in light of our bargaining framework. Our evaluations are reported in Figure 1, which indicates how these cities fall along a continuum in respect to the distribution of bargaining advantages. The figure suggests how bargaining advantages vary considerably among the cities along each dimension, confirming our earlier discussion. More important, this analysis enables us to identify two cities—Amsterdam and Detroit—that consistently fall at the extreme ends of all three continua.

Comparison of these two antipodal cities permits us to illustrate the cumulative consequences of differences in bargaining resources for political control of business development. To begin with market conditions, Amsterdam has a highly favorable market position because it is at the center of Holland's economic engine—a horseshoe shaped region called the Randstad. The cities of the Randstad (Amsterdam, Utrecht, Rotterdam, and the Hague) form a powerful and diversified conurbation that drives Holland's economy, its politics, and its sociocultural life. Amsterdam itself is the nation's political and financial capital. It also holds light industry, is a tourist and historic center, and is one of northern Europe's transportation hubs. Although Amsterdam has gone through significant deindustrialization (Jobse and Needham 1987) and has lost 21% of its population since 1960, it has transformed its economy to residential and postindustrial uses and is attractively positioned as one of the keystones of a united Europe.

Detroit's market conditions are dramatically less favorable. It is situated in what was once America's industrial heartland and what is now balefully called the Rustbelt. Known as America's Motor City, its economy revolved around automobile manufacture. Deindustrialization and foreign competition have taken a devastating toll. In just three decades, Detroit lost more than half its manufacturing jobs and 38% of its population

Figure 11.1 Government-Business Bargaining in Select Cities

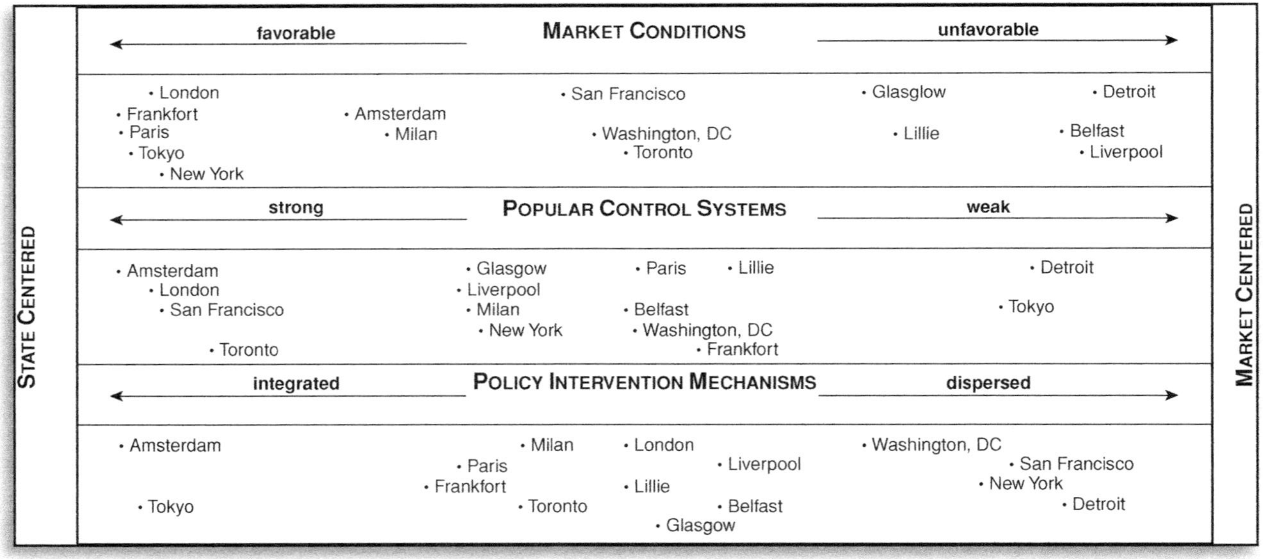
State Centered
Market Centered
favorable
Market Conditions
unfavorable
• London
• Frankfort
• Paris
• Tokyo
• New York
• Amsterdam
• Milan
• San Francisco
• Washington, DC
• Toronto
• Glasglow
• Lillie
• Detroit
• Belfast
• Liverpool
strong
Popular Control Systems
weak
• Amsterdam
• London
• San Francisco
• Toronto
• Glasgow
• Liverpool
• Milan
• New York
• Paris
• Lillie
• Belfast
• Washington, DC
• Frankfort
• Detroit
• Tokyo
integrated
Policy Intervention Mechanisms
dispersed
• Amsterdam
• Tokyo
• Milan
• Paris
• Frankfort
• Toronto
• London
• Liverpool
• Lillie
• Belfast
• Glasgow
• Washington, DC
• San Francisco
• New York
• Detroit

Sources: Compiled from Cheshire, Carbonaro, and Hay (1986); Nathan and Adams (1976, 1989); Kasarda and Dogan (1989); Parkinson, Foley, and Judd (1989); Tokyo Municipal Government (1978); Bestor (1989); and Frisken (1990).

(Darden et al. 1987). Nearly half the population lives below the poverty line, and one quarter is unemployed (Nethercutt 1987). Detroit has tried to come back to its former prominence by rebuilding its downtown and diversifying its economy for tourism and banking. But those efforts have not changed the city's market posture. Jobs and the middle class continue to move to surrounding suburbs, and any possible conversion of the Rustbelt economy appears slim when viewed against more attractive opportunities elsewhere.

The differences in popular control of these two cities are equally stark. Amsterdam is governed by a 45-member council that is elected by proportional representation (the council also elects a smaller body of aldermen) and is well organized and easily disciplined by the voters. Political parties have cohesive programs geared to conservative, social democratic, centrist, and left-wing orientations. Political accountability is reinforced by a system of elected district councils that represent different neighborhoods of the city. These councils participate in a host of decentralized services including land use, housing, and development.

In contrast, Detroit's government is poorly organized in respect to promoting popular control of economic development. A nine-member city council is elected at large and in nonpartisan balloting. Detroit's mayor, Coleman Young, has held power for 16 years and has based his administration on distributing selective benefits, especially city jobs and contracts, while focusing on downtown project development (Hill 1986; Rich 1991). The system affords scant opportunity for neighborhood expression, and the city's singular ethnic composition (Detroit is 75% black) is coupled to a politics of black symbolism that impedes programmatic accountability and pluralist opposition. Indeed, one scholar has described Detroit as ruled by a tight-knit elite (Ewen 1978); two other researchers believed that the city's power was exercised at the peaks of major sectors within the city (Jones and Bachelor 1986).

The two cities also differ dramatically in respect to modes of policy intervention. Like many European cities, Amsterdam is governed within an integrated national planning scheme. The Dutch rely on three-tier government, at the national, regional, and municipal levels. Goals are set at the uppermost levels, master plans are developed at the regional level, and allocation plans are implemented at the grass roots. A municipalities fund allocates financial support based on population, and over 90% of Amsterdam's budget is carried by the national treasury.

By contrast, Detroit stands very much alone. While "golden corridors" (drawn from Detroit's former wealth) have sprung up in affluent outskirts, the suburbs now resist the central city. Attempts at creating metropolitan mechanisms to share tax bases or to undertake planning have failed (Darden et al. 1987). Over the years, federal aid has shrunk and now accounts for less than 6% of the city's budget (Savitch and Thomas 1991). State aid has compensated for some of Detroit's shortfalls, but like most states, Michigan is at a loss to do anything about the internecine struggles for jobs and investment.

Given the cumulative differences along all three dimensions, the bargaining outcomes for each city are dramatically opposite. Under the planning and support of national and regional authorities, Amsterdam has managed its deindustrialization—first by moving heavy industry to specific subregions (called *concentrated deconcentration*) and later by locating housing and light commerce in abandoned wharves and depleted neighborhoods. The Dutch have accomplished this through a combination of infrastructure investment, direct subsidies, and the power to finance and build housing (Levine and Van Weesop 1988; Van Weesop and Wiegersma 1991). Amsterdam's capacity to construct housing is a particularly potent policy instrument and constitutes a countervailing alternative to private development. Between 50% and 80% of housing in Amsterdam is subsidized or publicly built. This puts a considerable squeeze on private developers, who face limitations of land availability as well as zoning, density, and architectural controls. As a condition of development, it is not uncommon for commercial investors to agree to devote a portion of their projects toward residential use (Van Weesop and Wiegersma 1991).

Indeed, the bargaining game in Holland is tilted toward the public sector in ways that seem unimaginable in the United States. Freestyle commercial development in Amsterdam has been restricted, so that most neighborhoods remain residential. Because of massive housing subsidies, neighborhoods have lacked the extremes of wealth or poverty. Even squatting has been declared legal. Abandoned buildings have been taken over by groups of young, marginal, and working-class populations—thus leading to lowerclass gentrification (Mamadouh 1990).

All this compares very differently to the thrust of development outcomes in Detroit. The case of Poletown provides a stark profile of Detroit's response to bargaining with the private sector (Fasenfest 1986). When General Motors announced that it was looking for a new plant site, the city invoked the state's "quick take" law, allowing municipalities to acquire property before actually reaching agreement with individual owners. To attract the plant and an anticipated 6,000 jobs, the city moved more than 3,000 residents and 143 institutions (hospitals, churches, schools, and businesses) and demolished more than 1,000 buildings. To strike this bargain, Detroit committed to at least $200 million in direct expenditures and a dozen years of tax abatements. In the end, the bargaining exchange resulted in one lost neighborhood and a gain of an automobile plant—all under what one judge labeled as the "guiding and sustaining, indeed controlling hand of the General Motors Corporation" (Jones and Bachelor 1986).

In many respects, Poletown reflects a larger pattern of bargaining. The city is now trying to expand its airport. At stake are 3,600 homes, more than 12,000 residents, and scores of businesses. The city and a local bank also have their sights set on a venerable auditorium called Ford Hall. The arrangement calls for razing Ford Hall and granting the developers an $18 million no-interest loan, payable in 28 years. When citizen protests stalled the project, developers threatened to move elsewhere. Since then, Detroit's city council approved the project (Rich 1991).

The polar cases of Amsterdam and Detroit reveal something about the vastly different development prizes and sacrifices that particular cities experience as a result of their accumulated bargaining advantages. Amsterdam is able to use public investment to extract concessions from investors and enforce development standards in a process conducted under public scrutiny. Detroit offers land, money, and tax relief to attract development in a process managed by a tight circle of political and economic elites.

Political Control of Urban Development

By examining urban development from a state-bargaining perspective, we are able to identify some critical forces that influence local governmental control over this area of policy. From this vantage point, public influence over urban development appears to be tied to differences in market conditions, popular-control mechanisms, and public policy systems because these interdependent spheres powerfully affect the ability of politicians to bargain with business. Cities vary considerably in their position within local, national, and global markets. Also affecting outcomes are the variability of economic goals, uneven capital mobility, the advantages of agglomeration, the extent of sunk capital, and the willingness of local populations to support economic growth.

Local governments also derive bargaining advantages from their ability to exploit popular-control systems as a bargaining resource. Differences in party systems, political cleavage, and programmatic politics influence the capacity of political leaders to mobilize popular support and legitimize the demands of business. Finally, policy intervention is a source of bargaining advantages for local government in the urban-development game. This resource increases in importance when local government is able to regulate market failures and draw on the political resources found in more nationally integrated regimes. By using our bargaining perspective, future researchers may be able to overcome the limitations of extant theory and better understand the actual political choices of local communities in economic development.

Note

1. Urban Summit Conference, New York City, 12 November 1990.

References

Almond, G. 1988. The return to the state. *American Political Science Review* 82:853–74.

Bachrach, P., and M. Baratz. 1962. The two faces of power. *American Political Science Review* 56:947–52.

Benjamin, R., and S. C. Elkin, eds. 1985. *The democratic state*. Lawrence: University Press of Kansas.

Bestor, T. 1989. *Neighborhood Tokyo*. Palo Alto, CA: Stanford Univ. Press.

Body-Gendrot, S. 1987. Grass roots mobilization in the Thirteenth Arrondissment: A cross national view. In *The politics of urban development*, edited by C. Stone and H. Sanders, 125–43. Lawrence: University Press of Kansas.

Capek, S., and J. Gilderbloom. 1992. *Community versus commodity*. Albany: State Univ. of New York Press.

Caro, R. 1974. *The power broker*. New York: Vintage.

Cheshire, P., G. Carbanaro, and D. Hay. 1986. Problems of urban decline and growth in EEC countries: Or measuring degrees of elephantness. *Urban Studies* 2:131–49.

Christensen, T. 1979. *Neighborhood survival*. London: Prism Press.

Crenson, M. 1971. *The un-politics of air pollution*. Baltimore, MD: Johns Hopkins Univ. Press.

Cummings, S., ed. 1988. *Business elites and urban development*. Albany: State Univ. of New York Press.

Dahl, R. 1971. *Polyarchy*. New Haven, CT: Yale Univ. Press.

Dahl, R., and C. E. Lindblom. 1965. *Politics, economics and welfare*. New Haven, CT: Yale Univ. Press.

Danielson, M. 1976. *The politics of exclusion*. New York: Columbia Univ. Press.

Darden, J., R. C. Hill, J. Thomas, and R. Thomas. 1987. *Race and uneven development*. Philadelphia: Temple Univ. Press.

Dreier, P. 1989. Economic growth and economic justice in Boston. In *Unequal partnerships*, edited by G. Squires, 35–58. New Brunswick, NJ: Rutgers Univ. Press.

Dreier, P., and W. D. Keating. 1990. The limits of localism: Progressive housing policies in Boston, 1984–1989. *Urban Affairs Quarterly* 26:191–216.

Elkin, S. 1987. State and market in city politics: Or, the real Dallas. In *The politics of urban development*, edited by C. Stone and H. Sanders, 25–51. Lawrence: University Press of Kansas.

Etzkowitz, H., and R. Mack. 1976. Emperialism in the First World: The corporation and the suburb. Paper presented at the Pacific Sociological Association meetings, San Jose, CA, March.

Evans, P., D. Rueschemeyer, and T. Skocpol. 1985. *Bringing the state back in*. New York: Cambridge Univ. Press.

Ewen, L. 1978. *Corporate power and the urban crisis in Detroit*. Princeton, NJ: Princeton Univ. Press.

Fainstein, S. S., N. I. Fainstein, R. C. Hill, D. Judd, and M. P. Smith. 1986. *Restructuring the city*. 2d ed. New York: Longman.

Fasenfest, D. 1986. Community politics and urban redevelopment. *Urban Affairs Quarterly* 22:101–23.

Feagin, J. 1988. *Free enterprise city*. New Brunswick, NJ: Rutgers Univ. Press.

Fogelsong, R. 1989. Do politics matter in the formulation of local economic development policy: The case of Orlando, Florida. Paper presented at the annual meeting of the American Political Science Association, Atlanta, GA, September.

Frisken, F. 1990. Planning and servicing the Greater Toronto area Working paper No. 12. Urban Studies Program, York University.

Governor turns down UAL. 1991. *Courier-Journal*, 18 October, 1.

Gurr, T., and D. King. 1987. *The state and the city*. Chicago: Univ. of Chicago Press.

Hill, R. 1989. Industrial restructuring, state intervention and uneven development in the United States and Japan. Paper presented at conference The Tiger by the Tail: Urban Policy and Economic Restructuring in Comparative Perspective, State University of New York, Albany, October.

Hill, R. C. 1986. Crisis in the Motor City: The politics of urban development in Detroit. In *Restructuring the city*. 2d ed., by S. S. Fainstein, N. I. Fainstein, R. C. Hill, D. Judd, and M. P. Smith. New York: Longman.

Horan, C. 1991. Beyond governing coalitions: Analyzing urban regimes. *Journal of Urban Affairs* 13:119–36.

Jobse, B., and B. Needham. 1987. The economic future of the Randstad, Holland. *Urban Studies* 25:282–96.

Jones, B., and L. Bachelor. 1986. *The sustaining hand*. Lawrence: University Press of Kansas.

Kantor, P. 1993. The dual city as political choice. *Journal of Urban Affairs* 15 (3): 231–44.

Kantor, P. (with S. David). 1988. *The dependent city*. Boston, MA: Scott, Foresman/Little, Brown.

Kasarda, V., and M. Dogan. 1989. *Cities in a global society*. Newbury Park, CA: Sage.

Krasner, S. 1984. Approaches to the state: Alternative conceptions and historical dynamics. *Comparative Politics* 16: 223–46.

Levine, M., and J. Van Weesop. 1988. The changing nature of urban planning in the Netherlands. *Journal of the American Planning Association* 54:315–23.

Lindblom, C. 1977. *Politics and markets*. New Haven, CT: Yale Univ. Press.

———. 1982. The market as a prison. *Journal of Politics* 44:324–36.

Logan, J., and H. Molotch. 1987. *Urban fortunes*. Berkeley: Univ. of California Press.

Logan, J., and T. Swanstrom, eds. 1990. *Beyond the city limits*. Philadelphia: Temple Univ. Press.

Mamadouh, V. 1990. Squatting, housing and urban policy in Amsterdam. Paper presented at the International Research Conference on Housing Debates and Urban Challenges, Paris, July.

Mollenkopf, J. 1983. *The contested city*. Princeton, NJ: Princeton Univ. Press.

Molotch, H., and S. Vicari. 1988. Three ways to build: The development process in the United States, Japan, and Italy. *Urban Affairs Quarterly* 24:188–214.

Muzzio, D., and R. Bailey. 1986. Economic development, housing and zoning. *Journal of Urban Affairs* 8:1–18.

Nathan, R., and C. Adams. 1976. Understanding central city hardship. *Political Science Quarterly* 91 (1): 47–62.

———. 1989. Four perspectives on urban hardship. *Political Science Quarterly* 104 (3): 483–509.

Nethercutt, M. 1987. *Detroit twenty years after: A statistical profile of the Detroit area since 1967*. Detroit, MI: Center for Urban Studies, Wayne State University.

Nordlinger, E. 1981. *On the autonomy of the democratic state*. Cambridge, MA: Harvard Univ. Press.

Noyelle, T., and T. M. Stanback. 1984. *Economic transformation of American cities*. New York: Conservation for Human Resources Columbia University.

Parkinson, M., B. Foley, and D. Judd. 1989. *Regenerating the cities*. Boston, MA: Scott, Foresman.

Peterson, P. 1981. *City limits*. Chicago: Univ. of Chicago Press.

Rich, W. 1991. Detroit: From Motor City to service hub. In *Big city politics in transition*, edited by H. V. Savitch and J. C. Thomas, 64–85. Newbury Park, CA: Sage.

Rosentraub, M., and D. Swindell. 1990. "Just say no"? The economic and political realities of a small city's investment in minor league baseball. Paper presented at the 20th annual meeting of the Urban Affairs Association, Charlotte, NC, April.

Sassen, S. 1988. *The mobility of capital and labor*. Cambridge: Cambridge Univ. Press.

Savitch, H. V. 1988. *Post-industrial cities: Politics and planning in New York, Paris and London*. Princeton, NJ: Princeton Univ. Press.

Savitch, H. V., and J. C. Thomas, eds. 1991. *Big city politics in transition*. Newbury Park, CA: Sage.

Squires, G., ed. 1988. *Unequal partnerships*. New Brunswick, NJ: Rutgers Univ. Press.

Stone, C. 1989. *Regime politics*. Lawrence: University Press of Kansas.

Stone, C., and H. Sanders, eds. 1987. *The politics of urban development*. Lawrence: University Press of Kansas.

Swanstrom, T. 1986. *The crisis of growth politics*. Philadelphia: Temple University Press.

Tokyo Municipal Government. 1978. *An administrative perspective of Tokyo*. Tokyo: Author.

UAL bidding goes on. 1991. *Courier-Journal*, 22 October, 1.

Van Weesop, J., and M. Wiegersma. 1991. Gentrification in the Netherlands. In *Urban housing for the better-off: Gentrification in Europe*, edited by J. Van Weesop and S. Musterd, 98–111. Utrecht, Netherlands: Bureau Stedellijke Netwerken.

Vaughn, R. 1979. *State taxation and economic development*. Washington, DC: Council of State Planning Agencies.

Vogel, R. 1990. The local regime and economic development. *Economic Development Quarterly* 4:101–12.

Walsh, A. 1978. *The public's business*. Cambridge: MIT Press.

Conclusion

Public Policy Applications: Downtown Development

Policy Then

An excellent example of an urban regime led by business elites pursuing a downtown development agenda is the one that arose in Baltimore during the 1950s. Asserting that the city needed to transition from an industrial to a downtown-centered postindustrial economy, Baltimore's business leaders commissioned a master plan to rejuvenate the aging central business district. The focal point of that plan was the Charles Center Project, a new complex of sleek office buildings, hotels, and public plazas connected by walkways and pedestrian bridges. Following the project's successful completion by the end of the 1960s, the regime embarked on a more ambitious initiative—the transformation of the adjoining Inner Harbor area with additional office towers and a revitalized waterfront that would become a major recreational and leisure destination for Baltimoreans as well as a catalyst for future development. That initiative commenced in the early 1970s with the reconstruction of the infrastructure surrounding the decaying harbor, including a thirty-five-foot-wide promenade around the perimeter of the Inner Harbor to improve public access to and enjoyment of the water. A host of amenities followed: an aquarium, a science center, a marina, historic ships, and a novel (for its time) festival marketplace containing restaurants, bars, and shops. The redevelopment of the Inner Harbor was a huge hit with the public. By 1982, it was attracting 20 million visitors a year, two-thirds of whom were area residents delighted with their city's new playground. The sudden influx of millions of tourists—a new phenomenon for Baltimore—stimulated a burst of hotel construction, along with new office and residential development. Downtown development produced thousands of jobs and millions of dollars in tax revenue each year.

G. Edward Johnson (http://EdwardJohnson.com/, http://creativecommons.org/licenses/by/3.0), via Wikimedia Commons

Inner Harbor, Baltimore

However, Baltimore's approach to urban revitalization has not been without criticism. Some scholars have cautioned about the shortcomings of creating a "tourist bubble"—a safe and sanitized enclave within a city for visitors but one that is essentially indistinguishable from generic theme parks. Such zones of inauthenticity have the further problem of sheltering visitors from the reality of life in other city neighborhoods where conditions are difficult at best. Tourist bubbles thus contribute to an out-of-sight, out-of-mind mentality that, in turn, reinforces policy neglect. The most trenchant criticism of Baltimore's Inner Harbor project is that it has done little to improve the well-being of residents of impoverished neighborhoods elsewhere in the city (in some cases, only a few blocks from the Inner Harbor). Notwithstanding the genuine gains associated with waterfront development, the city's unemployment and poverty rates remained high. Reflecting on the overall impact of downtown development, Mayor Kurt Schmoke observed, "Baltimore is prettier but poorer in 1989 than 1979."

Policy Now

The story of Baltimore's Inner Harbor is hardly unusual. Many American cities tried to promote economic growth through aggressive downtown development only to discover that many of the quality jobs created went to suburban commuters while city residents were left with low-skilled, low-paying positions at the other end of the postindustrial economy's employment structure. Furthermore, the increased tax revenue produced by new construction and rising downtown property values somehow did not flow to distressed communities beyond the flourishing central business district and a handful of gentrifying neighborhoods. In short, downtown development did not live up to its promise of generating prosperity for a majority of city residents; some thrived, but most did not.

Community activists demanded that city governments rethink their priorities. Instead of channeling such a large share of scarce public resources to downtown business districts, they insisted that more dollars be allocated to rebuild impoverished and long-neglected neighborhoods. Others, recognizing the value of downtown revitalization, were reluctant to "kill the goose that laid the golden egg" but sought to ensure a more equitable distribution of the policy's benefits. In San Francisco, activists argued that downtown development could be linked to community development and effectively pressured the city government to enact a series of so-called linkage policies. For example, the city imposed a stiff one-time fee of $5 per square foot on new commercial office development in the downtown district and set aside the proceeds to fund affordable housing production in outlying neighborhoods. Similar exactions were imposed on developers to subsidize public transit, child care, and job training and placement programs.

Other cities enacted their own variations of linkage policies. A community benefit agreement, for instance, is a contract entered into by a private developer who makes financial and/or programmatic commitments to a community in exchange for that community's backing for a proposed project; community benefit agreements are a vehicle for ensuring that promised benefits from a development actually materialize. Another mechanism for linking downtown development to the well-being of neighborhood residents is a living wage ordinance. Baltimore, perhaps not coincidentally because of its experiences with uneven development, was the pioneer in implementing a living wage ordinance in 1994 following determined organizing by a coalition of labor, religious, and community groups. The law passed in Baltimore required firms that are under municipal contract, many of which are located or operate downtown, to pay their employees at a rate above the federal minimum wage, which was considered inadequate to cover basic household needs. Baltimore's pathbreaking action triggered a living wage movement across the United States that has led to the enactment of similar ordinances in more than a hundred municipalities. Some laws sweep more broadly in applying to employees of any firm that has received public support or even all municipal employees; some mandate a living wage that is as much as twice the federal minimum wage.

Additional Resources

Carl Abbott, "Centers and Edges: Reshaping Downtown Portland," in *The Portland Edge: Challenges and Successes in Growing Communities*, ed. Connie P. Ozawa (Washington, DC: Island Press, 2004).

Eyes on the Prize: America's Civil Rights Movement—Keys to the Kingdom, 1974–1980. Profile of Atlanta's first black mayor, Maynard Jackson (WGBH Boston, 2006).

Richard C. Hula, "The Two Baltimores," in *Leadership and Urban Regeneration*, ed. Dennis R. Judd and Michael Parkinson (Newbury Park, CA: SAGE Publications, 1990).

Dennis R. Judd and Susan S. Fainstein, eds., *The Tourist City* (New Haven: Yale University Press, 1999).

Harold Meyerson, "LA Story," *American Prospect*, July/August 2013.

Martin L. Millspaugh, "The Inner Harbor Story," *Urban Land*, April 2003.

Douglas Rae, "Two Cheers for Very Unequal Incomes," in *Justice and the American Metropolis*, ed. Clarissa Rile Hayward and Todd Swanstrom (Minneapolis: University of Minnesota Press, 2011).

Urban Land Institute. An influential nonprofit organization representing the real estate development industry that has praised the revitalization of the Inner Harbor as "the model for post-industrial waterfront redevelopment around the world." www.uli.org.

Laura Wolf-Powers, "Community Benefit Agreements and Local Government: A Review of Recent Evidence," *Journal of the American Planning Association*, Spring 2010.

Discussion Questions

1. How has the revitalization of Baltimore's Inner Harbor affected that city's fortunes?

2. How do real estate developers and other pro-business organizations feel about linkage policies? In their view, what impact will these policies likely have on cities?

3. What kinds of cities are most likely to adopt equitable growth policies like linkage, community benefit agreements, and living wage ordinances? Why are some cities seemingly less affected by threats of capital mobility?

4. Why have governing regimes led by downtown business leaders been so common in U.S. cities?

5. Why is it so difficult for community-based organizations that are chronically overlooked by city government to challenge downtown-led regimes and establish their own governing coalitions?

Chapter 12

Race and Ethnicity in Contemporary Urban Politics

Introduction

The terrain of urban politics in the United States for people of color changed rapidly starting in the 1960s. The civil rights and Black Power movements, along with the other race-based identity movements that they inspired, motivated millions of citizens who had previously been marginalized, if not completely excluded, from positions of political authority in American cities to contemplate gaining control over the machinery of municipal government through the electoral process.[1] The transition from protest to politics was aided by demographic shifts—the continuing influx of blacks, Latinos, and Asians into urban areas and the ongoing flight of whites to the suburbs. In some cities, such as Newark, Atlanta, and Washington, D.C., minority residents represented a majority of the population; in many other cities, they constituted a strong plurality. Richard Hatcher of Gary, Indiana, and Carl Stokes of Cleveland, Ohio, made history in 1967 by becoming the first African Americans to be elected as mayors of large U.S. cities. Others soon followed: Kenneth Gibson of Newark, Coleman Young of Detroit, Maynard Jackson of Atlanta, and Marion Barry of Washington, D.C. By the mid-1980s, three of the four largest cities had black mayors. By 1993, sixty-seven cities with populations more than 50,000 were led by African Americans.[2]

The first wave of black mayors made important strides in substantially increasing jobs for people of color in city government, improving opportunities for minority businesses through affirmative action programs, implementing more equitable delivery of public services, strengthening support for social programs, and cracking down on police misconduct in minority communities.[3] However, hopes for broader changes in public policy collided with the unfortunate reality that cities during this period were confronting extraordinarily difficult circumstances. The new black mayors experienced as much frustration as their white counterparts in trying to overcome all the societal and political pressures working against cities during the 1970s. And then some black mayors also had to contend with the persistence of racial hostility within the general population and among white officials in city government and politics. For example, the head of the Democratic Party in Gary objected to Richard Hatcher's candidacy for mayor by lamenting that he was "not the right kind of Negro." The white-controlled city council in Chicago resisted nearly every initiative of that city's first black mayor, Harold Washington, prompting *The Wall Street Journal* to describe the internecine politics there as "Beirut by the Lake."[4]

Given the sky-high expectations that many blacks, Latinos, and Asian Americans held regarding the first minority mayors and other high-ranking officials in city government, it was inevitable that frustrations would mount over what seemed to be the halting pace of reform. Public policies did not seem to respond to their pressing needs and interests. Increasingly disillusioned, some even charged that the leaders in city hall were traitors to their race. Disappointment also spawned divisions among minority groups that had once been solidly united when challenging a white power structure. Accusations of incompetence and corruption became more commonplace.[5]

By the 1980s, a new generation of political leaders emerged within minority communities, particularly in cities in which white voters continued to represent a substantial portion of the voting population. Unlike the first generation of civil-rights-era leaders who forcefully called attention to issues of racial discrimination and inequality and appealed directly to racial solidarity, the succeeding wave of leadership, as Andra Gillespie recounts in **Reading 12-1**, ran their electoral campaigns and governed their cities by deemphasizing race. Mayoral candidates

like Wilson Goode of Philadelphia, Norm Rice of Seattle, and David Dinkins of New York avoided explicit references to race-based concerns and instead focused on racially transcendent issues like balancing the budget and
reducing crime. Stressing the competence that they would bring to city hall, they promised to push an agenda that
would benefit all groups.[6] Although deracialized campaigns and governing styles proved to be a winning formula
for getting elected in white-majority and racially diverse cities, some observers argued that by downplaying race,
critical issues related to racial injustice got swept under the rug and off the political agenda. Moreover,
deracialization had the effect of enabling some groups to claim that the civil rights movement had mostly solved
racial problems in America.[7] Others answered that deracialized politics was a welcome development because the
"incessant attention" to race by the first generation of black mayors had obscured what people of varied racial
and ethnic backgrounds have in common and undermined the potential for multiracial coalitions.[8]

The practitioners of deracialization in urban politics were likely to participate in governing coalitions with downtown business leaders of the type that Clarence Stone examined in *Regime Politics*. Andrew Young, once a close ally
of Martin Luther King during the civil rights movement, later chose to tamp down racially charged issues as the mayor
of Atlanta in the 1980s and collaborate with the business establishment. Such regimes sometimes worked to the
advantage of middle-class blacks who, as coalition partners, managed to secure material benefits through aggressive
downtown development; much of the rest of the African American community, however, was left out.[9] That outcome
led some scholars to criticize regime theory for failing to explain why so many black voters continued to support such
regimes, especially in cases where regime leaders had tried to avoid racialized appeals.[10] More broadly, why were
oppositional movements aimed at downtown-led regimes so hard to organize and sustain? Cynthia Horan argued that
Stone's emphasis on the difficulties of overcoming the fragmentation of urban neighborhoods—a collective action
problem—ignored the extent to which white-dominated institutions have systematically oppressed community-based
organizations in black communities. In this way, Stone, given his preoccupation with the relationship between the state
and the market, underestimated the role of race in theorizing power relations in American cities.[11]

The political scientist J. Philip Thompson took a closer look at the potential for alternatives to regimes led by black
mayors and supported by white business elites. He asserted that the construction of an alternative regime must begin
by building "civic capacity" within neglected communities. That entails developing a base of power grounded on a
coherent understanding of the source of problems and clear interests regarding possible remedies with the goal of
fostering organizations capable of electing insurgent candidates and holding them accountable once in office. Ideally,
a forward-looking mayor would utilize the resources of his or her office to strengthen organizations and institutions
in lower-income communities to promote "deep pluralism," but Thompson contended that black mayors often
choose just the opposite—the demobilization of the poor. They fear that grassroots mobilization might complicate
an already difficult governing process or perhaps even spark competition threatening to their leadership.[12]

Adolph Reed Jr. has been a perceptive analyst of the demobilization of black politics in U.S. cities for many years.
In **Reading 12-2**, he explains how the transition from street protest to governance has had a conservative effect on
black mayors. Not only must they contend with the fiscal pressures that constrain any city official, but they also come
to internalize a pragmatic, incrementalist approach to public administration. And, once elected, they value predictability
and continuity and thus shun strategies aimed at generating extensive political mobilization. In such a demobilized
environment, the prevailing discourse regarding the persistence of racial inequality focuses on the limitations of
individuals and the need for self-help initiatives rather than on structural and institutional flaws requiring aggressive
governmental action. All this, according to Reed, begets political passivity among the citizenry and reinforces the
tendency of black mayors to cooperate with business-led regimes whose programs exacerbate existing inequities.

At the same time, there have been notable departures from the pattern of deracialized politics with governing
coalitions dominated by downtown business elites. In Houston, where the business community has long been a
powerful force in city politics and where African Americans are a minority and a declining part of the city's
population, one would expect electoral campaigns to deemphasize race.[13] However, in a hotly contested mayoral

election in 1997, both candidates, Lee Brown, a black ex-police chief, and Bob Mosbacher, a prominent white businessman, frequently addressed issues relevant to blacks, Latinos, and Asians while talking openly about race.[14]

A more far-reaching deviation from the kind of deracialized and demobilized politics that Reed critiques occurred in Chicago beginning in the late 1970s. After he had lost an initial campaign for mayor in 1977 because of a lack of support in low-income neighborhoods, Congressman Harold Washington embarked on a community organizing initiative in conjunction with local activists to build the civic capacity of those neighborhoods. Washington also benefited from the mobilization efforts of Jesse Jackson's Operation PUSH (People United to Save Humanity) in preparation for his first presidential campaign in 1984. By 1983, 600,000 of 665,000 eligible black voters had been registered to vote, and a massive turnout helped sweep Washington into the mayor's office that year. Once in power, Washington departed from the norm by using his office to encourage widespread participation in policy making that would bring new resources to those neighborhoods while empowering their residents.[15]

However, examples of electoral and governing coalitions that explicitly address racial inequality and subordination might be seen as exceptions that prove the rule of deracialized politics and policy making.[16] Furthermore, even in cities where people of color have obtained political power and talk openly of racial injustice, a culture of distrust between whites and nonwhites inhibits productive action. The experiences of New Orleans since Hurricane Katrina in 2005 stand as a sobering case in point. **Reading 12-3** by Arnold Hirsch and A. Lee Levert reveals how racial conflict continues to permeate city politics, notwithstanding the election and reelection of the nation's first African American president and the hopes that such milestones had signaled the arrival of a postracial society.[17] Indeed, some scholars contend that race, more than any other factor such as class, ideology, or partisanship, tends to dominate the politics of American cities in the contemporary era.[18]

Notes

1. Rufus P. Browning, Dale Rogers Marshall, and David H. Tabb, *Protest Is Not Enough: The Struggle of Blacks and Hispanics for Equality in Urban Politics* (Berkeley: University of California Press, 1984).

2. Jeffrey S. Adler, "Introduction," in *African-American Mayors: Race, Politics, and the American City*, ed. David R. Colburn and Jeffrey S. Adler (Urbana: University of Illinois Press, 2001).

3. Rufus P. Browning, Dale Rogers Marshall, and David H. Tabb, *Racial Politics in American Cities*, 3rd ed. (New York: Longman, 2003).

4. Adler, "Introduction" and Arnold R. Hirsch, "Harold and Dutch Revisited: A Comparative Look at the First Black Mayors of Chicago and New Orleans," in *African-American Mayors*, ed. Colburn and Adler.

5. Colburn and Adler, *African-American Mayors*; Browning, Marshall, and Tabb, *Racial Politics in American Cities*.

6. Joseph P. McCormick and Charles E. Jones, "The Conceptualization of Deracialization: Thinking through the Dilemma," in *Dilemmas of Black Politics: Issues of Leadership and Strategy*, ed. Georgia A. Persons (New York: HarperCollins, 1993).

7. Robert C. Smith, "Ideology as the Enduring Dilemma of Black Politics," in *Dilemmas of Black Politics*, ed. Persons.

8. William J. Wilson, *The Bridge over the Racial Divide* (Berkeley: University of California Press, 1999).

9. Clarence N. Stone, *Regime Politics: Governing Atlanta, 1946–1988* (Lawrence: University Press of Kansas, 1989).

10. William Sites, "The Limits of Urban Regime Theory: New York City under Koch, Dinkins, and Giuliani," *Urban Affairs Review*, 32 (4), March 1997.

11. Cynthia Horan, "Racializing Regime Politics," *Journal of Urban Affairs*, 24 (1), 2002.

12. J. Phillip Thompson III, *Double Trouble: Black Mayors, Black Communities, and the Call for a Deep Democracy* (New York: Oxford University Press, 2006). See also Todd Shaw, *Now Is the Time! Detroit Black Politics and Grassroots Activism* (Durham, NC: Duke University Press, 2009).

13. Huey L. Perry, "Deracialization as an Analytical Construct in American Urban Politics," *Urban Affairs Quarterly*, 27 (2), 1991.

14. For example, Brown highlighted his leadership in establishing a multiracial police department and a hate-crime task force while Mosbacher courted Latinos by stressing his plans to nurture business ties with Latin America. The point is that both candidates organized their campaigns to showcase their commitment to distinct racial and ethnic groups. Matthew McKeever, "Interethnic Politics in the Consensus City," in *Governing American Cities: Inter-Ethnic Coalitions, Competition, and Conflict*, ed. Michael Jones-Correa (New York: Russell Sage Foundation, 2001). See also Ravi K. Perry, "Kindred Political Rhetoric: Black Mayors, President Obama, and the Universalizing of Black Interests," *Journal of Urban Affairs*, 33 (5), 2011.

15. Pierre Clavel and Wim Wiewel, eds., *Harold Washington and the Neighborhoods: Progressive City Government in Chicago, 1983–1987* (New Brunswick, NJ: Rutgers University Press, 1991).

16. Refer to Katherine Underwood, "Ethnicity Is Not Enough: Latino-Led Multiracial Coalitions in Los Angeles," *Urban Affairs Review*, 33 (1), 1997, which documents the deracialized electoral strategies of Latino candidates for the Los Angeles city council.

17. Refer to Wilbur C. Rich, *The Post-Racial Society Is Here: Recognition, Critics and the Nation-State* (New York: Routledge, 2013); for a critique of the notion of a postracial society in contemporary America, see Michael C. Dawson, *Not in Our Lifetimes: The Future of Black Politics* (Chicago: University of Chicago Press, 2011).

18. Zoltan Hajnal and Jessica Trounstine, "What Underlies Urban Politics? Race, Class, Ideology, Partisanship, and the Urban Vote," *Urban Affairs Review*, 50 (1), 2014.

12-1 "Meet the New Class: Theorizing Young Black Leadership in a 'Postracial' Era"*[1]

Andra Gillespie

Whose Black Politics? Cases in Post-Racial Black Leadership

Introduction

By all accounts, Americans are being introduced to a third generation of Black elected leadership. Ironically, this new phase, like the phases that preceded it, is called "new Black politics." What distinguishes this new batch of leaders from their predecessors is their generation (i.e., they were born or came of age after the Civil Rights Movement), their education (they were educated in Ivy League and other White institutions), and their potential (they have realistic chances of holding higher executive and legislative positions more frequently than any other generation of Black leaders) (Reed and Alleyne 2002).

This latest wave of Black politicians is not immune from criticism. Not least among critics' concerns is whether these new Black politicians will advance the substantive and strategic policy goals of the African-American community. Yes, some of these women and men can realistically become senators and president, as Barack Obama has so aptly demonstrated, but at what price? Will they have to sell out Black interests to gain the electoral advantage needed to attain high office (Martin 2003)?

Implicit in this discussion of new Black politicians is their relative chance for success and the means by which they emerge onto the political spectrum. Is the emergence of this cohort of leadership an organic development emanating from Black communities, or are these politicians overly ambitious instrumentalists who are exploiting their racial background for political

traction? What is more, does this cohort of elected leadership have a chance at developing a loyal base of Black voters, or are they being propped up by White elites seeking to divide and conquer Black communities?

The answers to these questions are important because the stakes are so high. The new cohort of Black elected officials receive such notoriety because their probability of attaining high office is greater than it has been for any generation of Blacks in the United States. If this cohort of elected leadership meets expectations, and continues to ascend in critical numbers to governors' mansions, the U.S. Senate, and the White House, what are the implications for Black communities? Clearly, these leaders will be in an unprecedented position to shape public policy. Thus, it seems that the big question is not just what pundits think about new Black politicians, but what constituents think about these candidates and whether the material conditions of African Americans will improve under their direction. . . .

New Black Politics throughout History

So far, there have been three iterations of new Black politics in the post-Civil Rights era: the widespread election of the first Black elected officials in the 1970s; the successes of Black candidates in major elections in large, majority White jurisdictions in the 1980s; finally, the current rise of young, Black moderates, many of whom challenge members of the earlier wave of Black elected officials in majority Black cities and Congressional districts. Each wave of Black politicians is significant for

Source: Andra Gillespie, "Meet the New Class: Theorizing Young Black Leadership in a 'Postracial' Era," in *Whose Black Politics? Cases in Post-Racial Black Leadership*, ed. Andra Gillespie. Published in 2010 by Routledge. Reprinted by permission of Taylor & Francis LLC Books.

*Some text and accompanying endnotes and references have been omitted. Please consult the original source.

the barriers that the politicians traversed. They are also important to study because the rise of each class of Black elected officials is concurrent with innovations in campaign strategy. However, despite the campaign innovations, scholars studying these waves of elected officials have been careful to question whether the programmatic agenda of these Black elected officials aligns with the interests of Black constituents.

New Black Politics: Phase I

Charles Hamilton notes that after the passage of [the] Voting Rights Act, the focus of Black politics, in a literal and academic sense, shifted from the judicial to the legislative/electoral arena. Now that Blacks largely had the franchise, the goal shifted to channel that electoral power into legislative policies that would benefit Blacks (Hamilton, 1982). Putting Black officials in office was a key first step in achieving that agenda. Indeed, from 1965 to 1988, there was a more than thirteen-fold increase in the number of Black elected officials (Tate 1994, 1; see also Williams 1987, 112).

The elected officials of the first wave of new Black politics faced tremendous obstacles. As trailblazers coming on the heels of the Civil Rights Movement, they had to run in still racially tense environments. Furthermore, they had to reconcile with the White portions of their constituency that may have been skeptical of them as leaders (Smith 1990).

Moreover, these new Black elected officials had difficulty implementing their agenda. As Linda Williams notes, "urban Blacks today have reached city hall precisely at the moment when the real power to deliver jobs, money, education and basic services is migrating to higher levels of government and the private sector" (Williams 1987, 129). She observes that first wave Black politicians came to power during a period of national economic decline and decreased federal aid to cities. As a result, first wave Black mayors were hampered in their efforts to provide redistributive relief to their constituents. What little aid they were able to provide tended to focus on ameliorative policies such as affirmative action and set-asides, which disproportionately benefited middle class Black residents. What is more, Blacks ascended to the mayoralty in cities which severely proscribed their power, limiting some from having control over important functions such as taxation (Williams 1987, 128–29).

William Nelson further notes that the notion of new Black politics being the collective agent for improvement of the whole Black community is easier said than done. Using Cleveland as an example, he notes that uniting Blacks around a permanent agenda is difficult. Carl Stokes was able to unite Blacks under one political banner. However, that union dissolved when Stokes stepped down as leader of Cleveland's Black political organization. Diversity of opinion and ambition, then, undermined some attempts for political unity (Nelson 1982). Moreover, Robert Smith observes that the legislative record of these officials, with respect to their progressive, Black politics agenda, has been limited. They were only able to develop downtown space, implement municipal affirmative action, and respond to police brutality (Smith 1990).

New Black Politics: Phase II

One of the distinguishing features of each wave of new Black politics has been the new Black candidates' campaign style. While candidates in each wave of new Black politics have had some measure of crossover appeal, observers have attributed more crossover appeal to each subsequent generation of new Black political candidates. For example, Ardrey and Nelson (1990) note that Black elected officials elected in new Black politics' first wave, who were largely civil rights leaders, transferred the confrontational style from the movement to the electoral and legislative arena.

Many scholars viewed 1989 as a watershed year for Black politics. In November 1989, Blacks ascended to the mayoralty for the first time in Seattle (Norm Rice), New Haven (John Daniels), Durham (Chester Jenkins), and New York City (David Dinkins). Most notably, Douglas Wilder was elected Governor of Virginia, making him the country's first Black governor since Reconstruction. This cluster of elections is particularly important given that these men were elected in majority White jurisdictions with at least 40 percent of the White vote (McCormick and Jones 1993, 66, 68).

With their elections, Wilder and his peers ushered in the second wave of new Black politics. The second wave is characterized by the prevalent use of a deracialized campaign strategy. McCormick and Jones define a deracialized campaign as one being ". . . in a stylistic fashion that diffuses the polarizing effects of race by avoiding explicit reference to race-specific issues, while at the same time emphasizing those issues that are perceived as racially transcendent, thus mobilizing a broad segment of the electorate" (McCormick and Jones 1993, 76). McCormick and Jones (1993) go further to articulate this strategy by noting that candidates employing such a strategy convey *"a nonthreatening image"* (76, original emphasis), "avoid employing direct racial appeals in organizing the Black community" (76), and *"should avoid emphasis of a racially specific issue agenda"* (77, original emphasis).

Douglas Wilder clearly exemplifies the deracialized strategy. Strickland and Whicker note that Wilder, "adopted mainstream and even fiscally conservative positions. He was also able to avoid discussing overtly racial issues" (Strickland and Whicker 1992, 210). For example, Wilder's campaign theme was "the 'New Virginia Mainstream," and he made law and order, drug enforcement, and his support for the death penalty a key part of his platform (Jones and Clemons 1993, 140).

While this strategy may be electorally effective, some find it normatively troubling and wonder what the implications are for the pursuit of a pro-Black political agenda. Earl Sheridan (1996), in his article, "The New Accommodationists," implicitly likens such a strategy to Booker T. Washington's infamous Atlanta Compromise speech when he writes that instead of lauding Black elected officials who deemphasize race to get elected, "America needs Black leaders who will continue the legacy of the 1960's, not the 1890's—men and women who will call for meaningful change in our society" (Sheridan 1996, 169). He fears that in an attempt to gain office by any means necessary, these officials would abandon the issues of concern to the Black community to get votes and would shortchange Black interests to stay in power (Sheridan 1996, 165, 166).

McCormick and Jones are a little less fearful of the implications of using a deracialized electoral strategy, but they, too, brace for less progressive politics as a result of the strategy. They write that "In the absence of such demands from a politically organized African American community, there is little reason to expect African American elected officials who capture office in predominantly White political jurisdictions to be in the vanguard of articulating racially-specific policy issues" (McCormick and Jones 1993, 78). That being said, they proffer that even these politicians will occasionally

have to make some explicitly racial overtures to their Black constituents, lest these officials lose an important base of support in their communities (McCormick and Jones 1993, 78).

However, much of the hand wringing over the implications of deracialization as a strategy of second-wave Black politicians was short-lived. Second wave politicians experienced a number of setbacks which prevented that cohort from making a long-term impact on the communities they represented. Some setbacks were structural. Doug Wilder, for instance, was constitutionally barred from seeking a second consecutive term as Governor of Virginia. Others, such as David Dinkins, had very short tenures in office due to poor public perceptions (see Kim 2000 for an example of Dinkins' alienation of Black constituents). However, a number of politicians in the second wave suffered electoral defeats that marked the end of their electoral pursuits. For instance, Harvey Gantt twice lost his bid to represent North Carolina in the U.S. Senate to Jesse Helms in what were racially vitriolic campaigns. Andrew Young[2] lost a bid to be Georgia's Governor by wasting time campaigning for White votes in southern Georgia at the expense of campaigning in his base in and around Atlanta. Thus, according to the various authors studying the rise of second wave politicians in the late 1980s and early 1990s, deracialized candidates overestimated racial goodwill outside of the Black community and paid a high electoral price for ignoring Black voters (Z. Wilson 1993; Davis and Willingham 1993; Pierannunzi and Hutcheson 1996).

Moreover, from an academic perspective, many authors challenged the notion that pure deracialization was even going on in the first place. Mary Summers and Phillip Klinkner, for instance, argue that John Daniels did not run a deracialized campaign in his successful bid to become New Haven's first Black mayor. They point to his progressive campaign platform, his integral role in introducing community policing to New Haven and his creation of a needle exchange program, in addition to his willingness to discuss his race on the campaign trail, as evidence that Daniels was not a deracialized candidate. Additionally, Lenneal Henderson studied Kurt Schmoke's ascendance to the mayoralty of Baltimore and reached similar conclusions. He contends that Schmoke's efforts at economic redevelopment were racially transcendent, but that Schmoke was not trying to distance himself from Black communities.

Thus, Schmoke was a transracialized Black politician and not a deracialized Black politician (Summers and Klinkner 1996; Henderson 1996).

New Black Politics: Phase III

The current wave of new Black politics very much resembles the second wave in that this wave is characterized by ambitious politicians with more moderate politics. What distinguishes this group from its predecessors is its youth and connection to civil rights history. The figures associated with the third wave of new Black politics were born after 1960,[3] immediately before or after the passage of all the major civil rights legislation (Traub 2002). For example, Barack Obama was born in 1961; Cory Booker was born in 1969; Harold Ford Jr. and Kwame Kilpatrick were born in 1970. As a result, these figures benefited from the fruits of the struggle and were able to grow up in integrated neighborhoods and attend predominantly White schools from kindergarten to graduate school. However, their youth also means that some perceive this generation as being less likely to relate to the Civil Rights struggle (Bositis 2001, 3–11). While second wave new Black politicians were charged with deliberately not having been active in the Civil Rights Movement, they at least had the benefit of having been eyewitness to the monumental changes that took place in the 1950s and 1960s (Sheridan 1996, 166).[4] In addition, at the beginning of the twenty-first century, some could legitimately view this generation as being untested and unable to point to any record upon which to base their claims of being better legislators or government executives or to a clear agenda around which to organize their candidacies (Martin 2003).

This perceived lack of identification with the struggle is what raises so much skepticism among older Black elites when evaluating this emerging generation of leadership. In an interview with *Savoy* magazine, Ronald Walters voiced the suspicion that this new generation was merely a tool of White elites who wanted to replace more acerbic, older Black leaders with less threatening, younger Black leaders:

> [The White power structure] would rather supplant [the old guard] with a far more accommodating leadership. They are going to pit them against the so-called old leadership because

they have been threatened by the interests and power of the Black leadership who really have the influence and control of Black people. (Walters, quoted in Martin 2003, 56)

In addition to having had their race consciousness questioned, this generation has also been accused of hubris. David Bositis acknowledged in an interview that young Black leaders "imagine themselves as governors, United States Senators, and even President" (Bositis, quoted in Martin 2003, 56). When Harold Ford Jr. ran to unseat Nancy Pelosi as House Minority Leader in 2003, his efforts were rebuffed even by members of the Congressional Black Caucus. Ford's attempted power grab failed, according to Walters, because he had not spent years currying favor and garnering support from his colleagues in the House Democratic Caucus. "To step out there because you've got a pretty face and no agenda," Walters said, "you're going to lose every time" (Walters, quoted in Martin 2003, 56).

If there is anything that does distinguish the third wave of new Black politics from the first two waves, it may be that it is the synthesis of the first and second waves. Where we witnessed civil rights activists turned legislators challenge the White power structure in the first wave, and where we witnessed second wave politicians attempt to join the White power structure, we now see third wave politicians who behave like second wave politicians and challenge first wave incumbents for power,[5] often in majority Black jurisdictions, and often with extensive mainstream media support. For instance, Alexandra Starr predicts that moderate politics would probably propel more Black candidates to national office (2002). James Traub goes so far as to say that the success of people like Cory Booker and Artur Davis against the Sharpe Jameses and Earl Hilliards of the world would be a "balm to White liberals, whose politics have been so heavily determined by an agonized sense of 'what Black people want,' as defined by the Black leadership class. And it will be a boon to the Democrats, for it will help heal the ideological rifts within the party" (Traub 2002, 1).

Analytical Concerns with Phases II and III of New Black Politics

The academy has not been immune from being infatuated with second and third wave new Black politics because of the nonthreatening dimension of their electoral strategy. Strickland and Whicker acquiesce to the reality of racism in American society and propose a crossover model for Black electoral success. This model calls for espousing conservative positions on issues, deemphasizing race, and working outside the Civil Rights Movement. While they do all this, these candidates are supposed to excite and maintain a Black voting base (Strickland and Whicker 1992, 208, 209).

Strickland and Whicker acknowledge that catering to Whites while not alienating Blacks is easier said than done. However, their key mistake is assuming that Black voters will be loyal to any Black candidate. While that is a gross overgeneralization of Black voting preferences in and of itself, Strickland and Whicker fail to account for the situation when two Blacks would run against each other. Who should Black voters choose, then? In their study of congressional elections, Canon, Schousen, and Sellers (1996) studied the electoral success of Black candidates pitted against other Black candidates in majority minority districts. They argue that when first wave new Black politicians run against second or third wave new Black politicians, the second or third wave new Black politician will win if Whites, who should be a sizable minority of the constituency, vote as a bloc. They assume that Whites are more likely to support moderate Blacks. However, they do concede that if Blacks vote as a bloc, the first wave new Black politician has a better chance of winning.

This focus on which Black candidates appeal to White voters (as opposed to which Black candidates can best represent the interests of Black voters) is what is so troubling to students of Black politics. Ronald Walter's aforementioned quote captures this concern (Martin, 2003, 56). Indeed, it is this fixation with keeping Whites happy that seems to be anathema to Black self-determination, if only because the focus on this type of Black politics shifts the focus away from Blacks and their policy interests.

Critics must respond to the question, though, of whether these candidates are out of touch. Reed and Alleyne note that the hallmark of third wave new Black politics is their "philosophic mix of political pragmatism, pro-business sensibility, and social progressivism" (Reed and Alleyne 2002, 84). Martin notes that, "today's Black elected official may be more concerned with closing the digital divide, increasing economic opportunities for people of color, and school vouchers . . ." (Martin 2003, 54). Are these positions really out of touch with the policy preferences of Black constituents? David Bositis would have to concede that these candidates may not be so out of touch with their constituents. Reporting the results of the Joint Center's 2002 National Opinion Poll, he notes that a majority of Blacks were in favor of vouchers, that younger Blacks identified less with the Democratic Party, and that Blacks are far more concerned about the economy, foreign affairs, and education than they are about racism (Bositis 2002, 7, 6, 10). What is more, when the Joint Center compared the political attitudes of Black elected officials to the Black electorate, they found that generational differences in attitudes among Blacks generally paralleled generational differences among Black elected officials (Bositis 2001, 21).

Skeptics need also to consider the substantive critiques levied against older generations of Black leadership. While Walters chided the younger generation of Black elected officials for being overly ambitious but substantively unfocused and proclaimed that the older generation of Black leaders "really have the influence and control of Black people" (Walters, quoted in Martin 2003, 56), he has also acknowledged elsewhere that the earlier vanguard of leadership encountered institutional barriers that limited their effectiveness in providing benefits for Blacks (Walters and Smith, 1999, 135). His colleague, Robert Smith, argued that post-Civil Rights elected officials assumed power but were co-opted by the establishment and thus accomplished very little of the programmatic agenda to improve the lives of African Americans. The reality that even the first wave of Black politicians sold out to some degree led Smith to boldly proclaim in the title of his book that *We Have No Leaders* (Smith 1996). This reality begs the questions of whether younger, postracial candidates really can do more harm than good, relative to the previous generation of leadership, for the advancement of an African-American agenda? . . .

Notes

1. This is adapted with permission from Andra Gillespie. 2009. The Third Wave: A Theoretical Introduction to the Post-Civil Rights Cohort of African American Leadership. *National Political Science Review* 12:139–161.

2. Andrew Young, like Jesse Jackson Sr., represents an interesting case of Phase I Black politicians who attempted to adopt a Phase II posture in order to pursue high elective office. Their evolution evinces the possibility that older Black politicians can shift phases depending on changes in their personal philosophy or in the office they were pursuing (for further discussion, see Pierannunzi and Hutcheson 1996; Davis and Willingham 1993; Tate 1995, 8–15). In general, though, most politicians maintain a particular posture throughout their careers.

3. My discussion of Phases I and II deliberately avoided defining the Phases by generation. That is because there is a generational overlap between Phases I and II. While most Phase I politicians were members of the Greatest (or World War II) Generation, there are some Baby Boomers who adopted a Phase I posture (e.g., Jesse Jackson Sr. in 1984). Similarly, while most Phase II Black politicians are members of the Silent and Baby Boom Generations, there were older Phase II politicians (e.g., Tom Bradley).

4. Sheridan uses Douglas Wilder as a [sic] example of a second wave politician who refused to identify with the civil rights struggle, saying that he opted to make money rather than advocate for change in the 1960s. Whatever one can say about Wilder's personal politics, given his age, no one can argue that he missed being personally affected by Jim Crow growing up in Richmond, Virginia (Sheridan 1996, 166).

5. To be sure, there are earlier examples of young, moderate Blacks challenging leaders from the older, Civil Rights generation. Ardrey and Nelson note that Michael White challenged the combative, divisive tactics of George Forbes and beat him for the mayoralty of Cleveland. There are other early examples of Black politicians competing against other Black politicians, such as former Detroit Mayor Dennis Archer (Ardrey and Nelson 1990; Nordlinger 2002).

References

Ardrey, Saundra C., and William E. Nelson. 1990. The maturation of Black political power: The case of Cleveland. *PS: Political Science and Politics* 23(2): 148–51.

Bositis, David. 2001. *Changing the guard: Generational difference among Black elected officials.* Washington, DC: Joint Center for Political and Economic Studies.

———. 2002. *2002 National opinion poll: Politics.* Washington, DC: Joint Center for Political and Economic Studies, http://www.jointcenter.org.

Canon, David T., Matthew Schousen, and Patrick Sellers. 1996. The supply side of congressional redistricting: Race and strategic politicians, 1972–1992. *The Journal of Politics* 58, no. 3: 846–62.

Davis, Marilyn, and Alex Willingham. 1993. Andrew Young and the Georgia state elections of 1990. In *Dilemmas of Black politics,* ed. Georgia Persons, 147–75. New York: HarperCollins.

Gillespie, Andra. 2009. The third wave: Assessing the post-civil rights cohort of Black elected leadership. *The National Political Science Review* 12: 139–61.

Hamilton, Charles V. 1982. Foreword. In *The new Black politics: The search for political power,* ed. Michael B. Preston, Lenneal J. Henderson Jr., and Paul Puryear, xvii–xx. New York: Longman.

Henderson, Lenneal J. Jr. 1996. The governance of Kurt Schmoke as mayor of Baltimore. In *Race, governance, and politics in the United States,* ed. Huey L. Perry, 165–78. Gainesville: University of Florida Press.

Jones, Charles E., and Michael Clemons. 1993. A model of racial crossover voting: An assessment of the Wilder victory. In *Dilemmas of Black politics,* ed. Georgia Persons, 128–46. New York: HarperCollins.

Kim, Claire. 2000. *Bitter fruit: The politics of Black-Korean conflict in New York City.* New Haven, CT: Yale University Press.

Martin, Roland. 2003. Ready or not. . . . *Savoy.* March, 52–56.

McCormick, Joseph II, and Charles E. Jones. 1993. The conceptualization of deracialization: Thinking through the dilemma. In *Dilemmas of Black politics,* ed. Georgia Persons, 66–84. New York: HarperCollins.

Nelson, William E. 1982. Cleveland: The rise and fall of the new Black politics. In *The new Black politics: The search for political power,* ed. Michael B. Preston, Lenneal J. Henderson Jr. and Paul Puryear, 187–208. New York: Longman.

Nordlinger, Jay. 2002. Some "dissident." Doin' the skin-color nasty. A bit of righteous kvetching. etc. *National Review Online,* May 28. LexisNexis Academic Universe. http://www.web.lexis-nexis.com/universe (accessed January 20, 2003).

Pierannunzi, Carol A., and John D. Hutcheson Jr. 1996. The rise and fall of deracialization: Andrew Young as mayor and gubernatorial candidate. In *Race, governance, and politics in the United States,* ed. Huey L. Perry, 96–105. Gainesville: University of Florida Press.

Reed, K. Terrell, and Sonia Alleyne. 2002. What it takes to win. *Black Enterprise*, November: 82–95.

Sheridan, Earl. 1996. The new accommodationists. *Journal of Black Studies* 27(2): 152–71.

Smith, Robert C. 1990. Recent elections and Black politics: The maturation or death of Black politics? PS: *Political Science and Politics* 23(2): 160–62.

———. 1996. *We have no leaders.* Albany: SUNY Press.

Starr, Alexandra. 2002. We shall overcome, too. *Business Week*, July 15. LexisNexis Academic Universe http://www.web.lexis-nexis.com/universe (accessed January 20, 2003).

Strickland, Ruth Ann, and Marcia Lynn Whicker. 1992. Comparing the Wilder and Gantt campaigns: A model for Black candidate success in statewide elections. *PS: Political Science and Politics* 25(2): 204–12.

Summers, Mary, and Phillip Klinkner. 1996. The election and governance of John Daniels as mayor of New Haven. In *Race, governance, and politics in the United States,* ed. Huey L. Perry, 127–50. Gainesville: University of Florida Press.

Tate, Katherine. 1994. *From protest to politics: The new Black voters in American elections.* New York and Cambridge, MA: Russell Sage Foundation/Harvard University Press.

Traub, James. 2002. The way we live now: 9-8-02; The last color line. *The New York Times Magazine*, September 8. LexisNexis Academic Universe. http://www.web.lexis-nexis.com/universe (accessed January 20, 2003).

Walters, Ronald, and Robert C. Smith. 1999. *African American leadership.* Albany: SUNY Press.

Williams, Linda. 1987. Black political progress in the 1980's: The electoral arena. In *The new Black politics: The search for political power.* 2nd ed., ed. Michael B. Preston, Lenneal J. Henderson Jr., and Paul Puryear, 97–136. New York and London: Longman.

Wilson, Zaphon. 1993. Gantt versus Helms: Deracialization confronts southern traditionalism. In *Dilemmas of Black politics,* ed. Georgia Persons, 176–93. New York: HarperCollins.

12-2 "Demobilization in the New Black Political Regime: Ideological Capitulation and Radical Failure in the Post-Segregation Era"*

Adolph Reed Jr.

Excerpt from *The Bubbling Cauldron: Race, Ethnicity, and the Urban Crisis*

It is ironic that the exponential increases in black public-office holding since the 1970s have been accompanied by a deterioration of the material circumstances of large segments of the black citizenry. Comment on that irony comes both from those on the Left who underscore the insufficiency of capturing public office and from those on the Right who disparage the pursuit of public action on behalf of blacks or push oblique claims about black incompetence. In the middle are liberal social scientists and journalists who construe this inverse association as a puzzling deviation from the orthodox narrative of American interest-group pluralism. The liberal and conservative tendencies especially are often elaborated through a rhetoric that juxtaposes black political power and white economic power, treating them almost as naturalized racial properties, rather than as contingent products of social and political institutions.

At the same time, a different anomaly bedevils those on the Left who presume that oppression breeds political resistance to power relations enforced through the state apparatus. The intensification of oppression over the 1980s—seen, for example, in worsening of material conditions and an expanding regime of social repression—has not produced serious oppositional political mobilization. This is the key problem for articulation of a progressive black urban politics in the 1990s.

Making sense of these anomalies requires examining critical characteristics of post-segregation-era black politics. Although the disparate fortunes of black officialdom and its constituents are not causally linked, their relation sheds light on popular demobilization. This relation connects with each of the three features of the contemporary political landscape that hinder progressive black mobilization: (1) political incorporation and its limits, (2) the hegemony of underclass discourse as a frame for discussing racial inequality and poverty, and (3) the Left's failure to think carefully and critically about black politics and the ways that it connects with the role of race in the American stratification system.

The Limits of Incorporation

Systemic incorporation along four dimensions has been the most significant development in black urban politics since the 1960s. First, enforcement of the Voting Rights Act has increased the efficacy of black electoral participation: invalidation of cruder forms of racial gerrymandering and biased electoral systems, as well as redress against intimidation, have made it easier for black voters to elect candidates.[1]

Second, a corollary of that electoral efficacy, has been the dramatic increase of black elected officials. Their existence has become a fact of life in U.S. politics and has shaped the modalities of race relations management. Black elected officials tend to operate within already existing governing coalitions at the local level and within the imperatives of the Democratic party's

---

*Some text and accompanying endnotes have been omitted. Please consult the original source.

internal politics, as well as with an eye to their constituents. The logic of incumbency, moreover, is race-blind and favors reelection above all else. Not surprisingly, black officeholders tend to be disposed to articulate their black constituents' interests in ways that are compatible with those other commitments.

Third, black people have increasingly assumed administrative control of the institutions of urban governance. Housing authorities, welfare departments, school systems, even public safety departments are ever more likely to be run by black officials, and black functionaries are likely to be prominent at all levels within those organizations.[2] Those agencies have their own attentive constituencies within the black electorate, radiating out into the family and friendship networks of personnel. And a substratum of professional, often geographically mobile public functionaries with commitments to public management ideologies may now constitute a relatively autonomous interest configuration within black politics. This dimension of incorporation short-circuits critiques of those agencies' operations crafted within the racially inflected language most familiar to black insurgency. A critique that pivots on racial legitimacy as a standard for evaluating institutional behavior cannot be effective—as a basis for either organizing opposition or stimulating critical public debate—in a situation in which blacks conspicuously run the institutions. Because they have their own black constituencies and greater access to resources for shaping public opinion, public officials have the advantage in any debate that rests simplistically on determining racial authenticity.

A fourth and related dimension of incorporation is the integration of private civil rights and uplift organizations into a regime of race relations management driven by incrementalist, insider negotiation.[3] The tracings of this process could be seen dramatically at the national level during the Jimmy Carter administration with the inclusion of Jesse Jackson's Operation Push and the National Urban League as line item accounts in Department of Labor budgets. The boundaries between state agendas and elites and those of black nongovernment organizations may even be more porous at the local level, where personnel commonly move back and forth from one payroll system to another and where close coordination

with local interest groupings is woven more seamlessly into the texture of everyday life.

An effect has arguably been further to skew the black politically attentive public toward the new regime of race relations management. On the one hand, generation of a professional world of public/private race relations engineers drawn from politically attentive elements of the black population channels issue-articulation and agenda-formation processes in black politics in ways reflecting the regime's common sense. On the other hand, insofar as the nongovernmental organizations and their elites carry the historical sediment of adversarial, protest politics, their integration into the new regime further ratifies its protocols as the only thinkable politics.

These trajectories of incorporation have yielded real benefits for the black citizenry. They have enhanced income and employment opportunity and have injected a greater measure of fairness into the distribution of public benefits in large and small ways. Black citizens have greater access now to the informal networks through which ordinary people use government to get things done—find summer jobs for their children, obtain zoning variances and building permits, get people out of jail, remove neighborhood nuisances, or site parks and libraries. Objectives that not long ago required storming city council meetings now can be met through routine processes. These accomplishments often are dismissed in some quarters on the Left as trivial and evidence of co-optation. Certainly, such characterizations are true "in the last analysis," but we don't live and can't do effective politics "in the last analysis." For them to function effectively as co-optation, for example, the fruits of incorporation cannot be trivial for those who partake or expect to be able to partake of them. The inclination to dismiss them reflects instead problematic tendencies within the Left to trivialize and simultaneously to demonize the exercise of public authority.

The new regime of race relations management as realized through the four-pronged dynamic of incorporation has exerted a *demobilizing* effect on black politics precisely by virtue of its capacities for delivering benefits and for defining what benefits political action can legitimately be used to pursue. Ease in voting and in producing desired electoral outcomes legitimizes that form as the primary means of political participation, which naturally seems attractive compared with others that require more extensive and intensive commitment of attention and effort. A result is to narrow the operative conception of political engagement to one form, and the most passive one at that.

Incumbent public officials generically have an interest in dampening the possibilities for new or widespread mobilization because of its intrinsic volatility. Uncontrolled participation can produce unpleasant electoral surprises and equally can interfere with the reigning protocols through which public agencies discharge their functions. As popular participation narrows, the inertial logic of incumbency operates to constrict the field of political discourse. Incumbents respond to durable interests, and they seek predictability, continuity, and a shared common sense. This translates into a preference for a brokered "politics as usual" that limits the number and range of claims on the policy agenda. Such a politics preserves the thrust of inherited policy regimes and reinforces existing patterns of systemic advantage by limiting the boundaries of the politically reasonable.[4] The same is true for the insider-negotiation processes through which the nongovernmental organizations now define their roles, and those organizations often earn their insider status by providing a convincing alternative to popular political mobilization.

Underclass Rhetoric and the Disappearance of Politics

Fueled largely by sensationalist journalism and supposedly tough-minded, policy-oriented social scientists, underclass rhetoric became over the 1980s the main frame within which to discuss inner-city poverty and inequality. The pundits and scholars who created this "underclass" define the stratum's membership in a variety of slightly differing ways; however, they all circle around a basic characterization that roots it among inner-city blacks and Hispanics, and they share a consensual assessment that the underclass makes up about 20 percent of the impoverished population in inner cities.[5]

The underclass notion is a contemporary extrapolation from a Victorian petit bourgeois fantasy world, and it is almost invariably harnessed to arguments for reactionary and punitive social policy. Even at its best—that is, when it is connected with some agenda

other than pure stigmatization and denial of public responsibility—this rhetoric is depoliticizing and thus demobilizing in at least three ways.

First, the underclass frame does not direct attention to the political-economic dynamics that produce and reproduce dispossession and its entailments but focuses instead on behavioral characteristics alleged to exist among the victims of those dynamics. The result is to immerse discussion of inequality poverty, and racial stratification in often overlapping rhetorics of individual or collective pathogenesis and knee-jerk moral evaluation. Conservatives bask in the simplicity of a discourse that revolves around racialized stigmatization of people as good, bad, or defective.[6] Even those versions propounded by liberals, like that offered by William Julius Wilson, which purport to provide structurally grounded accounts of inner-city inequality, describe the "underclass" in primarily behavioral terms.[7]

In both conservative and putatively liberal versions, the underclass rhetoric reinforces tendencies to demobilization by situating debate about poverty and inequality not in the public realm of politics—which would warrant examination of the role of public action in the reproduction of an unequal distribution of material costs and benefits (for example, federal and local housing and redevelopment policies that feed ghettoization and favor suburbs over inner cities, that favor homeowners over renters in the face of widespread and blatant racial discrimination in access to mortgages, and subsidies for urban deindustrialization and disinvestment)—but on the ostensibly private realm of individual values and behavior, pivoting specifically on images of male criminality and female slovenliness and irresponsible sexuality. The specter of drugs and gangs is omnipresent as well, underscoring the composite image of a wanton, depraved Other and automatically justifying any extreme of official repression and brutality. Even when acknowledged as unfounded, invocation of suspicion of the presence of drugs and gangs exculpates arbitrary violation of civil liberties in inner cities and police brutality to the extent of homicide.

Insofar as this focus opens to public policy at all, it tilts toward social and police repression, as in ubiquitous proposals for draconian "welfare reform" that seek only to codify the punitive moralism propelling the underclass narrative. That essentially racialized agenda is not likely to fuel broad political mobilization among black Americans, not in service to progressive agendas, at any rate.

Second, the underclass rhetoric reinforces demobilization because of its very nature as a third-person discourse. As a rhetoric of stigmatization, it is deployed about rather than by any real population. No one self-identifies as a member of the underclass. To that extent, as well as because the rhetoric presumes their incompetence, exhortations of the stigmatized population to undertake any concerted political action on their own behalf are unthinkable.

Its association with "self-help" ideology is in fact the third way that the underclass narrative undercuts popular mobilization. Because behavioral pathology appears in that narrative as at least the proximate source of poverty, inequality, and even contemporary racial discrimination, the programmatic responses that arise most naturally within its purview are those geared to correcting the supposed defects of the target population. This biases programmatic discussion toward bootstrap initiatives that claim moral rehabilitation of impoverished individuals and communities as part of their mission.

In this context two apparently different streams of neo-Jeffersonian romanticism—those associated respectively with the 1960s' New Left and Reaganism—converge on an orientation that eschews government action on principle in favor of voluntarist, "community-based" initiatives. Particularly when steeped in a language of "empowerment," this antistatist convergence overlaps current manifestations of a conservative, bootstrap tendency among black elites that stretches back at least through Booker T. Washington at the turn of the century. Indeed, it was the Reagan administration's evil genius to appeal to that tendency by shifting from a first-term tactic that projected combative black voices, like Thomas Sowell and Clarence Pendleton, to a more conciliatory style exemplified by Glenn Loury. In Reagan's second term the administration apparently opted for a different posture as a new group of its black supporters, led by Loury and Robert Woodson of the National Center for Neighborhood Enterprise, stepped into the spotlight. Although this wave of black Reaganauts could be pugnacious with adversaries, they were far more inclined than their predecessors to make overtures to the entrenched race relations elite. Those overtures disarmed partisan skepticism by emphasizing the black middle class's supposedly special responsibility for correcting the underclass and the problems associated with it.[8]

Underwriting this version of self-help are three interlocked claims: (1) that black inner cities are beset by grave and self-regenerative problems of social breakdown and pathology that have undermined the possibility of normal civic life, (2) that these problems are beyond the reach of positive state action, and (3) that they can be addressed only by private, voluntarist black action led by the middle class. Over the late 1980s and early 1990s these three claims—each dubious enough on its own, all justified at most by appeal to lurid anecdotes, self-righteous prejudices, and crackerbarrel social theory—congealed into hegemonic wisdom. Black public figures supposedly identified with the Left, like Jesse Jackson, Roger Wilkins, and Cornel West, have become as devout proselytizers of this catechistic orthodoxy as are rightists like Woodson, Loury, and Clarence Thomas.[9]

The rise and consolidation of the Democratic Leadership Council and the "New Liberalism" as dominant within the Democratic party no doubt reinforced and were reinforced by black self-help bromides' elevation to the status of conventional wisdom. On the one hand, black self-help rhetoric historically has been associated with presumptions that blacks have no hope for allies in pursuit of justice through public policy, and the successful offensive of Democratic "centrists" and neoliberals—predicated in large part on flight from identification with both perceived black interests and downwardly redistributive social policy—certainly lends credence to the impression that the federal government is not a dependable ally of black objectives. Even the celebrated declamations by New Liberal consciences Bill Bradley and John Kerry for racial justice and tolerance were mainly, after brief statements against bigotry, extended characterizations of impoverished inner cities as savage hearts of darkness, saturated in self-destructive violence and pathology; the speeches carried no particular warrant for action addressing inequality and its effects except calls for moral uplift.

Despite its foundation on notions of grassroots activism, the self-help regime is best seen as community mobilization for political demobilization. Each attempt by a neighborhood or church group to scrounge around the philanthropic world and the interstices of the federal system for funds to build low-income housing or day-care or neighborhood centers or to organize programs that compensate for inadequate school funding, public safety, or trash pickup, simultaneously concedes the point that black citizens cannot legitimately pursue those benefits through government. This is a very dangerous concession in an ideological context defined largely by a logic that, like that in the post-Reconstruction era of the last century, could extend to an almost genocidal expulsion of black citizens toward a "Bantustanized" periphery of society.

We cannot concede the important ground of black people's equal proprietorship of public institutions with all other citizens; affirming the legitimacy of black Americans' demands on the state—on an equal basis with those who receive defense contracts, homeownership subsidies, investment tax credits, flood protection, and a host of other benefits from government—is also affirming black Americans' equal membership in the polity. The more ground we give on this front, the more the latter-day versions of the Southern Redeemers will take. Frederick Douglass put it succinctly, "The limits of tyrants are prescribed by the endurance of those whom they oppress."

The problem with self-help ideology is that it reifies community initiative, freighting it with an ideological burden that reduces to political quietism and a programmatic mission it is ill equipped to fulfill. It is absurd to present neighborhood and church initiatives as appropriate responses to the effects of government-supported disinvestment, labor market segmentation, widespread and well-documented patterns of discrimination in employment and housing as well as in the trajectory of direct and indirect public spending, and an all-out corporate assault on the social wage.

Its endorsement by public officials is a particularly ironic aspect of the self-help rhetoric. That endorsement amounts to an admission of failure, an acknowledgment that the problems afflicting their constituents are indeed beyond the scope of the institutional apparatus under their control, that black officials are in fact powerless to provide services to inner-city citizens effectively through those institutions.

A key to overcoming the demobilizing effects of self-help ideology, as well as those of underclass rhetoric more generally, lies in stimulation of strategic debate—grounded in the relation between social

conditions affecting the black population and public policy and the larger political-economic tendencies to which it responds—within and about black political activity. This in turn requires attending to the complex dynamics of interest and ideological differentiation that operate within black politics, taking into account the who-gets-what-when-where-how dimension of politics as it appears among black political agents and interest configurations. In principle, the Left should be intimately engaged in this project, which is the stock-in-trade of Left political analysis.

The Left and Black Politics

By outlawing official segregation and discriminatory restrictions on political participation, the Voting Rights Act and the 1964 Civil Rights Act rendered obsolete the least common denominator—opposition to Jim Crow—that for more than a half-century had given black political activity coherence and a pragmatic agenda plausibly understood to be shared uniformly among the black citizenry.[10] (This effect no doubt is a factor—along with the spread of self-help ideology and the aging of the population that can recall the ancient regime—driving contemporary nostalgia for the sense of community that supposedly flourished under segregation. That perception was always more apparent than real; the coherence and cohesiveness were most of all artifacts of the imperatives of the Jim Crow system and the struggle against it. In black politics as elsewhere, what appears as political cohesiveness has been the assertion of one tendency over others coexisting and competing with it—in this case, first, white elites' successful projection of Booker T. Washington's capitulationist program and then, for the half-century after Washington's death, the primacy of the focus on attacking codified segregation.) The Voting Rights Act, additionally, ensued in opening new possibilities, concrete objectives and incentives for political action, and new, more complex relations with mainstream political institutions, particularly government and the Democratic party at all levels.

In the decade after 1965 black political activity came increasingly to revolve around gaining, enhancing, or maintaining official representation in public institutions and the distribution of associated material and symbolic benefits. The greatest increases in black elective-office holding occurred during those years. That period also saw the rise of black urban governance, both in black-led municipal regimes and in growing black authority in the urban administrative apparatus.

At the same time this shift exposed a long-standing tension in black political discourse between narrower and broader constructions of the practical agenda for realizing racially democratic interests. The narrower view has focused political objectives on singular pursuit of racial inclusion, either accepting the structure and performance of political and economic institutions as given or presuming that black representation is an adequate basis for correcting what might be unsatisfactory about them. The essence of this view was distilled, appropriately, in two pithy formulations in the late 1960s: the slogan demanding "black faces in previously all-white places" and the proposition that, as an ideal, black Americans should make up 12 percent of corporate executives, 12 percent of the unemployed, and 12 percent of everything in between.[11] The broader tendency is perhaps best seen as an ensemble of views joined by inclination toward structural critique. This tendency sees simple racial inclusion as inadequate and argues for tying political action to insurgent programs that seek either to transform existing institutions or to reject them altogether in favor of race nationalist or social revolutionary alternatives.

The tension between these two views has been a recurring issue in black politics, overlapping and crosscutting—and, arguably being mistaken for—other fault lines that appear more commonly in the historiography of black political debate (for example, the militant/moderate, protest/accommodationist, and integrationist/nationalist dichotomies).[12] In the 1960s, however, the combination of broad popular mobilization and heightened prospects for victory against legally enforced exclusion made this tension more prominent than at any prior time except during the 1930s and early 1940s, when Ralph Bunche and other Young Turks pushed sharp, Marxist-inspired critiques into the main lines of black debate.

Black accession to responsible positions in the apparatus of public management enabled for the first time—save for fleeting moments in Reconstruction a discourse focused on the concrete, nuts-and-bolts, incrementalist exercise of public authority. Three factors compel the new pragmatic orientation toward incrementalism. First, the inclusionist program had developed largely as an insider politics, seeking legitimacy in part through emphasis of loyalty, particularly in the cold war context, to prevailing political and economic arrangements except insofar as those were racially exclusionary. To that extent it has been predisposed to take existing systemic and institutional imperatives as given. Second, experience in War on Poverty and Great Society programs socialized the pool of potential black officials into the public management system's entrenched protocols and operating logic, initiating them into existing policy processes. This socialization spurred articulation of a rhetoric exalting realpolitik and keying strategic consideration only to advancement of black representation among beneficiaries within existing institutional regimes.[13] This notion of political pragmatism not only reinforces incrementalism, it also requires a shifting construction of "black" interests to conform to options set in a received policy and issue framework. For instance, Mayor Maynard Jackson strained to define one of the alternatives in a developers' fight over siting a new Atlanta airport as the black choice, although building a second airport on either location would have had no discernibly positive impact on black Atlantans; public support for the project on any site, moreover, would amount to a redistribution of fiscal resources away from the city's black population to developers and remote, generally hostile metropolitan economic interests.[14] Finally, inclusionist politics affords no larger vision around which to orient a critical perspective on either the operations and general functions of political institutions or the general thrust of public policy. This characteristic, which might appear as political myopia, is rationalizable as pragmatic; in any event, it further reinforces incrementalism by screening out broader issues and concerns.

The hegemony of incrementalism has facilitated elaboration of a political discourse that sidesteps a critical problem at the core of post-segregation-era black politics: the tension between black officials' institutional legitimation and their popular electoral legitimation. The institutions that black officials administer are driven by the imperatives of managing systemic racial subordination, but the expectations they cultivate among their constituents define the role of black administrative representation in those institutions as a de facto challenge to racial subordination.

So by the 1990s it was commonplace to see black housing authority directors' policy innovations run to advocating lockdowns and random police sweeps, black school superintendents discussing their duties principally through a rhetoric of discipline and calling for punishment of parents of transgressors in their charge, black mayors and legislators locked into a victim-blaming interpretive frame accenting drug abuse and criminality as the only actionable social problems—and all falling back on the bromides about family breakdown and moral crisis among their constituents to explain the inadequacy of public services. This rhetoric obscures their capitulation to business-led programs of regressive redistribution—tax breaks and other subsidies, as well as general subservience to development interests in planning and policy formulation—that contribute further to fiscal strain, thus justifying still further service cuts, which increase pressure for giving more to development interests to stimulate "growth" that supposedly will build the tax base, and so on. From this perspective, Sharon Pratt Kelly's Washington, D.C., mayoralty is emblematic; her tenure was distinguished only by repeated service and personnel cuts and her 1993 call for the National Guard to buttress municipal police efforts—even as the District of Columbia already has one of the highest police-to-citizen ratios in the United States. There could hardly be a more striking illustration of the extent to which minority public officials are the equivalent of Bantustan administrators. Incrementalism serves as blinders, sword, and shield. It blocks alternative courses from view, delegitimizes criticism with incantations of realpolitik, and provides a Pontius Pilate defense of any action by characterizing officials as incapable of acting on their circumstances.[15]

Continued debate with the oppositional tendency in black politics could have mitigated the corrosive effects of incrementalist hegemony. Such debate might have broadened somewhat the perspective from which black officials themselves define pragmatic agendas. It might have stimulated among black citizens a practical, policy-oriented public discourse that would either have supported black officials in the articulation of bold initiatives and/or held them accountable to autonomously generated programmatic agendas and concerns.

Yet few would dispute the argument that radicalism has been routed in post-segregation black politics. Some fit that fact into a naturalistic reading of incorporation: radicalism automatically wanes as avenues open for regular political participation. Others concede incrementalist, petit bourgeois hegemony in electoral politics but claim that radicalism's social base has not been destroyed but only displaced to other domains—dormant mass anger, Louis -Farrakhan's apparent popularity, rap music and other extrusions of youth culture, literary production, and the like—suggesting a need to reconceptualize politics to reflect the significance of such phenomena. Both sorts of response, however, evade giving an account of how the radical tendency was expunged from the black political mainstream, which is critically important for making sense of the limitations of inherited forms of black radicalism and for the task of constructing a progressive black politics in the present.

The oppositional tendency in post-segregation black politics was hampered by an aspect of its origin in black power ideology. Radicals—all along the spectrum, ranging from cultural nationalist to Stalinoid Marxist—began from a stance that took the "black community" as the central configuration of political interest and the source of critical agency. This stance grew from black power rhetoric's emphasis on "community control" and its projection of the "community" as touchstone of legitimacy and insurgent authenticity. This formulation is a presumptive claim for the existence of a racial population that is organically integrated and that operates as a collective subject in pursuit of unitary interests. That claim, which persists as a grounding principle in black strategic discourse, is problematic in two linked ways that bear on elaboration of a critical politics.

First, positing a black collectivity as an organic political agent preempts questions of interest differentiation. If the "community" operates with a single will and a single agenda, then there is neither need nor basis for evaluating political programs or policies with respect to their impact on differing elements of the black population. Any initiative enjoying conspicuous support from any group of black people can be said plausibly to reflect the community's preference or interest; the metaphorical organicism that drives the "black community" formulation presumes that what is good for one is good for all.

Similarly, because the organic black community is construed as naturalistic, the notion precludes discussion

of both criteria of political representation and the definition of constituencies. Those issues become matters for
concern when the relevant polity is perceived to be made
up of diverse and not necessarily compatible interests
and/or when the relation between representatives and
represented is seen as contingent and mediated rather
than cellular or isomorphic. By contrast, in the black
community construct those who appear as leaders or
spokespersons are not so much representatives as pure
embodiments of collective aspirations.

As the stratum of black public officials emerged,
black power radicalism's limitations became visible.
Blacks' accession to prominence within the institutional
apparatus of urban administration did not appreciably
alter the mission or official practices of the institutions
in their charge. Putting black faces in previously all-
white places was not sufficient for those who identified
with institutional transformation along populist lines
or who otherwise rejected the status quo of race
relations management. Yet, because black power's
communitarian premises reified group identity and
could not accommodate structural differentiation
among Afro-Americans, the only critical frame on
which radicals could draw consensually was the
language of racial authenticity.

By the end of the 1960s, black power's inadequacy
as a basis for concrete political judgment had begun to
fuel radicals' self-conscious turn to creation and adoption of "ideologies"—global political narratives
encompassing alternative vision, norms, and strategic
programs—that promised to provide definite standpoints for critical judgment and platforms for political
mobilization. This development underwrote a logic of
sectarianism that embedded a cleavage between
Marxists and cultural nationalists as the pivotal tension in black oppositional politics.

Ironically, the impetus propelling the ideological
turn—the need to compensate for the inadequacies of
black power's simplistic communitarianism—was
thwarted by failure to break with the essential flaw,
the stance positing the "black community" as the
source of political legitimation and its attendant rhetoric of authenticity. Indeed, the turn to ideology may
have reinforced propensities to rely on communitarian
mystification because the flight into theoreticism
made the need to claim connections with popular
action all the more urgent. . . .

In the current situation black (and white) radicalism
has retreated ever more hermetically into the university; and the unaddressed tendency to wish fulfillment
has reached new extremes, so that oppositional politics
becomes little more than a pose livening up the march
through the tenure ranks. The context of desperation
and utter defeat enveloping activist politics outside
the academy has not only reinforced the retreat to the
campus; it has also removed practical fetters on the
compensatory imagination guiding the creation of
intentionally oppositional academic discourses. In this
context the notion of radicalism is increasingly
removed from critique and substantive action directed
toward altering entrenched patterns of subordination
and inequality mediated through public policy.

The characteristics of this dynamic are mainly crystal-
lized in the turn to a rhetoric pivoting on an idea of
"cultural politics." The discourse of cultural politics does
not differentiate between public, collective activity explicitly challenging patterns of political and socioeconomic
hierarchy and the typically surreptitious, often privatistic
practices of "everyday resistance"—the mechanisms
through which subordinates construct moments of dignity and autonomy and enhance their options within
relations of oppression without attacking them head on.
The failure to make any such distinction—or making and
then eliding it—dramatizes the fate that befalls black
radicalism's separation of abstract theorizing from concrete political action when academic hermeticism eliminates the imperative to think about identifying and
mobilizing a popular constituency. Participating in youth
fads, maintaining fraternal organizations, vesting hopes
in prayer or root doctors, and even quilt making thus
become indistinguishable from slave revolts, activism in
Reconstruction governments, the Montgomery bus boycott, grassroots campaigns for voter registration, and
labor union or welfare rights agitation as politically
meaningful forms of "resistance. . . ."[20]

Notes

1. See Frank Parker, *Black Votes Count* (Chapel
Hill: University of North Carolina Press, 1990); James
W. Button, *Blacks and Social Change*
(Princeton, N.J.: Princeton University Press, 1989); and
Chandler Davidson and Bernard Grofman, eds., *Quiet
Revolution in the South* (Princeton, N.J.: Princeton
University Press, 1994).

2. Peter Eisinger, "Black Mayors and the Politics of Racial Economic Advancement," in *Readings in Urban Politics: Past, Present and Future*, ed. Harlan Hahn and Charles Levine (New York: Longman, 1984); Eisinger, "Black Empowerment in Municipal Jobs: The Impact of Black Political Power," *American Political Science Review* 76 (June 1982): 380–92.

3. Earl Picard, "New Black Economic Development Strategy," *Telos,* Summer 1984, 53–64.

4. See Clarence N. Stone, "Social Stratification, Nondecision-Making, and the Study of Community Power," *American Politics Quarterly* 10 (July 1982): 275–302.

5. For a critique, see Adolph Reed Jr., "The 'Underclass' as Myth and Symbol: The Poverty of Discourse about Poverty," *Radical America* 24 (Winter 1991/92): 21–40; Brett Williams, "Poverty among African Americans in the Urban United States," *Human Organization* 51 (Summer 1992): 164–74; Leslie Innis and Joe R. Feagin, "The Black 'Underclass' Ideology in Race Relations Analysis," *Social Justice* 16 (Winter 1989): 13–33.

6. See Lawrence Mead, *Beyond Entitlement: The Social Obligations of Citizenship* (New York: Free Press, 1986).

7. William Julius Wilson, *The Truly Disadvantaged: The Inner City, The Underclass, and Public Policy* (Chicago: University of Chicago Press, 1987).

8. See, for example, Murray Friedman, "The New Black Intellectuals," *Commentary* 69 (June 1980): 46–52; Glenn Loury, "Who Speaks for Black Americans?" *Commentary* 83 (January 1987): 34–38.

9. See Joint Center for Political Studies, *Black Initiative and Governmental Responsibility* (Washington, D.C.: JCPS, 1987); Eugene Rivers, "On the Responsibility of Intellectuals in the Age of Crack," *Boston Review,* September/October 1992; Anthony Appiah, Eugene Rivers, Cornel West, bell hooks, Henry Louis Gates Jr., Margaret Burnham, and special expert Glenn Loury, "On the Responsibility of Intellectuals (in the Age of Crack)," *Boston Review,* January/February 1993.

10. Bayard Rustin's famous essay, "From Protest to Politics," *Commentary* 39 (February 1965): 25–31, noted at the time the challenge that the civil rights movement's successes posed for progressive black interests.

11. See Nathan Wright, *Black Power and Urban Unrest* (New York: Hawthorn, 1967).

12. See Howard Brotz, *Negro Social and Political Thought, 1850–1920* (New York: Basic Books, 1966), 1–33.

13. Roberti Kerstem and Dennis R. Judd, "Achieving Less Influence with More Democracy: The Permanent Legacy of the War on Poverty," *Social Science Quarterly* 61 (September 1980): 208–20.

14. Adolph Reed Jr., "Critique of Neo-Progressivism in Theorizing about Development Policy: A Case from Atlanta," *in The Politics of Urban Development*, ed. Clarence N. Stone and Heywood Sanders (Lawrence: University of Kansas Press, 1987).

15. See "Murder Capital: A Mayor's Call for Help," *Newsweek,* November 1, 1993; Don Terry, "A Graver Jackson's Cry; Overcome the Violence," *New York Times,* November 13, 1993; William Raspberry. "Jesse Jackson Calls on Nation's Blacks to 'Tell It' Like It Is," *Chicago Tribune,* October 11, 1993.

20. See, for example, George Lipsitz, "The Mardi Gras Indians: Carnival and Counter-Narrative in Black New Orleans," *Cultural Critique*, Fall 1988, 99–121; Elsa Barkley-Brown, "African-American Women's Quilting: A Framework for Conceptualizing and Teaching African-American Women's History," *Signs* 14 (Summer 1989): 921–29; and Michelle Wallace and Gina Dent, eds., *Black Popular Culture* (Seattle, Wash.: Bay Press, 1992).

12-3 "The Katrina Conspiracies: The Problem of Trust in Rebuilding an American City"

Arnold R. Hirsch and A. Lee Levert

Journal of Urban History

The devastation wrought by Hurricane Katrina across the North American Gulf Coast left a stunned nation groping for explanations. Few—very few—went so far as the Idaho weatherman who pointed an accusatory finger at the Japanese mafia (Yakuza) for its use of an electromagnetic generator devised by the old Soviet Union "to create and control storms." A theory that unilaterally repealed the "second law of thermodynamics," while arguing that the inundation of New Orleans was payback for the incineration of Hiroshima sixty years before, did not find a wealth of believers.[1]

There were other theories and theorists, of course, of greater but still variable credibility. Crossing the political spectrum from the wacky Left to the radical Right, people offered, exchanged, and accepted tales of perfidy and betrayal on a scale that could scarcely be imagined.

African Americans heard from Nation of Islam leader Louis Farrakhan, for example, who emerged from a meeting with New Orleans mayor C. Ray Nagin demanding an investigation into alleged links between the Bush administration and a suspected plot to sabotage the levees. If established, such links would permit Farrakhan to press charges of mass murder.

Emanating from multiple sources, allegations that the levees had been deliberately breached to flood poor black areas and spare well-to-do white ones gained wide currency. Interviews with Katrina's refugees, both on the nightly news and in authoritative documentary films, reinforced such charges with conviction and belief. Eye- and earwitnesses seemingly confirmed the presence of strange figures scurrying about the levees in the hours between Katrina's passing and the flooding

of the Lower Ninth Ward. Even more heard at least one explosion. That the "big bang," it appears, came from a runaway barge that crashed into—and destroyed—what remained of the Industrial Canal levee still failed to sway locals from their belief in sabotage. One unidentified resident stated the case plainly: "They had a bomb. They bombed that sucker."[2]

Given the certainty of conviction, motives seemed self-evident. Whites, having only recently "lost" control of the city demographically and politically, seemed poised to "take over" once more. Dutch Morial had been elected the city's first black mayor in 1978; no white candidate had won that office since.[3] Black voting majorities had also recently (1985) produced a black majority on the City Council and, at least, the hope of a more responsive government. Complicating matters, elections for all of these offices loomed on the horizon just a few months away. With the forced, near total evacuation of the city, questions arose quickly as to the size, character, and mood of the electorate that would (or could) take part in the contest. Talk of a "whitening" of the city subsequently became election fodder for both groups.[4]

The perceived motives for the opportunistic breakup of black New Orleans extended beyond the political realm as well. Suspicions in the community ran to real estate interests and developers who coveted black-occupied land. Moreover, those seeking to gentrify the city at black expense were accompanied by the persistence, many African Americans believed, of the sort [of] mindless racism that simply wished to do them harm.

The significance of such conjecture lay not in the truth of the allegations but in their plausibility and

Source: Arnold R. Hirsch and A. Lee Levert, "The Katrina Conspiracies: The Problem of Trust in Rebuilding an American City," *Journal of Urban History*, vol. 35, no. 2, January 2009, pp. 207–19. Reprinted with permission from SAGE Publications, Inc.

acceptance, no matter how outlandish. It was also much more than a matter of laying blame or seeking "causes" for the magnitude of Katrina's horror. Whether fantasy or common sense, the conclusions drawn regarding the course of destruction that accompanied the storm were both rooted in history and determinative of the direction that recovery and reform would take. More than that, they compromised the chances for success as well. The utter lack of trust, and the inability to deal in good faith across racial lines, would short-circuit those attempts at reconstruction that challenged racial verities. Old patterns of thought and behavior—on the part of both blacks and whites—were simply inadequate to address the unprecedented situation in the Crescent City, and yet they preempted any new departures.

The opportunity to start over provides a chance to do better. What would the new New Orleans be like? Any attempt to answer that question requires, first of all, an appreciation for the enormity and complexity of the problems involved. Eighty percent of the city of New Orleans was under water after Lake Pontchartrain emptied into it, nearly 2,000 people had died (as best we can tell today), and its political, civic, and economic structures had virtually disappeared.[5] It had reverted almost to a state of nature—or at least as close to one as we are ever likely to see. Given the city's dysfunctional economic and political structures, its poverty and dearth of resources, it is hard to imagine any people asked to do more with less.

One need only make the comparison to another era of urban revitalization to see that the unprecedented scale and nature of the Katrina catastrophe is not well understood. The nation's flirtation with urban renewal in the 1950s and 1960s witnessed the development of projects and plans that were years in the making. Renewal cut a large swath through densely settled urban land, cost millions of dollars, called for the displacement and resettlement of thousands, and finally, had to confront the race issue in virtually every neighborhood it touched.[6]

In contrast, Katrina almost literally wiped the entire city of New Orleans off the map. There was no targeted selection of needy neighborhoods in New Orleans; there was, instead, the submersion of 80 percent of the city for a period of several weeks. The job facing post-Katrina New Orleanians did not involve

rehabilitation or renovation as much as it demanded a total reconstruction. The city's weak-kneed economy simply disappeared. Its politics (ineffectual, corrupt, and racially polarized) served the city as a cement life jacket, permitting not even a gulp of fresh air before submerging it in a toxic brew of problems for which it offered few solutions and less hope.[7]

Where urban renewal tried to build upon strengths and expand healthy areas, the recovery of post-Katrina New Orleans involved repopulating and rebuilding virtually the entire city. Even those neighborhoods that escaped relatively unscathed had the lives and daily routines of their residents deeply impacted. The physical resurrection of the Crescent City thus also had to be far more than a bricks-and-mortar program. Not only did the social revivification of the city involve reuniting families over a period of weeks, months, and yes, now years, but those who returned relatively quickly had to relearn the urban landscape. Where could you get a meal? Groceries? Gas for your car? How to run errands or begin to clean up with businesses open only a couple of hours a day, if at all (the lack of help and accessibility crippled even those eagerly trying to reopen their doors)? Urban renewal was never like this. And there were no ready-made plans that encompassed the rebuilding of an entire city, with earmarked resources, on an accelerated timetable.

Even after considering all of that, there was still the problem of race. One need only contemplate the post–World War II difficulties that ate at inner-city neighborhoods from blockbusting in Baltimore, to the selection of public-housing sites in Chicago, to the dearth of decent housing that pinched middle-class blacks everywhere, in order to see that such considerations overwhelmed the laser-like, focused programs that involved only the most carefully selected projects during the era of renewal.[8]

And the results? Even given the time, resources (political and economic), and seeming manageability of the problems facing it, urban renewal is neither regarded highly nor remembered fondly. Slums and so-called blight not only persisted but grew faster than they could be eradicated by any clearance or prevention program. Periodic, almost cyclical discussions of the various "pathologies" of the ghetto, represented by such concepts as the "culture of poverty" in the 1960s and the "underclass" of the 1980s and 1990s, reinforced conventional wisdom and left an idiosyncratic white perspective to direct ameliorative efforts.[9] Such developments did little but leave the intellectual cupboard bare of any potentially fresh approach to the problem. And that would explain, at least in part, the persistence and "invisibility" of the minority poor and their "rediscovery" in the reports emanating from the Louisiana Superdome and Convention Center.

Moreover, in the age of renewal, the announcement of a development sent shock waves rippling through the affected neighborhood. The displacement and relocation of the poorest African Americans into adjacent communities repeatedly triggered white resistance in myriad forms and contested virtually every effort to develop black living space, whether public or private.[10] The refusal to tolerate unfettered black mobility led each project to seek its own accommodation to local conditions. To address the problem today, it is understood that the effects of displacement on a New Orleans–Katrina scale could not be handled piecemeal, on a neighborhood-by-neighborhood basis. It would be necessary to tackle the whole thing at once. Who in this room would care to define and proclaim the racial homelands in our major cities? It is a problem that cannot even be faced, let alone resolved.

But it must still be said that Katrina represented opportunity as well as tragedy. That opportunity, however, had to be recognized before it could be seized—a prospect made all the more difficult by the city's unspeakable trauma. Familiar, comfortable patterns of thought and behavior would need to be jettisoned in favor of the untried and unknown. If such was not too much to ask, it certainly proved too much to expect.

The easy, uncritical bruiting about of rumors regarding the deliberate, malevolent destruction of the Industrial Canal levee testified to the prepositioning of those obstacles. Whites, of course, had their own cherished tales. They included accounts of rape, murder, child molestation, sniping, and looting. Lamentably, many such reports proved all too true, but inflammatory exaggerations and outright fabrications aggravated the situation.

Filmmaker Spike Lee devoted considerable attention to the "bombing" allegations emanating from the Ninth Ward by allowing local residents to voice their suspicions with little contradiction in his documentary *When the Levee Broke*. Uptown whites, particularly those who were fortunate enough to have laid claim to the high ground that edged the Mississippi River's banks above the French Quarter (the "sliver on the river" according to some, the "isle of denial" to others) thought it scandalous that anyone could think them capable of such crimes and, worse, prevent them from offering a defense. They could not see, however, that it was Lee's intention neither to make patently false accusations nor to defend whites against them. He was exposing a pattern of belief that was as real as the hurricane itself and one that could be ignored only at its own peril.

There were good reasons, moreover, for African Americans in New Orleans to expect the worst even as they hoped for better. First, they had history as a teacher. Not only had the political and economic elites of New Orleans coldly planned the intentional demolition of levees to flood neighboring parishes to save themselves, but they had actually already done so once before. Journalist John Barry recalled in *Rising Tide* (his detailed account of the great 1927 flood) that the U.S. Army Corps of Engineers had earlier advised the city's financial community to "blow a hole in the levee" should the river ever "threaten" the city. Ultimately, New Orleans's civic leadership took ten days and thirty-nine tons of explosives to punch a hole in the levee system in what later officials called an unnecessary attempt to relieve pressure on the city. When, in 1965, Hurricane Betsy ravaged the same area, including the black-occupied Lower Ninth Ward, the previously demonstrated willingness to flood out white residents in St. Bernard and Plaquemines parishes gave rise to rumors identical to those that swept the neighborhood in Katrina's wake forty years later. New Orleans's use of "bombs" to divert flooding may have been questionable, but it was hardly unknown. Such allegations were thus rooted in fact, renewed over the years, and reinforced by contemporary divisions. It did not take much to make such tales appear real.[11]

Such experiences raised new difficulties both during and after the crisis brought on by Katrina. The horrific conditions and televised human drama evident in the Louisiana Superdome and the city's convention center highlighted the callousness of government at every level and shocked most of the United States into recognizing the seemingly perpetually joined problems of poverty and race once more. Still, it apparently took nearly a week for the depth and scope of the tragedy to penetrate the Republican President's consciousness, and the Governor of Louisiana, Democrat Kathleen Blanco, barely made her presence felt beyond a Mayor Richard J. Daley-style warning . . . that the late-arriving National Guard would "shoot-to-kill."[12] New Orleans' black Democratic mayor, C. Ray Nagin, stepped into the yawning leadership vacuum and promptly disappeared after expressing hope for the "cavalry's" timely arrival.[13] Thus, there was an utter failure of leadership regardless of partisan affiliation, color, gender, or class.

It would be wrong to assume, however, that adversarial posturing represented the full extent of black/white interactions. Indeed, at the height of the crisis, to cite just a single example, the so-called Cajun Navy emerged from the swamps of south Louisiana with their own boats and equipment and, at great personal risk, engaged in systematic rescue efforts, plucking New Orleanians off the roofs of their flooded homes and out of the toxic waters that filled the city. A volunteer citizens' armada, they jumped in where the Federal Emergency Management Agency and other authorities feared to tread. The Cajun Navy was ultimately credited with rescuing some 4,000 endangered residents in eastern New Orleans.[14]

Conversely, the unquestionably heroic actions of uncounted African Americans also kept Katrina's death toll far below what it might have otherwise been. Proportionately, the greatest number of casualties and suffering could be found among the elderly, sick, and disabled who were unable to flee. Here, despite a highly publicized cases [sic] of a doctor and two nurses who were charged (the charges were later dropped) with murder and of another in which a pair of nursing-home operators were tried (and acquitted) for deserting their wards at the height of the crisis (several dozen of the home's residents drowned), there is also evidence of unusual selflessness in the service of (other-race) others. The anecdotal evidence is overwhelming that the large number of nurses, personal and professional, and other such service personnel employed in the city refused to leave their wards, often staying with and saving patients at the cost of being cut off from their own families.[15]

But those wisps of empathy and threads of a common humanity, though essential to the reknitting of New Orleans's society, remained subordinate to a dominant, reflexive fear and hostility. It is important to realize that in the first hours and days after the levees crumbled, the reactions of both whites and blacks were reflexive and, hence, especially revelatory. Just as surely as a knee will jerk upward when properly struck, New Orleans twitched violently along preconditioned lines in Katrina's wake. The earliest responses exposed fundamental assumptions and perceptions normally hidden from view—and those that would be buried again beneath the verbiage of later, more deliberate responses. Furthermore, despite the encouraging interracial initiatives noted above, the unmistakable intensity of an in-group, "we-versus-they" perspective seemed to deepen the closer [that one] stood in the path of the hurricane's eye.

Humanitarian needs, however, had to be immediately addressed by state and local authorities. If Governor Blanco and Mayor Nagin offered little help, a Republican congressman from Baton Rouge, Richard Baker, literally could not contain himself. Exuding the rank opportunism afforded by the moment, Baker plumbed new depths of cynicism with a statement wholly inappropriate in tone and substance. "We finally cleaned up public housing in New Orleans," he told the Wall Street Journal. "We couldn't do it, but God did."[16]

Even more blunt were the locally generated sentiments borne of the chaos, fear, and disorder that seemed to be everywhere. One white professional who could observe both looters and those he believed to be such from his uptown porch (observers often distinguished looters from those foraging for food, clothing, and medical necessities simply by the color of their skin) sat holding a small arsenal as he was interviewed. When asked about the source of New Orleans's problems, he volunteered, "Two blocks away from here people are living hand to mouth. . . . I don't know of another city where, if you're in a two-million-dollar house, you're not sure that everything around you for two miles is a two-million-dollar house."[17] Familiarity, under these conditions, bred not just contempt but a good deal of suspicion and fear as well.

It is impossible, in the limited allotments of time and space permitted here, to catalog the full range of difficulties revived and aggravated by the intersection of the hurricane's destructive force with New Orleans's racial history. But it is possible to expose and, at least, begin to explore one fundamental aspect of the city's race relations: who would repopulate the city, and how would that be done? As clearly implied by Congressman Baker and the white homeowner above, housing and the allocation of urban space would be two key issues receiving the closest scrutiny. Having endured a forced evacuation, the repopulation of New Orleans would necessarily be a conscious rather than a haphazard process. There was also something else. It would also be, of necessity, a political process. The quantity, cost, quality, and location of public housing; the desire to shrink the vulnerable city's "footprint"; the amount of and ease with which Louisiana residents could obtain state aid for their return home (Louisiana residents filing applications for such assistance remained scattered among some forty-five states more than two years after Katrina's landfall); and the selection of neighborhoods to be favored by the city's planning resources represented only a handful of the uncounted considerations that linked housing and race in post-Katrina New Orleans.

Finally, of course, there was the question of politics itself. The battles over housing, development, and access to aid and the land were viewed, by both blacks and whites, as a power struggle of signal importance. The seemingly "Pavlovian" statements made and actions taken during the immediate crisis and the cooler, more calculated ones later (sometimes masquerading as policy) with regard to housing and mobility issues revealed the now carefully hidden assumptions that not only cast a long shadow over any reconstruction proposal but also reified the racial divisions and interests that remained the greatest threat to the emergence of a new city.

A full understanding of these issues in New Orleans must come to grips with their multifaceted character. First, for African Americans, freedom of movement, the right to go where one pleases, is both evidence and symbolic of freedom itself. Although circumstances were quite different in the post-Katrina period compared with that following emancipation, the former slaves' ability to locate and relocate their families, flee to safety, travel in groups, and otherwise improve their lot, virtually defined freedom for them even as whites viewed such matters as security issues for themselves. Whether uprooted by war or natural disaster, the sheer movement of black people, their gathering in concentrated settlements, their encroachment on "white" territory, or their freedom simply to roam

about the countryside had, therefore, never gone uncontested or unregulated.[18] A subsequent pattern of instinctive, seemingly almost intuitive reactions on the part of local whites tended to isolate and confine blacks within the city rather than to whisk them to safety and extend humanitarian assistance. They also generated violent, or near violent, confrontations that fueled differing "racial" perceptions of Katrina's impact and significance.

The best known of these incidents involves the attempt of perhaps several hundred people (overwhelmingly black, though not exclusively so) to leave the rapidly deteriorating conditions around the Louisiana Superdome and to cross the Crescent City Connection (the bridge linking the city's east and west banks) on foot on September 1, 2005. A small contingent emerged from the town of Gretna, in Jefferson Parish, at the opposite end of the bridge, to cut them off. Gretna's defenders, led by a pair of uniformed Sheriff's deputies, greeted Katrina's neediest refugees with a shotgun blast over their heads and the vow that "there would be no Superdomes" in their city.[19]

Forced to back off the bridge at gunpoint, these storm victims still fared better than some of those Katrina refugees who tried to flee across the Industrial Canal's Danziger bridge to the east. There, on September 5, 2005, police rushed to the scene where snipers, it was erroneously reported, had wounded an officer. They opened fire on an unarmed group crossing the span, killing two and injuring four others. Governor Blanco went further, placing National Guard troops on other bridges and possible points where pedestrians might exit the city. Suburban Jefferson Parish similarly denied access to residents from neighboring Orleans Parish by setting up roadblocks. (This was a recurring practice. New Orleans Mayor Sidney Barthelemy had to endure Jefferson Parish Sheriff Harry Lee's blockage of streets crossing parish lines early in his 1986–1994 administration.)[20]

The quick resort to deadly violence in the face of rumored racial disorders made the Danziger incident reminiscent, perhaps, of the slave insurrection panics that erupted throughout the South in 1835 and in 1856 to 1857. At the least, it is not much of a stretch to hear in the contemporary complaints of local officials echoes of their postemancipation predecessors. Indeed, historian Leon Litwack noted that in the nineteenth century, municipal authorities tended to regard any influx of black migrants as an "inundation" of "vagrants, thieves, and indigents," who threatened to "place an intolerable burden on taxpayers and charitable services."[21] Those promising "no Superdomes" certainly understood those arguments.

Once the immediate crisis had passed, authorities and citizens alike pondered an uncertain future. Congressman Baker's opportunistic suggestion to let God handle public housing at least had the virtue of raising the key question in the context of public policy. Where are poor people to live? Not only did this issue have to be explicitly addressed, but it was clear that the outcome, whatever it might be, would result from conscious political discussion and choice.

On the local level, one particularly revealing effort tried desperately to dress up nineteenth-century thought in twenty-first-century science. St. Bernard Parish, perhaps more rural than suburban, and nearly all white, bumped up against the city's Ninth Ward on its southeastern border. It enjoyed a serious growth spurt in the late 1960s, spurred on by the twin incentives of court-ordered school desegregation in the city and the insurance settlements that were converted into down payments on new homes following Hurricane Betsy in 1965. Virtually leveled by Katrina forty years later, St. Bernard sought to control its future development by passing an ordinance that prohibited the owners of single-family homes that had not been rented out before the hurricane from renting to anyone who was not a blood relative. Ostensibly intended to "promote home ownership" and preserve the parish's "quality of life," the ordinance aimed, its proponents argued, at preventing monied interests from buying up large tracts of land and dumping cheap rental units on the market.[22]

Most observers failed to buy the cover story. The Greater New Orleans Fair Housing Center charged that it was an effort to "perpetuate segregation" and filed suit in U.S. District Court. Others simply pointed to the region's tangled racial history and noted, with almost palpable discomfort and certainly with cause, that enforcement would involve more than simple observation. One critic noted the need for DNA tests "on everyone who wants to rent a house."[23] Given such thin disguises and blunt actions, it is not surprising that New Orleans's African Americans would

question either the motives or the judgment of those offering such a "welcome home." And reasonable people who could not bring themselves to find a cosmic relationship between the middle passage and the path taken by many hurricanes across the Atlantic to punish the United States, or to see the similarities between the hulls of slave ships and the configuration of the Louisiana Superdome, may be forgiven for harboring some suspicions.[24]

Public housing was perhaps the policy area that best illustrated the damage done by the high degree of mutual distrust that sprang from racial polarization and adversarial politics. Certainly, Congressman Baker's public comments provided black New Orleanians cause for concern. Before Katrina, New Orleans was a city of just under 500,000 that had roughly 7,100 public-housing units, of which some 5,600 were occupied. Federal and local authorities were, in fact, already deep into discussions concerning the demolition of the city's largest remaining projects and their replacement by new mixed-income developments.

The evacuation, however, had emptied the projects, and initially, the federal government and the Housing Authority of New Orleans (HANO)—the former had taken control of the latter in 2002—did not permit the tenants to return. That a significant number of the apartments could have been repaired thus raised suspicions in the minds of the minority poor as to whether they would be welcomed back at all. Indeed, to the extent that Katrina lent any urgency at all to the long-standing housing crisis for the poor in the Crescent City, it was to speed ongoing negotiations on demolition not to press already existing, serviceable, affordable, and subsidized units into use. The result was that more than a year after Katrina cut her path of destruction across the Gulf Coast, only 1,600 HANO families had returned to the city, and another 400 units stood ready to be occupied. But HANO had also, by that time, contracted for the demolition of some 4,500 apartments in four remaining large projects.[25]

Government officials had determined, quite rightly, that it needed to surrender the policy of concentrating the poor in massive, segregated, and decaying projects in favor of more mixed developments. But there was a certain comfort level despite the poverty, crime, and other dangers found there. The close ties nurtured by familial and social networks often supplied those who called it "home" for generations what little help they could count on. The fear and insecurity of living on the margins outside of the projects provided the governing context.

Dubious tenants, therefore, responded with lawsuits, appeals, and Attorney William Quigley's argument that the government's permanent displacement of thousands represented an assault on the city's culture and history. While survival itself under such hostile conditions may well be celebrated, it was an essentially negative stance that contemplated only the prevention of the loss of existing housing. It was an argument that held no vision of a better future and represented an opportunity lost. Forced to play defense against virtually every aggressive initiative emanating from government or the private sector, well-meaning advocates for the poor had precious little to advocate.[26]

It is now nearly two and a half years into the post-Katrina era. Those who had been least affected are staggering toward a modest recovery. Here and there (especially if "there" is uptown or involves the centers of the tourist trade), there are some signs of revival and even new life. But vast, desolate stretches of an abandoned city remain; there are no "ruins" as such, only an emptiness where busy neighborhoods once stirred—and the darkness at night. Quality of life and, especially, safety issues are troublesome.

The federal government initially promised to provide "whatever it takes" to restore New Orleans. It has come up short. There are more expressions of disappointment and anger than surprise with regard to the president's lack of involvement; but the state and city were also the victims of bad timing and the ugly politics of the age. The two Louisiana congressional districts hit hardest by Katrina were the first and second districts—precisely those that covered most of metropolitan New Orleans. Republican Bob Livingston represented the first district and stood poised to become Speaker of the House in 1998 when the revelation of past personal improprieties forced his resignation. Democrat William Jefferson held the second district seat, and while he remains in Congress, Katrina's aftermath found him under investigation

and politically hobbled by the discovery of $90,000 in cash in his freezer. He has since been indicted on a variety of charges, including the solicitation of bribes. One can only imagine the difference in assistance that would have been forthcoming if these rising stars had tended to the district's business rather than their own. Whether taking the high road of bipartisanship or pursuing the narrow path of rigid party rule, New Orleans's delegation would have been well positioned to press its claims.

There was little relief to be had, moreover, from electoral politics on the local level. The pace of reconstruction remains glacially slow, and the trends revealed by two post-Katrina elections are not promising. In the spring of 2006, following an unstructured, twenty-three-candidate, nonpartisan, open primary, the city held its first post-Katrina mayoral election. In pitting African American incumbent C. Ray Nagin against the state's white Lieutenant Governor, Mitch Landrieu, New Orleans demonstrated how identity politics could be reduced to pure tactics, an empty vessel to be filled by the candidate du jour and the needs of the moment.

In 2002, Nagin won office running as a surrogate "white" candidate, a business executive who stood on a typical "good-government" platform.[27] He enjoyed solid backing from white civic and social elites and used their endorsements and funds to defeat the "black" candidate, police chief Richard Pennington. Nagin's white support (especially his largest donors) disappeared with Katrina's floodwaters, however, and following the April 2006 primary, he alone survived as the African American community's last, best hope against yet another feared "white takeover."

Nagin proved only too willing and able to shed the image of the reform-minded, elite-supported corporate executive. With the multicrisis brought on by Katrina providing the context, his campaign's use of the "race card" reflected the shrewd calculation of a tactician, not the commitment of an ideologue. His apparent determination (once he was dumped by big-money white contributors) was simply that racial polarization was the only way to keep his job. It was not a difficult calculation. He won in 2002 by collecting 90 percent of the white vote; he would attract but 6 percent in his post-Katrina reelection. This was the context for his Martin Luther King Jr. Day speech in which he tweaked white sensibilities and energized black troops with his claim that New Orleans was, and would remain, a "Chocolate City."

His capitulation to the politics of division, fear, and scarcity did not, however, make him a popular figure in the black community, nor did it provide him with an agenda. African Americans bore the brunt of his failures during the Katrina crisis itself, and his black opposition in the 2006 primary excoriated him. But his main black challenger, Pentacostal preacher Tom Watson, endorsed him in the general election after branding him a murderer responsible for the deaths of 1,200 storm victims in the primary. It was testimony not only to the depth and power of race as an issue but also to its ability to trump accountability. It also gave him enough votes to beat Mitch Landrieu.

For their part, Landrieu and most whites seemed content with the politics of displacement. Whether acting out of sheer opportunism, fear, or mistaken calculation, Landrieu's mayoral campaign relied more on the perceived iconic status of the candidate's father, Moon Landrieu, as a civil rights mayor to attract black votes than its own ability to make self-interested appeals. Clearly, there were elements in the black community that had been alienated from the current administration and could be wooed; even among many of those who eventually came around to vote for Nagin, there was no close personal connection. And after Nagin's victory, it quickly became apparent how lightly those racial ties bound him. He continued to take counsel from many of the same white developers, businessmen, and civic elites as before. Otherwise, he has kept a low profile, fighting few battles for "the race" even as events heat up in the street. As this is being written, protestors are placing themselves between bulldozers and those public-housing units facing imminent court-ordered demolition.[28] The mayor is nowhere to be found. And for those watching the buildings coming down, there are few convincing, credible voices contradicting the notion that it is all part of a grand design to prevent their families and friends from coming home.

Just as clearly, the liberal Landrieu feared losing white voters by appearing too eager in his pursuit of black ones. Ultimately, he looked at the city's post-Katrina demographics and tried to have it both ways. Landrieu carried nearly one in four black primary voters on the strength of his own liberal-moderate record, his father's role in advancing the early civil rights revolution, and the hurricane-induced reduction in black population, registration, and turnout. In the end, Landrieu and Nagin found themselves with few programmatic differences and applying the same campaign logic, if not tactics. Solidifying their own racial bases, they would rely on unity and turnout to produce a victory. Surely, such a course doomed any white candidate to defeat before Katrina, but now, white New Orleans believed a door had been opened. Uncertainty governed estimates of population size, composition, location, and commitment; it also governed the unusual voting procedures adopted under post-Katrina circumstances producing still more guesswork and hope for an unexpected victory. The difference came in means. Nagin had to heighten race consciousness and issues, while Landrieu preferred to mute them. Indeed, in the end, the elder Landrieu's civil rights record may have cost as many embittered white votes as it won grateful black ones.

Nagin eked out a narrow victory, and black New Orleans had its mayor. They enjoyed something less than a political honeymoon; it was more like a one-night stand. And just a month ago, in November 2007, the city held its first post-Katrina election for the City Council and a host of other local offices. Without a single black member until one was appointed to fill a vacancy in 1973, the seven-member council became majority black in 1985. It remained so until the first post-Katrina body was sworn in. Sporting a dominant 5–2 majority of women to men, it is also tilted in favor of whites by a 4–3 margin. Similarly, black district representatives who held seats in the state house and senate found themselves beaten by white challengers.[29]

One might wish the city's political forces were coherent and efficient enough to produce an intended result with some purpose behind it. But these results seem to fall in the realm of visceral reactions, the application of long-nursed grudges, and the utter inability of leadership to overcome the burden of the past even as unprecedented circumstances demanded it.[30] But, then, maybe that Idaho weatherman was onto something.

Notes

1. "Cold-War Device Used to Cause Katrina?," *USA Today*, September 20, 2005.

2. *When the Levees Broke: A Requiem in Four Acts*, directed by Spike Lee (Home Box Office, 2006).

3. Arnold R. Hirsch, "Simply a Matter of Black and White: The Transformation of Race and Politics in Twentieth-century New Orleans," in Arnold R. Hirsch and Joseph Logsdon, eds., *Creole New Orleans: Race and Americanization* (Baton Rouge, LA, 1992), chap. 6; Arnold R. Hirsch, "Race and Politics in Modern New Orleans: The Mayoralty of Dutch Morial," *Amerikastudien/American Studies* 35 (1990): 461–85.

4. "Whites Take a Majority on New Orleans' Council," *New York Times*, November 19, 2007.

5. "Blanco Tours New Orleans," *Times-Picayune*, September 7, 2005; "FEMA Denied State's Request for Rescue Rafts as Katrina Approached," *Times-Picayune*, January 30, 2006.

6. For background on urban renewal, see Mark Gelfand, *A Nation of Cities* (New York, 1975); John Mollenkopf, *The Contested City* (Princeton, NJ, 1983); Jon Teaford, *The Rough Road to Renaissance: Urban Revitalization in America, 1940–1985* (Baltimore, 1990); Robert Caro, *Robert Moses and the Fall of New York* (New York, 1974); Scott Greer, *Urban Renewal and American Cities* (Indianapolis, IN, 1964); and James Q. Wilson, ed., *Urban Renewal: The Record and the Controversy* (Cambridge, MA, 1966). Individual case studies abound, and a provocative review essay that covers recent housing policy historiography is D. Bradford Hunt, "Rethinking the Retrenchment Narrative in U.S. Housing Policy History," *Journal of Urban History* 32 (September 2006): 937–50.

7. For general histories of Hurricane Katrina and its aftermath, see Douglas Brinkley, *The Great Deluge: Hurricane Katrina, New Orleans, and the Mississippi Gulf Coast* (New York, 2006); Michael Eric Dyson, *Come Hell or High Water: Hurricane Katrina and the Color of Disaster* (Cambridge, MA, 2006); Ivor van Heerden and Mike Bryan, *The Storm: What Went Wrong and Why During Hurricane Katrina—The Inside Story from One Louisiana Scientist* (New York, 2007); and Center for Public Integrity Investigation, *City Adrift: New Orleans Before and After Katrina* (Baton Rouge, LA, 2007); See also Jed Horne, *Breach of Faith: Hurricane Katrina and the Near Death of a Great American City* (New York, 2006); Chester Hartman and Gregory D. Squires, eds., *There Is No Such Thing as a Natural Disaster: Race, Class and Hurricane Katrina* (New York, 2006); Sally Forman, *Eye of the Storm: Inside City Hall During Katrina* (Bloomington, IN, 2007); and Chris Rose, *One Dead in Attic* (New Orleans, 2005).

8. Edward Orser, *Blockbusting in Baltimore: The Edmondson Village Story* (Lexington, KY, 1994); Arnold R. Hirsch, *Making the Second Ghetto: Race and Housing in Chicago, 1940–1960* (Chicago, 1998); Mary Pattillo, *Black on the Block: The Politics of Race and Class in the City* (Chicago, 2007).

9. Michael B. Katz, ed., *The "Underclass" Debate* (Princeton, NJ, 1993); Oscar Lewis, "The Culture of Poverty," in G. Gmelch and W. Zenner, eds., *Urban Life: Readings in the Anthropology of the City* (Long Grove, IL, 1996); Nicholas Lemann, *The Promised Land: The Great Black Migration and How It Changed America* (New York, 1991).

10. Stephen Grant Meyer, *As Long as They Don't Move Next Door: Segregation and Racial Conflict in American Neighborhoods* (Lanham, MD, 2000); Hirsch, *Making the Second Ghetto*; Orser, *Blockbusting in Baltimore*; Kenneth D. Durr, *Behind the Backlash: White Working Class Politics in Baltimore, 1940–1980* (Chapel Hill, NC, 2003).

11. John M. Barry, *Rising Tide: The Great Mississippi Flood of 1927 and How It Changed America* (New York, 1997), 222, 257, 339.

12. "Blanco Demands Apology," *Times-Picayune*, September 1, 2005; "Troops Told 'Shoot to Kill' in New Orleans," *ABC News Online*, September 2, 2005.

13. "Mayor Nagin Speaks Out," *Times-Picayune*, September 10, 2005.

14. Brinkley, *Great Deluge*, 381.

15. A grand jury refused to indict Dr. Anna Pou on charges that she murdered nine of her patients in the days after Hurricane Katrina. Pou still faces four civil suits in connection with the deaths. "Grand Jury Refuses to Indict Anna Pou," *Times-Picayune*, July 25, 2007. Sal and Mabel Mangano also were "found innocent of negligent homicide in the drowning deaths of 25 elderly residents in their St. Bernard Parish nursing home during Hurricane Katrina." "Manganos Not Guilty in St. Rita's Nursing Home Case," *Times-Picayune*, September 7, 2007. For anecdotal evidence of the assistance extended across racial lines, see Eileen Guillory, "Facing the Storm: An Oral History of Elderly Survivors of Katrina" (paper presented at the Fifteenth International Oral

History Association Conference, Guadalajara, Mexico, September 23–26, 2008).

16. "Some GOP Legislators Hit Jarring Notes in Addressing Katrina," *Washington Post*, September 10, 2005.

17. Dan Baum, "Porch Duty: Report from Carrollton," *The New Yorker*, September 12, 2005.

18. Leon F. Litwack, *Been in the Storm So Long: The Aftermath of Slavery* (New York, 1979), 296–326.

19. Brinkley, *Great Deluge*, 469.

20. Lyle Kenneth Perkins, "Failing the Race: The Historical Assessment of New Orleans Mayor Sidney Barthelemy, 1986–1984" (MA thesis, Louisiana State University, 2002), 22–23.

21. Litwack, *Been in the Storm So Long*, 314.

22. "St. Bernard Sued over Rent Limit; Group Says New Law Upholds Segregation," *Times-Picayune*, October 4, 2006.

23. Ibid.

24. Black activist Daniel Buford lectures that "hurricanes follow the path of the slave ships." "Hurricanes Follow Path of Slave Ships," *Louisiana Weekly*, September 26, 2005. Jesse Jackson, upon seeing the Convention Center where thousands had been stranded for days after the storm, said, "This looks like the hull of a slave ship." "Katrina's Racial Storm," *Chicago Tribune*, September 8, 2005. On February 28, 2008, a federal judge ordered St. Bernard Parish to pay $32,500 in damages to the New Orleans Fair Housing Action Center and a local landowner who brought suit and challenged the September 2006 ordinance in court. Parish officials were not compelled to admit any "wrongdoing" and claimed "victory" on that basis. See "Judge OKs Accord in Housing Bias Suit," *Times-Picayune*, February 29, 2008.

25. "Far from Full: Lost in the Debate about the Demolition of N.O. Housing Developments Is One Fact: There Are Hundreds of Units Available Right Now," *Times-Picayune*, December 16, 2007.

26. "HANO Gets OK to Raise 4500 Units," *Times-Picayune*, September 22, 2007; "HANO Balks at Tearing Down Lafitte," *Times-Picayune*, December 11, 2007.

27. For a more detailed account of the 2006 mayoral election, see Arnold R. Hirsch, "Fade to Black: Hurricane Katrina and the Disappearance of Creole New Orleans," *Journal of American History* 34, no. 3 (December 2007): 752–61.

28. "Judge Puts Demolitions in Hands of Council," *Times-Picayune*, December 15, 2007.

29. "Election Results Reflect Racial Shift," *Times-Picayune*, November 19, 2007.

30. One straw in a cross-cutting political wind was the recent 7–0 vote of the City Council to demolish those contested public-housing units. Defying expectations that they would be racially divided, the Council's unity held forth the promise of a different future—if they could deliver not only on the demolition but also the subsequent provision of more and better affordable housing.

Conclusion

Public Policy Applications: Policing Strategies

Policy Then

Elections matter. Who controls city hall may have far-reaching consequences for people of color, even for relatively mundane matters such as routine service provision. In most cities, white residents may be able to count on regular trash pickup, street maintenance, and fire protection. But in some cities led by white mayors, there has been an ignominious history of municipal governments engaging in discriminatory behavior in the delivery of basic services. To give just one example, residents of some black neighborhoods have justifiably complained about the pattern of their streets being the last to be plowed after a major snowstorm. Alternatively, white-led administrations have sometimes devoted *excessive* attention to minority neighborhoods; overzealous law enforcement, for instance, has contributed to soaring incarceration rates for young black and Latino males, with devastating consequences for those individuals, their families, and their communities.

In New York City during the mid-1990s, Mayor Rudolph Giuliani responded to broad anxiety about a long-term escalation in violent crime by implementing innovative policing strategies. Influenced by the so-called broken windows theory of crime, which posited that an environment characterized by disorder breeds illicit activity, Giuliani and his police commissioner, William Bratton, directed police officers to crack down on those found to be committing minor crimes and misdemeanors. The assumption was that a reduction in even low-level offenses like loitering, public drinking, graffiti writing, panhandling, and subway turnstile jumping would lead to a more orderly atmosphere, make people feel safer, encourage more people to spend time outside, and thus deter more serious crime. The Giuliani administration also began to use new technologies like CompStat, a computer-based, crime-tracking program, to identify places where crime was spiking and then deploy additional law enforcement resources to those "hot spots." The new policing strategies seemed to work. New York City's crime rate soon began to decline at a startling rate, a trend that continued through the remainder of Giuliani's tenure in office and beyond.

One drawback of the Giuliani-Bratton approach to crime fighting, however, was that both quality of life policing and the reliance on CompStat led to a concentration of law enforcement activity in minority neighborhoods and a surge in reports of police harassment and abuse. Allegations of civil rights violations spiraled upward. As more and more young blacks and Latinos were arrested, prosecuted, and imprisoned, often for petty offenses, tensions between police and minority communities mounted.

Policy Now

Rudy Giuliani's successor as mayor of New York, Michael Bloomberg, relaxed the previous administration's emphasis on quality of life policing while continuing to rely heavily on computer-based technologies to target law enforcement efforts. Under pressure to preserve Giuliani's impressive progress in driving down violent crime, the Bloomberg administration significantly increased the use of another policing strategy that soon sparked considerable controversy. "Stop and frisk" is a procedure that allows a police officer to stop a person who is reasonably suspected of criminal activity, question that person, and pat down the person's outer clothing to determine whether he or she is carrying a concealed weapon or other contraband.

Bloomberg and his police commissioner, Ray Kelly, insisted that stop and frisk was an essential tool in their arsenal for removing thousands of guns from the streets and further reducing crime rates to historic lows. Critics charged that in practice police officers often employed stop and frisk indiscriminately, without any reasonable basis for believing that a crime had been or was about to be committed. Instead, they engaged in racial profiling when determining

Figure 12.1   Title Page of Complaint in *Floyd v. The City of New York* (2013)

UNITED STATES DISTRICT COURT
SOUTHERN DISTRICT OF NEW YORK

DAVID FLOYD and LALIT CLARKSON;   08 Civ. 01034 (SAS)

                    Plaintiffs,   COMPLAINT
                                         DEMAND FOR JURY TRIAL
        -against-

THE CITY OF NEW YORK; NEW YORK
CITY POLICE COMMISSIONER RAYMOND
KELLY, in his individual and official capacity;
MAYOR MICHAEL BLOOMBERG, in his
individual and official capacity; NEW YORK
CITY POLICE OFFICER RODRIGUEZ, in his
individual capacity; NEW YORK CITY
POLICE OFFICER GOODMAN, in his
individual capacity; NEW YORK CITY
POLICE OFFICER JANE DOE, in her
individual capacity; and NEW YORK CITY
POLICE OFFICERS, JOHN DOES ##1 and
2, in their individual capacities;

                    Defendants.

                PRELIMINARY STATEMENT

    1.   This is a civil rights action brought by Plaintiffs David Floyd and Lalit Clarkson to

seek relief for Defendants' violation of their rights, privileges, and immunities secured by the Civil

Rights Act of 1871, 42 U.S.C. § 1983, the Fourth and Fourteenth Amendments to the United States

Constitution, Title VI of the Civil Rights Act of 1964, 42 U.S.C. § 2000(d), *et seq.* ("Title VI"), and

the Constitution and laws of the State of New York.

    2.   The Defendants in this action, the City of New York ("City"), New York City Police

Commissioner Raymond Kelly ("Kelly"), the Mayor of the City of New York, Michael Bloomberg

("Bloomberg") and New York City Police Officers Rodriguez, Goodman, Jane Doe and John Does

Source: The Center for Constitutional Rights.

when and where to stop and frisk individuals; 83 percent of the 4.4 million stops conducted by New York police officers between January 2004 and June 2012 involved African Americans or Latinos (those groups constituted 52 percent of the city's resident population). Moreover, the intrusive and embarrassing nature of encounters with police officers provoked deepening distrust and antagonism between the police department and communities of color throughout New York.

The Bloomberg administration's growing reliance on the tactic, even as crime rates were falling, led civil rights organizations to file a class action lawsuit in federal court. In 2013, the court found that police officers had violated the constitutional rights of innocent people who had been stopped and frisked without any objective reason to suspect them of wrongdoing. The court went on to state that "the City [had] adopted a policy of indirect racial profiling by targeting racially defined groups for stops based on local crime suspect data. This has resulted in the disproportionate and discriminatory stopping of blacks and Hispanics in violation of the Equal Protection Clause."

New York's current mayor, Bill de Blasio, has promised to work with a court-appointed administrator to implement appropriate reforms. Is stop and frisk an inherently flawed policing strategy that should be eliminated? Or is it possible to implement a revised version of the policy to maintain an appropriate balance between crime control and the protection of civil liberties?

Additional Resources

Michelle Alexander, *The New Jim Crow: Mass Incarceration in the Age of Color Blindness*, rev. ed. (New York: New Press, 2012).

Brookings Institution. Web site devoted to research and commentary on the rebuilding of New Orleans after Hurricane Katrina. www.brookings.edu/research/topics/new-orleans.

Center for Constitutional Rights. The civil rights organization that filed the successful class action lawsuit challenging the constitutionality of New York City's stop and frisk policy. www.ccrjustice.org/Floyd.

Coming of Age with Stop and Frisk: Experiences, Self-Perceptions, and Public Safety. Vera Institute of Justice. Webcast. October 17, 2013. www.vera.org/videos/stop-and-frisk-video.

Bernard E. Harcourt, *Illusions of Order: The False Promise of Broken Windows Policing* (Cambridge, MA: Harvard University Press, 2001).

Street Fight. Documentary film on mayoral election in 2005 between thirty-two-year-old Cory Booker and four-term incumbent Sharpe James. Bullfrog Films, 2005.

James Q. Wilson and George L. Kelling Jr., "Broken Windows," *Atlantic Monthly,* March 1982. http://www.theatlantic .com/magazine/archive/1982/03/broken-windows/304465/; see also George Kelling and Catherine Coles, *Fixing Broken Windows: Restoring Order and Reducing Crime in our Communities* (New York: Free Press, 1996).

Discussion Questions

1. Scholars like Andra Gillespie have identified various styles of leadership of African American mayors during the past few decades. What leadership styles have been most effective in advancing black interests?

2. A common characteristic of the new breed of black leaders has been an inclination to play down the role of race in electoral campaigns and the administration of city government. Why has deracialized politics become more common? Is this evidence that racial discrimination and inequality have been subsiding in an increasingly postracial society?

3. What are the costs of a deracialized approach to urban politics and governance?

4. Are there ways to call attention to ongoing racial problems like the implementation of policing strategies in New York such as stop and frisk without provoking resentment from many white residents?

5. Is it possible to pursue a deracialized strategy without slighting black interests?

6. How might political mobilization within inner-city neighborhoods be achieved?

7. What are the prospects for sustained multiracial coalitions that address issues related to racial inequality in urban politics?

Chapter 13

Immigration and Contemporary Urban Politics

Introduction

For the first 125 years of American history, immigration was essentially unregulated, a consequence of the nation's developmental needs. The United States was rapidly expanding, both spatially and economically, and immigration was seen as necessary for growth. Nearly five million immigrants, mostly from Great Britain, Ireland, and Germany, came to the United States between 1820 and 1860 in search of jobs and economic opportunity and to escape extreme hardship arising from agricultural crises, famine, and political upheaval. Another massive wave of approximately twenty-four million immigrants, this time primarily from Southern and Central Europe and Russia, arrived between 1880 and 1920, drawn by further expansion of America's burgeoning industrial economy. By 1910, 14.5 percent of the nation's population was foreign born, and that percentage was far higher in the cities of the northeast and the midwest.[1]

Mass immigration eventually provoked a backlash among nativist groups, warning that the unprecedented influx of newcomers with their strange languages, religions, and customs threatened Anglo-American Protestant values and culture. Their oppositional voices were augmented by workers in the growing labor movement who claimed that the surge of immigrants had put downward pressure on wages and increased unemployment. In response, Congress enacted the Immigration Act of 1924 (or the National Origins Act), which established a limit of 154,000 entrants to the United States each year, the first legislative ceiling on immigration in the nation's history.[2] Moreover, the law set strict quotas on the number of immigrants from most countries, quotas that gave preferential treatment to immigrants from Western and Northern Europe at the expense of all other countries.[3]

With the rise of the civil rights movement four decades later, the Immigration Act of 1924 came under withering criticism—an immigration policy based on national origins was blatantly racist. One year after passage of the landmark Civil Rights Act, Congress adopted the Immigration Act of 1965, which eliminated the national origins quota system. The new law set annual limits of 170,000 entries for the eastern hemisphere and 120,000 for the western hemisphere, but at the same time, it allowed unlimited admission of children, parents, and spouses of U.S. citizens, which had the practical effect of significantly expanding immigration levels beyond those ceilings. The admission of immigrants would be based mainly on two criteria: (1) family reunification and (2) the nation's labor needs. The first criterion was accorded a higher priority; 74 percent of visas would be set aside for individuals seeking admission to the United States to be reunited with family members. The percentage of visas for individuals with needed labor skills was reduced from more than 50 percent to less than 20 percent.[4]

The impact of the 1965 act has been enormous. The volume of immigration jumped dramatically with each passing decade. The nation's immigrant population increased from 9.6 million in 1970 to 14.1 million in 1980, to 19.8 million in 1990, to 31.1 million in 2000, to 40 million in 2010. More people immigrated to America during the 1990s than in any other decade in U.S. history, eclipsing the previous record of 8.8 million between 1900 and 1910. The percentage of foreign-born residents in 2010 was 12.9 percent of the U.S. population, the highest figure since 1920.[5] The other major effect of the Immigration Act of 1965 concerns the composition of the immigrant stream. In the 1950s, more than half of all immigrants came from Europe, with Germany the top country of origin. By 2010, 53 percent of all immigrants came from Latin America (29 percent alone from Mexico) and another 28 percent from Asia, with Europe's contribution down to 12 percent. Since 1980, the leading countries of origin have been Mexico, the Philippines, China, the Dominican Republic, Vietnam, India, and Korea.[6]

With respect to destinations, immigrants have tended to congregate in six states—67 percent of all immigrants in the United States resided in California, New York, Texas, Florida, New Jersey, and Illinois in 2010. The most popular metropolitan areas have been Los Angeles, New York, Miami, Chicago, Washington, D.C., and San Francisco.[7] Since 1990, however, this pattern of concentrated settlement has been changing, with many new immigrants increasingly dispersing throughout the country, including many suburban and rural areas.[8] **Reading 13-1** by Audrey Singer provides a more detailed overview of the history of immigration in the United States.

As in the previous century, the more recent surge in immigration has generated considerable controversy, particularly over rising levels of undocumented immigrants. Like before, some warn that increased immigration fractures American society into increasingly separate and isolated enclaves, threatens long-standing linguistic traditions and values, and undermines the nation's civic culture.[9] Others argue that rising immigration, especially among workers with limited skills and education, keeps unemployment high and wages low. It also places a strain on local governments in destination cities trying to cope with heightened demands on overcrowded public schools and hospitals.[10] Others worry about the ability of new arrivals to thrive in an environment that may be much less hospitable than the ones that greeted earlier waves of immigrants. Unlike most of their predecessors in the nineteenth and early twentieth centuries, recent immigrants from Latin America and Asia do not share a common European heritage and are more visibly identifiable in what remains a white-dominated society. Furthermore, the transformation from an industrial to a postindustrial economy that rewards high levels of skill and educational attainment impedes many newcomers who possess neither. Although the previous immigrants encountered rampant discrimination and other obstacles, their path to assimilation was relatively steady and successful. The current influx of immigrants faces a more uncertain future.[11]

By the same token, immigration has yielded undeniable benefits, particularly for many cities. At a time when urban areas have undergone a debilitating loss of population, the influx of residents has provided a much-needed boost to the tax base, generated a new source of labor for struggling manufacturing plants, replenished the customer base for neighborhood retail establishments, and supplied new students for schools that might have otherwise closed because of falling enrollments. In short, immigration has revitalized entire communities.[12] With respect to urban economies, the new arrivals have filled employment gaps at both ends of the growing service sector. They are disproportionately represented in low-skilled, low-wage jobs in restaurants, hotels, and office buildings, but they are also well-represented in various professional fields such as health care and engineering. Their entrepreneurial success in running small businesses serving city neighborhoods continues to be a staple of the urban fabric.[13]

Political battles over immigration at the national level have been heated for many years. Congress sought to gain better control over illegal immigration by passing the Immigration Reform and Control Act of 1986, which imposed penalties on employers who hire undocumented workers while granting amnesty to those who came illegally but who had resided in the United States for many years and satisfied a number of conditions. Because of loopholes in the law, however, employer sanctions proved ineffective at stemming illegal immigration, and Congress has lacked the political will to pass new legislation in more recent years. Impatient with the federal government, some state and local governments have acted to deter illegal immigration by restricting or denying certain public services, including public education and health care, to undocumented immigrants. Some of these policies have been overturned in court on the ground that they violate the Equal Protection Clause of the United States or state constitutions or because they are preempted by the federal government, but other policies have been upheld by the courts.[14] In some locations, anti-immigrant policies have unleashed fervent mobilization campaigns by immigrants and their supporters that have exacted a heavy political toll on those who initiated such legislation in the first place.[15] In other places, however, restrictions on immigration remain popular with a majority of voters.

How has immigration affected politics within American cities? Urbanists are particularly interested in the degree to which immigrants have attained political incorporation in local governance. To what extent do immigrants have access to city officials? To what extent have they been able to shape political decision making? One key issue concerns the process of obtaining citizenship and the political rights that flow from that status. What factors either encourage or discourage immigrants from becoming naturalized citizens who are then able to vote? Once citizenship is obtained, do naturalized citizens participate effectively in city politics? Domenic Vitiello in **Reading 13-2** addresses these issues in his analysis of the political incorporation of immigrants.[16]

One would expect that the road to political incorporation would be somewhat smoother for immigrant groups with higher levels of socioeconomic status. Political scientists have long noted a causal relationship between resources such as income, wealth, and educational attainment and effective political participation.[17] Many studies have confirmed that immigrant groups with such resources are more likely to achieve visibility and influence in city politics.[18] Recent research, however, emphasizes the crucial role that social service organizations and advocacy groups play in mobilizing immigrants. One study of the political incorporation of Indian, Polish, and Mexican immigrants in Chicago found that the latter had obtained the greatest influence in local politics—notwithstanding their relative disadvantage in terms of material resources—because they benefited from an extensive network of preexisting community-based organizations.[19]

Since immigrant groups rarely constitute a majority of any one city's population, attaining political influence often requires the construction of coalitions with other urban groups. On the one hand, such coalition building would seem to be relatively easy based on the expectation that lower-income immigrants of different ethnic backgrounds would find common ground around similar economic interests.[20] Likewise, African Americans and many immigrant groups would presumably have ample reason to cooperate given their shared nonwhite racial status and vulnerability to persistent discrimination. Such groups have a "linked fate" in confronting racial barriers.[21] On the other hand, cohesion even within pan-ethnic groups is far from assured; given the variation regarding national origin and socioeconomic status, electoral alliances among Latinos or Asian Americans have often been difficult to sustain. Constructing multiracial coalitions that include African Americans has proved to be even more problematic. The competition among different racial and ethnic groups for good jobs and over the distribution of public services has sometimes fueled intense conflicts in American cities. The uprising in South Central Los Angeles in 1992 was triggered by an incident of police brutality, but many commentators pointed to increasing tensions between blacks and Latino and Asian immigrants living in impoverished neighborhoods as the key underlying source.[22] Even in a less combustible milieu, friction between diverse groups may render the task of building and maintaining electoral and governing coalitions a huge challenge. Zoltan Hajnal and Jessica Trounstine explore this theme further in **Reading 13-3**.[23]

Since interethnic coalitions are so critical to lasting political empowerment of immigrant groups, scholars have been interested in identifying factors that either facilitate or hinder their formation. A comparative case study of Los Angeles and New York is intriguing not only because both places are such major gateway and destination cities for immigrants but also because they have had dissimilar experiences with respect to immigrant political incorporation. Antonio Villaraigosa became the first Latino elected mayor of Los Angeles in 2005 and then was reelected in 2009. By contrast, New York voters have never elected a Latino mayor despite the large percentage of first- and second-generation immigrants in that city. In explaining the diverging outcomes, John Mollenkopf and Raphael Sonenshein note important differences in the two cities' political culture and structure. For example, while New York City's large, fifty-one-member city council increases the possibility that numerous ethnic groups will obtain representation, such an arrangement simultaneously engenders interethnic conflict, thus making consensus around one mayoral candidate difficult to achieve. In Los Angeles, a much smaller city council has the effect of blurring ethnic divisions, which, paradoxically, renders interethnic coalition building more manageable.[24] Such differences in the institutional composition of municipal governments help account for the varying fortunes of immigrant groups seeking an expanded role in urban politics.

Finally, incidents of black–brown conflict in urban affairs, a favorite target of media coverage, should not obscure what is perhaps the more routine pattern of interethnic cooperation. In many cities and suburbs with swelling minority populations, productive relationships have been forged, sometimes through intervention by religious institutions or national civil rights organizations but more often through a simple recognition of shared experience and interests.[25]

Notes

1. Refer to Maldwyn Allen Jones, *American Immigration*, 2nd ed. (Chicago: University of Chicago Press, 1992); Susan F. Martin, *A Nation of Immigrants* (New York: Cambridge University Press, 2011).

2. By comparison, the high point of annual immigration to the United States during this period came in 1907 with the arrival of 1.3 million newcomers. Jones, *American Immigration*.

3. The Immigration Act of 1924 did not apply to the western hemisphere due to pressure from agricultural interests in the west and southwest that anticipated an ever-increasing need for Mexican farmworkers. Prior to the 1920s, Congress had passed legislation to restrict immigration on two other occasions. Although Chinese immigrants in the western United States had provided a crucial source of labor during the mid-nineteenth century in gold mines, farms, and railroad construction, nativist opposition in California prompted Congress to enact the Chinese Exclusion Act in 1882, which prohibited the immigration of Chinese laborers. In 1907, it adopted legislation setting quotas on the immigration of Japanese workers. David Gerber, *American Immigration: A Very Short Introduction* (New York: Oxford University Press, 2011).

4. Aristide R. Zolberg, "Immigration Control Policy: Law and Implementation" in *The New Americans: A Guide to Immigration since 1965*, ed. Mary C. Waters and Reed Ueda with Helen B. Marrow (Cambridge, MA: Harvard University Press, 2007).

5. Alejandro Portes and Ruben G. Rumbaut, *Immigrant America: A Portrait*, 4th ed. (Berkeley: University of California Press, 2014).

6. Audrey Singer, "Contemporary Immigrant Gateways in Historical Perspective," *Daedalus, the Journal of the American Academy of Arts & Sciences*, 142 (3), 2013.

7. Portes and Rumbaut, *Immigrant America*; see also John R. Logan, "Settlement Patterns in Metropolitan America," in *The New Americans*, ed. Waters et al.

8. Douglas S. Massey, ed., *New Faces in New Places: The Changing Geography of American Immigration* (New York: Russell Sage Foundation, 2008); Jill H. Wilson and Nicole Prchal Svajlenka, "Immigrants Continue to Disperse, with Fastest Growth in the Suburbs," Brookings Institute report, October 29, 2014, www.brookings.edu/research/papers/2014/10/29-immigrants-disperse-suburbs-wilson-svajlenka.

9. Samuel Huntington, "The Hispanic Challenge," *Foreign Policy*, March–April 2004; Georgie Anne Geyer, *Americans No More: The Death of Citizenship* (New York: Atlantic Monthly Press, 1996).

10. Vernon Briggs, "Immigration Policy and the U.S. Economy: An Institutional Perspective," *Journal of Economic Issues*, 30 (2), 1996; but see also Neeraj Kaushal, Cordelia W. Reimers, and David M. Reimers, "Immigrants and the Economy," in *The New Americans*, ed. Waters et al.

11. Richard D. Alba, "Assimilation's Quiet Tide," *The Public Interest*, 119 (Spring), 1995; Min Zhou, "Growing Up American: The Challenge Confronting Immigrant Children and Children of Immigrants," *Annual Review of Sociology*, 23 (1997); but see also Joel Perlmann and Roger Waldinger, "Are the Children of Today's Immigrants Making It?" *The Public Interest*, 132 (Summer 1998). For a more positive report on how second-generation immigrants are faring in the United States, see Vivian Louie, *Keeping the Immigrant Bargain: The Costs and Rewards of Success in America* (New York: Russell Sage Foundation, 2012).

12. Refer to Alexander von Hoffman, *House by House, Block by Block: The Rebirth of Urban Neighborhoods* (New York: Oxford University Press, 2003).

13. Thomas Muller, *Immigrants and the American City* (New York: New York University Press, 1993). See also Portes and Rumbaut, *Immigrant America*.

14. Zolberg, "Immigration Control Policy."

15. For example, the Republican Party in California suffered crippling electoral defeats following its support in 1994 for Proposition 187, which denied nonemergency health care and primary schooling to undocumented immigrants. A massive effort to encourage Latino immigrants to become naturalized citizens and register to vote culminated in widespread gains by Democrats in the 1998 elections, and the GOP in California has suffered ever since. Lisa Garcia Bedolla, *Fluid Borders: Latino Power, Identity, and Politics in Los Angeles* (Berkeley: University of California Press, 2005). See also Kim Voss and Irene Bloemraad, *Rallying for Immigrant Rights: The Fight for Inclusion in 21st Century America* (Berkeley: University of California Press, 2011), which documents the explosion in grassroots activism in many parts of the United States following attempts by members of Congress to impose new restrictions on immigration.

16. For a helpful examination of the concept of political incorporation and how it differs from assimilation, see S. Karthick Ramakrishnan, "Incorporation versus Assimilation," in *Outsiders No More? Models of Immigrant Political Incorporation*, ed. Jennifer Hochschild, Jacqueline Chattopadhyay, Claudin Gay, and Michall Jones Correa (New York: Oxford University Press, 2013).

17. Refer to Sidney Verba, Kay Lehman Schlozman, and Henry E. Brady, *Voice and Equality: Civic Voluntarism in American Politics* (Cambridge, MA: Harvard University Press, 1995).

18. S. Karthick Ramakrishnan and Irene Bloemraad, "Making Organizations Count: Immigrant Civic Engagement in Ten California Cities," in *Civic Hopes and Political Realities: Immigrants, Community Organizations, and Political Engagement*, ed. S. Karthick Ramakrishnan and Irene Bloemraad (New York: Russell Sage Foundation, 2008).

19. Laurencio Sanguino, "Selective Service: Indians, Poles, and Mexicans in Chicago," in *Civic Hopes and Political Realities*, ed. Karthick Ramakrishnan and Bloemraad.

20. William Julius Wilson, *The Bridge over the Racial Divide: Rising Inequality and Coalitional Politics* (Berkeley: University of California Press, 1999).

21. Michael C. Dawson, *Behind the Mule: Race and Class in African American Politics* (Princeton: Princeton University Press, 1994).

22. Refer to Jack Miles, "Blacks v. Browns," *Atlantic Monthly*, October 1992.

23. See also Guillermo J. Grenier and Max Castro, "Blacks and Cubans in Miami: The Negative Consequences of the Cuban Enclave on Ethnic Relations," in *Governing American Cities: Interethnic Coalitions, Competition, and Conflict*, ed. Michael Jones-Correa (New York: Russell Sage Foundation, 2001); Alexandra Filindra and Marion Orr, "Anxieties of an Ethnic Transition: The Election of the First Latino Mayor in Providence, Rhode Island," *Urban Affairs Review*, 49 (1), 2013.

24. John H. Mollenkopf and Raphael Sonenshein, "The New Urban Politics of Integration: A View from the Gateway Cities," in *Bringing Outsiders In: Transatlantic Perspectives on Immigrant Political Incorporation*, ed. Jennifer L. Hochschild and John H. Mollenkopf (Ithaca, NY: Cornell University Press, 2009); see also Reuel Rogers, *Afro-Caribbean Immigrants and the Politics of Incorporation: Ethnicity, Exception or Exit* (Cambridge: Cambridge University Press, 2006).

25. Refer to Albert M. Camarillo, "Blacks, Latinos, and the New Racial Frontier in American Cities of Color: California's Emerging Minority-Majority Cities," in *African American Urban History since World War II*, ed. Kenneth L. Kusmer and Joe W. Trotter (Chicago: University of Chicago Press, 2009); see also Albert M. Camarillo, "Black and Brown in Compton: Demographic Change, Suburban Decline, and Intergroup Relations in a South Central Los Angeles Community, 1950 to 2000," in *Not Just Black and White: Historical and Contemporary Perspectives on Immigration, Race, and Ethnicity in the United States*, ed. Nancy Foner and George M. Fredickson (New York: Russell Sage Foundation, 2011).

13-1 "Contemporary Immigrant Gateways in Historical Perspective"

Audrey Singer

Daedalus, the Journal of the American Academy of Arts & Sciences

New immigrant settlement trends have reshaped communities across the United States. The history of immigrant urban enclaves has been fundamentally altered by the post–World War II restructuring of the U.S. economy, the decentralization of cities, and the growth of suburbs as major employment centers. The contemporary immigration "map" has multiple implications for the social, economic, civic, and political integration of immigrants.

Similar transformative processes also characterized the turn of the twentieth century, when the United States was shifting from an agrarian to an industrial economy, inducing both an exodus from rural areas to cities and mass immigration, mainly from Europe. At that time, immigrants significantly altered neighborhoods in burgeoning cities, some of which are still defined by the immigrants who settled there during that period.

Today, these processes are taking place in new geographies and through different industrial transitions. During both periods, the content and the location of working life changed. At the turn of the twentieth century, the U.S. economy moved from agriculture toward manufacturing, and the population shifted from rural to urban areas. The turn of the twenty-first century has been characterized by a transition from manufacturing to "new economy" technology and service jobs, and a population movement from urban to suburban and exurban areas.

The historical immigrant settlement narrative typically begins with immigrants arriving at Ellis Island or the ports of California, before making their way to ethnic neighborhoods in cities such as New York, Philadelphia, Baltimore, Chicago, St. Louis, or San Francisco. As these communities developed, immigrants worked in local establishments, started their own businesses, sent their children to local schools, and organized places of worship.

Building on this history, the contemporary story entails the arrival of immigrants to established immigrant gateways with well-defined service infrastructures and a receptivity that aids the integration process. But it also includes a large number of immigrants streaming to newer destinations. These new gateways have emerged over the past two decades, creating a different context for integration and eliciting a mixed response from local communities. In some areas, immigrants have been welcomed, while in others they have stimulated conflict. Rapid demographic shifts in the newest gateways often have an impact on public institutions, whose adjustments to the changes unfold across immigrant and native-born communities that may be unprepared for change. This article focuses on settlement trends of immigrants in the two periods that bookend the twentieth century, both eras of mass immigration. It compares settlement patterns in both periods, describing old and new gateways, the growth of the immigrant population, and geographic concentration and dispersion. The rise of suburban settlement patterns is examined in the contemporary period.

This analysis examines the size and distribution of the foreign-born population for the period between 1900 and 2010. Much of the analysis focuses on 1900, representing the beginning of the twentieth century, and 2010, representing the beginning of the twenty-first century. County-level data from decennial censuses for the years 1900 to 1950 and 1970 to 2000 were accessed via the Minnesota Population Center's National Historical Geographic Information System (NHGIS).[1] Due to sampling errors noted by the Minnesota Population Center, data for the year 1960 were extracted directly from Census Bureau digital uploads of the *U.S. Census of Population: 1960*, vol. 1, *Characteristics of the Population*.[2] For 2010, American Community Survey (ACS) 2006–2010 5-year estimates were accessed from the Census Bureau because comparable data at the county level are not available from 1-year estimates of the ACS.

While "metropolitan areas" as we know them today did not exist at the turn of the twentieth century, consistent metropolitan definitions based on 2010 Office of Management and Budget (OMB) definitions are used throughout the analysis in order to standardize data comparisons. Metropolitan immigration estimates were constructed from individual county-level data. Thus, metropolitan area definitions are applied to data from 1900, even though population was heavily concentrated in the cities of those areas, and suburbs were not yet well developed. Metropolitan areas are composed of counties or county equivalents and are ranked according to the one hundred most populous metro areas of each decade.

Two trends emerge from a review of the share of foreign-born populations residing in the primary urban counties of the metropolitan areas with the largest immigrant populations. For contemporary metropolitan areas that developed prior to World War II, the share of the immigrant population in the primary urban county is generally high in the first half of the century. As immigrants began to suburbanize in the second half of the century, this share diminished; St. Louis, Baltimore, and Portland, Oregon, follow this pattern. For newer metropolitan areas that experienced development after the advent of the automobile, the trend tends to be different. The share of immigrants in the primary urban county, often only a small city or town in the early twentieth century, is small, reflecting a more rural foreign-born population. The share of the immigrant population in the primary urban county increases over time, as the region surrounding the cities becomes denser. This pattern is particularly evident in states such as Texas, which shares a border with Mexico, and which has a significant Mexican immigrant population, especially in cities such as Houston and Austin. Areas that tend to have a consistently low share of immigrants residing in the primary urban county are those that have recently emerged or reemerged as immigrant gateways and that have a largely suburban population, such as Salt Lake City, Denver, and Sacramento.

Currently, the OMB defines 366 metropolitan areas in the United States, all of which are included in this study. Thirty-seven percent of U.S. counties (1,168) are located in metropolitan areas. In this analysis, "metropolitan area" is used to describe all urban places, including those at the beginning of the twentieth century. The 100 largest metropolitan areas in 2010 constitute "large metropolitan areas"; the remaining 266 are the "small metropolitan areas." The remainder of the population lives in rural or nonmetropolitan areas. The 100 largest metropolitan areas are defined by the Brookings Metropolitan Policy Program's State of Metropolitan America Indicator Map.[3] Primary cities are defined as the largest city in each metropolitan area, plus all other incorporated places with populations of at least 100,000. Suburbs are designated as the remainder of the metro areas outside primary cities.

The terms *immigrant* and *foreign born* are used interchangeably here to refer to persons born outside the United States, excluding those born to American citizens abroad. Immigrant status is determined by a question about birthplace in the census questionnaire. This question varies somewhat over the twentieth century, but foreign-born population and total population were determined for each year at the metropolitan level.

During the turn of both the twentieth and twenty-first centuries, immigration levels were high, and the share of the population that was foreign born was at a peak. In this regard, America at the turn of the twenty-first century bears some similarities to America at the turn of the twentieth century. In 1900, immigrants made up nearly 14 percent of the U.S. population; in 2010, they composed 13 percent of the total. However, in absolute terms, the number of immigrants has quadrupled, from 10 million in 1900 to nearly 40 million today.

For several decades prior to 1900, immigrants arrived in great numbers. Between 1860 and 1900, the immigrant population grew by more than 6 million persons, growing by 35 percent between 1860 and 1870 and then varying in growth rates between 12 and 38 percent per decade (see Table 1). Between 1900 and 1910, the immigrant population grew by a whopping 3.2 million, a rate of 31 percent, yielding a U.S. population in 1910 that was nearly 15 percent foreign born.

What followed were six decades of much lower immigration levels, as the Great Depression and two world wars curtailed immigration worldwide. This slow and, at times, negative growth of the immigrant population, coupled with restrictive immigration policy and the mid-century baby boom, rendered a nation that was almost entirely native born. By 1960, the share of the population that was foreign born was less than 5 percent, amounting to fewer than 10 million immigrants.

Between 1970 and 1980, immigration began to pick up again in earnest, increasing steadily over the four decades between 1970 and 2010. The greatest increase came in the 1990s, when more than 11.3 million immigrants arrived, a growth of 57 percent. Immigration in

Table 1   Foreign-Born Population, including Its Share of the Total Population and Its Change from the Previous Decade, 1860–2010

	Foreign Born	Share of Total	Change from Previous Decade	
			Number	Growth Rate
1860	4,138,697	13.2%	—	—
1870	5,567,229	14.4%	1,428,532	35%
1880	6,679,943	13.3%	1,112,714	20%
1890	9,249,547	14.8%	2,569,604	38%
1900	10,341,276	13.6%	1,091,729	12%
1910	13,515,886	14.7%	3,174,610	31%
1920	13,920,692	13.2%	404,806	3%
1930	14,204,149	11.6%	283,457	2%
1940	11,594,896	8.8%	−2,609,253	−18%
1950	10,347,395	6.9%	−1,247,501	−11%
1960	9,738,091	5.4%	−609,304	−6%
1970	9,619,302	4.7%	−118,789	−1%
1980	14,079,906	6.2%	4,460,604	46%
1990	19,767,316	7.9%	5,687,410	40%
2000	31,107,889	11.1%	11,340,573	57%
2010	39,955,854	12.9%	8,847,965	28%

Source: Author's calculations of 1860–2000 data via Campbell Gibson and Kay Jung, "Historical Census Statistics on the Foreign-Born Population of the United States: 1850–2000," Population Division Working Paper No. 81 (Washington, D.C.: U.S. Bureau of the Census, February 2006), http://www.census.gov/population/www/documentation/twps0081/twps0081.html; and 2010 ACS 1-year estimates, http://www.census.gov/acs/www.

the 2000s slowed a bit after the recession; still, nearly 9 million immigrants arrived, boosting the U.S. foreign-born population to nearly 13 percent, the highest share since 1920.

During the 1960s and 1970s, changes in U.S. admissions policy regarding national origins as well as political and economic conditions in sending countries affected the composition of immigrants entering the United States.[4] Thus, the two periods also differ greatly in the regional origins of immigrants. In 1900, the vast majority of the 10 million immigrants residing in the United States were from European countries, but by 2010, Europeans made up less than 13 percent of all immigrants (see Table 2). At the turn of the twentieth century, 11 percent of immigrants were from Northern America (in addition to Canada, this includes Bermuda, Greenland, and St. Pierre and Miquelon). Mexican immigrants then made up only 1 percent of the total, as did immigrants from all Asian countries combined. The remainder of Latin America, Africa, and Oceania each contributed less than 1 percent of the total. By 2010, however, immigrants from Mexico had the largest share of the total, at 30 percent. The rest of Latin

America contributed 23 percent and all Asian countries combined were another 28 percent of the total. Africans comprised 4 percent, Northern America 2 percent, and immigrants from Oceania less than 1 percent.

As the United States has urbanized and developed, the destinations of immigrants have shifted. While the United States developed from a largely rural to a largely urban society, the number and density of cities increased.[5] Eventually, the cities themselves expanded, growing from dense urban cores to metropolitan areas with large suburban areas extending outward.

Immigrant workers contributed mightily to the workforce during the industrial transformation of the U.S. economy. Sociologists Charles Hirschman and Elizabeth Mogford estimate that immigrants and their children held half of all U.S. manufacturing jobs by 1920.[6] Thus, the industrializing cities of the Northeast and Midwest attracted workers to manufacturing jobs in great numbers, and immigrants played a major role in the process of urbanization. Indeed, 67 percent of all immigrants lived in the largest metropolitan areas in 1900, as compared to just 44 percent of the native born (see Figure 1). Including small "metros," more than three-quarters of

Table 2 Foreign-Born Population by Region or Country of Birth, 1900 and 2010

Region or Country	1900		2010	
	Number	**Share**	**Number**	**Share**
Europe	8,881,548	86.0%	4,817,437	12.1%
Asia	120,248	1.2%	11,283,574	28.2%
Africa	2,538	<0.1%	1,606,914	4.0%
Oceania	8,820	0.1%	216,736	0.5%
Latin America (excluding Mexico)	34,065	0.3%	9,512,984	23.8%
Mexico	103,393	1.0%	11,711,103	29.3%
Northern America	1,179,922	11.4%	806,925	2.0%
Total	10,330,534		39,955,673	

The table excludes unreported country of birth (1900 only).

Source: Author's calculations of 1860–2000 data via Campbell Gibson and Kay Jung, "Historical Census Statistics on the Foreign-Born Population of the United States: 1850–2000," Population Division Working Paper No. 81 (Washington, D.C.: U.S. Bureau of the Census, February 2006), http://www.census.gov/population/www/documentation/twps0081/twps0081.html; and 2010 ACS 1-year estimates, http://www.census.gov/acs/www.

Figure 1   Metropolitan/Non-Metropolitan Residence by Nativity, 1900 and 2010

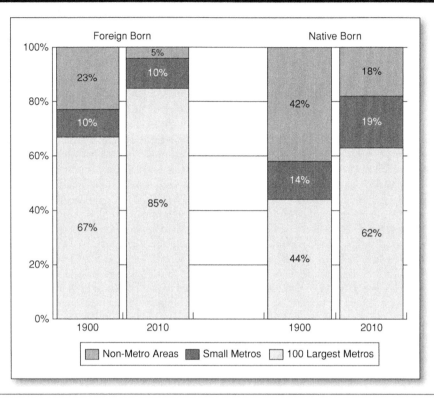

Source: Author's calculations of 1900 Decennial Census data accessed via Minnesota Population Center's National Historical Geographic Information System, http://www.nhgis.org; and 2006–2010 ACS 5-year estimates, http://www.census.gov/acs/www/.

immigrants lived in metropolitan areas and less than one-quarter lived in rural areas in 1900. In contrast, 58 percent of the native-born population lived in metro areas and 42 percent in non-metropolitan areas. By 2010, 95 percent of foreign-born residents lived in metropolitan America, as compared with only 81 percent of the native born. Among the large metropolitan areas in 1900, the majority of the foreign born lived in the Northeast (41 percent) and Midwest (20 percent). Only a small share lived in large metro areas in the South (3 percent) and the West (3 percent), and another 10 percent lived in smaller metropolitan areas (see Figure 2).

By 2010, however, the large metropolitan areas in the Northeast housed only 20 percent of the immigrant population and the Midwest dropped to only

9 percent of the total, reflecting broader population shifts to the South and West. Metropolitan areas in the South (25 percent) and the West (31 percent) are now home to more than half of all immigrants. Small metro areas make up another 10 percent of the total.

Immigrants were drawn to cities that were flourishing at the turn of the twentieth century. Indeed, metropolitan immigrant settlement was highly concentrated (see Figure 3).[7] For most of the century, just five cities ruled as major settlement areas, where half of all immigrants chose to live. New York is by far the dominant destination, garnering at least one-quarter of all immigrants for each decade throughout most of the century. No other metropolitan area comes close to that share until 1990, when Los Angeles matches New York's

Figure 2   Regional Share of Foreign Born in Large Metropolitan Areas, Small Metropolitan Areas, and Non-Metropolitan Areas, 1900 and 2010

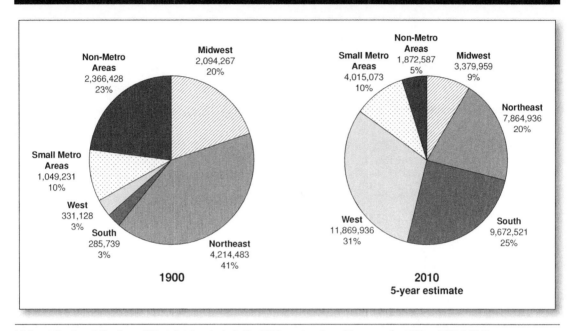

Midwest, Northeast, South, and West divisions include the 100 largest metropolitan areas for 1900 and 2006–2010.

Source: Author's calculations of 1900 Decennial Census data accessed via Minnesota Population Center's National Historical Geographic Information System, http://www.nhgis.org; and 2006–2010 ACS 5-year estimates, http://www.census.gov/acs/www/.

share at 19 percent, or 3.4 million immigrants each. Only New York and Chicago make the top-five list for every decade between 1900 and 2010. New York is ranked first (with the exception of 1990, when it shares that rank with Los Angeles) and Chicago ranks second all the way through 1960, after which Chicago drops in rank, though all the while gaining immigrants in absolute numbers.[8]

In the early decades of the twentieth century, industrial Philadelphia maintains a rank in the top five, but by 1940 it suffers a net loss of immigrants. Pittsburgh, another industrial city, also appears in the first three decades, only to be trumped by Detroit, which occupies a top spot from 1930 to 1960 as job opportunities there expanded. Boston maintains a continuous presence on the list through 1960, despite a net decline in the number of immigrants. San Francisco claims a strong and

growing share from 1970 to 2010, reflecting gains in immigrants from the Pacific Rim. Los Angeles rises from mid-century on to assert a large share of all immigrants living in metropolitan America. In a similar fashion, albeit with a smaller share among all metro areas, Miami stakes out third place in the last several decades due to an increase, first, in Cuban immigrants and, later, in immigrants from other Caribbean and Latin American countries.

The concentration of immigrants after 1990 is especially notable. After seven continuous decades—between 1930 and 1990—when just five metro areas housed about half of all immigrants living in metropolitan areas, the share declines to 45 percent in 2000 and 40 percent in 2010 as immigrant newcomers make their way to new metro areas, particularly in the South and West. If growth trajectories of dispersal

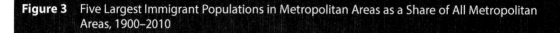

Figure 3   Five Largest Immigrant Populations in Metropolitan Areas as a Share of All Metropolitan Areas, 1900–2010

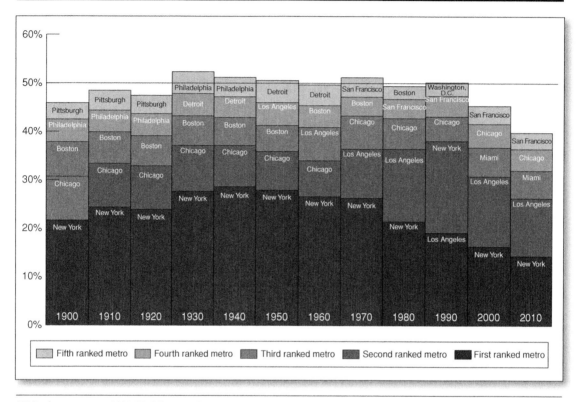

2010 values represent 2006–2010 5-year estimates.

Source: Author's calculations of 1900–1950 and 1970–2000. Decennial Census data accessed via Minnesota Population Center's National Historical Geographic Information System, http://www.nhgis.org; 1960 Decennial Census data accessed via U.S. Census Bureau, *U.S. Census of Population: 1960*, vol. 1, *Characteristics of the Population* (Washington, D.C.: U.S. Government Printing Office, 1963); and 2006–2010 ACS 5-year estimates, http://www.census.gov/acs/www/.

continue into the next decade, the immigrant population in the five largest metropolitan areas may only amount to slightly more than one-third of the total.

Mapping the largest immigrant populations within metropolitan areas in 1900 and 2010 reveals just how dispersed the foreign-born population has become (see Map 1). With the exception of San Francisco, all of the big immigrant destinations in 1900 were in the Midwest or Northeast, including cities in the Great Lakes region such as Buffalo, Detroit, Cleveland, Pittsburgh, and Milwaukee, which all share a manufacturing past

and no longer draw immigrants in great numbers. New England also drew immigrants to jobs in Worcester, Providence, New Haven, and Boston. The big magnets of Chicago, New York, and Philadelphia attracted large numbers of immigrants.

By 2010, the immigration map had been redrawn. While San Francisco, New York, Chicago, Boston, and Philadelphia are on both maps, more notable are the metro areas in the South and West that have risen to the top. Los Angeles, Riverside, Phoenix, Dallas, and Houston are among the metro areas in the Southwest

Map 1   Twenty Metropolitan Areas with the Largest Immigrant Populations, 1900 and 2010

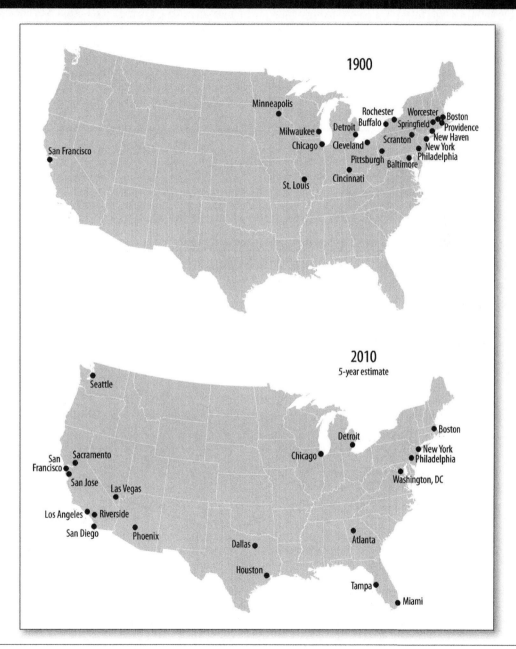

Source: Author's calculations of 1900 Decennial Census data accessed via Minnesota Population Center's National Historical Geographic Information System, http://www.nhgis.org; and 2006–2010 ACS 5-year estimates, http://www.census.gov/acs/www/.

that rank highly, along with Miami, Tampa, and Atlanta in the Southeast.

The body of work that analyzes contemporary immigrant gateways in historical perspective sheds further light on the stature and composition of today's destinations.[9] A typology of immigrant gateways reflects the size and geography of immigrant settlement patterns shaped by industrial histories, economic conditions, proximity to immigrant sending countries, and social networks.[10] In the contemporary period, they vary in size and national-origin composition, skills distribution, and neighborhood concentration. The share of the population that is foreign born, aggregated by gateway type, illustrates the long-term patterns of growth and decline within each type (see Figure 4).

Cities such as Cleveland, Milwaukee, and St. Louis, which had populations with a higher immigrant share

than the national average from 1900 to 1970, followed by a lower share in every decade since, are former immigrant gateways. New York, Boston, San Francisco, and Chicago are the quintessential immigrant destinations, having large and sustained immigrant populations over the entire twentieth century. These are the "major" continuous gateways responsible for much higher than average shares of immigrants for every decade of the twentieth century. In addition, the "minor" continuous gateways, like their larger counterparts, have had long histories of immigrant settlement, but the size of the immigrant population is historically smaller.

There are two groups of minor continuous gateways, most easily described by their geographies. The first group includes New England metro areas such as Hartford, New Haven, and Bridgeport that attracted

Figure 4   Percent of Foreign Born in Metropolitan Areas, by Gateway Type, 1900–2010

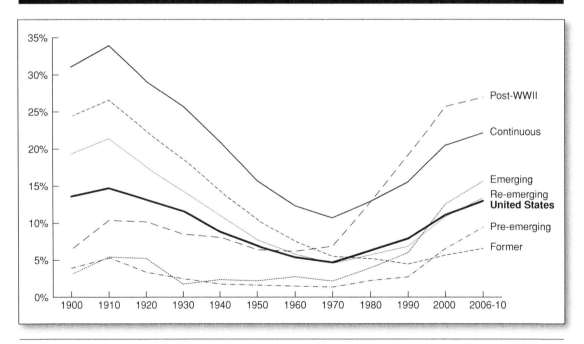

Source: Author's calculations of 1900–1950, 1970–2000 Decennial Census data accessed via Minnesota Population Center's National Historical Geographic Information System, http://www.nhgis.org; 1960 Decennial Census data accessed via U.S. Census Bureau, *U.S. Census of Population: 1960*, vol. 1, *Characteristics of the Population* (Washington, D.C.: U.S. Government Printing Office, 1963); and 2006–2010 ACS 5-year estimates.

Europeans in the early part of the twentieth century, and that now receive a mixture of Europeans, Caribbeans, and other groups. The other group of metropolitan areas is primarily located among border states, which have been long-term settlement areas for Mexican immigrants. These include Bakersfield and Fresno in the central valley of California and San Antonio and McAllen in Texas.[11]

Post–World War II immigrant gateways such as Miami, Los Angeles, Houston, and Washington, D.C., all emerged as major immigrant destinations in the second half of the twentieth century (albeit in different decades). Until the 1960s, these places had comparatively small immigrant populations making up small shares of their total population, but they grew rapidly thereafter, and now include some of the largest contemporary gateways. Their populations had lower shares of immigrants than the national average for the first six decades of the century, followed by spiking rates up to the present.

Due to expanding economic and housing opportunities in several regions—the Southeast and the Mountain West in particular—many metropolitan areas quickly drew immigrants to work in construction, real estate, health care, and service sector jobs. Many metropolitan areas that became new gateways at the turn of the twenty-first century also attracted domestic migrants in large numbers, outweighing the growth due to immigrants.[12] Atlanta, Las Vegas, and Phoenix lead the emerging gateways. These places saw immigrant growth rates exceed the national average during one of the last three decades of the twentieth century, but until then had small numbers of immigrants. The immigrant share in emerging gateways has been higher than the national average since 2000.

Similar to the continuous gateways, the reemerging gateways, including Seattle, the Twin Cities, and Baltimore, drew immigrants in large numbers in the early part of the twentieth century, but experienced low levels of immigration during the rest of the century. They then had fast immigrant growth at the very end of the twentieth century and into the 2000s, reemerging as significant destinations. Among all the gateways types, foreign-born shares in the reemerging gateways most closely mirror the national average. Other metro areas, such as Nashville, Charlotte, and

Columbus, have little history of immigration, but recently have seen extraordinary growth in their immigrant populations. Still relatively small in absolute terms and as a share of the population, the rates of growth in these "preemerging" gateways have been at least three times the national rate during the past two decades.

The newest gateways, designated "twenty-first-century gateways" elsewhere, differ from the more established continuous gateways and the former gateways in that they developed largely as auto-dependent metropolises and thus are very suburban in form.[13] They tend to be large and sprawling compared to the metropolitan areas with dense cities at their core that received immigrants in the early twentieth century. Growth patterns in areas such as metropolitan Atlanta and Washington, D.C., have led to extensive suburbs surrounding comparatively small central cities. Most of the population, including immigrants, lives in the suburbs. Other new destinations like Phoenix, Charlotte, and Austin are comprised of very large central cities resulting from annexation. Here, the official city limits encompass vast suburban-like areas.

Nonetheless, the geography of U.S. immigrant settlement is now decidedly suburban (see Figure 5). Just thirty years ago, similar shares of immigrants lived in the cities and the suburbs of the largest metropolitan areas in the United States (41 percent and 43 percent, respectively). By 2010, only 33 percent of U.S. immigrants lived in central cities of the 100 largest metro areas, while 51 percent lived in the suburbs of these cities. All the while, the immigrant population increased nearly threefold. Throughout this period, about 11 percent of immigrants lived in the smaller metro areas, and another 5 percent were in non-metropolitan or rural areas, while also growing in absolute terms.

The list of metropolitan areas with the largest suburban population reflects divergent trends (see Table 3). Slightly more than 20 million immigrants—about half of all immigrants in the United States—live in the suburbs of ten metropolitan areas. These ten places include many of the largest metropolitan areas in the country; although some are well-established continuous gateways such as New York, Chicago, and San Francisco, others are mid-century gainers such as

Figure 5   Residence of the Foreign-Born Population in the United States, 1980–2010

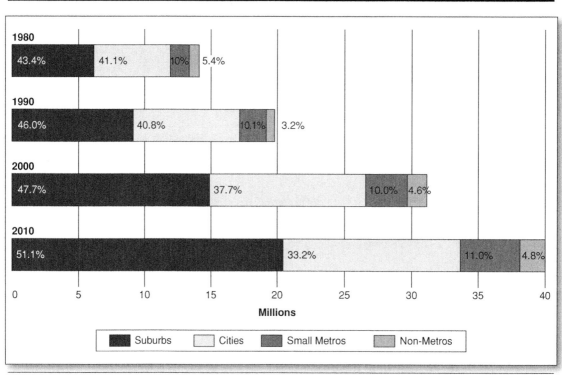

Cities and suburbs are defined for the 95 largest metropolitan areas based on the 2010 population. Primary cities are those that are named in metropolitan area title, as well as any incorporated places that had at least 100,000 in total population in 2010. The residual of the metro area is defined as suburban. In 5 of the 100 largest metropolitan areas, foreign-born population data at the city level are not available from the ACS. Thus, metro areas that are not in the top 95 are classified as "small metros."

Source: Author's calculations of Decennial Census data; and 2010 ACS 1-year estimates, http://www.census.gov/acs/www/.

Los Angeles, Miami, and Houston. Atlanta, a gateway that only recently emerged, is also on the list.

Atlanta also tops the list of metropolitan areas with the greatest proportion of immigrants living in the suburbs: 95 percent. This is not surprising due to its small central city population, as is the case with Washington, D.C., Detroit, and Cleveland, all of which also have vast majorities of the population in suburbs. On average, the metropolitan areas on this list have over 80 percent of immigrants residing in their suburbs, compared to an average of 60 percent across the 100 largest metro areas.

Not coincidentally, the fastest-growing suburban immigrant populations correspond to the metropolitan areas with the fastest-growing immigrant populations in the country. Eight of the ten areas with suburban immigration growth of at least 124 percent in the last decade were metro areas whose immigrant populations doubled during the same period.[14] The foreign-born population grew by 246 percent in Louisville's suburbs, Jackson's by 159 percent, and Knoxville's by 150 percent. All of the metropolitan areas on this list are newer destinations, or in the case of Scranton, reemergent ones. Seven of the ten are in the Southeast.

The history of immigration to the United States is intertwined with the American narrative. This story is often cast as the movement of people in search of economic opportunity, political and religious freedom, and

Table 3   Largest Number, Highest Share, and Fastest Growth of Immigrants in the Suburbs of the 100 Largest Metropolitan Areas, 2010

Largest Number of Immigrants Living in the Suburbs

Rank	Metro Area	Immigrants
1	Los Angeles, CA	2,639,567
2	New York, NY	2,330,889
3	Miami, FL	1,893,530
4	Chicago, IL	1,065,839
5	Washington, D.C.	1,055,461
6	San Francisco, CA	815,914
7	Riverside, CA	757,105
8	Houston, TX	726,498
9	Atlanta, GA	682,813
10	Dallas, TX	617,036
	All Large Metro Areas	20,401,330

Highest Share of Foreign-Born Population Living in the Suburbs

Rank	Metro Area	Share Foreign Born
1	Atlanta, GA	95.3%
2	Miami, FL	87.4%
3	Orlando, FL	87.0%
4	Detroit, MI	86.8%
5	Washington, D.C.	86.3%
6	Birmingham, AL	86.0%
7	Cleveland, OH	85.6%
8	Lakeland, FL	84.0%
9	McAllen, TX	83.0%
10	Dayton, OH	82.7%
	All Large Metro Areas	60.6%

Fastest Suburban Foreign-Born Growth Rate, 2000–2010

Rank	Metro Area	Growth Rate
1	Louisville, KY	246%
2	Jackson, MS	159%
3	Knoxville, TN	150%
4	Des Moines, IA	148%
5	Little Rock, AR	141%
6	Indianapolis, IN	141%
7	Birmingham, AL	140%
8	Scranton, PA	136%
9	Cape Coral, FL	133%
10	Austin, TX	124%
	All Large Metro Areas	27%

Source: Author's calculations of 2000 Decennial Census data; and 2010 ACS 1-year estimates, http://www.census.gov/acs/www/.

a better life for their children. These desires have not changed over time, but the U.S. locations where opportunity unfolds have been altered by industrial restructuring, changes in transportation, and new technology. No longer are immigrants confined to urban ethnic neighborhoods; rather, they are a strong presence in many suburbs. In this way, the history of immigration also parallels the history of American urbanization.

As immigrant settlement patterns have shifted alongside those of the native-born population, immigrant metropolitan settlement trends since 1990 have taken at least two new turns. For most of the twentieth century, the majority of immigrants were drawn to only a handful of established gateways. But new opportunities in metro areas with little history of receiving immigrants led to significant spikes in the foreign-born populations of these places.

In a second shift, immigrants began bypassing cities to settle directly in suburban areas. During industrialization in the early part of the twentieth century, immigrants moved to cities to be close to jobs. Now, as jobs have decentralized and suburban opportunities have opened up, there are more immigrants residing in suburbs than in cities. During the first decade of the twenty-first century, as regions experienced sluggish recovery following the recession, immigration to the United States slowed.

These new patterns are not without conflict and stress, especially as major institutions in the newest metropolitan destinations now confront the challenge of how to serve this diverse population. Many areas have yet to recover from the effects of the recession, and immigrants are often viewed as competitors for jobs and scarce public resources. In some of the metropolitan areas that recently experienced fast immigrant growth, state and local measures to control immigration, especially unauthorized immigration, have been proposed or legislated. But other areas have welcomed immigrants, including places with well-established foreign-born populations that have been integrating immigrants since mid-century or prior. Moreover, cities such as Detroit, Pittsburgh, and Dayton would like to attract and retain immigrants to stem population loss and to stimulate economic activity; those regions are putting out the welcome mat for immigrant newcomers. These distinct and shifting patterns of receptivity will no doubt yield future changes to twenty-first-century immigrant settlement patterns.

Notes

1. Minnesota Population Center, *National Historical Geographic Information System: Version 2.0* (Minneapolis: University of Minnesota, 2011), http://www.nhgis.org.

2. Census Bureau, "Social Characteristics of the Population, for Counties: 1960," *U.S. Census of Population: 1960*, vol. 1, *Characteristics of the Population* (Washington, D.C.: U.S. Government Printing Office, 1963), Table 82.

3. The Brookings Institution, "State of Metropolitan America Indicator Map," http://www.brookings.edu/research/interactives/state-of-metropolitan-america-indicator map#/?subject=7&ind=70&dist=0&data=Number&year=2010&geo=metro&zoom=0&x=0&y=0.

4. See Nancy Foner, *From Ellis Island to JFK: New York's Two Great Waves of Immigration* (New York: Russell Sage Foundation, 2000); and Aristide Zolberg, *A Nation by Design: Immigration Policy in the Fashioning of America* (New York: Russell Sage Foundation, 2006).

5. Sukkoo Kim and Robert A. Margo, "Historical Perspectives on U.S. Economic Geography," in *Handbook of Regional and Urban Economics*, 1st ed., vol. 4, eds. J. Vernon Henderson and Jacques-François Thisse (Amsterdam: Elsevier, 1986), chap. 66, 2981–3019.

6. Charles Hirschman and Elizabeth Mogford, "Immigration and the American Industrial Revolution from 1880 to 1920," *Social Science Research* 38 (2009): 897–920.

7. Figure 3 shows "metropolitan areas" for each decade. These are constructed at the county level and are consistent throughout. While metropolitan areas as we know them today did not exist in the early part of the twentieth century, full metropolitan area definitions for 2010 are used for the sake of making consistent comparisons. See the earlier methodology section for a more detailed discussion.

8. Data on absolute change not shown.

9. See Audrey Singer, "The Rise of New Immigrant Gateways" (Washington, D.C.: Brookings Institution Center on Urban and Metropolitan Policy, February 2004), http://www.brookings.edu/~/media/research/files/reports/2004/2/demographics%20singer/20040301_gateways.pdf; Audrey Singer, Susan W. Hardwick, and Caroline B. Brettell, eds., *Twenty-First Century Gateways: Immigrant Incorporation in Suburban America* (Washington, D.C.: Brookings Institution Press, 2008); and Matthew Hall, Audrey Singer, Gordon F. De Jong, and Deborah Roempke Graefe, "The Geography of Immigrant Skills: Educational Profiles of Metropolitan Areas" (Washington, D.C.: Brookings Institution Metropolitan Policy Program, June 2011), http://www.brookings.edu/~/media/research/files/papers/2011/6/immigrants%20singer/06_immigrants_singer.pdf.

10. Hall et al., "The Geography of Immigrant Skills."

11. See ibid. for listing of all metropolitan areas by gateway type.

12. Singer, "The Rise of New Immigrant Gateways."

13. Singer et al., *Twenty-First Century Gateways*.

14. See Jill H. Wilson and Audrey Singer, "Immigrants in 2010 Metropolitan America" (Washington, D.C.: Brookings Institution Metropolitan Policy Program, October 2011), http://www.brookings.edu/~/media/research/files/papers/2011/10/13%20immigration%20wilson%20singer/1013_immigration_wilson_singer.pdf. Only Des Moines and Austin did not double their immigrant populations between 2000 and 2010.

13-2 "The Politics of Immigration and Suburban Revitalization: Divergent Responses in Adjacent Pennsylvania Towns"*

Domenic Vitiello

Journal of Urban Affairs

For a generation, urban planners and regional scientists have promoted reinvestment in older working class suburbs that have lost population and jobs. The increase of immigration and the spread of immigrant settlement nationally since the 1990s, along with the suburbanization of immigrant settlement, raise important challenges and opportunities for these "first suburbs" (also known as "inner ring suburbs")[1] and their revitalization.[2] Local governments have responded to these changes in divergent ways, seeking to encourage or discourage immigration and the incorporation of newcomers, particularly of unauthorized immigrants.[3] Among other motivations, their responses reflect distinct experiences, fears, aspirations, and expectations regarding immigrants' integration and impacts upon economic and community development.

This article compares two adjacent towns in suburban Philadelphia, Norristown and Bridgeport, Pennsylvania, which share a common history of Italian, Irish, and Eastern European immigration, industrial growth and decline, and recent attempts at riverfront and main street revitalization. Wedged between the vast mall and office parks of the edge city of King of Prussia on one side, and the lifestyle center mall and affluent bedroom communities around Plymouth Meeting on the other, these towns exhibit the central features of economically distressed suburbs within a fragmented and unequal regional landscape of municipalities. Their respective policy responses to immigration also reflect the diversity of first suburbs' social politics and their politics of revitalization.

Mirroring national trends, the two towns' governments took opposite stances toward illegal immigration. In 2003, Norristown's council unanimously passed a form of "sanctuary law," a resolution recognizing the Mexican consular identification card as valid for accessing municipal services. Modeled after an act in the Detroit suburb of Pontiac, Michigan, it was coupled with a successful effort to convince local banks to recognize the card so undocumented immigrants could open accounts, partly to help curb payday robberies of workers paid in cash. Just across the Schuylkill River, in October 2006 Bridgeport's council voted unanimously to fine and revoke licenses of landlords and employers of illegal immigrants. This "illegal immigration relief act" copied that of Hazleton, Pennsylvania, passed earlier that summer, seeking "relief" for local government and taxpayers (other than illegal immigrants). As in other towns with such laws, it was paired with a resolution declaring English as Bridgeport's official language.

By mid-October 2006, 26 of the 49 illegal immigration relief acts introduced in municipalities across the United States were in Pennsylvania, almost all in declining industrial towns (Mansilla, 2006). The state became a central place in the nation's debate over immigration, and these acts helped keep alive recently energized national and local movements for immigration restriction, immigrant rights, and immigrant integration. . . . By contrast, a smaller number of Pennsylvania cities and towns passed laws or resolutions welcoming immigrants regardless of their status. These places, notably

---

Source: Domenic Vitiello, "The Politics of Immigration and Suburban Revitalization: Divergent Responses in Adjacent Pennsylvania Towns," *Journal of Urban Affairs*, 36 (3), August 2014. Reprinted with permission from John Wiley & Sons.

*Endnotes have been omitted. Please consult the original source.

Norristown, Lancaster, and Philadelphia, had also experienced deindustrialization, population loss, and recent Latino immigration. These patterns characterized many American cities and towns re-emerging as immigrant gateways in the 1990s and 2000s (Singer, Hardwick, & Brettell, 2008a).

The case of Norristown and Bridgeport raises questions of relevance for suburbs and metropolitan regions broadly. What accounts for different local responses to recent immigration, and what does this have to do with their revitalization? Specifically, what are the terms of debate regarding immigrants' integration and impacts in local economies and communities, their housing and labor markets? How do the social and economic pressures, and the recent social history, of these first suburbs help shape their politics of immigration? How do local governments navigate the challenges and opportunities of immigration and revitalization in places beyond the historic big city immigrant gateways?

Examining the politics of revitalization illuminates key dimensions of local immigration debates and policies beyond the terms law and order, which are important but not sufficient for understanding their motives, meanings, and impacts. This helps locate immigration in the history and politics of decline and renewal in urban and suburban America (see Jones-Correa, 2006; Roth, 2009; Carpio, Irazabal, Pulido, 2011; Carr, Lichter, & Kefalas, 2012). Newcomers' settlement presents opportunities to address first suburbs' struggles with economic decline and the loss of younger generations, but it also heightens fiscal stresses and fears in towns with weak tax bases and public sector capacity. Significantly, new immigrants' impacts on local housing, neighborhoods, and economies occupy a central place in arguments put forth by proponents of both restrictive and affirmative approaches. Indeed, opposing and (in fewer cases) welcoming unauthorized immigration have become key tools that distressed municipalities use to cope (if not always rationally) with urban and suburban decline, renewal, and associated changes.

Some of this divergence of local responses can be explained by the particularities of local histories of migration and revitalization. Although the authors of both illegal immigration relief acts and sanctuary laws repeat the rhetoric and laws of others, their responses are also based on their own experiences (or lack of experience) of newcomers and their impacts. Norristown experienced African American, Latino, and other migrant groups' settlement since the 1960s, while Bridgeport did not. This helped shape distinct perspectives on immigration's meanings for local communities and economies.

This study is based primarily on 23 semistructured interviews by the author and research assistants conducted between 2007 and 2011.[4] We interviewed local politicians, police, realtors, and bureaucrats in each town, including planning and code enforcement professionals in Norristown and the borough manager in Bridgeport, as well as representatives of local and regional civic organizations active in the two towns, including immigrant service providers, labor organizations, and a coalition promoting the interests of older suburbs in the region. Interviews focused on the two towns' histories of immigration and on the impetus and rationale for their laws. We also examined local newspaper coverage of immigration and of the laws, which included interviews with these and other politicians.

The article first reviews the diversity of immigration and local responses in American suburbs and towns. It then discusses Norristown's and Bridgeport's recent demographic and economic histories and the social politics they shaped. The next section examines the ways public and civic leaders parsed the issues behind the towns' different responses, exploring their diverse rationales and links to revitalization. The conclusion reflects upon the politics of immigration and revitalization in the metropolitan context.[5]

Suburbanization and Local Responses

Recent immigrants have settled in older working class suburbs in metropolitan America, helping some suburbs begin to grow again after decades of decline. The diversity of immigration intersects with the diversity of suburbs to produce a complex range of social and economic impacts, actual and perceived. As immigrants move to older suburbs, a variety of challenges and opportunities arise related to housing, labor, urban development, and public services. For a generation, these pressures and the metropolitan disparities they reflect have been the subject of scholarship concerned with regionalism (see Downs, 1994; Orfield, 1997; Dreier, Mollenkopf, & Swanstrom, 2001), though immigration has only recently entered this discussion as some of the research on immigrant suburbanization has examined first suburbs (Jones-Correa, 2006, 2008; Massey, 2008; Odom, 2008; Singer et al., 2008a; Carr et al., 2012).

Suburbanization and diversity are defining characteristics of immigration today. The majority of immigrants to the United States now move directly to the suburbs, settling everywhere from McMansion subdivisions in the exurbs to rowhomes and apartments in older, working class streetcar suburbs (Frey, 2006; Li & Skop, 2007; Singer et al., 2008a; Massey, 2008; Katz, Creighton, Amsterdam, & Chowkwanyun, 2010). Immigrants' impacts on suburbs are equally diverse, as renters, homeowners, and workers in construction, landscaping, and domestic services vital to suburban development and quality of life (Carter & Vitiello, 2011). Immigration also raises old fears about overcrowding and newcomers' economic and social integration (Myers, Baer, & Choi, 1996; Harwood & Myers, 2002; Adams & Osho, 2008; Roth, 2009; Vitiello, 2009).

These tensions and fragmented patterns highlight an issue of central importance to proponents of regionalism, namely the uneven distribution of costs and benefits of labor and housing markets between different sorts of suburbs. At the metropolitan level, the costs and benefits of immigrants (of diverse socioeconomic status) to the economy are not shared evenly between working-class towns and job centers or higher wealth residential suburbs (Smith & Edmonston, 1997; Singer, Vitiello, Katz, & Park, 2008b). The latter places reap their labor but generally do not pay for their children's schooling, the libraries and community centers that teach them English, or health clinics when they get sick.

Responding to these and other pressures, local governments in the United States have recently reacted in divergent ways to immigration, particularly of unauthorized Latinos (Harwood, 2005, 2009; National Immigration Law Center [NILC], 2005, 2008; Vazquez-Castillo, 2009; Ridgley & Steil, 2009; Martinez & Stowell, 2012). After Congress failed to pass immigration reform in early 2006, amidst mass protests in big cities by a newly invigorated immigrant rights movement, the former coalmining and ironworking town of Hazleton, Pennsylvania passed the nation's first municipal illegal immigration relief act

that summer. It imposed fines and penalties on landlords who rent to undocumented immigrants and businesses that employ them. Towns across the country copied this law, especially in Eastern Pennsylvania and largely in places devastated by deindustrialization a generation ago. Bridgeport was the second such place in suburban Philadelphia to copy it, after Riverside, New Jersey. Riverside later repealed its act, due to the costs of fighting legal challenges, business closures as immigrant customers left town, and embarrassment from the national media attention it received (Belson & Capuzzo, 2007). Bridgeport and other towns have been threatened with lawsuits by civil liberties and immigrant rights groups. They have waited to enforce their laws while legal challenges to Hazleton move through the courts.[6]

The spread of illegal immigration relief acts sharpened an already polarized landscape of local governments taking contradictory approaches to unauthorized immigration. By 2006, most major cities from Boston to Los Angeles had "sanctuary laws" forbidding local police from asking people about immigration status. They also issued resolutions affirming immigrants' access to city services like schools, libraries, and health clinics. Big cities support language access, immigrant businesses, and marketing campaigns to attract and retain newcomers, usually regardless of people's legal status (Vitiello, 2009). Some smaller city and town governments have also adopted welcoming stances that share the goals of promoting safety and prosperity, making this landscape of local responses to unauthorized immigration more complicated than just big cities with "sanctuary laws" versus small towns with illegal immigration relief acts.

Academic and popular observers have interpreted these responses principally in terms of law and order, public safety, and civil rights (see Harwood, 2009; Roth, 2009; Vazquez-Castillo, 2009; Ridgley & Steil, 2009; Carpio et al., 2011; Martinez & Stowell, 2012). Supporters of restrictive measures cite violent crimes committed by immigrants and associated costs to police departments among their chief motivations. They argue that these acts (should) give localities the power to impose law and order, relative to immigration violations and other laws, in the absence of federal action on immigration reform. Their critics point out that crime rates among undocumented immigrants are lower than the general population, a point substantiated by criminologists (see Sampson, 2008). Critics claim local immigration enforcement is unjust, and that it spreads fear among legal as well as unauthorized immigrants and native-born minorities, limiting communication between police and residents, particularly victims and witnesses of crime, which "sanctuary" policies seek to encourage (see Kirk, Papachristos, Fagan, & Tyler, 2012). Yet these are just some of the issues and arguments behind local laws, which typically reflect a variety of concerns, only some of which local authorities have power to influence.

Local measures related to illegal immigration are necessarily tied to national debates, which often obscure the particular experiences that motivate local authorities to act. The authors of both illegal immigration relief acts and "sanctuary laws" have often introduced these bills in reaction (positive or negative) to laws in other places, including some Pennsylvania towns' declaration of opposition to Hazleton's act (see Birkbeck, 2007). Yet, notwithstanding the widespread copying of rhetoric and legislation from elsewhere, local conditions and experiences also explain much of why certain towns take particular stances. Although first suburbs share similar economic pressures, their histories sometimes differ in ways that shape distinct politics of immigration and revitalization.

Local Histories and Social Politics

To understand immigration's implications for local planning and development, it is critical to understand the nuances of receiving communities' social, political economic, and neighborhood dynamics (Sandercock, 2003). Interviewees in Bridgeport and Norristown recounted the history of immigration to their towns in ways that help explain key aspects of their respective responses to recent immigration. Despite the similarities between these and other first suburbs and older industrial towns, their histories of race and migration differ in ways that impact the politics of local residents and government.

Like most of Philadelphia's working-class suburbs, Norristown and Bridgeport are former factory towns. Though both are older settlements, they grew with Irish, Italian, and Eastern European immigration in the nineteenth and early twentieth centuries. Most settled in Norristown, the county seat and a much larger town than Bridgeport, which in turn was populated largely by people moving over the bridge from Norristown.

In a familiar story across the Northeast and Midwest, after World War Two deindustrialization and mass suburbanization brought shuttered mills and population loss. Nearby residential, office park, and mall development helped make Norristown and Bridgeport relatively poor towns in a rich county. The close presence of the malls decimated the Main Street shopping district in Norristown, which also largely served as Bridgeport's commercial downtown. Today, it has a mix of law offices, construction supply shops, lawnmower repair shops, Mexican restaurants, and Italian funeral homes. Big employers in Norristown include the county, courts, and two hospitals, though most higher paid employees live in other suburbs. When a huge fire in Bridgeport (a much smaller place), consumed the industrial park on the river in 2000, it lost its main source of local jobs. For decades, regional planners have categorized both Bridgeport and Norristown as fiscally and economically distressed first suburbs (see Delaware Valley Regional Planning Commission [DVRPC], 1997; Gold, 2008).

Post–World War Two *out*-migration from both towns reflects the common story of families moving to new subdivisions and young people not returning after college (Table 1); however, the two towns' experiences of *in*-migration differed in composition and in timing (Table 2). In the 1960s and 1970s African Americans and Puerto Ricans came to Norristown from Philadelphia, New York, the South, and the Caribbean. Some Mariel Cubans were resettled there, partly because Puerto Ricans had established social services for Spanish speakers, though most soon moved on to Miami. Small numbers of Indians, Koreans, Jamaicans, Panamanians, and Filipinos also settled in Norristown in the 1980s. In total, more people departed than arrived, a pattern shared with most medium-to-large U.S. cities (Myers, 1999). Meanwhile, until the mid-1990s, Bridgeport's population was almost all white, its foreign-born residents aged Europeans who had come decades earlier (Tables 1, 2, and 3).

Table 1 Norristown and Bridgeport Population—Total and Percent Foreign-Born

		1970	1980	1990	2000	2010
Total population	Norristown	38,169	34,684	30,749	31,284	34,324
	Bridgeport	5,630	4,843	4,292	4,371	4,554
Percent FB	Norristown	6.3	6.0	5.2	10.2	19.6
	Bridgeport	9.6	6.5	3.2	7.3	n.d.[a]

[a]*Bridgeport is too small to achieve a statistically significant sample in the American Community Survey 5-year series.*

Source: U.S. Census and American Community Survey (2006–2010).

In the late 1990s, both towns' populations began growing, ending three decades of decline, largely due to Mexican immigration. Norristown's foreign-born population roughly doubled in the 1990s, from 5.2 to 10.2 percent, and again in the 2000s, to 19.6 percent (Table 1). In 2003, civic leaders estimated 12,000 Mexican residents in peak landscaping season each year (Gidjunis, 2003), in a town of some 31,000.[7] In 2010, over one quarter of residents identified as Hispanic (Table 4).

Across the river, in the mid-1990s Councilman Pizza noticed "a social change," as "children were growing up and moving out, old people were dying off," and new "people were moving in" (Interview 1, also 3, 4, 6, 7). By 2000, Bridgeport was home to Chinese, Indians, Mexicans, and Salvadorans, some of whom moved from Norristown as earlier immigrants had done. Their numbers were small but noticeable in a place of some 4,000 residents, as the foreign-born grew from 3.2 to 7.3 percent of the population in the 1990s. By

Table 2 Norristown Top 10 Foreign-Born (FB) Groups, 1990 and 2000

1990	#	% share of FB	2000	#	% share of FB
Italy	469	29.3	Mexico	1,397	43.9
Not reported	184	11.5	Vietnam	260	8.2
India	103	6.4	Korea	214	6.7
Korea	91	5.7	Italy	187	5.9
Jamaica	89	5.6	Jamaica	165	5.2
U.K.	84	5.2	India	126	4.0
Cuba	63	3.9	China	88	2.8
Poland	46	2.9	Haiti	68	2.1
Panama	41	2.6	Germany	55	1.7
Philippines	39	2.4	Greece	55	1.7
Total FB	1,603	100	Total FB	3,179	100

Source: U.S. Census and American Community Survey (2006–2010).

Table 3 Bridgeport Foreign-Born (FB) Groups, 1990 and 2000 (Top 10)

1990	#	% share of FB	2000	#	% share of FB
Europe	139	100	China	68	21.3
			Italy	60	18.8
			India	48	15.0
			Mexico	48	15.0
			Ukraine	30	9.4
			El Salvador	16	5.0
			Slovakia	9	2.8
			Philippines	9	2.8
			U.K.	7	2.2
			Austria	7	2.2
Total FB	139	100	Total FB	320	100

2010, it was 12.8 percent Hispanic, 2.8 percent Asian, and 0.3 percent black (Tables 1 and 4).

Recent immigrants have come to the area for many of the same reasons as native-born residents. Nearby King of Prussia/Valley Forge is Philadelphia's premier edge city, with the region's largest concentration of suburban jobs. This and other nearby job centers have two identifiable immigrant workforces. One, comprised mostly of South and East Asians, but also of Europeans and Latin Americans, works in pharmaceutical research, financial services, and other professions and lives in dispersed bedroom communities. The second immigrant workforce, made up mostly of Mexicans with some Africans, Brazilians, Central Americans, and others, works in restaurants, janitorial and security services, cleaning homes and offices, and landscaping and construction. They tend to live in the region's old working-class towns, finding affordable rental housing there and access to jobs serving the growth and quality of life in wealthier suburbs nearby. Immigrants, especially Mexicans, have changed the face of Norristown. (Their impact has been less visible in Bridgeport.) On Marshall Street in Norristown's West End, grocery, phone card, and clothing stores, bakeries, and a tortilla factory are the commercial spine of a "Little Mexico." The town's birthrate has risen, and the lower grades of its elementary schools have swelled with children of Mexican immigrants (Wortham, Mortimer, & Allard, 2009). In Bridgeport, although a few Latin American–owned stores have been established (usually with limited tenure), residential enclaves of new immigrants are difficult to discern, even for longtime residents who know a lot about their neighbors (Interviews 1, 2, 4–7).

Table 4 Norristown and Bridgeport Percent of Population by Race/Ancestry, 2010

	Black	Hispanic	Mexican	Non-Hispanic White
Norristown	35.9	28.3	18.2	31.6
Bridgeport	0.3	12.8	no data	79.8

These different experiences with newcomers figure prominently in civic leaders' explanations of why their town governments responded to Mexican immigration in opposite ways. "Blacks moved to Norristown decades ago," followed by "little waves" of migrants from the Caribbean and Asia, and over time whites grew accustomed to people of color settling there, well before Mexicans arrived (Interview 14, also 6, 8–12, 16, 20). Observers in and outside of Norristown routinely compare Italians and Mexicans in a favorable light, noting shared Catholicism, migration, and labor histories, including hard work in vital industries. They sometimes speculate about white landlords, employers, and neighbors preferring immigrants over blacks, a claim supported by some scholarship on labor and housing markets (Interviews 8–18, 20; Waldinger, 1997; Charles, 2006).

In Bridgeport it was not the local experiences of recent generations that provided the lens through which politicians and others viewed newcomers, but rather the collective memory of their immigrant ancestors. Echoing Hazleton Mayor Lou Barletta and other Italian American critics of illegal immigration today, they compared Italian immigrants' legal status and experiences of Americanization a century ago to their understanding of unauthorized Mexican immigrants today as a group not forced to assimilate (Vitiello, 2011). "Teddy Roosevelt said in the early 1900s that when you came to this country you were supposed to speak English, be able to read and write it and give up your allegiance to your home country," said Councilman John Pizza, one of the illegal immigration relief act's two sponsors, "which is basically what our grandparents did as Italian immigrants who had to learn English" (Interview 1, also 3, 4, 6).

Italian, Irish, and Eastern European Americans in both Bridgeport and Norristown draw upon the narratives of the white ethnic revival of the 1960s, including "appeals to the romantic icon of yesterday's European immigrant—downtrodden, hard-working, self-reliant, triumphant" (Jacobson, 2006, pp. 8–9; see also Luconi, 2001). Significantly, leaders and many of their native-born constituents in both Norristown and Bridgeport cast unauthorized immigrants from Mexico as hard-working. But only in Norristown did they also describe them as self-reliant and positive contributors to the town, particularly its revitalization along Marshall Street and adjacent neighborhoods (Interviews 1–12, 18–20).

Though narratives of the ethnic revival support both pro-and anti-immigration stances, Bridgeport's response to Mexican immigration is more characteristic of white ethnic receiving communities (Jacobson, 2006). It is especially prevalent in older industrial towns and their residents' early reactions to social change after decades of stagnation. For a long time, of course, Bridgeport residents have had some experience with immigrants and people of color around the Philadelphia region, including in Norristown, but rarely in their own neighborhoods. Two big Italian and Ukrainian ethnic parishes still shape old-timers' views of the town's social geography (Interviews 1–3, 6–7).

The experiences of Norristown and Bridgeport suggest that the settlement of Latinos and other people of color across generations helped forge a politics of welcoming recent Mexican immigrants, whereas its absence apparently limited such a development. This pattern appears consistent with the experiences of big "sanctuary cities" and towns with restrictive acts (Vazquez-Castillo, 2009). It complicates scholars' findings that, in places lacking traditional Latino presence, or in places manifesting prejudice across generations as in the Southwest, immigrant and receiving communities often have room to develop positive models of Latino immigrant identity and integration (see Wortham et al., 2009).

Race does matter in this story, but in more nuanced ways than critics of illegal immigration relief acts charge as they repeat familiar claims. Norristown-based legal aid, housing rights, and social service agencies protested Bridgeport's law as it moved through council. Eddie Cruz, then director of Latin American Community Action of Montgomery County (ACLAMO), stated: "It is obvious to me the ordinance could be used to foment an atmosphere of profiling" (Phucas, 2006a). A labor organizer averred the act was "scapegoating particular races" for broader problems (Interview 14). Bridgeport's politicians countered that these accusations of racism were unfounded, and that their opposition to illegal immigration was not just about Mexicans or any particular race (Interviews 1, 3, 6, 7). The merits of these claims and counter-claims aside, they obscured the more complex context and motivations behind both towns' laws.

Diverse and Divergent Rationales

Unpacking the particular reasons and rationales behind Norristown and Bridgeport's different laws reveals a multiplicity of concerns, again inspired by local experience and by developments in other places. In a broad sense, both towns' governments sought to gain a greater handle on undocumented immigration and its local impacts, and their leaders cited essentially the same set of issues. Crime and law and order appeared at the forefront of their concerns, yet these were just part of the story and in key ways were not as important as they seemed. At least as significant in both towns were interrelated issues of fiscal and economic vitality, newcomer integration, housing, and revitalization.

Bridgeport's illegal immigration relief act obscures its leaders' particular impetus to pass the law. In copying Hazleton's act, the borough council repeated the "finding":

> That unlawful employment, the harboring of illegal aliens in dwelling units in the Borough of Bridgeport, and crime committed by illegal aliens harm the health, safety and welfare of authorized US workers and legal residents in the Borough of Bridgeport. Illegal immigration leads to higher crime rates, subjects our hospitals to fiscal hardship and legal residents to substandard quality of care, contributes to other burdens on public services, increasing their cost and diminishing their availability to legal residents, and diminishes our overall quality of life. (Borough of Bridgeport, 2006)

Yet all of the local politicians and police interviewed acknowledged that crime by unauthorized immigrants in Bridgeport was not an issue. According to Borough Manager Anthony DiSanto, "Our chief of police had no records of the crime rate going up" (Interview 4, also interviews 1–3, 7). A police officer noted, "The complaints that the department might get [about Mexicans] would be overcrowding and parking, not drinking, yelling or cursing," nor other nuisances or more serious crimes (Interview 2). One interviewee in Bridgeport opined that Mexicans living there are "law abiding" and "good people" who "just want to work and live peacefully" (Interview 6). The other claims copied from Hazleton did not describe Bridgeport's experience, either, as the town has no hospital or health clinic and very few locally based jobs.

To the extent that "local" crime motivated Bridgeport's leaders, it was in the town next door. "You just have to look around and right over the bridge to Norristown and see that there are a lot of arrests that have been made and crime that happens . . . it turns out that it's an illegal immigrant," said Mayor Jerry Nicola, the town's former police chief. "The bridge doesn't really separate these people," he added (Interview 3). Nicola and his colleagues expressed apprehension about losing control of law and order, and of their town more generally, as some believed Norristown's old-timers had (Interviews 1, 3, 4, 6, 7). One politician presented the town's act as a proactive measure, noting, "Bridgeport doesn't want things happening that happen elsewhere" (Interview 7). Another interviewee even speculated that Mexicans had moved to Bridgeport for the purpose of "escaping the crime and problems of Norristown" (Interview 6).

Crime inspired Norristown's law in a more tangible sense—specifically, crimes *against*, not *by*, Mexicans. Local leaders' focus on curbing payday robberies of immigrants carrying cash repeated one of the central claims of sanctuary laws and their supporters. "If immigrants have cards, they won't be as fearful to report crimes or cooperate," claimed Norristown Council Vice President Olivia Brady (O'Toole, 2002). Recognition of the consular ID was a logical outgrowth of local government and civic efforts already under way to foster communication and public safety, which included police and town watch outreach at Spanish mass (Interviews 12, 14, 15). As one observer put it, in the early 2000s the police "were very conciliatory. They wanted that part of the community to report crimes, not make that part of the community ungovernable" (Interview 14).

Through their immigration acts, both Norristown and Bridgeport sought to impose greater law and order, though of course in different senses. Bridgeport's politicians emphasized that their opposition to illegal immigration was about the fact of being illegal and basic fairness to people who followed the rules of U.S. immigration law (Interviews 1–3, 6, 7). Norristown's leaders, by contrast, promoted law and order through newcomer incorporation and by seeking to regulate immigrants' impacts via other means.

Norristown council members cast their act as one step towards integrating unauthorized immigrants, especially in economic terms. Immigrants' ability to open bank accounts "puts money into the banking system rather than keeping it out on the streets," argued Councilwoman Brady on the eve of the bill's passage, adding, "the sooner we can get them to be taxpaying citizens, the better off we're going to be." She hoped that recognizing the consular ID card would help the town gain a fuller accounting of the Mexican population: "This will give us more knowledge of who's here, and it's better than pushing immigrants further underground and having less knowledge about them" (O'Toole, 2002). In the fall of 2006, as Pennsylvania towns debated Hazleton's law, Norristown's Council discussed but rejected the prospect of a similar act. "The Mexican community is becoming integral to Norristown," stated Council President Bill Procyson, "and we'd like to see what we can do to [better] integrate them" (Phucas, 2006b).

In Bridgeport, politicians expressed fear about the limits of unauthorized immigrants' social and economic integration, again in ways that repeated national narratives and referenced Norristown more than Bridgeport itself. "These immigrants have their own society and keep their own society," asserted Councilman Pizza, "you don't see American flags everywhere, you just see Mexican flags" in Norristown. "Illegal immigrants pay nothing and are a drain on your taxes for services," he continued. "I realize they are hardworking people but they are underground with no social security pay-ins, they have medical care for free and are a burden on the police department and social services and schools" (Interview 1, also interviews 3, 6, 7). Although politicians and residents in Norristown, too, were concerned about working-class immigrants' impacts on the fiscal and operational pressures already experienced by local schools and public services, they cast those impacts in more nuanced terms and as problems they could partially solve (Interviews 8–11, 16, 21; see also Gidjunis, 2003; Phucas, 2006b).

Echoing an old theme in debates about immigrants' integration and impacts in cities, overcrowded housing has been arguably the greatest concern for residents and government in both Bridgeport and Norristown. Complaints of overcrowding were the only specific incidents that interviewees in Bridgeport cited for their law. "Leading up to the ordinance we [City Council] got a lot of complaints of overcrowding," reported Councilman Pizza, "it would be a single family dwelling and have 15–20 renters so the neighbors would be complaining" (Interview 1, also interviews 2–7). Some in Bridgeport and Norristown questioned the scale, scope, and sometimes the veracity of complaints about overcrowding, reflecting conflicts and uncertainty typical of debates about overcrowding (Interviews 4, 6, 8, 9, 11, 14, 15, 22; Myers et al., 1996; Harwood & Myers, 2002; Roth, 2009).

In Norristown, taking overcrowding seriously became a key way that politicians sought to address some residents' fears about newcomers and to reframe those fears in more positive terms of community stability and vitality. In dismissing an illegal immigration relief act in 2006, Councilman Procyson was careful to add, "If people are aware of an overcrowding situation, they can call us (at the borough). . . . (Overcrowding) is not good for them or the community" (Phucas, 2006b). Local planners and Latino social service professionals also presented overcrowding as an issue of social and economic "neighborhood stability" (Interview 9, also 8, 11, 22; Phucas, 2006b). Reflecting a common pattern nationally, some homeowners lamented that renters do not pay property taxes, which bureaucrats and activists were quick to point out they do indirectly through their rent (Interviews 9, 11, 14, 15, 17, 20, 22).

Local immigrant housing issues are "really about landlords" and their impacts on neighborhoods, said one labor organizer (Interview 15). Sometimes the landlords who collect immigrants' rent (and employers that hire them) reside and reinvest their money locally, but often they do not. Absentee owners hold much of Norristown's property, particularly in immigrant neighborhoods, and are an important part of the local economy. The town's landlord class has grown dependent on immigrants for rental income as well as a tighter market buoying rental rates and property values. Owner occupancy continued to decline, from 46 to 43 percent between 2000 and 2006–2010, as population grew (U.S. Census). Homeowners often blame tenants for landlords' shortcomings, such as failure to keep up properties or willingness to rent to more people than occupancy laws allow (Interviews 4–6, 8, 9, 14–18). Norristown stepped up code enforcement, not only to mitigate these tensions but also to address in concrete fashion broader concerns about property values and the physical integrity of old neighborhoods (Interview 22). By contrast, Bridgeport's leaders and their constituents, again looking across the river, viewed their law as a way to prevent the growth of an absentee landlord class and its potential for neglect of property and community (Interviews 4–6, 14, 16).

Bridgeport largely lacked the civic and public sector capacity that Norristown had to forge a rhetorical politics as well as practical initiatives of revitalization in which immigration played a valued and constructive role. Norristown has a much larger local government, with a planning and municipal development director from Kenya and Latino and Asian American staff in planning and other agencies. Some of these people and their colleagues claim that their backgrounds predispose them to a more welcoming stance and help them understand the practical issues faced by immigrant and receiving communities.[8] In more tangible terms, they are able to implement modest yet visible community and economic development programs, from a Small Business Assistance Center to historic façade rehabilitation matching grants (Interviews 8, 9, 14, 16, 18). Bridgeport has no planning department and only a bare-bones bureaucracy. Local government officials noted it lacks the resources to defend its law in court or to translate official documents, making its English-only ordinance simply a gesture to "tweak people's noses" (Interview 4, also 7). In this light, the different sizes of these towns mattered considerably.

Beyond government itself, the political economy of urban development in and around Norristown has fostered a sort of "growth politics" of immigration (Interview 14). In explaining the town's stance towards immigrants, observers inside and outside of local government consistently pointed to West Marshall Street's revival and the growth of previously declining neighborhoods since Mexicans began arriving in large numbers. The revival of neighborhood-serving retail benefited old-timers as well as newcomers. Moreover, for most of the last two decades, the construction industry in surrounding suburbs has kept up a voracious appetite for the services of ethnic Italian–owned contractors based in Norristown, who rely heavily on Mexican labor. Several big landscaping companies in town have taken part in the federal seasonal guest worker program since the 1990s. The politics of immigration and revitalization in Norristown is thus rooted in and acknowledges the interdependency of employees and employers, renters and landlords, shopkeepers and customers, taxpayers and local government (Interviews 8–10, 14, 16, 18, 19, 22).

Revitalization also figured prominently in Bridgeport's politics of immigration, beyond the housing and fiscal issues already noted. Politicians and other residents spoke about the illegal immigration relief act as a way to help ensure the town is revitalized in a way that does not discomfort or push out longtime residents who are already anxious about the redevelopment of the old industrial park. The act passed in the early phases of a large mixed-use project there with some 900 planned housing units plus retail. "Redevelopment is coming," Councilman Pizza noted, "and there's going to be an influx of people that are going to turn the town into a yuppie town because the things being built are for upscale younger people" (Interview 1, also 2–4, 6, 7). Curbing illegal immigration and its perceived impacts seemed to enhance local government's influence over changes largely outside its control, in an effort to "get redevelopment right" (Interview 6).

The outcomes of Norristown and Bridgeport's laws, including their impacts upon community and economic development, have been unsurprising and largely consistent with their aims. As in other towns with illegal immigration relief acts, Bridgeport's law discourages Latin Americans from settling there. According to realtors, civil servants, and the staff of civic organizations, Mexicans and other Latinos left Bridgeport, although some still live there or have moved there recently (Interviews 4–6, 9, 11, 14). "It's funny the way everything stopped," said one realtor a year after the ordinance passed, as he stopped receiving calls from people who sounded Hispanic and some

Mexican tenants abruptly moved (Interview 5). Borough Manager DiSanto reported in late 2007, "three Mexican restaurants said that after the bill, they started to lose a lot of business, I guess especially from illegal Hispanics, and one has closed down" (Interview 4). These patterns of people leaving and businesses closing are typical in towns that pass illegal immigration relief acts (see Capuzzo, 2006; Belson & Capuzzo, 2007).

After its "sanctuary law" passed, Norristown kept growing thanks largely to migration from Mexico, and most of local government sustained its affirmative politics of immigration. When the federal Secure Communities program compelled local police to collaborate in deportation beginning in late 2008 (Immigration and Customs Enforcement [ICE], 2012), the borough manager and council still sought to protect unauthorized immigrants. At a recent community meeting, Borough Manager David Forrest promised Latino residents the town government would discipline local cops if they were found to be profiling Latinos. Councilwoman Linda Christian invited people who felt uneasy reporting crimes to the police to report them directly to any member of the council or the borough administration. Notwithstanding this stance, Mexican and native-born observers complained that the new federal law enforcement regime was bad for business and the local economy, suggesting that Latinos were taking their money elsewhere (Varela, 2012).

Norristown and Bridgeport continue to reflect the diversity, complexity, and polarization of immigration debates in the United States. The jumble of motivations behind the [sic] their divergent responses to unauthorized immigration show how inappropriate it can be to reduce explanations of local responses to questions of law and order versus racism, or any other single issue or false dichotomy. Bridgeport and Norristown also reveal many of the important community and economic development issues highlighted by immigration, and the degree to which immigration debates are revitalization debates, particularly in first suburbs and older industrial communities.

The Metropolitics of Immigration

In towns like Bridgeport, Norristown, and Hazleton, "immigration problems" (and opportunities) are tangled up, often inextricably, with everyday economic and social concerns, including issues of metropolitan equity and vitality. Residents sometimes conflate newcomers with larger fiscal and infrastructure pressures (Interviews 14–16). The "defensive localism" of Bridgeport reflects real concerns (Weir, 1994), including government's limited capacity to manage newcomer integration or revitalization in ways the public sector in Norristown to some extent can accomplish. Bridgeport followed a common pattern among places that have experienced deindustrialization, in which individuals and institutions sometimes exacerbate the pressures of decline and reinforce regional inequality by limiting outsiders' access and investment (Dreier et al., 2001; Gillette, 2005). Norristown took an approach more typical of big cities with more diverse populations, whose histories of deindustrialization and efforts at revitalization have produced growth politics in which immigration plays a constructive and increasingly vital role. And like their counterparts in big cities, politicians and bureaucrats in Norristown's borough hall also came to understand their problems and opportunities regionally.

The politics of immigration and revitalization in Norristown have enabled—and in turn been reinforced by—the participation of local government, civic organizations, and residents in building communities of interest beyond the town. The borough manager and community leaders have been active in the First Suburbs Alliance, a coalition of public and third sector groups formed in 2007 that advocates for state funding and reinvestment in towns outside of Philadelphia. Its members have discussed immigration and ways to foster "stable integration," though their advocacy campaigns have targeted issues of "broader appeal," such as school funding and healthcare—all this in a state whose legislators have continued to push bills cracking down on illegal immigrants (Interview 14, also 16, 20, 21, 23). Another town's mayor, active in First Suburbs, characterized its members as those who want to explore cooperation with other groups and towns, not those with defensive politics (Interview 21). In addition, Norristown's government, civic groups, and immigrant and native-born residents find political, social, and material support among social service providers in the Montgomery County Collaborative as well as regional labor organizers, legal services, and immigrant rights groups such as the New Sanctuary Movement Coalition of Faith Communities (Interviews 9, 14, 16, 20, 23). Norristown's greater infrastructure of public and civic institutions, along with its politics of immigration and revitalization, help it connect to these resources.

Regional initiatives, however, have limited ability to resolve U.S. governments' and communities' conflicts over unauthorized immigration. Bridgeport remains relatively isolated from regional networks (Interviews 6, 11, 14–17, 23), though it is part of a larger network of mostly small town leaders and state legislators seeking to restrict illegal immigration at the sub-national level. And, of course, federal opposition to state and local immigration laws and federal deportation policies and programs have undermined both Bridgeport and Norristown's acts, and others like them.

Yet the politics of immigration are worth understanding in regional context, partly to help illuminate the social and material issues at stake in different local responses. The "heterolocal" nature of immigration—the diverse patterns of people working, shopping, residing, and consequently paying different sorts of taxes as well as seeking services in different municipalities (Zelinsky & Lee, 1998)—renders the distribution of immigration's local costs and benefits difficult to measure and presumably more uneven. This exacerbates the inequities produced by metropolitan fragmentation and can heighten the pressures on first suburbs with already limited tax bases and high demand for services.

At the same time, immigration presents important opportunities for metropolitan regions and their first suburbs' revitalization, a more promising form of "relief" from these pressures for the long term. Understanding and being able to manage some of immigration's impacts in suburban and small town housing and labor markets is increasingly relevant to the future of these places. Approaching these issues as challenges and opportunities for integration and revitalization offers a more constructive framework to manage change than disputes over law and order or racism. Such disputes, notwithstanding their truths, tend to be dead-end debates, further polarizing people and places. Instead, grappling with immigration's implications for revitalization allows local governments and their constituents to take seriously the pressures they face, with immigration as more than a zero-sum proposition. This is a key step for policy makers, planners, and others seeking to manage immigration to the advantage of cities, suburbs, and regions.

References

Adams, M., & Osho, G. (2008). Migration, immigration and the politics of space: Immigration and local housing issues in the United States. *Research Journal of International Studies, 8,* 5–12.

Belson, K., & Capuzzo, J. P. (2007). Towns rethink laws against illegal immigrants. *New York Times,* September 26.

Birkbeck, M. (2007). Appeals expected in Hazleton case after judge strikes down law regulating illegal immigrants. *The Morning Call,* July 27.

Borough of Bridgeport. (2006). *Illegal Immigration Relief Act.* Retrieved August 30, 2013, from http://ecode360 .com/10371205.

Capuzzo, J. P. (2006). Town battling illegal immigration is emptier now. *New York Times,* July 28.

Carpio, G., Irazabal, C., & Pulido, L. (2011). Right to the suburb? Rethinking Lefebvre and immigrant activism. *Journal of Urban Affairs, 33,* 185–208.

Carr, P. J., Lichter, D. T., & Kefalas, M. J. (2012). Can immigration save small-town America? Hispanic boom-towns and the uneasy path to renewal. *The Annals of the American Academy of Political and Social Science, 641,* 38–57.

Carter, T., & Vitiello, D. (2011). Immigrants, refugees and housing: The North American experience. In C. Teixeira, W. Li, & A. Kobayashi (Eds.), *Immigrant geographies of North American cities* (pp. 91–111). Toronto: Oxford University Press.

Charles, C. (2006). *Won't you be my neighbor? Race, class, and residence in Los Angeles.* New York: Russell Sage.

Delaware Valley Regional Planning Commission (DVRPC). (1997). *The future of first-generation suburbs in the Delaware Valley Region.* Philadelphia: DVRPC.

Downs, A. (1994). *New visions for metropolitan America.* Washington, DC: Brookings Institution Press.

Dreier, P., Mollenkopf, J., & Swanstrom, T. (2001). *Place matters: Metropolitics for the twenty-first century.* Lawrence: University Press of Kansas.

Frey, W. (2006). *Diversity spreads out: Metropolitan shifts in Hispanic, Asian, and Black populations since 2000.* Washington, DC: Brookings Institution Press.

Gidjunis, J. (2003). Straining the system. *Times Herald,* October 8.

Gillette, H. F. (2005). *Camden after the fall: Decline and renewal in a postindustrial city.* Philadelphia: University of Pennsylvania Press.

Gold, A. (2008). *Norristown: The best argument for reducing local government fragmentation in PA.* Philadelphia: Economy League of Greater Philadelphia.

Harwood, S. (2005). Struggling to embrace difference in land-use decision making in multicultural communities. *Planning Research and Practice, 20,* 355–371.

Harwood, S. (2009). Immigration and racialized regulation: Planning in the face of anti-immigrant sentiment. *Progressive Planning, 178,* 8–9.

Harwood, S., & Myers, D. (2002). The dynamics of immigration and local governance in Santa Ana: Neighborhood activism, overcrowding and land-use policy. *Policy Studies Journal, 20,* 70–91.

Immigration and Customs Enforcement (ICE). (2012). *Secure communities: Activated jurisdictions.* Washington, DC: U.S. Department of Homeland Security. Retrieved October 24, 2012, from http://www.ice.gov/doclib/secure-communities/pdf/sc-activated.pdf

Jacobson, M. F. (2006). *Roots too: White ethnic revival in post-civil rights America.* Cambridge, MA: Harvard University Press.

Jones-Correa, M. (2006). Reshaping the American dream: Immigrants and the politics of the new suburbs. In K. M. Kruse & T. J. Sugrue (Eds.), *The new suburban history* (pp. 183–204). Chicago: University of Chicago Press.

Jones-Correa, M. (2008). Immigrant incorporation in the suburbs: Differential pathways, arenas and intermediaries. In L. M. Hanley, B. A. Ruble, & A. Garland (Eds.), *Immigration and integration in urban communities: Renegotiating the city* (pp. 19–47). Baltimore: Johns Hopkins University Press.

Katz, M. B., Creighton, M. J., Amsterdam, D., & Chowkwanyun, M. (2010). Immigration and the new metropolitan geography. *Journal of Urban Affairs, 32,* 523–547.

Kirk, D. S., A. Papachristos, J. Fagan, & T. R. Tyler. (2012). The paradox of law enforcement in immigrant communities: Does tough immigration enforcement undermine public safety? *The Annals of the American Academy of Political and Social Science, 641,* 79–98.

Li, W., & Skop, P. (2007). Enclaves, ethnoburbs, and new patterns of settlement among Asian immigrants. In Zhou, M., & Gatewood, J. (Eds.), *Contemporary Asian America: A multi-disciplinary reader* (2nd ed., pp. 222–236), New York: New York University Press.

Luconi, S. (2001). *From paesani to white ethnics: The Italian experience in Philadelphia.* Albany: State University of New York Press.

Mansilla, P. (2006). Penoso record para Pensilvania. *Al Dia,* October 15, 1.

Martinez, R., Jr., & Stowell, J. I. (2012). Extending immigration and crime studies: National implications and local settings. *The Annals of the American Academy of Political and Social Science, 641,* 174–191.

Massey, D. (Ed.). (2008). *New faces in new places.* New York: Russell Sage Foundation.

Myers, D. (1999). Immigration: Fundamental force in the American city. *Housing Facts and Findings, 1,* 3–5.

Myers, D., Baer, W., & Choi, S. (1996). The changing problem of overcrowded housing. *Journal of the American Planning Association, 62,* 66–84.

National Immigration Law Center (NILC). (2005). *Pro-immigrant measures available to state or local governments: A quick menu of affirmative ideas.* Retrieved January 3, 2009, from http://www.nilc.org/immlawpolicy/misc/affirmstatelocalmenu_2005-09-13.pdf

National Immigration Law Center (NILC). (2008). *Laws, resolutions and policies instituted across the U.S. limiting enforcement of immigration laws by state and local authorities.* Retrieved January 3, 2009, from http://www.nilc.org/immlawpolicy/LocalLaw/locallaw-limiting-tbl-2008-12-03.pdf

Odom, M. E. (2008). Unsettled in the suburbs: Latino immigration and ethnic diversity in metro Atlanta. In A. Singer, S. Harwood, and C. Brettel (Eds.), *Twenty-first century gateways* (pp. 105–136). Washington, DC: Brookings Institution Press.

Orfield, M. (1997). *Metropolitics: A regional agenda for community and stability.* Washington, DC: Brookings Institution Press.

O'Toole, S. (2002). Norristown ready to recognize Mexican IDs. *Times Herald,* December 30.

Phucas, K. (2006a). Illegal-alien ban adopted. *King of Prussia Courier,* November 2.

———— (2006b). Norristown decides against alien ban. *Times Herald*, November 14.

Ridgley, J., & Steil, J. (2009). Controlling immigrants by controlling space: Current issues in historical perspective. *Progressive Planning, 178*, 14–17.

Roth, B. (2009). Housing overcrowding in the suburbs: The politics of space and the social exclusion of immigrants. *Progressive Planning, 178*, 18–20.

Saito, L. T. (1998). *Race and politics: Asian Americans, Latinos, and Whites in a Los Angeles suburb*. Urbana: University of Illinois Press.

Sampson, R. (2008). Rethinking crime and immigration. *Contexts, 7*, 28–33.

Sandercock, L. (2003). *Cosmopolis II: Mongrel cities of the twenty-first century*. New York: Continuum.

Singer, A., Hardwick, S., & Brettell, C. (Eds.). (2008a). *Twenty-first century gateways: Immigrant incorporation in suburban America*. Washington, DC: Brookings Institution Press.

Singer, A., Vitiello, D., Katz, M. & Park, D. (2008b). *Recent immigration to Philadelphia: Regional change and response*. Washington, DC: Brookings Institution Press.

Smith, J., & Edmonston, B. (Eds.). (1997). *The new Americans: Economic, demographic, and fiscal effects of immigration*. Washington, DC: National Academies Press.

Varela, A. (2012). Abuso contra Latinos en Norristown. *Al Dia*, September 23, 4–7.

Vazquez-Castillo, M.-T. (2009). Anti-immigrant, sanctuary, and repentance cities. *Progressive Planning, 178*, 10–13.

Vitiello, D. (2009). The migrant metropolis and American planning. *Journal of the American Planning Association, 75*, 245–255.

Vitiello, D. (2011, April). *The politics of place in immigrant and receiving communities*. Paper presented at the Massachusetts Historical Society conference, *What's new about the new immigration?*, Boston, MA.

Waldinger, R. (1997). Black/immigrant competition re-assessed: New evidence from Los Angeles. *Sociological Perspectives, 40*, 365–386.

Weir, M. (1994). Urban poverty and defensive localism. *Dissent* (Summer), 337–342.

Wortham, S., Mortimer, K., & Allard, E. (2009). Mexicans as model minorities in the New Latino Diaspora. *Anthropology and Education Quarterly, 40*, 388–404.

Zelinsky, W., & Lee, B. A. (1998). Heterolocalism: An alternative model of the sociospatial behaviour of immigrant ethnic communities. *International Journal of Population Geography, 4*, 281–298.

13-3 "What Underlies Urban Politics? Race, Class, Ideology, Partisanship, and the Urban Vote"*

Zoltan Hajnal and Jessica Trounstine

Urban Affairs Review

One of the core questions behind the study of urban politics is as follows: What is urban politics really about? Is it largely a competition across cities each with limited local control, limited issues, and limited local politics as Peterson (1981) and others argued (J. E. Oliver 2012; Tiebout 1956)? Or is it more likely to be a ubiquitous struggle between racial groups to control local decision making as any number of studies have suggested (Barreto 2007; Collet 2005; Hajnal 2006; Kaufmann 2004; Liu and Vanderleeuw 2007)? Perhaps local politics is principally a class-based conflict between haves and have-nots (Bridges 1997; Trounstine 2008). Alternatively, does local electoral politics mirror national-level politics where ideological battles between liberals and conservatives and partisan contests between Democrats and Republicans dominate (Abrajano and Alvarez 2005)? Or are the contenders defined more by religion and morality, gender, and age (Bailey 1999; DeLeon and Naff 2004; Sharp 2002)? These questions have dominated scholarly attention on urban politics for decades. The results of these efforts have been illuminating and somewhat contradictory. We know that all of these different accounts of urban politics apply in some cities and contexts but we know less about the relative roles of each factor across a wide range of cases.

In this article, we focus on one core aspect of the debate. In the typical electoral contest, how do these potentially interacting and potentially overlapping divisions play out? Ultimately, when we consider a number of different potential factors, what tends to drive urban politics today? We attempt to answer these questions and to adjudicate between these different views of what shapes urban politics with two innovations. First, unlike most existing studies, we explicitly compare divisions across the different dimensions of race, class, ideology, partisanship, and other demographic characteristics in electoral contests. Given that race, class, partisanship, ideology, and other factors purported to drive urban politics are often highly correlated with each other, we cannot know which factors truly matter until we have a test that considers all of the alternatives in a single empirical model of vote choice.

Second, we include a wide range of elections in which to assess the question of what drives urban politics. One real concern is that many of the existing studies are limited to an analysis of a single election in one city or at most to a number of respondents in [a] handful of cities. They offer keen insight into a particular locale but it is difficult to offer meaningful generalizations about urban politics based on analyses that do not incorporate patterns from more than a few cities or elections. To address this concern, we generate two different data sets—one that includes data on all elections in all available exit polls in 5 of the nation's largest cities and one that includes every available mayoral primary and general election over the past 20 years in the nation's largest 25 cities.

A larger number and a more diverse array of cases serve two purposes. With a broader array and an at least somewhat more representative set of cases, we

Source: Zoltan Hajnal and Jessica Trounstine, "What Underlies Urban Politics? Race, Class, Ideology, Partisanship, and the Urban Vote," *Urban Affairs Review*, vol. 50, no. 1, January 2014. Reprinted with permission from SAGE Publications, Inc.

*Endnotes and appendix have been omitted. Please consult the original source.

increase our confidence in the generalizability of the results. The other purpose of a larger, more diverse sample is that we can begin to assess and understand patterns in where and when race matters. Although we seek to provide the big picture, we are also well aware that patterns in the vote are likely to vary substantially from place to place and election to election. There is no single story that describes all urban elections.

An important element of this article will be to put forward and test a theory of racial politics that begins to help us understand the factors that make race more or less central features of the urban political arena. Our theory highlights the role that realistic group conflict can play in explaining patterns in the vote. To a significant extent, whether individual members of different racial and ethnic groups stand with or against each other depends on the size and perceived threat posed by the other group.

In what follows, we review the existing research on the urban vote and note its limitations. We then outline an empirical strategy for advancing our knowledge of the urban vote. The following section details our analysis of the vote not only highlighting the relatively large role played by race in the urban electoral arena but also illustrating how a range of other political and demographic features impact the vote. We end the analysis by examining and seeking to understand variation in the urban vote across different contexts. The article concludes with the implications of our findings for how we perceive local politics.

Existing Evidence

A wide range of research has illustrated the divergent preferences of black and white voters in local contests (Browning, Marshall, and Tabb 1984; DeLorenzo 1997; McCrary 1990; Pinderhughes 1987; Sonenshein 1993; L. Stein and Kohfeld 1991). And there is not only evidence that black–white divisions persist but also that the racial divide extends to other groups (Bobo and Johnson 2000; Joyce 2003; Kim 2000; Meier et al. 2004; Rocha 2007). In particular, there is clear evidence of significant racial solidarity among Latino (Barreto 2007) and Asian-American voters (Collet 2005) when coethnics are on the ballot.

But recent research is far from unanimous in its findings on the centrality of race in the local political arena. A number of other studies have found wide variation in the significance of race across different electoral contests (DeLeon and Naff 2004; Hajnal 2006; Kaufmann 2004; Liu 2003; Logan and Mollenkopf 2003; R. M. Stein, Ulbig, and Post 2005). Moreover, much of the most prominent research on local politics either does not include race in models of voter behavior or finds it insignificant (e.g., Berry and Howell 2007; Clingermayer and Feiock 2001; Krebs 1998; J. E. Oliver and Ha 2007; Wald, Button, and Rienzo 1996).

Even more importantly, there is evidence that many urban politics contests are shaped by dimensions other than race. Among others, Krebs (1998), J. E. Oliver and Ha (2007), and Ramakrishnan and Wong (2010) found that partisanship can dramatically shape local politics. A different set of scholars suggest that ideology can trump other factors in local democracy (Abrajano and Alvarez 2005; DeLeon 1991). Still others point to class as a primary dividing line in local governance (Bridges 1997; DeLeon and Naff 2004; Trounstine 2008). Sexuality, religion, age, and gender have also, at times, been linked to outcomes in the local arena (Bailey 1999; Sharp 2002; Wald, Button, and Rienzo 1996).

Concerns

Five issues inform the conclusions we can draw from these studies. First, given that different divisions appear to dominate in different sets of studies, it is difficult, if not impossible, to come up with an overall assessment of the importance of America's urban racial divides. Second, and perhaps most importantly, few studies explicitly incorporate and compare the effects of race with each of the other demographic or political dimensions (for two important exceptions, see Abrajano and Alvarez 2005 and Lieske and Hillard 1984). It is hard to judge if racial divisions are large unless they are compared with divisions across other demographic groups and it is harder still to know if race is the primary factor behind the vote, if we do not simultaneously control for other key demographic characteristics. Especially given strong correlations between race, class, ideology, and partisanship—the four factors most regularly cited as the main driving force in local politics—any model that does not simultaneously test all of these different factors is incomplete.

Also, most of the research is limited in breadth. Much of the research is focused on a single election in one city or at best on a series of elections in a couple of cities. Logan and Mollenkopf (2003); Liu and Vanderleeuw (2007); R. M. Stein, Ulbig, and Post (2005); Sonenshein (1993); and Hero (1989) provided excellent in-depth assessments of racial voting patterns but they all did so in only one city.[1] Other studies only improve matters slightly by looking at one or two cities (Kaufmann 2004). Large-N comparisons across multiple cities are rare (see J. E. Oliver 2012).

Another issue specific to the studies that examine racial divides is that they focus almost exclusively on biracial elections. Almost all of this research aims to assess the vote when there is one white candidate and one minority candidate (e.g., Hajnal 2006). This is crucial for establishing the willingness of members of each racial group to vote for candidates of another racial group but it may lead us to significantly overstate the role of race in the urban arena. If we want to see how much race matters in the urban arena, we need to look at the entire range of elections.

Finally, in light of how immigration is transforming the racial landscape of America's cities, there are also a series of important, largely unanswered questions about how racial diversity impacts local democracy. Perhaps the most obvious question is where voters from the two relatively new groups fit into the racial mosaic? Do Latino or Asian-American voters even form cohesive voting blocs? Given a wide range of divergent national origin experiences, an array of different immigrant experiences, and often divergent socioeconomic outcomes, it is far from certain that individual members of these two pan-ethnic groups will feel strong attachment to their coethnics or sufficient motivation for voting as a collective (de la Garza 1992; Lien, Conway, and Wong 2004). If, however, Latinos and Asian-Americans are able to overcome these differences, against whom will they be competing and with whom will they form coalitions? And how stark are those patterns of competition and cooperation? Furthermore, how has this increasingly complex racial picture affected the gap between white and black voters? Thus, a significant final concern is that existing studies are rarely able to examine the voting preferences of all four racial and ethnic groups (see DeLeon 1991; Logan and Mollenkopf 2003). This is understandable given that few cities have sizable populations of Latinos, Asian-Americans, African-Americans, and

whites. Nevertheless, it means that it is extremely difficult to offer conclusions about the relative size of the divides across different groups. It also makes it difficult to establish evidence about which groups are most likely to form voting alliances. In short, we fail to get the entire, complex picture of intergroup dynamics.

The end result is a mix of important and illuminating studies that nevertheless fail to lead to an overarching set of conclusions about the nature of racial divisions in the urban political arena. We know a lot about particular groups in particular cities in particular types of biracial elections but we have not yet been able to come up with an assessment of the larger patterns of competition and cooperation that undergird local democracy. By examining racial differences across a larger sample of cases and elections and by explicitly comparing each of the different racial divisions with other potentially relevant demographic and political factors, we hope to offer firmer conclusions about the underlying dimensions of urban politics.

Where and When Does Race Matter?

Providing an understanding of variation in voting patterns across cities and contexts is, in many ways, just as important as offering an overall picture of the urban vote. Thus, in the latter stages of this article, we begin to assess changes in patterns of the urban vote across different cases.

We do not claim to offer a full-fledged theory of urban politics that can explain any and all of the variation in the vote. We do, however, believe that a realistic group conflict account of race relations can help to predict when and where racial considerations are more pronounced. Drawing on the work of Bobo (1983), Bobo and Johnson (2000), Key (1984), Blalock (1967), and others, we believe that members of different racial and ethnic groups often feel a strong sense of competition with other groups over a range of political, economic, and social resources. That sense of competition or conflict is not constant but rather is likely to vary as the perceived threat posed by another group increases. In particular, two key factors are likely to structure the degree of threat and conflict. First, as any number of previous studies have demonstrated, larger out-groups can represent a greater threat that spurs greater action (Baybeck 2006; Key 1984; Taylor 1998). This relationship is pronounced for black–white interactions.[2] Whether group context or group size governs relations between other racial and ethnic groups is a more open question (Gay 2006; Ha and Oliver 2010; Hopkins 2010; Taylor 1998). Second, minority efforts at political empowerment have been shown to trigger threat and motivate action (Hajnal 2006; Olzak 1992). In this sense, it is not surprising that studies find that the presence of minority candidates on the ballot can be influential (Barreto 2007, 2011; Collet 2005).[3] If racial threat and group conflict do govern intergroup relations in the local political arena, these two factors should help to predict racial divisions in the vote.

In addition, there are a number of other factors that previous research has identified as structuring local politics that we need to incorporate into our analysis. Specifically, the literature highlights at least three other nonracial sets of factors that could shape the racial vote in urban contests: (1) local institutional structure, (2) economic conditions, and (3) local political leaning.

A well-worn finding in the urban politics literature is that local institutions can play a major role in limiting or facilitating minority representation (Bullock and MacManus 1990; Karnig and Welch 1980; Kaufmann 2004). As such, we might also expect certain local structures to impact patterns in the vote as well. Specifically, logic suggests that parties would be less important in nonpartisan contests and as a result, we might see heightened racial divides in nonpartisan contests (Bridges 1997; Karnig and Welch 1980).[4] It is also well known that local economic conditions can exacerbate group tensions (Branton and Jones 2005). Given these findings, we might predict heightened racial divides under conditions of economic stress. One other feature of the local population—the attitudes and political leanings of residents—may also influence the vote. Given that minorities often align with liberal whites in national and local politics, cities with more liberal populations might be expected to generate more limited racial gaps in the vote (Sonenshein 1993).[5]

Data

The key to providing a realistic assessment of the dimensions underlying the urban vote is incorporating each of the potentially relevant demographic and political divisions in a single model. This is really only possible if we have detailed data on large numbers of individual voters—a condition that at the local level requires raw exit poll data. To ensure that we have as broad a sample as possible, we assembled data from every available exit poll in large American cities. That effort led to a data set that includes the vote choice for 56,000 respondents across 63 elections for different local offices in five cities (New York, Los Angeles, Chicago, Houston, and Detroit) between 1985 and 2005—hereafter called the "Exit Poll Data Set." The Exit Poll Data Set includes not only mayoral vote choice (23 elections) but also candidate choices in city council (26 contests), city comptroller (2), city attorney (2), city clerk (1), and public advocate elections (2) and preferences on six ballot propositions.

This is obviously a small number of cities and by some dimensions an unrepresentative sample of cities. These cities are relatively representative of large American cities in terms of most economic characteristics and the five cities do represent different regions, different racial mixes, and different socioeconomic circumstances. But the five cities are generally larger and less white than the national urban population. Thus, our results cannot confidently be generalized to the entire urban arena.

Given concerns about generalizability, we endeavored to assess divisions across a much larger set of elections. Specifically, we collected the vote by race for mayor in all available primary and general elections in the nation's 25 largest cities over the past 20 years.[6] This process led to a data set with the aggregate vote by race for 254 candidates in 96 elections that represent a fairly wide range of cities and electoral contexts—hereafter called the "Mayoral Elections Data Set." The cities are Austin, Baltimore, Boston, Chicago, Columbus, Dallas, Denver, Detroit, El Paso, Houston, Indianapolis, Jacksonville, Los Angeles, Memphis, Milwaukee, Nashville, New York, Philadelphia, Phoenix, San Antonio, San Diego, San Francisco, San Jose, Seattle, and Washington. The online appendix presents a list of the 96 elections and includes a few core features of each contest.

The data in this larger data set are also far from perfect. For one, these 25 cities are also not fully representative of the urban population. They are larger and less white than the average American city. However, two factors suggest that they can tell us a lot about basic patterns in the urban vote. First, they account for roughly 30% of the nation's urban population. Thus, they offer a fairly broad window into the urban electorate. Second, these cities are fairly representative in terms of education outcomes and economic characteristics like employment rates and housing values. . . .

Basic Divides

In Table 1, we get our first glance at the size of the underlying divisions in the urban vote across 63 elections in the data set.[10] The table presents data on electoral divisions across each of the major demographic and political factors that previous research has suggested represent important dividing lines in local politics. For each election, we proceed with the following steps. First, we get the proportion of respondents from a given group (e.g., blacks) that supports the winning candidate. We then subtract the proportion of respondents from a second group (e.g., white respondents) that supported the same winning candidate. We then pool all of the elections and take the mean of the absolute value of the group difference (e.g., black support minus white support).

To allow comparability across different demographic and political factors, for each election, we recorded the biggest gap between any two categories within that particular demographic or political characteristic. For example, with religion, rather than always record the gap between one particular religious denomination (e.g., Catholics) and one other denomination (e.g., Protestants), we recorded the size of the largest gap between any of the six religious categories in each election. Likewise, for race, we record the biggest racial gap in the vote for the winner between any of the four racial and ethnic groups.[11] This ensures that the key division within each demographic or political characteristic in each election is recorded in Table 1 and allows us to determine which characteristics tend to produce the largest divisions.[12]

Perhaps the most striking feature of Table 1 is the degree to which the racial divide overshadows other demographic divides. Across all of the elections in this

| Table 1 | Racial, Demographic, and Political Divisions in Urban Elections |

	Average Divide in Vote for Winning Candidate (SD)
Race	38.3 (22.1)
Class	
Income	19.6 (12.8)
Education	18.2 (10.4)
Employment status	8.3 (3.7)
Other demographics	
Age	21.4 (11.8)
Gender	5.8 (5.0)
Religion	29.9 (16.0)
Sexuality	14.9 (7.3)
Marital status	6.4 (6.9)
Union membership	7.1 (3.1)
Children	5.1 (3.6)
Political orientation	
Liberal–conservative	27.4 (13.8)
Ideology	
Party identification	33.0 (18.7)

Source: Exit Poll Data Set—Elections for mayor, council, advocate, comptroller, clerk, city attorney, and ballot propositions in New York, Los Angeles, Chicago, Houston, and Detroit.

Exit Poll Data Set, the average maximum racial divide is a massive 38.3 percentage points. To illustrate that number more clearly, we provide the following example. A 38.3 point gap between racial groups could translate to overwhelming support for one candidate by one racial group (e.g., 75% support) and clear opposition to that candidate by a second racial group (e.g., only 36.7% support). In other words, a 38.3 point gap means that the typical urban election pits two racial groups against each other.[13]

Although some maintain that class is still the main driving force in politics, in these elections, class divides are typically much smaller than racial divides

(Evans 2000). The average income gap in the vote is 19.6 percentage points—sizable but only about half of the typical racial divide. In these contest [*sic*], *t*-tests indicate that class divides are significantly smaller than racial divides. Educational divides are also generally half as small as racial divides in these contests.[14] And aside from class, few major demographic divides emerge.[15] Differences across gender, employment status, marital status, union membership, and parental status are all dwarfed by racial divides. Interestingly, some of the largest demographic divides aside from race are between different religious affiliations, across different age groups, and between gay and straight voters. The largest religious divide in these contests averages 29.9 percentage points making religion the second most important demographic variable.[16] Age also factored into these contests in a significant way. The average maximum age gap that was generally between the oldest and youngest voters was 21.4 percentage points. Finally, in the few exit polls that asked about sexuality, there was a reasonably large 14.9 point divide between gay and straight voters.

Importantly, Table 1 also indicates that racial divisions significantly surpass partisan and ideological divides.[17] The 38 point racial gap in urban elections exceeds the average 27.4 point gap between liberal and conservative voters and the average 33 point gap between Democratic and Republic voters. Moreover, in less than a third of the elections is the partisan or ideological divide greater than the racial divide.[18] This is perhaps the starkest evidence yet that race is still a central driving force in urban politics. Party and ideology do shape the mayoral vote but race is the more dominant factor.

Another way to get at the importance of race is to focus on contests that involved two candidates of the same race. In doing so, we can see if race is only important when candidates from two different racial groups square off against each other. When we split the sample into two and focus only on non-biracial contests, average racial divides were substantially smaller but still large—on average 26.7 point gap.[19] Furthermore, we find that even in non-biracial contests, the racial divide dwarfed most other demographic divides and was roughly on par with the

liberal–conservative and the Democrat–Republican divides (23.6 and 27.1 point gaps, respectively, in single-race contests). Racial divisions are not isolated to a few biracial contests but are rather a much more pervasive aspect of the urban political arena.

A Closer Look at Racial/Ethnic Divisions

Given the prominence of racial divisions in the urban vote, we further explored the data to see exactly which racial and ethnic groups differed most in their preferences from each other and which most often favored the same candidates. Table 2 presents figures for the average divide between each racial and ethnic group across the entire set of local elections. Specifically, the table shows the average absolute difference in the percentage favoring the winning candidate.

As evidenced by Table 2, there is considerable variation in the size of racial and ethnic divisions across different pairs of groups.[20] The black–white gap, as past research might lead us to expect, is the largest. In the typical case, the percentage of blacks who supported the winning candidate differed by 31.6 points from the percentage of white voters supporting that same candidate. In one election, that gap grew to 84 points and in only a quarter of the cases did it fall below 10 points. In short, it was unusual when black and white voters favored the same candidates at the local level.

Table 2   Racial Divisions in Urban Politics

	Average Divide in Vote (SD)
Black–white	31.6 (25.0)
Black–Latino	24.1 (18.3)
Black–Asian-American	20.8 (14.8)
White–Latino	22.5 (17.8)
White–Asian-American	15.0 (10.4)
Latino–Asian-American	19.6 (15.2)

Source: Exit Poll Data Set—Elections for mayor, council, advocate, comptroller, clerk, city attorney, and ballot propositions in New York, Los Angeles, Chicago, Houston, and Detroit.

Another interesting set of patterns that emerges relates to the large divides between racial and ethnic minorities. The growth of the minority community has not, as some had hoped, paved the way for an interminority coalition that is challenging white control. Instead, blacks, Latinos, and Asian-Americans appear to be regularly competing for the often meager political and economic prizes that are available in the local political arena. Blacks and Latinos, the two groups that are often seen as having common economic and racial interests and as being potential coalition partners, seldom support the same candidates. The black–Latino divide is, in fact, the largest divide within the minority population. In the typical case, the percentage of blacks who supported the winning candidate differed by 24.1 points from the percentage of Latino voters supporting that same candidate. From these results, it is apparent that Latinos and African-Americans could see themselves more often as competitors than as partners. This lends credence to accounts highlighting conflict between these two groups (Meier and Stewart 1991; M. L. Oliver and Johnson 1984; Vaca 2004). Other intraminority divisions were also stark. In particular, black voters differed sharply from Asian-American voters. Here, the average divide was 20.8 percentage points. For whatever reason, these three groups have not consistently worked together to get candidates elected.

Combined, all of these patterns highlight the distinctiveness of the black community. The black vote differs sharply not just from the white vote but also from the Latino and Asian-American votes. In many contests, the black community is competing against the white community and challenging the Latino and Asian-American communities.[21]

There are few signs of a close, enduring coalition in Table 2 but of all the groups, whites and Asian-Americans appear to have the closest preferences in the urban electoral arena. The average divide between white and Asian-American voters is a relatively small 15 points and exceeds 20 points in under half of the cases.

Assessing Relative Contributions

Although these bivariate results are compelling, they ignore the fact that race, political orientation, and other demographic characteristics are all likely to be correlated. It is difficult to determine the individual contribution of one of the demographic or racial characteristic without controlling for other potentially relevant characteristics. So in Table 3, we present results from a series of regressions that do exactly that.

Table 3   Regression-Based Estimate of Racial, Demographic, and Political Divisions in Urban Elections

	Average Marginal Effect (SD)	% of Coefficients Significant at .05
Race		
Blacks	0.280 (0.203)	80
Latino	0.194 (0.158)	55
Asian-American	0.115 (0.106)	20
Class		
Income	0.038 (0.061)	31
Education	0.029 (0.026)	30
Employment status	0.060 (0.057)	16
Other demographics		
Age	0.032 (0.034)	31
Sexuality	0.086 (0.081)	37
Marital status	0.030 (0.026)	16
Protestant	0.086 (0.060)	35
Catholic	0.114 (0.088)	54
Jewish	0.125 (0.084)	54
Political orientation		
Democrat	0.191 (0.147)	73
Independent	0.113 (0.087)	50
Liberal	0.176 (0.098)	73
Moderate	0.106 (0.094)	46

Note: Dependent variable—Support for the winning candidate

Source: Exit Poll Data Set—Elections for mayor, council, advocate, comptroller, clerk, city attorney, and ballot propositions in New York, Los Angeles, Chicago, Houston, and Detroit.

Specifically, for each election in the data set, we run a single logistic regression with all of the individual voters in the exit poll as cases predicting support for the winning candidate. Then for each election, we use Clarify to calculate the marginal effect of shifting from one category (e.g., black respondent) to the comparison category (e.g., white respondent) for each independent variable in each election. We then calculate the average predicted effect of each independent variable across the different elections in the Exit Poll Data Set.[22] Table 3 displays the means and standard deviations for the predicted effects for each independent variable across the elections. The last column of the table indicates how often each coefficient is significant across the elections.

As independent variables, we include all of the relevant racial, demographic, and political variables that are available for that particular election.[23] To assess race, we include dummy variables for black, Latino, and Asian-American respondents with whites as the baseline comparison category. For party, the regressions include dummy variables for Democrats and Independents with Republicans as the base. Similarly, for ideology, it is liberals and moderates with conservatives as the comparison. The omitted category for religion is atheist.[24] Education and income are 4- or 5-point scale (depending on the exit poll). All variables are coded on a scale from 0 to 1.

The results in Table 3 indicate that even after controlling for a host of other potentially important factors, race still matters. The coefficients for each racial group vary considerably from election to election, as we would expect from Table 2, but overall race is one of the most predictive factors in Table 3. And among the racial variables, black voters once again stand out. Even after controlling for all of the other demographic and political factors, the average predicted gap between the black vote and the white vote is 27.6 points. Perhaps more importantly, across the different election-specific regressions, the black–white divide is almost always significant. In fully 80% of the contests, the coefficient on black voters is significant indicating that the black vote differs significantly from the white vote. As we saw before with the bivariate results, there is a substantial but smaller divide between Latino and white voters and a relatively small difference between

the preferences of Asian-American and white voters. Once again, it is black voters who stand out and it is whites and Asian-Americans who appear to be the most likely candidates for an interracial coalition.

The results for the rest of the demographic characteristics in Table 3 also mirror what we saw with the bivariate results. Factors like class, age, sexuality, and religion have a smaller and less consistently significant effect than race. Income and education, in particular, are only a significant factor in about 30% of the elections and their coefficients are about one-tenth the size of the black–white divide.

The other important finding here is the central role that politics plays in the urban political arena. Despite some claims that urban politics is issueless and that traditional ideology is largely irrelevant in the typical urban contest, these results suggest that ideology matters. Indeed, in 73% of the elections, there was a significant divide between liberal and conservative voters. And the average difference between ideological groups was substantial with the average predicted gap of 18.0 points between liberals and conservatives. Moreover, the fact that most of these elections are nonpartisan does not mean that partisanship is inconsequential. Democrats vote significantly differently from Republicans in 73% of the contest and again that gap tends to be large (an average predicted gap of 19.2 points). After instituting a range of controls, race remains the most robust factor in the urban electoral arena but political dimensions like party and ideology also very strongly shape the vote.[25]

Importantly, conclusions about the relatively central role of race hold even if we focus exclusively on contests involving two candidates of the same race. Even in contests where voters cannot choose on the basis of the race of the candidates, the average effect of race remains far more important than other demographic characteristics and continues to be on par with party and ideology.[26]

The Mayoral Elections Data Set Results

The results to this point highlight the centrality of race in the urban political arena but the findings are admittedly based on a relatively small number of elections across a small number of cities. Given concerns about the generalizability of this first data set, we sought to evaluate the role of race in a larger and more diverse set of elections. Specifically, we present data on the vote by race for mayor in all available primary and general mayoral elections in the nation's 25 largest cities over the past 20 years. The goals here are twofold. The first is to attempt to reconfirm the important impact that race and ethnicity have in urban elections. The second is to delve deeper into racial patterns in the vote. In addition to identifying possible coalition partners and potential competitors, we can also assess more fundamental factors like the internal cohesiveness of each group. Given a wide range of divergent national origin experiences, an array of different immigrant experiences, and often divergent socioeconomic outcomes, one might reasonably wonder whether Latino or Asian-American voters typically form cohesive voting blocs. Unfortunately, by expanding the set of elections to cases without raw exit poll data, we lose the ability to incorporate data on other demographic or political characteristics.[27] Thus, our focus in the next section is exclusively on race.

We begin the analysis of the larger data set by reexamining racial divisions in the vote. Table 4 presents figures for the average divide between each racial and ethnic group across the entire set of 96 mayoral elections. As with Table 2, this table shows the average

Table 4   Racial Divisions in Mayoral Politics

	Average Divide in Mayoral Vote	
	All Elections (%)	Two-Candidate Elections (%)
Black–white	43.4	46.7
Black–Latino	32.9	34.7
Black–Asian-American	24.8	26.9
White–Latino	22.0	22.7
White–Asian-American	20.5	22.1
Latino–Asian-American	15.6	16.8

Source: Mayoral Elections Data Set—Mayoral elections in the nation's largest 25 cities over the past two decades.

absolute difference in the percentage favoring the winning candidate.

The results are clear and confirm our earlier findings. Across this broader set of cities, this longer time frame, and this greater number of elections, race continues to greatly shape the urban vote. There are considerable gaps between the vote of the white, Latino, black, and Asian-American electorates. There is also, once again, considerable variation in the size of those gaps across groups. The black–white gap continues to be the largest racial gap. In the average election, the percentage of blacks who supported the winning candidate differed by 43 points from the percentage of white voters supporting that same candidate. This grows to a 47 point gap in elections with only two candidates—about half the contests. Assessed another way, across the entire set of elections, the black vote was significantly and negatively correlated with the white vote ($r = -.24$, $p < .05$). Black and white voters generally did not support the same candidates.

Once again, the results reveal substantial gaps between different minority voters and reinforce the notion of a uniquely isolated African-American electorate. Blacks and Latinos are, as before, the two minority groups whose voting patterns are most distant from each other. On average, the black vote differs from the Latino vote by 33 points, again reaffirming the existence of conflict between these two disadvantaged minority groups (Meier and Stewart 1991; M. L. Oliver and Johnson 1984; Vaca 2004). The mayoral vote also separates black voters from Asian-American voters. Here, the average divide was 22.5 percentage points (21.7 points in two candidate elections). There is, in short, little evidence of a grand interminority coalition seeking to control the local political arena.

There are, however, prospects for different kinds of coalitions. Just as we saw in Table 2, differences between white and Asian-American voters are smaller than for any other pair of racial groups. White and Asian-American voters differed in their preferences by only 17.2 points on average (15.4 in two candidate contests). One might also highlight the relatively small divides between Latinos and Asian-Americans and to a slightly lesser extent the divide between white and Latino voters.[28] Thus, judging by the vote, whites,

Latinos, and Asian-Americans appear to be the three groups most likely to form a viable rainbow coalition. This potential coalition is perhaps best illustrated by looking at correlations in the vote across elections. Across the entire set of mayoral elections, the white vote was fairly closely correlated with the Asian-American vote ($r = .73$, $p < .01$) and the Latino vote ($r = .64$, $p < .01$). Similarly, the Latino and Asian-American votes correlated at .67 ($p < .01$). In short, these three racial and ethnic groups often seem to want the same things, or at least the same candidates.

Racial Cohesion

One, perhaps, prefatory question we might have asked about the racial vote in urban elections is whether these four populations are really groups at all? Put more succinctly, does each group vote cohesively? This is less of a question with black voters where existing research tends to show high levels of cohesiveness in the political arena. But it remains an open question for white voters who at least in national elections are often sharply divided by partisanship, ideology, and demographic factors like class (Miller and Shanks 1996). And this is especially important to establish for the Latino and Asian-American cases where differences of national origin, socioeconomic standing, and length of time in the United States could serve to divide the larger pan-ethnic vote (de la Garza 1992; Lien, Conway, and Wong 2004; Tam 1995).

Thus, in Table 5, we assess intragroup dynamics by looking at voting cohesion across the set of 96 mayoral elections. The table displays the percentage of voters from each racial/ethnic group that supported the group's preferred candidate. If a group was wholly united, the measure would equal 100. A totally divided group would score 50 in a two-candidate contest and 25 in a four-person contest. As cohesion could depend greatly on the number of candidates, the table presents results for all elections as well as those with only two candidates. Also, because assessments of cohesion will be affected by the competitiveness of a given election, it is important to note that most of these mayoral elections are far from landslides. The average winning candidate received only 56.7% of the vote. Moreover, as the candidate preferred by minority voters is not the winning candidate in many of these

| **Table 5** Intragroup Cohesion in Mayoral Politics |

Average Support for Each Group's Preferred Candidate		
	All Elections (%)	**Two-Candidate Elections (%)**
African-Americans	76.3	76.2
Latinos	68.7	67.9
Whites	71.7	72.1
Asian-Americans	64.9	63.0

Source: Mayoral Elections Data Set—Mayoral elections in the nation's largest 25 cities over the past two decades.

elections, the margin of victory is essentially unrelated to minority cohesion.[29]

The main conclusion to emerge from this analysis is that it *is* possible to talk about racial group voting blocs.[30] The results of *t*-tests indicate that all four racial and ethnic groups are significantly more cohesive than a vote evenly divided among the candidates. Even among the least cohesive group, Asian-Americans, 64.9% of the group's voters support the group's favorite candidate. This is not only far from a wholly united vote but it is also far from evenly divided. Moreover, Latinos, whites, and African-Americans are all more apt to vote as a bloc. Importantly, this within-group cohesion persists when the candidates in the election are all from the same race. Cohesion drops for all four groups in single-race contests but remains high. Cohesion in these single-race elections is 69.4% for blacks, 67.5% for whites, 61.5% for Latinos, and 63.1% for Asian-Americans. Cohesion is not simply a function of choosing a candidate of your own race. Racial group cohesion is also not simply a function of partisanship. When we split the sample into partisan and nonpartisan contests and focus on contests in which political parties are not on the ballot, there is little drop in the levels of cohesion. Overall, these results suggest that race is fairly ubiquitous in the urban arena. America's four main racial and ethnic groups do represent somewhat cohesive communities. Mayoral voting is at least in part the story of four different racial and ethnic groups sorting out their preferences.

This cohesion is perhaps most surprising for Asian-Americans. The fact that only a little over third of the Asian-American electorate opposes the candidate favored by the majority of Asian-Americans means that in the arena of urban politics, the Asian-American community is often able to at least partially overcome differences of national origin group, immigration status, and socioeconomic status. We still cannot think of Asian-Americans as a monolithic voting bloc but we should probably consider them as more of a voting bloc than many accounts suggest (Espiritu 1992; Lien, Conway, and Wong 2004).[31]

The other conclusion that is evident from Table 5 is that cohesion varies substantially across groups. On one end of the spectrum, African-American voters are highly unified. There is some difference of opinion within the black community, but at the local level, it is generally clear who the "black" candidate is and who the "black" candidate is not and the vast majority of the black community support their group's candidate. Despite growing class divisions and by some accounts, the diminishing importance of race, electoral politics still appears to bring blacks together. Whites, perhaps somewhat surprisingly given intragroup divisions in national elections, are the next most cohesive voting bloc in urban elections. On average, roughly 72% of white voters end up supporting that same candidate. Latinos vote together about 68% of the time in these urban elections. For an ethnic group that is often viewed as being sharply divided by national origin group and immigrant status, cohesion in the voting booth is surprisingly high. The issues, candidates, and choices that are put forward in local contests enable Latino voters to overcome at least some of their internal divisions. Finally, Asian-Americans anchor the far end of the cohesiveness spectrum.

When Does Race Matter?

A closer look at the data reveals, however, that these overall assessments of the vote hide substantial variation in the vote across different cities and contexts. The multilevel mixed-effects regressions in Table 3 reveal that race while usually significant is in several cases far less relevant. Table 3 also shows similar variation in the significance of other factors like party and ideology. Moreover, the standard deviations listed in Tables 1 through 3 demonstrate quite clearly that there is considerable variation in the impact of race and all of the other factors that we have examined. Standard deviations are reasonably high for almost every factor but for race they are particularly large. In more concrete terms, it means that in the Mayoral Elections Data Set, the size of the black–white divide ranges from 2 to 93 percentage points whereas the size of the Latino–Asian-American divide ranges from 0 to 59 percentage points. Clearly, there is not one urban election but instead many different kinds of urban contests that separate different kinds of voters in different ways.

This range in outcomes inevitably raises questions about why race matters in some cases and not others. With a large number of potential explanations and a limited number of elections and cities, rigorous testing of all of the various hypotheses is difficult. In lieu of a complete model, we run a series of regressions that include a single measure for each of the five factors that are arguably most likely to be linked to racial divisions. In alternate tests, we do, however, substitute in alternate measures for each of the five different theories. Table 6 presents three regression models that predict the black–white divide, the Latino–white divide, and the black–Latino divide using cases from the Mayoral Elections Data Set.

The regressions in Tables 6 indicate that the impact of race does vary in predictable and understandable ways. In particular, different elements of the realistic group conflict theory of racial group relations seem to garner considerable support. Both of the different measures of realistic group conflict that we use here—candidate race and group size—strongly impact racial divisions. As predicted, biracial contests involving candidates from the two racial groups in question were fundamentally different from other elections. For example, having a black and a white candidate increased the black–white divide by just over 14 points. Likewise, the presence of a Latino and a white candidate was linked to a 23 point jump in the Latino–white divide. The comparable figure for the combination of a black and a Latino candidate was 22 points for the black–Latino voting gap. In this

Table 6   Understanding Variation in Racial Divisions in Mayoral Elections

	Black–White Divide	Latino–White Divide	Black–Latino Divide
Realistic group conflict			
Candidate race			
Biracial election	0.14 (.04)**	0.21 (.07)**	0.24 (.10)*
Racial demographics			
Proportion black	0.88 (.45)*	−0.49 (.44)	1.13 (.43)**
Proportion Latino	0.59 (.47)	−0.28 (.45)	1.07 (.45)*
Proportion white	0.09 (.52)	−0.14 (.49)	0.42 (.50)
Local institutions			
Nonpartisan elections	−0.02 (.09)	−0.21 (.09)*	0.25 (.08)**
Local ideology			
% Democratic	−0.08 (.34)	−0.33 (.33)	0.40 (.33)
Economic conditions			
% poor	−0.78 (.75)	1.81 (.74)*	−0.43 (.69)
Controls			
Primaries (vs. runoffs)	−0.13 (.05)**	0.05 (.04)	−0.03 (.04)
Number of candidates	−0.06 (.02)*	−0.03 (.02)	−0.08 (.02)**
Year	−0.01 (.01)	−0.00 (.01)	−0.00 (.01)
South	−0.14 (.08)	0.03 (.07)	−0.04 (.07)
Constant	13.2 (9.8)	11.7 (8.1)	9.0 (8.8)
Number of observations	121	110	109
Number of groups	19	17	17
Wald χ^2	101**	29.6**	75.0**

Source: Mayoral Elections Data Set—Mayoral elections in the nation's largest 25 cities over the past two decades.

Note: Multilevel mixed-effects linear regression with random intercepts for city.

*$p < .05$. **$p < .01$.

sense, candidates matter greatly and the presence of minority candidates can do a lot to increase intra-group cohesiveness and expand the divide between America's different racial and ethnic voting blocs.[32]

The second important aspect of the realistic group conflict theory is the size of each racial and ethnic group. Looking across the regressions, it is readily apparent that the larger a group, the more it tends to be divided from other groups. Often the effect is substantial. A two-standard-deviation jump in percentage black is, for example, associated with a 35 point increase in the black–white divide and a 47 point increase in the black–Latino divide. A larger Latino population was also tied to a larger black–Latino divide. All of these results fit neatly with a realistic group conflict view of urban politics and imply that individual members of America's different racial and ethnic groups do feel a sense of racial competition that can be activated under predictable circumstances. However, as we do not directly measure intergroup attitudes here, the results are at best suggestive. In that light, it is important to note other studies focusing directly on individual attitudes have found that larger group size and efforts at minority empowerment often incite more negative intergroup attitudes (Baybeck 2006; Bobo and Hutchings 1996; Gay 2006; Hajnal 2006; Taylor 1998; but see Ha and Oliver 2010).

No other element of the local political arena compared in size or significance to the two measures associated with realistic group threat but the three regressions in Table 6 hint at the role that local institutional structure can play. Nonpartisan elections mattered in two of the three cases, increasing the black–Latino divide in one case and diminishing the white–Latino divide in the other. Presumably, when black and Latino voters were not united by allegiance to Democratic Party candidates, their voting preferences tended to diverge. Similarly, when Asian-American and white voters were not divided by their partisan allegiances (Latinos leaning largely Democratic and whites leaning primarily Republican), their voting choices were more aligned. Two other institutional structures showed some signs of affecting the vote in alternate tests. The mayoral-council form of government tended to foster greater black–white and black–Latino divides than the city manager form of government. Similarly, when city council elections are not staggered, they are linked to larger divides between blacks and Latinos and blacks and whites. The substantive effects for these other institutional features were less meaningful and the results were not always significant, but the overall pattern suggests that when more is at stake in the local electoral arena, America's racial and ethnic groups may be more divided.

Perhaps surprisingly, the overall ideology of the city's residents did not appear to be related to divisions in the vote. More liberal cities were just as racially divided as less liberal cities. Furthermore, in alternate tests, when we substituted in a proxy for racial tolerance—the percentage of residents with a college degree—we found no additional link to the vote. It is certainly possible that these measures are not precise enough to show effects, but the results to this point suggest that political ideology and racial tolerance may do less to shape racial divides than group demographics and descriptive representation. Economic conditions, no matter how we measured them, also had little noticeable impact on racial divides. In the three regressions in Table 6, the proportion of the population that is poor was insignificant, and in alternate tests, various measures of income (median household income, per capita income), the unemployment rate, and inequality revealed few clear effects. Finally, among the control variables, we found that fewer candidates and primary elections sometimes meant smaller racial divides while year and region had no clear impact.

With fewer cases, we have much less confidence in our analysis of the divisions between Asian-American voters and other groups. However, it is interesting to note that realistic group conflict also appeared to play a role in shaping divisions between Asian-Americans and others. Regressions with the same basic model suggest that candidate race is also significant to the Asian-American vote. All else equal, the presence of an Asian-American candidate increases the Asian-American–white divide by an estimated 19 points and the Asian-American–Latino divide by 8 points. Likewise, the Asian-American–black divide grows significantly when a black candidate is on the ballot. The Asian-American regressions also tend to confirm the limited role played by local economic conditions, the political leaning of local voters, and the mean educational level or racial tolerance of the city. The one exception is that group demographics play less of a role in shaping the divide between Asian-American voters and other groups. If anything, there are even some limited signs that a larger Asian-American population breeds less group conflict.[33]

Importantly, the basic conclusions presented here endure if we instead analyze the smaller Exit Poll Data Set. Across these 63 contests, realistic group conflict again appeared to shape the vote. Racial divisions tended to be larger in biracial contests and in cities with larger black and Latino populations.

With the Exit Poll Data Set, we can also look at variation across different types of contests (e.g., mayoral vs. council vs. proposition) and at variation in the role that partisan and ideological divides play. In terms of election type, the *Exit Poll* data show that racial divides are especially heightened in mayoral contests, much reduced in city council elections, and even lower when residents are voting on ballot propositions. The black–white divide, for example, drops from an average of 46.3% in mayoral contests to 16.3% in council elections, and finally to 14.5% on ballot propositions. Likewise, the Latino–white divide falls from 26.9 to 22.3 points, and 9.6 points across the three types of contests. Perhaps the importance of the mayoral post and the fact that it is essentially an at-large contest for control of the city is the reason why mayoral politics stirs greater racial division than city council politics. The even lower racial divisions for ballot propositions suggest that race is less important when the battle is over policy than when the fight is between candidates.[34] In other words, America's different racial and ethnic groups may not disagree as strongly over concrete policy objectives as many local electoral contests suggest.

By contrast, if we shift the focus to divisions in the vote between Democrats and Republicans (or between liberals and conservatives), a very different pattern of results emerges. Although it is beyond the scope of this article to try to explain all of the factors that increased the impact of political divisions like partisanship and political ideology, it is interesting to note some of the key differences we found. First, while party is a less robust factor than race in most elections, partisan divisions tend to dominate racial divisions in direct democracy. Issues—more than candidates—may divide members of the two major political parties. Also, unlike our earlier findings, biracial elections tended to reduce the size of the partisan divide. When the contest was not about descriptive representation, party allegiances held more sway. Finally, as one would expect, party ties tended to matter more than race in the minority of local elections that are partisan contests.

Conclusion

The patterns illustrated in this article offer a telling account of race and other divisions in the local political arena. Judged by these electoral contests—albeit a limited set of elections in a sample of cities—the local political arena is one that is in no small part defined by race

and ethnicity. Growing racial and ethnic diversity does not appear to be leading to racial harmony. Instead, blacks, Latinos, Asian-Americans, and whites tend to vote as blocs and often as competing blocs. Within-group cohesion and across-group division strongly shape urban politics.

Of all the groups, African-Americans stand out— both for the unity with which the black community votes and for the distinctiveness of the black vote. When racial and ethnic groups compete in the local political arena, often it is black voters who are competing against everyone else. This obviously does not put black voters in a favorable position and is likely to lead to regular electoral defeat (Hajnal 2009).[35] The flip side of this black/nonblack divide is the possibility of a rainbow coalition of whites, Latinos, and Asian-Americans. These three groups regularly support the same candidates and thus appear to have the potential to form a viable, long-lasting coalition. Importantly, our results also highlight the unity within each of these groups. Even for Asian-Americans and Latinos, groups that are often seen as extremely diverse and internally divided, urban elections tend to foster a cohesive vote.

Moreover, it is clear from the analysis that racial divisions tend to overshadow other divisions. Race divides us much more than any other demographic characteristic. The urban electorate is shaped in part by class, religion, sexuality, age, gender, and a host of other demographic measures, but race seems to be more central and more decisive than all of these other factors. Perhaps even more importantly, in these elections, race often divides more than conventional politics. Most accounts of politics at the local or national level point to party identification or ideology as the main driving forces in American politics (Campbell et al. 1960; Green et al. 2002; Miller and Shanks 1996). But the results presented here suggest otherwise. Party identification certainly matters. And ideology greatly helps to predict vote choice. But in local democracy, it is race more than anything else that tends to dominate voter decision making.

Importantly, hidden beneath these aggregate patterns is wide variation in the impact of race across different elections. For every two racial and ethnic groups, there are cases in which the two groups voted together as a coalition and other cases in which they were almost totally opposed to each other. Our exploratory efforts at understanding this variation reinforce at least one existing theory about the dynamics of race. Race matters more when minority candidates enter the electoral arena and when minority groups represent a larger fraction of the population suggesting that realistic group threat may be a helpful way of thinking about racial relations in the urban political arena.

More works need to be done across a wide range and number of elections, but the underlying variation in the racial vote suggests there [sic] race need not always be the main driving force behind urban politics. Straightforward solutions are far from evident but institutional reform is at least one area where we could look for levers to bring groups together. But for now, it is important to admit that stark racial divides continue to help define the urban electorate.

References

Abrajano, M., and R. M. Alvarez. 2005. A natural experiment of race-based and issue voting: The 2001 city of Los Angeles elections. *American Politics Quarterly* 58 (2): 203–18.

Bailey, R. W. 1999. *Gay politics, urban politics: Identity and economics in the urban setting.* New York: Columbia Univ. Press.

Barreto, M. 2007. Si Se Puede! Latino candidates and the mobilization of Latino voters. *American Political Science Review* 101 (3): 425–41.

Barreto, M. 2011. *Ethnic cues: The role of shared ethnicity in Latino political participation.* Ann Arbor: Univ. of Michigan Press.

Baybeck, B. 2006. Sorting out the competing effects of racial context. *Journal of Politics* 68 (2): 386–96.

Berry, C., and W. Howell. 2007. Accountability and local elections: Rethinking retrospective voting. *Journal of Politics* 69 (3): 844–58.

Blalock, H. M. 1967. *Toward a theory of minority-group relations.* New York: Wiley.

Bobo, L. D. 1983. Whites' opposition to busing: Symbolic racism or realistic group conflict. *Journal of Personality and Social Psychology* 45 (6): 1196–210.

Bobo, L. D., and V. Hutchings. 1996. Perceptions of racial group competition: Extending Blumer's theory of group position to a multiracial social context. *American Sociological Review* 61 (6): 951–71.

Bobo, L. D., and D. Johnson. 2000. Racial attitudes in a prismatic metropolis: Mapping identity, stereotypes, competition, and views on affirmative action. In *Prismatic metropolis: Inequality in Los Angeles*, edited by L. Bobo, M. Oliver, J. Johnson, and A. Valenzuela. New York: Russell Sage Foundation.

Branton, R., and B. S. Jones. 2005. Re-examining racial attitudes: The conditional relationship between diversity and socio-economic environment. *American Journal of Political Science* 49 (2): 359–72.

Bridges, A. 1997. *Morning glories: Municipal reform in the southwest.* Princeton: Princeton Univ. Press.

Browning, R. R., D. R. Marshall, and D. H. Tabb. 1984. *Protest is not enough.* Berkeley: Univ. of California Press.

Bullock, C. S., and S. A. MacManus. 1990. Structural features of municipalities and the incidence of Hispanic council members. *Social Science Quarterly* 71 (4): 665–81.

Campbell, A., P. E. Converse, W. E. Miller, and D. E. Stokes. 1960. *The American voter.* Chicago: Univ. of Chicago Press.

Cho, W. K. T., and B. J. Gaines. 2004. The limits of ecological inference: The case of split ticket voting. *American Journal of Political Science* 48 (1): 152–71.

Clingermayer, J. C., and R. C. Feiock. 2001. *Institutional constraints and policy choice: An exploration of local governance.* Albany: State Univ. of New York.

Collet, C. 2005. Bloc voting, polarization and the panethnic hypothesis: The case of Little Saigon. *Journal of Politics* 67 (3): 907–33.

de la Garza, R. O., ed. 1992. *Latino voices: Mexican, Puerto Rican, and Cuban perspectives on American politics.* Boulder: Westview Press.

DeLeon, R. 1991. The progressive urban regime: Ethnic coalitions in San Francisco. In *Racial and ethnic politics in California*, edited by B. O. Jackson and B. Cain, 157–92. Berkeley: Institute for Governmental Studies.

DeLeon, R., and K. C. Naff. 2004. Identity politics and local political culture. *Urban Affairs Review* 39 (6): 689–719.

Delorenzo, L. C. 1997. The impact of cross-racial voting on St. Louis primary election results. *Urban Affairs Review* 33:120–33.

Dixon, J. C., and M. S. Rosenbaum. 2004. Nice to know you? Testing contact, cultural, and group threat theories of anti-black and anti-Hispanic stereotypes. *Social Science Quarterly* 85 (2): 257–80.

Espiritu, Y. L. 1992. *Asian American panethnicity: Bridging institutions and identities.* Philadelphia: Temple Univ. Press.

Evans, G. 2000. The continued significance of class voting. *Annual Review of Political Science* 3: 401–17.

Ferree, K. E. 2004. Iterative approaches to R × C ecological inference problems: Where they can go wrong and one quick fix. *Political Analysis* 12 (2): 143–59.

Gay, C. 2006. Seeing difference: The effect of economic disparity on black attitudes toward Latinos. *American Journal of Political Science* 50 (4): 982–97.

Green, D. P., B. Palmquist, E. Schickler, and G. Bruno. 2002. *Partisan hearts and minds: Political parties and the social identity of voters*. New Haven: Yale Univ. Press.

Ha, S. E., and J. E. Oliver. 2010. The consequences of multiracial contexts on public attitudes toward immigration. *Political Research Quarterly* 63 (1): 29–42.

Hajnal, Z. L. 2006. *Changing white attitudes toward black political leadership*. New York: Cambridge Univ. Press.

Hajnal, Z. L. 2009. *America's uneven democracy: Turnout, race, and representation in city politics*. Cambridge: Cambridge Univ. Press.

Hero, R. 1989. Multiracial coalitions in city elections involving minority candidates: Some evidence from Denver. *Urban Affairs Quarterly* 25 (2): 342–51.

Hopkins, D. J. 2009. No more wilder effect, never a Whitman effect: When and why polls mislead about black and female candidates. *Journal of Politics* 71 (3): 769–71.

Hopkins, D. J. 2010. Politicized places: Explaining where and when immigrants provoke local opposition. *American Political Science Review* 104 (1): 40–60.

Joyce, P. D. 2003. *No fire next time: Black-Korean conflicts and the future of American cities*. Ithaca: Cornell Univ. Press.

Karnig, A. K., and S. Welch. 1980. *Black representation and urban policy*. Chicago: The Univ. of Chicago Press.

Kaufmann, K. 2004. *The urban voter: Group conflict and mayoral voting in American cities*. Ann Arbor: Univ. of Michigan Press.

Key, V. O. 1984. *Southern politics in state and nation*. Knoxville: Univ. of Tennessee Press.

Kim, C. J. 2000. *Bitter fruit: The politics of black-Korean conflict in New York City*. New Haven: Yale Univ. Press.

Kinder, D., and T. Mendelberg. 1995. Cracks in American apartheid: The political impact of prejudice among desegregated whites. *Journal of Politics* 57 (2): 402–24.

Krebs, T. B. 1998. The determinants of candidates' vote share and advantages of incumbency in city council elections. *American Journal of Political Science* 42 (July): 921–35.

Lien, P.-t., M. M. Conway, and J. Wong. 2004. *The politics of Asian Americans: Diversity and community*. New York: Routledge.

Lieske, J., and J. W. Hillard. 1984. The racial factor in urban elections. *Western Political Quarterly* 37:545–63.

Liu, B. 2003. Deracialization and urban racial contexts. *Urban Affairs Review* 38 (4): 572–91.

Liu, B., and J. M. Vanderleeuw. 2007. *Race rules: Electoral politics in New Orleans, 1965–2006*. Lanham: Lexington.

Logan, J., and J. Mollenkopf. 2003. *People and politics in America's big cities*. New York City: Center for Urban Research, City University.

McCrary, P. 1990. Racially polarized voting in the South: Quantitative evidence from the courtroom. *Social Science History* 14 (4): 507–31.

Meier, K. J., P. D. McClain, J. L. Polinard, and R. D. Wrinkle. 2004. Divided or together? Conflict and cooperation between African Americans and Latinos. *Political Research Quarterly* 57 (3): 399–409.

Meier, K. J., and J. Stewart, Jr., 1991. Cooperation and conflict in multiracial school districts. *Journal of Politics* 53 (4): 1123–33.

Miller, W. E., and J. M. Shanks. 1996. *The new American voter*. Cambridge: Harvard Univ. Press.

Oliver, J. E. 2012. *Local elections and the politics of small-scale democracy*. Princeton: Princeton Univ. Press.

Oliver, J. E., and S. E. Ha. 2007. Vote choice in suburban elections. *American Political Science Review* 101 (3): 393–408.

Oliver, J. E., and J. Wong. 2003. Intergroup prejudice in multiethnic settings. *American Journal of Political Science* 47 (4): 567–82.

Oliver, M. L., and J. H. Johnson. 1984. Inter-ethnic conflict in an urban ghetto: The case of blacks and Latinos in Los Angeles. *Social Movements, Conflicts, and Change* 6:57–94.

Olzak, S. 1992. *The dynamics of ethnic competition and conflict*. Stanford: Stanford Univ. Press.

Perry, H. L. 1991. Deracialization as an analytical construct in American urban politics. *Urban Affairs Quarterly* 27 (2): 181–91.

Peterson, P. E. 1981. *City limits*. Chicago: Univ. of Chicago Press.

Pinderhughes, D. 1987. *Race and ethnicity in Chicago politics*. Urbana: Univ. of Illinois.

Ramakrishnan, S. K., and T. Wong. 2010. Partisanship, not Spanish: Explaining municipal ordinances affecting undocumented immigrants. In *Taking local control: Immigration policy activism in U.S. cities and states*, edited by M. Varsanyi, 73–92. Palo Alto: Stanford Univ. Press.

Rocha, R. R. 2007. Black-brown coalitions in local school board elections. *Political Research Quarterly* 60 (2): 315–27.

Segura, G. 2012. *How the exit polls misrepresent Latino voters, and badly*. Report by Latino Decisions. http://www.latinodecisions.com/blog/2012/11/01/howthe-exit-polls-misrepresent-latino-voters-and-badly/ (accessed April 3, 2013).

Sharp, E. B. 2002. Culture, institutions, and urban official's responses to morality issues. *Political Research Quarterly* 55 (4): 861–83.

Sonenshein, R. J. 1993. *Politics in black and white: Race and power in Los Angeles*. Princeton: Princeton Univ. Press.

Stein, L., and C. W. Kohfeld. 1991. St. Louis's black-white elections: Products of machine factionalism and polarization. *Urban Affairs Quarterly* 27 (2): 227–48.

Stein, R. M., S. G. Ulbig, and S. S. Post. 2005. Voting for minority candidates in multi-racial/ethnic communities. *Urban Affairs Review* 41 (2): 157–81.

Stowers, G. N. L., and R. K. Vogel. 1994. Racial and ethnic voting patterns in Miami. In *Big city politics, governance, and fiscal constraints*, edited by G. E. Peterson, 61–85. Urbana: Univ. of Illinois.

Tam, W. K. 1995. Asians—A monolithic voting bloc? *Political Behavior* 17 (2): 223–49.

Taylor, M. C. 1998. How white attitudes vary with the racial composition of local populations: Numbers count. *American Sociological Review* 63 (August): 512–35.

Tiebout, C. 1956. A pure theory of local expenditures. *Journal of Political Economy* 64: 416–24.

Trounstine, J. 2008. *Political monopolies in American cities: The rise and fall of bosses and reformers*. Chicago: Univ. of Chicago Press.

Vaca, N. C. 2004. *The presumed alliance: The unspoken conflict between Latinos and blacks and what it means for America*. New York: HarperCollins Publishers.

Wald, K. D., J. W. Button, and B. A. Rienzo. 1996. The politics of gay rights in American communities: Explaining antidiscrimination ordinances and policies. *American Journal of Political Science* 40 (November): 1152–78.

Conclusion

Public Policy Applications: Anti-immigrant Policies

Policy Then

Amid rising public concern over illegal immigration to the United States, members of Congress introduced legislation in 2005 that would strengthen border security and give state and local authorities more responsibility for immigration enforcement by criminalizing violations of federal immigration law, including illegal presence. The prospect of local police officers stopping, questioning, and arresting undocumented individuals, and anyone who they felt might look like an undocumented individual, motivated millions of immigrants and their supporters to take to the streets in cities all over the country during the spring of 2006 to voice their opposition. The bill was eventually defeated.

However, popular frustration about the lack of action by Congress on comprehensive immigration reform prompted many state and local governments to enact their own laws seeking to deter illegal immigration. The earliest municipal ordinances were adopted in Hazleton, Pennsylvania, and Farmers Branch, Texas, in 2006. Each required private landlords to determine the immigration status of prospective tenants and penalized them for renting to undocumented immigrants. Within a year, almost a hundred more municipalities throughout the United States had proposed anti-immigrant ordinances. Some authorized the local police to check people's immigration status; others obligated employers to act as federal immigration officers and verify the immigration status of their employees and job applicants, while still others required all city business to take place in English only.

As for the impact of these ordinances, it is not clear whether they inhibited any illegal immigration to the United States, but in many cities, they did drive away segments of the immigrant community, including naturalized citizens and other legal residents, who no longer felt welcome in their communities. Their exodus, in turn, had deleterious effects on the local economy as retail shops lost customers and neighborhood churches and schools suffered declines in their congregations and student populations. Most important, increased racial profiling and discrimination against anyone who appeared to look or sound foreign sowed distrust and hard feelings among people who had previously lived together in relative stability, if not always in harmony.

Civil rights organizations and immigrant advocacy groups filed numerous lawsuits contesting the legality of local anti-immigrant ordinances, and before long a steady stream of federal courts struck down most of the laws as an illegal usurpation of the federal government's exclusive power over immigration. In 2014, the U.S. Supreme Court declined to review appeals of the lower federal court decisions striking down the ordinances passed in Hazleton and Farmers Branch, which discouraged the practice of anti-immigrant legislation at the local level.

Policy Now

Another manifestation of anti-immigrant sentiment in American politics and policy in recent years has been a wave of initiatives and laws that restrict or eliminate bilingual education programs in public schools. A crest in that movement came in 1998 with the passage of Proposition 227, a ballot initiative in California that confined bilingual teaching to students with limited English skills to one year before placing them in the mainstream. Supporters of the initiative appeared to be motivated mainly by the conviction that "if you live in America, you need to speak English."

There have been notable departures from the English-only movement, however. Just as California was embracing restrictive language policies, the Miami-Dade County school district, the fourth-largest school district in the nation, with 347,000 students and a pioneer in the development of bilingual education, was moving in the opposite direction. In 1998, its school board voted to expand bilingual education for all students and not just for those with limited proficiency in English. Miami-Dade offers a variety of options for promoting English proficiency and preserving heritage languages. For example, in some of its schools, students may spend 40 percent of the day

---

| Box 13.1 | **Anti-immigrant Ordinance, Hazleton, Pennsylvania** |

ORDINANCE 2006-18
ILLEGAL IMMIGRATION RELIEF ACT ORDINANCE
BE IT ORDAINED BY THE COUNCIL OF THE CITY OF HAZLETON AS FOLLOWS:

. . .

SECTION 2. FINDINGS AND DECLARATION OF PURPOSE

The People of the City of Hazleton find and declare:

. . .

C. That unlawful employment, the harboring of illegal aliens in dwelling units in the City of Hazleton, and crime committed by illegal aliens harm the health, safety and welfare of authorized US workers and legal residents in the City of Hazleton. Illegal immigration leads to higher crime rates, subjects our hospitals to fiscal hardship and legal residents to substandard quality of care, contributes to other burdens on public services, increasing their cost and diminishing their availability to legal residents, and diminishes our overall quality of life.

D. That the City of Hazleton is authorized to abate public nuisance and empowered and mandated by the people of Hazleton to abate the nuisance of illegal immigration by diligently prohibiting the acts and policies that facilitate illegal immigration in a manner consistent with federal law and the objectives of Congress.

. . .

SECTION 5. HARBORING ILLEGAL ALIENS

A. It is unlawful for any person or business entity that owns a dwelling unit in the City to harbor an illegal alien in the dwelling unit, knowing or in reckless disregard of the fact that an alien has come to, entered, or remains in the United States in violation of law, unless such harboring is otherwise expressly permitted by federal law.

(1) For the purposes of this section, to let, lease, or rent a dwelling unit to an illegal alien, knowing or in reckless disregard of the fact that an alien has come to, entered, or remains in the United States in violation of law, shall be deemed to constitute harboring. . . .

Source: City of Hazleton Illegal Immigration Relief Act Ordinance, Ordinance 2006-18, Hazleton, Pennsylvania, 2006.

---

obtaining instruction in core subjects in Spanish and 60 percent in English. The district also features a number of secondary magnet programs organized around the curricula of other countries like Spain or Italy. Additional programs ensure that other students in the district are fully exposed to a "two-way" bilingual education that immerses them in both English and another language.

The results have been impressive, particularly for a large urban school district in which 65 percent of the students are Latino and 54 percent speak Spanish at home (and significant percentages speak Haitian Creole, French, and Portuguese). Miami-Dade's fourth and eighth grade Latino students have earned above-average scores in math and reading on the National Assessment of Education Progress, and the gaps between white and Latino students in these subjects are smaller than they are for other large urban school districts and the nation as a whole. Finally,

Miami-Dade ranks first in the United States in both the number of Advanced Placement exams taken by Latino students and the percentage of Latino students who score a three or better out of a possible five on the exam.

In accounting for its success, Miami-Dade benefits from having many years of experience with bilingual education, a high percentage of teachers and administrators who are familiar with the languages and cultures of their students, a political environment in which Latinos represent a substantial part of the population and exercise considerable political clout, and a broad consensus among the city's civic and business leaders that teaching both English and another language serves the city's long-term interests.

Additional Resources

Brookings Institution, Research and commentary on immigration in the United States. www.brookings.edu/research/topics/immigration.

Peter J. Duignan, "Bilingual Education: A Critique," Report issued by the Hoover Institution. September 1, 1998. http://www.hoover.org/research/biligual-education-critique.

Federation for American Immigration Reform (FAIR). A national nonprofit organization that advocates for improved border security, a halt to illegal immigration, and reduced annual immigration to about 300,000 per year. www.fairus.org.

Joel Kotkin, "Movers and Shakers: How Immigrants Are Reviving Neighborhoods Given Up for Dead," *Reason Magazine*, December 2000.

Mexican American Legal Defense and Educational Fund (MALDEF). The nation's most prominent civil rights organization on behalf of Latinos. www.maldef.org.

National Immigration Law Center. A public interest group that seeks to defend and advance the rights and opportunities of low-income immigrants and their families. www.nilc.org.

Discussion Questions

1. What kinds of cities are most likely to experience outbursts of anti-immigrant fervor?

2. What factors might warrant a city to take steps to discourage an influx of immigrants? Alternatively, why might urban policymakers seek to encourage immigrants to move to their cities?

3. Miami-Dade County has been a leader in promoting bilingual education programs in public schools. Why have other cities been hesitant about following its lead?

4. In the realm of big-city politics, blacks and Latinos would seem to have many common experiences and share many common interests. And yet the two groups have often struggled to form unified electoral and governing coalitions. Why?

5. Why have some political leaders succeeded in building enduring alliances among various racial and ethnic groups?

6. Looking to the future, do you expect more or less cooperation among African Americans, Latinos, and Asian Americans in the quest for political power in U.S. cities? Why?

Chapter 14

Contemporary Approaches to Urban Governance

Introduction

One of the recurring themes of this book concerns the myriad societal and political constraints that limit how mayors and other local officials go about governing their cities. And yet most urban politics specialists agree that notwithstanding such limitations, policymakers have some flexibility in charting distinctive political directions. In making their choices, constrained as they may be, city leaders are generally guided by an underlying set of ideas, values, and beliefs about politics and society, an ideological orientation that predisposes them to prefer one approach to governance over others. A similar orientation operates among ordinary citizens who participate in the political sphere, either on a regular or an episodic basis. In other words, a particular "vision of politics" tends to animate political activity in cities at both the elite level and the grassroots.

More specifically, scholars have examined electoral and governing coalitions organized by political leaders from the top down and community activists from the bottom up. Some types of coalitions have been more common than others. The earlier analysis of urban regimes revealed that a governing coalition led by the downtown business establishment and pressing a pro-growth agenda purporting to benefit all city residents has been a familiar actor in the urban political landscape in recent decades. But electoral and governing alliances have taken other forms as well, with important ramifications for the critical question of who gets what, when, where, and how.

This chapter explores some of the varied approaches to politics and governance that have attained prominence in contemporary American cities. It does so by employing an analytical framework that highlights diverging perspectives on two of the most fundamental issues in a democracy: Who should rule? And what is the appropriate role of government? Answers to these venerable questions yield four separate visions of politics or four distinct ways in which city leaders, interest groups, community-based organizations, and neighborhood residents might coalesce in support of a common approach to governing a city.[1]

An appropriate place to start is to ask "Who should govern?" This is a question that has preoccupied political thinkers for millennia and one that has captivated scholars in our era.[2] For some, decision making about the intricacies of administering city government, including the complicated allocation of goods and services, should be entrusted to individuals who are the most capable. Some of the most influential framers of the U.S. Constitution, such as Alexander Hamilton and John Adams, subscribed to this view, as did the progressive reformers from a century ago who sought to restructure machine-dominated municipal governments lacking in honesty, efficiency, and productivity.[3] A preference for rule by the best and brightest continues today among those who believe that government should be run like a business with a clear chain of command and an emphasis on public accountability. Such an organizational structure overseen by leaders with experience and expertise will most likely produce public policy that furthers the public interest.

At the other end of the spectrum are those who reject any manifestation of elite rule or any notion that well-educated and highly skilled individuals possess a special ability to ascertain and pursue the public interest. In their view, individuals who make such claims are just as likely to follow their own self-interest as anyone else. Such sentiments were common among the Antifederalists who dismissed the Federalists' faith in a national aristocracy of well-bred gentlemen to lead the nation and among the skeptics of progressive reformers such as George Washington

Plunkitt and latter-day scholars such as Samuel Hays.[4] In recent years, critics of elite rule have harped on the dangers of concentrating power in the hands of a few, whether they are top city officials or the chief executive officers of Fortune 500 corporations based in the downtown core. They look with suspicion on any large institution—big government or big business—because they inevitably come under the control of elites whose interests rarely coincide with the needs and desires of people in the neighborhoods.[5] The preferred alternative to elite rule is popular empowerment. However, giving a wide variety of people a meaningful opportunity to participate in city government is fraught with risks. The policy-making process may bog down or even grind to a halt while fractious groups grapple with hard issues. Citizens may lack the knowledge that is often conducive to quality decision making. Advocates of popular rule respond that over time citizens develop skills and acquire expertise while learning on the job. Moreover, political participation cultivates virtuous citizenship; through close interaction with diverse groups, people gain a deeper understanding of alternative perspectives and a heightened ability to reach compromises on behalf of the common good.[6]

The second fundamental issue addressed in this chapter is "What is the proper role of government in urban affairs?" There is a long and respected tradition in American political history dating at least back to Thomas Jefferson of a preference for limited government. According to this perspective, society is simply too complex to be analyzed and reformed by even the most enlightened and well-intentioned public officials. Indeed, governmental meddling into societal affairs often results in more harm than good. The better option is to allow powerful forces within the private sector to run their course; over the long term, improvements in the quality of life are more likely to result from the unplanned and unintended consequences of normal human activity than from instrumental government action. Of all private sector forces, the economic marketplace is particularly effective at producing an efficient and just distribution of goods and greater overall prosperity than any one system of governmental control.[7]

Proponents of an expansive role for government dismiss the proposition that an uncontrolled private sector yields prosperity for the general population. The actual experience of cities that have limited the role of their governments to encouraging business investment in downtown development while minimizing redistributive policies belies the libertarian faith in the magic of the marketplace. Instead, such an approach to urban governance has time and again engendered a tale of two cities: a thriving downtown core surrounded by struggling or impoverished neighborhoods.[8] What is needed is an activist government capable of using its powers and resources to effect a more equitable allocation of the costs and benefits of urban growth. Striking a balance between promoting capital investment and equitable treatment of a city's residents through purposeful governmental intervention is the more reliable path to a fully prosperous and just society.[9]

Combining the two key issues—Who should govern? and What is the appropriate role of government?—yields four different ideological orientations in thinking about how to govern a city (Table 14.1).

First, a political system led by knowledgeable and experienced elites who seek to limit the role of government represents the most common form of municipal governance. Such a *privatist* vision of politics reflects the governing coalition that ruled Atlanta throughout the post–World War II era, according to Clarence Stone, and can be found in

Table 14.1   Approaches to Urban Governance

		Source of Power	
		Elite	*Mass*
Scope of Government	*Limited*	Privatism	Populism
	Broad	Managerialism	Progressivism

numerous cities today.[10] **Reading 14-1** by Larry Bennett evaluates the longtime mayor of Chicago, Richard M. Daley, whose privatist approach to governance produced a record that was consistently popular with a majority of voters.

Second, a *populist* vision of politics that features a commitment to limited government but broad opportunities for citizens to participate in and influence the policy-making process is less common. The famed community organizer, Saul Alinsky, would have been comfortable with a populist political system, and mayors such as Stephen Goldsmith of Indianapolis have succeeded in implementing such an approach, as he, himself, elaborates in **Reading 14-2**.[11]

Third, advocates of a vigorous role for government to bring about greater equity but a government guided by professionals capable of ensuring honest, efficient, and effective administration of public policies are associated with a *managerial* vision of politics. Progressive reformers of the early twentieth century were practitioners of this approach.[12] A prominent subscriber of managerialism was New York City's recent mayor, Michael Bloomberg.[13] His governing outlook is examined in **Reading 14-3** by Julian Brash.

Finally, a *progressive* vision of politics calls for an expansive and energetic government under the control of an actively engaged citizenry. Progressive politics has flourished in San Francisco, Boston, Seattle, and Portland, Oregon, and may be gathering momentum in the nation's two largest cities, New York and Los Angeles.[14] In **Reading 14-4**, Thad Williamson considers how progressivism might be implemented in the city of Richmond, Virginia.

The following readings offer case studies of each approach to urban governance. What are the strengths and weaknesses of each? Under what conditions would it be feasible to pursue each approach in any given city?

Notes

1. The analytical structure applied here was first utilized in Stephen J. McGovern, *The Politics of Downtown Development: Dynamic Political Cultures in San Francisco and Washington, D.C.* (Lexington: University Press of Kentucky, 1998) and is loosely based on a clever way of thinking about urban politics developed by Peter J. Steinberger in his book *Ideology and the Urban Crisis* (Albany: State University of New York Press, 1985).

2. Aristotle's classification of constitutional schemes of government was grounded in part on his consideration of appropriate sources of power. One of the most influential books in the annals of twentieth-century political science was Robert Dahl's *Who Governs? Democracy and Power in an American City* (New Haven: Yale University Press, 1961), which examined who wields power in New Haven, Connecticut. It stimulated a contentious and long-running debate between pluralists and elitists over power relations in American politics at large. Refer to C. Wright Mills, *The Power Elite* (New York: Oxford University Press, 1956); Nelson W. Polsby, *Community Power and Political Theory* (New Haven: Yale University Press, 1963); Peter Bachrach and Morton S. Baratz, *Power and Poverty: Theory and Practice* (New York: Oxford University Press, 1970); G. William Domhoff, *The Power Elite and the State: How Policy Is Made in America* (New York: A. de Gruyter, 1990).

3. Steinberger, *Ideology and the Urban Crisis*.

4. See Readings 3-1 and 4-4.

5. A populist orientation is embodied in the community organizing of Saul Alinsky (see Reading 10-1) and his followers (see Reading 10-2) and the politics of the consumer advocate, Ralph Nader.

6. Jane Mansbridge, "On the Idea That Participation Makes Better Citizens," in *Citizen Competence and Democratic Institutions*, ed. Stephen L. Elkin and Karol Edward Soltan (University Park: Penn State University Press, 1999); Frank M. Bryan, *Real Democracy: The New England Town Meeting and How It Works* (Chicago: University of Chicago Press, 2004).

7. Refer to Milton Friedman, *Capitalism and Freedom* (Chicago: University of Chicago Press, 1962); Friedrich A. von Hayek, *The Road to Serfdom* (Chicago: University of Chicago Press, 1944).

8. Susan S. Fainstein, *The City Builders: Property Development in New York and London, 1980–2000*, 2nd ed. (Lawrence: University Press of Kansas, 2001); Gregory D. Squires, ed., *Unequal Partnerships: The Politcal Economy of Urban Redevelopment in Postwar America* (New Brunswick, NJ: Rutgers University Press, 1989).

9. Clarissa Rile Hayward and Todd Swanstrom, eds., *Justice and the American Metropolis* (Minneapolis: University of Minnesota Press, 2011). See also Susan S. Fainstein, *The Just City* (Ithaca, NY: Cornell University Press, 2010).

10. Refer to Steven P. Erie, Vladimir Kogan, and Scott A. MacKenzie, "Redevelopment, San Diego Style: The Limits of Public-Private Partnerships," *Urban Affairs Review*, 45 (5), 2010; Howard Gillette Jr., *Camden after the Fall: Decline and Renewal in a Post-industrial City* (Philadelphia: University of Pennsylvania Press, 2005); and Alice O'Connor, "The Privatized City: The Manhattan Institute, the Urban Crisis, and the Conservative Counterrevolution in New York," *Journal of Urban History*, 34 (2), 2007.

11. Saul D. Alinsky, *Reveille for Radicals* (New York: Random House, 1946); Robert Fisher, *Let the People Decide: Neighborhood Organizing in America* (New Brunswick, NJ: Rutgers University Press, 1984); Stephen J. McGovern, "Ideology, Consciousness, and Inner-City Revitalization: The Case of Stephen Goldsmith's Indianapolis," *Journal of Urban Affairs*, 25 (1), 2003.

12. Refer to Carl S. Smith, *The Plan of Chicago: Daniel Burnham and the Remaking of the American City* (Chicago: University of Chicago Press, 2006).

13. Many city officials strive to "run their city like a business." However, relatively few apply a truly managerial emphasis on the power of government and professional expertise. For another study of Michael Bloomberg, see Joyce Purnick, *Mike Bloomberg: Money, Power, Politics* (New York: Public Affairs, 2009).

14. Pierre Clavel, *Activists in City Hall: The Progressive Response to the Reagan Era in Boston and Chicago* (Ithaca, NY: Cornell University Press, 2010); McGovern, *The Politics of Downtown Development*; Peter Dreier, "Urban Politics and Progressive Housing Policy: Ray Flynn and Boston's Neighborhood Agenda," in *Revitalizing Urban Neighborhoods*, ed. W. Dennis Keating, Norman Krumholz, and Philip Star (Lawrence: University of Kansas Press, 1996); Robert Gottlieb, Mark Vallianatos, Regina M. Freer, and Peter Dreier, *The Next Los Angeles: The Struggle for a Livable City* (Berkeley: University of California Press, 2005); Jarrett Murphy, "Bill de Blasio's Great Experiment," *The Nation*, May 5, 2014.

14-1 "The Mayor among His Peers: Interpreting Richard M. Daley"*

Larry Bennett

The City Revisited: Urban Theory from Chicago, Los Angeles, and New York

Richard M. Daley was nearing his thirteenth birthday when Richard J. Daley defeated Robert Merriam in the mayoral election of April 5, 1955. The younger Richard Daley grew up in the Bridgeport neighborhood, home of his parents for the entirety of their lives. Richard M. left Chicago to attend Providence College, but he soon returned, completing his bachelor's degree at DePaul University. He also earned a law degree from DePaul. The younger Daley won his first elective office in 1969, when he was chosen as a delegate to the convention writing a new state constitution for Illinois.[28] For most of the 1970s, Daley served as a senator in the Illinois General Assembly. As a state legislator, Daley was not universally admired. In 1977, *Chicago* magazine published an article—based on a survey of twenty state capitol insiders—identifying the ten best and worst members of the general assembly. Richard M. Daley was ranked among the latter, described as "shrewd" but also "shark-like."[29]

Mayor Richard M. Daley regularly asserts his nonpartisanship, so it is of some interest that he served as 11th ward Democratic Party committeeman for a few years following his father's death. However, by 1980 Daley found himself in the unlikely position of running against the Democratic Party's endorsed candidate in the primary election for Cook County state's attorney. In this race, Chicago Mayor Jane Byrne had backed another young politician with deep family roots in the Democratic Party, 14th ward alderman Ed Burke. Daley defeated Burke, won the general election, and was reelected state's attorney in 1984 and 1988. During the 1980s, Daley also experienced the only electoral defeat of his political career, finishing a close third in the three-way Democratic mayoral primary of 1983 that was won by Harold Washington. Yet Daley did achieve a kind of victory in 1983. Campaigning as a "moderate, good government reformer," he won the endorsement of several prominent Democrats who had previously opposed his father.[30] Even more important, he distanced himself from the racially polarizing rhetoric of the more vociferous anti-Washington Democrats.

In 1989 Daley defeated the incumbent mayor, Eugene Sawyer—selected by the city council to serve as interim mayor following Harold Washington's sudden death in late 1987—in the special election primary, then triumphed over Ed Vrdolyak (until recently a Democrat, running as the Republican Party nominee) and Timothy Evans (qualifying for the election as the standard-bearer of the short-lived Harold Washington Party) in the general election. Daley has been reelected mayor five times, in 1991, 1995, 1999, 2003, and 2007. His original voting base was a "white/brown" coalition of working-class Democratic Party loyalists and Latinos. Until the mid-1990s there were recurring efforts by African-American activists to rejuvenate the "Harold Washington coalition" and unite behind an African-American candidate for mayor.[31] In fact, over the span of Daley's five reelection campaigns he has substantially increased his support among black voters. Until the emergence in 2004 of the series of corruption scandals that have substantially tarnished his administration, the one sign of Richard M. Daley's political weakness has been his declining ability to mobilize the electorate.[32] Like his father, Richard

---

Source: "Larry Bennett, "The Mayor among His Peers: Interpreting Richard M. Daley," in *The City Revisited: Urban Theory from Chicago, Los Angeles, and New York*, ed. Dennis R. Judd and Dick Simpson. Copyright © 2011 by the Regents of the University of Minnesota.

*Some text and accompanying endnotes have been omitted. Please consult the original source.

M. Daley has been an incumbent whose reelection victories have combined impressive winning percentages and diminished voter turnouts. In the younger Daley's "landslide" election of 2007, he drew 250,000 fewer votes than in his special election victory of 1989.

Richard M. Daley—by all accounts—has been a very successful political leader. Apart from his string of election victories, he has reasserted mayoral control over what had been, in the 1980s, a very fractious city council. Moreover, he has extended mayoral control and generated visible results from various of the city's nonmunicipal, independent agencies, including the Chicago Public Schools, the Chicago Housing Authority, and the Chicago Park District. The national press has frequently and favorably commented on his record, and a variety of governmental, civic, and environmental groups have honored him. The latter have included the U.S. Conference of Mayors, the National Trust for Historic Preservation, and the National Arbor Day Foundation. In designating Daley as a Public Official of the Year for 1997, *Governing* editor Alan Ehrenhalt commented: "He has been patient and skillful in mastering the details of local government, and remarkably creative in devising pragmatic solutions to the most complex problems."[33] As such, Richard M. Daley fits comfortably among the prototype post–federal era mayors described by Peter Eisinger.

Though Eisinger's characterization of new-style mayors—which is of a piece with *Governing's* paean to Richard M. Daley—links their "mastering the details" to a withdrawal from the "bully pulpit," the Richard M. Daley administration, over time, has advanced a discernible and far from timid mayoral program. The three fundamental components of this program include promotion of Chicago as a global city, the reorganization of a variety of municipal and independent agency service functions, and social inclusivity at the elite level.

The Daley administration's promotion of Chicago as a global or world-class city is in no way a striking or innovative policy preference. One only needs to recall the bright-eyed Flint, Michigan, officials who were interviewed by Michael Moore in *Roger and Me* (1989) to recognize that the dream of postindustrial transcendence to the friendly skies of mass tourism and the leisure economy is an impulse driving many municipal leaders. The Daley administration, nevertheless, has pursued this goal in a plausibly strategic fashion. On the one hand, efforts to expand both O'Hare Airport and the downtown McCormick Place convention complex seek to build on demonstrated Chicago assets: geographic and transportation network centrality and extensive facilities to support trade shows and conventions. Likewise, the Daley administration's redevelopment of Navy Pier at the northeastern end of the downtown area, and the creation of the Millennium Park complex, have forged two powerful tourist magnets. Chicago's unsuccessful campaign to host the 2016 Olympic Games nonetheless served to reinforce the city's image as a primary global node.[34]

Less dramatically, but possibly more consequentially, Richard M. Daley [and] city planners have implemented numerous small-scale infrastructure and beautification improvements, sped up approval processes, and reimagined local neighborhood identities in such a fashion so as to add momentum to the ongoing industrial to commercial/residential transformation of the city's Near West and Near South Sides. So far, the gentrification of these areas has engendered relatively little neighborhood resistance. From the standpoint of Chicago's image as a global city, this expanded cityscape of "upscale boutiques and stylish restaurants" represents both a talent-drawing amenity and a marker of Chicago's progressive, postindustrial character.[35]

Richard M. Daley has also been an aggressive reorganizer of local government bureaucracies. In 1995, he won state legislation enabling him to replace the school board and top administration at the Chicago Public Schools (CPS). Daley selected his budget director, Paul Vallas, to assume the new post as CEO of the schools. Vallas pulled back authority from the parent-dominated Local School Councils (elected to govern each Chicago public school), moved to standardize the curriculum, and pushed hard for improvement in student performance on academic achievement tests. Mayor Daley, in turn, poured immense resources into a program of school construction and rehabilitation. Since the mid-1990s, Chicago school system standardized test performance has generally moved upward, though slowly and unevenly across grades and testing fields. In June 2004, Daley and then-CPS CEO Arne Duncan (appointed to replace Vallas in 2001) announced Renaissance 2010, a proposal to close poorly performing schools and to replace them with one hundred new schools. Many of the latter are independent charter schools.[36]

No less sweeping has been Daley's makeover of the Chicago Housing Authority (CHA). Following the U.S. Department of Housing and Urban Development's takeover of the CHA between 1995 and 1999, Daley appointees initiated an agency restructuring called the Plan for Transformation. This plan aims to reduce the number of local public housing units from approximately 40,000 to 25,000 (with 10,000 units reserved for senior citizens), rehabilitate or build anew each of those 25,000 units, turn over day-to-day property management and social service provision to private vendors, and site most public housing in mixed-income developments. As a rule, these mixed-income developments adhere to a one-third/one-third/one-third proportioning of public housing, affordable housing (mainly rental, some for sale), and market-rate housing.[37]

The CHA's track record in implementing the Plan for Transformation has been very mixed. At some developments, resident acceptance of the new CHA vision has been forthcoming, at other developments—including the famous Cabrini-Green complex on the Near North Side—there has been substantial resident resistance. One of the most significant process challenges involved in a planning effort of this magnitude is resident relocation, both temporary moves as developments are rebuilt and permanent relocations from public housing. On both counts, the CHA's performance has been poor. At developments such as the ABLA Homes on the Near West Side, planning and project execution spanned more than a decade, during which time the inconveniences visited upon residents were extraordinary. For former public housing residents across the city, CHA-contracted relocation services have been spotty. The findings of researchers who have examined where former CHA residents have found new places to live are disturbingly uniform: in overwhelmingly African-American neighborhoods nearly as poor as the public housing communities from which they departed.[38]

Richard M. Daley's other major public service reorganization has been within the city government. In 1994 the police department implemented a citywide program of community policing known as the Chicago Alternative Policing Strategy (CAPS). The CAPS initiative has put more patrol officers onto Chicago's sidewalks, and via nearly three hundred monthly "beat" meetings brings together police personnel and community residents to discuss local, crime-related issues. During the later 1990s and into the current decade, Chicago's crime rate has paralleled the pattern of decline achieved in many cities. The Daley administration has not hesitated to attribute the local decline to the effective implementation of CAPS.[39]

The third component of the Daley program is elite social inclusivity. As mayor, Richard M. Daley has routinely filled important administrative positions with Latinos, African Americans, and women. Although his 1989 voting base included few African Americans, since that time Daley has worked hard to solidify his relationship with leading black political figures such as the late John Stroger, president of the Cook County Board of Commissioners from 1994 until 2006. Daley has also cultivated the city's business and civic leadership, which, for its part, has been warmly grateful to the mayor for Chicago's resurgent reputation. And not least, in a stunning departure from his father's politics, Richard M. Daley has courted formerly marginal constituencies such as gay rights and environmental activists. Richard M. Daley most strikingly distinguishes himself from his father—in terms of worldview, his sense of the city, and his coalition-building inclinations—through his appearances at the annual Gay Pride Parade.

Nevertheless, the current Mayor Daley's approach to social inclusivity is a matter of communication and consultation at the elite level. In a 1999 assessment of Daley's record, journalist David Moberg observed: "The mayor has done everything he could to discourage any popular involvement in civic affairs that would compromise his hold on power. Despite preserving many of the reforms that emerged during Harold Washington's brief tenure, he has largely rejected Washington's belief in community participation in planning and implementing public policy."[40] Daley planners, in effect, dictated the terms of public housing redevelopment, and since the mayor's asserting his control of the Chicago Public Schools in 1995, there has been a substantial erosion of influence exercised by the neighborhood-based, elected local school councils. Even the mayor's admirers agree that he is a reclusive decision maker who relies on the advice of a handful of close advisors. In short, Daley promotes Chicago as a prospective home and workplace for all, though as the chief executive he has depended on a very narrow stream of local information gathering, expertise, and counsel.

The preceding review of the basic features of the Richard M. Daley program has, in its retrospectiveness and thematization of particular initiatives, also tended to exaggerate the program's coherence and the degree of rationalistic forethought that shaped it. Daley's candidacy in 1989 was described as a "cautious, scripted campaign," and his April 1989 inaugural address was brief though richly platitudinous:

> Our common opponents are crime and ignorance, waste and fraud, poverty and disease, hatred and discrimination. And we either rise up as one city and make the special effort required to meet these challenges, or sit back and watch Chicago decline. As one who loves Chicago, I'm ready to make that special effort—and to ask everyone in our city to do the same. Business as usual is a prescription for failure. The old ways of doing things simply aren't adequate to cope with the new challenges we face. In times of limited resources, government must be more creative and productive than ever before. We must do a better job with the resources we have.[41]

In a subsequent passage—which was also the only section of the speech addressing a specific local government function—Daley turned to Chicago's public schools. Education reform, of course, has become a signature Richard M. Daley initiative, but his crucial move in this policy area—which was to seek state government approval for reorganizing the Chicago Public Schools—would wait for another six years, following his reelection to a second four-year term as mayor. In the pages to follow, I attempt to explain how Richard M. Daley's program emerged, and in so doing, link his mayoralty to recent trends in American mayoral practice and specify some of its more individualistic sources.

Richard M. Daley Reconsidered

A generation ago, political scientist John W. Kingdon published a book entitled *Agendas, Alternatives, and Public Policies*, in which he offered a "loose, messy" decision-making model as a more realistic alternative to "the tight, orderly process that a rational approach specifies." Even my unadorned summary of Richard M. Daley's main initiatives *suggests* a degree of rationality in policy selection that is

at odds with reality. In this reconsideration of Daley's program, I propose an interpretive framework that is loosely drawn from Kingdon's triad of public agenda sources: "problems, policies, and politics."[42]

The Richard M. Daley administration's approach to governing Chicago bears the mark of five shaping forces. These forces are a mixed bag, but also represent a constellation of influences structuring the action of any big-city mayor: broad-scale economic and social conditions; the mayor's personal inclinations as a municipal leader; opportunities presented by emerging situations or trends in public policy; the laundry list of prospective projects (usually, physical projects) circulating among local elites and begging the mayor's attention; and what I term "politically usable policies" that emerge as priorities due to their strategic constituent appeal. As we walk through this funhouse of potential action, I believe we can begin to understand more readily both the coherence and incoherences of the Daley program, even as we also gain a deeper sense of why his particular program emerged.

In terms of understanding the main threads of Richard M. Daley's programmatic action, the simplest of the five shaping forces to identify are the pair of basic structural conditions that in 1989 loomed over both Chicago and his nascent mayoralty. The first of these was the massive economic restructuring that had undermined Chicago's industrial economy since the 1960s. The second was carryover racial polarization, initially produced by the city's wrenching neighborhood transitions and the politics of civil rights activism and resistance in the 1960s, then reignited during the election of 1983 and the subsequent Harold Washington mayoralty.

In reference to economic restructuring, with the exception of Harold Washington—an outlier not just among the ranks of Chicago chief executives—the dream of every Chicago mayor running back to Richard J. Daley has been the transformation of central Chicago into a more formidable corporate management district and upscale residential enclave. This reworking of the central city's physical environment has been promoted both to compensate for the decline of the manufacturing economy and to boost the Loop and its environs as generators of tax revenue. In effect, local leaders since the 1950s have sought what is literally unspeakable in the proud city of Chicago, the Manhattanization of the Loop and the adjoining Near North, West, and South Sides. Richard M. Daley's contribution to the achievement of this dream—apart from holding the mayoralty at a time when the real estate market was moving very briskly along a parallel course—has been to skillfully use public works to environmentally enhance central Chicago and deploy an array of planning tools intended to lubricate private investment. Mayor Daley's efforts to expand O'Hare Airport and the McCormick Place convention complex, likewise, have sought to boost Chicago advantages as a transportation node and tourist/trade show destination.

Traditional infrastructure and central city development initiatives have not been Richard M. Daley's only gambit to economically reposition Chicago. In the early 2000s, his CivicNet initiative sought to build a citywide fiber optic network, and although the city government was unable to find a private-sector partner for CivicNet, the Daley administration has continued its efforts to enhance telecommunications access across Chicago.[43] Daley's city government has also sought to protect viable portions of the city's residual industrial economy.[44] Nevertheless, in terms of resources committed and publicity generated, not just the rebuilding, but more grandly, the reimagining of central Chicago, has grown out of Richard M. Daley's particular approach to his city's long arc of economic transformation running back to the 1960s.

Also attuned to conditions originating in the 1960s has been Richard M. Daley's commitment to elite social inclusivity. Richard M. Daley is neither a political natural—in the sense of embracing crowds and seizing the opportunity to speak from the stump—nor is he a philosophical populist. Yet recognizing the racially divided electorate of the 1980s—and more fundamentally, Chicago's unresolved social conflicts dating from the 1960s—Daley has moved to co-opt key figures representing various dissident constituencies, notably African Americans and anti-Richard J. Daley "independent" Democrats. He has also reached out to the city's corporate and civic leadership while cultivating new constituencies such as gays and environmentalists. Daley is not a warm politician in the style of a Harold Washington or Fiorello La Guardia, but through high-level consultation and careful observance of the city's

civic protocols he has projected the image of a publicly attentive, if not personally accessible chief executive.

Then there are Richard M. Daley's personal inclinations as mayor, which admittedly constitute an amorphous subject for analysis. Nevertheless, various of the mayor's biographical details do permit a plausible explanation of one of his administration's most persistent commitments, its diversified campaign of civic beautification. My cautiously offered explanation of this Daley inclination begins by noting his coming of age during the 1960s, and more pertinently, during the latter half of his father's administration. During that period, the Chicago cityscape was badly damaged: by civil unrest that destroyed scores of buildings along major South Side and West Side commercial corridors; by fires, housing abandonment, and demolitions in many residential areas; by deferred maintenance of public structures such as schools, transit stations, and, most notably, public housing developments.[45]

Given the proprietorial mindset that Richard M. Daley does seem to share with his late father, his persistence in repairing—or rebuilding more grandly—basic infrastructure such as roadways, bridges, schools, libraries, and parks buildings brings to mind the heir to a once great estate who aspires to restore its past glory. Moreover, Daley has determined that there is an economic payoff to urban beautification. The following comment drawn from his address to the Urban Parks Institute's "Great Parks/Great Cities" conference in 2001 makes the point quite succinctly: "The nice thing is, if you improve the quality of life for the people who live in your city, you will end up attracting new people and new employers."[46] Other factors that surely have stoked Daley's commitment to physically restore Chicago include his mingling with the likes of John Norquist at U.S. Conference of Mayors events, as well as his extensive international travels. Unlike his father, the younger Mayor Daley is a geographic and urban cosmopolitan.

Among the striking elements of the Richard M. Daley beautification campaign is the multitude of small-scale physical improvements one observes across Chicago. Much press coverage has been devoted to Daley's big projects such as Millennium Park, but for rank-and-file Chicagoans, the mayor's most lasting contribution to physical Chicago has been the installation of hundreds of sidewalk bicycle racks, the planting of perennial flowers and shrubs in previously neglected traffic islands, the rebuilding of neighborhood public libraries, and the like. Daley's urban design inclinations, typically street-level in their focus, have clearly been influenced by the thinking of celebrated urbanist Jane Jacobs. They are the sorts of microscale physical improvements that may often spring to Mayor Daley's mind as his chauffeur-driven automobile navigates Chicago's streets.

Richard M. Daley has also been an opportunistic mayoral leader, responding in imaginative ways to unforeseen situations or even programmatic setbacks. Political scientist Joel Rast has proposed that the Daley administration's reengagement with a previously dismissed policy option—neighborhood economic development, which was initially viewed as too closely associated with Harold Washington's administration—was just such an opportunistic policy selection. Having experienced the political undoing of several large-scale public works proposals, notably a South Side airport plan and a near-Loop casino project, and having suffered through the embarrassing "Loop flood" of 1992 (when tunnels running beneath downtown office towers filled with water escaping from the main channel of the Chicago River), Daley and his planners determined that basic infrastructure improvements should be given greater attention.[47]

Between 2004 and 2008, the Daley administration signed long-term leasing agreements with private vendors to operate several city-owned facilities and physical assets: the Chicago Skyway, a South Side toll highway; municipal parking garages and parking meters; and Midway Airport. In the face of a growing city budget deficit, these lease agreements promised to generate more than five billion dollars in immediate revenues. In turn, the firms operating the skyway and the city's parking meter network announced plans to substantially increase user fees. In the long run, it is both uncertain how responsibly these properties will be managed and physically maintained, as well as how the Daley administration will use the cash generated by these deals. Also noteworthy was the lack of either public discussion or city council involvement as these leasing arrangements were worked out.[48]

Though community policing in Chicago is repeatedly invoked as a mayoral initiative, it was, in fact, a grassroots movement—the Chicago Alliance for Neighborhood Safety—that initially promoted intensified street-patrolling and closer cooperation between the police department and neighborhood residents.[49] The Daley administration has certainly been a leader in promoting public school and public housing restructuring, but these are also policy areas in which there had been years of national debate preceding the advent of local action.[50] Once more, it bears mentioning that Richard M. Daley has been an active participant in national organizations whose agendas have, in part, been directed to discussion of just such policy innovations.

In years to come, Chicago's many visitors will principally celebrate Richard M. Daley's accomplishments as an urban builder. In central Chicago, his term in office has coincided, most notably, with the redevelopment of Navy Pier as a tourist/entertainment attraction, the reconstruction of Wacker Drive paralleling the main and south branches of the Chicago River, the development of Millennium Park, the rerouting of Lake Shore Drive (which permits uninterrupted pedestrian movement between the Field Museum, Shedd Aquarium, and Adler Planetarium, the area now known as the Museum Campus), the rebuilding of Soldier Field, and several expansions of McCormick Place. The Daley administration has won much praise for seeing these projects through to completion, but the roots of several of these initiatives precede Daley's mayoralty. Plans to convert the then-derelict Navy Pier into a public promenade date from the 1980s.[51] From about the same time, the Chicago Bears National Football League franchise, Soldier Field's principal tenant, had lobbied for a stadium upgrade.[52] Historian Timothy Gilfoyle, in his account of the creation of Millennium Park, notes that even this public works extravaganza—which is so closely identified with Richard M. Daley—grew out of preceding efforts by several of Chicago's civic notables to create a "Lakefront Gardens" performing arts complex.[53]

There is, however, an overriding logic that has yielded this clustering of public works initiatives, and which is attributable to Richard M. Daley. In a fashion that mimics the approach to civic enhancement—if not invariably the classically inspired architectural monumentality—associated with the early twentieth-century City Beautiful Movement, Daley has devoted billions of dollars to dignifying those portions of his city most accessible to visitors, but which might also be considered a civic common ground for Chicagoans. And judging by the popularity of these sites, this effort to create a memorable civic gathering place for all Chicago has been successful. For Richard M. Daley—personally speaking—there is good reason to suppose that this mammoth program of civic refurbishment is also a satisfying exercise in erasing physical reminders of Chicago's sad decline in the 1960s and 1970s.

In short, Richard M. Daley, the urban builder, has pursued a course of action that has general sources—the dreams of nearly all ambitious mayors include large-scale public works accomplishments—but is also reflective of his proprietorial view of Chicago, and as well, persistent opportunism. Practically speaking, the Daley public works program has involved picking a group of projects—several of which were already in the civic/municipal pipeline—and bringing them to fruition. This taking on and completing initiatives that antedate one's administration is a characteristic feature of successful public works execution, but it is a form of action not limited to infrastructure and public buildings. Richard M. Daley's movement into public school reform, from the standpoints of political action and policy choice, has followed an analogous course. Toward the end of Harold Washington's mayoralty, parent groups, a civic/business alliance known as Chicago United, and members of the mayor's administration began to promote an overhaul of the Chicago Public Schools. Ironically, the fruit of their work was state legislation passed in 1989 that dramatically decentralized CPS operations by vesting new powers in the local school councils. Daley's "takeover" of the CPS in 1995, in one sense, carried on reform efforts that had begun in the previous decade, even as, in another sense, these reforms were reversed by Paul Vallas's recentralization of CPS decision making.[54]

If Rudolph Giuliani can be characterized as an immoderate centrist, the equivalent designation for Richard M. Daley might be eccentric relativist. Among Daley's arsenal of politically usable policy stances has been a bewildering series of moral issue endorsements: neighborhood referenda to de-license "problem" taverns, official recognition of same-sex marriages, online identification of sex offenders.[55] There appears to be little philosophical coherence to Daley's expressed commitments on these matters, but there is a discernible political logic. Over his two-decade mayoralty, Daley has persistently sought to broaden his initially white/brown electoral (and racially/ethnically inflected) coalition. This strategy has involved reaching out to African-American ministers, who are often vigorous proponents of strict moral standards, and it has also involved catering to Chicago's substantial gay population. It is a strategy that clearly incorporates some of the mayor's particular inclinations, especially his support of urban bicycling and various green measures such as rooftop gardens. Each of these constituencies—socially conservative African Americans, gays and lesbians, outdoors enthusiasts and environmentalists—represents a relatively small increment of support, but conjoined they have allowed Richard M. Daley to expand his base of support well beyond his initial voting coalition.

The most encompassing of Richard M. Daley's politically usable policies has been his personal identification with managerial innovation. Apart from the real policy reorientations evident in the Chicago Public Schools, Chicago Housing Authority, and the police department, Daley has steadfastly presented himself as a mayor above politics. As he explained to a reporter in 1994: "If I had to worry about my election, I'd never make a decision here and my role is to make decisions. I don't consume this political stuff.... I'm not a political junkie. [Working in government] is where you get things done."[56] It has been many years since Daley served as 11th ward Democratic committeeman, and as a rule, he has adopted a neutral pose in the face of internecine Democratic Party disputes. Yet it is also evident that Daley's posture as manager rather than politician has served a useful political purpose. Until the spate of corruption scandals rocked his administration in 2004, Daley routinely deflected criticism by asserting that efficiency and calculation of the public good were his first—and only—executive considerations. The following is his response to criticism that had been directed at the Chicago Public Schools in early 2006:

There is nothing wrong with people giving me their ideas, whether Congressman [Luis] Gutierrez or you or anyone else.... That is what you do as a public official. You listen. You take their criticism, you take their evaluation. . . . I had the vision, I had the will and I had the character to do it, and the courage. . . . I said we are going to make a difference, and there has been a difference. I am the only mayor in the United States who would take that political responsibility. Every other mayor ran out left and right.[57]

In this representation by Daley of his own aims and means, executive wisdom and courage are contrasted with the small-minded carping that is the presumed stock-in-trade of politicians such as Congressman Gutierrez.

Richard M. Daley and Municipal Neoliberalism

Despite holding Chicago's mayoralty for two decades, Richard M. Daley remains a surprisingly enigmatic figure, the object of widely varying appraisals. For some commentators, the scope of his local political dominance combines with certain of his personal attributes—notably his colossal temper and maladroit public speaking—to establish a direct link to his father. The result is an interpretative stance presenting Richard M. Daley as the most recent in Chicago's long line of political bosses. Almost perfectly at odds with Daley-the-boss is another widely circulated image, Richard M. Daley the nuts-and-bolts manager and administrative innovator. A variant of the latter image is the view of Daley accepted by many of Chicago's corporate leaders, "The CEO of City Hall."[58]

The contention that Richard M. Daley is a contemporary political boss typically does not come to terms with two fundamental features of Chicago's early twenty-first century political landscape: the decline of most of the Democratic Party ward organizations as voter mobilizers; the rise of media-directed, fund-raising–dependent local campaigning. Richard M. Daley has been a tremendously effective fund-raiser and has used his campaign war chest to win the loyalty of many subordinate elected officials (notably city council members).[59] Just as crucially, Daley triumphs in municipal elections attracting fewer than 40 percent of the registered voters and in which there is no cohesive opposition party. The much-vaunted Cook County Democratic machine, these days, is a paper tiger, but

riding astride this ghost of machines past is a mayor who has achieved a powerful personal hold on the local electorate and government.

In the wake of the overlapping city hall patronage and "Hired Truck" contracting scandals between 2004 and 2006, Mayor Daley has himself backed off from his previous self-presentation as the ultravigilant manager: "I wish I could be on top of every detail. I'm aware that the prevailing perception is that I am. Obviously, in an organization as large and multilayered as city government, that's impossible."[60] Ultimately, Daley's success as Chicago's administrator-in-chief does not appear to be a function of anything particularly distinctive in his management style, nor even of an uncanny knowledge of municipal arcana. The mayor has elicited strong performance from many subordinates due to some currently unfashionable executive strengths: his stranglehold on reelection, which produces the widely held presumption that the man at the top will be in charge so long as he wishes to be, and ruthlessness in punishing subordinates in the wake of publicized performance breakdowns. Even the Daley administration's recent spate of privatization activity—contracting out Chicago Skyway, parking garage, parking meter, and Midway Airport operations (the latter agreement was subsequently withdrawn)—appears to be an impromptu escape from deficit ambush as opposed to a studied reordering of municipal priorities.

It is noteworthy that Richard M. Daley's approach to managing city services has also been the source of some of the most pointed criticisms of his administration. Sociologist Eric Klinenberg's study of the mid-1995 Chicago temperature spike and its deadly aftermath, Heat Wave, identifies Daley administration-implemented social service privatization and police and fire department emergency services reorganization as amplifiers of the temperature-induced health crisis.[61] Fellow sociologist David Pellow, in Garbage Wars, his examination of Chicago's since-terminated "blue-bag" recycling program, reaches conclusions that are directly analogous to Klinenberg's. Chicago's recycling rate stalled at well below 10 percent, and the private firm in charge of the blue-bag program from its initiation in 1995, Waste Management, Inc., was poorly regarded both in terms of its environmental record and labor/management practices. In effect, quite like the municipal government's privatization of social services, favorable publicity for presumably cutting-edge management practice—that is, contracting with private vendors—masked underlying performance deficiencies.[62]

Though Richard M. Daley's considerable ego does not allow for much acknowledgement of influences, he is a mayor who has learned from the practice of peers such as Rudolph Giuliani, Ed Rendell, and John Norquist. Whereas Daley's father by the late 1960s had become the self-conscious defender of an older urban order—a Chicago in which family and community allegiances were presumed to be fundamental sources of identity, the city of journalist Mike Royko's primal, ethnic "nation states"—the second mayor Daley is self-consciously an innovator, catching the wave of new trends in city management and planning (even if the latter, like new urbanism, are themselves explicitly traditionalist). Of particular significance—for Chicago, and as an exemplar of the new form of urban governance that has taken shape across the United States in the last two decades—is how Richard M. Daley's administration has recast the aims of municipal administration. No longer the direct provider of the full slate of essential local services and with no aspiration whatsoever to equalizing individual and family opportunity through redistributive means, Daley's municipal government *facilitates* economic entrepreneurship, neighborhood redevelopment, and privately devised policy innovation (for example, charter schools). This redirection of municipal policy has not produced an appreciably smaller city government—public works are expensive and over the years the Daley administration payroll has dipped only slightly—but it has substantially narrowed its aims. In effect, municipal government in Chicago has become the collaborator with major firms and key investors in advancing *their agendas*, promoter of the city's overall image (and in particular instances, the fortunes of promising neighborhoods), and the provider of a residue of traditional services such as police and fire protection, sanitation, and basic physical infrastructure.

By shedding redistributive functions while emphasizing physical enhancements, stripped-down municipal custodianship, and attention-garnering mega-events, Richard M. Daley has turned Chicago's municipal government into a public sector agent in support of corporate investment, upscale residential development, and associated arts, entertainment, and leisure-sector functions. This basic policy emphasis has been developed while on the job, both as a result of local lessons learned and via the shared experience of peer mayors and their cities. Given the widespread admiration of Richard M. Daley's mayoralty, and the similarly widespread perception of Chicago as a city that has successfully made the industrial-to-postindustrial transition, Daley-style mayoring is likely to be carried to other cities in the coming years. Yet at root, Daley-style mayoring operates within a political economic framework—neoliberalism—whose sources transcend the local milieu: "urban policy [that] . . . shift [s] away from an explicit concern with social and spatial equity, full employment and welfare programmes and toward initiatives aimed at promoting workforce flexibility and the economic competitiveness of the private sector."[63] Richard M. Daley is certainly the product of a particular place, but his approach to municipal governance is very much a function of his time and the globalized capitalism that shapes prevailing understandings of what can and cannot be accomplished by even the most efficacious of municipal chief executives.

Notes

28. A biographical essay on Richard M. Daley, a list of his honorary citations, and various of his public statements can be accessed at the City of Chicago Web site: http://www.ci.chi.il.us/city/webportal/home.do. Other profiles of Richard M. Daley include Thomas Hardy, "His Goal: Make His Own Name," *Chicago Tribune*, April 5, 1989, sec. 2; James Atlas, "The Daleys of Chicago," *New York Times Magazine*, August 25, 1996, 37–39, 52, 56–58; Evan Osnos, "The Daley Show," *The New Yorker*, March 8, 2010, 38–51.

29. Henry Hansen, "Ten to Keep Around, Ten to Kick Around," *Chicago*, November 1977, 146–47.

30. David Moberg, "Can You Find the Reformer in This Group?" *The Reader* (Chicago), February 18, 1983.

31. Thomas Byrne Edsall, "Black vs. White in Chicago," *New York Review of Books*, April 13, 1989, 21–23.

32. Shane Tritsch, "The Mystery of Mayor Daley," *Chicago*, July 2004, 58–63, 88–93; Gary Washburn and Ray Long, "Daley Will Kill Scandal-Torn Hired Truck,"

Chicago Tribune, Feb. 9, 2005; Rudolph Bush and Dan Mihalopoulos, "Daley Jobs Chief Guilty," *Chicago Tribune*, July 7, 2006.

33. Alan Ehrenhalt, "Master of the Detail," *Governing*, December 1997, 22.

34. Larry Bennett, Michael Bennett, and Stephen Alexander, "Chicago and the 2016 Olympics: Why Host the Games? How Should We Host the Games? What Should We Accomplish by Hosting the Games?" (research report, Egan Urban Center, DePaul University, Chicago, November 2008).

35. Saskia Sassen, "A Global City," in Charles Madigan, ed., *Global Chicago* (Urbana: University of Illinois Press, 2004), 29. At a presentation by Sassen a number of years ago, she referred to these gentrifying areas of Chicago as the city's "glamour zone."

36. Anthony S. Bryk, David Kerbow, and Sharon Rollow, "Chicago School Reform," in Diane Ravitch and Joseph Viteritti, eds., *New Schools for a New Century* (New Haven: Yale University Press, 1997), 164–200; Tracy Dell'Angela and Gary Washburn, "Daley Set to Remake Troubled Schools," *Chicago Tribune*, June 25, 2004; Tracy Dell'Angela, "12 Years In, School Reforms Mixed," *Chicago Tribune*, February 5, 2007, sec. 2.

37. Chicago Housing Authority, "Plan for Transformation," *Chicago*, January 6, 2000; Larry Bennett, Janet S. Smith, and Patricia A. Wright, eds., *Where Are Poor People to Live? Transforming Public Housing* (Armonk, N.Y.: M.E. Sharpe, 2006).

38. Paul Fischer, "Section 8 and the Public Housing Revolution: Where Will the Families Go?" (Chicago: The Woods Fund, September 4, 2001); Paul Fischer, "Where Are the Public Housing Families Going? An Update" (unpublished paper, January 2003); Susan Popkin and Mary K. Cunningham, "CHA Relocation Counseling Assessment," (Washington, D.C., The Urban Institute, July 2002); Thomas P. Sullivan, "Independent Monitor's Report No. 5 to the Chicago Housing Authority and the Central Advisory Council," *Chicago*, January 8, 2003. Sullivan writes on CHA relocation activities in summer and early fall of 2002: "In July, August and September 2002, the large number of HCV [housing choice voucher]-eligible families still in the CHA buildings, coupled with imminent building-empty dates, and the relatively small number of relocation counselors, caused a rush to place families in rental units. This in turn led inevitably to placing families hurriedly, and to relocating families into racially segregated areas already overwhelmingly populated by low-income families. Housing quality was overlooked or given little attention," 22; also see Dan A. Lewis and Vandna Sinha, "Moving Up and Moving Out?: Economic and Residential Mobility of Low-Income Chicago Families," *Urban Affairs Review* 43, no. 2 (Nov. 2007): 139–70.

39. Wesley G. Skogan and Susan M. Hartnett, *Community Policing, Chicago Style* (New York: Oxford University Press, 1997); Wesley G. Skogan et al., "Taking Stock: Community Policing in Chicago," (Washington, D.C.: National Institute of Justice, July 2002).

40. David Moberg, "How Does Richie Rate?" *The Reader* (Chicago), February 19, 1999.

41. The characterization of the 1989 Daley campaign appeared in Hardy, "His Goal: Make His Own Name"; Richard M. Daley, "Inaugural Address," *Chicago*, April 24, 1989, http://www.chipublib.org/cplb00k5m-0vie5/cpl5rchive/mayors/rm_daley_inaug01.php (accessed 6 September 2010).

42. John W. Kingdon, *Agendas, Alternatives, and Public Policies* (Boston: Little, Brown, 1984), 83, 93. Although his subject is mayoral leadership rather than the sources of mayoral programmatic action, my argument also parallels the main lines of Richard Flanagan's analysis in "Opportunities and Constraints in Mayoral Behavior: A Historical-Institutional Approach," *Journal of Urban ffairs* 26, no. 1 (2004): 43–65.

43. Paul Merrion, "City's Internet Project Becomes a Daley Double," *Crain's Chicago Business*, Jan. 14, 2002, 9; Jon Van, "Broadband Picture Not Finished," *Chicago Tribune*, Sept. 9, 2007, sec. 3; Report of the Mayor's Advisory Council on Closing the Digital Divide, "The City that Networks: Transforming Society and Economy Through Digital Excellence," *Chicago*, May 2007.

44. Joel Rast, *Remaking Chicago: The Political Origins of Urban Industrial Change* (DeKalb: Northern Illinois University Press, 1999), 132–57.

45. Amanda Seligman, *Block by Block: Neighborhoods and Public Policy on Chicago's West Side* (Chicago: University of Chicago Press, 2005), 63. By the mid-1960s, some local civic activists began to express the view that the aggressiveness of city government-initiated building demolition activity itself posed a threat to neighborhood stability.

46. Richard M. Daley, "Revitalizing Chicago through Parks and Public Spaces," July 31, 2001, http://www/pps.org/daleyspeech/ (accessed 6 September 2010).

47. Rast, *Remaking Chicago*, 149–50.

48. Dan Mihalopoulos, "Group Pays for Skyway Lease," *Chicago Tribune*, Jan. 25, 2005, sec. 2; Ben Joravsky, "Easy Money," *Chicago Reader*, October 16, 2008; Dan Mihalopoulos and Hal Dardick, "Pain in the Meter," *Chicago Tribune*, Dec. 3, 2008; Dan Mihalopoulos and Hal Dardick, "Parking Meter Deal Okd: Rates Going Up," *Chicago Tribune*, Dec. 5, 2008.

49. Skogan, *Community Policing, Chicago Style*, 138.

50. Clarence N. Stone et al., *Building Civic Capacity: The Politics of Reforming Urban Schools* (Lawrence: University Press of Kansas, 2001); Janet L. Smith, "Public Housing Transformation: Evolving National Policy," and Yan Zhang and Gretchen Weismann, "Public Housing's Cinderella: Policy Dynamics of HOPE VI in the Mid-1990s," in Bennett, Smith, and Wright, *Where Are Poor People to Live?*, 19–67.

51. James M. Smith, "Special-Purpose Governance in Chicago: Institutional Independence and Political Interdependence at the Municipal Pier and Exposition Authority" (paper presented at the annual meeting of the Urban Affairs Association, Montreal, April 2006) 9–10.

52. Robert A. Baade and Allen R. Sanderson, "Bearing Down on Chicago," in Roger G. Noll and Andrew Zimbalist, eds., *Sports, Jobs, and Taxes: The Economic Impact of Sports Teams and Stadiums* (Washington, D.C.: Brookings Institution Press, 1997), 324–54.

53. Timothy J. Gilfoyle, *Millennium Park: Creating a Chicago Landmark* (Chicago: University of Chicago Press, 2006), 63–76.

54. Jeffrey Mirel, "School Reform, Chicago Style: Educational Innovation in a Changing Urban Context, 1976–1991," *Urban Education* 28, no. 2 (July 1993): 116–149; Dorothy Shipps, *School Reform, Corporate Style: Chicago, 1880–2000* (Lawrence: University Press of Kansas, 2006), 130–69.

55. Gary Washburn and John Chase, "Daley Puts on a Press for Liquor Proposals," *Chicago Tribune*, Oct. 22, 1998, sec. 2; Kathryn Masterson, "Gay-marriage Backers Get Daley's Signature," *Chicago Tribune*, Oct. 29, 2004, sec. 2; John Chase, "City to Put List of Sex Offenders On-line," *Chicago Tribune*, Nov. 23, 1998, sec. 2.

56. David H. Roeder, "Mayor Daley as Conciliator," *Illinois Issues*, April 1994, 23. The brackets appear in Roeder's text.

57. Gary Washburn, "Daley Quick to Defend His Record," *Chicago Tribune*, May 10, 2006, sec. 2.

58. See Joseph Weber, "The CEO of City Hall," *BW Chicago*, premier issue, 2007.

59. Anthony Gierzynski, Paul Kleppner, and James Lewis, "The Price of Democracy: Financing Chicago's 1995 City Elections" (Chicago: Chicago Urban League and the Office for Social Policy Research, Northern Illinois University, September 1996).

60. Tritsch, "The Mystery of Mayor Daley," 63.

61. Eric Klinenberg, *Heat Wave: A Social Autopsy of Disaster in Chicago* (Chicago: University of Chicago Press, 2003), 129–64.

62. David Naguib Pellow, *Garbage Wars: The Struggle for Environmental Justice in Chicago* (Cambridge, Mass.: MIT Press, 2002); also see Dan Mihalopoulos and Gary Washburn, "City to Wave White Flag on Blue Bags," *Chicago Tribune*, Oct. 25, 2006.

63. Joe Painter, "Regulation Theory, Post-Fordism, and Urban Politics," in David Judge, Gerry Stoker, and Harold Wolman, eds., *Theories of Urban Politics* (Thousand Oaks, Calif.: SAGE Publications, 1995), 286–87; Peter Eisinger, "The Politics of Bread and Circuses: Building the City for the Visitor Class," *Urban Affairs Review* 35, no. 3 (Jan. 2000): 316–33; Neil Brenner and Nik Theodore, eds., *Spaces of Neoliberalism: Urban Restructuring in North America and Western Europe* (Malden, Mass.: Blackwell, 2002); David Harvey, *A Brief History of Neoliberalism* (New York: Oxford University Press, 2005); Jason Hackworth, *The Neoliberal City: Governance, Ideology, and Development in American Urbanism* (Ithaca, N.Y.: Cornell University Press, 2007).

14-2 "The Story of America's Cities" and "Making a Market"

Stephen Goldsmith

The Twenty-first Century City: Resurrecting Urban America

The Story of America's Cities

. . . For two hundred years, America built great cities. People flocked to cities because they were places of limitless opportunity. Despite pockets of poverty, and even slums, many urban neighborhoods were home to vibrant civic organizations and communities of faith. The unemployed and the working poor shared their neighborhoods with large numbers of middle-class families, who provided positive role models and support for struggling neighbors. Strong families, churches, and schools worked together to instill a sense of unity and a shared set of values. Cities were where people went to pursue the American dream.

Today, the American dream for many is to escape the city for the comforts of the suburbs. Cities are losing population, and businesses increasingly locate outside city limits. Badly deteriorated inner-city neighborhoods are places of widespread unemployment and intolerably high rates of crime.

Ed Rendell, the Democratic mayor of Philadelphia, is fond of quoting a rather glum prediction by Professor Theodore Hershberg of his city's University of Pennsylvania:

All of America's cities are on greased skids. What differentiates one from another is the angle of descent. And unless there is a major shift in public policy, America will lose all its major cities.

Hershberg was correct. Not only are cities on skids, but in most cases government itself is the grease that has hastened the pace of decay. Urban programs based on the principle of wealth redistribution trapped those who did not work in a web of dependency, inflicted poor families who did work with the highest marginal tax rates in the country, and isolated both groups in inner cities by driving out the middle class with higher taxes.

By making teen pregnancy and illegitimacy economically viable through welfare, while abdicating responsible enforcement of child support laws, government subsidized the breakup of the family, with disastrous consequences.

Ineffective urban school systems failed to equip an entire generation of youths with the skills they needed to succeed in the workplace, while at the same time preserving a monopoly that denied poor families the option to escape that is available to middle-class families. Meanwhile, forced busing destroyed the fabric of many neighborhoods, and the often accurate perception of substandard schools provided yet another reason for families to head for the suburbs.

Instead of sending strong messages to youths when they first got into trouble, a nonexistent juvenile justice system waited to deal with them until they were hardened and unreformable, to the benefit of neither society nor the individual.

Many point to the War on Poverty as the turning point. The program signaled the beginning of an era in which government would attempt to solve the problems of inner cities through massive wealth redistribution. As government attempted to buy cities out of poverty through impersonal programs, it supplanted private efforts and raised taxes in the process. Worse, while government spent billions on an ever-increasing array of social programs, it neglected its core responsibilities of public safety and infrastructure.

Excessive taxation, crumbling infrastructure, bad schools, and rising crime rates prompted an exodus of

---

those who could afford to leave, robbing poor residents of the benefit of these strong families and weakening stabilizing institutions such as churches and neighborhood associations. This flight of wealth left a smaller, poorer tax base and caused chronic revenue shortfalls. Predictably, government's solution was to raise taxes further and pour more money into programs, and a vicious cycle began.

Jane Jacobs, in her classic *The Death and Life of Great American Cities,* understood in 1961 that the War on Poverty would fail:

> There is a wistful myth that if only we had enough money to spend—the figure is usually put at a hundred billion dollars—we could wipe out all of our slums in ten years, reverse decay in great, dull, gray belts that were yesterday's and day-before yesterday's suburbs, anchor the wandering middle class and its wandering tax money, and perhaps even solve the traffic problem.
>
> But look what we have built with the first several billion: low-income projects that become worse centers of delinquency, vandalism, and general social hopelessness than the slums they were supposed to replace.

The War on Poverty was rooted in the notion that government knows better than people what is in their best interests and that government must solve social problems. Big-city mayors bought into this doctrine as well, attempting to address the problems facing their cities through what Milwaukee Mayor John Norquist disdainfully calls "the pity strategy." This strategy led mayors to Washington, tin cups in hand, saying, "Pity me, we have awful problems, I need financial help." The bigger the problem, the bigger the handout, the worse the outcome.

A Smaller Government Approach

As urban problems continued to worsen, the days of simply pouring more money into failed programs inevitably came to an end. Fiscal crises forced several mayors to reexamine the way they did business, with many turning to privatization and other efficiency measures in hopes of getting more value out of fewer

tax dollars. The best of these efforts produced notable successes, some of which are described in such excellent books as *Reinventing Government* by David Osborne and Ted Gaebler, and *Revolution at the Roots* by John O'Leary and Bill Eggers.

Part of what distinguishes our experience in Indianapolis from some of these other efforts is that we were not prompted to change because of a crisis. While Indianapolis has its share of big-city problems, the city also benefits from more than twenty years of enlightened corporate involvement and strong leadership by mayors Richard G. Lugar and William H. Hudnut.

When I came into office in 1992, Indianapolis's finances were sound: taxes were relatively low, our public workforce seemed lean, and the city boasted a healthy bond rating. Rather than adopting a fire-sale privatization approach, we implemented a comprehensive approach to city management based on a belief that smaller government is just plain better.

At every juncture, a few simple principles guided our decision making:

- People know better than government what is in their best interest.
- Monopolies are inefficient, and government monopolies are particularly inefficient.
- Wealth needs to be created, not redistributed.
- Government should do a few things well.
- Cities must not raise taxes or price themselves out of competition with excessive regulations.

We made mistakes, as well as our share of adversaries, in the process. As in the Metro story, we dealt with intransigent middle managers, stubborn federal bureaucrats, self-interested advocates of the status quo, distrust from residents of long-neglected neighborhoods, and other obstacles to change.

Yet we remain optimistic. From 1992 to 1997 our efforts to move city services into the competitive marketplace saved $230 million. During that period we cut the city budget each year. We did not just cut the rate of growth, we actually spent less. Our budget in 1997 was 7 percent lower than the budget when I took office. We reduced the nonpublic safety work force (everybody but police officers and firefighters) by more than 40 percent. At the same time, we made the largest infrastructure investment in the city's history—more than three-quarters of a billion dollars—and put one hundred more police officers on city streets, while reducing taxes slightly.

Today, more people are moving into Indianapolis than at any time in decades. The city has enjoyed four consecutive years of record job creation and record numbers of new homes built. Unemployment recently dropped below 3 percent, the lowest level since such statistics have been kept.

As word of our approach spread to public officials and other observers of urban policy, we quickly discovered that there was a market for our experiences. Our efforts drew hundreds of public managers to the city for seminars and tours, talented individuals who brought with them scores of additional good ideas. In 1993 I had the good fortune to meet Larry Mone, president of the Manhattan Institute, and Myron Magnet, editor of the institute's outstanding *City Journal* (probably the best source of good ideas on urban policy), who encouraged us to collect our experiences in a book, in the hope that an overview of our successes and failures and the policies that produced them might prove useful. This book is the result; it describes an approach, under way in Indianapolis, to prepare cities for the twenty-first century through an explicit policy of reducing the size of government, creating wealth through the marketplace, and rebuilding civility by giving authority back to families, churches, and neighborhood associations. . . .

Making a Market

Cities no longer compete against each other for businesses and families. They compete against their suburbs, and they are losing badly. Virtually every large, older city has lost population over the past thirty years.

Every time a family moves out, every time a business relocates, every time a new business starts up in the suburbs, the central city loses a little bit of its tax base. This creates pressure for more revenue, and increases the temptation to raise tax rates, driving more businesses and homeowners away. It is an ugly downward spiral, and cities all across the country are caught in it.

Robert Inman, professor of finance and economics at the Wharton School of Business, describes the phenomenon in bleak terms:

The jobs and families that leave the city as taxes rise are likely to be the best paying jobs and the wealthier families. The loss of high-wage firms is likely to discourage educational investments by current residents and to deter the in-migration of good jobs and skilled workers in the future. As the population of the city becomes less skilled, average wages are likely to decline, and falling incomes often create additional pressure for local government services. Rising service demands and falling tax bases mean more, not less, pressure on the city's deficit.

Public officials are only now recognizing that holding the line on taxes is more than just a campaign slogan—it is an economic necessity. They are reacting by searching more aggressively than ever for solutions that do not involve higher taxes. . . .

. . . [A]n emerging solution for many policymakers is to turn over the delivery of many services to private sector firms.

"Privatization," as it is called, describes the process of turning over to the private sector the job of running public services that are ordinarily, and often exclusively, provided by the government. The term was coined in the mid-1970s by Robert Poole, who today runs the Reason Foundation in Los Angeles, a think tank that boasts some of the nation's best-known experts on privatization. . . .

[W]hen I took office in 1992 the question remained whether privatization could work in heavily urban areas, where resources were scarce, the demand for services was great, and the bureaucracy was thoroughly entrenched.

We came into office betting that yes, it could.

Competition, Not Privatization

Fortunately, as revolutionaries go, we tended toward the button-down, Midwest, Republican variety. In order to learn how privatization really worked, we decided early on that we would start with a small, doable project that would not attract much political resistance.

One of the first services we attempted to privatize was the billing of the city's sewer users. In Indianapolis, the sewers are run by the Department of Public Works (public works). Naturally enough, public works employees mail out and collect sewer bills. Privatizing this function seemed a perfect test case for several reasons.

First, it seemed to cost too much. In 1992 the city spent nearly $3 million to collect $40 million in sewer bills.

Second, there was an obvious private partner. Sewer bills are based on the amount of water used as determined by the Indianapolis Water Company (IWC), a private utility that provides Indianapolis residents with drinking water. The water company also turns off water lines for the city when sewer users do not pay their bills. Even better, the company was preparing to open a new customer service center.

We approached the water company about taking over sewer billing. The company agreed enthusiastically, and offered to do the job for 5 percent less than our cost of $3 million.

We were disappointed. While we had committed to starting with a small project, we were hoping for more than small savings. In retrospect, however, we should not have been surprised. After all, our plan amounted to this: In the name of privatization, we were going to replace a public monopoly with a private monopoly. For that we expected to reap huge savings?

The truth is that although "privatization" seemed like a useful piece of shorthand for what we wanted to do, it was actually misleading and threw us off track. The key issue, we soon discovered, was not whether tasks were performed by public or private institutions. A private monopoly, like the water company, might be less bureaucratic and more efficient than a government monopoly. But without the spur of competition, the difference in what we could expect in price and service would be distinctly unrevolutionary.

We approached sewer billing in a different way, contacting every utility in central Indiana and asking them to compete for the sewer bill job. Forced by competition to further effort, the water company returned with a new proposal to collect sewer bills for $2 million annually, for a savings of 30 percent—six times the amount it had offered originally.

More impressive from our perspective, IWC went a step further by offering to find unbilled or underbilled sewer users, collect the missing revenue, and share the earnings with the city. The company offered the first $500,000 in collections to the city, and proposed to split additional collections evenly. So without hiring any more employees, conducting any studies, or installing any more auditors, the city has earned savings and

revenues from this small example of more than $10.6 million to date.

Dramatically lower costs coincided with better service. Sewer and water bills now appear on one statement, so our customers have one less monthly check to write. In addition, customers have one office to call for sewer and water service and billing information. The office also stays open longer, which improves customer service.

Our experience with sewer billing made an immediate impact on our thinking about privatization. Competition, not privatization, made the difference. Competition drives private firms—and, as we soon discovered, public agencies—to constantly seek ways to reduce costs and improve service. The pressure exerted by customers and the threat of losing out to competitors are what spur innovation and overcome the natural bureaucratic resistance to change in public or private institutions.

Creating Markets

The second event that changed our thinking about privatization occurred when we decided to seek competitive bids for the maintenance of a small section of the city's streets. When our Department of Transportation workers learned that they would have to compete to keep the work, amazing things happened.

To be honest, we thought our city workers had no chance of defeating private companies in direct competition. Traditional notions of government workers as bureaucratic and even lazy led us to believe that public employees faced an uphill battle in competing with the lean, mean private sector.

Transportation workers were skeptical too, but for a very different reason. They did not think we were serious about letting them bid. They thought we were setting them up for failure. And when they insisted that we talk seriously about the problems they faced in competing with private firms, it turned out they had a point.

The workers complained they could not possibly compete while carrying unreasonable overhead in the form of managers' salaries. For a mere ninety-four workers in the street repair division there were thirty-two politically appointed supervisors—an absurd ratio, especially considering that most of the supervisors were relatively highly paid. In part to call my bluff, union employees told us that if we were serious about competition we would eliminate several of these supervisors to give the union a real chance to compete.

By normal political standards the union's demand would have been a show stopper. The supervisors were all registered Republicans. I was a Republican mayor. These managers, and their patrons in the party, had supported my election. The union had supported the opposition and campaigned strongly against me. Now the union wanted me to fire politically connected Republicans to help a Democratic union look good.

We did it. We had to. If I had blinked and shielded my fellow Republicans, the message would have been clear: we were not serious about competition. In addition to laying off or transferring fourteen of the thirty-two supervisors, we provided the workers with a consultant to help them prepare their bid.

The union was surprised, impressed, and probably nervous. Workers now knew that they, too, would be finding new jobs if they failed to draw up a competitive plan.

Making workers responsible for their own destiny sent a clear message that for the first time in ages management recognized that the men and women who do the job know better than anyone what it takes to get it done. Simply empowering these workers transformed them into efficiency experts overnight. They became incredibly creative in imagining how they could do their work more cost effectively. As Todd Durnil, the deputy administrator of street maintenance, observed, "We took the shackles off the guys. We tapped their knowledge and experience instead of telling them what to do."

For example, street repair crews previously consisted of an eight-man team that used two trucks to haul a patching device and a tar kettle. Once in charge, the city workers saw that by remounting the patching equipment they could eliminate one of the trucks, and by doing so reduce the crew from eight to five.

The city employees bid significantly below their private competitors and won the job decisively. While the city previously spent $425 per ton filling potholes with hot asphalt, the new proposal reduced the city's cost to $307 per ton—a 25 percent savings.

We were shocked. In fact, many within city government doubted the union proposal. But the city's employees not only met the bid price, they beat it—by

$20,000. They increased the average production of a work crew from 3.1 to 5.2 lane miles per day—a 68 percent efficiency increase.

Union leaders declared that the bidding process brought them "from darkness into daylight." Isaac Sanders, a crew leader responsible for street repair, said that before the bidding process, "we didn't give a hoot what anything cost," but because of competition "we got efficient real quick."

The pothole competition confirmed that a preoccupation with privatization is unproductive. Contrary to their poor public image, most civil servants are hardworking and talented—and they know a lot more than their mayors do about how to do their jobs well. The problem is that they have been trapped in a system that punishes initiative, ignores efficiency, and rewards big spenders.

Our experiences with sewer bills and street repair led us to adopt an explicit model of competition between private firms and public employees. From the taxpayers' point of view, the ideal situation occurs when the most efficient private sector service provider goes head-to-head with a government division operating at its most efficient level.

This new appreciation of the importance of competition shifted our focus away from privatization and toward what we began to call "marketization." For us, marketization meant creating a market where none previously existed. Today, throughout city government, we are trying to create a true market, a place where competition continually generates lower costs, better service, and new ideas for helping citizens. . . .

The Yellow Pages Test

Making the distinction between privatization and competition provided us with an important new understanding of how to use the marketplace to improve city services. Having made two successful forays into competitive contracting, we began to seek out other city services that could benefit from being moved into the evolving city market.

We quickly discovered that some services are more obvious candidates for competition than others, and that identifying the "low-hanging fruit" can provide governments with lucrative and relatively straightforward competitive initiatives. There are, we learned, a few basic ways to determine a given service's ripeness for competition.

It is useful, for example, to determine whether an activity requires the making of policy, or merely the implementation of policy that has already been established. Deciding which streets to repair in a given summer is a policy decision; laying the asphalt is implementation. This is similar to the distinction Osborne and Gaebler make between "steering" and "rowing" in *Reinventing Government*. We found that services that involved "rowing" were good candidates for competition.

Another issue worth addressing was whether the activity represented a core service that government must provide for citizens, or only supported the provision of these core services. We learned that support services, such as mailing sewer bills, usually had direct private sector counterparts and often resulted in privatization. Core services such as street repair, on the other hand, often resulted in successful bids by our own employees.

Our early rule of thumb was simple and is still probably the best guide. Look at the city's yellow pages. If the phone book lists three companies that provide a certain service, the city probably should not be in that business, at least not exclusively. If there are five florists in Indianapolis, the city probably does not need its own hothouse; if window-cleaning services are booming, why should the city operate its own? The best candidates for marketization are those for which a bustling competitive market already exists. Using the yellow pages test, we could take advantage of markets that had been operating for years.

Printing was a great example. Before 1993 the city spent $1.4 million annually to run three print shops and operate more than two hundred copiers.

Yet the yellow pages contained scores of private printers, entrepreneurs whose first thought in the morning and last thought at night was how to shave a hundredth of a penny off the cost of a copy. Several vendors came in with bids that would save us almost 30 percent of our cash cost.

We selected Pitney-Bowes Management Services, a vendor that would provide all our copying services, plus everything the print shops had been doing for us, for only $1 million—a savings of almost $400,000 a year, or 27 percent. But that was only the beginning. The competition for the city's business was so fierce that we were able to press for additional benefits.

Pitney-Bowes set up an in-house copy center, renting space in the basement of the City-County Building. The company established 120 pickup points throughout city offices for copy and print requests. Throughout the day, Pitney employees visit these locations on a preset schedule to pick up work and drop off finished products.

There are still 160 copy machines available in city offices for fast copies and short documents—which Pitney restocks each morning with paper and toner—but the new copy center now produces 78 percent of all of the city's copies, saving hundreds of clerical hours each year.

Finally, Pitney-Bowes generated unexpected savings when it helped us conduct a "red tape" initiative to reduce the number of forms produced by city departments.

The yellow pages test produced dramatic results. Over the years even the prudently managed city of Indianapolis had ventured far afield. The city ran golf courses, tree nurseries, and even a window-washing service. We had done these things for so long that they seemed like obvious government functions even though to an outside observer they might seem absurd. Tree nurseries?

Do what is easy. That is the first thing we learned and the first thing a city should do. The easy stuff will not turn a city around tomorrow, but it is a start. As a wise man once said, "The greatest difference in the world is the difference between somewhat better and somewhat worse."

So pick up the yellow pages. And let your fingers do the walking to better service and lower costs.

14-3 "Running Government like a Business"*

Julian Brash

Bloomberg's New York: Class and Governance in the Luxury City

Michael Bloomberg portrayed the CEO as the ultimate locus of responsibility and decision-making, and he asked to be judged on his accomplishments rather than on the basis of partisanship or political ideology. "In the end, it's one person's decision, one person's responsibility," Bloomberg writes in his autobiography. "A major part of the CEO's responsibilities is to be the ultimate risk taker and decision maker" (Bloomberg and Winkler 2001, 182). In return, employees must trust the CEO's judgment and fall in line with his decisions: "Either they believe in me, trust me, and are willing to take the risk that I will deliver success, or they don't. It's that simple. There's no haggling. I don't negotiate" (Bloomberg and Winkler 2001, 46–47). The CEO's acceptance of ultimate responsibility creates an obligation: leadership implies deference and loyalty on the part of those being led. This relationship between the leader and the led hinges on the notion of performance: It is the CEO's performance in the face of competition that generates the obligation to follow and that legitimizes his power.

As a CEO of a privately held company, Bloomberg in fact enjoyed a relative lack of accountability. In his autobiography he discusses the possibility of converting his company to public ownership: "Go Public? And have to answer to more partners, stockholders, and securities analysts? . . . For the moment, *answering to no one is the ultimate situation*" (Bloomberg and Winkler 2001, 187, emphasis added). As mayor, Bloomberg was now directly accountable to the voters of New York in a way he had never been accountable to anyone in his business career. However, aside from electoral "accountability moments," to borrow George

W. Bush's term, Bloomberg's vision of mayoral leadership very much reflected his private-sector experience. He demanded of the city's citizenry—including city council members, members of community boards, and others—the kind of deference to his decisions that he had once demanded from his company's employees. As the CEO mayor, he needed unconstrained freedom to make decisions based on his own judgments of the best interests of the city.

But if the CEO mayor needed such autonomy, he also had to ensure that his achievements were visible to the public. At Bloomberg LP, Bloomberg had stressed transparency and openness. The most obvious example of this was the company's "bullpen" office layout, in which all employees, including the CEO, sat in an open arrangement of desks separated only by waist-high dividers. According to Bloomberg, this configuration served to facilitate teamwork, but more pertinently it allowed the monitoring of employees by management, by each other, and by office visitors, preventing bad work habits and undercutting intraoffice politics. "As is true with markets," he writes, "transparency produces fairness" (Bloomberg and Winkler 2001, 163). This physical layout symbolized a broader approach: as Bloomberg told one interviewer, "My whole business life has been out in the open" (Gimein 2002). In fact, Bloomberg took great care to manage and limit scrutiny of many aspects of his business life, made possible by his firm's private ownership. But the appearance of transparency was indispensable to Bloomberg's status as a charismatic CEO, as it allowed him to cultivate his image as an individual of extraordinary capabilities and potency.

Source: "Running Government like a Business," in *Bloomberg's New York: Class and Governance in the Luxury City* by Julian Brash. Copyright © 2011 by The University of Georgia Press. Reprinted with permission from the publisher.

*Endnotes and references have been omitted. Please consult the original source.

In short, the dual notion of performance central to the notion of the CEO mayor translated into twin imperatives of autonomy and transparency. In fact, Bloomberg faced significant constraints on his autonomy as mayor. Most land use decisions and planning projects would be subject to ULURP (Uniform Land Use Review Procedure). The New York City Council, while weak in many regards, had the power to pass local laws, vote yes or no on land use changes, and override mayoral vetoes. There were also a number of intergovernmental constraints on the city government's autonomy, such as New York State's control of its education system, the various State authorities that had significant power over land use decisions (especially in regards to state-owned land), the various financing and subsidy programs related to economic development policy, and the strings attached to various federal funding streams. An additional factor was the vulnerability of the city's economy to broader economic trends.

Nevertheless, the mayor was resolute in his belief that, as he said during his 2001 campaign with reference to the process of rebuilding the World Trade Center site, "the city should be responsible for its own destiny" (Nagourney 2001). He demanded and received control of the city's schools. The administration acted to circumvent the federal government's often incompetent and underfunded efforts to protect the city against further terrorist attacks after 9/11, as Police Commissioner Raymond Kelly built up an anti-terrorism unit in the city's police department whose capabilities were extremely well regarded among counterterrorism experts worldwide (Finnegan 2005). Other attempts to assert the financial and political autonomy of the city were less successful, including efforts to have the state legislature allow the city to reinstate a commuter tax, to have the federal government change its formulas for terrorism funding to the city's benefit, and to have the state legislature reduce the city's portion of its Medicaid bill.

The new mayor vowed that his administration would be transparent and open. On a symbolic level, the bullpen layout was introduced into city hall. More substantively, a series of steps were taken to make available data that would allow for the evaluation of mayoral performance by both the public and the administration itself. Drawing on "best practices" in governmental management and on the corporate experience of its members, the administration developed a comprehensive system of measurement and reporting aimed at supplying different "audiences"—the public, agency managers, and "senior executives" (that is, the mayor and his deputy mayors)—with data of appropriate detail and frequency. The great majority of these data, in keeping with the private-sector faith in ostensibly objective "benchmarks," were quantitative in form. This system included the Citywide Accountability Program, an internal program founded in 2001 to provide detailed and frequently updated information that agency managers could use to "monitor and improve performance" (City of New York 2002b). In addition, it included the new 311 telephone system, which provided citizens with an easy way to report complaints and also served as a new source of data about public services. Later, in keeping with Bloomberg's long-held commitment to customer service, the administration sought to create "a comprehensive citywide customer satisfaction survey" to gauge how city residents judged the responsiveness and performance of city employees and agencies (Gardiner 2007). Finally, the administration revamped the *Mayor's Management Report*. Introduced as a 150-page tool of managerial efficiency and transparency after the 1970s fiscal crisis, this report had by 2001 degenerated into an unusable three-volume, 1,000-page grab bag of over 4,000 statistical indicators. In September 2002, the administration released its first version of the revised report, which was now conceptualized as a "Public Report Card?" The number of statistical indicators was reduced and the mix of indicators reoriented "toward reporting on 'outcome' or results-oriented statistics that demonstrate success or failure" (City of New York 2002b, 4). Indicators were made available on the city's Web site, with an easy-to-use mapping function that allowed citizens to evaluate city services in their neighborhoods. Finally, "based on best practices in performance reporting," the 2002 report contained a series of goals and targets against which important indicators could be measured. These "provide[d] a clear frame of reference for assessing performance and may take several forms . . . including . . . nationally recognized standards and the benchmarking of performance against other large cities" (City of New York 2002b, 4). While some criticized particular measurements or absences in the report (McIntyre 2004; Pasanen 2004), the *Mayor's Management Report* cannot be easily dismissed. Indicators in the 2002 and subsequent reports were often unflattering to the administration, and the mayor publicly acknowledged the areas in which the city's performance could improve. Whatever its flaws, the *Mayor's Management Report*, along with other publicly available forms of evaluation, were important steps toward the fulfillment of the CEO mayor's promise of transparency.

Besides the autonomy to make decisions and the transparency necessary for the public to judge his achievements, a third element was necessary for the CEO mayor's political success: governmental capacity. He needed a well-structured organization, staffed by capable people, that could get things done. And in the early months of Bloomberg's first term, the administration was taking steps to transform city government into just such an organization.

Hiring the "Right People"

A few months after entering office, Mayor Bloomberg discussed how he had approached staffing his administration. "I'm a big believer in picking good people, giving them the tools, removing barriers to cooperation, promoting, and protecting them, and letting the professionals go and do what they do well," he said, before concluding: "I think I put exactly the right people in place" (2002a). Indeed, in his biography, Bloomberg had made it clear that while the CEO was "the ultimate risk taker and decision maker," it was crucial that he surround himself with creative, intelligent, and skilled employees and give them the freedom to think and act freely in pursuit of the goals he had established (Bloomberg and Winkler 2001, 182, 163–167). At Bloomberg LP, loyalty to the CEO was paired with respect for employees and their expertise and a stress on meritocracy. The company was perceived as a rewarding, if demanding, place to work, and it was known for low rates of employee turnover (Loomis 2007; Mnookin 2008). This ethos of meritocracy and loyalty shaped the staffing of Bloomberg's campaign and administration.

Even early on in his campaign Bloomberg took a different approach to hiring than had successful New York City mayoral candidates, at least since John Lindsay,

whose administration had a deep technocratic and meritocratic streak. Mayors Abe Beame, Ed Koch, and David Dinkins all were politicians' politicians, with deep roots in Democratic Party politics, and they staffed key positions in their campaigns and administrations with government insiders and party players. The key positions in Rudy Giuliani's campaign and administration were filled largely on the basis of personal and political loyalty. In contrast, Bloomberg's campaign—and later his administration—drew heavily on political outsiders, particularly, but not solely, from the private sector. Bloomberg's two key campaign advisors came from Bloomberg LP: Patricia Harris, who after an early stint in government had directed the company's philanthropic activity; and Kevin Sheekey, who after working as the chief of staff for New York Senator Daniel Patrick Moynihan had directed Bloomberg LP's government relations office. This reliance on individuals with private-sector experience and close personal connections to Bloomberg was paired with a reliance on urban experts of various sorts. Early on, the campaign asked a wide array of such experts for background policy papers for the candidate's edification; later, important positions in Bloomberg's campaign policy team were filled by a small but eclectic group of well-respected academics and other political novices, as well as a few experienced government insiders. In sum, the 2001 Bloomberg campaign relied on corporate networks for its top-level decision makers while demonstrating a respect for professional expertise in developing policy specifics.

Once elected, Bloomberg's stated priority was finding "good people" and the "right people" (2002a). Looking back on his first 100 days in office, Bloomberg said:

> I think . . . I have put together a great team. . . . It's a diverse group of people, with lots of ideas, a mixture of government experience and private-sector experience. . . . I tried to have a balance, a lot of people who had been in government before, some of whom had gone off to the private sector and were coming back, and some absolute new faces who never had to deal with the problems and restrictions the government places on you. I think that kind of a dynamic and that kind of interaction—some people saying, "Why can't

we do it," and others saying "here's why you can't"—having them fight it out in the road is a very good thing. (2002a)

The new mayor's deputy mayors, policy advisors, and commissioners were drawn from diverse backgrounds and sectors, and all had strong professional experience and expertise relevant to their new positions. Nevertheless, the staffing of his administration displayed the same pattern as his campaign, as individuals with private-sector experience, and often with social or business connections to Bloomberg, tended to fill the high-level positions closest to the mayor. Along with the aforementioned Patricia Harris, who was appointed to serve as deputy mayor for administration, and Kevin Sheekey, who served as the mayor's key political advisor, a number of other Bloomberg LP executives joined the administration. Bloomberg also tapped Joel Klein, who had served as the corporate counsel to Bertelsmann AG after serving in the Clinton administration in various positions, to be chancellor of the city's school system. However, the most important corporate executives who entered the administration filled key positions related to economic and urban development. . . .

Making Performance Possible: Increasing Organizational Capacity

With "exactly the right people in place," the task now was to achieve the economic and fiscal goals Bloomberg had set out in his campaign. In the expansive area of economic and urban development policy, this required the organizational capacity to develop and implement a coherent and comprehensive strategy. The effort to increase the capacity of the city government's development apparatus demonstrated in concrete terms what the idea of "running the city like a business" meant to ex–corporate executives like Bloomberg, Doctoroff, and Alper, as it entailed the importing of a number of corporate management practices directly into city government.

The best publicized of these corporate practices was the physical rearrangement of the mayor's offices in city hall to resemble the "bullpen" layout used in Bloomberg LP. However, this was just the tip of the iceberg: such practices were implemented in a far more

thoroughgoing manner, especially in agencies headed by Deputy Mayor Doctoroff. Weeks into Mayor Bloomberg's first term, shortly after he hired Daniel Doctoroff, an important—if largely unnoticed—bureaucratic reshuffling took place: all city agencies relating to economic and urban development would now be under the control of the new deputy mayor for economic development and rebuilding. In previous administrations, these agencies—including the EDC, the DCP, the Department of Business Services (soon to be renamed the "Department of Small Business Services"), and the department of housing preservation and development—had reported to a variety of deputy mayors. Now one man, Daniel Doctoroff, would exercise a degree of bureaucratic control over development policies and projects unprecedented since the days of Robert Moses. Everything from the tiniest infractions of the city's signage regulations by small businesses to multimillion-dollar incentive deals for the city's biggest corporations, from the smallest neighborhood rezoning to redevelopment of the former World Trade Center site—all would be under Doctoroff's purview.

With the mayor's backing, Doctoroff quickly acted to ensure that these agencies would work in tandem by creating the Economic Development Agency Council. In the council's reportedly well-attended, engaging, and lively weekly or biweekly meetings, commissioners and other executives of agencies reporting to the deputy mayor met to discuss agency activities and interagency issues. EDAC, in combination with occasional corporate-style retreats, was apparently effective in "removing barriers to cooperation." In interviews with me and in other venues, commissioners and other city officials repeatedly highlighted increased interagency cooperation and its benefits. As CPC Chair Amanda Burden said of the interagency cooperation that the council helped bring about, "That's how you get things done, and that's what the Mayor is all about. It's about executive decisions and performance" (2004).

The establishment of the council also provided a forum for Doctoroff to assert bureaucratic control over the agencies under his command. He required each to develop a strategic plan in PowerPoint, the presentation software de rigueur in the private sector. These strategic plans included the agency's mission, agency-specific goals and initiatives to meet them, quarterly targets for progress, and so on. They served as both a comprehensive policy development tool used to coordinate the goals of each agency and a technique to encourage efficient management and to hold commissioners accountable for their agencies' performance. In the words of EDC President Alper, no stranger to such corporate management techniques, they provided "a road map to how to spend our time and our capital" and "a mechanism to ensure and measure success" with "metrics built into it to make sure that we're in fact doing what we say we're going to do" (2003b).

Such practices were not altogether novel at the EDC, which had long had close connections to the private sector and something of a corporate ethos. Nevertheless, the administration's explicitly corporate approach led to drastic changes in management and policy there, as EDC President Alper "set out to restructure EDC and instill a private sector focus [by] applying what he learned running Goldman's Investment Banking Division" (University of Chicago Graduate School of Business 2004). One example of this was the introduction of strict cost-benefit analysis to judge the worthiness of various subsidy programs and development projects. Another, more important, example was the agency's "reorganiz[ation] with a new 'client-centered' approach to retain and attract companies," as Bloomberg put it in his 2002 State of the Union address (2002c).

In April 2002, Alper announced an internal restructuring of his agency, which would "enable EDC to function more efficiently, empower decision-making at all levels, encourage horizontal collaboration and establish short- and long-term strategic goals" (New York City Economic Development Corporation 2002). The agency's structure was simplified and certain functions, including strategic planning and long-term infrastructure maintenance and development, were strengthened. As well as facilitating internal efficiency, the reorganization enhanced the EDC's capacity to approach economic and urban development in a comprehensive and proactive way, a real change at an agency that, as one long-time EDC official told me, "always had a short-term transaction culture—sell the land, get construction going, get a new factory, get new jobs."

The centerpiece of this reorganization was the creation of the Client Coverage Operating Division. This new division would be organized on the basis of, as

one of Doctoroff's aides told me, a "client coverage model, obvious to any investment bank, but less obvious to a lot of city governments." In the private sector, this model consists of a series of "desks" staffed by experts responsible for a number of industry-specific tasks: monitoring events and developments, serving as the identifiable and trusted face of the company, and maintaining open communication. The consolidation of responsibility for expertise and outreach in one employee or group of employees allows the company to cull information that permits it to better serve current clients and target potential clients. The EDC's Client Coverage Operating Division reflected this, as indicated by the words of Doctoroff's aide:

> There is a person who is the media desk, whose job it is to understand what's going on with media companies [and] to keep tabs on who might be relocating, who's looking for space. When we get a call from a major media company saying we're thinking about relocating this guy at the media desk [can give] us information in terms of here's how much space they have, how many employees they have, here's what we've done for them, here's what we hear. We want [him] to understand not just real estate, but the peculiarities of the real estate needs facing a media company. Do they need large floor plate? How much are they willing to pay? Where are their employees located?

Serving as a source of expertise and a point of contact with a particular sector, the desk staff would be able to better understand the strengths and weaknesses of New York City as a place for business and, in EDC President Alper's words, "to make sure that we have proactive relationships and dialogues with companies and industries big and small throughout the five boroughs to make sure that we're being responsive" (2002b). To ensure that the division remained true to its private-sector origins, Alper hired a former Goldman Sachs colleague to oversee the industry desks.

The EDC adopted not just organizational aspects of the client coverage model but conceptual ones as well. Businesses were conceived of as "clients" as expressed succinctly by Deputy Mayor Doctoroff in a 2004 speech describing the creation of the Client Coverage Operating Division: "We began to think about covering our clients—the companies in this city who pay taxes and generate jobs—the way an investment bank or a commercial bank would" (2004a). Another of the division's aims was to understand how city government, and the city itself, could "add value" for these clients, just as a private-sector firm might do in providing a service or product. "We need to develop expertise and relationships in those industries that are growing" EDC President Alper told the city council in 2002, "to understand how we, as a City, can add value to their businesses and make sure we are a better host . . . for them" (2002a).

These various practices and conceptions, all "reminiscent of a private sector mentality," as one informant put it to me, were crucial to the development and implementation of a coherent and comprehensive development strategy. CPC Chair Burden expressed this in a 2004 speech. "Early on, in January 2002, Deputy Mayor Doctoroff instructed one of his agencies to develop a Strategic Plan in PowerPoint," she said. "City Planning didn't know what a PowerPoint was! But we learned fast. He wanted strategic planning benchmarks—month-to-month benchmarks for two years about what we were going to achieve and when we were going to achieve it. And he held us to those benchmarks and we got judged by those plans all the time and those benchmarks, and we've kept to them" (2004). DCP's benchmarks consisted of a series of rezonings of an ambition and quantity unimaginable under previous administrations, which in fact were in large part successfully implemented over the next few years. Likewise, the EDC's corporate-inflected reorganization would permit it to effectively understand the city's "value proposition" and use this as a guide for economic development policy. Finally, the centralization of Doctoroff's control would allow for coordination and cooperation between agencies necessary for both the construction of a broad development agenda and the successful implementation of complex and multifaceted projects that were a part of it.

It was not just the development and implementation of this agenda that were important here but its communication as well. While seemingly a small detail, the use of PowerPoint, with its (at times deceptive) ability to present information neatly and simply, was in fact quite important. Administration officials used the PowerPoint presentations, embellished with attractive graphics and illustrations, as crucial public relations tools in speeches and presentations to various groups across the city. The presentations allowed officials to clearly and concisely communicate the tenets and goals of the administration's economic development policy, the ways in which their agencies' initiatives related to these goals, and progress toward them. Once again, we see the importance of the double notion of performance to the Bloomberg Way—the necessity to make good on the proposition that the skills and experience of the postindustrial elites moving into city hall would push the city toward economic growth and prosperity and the imperative of demonstrating this to the broader public.

Running Government Like a Business: From Theory to Practice

The early months of the Bloomberg administration provided a unique illustration of what "running government like a business" might mean to those who had actually done so. Unlike the typical neoliberal case, in which entrepreneurial or managerial logics are applied to particular and isolated policy realms, or what is called "businesslike governance" actually comprises enhancing the business climate, in the Bloomberg administration "running the city like a business" had profound impacts on concrete practices of urban governance such as hiring, bureaucratic organization, and evaluation.

However, this was not merely a dispassionate application of managerial expertise toward the ends of efficiency and good government. In fact, the importation of private-sector conceptions and practices into municipal government constituted a claim of legitimacy for the wealth and power—and now state power—wielded by members of the city's postindustrial elite. Various forms of expertise, experience, and skill were brought into city government, and the successful application of these forms to the city's problems would be the ultimate vindicator of such claims to class power. But these claims had to be recognized by New Yorkers at large. Successful governance had to be performed and communicated via a plethora of means: 311, the *Mayor's Management Report,* a redesigned city government Web site, customer service surveys, PowerPoint presentations, and the like.

But if "running the government like a business" constituted a class project in and of itself, it also was a means to an end. Bob Jessop argues that cities can only be held to be truly entrepreneurial in certain cases: "From a strategic viewpoint [an 'entrepreneurial city'] would be one that has achieved the capacity to act entrepreneurially. It may then itself directly act as an economic entrepreneur, targeting one or more . . . facets of the urban 'product'" (1998, 87). "Running the city like a business" created the capacity for the city government to act entrepreneurially by developing and implementing an aggressive and ambitious development agenda that approached the city as a product to be branded and marketed. . . .

14-4 "Justice, the Public Sector, and Cities: Relegitimating the Activist State"*

Thad Williamson

Justice and the American Metropolis

The assault on egalitarian social justice in the United States over the past forty years has also been an assault on the legitimacy of vigorous public action to forward substantive goals. This is no coincidence: egalitarian conceptions of social justice invariably assume that the state will be the principal mechanism for establishing just social arrangements and rectifying inequalities (Rawls 1971; Dworkin 2000). In contrast, neoliberal conceptions of governance aim to both straitjacket the public sector and stymie efforts toward meaningful egalitarian redistribution. Given this strong internal connection between attractive conceptions of social justice and the idea of an active, competent public sector, advocates of urban social justice need to develop an account of how public-sector leadership on behalf of normatively desirable ends can be relegitimated. In this chapter, I focus on how we might begin to rehabilitate the idea of a vigorous public sector at the local level, given the existing political climate. As theorists since Tocqueville have recognized, local-level democratic practice is the building block (for better or worse) of larger-scale democracy, and (to use Rawlsian terminology) a society cannot be well ordered, stable, and just if local political and economic life is characterized by large inequalities and the predominance of private interests over public concerns.[1]

This chapter proceeds in two parts. In the first section, I argue that rehabilitating a vigorous public sector will require establishing a practical conception of the "public interest" that is capable of guiding policymakers and citizens. After discussing the relationship between ideas of social justice and the public interest, I go on to introduce conceptions of effective public-sector leadership—the "New Public Service"—developed by contemporary theorists of public administration in response to the neoliberal assault on the state. This engagement with theory is driven by a practical question: how can we begin at the local level to relegitimate the idea of a vibrant public sector that has the ability to curb private interests and advance social justice?

In the second section, I introduce a case study of creative public leadership in Richmond, Virginia, that corresponds to the "New Public Service" in important respects. Specifically, I examine how a city planner (Rachel Flynn) used a participatory process to galvanize public support for a new downtown master plan that vigorously challenges the traditional prerogative of developers in the city by calling for public control of riverfront property. The relative success of that effort, the resistance it has encountered, and its inherent limitations all shed light on the challenges involved in rehabilitating an activist public sector in inhospitable settings.

Social justice advocates who presume that the state will be a principal mechanism for rectifying injustice must develop an account of how the public sector can play this constructive role. In particular, those concerned with advancing social justice at the metropolitan level must wrestle with four critical issues: First, predominant theories of public management and urban public leadership generally are not predicated on the idea of an activist public sector acting to rectify inequalities and injustices. Second, government policy and actions have often taken a direct role in constituting or reinforcing social injustices, and in many cases, small- and large-scale public action at the local level has been biased toward the interests of business elites (Holland et al. 2007). Third, as presently constituted, local public sectors often lack the capacity to undertake the agendas frequently proposed by social justice advocates and green urbanists. In particular, we have relatively few examples of effective large-scale public action that also exhibits the virtues of transparency, openness to civic participation, and sensitivity toward all affected groups. Fourth, the public sector too often displays incompetence in the tasks that it already takes on, and corruption of various kinds is a recurrent problem in municipal government.

Social justice advocates need to explain why we should believe, despite these challenges, that the state is capable of acting in a vigorous way to correct social injustices and advance the public interest (especially our massive ecological challenges). This account should have two major components. The first is a *constitutional* theory of how to organize local and metropolitan government, including specification of the powers government should have vis-à-vis private actors, specification of the division of labor between more local and metropolitan-wide governments, and specification of the mechanisms by which government will be rendered inclusive, democratic, and accountable. The second needed component, and the focus of this chapter, is an account of how the public sector, once constituted, can or should go about acting on behalf of social justice and the public interest. What is needed is a positive theory of public administration on behalf of normatively desirable ends. Central to such an account must be a workable conception of what "the public interest" is and how it is to be pursued in practice.

Social Justice and the Public Interest

In its simplest sense, the public interest is to be distinguished from factional rule or domination by one segment of the community. To appeal to the "public interest" as a normative standard for evaluating public policy is to insist that the advocates of a given proposal explain why such an action is to the benefit of the larger community and not just the interests (material or otherwise) of its advocates. This does not mean that a proposal needs to directly benefit every member of the community, or even most of them, to be in accord with the public interest. For example, when disadvantaged groups press for more resources, they need not be forced to show that their demands would maximize the community's aggregate utility. Instead, they can reasonably appeal to the public interest that the community as a whole has in all citizens having adequate resources to develop themselves and pursue their aims. In other words, disadvantaged groups should be able to appeal to substantive conceptions of social justice in making arguments about why they should get more resources. This is the primary impetus motivating John Rawls's conception of social justice: to move away from utilitarian methods for measuring what the public interest is and to insist upon the normative priority of improving—maximizing—the position of the least well off (Rawls 1971). . . .

Relegitimating the Public Sector

[Stephen] Elkin's [2006] account stipulates that local politics should have the following features: a culture of civic participation and deliberation; an active public sector with the competence, resources, and legitimacy to act on behalf of the community as a whole; and competent public officials who attempt to discern the public interest and act upon it. Each of these requirements contradicts neoliberal accounts of public sector management that have become predominant in recent decades. Persistent fiscal strains, the privatization wave, and ideological attacks on bureaucrats have combined both to constrain government action and undermine its legitimacy.

In this context, two new ideologies of public management have emerged, offering a critique of traditional "command-and-control" government. Drawing on the observation that bureaucracies often must perform ambiguous tasks in ways that are shaped more by politics than by efficiency, these approaches assume that government is least inefficient and most effective when organized so as to mimic the market. "New Public Management" theories call for turning government control of resources and provision of services to private firms when possible and adopting a government-by-contract model. The strong assumption is that government is inherently inefficient because it lacks market account-ability; consequently, privatization of government functions whenever feasible is normatively desirable (Morgan, England, and Pelissero 2006). The second approach, "Reinventing Government," calls on public officials to act as entrepreneurs and find new ways to generate revenue and hold down costs (Gaebler and Osborne 1992). For both approaches, the default assumption is that government ought to be "run like a business"; New Public Management holds the further assumption that government action is legitimate only in cases of "market failure." While the Reinventing Government framework sanctions innovative public-sector entrepreneurial activity in potentially interesting ways, neither approach envisages an active public sector capable of taking aggressive action to forward the public interest and rectify social injustice. Yet each of these frameworks has had a substantial impact on the practice of public management in American cities (Doherty and Stone 1999; Morgan, England, and Pelissero 2007; Holland et al. 2007).

Janet and Robert Denhardt's work provides the most systematic attempt to date to provide a positive theory of public administration as an alternative to both command-and-control and market-based paradigms. Denhardt and Denhardt's notion of the "New Public Service" aims to recover and rearticulate the notion that public officials can and should be publicly minded and concerned with advancing the public interest and that this is best done by inculcating among officials an ethic of serving the public, as opposed to imposing one's will on others. This conception of public service stands in direct contrast to public choice theory's assumption that all actors, including public officials, are ultimately motivated by self-interest (whether narrowly or expansively defined). Denhardt and Denhardt's highly plausible claim is that the reductive public choice account of public-official behavior can become a self-fulfilling prophecy (witness the federal response to Hurricane Katrina) and that, conversely, sustaining a culture and ethos of public-minded behavior within public institutions requires being very explicit about the value of public service and developing a theoretical account of how public-minded officials can and should act (Denhardt and Denhardt 2003).

Denhardt and Denhardt thus approvingly cite Jeffrey Luke's conception of "catalytic leadership" as an appropriate model for the public sector. In this model, the tasks of "leaders" (public officials) are fourfold. First, public leaders must call attention to a specific issue and problem in order to "[create] a sense of urgency about its solution, and [trigger] broad public interest." Second, leaders need to get all stakeholders engaged in the issue, with a particular focus on ensuring diverse interests and perspectives are at the table. Third, working in concert with assembled citizens, alternative strategies for action need to be explored. Fourth, once action in a particular direction is under way, leaders must "build support" for it "among 'champions,' power holders, advocacy groups, and those holding important resources. The leader must then turn to institutionalizing cooperative behavior and becoming a network facilitator" (Denhardt and Denhardt 2003, 151; adapted from Luke 1998, 37–148).

This approach is an admirable attempt to specify a positive account of democratically minded, justice-inclined public administration. Especially important is the internal connection drawn between the legitimacy and long-term effectiveness of public actions and the willingness and ability to engage affected and interested citizens in the process. Nonetheless, we might doubt whether public officials learning how to incorporate citizen participation and involvement in the policy process is sufficient to redress background structural inequalities in a meaningful way. The work of Richard Box offers an important corrective on this point. Box calls on public administrators to understand from the outset the nature of the political-economic system in which they operate and to see themselves as subversives—that is, as agents fighting against the dominant logic of the existing political-economic system. The ideal public-sector worker, in his view, is not only the civic-minded public servant but also the official who uses her position and the resources available to her to struggle against both the tendency of state power to reinforce background inequalities and background inequalities themselves (Box 2004).

Case Study: Downtown Planning in Richmond, Virginia

Taken together, Denhardt and Denhardt's and Box's respective conceptions of public leadership call for catalytic leadership from public officials who are capable of mobilizing and collaborating with civic groups and who understand the political environment in which they operate. Leadership in this vein has at least a chance of harnessing public power toward normatively desirable and democratically legitimate ends. How might these conceptions work in practice? The following section considers the work of Richmond's community planning director Rachel Flynn, who devised and attempted to implement a new downtown master plan for the city. Flynn's efforts approximate most closely the idea of "catalytic leadership" but also incorporate aspects of Box's approach.

Richmond, Virginia, is hardly promising terrain for innovative public-sector leadership. The metropolitan area is a classic case of a central city with a majority African-American population and high levels of poverty (nearly 25 percent) surrounded by more affluent suburbs. Due to the geographic and political separation of cities and counties in Virginia, meaningful regional cooperation among the metropolitan area's governments is limited in scope, and there are no cooperative arrangements with a significant redistributive content. Politics in the city proper have generally been dominated by powerful local business interests such as local corporations and the real estate industry. Civic participation in the city is generally weak and usually racially divided and continues to be hampered by a long history of mutual racial distrust (Corcoran 2010); participation in public meetings and other efforts to lobby public officials is often disproportionately white. There are no powerful cross-racial organizations operating in the city and Industrial Areas Foundation-style community-organizing efforts to date have had very limited impact. Land use and redevelopment issues in the city have traditionally been the prerogative of developers and real estate interests (Silver 1984).

The case study that follows concerns both the public interest and distributive justice, though not in the more common sense of policies and practices affecting the least well off. Rather, this is a case of mobilizing the public at large to prevent powerful economic interests from imposing their will on the political process and claiming the most valuable real estate in the city. It is also about an attempt to reassert the legitimacy of direct public action for public ends and of city planning in a relatively conservative political context that has often been hostile to both ideas.

Starting in 2007, Flynn spearheaded a process leading to the adoption and implementation of a new master plan for downtown Richmond. Flynn is an experienced urban planner with progressive sensibilities who previously worked in Lynchburg, Virginia (doing political battle, on occasion, with Jerry Falwell and Liberty University). Flynn was hired by then-mayor L. Douglas Wilder in March 2006 and charged with revitalizing Richmond's downtown, which has been decaying as a commercial center and residential location for decades. Despite the presence of the state capital, a branch of the Federal Reserve, numerous law and financial firms, a major state university, and a historically significant river, large swaths of the city's downtown remain underused or vacant, with few recognized and widely used spaces or pedestrian attractions.

The substance of Flynn's work has consisted of initiating a process to transform downtown into a more pedestrian-friendly, urbanist environment with expanded public space, dramatically improved public access to the James River, and more green amenities, such as trees. At the heart of Flynn's strategy for downtown is a renewed focus on capitalizing on its urbanist strengths, such as its small blocks and tight grid. This means focusing on storefront commerce, moving parking lots underground, lowering the parking space requirement for new buildings, putting an end to high-speed one-way streets, and in general encouraging pedestrian activity and alternative forms of transportation such as biking and (potentially) streetcars. The boldest part of the plan, however, is a proposal to construct a continuous riverfront park alongside the James River running through the heart of the city, anchored by a large public park to be located on currently vacant (but privately owned) land. Currently public access to the river is limited and uneven, and much of the riverfront area is unattractive; transforming the James River into Richmond's "great, wet Central Park" became one of the plan's catchphrases. Taken as a whole, the downtown plan is a thinly veiled criticism of decades of haphazard development and the city's failure to capitalize on its most outstanding asset, the James River, and an explicit claim that the public can do better by moving aggressively to purchase key properties and build an attractive new waterfront park accessible to all by foot.

Flynn built public support for this approach by providing extensive opportunities for civic participation in the formation of the plan. In summer of 2007, a series of planning charrettes were held, in which citizens were asked about their ideas for downtown and the general outcomes they would like to see the master plan realize. At least eight hundred residents (of roughly 195,000) participated in at least one of these meetings (exceeding Flynn's expectations). These discussions did not begin on a blank slate—Flynn's urbanist principles were used as a takeoff point—but in theory at least, "everything" with respect to land use, development, and streetscapes was on the table. As the plan was drafted, further meetings were held to solicit citizen feedback, and citizens were given the chance to interact directly with planning staff. Over a one-week period, an ongoing open house was held, allowing citizens to see the plans in formation, ask questions of city planning staff and design firm Dover, Kohl and Partners, and provide input. This process was intended both to generate input for the plan and to create a constituency of engaged citizens willing and able to advocate publically on behalf of the plan. This participatory approach, along with Flynn's perceived competence, played a major role in bolstering her credibility and political security and in winning support for the plan from much of the mainstream business and real estate leadership in the city (outside of affected development interests).

But Flynn has not just enlisted citizens in a planning exercise; she has acted self-consciously as a *political* agent in mobilizing support for the plan. Flynn has worked in concert with local smart growth and preservationist organizations to promote the plan and to solicit citizens willing to speak on behalf of the plan before city council and in public forums and also has spent extensive time consulting with experienced political observers and civic leaders in the city, strategizing about how to navigate the plan through the political process and an often developer-friendly city council. Indeed, the danger with the master plan all along has been that its teeth would be cut out at the implementation stage under pressure from developers negatively affected by the proposals. Flynn took steps throughout this process to prepare for a fight, and in 2009, a fight arrived.

The conflict derives from the contradiction between the aspirations of the master plan and a private developer's proposals to build high-rise luxury condos along the James River (the "Echo Harbour" project), permanently impacting the view of the river from atop historic Church Hill, on exactly the parcel of land designated by the city for a riverfront park. The project would simultaneously squash the possibility of an attractive, continuous public riverfront park and impede the view of the James River for which the city is named.[4] Lawyer James Theobald, representing development firm USP Rocketts, sharply criticized the master plan and the process as disrespectful of property rights in a series of public hearings in 2008 and 2009. Immediately after the passage of the plan by the city council in October 2008, council member Bruce Tyler, an architect for one of the firms involved in the Echo Harbour proposal, announced he would seek amendments to the plan in coming months.

Spring and summer 2009 saw a protracted struggle over Tyler's attempts to amend the plan so as to weaken its commitment to a continuous public riverfront park and weaken the standards by which future special use-permit requests will be judged. For instance, in the original plan, the public option for establishing a park is listed first; in the revised plan, a private development option for the property in question is listed first. More important, Tyler favored striking out a provision mandating that all special-use permits be evaluated in terms of the specific character and zoning designation of the land under question. This is significant because the proposed height of the condominium proposal violates existing zoning for riverfront property, and the developers would need a special-use permit (under both current zoning and the new plan) to go forward. Planning commission and city council meetings throughout 2009 featured citizens overwhelmingly speaking out against the condominium proposal, but Theobald and USP Rocketts continued to lobby on behalf of the proposal. Behind the scenes, the firm made extensive efforts to sway planning commission and city council members (almost all council members receive significant campaign funding from development interests). After months of hearings and delays, the revised plan was approved on July 27, 2009; the amendment backed by Tyler to weaken special-use permit language failed by one vote.

What is the public interest in this case? Proponents of the Echo Harbour development have made two kinds of arguments: a property rights–based argument that, in effect, developers and property owners should be allowed to do what they want, and an argument that the development will create jobs and tax revenues and not disrupt public access to the river. Theobald and USP Rocketts have made almost no effort to argue that the condominium plan in fact fits the aspirations of the downtown plan strongly endorsed by citizens and approved by the city council. Those aspirations are for the city to use the James River to reestablish the city's identity and to make public space and public access to the river the heart of that identity. The force of the argument for the public park proposal and against riverfront condominiums is not simply about providing more or better recreational or aesthetic amenities to citizens or about providing a better way to stimulate downtown economic activity (though the downtown plan embraces both those goals as well) but about creating a signature location that people can identify with the city. This in turn is seen to be in the public interest because it would bolster the city's unique identity, give residents a new shared space to be proud of, and reinvigorate pride and interest in Richmond's unique qualities. Further, the long process by which the new master plan was adopted and the civic participation it engendered lends the specifics of the plan credibility as an expression of what the community (more precisely, the civically active part of the community) would like to see happen.

The alternative proposal for the land in question has none of these qualities; it is a proposal, largely unwanted by city residents, to build a fairly generic, high-rise condo and create a space that will be the terrain of high-end residents and consumers, taking much of the best riverfront view and access in the process. Approval of the Echo Harbour proposal would further send a strong signal that no matter what the public says it wants, developers have sufficient influence and political muscle to impose their will on land-use planning. That in turn has very negative implications for the future of democratic politics in Richmond. Advocates for the downtown master plan can thus contend that there is both a smaller-order public interest in this case in seeing the public's aspirations for a large riverside park realized because of the specific public goods that that project is expected to provide and a larger-order public interest in seeing the expressed will of the community and overwhelming views of local residents honored because of the implications that carries for where political power really lies in the city.

In the process of this debate, Flynn has emerged as a lightning-rod figure: a hero to almost all the citizens

involved in the process, who view her as a champion for the public good, but an arrogant annoyance to several members of city council. After an April 2009 planning commission meeting in which Flynn flatly refused a commissioner's request to seek an accommodation with Echo Harbour developers about the project, saying it was not her job to compromise what the public wanted and the principles of the plan, at least three council members wrote to the mayor requesting Flynn's termination. Flynn withstood this pressure and continued in her job for the next two years as an advocate for the plan's goals. The future of the proposal to create a true riverfront park remains uncertain, however. City council removed money set aside by the mayor to buy up riverfront properties from both the fiscal 2009–10 and fiscal 2010–11 budgets, meaning Flynn and the city could not act to acquire the properties needed to establish the proposed park. In the meantime, despite losing on the downtown plan amendment language, Theobald and USP Rocketts have not withdrawn the project or abandoned hope of obtaining a special-use permit for it. As of April 2011, the fate of the contested riverfront possibility is still undecided.[5] Flynn herself announced her resignation from city government in March 2011 to take a consulting position in Abu Dhabi.

While this example of public-sector leadership contains significant flaws and a still-uncertain outcome, the downtown plan process represents a breakthrough in contemporary Richmond politics. Flynn's work changed the discourse about downtown development in Richmond and shown [sic] that there is fairly wide citizen support for strong public action on behalf of urbanism. The idea that the city should be shaped by the public, not the developers, has been widely embraced. Because of the way citizens have been mobilized and the legitimacy the planning process has commanded, Flynn has been able to take strong stands and directly criticize powerful interests and figures in the city.

Nonetheless, Flynn's efforts were hampered by the relatively weak level of civic organization in Richmond. White, well-educated persons represent the overwhelming majority of persons involved both in the charrette-based public-planning process and in advocacy groups like Partnership for Smarter Growth and the Alliance to Conserve Old Richmond Neighborhoods. This is highly problematic in a city that is majority African-American and has allowed critics like Tyler to claim that the downtown plan process reflected the views of a small group of self-selected people. Although the city government and some activists did reach out to African-American organizations and the plan was endorsed by some important African-American leaders (including new mayor Dwight Jones, who succeeded Wilder in 2009), success in generating extensive African-American participation was limited.[6]

In this regard, the debate over the downtown plan has reenacted a recurrent dilemma for social justice advocates in Richmond: the political mismatch between the task of promoting justice within the metropolitan region as a whole and the task of promoting justice within the city itself. There is good reason to think the downtown plan, if enacted, would draw more people back into living downtown, in turn stimulating commercial development in the currently dilapidated Broad Street corridor. Such resettlement of downtown would strengthen the city's tax base and allow it to capture a greater proportion of regional economic growth. Yet while the plan may benefit the city as a whole, its promised benefits for the least well off in Richmond are either indirect (e.g., possible access to jobs created by increases in commercial activity downtown) or intangible (e.g., the benefit of living in a more pedestrian-friendly city). From the perspective of the least well off, the downtown plan looks like just another effort to make life more comfortable for middle-class urban dwellers.

Likewise, the relative success of the downtown planning process has depended precisely on the fact that it has been perceived simultaneously as progressive and nonthreatening. As noted, most mainstream business groups in the city have been broadly supportive, as have those developers who stand to benefit from opportunities to build higher-density mixed-use developments within the downtown study area. But it is much more difficult to imagine an initiative in the Richmond metropolitan area aimed at directly benefitting "the least well off"—that is, directly attacking poverty in the city via a substantial outlay of public resources—gaining such widespread support. Indeed, Richmond's metropolitan structure makes such an initiative extremely difficult, since it would involve making a claim on resources controlled by politically distinct suburban counties.

This case thus illustrates both the possibilities and limitations of "New Public Service"-type public leadership in helping to reinvigorate the public sector. Succinctly put, leadership that seeks to engage citizens and calls attention to positive possibilities for significantly improving the city can, in fact, call into being civic forces that were previously dormant and draw new people into the policy-making process. When combined with shrewd and, at times, forceful political judgment, activist public leaders can also shepherd proposals to change the way the city is developed through the political process, compromising on some details but not the essentials. But public leadership alone cannot overcome inherent structural flaws in the metropolis. In the Richmond case specifically, despite efforts to engage the African-American population (which led to the inclusion of affordable housing language in the final plan) and support from several key African-America [sic] leaders, grassroots participation in the debate about the downtown plan remained disproportionately white and middle class. While the process Flynn initiated was not inherently exclusionary, it did not do nearly enough to overcome or alter long-standing inequalities of political participation and voice in the city.

The second limitation refers to the fact that Richmond's metropolitan governance structure—or lack thereof—means that, at present, challenging fundamental structural inequalities is simply off the political table. There is no plausible way by which another Rachel Flynn could initiate a process intended to fundamentally rectify inequalities of public education in the metropolis, since each school district is separate and suburban residents have no interest in such reform (Ryan 2010). What city officials can and cannot do is thus shaped by the structure of metropolitan governance already in place—hence, the importance for metropolitan social justice to establish both (a) an account of what a just metropolitan constitution for American's urban areas would look like and (b) a more-than-wishful-thinking account of how sharply divided metropolises might meaningfully move in that direction in the future.

Importantly, this does not mean that city officials in Richmond or elsewhere have no capacity to attempt to improve the city's position and promote the shared interests of its citizens. Flynn found an opportunity to do so in the fact that a major, unique natural resource of the city (the James River) has yet to be fully tapped as a signature attraction and central community location for the city and there is reason to believe that if the vision of the plan were fully realized, then the city would reap multiple benefits and be in a stronger position relative to its suburban neighbors. Moreover, and central to our concern here, it would help rehabilitate the idea that the public sector can act successfully on behalf of public aims. But while the public aims involved in the downtown master plan are significant and worth fighting to achieve, they simply do not address the fundamental structural inequalities characterizing the Richmond metropolitan area.

Conclusion

This assessment naturally raises a question: what would the politics capable of addressing such fundamental inequalities and injustices look like in a place like Richmond, especially given the area's very unfavorable metropolitan political structure? One prerequisite of such a politics, and the focus of this chapter, is public support for using public power to constrain private actors and regulate market processes in order to achieve substantive public goals. This idea is fundamental to almost all attractive conceptions of social justice, and it is an idea that has been under attack in the United States at all levels of government in recent decades. Despite its inherent limitations, the effort to create a new downtown master plan in Richmond has had significant success in beginning to rehabilitate that basic idea. Indeed, perhaps the most promising aspect of the downtown master-plan debate in Richmond is that Flynn's core assertion—that the public should have the first claim on the best and most valuable undeveloped land in the city—found significant resonance in a city that has traditionally been deferential to private developers.

But reestablishing the legitimacy of meaningful public sector action is not enough if larger-order social justice issues are to be tackled. The next step in Richmond must involve the forging of the kind of coalition that was almost completely absent in the struggle over the downtown plan: a genuinely multiracial coalition committed to establishing not just public space and other public goods but also more direct steps to address poverty and improve the position of the "least well off." It is possible that one or more local public officials might play a catalytic role in helping

mobilize low-income residents in the city in a more direct fashion and help forge a coalition between middle-class and low-income residents on behalf of a concrete goal. The most promising candidate issue in this respect is dramatically improving public transportation in the city, an issue that directly affects low-income residents in the city and is a goal supported by almost all the advocates who mobilized on behalf of the downtown master plan. Improving public transportation is also a regional issue (transit to Richmond's suburbs is generally limited, meaning many jobs are out of reach of carless Richmond residents). A strong, cross-class, multiracial coalition of Richmonders and supportive suburban residents could potentially challenge the regional status quo and begin correcting one very significant social injustice (unequal access to employment).

Regardless of whether creative public-sector leadership in support of that goal is forthcoming, the burden of building a truly multiracial coalition on behalf of social justice must rest with civic and grassroots activists committed to creating and sustaining long-term solidarity across difference. At particular historical moments, public-sector leaders can play a critical role in framing issues and mobilizing constituents to address key problems, but they cannot create powerful, cross-cutting social movements out of whole cloth. That job falls to citizens.

Notes

Discussions with Planning Commission member Amy Howard, John Moeser (Virginia Commonwealth University professor of urban planning emeritus), and numerous citizen participants in the process have helped inform this chapter. Informal conversations with Rachel Flynn in 2008 and 2009 and an extensive formal interview with Flynn in June 2010 have provided additional insight into the process. The author has also attended or participated in several public hearings related to the downtown plan.

1. With the advent of the Obama administration, some Progressives such as Peter Dreier believe that attention should shift to national-level policy (Dreier 2009). While better national policies would have many positive ramifications for cities, to date there is little evidence that the large-scale stimulus programs or any of the other initiatives of the Obama administration has or will materially change public attitudes toward the

state and the legitimacy of public action. While it remains possible that a large-scale, federal domestic project, successfully implemented, might have that effect, continued attention to local and metropolitan structures of democratic practice remains essential— independent of the future direction of federal policy.

4. William Byrd II named the city "Richmond" in 1737 because the view of the James River from atop Church Hill closely resembled the view of the River Thames from Richmond Hill outside London; the location today is considered a historical site and is a prime attraction for visitors to the city.

5. In August 2010, Mayor Dwight Jones announced plans to commission a new $500,000 study of how to "improve and expand access along the downtown riverfront," inclusive of the land involved in the Echo Harbour controversy (Jones 2010).

6. Notably, in June 2010, the charrette technique was again used in Richmond to launch a significant planning effort, this time regarding the revitalization of the area around the Bon Secours Richmond Community Hospital in the city's overwhelmingly poor and African-American East End. These charrettes, cosponsored by Bon Secours, the city, and the Richmond Redevelopment and Housing Authority, were well attended by African-Americans and heavily publicized in the local African-American media.

References

Biegelesen, Amy. 2007a. "Master Plan Sessions Confront Race, Push Details." *Style Weekly,* August 12.

———. 2007b. "Master Planners Return to Dispel "Sea of Whiteness."" *Style Weekly,* September 19.

———. 2008. "In Like Flynn." *Style Weekly,* January 16.

———. 2008. "Master Panned." *Style Weekly,* October 28.

———. 2009. "Flynn's Last Stand?" *Style Weekly,* May 7.

Box, Richard C. 2004. *Critical Social Theory in Public Administration.* Armonk, N.Y.: M. E. Sharpe.

Church Hill People's News. n.d. http: //www.chpn.net.

Corcoran, Rob. 2010. *Trustbuilding: An Honest Conversation on Race, Reconciliation, and Responsibility.* Charlottesville: University of Virginia Press.

Denhardt, Janet V., and Robert B. Denhardt. 2003. *The New Public Service: Serving, Not Steering.* Armonk, N.Y.: M. E. Sharpe.

Doherty, Kathryn M., and Clarence N. Stone. 1999. "Local Practice in Transition: From Government to Governance." In *Dilemmas of Scale in America's Federal Democracy,* ed. Martha Derthick. Cambridge: Cambridge University Press.

Dreier, Peter. 2009. "There Is No Urban Crisis: Progressive Politics and Urban Policy in the Obama Era." Paper presented at "Justice and the American Metropolis" conference, St. Louis, MO, May 9, 2009.

Dworkin, Ronald. 2000. *Sovereign Virtue: The Theory and Practice of Equality.* Cambridge: Cambridge University Press.

Elkin, Stephen L. 2006. *Reconstructing the Commercial Republic: Constitutional Theory after Madison.* Chicago: University of Chicago Press.

Freeman, Samuel. 2007. *Rawls.* New York Routledge.

Fung, Archon. 2004. *Empowered Participation: Reinventing Urban Democracy.* Princeton, N.J.: Princeton University Press.

Gaebler, Ted, and David Osborne. 1992. *Reinventing Government: How the Entrepreneurial Spirit Is Transforming the Public Sector.* Reading, Mass.: Addison-Wesley.

Holland, Dorothy, Catherine Lutz, Donald Nonini, Lesley Bartlett, Marla FrederickMcGlathery, Thaddeus Gulbrandsen, and Enrique Murillo Jr. 2007. *Local Democracy under Siege: Activism, Public Interests, and Private Politics.* New York: New York University Press.

Jones, Will. 2010. "Study to Explore Expanding Access to Richmond's Riverfront." *Richmond Times-Dispatch,* August 15.

Luke, Jeffrey. 1998. *Catalytic Leadership.* San Francisco: Jossey-Bass.

Morgan, David R., Robert E. England, and John P. Pelissero. 2006. *Managing Urban America.* 6th ed. Washington, D.C.: CQ Press.

Rawls, John. 1971. *A Theory of Justice.* Cambridge, Mass.: Harvard University Press.

Richmond, Virginia. 2008. Richmond Downtown Plan. *Official Richmond Web site,* October. http://www .cisichmond.va.us/forms/DowntownPlan.aspx.

Ryan, James. 2010. *Five Miles Away, A World Apart: One City, Two Schools, and the Story of Educational Opportunity in Modern America.* New York: Oxford University Press.

Sarvay, John. n.d. *Buttermilk & Molasses.* http://floricane .typepad.com/buttermilk/richmonds_downtown_plan/ index.html.

Silver, Christopher. 1984. *Twentieth Century Richmond: Politics, Planning, and Race.* Knoxville: University of Tennessee Press.

Williamson, Thad. 2009. "Echo Chamber." *Style Weekly,* April 28.

Young, Iris Marion. 1990. *Justice and the Politics of Difference.* Princeton, N.J.: Princeton University Press.

Conclusion

Public Policy Applications: Waterfront Development

Policy Then

Few mayors in recent years have had a more sweeping vision of how to transform their cities than Michael Bloomberg of New York, who occupied city hall from 2002 until 2014. His administration rezoned over 12,000 blocks, or 40 percent, of the city, an unprecedented undertaking that facilitated a surge in the development of office buildings, hotels, and residential towers mainly on the west side of Manhattan, Brooklyn, and Queens. Bloomberg trumpeted the economic benefits that accrued to the city from the construction boom. However, urbanists also credit the mayor with reshaping the city in ways that made New York a more pleasant place to live. Prominent in this regard was the creation of remarkable public spaces and parks such as the widely praised High Line, a mile-long greenway reconstructed from a derelict elevated rail track, and the sprawling 2,200-acre Freshkills Park in Staten Island, the largest park established in New York in over a century. Some veteran observers of New York believe that Bloomberg's most important legacy was restoring the public's faith that a polity can effect massive changes in its physical landscape, that citizens are not necessarily trapped by the development decisions of past generations.

Bloomberg's approach to waterfront revitalization illustrates the point. Early on, the mayor and city planners recognized the enormous potential of reclaiming extended stretches of vacant, deteriorating, and polluted industrial sites along the city's 520 miles of shoreline and opening up that land to residential, recreational, and commercial uses. This was a golden opportunity to reconnect neighborhoods to the water through parks and

Playground in Brooklyn Bridge Park, New York

© Julienne Schaer

548

esplanades and tie new developments and emerging communities together through commuter ferries, water taxis, and leisure boating. The administration's award-winning comprehensive plan for the waterfront quickly led to numerous proposals for high-rise condominiums, retail and entertainment businesses, and civic spaces, often with breathtaking views of the Manhattan skyline. The crown jewel was Brooklyn Bridge Park, an 85-acre expanse along the Brooklyn waterfront with imaginative playgrounds; a carousel; athletic fields for soccer, lacrosse, rugby, and ultimate frisbee; lawns and greenways; volleyball, handball, and basketball courts; restaurants; and picnic areas, all of which would be lined by new residential complexes capable of generating the revenue needed to maintain park operations in future years.

The key question regarding Bloomberg's waterfront development is who benefits from the proliferation of residential towers. Most of the new housing was market rate, which along the New York waterfront translated into price tags far in excess of what most residents of surrounding communities could afford. Even many of the new parks seemed to cater to the affluent denizens of the splashy waterfront high-rises. The Bloomberg administration hotly contested charges that its policies were spawning a luxury city increasingly unaffordable to all but the wealthy by pointing out that it had created 160,000 units of affordable housing over a twelve-year period. However, only about two-thirds of that total consisted of newly constructed units (as opposed to older units that had been renovated). Little new housing along the waterfront was affordable to the city's poor, working class, or even middle class. And the "affordable" housing that was constructed was sometimes separated from the market-rate housing in less desirable settings or was small in scale (e.g., studio or one-bedroom apartments) and thus unsuitable for families.

Policy Now

As a candidate for mayor of New York in 2013, the city's public advocate Bill de Blasio made inequality his defining issue. He warned that more and more sections of the city resembled exclusive, gated communities instead of places of opportunity for all members of society. The dearth of decent, affordable housing was becoming a particularly onerous problem for many New Yorkers. De Blasio argued that with soaring rents outpacing stagnant wages, a rising percentage of city residents were paying 50 percent or more of their incomes on rent and utilities, a severe and unsustainable burden.

After his election as mayor, de Blasio promised to significantly enlarge the supply of affordable housing by demanding more of residential developers. The Bloomberg administration had tried to entice developers to include affordable housing units in new, market-rate developments by offering subsidies and incentives, but that voluntary inclusionary housing policy only produced about 2,700 affordable units since 2005, and many of those were actually well beyond the price range of poor and working-class New Yorkers. By contrast, de Blasio adopted a *mandatory* inclusionary housing policy in which developers would be required to set aside 20 percent of their units as affordable in any area that had been rezoned for residential use. If developers provided additional units of affordable housing above and beyond the 20 percent set aside, the city would reward them by allowing them to build projects taller or denser than what the zoning code permitted (and since de Blasio advocates high-density development as a core strategy for expanding affordable housing, the awarding of density bonuses was anticipated to be a common practice). The mayor predicted 80,000 units of newly constructed affordable housing by 2024, twice the average annual rate of the previous twenty-five years. That amount, together with the additional 120,000 units that would be preserved under the city's housing rehabilitation programs, was expected to provide affordable housing for a half-million city residents.

An application of de Blasio's mandatory inclusionary housing policy concerns the Astoria Cove development on the Queens waterfront. The centerpiece of that 2014 proposal is a residential complex consisting of 1,700 units with one-bedroom, market-rate units renting at $2,700/month—far above the reach of area residents whose annual median income (AMI) is $65,000. In light of de Blasio's "muscular" approach to residential development, the developer agreed to set aside 27 percent of the units as affordable (i.e., 5 percent for tenants earning 60 percent of AMI, 15 percent for those at 80 percent of AMI, and 7 percent for those at 125 percent of AMI). In addition, the developer will finance the renovation of a local park and build a grocery store and public school. Representatives within the real estate industry cautioned that de Blasio's tough stance with developers might deter other projects, but all indications suggest that the demand for affordable and market-rate housing in New York remains very strong.

Additional Resources

Brooklyn Bridge Park Web site. www.brooklynbridgepark.org.

City Observatory. Think tank based in Portland, Oregon, devoted to data-driven analysis of cities and urban policy. www.cityobservatory.org.

Pierre Clavel and Wim Wiewel, eds., *Harold Washington and the Neighborhoods: Progressive City Government in Chicago, 1983–1987* (New Brunswick, NJ: Rutgers University Press, 1991).

Ryan Holeywell, "Building Blocks," *Governing*, 26 (6), March 2013. A favorable assessment of Mayor Michael Bloomberg.

Manhattan Institute. Think tank that offers a conservative perspective on urban politics and policy. www.manhattan-institute.org.

Stephen J. McGovern, "Ideology, Consciousness, and Inner-City Revitalization: The Case of Stephen Goldsmith's Indianapolis," *Journal of Urban Affairs*, 25 (1), 2003.

Harold Meyerson, "The Revolt of the Cities," *American Prospect*, May/June 2014.

Urban Institute. Research institute that emphasizes academic rigor and collaboration with cities, communities, and the private sector in the search for policy solutions to challenging problems. www.urban.org.

Vision 2020: New York City Comprehensive Waterfront Plan. www.nyc.gov/html/dcp/pdf/cwp/vision2020_nyc_cwp.pdf.

Discussion Questions

1. Why was Mayor Michael Bloomberg able to transform his city's physical landscape more extensively than anyone since (and perhaps including) New York's legendary builder, Robert Moses?

2. Mayor Bill de Blasio seems to be willing and able to drive hard bargains with private developers with respect to extracting public benefits. Is this a viable strategy for most U.S. cities?

3. Apart from promoting affordable housing along a city's waterfront, are there any other ways to ensure that the waterfront does not become the relatively exclusive domain of privileged groups?

4. Finding public funds to create and maintain public parks is always a dilemma for most cities. New York has been in the forefront of an alternative model, as exemplified by the successful Brooklyn Bridge Park. In that case, market-rate residential development (really luxury residential development) along the perimeter of the park has been used to generate operational revenue for the park. Should more cities pursue this mechanism of financing public parks?

5. Enacting inclusionary zoning policies represents one strategy for producing more affordable housing. Another, favored by both Michael Bloomberg and Bill de Blasio, is simply to promote much more high-density residential development. The assumption is that a robust expansion in the volume of residential development will inevitably yield more housing for everyone. Do you agree? What are the potential costs of encouraging taller and denser residential buildings?

6. What should happen when there is a conflict between the expertise of professional planners and the desires of a perhaps less-informed mass public? Whose views should prevail in the policy-making process?

7. Richard M. Daley was elected and reelected as mayor of Chicago several times. Why did a majority of voters perceive him as so effective? Is that judgment warranted?

8. How does Mayor Stephen Goldsmith of Indianapolis differ from Daley in his approach to urban governance? Does that variation constitute a significant improvement or not? What vision of urban politics is most likely to improve the condition of American cities?

Printed in Great Britain
by Amazon